Get Connected.

Interactive Presentations

Connect Business's **Interactive Presentations** teach each chapter's core learning objectives and concepts through an engaging, hands-on presentation, bringing the text content to life. Interactive Presentations harness the full power of technology to truly engage and appeal to all learning styles. Interactive Presentations are ideal in all class formats—online, face-to-face, or hybrid.

Interactive Applications

Connect Business's **Interactive Applications** offer students a variety of tools to help engage students in application level thinking about the core contents. Interactive Application exercises include: Drag and Drops, Case Analyses, Sequencing, Video Cases, and Decision Generators, which are all auto-gradable. After completing an activity, students receive immediate feedback and can track their progress through a personalized report, while instructors are provided detailed results on how each student in their course is performing.

Get Engaged.

eBook

Connect Plus includes a media-rich eBook that allows you to share your notes with your students. Your students can insert and review their own notes, highlight the text, search for specific information, and interact with media resources. Using an eBook with *Connect Plus* gives your students a complete digital solution that allows them to access their materials from any computer.

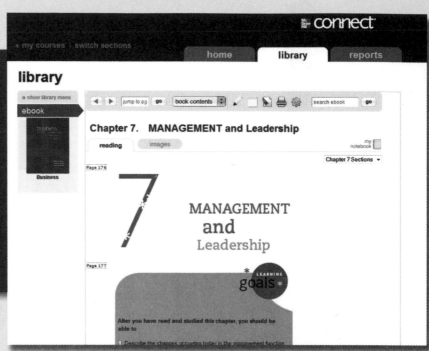

Lecture Capture

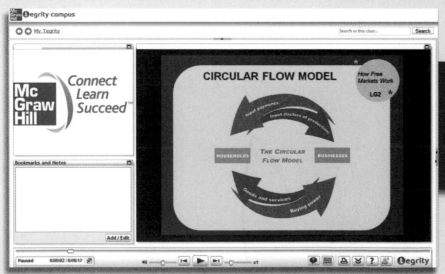

Make your classes available anytime, anywhere. With simple, one-click recording, students can search for a word or phrase and be taken to the exact place in your lecture that they need to review.

business:

CONNECTING
PRINCIPLES
TO PRACTICE

business:

second edition

CONNECTING
PRINCIPLES
TO PRACTICE

William G. Nickels
University of Maryland

James M. McHugh
St. Louis Community College at Forest Park

Susan M. McHugh
Applied Learning Systems

The McGraw-Hill Companies

McGraw-Hill
Irwin

BUSINESS: CONNECTING PRINCIPLES TO PRACTICE, SECOND EDITION

1 2 3 4 5 6 7 8 9 0 QVR/QVR 1 0 9 8 7 6 5 4 3

ISBN   978-0-07-802314-9
MHID   0-07-802314-9

Senior Vice President, Products & Markets: *Kurt L. Strand*
Vice President, Content Production & Technology Services: *Kimberly Meriwether David*
Managing Director: *Paul Ducham*
Senior Brand Manager: *Anke Braun Weekes*
Executive Director of Development: *Ann Torbert*
Development Editor II: *Kelly L. Delso*
Executive Marketing Manager: *Michael Gedatus*
Marketing Specialist: *Elizabeth Steiner*
Lead Project Manager: *Christine A. Vaughan*
Senior Buyer: *Carol A. Bielski*
Lead Designer: *Matthew Baldwin*
Cover Designer: *Laurie Entringer*
Senior Content Licensing Specialist: *Jeremy Cheshareck*
Photo Researcher: *Jennifer Blankenship*
Lead Media Project Manager: *Brian Nacik*
Media Project Manager: *Ron Nelms*
Typeface: *11/13 Times Roman*
Compositor: *Laserwords Private Limited*
Printer: *Quad/Graphics*

Library of Congress Cataloging-in-Publication Data
Nickels, William G.
    Business : connecting principles to practice / William G. Nickels, University of Maryland, James
    M. McHugh, St. Louis Community College at Forest Park, Susan M. McHugh, Applied Learning
Systems.—Second edition.
        p. cm.
    Includes index.
    ISBN 978-0-07-802314-9 (alk. paper)—ISBN 0-07-802314-9 (alk. paper)
    1. Industrial management. 2. Business. I. McHugh,
James M. II. McHugh, Susan M. III. Title.
HD31.N4895 2014
658—dc23

                                                                            2012046437

www.mhhe.com

dedication

To our families—Marsha, Joel, Carrie, Casey, Dan, Molly, Michael, Colin, and Quinn. You continue to be our inspiration!

and

To the team that made this edition possible, especially the instructors and students who gave us such valuable guidance as we revised the text and package.

ABOUT THE
authors

Bill Nickels is emeritus professor of business at the University of Maryland, College Park. He has over 30 years' experience teaching graduate and undergraduate business courses, including introduction to business, marketing, and promotion. He has won the Outstanding Teacher on Campus Award four times and was nominated for the award many other times. He received his M.B.A. degree from Western Reserve University and his Ph.D. from The Ohio State University. He has written a marketing communications text and two marketing principles texts in addition to many articles in business publications. He has taught many seminars to businesspeople on subjects such as power communications, marketing, non-business marketing, and stress and life management. His son, Joel, is a Professor of English at the University of Miami (Florida).

Jim McHugh holds an M.B.A. degree from Lindenwood University and has had broad experience in education, business, and government. As chairman of the Business and Economics Department of St. Louis Community College/Forest Park, Jim coordinated and directed the development of the business curriculum. In addition to teaching several sections of Introduction to Business each semester for nearly 30 years, Jim taught in the marketing and management areas at both the undergraduate and graduate levels. Jim enjoys conducting business seminars and consulting with small and large businesses. He is actively involved in the public service sector and served as chief of staff to the St. Louis County Executive.

Susan McHugh is a learning specialist with extensive training and experience in adult learning and curriculum development. She holds an M.Ed. degree from the University of Missouri and completed her course work for a Ph.D. in education administration with a specialty in adult learning theory. As a professional curriculum developer, she has directed numerous curriculum projects and educator training programs. She has worked in the public and private sectors as a consultant in training and employee development. While Jim and Susan treasure their participation in writing projects, their greatest accomplishment is their collaboration on their three children. Casey is carrying on the family's teaching tradition as an adjunct professor at Washington University. Molly and Michael are carrying on the family writing tradition by contributing to the development of several supplementary materials for this text.

We've listened to you and your students in revising this edition and that's helped us offer you:

Resources that were developed based directly on *your* feedback—all geared to make the most of your time and to help students succeed in this course. All the supplemental resources for *Business: Connecting Principles to Practice* are carefully reviewed by Bill, Jim, and Susan to ensure cohesion with the text.

Technology that leads the way and is consistently being updated to keep up with you and your students. *Connect® Business* offers students a truly interactive and adaptive study arena. *Interactive Presentations, Interactive Applications*, and *LearnSmart* are designed to engage students and have been proven to increase grades by a full letter.

Support that is always available to help you in planning your course, working with technology, and meeting the needs of you and your students.

KEEPING UP WITH WHAT'S NEW

Users of *Business: Connecting Principles to Practice* have always appreciated the currency of the material and the large number of examples from companies of all sizes and industries (e.g., service, manufacturing, nonprofit, and profit) in the United States and around the world. A glance at the Chapter Notes will show you that almost all of them are from 2011 or 2012. Accordingly, this edition features the latest business practices and other developments affecting business including:

- Career Outlook sections have been added at the end of each part to identify current career opportunities and to help illustrate how students can transfer their skills to a career in business. Well-crafted cover letters, résumés, and responses to interview questions highlight how to present transferable skills to potential employers.
- The Prologue and Epilogue provided at the beginning and end of the text are designed to help students succeed not only in this course, but also in the business world. Students are offered study tips, best practices in interviewing, and résumé-building skills.
- Key concepts are explained through brief animated "iSee It!" videos geared specifically toward students. These videos are accessed through the use of QR codes in the text margin near where each concept is covered.
- 2012 Supreme Court decision on the Patient Protection and Affordable Care Act (PPACA, also known as Obamacare).
- Using social media in business (integrated throughout the text and featured in new themed boxes).
- Growing economic importance of China.
- European debt crisis and its affect on the U.S. economy.
- COMESA, the African trading bloc.
- BRIC economies.
- Dodd-Frank Wall Street Reform and Consumer Protection Act.
- Socially conscious research organizations.

- Recent conflicts between governments and public sector labor unions.
- Economic crisis—its causes, effects, and attempted remedies, including TARP and the stimulus package.
- NYSE Euronext ownership changes.
- Credit Card Responsibility, Accountability, and Disclosure Act.
- Taxing online purchases.
- Millennials in the workplace.
- And much, much more.

CONNECTING TO STUDENTS THROUGH ADAPTIVE LEARNING

 McGraw-Hill *Connect*® is the leading online assignment and assessment solution that connects students with the tools and resources they need to achieve success while providing instructors with tools to quickly pick content and assignments according to the learning objectives they want to emphasize.

Connect improves student learning and retention with engaging presentations and activities that prepare students for class and help them master concepts and review for exams.

Interactive Presentations within *Connect* are designed to reinforce learning by offering a visual presentation of the Learning Goals highlighted in every chapter of the text. Interactive presentations are engaging, online, professional presentations (fully Section 508 compliant) covering the same core concepts directly from the chapter, while offering additional examples and graphics. *Interactive Presentations* teach students Learning Goals in a multimedia format, bringing the course and the book to life. *Interactive Presentations* are a great prep tool for students—when students are better prepared, they are more engaged and better able to participate in class.

LearnSmart within *Connect* is an adaptive learning system designed to help students learn faster, study more efficiently, and retain more knowledge for greater success. *LearnSmart* is the premier learning system designed to effectively assess a student's knowledge of course content through a series of adaptive questions, intelligently pinpointing concepts the student does not understand and mapping out a personalized study plan for success. LearnSmart prepares students, allowing instructors to focus valuable class time on higher-level concepts.

Key Benefits include:

- Provides just-in-time material for efficient study to save students time.
- At-a-glance view of student strengths and weaknesses.
- Web-based technology, so there is nothing to download or backup.
- Prepares students well for upcoming lectures or exams.
- Students can access anytime via an Internet connection, even on their iPhone or iPod Touch.
- Intuitive interface builds student engagement.
- Provides instructors with comprehensive reports of student performance by individual, topic, or learning objective to help gauge student learning.

LearnSmart adaptively assesses students' skill levels to determine which topics students have mastered and which require further practice by way of personalized learning.

Interactive Applications within *Connect* offer students a variety of tools to help them assess their understanding. All *Interactive Applications* require students to APPLY what they have learned from the text to these assignments, and other than the Comprehension Cases, are all auto-graded. Some of the *Interactive Application* exercises include: video cases, decision generators, comprehensive cases, and case analyses.

Click and drag exercises allow students to reinforce key models/processes by requiring students to label key illustrations and models from the text or build a process, and then demonstrate application-level knowledge. . . . .

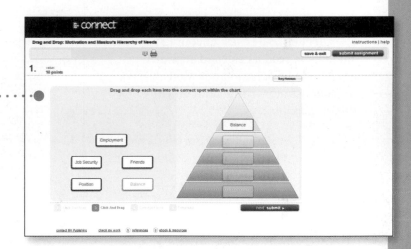

Video cases give students the opportunity to watch case videos and apply chapter concepts to a real-world business scenario as the scenario unfolds. . . . .

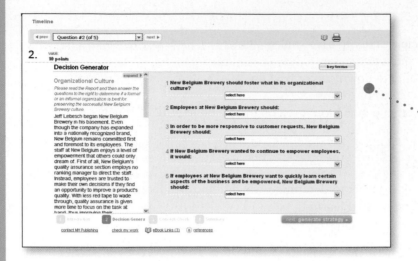

Decision generators require students to make real business decisions based on specific real-world scenarios and cases.

Comprehensive cases encourage students to read a case and answer open-ended discussion questions to demonstrate writing and critical-thinking skills.

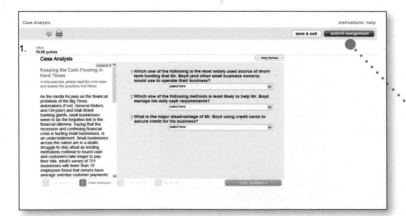

Case analyses like comprehensive cases ask students to read a case and answer questions. Students choose an option in a multiple-choice fashion to generate a response that can be auto-graded.

Student Online Learning Center (www.mhhe.com/P2P2e)

The Online Learning Center will help students use *Business: Connecting Principles to Practice* effectively. Some features on the website are:

- Manager's HotSeat Online—The Manager's HotSeat Online (www.mhhe.com/mhs) is an interactive application that allows students to watch 15 real managers apply their years of experience in confronting certain management and organizational behavior issues. Students assume the role of the manager as they watch the video and answer multiple-choice questions that pop up during the segment, forcing them to make decisions on the spot. Students learn from the managers' mistakes and successes, and then do a report critiquing the managers' approach by defending their reasoning. An Instructor's Manual is also offered on the Online Learning Center.
- Investment Trader—The Investment Trader gives students access to a hypothetical $100,000 account to buy and sell stocks and mutual funds. They use real company data in conjunction with the text content on investments to compete with students around the world. An instructor's guide is also offered on the Online Learning Center.
- Casing the Web—short cases that allow students to practice managerial decision making. These discussion starters are provided for every chapter and are intended to replace comprehensive cases that can consume class time.
- Multiple-choice questions—quizzes focusing on key concepts and providing immediate feedback offer students the opportunity to determine their level of understanding.
- Student Assessment and Learning Guide—questions, key term review, practice tests with answer key, and Internet exercises to help students succeed in their course.

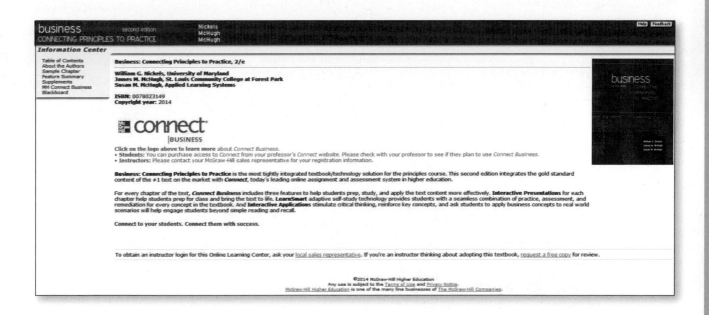

CONNECTING THROUGH STUDENT-FRIENDLY FEATURES

Learning Goals Everything in the text and supplements package ties back to the chapter learning goals. The learning goals listed throughout the chapter help students preview what they should know after reading the chapter. Chapter summaries test students' knowledge by asking questions related to the learning goals. The Test Bank, Instructor's Manual, PowerPoints, Online Course, and *Connect* are all organized according to the learning goals.

Connecting with Business Professionals Every chapter in the text opens with the profile of a business professional whose career relates closely to the material in the chapter. These business professionals work for a variety of businesses from small businesses to nonprofit organizations to large corporations. These career profiles are an engaging way to open the chapter and to introduce students to a variety of business career paths.

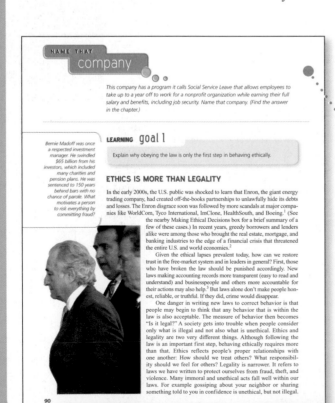

Name That Company Every text chapter opens with a Name That Company challenge. The answer for the challenge can be found somewhere in the chapter.

Career Outlook sections can be found at the close of each part. There are six portfolios featuring a potential job applicant. Each scenario includes a sample cover letter and résumé highlighting best practices in an effort to further prepare students to enter the workforce. The Career Outlook sections also include descriptions (including salary potential and skills needed) for careers in the fields featured in the part as well as sample interview questions and potential responses..

The *Prologue and Epilogue* offer students tips for succeeding in college, as well as in the workforce.

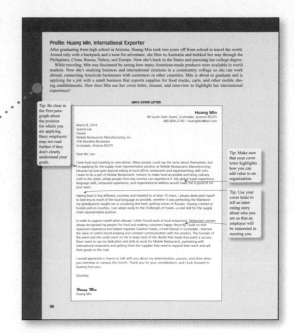

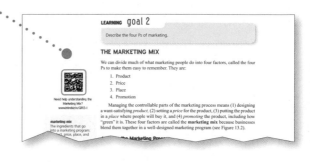

progress assessment

- What led to the emergence of socialism?
- What are the benefits and drawbacks of socialism?
- What countries still practice communism?
- What are the characteristics of a mixed economy?

Progress Assessments help students understand and retain the material in the chapters. Progress Assessment questions stop them at important points in the chapter to assess what they've learned before they continue reading.

New to this Edition! iSee It! Videos are provided in select chapters to point students to 90-second animated video clips designed to further explain key concepts by using memorable, relatable examples.

NEW to This Edition! **Connecting Through Social Media** boxes ask students to consider the impact social media have on the way they communicate and the way companies conduct business as a result. . . . .

Making the Green Connection boxes highlight corporate responsibility and help students understand the various ways business activities affect the environment. . . . .

Connecting with Small Business boxes feature how the concepts in the chapter relate to small businesses. . . . .

Connecting Across Borders boxes focus on global issues surrounding business. . . . .

Making Ethical Decisions boxes offer students ethical dilemmas to consider. . . . .

CONNECTING TO INSTRUCTORS THROUGH PREMIUM RESOURCES

Connect offers instructors auto-gradable material in an effort to facilitate learning and save time.

Student Progress Tracking

Connect keeps instructors informed about how each student, section, and class is performing, allowing for more productive use of lecture and office hours. The progress-tracking function enables instructors to:

- View scored work immediately and track individual or group performance with assignment and grade reports.
- Access an instant view of student or class performance relative to learning objectives.
- Collect data and generate reports required by many accreditation organizations, such as AACSB.

Online Learning Center for Instructors www.mhhe.com/P2P2e

The Online Learning Center offers instructors a one-stop, secure site for essential course materials, allowing instructors to save prep time before class. The instructor site offers:

- Instructor's Manual—The authors have carefully reviewed all resources provided in the Instructor's Manual to ensure cohesion with the text. The Instructor's Manual contains everything an instructor needs to prepare a lecture, including lecture outlines, discussion questions, and teaching notes. An Instructor's CD is also available.
- *Connect* Instructor's Manual—This Instructor's Manual offers instructors what they need to set up *Connect* for their courses. It explains everything from how to get started to suggestions of what to assign and ideas about assigning credit. This tool was developed by instructors who have used and continue to use *Connect* successfully in their courses. This Instructor's Manual can be found in *Connect*, on the Instructor's Resource CD, and on the OLC.
- PowerPoint® Presentations—More than 900 PowerPoint slides offer material from the text, as well as expanded coverage to supplement discussion. These slides offer useful teaching notes and feature new examples not offered in the text as designated by use of a purple background.
- Test Bank/EZ Test—The Test Bank and Computerized Test Bank offer over 8,000 multiple-choice, true/false, short answer, essay, and application questions.

- Videos/DVD—Chapter-specific videos are provided to complement each chapter of the text. Eleven of the 20 videos have been updated to include interesting companies that students will identify with such as Redbox, Zappos, and Groupon.
- Video Guide—This guide (available on the Online Learning Center) includes detailed teaching notes to accompany the chapter videos, as well as essay-style and multiple-choice questions.
- Monthly Newsletters—Each month, instructors using *Business: Connecting Principles to Practice* receive a newsletter that includes many of the hottest topics in business today. Each newsletter contains 10 or more abstracts of current business articles and videos along with discussion questions and answers, and a chart that identifies the chapters the material complements.

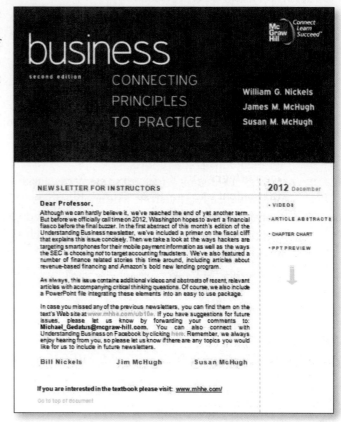

business
second edition

CONNECTING
PRINCIPLES
TO PRACTICE

McGraw Hill — Connect Learn Succeed

William G. Nickels
James M. McHugh
Susan M. McHugh

NEWSLETTER FOR INSTRUCTORS   2012 December

Dear Professor,

Although we can hardly believe it, we've reached the end of yet another term. But before we officially call time on 2012, Washington hopes to avert a financial fiasco before the final buzzer. In the first abstract of this month's edition of the Understanding Business newsletter, we've included a primer on the fiscal cliff that explains this issue concisely. Then we take a look at the ways hackers are targeting smartphones for their mobile payment information as well as the ways the SEC is choosing not to target accounting fraudsters. We've also featured a number of finance related stories this time around, including articles about revenue-based financing and Amazon's bold new lending program.

As always, this issue contains additional videos and abstracts of recent, relevant articles with accompanying critical thinking questions. Of course, we also include a PowerPoint file integrating these elements into an easy to use package.

In case you missed any of the previous newsletters, you can find them on the text's Web site at www.mhhe.com/ub10e. If you have suggestions for future issues, please let us know by forwarding your comments to: Michael_Gedatus@mcgraw-hill.com. You can also connect with Understanding Business on Facebook by clicking here. Remember, we always enjoy hearing from you, so please let us know if there are any topics you would like for us to include in future newsletters.

Bill Nickels   Jim McHugh   Susan McHugh

If you are interested in the textbook please visit: www.mhhe.com/

Go to top of document

- VIDEOS
- ARTICLE ABSTRACTS
- CHAPTER CHART
- PPT PREVIEW

TEACHING OPTIONS AND SOLUTIONS

The Best of Both Worlds

McGraw-Hill Higher Education and Blackboard have teamed up. What does this mean for you?

1. **Your life, simplified. Single Sign-On:** A single login and single environment provide seamless access to all course resources—all McGraw-Hill's resources are available within the Blackboard Learn platform.

2. **Deep integration of content and tools. Deep Integration:** One-click access to a wealth of McGraw-Hill content and tools—all from within Blackboard Learn.™

3. **Seamless Gradebooks. One Gradebook:** Automatic grade synchronization with Blackboard gradebook. All grades for McGraw-Hill *Connect* assignments are recorded in the Blackboard gradebook automatically.

4. **A solution for everyone. Openness:** Unique in higher education, the partnership of McGraw-Hill Higher Education and Blackboard preserves the spirit of academic freedom and openness. Blackboard remains publisher independent, and McGraw-Hill remains LMS independent. The result makes our content, engines, and platform more usable and accessible, with fewer barriers to adoption and use.

5. **100% FERPA-**compliant solution protects student privacy.

6. **McGraw-Hill and Blackboard** can now offer you easy access to industry-leading technology and content, whether your campus hosts it, or we do. Be sure to ask your local McGraw-Hill representative for details.

McGraw-Hill reinvents the textbook-learning experience for today's students with *Connect Plus Business*. A seamless integration of an eBook and *Connect* provides all of the *Connect* features plus the following:

- An integrated eBook, allowing for anytime, anywhere online access to the textbook.
- Dynamic links between the problems or questions assigned to students and the location in the eBook where that problem or question is covered.
- Powerful search function to pinpoint and connect key concepts in a snap.

For more information about *Connect*, go to connect.mcgraw-hill.com, or contact your local McGraw-Hill sales representative.

CourseSmart

CourseSmart is a new way for faculty to find and review eTextbooks. It's also a great option for students who are interested in accessing their course materials digitally, and saving money.

CourseSmart offers thousands of the most commonly adopted textbooks across hundreds of courses from a wide variety of higher education publishers. It is the only place for faculty to review and compare the full text of a textbook online, providing immediate access without the environmental impact of requesting a print exam copy.

With the CourseSmart eTextbook, students can save up to 45 percent off the cost of a printed book, reduce their impact on the environment, and access powerful web tools for learning. CourseSmart is an online eTextbook, which means users access and view their textbook online when connected to the Internet. Students can also print sections of the book for maximum portability. CourseSmart eTextbooks are available in one standard online reader with full text search, notes, and highlighting, and e-mail tools for sharing notes between classmates. For more information on CourseSmart, go to **http://www.coursesmart.com.**

 Instructors can now tailor their teaching resources to match the way they teach! With McGraw-Hill Create, **www.mcgrawhillcreate.com,** instructors can easily rearrange chapters, combine material from other content sources, and quickly upload and integrate their own content, like course syllabi or teaching notes. Find the right content in Create by searching through thousands of leading McGraw-Hill textbooks. Arrange the material to fit your teaching style. Order a Create book and receive a complimentary print review copy in 3–5 business days or a complimentary electronic review copy (eComp) via e-mail within one hour. Go to **www.mcgrawhillcreate.com** today and register.

 Tegrity Campus is a service that makes class time available 24/7 by automatically capturing every lecture in a searchable format for students to review when they study and complete assignments. With a simple one-click start-and-stop process, you capture all computer screens and corresponding audio. Students can replay any part of any class with easy-to-use browser-based viewing on a PC or Mac.

Educators know that the more students can see, hear, and experience class resources, the better they learn. In fact, studies prove it. With patented Tegrity "search anything" technology, students instantly recall key class moments for replay online, or on iPods® and mobile devices. Instructors can help turn all their students' study time into learning moments immediately supported by their lecture.

To learn more about Tegrity watch a 2-minute Flash demo at **http://tegritycampus.mhhe.com.**

Assurance of Learning Ready

Many educational institutions today are focused on the notion of *assurance of learning,* an important element of some accreditation standards. *Business: Connecting Principles to Practice* is designed specifically to support instructors' assurance of learning initiatives with a simple, yet powerful solution.

Each test bank question for *Business: Connecting Principles to Practice* maps to a specific chapter learning outcome/objective listed in the text. Instructors can use our test bank software, EZ Test and EZ Test Online, to easily query for learning outcomes/objectives that directly relate to the learning objectives for their course. Instructors can then use the reporting features of EZ Test to aggregate student results in similar fashion, making the collection and presentation of assurance of learning data simple and easy.

 The McGraw-Hill Companies is a proud corporate member of AACSB International. Understanding the importance and value of AACSB accreditation, *Business: Connecting Principles to Practice* recognizes the curricula guidelines detailed in the AACSB standards for business accreditation by connecting selected questions in the text and the test bank to the six general knowledge and skill guidelines in the AACSB standards.

The statements contained in *Business: Connecting Principles to Practice* are provided only as a guide for the users of this textbook. The AACSB leaves content coverage and assessment within the purview of individual schools, the mission of the school, and the faculty. While the *Business: Connecting Principles to Practice* teaching package makes no claim of any specific AACSB qualification or evaluation, we have within *Business: Connecting Principles to Practice* labeled selected questions according to the six general knowledge and skills areas.

McGraw-Hill Customer Experience Group Contact Information

At McGraw-Hill, we understand that getting the most from new technology can be challenging. That's why our services don't stop after you purchase our products. You can e-mail our Product Specialists 24 hours a day to get product training online. Or you can search our knowledge bank of Frequently Asked Questions on our support website. For Customer Support, call **800-331-5094,** e-mail **hmsupport@mcgraw-hill.com**, or visit **www.mhhe.com/support**. One of our Technical Support Analysts will be able to assist you in a timely fashion.

acknowledgments

Our editorial director, Paul Ducham and our senior brand manager, Anke Weekes, led the talented team at Irwin/McGraw-Hill. We appreciate their dedication to the success of the project and their responsiveness to the demands of the market. Kelly Delso served as our developmental editor and kept everyone on task and on schedule. Michael McHugh contributed the engaging new boxes and profiles. Lindsay Toler developed the creative new Career Outlook sections at the end of each Part. Sharon Cannon of UNC Kengan-Flagler shared her expertise by editing these career sections. Michael Hannon provided much-appreciated research assistance. Matt Baldwin created the new fresh, open interior design and extraordinary cover. Jeremy Cheshareck and Jen Blankenship carried out the extensive research for photos that was necessary to effectively reflect the concepts presented in the text. Lead project manager, Christine Vaughan, did a splendid job of keeping the production of the text on schedule. Brian Nacik expertly supervised the supplements and media assets and Chris Nowack assisted in the delivery of *Connect* materials. Becky Komro's remarkable attention to detail as she proofread our "final revised" pages amazed us.

Many dedicated educators made extraordinary contributions to the quality and utility of this text and package. For this edition, Molly McHugh did an exceptional job in preparing the Test Bank and creating the quizzes for the Online Learning Center and *Connect*. Molly also did a superb job of creating the PowerPoint slides and worked to provide a useful and current Instructor's Resource Manual. A special thanks to Robin James of Harper College for her work on selecting the Student PowerPoints. We also recognize the efforts of Tim Rogers at Ozarks Technical Community College, Barbara Barrett of St. Louis Community College, Donna Haeger of Monroe Community College, John Striebich of Monroe Community College, Grace McLaughlin of University of California, Irvine, Colette Wolfson of Ivy Tech Community College of Indiana, and Linda Hoffman of Ivy Tech Community College of Indiana who contributed to the creation of *Connect* materials, and to our LearnSmart "team" at Monroe Community College, Judy Bulin John Striebich, and Donna Haeger, who tirelessly worked to review and perfect LearnSmart content. Thank you to Len Davis, Kelly Yee, and the crew of Pure Imagination for the fabulous new videos they produced. We'd also like to thank Kelly Luchtman at Lightfellow for providing two new videos to accompany this edition. We'd also like to thank Anthony Chelte of University of Arkansas, Little Rock, for his work in revising the Video Guide for this edition. Thank you to Donna Haeger at Monroe Community College, Tim Rogers at Ozarks Technical Community College, and Robin James at Harper College for their work in authoring the *Connect* Instructor's Manual. Thank you to the Digital Faculty Consultants who have helped to train and support so many instructors in the Introduction to Business course, as well as assist them in successfully implementing *Connect* into their courses: Chris Finnin, Drexel University; Julie Hansen, Grossmont College; Todd Korol, Monroe Community College; John Striebich, Monroe Community College; and Marie Lapidus, Oakton Community College.

Our outstanding marketing manager, Michael Gedatus was up to the challenge of keeping us connected with instructors, students, and sales reps. We appreciate his commitment and the renowned product knowledge, service, and dedication of the McGraw-Hill/Irwin sales reps. We want to thank the many instructors who contributed to the development of *Business: Connecting Principles to Practice.*

REVIEWERS

We would also like to thank those who reviewed the First Edition, as well as the new features in the current edition.

Chi Anyansi-Archibong, *North Carolina A&T State University*

Lisa Augustyniak, *Lake Michigan College*

Deborah Barbe, *Nunez Community College*

Patricia Beckenholdt, *University of Maryland University College*

Fred Bounds, *Georgia Perimeter College*

Harry Dalmaso, *Onondaga Community College*

Donna Davisson, *Cleveland State University*

Carole Hollingsworth, *Georgia Perimeter College*

Mary Carole Hollingsworth, *Georgia Perimeter College*

Ralph Jagodka, *Mt. San Antonio College*

Janice Karlen, *LaGuardia Community College*

Tom McFarland, *Mt. San Antonio College*

Christopher C. O'Suanah, *J. Sargeant Reynolds Community College and University of Phoenix*

Anne Payne, *Hartwick College*

Sandra Robertson, *Thomas Nelson Community College*

Ingrid Sellers, *Georgia Perimeter College*

Sally Wells, *Columbia College*

Joe Zwiller, *Lake Michigan College*

We would like to thank the following instructors for sharing their opinions with us in an effort to improve the previous edition:

Nikolas Adamou, *Borough of Manhattan Community College*

Cathy Adamson, *Southern Union State Community College*

Ashraf Almurdaah, *Los Angeles City College*

Gary Amundson, *Montana State University–Billings*

Kenneth Anderson, *Mott Community College*

Kenneth Anderson, *Borough of Manhattan Community College*

Lydia Anderson, *Fresno City College*

Narita Anderson, *University of Central Oklahoma*

Roanne Angiello, *Bergen Community College*

Chi Anyansi-Archibong, *North Carolina A&T State University*

Maria Aria, *Camden County College*

Michael Atchison, *University of Virginia–Charlottesville*

Michael Aubry, *Cuyamaca College*

Andrea Bailey, *Moraine Valley Community College*

Sandra Bailey, *Ivy Tech Community College of Indiana*

Scott Bailey, *Troy University*

Wayne Ballantine, *Prairie View A&M University*

Frank Barber, *Cuyahoga Community College*

Ruby Barker, *Tarleton State University*

Rosalia (Lia) Barone, *Norwalk Community College*

Barbara Barrett, *St. Louis Community College–Meramec*

Barry Barrett, *University of Wisconsin–Milwaukee*

Richard Bartlett, *Columbus State Community College*

Lorraine Bassette, *Prince George's Community College*

Robb Bay, *College of Southern Nevada–West Charleston*

Jim Beard, *University of Arkansas–Fort Smith*

Amy Beattie, *Champlain College*

Charles Beavin, *Miami Dade College North*

Charles Beem, *Bucks County Community College*

Cathleen Behan, *Northern Virginia Community College*

Lori Bennett, *Moorpark College*

Robert Bennett, *Delaware County Community College*

Ellen Benowitz, *Mercer Community College*

Michael Bento, *Owens Community College*

George H. Bernard, *Seminole State College of Florida*

Patricia Bernson, *County College of Morris*

Marilyn Besich, *Montana State University–Great Falls*

William Bettencourt, *Edmonds Community College*

Robert Blanchard, *Salem State College*

Mary Jo Boehms, *Jackson State Community College*

James Borden, *Villanova University*

Michael Bravo, *Bentley College*

Dennis Brode, *Sinclair Community College*

Kathy Broneck, *Pima Community College*

Harvey Bronstein, *Oakland Community College–Farmington Hills*

Colin Brooks, *University of New Orleans*

Deborah Brown, *North Carolina State University–Raleigh*

Aaron A. Buchko, *Bradley University*

Jerri Buiting, *Baker College–Flint*

Laura Bulas, *Central Community College–Hastings*

Judy Bulin, *Monroe Community College*

Barry Bunn, *Valencia Community College–West Campus*

Bill Burton, *Indiana Wesleyan University*

Paul Callahan, *Cincinnati State Technical and Community College*

William Candley, *Lemoyne Owen College*

Nancy Carr, *Community College of Philadelphia*

Ron Cereola, *James Madison University*

Bonnie Chavez, *Santa Barbara City College*

Susan Cisco, *Oakton Community College*

Margaret (Meg) Clark, *Cincinnati State Technical and Community College*

Savannah Clay, *Central Piedmont Community College*

David Clifton, *Ivy Tech Community College of Indiana*

C. Cloud, *Phoenix College*

Paul Coakley, *Community College of Baltimore County*

Doug Cobbs, *JS Reynolds Community College*

Debbie Collins, *Anne Arundel Community College*

Patrick Conroy, *Delgado Community College*

Andrew Cook, *Limestone College*

Bob Cox, *Salt Lake Community College*

Susan Cremins, *Westchester Community College*

Julie Cross, *Chippewa Valley Tech College*

Geoffrey Crosslin, *Kalamazoo Valley Community College*

Douglas Crowe, *Bradley University*

James Darling, *Central New Mexico Community College*

John David, *Stark State College of Technology*

Peter Dawson, *Collin County Community College*

Joseph Defilippe, *Suffolk County Community College–Brentwood*

Tim DeGroot, *Midwestern State University*

Len Denault, *Bentley College*

Frances Depaul, *Westmoreland County Community College*

Donna Devault, *Fayetteville Tech Community College*

Sharon Dexter, *Southeast Community College–Beatrice*

John Dilyard, *St. Francis College*

Barbara Dinardo, *Owens Community College*

George Dollar, *St. Petersburg College*

Glenn Doolittle, *Santa Ana College*

Ron Dougherty, *Ivy Tech Community College of Indiana*

Michael Drafke, *College of DuPage*

Joseph Dutka, *Ivy Tech Community College of Indiana*

Karen Eboch, *Bowling Green State University*

Brenda Eichelberger, *Portland State University*

Kelvin Elston, *Nashville State Tech Community College*

Robert Ettl, *Stony Brook University*

Nancy Evans, *Heartland Community College*

Michael Ewens, *Ventura College*

Hyacinth Ezeka, *Coppin State University*

Bob Farris, *Mt. San Antonio College*

Karen Faulkner, *Long Beach City College*

Gil Feiertag, *Columbus State Community College*

Joseph Flack, *Washtenaw Community College*

Lucinda Fleming, *Orange County Community College*

Jackie Flom, *University of Toledo*

Andrea Foster, *John Tyler Community College*

Michael Foster, *Bentley College*

Leatrice Freer, *Pitt Community College*

Alan Friedenthal, *Kingsborough Community College*

MaryBeth Furst, *Howard Community College*

Charles Gaiser, *Brunswick Community College*

Wayne Gawlik, *Joliet Junior College*

Ashley Geisewite, *Southwest Tennessee Community College*

Katie Ghahramani, *Johnson County Community College*

Debora Gilliard, *Metropolitan State College–Denver*

Ross Gittell, *University of New Hampshire*

James Glover, *Community College of Baltimore County–Essex*

Constance Golden, *Lakeland Community College*

Doug Greiner, *University of Toledo–Scott Park*

Toby Grodner, *Union County College*

John Guess, *Delgado Community College*

Lisa E. Hadley, *Southwest Tennessee Community College*

Clark Hallpike, *Elgin Community College*

Geri Harper, *Western Illinois University*

Frank Hatstat, *Bellevue Community College*

Spedden Hause, *University of Maryland–University College*

Karen Hawkins, *Miami-Dade College–Kendall*

Travis Hayes, *Chattanooga State Technical Community College*

Jack Heinsius, *Modesto Junior College*

Charlane Held, *Onondaga Community College*

Nancy Hernandez, *Howard College*

James Hess, *Ivy Tech Community College of Indiana*

Steve Hester, *Southwest Tennessee Community College–Macon Campus*

William Hill, *Mississippi State University*

Nathan Himelstein, *Essex County College*

Paula Hladik, *Waubonsee Community College*

David Ho, *Metropolitan Community College*

Douglas Hobbs, *Sussex County Community College*

Maryanne Holcomb, *Antelope Valley College*

Mary Carole Hollingsworth, *Georgia Perimeter College*

Russell Holmes, *Des Moines Area Community College*

Scott Homan, *Purdue University–West Lafayette*

Stacy Horner, *Southwestern Michigan College*

Dennis Hudson, *University of Tulsa*

Jo Ann Hunter, *Community College Allegheny County in Pittsburgh*

Kimberly Hurns, *Washtenaw Community College*

Victor Isbell, *University of Nevada–Las Vegas*

Deloris James, *University of Maryland–University College*

Pam Janson, *Stark State College of Technology*

William Jedlicka, *Harper College*

Carol Johnson, *University of Denver*

Gwendolyn Jones, *University of Akron*

Kenneth Jones, *Ivy Tech Community College of Indiana*

Marilyn Jones, *Friends University*

Michael Jones, *Delgado Community College*

Dmitriy Kalyagin, *Chabot College*

Jack Kant, *San Juan College*

Janice Karlen, *La Guardia Community College*

Jimmy Kelsey, *Seattle Central Community College*

Robert Kemp, *University of Virginia–Charlottesville*

David Kendall, *Fashion Institute of Technology*

Kristine Kinard, *Shelton State Community College*

Sandra King, *Minnesota State University–Mankato*

John Kurnik, *Saint Petersburg College*

Jeff LaVake, *University of Wisconsin–Oshkosh*

Robert Lewis, *Davenport University*

Byron Lilly, *DeAnza College*

Beverly Loach, *Central Piedmont Community College*

Boone Londrigan, *Mott Community College*

Ladonna Love, *Fashion Institute of Technology*

Ivan Lowe, *York Technical College*

Yvonne Lucas, *Southwestern College*

Robert Lupton, *Central Washington University*

Megan Luttenton, *Grand Valley State University*

Elaine Madden, *Anne Arundel Community College*

Lawrence Maes, *Davenport University*

Niki Maglaris, *Northwestern College*

James Maniki, *Northwestern College*

James W. Marco, *Wake Technical Community College*

Martin Markowitz, *College of Charleston*

Theresa Mastrianni, *Kingsborough Community College*

Fred Mayerson, *Kingsborough Community College*

Stacy McCaskill, *Rock Valley College*

Vershun L. McClain, *Jackson State University*

Gina McConoughey, *Illinois Central College*

Patricia McDaniel, *Central Piedmont Community College*

Pam McElligott, *St. Louis Community College–Meramec*

Tom McFarland, *Mt. San Antonio College*

Bill McPherson, *Indiana University of Pennsylvania*

Michelle Meyer, *Joliet Junior College*

Catherine Milburn, *University of Colorado–Denver*

Ginger Moore, *York Technical College*

Sandy Moore, *Ivy Tech Community College of Indiana*

Jennifer Morton, *Ivy Tech Community College of Indiana*

Peter Moutsatson, *Central Michigan University*

Rachna Nagi-Condos, *American River College*

Darrell Neron, *Pierce College*

Mihia Nica, *University of Central Oklahoma*

Charles Nichols, *Sullivan University*

Frank Novakowski, *Davenport University*

Mark Nygren, *Brigham Young University–Idaho*

Paul Okello, *Tarrant County College*

David Oliver, *Edison Community College*

Faviana Olivier, *Bentley College*

John Olivo, *Bloomsburg University of Pennsylvania*

Teresa O'Neill, *International Institute of the Americas*

Cathy Onion, *Western Illinois University*

Susan Ontko, *Schoolcraft College*

Glenda Orosco, *Oklahoma State University Institute of Technology*

Christopher O'Suanah, *J. Sargeant. Reynolds Community College*

Daniel Pacheco, *Kansas City Kansas Community College*

Esther Page-Wood, *Western Michigan University*

Lauren Paisley, *Genesee Community College*

John Pappalardo, *Keene State College*

Ron Pardee, *Riverside Community College*

Jack Partlow, *Northern Virginia Community College*

Dyan Pease, *Sacramento City College*

Jeff Pepper, *Chippewa Valley Tech College*

Sheila Petcavage, *Cuyahoga Community College Western–Parma*

Roy Pipitone, *Erie Community College*

Lana Powell, *Valencia Community College–West Campus*

Dan Powroznik, *Chesapeake College*

Litsa Press, *College of Lake County*

Sally Proffitt, *Tarrant County College–Northeast*

Vincent Quan, *Fashion Institute of Technology*

Michael Quinn, *James Madison University*

Anthony Racka, *Oakland Community College*

Larry Ramos, *Miami-Dade Community College*

Greg Rapp, *Portland Community College–Sylvania*

Robert Reese, *Illinois Valley Community College*

David Reiman, *Monroe County Community College*

Gloria Rembert, *Mitchell Community College*

Levi Richard, *Citrus College*

Clinton Richards, *University of Nevada–Las Vegas*

Patricia Richards, *Westchester Community College*

Susan Roach, *Georgia Southern University*

Sandra Robertson, *Thomas Nelson Community College*

David Robinson, *University of California–Berkeley*

Catherine Roche, *Rockland Community College*

Tim Rogers, *Ozark Technical College*

Sam Rohr, *University of Northwestern Ohio*

Pamela Rouse, *Butler University*

Carol Rowey, *Community College of Rhode Island*

Jeri Rubin, *University of Alaska–Anchorage*

Storm Russo, *Valencia Community College*

Mark Ryan, *Hawkeye Community College*

Richard Sarkisian, *Camden County College*

Andy Saucedo, *Dona Ana Community College–Las Cruces*

James Scott, *Central Michigan University*

Janet Seggern, *Lehigh Carbon Community College*

Sashi Sekhar, *Purdue University–Calumet-Hammond*

Pat Setlik, *Harper College*

Swannee Sexton, *University of Tennessee–Knoxville*

Phyllis Shafer, *Brookdale Community College*

Richard Shortridge, *Glendale Community College*

Rieann Spence-Gale, *Nova Community College*

Louise Stephens, *Volunteer State Community College*

Desiree Stephens, *Norwalk Community College*

Clifford Stalter, *Chattanooga State Technical Community College*

Kurt Stanberry, *University of Houston–Downtown*

Martin St. John, *Westmoreland County Community College*

John Striebich, *Monroe Community College*

David Stringer, *DeAnza College*

Ron Surmacz, *Duquesne University*

William Syvertsen, *Fresno City College*

Scott Taylor, *Moberly Area Community College*

Marguerite Teubner, *Nassau Community College*

Rod Thirion, *Pikes Peak Community College*

Jim Thomas, *Indiana University Northwest*

Deborah Thompson, *Bentley College*

Evelyn Thrasher, *University of Massachusetts–Dartmouth*

Jon Tomlinson, *University of Northwestern Ohio*

Bob Trewartha, *Minnesota School of Business*

Bob Urell, *Irvine Valley College*

Dan Vetter, *Central Michigan University*

Andrea Vidrine, *Baton Rouge Community College*

Daniel Viveiros, *Johnson & Wales University*

William J. Wardrope, *University of Central Oklahoma*

Joann Warren, *Community College of Rhode Island–Warwick*

David Washington, *North Carolina State University*

R. Patrick Wehner, *Everest University*

Sally Wells, *Columbia College*

Mildred Wilson, *Georgia Southern University*

Karen Wisniewski, *County College of Morris*

Greg Witkowski, *Northwestern College*

Colette Wolfson, *Ivy Tech Community College of Indiana*

Deborah Yancey, *Virginia Western Community College*

Mark Zarycki, *Hillsborough Community College*

Lisa Zingaro, *Oakton Community College*

Mark Zorn, *Butler County Community College*

This edition continues to improve due to the involvement of these committed instructors and students. We thank them all for their help, support, and friendship.

Bill Nickels   Jim McHugh   Susan McHugh

brief
CONTENTS

Prologue: Getting Ready for This Course and Your Career   P-1

part 1

Business Trends: Cultivating a Business in Diverse, Global Environments

1 Connecting to the Dynamic Business Environment 2
2 Understanding Economics and How It Affects Business 28
3 Doing Business in Global Markets 58
4 Demanding Ethical and Socially Responsible Behavior 88

Career Outlook: Part 1 Conclusion–Business Trends

part 2

Business Ownership: Starting a Small Business

5 How to Form a Business 120
6 Entrepreneurship and Starting a Small Business 152

Career Outlook: Part 2 Conclusion–Business Ownership

part 3

Business Management: Empowering Employees to Satisfy Customers

7 Management and Leadership 190
8 Structuring Organizations for Today's Challenges 214
9 Production and Operations Management 244

Career Outlook: Part 3 Conclusion–Business Management

part 4

Management of Human Resources: Motivating Employees to Produce Quality Goods and Services

10 Motivating Employees 276
11 Human Resource Management: Finding and Keeping the Best Employees 306
12 Dealing with Union and Employee–Management Issues 340

Career Outlook: Part 4 Conclusion–Management of Human Resources

part 5

Marketing: Developing and Implementing Customer-Oriented Marketing Plans

13 Marketing: Helping Buyers Buy 374
14 Developing and Pricing Goods and Services 402
15 Distributing Products 432
16 Using Effective Promotions 462

Career Outlook: Part 5 Conclusion–Marketing

part 6

Managing Financial Resources

17 Understanding Accounting and Financial Information 496
18 Financial Management 526
19 Using Securities Markets for Financing and Investing Opportunities 554
20 Money, Financial Institutions, and the Federal Reserve 586

Career Outlook: Part 6 Conclusion–Financial Management

Appendixes

1 Working within the Legal Environment A1
2 Managing Personal Finances A2

Epilogue: Getting the Job You Want   E

Bonus Chapters (Online Olny)

A Using Technology to Manage Information
B Managing Risk

Chapter Notes N

Glossary G-1

Photo Credits PC-1

Name Index I-1

Organization Index I-8

Subject Index I-12

contents

Prologue: Getting Ready for This Course and Your Career P-1

part 1
Business Trends: Cultivating a Business in Diverse, Global Environments

Chapter One

2 Connecting to the Dynamic Business Environment

Profile: Connecting with Terry Pham, Founder of Fat Straws   3

Entrepreneurship and Wealth Building   4

Revenues, Profits, and Losses   4

Matching Risk with Profit   5

Standard of Living and Quality of Life   5

Responding to the Various Business Stakeholders   6

Using Business Principles in Nonprofit Organizations   7

Entrepreneurship versus Working for Others   8

Opportunities for Entrepreneurs   8

Connecting with Small Business: Making the Most of a Stinky Situation   9

The Importance of Entrepreneurs to the Creation of Wealth   9

The Business Environment   11

The Economic and Legal Environment   12

Making Ethical Decisions: Ethics Begins with You   13

Connecting Through Social Media: Using Smartphones to Connect with Customers   14

The Technological Environment   14

The Competitive Environment   16

The Social Environment   17

The Global Environment   18

Making the Green Connection: Green Up Your Life   20

The Evolution of U.S. Business   20

Progress in the Agricultural and Manufacturing Industries   20

Progress in Service Industries   21

Your Future in Business   21

Video Case: Redbox Focusing on Customer Needs   26

Chapter Two

28 Understanding Economics and How It Affects Business

Profile: Connecting with Steven Levitt and Stephen Dubner, Authors of *Freakonomics*   29

How Economic Conditions Affect Businesses   30

What Is Economics?   30

The Secret to Creating a Wealthy Economy   31

Making the Green Connection: It's Not Always Greener   32

Adam Smith and the Creation of Wealth   33

How Businesses Benefit the Community   33

Making Ethical Decisions: How Corruption Harms the Economy   34

Understanding Free-Market Capitalism   34

The Foundations of Capitalism   35

Connecting with Small Business: Small Loan, Big Opportunity   36

How Free Markets Work   36

How Prices Are Determined   37

The Economic Concept of Supply   37

The Economic Concept of Demand   37

The Equilibrium Point, or Market Price   37

Competition within Free Markets   39

Benefits and Limitations of Free Markets   40

Understanding Socialism   41

The Benefits of Socialism   41

The Negative Consequences of Socialism   42

Understanding Communism   42

The Trend toward Mixed Economies   43

Connecting Across Borders: Africa's Evolving Economy   44

Understanding the U.S. Economic System 46

Key Economic Indicators 46

Productivity in the United States 48

Productivity in the Service Sector 48

The Business Cycle 49

Stabilizing the Economy through Fiscal Policy 50

Fiscal Policy in Action during the Economic Crisis That Began in 2008 51

Using Monetary Policy to Keep the Economy Growing 51

Video Case: Opportunity International: Giving the Poor a Working Chance 56

Chapter Three

58 Doing Business in Global Markets

Profile: Connecting with Bill Johnson, President and CEO of Heinz 59

The Dynamic Global Market 60

Why Trade with Other Nations? 61

The Theories of Comparative and Absolute Advantage 62

Getting Involved in Global Trade 63

Importing Goods and Services 63

Exporting Goods and Services 63

Connecting with Small Business: Improving Sight through Entrepreneurship 64

Measuring Global Trade 64

Strategies for Reaching Global Markets 66

Licensing 66

Exporting 68

Franchising 68

Contract Manufacturing 68

Connecting Across Borders: McDonald's: Over 100 Cultures Served 69

International Joint Ventures and Strategic Alliances 70

Foreign Direct Investment 70

Forces Affecting Trading in Global Markets 72

Sociocultural Forces 72

Economic and Financial Forces 73

Legal and Regulatory Forces 75

Physical and Environmental Forces 75

Trade Protectionism 76

The World Trade Organization 77

Common Markets 77

The North American and Central American Free Trade Agreements 79

The Future of Global Trade 80

The Challenge of Offshore Outsourcing 81

Globalization and Your Future 82

Making Ethical Decisions: Need an Operation? Take a Vacation 83

Video Case: CH2M Hill: A Global Company 87

Chapter Four

88 Demanding Ethical and Socially Responsible Behavior

Profile: Connecting with Brenda Palms Barber, CEO of Sweet Beginnings 89

Ethics Is More Than Legality 90

Making Ethical Decisions: Cost of Corruption 91

Ethical Standards Are Fundamental 92

Ethics Begins with Each of Us 92

Connecting Through Social Media: Facebook or Fakebook? 93

Managing Businesses Ethically and Responsibly 94

Setting Corporate Ethical Standards 96

Corporate Social Responsibility 98

Responsibility to Customers 100

Responsibility to Investors 101

Responsibility to Employees 102

Responsibility to Society and the Environment 103

Making the Green Connection: Who's the Greenest of Them All? 104

Social Auditing 104

International Ethics and Social Responsibility 106

Connecting Across Borders: When a House Is Not a Home 108

Video Case: Going Beyond Legality 112

Career Outlook: Part 1 Conclusion—Business Trends

part 2

Business Ownership: Starting a Small Business

Chapter Five

120 How to Form a Business

Profile: Connecting with David Overton, CEO of The Cheesecake Factory 121

Basic Forms of Business Ownership 122

Sole Proprietorships 123

Advantages of Sole Proprietorships 123

Disadvantages of Sole Proprietorships 124

Partnerships 125

Advantages of Partnerships 126

Disadvantages of Partnerships 127

Making Ethical Decisions: Good Business, Bad Karma? 128

Corporations 129

Advantages of Corporations   129

Disadvantages of Corporations   131

Individuals Can Incorporate   132

S Corporations   133

Limited Liability Companies   134

Corporate Expansion: Mergers and Acquisitions   136

Franchises   138

Advantages of Franchises   140

Disadvantages of Franchises   140

Connecting with Small Business: Keeping Franchises in the Family   142

Diversity in Franchising   142

Home-Based Franchises   143

E-Commerce in Franchising   143

Using Technology in Franchising   144

Franchising in Global Markets   144

Connecting Through Social Media: From Facebook Friends to Franchisees   145

Cooperatives   146

Which Form of Ownership Is for You?   146

Video Case: PODS: The Evolution of a Small Business   151

Chapter Six

152   Entrepreneurship and Starting a Small Business

Profile: Connecting with Aviva Weiss, Co-Founder of Fun and Function   153

The Age of the Entrepreneur   154

The Job-Creating Power of Entrepreneurs in the United States   154

Connecting with Small Business: Business Has No Age Limit   155

Why People Take the Entrepreneurial Challenge   156

What Does It Take to Be an Entrepreneur?   156

Turning Your Passions and Problems into Opportunities   157

Entrepreneurial Teams   158

Micropreneurs and Home-Based Businesses   158

Web-Based Businesses   161

Entrepreneurship within Firms   163

Encouraging Entrepreneurship: What Government Can Do   163

Getting Started in Small Business   164

Small versus Big Business   165

Importance of Small Businesses   165

Small-Business Success and Failure   166

Learning about Small-Business Operations   167

Learn from Others   167

Get Some Experience   167

Making Ethical Decisions: Should You Stay or Should You Go?   168

Take Over a Successful Firm   168

Managing a Small Business   169

Begin with Planning   169

Writing a Business Plan   170

Getting Money to Fund a Small Business   170

Connecting Through Social Media: Peer-to-Peer Lending   173

The Small Business Administration (SBA)   173

Making the Green Connection: Going Locavore   175

Knowing Your Customers   175

Managing Employees   176

Keeping Records   176

Looking for Help   176

Going Global: Small-Business Prospects   178

Video Case: Launching a Business: Pillow Pets   182

Career Outlook: Part 2 Conclusion—Business Ownership

part 3

Business Management: Empowering Employees to Satisfy Customers

Chapter Seven

190   Management and Leadership

Profile: Connecting with Kathy Ireland, CEO of Kathy Ireland Worldwide   191

Managers' Roles Are Evolving   192

The Four Functions of Management   193

Planning and Decision Making   195

Decision Making: Finding the Best Alternative   198

Organizing: Creating a Unified System   199

Connecting Across Borders: Breaking the Language Barrier   201

Tasks and Skills at Different Levels of Management   201

Staffing: Getting and Keeping the Right People   202

Leading: Providing Continuous Vision and Values   203

Making Ethical Decisions: To Share or Not to Share   204

Leadership Styles   204

Connecting Through Social Media: Caring for Customers by Tracking Tweets   206

Empowering Workers   206

Managing Knowledge   207

Controlling: Making Sure It Works 207

A Key Criterion for Measurement:
Customer Satisfaction 208

Video Case: Zappos' Team Approach 213

Chapter Eight

214 Structuring Organizations for Today's
Challenges

**Profile: Connecting with Dave Bing, Mayor of
Detroit 215**

Everyone's Reorganizing 216

Building an Organization from the Bottom Up 216

*Making Ethical Decisions: Would You Sacrifice Safety
for Profits? 217*

The Changing Organization 218

The Development of Organization Design 218

Turning Principles into Organization Design 220

**Decisions to Make in Structuring
Organizations 222**

Choosing Centralized or Decentralized Authority 222

Choosing the Appropriate Span of Control 223

Choosing between Tall and Flat Organization
Structures 223

Weighing the Advantages and Disadvantages of
Departmentalization 224

Organizational Models 227

Line Organizations 227

Line-and-Staff Organizations 228

Matrix-Style Organizations 228

Cross-Functional Self-Managed Teams 230

Going Beyond Organizational Boundaries 230

Managing the Interactions among Firms 231

Transparency and Virtual Organizations 231

*Connecting with Small Business: Starting Up with a
Smaller Staff 232*

Benchmarking and Core Competencies 232

*Connecting Through Social Media: When Twitter and
Facebook Are Old School 234*

Adapting to Change 234

Restructuring for Empowerment 235

Creating a Change-Oriented Organizational
Culture 236

Managing the Informal Organization 237

**Video Case: Open-Book Management at New
Belgium Brewery 242**

Chapter Nine

244 Production and Operations Management

**Profile: Connecting with Virginia Rometty,
President and CEO of IBM 245**

Manufacturing and Services in Perspective 246

*Making the Green Connection: Sustaining Our Planet
for the Future 247*

Manufacturers and Service Organizations
Become More Competitive 248

From Production to Operations Management 248

*Connecting Across Borders: How Germany's Economy
Remains Mighty with Manufacturing 249*

Operations Management in the Service Sector 250

Production Processes 251

The Need to Improve Production Techniques
and Cut Costs 252

Computer-Aided Design and Manufacturing 252

Flexible Manufacturing 253

Lean Manufacturing 253

Connecting with Small Business: Designed by You,
Enjoyed by Many 254

Mass Customization 254

Operations Management Planning 255

Facility Location 255

Facility Location for Manufacturers 256

Making Ethical Decisions: Stay or Leave? 257

Taking Operations Management to the Internet 257

Facility Location in the Future 258

Facility Layout 258

Materials Requirement Planning 259

Purchasing 259

Just-in-Time Inventory Control 260

Quality Control 261

The Baldrige Awards 262

ISO 9000 and ISO 14000 Standards 262

Control Procedures: Pert and Gantt Charts 263

Preparing for the Future 264

Video Case: Keeping Your Eye on Ball 269

*Career Outlook: Part 3 Conclusion—Business
Management*

part 4

**Management of Human Resources:
Motivating Employees to Produce Quality
Goods and Services**

Chapter Ten

276 Motivating Employees

**Profile: Connecting with Jim Goodnight, CEO
of SAS 277**

The Value of Motivation 278

Frederick Taylor: The Father of Scientific
Management 279

Elton Mayo and the Hawthorne Studies 280

Motivation and Maslow's Hierarchy of Needs   281
Herzberg's Motivating Factors   283
McGregor's Theory X and Theory Y   285
    Theory X   285
    Theory Y   285
Ouchi's Theory Z   286
Goal-Setting Theory and Management by Objectives   288
Meeting Employee Expectations: Expectancy Theory   289
Reinforcing Employee Performance: Reinforcement Theory   290
Treating Employees Fairly: Equity Theory   290
Putting Theory into Action   291
    Motivation through Job Enrichment   291
    Motivating through Open Communication   292
    Connecting Through Social Media: Make the World Your Office   293
    Applying Open Communication in Self-Managed Teams   294
    Recognizing a Job Well Done   294
Personalizing Motivation   295
    Connecting with Small Business: A Little Fun Can Be a Big Motivator   296
    Motivating Employees across the Globe   296
    Connecting Across Borders: Respecting Cross-Cultural Boundaries   297
    Motivating Employees across Generations   297
Video Case: Management Philosophy at The Container Store   304

Chapter Eleven

306   Human Resource Management: Finding and Keeping the Best Employees

Profile: Connecting with Kim Jordan, CEO of New Belgium Brewing Company   307
Working with People Is Just the Beginning   308
    Developing the Ultimate Resource   308
    The Human Resource Challenge   309
Laws Affecting Human Resource Management   311
    Laws Protecting Employees with Disabilities and Older Employees   312
    Effects of Legislation   313
Determining a Firm's Human Resource Needs   314
Recruiting Employees from a Diverse Population   315
    Connecting with Small Business: Attracting Big Players to Your Small Business   317
Selecting Employees Who Will Be Productive   318
    Hiring Contingent Workers   319

Training and Developing Employees for Optimum Performance   320
    Making Ethical Decisions: Intern or Indentured Servant?   321
    Management Development   323
    Networking   324
    Diversity in Management Development   324
Appraising Employee Performance to Get Optimum Results   325
Compensating Employees: Attracting and Keeping the Best   326
    Pay Systems   327
    Compensating Teams   327
    Fringe Benefits   328
Scheduling Employees to Meet Organizational and Employee Needs   329
    Connecting Across Borders: Coping with Cultural Challenges   330
    Flextime Plans   330
    Home-Based Work   331
    Job-Sharing Plans   332
Moving Employees Up, Over, and Out   333
    Promoting and Reassigning Employees   333
    Terminating Employees   333
    Connecting Through Social Media: HR on the Go   334
    Retiring Employees   334
    Losing Valued Employees   334
Video Case: Human Resource Management at SAS   339

Chapter Twelve

340   Dealing with Union and Employee–Management Issues

Profile: Connecting with David Stern, Commissioner of the NBA   341
Employee–Management Issues   342
Labor Unions from Different Perspectives   343
    The History of Organized Labor   344
    Connecting with Small Business: The Triangle Fire   345
    Public Sector Union Membership   346
Labor Legislation and Collective Bargaining   346
    Union Organizing Campaigns   347
    Objectives of Organized Labor over Time   349
    Resolving Labor–Management Disagreements   351
    Mediation and Arbitration   352
Tactics Used in Labor–Management Conflicts   352
    Union Tactics   352
    Management Tactics   353

Making Ethical Decisions: Would You Cross the Line? 354

The Future of Unions and Labor–Management Relations 354

Controversial Employee–Management Issues 356

Executive Compensation 356

Connecting Across Borders: Executive Compensation around the World 357

Pay Equity 358

Sexual Harassment 359

Child Care 360

Elder Care 361

Drug Testing 362

Violence in the Workplace 362

Video Case: United We Stand 366

Career Outlook: Part 4 Conclusion—Management of Human Resources

part 5
Marketing: Developing and Implementing Customer-Oriented Marketing Plans

Chapter Thirteen

374 Marketing: Helping Buyers Buy

Profile: Connecting with Cesar Conde, President of Univision 375

What Is Marketing? 376

The Evolution of Marketing 377

Nonprofit Organizations and Marketing 379

Making the Green Connection: Are Your Blue Jeans "Green" Jeans? 380

The Marketing Mix 380

Applying the Marketing Process 380

Designing a Product to Meet Consumer Needs 381

Setting an Appropriate Price 382

Getting the Product to the Right Place 383

Developing an Effective Promotional Strategy 383

Connecting Through Social Media: Getting Attention through Mobile Marketing 384

Providing Marketers with Information 384

The Marketing Research Process 385

The Marketing Environment 387

Global Factors 387

Technological Factors 387

Sociocultural Factors 388

Competitive Factors 388

Connecting Across Borders: As Population Booms, Marketers Target Hispanics 389

Economic Factors 389

Two Different Markets: Consumer and Business-to-Business (B2B) 390

The Consumer Market 390

Segmenting the Consumer Market 391

Reaching Smaller Market Segments 392

Moving toward Relationship Marketing 393

The Consumer Decision-Making Process 393

The Business-to-Business Market 395

Your Prospects in Marketing 396

Video Case: Using the 4 Ps at Energizer 400

Chapter Fourteen

402 Developing and Pricing Goods and Services

Profile: Connecting with Randy Hetrick, CEO of Fitness Anywhere 403

Product Development and the Total Product Offer 404

Connecting Through Social Media: Settling Up Simply through Social Media 405

Distributed Product Development 406

Developing a Total Product Offer 406

Product Lines and the Product Mix 407

Making the Green Connection: Thinking Outside the Bottle 408

Product Differentiation 409

Marketing Different Classes of Consumer Goods and Services 409

Marketing Industrial Goods and Services 410

Packaging Changes the Product 412

The Growing Importance of Packaging 412

Branding and Brand Equity 413

Connecting Across Borders: What's in a Name? 414

Brand Categories 414

Generating Brand Equity and Loyalty 415

Creating Brand Associations 416

Brand Management 416

The New-Product Development Process 416

Generating New-Product Ideas 417

Product Screening 417

Connecting with Small Business: Keep on Food Truckin' 418

Product Analysis 418

Product Development and Testing 418

Commercialization 419

The Product Life Cycle 419

Example of the Product Life Cycle 419

Using the Product Life Cycle 420

Competitive Pricing 422

Pricing Objectives 422

Cost-Based Pricing 423

Demand-Based Pricing   423

Competition-Based Pricing   423

Break-Even Analysis   424

Other Pricing Strategies   424

How Market Forces Affect Pricing   425

Nonprice Competition   425

Video Case: Dream Dinners Food-to-Go   430

Chapter Fifteen

432   Distributing Products

Profile: Connecting with Charlie Chanaratsopon, Founder of Charming Charlie   433

The Emergence of Marketing Intermediaries   434

Making the Green Connection: Saving on Shipping with Paper and Plastic Pallets   435

Why Marketing Needs Intermediaries   435

How Intermediaries Create Exchange Efficiency   436

The Value versus the Cost of Intermediaries   437

The Utilities Created by Intermediaries   439

Form Utility   439

Time Utility   439

Place Utility   439

Possession Utility   440

Information Utility   440

Service Utility   440

Wholesale Intermediaries   441

Merchant Wholesalers   441

Agents and Brokers   442

Retail Intermediaries   443

Retail Distribution Strategy   443

Connecting with Small Business: Pop Goes the Retail Store   444

Nonstore Retailing   445

Electronic Retailing   445

Telemarketing   446

Vending Machines, Kiosks, and Carts   446

Direct Selling   446

Multilevel Marketing   447

Direct Marketing   447

Building Cooperation in Channel Systems   448

Corporate Distribution Systems   448

Contractual Distribution Systems   448

Administered Distribution Systems   448

Supply Chains   449

Connecting Across Borders: The Globe's Growing Service Supply Chain   450

Logistics: Getting Goods to Consumers Efficiently   451

Trains Are Great for Large Shipments   452

Trucks Are Good for Small Shipments to Remote Locations   453

Water Transportation Is Inexpensive but Slow   453

Pipelines Are Fast and Efficient   454

Air Transportation Is Fast but Expensive   454

Intermodal Shipping   454

The Storage Function   454

Tracking Goods   455

What All This Means to You   455

Video Case: Making Life Easier   460

Chapter Sixteen

462   Using Effective Promotions

Profile: Connecting with Shama Kabani, President of The Marketing Zen Group   463

Promotion and the Promotion Mix   464

Connecting with Small Business: Turning Customers into Spokespeople   465

Advertising: Informing, Persuading, and Reminding   465

Television Advertising   469

Product Placement   469

Infomercials   470

Online Advertising   470

Making Ethical Decisions: Pay-Per-Tweet   471

Using Social Media to Monitor Ad Effectiveness   472

Global Advertising   473

Connecting Across Borders: What's in Your Oreo?   474

Personal Selling: Providing Personal Attention   474

Steps in the Selling Process   475

The Business-to-Consumer Sales Process   477

Public Relations: Building Relationships   478

Publicity: The Talking Arm of PR   478

Sales Promotion: Giving Buyers Incentives   479

Word of Mouth and Other Promotional Tools   481

Connecting Through Social Media: The Dark Side of Yelp   482

Viral Marketing   482

Blogging   483

Podcasting   483

E-Mail Promotions   483

Mobile Media   483

Managing the Promotion Mix: Putting It All Together   484

Promotional Strategies   484

Video Case: Integrated Marketing Communications at Groupon   489

Career Outlook: Part 5 Counclusion— Marketing

part 6
Managing Financial Resources

Chapter Seventeen

496 Understanding Accounting and Financial Information

Profile: Connecting with Roxanne Coady, Founder of R.J. Julia Booksellers 497

The Role of Accounting Information 498

What Is Accounting? 498

Accounting Disciplines 499

Managerial Accounting 499

Financial Accounting 500

Auditing 501

Tax Accounting 502

Government and Not-for-Profit Accounting 502

The Accounting Cycle 503

Accounting Technology 504

Understanding Key Financial Statements 505

The Fundamental Accounting Equation 506

The Balance Sheet 506

Classifying Assets 506

Liabilities and Owners' Equity Accounts 508

The Income Statement 509

Revenue 510

Cost of Goods Sold 510

Operating Expenses 511

Net Profit or Loss 511

Connecting with Small Business: LIFO or FIFO? 512

The Statement of Cash Flows 512

The Need for Cash Flow Analysis 514

Making Ethical Decisions: Would You Cook the Books? 515

Analyzing Financial Performance Using Ratios 515

Liquidity Ratios 516

Leverage (Debt) Ratios 516

Profitability (Performance) Ratios 517

Activity Ratios 518

Connecting Across Borders: Speaking a Universal Accounting Language 519

Video Case: The Accounting Function at Goodwill Industries 524

Chapter Eighteen

526 Financial Management

Profile: Connecting with James Reinhart, CEO of thredUP 527

The Role of Finance and Financial Managers 528

The Value of Understanding Finance 529

What Is Financial Management? 530

Financial Planning 531

Forecasting Financial Needs 531

Working with the Budget Process 532

Establishing Financial Controls 533

The Need for Operating Funds 534

Managing Day-by-Day Needs of the Business 535

Controlling Credit Operations 535

Making Ethical Decisions: Good Finance or Bad Medicine? 536

Acquiring Needed Inventory 536

Making Capital Expenditures 536

Alternative Sources of Funds 537

Obtaining Short-Term Financing 537

Trade Credit 538

Family and Friends 538

Commercial Banks 538

Different Forms of Short-Term Loans 539

Connecting Through Social Media: Finding Funding Online 540

Factoring Accounts Receivable 541

Commercial Paper 542

Credit Cards 542

Obtaining Long-Term Financing 543

Debt Financing 543

Connecting Across Borders: Investing Domestically in the Middle East 544

Equity Financing 545

Comparing Debt and Equity Financing 547

Lessons from the Financial Crisis 548

Video Case: Starting Up: Tom and Eddie's 553

Chapter Nineteen

554 Using Securities Markets for Financing and Investing Opportunities

Profile: Connecting with Maria Bartiromo of CNBC 555

The Function of Securities Markets 556

The Role of Investment Bankers 557

Stock Exchanges 557

Connecting with Small Business: You Are Not Too Small to Trade 559

Securities Regulations and the Securities and Exchange Commission 559

Foreign Stock Exchanges 560

How Businesses Raise Capital by Selling Stock 561

Advantages and Disadvantages
of Issuing Stock   561

Issuing Shares of Common Stock   562

Issuing Shares of Preferred Stock   562

**How Businesses Raise Capital
by Issuing Bonds   563**

Learning the Language of Bonds   563

Advantages and Disadvantages
of Issuing Bonds   564

Different Classes of Bonds   564

Special Bond Features   565

How Investors Buy Securities   566

Investing through Online Brokers   566

*Making Ethical Decisions:
Money Going Up in Smoke   567*

Choosing the Right Investment Strategy   567

*Connecting Across Borders: Investment Opportunities
Home and Away   568*

Reducing Risk by Diversifying Investments   568

Investing in Stocks   569

Stock Splits   570

Buying Stock on Margin   571

Understanding Stock Quotations   571

Investing in Bonds   572

Investing in High-Risk (Junk) Bonds   572

Understanding Bond Quotations   573

**Investing in Mutual Funds and
Exchange-Traded Funds   573**

Understanding Mutual Fund Quotations   575

Understanding Stock Market Indicators   576

Riding the Market's Roller Coaster   577

Investing Challenges in the 21st-Century Market   579

Video Case: Where Did All My Money Go?   584

Chapter Twenty

586   Money, Financial Institutions, and the Federal
Reserve

**Profile: Connecting with Ben Bernanke, Chairman
of the Federal Reserve   587**

Why Money Is Important   588

What Is Money?   589

What Is the Money Supply?   590

Managing Inflation and the Money Supply   590

The Global Exchange of Money   591

Control of the Money Supply   591

Basics about the Federal Reserve   591

The Reserve Requirement   593

Open-Market Operations   593

The Discount Rate   593

The Federal Reserve's Check-Clearing Role   594

**The History of Banking and the Need for
the Fed   595**

Banking and the Great Depression   596

The U.S. Banking System   597

Commercial Banks   597

Services Provided by Commercial Banks   597

*Connecting Through Social Media: Banking On the
Go   598*

Services to Borrowers   598

Savings and Loan Associations (S&Ls)   598

Making Ethical Decisions: Would You Tell the Teller?   599

Credit Unions   599

Other Financial Institutions (Nonbanks)   600

*Connecting with Small Business:
The Rise of the Nonbank   601*

**The Recent Banking Crisis and How the
Government Protects Your Money   601**

Protecting Your Funds   602

The Federal Deposit Insurance Corporation (FDIC)   602

The Savings Association Insurance Fund (SAIF)   603

The National Credit Union Administration (NCUA)   603

**Using Technology to Make Banking More
Efficient   603**

Online Banking   605

**International Banking and
Banking Services   605**

Leaders in International Banking   605

The World Bank and the International Monetary Fund
(IMF)   606

*Connecting Across borders: Troubles Facing the
World's Financial Watchdogs   607*

Video Case: The Financial Crisis   612

*Career Outlook: Part 6 Conclusion—Financial
Management*

Appendix 1

A1   Working within the Legal Environment

**Profile: Connecting with Kenneth C. Frazier,
CEO of Merck   A1-1**

The Case for Laws   A1-2

Statutory and Common Law   A1-3

Administrative Agencies   A1-3

Tort Law   A1-4

Product Liability   A1-4

**Legally Protecting Ideas: Patents,
Copyrights, and Trademarks   A1-6**

**Sales Law: The Uniform Commercial
Code   A1-8**

Warranties   A1-8

Negotiable Instruments   A1-9

Contract Law   A1-9

Breach of Contract   A1-10

Promoting Fair and Competitive Business Practices   A1-11

The History of Antitrust Legislation   A1-11

Laws to Protect Consumers   A1-13

Tax Laws   A1-14

Bankruptcy Laws   A1-15

Deregulation versus Regulation   A1-17

Appendix 2

A2   Managing Personal Finances

Profile: Connecting with Carmen Wong Ulrich, Personal Finance Expert   A2-1

The Need for Personal Financial Planning   A2-2

Financial Planning Begins with Making Money   A2-2

Six Steps to Controlling Your Assets   A2-3

Building Your Financial Base   A2-6

Real Estate: Historically, a Relatively Secure Investment   A2-7

Tax Deductions and Home Ownership   A2-7

Where to Put Your Savings   A2-8

Learning to Manage Credit   A2-8

Protecting Your Financial Base: Buying Insurance   A2-10

Health Insurance   A2-11

Homeowner's or Renter's Insurance   A2-12

Other Insurance   A2-12

Planning Your Retirement   A2-12

Social Security   A2-12

Individual Retirement Accounts (IRAs)   A2-13

Simple IRAs   A2-14

401(k) Plans   A2-15

Keogh Plans   A2-15

Financial Planners   A2-15

Estate Planning   A2-16

Epilogue: Getting the Job You Want   E

Bonus Chapter A: Using Techonology to Manage Information   Online

Bonus Chapter B: Managing Risk   Online

Chapter Notes   N

Glossary   G-1

Photo Credits   PC-1

Name Index   I-1

Organization Index   I-8

Subject Index   I-12

getting ready for this course and your career

Top 10 Reasons to Read This Introduction

(Even If It Isn't Assigned)

10 What the heck—you already bought the book, so you might as well get your money's worth.

9 You don't want the only reason you get a raise to be that the government has increased the minimum wage.

8 Getting off to a good start in the course can improve your chances of getting a higher grade, and your Uncle Ernie will send you a dollar for every A you get.

7 Your friends say that you've got the manners of a troll and you want to find out what the heck they're talking about.

6 How else would you find out a spork isn't usually one of the utensils used at a business dinner?

5 You don't want to experience the irony of frantically reading the "time management" section at 3:00 a.m.

4 Like the Boy Scouts, you want to be prepared.

3 It must be important because the authors spent so much time writing it.

2 You want to run with the big dogs someday.

And the number one reason for reading this introductory section is . . .

1 It could be on a test.

LEARNING THE SKILLS YOU NEED TO SUCCEED TODAY AND TOMORROW

Your life is full. You're starting a new semester, perhaps even beginning your college career, and you're feeling pulled in many directions. Why take time to read this introduction? We lightheartedly offer our top 10 reasons on page P-l, but the real importance of this section is no joking matter.

Its purpose, and that of the entire text, is to help you learn principles, strategies, and skills for success that will serve you not only in this course but also in your career and your life. Whether you learn them is up to you. Learning them won't guarantee success, but not learning them—well, you get the picture.

This is an exciting and challenging time. Success in any venture comes from understanding basic principles and knowing how to apply them effectively. What you learn now could help you be a success—for the rest of your life. Begin applying these skills now to gain an edge on the competition. READ THIS SECTION BEFORE YOUR FIRST CLASS and make a great first impression! Good luck. We wish you the best.

Bill Nickels   **Jim McHugh**   **Susan McHugh**

USING THIS COURSE TO PREPARE FOR YOUR CAREER

Since you've signed up for this course, we're guessing you already know the value of a college education. The holders of bachelor's degrees make an average of $46,000 per year compared to $30,000 for high school graduates.[1] That's 53 percent more for college graduates than those with just a high school diploma. Compounded over the course of a 30-year career, the average college grad will make nearly a half million dollars more than the high school grad! Thus, what you invest in a college education is likely to pay you back many times. See Figure P.1 for more of an idea of how much salary difference a college degree makes by the end of a 30-year career. That doesn't mean there aren't good careers available to non–college graduates. It just means those with an education are more likely to have higher earnings over their lifetime.

The value of a college education is more than just a larger paycheck. Other benefits include increasing your ability to think critically and communicate your ideas to others, improving your ability to use technology, and preparing yourself to live in a diverse world. Knowing you've met your goals and earned a college degree also gives you the self-confidence to work toward future goals.

Experts say today's college graduates will likely hold seven or eight different jobs (often in several different careers) in their lifetime. Many returning students are changing their careers and their plans for life. In fact, over 30 percent of the people enrolled in college today are 25 or older. In addition, over 60 percent of all part-time college students are 25 or older.[2]

You too may want to change careers someday. It can be the path to long-term happiness and success. That means you'll have to be flexible and adjust your strengths and talents to new opportunities.[3] Learning has become a lifelong job. You'll constantly update your skills to achieve and remain competitive.

If you're typical of many college students, you may not have any idea what career you'd like to pursue. That isn't necessarily a big disadvantage in today's fast-changing job market. After all, many of the best jobs of the future don't even exist today. Figure P.2 lists 10 careers that didn't exist 10 years ago. There are no perfect or certain ways to prepare for the most interesting and challenging jobs

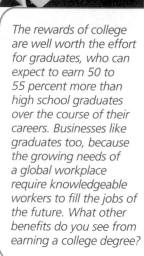

The rewards of college are well worth the effort for graduates, who can expect to earn 50 to 55 percent more than high school graduates over the course of their careers. Businesses like graduates too, because the growing needs of a global workplace require knowledgeable workers to fill the jobs of the future. What other benefits do you see from earning a college degree?

figure P.1

SALARY COMPARISON OF HIGH SCHOOL VERSUS COLLEGE GRADUATES

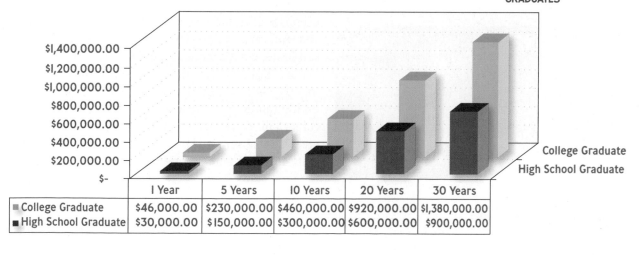

	1 Year	5 Years	10 Years	20 Years	30 Years
College Graduate	$46,000.00	$230,000.00	$460,000.00	$920,000.00	$1,380,000.00
High School Graduate	$30,000.00	$150,000.00	$300,000.00	$600,000.00	$900,000.00

figure P.2

NEW CAREERS

NEW CAREERS

These careers didn't exist 10 years ago:

- Bloggers
- Community managers or content managers
- Green funeral directors
- Interior redesigners
- Patient advocates
- Senior move management
- Social media strategists
- User experience analyst
- Video journalist
- Virtual business service providers

Source: Rachel Zupek, "10 Careers That Didn't Exist 10 Years Ago," www.careerbuilder.com, accessed June 2011.

of tomorrow. Rather, you should continue your college education, develop strong computer and Internet skills, improve your verbal and written communication skills, and remain flexible while you explore the job market.

One of the objectives of this class, and this book, is to help you choose an area in which you might enjoy working and have a good chance to succeed. You'll learn about economics, global business, ethics, entrepreneurship, management, marketing, accounting, finance, and more. At the end of the course, you should have a much better idea which careers would be best for you and which you would not enjoy.

But you don't have to be in business to use business principles. You can use marketing principles to get a job and to sell your ideas to others. You can use your knowledge of investments to make money in the stock market. You'll use your management skills and general business knowledge wherever you go and in whatever career you pursue—including government agencies, charities, and social causes.

ASSESSING YOUR SKILLS AND PERSONALITY

The earlier you can do a personal assessment of your interests, skills, and values, the better it can help you find career direction. Hundreds of schools use software exercises like the System for Interactive Guidance and Information (SIGI) and DISCOVER to offer self-assessment exercises, personalized lists of occupations based on your interests and skills, and information about different careers and the preparation each requires. Visit your college's placement center, career lab, or library soon and learn what programs are available for you. Even if you're a returning student, an assessment of your skills will help you choose the right courses and career path to follow next.

Self-assessment will help you determine the kind of work environment you'd prefer (technical, social service, or business); what values you seek to fulfill

Networking provides you with an array of personal contacts on whom you can call for career advice and help. Have you begun creating your network yet? Are you part of someone else's?

in a career (security, variety, or independence); what abilities you have (creative/artistic, numerical, or sales); and what job characteristics matter to you (income, travel, or amount of job pressure versus free time).

USING PROFESSIONAL BUSINESS STRATEGIES RIGHT NOW

Here are two secrets to success you can start practicing now: *networking* and *keeping files on subjects important to you.*

Networking is building a personal array of people you've met, spoken to, or corresponded with who can offer you advice about and even help with your career options. Start with the names of your professors, both as employment references and as resources about fields of interest to you. Add additional contacts, mentors, and resource people, and keep the notes you make when talking with them about careers including salary information and courses you need to take.

All students need a way to retain what they learn. An effective way to become an expert on almost any business subject is to set up your own information system. You can store data on your computer and cell phone (back these files up!), or you can establish a comprehensive filing system on paper, or you can use a combination of the two. Few college students make this effort; those who don't lose much of the information they read in college or thereafter.

Keep as many of your textbooks and other assigned readings as you can, as well as your course notes. Read a national newspaper such as *The Wall Street Journal, The New York Times,* or *USA Today.* Read your local newspaper. Each time you read a story that interests you, save a paper copy or add a link to the story online in your electronic file, under a topic heading like *careers, small business, marketing, economics,* or *management.* You'll easily find the latest data on almost any subject on the Internet. Don't rely on just one site for information (and be especially wary of Wikipedia)! Get familiar with a variety of sources and use them.

Start a file for your résumé. In it, keep a copy of your current résumé along with reference letters and other information about jobs you may have held, including projects accomplished and additions to your responsibilities over time. Soon you'll have a tremendous amount of information to help you prepare a polished résumé and answer challenging job interview questions with ease.

Watching television shows about business, such as *Nightly Business Report* and Jim Cramer's *Mad Money,* is like getting a free graduate education in business. Try viewing some of these shows or listening to similar ones on the radio, and see which ones you like best. Take notes and put them in your files. Keep up with business news in your area so that you know what jobs are available and where. You may also want to join a local business group to begin networking with people and learning the secrets of the local business scene. Many business groups and professional societies accept student members.

LEARNING TO BEHAVE LIKE A PROFESSIONAL

There's a reason good manners never go out of style. As the world becomes increasingly competitive, the gold goes to teams and individuals with that extra bit of polish. The person who makes a good impression will be the one who gets the job, wins the promotion, or clinches the deal. Good manners and professionalism are not difficult to acquire; they're second nature to those who achieve and maintain a competitive edge.

Many businesses have adopted business casual as the proper work attire, but others still require traditional clothing styles. How does your appearance at work affect both you and your company?

Not even a great résumé or designer suit can substitute for poor behavior, including verbal behavior, in an interview.[4] Say "please" and "thank you" when you ask for something. Open doors for others, stand when an older person enters the room, and use a polite tone of voice. You may want to take a class in etiquette to learn the proper way to eat in a nice restaurant, what to do at a formal party, and so on. Of course, it's also critical to be honest, reliable, dependable, and ethical at all times.

Some rules are not formally written anywhere; instead, every successful businessperson learns them through experience. If you follow these rules in college, you'll have the skills for success when you start your career. Here are the basics:

1. **Making a good first impression.** An old saying goes, "You never get a second chance to make a good first impression." You have just a few seconds to make an impression. Therefore, how you dress and how you look are important. Take your cue as to what is appropriate at any specific company by studying the people there who are most successful. What do they wear? How do they act?

2. **Focusing on good grooming.** Be aware of your appearance and its impact. Wear appropriate, clean clothing and a few simple accessories. Revealing shirts, nose rings, and tattoos may not be appropriate in a work setting. Be consistent, too; you can't project a good image by dressing well a few times a week and then showing up looking like you're getting ready to mow a lawn.

   Many organizations have adopted "business casual" guidelines, but others still require traditional attire, so ask what the organization's policies are and choose your wardrobe accordingly. Casual doesn't mean sloppy or shabby. Wrinkled clothing, shirttails hanging out, and hats worn indoors are not usually appropriate. For women, business casual attire includes simple skirts and slacks (no jeans), cotton shirts, sweaters (not too tight), blazers, and low-heeled shoes or boots. Men may wear khaki trousers, sport shirts with collars, sweaters or sport jackets, and casual loafers or lace-up shoes.

3. **Being on time.** When you don't come to class or work on time, you're sending this message to your teacher or boss: "My time is more important than your time. I have more important things to do than be here." In addition to showing a lack of respect to your teacher or boss, lateness rudely disrupts the work of your colleagues.

   Pay attention to the corporate culture. Sometimes you have to come in earlier than others and leave later to get that promotion you desire. To develop good work habits and get good grades, arrive in class on time and avoid leaving (or packing up to leave) early.

4. **Practicing considerate behavior.** Listen when others are talking—for example, don't read the newspaper or eat in class. Don't interrupt others when they are speaking; wait your turn. Eliminate profanity from your vocabulary. Use appropriate body language by sitting up attentively and not slouching. Sitting up has the added bonus of helping you stay awake! Professors and managers alike get a favorable impression from those who look and act alert.

5. **Practicing good e-mail etiquette.** The basic rules of courtesy in face-to-face communication also apply to e-mail exchanges. Introduce yourself at the beginning of your first e-mail message. Next, let your recipients

know how you got their names and e-mail addresses. Then proceed with your clear but succinct message, and always be sure to type full words (*ur* is not the same thing as *your*). Finally, close the e-mail with a signature. Do not send an attachment unless your correspondent has indicated he or she will accept it. Ask first! You can find much more information about proper Internet etiquette, or netiquette, online—for example, at NetManners.com.

6. **Practicing good cell phone manners.** Your Introduction to Business class is not the place to be arranging a date for tonight. Turn off the phone during class or in a business meeting unless you are expecting a critical call. If you are expecting such a call, let your professor know before class. Turn off your ringer and put the phone on vibrate. Sit by the aisle and near the door. If you do receive a critical call, leave the room before answering it. Apologize to the professor after class and explain the situation.

Behavior that's taken for granted in other countries might be unusual in the United States. In some cultures bowing is a form of greeting to show respect. How can you learn the appropriate business etiquette for the countries in which you do business?

7. **Practicing safe posting on social media.** Be careful what you post on your Facebook page or any other social media. While it may be fun to share your latest adventures with your friends, your boss or future boss may not appreciate your latest party pictures. Be aware that those pictures may not go away even if you delete them from your page. If anyone else downloaded them, they are still out there waiting for a recruiter to discover. Make sure to update your privacy settings frequently. It's a good idea to separate our list of work friends and limit what that group can view. Also be aware that some work colleagues aren't interested in becoming your Facebook friends. To avoid awkwardness, wait for work associates to reach out to you first.[5] Make sure you know your employer's policy on using social media on company time. Obviously, they will probably frown on using it for personal use on company time, but there may be rules about sharing technical matter, etc. Be mindful that social media accounts time-stamp your comments.[6]

8. **Being prepared.** A businessperson would never show up for a meeting without having read the appropriate materials and being prepared to discuss the topics on the agenda. For students, acting like a professional means reading assigned materials before class, asking and responding to questions in class, and discussing the material with fellow students.

Just as traffic laws enable people to drive more safely, business etiquette allows people to conduct business with the appropriate amount of consideration. Sharpen your competitive edge by becoming familiar with its rules. If your job or career requires you to travel internationally, learn the proper business etiquette for each country you visit. Customs differ widely for such everyday activities as greeting people, eating, giving gifts, presenting and receiving business cards, and conducting business in general. In Japan, businesspeople typically bow instead of shaking hands, and in some Arab countries it is insulting to sit so as to show the soles of your shoes. Honesty, high ethical standards, and reliability and trustworthiness are important for success in any country.

Having a reputation for integrity will enable you to be proud of who you are and contribute a great deal to your business success. Unethical behavior can ruin your reputation; so think carefully before you act. When in doubt, don't! Ethics is so important to success that we include discussions about it throughout the text.

DOING YOUR BEST IN SCHOOL

The skills you need to succeed in life after college are the same ones that will serve you well in your studies. Career, family, and hobbies all benefit from organizational and time management skills you can apply right now. Here are some tips for improving your study habits, taking tests, and managing your time.

Study Hints

For the remainder of your college career, consider studying to be your business. Though you may hold another job while enrolled in this class, you're in school because you want to advance yourself. So until you get out of school and into your desired occupation, studying is your business. And like any good businessperson, you aim for success. Follow these strategies:

1. **Go to class.** It's tempting to cut a class on a nice day or when there are other things to do. But nothing is more important to doing well in school than going to class every time. If possible, sit in the front near the instructor. This will help you focus better and avoid distractions in the room.

2. **Listen well.** It's not enough to show up for class if you use the time for a nap. Make eye contact with the instructor. In your mind, form a picture of what he or she is discussing. Include your existing knowledge and past experiences in your picture. This ties new knowledge to what you already know.

3. **Take careful notes.** Make two columns in your notebook or on your laptop. On one side write down important concepts, and on the other examples or more detailed explanations. Use abbreviations and symbols whenever possible and wide spacing to make the notes easier to read. Edit your notes after class to make them easier to read. Rereading and rewriting help store the information in your long-term memory. Learn the concepts in your courses the same way you learn the words to your favorite song: through repetition and review.

4. **Find a good place to study.** Find a place with good lighting and a quiet atmosphere. Some students do well with classical music or other music without lyrics playing in the background. Keep your study place equipped with extra supplies such as pens, pencils, calculator, folders, and paper so you don't have to interrupt studying to hunt for them.

5. **Read the text using a strategy such as "survey, question, read, recite, review" (SQ3R).**

   a. *Survey* or scan the chapter first to see what it is all about. This means looking over the table of contents, learning goals, headings, photo essays, and charts so you get a broad idea of the content. The summaries at the end of each chapter in this text provide a great overview of the concepts in the chapter. Scanning will provide an introduction and help get your mind in a learning mode.

The SQ3R study system recommends that you "survey, question, read, recite, and review" to stay up-to-date with assignments and shine in class every day. Have you adopted this system?

b. Write *questions,* first by changing the headings into questions. For example, you could change the heading of this section to "What hints can I use to study better?" Read the questions that appear throughout each chapter in the Progress Assessment sections to give yourself a chance to recall what you've read.

c. *Read* the chapter to find the answers to your questions. Be sure to read the boxes as well. They offer extended examples or discussions of the concepts in the text. You've probably asked, "Will the material in the boxes be on the tests?" Even if your instructor chooses not to test over them directly, they are often the most interesting parts of the chapter and will help you retain the concepts better.

d. *Recite* your answers to yourself or to others in a study group. Make sure you say the answers in your own words so that you clearly understand the concepts. Research has shown that saying things is a more effective way to learn them than seeing, hearing, or reading about them. While often used in study groups, recitation is also good practice for working in teams in the work world.

e. *Review* by rereading and recapping the information. The chapter summaries are written in a question-and-answer form, much like a classroom dialogue. They're also tied directly to the learning goals so that you can see whether you've accomplished the chapter's objectives. Cover the written answers and see whether you can answer the questions yourself first.

6. **Use flash cards.** You'll master the course more easily if you know the language of business. To review the key terms in the book, write any terms you don't know on index cards and go through your cards between classes and when you have other free time.

7. **Use this text's Online Learning Center.** Using the Online Learning Center (OLC) on this text's website (www.mhhe.com/P2P2e) is a great way to practice your test-taking skills. The OLC contains sample test questions, review work that allows you to gauge what material you have mastered, and other material you may need to review again.

8. **Use *Connect* Introduction to Business**. (if your professor has recommended it for your course). *Connect's* online features include interactive presentations, *LearnSmart* (intelligent flash cards that offer feedback and direct you back to the text based on your performance), and interactive applications.

9. **Go over old exams, if possible.** If old exams are not available from your professor, ask how many multiple-choice, true/false, and essay questions will be on your test. It's acceptable to ask your professor's former students what kind of questions are given and what material is usually emphasized. It is unethical, though, to go over exams you obtain illegally.

10. **Use as many of your senses in learning as possible.** If you're an auditory learner—that is, if you learn best by hearing—record yourself reading your notes and answering the questions you've written. Listen to the tape while you're dressing in the morning. You can also benefit from reading or studying aloud. If you're a visual learner, use pictures, charts, colors, and graphs. Your professor has a set of videos that illustrate the concepts

in this text. If you're a kinesthetic learner, you remember best by doing, touching, and experiencing. Do some of the Developing Workplace Skills exercises at the end of each chapter.

Test-Taking Hints

Often students will say, "I know this stuff, but I'm just not good at taking multiple-choice (or essay) tests." Other students find test taking relatively easy. Here are a few test-taking hints:

1. **Get plenty of sleep and have a good meal.** It's better to be alert and awake during an exam than to study all night and be groggy. If you keep up with your reading and your reviews, you won't need to pull an all-nighter. Proper nutrition plays an important part in your brain's ability to function.

2. **Bring all you need for the exam.** Sometimes you'll need No. 2 pencils, erasers, and a calculator. Ask beforehand.

3. **Relax.** At home before the test, take deep, slow breaths. Picture yourself in the testing session, relaxed and confident. Reread the chapter summaries. Get to class early to settle down. If you start to get nervous during the test, stop and take a few deep breaths. Turn the test over and write down information you remember. Sometimes this helps you connect the information you know to the questions on the test.

4. **Read the directions on the exam carefully.** You don't want to miss anything or do something you're not supposed to do.

5. **Read all the answers in multiple-choice questions.** Even if there is more than one correct-sounding answer to a multiple-choice question, one is clearly better. Read them all to be sure you pick the best. Try covering up the choices while reading the question. If the answer you think of is one of the choices, it is probably correct. If you are still unsure of the answer, start eliminating options you know are wrong. Narrowing the choices to two or three improves your odds.

6. **Answer all the questions.** Unless your instructor takes off more for an incorrect answer than for no answer, you have nothing to lose by guessing. Also, skipping a question can lead to inadvertently misaligning your answers on a scan sheet. You could end up with all your subsequent answers scored wrong!

7. **Read true/false questions carefully.** All parts of the statement must be true or else the entire statement is false. Watch out for absolutes such as *never, always,* and *none.* These often make a statement false.

8. **Organize your thoughts before answering essay questions.** Think about the sequence in which to present what you want to say. Use complete sentences with correct grammar and punctuation. Explain or defend your answers.

9. **Go over the test at the end.** Make sure you've answered all the questions, put your name on the exam, and followed all directions.

Time Management Hints

The most important management skill you can learn is how to manage your time. Now is as good an opportunity to practice as any. Here are some hints other students have learned—often the hard way:

1. **Write weekly goals for yourself.** Make certain your goals are realistic and attainable. Write the steps you'll use to achieve each goal. Reward yourself when you reach a goal.

Keeping a daily schedule is only one of the many strategies that will help you manage your time. You should also keep a running list of goals and things you need to do each week. In what other ways can you defend your study time?

2. **Keep a "to do" list.** It's easy to forget things unless you write them down. Jot tasks down as soon as you know of them. That gives you one less thing to do: remembering what you have to do.

3. **Prepare a daily schedule.** Use a commercial printed or electronic daily planner or create your own. Write the days of the week across the top of the page. Write the hours of the day from the time you get up until the time you go to bed down the left side. Draw lines to form columns and rows and fill in all the activities you have planned in each hour. Hopefully, you will be surprised to see how many slots of time you have available for studying.

4. **Prepare for the next day the night before.** Having everything ready to go will help you make a quick, stress-free start in the morning.

5. **Prepare weekly and monthly schedules.** Use a calendar to fill in activities and upcoming assignments. Include both academic and social activities so that you can balance your work and fun.

6. **Space out your work.** Don't wait until the last week of the course to write all your papers and study for your exams. If you do a few pages a day, you can write a 20-page paper in a couple of weeks with little effort. It is really difficult to push out 20 pages in a day or two.

7. **Defend your study time.** Study every day. Use the time between classes to go over your flash cards and read the next day's assignments. Make it a habit to defend your study time so you don't slip.

8. **Take time for fun.** If you have some fun every day, life will be full. Schedule your fun times along with your studying so that you have balance.

"Time is money," the saying goes. Some, however, would argue that time is more valuable than money. If your bank account balance falls, you might be able to build it back up by finding a better-paying job, taking a second job, or even selling something you own. But you only have a limited amount of time and there is no way to make more. Learn to manage your time well, because you can never get it back.

MAKING THE MOST OF THE RESOURCES FOR THIS COURSE

College courses and textbooks are best at teaching you concepts and ways of thinking about business. However, to learn firsthand how to apply those ideas to real business situations, you need to explore and interact with other resources. Here are seven basic resources for the class in addition to the text:

1. **The professor.** One of the most valuable facets of college is the chance to study with experienced professors. Your instructor is a resource who's there to answer some questions and guide you to answers for others. Many professors get job leads they can pass on to you and can provide letters of recommendation too. Thus it's important to develop a friendly relationship with your professors.

2. **The supplements that come with this text.** The Online Learning Center (at www.mhhe.com/P2P2e) and *Connect* Introduction to Business online course material (if your professor has recommended it for your course) will help you review and interpret key material and give you practice answering test questions. Even if your professor does not assign these materials, you may want to use them anyhow. Doing so will improve your test scores and help you compete successfully with the other students.

3. **Outside readings.** One secret to success in business is staying current. Review and become familiar with the following magazines and newspapers during the course and throughout your career: *The Wall Street Journal, Forbes, Barron's, Bloomberg Businessweek, Fortune, Money, Hispanic Business, Smart Money, Harvard Business Review, Black Enterprise, BtoB, Inc.,* and *Entrepreneur.* You may also want to read your local newspaper's business section and national news magazines such as *Time* and *Newsweek.* You can find them in your school's learning resource center or the local public library. Some are also available online free.

4. **Your own experience and that of your classmates.** Many college students have had experience working in business or nonprofit organizations. Hearing and talking about those experiences exposes you to many real-life examples that are invaluable for understanding business. Don't rely exclusively on the professor for answers to the cases and other exercises in this book. Often there is no single "right" answer, and your classmates may open up new ways of looking at things for you.

   Part of being a successful businessperson is knowing how to work with others. Some professors let their students work together and build teamwork as well as presentation and analytical skills. Students from other countries can help you learn about different cultures and different approaches to handling business problems. There is strength in diversity, so seek out people different from you to work with on teams.

5. **Outside contacts.** Who can tell you more about what it's like to start a career in accounting than someone who's

Your college professors are among the most valuable resources and contacts you'll encounter as you develop your career path. How many of your professors have you gotten to know so far?

doing it now? One of the best ways to learn about different businesses is to visit them in person. The world can be your classroom.

When you go shopping, think about whether you would enjoy working in and managing a store. Think about owning or managing a restaurant, an auto body shop, a health club, or any other establishment you visit. If something looks interesting, talk to the employees and learn more about their jobs and the industry. Be constantly on the alert to find career possibilities, and don't hesitate to talk with people about their careers. Many will be pleased to give you their time.

6. **The Internet.** The Internet offers more material than you could use in a lifetime. Throughout this text we present information and exercises that require you to use the Internet. Information changes rapidly, and it is up to you to stay current.

7. **The library or learning resource center.** The library is a great complement to the Internet and a valuable resource. Work with your librarian to learn how to best access the information you need.

Getting the Most from This Text

Many learning aids appear throughout this text to help you understand the concepts:

1. **List of Learning Goals at the beginning of each chapter.** Reading through these goals will help you set the framework and focus for the chapter material. Since every student at one time or other has found it difficult to get into studying, the Learning Goals are there to provide an introduction and to get your mind into a learning mode.

2. **Opening Profile and Name That Company features.** The opening profiles offer stories that will help you get to know professionals who successfully use the concepts presented in the chapters. The Name That Company feature at the beginning of each chapter challenges you to identify a company discussed in the chapter.

3. **Photo essays**. The photos offer examples of the concepts in the chapter. Looking at the photos and reading the photo essays (captions) before you read the chapter will give you a good idea of what the chapter is all about.

4. **Self-test questions.** Periodically, within each chapter, you'll encounter set-off lists of questions called Progress Assessment. These questions give you a chance to pause, think carefully about, and recall what you've just read.

5. **Key terms.** Developing a strong business vocabulary is one of the most important and useful aspects of this course. To assist you, all key terms in the book are highlighted in boldface type. Key terms are also defined in the margins, and page references to these terms are given at the end of each chapter. A full glossary is located in the back of the book. You should rely heavily on these learning aids in adding new terms to your vocabulary.

6. **Boxes.** Each chapter contains a number of boxed extended examples or discussions that cover major themes of the book: *(a)* ethics (Making Ethical Decisions); *(b)* small business (Connecting with Small Business); *(c)* global business (Connecting Across Borders); *(d)* environmental issues (Making the Green Connection) and *(e)* social media (Connecting Through Social Media). They're interesting to read; we hope you enjoy and learn from them.

7. **End-of-chapter summaries.** The chapter summaries are directly tied to the chapter Learning Goals so that you can see whether you've accomplished the chapter's objectives.

8. **Critical Thinking questions.** The end-of-chapter questions help you relate the material to your own experiences.

9. **Developing Workplace Skills exercises.** To really remember something, it's best to do it. That's why Developing Workplace Skills sections at the end of each chapter suggest small projects that help you use resources, develop interpersonal skills, manage information, understand systems, and sharpen computer skills.

10. **Taking It to the Net exercises.** These exercises direct you to dynamic outside resources that reinforce the concepts introduced in the text. You might want to bookmark some of the websites you'll discover. They appear on the Online Learning Center at www.mhhe.com/P2P2e.

11. **Casing the Web cases.** These cases give you another chance to think about the material and apply it in real-life situations. They also appear on the Online Learning Center at www.mhhe.com/P2P2e.

12. **Video Cases.** These cases feature companies, processes, practices, and managers that bring to life the key concepts in the chapter and give you real-world information to think over and discuss.

13. **Career Outlook sections.** These special sections that appear at the end of each Part in the text contain overviews of the careers, and the skills needed to succeed in those careers, that use the concepts you learned in the preceding chapters. They also contain profiles of individuals applying for positions in the field, including their cover letters, résumés, and interview answers. The Career Outlook material will help you identify a potential career and help you prepare to apply for a job.

If you use the suggestions we've presented here, you'll actively participate in a learning experience that will help you greatly in your chosen career. The most important secret to success may be to enjoy what you're doing and do your best in everything. To do your best, take advantage of all the learning aids available to you.

Business Trends:
CULTIVATING A BUSINESS IN DIVERSE, GLOBAL ENVIRONMENTS

In order to succeed in any business, you must constantly adapt to changes in the market. This means that you must understand business and all of the elements that affect it, including economic and legal issues, new technology, the competitive environment, social factors, and global influences.

In the chapters in this part, you will learn about how businesses contribute to the standard of living and quality of life in local, national, and global communities. You will explore the various economic systems and learn the basics of how each works, examine many of the opportunities and hurdles in global trade, and discuss how ethical and socially responsible behavior influences the success or failure of individuals and businesses.

LOOKING
Ahead

CHAPTER 1 Connecting to the Dynamic Business Environment

CHAPTER 2 Understanding Economics and How It Affects Business

CHAPTER 3 Doing Business in Global Markets

CHAPTER 4 Demanding Ethical and Socially Responsible Behavior

Connecting TO THE Dynamic Business ENVIRONMENT

LEARNING goals

After you have read and studied this chapter, you should be able to

1 Describe the relationship between profit and risk, and show how businesses and nonprofit organizations can raise the standard of living for all.

2 Compare and contrast being an entrepreneur and working for others.

3 Analyze the effects of the economic environment and taxes on businesses.

4 Describe the effects of technology on businesses.

5 Demonstrate how businesses can meet and beat competition.

6 Analyze the social changes affecting businesses.

7 Identify what businesses must do to meet global challenges, including war and terrorism.

8 Review how past trends are being repeated in the present and what those trends mean for tomorrow's college graduates.

For many budding entrepreneurs, choosing the right time to start a business can be difficult. The recent recession hasn't made the idea of building a company from the ground up any more appealing, either. In reality, though, there's no such thing as a perfect moment to start a business. Economic climates can change from good to bad (and vice versa) at any time. The best companies are able to thrive in any situation, no matter what obstacles get in their way.

Terry Pham knows a thing or two about keeping a business afloat in troubled times. In 2002 he founded Fat Straws in Dallas, Texas, when the dot-com bust of the late 90s was still taking a toll on the nation. But Pham was less concerned with economic bubbles than he was with his company's product, bubble tea. While popular in East Asian countries, bubble tea had yet to make a big impact in the United States The drink has a distinctly foreign flavor. Bubble tea starts out familiar enough, as a tea base gets shaken up with a mixture of fruit flavors or milk, creating a frothy, bubbly beverage. Things get a bit unusual, however, once the "pearls" are added. These chewy balls of tapioca float at the bottom of the drink until they get sucked up through wide straws, which provide the namesake for Pham's company.

It's safe to say that most people wouldn't call opening a niche tea shop deep in the heart of Texas during a downturn a good idea. Pham had the confidence of experience on his side, though. The son of Vietnamese immigrants, Pham moved with his mother and siblings to Garland, Texas, after the sudden death of his father. Pham's mother found work behind the counter of a 7-Eleven convenience store. She soon worked her way up to field consultant, where she managed several stores. By her side all that time was her son Terry, helping around the shop and learning the business. "I was a kid of 7-Eleven, cleaning shelves and mopping floors," Pham says.

By 2002 Pham felt he had gathered enough know-how to start his own business. He learned important lessons from his time at 7-Eleven, namely that keeping things simple could be the key to success. For instance, many bubble tea shops overwhelm their customers with more than 150 flavors to choose from. Pham decided to launch with only about 15 to 20 basic teas that would be the most appetizing to his customer base. Also, since tea isn't very expensive, Fat Straws was able to open with low overhead costs. "We didn't need a ton of capital to build out and get started," Pham says. "We were able to launch and be profitable early on, growing every year 15 to 20 percent." Meanwhile, Fat Straws' laid-back atmosphere ensured that many of its young customers would come back. Pham decked out his shop with comfortable couches that encouraged lounging and reflected the carefree nature of the company's signature product.

Fat Straws continued to grow so steadily that by 2007 Pham opened a second location in north Dallas. The next year, though, the stock market bottomed out as a result of the credit crunch, and the economy turned upside-down. Pham started hearing rumors that neighboring restaurants were losing as much as 20 percent of their pre-recession business. Rather than scrambling to cut costs, Pham instead refocused his company on quality control and service. "People were losing their jobs and homes," he says. "If they chose to come in here and spend five dollars on a drink, we wanted to make the experience everything they expected—and then some." So even as Pham watched nearby businesses close their doors, Fat Straws survived and continued to go strong.

The business environment is constantly changing, as evidenced by the recent economic decline, but along with those changes come opportunities for new entrepreneurs like Pham. The purpose of this chapter, and this text, is to introduce you to the dynamic world of business and to some of the people who run those businesses. You'll learn about all phases of business from planning to management, production, marketing, finance, accounting, and more. You'll also learn about all kinds of businesses: small, large, nonprofit, local, national, and international. Through your studies, you should be able to find attractive career possibilities.

We begin by looking at some key terms you will need to know, like *profit* and *loss* and *risk*. Entrepreneurs like Terry Pham contribute much to the communities they serve, and they also make a good living doing so. That's what business is all about.

Sources: Rich Karpinski, "How to Start a Business in a Recession," *Entrepreneur*, September 27, 2011; Emily Toman, "Fat Straws Bubble Tea," *Far North Dallas Advocate*, July 22, 2010; www.fatstraws.net/about.html, accessed March 6, 2012.

CONNECTING WITH

X   *Terry Pham*

Founder of Fat Straws

This microlending organization provides small loans to entrepreneurs too poor to qualify for traditional loans. The person who started the organization has started 30 of what he calls social businesses that do not have profit as their goal. Name that organization and its founder. (Find the answers in the chapter.)

LEARNING **goal 1**

Describe the relationship between profit and risk, and show how businesses and nonprofit organizations can raise the standard of living for all.

business
Any activity that seeks to provide goods and services to others while operating at a profit.

goods
Tangible products such as computers, food, clothing, cars, and appliances.

services
Intangible products (i.e., products that can't be held in your hand) such as education, health care, insurance, recreation, and travel and tourism.

entrepreneur
A person who risks time and money to start and manage a business.

revenue
The total amount of money a business takes in during a given period by selling goods and services.

profit
The amount of money a business earns above and beyond what it spends for salaries and other expenses.

loss
When a business's expenses are more than its revenues.

ENTREPRENEURSHIP AND WEALTH BUILDING

One thing you can learn from the chapter-opening Profile is that success in business is based on constantly adapting to the market. A **business** is any activity that seeks to provide goods and services to others while operating at a profit. To earn that profit, you provide desired goods, jobs, and services to people in the area. **Goods** are *tangible* products such as computers, food, clothing, cars, and appliances. **Services** are *intangible* products (i.e., products that can't be held in your hand) such as education, health care, insurance, recreation, and travel and tourism. Once you have developed the right goods and services, based on consumer wants and needs, you need to reach those consumers using whatever media they prefer, including blogs, tweets, Facebook, TV advertising, and more.[1]

Although you don't need to have wealth as a primary goal, one result of successfully filling a market need is that you can make money for yourself, sometimes a great deal, by giving customers what they want. Sam Walton of Walmart began by opening one store in Arkansas and, over time, became one of the richest people in the United States.[2] There are over 11 million millionaires in the world.[3] Maybe you will be one of them someday if you start your own business. An **entrepreneur** is a person who risks time and money to start and manage a business.

Revenues, Profits, and Losses

Revenue is the total amount of money a business takes in during a given period by selling goods and services. **Profit** is the amount of money a business earns above and beyond what it spends for salaries and other expenses needed to run the operation. A **loss** occurs when a business's expenses are more than its revenues. If a business loses money over time, it will likely have to close, putting its employees out of work. About 80,000 businesses in the United States close each year; even more close during a slowdown like the United States experienced starting in 2008.[4]

As noted above, the business environment is constantly changing. What seems like a great opportunity one day—for example, online grocery shopping or

SUVs—may become a huge failure when the economy changes. Starting a business may thus come with huge risks.[5] But huge risks often result in huge profits. We'll explore that concept next.

Matching Risk with Profit

Risk is the chance an entrepreneur takes of losing time and money on a business that may not prove profitable. Profit, remember, is the amount of money a business earns *above and beyond* what it pays out for salaries and other expenses. For example, if you were to start a business selling hot dogs from a cart in the summer, you would have to pay for the cart rental. You would also have to pay for the hot dogs and other materials and for someone to run the cart while you were away. After you paid your employee and yourself, paid for the food and materials you used, paid the rent on the cart, and paid your taxes, any money left over would be profit.

Keep in mind that profit is over and above the money you pay yourself in salary. You could use any profit to rent or buy a second cart and hire other employees. After a few summers, you might have a dozen carts employing dozens of workers.

Not all enterprises make the same amount of profit. Those that take the most risk may make the most profit. There is high risk, for example, in making a new kind of automobile.[6] It's also risky to open a business in an inner city, because insurance and rent are usually higher than in suburban areas, but reduced competition makes substantial profit possible. Irish entrepreneur Denis O'Brien, of Digicel, makes billions of dollars selling cell phones in the poorest, most violent countries in the world. Big risk, big profits.

Standard of Living and Quality of Life

Entrepreneurs such as Sam Walton (Walmart) and Bill Gates (Microsoft) not only became wealthy themselves; they also provided employment for many other people. Walmart is currently the nation's largest private employer.

Businesses and their employees pay taxes that the federal government and local communities use to build hospitals, schools, libraries, playgrounds, roads, and other public facilities. Taxes also help to keep the environment clean, support people in need, and provide police and fire protection. Thus, the wealth businesses generate and the taxes they pay help everyone in their communities. A nation's businesses are part of an economic system that contributes to the standard of living and quality of life for everyone in the country (and, potentially, the world). How has the recent economic slowdown affected the standard of living and quality of life in your part of the world?

The term **standard of living** refers to the amount of goods and services people can buy with the money they have. For example, the United States has one of the highest standards of living in the world, even though workers in some other countries, such as Germany and Japan, may on average make more money per hour. How can that be? Prices for goods and services in Germany and Japan are higher than in the United States, so a person in those countries can buy less than what a person in the United States can buy with the same amount of money. For example, a bottle of beer may cost $7 in Japan and $3 in the United States.

Often, goods cost more in one country than another because of higher taxes and stricter government regulations. Finding the right level of taxes and regulation is important in making a country or city prosperous. We'll explore that issue more deeply in Chapter 2. At this point, it is enough to understand that

risk
The chance an entrepreneur takes of losing time and money on a business that may not prove profitable.

standard of living
The amount of goods and services people can buy with the money they have.

Mary Kate and Ashley Olsen are now the head designers of their company Dualstar, which has three clothing lines ranging from the high-end to the more affordable. Today the business is worth over $1 billion. What risks and rewards did the twins face when they started their business?

the United States enjoys a high standard of living largely because of the wealth created by its businesses.

The term **quality of life** refers to the general well-being of a society in terms of its political freedom, natural environment, education, health care, safety, amount of leisure, and rewards that add to the satisfaction and joy that other goods and services provide. Maintaining a high quality of life requires the combined efforts of businesses, nonprofit organizations, and government agencies. The more money businesses create, the more is potentially available to improve the quality of life for everyone. It's important to be careful, however. Working to build a higher standard of living may lower the quality of life if it means less time with family or more stress.[7]

Responding to the Various Business Stakeholders

Stakeholders are all the people who stand to gain or lose by the policies and activities of a business and whose concerns the business needs to address.[8] They include customers, employees, stockholders, suppliers, dealers (retailers), bankers, people in the surrounding community, the media, environmentalists, and elected government leaders (see Figure 1.1).

A primary challenge for organizations of the 21st century will be to recognize and respond to the needs of their stakeholders. For example, the need for the business to make profits may be balanced against the needs of employees to earn sufficient income or the need to protect the environment.[9] Ignore the media, and they might attack your business with articles that hurt sales. Oppose the local community, and it may stop you from expanding.

Staying competitive may call for outsourcing. **Outsourcing** means contracting with other companies (often in other countries) to do some or all the functions of a firm, like its production or accounting tasks. Outsourcing has had serious

quality of life
The general well-being of a society in terms of its political freedom, natural environment, education, health care, safety, amount of leisure, and rewards that add to the satisfaction and joy that other goods and services provide.

stakeholders
All the people who stand to gain or lose by the policies and activities of a business and whose concerns the business needs to address.

outsourcing
Contracting with other companies (often in other countries) to do some or all of the functions of a firm, like its production or accounting tasks.

figure 1.1

A BUSINESS AND ITS STAKEHOLDERS

Often the needs of a firm's various stakeholders will conflict. For example, paying employees more may cut into stockholders' profits. Balancing such demands is a major role of business managers.

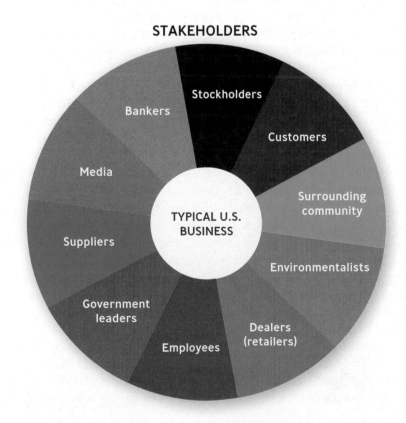

STAKEHOLDERS

consequences in some states where jobs have been lost to overseas competitors. We discuss outsourcing in more detail in Chapter 3.

The other side of the outsourcing coin is *insourcing*.[10] Many foreign companies are setting up design and production facilities here in the United States. For example, Korea-based Hyundai operates design and engineering headquarters in Detroit, Michigan, and produces cars in Montgomery, Alabama. Japanese automakers Honda and Toyota have been producing cars in the United States for years. Insourcing creates many new U.S. jobs and helps offset those being outsourced.[11]

It may be legal and profitable to outsource, but is it best for all the stakeholders? Business leaders must make outsourcing decisions based on all factors. Pleasing stakeholders is not easy and often calls for trade-offs.

Using Business Principles in Nonprofit Organizations

Despite their efforts to satisfy their stakeholders, businesses cannot do everything needed to make a community all it can be. Nonprofit organizations—such as public schools, civic associations, charities like United Way and Salvation Army, and groups devoted to social causes—also make a major contribution to the welfare of society. A **nonprofit organization** is an organization whose goals do not include making a personal profit for its owners or organizers. Nonprofit organizations often do strive for financial gains, but they use them to meet their social or educational goals rather than for personal profit.[12]

Social entrepreneurs are people who use business principles to start and manage not-for-profits and help address social issues. Muhammad Yunus won the Nobel Prize for starting the Grameen Bank, a microlending organization that provides small loans to entrepreneurs too poor to qualify for traditional loans. Yunus has started 30 of what he calls social businesses that do not have profit as their goal. One, for example, provides cataract operations for a fraction of the usual cost.[13]

Your interests may lead you to work for a nonprofit organization such as those started by Yunus. That doesn't mean, however, that you shouldn't study business in college. You'll still need to learn business skills such as information management,

nonprofit organization
An organization whose goals do not include making a personal profit for its owners or organizers.

The goals of nonprofit organizations are social and educational, not profit-oriented. The Red Cross, for instance, provides assistance to around 30 million people annually from refugees to victims of natural disasters. Why do good management principles apply equally to businesses and nonprofit organizations?

leadership, marketing, and financial management. The knowledge and skills you acquire in this and other business courses are useful for careers in any organization, including nonprofits. We'll explore entrepreneurship in more detail right after the Progress Assessment.

progress assessment

- What is the difference between *revenue* and *profit?*
- What is the difference between *standard of living* and *quality of life?*
- What is risk, and how is it related to profit?
- What do the terms *stakeholders, outsourcing,* and *insourcing* mean?

LEARNING goal 2

Compare and contrast being an entrepreneur and working for others.

ENTREPRENEURSHIP VERSUS WORKING FOR OTHERS

To create wealth for its citizens, a country requires more than natural resources. It needs the efforts of entrepreneurs and the skill and knowledge to produce goods and services. How can government support entrepreneurship and the spread of knowledge?

There are two ways to succeed in business. One is to rise through the ranks of large companies. The advantage of working for others is that somebody else assumes the company's entrepreneurial risk and provides you with benefits like paid vacation time and health insurance.[14] It's a good option, and many people choose it.

The other, riskier path is to become an entrepreneur. The national anthem, "The Star Spangled Banner," says that the United States is the "land of the free and the home of the brave." Part of being free is being able to own your own business and reap the profits from it. But freedom to succeed also means freedom to fail, and many small businesses fail each year. It takes a brave person to start one. As an entrepreneur, you don't receive any benefits such as paid vacation time, day care, a company car, or health insurance. You have to provide them for yourself! But what you gain—freedom to make your own decisions, opportunity, and possible wealth—is often worth the effort. Before you take on the challenge, you should study successful entrepreneurs to learn the process. You can talk to them personally and read about them in Chapter 6, as well as in other books and magazines.

Opportunities for Entrepreneurs

Millions of people from all over the world have taken the entrepreneurial challenge and succeeded. For example, the number of Hispanic-owned businesses in the United States has grown dramatically (Hispanics are now the largest ethnic group in the United States). Both Hispanic men and women are doing particularly well. Similar successes are true of businesses owned by Asians, Pacific Islanders, Native Americans, and Alaskan Natives.

Making the Most of a Stinky Situation

Some of the best business ideas come from solutions to everyday problems. For Marie Gelin, getting her active son to bathe was a struggle. She would often hear him running the shower only to catch him playing video games or reading instead of washing. Although adults might wrinkle their noses at being so dirty, there was no incentive for Gelin's son to smell better. He only cared about playing.

That gave Gelin an idea: What if she could convince her son that bathtime was just a continuation of playtime? She decided to package soaps and shampoos into the shape of baseballs, footballs, and soccer balls. Her son loved the new containers, and eventually she started

selling the products under the brand name Stinky Boyz. Gelin discovered that not only had she come up with a unique idea, but she also had tapped into a relatively unexplored market. While there are plenty of hygiene products available for young girls, boys don't have a lot of brands targeted toward them. Soon, though, Stinky Boyz will be available in as many as 4,000 supermarkets and drugstore chains, sparing the noses of countless parents across the country from unwelcome odors.

Sources: Michelle Juergen, "A Mom Sees and Fills a Need in the Marketplace: Personal Hygiene Products for Boys," *Entrepreneur,* May 24, 2011, and www .stinky-boyz.com, accessed May 3, 2012.

Women now own over a third of all businesses. Names you may know include Oprah Winfrey, Donna Karan, and Lillian Vernon. The world's most powerful women include Ho Ching, the chief executive of Temasek Holdings in Singapore; Indra Nooyi, chief executive of PepsiCo, U.S.; and Cynthia Carroll, chief executive of Anglo American in the United Kingdom.[15]

Businesses owned by minority women are growing faster than those owned by men or nonminority women. Women of color are establishing businesses at twice the rate of their male counterparts and more than four times that of nonminority entrepreneurs. Read the nearby Connecting with Small Business box to learn more about minority entrepreneurs.

The Importance of Entrepreneurs to the Creation of Wealth

Have you ever wondered why some countries are relatively wealthy and others poor? Economists have been studying the issue of wealth creation for many years. They began by identifying five **factors of production** that seemed to contribute to wealth (see Figure 1.2):

factors of production
The resources used to create wealth: land, labor, capital, entrepreneurship, and knowledge.

1. Land (or natural resources).
2. Labor (workers).
3. Capital. (This includes machines, tools, buildings, or whatever else is used in the production of goods. It may not include money; money is used to buy factors of production but is not always considered a factor by itself.)
4. Entrepreneurship.
5. Knowledge.

figure 1.2

THE FIVE FACTORS
OF PRODUCTION

Land

Land and other natural resources are used to make homes, cars, and other products.

Labor

People have always been an important resource in producing goods and services, but many people are now being replaced by technology.

Capital

Capital includes machines, tools, buildings, and other means of manufacturing.

Entrepreneurship

All the resources in the world have little value unless entrepreneurs are willing to take the risk of starting businesses to use those resources.

Knowledge

Information technology has revolutionized business, making it possible to quickly determine wants and needs and to respond with desired goods and services.

Traditionally, business and economics textbooks emphasized only four factors of production: land, labor, capital, and entrepreneurship. But the late management expert and business consultant Peter Drucker said the most important factor of production in our economy is and always will be *knowledge.*

What do we find when we compare the factors of production in rich and poor countries? Some poor countries have plenty of land and natural resources. Russia, for example, has vast areas of land with many resources such as timber and oil, but it is not considered a rich country (yet). Therefore, land isn't the critical element for wealth creation.

Most poor countries, such as Mexico, have many laborers, so it's not labor that's the primary source of wealth today. Laborers need to find work to make a contribution; that is, they need entrepreneurs to create jobs for them. Furthermore, capital—machinery and tools—is now fairly easy for firms to find in world markets, so capital isn't the missing ingredient either. Capital is not productive without entrepreneurs to put it to use.

What makes rich countries rich today is a combination of *entrepreneurship* and the effective use of *knowledge.* Entrepreneurs use what they've learned (knowledge) to grow their businesses and increase wealth. Economic and political freedom also matter.

The business environment either encourages or discourages entrepreneurship. That helps explain why some states and cities in the United States grow rich while others remain relatively poor. In the following section, we'll explore what makes up the business environment and how to build an environment that encourages growth and job creation.

progress assessment

- What are some of the advantages of working for others?
- What benefits do you lose by being an entrepreneur, and what do you gain?
- What are the five factors of production? Which ones seem to be the most important for creating wealth?

figure 1.3

TODAY'S DYNAMIC BUSINESS ENVIRONMENT

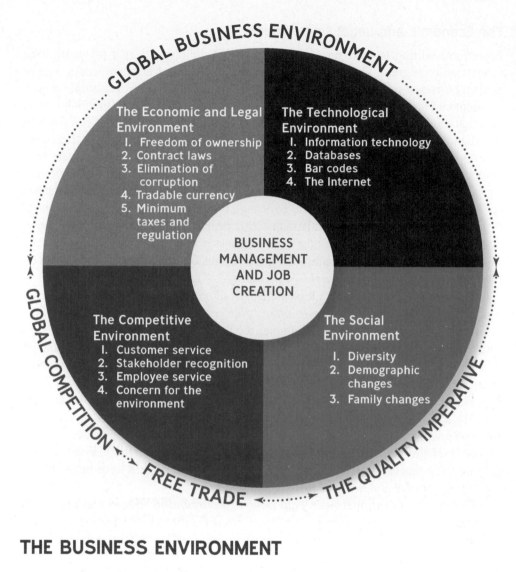

GLOBAL BUSINESS ENVIRONMENT

The Economic and Legal Environment
1. Freedom of ownership
2. Contract laws
3. Elimination of corruption
4. Tradable currency
5. Minimum taxes and regulation

The Technological Environment
1. Information technology
2. Databases
3. Bar codes
4. The Internet

BUSINESS MANAGEMENT AND JOB CREATION

The Competitive Environment
1. Customer service
2. Stakeholder recognition
3. Employee service
4. Concern for the environment

The Social Environment
1. Diversity
2. Demographic changes
3. Family changes

GLOBAL COMPETITION
FREE TRADE
THE QUALITY IMPERATIVE

Need help understanding standard of living vs. quality of life? www.introbiz.tv/QR1-1 Can't Scan? Try ScanLife at your app store.

THE BUSINESS ENVIRONMENT

The **business environment** consists of the surrounding factors that either help or hinder the development of businesses. Figure 1.3 shows the five elements in the business environment:

1. The economic and legal environment.
2. The technological environment.
3. The competitive environment.
4. The social environment.
5. The global business environment.

Businesses that create wealth and jobs grow and prosper in a healthy environment. Thus, creating the right business environment is the foundation for social benefits of all kinds, including good schools, clean air and water, good health care, and low rates of crime. Businesses normally can't control their environment, but they need to monitor it carefully and do what they can to adapt as it changes.

business environment
The surrounding factors that either help or hinder the development of businesses.

LEARNING goal 3

Analyze the effects of the economic environment and taxes on businesses.

The Economic and Legal Environment

People are willing to start new businesses if they believe the risk of losing their money isn't too great. The economic system and the way government works with or against businesses can have a strong impact on that level of risk. For example, a government can *minimize spending* and *keep taxes and regulations to a minimum,* policies that tend to favor business. Much of the debate in recent elections has focused on whether or not to raise taxes and how to lower government spending.[16] President Obama increased government spending with the idea of getting the economy moving faster. Some economists agreed with such a stimulus, but some did not.[17] One way for government to actively promote entrepreneurship is to *allow private ownership of businesses.* In some countries, the government owns most businesses, and there's little incentive for people to work hard or create profit. Around the world today, however, some governments are selling those businesses to private individuals to create more wealth. One of the best things the governments of developing countries can do is to *minimize interference with the free exchange of goods and services.*

The government can further lessen the risks of entrepreneurship by *passing laws that enable businesspeople to write enforceable contracts.* In the United States, the Uniform Commercial Code, for example, regulates business agreements like contracts and warranties so that firms know they can rely on one another. In countries that don't yet have such laws, the risks of starting a business are that much greater. You can read more about business laws in Appendix A at the end of this book.

The government can also *establish a currency that's tradable in world markets.* That is, the currency lets you buy and sell goods and services anywhere in the world when it is easily exchanged for that of the other countries where you do business. If the Chinese did not want to trade their yuan for the U.S. dollar, for instance, it's hard to imagine how Coca-Cola or Disney would have been able to sell their products and services there.

Finally, the government can help *minimize corruption* in business and in its own ranks. Where governments are corrupt, it's difficult to build a factory or open a store without a government permit, which is obtained largely through bribery of

Starting a business is much harder in some countries than in others. In India, for example, it requires a time-consuming and bureaucratic process to obtain government permission. Nonetheless, new businesses can become a major source of wealth and employment; this sari shop is one small example. What do you think would be the effect of a little more freedom to create business opportunities in this country of over a billion people?

MAKING ethical decisions

Ethics Begins with You

It is easy to criticize the ethics of people whose names appear in the headlines. It is more difficult to see the moral and ethical misbehavior of your own social group. Do you find some of the behaviors of your friends morally or ethically questionable?

A survey found that the number of employees calling in sick had reached a five-year high, and three-fifths were not sick at all. Other employees have been caught conducting personal business at work, such as doing their taxes. And others play video games on their work computers. We're sure you can add many more examples.

Many companies today are creating ethics codes to guide their employees' behavior. We believe the trend toward improving ethical behavior is so important that

we've made it a major theme of this book. Throughout the text you'll see boxes like this one, called Making Ethical Decisions, that pose ethical dilemmas and ask what you would do to resolve them. The idea is for you to think about the moral and ethical dimensions of every decision you make.

Here is your first one: You have become addicted to your electronic gadgets. Some days at work you spend most of the time playing games, watching TV, texting, sending e-mails to friends, or reading a book or magazine on your devices. What is the problem in this situation? What are your alternatives? What are the consequences of each alternative? Which alternative will you choose? Is your choice ethical?

---

public officials. Among businesses themselves, unscrupulous leaders can threaten their competitors and unlawfully minimize competition.

Many laws in the United States attempt to minimize corruption. Nonetheless, corrupt and illegal activities at some companies do negatively affect the business community and the economy as a whole.[18] The news media widely report these scandals. Ethics is so important to the success of businesses and the economy as a whole that we feature stories about ethics in most chapters and devote Chapter 4 to the subject.

The capitalist system relies heavily on honesty, integrity, and high ethical standards. Failure of those fundamentals can weaken the whole system. The faltering economy that began in 2008 was due in large part to such failure. Some mortgage lenders, for instance, failed to do the research necessary to ensure their borrowers' creditworthiness. Many subprime borrowers (people with low credit ratings) forfeited their loans. The ripple effects of these unpaid debts not only cost many people their homes but also reduced the value of housing across the world and made it difficult even for business borrowers to get new loans. Part of the blame for this economic disaster can be placed on the borrowers who didn't tell the truth about their income or who otherwise deceived the lenders.

It is easy to see the damage caused by the poor moral and ethical behavior of some businesspeople.[19] What is not so obvious is the damage caused by the moral and ethical lapses of the everyday consumer—that is, you and me. The Making Ethical Decisions box discusses that issue in more depth.

LEARNING goal 4

Describe the effects of technology on businesses.

Using Smartphones to Connect with Customers

Nothing highlights the dynamic nature of business more than the number of new electronic devices people carry today, including iPads, e-readers, and smartphones of all kinds. People seem to be constantly texting, tweeting, and talking to each other. You cannot help but notice them in restaurants, on buses, and even walking down the street. Hopefully, though, you don't see them doing it while they're driving.

As the generation that grew up with smartphones gets older, retailers are trying to figure out ways to connect with them through technology. For instance, the Northeastern supermarket chain Stop & Shop recently began offering its own smartphone app to customers at select locations. The app links directly to the customer's rewards card, which grants them various coupons and discounts. Using Quick Response Codes (QRCs) like the ones seen throughout this text, customers scan the items they place in their cart. The app then targets special offers and coupons to the customer for products they like.

Stop & Shop's idea is by no means a new one. For years the supermarket provided special scanning devices for customers to use in the store. Now that smartphones are so common, though, the company saves a bundle on buying and maintaining the unwieldy old scanners. Stop & Shop also hopes its scanning strategy will save money on labor costs as the years go by. After all, when a smartphone can answer a question clearly within a matter of seconds, there's no reason to clutter the sales floor with as many staff.

Another retail app, AisleBuyer, could prove even more revolutionary. Besides offering coupons, the app allows customers to check out directly from their phones. All they need to do is scan their items, press a button, maybe show their digital receipt to an employee, and then head home. As more apps like Stop & Shop's and AisleBuyer become available, experts predict that scanning products while shopping could become just as common as smartphones themselves.

Sources: Dana Mattioli, "Grocers Testing Smartphones," *The Wall Street Journal,* October 11, 2011; and Hiawatha Bray, "Smartphone Apps May Help Retail Scanning Catch On," *The Boston Globe,* March 12, 2012.

The Technological Environment

Since prehistoric times, humans have felt the need to create tools that make work easier. Few technological changes have had a more comprehensive and lasting impact on businesses, however, than the emergence of information technology (IT): computers, networks, cell phones, and especially the Internet.

The iPad, iPhone, BlackBerry, and other smartphones, as well as social media like Facebook and Twitter, have completely changed the way people communicate with one another. Advertisers and other businesspeople have created ways of using these tools to reach their suppliers and customers. Even politicians have harnessed the power of the Internet to advance their causes. See the nearby Connecting Through Social Media box for an example of how some grocery stores use these tools to interact with customers.

IT is such a major force in business today that we discuss its impact on businesses throughout the entire text.

How Technology Benefits Workers and You   One of the advantages of working for others is that the company often provides the tools and technology to make your job more productive. **Technology** means everything from phones and copiers

technology
Everything from phones and copiers to computers, medical imaging devices, personal digital assistants, and the various software programs that make business processes more effective, efficient, and productive.

Technology makes workers more productive. Instead of spending hours traveling to meet, for instance, these employees use teleconferencing to share information and make decisions. Are some workers likely to be more comfortable with new technology than others?

to computers, medical imaging devices, and the various software programs that make business processes more effective, efficient, and productive. *Effectiveness* means producing the desired result. *Efficiency* means producing goods and services using the least amount of resources.

Productivity is the amount of output you generate given the amount of input, such as the number of hours you work. The more you can produce in any given period, the more money you are worth to companies. The average worker in the United States contributes $63,885 to GDP, making U.S. workers some of the world's most productive employees. The problem with productivity today is that workers are so productive that fewer are needed, and that is contributing to the high unemployment rate we are now experiencing.[20]

Technology affects people in all industries. For example, Don Glenn, a farmer in Decatur, Alabama, uses his personal computer to compare data from the previous year's harvest with infrared satellite photos of his farm that show which crops are flourishing. He has a desktop terminal called a DTN that allows him to check the latest grain prices, and he uses AgTalk, a web-based bulletin board, to converse with other farmers from all over the world. He also bids for bulk fertilizer on XSAg.com, an online agricultural exchange. High-tech equipment tells Glenn how and where to spread fertilizer and seed, tracks yields yard by yard, and allows him to maintain high profit margins.

The Growth of E-Commerce **E-commerce** is the buying and selling of goods over the Internet. There are two major types of e-commerce transactions: business-to-consumer (B2C) and business-to-business (B2B). As important as the Internet has been to retailers like Amazon.com in the consumer market, it has become even more important in the B2B market, where businesses sell goods and services to one another, such as IBM selling consulting services to a local bank. Websites have become the new stores.[21]

Traditional businesses must deal with the competition from B2B and B2C firms, and vice versa. Many new parents would just as soon buy used items posted on Craigslist than shop in a baby-goods store. Starting a business on eBay has never been easier. More than 450 million Chinese citizens are using the Internet. This is about double the number of U.S. users.[22] And what did people do before they could google? E-commerce has become so important that we will discuss it throughout the text.

productivity
The amount of output you generate given the amount of input (e.g., hours worked).

e-commerce
The buying and selling of goods over the Internet.

database
An electronic storage file
for information.

identity theft
The obtaining of
individuals' personal
information, such as
Social Security and credit
card numbers, for illegal
purposes.

Using Technology to Be Responsive to Customers   A major theme of this text is that those businesses most responsive to customer wants and needs will succeed. That realization points to one way in which even traditional retailers can use Internet technology. For example, businesscs use bar codes to identify products you buy and their size, quantity, and color. The scanner at the checkout counter identifies the price but can also put all your purchase information into a **database,** an electronic storage file for information.

Databases enable stores to carry only the merchandise their local population wants. But because companies routinely trade database information, many retailers know what you buy and from whom you buy it. Thus they can send you catalogs and other direct mail advertising offering the kind of products you might want, as indicated by your past purchases. We discuss other ways businesses use technology to be responsive to consumers throughout the text.

Unfortunately, the legitimate collection of personal customer information also opens the door to identity theft. **Identity theft** is the obtaining of individuals' personal information, such as Social Security and credit card numbers, for illegal purposes. The Federal Trade Commission says millions of U.S. consumers are victims of identity theft each year. What you should learn from these examples is to limit those to whom you give personal information. You also need antivirus software on your computer as well as a firewall and antispyware software. You may also want to monitor your credit report. It is important for you to understand identity theft, security, privacy, stability, and other important IT issues.[23]

LEARNING goal 5

Demonstrate how businesses can meet and beat competition.

The Competitive Environment

Competition among businesses has never been greater. Some have found a competitive edge by focusing on quality. The goal for many companies is zero defects—no mistakes in making the product. However, even achieving a rate of zero defects isn't enough to stay competitive in world markets. Companies now have to offer both high-quality products and good value—that is, outstanding service at competitive prices.

Competing by Exceeding Customer Expectations   Today's customers want not only good quality at low prices but great service as well. Every manufacturing and service organization in the world should have a sign over its door telling its workers that the customer is king. Business is becoming customer-driven, not management-driven as often occurred in the past. Successful organizations must now listen more closely to customers to determine their wants and needs, and then adjust the firm's products, policies, and practices accordingly. We will explore these ideas in more depth in Chapter 13.

Competing by Restructuring and Empowerment   To meet the needs of customers, firms must give their frontline workers—for example, office clerks, front-desk people at hotels, and salespeople—the responsibility, authority, freedom, training, and equipment they need to respond quickly to customer requests. They also must allow workers to make other decisions essential to producing high-quality goods and services. The process is called **empowerment,** and we'll be talking about it throughout this book.

As many companies have discovered, it sometimes takes years to restructure an organization so that managers can and will give up some of their authority and employees will assume more responsibility. We'll discuss such organizational changes in Chapter 8.

empowerment
Giving frontline workers the responsibility, authority, freedom, training, and equipment they need to respond quickly to customer requests.

LEARNING goal 6

Analyze the social changes affecting businesses.

The Social Environment

Demography is the statistical study of the human population with regard to its size, density, and other characteristics such as age, race, gender, and income. In this text, we're particularly interested in the demographic trends that most affect businesses and career choices. The U.S. population is going through major changes that are dramatically affecting how people live, where they live, what they buy, and how they spend their time. Furthermore, tremendous population shifts are leading to new opportunities for some firms and to declining opportunities for others. For example, there are many more retired workers than in the past, creating new markets for all kinds of goods and services.[24]

demography
The statistical study of the human population with regard to its size, density, and other characteristics such as age, race, gender, and income.

Managing Diversity *Diversity* has come to mean much more than recruiting and keeping minority and female employees. Diversity efforts now include seniors, people with disabilities, homosexuals, atheists, extroverts, introverts, married people, singles, and the devout. It also means dealing sensitively with workers and cultures around the world.

Legal and illegal immigrants have had a dramatic effect on many cities. Schools and hospitals have been especially affected. Some local governments are making every effort to adapt, including changing signs, brochures, websites, and forms to include other languages. Has your city experienced such changes? What are some of the impacts you've noticed?

The United States boasts enormous ethnic and racial diversity. Its workforce is also widely diverse in terms of age, which means managers must adapt to the generational demographics of the workplace. What are some challenges of working with someone much younger or much older than yourself?

The Increase in the Number of Older Citizens People ages 65 to 74 are currently the richest demographic group in the United States. They thus represent a lucrative market for companies involved with food service, transportation, entertainment, education, lodging, and so on. By 2020, the percentage of the population over 60 will be 22.8 percent (versus 16 percent in 2000). What do these changes mean for you and for businesses in the future? Think of the products and services that middle-aged and elderly people will need—medicine, nursing homes, assisted-living facilities, adult day care, home health care, recreation, and the like—and you'll see opportunities for successful businesses of the 21st century. Don't rule out computer games and Internet services, even Wii. Businesses that cater to older

consumers will have the opportunity for exceptional growth in the near future. The market is huge.[25]

On the other hand, retired people will be draining the economy of wealth. Social Security has become a major issue. The pay-as-you-go system (in which workers today pay the retirement benefits for today's retirees) operated just fine in 1940, when 42 workers supported each retiree; but by 1960, there were only 5 workers per retiree, and today, as the baby-boom generation (born between 1946 and 1964) begins to retire, that number is under 3 and dropping. In addition, the government has been spending the accumulated Social Security money instead of leaving it in a Social Security account.

Soon, less money will be coming into Social Security than will be going out. The government will have to do something to make up for the shortfall: raise taxes, reduce Social Security benefits (e.g., raise the retirement age at which people qualify for payments), reduce spending elsewhere (e.g., in other social programs like Medicare or Medicaid), or borrow on the world market.

In short, paying Social Security to senior citizens in the future will draw huge amounts of money from the working population. That is why there is so much discussion in the media today about what to do with Social Security.

More and more working families consist of single parents who must juggle the demands of a job and responsibilities of raising children. What can managers do to try to retain valued employees who face such challenges?

The Increase in the Number of Single-Parent Families   It is a tremendous task to work full-time and raise a family. Thus, the rapid growth of single-parent households has also had a major effect on businesses. Single parents, including those forced by welfare rules to return to work after a certain benefit period, have encouraged businesses to implement programs such as family leave (giving workers time off to attend to a sick child or elder relative) and flextime (allowing workers to arrive or leave at selected times). You will read about such programs in more detail in Chapter 11.

LEARNING goal 7

Identify what businesses must do to meet global challenges, including war and terrorism.

The Global Environment

The global environment of business is so important that we show it as surrounding all other environmental influences (see again Figure 1.3). Two important changes here are the growth of global competition and the increase of free trade among nations.

World trade, or *globalization,* has grown thanks to the development of efficient distribution systems (we'll talk about these in Chapter 15) and communication advances such as the Internet. Globalization has greatly improved living standards around the world. China and India have become major U.S. competitors.

Lenovo, a Chinese firm, bought IBM's PC unit. Shop at Walmart and most other U.S. retail stores, and you can't help but notice the number of "Made in China" stickers you see. Call for computer help, and you are as likely to be talking with someone in India as someone in the United States.

World trade has its benefits and costs. You'll read much more about its importance in Chapter 3 and in the Connecting Across Borders boxes throughout the text.

War and Terrorism   The wars in Iraq and Afghanistan have drawn billions of dollars from the U.S. economy. Some companies—like those that make bullets, tanks, and uniforms—have benefited greatly. Others, however, have lost workers to the armed forces, and still others (e.g., tourism) have grown more slowly as money has been diverted to the war effort. The threat of other wars and terrorism leads the government to spend even more money on the military. Such expenditures are subject to much debate, especially as the United States responds to an economic recession. Note the increased unrest in the world as people in other nations are demanding more freedom.

The threat of terrorism also adds greatly to organizational costs, including the cost of insurance. In fact, some firms are finding it difficult to get insurance against terrorist attacks. Security, too, is costly. Airlines, for example, have had to install stronger cockpit doors and add more passenger screening devices.

Like all citizens, businesspeople benefit from a peaceful and prosperous world. One way to lessen international tensions is to foster global economic growth among both profit-making and nonprofit organizations.

How Global Changes Affect You   As businesses expand to serve global markets, new jobs will be created in both manufacturing and service industries. Global trade also means global competition. The students who will prosper will be those prepared for the markets of tomorrow. Rapid changes create a need for continuous learning, so be prepared to continue your education throughout your career. You'll have every reason to be optimistic about job opportunities in the future if you prepare yourself well.

The Ecological Environment   Few issues have captured the attention of the international business community more than climate change. **Climate change** is the movement of the temperature of the planet up or down over time. The issue now is global warming, but the issue may become global cooling. Some of the world's largest firms—including General Electric, Coca-Cola, Shell, Nestlé, DuPont, Johnson & Johnson, British Airways, and Shanghai Electric—say the evidence for climate change is overwhelming. Saving energy and producing products that cause less harm to the environment is a trend called **greening**.[26] Greening has become such a pervasive issue that we devote boxes to that subject throughout the text. (See the Making the Green Connection box for things you can do to contribute to the cause.)

climate change
The movement of the temperature of the planet up or down over time.

greening
The trend toward saving energy and producing products that cause less harm to the environment.

progress assessment

- What are four ways the government can foster entrepreneurship?
- What's the difference between effectiveness, efficiency, and productivity?
- What is *empowerment?*
- What are some of the major issues affecting the economy today?

MAKING THE GREEN
connection

http://sustainability.publicradio.org/
consumed/tips.html

Green Up Your Life

There is little doubt humans can take action to protect the environment. What can we do now to start?

It's not necessary to change your lifestyle radically in order to make a difference. Simply heating or cooling your apartment or house more efficiently is a good start. Why not buy a reusable grocery bag? You can recycle paper and containers. You can walk or ride a bike instead of driving. You can reduce your use of electrical equipment and of water (pumping water takes a lot of electricity). Buy produce that is grown locally to save the energy used in shipping food from faraway places. If you're in the market for a car, you could "go green" by buying a hybrid or a small, fuel-efficient car.

The idea is to become more ecologically aware and join others throughout the world in using less energy and emitting less carbon into the atmosphere. Everyone benefits when the air is cleaner. That's part of what the green movement is all about.

LEARNING **goal 8**

Review how past trends are being repeated in the present and what those trends mean for tomorrow's college graduates.

THE EVOLUTION OF U.S. BUSINESS

Businesses in the United States have become so productive that they need fewer workers than ever before to produce goods. If global competition and improved technology are putting skilled people out of work, should we be concerned about the prospect of high unemployment rates and low incomes? Where will the jobs be when you graduate? These important questions force us all to look briefly at the U.S. economy and its future.

Progress in the Agricultural and Manufacturing Industries

The United States has experienced strong economic development since the 1800s. The agricultural industry led the way, providing food for the United States and much of the world. Cyrus McCormick's invention of the harvester in 1834, other inventions such as Eli Whitney's cotton gin, and modern improvements on such equipment did much to make large-scale farming successful. Technology has made modern farming so efficient that the number of farmers has dropped from about 33 percent of the population to about 1 percent today. However, average farm size is now about 450 acres versus 160 acres in the past.

Agriculture is still a major industry in the United States. What has changed is that the millions of small farms that existed previously have been replaced by some huge farms, some merely large farms, and some small but highly specialized farms. The loss of farm workers over the past century is not a negative sign. It is instead an indication that U.S. agricultural workers are the most productive in the world.

Most farmers who lost their jobs during the 19th and 20th centuries went to work in factories springing up around the country. Manufacturers, like farms, began using technology like tools and machines to become more productive. Eventually the consequence in manufacturing, as in farming, was the elimination of many jobs.

Again, the loss to society is minimized if the wealth created by increased productivity and efficiency creates new jobs elsewhere—and that's exactly what has happened over the past 50 years. Many workers in the industrial sector found jobs in the growing service sector. Most of those who can't find work today are people who need retraining and education to become qualified for jobs that now exist or will exist in the near future, like building wind farms or making electric automobiles. We'll discuss the manufacturing sector and production in more detail in Chapter 9.

Agriculture is one of the largest and most important industries in the United States Technology has increased productivity and made farmers more efficient, allowing for larger farms. This trend has reduced the price of food for consumers, but has also reduced the number of small, family-run farms. Does the new technology also help smaller farms compete? How?

Progress in Service Industries

In the past, the fastest-growing industries in the United States produced goods like steel, automobiles, and machine tools. Today, the fastest-growing firms provide services in areas like law, health, telecommunications, entertainment, and finance.

Together, services make up over 70 percent of the value of the U.S. economy. Since the mid-1980s, the service industry has generated almost all the increases in employment. Although service-sector growth has slowed, it remains the largest area of growth. Chances are very high that you'll work in a service job at some point in your career. Figure 1.4 lists many service-sector jobs; look it over to see where the careers of the future are likely to be. Retailers like American Eagle are part of the service sector. Each new retail store can create managerial jobs for college graduates.

Another bit of good news is that there are *more* high-paying jobs in the service sector than in the goods-producing sector. High-paying service-sector jobs abound in health care, accounting, finance, entertainment, telecommunications, architecture, law, software engineering, and more. Projections are that some areas of the service sector will grow rapidly, while others may have much slower growth. The strategy for college graduates is to remain flexible, find out where jobs are being created, and move when appropriate.[27]

Your Future in Business

Despite the growth in the service sector we've described above, the service era now seems to be coming to a close as a new era is beginning. We're in the midst of an information-based global revolution that will alter all sectors of the economy: agricultural, industrial, and service. It's exciting to think about the role you'll play in that revolution. You may be a leader who will implement the changes and accept the challenges of world competition based on world quality standards. This book will introduce you to some of the concepts that make such leadership possible, not just in business but also in government agencies and nonprofit organizations. Business can't prosper in the future without the cooperation of government and social leaders throughout the world.

There's much talk about the service sector, but few discussions actually list what it includes. Here's a representative list of services as classified by the government:

Lodging Services

Hotels, rooming houses, and other lodging places
Sporting and recreation camps
Trailer parks and campsites for transients

Personal Services

Laundries	Child care
Linen supply	Shoe repair
Diaper service	Funeral homes
Carpet cleaning	Tax preparation
Photographic studios	Beauty shops
Health clubs	

Business Services

Accounting	Exterminating
Ad agencies	Employment agencies
Collection agencies	Computer programming
Commercial photography	Research & development labs
Commercial art	Management services
Stenographic services	Public relations
Window cleaning	Detective agencies
Consulting	Interior design
Equipment rental	Web design
Tax preparation	Trash collection

Automotive Repair Services and Garages

Auto rental	Tire retreading
Truck rental	Exhaust system shops
Parking lots	Car washes
Paint shops	Transmission repair

Miscellaneous Repair Services

Radio and television	Welding
Watch	Sharpening
Reupholstery	Septic tank cleaning

Motion Picture Industry

Production	Theaters
Distribution	Drive-ins

Amusement and Recreation Services

Restaurants	Racetracks
Symphony orchestras	Golf courses
Pool halls	Amusement parks
Bowling alleys	Carnivals
Fairs	Ice skating rinks
Botanical gardens	Circuses
Video rentals	Infotainment

Health Services

Physicians	Nursery care
Dentists	Medical labs
Chiropractors	Dental labs

Legal Services

Educational Services

Libraries	Computer schools
Schools	Online schools

Social Services

Child care	Family services
Job training	Elder care

Noncommercial Museums, Art Galleries, and Botanical and Zoological Gardens

Selected Membership Organizations

Business associations	Civic associations

Financial Services

Banking	Real estate agencies
Insurance	Investment firms
(brokers)	

Miscellaneous Services

Architectural	Surveying
Engineering	Utilities
Telecommunications	Lawn care
Vending	Delivery

figure 1.4

WHAT IS THE SERVICE SECTOR?

progress assessment

- What major factor caused people to move from farming to manufacturing and from manufacturing to the service sector?
- What does the future look like for tomorrow's college graduates?

summary

Learning Goal 1. Describe the relationship between profit and risk, and show how businesses and nonprofit organizations can raise the standard of living for all.

- **What is the relationship of businesses' profit to risk assumption?**

Profit is money a business earns above and beyond the money that it spends for salaries and other expenses. Businesspeople make profits by taking risks. *Risk* is the chance an entrepreneur takes of losing time and money on a business that may not prove profitable. A loss occurs when a business's costs and expenses are higher than its revenues.

- **Who are stakeholders, and which stakeholders are most important to a business?**

Stakeholders include customers, employees, stockholders, suppliers, dealers, bankers, the media, people in the local community, environmentalists, and elected government leaders. The goal of business leaders is to try to recognize and respond to the needs of these stakeholders and still make a profit.

Learning Goal 2. Compare and contrast being an entrepreneur and working for others.

- **What are the advantages and disadvantages of entrepreneurship?**

Working for others means getting benefits like paid vacations and health insurance. Entrepreneurs take more risks and lose those benefits. They gain the freedom to make their own decisions, more opportunity, and possible wealth.

- **What are the five factors of production?**

The five factors of production are land, labor, capital, entrepreneurship, and knowledge. Of these, the most important are entrepreneurship and knowledge. Entrepreneurs are people who risk time and money to start and manage a business. What makes rich countries rich today is a combination of *entrepreneurship* and the effective use of *knowledge.*

Learning Goal 3. Analyze the effects of the economic environment and taxes on businesses.

- **What can governments in developing countries do to reduce the risk of starting businesses and thus help entrepreneurs?**

The government may allow private ownership of businesses, pass laws that enable businesspeople to write contracts that are enforceable in court, establish a currency that's tradable in world markets, help to lessen corruption in business and government, and keep taxes and regulations to a minimum. From a business perspective, lower taxes mean lower risks, more growth, and thus more money for workers and the government.

Learning Goal 4. Describe the effects of technology on businesses.

- **How has technology benefited workers, businesses, and consumers?**

Technology enables workers to be more effective, efficient, and productive. *Effectiveness* means doing the right thing in the right way. *Efficiency* means producing items using the least amount of resources. *Productivity* is the amount of output you generate given the amount of input (e.g., hours worked).

Learning Goal 5. Demonstrate how businesses can meet and beat competition.

- **What are some ways in which businesses meet and beat competition?**

Some companies have found a competitive edge by focusing on making high-quality products, all the way to zero defects. Companies also aim to exceed customer expectations. Often that means *empowering* frontline workers by giving them more training and more responsibility and authority.

Learning Goal 6. Analyze the social changes affecting businesses.

- **How have social changes affected businesses?**

Diversity has come to mean much more than recruiting and keeping minority and female employees. Diversity efforts now include seniors, disabled people, homosexuals, atheists, extroverts, introverts, married people, singles, and the devout. It also means dealing sensitively with workers and cultures around the world. Providing Social Security benefits to senior citizens in the future will draw huge amounts of money from the working population. That is why there is so much discussion about Social Security in the media today.

Learning Goal 7. Identify what businesses must do to meet global challenges, including war and terrorism.

- **Which countries are creating the greatest challenges?**

China and India are two major competitors.

- **What will be the impacts of future wars and terrorism?**

Some businesses, such as those in the defense industry, may prosper. Others, such as tourism, may suffer. One way to minimize world tensions is to help less developed countries to become more prosperous.

Learning Goal 8. Review how past trends are being repeated in the present and what those trends mean for tomorrow's college graduates.

- **What is the history of our economic development in the United States, and what does it tell us about the future?**

Agricultural workers displaced by improved farm technology went to work in factories. Improved manufacturing productivity and increased competition from foreign firms contributed to the development of a service economy in the United States. The service era is now giving way to an information-based global revolution that will affect all sectors of the economy. The secret to long-term success in such an economy is flexibility and continuing education to be prepared for the opportunities that are sure to arise.

- **What job opportunities for college graduates exist in the service sector?**

Check over Figure 1.4, which outlines the service sector. That is where you are most likely to find the fast-growing firms of the future.

key terms

business 4	e-commerce 15	greening 19
business environment 11	empowerment 17	identity theft 16
climate change 19	entrepreneur 4	loss 4
database 16	factors of production 9	nonprofit organization 7
demography 17	goods 4	outsourcing 6

productivity 15	**revenue** 4	**stakeholders** 6
profit 4	**risk** 5	**standard of living** 5
quality of life 6	**services** 4	**technology** 14

critical thinking

Imagine you are thinking of starting a restaurant in your community. Answer the following questions:

1. Who will be the various stakeholders of your business?
2. What are some of the things you can do to benefit your community other than providing jobs and tax revenue?
3. How will you establish good relationships with your suppliers? With your employees?
4. Do you see any conflict between your desire to be as profitable as possible and your desire to pay employees a living wage?
5. Which of the environmental factors outlined in this chapter might have the biggest impact on your business? How?

developing workplace skills

1. Poll the class and determine which students believe that climate change is primarily caused by humans and which believe that other factors, such as climate cycles or sun spots, are the primary cause. Discuss what students can do to minimize human effects on the environment regardless of the primary causes of climate change. Are there any negative consequences to trying to minimize humans' impact on the environment?

2. Imagine you are a local businessperson who has to deal with the issue of outsourcing. You want to begin with the facts. How many, if any, jobs have been lost to outsourcing in your area? Are there any foreign firms in your area that are creating jobs (insourcing)? You may want to use the Internet to find the data you need.

3. What indicates that you and other people in the United States have a high standard of living? What are some signs that maintaining such a high standard of living may have a negative impact on quality of life?

4. Look through your local phone book to find five businesses that provide services in your area. List those businesses and, for each, describe how social trends might affect them in both positive and negative ways. Be prepared to explain your descriptions.

5. Form into teams of four or five and discuss the technological and e-commerce revolutions. How many students now shop for goods and services online? What have been their experiences? What other high-tech equipment do they use (smartphones, tablets, laptops, etc.)?

taking it to the net

Purpose

To learn what changes are occurring in the business environment today and how those changes are affecting businesses.

Exercise

1. Go to the National Taxpayers Union website (**www.ntu.org**) "Who Pays Income Taxes? See Who Pays What." Study the tables showing what percent of taxes the various income groups pay. Do you think that businesspeople pay their fair share? What percent of taxes does the top 1 percent of earners pay? What about the top 5 percent? The lowest 50 percent? How do such tax rates affect incentives to become a successful entrepreneur?

2. Go to the Census Bureau's website (**www.census.gov**) and learn what the population of the United States is at this moment. While at the site, you may want to look up the population in your town or city. Explore what other data are available at this site. What trends seem most important to you and to businesspeople in general?

3. Do a Google search for "business blogs" and check out some of the available results. Go to one of the blogs that seems interesting to you and write a brief paragraph about it—including such things as who sponsors it, who contributes the posts, and what other features it has—and how it may help a student in an introductory business course.

casing the web

To access the case "Moving Up the Corporate Ladder," visit
www.mhhe.com/P2P2e

video case

Redbox: Focusing on Customer Needs

Redbox currently has over 27,800 kiosks across the country dispensing DVDs, Blu-Ray, and video games. According to company executive Gary Cohen, Redbox began in an effort to solve a problem, and the problem focused on customer needs. Cohen puts it this way: "The consumer was asking, 'Why can't I rent a movie where I shop every day and why is rental so expensive?'" Redbox is the answer to both of those questions. Located conveniently in over 400 retail partnerships, consumers can rent a DVD for only $1 per day.

Convincing retailers to partner with Redbox has been a goal. McDonald's, for example, had an excellent breakfast and lunch business, but did not have a very robust dinner business. Redbox's research showed that over 90% of the households in the United States watch movies; further, movies are typically rented between the hours of 4:00 and 9:00 p.m. McDonald's, typical of most retailers, is interested in same-store traffic. By having a Redbox kiosk at McDonald's, individuals renting from that location would tend to return the DVD to the same location, thus increasing the probability that the customer would also purchase food or other products from the retailer at the kiosk location. Redbox initially had difficulty partnering with retailers, so it sought out a business partner, Coinstar, that already had established relationships with retailers across the country.

Redbox's business strategy focuses on success at every step. For example, the company first focused on making a single kiosk profitable, then moved to a region of kiosks, and finally expanded to the rest of the country. The key is to succeed at one step before moving on to the next one.

Customers are Redbox's primary stakeholders. The product mix in each kiosk is largely determined by the type of retail partner where the kiosk is located. For example, at a grocery store, the mix tends to focus on women, middle-aged or older, whereas at a 7-Eleven, the mix would be oriented toward a younger demographic.

Redbox is a technology-intensive business. Each kiosk has more than 800 components that are required to identify and vend the selected DVD. The company also maintains a diverse workforce that mirrors its customer base. It feels it learns about its diverse customers through its diverse workforce. While the company was not profitable in its first two years, due to the capital-intensive nature of the inventory, it has emerged as America's number one video rental business.

Thinking It Over

1. *Identify the major risks in the Redbox start-up that prevented venture capitalists from investing in the company.*
2. *How does Redbox influence the decision of a potential retail partner to host a kiosk at its location?*
3. *Provide an example of how Redbox focuses on customer needs.*

Understanding ECONOMICS and HOW IT AFFECTS Business

After you have read and studied this chapter, you should be able to

1 Explain basic economics.

2 Explain what capitalism is and how free markets work.

3 Compare socialism and communism.

4 Analyze the trend toward mixed economies.

5 Describe the economic system of the United States, including the significance of key economic indicators (especially GDP), productivity, and the business cycle.

6 Contrast fiscal policy and monetary policy, and explain how each affects the economy.

LEARNING goals →

profile

Like many academic fields, economics can be dense and uninviting to newcomers. At economics' highest level, scholars analyze enormous amounts of data with complex mathematical equations that can seem like an alien language to the uninitiated. Even the government's leading financial advisors appear to have trouble agreeing on what's happening in the economy at any given time.

Still, each one of us participates in the economy every day. We should all at least have a basic understanding of the system we engage with on a daily basis. At its best economics can teach us more about ourselves rather than just the mechanics of supply and demand. That's exactly what Steven Levitt and Stephen Dubner set out to prove with their best-selling book *Freakonomics: A Rogue Economist Explores the Hidden Side of Everything*. In the book, the authors combined economic analysis with elements of pop culture and sociology in order to gain a better understanding of how our world works. For instance, one chapter analyzed data about Japanese sumo wrestling to expose the rampant culture of corruption that had taken hold of the sport. Another chapter took a serious look at the economics of drug dealing and found the wages to be poor and the working conditions unlivable.

With unusual and interesting studies like these, Levitt and Dubner went on to sell four million copies of *Freakonomics* in 35 languages. So how did this book on economics turn into such a blockbuster? Surprisingly, it almost wasn't written at all. The authors were not colleagues before collaborating on this project. Steven Levitt was a respected economist at the University of Chicago who had earned degrees from prestigious institutions like Harvard University and M.I.T. Stephen Dubner, on the other hand, took a slightly different route to professional success. He had been set on becoming a writer since age 11, when he had his first piece published in *Highlights* magazine. However, his life took a bit of a detour when he formed a band while studying at Appalachian State University. The band was signed by Arista Records, which brought Dubner to New York City. Although he eventually bowed out of the music business, Dubner used his time in the Big Apple to get a master's degree in writing from Columbia University. Along with working for several high-profile publications, Dubner also penned a number of books.

By the early 2000s, Dubner was working on a manuscript about the "psychology of money" when an editor for *The New York Times Magazine* suggested he write a profile of Steven Levitt. Dubner was reluctant to take the project since he didn't think Levitt could provide much information for the book. "Fact is that Levitt has almost no interest in either psychology or money," says Dubner. After reading some of Levitt's scholarly papers, though, Dubner realized he wasn't dealing with any ordinary economist. "He was as creative and clever as an economist as I'd always tried to be as a writer, but he was much more successful!" says Dubner. The resulting profile created so much buzz that both men were approached to write books on the unexplored aspects of social economics. Rather than compete, in 2005 the two joined forces to create *Freakonomics*.

Once the book became a massive success, Levitt and Dubner turned their concept into a successful brand. Along with releasing a documentary film feature and 2009's book sequel *Superfreakonomics*, the pair also operate a *Freakonomics* blog, radio show, and popular podcast. Through these outlets, Levitt and Dubner can continue to study "the hidden side of everything" in the fast-paced world of online publishing. Furthermore, should the two decide to collaborate on another book, their brand name will remain fresh in the public's mind.

Outside of the *Freakonomics* spectrum, Levitt is the co-founder of The Greatest Good, a business and philanthropy consulting company. "Unfortunately, the way philanthropy is currently done, it is difficult to know what impact you'll have," says Levitt. "Very few charities engage in measuring their impact in a meaningful way." Using data analysis similar to Levitt's research in *Freakonomics*, The Greatest Good aims to use cutting-edge economic methods to solve the philanthropy world's biggest problems.

Many people don't realize the importance of the economic environment to the success of business. That is what this chapter is all about. You will learn to compare different economic systems to see the benefits and the drawbacks of each. You will learn how the free-market system of the United States works. And you will learn more about what makes some countries rich and other countries poor. By the end of the chapter, you should understand the direct affect economic systems have on the wealth and happiness of communities throughout the world.

CONNECTING WITH
X
Steven Levitt and Stephen Dubner,
Authors of *Freakonomics*

Sources: Don Schwabel, "Stephen Dubner on the Freakonomics Phenomenon," *Forbes*, January 30, 2012; David Futrelle, "The Man Who Made Economics Freaky," *Money Magazine*, June 14, 2010; www.freakonomics.com/about, accessed March 13, 2012; www.stephenjdubner.com/bio.html. accessed March 13, 2012; and www.greatestgood.com, accessed March 13, 2012.

This organization lends small amounts of money to people in poor countries. For example, it loaned a woman in Uganda enough to buy a refrigerator. She was able to sell fresh food from the refrigerator and make enough money for her family to succeed. Name this organization. (The answer is in the chapter.)

LEARNING goal 1

Explain basic economics.

HOW ECONOMIC CONDITIONS AFFECT BUSINESSES

Compared to, say, Mexico, the United States is a relatively wealthy country. Why? Why is South Korea comparatively wealthy and North Korea suffering economically, with many of its people starving?[1] Such questions are part of the subject of economics. In this chapter, we explore the various economic systems of the world and how they either promote or hinder business growth, the creation of wealth, and a higher quality of life for all.

A major part of the United States' business success in the past was due to an economic and social climate that allowed most businesses to operate freely. People were free to start a business anywhere, and just as free to fail and start again. That freedom motivated people to try until they succeeded because the rewards were often so great.[2]

Any change in the U.S. economic or political system has a major influence on the success of the business system. For example, the recent increase in government involvement in business will have an economic effect.[3] What that effect will be in the long run, however, remains to be seen.

Global economics and global politics also have a major influence on businesses in the United States. Therefore, to understand business, you must also understand basic economics and politics. This is especially true of new college graduates looking for jobs.

What Is Economics?

Economics is the study of how society chooses to employ resources to produce goods and services and distribute them for consumption among various competing groups and individuals. There are two major branches of economics: **macroeconomics** looks at the operation of a nation's economy as a whole (the whole United States), and **microeconomics** looks at the behavior of people and organizations in markets for particular products or services. A question in macroeconomics might be: What should the United States do to lower its national debt?[4] Macroeconomic topics in this chapter include gross domestic product (GDP), the

economics
The study of how society chooses to employ resources to produce goods and services and distribute them for consumption among various competing groups and individuals.

macroeconomics
The part of economics study that looks at the operation of a nation's economy as a whole.

microeconomics
The part of economics study that looks at the behavior of people and organizations in particular markets.

unemployment rate, and price indexes. A question in microeconomics might be: Why do people buy smaller cars when gas prices go up?

Some economists define economics as the study of the allocation of *scarce* resources. They believe resources need to be carefully divided among people, usually by the government. However, there's no way to maintain peace and prosperity in the world by merely dividing the resources we have today among the existing nations. There aren't enough known resources to do that. **Resource development** is the study of how to increase resources (say, by getting oil and gas from shale and tar sands) and create conditions that will make better use of them (like recycling and conservation).[5]

Businesses can contribute to an economic system by inventing products that greatly increase available resources. For example, they can discover new energy sources (hydrogen fuel for autos), new ways of growing food (hydroponics), and new ways of creating needed goods and services (nanotechnology). Mariculture, or raising fish in pens out in the ocean, could lead to more food for everyone and more employment. It is believed that the United States could monopolize the shrimp industry using aquaculture.[6] Now we import about a billion pounds of shrimp a year.[7] As sustainability remains a high priority in many U.S. industries, some companies try to appear greener than they are. See the nearby Making the Green Connection box for an example.

The Secret to Creating a Wealthy Economy

Imagine the world when kings and other rich landowners had most of the wealth, and the majority of the people were peasants. The peasants had many children, and it may have seemed a natural conclusion that if things went on as usual there would soon be too many people and not enough food and other resources. Economist

The economic contrast is remarkable. Business is booming in Seoul, South Korea (pictured on the left). But North Korea, a communist country, is not doing well, as the picture on the right of thousands of workers using old-fashioned tools in a work-for-food program shows. What do you think accounts for the dramatic differences in the economies of these two neighboring countries?

resource development
The study of how to increase resources and to create the conditions that will make better use of those resources.

It's Not Always Greener

With public concern over the environment at an all-time high, companies are constantly looking for more eco-friendly ways of doing business. Some, however, only want to appear green while still maintaining the same business practices.

These corner-cutting companies have been accused of "greenwashing," or using deceptive marketing and advertising that portray their businesses as environmentally responsible. For example, many paint brands claim to be low in eco-unfriendly volatile organic compounds (VOCs), but when colorant is added to the paint at stores, VOCs are added, too, and the count jumps to dangerous levels. Other products simply offer irrelevant information to appear green, such as aerosol cans with green dots to show the product has no ozone-depleting chlorofluorocarbons (CFCs). In fact, no aerosol spray contains CFCs, because the chemicals were banned in 1978.

Since most greenwashed ads are subtle, they fall short of being illegal and fly under the radar of most consumers. To combat this marketing strategy, independent organizations such as Consumer Reports' greenerchoices .org and the University of Oregon's greenwashingindex .com screen hundreds of ads and determine which are genuinely green and which are greenwashing. For more information, visit these sites, and keep in mind that not everything's as green as it seems.

Sources: Irene Park, "Chicago Shoppers Wary of Green Labeling by Marketers," *Medill Reports Chicago*, March 10, 2011; "Sherwin-Williams Zero-VOC Claim Misleading," *Environmental Building News*, January 21, 2011; and "What Is Greenwashing and How You Can Avoid It," *GreenAnswers.com*, March 4, 2011.

Thomas Malthus made this argument in the late 1700s and early 1800s, leading the writer Thomas Carlyle to call economics "the dismal science."

Followers of Malthus today (who are called neo-Malthusians) still believe there are too many people in the world and that the solution to poverty is radical birth control, including forced abortions and sterilization. The latest world statistics, however, show population growing more slowly than expected. In some industrial countries—like Japan, Germany, Italy, Russia, and the United States—population growth may be so slow that eventually there will be too many old people and too few young people to care for them.[8] In the developing world, on the other hand, population will climb relatively quickly and may lead to greater poverty and more unrest. Studies about the effects of population growth on the economy are part of macroeconomics.

Some macroeconomists believe that a large population, especially an educated one, can be a valuable resource. You've probably heard the saying "Give a man a fish and you feed him for a day, but teach a man to fish and you feed him for a lifetime." You can add to that: "Teach a person to start a fish farm, and he or she will be able to feed a village for a lifetime." *The secret to economic development is contained in this last statement.* Business owners provide jobs and economic growth for their employees and communities as well as for themselves.

The challenge for macroeconomists is to determine what makes some countries relatively wealthy and other countries relatively poor, and then to implement policies

New ways of producing goods and services add resources to the economy and create more employment. Fish farms, for instance, create both food and jobs. Can you think of other innovations that can help increase economic development?

and programs that lead to increased prosperity for everyone in all countries. One way to begin understanding this challenge is to consider the theories of Adam Smith.

Adam Smith and the Creation of Wealth

Rather than believing fixed resources had to be divided among competing groups and individuals, Scottish economist Adam Smith envisioned creating more resources so that everyone could become wealthier. Smith's book *An Inquiry into the Nature and Causes of the Wealth of Nations* (often called simply *The Wealth of Nations*) was published in 1776.

Smith believed *freedom* was vital to the survival of any economy, especially the freedom to own land or property and to keep the profits from working the land or running a business.[9] He believed people will work long and hard if they have incentives for doing so—that is, if they know they'll be rewarded. As a result of those efforts, the economy will prosper, with plenty of food and all kinds of products available to everyone.[10] Smith's ideas were later challenged by Malthus and others who believed economic conditions would only get worse, but Smith, not Malthus, is considered the *father of modern economics.*

How Businesses Benefit the Community

In Adam Smith's view, businesspeople don't necessarily deliberately set out to help others. They work primarily for their own prosperity and growth. Yet as people try to improve their own situation in life, Smith said, their efforts serve as an "invisible hand" that helps the economy grow and prosper through the production of needed goods, services, and ideas. Thus, the phrase **invisible hand** is used to describe the process that turns self-directed gain into social and economic benefits for all.

How do people working in their own self-interest produce goods, services, and wealth for others? The only way farmers can become wealthy is to sell some of their crops to others. To become even wealthier, they have to hire workers to produce more food. So the farmers' self-centered efforts to become wealthy lead to jobs for some and food for almost all. Think about that process for a minute, because it is critical

invisible hand
A phrase coined by Adam Smith to describe the process that turns self-directed gain into social and economic benefits for all.

According to Adam Smith's theory, business owners are motivated to work hard because they know they will earn, and keep, the rewards of their labor. When they prosper, as the owner of this restaurant has, they are able to add employees and grow, indirectly helping the community and the larger economy grow in the process. What might motivate you to start your own business?

MAKING ethical decisions

How Corruption Harms the Economy

There are numerous forces in poor countries that hinder economic growth and development. One of those forces is corruption. In many countries, a businessperson must bribe government officials to get permission to own land, build on it, and conduct normal business operations.

The United States has seen much corruption among businesspeople, such as use of prostitutes, illegal drug use, alcohol addiction, and gambling. Imagine you need a permit to add liquor to your restaurant menu to increase your profit. You have tried for years to get one, with no results. You have a friend in the government who offers to help you if you make a large contribution to his or her reelection campaign. Would you be tempted to make a campaign contribution? What are your alternatives? What are the consequences of each?

Sources: Alina Dizik, "Social Concerns Gain New Urgency," *The Wall Street Journal,* March 4, 2010; Carol Loomis, "The $600 Billion Challenge," *Fortune,* July 5, 2010; and Max Bazerman and Ann E. Tenbrunsel, "Ethical Breakdowns," *Harvard Business Review,* April 2011.

to understanding economic growth in the United States and other free countries. The same principles apply to everything from clothing to houses to iPads.

Smith assumed that as people became wealthier, they would naturally reach out to help the less fortunate in the community. That has not always happened. Today, however, many businesspeople are becoming more concerned about social issues and their obligation to return to society some of what they've earned.[11] As we mentioned in Chapter 1, it is important for businesses to be ethical as well as generous. Unethical practices undermine the whole economic system. The Making Ethical Decisions box explores the effects of corruption.

progress assessment

- What is the difference between macroeconomics and microeconomics?
- What is better for an economy than teaching a man to fish?
- What does Adam Smith's term *invisible hand* mean? How does the invisible hand create wealth for a country?

LEARNING goal 2

Explain what capitalism is and how free markets work.

UNDERSTANDING FREE-MARKET CAPITALISM

Basing their ideas on free-market principles such as those of Adam Smith, businesspeople in the United States, Europe, Japan, Canada, and other countries began to create more wealth than ever before. They hired others to work on their farms and in their factories, and their nations began to prosper as a result. Businesspeople soon became the wealthiest people in society.

However, great disparities in wealth remained or even increased. Many businesspeople owned large homes and fancy carriages while most workers lived in humble surroundings. Nonetheless, there was always the promise of better times. One way to be really wealthy was to start a successful business of your own. Of course, it wasn't that easy—it never has been. Then and now, you have to accumulate some money to buy or start a business, and you have to work long hours to make it grow. But the opportunities are there.[12]

The economic system that has led to wealth creation in much of the world is known as capitalism.[13] Under **capitalism** all or most of the factors of production and distribution—such as land, factories, railroads, and stores—are owned by individuals. They are operated for profit, and businesspeople, not government officials, decide what to produce and how much, what to charge, and how much to pay workers. They also decide whether to produce goods in their own countries or have them made in other countries. No country is purely capitalist, however. Often the government gets involved in issues such as determining minimum wages, setting farm prices, and lending money to some failing businesses—as it does in the United States. But capitalism is the *foundation* of the U.S. economic system, and of the economies of England, Australia, Canada, and most other industrialized nations. There have been many suggestions as to how the United States could improve its capitalist system, especially given the recession that began in 2008.[14]

Some countries are practicing state capitalism. *State capitalism* is where the state runs some businesses instead of private owners. The most obvious example is China, but the same concepts are being used in Russia and some of the Arab nations of the Middle East.[15] These countries have experienced some success using capitalist principles, but the future is still uncertain.[16]

The root word of *capitalism* is "capital." The Connecting with Small Business box shows how a little capital can help small businesses grow in the poorest countries in the world.

capitalism
An economic system in which all or most of the factors of production and distribution are privately owned and operated for profit.

The Foundations of Capitalism

Under free-market capitalism people have four basic rights:

1. *The right to own private property.* This is the most fundamental of all rights under capitalism. Private ownership means that individuals can buy, sell, and use land, buildings, machinery, inventions, and other forms of property. They can also pass property on to their children. Would farmers work as hard if they didn't own the land and couldn't keep the profits from what they earned? More than 90 percent of Egyptians hold their property without legal title. This is one reason they can't build wealth and why they protested in the streets.[17]

2. *The right to own a business and keep all that business's profits.* Recall from Chapter 1 that profits equal revenues minus expenses (salaries, materials, taxes). Profits act as important incentives for business owners.

The right to own private property and the right to own a business and keep its profits are two of the fundamental rights that exist in the economic system called free-market capitalism. Would either of these rights be viable without the other?

Small Loan, Big Opportunity

One way people in industrialized countries can help people in developing countries is to create a local "bank" that lends money to budding entrepreneurs so they can begin or expand their business. The entrepreneurs must pay the money back, with interest, and often must keep some money in the bank. Such banks don't necessarily have to be in a bank building. Village women often assume the role of banker and decide which women will get the loans. The "bankers" meet in a community building of some sort.

Such banks are sponsored by the Foundation for International Community Assistance (FINCA). In its 10-year history, FINCA has loaned more than $447 million to over 600,000 small-scale entrepreneurs in some of the world's poorest countries. Its borrowers have a 97.6 percent loan repayment rate.

The story of one small entrepreneur will help you understand the process. Pros Magaga lives in Kampala, Uganda. She had a tiny shop in town, but it carried very little inventory. She did not make enough to send her four children to school or to feed them more than once a day. FINCA lent her $50; she used it to buy a refrigerator, which allowed her to carry fresh foods and cold snacks. Later she added a freezer. Now her children are all in school, and the family enjoys two meals a day. Magaga has built a small home with two rooms and plans to add another room soon. She can borrow more money from FINCA because she has already paid back her $50 loan.

Sources: Ruth David, "In a Microfinance Boom, Echoes of Subprime," *Bloomberg Businessweek*, June 21–June 27, 2010; Daniel Fisher, "Bullish on Harare," *Forbes*, November 22, 2010; and "Meet Our Millionth Savings Client," *Impact*, Summer 2012.

3. *The right to freedom of competition.* Within certain guidelines established by the government, individuals are free to compete with other individuals or businesses in selling and promoting goods and services.

4. *The right to freedom of choice.* People are free to choose where they want to work and what career they want to follow. Other choices people are free to make include where to live and what to buy or sell.

One benefit of the four basic rights of capitalism is that people are willing to take more risks than they might otherwise. President Franklin Roosevelt believed four additional freedoms were essential to economic success: freedom of speech and expression, freedom to worship in your own way, freedom from want, and freedom from fear. Do you see the benefits of these additional freedoms?

Now let's explore how the free market works. What role do consumers play in the process? How do businesses learn what consumers need and want? These questions and more are answered next.

How Free Markets Work

A free market is one in which decisions about what and how much to produce are made by the market—by buyers and sellers negotiating prices for goods and services. You and I and other consumers send signals to tell producers what to make, how many, in what color, and so on. We do that by choosing to buy (or not to buy) certain products and services.

For example, if all of us decided we wanted T-shirts supporting our favorite baseball team, the clothing industry would respond in certain ways. Manufacturers and retailers would increase the price of those T-shirts, because they know people are willing to pay more for the shirts they want. They would also realize they could make more money by making more of those T-shirts. Thus, they have an incentive to pay workers to start earlier and end later. Further, the number of companies making T-shirts would increase. How many T-shirts they make depends on how many we request or buy in the stores. Prices and quantities will continue to change as the number of T-shirts we buy changes.

The same process occurs with most other products. The *price* tells producers how much to produce. If something is wanted but isn't available, the price tends to go up until someone begins making more of that product, sells the ones already on hand, or makes a substitute. As a consequence, there's rarely a long-term shortage of goods in the United States.

How Prices Are Determined

In a free market, prices are not determined by sellers; they are determined by buyers and sellers negotiating in the marketplace. A seller may want to receive $50 for a T-shirt, but the quantity buyers demand at that high price may be quite low. If the seller lowers the price, the quantity demanded is likely to increase. How is a price determined that is acceptable to both buyers and sellers? The answer is found in the microeconomic concepts of supply and demand. We shall explore both next.

The Economic Concept of Supply

Supply refers to the quantities of products manufacturers or owners are willing to sell at different prices at a specific time. Generally speaking, the amount supplied will increase as the price increases, because sellers can make more money with a higher price.

Economists show this relationship between quantity supplied and price on a graph. Figure 2.1 shows a simple supply curve for T-shirts. The price of the shirts in dollars is shown vertically on the left of the graph. The quantity of shirts sellers are willing to supply is shown horizontally at the bottom of the graph. The various points on the curve indicate how many T-shirts sellers would provide at different prices. For example, at a price of $5 a shirt, a T-shirt vendor would provide only 5 shirts, but at $50 a shirt the vendor would supply 50 shirts. The supply curve indicates the relationship between the price and the quantity supplied. All things being equal, the higher the price, the more the vendor will be willing to supply.

The Economic Concept of Demand

Demand refers to the quantity of products that people are willing to buy at different prices at a specific time. Generally speaking, the quantity demanded will increase as the price decreases. Again, we can show the relationship between price and quantity demanded in a graph. Figure 2.2 shows a simple demand curve for T-shirts. The various points on the graph indicate the quantity demanded at various prices. For example, at $45, buyers demand just 5 shirts, but at $5, the quantity demanded would increase to 35 shirts. All things being equal, the lower the price, the more buyers are willing to buy.

The Equilibrium Point, or Market Price

You might realize from Figures 2.1 and 2.2 that the key factor in determining the quantities supplied and demanded is *price*. If you were to lay the two graphs one on top of the other, the supply curve and the demand curve would cross where quantity

supply
The quantity of products that manufacturers or owners are willing to sell at different prices at a specific time.

Need help understanding Supply and Demand?
www.introbiz.tv/QR2-1
Can't Scan? Try ScanLife at your app store.

demand
The quantity of products that people are willing to buy at different prices at a specific time.

figure 2.1

THE SUPPLY CURVE AT VARIOUS PRICES

The supply curve rises from left to right. Think it through. The higher the price of T-shirts goes (the vertical axis), the more sellers will be willing to supply.

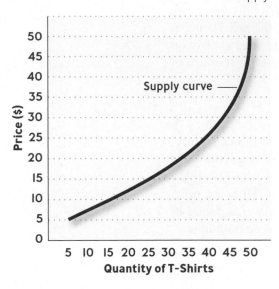

figure 2.2

THE DEMAND CURVE AT VARIOUS PRICES

This is a simple demand curve showing the quantity of T-shirts demanded at different prices. The demand curve falls from left to right. It is easy to understand why. The lower the price of T-shirts, the higher the quantity demanded.

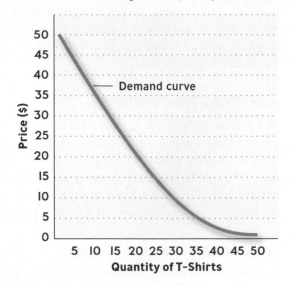

figure 2.3

THE EQUILIBRIUM POINT

The place where quantity demanded and quantity supplied meet is called the equilibrium point. When we put both the supply and demand curves on the same graph, we find that they intersect at a price where the quantity supplied and the quantity demanded are equal. In the long run, the market price will tend toward the equilibrium point.

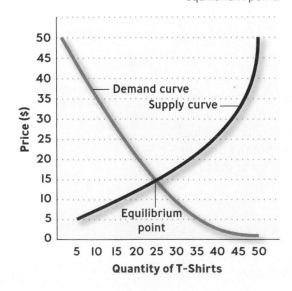

demanded and quantity supplied are equal. Figure 2.3 illustrates that point. At a price of $15, the quantity of T-shirts demanded and the quantity supplied are equal (25 shirts). That crossing point is known as the *equilibrium point* or *equilibrium price*. In the long run, that price will become the market price. **Market price,** then, is determined by supply and demand. It is the price toward which the market will trend.

Proponents of a free market argue that, because supply and demand interactions determine prices, there is no need for the government to set prices. If quantity supplied exceeds quantity demanded, the resulting surplus signals sellers to lower the price. If shortages develop because the quantity supplied is less than quantity demanded, it signals sellers to increase the price. Eventually, supply will again equal demand if nothing interferes with market forces.

When supplies of oil were lower because of the Gulf oil spill in 2010, for instance, the price of gasoline went up. When supplies were again plentiful, the price of gas fell a little. The price of gas rose again when there was turmoil in the Middle East (e.g., Libya) and the supply of oil was suspect. Note, too, how many alternative fuel sources (wind, solar, tar sands, shale gas, etc.) were tried when the price of gas approached $4 a gallon.[18]

In countries without a free market, there is no mechanism to reveal to businesses (via price) what to produce and in what amounts, so there are often shortages (not enough products)

The economic concept of demand measures the quantities of goods and services that people are willing to buy at a given price. Judging from this photo of people waiting to buy the iPad on the first day it was available for sale, how would you describe the demand for this product? Did the introduction of newer iPads generate similar demand?

or surpluses (too many products). In such countries, the government decides what to produce and in what quantity, but without price signals it has no way of knowing what the proper quantities are. Furthermore, when the government interferes in otherwise free markets, such as when it subsidizes farm goods, surpluses and shortages may develop. Competition differs in free markets, too. We shall explore that concept next.

market price
The price determined by supply and demand.

Competition within Free Markets

Economists generally agree there are four different degrees of competition: (1) perfect competition, (2) monopolistic competition, (3) oligopoly, and (4) monopoly.

Perfect competition exists when there are many sellers in a market and none is large enough to dictate the price of a product. Sellers' products appear to be identical, such as agricultural products like apples, corn, and potatoes. There are no true examples of perfect competition. Today, government price supports and drastic reductions in the number of farms make it hard to argue that even farming represents perfect competition.

perfect competition
The degree of competition in which there are many sellers in a market and none is large enough to dictate the price of a product.

Under **monopolistic competition** a large number of sellers produce very similar products that buyers nevertheless perceive as different, such as hot dogs, sodas, personal computers, and T-shirts. Product differentiation—the attempt to make buyers think similar products are different in some way—is a key to success. Think about what that means. Through advertising, branding, and packaging, sellers try to convince buyers that their products are different from competitors', though they may be very similar or even interchangeable. The fast-food industry, with its pricing battles among hamburger offerings and the like, offers a good example of monopolistic competition.[19]

monopolistic competition
The degree of competition in which a large number of sellers produce very similar products that buyers nevertheless perceive as different.

An **oligopoly** is a degree of competition in which just a few sellers dominate a market, as we see in tobacco, gasoline, automobiles, aluminum, and aircraft. One reason some industries remain in the hands of a few sellers is that the initial

oligopoly
A degree of competition in which just a few sellers dominate the market.

investment required to enter the business often is tremendous. Think, for example, of how much it would cost to start a new airplane manufacturing facility.

In an oligopoly, products from different companies tend to be priced about the same. The reason is simple: Intense price competition would lower profits for everyone, since a price cut by one producer would most likely be matched by the others. As in monopolistic competition, product differentiation, rather than price, is usually the major factor in market success in an oligopoly. Note, for example, that most cereals are priced about the same, as are soft drinks. Thus, advertising is a major factor determining which of the few available brands consumers buy, because often it is advertising that creates the perceived differences.[20]

monopoly
A degree of competition in which only one seller controls the total supply of a product or service, and sets the price.

A **monopoly** occurs when one seller controls the total supply of a product or service, and sets the price. In the United States, laws prohibit the creation of monopolies. Nonetheless, the U.S. legal system has permitted monopolies in the markets for public utilities that sell natural gas, water, and electric power. These companies' prices and profits are usually controlled by public service commissions to protect the interest of buyers. For example, the Florida Public Service Commission is the administering agency over the Florida Power and Light utility company. Legislation ended the monopoly status of utilities in some areas, letting consumers choose among providers. The intention of such *deregulation* is to increase competition among utility companies and, ultimately, lower prices for consumers.

Benefits and Limitations of Free Markets

One benefit of the free market is that it allows open competition among companies. Businesses must provide customers with high-quality products at fair prices with good service. If they don't, they lose customers to businesses that do. Do government services have the same incentives?

The free market—with its competition and incentives—was a major factor in creating the wealth that industrialized countries now enjoy. Some people even talk of the free market as an economic miracle. Free-market capitalism, more than any other economic system, provides opportunities for poor people to work their way out of poverty. Capitalism also encourages businesses to be more efficient so they can successfully compete on price and quality.

Yet, even as free-market capitalism has brought prosperity to the United States and to much of the rest of the world, it has brought inequality as well.[21] Business owners and managers usually make more money and have more wealth than lower-level workers. Yet people who are old, disabled, or sick may not be able to start and manage a business, and others may not have the talent or the drive. What should society do about such inequality? Not everyone in the United States is as generous as Bill Gates, founder of Microsoft, who with his wife has established the Bill and Melinda Gates Foundation to support world health and education.[22] In fact, the desire to create as much wealth as possible has led some businesspeople throughout history, and still today, to exploit such practices as slavery and child labor.

One of the dangers of free markets is that some people let greed dictate how they act. Criminal charges brought against some big businesses in banking, oil, accounting, telecommunications, insurance, and pharmaceuticals indicate the scope of the potential problem. Some businesspeople have deceived the public about their products; others have deceived stockholders about the value of their stock, all in order to increase executives' personal assets.[23]

Clearly, some government laws and regulations are necessary to protect businesses' stakeholders and make sure people who cannot work get the basic care they need.[24] To overcome some of capitalism's limitations, some countries have adopted an economic system called socialism. It, too, has its good and bad points. We explore these after you review the following Progress Assessment questions.

progress assessment

- What are the four basic rights that people have under free-market capitalism?
- How do businesspeople know what to produce and in what quantity?
- How are prices determined?
- What are the four degrees of competition, and what are some examples of each?

LEARNING goal 3

Compare socialism and communism.

socialism
An economic system based on the premise that some, if not most, basic businesses should be owned by the government so that profits can be more evenly distributed among the people.

UNDERSTANDING SOCIALISM

Socialism is an economic system based on the premise that some, if not most, basic businesses (e.g., steel mills, coal mines, and utilities) should be owned by the government so that profits can be more evenly distributed among the people. Entrepreneurs often own and run smaller businesses, and individuals are often taxed relatively steeply to pay for social programs. The top federal personal income tax rate in the United States, for example, was 35 percent recently, but in some socialist countries the top rate can be as much as 60 percent. While U.S. shoppers pay sales taxes ranging from over 10 percent in Chicago to zero in Delaware, socialist countries charge a similar value-added tax of 15 to 20 percent or more. Socialists acknowledge the major benefit of capitalism—wealth creation—but believe that wealth should be more evenly distributed than occurs in free-market capitalism. They believe the government should carry out the distribution and be much more involved in protecting the environment and providing for the poor.

Socialism has been more successful in some countries than in others. This photo shows Denmark's clean and modern public transportation system. In Greece, overspending caused a debt crisis that forced the government to impose austerity measures that many Greeks oppose. What other factors might lead to slower growth in socialist countries?

The Benefits of Socialism

The major benefit of socialism is supposed to be social equality. Ideally it comes about because the government takes income from wealthier people, in the form of taxes, and redistributes it to poorer people through various government programs.[25] Free education through college, free health care, and free child care are some of the benefits socialist governments, using the money from taxes, may provide to their people. Such education benefits helped Finland become the world leader in student achievement.[26] Workers in socialist countries

usually get longer vacations, work fewer hours per week, and have more employee benefits (e.g., generous sick leave) than those in countries where free-market capitalism prevails.

The Negative Consequences of Socialism

Socialism may create more equality than capitalism, but it takes away some of businesspeople's incentives. For example, tax rates in some socialist nations once reached 83 percent. Today, doctors, lawyers, business owners, and others who earn a lot of money pay very high tax rates. As a consequence, many of them leave socialist countries for capitalistic countries with lower taxes, such as the United States. This loss of the best and brightest people to other countries is called a **brain drain.**

Imagine an experiment in socialism in your own class. Imagine that after the first exam, those with grades of 90 and above have to give some of their points to those who make 70 and below so that everyone ends up with grades in the 80s. Would those who got 90s study as hard for the second exam? What about those who got 70s? Can you see why workers may not work as hard or as well if they all get the same benefits regardless of how hard they work?

Socialism also tends to result in fewer inventions and less innovation, because those who come up with new ideas usually don't receive as much reward as they would in a capitalist system. Communism may be considered a more intensive version of socialism. We shall explore that system next.

UNDERSTANDING COMMUNISM

Communism is an economic and political system in which the government makes almost all economic decisions and owns almost all the major factors of production. It intrudes further into the lives of people than socialism does. For example, some communist countries have not allowed their citizens to practice certain religions, change jobs, or move to the town of their choice.

One problem with communism is that the government has no way of knowing what to produce, because prices don't reflect supply and demand as they do in free markets. The government must guess what the people need. As a result, shortages of many items, including food and clothing, may develop. Another problem is that communism doesn't inspire businesspeople to work hard because the incentives are not there. Therefore, communism is slowly disappearing as an economic form.

Most communist countries today are suffering severe economic depression. In North Korea, many people are starving. In Cuba, people suffer a lack of goods and services readily available in most other countries, and some fear the government.

While some parts of the former Soviet Union remain under communist ideals, Russia itself now has a flat tax of only 13 percent. Yet this low rate increased the government's tax revenues by nearly 30 percent, because more people were willing to pay. The trend toward free markets is growing in Vietnam and parts of China as well. The regions of China that are most free have prospered rapidly, while the rest of the country has grown relatively slowly. Remnants of China's communist system, such as political and religious oppression, still exist, however.

brain drain
The loss of the best and brightest people to other countries.

communism
An economic and political system in which the government makes almost all economic decisions and owns almost all the major factors of production.

LEARNING **goal 4**

Analyze the trend toward mixed economies.

THE TREND TOWARD MIXED ECONOMIES

The nations of the world have largely been divided between those that followed the concepts of capitalism and those that adopted the concepts of communism or socialism. We can now contrast the two major economic systems as follows:

1. **Free-market economies** exist when the market largely determines what goods and services get produced, who gets them, and how the economy grows. *Capitalism* is the popular term for this economic system.

2. **Command economies** exist when the government largely decides what goods and services will be produced, who gets them, and how the economy will grow. *Socialism* and *communism* are variations on this economic system.

Although all countries actually have some mix of the two systems, neither free-market nor command economies have resulted in optimal economic conditions. Free-market mechanisms don't seem to respond enough to the needs of the poor, the old, or the disabled. Some people also believe that businesses in free-market economies have not done enough to protect the environment. (We shall discuss that issue throughout the text.) Over time, voters in mostly free-market countries, such as the United States, have elected officials who have adopted many social and environmental programs such as Social Security, welfare, unemployment compensation, and various clean air and water acts. What new or enhanced social policies do you know of that are being considered today?

Socialism and communism haven't always created enough jobs or wealth to keep economies growing fast enough. Thus, communist governments are disappearing, and some socialist governments have been cutting back on social programs and lowering taxes on businesses and workers to generate more business growth and more revenue.[27]

The trend, then, has been for mostly capitalist countries (like the United States) to move toward socialism (i.e., more government involvement in health care), and for some socialist countries to move toward capitalism (more private businesses, lower taxes). All countries have some mix of the two systems. Thus, the long-term global trend is toward a blend of capitalism and socialism. This trend likely will increase with the opening of global markets made easier by the Internet. The net effect is the emergence throughout the world of mixed economies (see the Connecting Across Borders box).

Mixed economies exist where some allocation of resources is made by the market and some by the government. Most countries don't have a name for such a system. If free-market mechanisms allocate most resources, the leaders call their system capitalism. If the government allocates most resources, the leaders call it socialism. Figure 2.4 compares the various economic systems.

Since the communist system in Russia has largely collapsed, the country has been moving toward a viable market economy. As poverty begins to decline, a middle class is emerging, but many of the country's vast natural resources are difficult to tap. Laws that help promote business are few, and there is an active black market for many goods. Many observers are optimistic that Russia can prosper. What do you think?

free-market economies
Economic systems in which the market largely determines what goods and services get produced, who gets them, and how the economy grows.

command economies
Economic systems in which the government largely decides what goods and services will be produced, who will get them, and how the economy will grow.

mixed economies
Economic systems in which some allocation of resources is made by the market and some by the government.

borders

Africa's Evolving Economy

For much of the 20th century, stories about Africa's economy inevitably focused on the continent's rampant poverty. The end of colonial rule in Africa brought military dictatorships and other oppressive forces to power in many countries. Coupled with disease and an almost nonexistent infrastructure, Africa's economy and its people suffered horribly.

Thankfully, the 21st century has been brighter for many Africans. A booming commodities market along with expanding manufacturing and service economies are leading to unprecedented growth. Over the last decade, six of the world's 10 fastest-growing countries were African. In eight of those years, Africa has even outpaced the growth of East Asia, including Japan. The International Monetary Fund estimated that the African economy would grow by 6 percent by the end of 2012 and further expand by the same amount in 2013.

Much of this economic expansion has happened thanks to the manufacturing might of countries like South Africa. With the largest economy on the continent, South Africa finished 2011's final quarter with a 3.2 percent growth in GDP. Even small, formerly war-torn nations are now experiencing economic improvements. For instance, in the 1990s Rwanda suffered a horrific civil war and genocide that claimed the lives of hundreds of thousands of citizens. Subsequent years of peace and a relatively stable government have since turned the country around significantly. Unlike many African nations, Rwandan businesses face little corruption and enjoy ever-improving infrastructure. Although skilled labor is in short supply in Rwanda and other emerging nations, population growth is set to double in the coming years. Experts hope that this younger generation will take advantage of improving educational opportunities and ensure Africa's place on the global economic stage.

Sources: Andres R. Martinez, "South African Economy Expands 3.2% as Manufacturing Rebounds," *Bloomberg Businessweek*, February 28, 2012; "Business in Rwanda: Africa's Singapore?" *The Economist*, February 25, 2012; and "The Hopeful Continent: Africa Rising," *The Economist*, December 3, 2011.

Like most other nations of the world, the United States has a mixed economy. The U.S. government has now become the largest employer in the country, which means there are more workers in the public sector (government) than in any of the major businesses in the United States. Do you see the government growing or declining in the coming years?

progress assessment

- What led to the emergence of socialism?
- What are the benefits and drawbacks of socialism?
- What countries still practice communism?
- What are the characteristics of a mixed economy?

LEARNING goal 5

Describe the economic system of the United States, including the significance of key economic indicators (especially GDP), productivity, and the business cycle.

	CAPITALISM* (United States)	SOCIALISM (Sweden)	COMMUNISM (North Korea)	MIXED ECONOMY (Germany)
Social and Economic Goals	Private ownership of land and business. Liberty and the pursuit of happiness. Free trade. Emphasis on freedom and the profit motive for economic growth.	Public ownership of major businesses. Some private ownership of smaller businesses and shops. Government control of education, health care, utilities, mining, transportation, and media. Very high taxation. Emphasis on equality.	Public ownership of all businesses. Government-run education and health care. Emphasis on equality. Many limitations on freedom, including freedom to own businesses and to assemble to protest government actions.	Private ownership of land and business with government regulation. Government control of some institutions (e.g., mail). High taxation for defense and the common welfare. Emphasis on a balance between freedom and equality.
Motivation of Workers	Much incentive to work efficiently and hard because profits are retained by owners. Workers are rewarded for high productivity.	Capitalist incentives exist in private businesses. Government control of wages in public institutions limits incentives.	Very little incentive to work hard or to produce quality goods or services.	Incentives are similar to capitalism except in government-owned enterprises, which may have fewer incentives.
Control over Markets	Complete freedom of trade within and among nations. Some government control of markets.	Some markets are controlled by the government and some are free. Trade restrictions among nations vary and include some free-trade agreements.	Total government control over markets except for illegal transactions.	Some government control of trade within and among nations (trade protectionism).
Choices in the Market	A wide variety of goods and services is available. Almost no scarcity or over-supply exists for long because supply and demand control the market.	Variety in the marketplace varies considerably from country to country. Choice is directly related to government involvement in markets.	Very little choice among competing goods.	Similar to capitalism, but scarcity and oversupply may be caused by government involvement in the market (e.g., subsidies for farms).
Social Freedoms	Freedom of speech, press, assembly, religion, job choice, movement, and elections.	Similar to mixed economy. Governments may restrict job choice, movement among countries, and who may attend upper-level schools (i.e., college).	Very limited freedom to protest the government, practice religion, or change houses or jobs.	Some restrictions on freedoms of assembly and speech. Separation of church and state may limit religious practices in schools.

*The United States is a mixed economy based on a foundation of capitalism.

figure 2.4
_____

COMPARISONS OF KEY ECONOMIC SYSTEMS

Need help understanding Basic
Economic Systems?
www.introbiz.tv/QR2-2

gross domestic product (GDP)
The total value of final
goods and services
produced in a country in a
given year.

unemployment rate
The number of civilians at
least 16 years old who are
unemployed and tried to
find a job within the prior
four weeks.

*The overall
unemployment rate in the
United States fluctuates.
Over the last decade, it
has been as low as less
than 5 percent and as
high as more than 10
percent. Unemployment
insurance goes only so
far to relieve the loss of
income caused by losing
your job. How high is the
unemployment rate in
your area today?*

UNDERSTANDING THE U.S. ECONOMIC SYSTEM

The following sections will introduce the terms and concepts that you, as an informed citizen, will need to understand in order to grasp the issues facing government and business leaders in the United States.

Key Economic Indicators

Three major indicators of economic conditions are (1) the gross domestic product (GDP), (2) the unemployment rate, and (3) price indexes. Another important statistic is the increase or decrease in productivity. When you read business literature, you'll see these terms used again and again. Let's explore what they mean.

Gross Domestic Product   **Gross domestic product (GDP),** which we mentioned briefly in Chapter 1, is the total value of final goods and services produced in a country in a given year. Both domestic and foreign-owned companies can produce the goods and services included in GDP, as long as the companies are located within the country's boundaries. For example, production values from Japanese automaker Honda's factory in Ohio are included in U.S. GDP. Revenue generated by Ford's factory in Mexico is included in Mexico's GDP, even though Ford is a U.S. company.

Almost every discussion about a nation's economy is based on GDP. If growth in GDP slows or declines, businesses may feel many negative effects, such as the slowdown in retail sales experienced beginning in 2008. A major influence on the growth of GDP is the productivity of the workforce—that is, how much output workers create with a given amount of input. The total U.S. GDP is over $14 trillion. The level of U.S. economic activity is actually larger than the GDP figures show, because those figures don't take into account illicit activities such as sales of illegal drugs. The high GDP in the United States is what enables its citizens to enjoy a high standard of living.

The Unemployment Rate   The **unemployment rate** refers to the percentage of civilians at least 16 years old who are unemployed *and tried to find a job within the prior four weeks*. In 2000, the U.S. unemployment rate reached its lowest point in over 30 years, falling as low as 3.9 percent, but by 2010 the rate had risen to over 9.5 percent (see Figure 2.5). The unemployment rate fell to about 8 percent in 2012, but many people had given up looking for jobs (people who are not actively looking for work are not included in the unemployment figures).[28]

Figure 2.6 describes the four types of unemployment: frictional, structural, cyclical, and seasonal. The United States tries to protect those who are unemployed because of recessions (defined later in the chapter), industry shifts, and other cyclical factors. Nonetheless, the *underemployment* figure in 2012 was about 17 percent (this includes those who are working part time and want to work full time and those who stopped looking for work).

If you worry about the U.S. unemployment rate, consider this: the unemployment rate in Zimbabwe was way over 80 percent, and the inflation rate was

figure 2.5

U.S. UNEMPLOYMENT RATE 1989–2012

spectacular. You would have enjoyed cashing in your dollars in Zimbabwe; one dollar got you billions of Zimbabwean dollars. Actually, the situation got much worse. Do you suppose Zimbabwe is a capitalist economy?

Inflation and Price Indexes   Price indexes help gauge the health of the economy by measuring the levels of inflation, disinflation, deflation, and stagflation. **Inflation** is a general rise in the prices of goods and services over time. The official definition is "a persistent increase in the level of consumer prices or a persistent decline in the purchasing power of money, caused by an increase in available currency and credit beyond the proportion of goods and services." Thus, it is also described as "too many dollars chasing too few goods." Go back and review the laws of supply and demand to see how that works. Rapid inflation is scary. If the prices of goods and services go up by just 7 percent a year, they will double in about 10 years. Think of how much fear was generated by the rapid increase in the price of gasoline in 2011 to early 2012.

    Disinflation occurs when price increases are slowing (the inflation rate is declining). That was the situation in the United States throughout the 1990s. **Deflation** means that prices are declining.[29] It occurs when countries produce so

inflation
A general rise in the prices of goods and services over time.

disinflation
A situation in which price increases are slowing (the inflation rate is declining).

deflation
A situation in which prices are declining.

figure 2.6

FOUR TYPES OF UNEMPLOYMENT

- *Frictional unemployment* refers to those people who have quit work because they didn't like the job, the boss, or the working conditions and who haven't yet found a new job. It also refers to those people who are entering the labor force for the first time (e.g., new graduates) or are returning to the labor force after significant time away (e.g., parents who reared children). There will always be some frictional unemployment because it takes some time to find a first job or a new job.

- *Structural unemployment* refers to unemployment caused by the restructuring of firms or by a mismatch between the skills (or location) of job seekers and the requirements (or location) of available jobs (e.g., coal miners in an area where mines have been closed).

- *Cyclical unemployment* occurs because of a recession or a similar downturn in the business cycle (the ups and downs of business growth and decline over time). This type of unemployment is the most serious.

- *Seasonal unemployment* occurs where demand for labor varies over the year, as with the harvesting of crops.

stagflation
A situation when the economy is slowing but prices are going up anyhow.

consumer price index (CPI)
Monthly statistics that measure the pace of inflation or deflation.

producer price index (PPI)
An index that measures prices at the wholesale level.

many goods that people cannot afford to buy them all (too few dollars are chasing too many goods). **Stagflation** occurs when the economy is slowing but prices are going up anyhow. Some economists fear the United States may face stagflation in the near future.[30]

The **consumer price index (CPI)** consists of monthly statistics that measure the pace of inflation or deflation. The government computes costs of goods and services—including housing, food, apparel, and medical care—to see whether they are going up or down (see Figure 2.7). The CPI is an important figure because some wages and salaries, rents and leases, tax brackets, government benefits, and interest rates are based on it. You may see the term *core inflation*. That means the CPI minus food and energy costs. Since food and energy have been going up rapidly, the core inflation figure is actually much lower than the real CPI.

The **producer price index (PPI)** measures prices at the wholesale level. Other indicators of the economy's condition include housing starts, retail sales, and changes in personal income. You can learn more about such indicators by reading business periodicals, listening to business broadcasts on radio and television, and exploring business sites on the Internet.

Productivity in the United States

An increase in productivity means a worker can produce more goods and services than before in the same time period, usually thanks to machinery or other equipment. Productivity in the United States has risen because computers and other technology have made production faster and easier. The higher productivity is, the lower the costs are of producing goods and services, and the lower prices can be. Therefore, businesspeople are eager to increase productivity. Remember, however, that high productivity can lead to high unemployment.[31] Certainly, that is what the United States in now experiencing.

Now that the U.S. economy is a service economy, productivity is an issue because service firms are so labor-intensive. Spurred by foreign competition, productivity in the manufacturing sector is rising rapidly. In the service sector, productivity is growing more slowly because service workers—like teachers, clerks, lawyers, and barbers—have fewer new technologies available than there are for factory workers.

Productivity in the Service Sector

One problem with the service industry is that an influx of machinery may add to the *quality* of the service provided but not to the *output per worker.* For example, you've probably noticed how many computers there are on college campuses. They add to the quality of education but don't necessarily boost professors' productivity. The

figure 2.7

HOW THE CONSUMER PRICE INDEX IS PUT TOGETHER

1. 400 data collectors visit stores and gather 80,000 retail price quotes and 5,000 housing rent quotes, transmitting data daily to Washington.

2. 40 commodity analysts at the Bureau of Labor Statistics review about a quarter of this avalanche of price data.

3. About nine days before the release of the CPI, the office is locked down—with bright red RESTRICTED AREA signs posted on all the doors.

4. 90 people—a mix of commodity analysts and other economists who specialize in assembling the CPI—compute basic indexes for 211 item categories, which are divided into 38 index areas.

5. Final results are released at 8:30 a.m., Eastern time, about two weeks after the end of the month in question.

same is true of some equipment in hospitals, such as CAT scanners, PET scanners, and MRI scanners. They improve patient care but don't necessarily increase the number of patients doctors can see. In other words, today's productivity measures in the service industry fail to capture the increase in quality caused by new technology.

Clearly, the United States and other countries need to develop new measures of productivity for the service economy that include quality as well as quantity of output. Despite productivity improvement, the economy is likely to go through a series of ups and downs, much as it has over the past few years. We'll explore that process next.

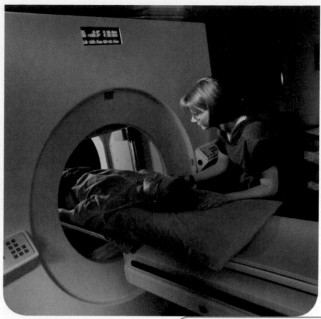

The Business Cycle

Business cycles are the periodic rises and falls that occur in economies over time. Economists look at a number of business cycles, from seasonal cycles that occur within a year to cycles that occur every 48–60 years.

Economist Joseph Schumpeter identified the four phases of long-term business cycles as boom–recession–depression–recovery:

1. An *economic boom* is just what it sounds like—business is booming.

2. **Recession** is two or more consecutive quarters of decline in the GDP. In a recession prices fall, people purchase fewer products, and businesses fail. A recession brings high unemployment, increased business failures, and an overall drop in living standards. The recession that started in 2008 is an example.

3. A **depression** is a severe recession, usually accompanied by deflation. Business cycles rarely go through a depression phase. In fact, while there were many business cycles during the 20th century, there was only one severe depression (1930s). Nonetheless some economists are predicting a depression in the coming years.

4. A *recovery* occurs when the economy stabilizes and starts to grow. This eventually leads to an economic boom, starting the cycle all over again.

One goal of some economists is to predict such ups and downs. That is very difficult to do. Business cycles are identified according to facts, but we can explain those facts only by using theories. Therefore, we cannot predict with certainty. But one thing is certain: over time, the economy *will* rise and fall as it has done lately.

Since dramatic swings up and down in the economy cause all kinds of disruptions to businesses, the government tries to minimize such changes. It uses fiscal policy and monetary policy to try to keep the economy from slowing too much or growing too rapidly.

LEARNING goal 6

Contrast fiscal policy and monetary policy, and explain how each affects the economy.

It can be difficult to measure productivity in the service sector. New technology can improve the quality of services without necessarily increasing the number of people served. A doctor can make more-accurate diagnoses with scans, for instance, but still can only see so many patients in a day. How can productivity measures capture improvements in the quality of service?

business cycles
The periodic rises and falls that occur in economies over time.

recession
Two or more consecutive quarters of decline in the GDP.

depression
A severe recession, usually accompanied by deflation.

Stabilizing the Economy through Fiscal Policy

fiscal policy
The federal government's efforts to keep the economy stable by increasing or decreasing taxes or government spending.

Fiscal policy refers to the federal government's efforts to keep the economy stable by increasing or decreasing taxes or government spending.[32] The first fiscal policy tool is taxation. Theoretically, high tax rates tend to slow the economy because they draw money away from the private sector and put it into the government. High tax rates may discourage small-business ownership because they decrease the profits businesses can earn and make the effort less rewarding. It follows, then, that low tax rates will theoretically give the economy a boost. When you count all fees, sales taxes, and more, taxes on the highest-earning U.S. citizens could exceed 50 percent. Is that figure too high or not high enough in your opinion? Why?

national debt
The sum of government deficits over time.

The second fiscal policy tool is government spending on highways, social programs, education, infrastructure (e.g., roads and utilities), defense, and so on. The *national deficit* is the amount of money the federal government spends beyond what it gathers in taxes for a given fiscal year. The deficit is expected to be over $1 trillion for the next several years. Such deficits increase the national debt. The **national debt** is the sum of government deficits over time. Recently, the national debt was over $16 trillion (see Figure 2.8). That is a rather misleading number, however, since the unfunded obligation for Medicare alone is over $34 trillion. The unfunded debt to Social Security is on top of that. If the government takes in more revenue than it spends (i.e., tax revenues exceed expenditures), there is a *national surplus*. That is not likely to happen soon.

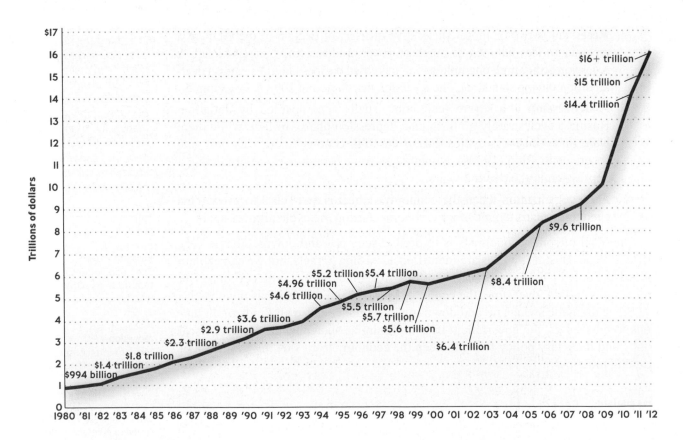

figure 2.8

THE NATIONAL DEBT

One way to lessen deficits is to cut government spending. Many presidents and those in Congress have promised to make the government "smaller," that is, to reduce government spending—but that doesn't happen very often. There seems to be a need for more social programs or more defense spending (such as for the wars in Iraq, Afghanistan, and Libya) each year, and thus the deficits continue and add to the national debt. Some people believe that government spending helps the economy grow. Others believe that the money the government spends comes out of the pockets of consumers and businesspeople, and thus slows growth. What do you think?

Fiscal Policy in Action during the Economic Crisis That Began in 2008

For most of his presidency, George W. Bush followed the basic economic principles of free markets. By the end of his term, however, the economy was facing a dire economic crisis and President Bush approved the spending of almost $1 trillion of government money in an effort to revive the failing economy (including helping out banks, the auto industry, and others). (A trillion dollars is about $3,272 per person in the United States.) President Barack Obama promised to spend additional funds. Both presidents were following the basic economic theory of John Maynard Keynes.[33] **Keynesian economic theory** is the theory that a government policy of increasing spending and cutting taxes could stimulate the economy in a recession.

The economic crisis beginning in 2008 caused much anguish among Wall Street workers and people in general. How effective was the government's response?

Using Monetary Policy to Keep the Economy Growing

Have you ever wondered what organization adds money to or subtracts money from the economy? The answer is the Federal Reserve Bank (the Fed). The Fed is a semiprivate organization that is not under the direct control of the government but does have members appointed by the president. We will discuss the Fed in detail when we look at banking in Chapter 20. Now we simply introduce monetary policy and the role of the Fed in controlling the economy.

Monetary policy is the management of the money supply and interest rates by the Federal Reserve Bank. The Fed's most visible role is the raising and lowering of interest rates. When the economy is booming, the Fed tends to raise interest rates. This makes money more expensive to borrow. Businesses thus borrow less, and the economy slows as businesspeople spend less money on everything they need to grow, including labor and machinery. The opposite is true when the Fed lowers interest rates. Businesses tend to borrow more, and the economy is expected to grow. Raising and lowering interest rates should therefore help control the rapid ups and downs of the economy.[34] In 2010–2012, the Fed kept interest rates near zero, but the economy remained sluggish. You can imagine the pressure that put on the head of the Federal Reserve.[35]

The Fed also controls the money supply. A simple explanation of this function is that the more money the Fed makes available to businesspeople and others, the

Keynesian economic theory
The theory that a government policy of increasing spending and cutting taxes could stimulate the economy in a recession.

monetary policy
The management of the money supply and interest rates by the Federal Reserve.

faster the economy is supposed to grow. To slow the economy (and prevent inflation), the Fed lowers the money supply. The Fed poured money into the economy
in 2008–2012. What would you expect the result to be?

To sum up, there are two major tools for managing the economy of the United
States: fiscal policy (government taxes and spending) and monetary policy (the
Fed's control over interest rates and the money supply). The goal is to keep the
economy growing so that more people can rise up the economic ladder and enjoy a
higher standard of living and quality of life.

progress assessment

- Name the three economic indicators and describe how well the United States
  is doing based on each indicator.
- What's the difference between a recession and a depression?
- How does the government manage the economy using fiscal policy?
- What does the term *monetary policy* mean? What organization is responsible
  for monetary policy?

summary

Learning Goal 1. Explain basic economics.

- **What is economics?**

Economics is the study of how society chooses to employ resources to produce
goods and services and distribute them for consumption among various competing groups and individuals.

- **What are the two branches of economics?**

There are two major branches of economics: macroeconomics studies the
operation of a nation's economy as a whole, and microeconomics studies the
behavior of people and organizations in particular markets (e.g., why people
buy smaller cars when gas prices go up).

- **How can we be assured of having enough resources?**

Resource development is the study of how to increase resources and create the
conditions that will make better use of them.

- **How does capitalism create a climate for economic growth?**

Under capitalism, businesspeople don't often deliberately set out to help others; they work mostly for their own prosperity and growth. Yet people's efforts
to improve their own situation in life act like an *invisible hand* to help the
economy grow and prosper through the production of needed goods, services,
and ideas.

Learning Goal 2. Explain what capitalism is and how free markets work.

- **What is capitalism?**

Capitalism is an economic system in which all or most of the means of
production and distribution are privately owned and operated for profit.

- **Who decides what to produce under capitalism?**

In capitalist countries, businesspeople decide what to produce, how much to pay workers, and how much to charge for goods and services. They also decide whether to produce certain goods in their own countries, import those goods, or have them made in other countries.

- **What are the basic rights people have under capitalism?**

The four basic rights under capitalism are (1) the right to own private property, (2) the right to own a business and to keep all of that business's profits after taxes, (3) the right to freedom of competition, and (4) the right to freedom of choice. President Franklin D. Roosevelt felt that other economic freedoms were also important: the right to freedom of speech and expression, the right to worship in your own way, and freedom from want and fear.

- **How does the free market work?**

The free market is one in which buyers and sellers negotiating prices for goods and services influence the decisions about what gets produced and in what quantities. Buyers' decisions in the marketplace tell sellers what to produce and in what quantity. When buyers demand more goods, the price goes up, signaling suppliers to produce more. The higher the price, the more goods and services suppliers are willing to produce. Price is the mechanism that allows free markets to work.

Learning Goal 3. Compare socialism and communism.

- **What is socialism?**

Socialism is an economic system based on the premise that some businesses should be owned by the government.

- **What are the advantages and disadvantages of socialism?**

Socialism intends to create more social equity. Workers in socialist countries usually receive more education, health care, and other benefits and also work fewer hours, with longer vacations. The major disadvantage of socialism is that it lowers the incentive to start a business or to work hard. Socialist economies tend to have a higher unemployment rate and a slower growth rate than capitalist economies.

- **How does socialism differ from communism?**

Under communism, the government owns almost all major production facilities and dictates what gets produced and by whom. Communism is also more restrictive when it comes to personal freedoms, such as religious freedom.

Learning Goal 4. Analyze the trend toward mixed economies.

- **What is a mixed economy?**

A mixed economy is part capitalist and part socialist. Some businesses are privately owned, but taxes tend to be high to distribute income more evenly among the population.

- **What countries have mixed economies?**

The United States has a mixed economy, as do most other industrialized countries.

- **What are the benefits of mixed economies?**

A mixed economy has most of the benefits of wealth creation that free markets bring plus the benefits of greater social equality and concern for the environment that socialism promises.

Learning Goal 5. Describe the economic system of the United States, including the significance of key economic indicators (especially GDP), productivity, and the business cycle.

- **What are the key economic indicators in the United States?**

Gross domestic product (GDP) is the total value of final goods and services produced in a country in a given year. The *unemployment rate* refers to the percentage of civilians at least 16 years old who are unemployed and tried to find a job within the most recent four weeks. The *consumer price index (CPI)* measures changes in the prices of about 400 goods and services that consumers buy.

- **What are the four phases of business cycles?**

In an *economic boom,* businesses do well. A *recession* occurs when two or more quarters show declines in the GDP, prices fall, people purchase fewer products, and businesses fail. A *depression* is a severe recession. *Recovery* occurs when the economy stabilizes and starts to grow.

Learning Goal 6. Contrast fiscal policy and monetary policy, and explain how each affects the economy.

- **What is fiscal policy?**

Fiscal policy consists of government efforts to keep the economy stable by increasing or decreasing taxes or government spending.

- **What is the importance of monetary policy to the economy?**

Monetary policy is the management of the money supply and interest rates. When unemployment gets too high, the Federal Reserve Bank (the Fed) may put more money into the economy and lower interest rates. That is supposed to provide a boost to the economy as businesses borrow and spend more money and hire more people.

key terms

brain drain 42
business cycles 49
capitalism 35
command economies 43
communism 42
consumer price index
 (CPI) 48
deflation 47
demand 37
depression 49
disinflation 47
economics 30
fiscal policy 50
free-market
 economies 43

gross domestic product
 (GDP) 46
inflation 47
invisible hand 33
Keynesian economic
 theory 51
macroeconomics 30
market price 38
microeconomics 30
mixed economies 43
monetary policy 51
monopolistic
 competition 39
monopoly 40
national debt 50

oligopoly 39
perfect competition 39
producer price index
 (PPI) 48
recession 49
resource
 development 31
socialism 41
stagflation 48
supply 37
unemployment rate 46

critical thinking

The U.S. Supreme Court ruled that cities could have school voucher programs that give money directly to parents, who could then choose between competing schools, public or private. The idea was to create competition among schools. Like businesses, schools were expected to improve their services (how effectively they teach) to win students from competitors. The result would be improvement in all schools, private and public, to benefit many students.

1. Do you believe economic principles like competition apply in both private and public organizations? Be prepared to defend your answer.
2. Are there other public functions that might benefit from more competition, including competition from private firms?
3. Many people say that businesspeople do not do enough for society. Some students choose to go into the public sector instead of business because they want to help others. However, businesspeople say that they do more to help others than nonprofit groups do because they provide jobs for people rather than giving them charity. Furthermore, they believe businesses create all the wealth that nonprofit groups distribute.

   a. How can you find some middle ground in this debate to show that both businesspeople and those who work for nonprofit organizations contribute to society and need to work together more closely to help people?

   b. How could you use the concepts of Adam Smith to help illustrate your position?

developing workplace skills

1. In teams, develop a list of the advantages of living in a capitalist society. Then develop lists headed "What are the disadvantages?" and "How could such disadvantages be minimized?" Describe why a poor person in a socialist country might reject capitalism and prefer a socialist state.

2. Show your understanding of the principles of supply and demand by looking at the oil market today. Why does the price of gas fluctuate so greatly? What will happen as more and more people in China and India decide to buy automobiles? What would happen if most U.S. consumers decided to drive electric cars?

3. This exercise will help you understand socialism from different perspectives. Form three groups. Each group should adopt a different role in a socialist economy: one group will be the business owners, another group will be workers, and another will be government leaders. Within your group discuss and list the advantages and disadvantages to you of lowering taxes on businesses. Then have each group choose a representative to go to the front of the class and debate the tax issue with the representatives from the other groups.

4. Draw a line and mark one end "Free-Market Capitalism" and the other end "Central Planning." Mark where on the line the United States is now. Explain why you marked the spot you chose. Students from other countries may want to do this exercise for their own countries and explain the differences to the class.

5. Break into small groups. In your group discuss how the following changes have affected people's purchasing behavior and attitudes toward the United States and its economy: the wars in Iraq and Afghanistan, the increased amount spent on homeland security, the government involvement in banking and other industries, and the growth of the Internet. Have a group member prepare a short summary for the class.

taking it to the net

Purpose

To familiarize you with the sources of economic information that are important to business decision makers.

Exercise

Imagine that your boss asked you to help her to prepare the company's sales forecast for the coming two years. In the past, she felt that trends in the nation's GDP, U.S. manufacturing, and manufacturing in Illinois were especially helpful in forecasting sales. She would like you to do the following:

1. Go to the Bureau of Economic Analysis's website (**www.bea.gov**) and locate the gross domestic product data. Compare the annual figure for the last four years. What do the figures indicate for the next couple of years?

2. At the Bureau of Labor Statistics' website (**www.bls.gov**) under Industries, click on Industries at a Glance to find the information about the manufacturing industry. What is the employment trend in manufacturing over the last four years (percentage change from preceding period)?

3. Return to the Bureau of Labor Statistics' home page and use the Search feature to find trends in employment for the state of Illinois. Look around the website to see what other information is available. Plot the trend in manufacturing employment in Illinois over the last four years. On your own, discuss what economic changes may have influenced that trend.

4. Based on the information you have gathered, write a brief summary of what may happen to company sales over the next couple of years.

casing the web

To access the case "The Rule of 72," visit **www.mhhe.com/P2P2e**

video case

Opportunity International: Giving the Poor a Working Chance

Billions of people in the world make $2 a day or less. In fact, a billion people make less than $1 a day. In such places, a loan of $100 or $200 makes a huge difference. That's where microloans from organizations such as Opportunity International come in.

Opportunity International is an organization that grants microloans to people, mostly women, in developing countries so they can invest in a business. Those investments often lead to community growth and employment, and help the owners themselves to prosper on a moderate scale. The borrowers must pay back the money with interest—when they do, they can borrow more and keep growing. Opportunity International, unlike some other microlending organizations, also provides a banking function where entrepreneurs can safely put their money. They can also buy some insurance to protect themselves against loss.

Opportunity International helps over a million people in over 28 countries, giving them the opportunity to change their lives for the better. This video introduces you to some of those people, but primarily explains how freedom and a little money can combine to create huge differences in people's lives.

Adam Smith was one of the first people to point out that wealth comes from freedom, the ability to own land, and the ability to keep the profits from what you do on that land. When people try to maximize profits, they have to hire other people to help them do the work. This provides jobs for others and wealth for the entrepreneur. And, like an invisible hand, the whole community benefits from the entrepreneurs' desire to earn a profit. In the video, you can see a woman in Uganda who has applied those principles to benefit her family, provide employment, and help her community.

Free-market capitalism is the system where people can own their own land and businesses and keep the profits they earn. Such a system demands that people can (1) own their own property (not a reality in many developing nations); (2) keep the profits from any business they start; (3) compete with other businesses (it is difficult to compete with the government); and (4) work wherever and whenever they want. The key word in capitalism is *freedom*— freedom of religion, freedom to own land, and freedom to prosper and grow. Opportunity International is making an attempt to show people how freedom plus a few dollars can make a huge difference in an economy.

In a free-market economy, price is determined by buyers and sellers negotiating over the price of a good or service. The equilibrium point is the place where buyers and sellers agree to an exchange; it is also called the market price. Without free markets, there is no way of knowing what buyers need and what sellers need to produce. Thus, in command economies, where there is no supply-and-demand mechanism in operation, there can be shortages or surpluses in food, clothing, and other necessities.

Socialism and communism are alternatives to a free-market economy. Under such systems, people are more likely to have a bit of equality, but there are fewer incentives to work hard, and entrepreneurs are often lured to countries where they can make more money by working harder. The result is called a brain drain, where the best and the brightest often move to free-market countries. There are advantages to socialism and communism, such as free schools, free health care, free day care, etc. But the taxes are higher, and there is usually less innovation and higher unemployment.

The trend in the world is toward mixed economies, where most of the economy is based on free-market principles, but the government gets involved in things such as education, health care, and welfare. The United States has been basically a free-market economy, but it is clear that there is a movement toward more government involvement. On the other hand, some countries are reducing the role of government in society and moving toward freer markets. Thus the world is moving toward mixed economies.

The United States government tries to control the money supply through the Federal Reserve and fiscal policy. Fiscal policy has to do with taxes and spending. The less the government spends, the more that is available for businesses to invest. And the lower the tax rates on entrepreneurs, the more they will invest in businesses and the faster the economy will grow.

Opportunity International shows the poorest of the poor how important entrepreneurs, freedom, opportunity, and a little bit of money are to economic growth and prosperity. You are encouraged in this video to participate in helping poor people around the world. You can do this by contributing time and money to organizations like Opportunity International. You can join the Peace Corps or other groups designed to assist less-developed countries.

Thinking It Over

1. *Why is there a need for organizations like Opportunity International? Can't poor people get loans from banks and other sources?*

2. *Identify the four major requirements necessary for a free-market system to operate.*

3. *What is the main difference between capitalism and a mixed economy? Which model is used in the United States?*

Doing BUSINESS IN
Global Markets

After you have read and studied this chapter, you should be able to

LEARNING
goals

1 Discuss the importance of the global market and the roles of comparative advantage and absolute advantage in global trade.

2 Explain the importance of importing and exporting, and understand key terms used in global business.

3 Illustrate the strategies used in reaching global markets and explain the role of multinational corporations.

4 Evaluate the forces that affect trading in global markets.

5 Debate the advantages and disadvantages of trade protectionism.

6 Discuss the changing landscape of the global market and the issue of offshore outsourcing.

profile

In today's global economy, doing business in emerging markets like India and China is becoming a necessity. Growth in the established economies of Western Europe and North America has slowed over the last few years. Meanwhile, in the so-called "BRIC bloc" of Brazil, Russia, India, and China, improvements to local infrastructure and growing middle classes are leading to a consumer revolution. That's why companies of all kinds are scrambling overseas for a piece of the action.

At Heinz, however, doing business in these countries is nothing new. The nearly 150-year-old food company has been active in emerging markets since the early 1990s thanks to the work of its current CEO, Bill Johnson. Under his leadership, Heinz now boasts the number-one- and number-two-selling products in as many as 50 countries. After seeing 12 percent growth in emerging markets in 2011, Johnson estimated that by the end of 2012, emerging market sales would account for more than 20 percent of the company's total business.

CONNECTING WITH
Bill Johnson
President and CEO of Heinz

After earning an undergraduate degree from UCLA and an MBA from the University of Texas, Johnson started at Heinz in 1982 as a general manager in charge of new business. In this position he became an expert at integrating changes into the company structure. After climbing the ladder throughout the 1980s, by 1993 he had assumed leadership of Heinz's Asia/Pacific operations. At that time revenues from the region barely registered on the company's bottom line. But during his first visits to Southeast Asia, Johnson could tell that these markets represented the future of Heinz's business. Although things like China's rickety public transport and shoddy roads surprised him, he nevertheless saw the makings of a budding middle class in the busy public markets. He also knew that growth in developed economies was bound to slow down sooner or later. With this information on hand, he began Heinz's first big push into the emerging world.

Johnson didn't take Heinz to this level of global dominance by only selling ketchup. By the time Johnson became CEO in 1996, he and his team had developed their long-term emerging market strategy. The system stressed what Johnson called the Three A's: applicability, availability, and affordability. The first "A" represents one of the core principles of doing business in other cultures. For a product to succeed, it must be in step with the typical tastes and preferences of the market. For instance, most Americans immediately associate Heinz's brand name with tomato ketchup. On Johnson's first trip to the Philippines, though, he discovered that people preferred their ketchup to be made from bananas. Also, while Heinz does sell some of its flagship product in China, the country's most popular condiment is soy sauce. Johnson knew that if Heinz was to take full advantage of these markets, they would have to offer the products that fit these cultures.

Simply producing the foods that consumers understood was only step one. The next "A," availability, ensured that the public could actually purchase Heinz's goods at established locations. In the United States this task is easy since nearly the entire population has access to any number of grocery stores and supercenters. Johnson knew this wasn't the case in emerging markets after only a few trips abroad.

In Indonesia most people rely on large open-air markets and tiny corner stores for their shopping. Less than a third of the consumers regularly visit grocery stores. Still, before Heinz could stock its products in these places there was another "A" to deal with. Americans often think nothing of buying jumbo portions of products that they can just throw in the fridge or the pantry. For many foreign consumers, however, not only are super-sized products hard to store, they're often outright unaffordable. That's why in Indonesia, Heinz sells billions of 3-cent soy sauce packets that would surely draw confused looks if they appeared on Western store shelves.

As Heinz's foreign business began to grow, by the 2000s Johnson had added another "A" to his list—affinity. Getting the right products in the right places at the right price was a good start, but Johnson wanted his local customers to feel close to the brands they were buying. After all, dependable products can become a lifelong fixture on many peoples' shopping lists. Building this trust between consumers and the Heinz brand has been Johnson's biggest challenge yet. Regardless, Heinz's stellar global performance and Johnson's personal accomplishments speak for themselves. Along with a number of other accolades, in 2006 he received the Marco Polo Award, the highest honor bestowed by the Chinese government to foreign business leaders, for his work in developing the Chinese food industry.

Bill Johnson is an example of an emerging global businessperson. He has learned to speak languages, understands cultural and economic differences, and knows how to adapt to changes successfully. This chapter explains the opportunities and challenges businesspeople like Johnson face every day in dealing with the dynamic environment of global business.

Sources: Bill Johnson, "The CEO of Heinz on Powering Growth in Emerging Markets," *Harvard Business Review,* October 2011; Paul Ziobro, "Heinz Sees Emerging Markets Driving Growth," *The Wall Street Journal,* May 26, 2011; "Heinz Company Business Fact Sheet," accessed March 21, 2012; and "William R. Johnson Bio," www.heinz.com, accessed March 21, 2012.

We franchise 36,000 of our KFC, Taco Bell, and Pizza Hut restaurants in 117 countries around the world. It didn't take us long to learn that customers around the globe have very different tastes when it comes to their food. We found in Japan that a favorite pizza enjoyed by our patrons was topped with squid and sweet mayonnaise. In China it's a must to serve a "dragon twister" with our world-famous chicken. Name our company. (Find the answer in the chapter.)

LEARNING goal 1

Discuss the importance of the global market and the roles of comparative advantage and absolute advantage in global trade.

THE DYNAMIC GLOBAL MARKET

Have you dreamed of traveling to cities like Paris, London, Rio de Janeiro, or Moscow? Today, over 90 percent of the companies doing business globally believe it's important for their employees to have experience working in other countries.[1] The reason is not surprising—although the United States is a market of over 313

The Houston Rockets and the New Jersey Nets christened the new Guangzhou International Sports Arena with a preseason game in 2010. The NBA now plays games in several countries around the world. What cultural factors must U.S. sports franchises overcome to increase popularity abroad?

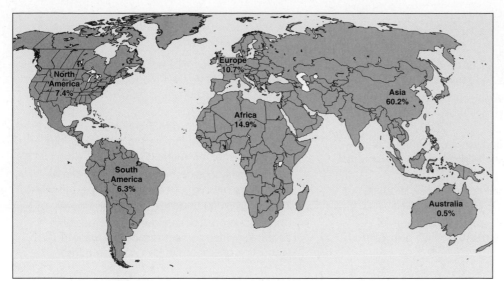

figure 3.1

WORLD POPULATION BY CONTINENT

million people, there are over 7 *billion* potential customers in the 194 countries that make up the global market.[2] That's too many people to ignore! (See Figure 3.1 for a map of the world and important statistics about world population.)

Today U.S. consumers buy billions of dollars' worth of goods from China.[3] United Parcel Service (UPS) has experienced double-digit market growth in its global operations and Walmart is planning to expand into Africa.[4] Major League Baseball opened its 2008 season in Japan and the National Basketball Association (NBA) and the National Football League (NFL) play games in Mexico, Italy, England, and elsewhere. Chinese-born Yao Ming, formerly of the NBA's Houston Rockets, was a seven-time NBA All-Star and Paul Gasol of Spain helped the L.A. Lakers win championships in 2009–2010.[5] U.S. film stars Johnny Depp, Will Smith, and Julia Roberts draw crowds to movie theaters around the globe.[6]

Because the global market is so large, it is important to understand the language used in global trade. For example, **importing** is buying products from another country. **Exporting** is selling products to another country. As you might suspect, competition among exporting nations is intense. The United States is the largest importing nation in the world and is the second-largest exporting nation, behind China.[7]

This chapter will familiarize you with global business and its many challenges. As competition in global markets intensifies, the demand for students with training in global business is almost certain to grow. If you choose such a career, prepare yourself to work hard and always be ready for new challenges.

importing
Buying products from another country.

exporting
Selling products to another country.

WHY TRADE WITH OTHER NATIONS?

No nation, not even a technologically advanced one, can produce all the products its people want and need. Even if a country did become self-sufficient, other nations would seek to trade with it to meet the needs of their own people. Some nations, like Venezuela and Russia, have an abundance of natural resources but limited technological know-how. Other countries, such as Japan and Switzerland, have sophisticated technology but few natural resources. Global trade enables a nation to produce what it is most capable of producing and buy what it needs from others in a mutually beneficial exchange relationship. This happens through the process called free trade.[8]

PROS	CONS
• The global market contains over 7 billion potential customers for goods and services.	• Domestic workers (particularly in manufacturing-based jobs) can lose their jobs due to increased imports or production shifts to low-wage global markets.
• Productivity grows when countries produce goods and services in which they have a comparative advantage.	• Workers may be forced to accept pay cuts from employers, who can threaten to move their jobs to lower-cost global markets.
• Global competition and less-costly imports keep prices down, so inflation does not curtail economic growth.	• Moving operations overseas because of intense competitive pressure often means the loss of service jobs and growing numbers of white-collar jobs.
• Free trade inspires innovation for new products and keeps firms competitively challenged.	• Domestic companies can lose their comparative advantage when competitors build advanced production operations in low-wage countries.
• Uninterrupted flow of capital gives countries access to foreign investments, which help keep interest rates low.	

figure 3.2

THE PROS AND CONS OF FREE TRADE

free trade
The movement of goods and services among nations without political or economic barriers.

comparative advantage theory
Theory that states that a country should sell to other countries those products that it produces most effectively and efficiently, and buy from other countries those products that it cannot produce as effectively or efficiently.

absolute advantage
The advantage that exists when a country has a monopoly on producing a specific product or is able to produce it more efficiently than all other countries.

Free trade is the movement of goods and services among nations without political or economic barriers. It has become a hotly debated concept.[9] In fact, many in the United States take the position "fair trade, not free trade."[10] Figure 3.2 offers some of the pros and cons of free trade.

The Theories of Comparative and Absolute Advantage

Countries exchange more than goods and services, however. They also exchange art, sports, cultural events, medical advances, space exploration, and labor. Comparative advantage theory, suggested in the early 19th century by English economist David Ricardo, was the guiding principle that supported the idea of free economic exchange.[11]

Comparative advantage theory states that a country should sell to other countries those products it produces most effectively and efficiently, and buy from other countries those products it cannot produce as effectively or efficiently. The United States has a comparative advantage in producing goods and services, such as software and engineering services. In contrast, it lacks a comparative advantage in growing coffee or making shoes; thus, we import most of the shoes and coffee we consume. By specializing and trading, the United States and its trading partners can realize mutually beneficial exchanges.[12]

A country has an **absolute advantage** if it has a monopoly on producing a specific product or is able to produce it more efficiently than all other countries. However, absolute advantage in natural resources does not last forever; for instance, South Africa once had an absolute advantage in diamond production, but that is no longer the case. Global competition also causes other absolute advantages to fade. Today there are very few instances of absolute advantage in global markets.

LEARNING goal 2

Explain the importance of importing and exporting, and understand key terms used in global business.

GETTING INVOLVED IN GLOBAL TRADE

People interested in a job in global business often think they are limited to firms like Boeing, Caterpillar, or IBM, which have large multinational accounts. However, real global job potential may be with small businesses.[13] In the United States, only 1 percent of the 29 million small businesses export yet they account for about 30 percent of the total U.S. exports. President Obama wants small businesses to think big and help double exports by 2015. With the support of the U.S. Department of Commerce, it's expected that almost half of these businesses will become involved in global trade.[14]

Getting started globally is often a matter of observing, being determined, and taking risks. For example, several years ago a U.S. traveler in an African country noticed there was no ice available for drinks or for keeping foods fresh. Research showed there was no ice factory for hundreds of miles, yet the market seemed huge. The man returned to the United States, found some investors, and returned to Africa to build an ice-making plant. The job was tough; much negotiation was necessary with local authorities (much of which was done by local citizens and businesspeople who knew the system). But the plant was built, and this forward-thinking entrepreneur gained a considerable return on his idea, while the people gained a needed product. The Connecting with Small Business box highlights how a small nonprofit business hopes to bring better sight to the world.

Importing Goods and Services

Students attending colleges and universities abroad often notice that some products widely available in their countries are unavailable or more expensive elsewhere. By working with producers in their native country, finding some start-up financing, and putting in long hours of hard work, many have become major importers while still in school.

Howard Schultz, CEO of Starbucks, found his opportunity while traveling in Italy. Schultz was enthralled with the ambience, the aroma, and especially the sense of community in the 200,000 Italian neighborhood coffee and espresso bars that stretched across the country. He felt such gathering places would be great in the United States. Schultz bought the original Starbucks coffee shop in Seattle and transformed it according to his vision.[15] Because the Italian coffee bars caught his attention, U.S. coffee lovers now know what a grande latte is.

Exporting Goods and Services

Who would think U.S. firms could sell beer in Germany, home of so many good beers? Well, around the corner from a famous beer hall in Munich you can buy Samuel Adams Boston Lager. If this surprises you, imagine selling sand in the Middle East. Meridan Group exports a special kind of sand used in swimming pool filters that sells well there.

The fact is, you can sell just about any good or service used in the United States to other countries—and sometimes the competition is not nearly so intense as it is at home. For example, you can sell snowplows to Saudi Arabians, who use them to clear sand off their driveways. In China, sales of men's cosmetic products is growing at twice the rate of women's due to their

Things may not have started off "pretty" for Ugly Dolls, a venture founded almost by accident, but the two-person company has grown into a global business selling its products in over 1,000 stores around the world. The original dolls have been joined by books, calendars, action figures, and T-shirts. Does a career in exporting or importing sound appealing to you?

Improving Sight through Entrepreneurship

When optometrist Jordan Kassalow made an aid trip to Mexico, he learned firsthand how the lack of glasses affected the local workers. "Losing eyesight is a silent robber of economic activity," said Kassalow. "Hundreds of millions of poor people lose their livelihood in their prime working years."

Kassalow wanted to help the people he met, but he didn't like the idea of relying solely on donations to achieve his goals. So Kassalow and a partner founded VisionSpring, a business that is part charity and part small franchisor. Kassalow employs mostly women needing additional income to travel around their villages selling glasses. The women buy glasses at cost from VisionSpring for $2.50 a pair and then sell them for $4 to $7 apiece. This way Kassalow is not only giving sight to those who need it most, but he's also stimulating the local economy. So far VisionSpring has sold 600,000 pairs of basic reading glasses in seven countries.

VisionSpring still operates at a loss, however, making charitable donations a necessary part of the company's income. Kassalow is making strides toward profitability though. VisionSpring recently opened its first store that sells higher-priced prescription glasses in El Salvador. A $15 pair of prescription glasses yields about $4.50 in profit, including a $1 finder's fee to Kassalow's local salespeople. The store made money in its first year of operation, putting Kassalow one step closer to his dream of a sustainable, market-driven solution for vision problems in the developing world.

Sources: Helen Coster and Jason Daley, "The Vision Thing," *Entrepreneur,* March 2010; "New Vision for Nonprofits," *Forbes,* February 14, 2011; and VisionSpring, www.visionspring.com, accessed May 2012.

---

desire to project an image of success.[16] Exporting also provides a terrific boost to the U.S. economy. C. Fred Bergsten, director of the Peterson Institute for International Economics, states that U.S. exports of $1.5 trillion goods and services create approximately 10 million well-paid jobs in our economy. He also estimates that every $1 billion in additional U.S. exports generates over 7,000 jobs at home.[17] But selling in global markets and adapting products to global customers are by no means easy tasks. We discuss key forces that affect global trading later in this chapter.

If you are interested in exporting, send for "The Basic Guide to Exporting," a brochure from the U.S. Government Printing Office, Superintendent of Documents, Washington, DC 20402. More advice is available at websites such as those sponsored by the U.S. Department of Commerce (www.doc.gov), the Bureau of Export Administration (www.bea.gov), the Small Business Administration (www.sba.gov), and the Small Business Exporters Association (www.sbea.org).

Measuring Global Trade

In measuring global trade, nations rely on two key indicators: balance of trade and balance of payments. The **balance of trade** is the total value of a nation's exports compared to its imports measured over a particular period. A *favorable* balance of trade, or **trade surplus,** occurs when the value of a country's exports exceeds that of its imports. An *unfavorable* balance of trade, or **trade deficit,** occurs when the value of a country's exports is less than its imports. It's easy to understand why countries prefer to export more than they import. If I sell you $200 worth of goods and buy only $100 worth, I have an extra $100 available to buy other things. However, I'm in an unfavorable position if I buy $200 worth of goods from you and sell you only $100.

balance of trade
The total value of a nation's exports compared to its imports measured over a particular period.

trade surplus
A favorable balance of trade; occurs when the value of a country's exports exceeds that of its imports.

trade deficit
An unfavorable balance of trade; occurs when the value of a country's imports exceeds that of its exports.

The United States imports most of its toys from China—and so does the rest of the world. China now produces and exports 80 percent of the toys manufactured in the world. The highest U.S. trade deficit is with China. What products do you use that are imported from China?

The **balance of payments** is the difference between money coming into a country (from exports) and money leaving the country (for imports) plus money flows coming into or leaving a country from other factors such as tourism, foreign aid, military expenditures, and foreign investment. The goal is to have more money flowing into the country than out—a *favorable* balance of payments. Conversely, an *unfavorable* balance of payments exists when more money is flowing out of a country than coming in.

In the past, the United States exported more goods and services than it imported. However, since 1975 it has bought more goods from other nations than it has sold and thus has a trade deficit.[18] Over the past few years, the United States ran its highest trade deficits with China.[19] Still the United States remains one of the world's largest *exporting* nations even though the U.S. exports a much lower *percentage* of its products than other countries, such as China, Japan, and Germany. Improving that percentage by expanding exports is a goal the United States hopes to achieve by 2015.[20] (Figure 3.3 lists the major trading countries in the world and the leading U.S. trading partners.)

balance of payments
The difference between money coming into a country (from exports) and money leaving the country (for imports) plus money flows from other factors such as tourism, foreign aid, military expenditures, and foreign investment.

Need help understanding balance of trade?
www.introbiz.tv/QR3-1

figure 3.3

THE LARGEST EXPORTING NATIONS IN THE WORLD AND THE LARGEST U.S. TRADE PARTNERS

World's Largest Exporting Nations

China
United States
Germany
Japan
France
South Korea
Netherlands
Italy
Russia
United Kingdom

Top U.S. Trading Partners

COUNTRY	2011 TOTAL TRADE (IN BILLIONS)
1. Canada	$597
2. China	$503
3. Mexico	$460
4. Japan	$195
5. Germany	$147
6. U.K.	$107
7. South Korea	$100
8. Brazil	$ 74
9. Saudi Arabia	$ 68
10. France	$ 67

dumping
Selling products in a foreign country at lower prices than those charged in the producing country.

In supporting free trade, the United States, like other nations, wants to make certain global trade is conducted fairly. To ensure a level playing field, countries prohibit unfair practices such as dumping. **Dumping** is selling products in a foreign country at lower prices than those charged in the producing country. This predatory pricing tactic is sometimes used to reduce surplus products in foreign markets or to gain a foothold in a new market. Some governments may offer financial incentives to certain industries to sell goods in global markets for less than they sell them at home. China, Brazil, and Russia, for example, have been penalized for dumping steel in the United States.[21] U.S. laws against dumping are specific and require foreign firms to price their products to include 10 percent overhead costs plus an 8 percent profit margin.

Now that you understand some of the basic terms used in global business, we can look at different strategies for entering global markets. First, let's assess your progress so far.

progress assessment

- What are two of the main arguments favoring the expansion of U.S. businesses into global markets?
- What is comparative advantage, and what are some examples of this concept at work in global markets?
- How are a nation's balance of trade and balance of payments determined?
- What is meant by the term *dumping* in global trade?

LEARNING goal 3

Illustrate the strategies used in reaching global markets and explain the role of multinational corporations.

STRATEGIES FOR REACHING GLOBAL MARKETS

Businesses use different strategies to compete in global markets. The key strategies include licensing, exporting, franchising, contract manufacturing, international joint ventures and strategic alliances, foreign subsidiaries, and foreign direct investment. Each provides different economic opportunities, along with specific commitments and risks. Figure 3.4 places the strategies on a continuum showing the amount of commitment, control, risk, and profit potential associated with each. Take a few minutes to look over Figure 3.4 before you continue.

Licensing

licensing
A global strategy in which a firm (the licensor) allows a foreign company (the licensee) to produce its product in exchange for a fee (a royalty).

A firm (the licensor) may decide to compete in a global market by **licensing** the right to manufacture its product or use its trademark to a foreign company (the licensee) for a fee (a royalty). A company with an interest in licensing generally sends company representatives to the foreign company to help set up operations. The licensor may also assist or work with a licensee in such areas as distribution, promotion, and consulting.

A licensing agreement can benefit a firm in several ways. First, the firm can gain revenues it would not otherwise have generated in its home market. Also, foreign licensees often must purchase start-up supplies, materials, and consulting

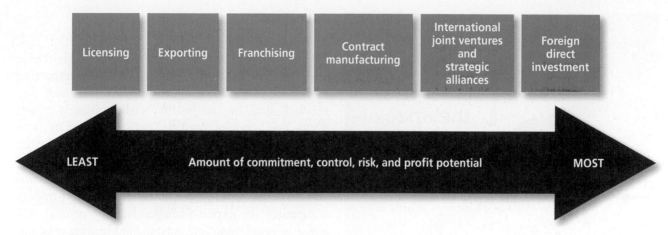

| Licensing | Exporting | Franchising | Contract manufacturing | International joint ventures and strategic alliances | Foreign direct investment |

LEAST   Amount of commitment, control, risk, and profit potential   MOST

figure 3.4

STRATEGIES FOR REACHING GLOBAL MARKETS

services from the licensing firm. Coca-Cola has entered into global licensing agreements with over 300 licensees that have extended into long-term service contracts that sell over $1 billion of the company's products each year.[22] Service-based companies are also active in licensing. For example, retailer Frederick's of Hollywood recently entered into a licensing agreement with Emirates Associated Business Group to build and operate Frederick's of Hollywood stores in the Middle East.[23]

A final advantage of licensing is that licensors spend little or no money to produce and market their products. These costs come from the licensee's pocket. Therefore, licensees generally work hard to succeed. However, licensors may also experience problems. Often a firm must grant licensing rights to its product for an extended period, 20 years or longer. If a product experiences remarkable growth in the foreign market, the bulk of the revenues belong to the licensee. Perhaps even more threatening is that the licensing firm is actually selling its expertise. If a foreign licensee learns the company's technology or product secrets, it may break the agreement and begin to produce a similar product on its own. If legal remedies are not available, the licensing firm may lose its trade secrets, not to mention promised royalties.

Warner Bros. has licensed hundreds of companies to make products related to its series of hit films based on the best-selling Harry Potter books, which have been translated into dozens of languages. Do you think Potter-licensed products will maintain their global popularity with new generations of young readers and viewers?

맛도, 가격도
더 스페셜
the special
피자

정말 맛있는 5가지 피자

15,900원

크림치킨   까망베르   데미그라스 비프   바질씨푸드   갈릭토마토

Pizza Hut

Tired of studying and want a quick snack? How about a piping hot Pizza Hut pizza with shrimp and mayonnaise? Pizza Hut serves pizzas around the globe that appeal to different tastes. How can franchises ensure their products are appropriate for global markets?

contract manufacturing
A foreign company's production of private-label goods to which a domestic company then attaches its brand name or trademark; part of the broad category of outsourcing.

Exporting

To meet increasing global competition, the U.S. Department of Commerce created Export Assistance Centers (EACs). EACs provide hands-on exporting assistance and trade-finance support for small and medium-sized businesses that wish to directly export goods and services. An EAC network exists in more than 109 U.S. cities and 80 countries, with further expansion planned.[24]

U.S. firms that are still hesitant can engage in *indirect* exporting through specialists called export-trading companies (or export-management companies) that assist in negotiating and establishing trading relationships. An export-trading company not only matches buyers and sellers from different countries but also deals with foreign customs offices, documentation, and even weights and measures conversions to ease the process of entering global markets. It also can assist exporters with warehousing, billing, and insuring. If you are considering a career in global business, export-trading companies often provide internships or part-time opportunities for students.

Franchising

Franchising is a contractual agreement whereby someone with a good idea for a business sells others the rights to use the business name and sell a product or service in a given territory in a specified manner. Franchising is popular domestically and internationally. (We discuss it in depth in Chapter 5.) Major U.S. franchisors such as Subway, Holiday Inn, and Dunkin' Donuts have many global units operated by foreign franchisees, but global franchising isn't limited to large franchisors. For example, Rocky Mountain Chocolate Factory, a Colorado-based producer of premium chocolates, has franchising agreements with the Al Muhairy Group of the United Arab Emirates, where chocolate is considered a gourmet luxury much like caviar in the United States.[25] Foreign franchisors also may look to expand to the U.S. market. Vietnamese entrepreneur Ly Qui Trung hopes to introduce his Pho24 franchises to the United States soon.[26]

Franchisors have to be careful to adapt their product or service to the countries they serve. Yum! Brands has 36,000 of its KFC, Taco Bell, and Pizza Hut restaurants in 117 countries around the world.[27] They learned quickly that preferences in pizza toppings differ globally. Japanese customers, for example, enjoy squid and sweet mayonnaise pizza. In the company's KFC restaurants in China, the menu is chicken with Sichuan spicy sauce and rice, egg soup, and a "dragon twister" (KFC's version of a traditional Beijing duck wrap).[28] Read the nearby Connecting Across Borders box that highlights another franchise champion, McDonald's.

Contract Manufacturing

In **contract manufacturing** a foreign company produces private-label goods to which a domestic company then attaches its own brand name or trademark. For example, contract manufacturers make circuit boards and components used in

McDonald's: Over 100 Cultures Served

For decades the undisputed king of global food franchising has been McDonald's. With more than 33,000 restaurants in 119 countries, Mickey D's serves more than 60 million customers every day.

So how did McDonald's become such a global powerhouse? It certainly didn't get there through hamburgers alone. Since it first began expanding overseas, McDonald's has been careful to include regional tastes on its menus along with the usual Big Mac and French fries. For instance, in Thailand patrons can order the Samurai Burger, a pork-patty sandwich marinated in teriyaki sauce and topped with mayonnaise and a pickle. If fish is more your taste, try Norway's salmon burger called the McLaks, or the Ebi Filet-o shrimp sandwich from Japan.

McDonald's is also careful to adapt its menus to local customs and culture. In Israel, all meat served in the chain's restaurants is 100 percent kosher beef. The company also closes many of its restaurants on the Sabbath and religious holidays. McDonald's pays respect to religious sentiments in India as well by not including any beef or pork on its menu. For more examples, go to www.mcdonalds .com and explore the various McDonald's international franchises websites. Notice how the company blends the culture of each country into the restaurant's image.

McDonald's main global market concern as of late has been China. So far McDonald's strategy seems to be working. In Shanghai the company's Hamburger University attracts top-level college graduates to be trained for management positions. Only about eight out of every 1,000 applicants makes it into the program, an acceptance rate even lower than Harvard's. McDonald's also found a boost of prestige in Hong Kong with its so-called McWeddings. Matrimony is a big deal in the city, with many young people saving for years or going deeply into debt to fund lavish ceremonies that cost around $29,000 for the average couple. A McWedding, on the

other hand, starts at $1,280 and includes drinks and food for 50 people along with gifts and invitations. The affordable wedding package even comes with a "cake" made out of a stack of McDonald's signature apple pies.

On that note, McDonald's continues to battle controversies over the fat content of its food as well as the safety of its production methods. In 2010, for instance, the company instituted a recall of its promotional line of *Shrek Forever After* glassware after reports of cadmium poisoning surfaced. In the end, one can only hope that McDonald's remains dedicated to quality as it continues adapting and expanding into the global market.

Sources: Bloomberg News, "Getting into Harvard Easier Than McDonald's University in China," *Bloomberg,* January 25, 2011; Joyce Hor-Chung Lau, "Raising a Milkshake to the Bride and Groom," *The New York Times,* February 27, 2011; Leslie Patton, "McDonald's to Almost Double China Employees as Gears Up," *Bloomberg,* May 16, 2012, and McDonald's, www.mcdonalds.com, accessed May 2012.

computers, printers, cell phones, medical products, airplanes, and consumer electronics for companies such as Dell, Xerox, and IBM.[29] Nike has more than 700 contract factories around the world that manufacture all its footwear and apparel. The worldwide contract manufacturing business is estimated to be a $250 billion industry that's expected to grow to $325 billion by 2013.[30]

Contract manufacturing enables a company to experiment in a new market without incurring heavy start-up costs such as building a manufacturing plant. If the brand name becomes a success, the company has penetrated a new market with relatively low risk. A firm can also use contract manufacturing temporarily to meet an unexpected increase in orders, and, of course, labor costs are often very low. Contract manufacturing falls under the broad category of *outsourcing,* which we defined in Chapter 1 and will discuss in more depth later in this chapter.

International Joint Ventures and Strategic Alliances

joint venture
A partnership in which two or more companies (often from different countries) join to undertake a major project.

A **joint venture** is a partnership in which two or more companies (often from different countries) join to undertake a major project. Joint ventures are often mandated by governments such as China as a condition of doing business in their country. For example, Disney and state-owned Shanghai Shendi Group entered a joint venture to create a Disneyland theme park in Shanghai that is expected to open in 2015.[31]

Joint ventures are developed for many different reasons. Marriott International and AC Hotels in Spain entered a joint venture to create AC Hotels by Marriott to increase their global footprint and future growth.[32] PepsiCo agreed to a joint venture with Tata Global Beverages of India to develop packaged health and wellness beverages for the mass consumer market in India.[33] Joint ventures can also be truly unique, such as the University of Pittsburgh's Medical Center and the Italian government's joint venture that brought a new medical transplant center to Sicily. The transplant center in Palermo called ISMETT recently celebrated its fifteenth year of operation.[34]

The benefits of international joint ventures are clear:

1. Shared technology and risk.
2. Shared marketing and management expertise.
3. Entry into markets where foreign companies are often not allowed unless goods are produced locally.

The drawbacks of joint ventures are not so obvious but are important. One partner can learn the other's technology and business practices and then use what it has learned to its own advantage. Also, a shared technology may become obsolete, or the joint venture may become too large to be as flexible as needed.

strategic alliance
A long-term partnership between two or more companies established to help each company build competitive market advantages.

The global market is also fueling the growth of strategic alliances. A **strategic alliance** is a long-term partnership between two or more companies established to help each company build competitive market advantages. Unlike joint ventures, strategic alliances don't share costs, risks, management, or even profits. Such alliances provide broad access to markets, capital, and technical expertise. Thanks to their flexibility, strategic alliances can effectively link firms from different countries and firms of vastly different sizes. Hewlett-Packard has strategic alliances with Hitachi and Samsung, and Coca-Cola and Nestlé have had an alliance since early 1990 to distribute ready-to-drink tea and coffee.

Foreign Direct Investment

foreign direct investment (FDI)
The buying of permanent property and businesses in foreign nations.

Foreign direct investment (FDI) is the buying of permanent property and businesses in foreign nations. The most common form of FDI is a **foreign subsidiary,** a company owned in a foreign country by another company, called the *parent company.* The subsidiary operates like a domestic firm, with production, distribution, promotion, pricing, and other business functions under the control of the subsidiary's management. The subsidiary also must observe the legal requirements of both the

foreign subsidiary
A company owned in a foreign country by another company, called the *parent company.*

country where the parent firm is located (called the *home country*) and the foreign country where the subsidiary is located (called the *host country*).

The primary advantage of a subsidiary is that the company maintains complete control over any technology or expertise it may possess. The major shortcoming is the need to commit funds and technology within foreign boundaries. Should relationships with a host country falter, the firm's assets could be *expropriated* (taken over by the foreign government). Swiss-based Nestlé has many foreign subsidiaries. The consumer-products giant spent billions of dollars acquiring foreign subsidiaries such as Jenny Craig (weight management), Ralston Purina, Chef America (maker of Hot Pockets), and Dreyer's Ice Cream in the United States as well as Perrier in France. Nestlé employs over 280,000 people and has operations in almost every country in the world.[35]

Nestlé is a **multinational corporation,** one that manufactures and markets products in many different countries and has multinational stock ownership and management. Multinational corporations are typically extremely large corporations like Nestlé, but not all large global businesses are multinationals. For example, a corporation could export everything it produces, deriving 100 percent of its sales and profits globally, and still not be a multinational corporation. Only firms that have *manufacturing capacity* or some other physical presence in different nations can truly be called multinational. Figure 3.5 lists the 10 largest multinational corporations in the world.

One of the fastest-growing forms of foreign direct investment is the use of **sovereign wealth funds (SWFs),** investment funds controlled by governments holding large stakes in foreign companies. SWFs from Kuwait, Singapore, and China have purchased significant portions of U.S. companies such as Citigroup. The size of SWFs and government ownership make some fear they might be used for achieving geopolitical objectives, gaining control of strategic natural resources, or obtaining sensitive technologies. SWFs could also undermine the management of the companies in which they invest. In contrast, some experts see foreign investment through SWFs as a vote of confidence in the U.S. economy and a way to create thousands of U.S. jobs.

The United States has been and remains a popular global spot for foreign direct investment. Global automobile manufacturers like Toyota, Honda, and Mercedes have spent millions of dollars building facilities in the United States, like the Mercedes plant in Tuscaloosa, Alabama, pictured here. Do you consider a Mercedes made in Alabama to be an American car or a German car?

multinational corporation
An organization that manufactures and markets products in many different countries and has multinational stock ownership and multinational management.

figure 3.5

THE LARGEST MULTINATIONAL CORPORATIONS IN THE WORLD

COMPANY	COUNTRY	WEBSITE
1. Wal-Mart Stores	United States	walmartstores.com
2. Royal Dutch Shell	Netherlands	shell.com
3. ExxonMobil	United States	exxonmobil.com
4. BP	Britain	bp.com
5. Sinopec Group	China	sinopecgroup.com
6. China National Petroleum	China	cnpc.com.cn
7. State Grid	China	sgcc.com.cn
8. Toyota Motor	Japan	toyota.co.jp
9. Japan Post Holdings	Japan	japanpost.jp
10. Chevron	United States	chevron.com

Source: *Fortune,* July 25, 2011.

sovereign wealth funds (SWFs)
Investment funds controlled by governments holding large stakes in foreign companies.

Entering global business requires selecting an entry strategy that best fits your business goals. The different strategies we've discussed reflect different levels of ownership, financial commitment, and risk. However, this is just the beginning. You should also be aware of market forces that affect a business's ability to thrive in global markets. After the Progress Assessment, we'll discuss them.

progress assessment

- What are the advantages to a firm of using licensing as a method of entry in global markets? What are the disadvantages?
- What services are usually provided by an export-trading company?
- What is the key difference between a joint venture and a strategic alliance?
- What makes a company a multinational corporation?

LEARNING goal 4

Evaluate the forces that affect trading in global markets.

FORCES AFFECTING TRADING IN GLOBAL MARKETS

The hurdles to success are higher and more complex in global markets than in domestic markets. Such hurdles include dealing with differences in sociocultural forces, economic and financial forces, legal and regulatory forces, and physical and environmental forces. Let's analyze each of these market forces to see how they challenge even the most established and experienced global businesses.

Sociocultural Forces

The word *culture* refers to the set of values, beliefs, rules, and institutions held by a specific group of people. Culture can include social structures, religion, manners and customs, values and attitudes, language, and personal communication. If you hope to get involved in global trade, it's critical to be aware of the cultural differences among nations. Unfortunately, while the United States is a multicultural nation, U.S. businesspeople are often accused of *ethnocentricity,* an attitude that your own culture is superior to other cultures.[36]

In contrast, many foreign companies are very good at adapting to U.S. culture. Think how effectively German, Japanese, and Korean carmakers adapted to U.S. drivers' wants and needs in the auto industry.[37] In contrast, for many years U.S. auto producers didn't adapt automobiles to drive on the left side of the road and printed owner's manuals only in English. Liberia, Myanmar, and the United States are the only nations in the world that have not conformed to the metric system of measurement. Let's look at other hurdles U.S. businesses face in adapting to social and cultural differences in global markets.

Religion is an important part of any society's culture and can have a significant impact on business operations. Consider the violent clashes between religious communities in India, Pakistan, and the Middle East—clashes that have wounded these areas' economies. Even successful global companies sometimes ignore religious implications in making business decisions. For example, in honor of nations competing in the World Cup, both McDonald's and Coca-Cola decided to reprint the flags of the participating countries on their packaging. Muslims were offended when the Saudi Arabian flag was put on their packaging because the flag's design contains a passage from the Koran, and Muslims believe their holy writ should never be wadded up and thrown away.

In another classic story, a U.S. manager in Islamic Pakistan toured a new plant under his control. While the plant was in full operation, he went to his office to make some preliminary production forecasts. Suddenly all the machinery in the plant stopped. The manager rushed out, suspecting a power failure, only to find his production workers on their prayer rugs. Upon learning that Muslims are required to pray five times a day, he returned to his office and lowered his production estimates.

Understanding sociocultural differences is also important in managing employees. In some Latin American countries, workers believe managers are in positions of authority to make decisions concerning the well-being of the workers under their control. Consider the U.S. manager in Peru who was unaware of this cultural characteristic and believed workers should participate in managerial functions. He was convinced he could motivate his workers to higher levels of productivity by instituting a more democratic decision-making style. Workers instead began quitting in droves. When asked why, they said the new manager did not know his job and was asking the workers what to do. All stated they wanted to find new jobs, since this company was doomed due to its incompetent management.

Many U.S. companies still fail to think globally. Even something like the color of flowers can have different meanings in different cultures.[38] A sound philosophy is: *Never assume what works in one country will work in another.* Intel, Nike, IBM, Apple, Honda, KFC, and Walmart have developed brand names with widespread global appeal and recognition, but even they often face difficulties. To get an idea of the problems companies have faced with translations of advertising, take a look at Figure 3.6.

Economic and Financial Forces

Economic differences can muddy the water in global markets. It's hard for us to imagine buying chewing gum by the stick. Yet this behavior is commonplace in economically depressed nations like Haiti, where customers can afford only small

---

- PepsiCo attempted a Chinese translation of "Come Alive, You're in the Pepsi Generation" that read to Chinese customers as "Pepsi Brings Your Ancestors Back from the Dead."
- Coors Brewing Company put its slogan "Turn It Loose" into Spanish and found it translated as "Suffer from Diarrhea."
- Perdue Chicken used the slogan "It Takes a Strong Man to Make a Chicken Tender," which was interpreted in Spanish as "It Takes an Aroused Man to Make a Chicken Affectionate."
- KFC's patented slogan "Finger-Lickin' Good" was understood in Japanese as "Bite Your Fingers Off."
- On the other side of the translation glitch, Electrolux, a Scandinavian vacuum manufacturer, tried to sell its products in the U.S. market with the slogan "Nothing Sucks Like an Electrolux."

figure 3.6

OOPS, DID WE SAY THAT?

A global marketing strategy can be very difficult to implement. Look at the problems these well-known companies encountered in global markets.

When the dollar is "up," foreign goods and travel are a bargain for U.S. consumers. When the dollar trades for less foreign currency, however, foreign tourists like these often flock to U.S. cities to enjoy relatively cheaper vacations and shopping trips. Do U.S. exporters profit more when the dollar is up or when it is down?

exchange rate
The value of one nation's currency relative to the currencies of other countries.

devaluation
Lowering the value of a nation's currency relative to other currencies.

countertrading
A complex form of bartering in which several countries may be involved, each trading goods for goods or services for services.

quantities. You might suspect with over 1 billion people each, India and China would be dream markets for companies like Pepsi-Cola and Procter & Gamble (P&G). Unfortunately, Indians consume an average of three soft drinks per person a year and China's 1.3 billion customers spend just $3 per year on P&G products due to low per-capita income.[39]

Mexicans shop with pesos, Chinese with yuan, South Koreans with won, Japanese with yen, and U.S. consumers with dollars. Globally, the U.S. dollar is considered a dominant and stable currency.[40] However, it doesn't always retain the same market value. In a global transaction today, a dollar may be exchanged for eight pesos; tomorrow you may get seven. The **exchange rate** is the value of one nation's currency relative to the currencies of other countries.

Changes in a nation's exchange rates have effects in global markets. A *high value of the dollar* means a dollar is trading for more foreign currency than previously. Therefore, foreign products become cheaper because it takes fewer dollars to buy them. However, U.S.-produced goods become more expensive because of the dollar's high value. Conversely, a *low value of the dollar* means a dollar is traded for less foreign currency—foreign goods become more expensive because it takes more dollars to buy them, but U.S. goods become cheaper to foreign buyers because it takes less foreign currency to buy them.

Global financial markets operate under a system called *floating exchange rates,* which means that currencies "float" in value according to the supply and demand for them in the global market for currency. This supply and demand is created by global currency traders who develop a market for a nation's currency based on the country's perceived trade and investment potential.

Changes in currency values can cause many problems globally.[41] For instance, labor costs for multinational corporations like Nestlé, General Electric, and Sony can vary considerably as currency values shift, causing them to juggle production from one country to another. The same is true for medium-sized companies like H. B. Fuller of St. Paul, Minnesota, which has 3,100 employees in 38 countries. Like their larger counterparts, H. B. Fuller learned to use currency fluctuations to their advantage in dealing with their global markets.

Currency valuation problems can be especially harsh on developing economies.[42] At times a nation's government will intervene and readjust the value of its currency, often to increase the export potential of its products. **Devaluation** lowers the value of a nation's currency relative to others. Sometimes, due to a nation's weak currency, the only way to trade is *bartering,* the exchange of merchandise for merchandise or service for service with no money traded.

Countertrading is a complex form of bartering in which several countries each trade goods or services for other goods or services. Let's say a developing country such as Jamaica wants to buy vehicles from Ford Motor Company in exchange for bauxite, a mineral compound that is a source of aluminum ore. Ford does not need Jamaican bauxite, but it does need compressors. In a countertrade, Ford may trade vehicles to Jamaica, which trades bauxite to another country, say India, which exchanges compressors with Ford. All three parties benefit and avoid some of the financial problems and currency constraints in global markets. Estimates are that countertrading accounts for over 20 percent of all global exchanges, especially with developing countries.[43]

Legal and Regulatory Forces

In any economy, the conduct and the direction of business are firmly tied to the legal and regulatory environment. In global markets, no central system of law exists, so different systems of laws and regulations may apply in different places. This makes conducting global business difficult as businesspeople navigate a sea of laws and regulations that are often inconsistent. Antitrust rules, labor relations, patents, copyrights, trade practices, taxes, product liability, child labor, prison labor, and other issues are governed differently country by country.

U.S. businesses must follow U.S. laws and regulations in conducting business globally, although legislation such as the Foreign Corrupt Practices Act of 1978 can create competitive disadvantages. This law prohibits "questionable" or "dubious" payments to foreign officials to secure business contracts.[44] That runs contrary to practices in many countries, where corporate or government bribery is not merely acceptable but perhaps the only way to secure a lucrative contract. The Organization for Economic Cooperation and Development (OECD) and Transparency International have led a global effort to fight corruption and bribery in global business, with limited success.[45] Figure 3.7 shows a partial list of countries where bribery or other unethical business practices are most common.

The cooperation and sponsorship of local businesspeople can help a company penetrate the market and deal with laws, regulations, and bureaucratic barriers in their country.

Physical and Environmental Forces

Physical and environmental forces certainly affect a company's ability to conduct global business. Some developing countries have such primitive transportation and storage systems that international distribution is ineffective, if not impossible, especially for perishable food. Add unclean water and lack of effective sewer systems, and you can see the intensity of the problem.

Technological differences also influence the features of exportable products. For example, residential electrical systems in most developing countries do not match those of U.S. homes, in kind or capacity. Computer and Internet use in many developing countries is thin or nonexistent. These facts make for a tough environment for business in general and for e-commerce in particular. After the Progress Assessment, we'll explore how another force, trade protectionism, affects global business.

figure 3.7

COUNTRIES RATED HIGHEST ON CORRUPT BUSINESS

1. Somalia
2. North Korea
3. Myanmar
4. Afghanistan
5. Uzbekistan
6. Turkmenistan
7. Sudan
8. Iraq
9. Haiti
10. Venezuela

Source: Transparency International, 2012.

progress assessment

- What are four major hurdles to successful global trade?
- What does *ethnocentricity* mean, and how can it affect global success?
- How would a low value of the dollar affect U.S. exports?
- What does the Foreign Corrupt Practices Act prohibit?

LEARNING goal 5

Debate the advantages and disadvantages of trade protectionism.

trade protectionism
The use of government regulations to limit the import of goods and services.

tariff
A tax imposed on imports.

Some workers believe that too many U.S. jobs have been lost due to the growing number of imported products. Should governments protect their industries by placing tariffs on imported products? Why or why not?

TRADE PROTECTIONISM

As we discussed in the previous section, sociocultural, economic and financial, legal and regulatory, and physical and environmental forces are all challenges to global trade. What is often a much greater barrier to global trade, however, is trade protectionism. **Trade protectionism** is the use of government regulations to limit the import of goods and services. Advocates of protectionism believe it allows domestic producers to survive and grow, producing more jobs. Other countries use protectionist measures because they are wary of foreign competition in general. To understand how protectionism affects global business, let's briefly review a bit of global economic history.

Business, economics, and politics have always been closely linked. Economics was once referred to as *political economy,* indicating the close ties between politics (government) and economics. In the 17th and 18th centuries, businesspeople and government leaders endorsed an economic policy called *mercantilism.*[46] The idea was for a nation to sell more goods to other nations than it bought from them, that is, to have a favorable balance of trade. According to mercantilists, this resulted in a flow of money to the country that sold the most globally. The philosophy led governments to implement **tariffs,** taxes on imports, making imported goods more expensive to buy.

There are two kinds of tariffs: protective and revenue. *Protective tariffs* (import taxes) raise the retail price of imported products so that domestic goods are more competitively priced. These tariffs are meant to save jobs for domestic workers and keep industries—especially infant industries that have companies in the early stages of growth—from closing down because of foreign competition. *Revenue tariffs* are designed to raise money for the government.

An **import quota** limits the number of products in certain categories a nation can import. The United States has import quotas on a number of products, including sugar and shrimp, to protect U.S. companies and preserve jobs. Nations also prohibit the export of specific products. Antiterrorism laws and the U.S. Export Administration Act of 1979 prohibit exporting goods such as high-tech weapons that could endanger national security. An **embargo** is a complete ban on the import or export of a certain product, or the stopping of all trade with a particular country. Political disagreements have caused many countries to establish embargoes, such as the U.S. embargo against Cuba, in effect since 1962.[47]

Nontariff barriers are not as specific or formal as tariffs, import quotas, and embargoes but can be as detrimental to free trade. For example, India imposes a number of restrictive standards like import licensing, burdensome product testing requirements, and lengthy customs procedures that inhibit the sale of imported products. China omits many American-made products from its government catalogs that specify what products may be purchased by its huge government sector. Other countries detail exactly how a product must be sold in a country. South Korea sells almost 450,000 cars to the United States each year but imports fewer than 6,000 due to nontariff barriers such as the size of the engine.[48] Hopefully the 2012 free trade agreement with South Korea will eliminate such nontariff barriers and open the market to U.S. producers.

Would-be exporters might view such trade barriers as good reasons to avoid global trade, but overcoming constraints creates business opportunities. Next, we'll look at organizations and agreements that attempt to eliminate trade barriers.

This Indian family used to use bullocks to pull their plow, but had to sell them because the cost to maintain the animals is now too high. Do you think a Doha resolution regarding tariff protection would help families like these?

The World Trade Organization

In 1948, government leaders from 23 nations formed the **General Agreement on Tariffs and Trade (GATT),** a global forum for reducing trade restrictions on goods, services, ideas, and cultural programs. In 1986, the Uruguay Round of the GATT convened to renegotiate trade agreements. After eight years of meetings, 124 nations voted to lower tariffs an average of 38 percent worldwide and to expand new trade rules to areas such as agriculture, services, and the protection of patents.

The Uruguay Round also established the **World Trade Organization (WTO)** to mediate trade disputes among nations. The WTO, headquartered in Geneva, is an independent entity of 153 member nations whose purpose is to oversee cross-border trade issues and global business practices.[49] Trade disputes are presented by member nations with decisions made within a year, rather than languishing for years as in the past; member nations can appeal a decision.[50]

The WTO has not solved all global trade problems. Legal and regulatory differences (discussed above) often impede trade expansion. Also a wide gap persists between developing nations (80 percent of the WTO membership) and industrialized nations like the United States. The WTO meetings in Doha, Qatar, begun in 2001 to address dismantling protection of manufactured goods, eliminating subsidies on agricultural products, and overturning temporary protectionist measures, have still not resulted in any significant agreements.[51]

Common Markets

An issue not resolved by the GATT or the WTO is whether common markets create regional alliances at the expense of global expansion. A **common market** (also called a *trading bloc*) is a regional group of countries with a common external tariff, no internal tariffs, and coordinated laws to facilitate exchange among members. The European Union (EU), Mercosur, the Association of Southeast Asian Nations (ASEAN) Economic Community, and the Common Market for Eastern and Southern Africa (COMESA) are common markets.

import quota
A limit on the number of products in certain categories that a nation can import.

embargo
A complete ban on the import or export of a certain product, or the stopping of all trade with a particular country.

General Agreement on Tariffs and Trade (GATT)
A 1948 agreement that established an international forum for negotiating mutual reductions in trade restrictions.

World Trade Organization (WTO)
The international organization that replaced the General Agreement on Tariffs and Trade and was assigned the duty to mediate trade disputes among nations.

figure 3.8

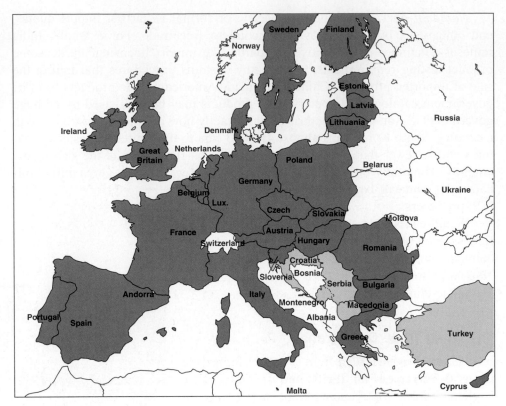

common market
A regional group of countries that have a common external tariff, no internal tariffs, and a coordination of laws to facilitate exchange; also called a *trading bloc*. An example is the European Union.

The EU began in the late 1950s as an alliance of six trading partners (then known as the Common Market and later the European Economic Community). Today it is a group of 27 nations (see Figure 3.8) with a population of over 500 million and a GDP of $16.4 trillion. France, Germany, Italy, the Netherlands, Poland, Spain, and the U.K. account for almost 80 percent of EU GDP.[52] The EU sees continued economic integration as the major way to compete for global business, particularly with the United States, China, and Japan.[53]

European unification was not easy, but in 1999 the EU took a significant step by adopting the euro as a common currency. The euro helped EU businesses save billions by eliminating currency conversions. It has also proven to be a worthy challenger to the U.S. dollar's dominance in global markets. In 2010–2011, the EU faced debt, deficit, and growth problems due to financial difficulties in member nations Greece, Ireland, Portugal, and Spain.[54] EU officials are moving forward with a broad economic-policy overhaul to try to ensure the stability of the union.[55]

Mercosur unites Brazil, Argentina, Paraguay, Uruguay, and associate members Bolivia, Chile, Colombia, Ecuador, and Peru in a trading bloc that encompasses more than 250 million people. Its economic goals also include the establishment of a single currency among member nations.[56]

The ASEAN Economic Community was established in 1967 in Thailand to create economic cooperation among its five original members (Indonesia, Malaysia, the Philippines, Singapore, and Thailand). ASEAN has expanded to include Brunei, Cambodia, the Lao People's Democratic Republic, Myanmar, and Vietnam, creating a trade association with a population of approximately 600 million and a GDP of $1.8 trillion.[57] COMESA is a 19-member African trading bloc. In 2008, COMESA joined with the Southern African Development Community

(SADC) and the East Africa Community (EAC) to form an expanded free-trade zone that has a GDP of $740 billion and a population of 533 million.

The North American and Central American Free Trade Agreements

A widely debated issue of the early 1990s was the **North American Free Trade Agreement (NAFTA),** which created a free-trade area among the United States, Canada, and Mexico. Opponents warned of the loss of U.S. jobs and capital. Supporters predicted NAFTA would open a vast new market for U.S. exports and create jobs and market opportunities in the long term.

NAFTA's objectives were to (1) eliminate trade barriers and facilitate cross-border movement of goods and services, (2) promote conditions of fair competition, (3) increase investment opportunities, (4) provide effective protection and enforcement of intellectual property rights (patents and copyrights), (5) establish a framework for further regional trade cooperation, and (6) improve working conditions in North America. Today, the three NAFTA countries have a combined population of over 450 million and a gross domestic product (GDP) of $17 trillion.[58]

NAFTA promises to remain a hotly debated issue. On the positive side, trade volume in goods and services among the three partners has expanded from $289 billion in 1994 to over $1 trillion today. On the downside, almost 750,000 U.S. jobs have been lost since enacting NAFTA; unfortunately most were in the high-paying manufacturing sector. Illegal immigration remains a major problem since annual per capita income in Mexico still lags considerably behind that of the United States.[59] NAFTA critics also argue that working conditions in Mexico are less safe than before NAFTA, especially in southern Mexico.

NAFTA controversies have not changed the U.S. commitment to free trade agreements. In 2005, the Central American Free Trade Agreement (CAFTA) was signed into law, creating a free-trade zone with Costa Rica, the Dominican Republic, El Salvador, Guatemala, Honduras, and Nicaragua. Again, supporters claimed CAFTA would open new markets, lower tariffs, and ease regulations between the member nations. Critics countered the measure would cost U.S. jobs, especially in the sugar and textile industries. Today, free trade agreements are being negotiated with South Korea, Colombia, and Panama.[60] The United States is also considering an agreement with a nine-nation free-trade bloc called the Trans-Pacific Partnership.[61]

Common markets and free-trade areas will be debated far into the future. While some economists resoundingly praise such efforts, others are concerned the world is dividing into major trading blocs (EU, NAFTA, etc.) that will exclude poor and developing nations. After the Progress Assessment, we'll look at the future of global trade and the issue of outsourcing.

North American Free Trade Agreement (NAFTA)
Agreement that created a free-trade area among the United States, Canada, and Mexico.

progress assessment

- What are the advantages and disadvantages of trade protectionism and of tariffs?
- What is the primary purpose of the WTO?
- What is the key objective of a common market like the EU?
- What three nations comprise NAFTA?

LEARNING goal 6

Discuss the changing landscape of the global market and the issue of off-shore outsourcing.

THE FUTURE OF GLOBAL TRADE

Global trade opportunities grow more interesting and more challenging each day. After all, 7 billion potential customers are attractive.[62] However, terrorism, nuclear proliferation, rogue states, and other issues cast a dark shadow on global markets. Let's conclude this chapter by looking at issues certain to influence global markets, and perhaps your business career.

With more than 1.3 billion people and incredible exporting prowess, China has transformed the world economic map. However, not long ago, foreign direct investment in China was considered risky and not worth the risk. In 2010, China attracted $105 billion in foreign direct investment.[63] Today, 400 of the Fortune 500 companies (the world's largest companies) have invested in over 2,000 projects in China. China has dethroned Germany as the world's largest exporter and surpassed Japan as the second-largest economy in the world. According to Goldman Sachs Group economist Jim O'Neill, China could overtake the United States as the world's largest economy by 2027.[64]

Since 2009 China has been the largest motor vehicle market in the world with sales and production topping 18 million in 2010. It's estimated that the Chinese car market will grow tenfold during the period 2005–2030, which means there could be more cars on the road in China than all the cars in the world today.[65] Walmart began operations in China in 1996 and now has over 200 stores with plans to open more. Newcomers like IMAX Corporation are also expanding in this fast-growing market. Imax plans to open 80 movie theaters in the next few years to get a share of a market that could rival the United States by 2016.[66]

China's economy is booming, and a highly educated middle class with money to spend is emerging, especially in the cities. Many observers believe China will continue its rapid growth and play a major role in the global economy. Are U.S. firms prepared to compete?

Many view China as a free trader's dream, where global investment and entrepreneurship will lead to wealth. However, concerns remain about China's one-party political system, human rights abuses, currency issues, and increasing urban population growth. China's underground economy also generates significant product piracy and counterfeiting, although China has been more responsive to these problems since its admission to the WTO. While the global economic downturn beginning in 2008 slowed China's economy down a bit, it is now a key driver of the world economy along with Japan, the EU, and the United States.

While China attracts most of the attention in Asia, India's population of 1.1 billion presents a tremendous opportunity. With 600 million of its population under 25, India's working-age population will continue to grow while the United States, China, and the EU see a possible decline in the 2020s.[67] Already India has seen huge growth in information technology and biotechnology, and its pharmaceutical business is expected to grow to $30 billion, a jump of over 150 percent by 2020. Still, it remains a nation with difficult trade laws and an inflexible bureaucracy.

Russia is an industrialized nation with large reserves of oil, gas, and gold. Multinationals like Chevron, ExxonMobil, and BP are intent on developing Russia's oil reserves.[68] Other multinationals, including Ford, General Motors, Toyota, and Volkswagen, have announced investments to boost auto production in Russia.[69] Unfortunately, Russia is plagued by political, currency, and social problems and is considered by Transparency International as the world's most corrupt major economy.[70]

Brazil is an emerging nation that along with China, India, and Russia is expected to be one of the wealthier global economies by 2030. In fact, the term *BRIC* has been used as an acronym for the economies of Brazil, Russia, India, and China. Expectations are that Brazil and Russia will dominate global business as suppliers of raw materials and China and India will be the leading global suppliers of manufactured goods and services. Today, Brazil is the largest economy in South America and the seventh-largest economy in the world with well-developed agriculture, mining, manufacturing, and service sectors. Its rapidly growing consumer market of 200 million people is a target for major exporters like the United States and China.

The *BRIC* economies are certainly not the only areas of opportunity in the global market. The developing nations of Asia, including Indonesia, Thailand, Singapore, the Philippines, Korea, Malaysia, and Vietnam, also offer great potential for U.S. businesses. Africa, especially South Africa, has only begun to emerge as a center for global economic growth. Business today is truly global and your role in it is up to you.

The Challenge of Offshore Outsourcing

Outsourcing, as noted in Chapter 1, is the process whereby one firm contracts with other companies, often in other countries, to do some or all of its functions. In the United States, companies have outsourced payroll functions, accounting, and some manufacturing operations for many years. However, the shift to primarily low-wage global markets, called *offshore outsourcing,* has remained a major issue in the United States. Take a look at the pros and cons of offshore outsourcing in Figure 3.9.

As lower-level manufacturing became more simplified, U.S. companies like Levi Strauss and Nike outsourced manufacturing offshore. Today, economists suggest, we are moving into the "second wave" of offshore outsourcing, shifting from product assembly to design and architecture. This process is proving more disruptive to the U.S. job market than the first, which primarily affected manufacturing

figure 3.9

THE PROS AND CONS OF
OFFSHORE OUTSOURCING

PROS

1. Less-strategic tasks can be outsourced globally so that companies can focus on areas in which they can excel and grow.

2. Outsourced work allows companies to create efficiencies that in fact let them hire more workers.

3. Consumers benefit from lower prices generated by effective use of global resources and developing nations grow, thus fueling global economic growth.

CONS

1. Jobs may be lost permanently and wages fall due to low-cost competition offshore.

2. Offshore outsourcing may reduce product quality and can therefore cause permanent damage to a company's reputation.

3. Communication among company members, with suppliers, and with customers becomes much more difficult.

jobs. Today, increasing numbers of skilled, educated, middle-income workers in service-sector jobs such as accounting, law, finance, risk management, health care, and information technology are seeing their jobs outsourced offshore.

While loss of jobs is a major concern, it's not the only worry. Nations such as China have a spotty safety record in manufacturing toys, food, and drugs. Today, concerns are mounting about companies like Medtronic and Siemens shifting production of sensitive medical devices such as MRI and CT machines to China. IBM is setting up research facilities in offshore locations. U.S. airlines have even outsourced airline maintenance to countries such as El Salvador. India at one time was the center for telemarketing, data entry, call centers, billing, and low-end software development. Today—with its well-educated, deep pool of scientists, software engineers, chemists, accountants, lawyers, and physicians—India is providing more sophisticated services. For example, radiologists from Wipro Health Science read CAT scans and MRIs for many U.S. hospitals. Some medical providers are shifting surgical procedures to India and other nations. The nearby Making Ethical Decisions box offers an interesting ethical question about this process.

As technical talent grows around the globe, offshore outsourcing will increase. To stay competitive, education and training will be critical for U.S. workers to preserve the skill premium they possess today and to stay ahead in the future.

Globalization and Your Future

Whether you aspire to be an entrepreneur, a manager, or some other type of business leader, think globally in planning your career. By studying foreign languages, learning about foreign cultures, and taking business courses (including a global business course), you can develop a global perspective on your future. As you progress through this text, keep two things in mind: globalization is real, and economic competition promises to intensify.

Also keep in mind that global market potential does not belong only to large, multinational corporations. Small and medium-sized businesses have a world of opportunity in front of them. In fact, these firms are often better prepared to leap into global markets and react quickly to opportunities than are large businesses. Finally, don't forget the potential of franchising, which we examine in more detail in Chapter 5.

Need an Operation? Take a Vacation

The recent health care reform bill may bring some relief to astronomical insurance costs. But as premiums continue to rise at home, overseas in countries like Thailand, South Korea, and India, health care is not only affordable, it's also high quality.

For instance, in the United States it costs approximately $144,000 to perform a heart bypass. At a foreign medical center like Bumrungrad International Hospital in Bangkok, Thailand, the same procedure runs only about $15,000. "That's the difference between putting it on your credit card or going into bankruptcy," said Ruben Toral, the former marketing director of Bumrungrad. Hospitals like Severance in South Korea or Bumrungrad's competitor Parkway in Thailand also include top-flight teams of doctors and state-of-the-art facilities, better than those in some U.S. hospitals. As a result, these hospitals are seeing an influx of foreign visitors seeking cheap, first-rate health care. Bumrungrad even has an adjoining hotel for recovering patients as well as several restaurants. "This doesn't look like a hospital. It feels more like a hotel or an upscale mall," said Toral.

Though few American companies include medical tourism in their health care plans, a study by the National Business Group on Health found that 40 percent of companies surveyed are planning to include it. It's even expected to become a $100 billion a year industry in 2012 with worldwide annual growth estimated between 20 and 30 percent. Would it be ethical to force patients to travel thousands of miles and be separated from friends and family in a time of crisis in order to save money?

Sources: Medical Tourism Association, "Medical Tourism Sample Surgery Cost Chart," www.medicaltourismassociation.com/en/for-patients.html, accessed March 20, 2011; Ira Mellman, "Concerns over Medical Tourism in Asia," *Voice of America,* March 1, 2011; Anne Kates Smith, "Health Care Bargains Abroad," *Kiplinger's Personal Finance,* January 2012; and "A Global Guide to Medical Tourism," *Kiplinger's Personal Finance,* January 2012.

progress assessment

- What are the major threats to doing business in global markets?
- What key challenges must India and Russia face before becoming global economic leaders?
- What does the acronym *BRIC* stand for?
- What are the two primary concerns associated with offshore outsourcing?

summary

Learning Goal 1. Discuss the importance of the global market and the roles of comparative advantage and absolute advantage in global trade.

- **Why should nations trade with other nations?**

(1) No country is self-sufficient, (2) other countries need products that prosperous countries produce, and (3) natural resources and technological skills are not distributed evenly around the world.

- **What is the theory of comparative advantage?**

The theory of comparative advantage contends that a country should make and then sell those products it produces most efficiently but buy those it cannot produce as efficiently.

- **What is absolute advantage?**

Absolute advantage means that a country has a monopoly on a certain product or can produce the product more efficiently than any other country. There are few examples of absolute advantage in the global market today.

Learning Goal 2. Explain the importance of importing and exporting, and understand key terms used in global business.

- **What kinds of products can be imported and exported?**

Though it is not necessarily easy, just about any kind of product can be imported or exported.

- **What terms are important in understanding world trade?**

Exporting is selling products to other countries. *Importing* is buying products from other countries. The *balance of trade* is the relationship of exports to imports. The *balance of payments* is the balance of trade plus other money flows such as tourism and foreign aid. *Dumping* is selling products for less in a foreign country than in your own country. See the Key Terms list at the end of this chapter to be sure you know the other important terms.

Learning Goal 3. Illustrate the strategies used in reaching global markets and explain the role of multinational corporations.

- **What are some ways in which a company can engage in global business?**

Ways of entering world trade include licensing, exporting, franchising, contract manufacturing, joint ventures and strategic alliances, and direct foreign investment.

- **How do multinational corporations differ from other companies that participate in global business?**

Unlike companies that only export or import, multinational corporations also have manufacturing facilities or other physical presence abroad.

Learning Goal 4. Evaluate the forces that affect trading in global markets.

- **What are some of the forces that can discourage participation in global business?**

Potential stumbling blocks to global trade include sociocultural forces, economic and financial forces, legal and regulatory forces, and physical and environmental forces.

Learning Goal 5. Debate the advantages and disadvantages of trade protectionism.

- **What is trade protectionism?**

Trade protectionism is the use of government regulations to limit the import of goods and services. Advocates believe it allows domestic producers to grow, producing more jobs. The key tools of protectionism are tariffs, import quotas, and embargoes.

- **What are tariffs?**

Tariffs are taxes on foreign products. Protective tariffs raise the price of foreign products and protect domestic industries; revenue tariffs raise money for the government.

- **What is an embargo?**

An embargo prohibits the importing or exporting of certain products.

- **Is trade protectionism good for domestic producers?**

That is debatable. Trade protectionism offers pluses and minuses.

- **Why do governments continue such practices?**

The theory of mercantilism started the practice of trade protectionism and it has persisted, though in a weaker form, ever since.

Learning Goal 6. Discuss the changing landscape of the global market and the issue of offshore outsourcing.

- **What is offshore outsourcing? Why is it a major concern for the future?**

Outsourcing is the purchase of goods and services from outside a firm rather than providing them inside the company. Today, more businesses are outsourcing manufacturing and services offshore. Many fear that growing numbers of jobs in the United States will be lost due to offshore outsourcing and that the quality of products produced could be inferior.

key terms

absolute advantage 62	exporting 61	multinational corporation 71
balance of payments 65	foreign direct investment (FDI) 70	North American Free Trade Agreement (NAFTA) 79
balance of trade 64	foreign subsidiary 70	
common market 78	free trade 62	sovereign wealth funds (SWFs) 72
comparative advantage theory 62	General Agreement on Tariffs and Trade (GATT) 77	strategic alliance 70
contract manufacturing 68	importing 61	tariff 76
countertrading 74	import quota 77	trade deficit 64
devaluation 74	joint venture 70	trade protectionism 76
dumping 66	licensing 66	trade surplus 64
embargo 77		World Trade Organization (WTO) 77
exchange rate 74		

critical thinking

1. About 95 percent of the world's population lives outside the United States, but many U.S. companies, especially small businesses, still do not engage in global trade. Why not? Do you think more small businesses will participate in global trade in the future? Why or why not?
2. Countries like the United States that have a high standard of living are referred to as *industrialized nations*. Countries with a lower standard of living and quality of life are called *developing countries* (or *underdeveloped* or *less developed countries*). What factors prevent developing nations from becoming industrialized nations?
3. What can businesses do to prevent unexpected problems in dealing with sociocultural, economic and financial, legal and regulatory, and physical and environmental forces in global markets?
4. How would you justify the use of revenue or protective tariffs in today's global market?

developing workplace skills

1. Find out firsthand the global impact on your life. How many different countries' names appear on the labels in your clothes? How many languages do your classmates speak? List the ethnic restaurants in your community. Are they family-owned or corporate chains?

2. Call, e-mail, or visit a local business that imports foreign goods (perhaps a wine or specialty foods importer). Ask the owner or manager about the business's participation in global trade, and compile a list of the advantages and disadvantages he or she cites. Compare notes with your classmates about their research.

3. Visit four or five public locations in your community such as schools, hospitals, city/county buildings, or airports. See how many signs are posted in different languages (don't forget the restrooms) and look for other multilingual information, such as brochures or handouts. Do any of the locations fly flags from different nations? In what other ways do they recognize the diversity of employees or students? What does your search tell you about your community?

4. Suppose Representative I. M. Wright delivers a passionate speech at your college on tariffs. He argues tariffs are needed to

   a. Protect our young industries.
   b. Encourage consumers to buy U.S.-made products because it's patriotic.
   c. Protect U.S. jobs and wages.
   d. Achieve a favorable balance of trade and balance of payments.

   Do you agree with Representative Wright? Evaluate each of his major points and decide whether you consider it valid. Be sure to justify your position.

5. Form an imaginary joint venture with three classmates and select a product, service, or idea to market to a specific country. Have each team member select a key global market force in that country (sociocultural, economic and financial, legal and regulatory, or physical and environmental) to research. Have each report his or her findings. Then, as a group, prepare a short explanation of whether the market is worth pursuing.

taking it to the net

Purpose

To compare the shifting exchange rates of various countries and to predict the effects of such exchange shifts on global trade.

Exercise

One of the difficulties of engaging in global trade is the constant shift in exchange rates. How much do exchange rates change over a 30-day period? Research this by choosing five currencies (say, the euro, the British pound, the Japanese yen, the Mexican peso, the Saudi Arabian riyal) and recording their exchange rates relative to the U.S. dollar for 30 days. The rates are available on the Internet at Yahoo Finance's Currency Center (http://finance.yahoo.com/currency). At the end of the tracking period, choose a company and describe what effects the currency shifts you noted might have on this company's trade with each of the countries or areas whose currency you chose.

video case

CH2M Hill: A Global Company

CH2M Hill was founded by a professor and three students at Oregon State University in 1946. Originally, the company was an engineering firm that over the last 60 years has developed into an engineering and construction company. CH2M Hill is truly a global company, with a presence all over the world. The company focuses on developing solutions to problems concerning water quality and waste management. Since its founding in 1946, the company has continued to grow to more than 30,000 employees worldwide.

CH2M Hill is a publicly traded concern, headquartered in the United States with more than 18,000 shareholders. It is a $7 billion firm operating globally in a world with more than 7 billion people. The company successfully navigates the various issues and challenges associated with operating globally, including different legal and regulatory environments, sociocultural differences from country to country, and differing degrees of technological sophistication in countries where it operates.

The company's primary customers include governments, industry, and energy companies. Part of its global success is due to the intellectual capital that it has amassed over the past 60 years. Operating successfully in vastly different cultures is challenging, particularly with respect to cultural and regulatory differences. Being successful in a global marketplace requires a high level of adaptability. To help successfully navigate the many global differences, the company favors joint ventures and strategic alliances. These approaches leverage the talent and expertise of CH2M Hill as well as the resources and local knowledge, customs, and credibility of the business partners in various areas throughout the world. These approaches help to mitigate the potential challenges global companies often face due to trade protectionism around the world.

In a global economy, business success is defined by a company's ability to expand and adapt to the many cultural, regulatory, technological, and comparative advantages of a truly global marketplace. With over 7 billion people on the planet, CH2M Hill is well positioned to continue providing solutions to problems facing people and countries that make life better and more sustainable.

Thinking It Over

1. *What is comparative advantage?*
2. *Identify the key strategies that companies can use to enter global markets.*
3. *What is trade protectionism and what types of protectionism may countries use?*

Demanding ETHICAL AND SOCIALLY **Responsible** Behavior

After you have read and studied this chapter, you should be able to

LEARNING goals

1 Explain why obeying the law is only the first step in behaving ethically.

2 Ask the three questions you need to answer when faced with a potentially unethical action.

3 Describe management's role in setting ethical standards.

4 Distinguish between compliance-based and integrity-based ethics codes, and list the six steps in setting up a corporate ethics code.

5 Define *corporate social responsibility* and compare corporations' responsibilities to various stakeholders.

6 Analyze the role of U.S. businesses in influencing ethical behavior and social responsibility in global markets.

www.sweetbeginningsllc.com

As the executive director at the North Lawndale Employment Network (NLEN), Chicago activist and entrepreneur Brenda Palms Barber helps find work for former prison inmates. Located in a community where 57 percent of the population has been incarcerated, Palms Barber certainly doesn't lack clients looking for work. But when Palms Barber took charge of NLEN in 2000, she quickly learned that many businesses weren't as keen on giving second chances as she was. After a few frustrating years, she decided to cut out the middleman and start a business of her own where her ex-con clients could hone their job skills.

CONNECTING WITH

Brenda Palms Barber

CEO of Sweet Beginnings

Starting a company from scratch is no simple task, however. Palms Barber had earned a degree in Business Management from the University of Phoenix to complement her years of experience managing non-profits. Still, in the entrepreneurial world, education and experience don't add up to much without a good idea to go on. Palms Barber considered several business plans including a landscaping company, a temp agency, and a delivery service. With these types of companies, though, she feared that potential customers would be just as wary of hiring her employees as local businesses were. Then, an NLEN board member suggested beekeeping. "He told me beekeeping was a profession passed on by word of mouth," says Palms Barber. "I liked that, because people learn well by storytelling, especially when they have academic challenges." While some objected to the unorthodox idea, one supporter at NLEN said it would be a "sweet beginning" for many ex-cons. And with that, Palms Barber had her business plan and a charming name to boot.

Thanks in part to a $140,000 investment from the Illinois Department of Corrections, in 2007 Palms Barber formed Sweet Beginnings as a for-profit subsidiary of NLEN. She found a tiny lot surrounded by a chain-link fence among a number of vacant and boarded-up buildings where she could keep the beehives. In this urban environment, Sweet Beginnings' honey takes on a flavor of its own because of the unique plant growth in the city. At first the company focused on selling only its honey. However, sales weren't high enough to reach one of Palms Barber's primary goals: to create a steady source of income for NLEN. Living from grant to grant can make running a nonprofit an uneasy enterprise for many people. With consistent cash flow, NLEN could

help even more people find work. Palms Barber decided to convert the honey to honey-infused skin care products, thinking such products would be more profitable for Sweet Beginnings. Her decision paid off, and now Sweet Beginnings sells $100,000 worth of beauty products each year with projected sales over the next five years estimated at $2 million.

In many ways Sweet Beginnings' employees are more important than its profit margins. Since its opening, more than 200 former inmates have worked at the company. Potential staffers must complete a job-readiness program before they're hired. Once they get on board, employees can earn their money tending to the bees or learning important job skills in areas like manufacturing, website management, sales, and customer service. Most stay on for 90-day terms and receive job-placement services as their time at the company ends. Although this creates a high rate of turnover, it's the best way to ensure that as many people as possible get valuable résumé entries and experience. Approximately 85 percent of employees find a job afterwards, compared to 50 percent of NLEN clients who haven't worked at Sweet Beginnings. Perhaps most significantly, though, the recidivism rate at the company is at just 4 percent, far below the national average of 65 percent.

As a result of all her good work, Palms Barber has received a number of awards and accolades from the Chicago community. Although they may not receive as much media attention as fraudulent businesspeople, ethical entrepreneurs like Brenda Palms Barber are the backbone of the business world. In this chapter, we explore the responsibility of businesses to their stakeholders: customers, investors, employees, and society. We look at the responsibilities of individuals as well. After all, responsible business behavior depends on the integrity of each person in the business.

Sources: Leigh Buchanan, "Finding Jobs for Ex-Offenders," *Inc.,* May 2011; Maudlyne Ihejirika, "Honeybee Program Taking Off at O'Hare," *Chicago Sun-Times,* July 5, 2011; and www.sweetbeginningsllc.com, accessed March 22, 2012.

This company has a program it calls Social Service Leave that allows employees to take up to a year off to work for a nonprofit organization while earning their full salary and benefits, including job security. Name that company. (Find the answer in the chapter.)

Bernie Madoff was once a respected investment manager. He swindled $65 billion from his investors, which included many charities and pension plans. He was sentenced to 150 years behind bars with no chance of parole. What motivates a person to risk everything by committing fraud?

LEARNING goal 1

Explain why obeying the law is only the first step in behaving ethically.

ETHICS IS MORE THAN LEGALITY

In the early 2000s, the U.S. public was shocked to learn that Enron, the giant energy trading company, had created off-the-books partnerships to unlawfully hide its debts and losses. The Enron disgrace soon was followed by more scandals at major companies like WorldCom, Tyco International, ImClone, HealthSouth, and Boeing.[1] (See the nearby Making Ethical Decisions box for a brief summary of a few of these cases.) In recent years, greedy borrowers and lenders alike were among those who brought the real estate, mortgage, and banking industries to the edge of a financial crisis that threatened the entire U.S. and world economies.[2]

Given the ethical lapses prevalent today, how can we restore trust in the free-market system and in leaders in general? First, those who have broken the law should be punished accordingly. New laws making accounting records more transparent (easy to read and understand) and businesspeople and others more accountable for their actions may also help.[3] But laws alone don't make people honest, reliable, or truthful. If they did, crime would disappear.

One danger in writing new laws to correct behavior is that people may begin to think that any behavior that is within the law is also acceptable. The measure of behavior then becomes "Is it legal?" A society gets into trouble when people consider only what is illegal and not also what is unethical. Ethics and legality are two very different things. Although following the law is an important first step, behaving ethically requires more than that. Ethics reflects people's proper relationships with one another: How should we treat others? What responsibility should we feel for others? Legality is narrower. It refers to laws we have written to protect ourselves from fraud, theft, and violence. Many immoral and unethical acts fall well within our laws. For example gossiping about your neighbor or sharing something told to you in confidence is unethical, but not illegal.

MAKING ethical decisions

Cost of Corruption

News stories of corporate fraud and corruption are all too common. White-collar criminals often assume the complexity of the financial system will hide their crimes, leaving them free to embezzle to their heart's content. But people tend to notice when a few billion dollars suddenly go missing. Eventually, even the most careful corporate criminals must pay the piper.

When the credit crunch hit in 2008, it unexpectedly exposed one of history's most shameful financial felons. Since the early 1970s, Bernie Madoff ran his exclusive wealth management firm as a gigantic Ponzi scheme. Legitimate money managers invest their client's money in various ventures and pay them back on their returns, minus a commission. With a Ponzi scheme, however, the fraudsters don't invest the money. They simply pass money contributed by new investors on to early investors (minus a healthy sum held back for their own personal use, of course), claiming the money as profits from the existing clients' "investments." The steady income fools the investors into thinking their wealth is growing when in reality it is being siphoned from other people. Obviously the scheme depends upon being able to continuously attract new "investors."

Once the bubble burst on Wall Street, the jig was up for Madoff. He confessed his crimes to his sons, who then contacted police. Though exact estimates are still uncertain, Madoff swindled approximately $65 billion from his investors, including $20 billion in cash losses that can never be recovered. In June 2009, a judge sentenced Madoff to 150 years behind bars with no chance of parole.

Before Madoff, though, the Enron scandal of the early 2000s was the gold standard of American corporate deception. Former Enron chairman and chief executive officer (CEO) Kenneth Lay, former CEO Jeffrey Skilling, and chief accounting officer Richard Causey were convicted of committing accounting fraud by setting up partnerships that the company used to improperly enhance profits while removing billions of dollars of debt off its balance sheet. That made the company's financial picture look better than it was and artificially inflated the company's stock and bond prices.

The company's pension regulations prohibited regular employees from selling their stock, but the executives sold millions of dollars' worth of shares just before the fraud became public. They bankrupted the company, yet made fortunes while the employees and other small investors lost millions.

Skilling is serving a 24-year prison sentence in Minnesota and must pay a $45 million fine. His lawyers are still working to have his conviction overturned. Causey entered a guilty plea and received a shorter sentence than Skilling. He was released from prison in October 2011. Lay suffered a heart attack and passed away before his sentencing. All his convictions were thrown out.

Around the time of the Enron scandal, the communications multinational WorldCom admitted that intentional accounting irregularities made the company look almost $4 billion more profitable than it was. Further scrutiny of the company's books revealed WorldCom's practice of counting revenue twice dated as far back as 1999, that additional debt continued to be undisclosed, and that revenue not received was entered in the books—pushing the irregularities to more than $11 billion.

In 2005, former CEO Bernie Ebbers was convicted of fraud, conspiracy, and making false regulatory filings. He was sentenced to 25 years in federal prison. The company has emerged from bankruptcy and now operates under the name of MCI Inc. Ebbers is in Oakdale Federal Correctional Institution in Louisiana and is expected to be released in July 2028.

Do you think the sentences of these fraudsters fit their crimes?

Sources: "Top 10 Crooked CEOs," Time.com, accessed July 2012; and Diana B. Henriques, "From Prison, Madoff Says Banks 'Had to Know' of Fraud," *The New York Times,* February 15, 2011.

Ethical Standards Are Fundamental

ethics
Standards of moral behavior, that is, behavior accepted by society as right versus wrong.

We define **ethics** as society's accepted standards of moral behavior, that is, behaviors accepted by society as right rather than wrong. Many Americans today have few moral absolutes. Many decide situationally whether it's OK to steal, lie, or drink and drive. They seem to think that what is right is whatever works best for the individual—that each person has to work out for himself or herself the difference between right and wrong. Such thinking may be part of the behavior that has led to the recent scandals in government and business.

This isn't the way it always was. When Thomas Jefferson wrote that all men have the right to life, liberty, and the pursuit of happiness, he declared it to be a self-evident truth. Going back even further in time, the Ten Commandments were not called the "Ten Highly Tentative Suggestions."

In the United States, with so many diverse cultures, you might think it is impossible to identify common standards of ethical behavior. However, among sources from many different times and places—such as the Bible, Aristotle's *Ethics,* the Koran, and the *Analects* of Confucius—you'll find the following common statements of basic moral values: Integrity, respect for human life, self-control, honesty, courage, and self-sacrifice are right. Cheating, cowardice, and cruelty are wrong. Furthermore, all the world's major religions support a version of what some call the Golden Rule: Do unto others as you would have them do unto you.[4]

LEARNING goal 2

Ask the three questions you need to answer when faced with a potentially unethical action.

Plagiarizing from the Internet is one of the most common forms of cheating in colleges today. Have you ever been tempted to plagiarize a paper or project? What are the possible consequences of copying someone else's material?

Ethics Begins with Each of Us

It is easy to criticize business and political leaders for moral and ethical shortcomings, and in a recent study both managers and workers cited low managerial ethics as a major cause of U.S. businesses' competitive woes.[5] But employees also reported frequently violating safety standards and goofing off as much as seven hours a week. U.S. adults in general are not always as honest or honorable as they should be. Even though volunteerism is at an all-time high according to the U.S. Census Bureau, three of every four citizens do not give any time to the community in which they live.[6]

Plagiarizing material from the Internet, including cutting and pasting information from websites without giving credit, is the most common form of cheating in schools today. To fight this problem, many instructors now use services like TurnItIn.com, which scans students' papers against more than 20 billion online sources to provide evidence of copying in seconds.[7]

In a recent study, most teens said they were prepared to make ethical decisions in the workforce, but an alarming 38 percent felt that lying, cheating, plagiarizing, or behaving violently is sometimes necessary.

"I don't know what plagiarizing is, so I'm gonna take the easy way out and just copy something off the internet."

social media

Facebook or Fakebook?

Facebook is so much a part of our culture that many people see their online profiles as extensions of themselves. It only takes an e-mail address to set up a Facebook account. Such accessibility allows for scammers to take advantage of the trust Facebook's users have in the online community.

With the site's massive collection of pictures and data, con artists can set up fake Facebook accounts with little difficulty. For example, a few scammers copied pictures of military servicemen from their profiles and set up dummy accounts. From there they established relationships with women by playing the part of lonely soldiers looking for love. Soon enough, the imposters asked their victims for money to pay for phone calls or visits home. With cash in hand, the scammers then severed contact with their prey and deleted the fake account, likely to start the whole process over again with a new victim.

Other Facebook scams may not be as dastardly, but are just as dangerously creative. In one instance, a banner ad offered an application called "Creeper Tracker" that supposedly lets users know who's looking at their Facebook page the most. Although this method is relatively common among fraudsters, this particular scheme came with an added element. After the victims filled out a survey that generated money for the scammer, they were directed to a new page where they could purchase a toolkit that provided step-by-step instructions on how to create their own scam. So Facebookers beware, because in this social media driven world even acts of fraud can go viral.

Some people create fake Facebook identities for less criminal activities—to prank friends or harass foes. Do you think it is ethical to create such fake online identities? Why or why not?

Sources: Bruce Schreiner and Janet Cappiello Blake, "Soldier Impersonators Hit the Web," Associated Press, February 27, 2011; Matt Liebowitz, "Malicious Facebook Trick Has Users Create Their Own Scam," MSNBC, February 8, 2011; and Jessica Bock, "Clayton High's Principal Resigns amid Facebook Mystery," *St. Louis Post-Dispatch,* May 6, 2012.

Studies have found a strong relationship between academic dishonesty among undergraduates and dishonesty at work.[8] In response, many schools are establishing heavier consequences for cheating and requiring students to perform a certain number of hours of community service to graduate. Do you think such policies make a difference in student behavior? The Connecting Through Social Media box deals with ethical behavior and online profiles.

Choices are not always easy, and the obvious ethical solution may have personal or professional drawbacks. Imagine that your supervisor has asked you to do something you feel is unethical. You've just taken out a mortgage on a new house to make room for your first baby, due in two months. Not carrying out your supervisor's request may get you fired. What should you do? Sometimes there is no easy alternative in such *ethical dilemmas* because you must choose between equally unsatisfactory alternatives.

It can be difficult to balance ethics and other goals, such as pleasing stakeholders or advancing in your career. According to management writer Ken Blanchard and religious leader Norman Vincent Peale, it helps to ask yourself the following questions when facing an ethical dilemma.[9]

1. *Is my proposed action legal?* Am I violating any law or company policy? Whether you're thinking about having a drink and driving home, gathering marketing intelligence, designing a product, hiring or firing employees, getting rid of industrial waste, or using a questionable nickname for an employee, think about the legal implications. This is the most basic question in business ethics, but it is only the first.

2. *Is it balanced?* Am I acting fairly? Would I want to be treated this way? Will I win everything at the expense of another? Win–lose situations often become lose–lose situations and generate retaliation from the loser. Not every situation can be completely balanced, but the health of our relationships requires us to avoid major imbalances over time. An ethical businessperson has a win–win attitude and tries to make decisions that benefit all.

3. *How will it make me feel about myself?* Would I feel proud if my family learned of my decision? My friends? Could I discuss the proposed situation or action with my supervisor? The company's clients? Will I have to hide my actions? Has someone warned me not to disclose them? What if my decision were announced on the evening news? Am I feeling unusually nervous? Decisions that go against our sense of right and wrong make us feel bad—they erode our self-esteem. That is why an ethical businessperson does what is proper as well as what is profitable.

Individuals and companies that develop a strong ethics code and use the three questions above have a better chance than most of behaving ethically. If you would like to know which style of recognizing and resolving ethical dilemmas you favor, fill out the ethical orientation questionnaire in Figure 4.1.

progress assessment

- What are ethics?
- How do ethics differ from legality?
- When faced with ethical dilemmas, what questions can you ask yourself that might help you make ethical decisions?

LEARNING goal 3

Describe management's role in setting ethical standards.

MANAGING BUSINESSES ETHICALLY AND RESPONSIBLY

Ethics is caught more than it is taught. That is, people learn their standards and values from observing what others do, not from hearing what they say. This is as true in business as it is at home. Organizational ethics begins at the top, and the leadership and example of strong managers can help instill corporate values in employees. The majority of CEOs surveyed recently attributed unethical employee conduct to leadership's failure to establish ethical standards and culture.[10]

Please answer the following questions.
1. Which is worse?
   A. Hurting someone's feelings by telling the truth.
   B. Telling a lie and protecting someone's feelings.

2. Which is the worse mistake?
   A. To make exceptions too freely.
   B. To apply rules too rigidly.

3. Which is it worse to be?
   A. Unmerciful.
   B. Unfair.

4. Which is worse?
   A. Stealing something valuable from someone for no good reason.
   B. Breaking a promise to a friend for no good reason.

5. Which is it better to be?
   A. Just and fair.
   B. Sympathetic and feeling.

6. Which is worse?
   A. Not helping someone in trouble.
   B. Being unfair to someone by playing favorites.

7. In making a decision you rely more on
   A. Hard facts.
   B. Personal feelings and intuition.

8. Your boss orders you to do something that will hurt someone. If you carry out the order, have you actually done anything wrong?
   A. Yes.
   B. No.

9. Which is more important in determining whether an action is right or wrong?
   A. Whether anyone actually gets hurt.
   B. Whether a rule, law, commandment, or moral principle is broken.

To score: The answers fall in one of two categories, J or C. Count your number of J and C answers using this key:
1. A = C; B = J; 2. A= J; B = C; 3. A = C; B = J; 4. A = J; B = C; 5. A = J; B = C; 6. A = C; B = J; 7. A = J; B = C; 8. A = C; B = J; 9. A = C; B = J

What your score means: The higher your J score, the more you rely on an ethic of *justice*. The higher your C score, the more you prefer an ethic of *care*. Neither style is better than the other, but they are different. Because they appear so different, they may seem opposed to one another, but they're actually complementary. In fact, your score probably shows you rely on each style to a greater or lesser degree. (Few people end up with a score of 9 to 0.) The more you can appreciate both approaches, the better you'll be able to resolve ethical dilemmas and to understand and communicate with people who prefer the other style.

An ethic of justice is based on principles like justice, fairness, equality, or authority. People who prefer this style see ethical dilemmas as conflicts of rights that can be solved by the impartial application of some general principle. The advantage of this approach is that it looks at a problem logically and impartially. People with this style try to be objective and fair, hoping to make a decision according to some standard that's higher than any specific individual's interests. The disadvantage of this approach is that people who rely on it might lose sight of the immediate interests of particular individuals. They may unintentionally ride roughshod over the people around them in favor of some abstract ideal or policy. This style is more common for men than women.

An ethic of care is based on a sense of responsibility to reduce actual harm or suffering. People who prefer this style see moral dilemmas as conflicts of duties or responsibilities. They believe that solutions must be tailored to the special details of individual circumstances. They tend to feel constrained by policies that are supposed to be enforced without exception. The advantage of this approach is that it is responsive to immediate suffering and harm. The disadvantage is that, when carried to an extreme, this style can produce decisions that seem not simply subjective, but arbitrary. This style is more common for women than men.

To learn more about these styles and how they might relate to gender, go to www.ethicsandbusiness.org/kgl.htm.

Source: Thomas I. White, *Discovering Philosophy—Brief Edition*, 1e, © Copyright 1996. Adapted by permission of Pearson Education, Inc., Upper Saddle River, NJ.

figure 4.1

ETHICAL ORIENTATION QUESTIONNAIRE

Trust and cooperation between workers and managers must be based on fairness, honesty, openness, and moral integrity. The same applies to relationships among businesses and between nations. A business should be managed ethically for many reasons: to maintain a good reputation; to keep existing customers and attract new ones; to avoid lawsuits; to reduce employee turnover; to avoid government intervention in the form of new laws and regulations controlling business activities; to please customers, employees, and society; and simply to do the right thing.

**compliance-based
ethics codes**
Ethical standards that
emphasize preventing
unlawful behavior by
increasing control and by
penalizing wrongdoers.

**integrity-based
ethics codes**
Ethical standards that
define the organization's
guiding values, create an
environment that supports
ethically sound behavior,
and stress a shared
accountability among
employees.

Some managers think ethics is a personal matter—either individuals have ethical principles or they don't. These managers feel that they are not responsible for an individual's misdeeds and that ethics has nothing to do with management. But a growing number of people think ethics has everything to do with management. Individuals do not usually act alone; they need the implied, if not the direct, cooperation of others to behave unethically in a corporation.

For example, there have been reports of cell phone service sales representatives who actually lie to get customers to extend their contracts—or even extend their contracts without the customers' knowledge. Some phone reps intentionally hang up on callers to prevent them from canceling their contracts. Why do these sales reps sometimes resort to overly aggressive tactics? Because poorly designed incentive programs reward them for meeting certain goals, sometimes doubling or tripling their salaries with incentives. Do their managers say directly, "Deceive the customers"? No, but the message is clear. Overly ambitious goals and incentives can create an environment in which unethical actions like this can occur.[11]

LEARNING goal 4

Distinguish between compliance-based and integrity-based ethics codes, and list the six steps in setting up a corporate ethics code.

Setting Corporate Ethical Standards

More and more companies have adopted written codes of ethics. Figure 4.2 offers Johnson & Johnson's as a sample. Although these codes vary greatly, they can be placed into two categories: compliance-based and integrity-based (see Figure 4.3). **Compliance-based ethics codes** emphasize preventing unlawful behavior by increasing control and penalizing wrongdoers. **Integrity-based ethics codes** define the organization's guiding values, create an environment that supports ethically sound behavior, and stress shared accountability.

Here are six steps many believe can improve U.S. business ethics:[12]

1. Top management must adopt and unconditionally support an explicit corporate code of conduct.

2. Employees must understand that expectations for ethical behavior begin at the top and that senior management expects all employees to act accordingly.

3. Managers and others must be trained to consider the ethical implications of all business decisions.

4. An ethics office must be set up with which employees can communicate anonymously. **Whistleblowers** (insiders who report illegal or unethical behavior) must feel protected from retaliation. The Sarbanes-Oxley Act protects whistleblowers by requiring all public corporations to allow employee concerns about accounting and auditing to be submitted confidentially and anonymously. The act also requires reinstatement and back pay to people who were punished by their employers for passing information about fraud on to authorities. (We cover

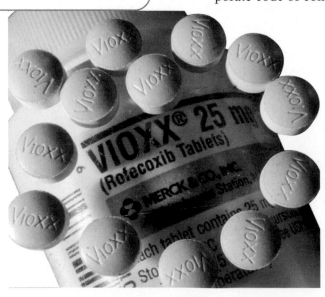

H. Dean Steinke blew the whistle on his former employer, drug company Merck, maker of Vioxx and Zocor, charging that it gave doctors excessive financial incentives to prescribe the drugs and discounts unavailable to government health programs. Steinke was awarded $68 million for reporting the misconduct. What motivates whistleblowers?

Written in 1943 by long-time Chairman General Robert Wood Johnson, the Johnson & Johnson Credo serves as a conscious plan that represents and encourages a unique set of values. Our Credo sums up the responsibilities we have to the four important groups we serve:

- Our customers—We have a responsibility to provide high-quality products they can trust, offered at a fair price.
- Our employees—We have a responsibility to treat them with respect and dignity, pay them fairly and help them develop and thrive personally and professionally.
- Our communities—We have a responsibility to be good corporate citizens, support good works, encourage better health and protect the environment.
- Our stockholders—We have a responsibility to provide a fair return on their investment.

The deliberate ordering of these groups—customers first, stockholders last–proclaims a bold business philosophy: If we meet our first three responsibilities, the fourth will take care of itself. . . . To ensure our adherence to Credo values, we periodically ask every employee to evaluate the company's performance in living up to them. We believe that by monitoring our actions against the ethical framework of Our Credo, we will best ensure that we make responsible decisions as a company.

figure 4.2

OVERVIEW OF JOHNSON & JOHNSON'S CODE OF ETHICS

This is an overview of Johnson & Johnson's code of ethics, what it calls its Credo. To see the company's complete Credo, go to www.jnj.com/connect/about=jnj/jnj=credo and click on "Our Credo Values."

FEATURES OF COMPLIANCE BASED ETHICS CODES		FEATURES OF INTEGRITY-BASED ETHICS CODES	
Ideal:	Conform to outside standards (laws and regulations)	Ideal:	Conform to outside standards (laws and regulations) and chosen internal standards
Objective:	Avoid criminal misconduct	Objective:	Enable responsible employee conduct
Leaders:	Lawyers	Leaders:	Managers with aid of lawyers and others
Methods:	Education, reduced employee discretion, controls, penalties	Methods:	Education, leadership, accountability, decision processes, controls, and penalties

figure 4.3

STRATEGIES FOR ETHICS MANAGEMENT

Integrity-based ethics codes move beyond legal compliance to create a "do-it-right" climate that emphasizes core values such as honesty, fair play, good service to customers, a commitment to diversity, and involvement in the community. These values are ethically desirable, but not necessarily legally mandatory.

Sarbanes-Oxley in more detail in Chapter 17.) In 2010 the Dodd-Frank Wall Street Reform and Consumer Protection Act was signed into law. The new law includes a "bounty" provision that allows corporate whistleblowers who provide information that leads to a successful enforcement action to collect 10–30 percent of the total penalty for violations that exceed $1 million. In 2011, a whistleblower in the Enron case received a $1 million reward from the IRS (and, yes, it is taxable).

5. Outsiders such as suppliers, subcontractors, distributors, and customers must be told about the ethics program. Pressure to put aside ethical considerations often comes from the outside, and it helps employees resist such pressure when everyone knows what the ethical standards are.

6. The ethics code must be enforced with timely action if any rules are broken. That is the most forceful way to communicate to all employees that the code is serious.

whistleblowers
Insiders who report illegal or unethical behavior.

This last step is perhaps the most critical. No matter how well intended a company's ethics code, it is worthless if not enforced.[13] Enron had a written code of ethics. By ignoring it, Enron's board and management sent employees the message that rules could be shelved when inconvenient. In contrast, Johnson & Johnson's response to a cyanide poisoning crisis in the 1980s shows that enforcing ethics codes can enhance profit. Although not legally required to do so, the company recalled its Tylenol products and won great praise and a reputation of corporate integrity.

An important factor in enforcing an ethics code is selecting an ethics officer. The most effective ethics officers set a positive tone, communicate effectively, and relate well to employees at every level. They are equally comfortable as counselors and investigators and can be trusted to maintain confidentiality, conduct objective investigations, and ensure fairness. They can demonstrate to stakeholders that ethics are important in everything the company does.[14]

progress assessment

- What are compliance-based and integrity-based ethics codes?
- What are the six steps to follow in establishing an effective ethics program in a business?

LEARNING goal 5

Define *corporate social responsibility* and compare corporations' responsibilities to various stakeholders.

CORPORATE SOCIAL RESPONSIBILITY

corporate social responsibility (CSR)
A business's concern for the welfare of society.

Just as you and I need to be good citizens, contributing what we can to society, corporations need to be good citizens as well. **Corporate social responsibility (CSR)** is the concern businesses have for the welfare of society, not just for their owners. CSR goes well beyond being ethical. It is based on a commitment to integrity, fairness, and respect.

You may be surprised to know that not everyone thinks that CSR is a good thing. Some critics of CSR believe that a manager's sole role is to compete and win in the marketplace. The late U.S. economist Milton Friedman made the famous statement that the only social responsibility of business is to make money for stockholders. He thought doing anything else was moving dangerously toward socialism. Other CSR critics believe that managers who pursue CSR are doing so with other people's money—which they invested to make more money, not to improve society. In this view spending money on CSR activities is stealing from investors.[15]

CSR defenders, in contrast, believe that businesses owe their existence to the societies they serve and cannot succeed in societies that fail. Firms have access to society's labor pool and its natural resources, in which every member of society has a stake. Even Adam Smith, the father of capitalism, believed that self-interested pursuit of profit was wrong and that benevolence was the highest virtue. CSR defenders acknowledge that businesses have deep obligations to investors and should not attempt government-type social responsibility projects. However, they also argue that CSR makes more money for investors in the long run. Studies show that companies with good ethical reputations attract and retain better employees, draw more customers, and enjoy greater employee loyalty.[16]

The social performance of a company has several dimensions:

- **Corporate philanthropy** includes charitable donations to nonprofit groups of all kinds. Eighty percent of the business leaders surveyed in a recent study said that their companies participate in philanthropic activities. Some make long-term commitments to one cause, such as McDonald's Ronald McDonald Houses for families whose critically ill children require treatment away from home. The Bill & Melinda Gates Foundation is by far the nation's largest philanthropic foundation, with assets of approximately $37 billion.[17]

- **Corporate social initiatives** include enhanced forms of corporate philanthropy. Corporate social initiatives differ from traditional philanthropy in that they are more directly related to the company's competencies. For example, logistics giant TNT keeps a 50-person emergency response team on standby to go anywhere in the world at 48 hours' notice to provide support in aviation, warehousing, transportation, reporting and communications. Since 2005, 225 TNT employees have been involved in 17 emergency response activities.[18]

- **Corporate responsibility** includes everything from hiring minority workers to making safe products, minimizing pollution, using energy wisely, and providing a safe work environment—essentially everything that has to do with acting responsibly within society.

- **Corporate policy** refers to the position a firm takes on social and political issues. For example, Patagonia's corporate policy includes this statement: "A love of wild and beautiful places demands participation in the fight to save them, and to help reverse the steep decline in the overall environmental health of our planet. We donate our time, services and at least 1% of our sales to hundreds of grassroots environmental groups all over the world who work to help reverse the tide."[19]

The problems corporations cause get so much news coverage that people tend to get a negative view of their impact on society. But businesses make positive

corporate philanthropy
The dimension of social responsibility that includes charitable donations.

corporate social initiatives
Enhanced forms of corporate philanthropy directly related to the company's competencies.

corporate responsibility
The dimension of social responsibility that includes everything from hiring minority workers to making safe products.

corporate policy
The dimension of social responsibility that refers to the position a firm takes on social and political issues.

Timberland is a company with a long-standing commitment to community service. The company's "Path of Service" program offers employees 40 hours of paid time off each year to serve their communities. Here at a sales meeting in Jacksonville, Florida, employees gather for a day of community service. Do companies have responsibilities to the environment beyond obeying environmental laws?

contributions too. Few people know, for example, that a Xerox program called Social Service Leave allows employees to take up to a year to work for a nonprofit organization while earning their full Xerox salary and benefits, including job security.[20] IBM and Wells-Fargo Bank have similar programs.

In fact, many companies allow employees to give part-time help to social agencies of all kinds. The recent recession has changed the way that many corporations approach corporate philanthropy. According to a survey by the Committee Encouraging Corporate Philanthropy, 60 percent of companies cut their philanthropic donations since 2008, most of them by more than 10 percent. That doesn't mean that they stopped giving. Now they are more likely to give time and goods rather than money. When asked how the recession has changed their philanthropy, the largest number said they were encouraging employees to volunteer more.[21] NetworkforGood.org, 1-800-Volunteer.org, and VolunteerMatch.org are web-based services that link volunteers with nonprofit and public sector organizations around the country. Volunteers enter a zip code or indicate the geographic area in which they'd like to work, and the programs list organizations that could use their help.

Two-thirds of the MBA students surveyed by a group called Students for Responsible Business said they would take a reduced salary to work for a socially responsible company.[22] But when the same students were asked to define *socially responsible,* things got complicated. Even those who support the idea of social responsibility can't agree on what it is. Let's look at the concept through the eyes of the stakeholders to whom businesses are responsible: customers, investors, employees, and society in general.

Responsibility to Customers

President John F. Kennedy proposed four basic rights of consumers: (1) the right to safety, (2) the right to be informed, (3) the right to choose, and (4) the right to be heard. These rights will be achieved only if businesses and consumers recognize them and take action in the marketplace.

A recurring theme of this book is the importance of pleasing customers by offering them real value. Since three of five new businesses fail, we know this responsibility is not as easy to meet as it seems. One sure way of failing to please customers is to be less than honest with them. The payoff for socially conscious behavior, however, can be new customers who admire the company's social efforts—a powerful competitive edge. Consumer behavior studies show that, all else being equal, a socially conscious company is likely to be viewed more favorably than others.[23]

Given the value customers place on social efforts, how do companies make customers aware of such efforts? One tool many companies use to raise awareness of their social responsibility efforts is social media. More than 70 percent of the executives surveyed report the primary value of using social media to communicate their CSR efforts is that it allows them to reach broad and diverse groups, allows them to connect directly with customers in a low-cost, efficient way, and enables them to interact with specific groups more easily than through more traditional efforts.[24]

It's not enough for companies to brag about their social responsibility efforts; they must live up to the expectations they raise or face the consequences. When herbal tea maker Celestial Seasonings ignored its advertised image of environmental stewardship by poisoning prairie dogs on its property, it incurred customers' wrath. Customers prefer to do business with companies they trust and, even more important, don't want to do business with those they don't trust. Companies earn customers' trust by demonstrating credibility over time; they can lose it at any point.

Responsibility to Investors

Ethical behavior doesn't subtract from the bottom line; it adds to it. In contrast, unethical behavior, even if it seems to work in the short term, does financial damage. Those cheated are the shareholders themselves. For example, in just 11 business days in June 2002, 44 CEOs left U.S. corporations amid accusations of wrongdoing, and the stock prices of their companies plummeted.

Some people believe that you must make money before you can do good; others believe that by doing good, you can also do well. Bagel Works, a New England–based chain of bagel stores, has a dual-bottom-line approach that focuses on the well-being of the planet in addition to profits. Each store not only employs environmentally protective practices such as in-store recycling, composting, and the use of organically grown ingredients and nontoxic cleaners, it also includes donations for community causes in its budget. The company donates 10 percent of its pretax profits to charities each year and has earned national recognition for social responsibility.

Many investors believe that it makes financial as well as moral sense to invest in companies that plan ahead to create a better environment. By choosing to put their money into companies whose goods and services benefit the community and the environment, investors can improve their own financial health while improving society's.[25]

A few investors, however, have chosen unethical means to improve their financial health. For example, **insider trading** uses private company information to further insiders' own fortunes or those of their family and friends. In 2011, one of the biggest insider trading cases in history went to trial in New York. Billionaire Raj Rajaratnam was convicted of masterminding an insider trading ring that made his Galleon Group hedge fund $64 million richer. Of course, he didn't do this all by himself. More than three dozen former traders, executives, and lawyers have pled guilty or face charges that they helped Rajaratnam trade illegally on more than 35 stocks, including Intel, Hilton, IBM, and eBay.[26]

Insider trading isn't limited to company executives and their friends. Before it was publicly known that IBM was going to take over Lotus Development, an IBM secretary told her husband, who told two co-workers, who told friends, relatives, business associates, and even a pizza delivery man. A total of 25 people traded illegally on the insider tip within a six-hour period. When the deal was announced publicly, Lotus stock soared 89 percent. One of the inside traders, a stockbroker who passed the information to a few customers, made $468,000 in profits. The U.S. Securities and Exchange Commission (SEC) filed charges against the secretary, her husband, and 23 others. Four defendants settled out of court by paying penalties of twice their profits. Prosecutors are increasingly pursuing insider trading cases to ensure that the securities market remains fair and equally accessible to all.

After the deluge of insider trader cases was made public in the early

insider trading
An unethical activity in which insiders use private company information to further their own fortunes or those of their family and friends.

Billionaire Raj Rajaratnam, co-founder of Galleon Group hedge fund, was found guilty in the largest insider trading case in a generation. Rajaratnam gained $64 million trading on illegal tips from corporate executives, bankers, consultants, traders, and directors of public companies. More than 40 people have pleaded guilty or face criminal charges or civil lawsuits stemming from the case.

2000s, the SEC adopted a new rule called Regulation FD (for "fair disclosure"). The rule doesn't specify what information can and cannot be disclosed. It simply requires companies that release any information to share it with everybody, not just a few select people. In other words, if companies tell anyone, they must tell everyone—at the same time.

Some companies have misused information for their own benefit at investors' expense. When WorldCom admitted to accounting irregularities misrepresenting its profitability, investors who had purchased its stock on the basis of the false financial reports saw share prices free-fall from the mid-teens in January 2002 to less than a dime the following July. The pain was even greater for long-term investors, who had bought the stock at around $60 in 1999.

Responsibility to Employees

It's been said that the best social program in the world is a job. Businesses have a responsibility to create jobs if they want to grow. Once they've done so, they must see to it that hard work and talent are fairly rewarded. Employees need realistic hope of a better future, which comes only through a chance for upward mobility. Studies have shown that what most influences a company's effectiveness and financial performance is responsible human resource management.[27] We'll discuss this in Chapter 11.

If a company treats employees with respect, those employees usually will respect the company as well. Mutual respect can make a huge difference to a company's profit. In their book *Contented Cows Give Better Milk,* Bill Catlette and Richard Hadden compared "contented cow" companies with "common cow" companies. The companies with contented employees outgrew their counterparts by four to one for more than 10 years. They also out-earned the "common cow" companies by nearly $40 billion and generated 800,000 more jobs. Catlette and Hadden attribute this difference in performance to the commitment and caring the outstanding companies demonstrated for their employees.[28]

One way a company can demonstrate commitment and caring is to give employees salaries and benefits that help them reach their personal goals. The wage and benefit packages offered by warehouse retailer Costco are among the best in hourly retail. Even part-time workers are covered by Costco's health plan, and the workers pay less for their coverage than at other retailers such as Walmart. Increased benefits reduce employee turnover, which at Costco is less than a third of the industry average.[29] The U.S. Department of Labor estimates that replacing employees costs between 150 and 250 percent of their annual salaries, so retaining workers is good for business as well as morale.

Getting even is one of the most powerful incentives for good people to do bad things. Few disgruntled workers are desperate enough to commit violence in the workplace, but a great number relieve their frustrations in subtle ways: blaming mistakes on others, not accepting responsibility, manipulating budgets and expenses, making commitments they intend to ignore, hoarding resources, doing the minimum needed to get by, and making results look better than they are.

The loss of employee commitment, confidence, and trust in the company and its management can be costly indeed. Employee fraud costs U.S. businesses approximately 5 percent of annual revenue and causes 30 percent of all business failures, according to the Association of Certified Fraud Examiners.[30] You'll read more about employee–management issues like pay equity, sexual harassment, child and elder care, drug testing, and violence in the workplace in Chapter 12.

BREWING
a better world
· ·
GMCR

Green Mountain Coffee Roasters calls itself "a force for good in the world," and claims: "We celebrate and support the power of businesses and individuals to bring about positive changes, locally and globally." The company sets aside 5 percent of pretax earnings each year for good causes and produces an annual corporate social responsibility report. Do companies owe their investors a responsibility to be profitable, or to do good? Can they do both?

Responsibility to Society and the Environment

More than a third of U.S. workers receive salaries from nonprofit organizations that receive funding from others, that in turn receive their money from businesses. Foundations, universities, and other nonprofit organizations own billions of shares in publicly held companies. As stock prices of those firms increase, businesses create more wealth to benefit society.

Businesses are also partly responsible for promoting social justice. Many companies believe they have a role in building communities that goes well beyond simply "giving back." To them, charity is not enough. Their social contributions include cleaning up the environment, building community toilets, providing computer lessons, caring for the elderly, and supporting children from low-income families.

As concern about climate change increased, the green movement emerged in nearly every aspect of daily life. What makes a product green? Some believe that a product's carbon footprint (the amount of carbon released during production, distribution, consumption, and disposal) defines how green it is. Many variables contribute to a product's carbon footprint. The carbon footprint of a package of, say, frozen corn includes not only the carbon released by the fertilizer to grow the corn but also the carbon in the fertilizer itself, the gas used to run the farm equipment and transport the corn to market, the electricity to make the plastic packages and power the freezers, and so on.

No specific guidelines define the carbon footprints of products, businesses, or individuals or outline how to communicate them to consumers. PepsiCo presents carbon information with a label on bags of cheese-and-onion potato chips, for example, that says "75 grams of CO_2." Simple enough, but what does it mean? (We don't know either.)

The green movement has provided consumers with lots of product choices. However, making those choices means sorting through the many and confusing claims made by manufacturers. (See the Making the Green Connection box for a discussion about how companies promote their green initiatives.) The noise in the marketplace challenges even the most dedicated green activists, but taking the easy route of buying what's most readily available violates the principles of the green movement.

Environmental efforts may increase a company's costs, but they also allow the company to charge higher prices, increase market share, or both. Ciba Specialty Chemicals, a Swiss textile-dye manufacturer, developed dyes that require less salt than traditional dyes. Since used dye solutions must be treated before being released into rivers or streams, less salt means lower water-treatment costs. Patents protect Ciba's low-salt dyes, so the company can charge more for its dyes than other companies can charge for theirs. Ciba's experience illustrates that, just as a new machine enhances labor productivity, lowering environmental costs can add value to a business.

Not all environmental strategies are as financially beneficial as Ciba's, however. In the early 1990s, tuna producer StarKist responded to consumer concerns about dolphins in the eastern Pacific dying in nets set out for yellow fin tuna. The company announced it would sell only skipjack tuna from the western Pacific, which do not swim near dolphins. Unfortunately, customers were unwilling to pay a premium for dolphin-safe tuna and considered the taste of skipjack inferior. Nor was there a clear environmental gain: for every dolphin saved in the eastern Pacific, thousands of immature tuna and dozens of sharks, turtles, and other marine animals died in the western Pacific fishing process.

The green movement can have a positive impact on the U.S. labor force. Emerging renewable-energy and energy-efficiency industries currently account for 9 million jobs and by 2030 may create as many as 40 million more in engineering,

connection

Who's the Greenest of Them All?

In today's business climate, going green has become normal practice. Sustainability displays a company's commitment to the environment that customers respect. It also helps reduce the cost of doing business. As green policies grow more common, companies want to make sure their stakeholders know just how environmentally conscious they are. However, measuring the greenness of a company is not so simple.

As going green becomes more popular, a mass of data-collecting companies has emerged to track green business practices. These agencies flood companies with data requests regarding their environmental sustainability. Often the inquiries come in too fast to address. For example, the tech company Intel receives dozens of requests a year from analysts and nonprofits about green topics like water usage and carbon emissions. Many of the questions can be answered directly from Intel's sustainability report while others may take a while to track down. As the requests start to stack up, Intel could miss one and end up scoring poorly in a sustainability study.

It is difficult to determine the worth of one study versus another. The most prominent green survey in operation is the Global Reporting Initiative (GRI). This study advises companies about the most important environmental facts to share with the public. Eighty percent of the world's 250 biggest companies base their sustainability reports on the GRI. But since companies can decide which stats they include in the survey, other factors like use of recycled materials or toxic waste spills can be omitted from their score.

In the end, companies may be better off developing their own sustainability initiatives. Walmart did just that with its Sustainability Consortium. The nonprofit brings together retailers, suppliers, and researchers to develop a set of green standards for consumer products. So far the Sustainability Consortium has determined standards for cotton towels, TVs, yogurt, and 50 other consumer categories. It takes every step of the production process into account when making these decisions. For instance, laptops make their most significant carbon footprint in the manufacturing process, so the Sustainability Consortium addresses that factor in its standards. Hopefully more companies can take a cue from Walmart and begin to develop their own set of green standards rather than wait for someone outside the operation to do it.

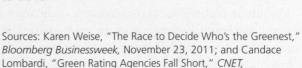

Sources: Karen Weise, "The Race to Decide Who's the Greenest," *Bloomberg Businessweek,* November 23, 2011; and Candace Lombardi, "Green Rating Agencies Fall Short," *CNET,* February 24, 2011.

manufacturing, construction, accounting, and management, according to a green-collar job report by the American Solar Energy Society.[31]

Environmental quality is a public good; that is, everyone gets to enjoy it regardless of who pays for it. The challenge for companies is to find the public goods that will appeal to their customers. Many corporations are publishing reports that document their net social contribution. To do that, a company must measure its positive social contributions and subtract its negative social impacts. We discuss that process next.

Social Auditing

Can we measure whether organizations are making social responsibility an integral part of top management's decision making? The answer is yes, and the term that represents that measurement is *social auditing*.

A **social audit** is a systematic evaluation of an organization's progress toward implementing socially responsible and responsive programs. One of the major problems of conducting a social audit is establishing procedures for measuring a firm's activities and their effects on society. What should a social audit measure? Many consider workplace issues, the environment, product safety, community relations, military weapons contracting, international operations and human rights, and respect for the rights of local people.

It remains a question whether organizations should add up positive actions like charitable donations and pollution control efforts, and then subtract negative effects like layoffs and overall pollution created, to get a net social contribution. Or should they just record positive actions? What do you think? However they are conducted, social audits force organizations to consider their social responsibility beyond the level of just feeling good or managing public relations.

In addition to social audits conducted by companies themselves, five types of groups serve as watchdogs to monitor how well companies enforce their ethical and social responsibility policies:

1. *Socially conscious investors* insist that a company extend its own high standards to its suppliers. Social responsibility investing (SRI) is on the rise, with nearly $3 trillion invested in SRI funds in the United States already.[32]

2. *Socially conscious research organizations,* such as Ethisphere, analyze and report on corporate social responsibility efforts.[33]

3. *Environmentalists* apply pressure by naming companies that don't abide by environmentalists' standards. After months of protests coordinated by the San Francisco–based Rainforest Action Network (RAN), JPMorgan Chase & Co. adopted guidelines that restrict its lending and underwriting practices for industrial projects likely to have a negative impact on the environment. RAN activists first go after an industry leader, like JPMorgan, then tackle smaller companies. "We call it, 'Rank 'em and spank 'em,'" says RAN's executive director.[34]

4. *Union officials* hunt down violations and force companies to comply to avoid negative publicity.

5. *Customers* make buying decisions based on their social conscience. Half of the companies surveyed recently said that they were adjusting their environmental and social responsibility strategies because of the number of customers that factor these into their buying decisions.[35]

Bob McDonald, Chairman of the Board, President, and CEO of Procter and Gamble, described the importance of corporate social responsibility this way: "I don't believe sustainability is optional anymore. The world today is so flat, so transparent with the Internet, and the impact of individuals is so heightened because of the ability to blog and Tweet and other things, that consumers want to know what they're buying into when they buy your brand. They want to know the company behind that brand. They want to know what that company stands for, and they want to know how that company takes care of the environment."[36] As you can see, it isn't enough for a company to be right when it comes to ethics and social responsibility—it also has to convince its customers and society that it's right.

RAINFOREST ACTION NETWORK

The goal of the Rainforest Action Network, an environmental activist group, is to show companies that it is possible to do well by doing good. It conducts public campaigns designed to put consumer pressure on companies that refuse to adopt responsible environmental policies. RAN has helped convince dozens of corporations including Home Depot, Citigroup, Boise Cascade, and Goldman Sachs to change their practices.

social audit
A systematic evaluation of an organization's progress toward implementing socially responsible and responsive programs.

- What is corporate social responsibility, and how does it relate to each of a business's major stakeholders?
- What is a social audit, and what kinds of activities does it monitor?

LEARNING **goal 6**

Analyze the role of U.S. businesses in influencing ethical behavior and social responsibility in global markets.

INTERNATIONAL ETHICS AND SOCIAL RESPONSIBILITY

Ethical problems and issues of social responsibility are not unique to the United States. Influence-peddling or bribery charges have been brought against top officials in Japan, South Korea, China, Italy, Brazil, Pakistan, and Zaire. What is new about the moral and ethical standards by which government leaders are being judged? They are much stricter than in the past. Top leaders are now being held to higher standards.

Many U.S. businesses also demand socially responsible behavior from their international suppliers, making sure they don't violate U.S. human rights and environmental standards. Sears will not import products made by Chinese prison labor. Clothing manufacturer Phillips–Van Heusen will cancel orders from suppliers that violate its ethical, environmental, and human rights code. Dow Chemical expects suppliers to conform to tough U.S. pollution and safety laws rather than just to local laws of their respective countries. McDonald's denied rumors that one of its suppliers grazes cattle on cleared rain-forest land but wrote a ban on the practice anyway.

In contrast are companies criticized for exploiting workers in less developed countries. Nike, the world's largest athletic shoe company, has been accused by human rights and labor groups of treating its workers poorly while lavishing millions of dollars on star athletes to endorse its products. Cartoonist Garry Trudeau featured an anti-Nike campaign in his popular syndicated series *Doonesbury.* In 1998, even Nike CEO Phil Knight acknowledged, "Nike product has become synonymous with slave wages, forced overtime, and arbitrary abuse."[37]

Nike has been working hard to improve its reputation. In the late 1990s, Nike began monitoring efforts to improve labor conditions in its 700 contract factories that are subject to local culture and economic conditions. In 2005, Nike released the names and locations of its factories, both as a show of transparency and to encourage its competitors to work on improving conditions as well. The company shared its audit data with a professor at MIT's Sloan School of Management, who released his findings in 2006. He concluded that despite "significant efforts and investments by Nike . . . workplace conditions in almost 80% of its suppliers have either remained the same or worsened over time."

Why has Nike's monitoring program not been as successful as the company hoped? One reason is that in emerging economies, government regulations tend to be weak, which leaves companies to police their suppliers. That's a major task for a company like Nike, which produces 98 percent of its shoes in hundreds of

Nike has outsourced the manufacture of its products to plants in other countries and has weathered much criticism for operating in low-wage countries where child labor is common. The company has taken many corrective measures, including working with other companies and advocacy groups on a set of common labor standards and factory guidelines. Can a successful firm overcome past ethical errors?

factories in many different countries. Another reason is that as a buyer, Nike has different degrees of leverage. This leverage is based on how long Nike has worked with a supplier or how much of the factory's revenue depends on Nike alone.

Nike is now trying to change its outsourcing model by helping convert suppliers from using low-skilled assembly lines to lean manufacturing, which organizes workers into multitasking teams (see Chapter 9 for more on lean manufacturing). This requires more on-the-job training, which in turn can motivate factory owners to improve conditions in order to hold onto their high-skilled laborers.[38]

The fairness of requiring international suppliers to adhere to U.S. ethical standards is not as clear-cut as you might think. For example, a gift in one culture can be a bribe in another. Is it always ethical for companies to demand compliance with the standards of their own countries? What about countries where child labor is accepted and families depend on children's salaries for survival? Should foreign companies doing business in the United States expect U.S. companies to comply with their ethical standards? Since multinational corporations span different societies, should they conform to any society's standards? Why is Sears applauded for not importing goods made in Chinese prisons when there are many prison-based enterprises in the United States? None of these questions are easy to answer, but they suggest the complexity of social responsibility in international markets. (See the nearby Connecting Across Borders box for an example of an ethical culture clash.)

In the 1970s, the Foreign Corrupt Practices Act (discussed in Chapter 3) sent a chill throughout the U.S. business community by criminalizing the act of paying foreign business or government leaders to get business. Many U.S. executives complained that this law put their businesses at a competitive disadvantage when bidding against non-U.S. companies, since foreign companies don't have to abide by it.[39]

To identify some form of common global ethic and fight corruption in global markets, partners in the Organization of American States signed the Inter-American Convention Against Corruption.[40] The United Nations adopted a formal condemnation of corporate bribery, as did the European Union and the Organization for Economic Cooperation and Development. In 2010, the International Organization for Standardization (ISO) published a standard on social responsibility called ISO 26000, with guidelines on product manufacturing, fair pay rates, appropriate

When a House Is Not a Home

Now that corporations have expanded into communities all over the globe, it raises the question: For which communities are they responsible?

Take communications and electronics giant Motorola. Almost half its employees live outside the United States, and more than half its revenues come from non-U.S. markets. Is it difficult for Motorola employees to adhere to the company's ethical values while at the same time respecting the values of the host countries in which Motorola manufactures and markets its products?

Here's an example of how corporate ethics can clash with cultural ethics. Joe, the oldest son of a poor South American cloth peddler, managed to move to the United States, earn an engineering degree, and get a job with Motorola.

After five years, Joe seemed to have bought into the Motorola culture and was happy to be granted a transfer back to his home country. He was told that the company expected him to live there in a safe and presentable home of his choice. To help him afford such a residence, Motorola agreed to reimburse him a maximum of $2,000 a month for the cost of his rent and servants. Each month Joe submitted rental receipts for exactly $2,000. The company later found out that Joe was living in what was, by Western standards, a shack in a dangerous area of town. Such a humble home could not have cost more than $200 a month. The company was concerned for Joe's safety as well as for the effect his residence would have on Motorola's image. The human resource manager was also worried about Joe's lack of integrity, given he had submitted false receipts for reimbursement.

Joe was upset with what he considered the company's invasion of his privacy. He argued he should receive the full $2,000 monthly reimbursement all employees received. He explained his choice of housing by saying he was making sacrifices so he could send the extra money to his family and put his younger siblings through school. This was especially important since his father had died and his family had no one else to depend on. "Look, my family is poor," Joe said, "so poor that most Westerners wouldn't believe our poverty even if they saw it. This money means the difference between hope and despair for all of us. For me to do anything less for my family would be to defile the honor of my late father. Can't you understand?"

Often it is difficult to understand what others perceive as ethical. Different situations often turn the clear waters of "rightness" downright muddy. Joe was trying to do the honorable thing for his family. Yet Motorola's wish to have its higher-level people live in safe housing is not unreasonable, given the dangerous conditions of the city in which Joe lived. The policy of housing reimbursement supports Motorola's intent to make its employees' stay in the country reasonably comfortable and safe, not to increase their salaries. If Joe worked in the United States, where he would not receive a housing supplement, it would be unethical for him to falsify expense reports in order to receive more money to send to his family. In South America, though, the issue is not so clear.

Sources: R. S. Moorthy, Robert C. Solomon, William J. Ellos, and Richard T. De George, "Friendship or Bribery?" *Across the Board,* January 1999; Yale Political Union, "Should Corporations Be Responsible to More Than Their Shareholders?" *The Huffington Post,* October 27, 2009; and "Americans Want Companies to Put Employees before Stockholders, Executives," *The Huffington Post,* accessed May 2012.

employee treatment, and hiring practices. These standards are advisory only and will not be used for certification purposes. The formation of a single set of international rules governing multinational corporations is unlikely in the near future. In many places "Fight corruption" remains just a slogan, but even a slogan is a start.

progress assessment

- How are U.S. businesses demanding socially responsible behavior from their international suppliers?
- Why is it unlikely that there will be a single set of international rules governing multinational companies soon?

summary

Learning Goal 1. Explain why obeying the law is only the first step in behaving ethically.

- **How is legality different from ethics?**

Ethics goes beyond obeying laws to include abiding by the moral standards accepted by society. Ethics reflects people's proper relationships with one another. Legality is more limiting; it refers only to laws written to protect people from fraud, theft, and violence.

Learning Goal 2. Ask the three questions you need to answer when faced with a potentially unethical action.

- **How can we tell if our business decisions are ethical?**

We can put our business decisions through an ethics check by asking three questions: (1) Is it legal? (2) Is it balanced? and (3) How will it make me feel?

Learning Goal 3. Describe management's role in setting ethical standards.

- **What is management's role in setting ethical standards?**

Managers often set formal ethical standards, but more important are the messages they send through their actions. Management's tolerance or intolerance of ethical misconduct influences employees more than any written ethics codes.

Learning Goal 4. Distinguish between compliance-based and integrity-based ethics codes, and list the six steps in setting up a corporate ethics code.

- **What's the difference between compliance-based and integrity-based ethics codes?**

Whereas compliance-based ethics codes are concerned with avoiding legal punishment, integrity-based ethics codes define the organization's guiding values, create an environment that supports ethically sound behavior, and stress a shared accountability among employees.

Learning Goal 5. Define *corporate social responsibility* and compare corporations' responsibilities to various stakeholders

- **What is corporate social responsibility?**

Corporate social responsibility is the concern businesses have for society.

- **How do businesses demonstrate corporate responsibility toward stakeholders?**

Business is responsible to four types of stakeholders: (1) it must satisfy *customers* with goods and services of real value; (2) it must make money for its *investors;* (3) it must create jobs for *employees,* maintain job security, and see that hard work and talent are fairly rewarded; and (4) it must create new wealth for *society,* promote social justice, and contribute to making its own environment a better place.

- **How are a company's social responsibility efforts measured?**

A corporate social audit measures an organization's progress toward social responsibility. Some people believe the audit should add together the organization's positive actions and then subtract the negative effects to get a net social benefit.

Learning Goal 6. Analyze the role of U.S. businesses in influencing ethical behavior and social responsibility in global markets.

- **How can U.S. companies influence ethical behavior and social responsibility in global markets?**

Many U.S. businesses are demanding socially responsible behavior from their international suppliers by making sure their suppliers do not violate U.S. human rights and environmental standards. Companies like Sears, Phillips–Van Heusen, and Dow Chemical will not import products from companies that do not meet their ethical and social responsibility standards.

key terms

compliance-based ethics codes 96

corporate philanthropy 99

corporate policy 99

corporate responsibility 99

corporate social initiatives 99

corporate social responsibility (CSR) 98

ethics 92

insider trading 101

integrity-based ethics codes 96

social audit 104

whistleblowers 97

critical thinking

Think of a situation that tested your ethical behavior. For example, maybe your best friend forgot about a term paper due the next day and asked if he could copy a paper you wrote for another instructor last semester.

1. What are your alternatives, and what are the consequences of each?

2. Would it have been easier to resolve the dilemma if you had asked yourself the three questions listed in the chapter? Try answering them now and see whether you would have made a different choice.

developing workplace skills

1. What sources have helped shape your personal code of ethics and morality? What influences, if any, have ever pressured you to compromise those standards? Think of an experience you had at work or school that tested your ethical standards. How did you resolve your dilemma? Now that time has passed, are you comfortable with the decision you made? If not, what would you do differently?

2. Do a little investigative reporting of your own. Identify a public interest group in your community and identify its officers, objectives, sources and amount of financial support, and size and characteristics of membership. List some examples of its recent actions and/or accomplishments. You should be able to choose from environmental groups, animal protection groups, political action committees, and so on. Call the local chamber of commerce, the Better Business Bureau, or local government agencies for help. Try using the Internet to help you find more information.

3. You're the manager of a coffeehouse called the Morning Cup. One of your best employees desires to be promoted to a managerial position; however, the owner is grooming his slow-thinking son for the job. The owner's nepotism may hurt a valuable employee's chances for advancement, but complaining may hurt your own chances for promotion. What do you do?

4. Contact a local corporation and ask for a copy of its written ethics code. Would you classify its code as compliance-based or integrity-based? Explain.

5. What effects have the new laws protecting whistleblowers had on the business environment? Use the Internet or the library to research individuals who reported their employers' illegal and/or unethical behavior. Did the companies change their policies? If so, what effect have these policies had on the companies' stakeholders? What effect did reporting the problems have on the whistleblowers themselves?

taking it to the net

Purpose

To demonstrate the level of commitment one business has to social responsibility.

Exercise

Richard Foos of Rhino Records built a multimillion-dollar entertainment experience out of a pile of dusty old records—by sticking to his ideals. Foos fosters ethical practices in Rhino's day-to-day business, supporting numerous charitable groups and promoting community service by Rhino employees. See for yourself how Foos responds to social and environmental issues by going to Rhino's website at www.rhino.com and exploring the "About Rhino" links. Then answer the following questions:

1. What is the social mission of Rhino Records?

2. What does the Social and Environmental Responsibility Team (SERT) do to implement this mission?

3. How does Rhino Records encourage its employees to get involved in community service?

4. How do Rhino employees communicate the company's social mission to their customers?

casing the web

To access the case "Got a Deadline? Click Here," visit
www.mhhe.com/P2P2e

video case

Going Beyond Legality

Recently, there was a debate on a television show about one of the most sensitive moral issues facing the United States today. One of the debaters said loudly, "But everything he did was legal!" Clearly some adults today still look at legality as the proper measure of behavior. "It's okay if it's legal" seems to be their motto.

Sometimes young people will surprise you with their insight and wisdom. They seem to know intuitively that legality is not the proper measure of morality. They know that doing the right thing is important, and the law has nothing (or almost nothing) to do with it. For example, two young people (a brother and sister named Brittany and Robbie) noticed that U.S. troops were having difficulty communicating with their loved ones—spouses, children, parents, etc. "What could a citizen do to help?" they wondered.

The answer was a project called Cell Phones for Soldiers (cellphonesforsoldiers.com). Why not make it possible for our military to use cell phones

to make calls? Sounds reasonable, so why not do it? It certainly would be the moral and ethical thing to do. The question of legality hardly enters the picture. Rather the questions "Would I want to be treated this way?" and "How would it make me feel about myself?" dominated the thoughts of Brittany and Robbie.

They decided to form a nonprofit organization and gather funds to send phones to the military. All corporations could learn how to make such ethical decisions. It begins by developing a code of conduct, where all employees must understand what is expected of them—managers included. This usually calls for some training. An ethics office should be established for communication purposes, and outside stakeholders informed. Finally, the ethical behavior must be performed. In this case, it meant sending cell phones to the military.

No businesses should neglect the responsibilities they have to all stakeholders, including the community. Employees like to work for companies that have an ethical base. It has been argued that the only responsibility of business is to make money. But who says that doing the right and ethical thing does not result in making more money?

And money is not the only measure of success and happiness. Making a difference in the world has motivated some of the richest people in the world, including Bill Gates and Warren Buffett. In contrast, this video shows that you don't have to be rich and famous to make a huge difference in the world. We salute these young entrepreneurs who saw a need and filled it. That should be the goal of every business. And the goal should also include doing it in a moral and ethical way. Young people know that; why doesn't everyone?

Thinking It Over

1. *Discuss the present state of morality and ethics in the United States with others in your class. What is their impression? Do they believe that businesses add or subtract from the overall ethical base? Why? What do they recommend doing about it?*

2. *Ethics begins at home. What moral and ethical problems do you observe around your school? What seems to be causing the collapse of values, if that is what you perceive? Or what keeps students on a moral and ethical journey?*

3. *What are the four elements associated with corporate social responsibility?*

Career Outlook
Part 1 Conclusion—Business Trends

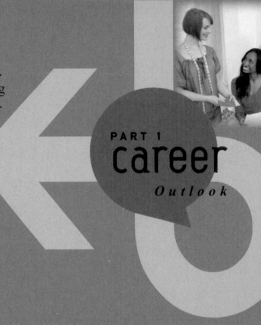

Business is a wide-ranging, ever-expanding, and challenging field. Whether you're building a skyscraper or working in one, growing vegetables or serving them in a restaurant, sewing dresses or marketing them, you are part of the collective world of business.

While opportunities in business are growing, the world itself is shrinking. As more people worldwide have access to the Internet, businesses find new opportunities to sell, work, market, analyze, manage, and create in new countries and markets. The possibilities are endless!

PART 1
career
Outlook

SKILLS NEEDED
POSSIBLE POSITIONS
PROFILE
COVER LETTER
RESUME
INTERVIEW

Skills Needed

Jobs in the field of business are diverse, but in order to succeed you'll need to be:

- **Motivated**—What drives you? Your ambition? Your family? Why would you succeed in business, if given a chance?

- **Educated**—Most business careers require bachelor's degrees, but every job requires training and experience of some kind.

- **A good communicator**—Are you a social butterfly, always meeting and talking to people? Or are you more behind the scenes, writing or making videos?

- **Determined**—Opportunities aren't always easy to find. What are your goals? What do you need to do to achieve them?

- **Flexible**—Can you change or alter your approach as the market changes?

Possible Positions

POSSIBLE POSITIONS IN BUSINESS

OPPORTUNITY	MEDIAN SALARY	DUTIES	REQUIREMENTS	GROWTH
Top Executives	$101,250 per year	Devise strategies and policies for a business	Vary widely, but at least a bachelor's degree and work experience	Slower than average growth
Agent for Artists and Athletes	$63,130 per year	Represent and promote artists and athletes, negotiate contracts	Bachelor's degree; 1–5 years in a related occupation	Average growth
Credit Analyst	$58,850 per year	Analyze credit for people or businesses to determine risk for lending money	Bachelor's degree	Faster than average growth
Retail Sales Supervisor	$35,820 per year	Supervise retail sales workers; budgeting, accounting, and personnel work	High school diploma or equivalent; 1–5 years of related work experience	Slower than average growth

Source: Bureau of Labor Statistics, *Occupational Outlook Handbook*, 2012–13 Edition.

Profile: Huang Min, International Exporter

After graduating from high school in Arizona, Huang Min took two years off from school to travel the world. Armed only with a backpack and a taste for adventure, she flew to Australia and trekked her way through the Philippines, China, Russia, Turkey, and Europe. Now she's back in the States and pursuing her college degree.

While traveling, Min was fascinated by seeing how many American-made products were available in world markets. Now she's studying business and international relations in a community college so she can work abroad, connecting American businesses with customers in other countries. Min is about to graduate and is applying for a job with a small business that exports supplies for food trucks, carts, and other mobile dining establishments. How does Min use her cover letter, résumé, and interview to highlight her international experience?

MIN'S COVER LETTER

> Tip: Be clear in the first paragraph about the position for which you are applying. Busy employers may not read further if they don't clearly understand your goals.

> Tip: Make sure that your cover letter highlights how you can add value to an organization.

> Tip: Use your cover letter to tell an interesting story about who you are so that an employer will be interested in meeting you.

Huang Min
48 South Sixth Street, Scottsdale, Arizona 85225
480-894-2740 - HuangMin@aol.com

March 8, 2014
Joanna Lee
Owner
Mobile Restaurants Manufacturing, Inc.
358 Alondres Boulevard
Scottsdale, Arizona 85225

Dear Ms. Lee:

I love food and traveling to new places. Many people could say the same about themselves, but I'm applying for the supply chain representative position at Mobile Restaurants Manufacturing because my love goes beyond eating at local ethnic restaurants and experimenting with tofu. I want to be a part of Mobile Restaurants' mission to make food accessible and bring culinary craft to the street, where people from any country can experience it. My global travel experience, language skills, restaurant experience, and organizational abilities would make me a good fit for your team.

Having lived in five different countries and traveled to at least 10 more, I always dedicated myself to learning as much of the local language as possible, whether it was perfecting the Mandarin my grandparents taught me or vocalizing the hard, spitting noises of Russian. Having crashed at hostels and on couches, I can adapt easily to the challenges of travel—a vital skill for the supply chain representative position.

In order to support myself when abroad, I often found work at local restaurants. Restaurant owners always recognized my passion for food and making customers happy. Recently, I built on that restaurant experience and helped organize Outdoor Feasts, a food festival in Scottsdale. I learned the value of careful record keeping and constant communication with the vendors. The founder of the event said she could count on me to keep track of the details that made that event a success. Now I want to use my dedication and skills to work for Mobile Restaurants, partnering with international restaurants and getting them the supplies they need to expand their reach and sell their goods on the road.

I would appreciate a chance to talk with you about my determination, passion, and drive when you interview on campus this month. Thank you for your consideration, and I look forward to hearing from you.

Sincerely,

Huang Min
Huang Min

MIN'S RESUME

Huang Min
48 South Street, Scottsdale, Arizona 85225
480-894-2740 email: huangmin@aol.com

Education

Scottsdale Area Community College   GPA: 3.48/4.00
Associate's Degree, cum laude, Business and International Relations   Anticipated: May 2014

Professional Experience

Blogger/Ad Salesperson
WhereisMin.com (June 2008–Present)

- Write and design travel/food blog based on my international and regional travels; readership has grown to over 3000 followers.
- Generated $3000 in advertising last year from travel-related businesses.

Part-time Administrative Assistant
Outdoor Feasts, Scottsdale, Arizona (2011–2012)

- Maintained relationships and managed expenses with reputable food vendors.
- Developed Excel spreadsheets to keep logistical details organized.
- Updated event website to highlight each day's events.
- Wrote press releases to promote Outdoor Feasts.
- Provided Twitter updates to keep the public interested.
- Initiated a Facebook page to develop followers before the event.

Various Restaurant Positions
Experience gained during international travel (June 2008–May 2010)

- Waitress, Café Orleans, Lyon, France (March–May 2010)
  —Marketed baked goods to students at my French language school.
- Hostess and Greeter, Hamdi Restaurant, Istanbul, Turkey (September–December 2009)
- Waitress, Starlite Diner, Moscow, Russia (May–September 2009)
- Hostess, Wei Hong Restaurant, Beijing, China (December 2008–May 2009)
  —Collaborated with restaurant owner to create mobile food cart to increase restaurant visibility.
- Waitress, Pancakes on the Rocks, Sydney, Australia (June–October 2008)

Language Skills

Fluent (Written and Oral): English, Mandarin Chinese
Proficient (Oral): French, Turkish
Conversational Basics: German, Spanish, Russian

Min's Interview

Question: Why did you decide to travel for two years after high school?

Poor answer: I've always wanted to travel and didn't want to be one of those Americans who is ignorant about the world. I couldn't believe some of the typical American tourists I saw when I was abroad. It was embarrassing.

Great answer: It was a big decision, and I'll admit that it scared my mother, but I knew I wanted to learn more about the world and myself before I continued on with school. In the end, my family supported me because they realized I'd have a better idea about what type of college program to choose after this type of learning experience. Memories of my trip motivate me to succeed when I get frustrated. I came to understand the value of an education after seeing so many people in the world who aren't fortunate enough to get this type of opportunity. I'm a more mature student as a result.

Tip: Talk about yourself. The employer isn't interested in what "typical Americans" are like. She is interested in what YOU are like. Stick to the facts about your own life and personality.

Question: Why should we hire you?

Poor answer: Like I said in my cover letter, I really love food and international travel, so I think I could be good at this. Um, I'm not sure what else to say. That's it.

Great answer: I know I'm new. I'm just out of college and new to this business, but it seems like this is where I belong, and I'd like a chance to prove it to you. You need someone who can travel, negotiate with clients, and make sure they are satisfied with your products. After my traveling experience, I feel you could drop me in any city in any country, and I could get whatever you needed done.

Tip: Stay confident. If you are shy or better at writing than speaking, then rehearse your answers before your interview. Ask a friend to pretend to be the employer. Interviewing is a skill, and it's a good idea to practice. Even if you think you interview well, practice and feedback from others will give you an edge in confidence and in being able to craft effective answers quickly.

Question: Why did you decide to get your degrees in business and international relations?

Poor answer: Oh, I like business. And I've traveled to other countries, so international relations seemed like a good idea.

Great answer: Living on my own for two years, I saw how business makes the world go round. Anyone with business experience seemed to have the jobs that I wanted. I've loved being a waitress, but I have bigger ideas, bigger passions than just serving food. I knew that a degree was the best way for me to get where I want to go in life. Now I see the potential for combining what I'm learning in the classroom with my travel experience to help a business like yours be more successful.

Tip: Find the balance between talking too much and not talking enough. Use each question as a chance to tell the employer something about yourself. One-word answers usually won't help you. And remember to use the information that you provide about yourself to answer the hidden question behind every interview question: "Why should I hire you?"

Business Ownership:
STARTING A SMALL BUSINESS

D o you think you have what it takes to start and manage a business? In the chapters in this part, you will examine the characteristics of entrepreneurs (those who choose to accept the risk of starting and running a business). You will learn about the various forms of business ownership and the advantages and disadvantages of each, where to go for funding and start-up advice, and what is involved with running a business.

After reading these chapters, you will have a better idea if entrepreneurship is for you or whether you would be more comfortable working for someone else.

LOOKING
Ahead

CHAPTER 5 How to Form a Business

CHAPTER 6 Entrepreneurship and Starting a Small Business

5

HOW TO FORM A Business

LEARNING goals

After you have read and studied this chapter, you should be able to

1 Compare the advantages and disadvantages of sole proprietorships.

2 Describe the differences between general and limited partners, and compare the advantages and disadvantages of partnerships.

3 Compare the advantages and disadvantages of corporations, and summarize the differences between C corporations, S corporations, and limited liability companies.

4 Define and give examples of three types of corporate mergers, and explain the role of leveraged buyouts and taking a firm private.

5 Outline the advantages and disadvantages of franchises, and discuss the opportunities for diversity in franchising and the challenges of global franchising.

6 Explain the role of cooperatives.

As the founder, president, and CEO of The Cheesecake Factory, David Overton heads one of the most successful restaurant chains. But working in food service wasn't Overton's dream as a young man. Growing up in Detroit in the 1950s, Overton made a penny for every cake box he folded for his mother and father's small cheesecake business. Playing the drums was his real passion, though. By the time he was 15, Overton was earning money drumming in a band rather than folding boxes in his parents' basement. After graduating from Wayne State University in 1967, he decided to have a go at drumming as a career and moved to San Francisco for the music scene.

CONNECTING WITH

David Overton

X

CEO of The Cheesecake Factory

With all their kids grown up and moved out, Overton's parents grew lonely in Detroit and wanted to live closer to their children. Since Los Angeles was bigger than San Francisco, Overton convinced his folks that the city would make a good market for their famous cheesecakes. So in 1972, Mr. and Mrs. Overton packed their car and drove west to open a wholesale bakery with the last of their savings. Getting the business off the ground turned out to be a struggle as the two regularly worked 18-hour days baking and trying to land new accounts. By 1975 their hard work had finally started to pay off. The Overtons moved into a bigger bakery and soon had 20 different varieties of cheesecake and other delicious desserts available for sale.

Meanwhile in San Francisco, David Overton came to the realization that he probably wasn't going to become a rock star. Knowing his parents could use the help, he moved to Los Angeles to work at the new bakery. Although the business was doing well, Overton didn't think it was growing as fast as it deserved. To him, the wholesale format wasn't suitable to the "Cadillac of cheesecakes" that his parents were making. Instead, he came up with the idea of opening a restaurant built around the cheesecake. The food would be simple American fare like macaroni and cheese and burgers that would draw people in but not distract them from the real attraction—the dessert. Overton told the family accountant about the plan, who simply replied, "I'll raise the money." Pretty soon the Overtons had gathered $125,000 from investors to start the restaurant.

Overton opened the first Cheesecake Factory in 1978 in Beverly Hills. He figured that such a high-class locale would reflect the quality of his parents' cheesecake. Plus, with so many upscale restaurants in the area, The Cheesecake Factory wouldn't have that many casual eateries to compete with. Overton's gamble paid off handsomely. Without so much as a sign, the restaurant filled up within 10 minutes of opening its doors. Business was so good that within five years the family had opened three more restaurants, two in California and the other in Washington, D.C. His parents were able to semi-retire and his investors were earning loads of money. By 1992, interest in the Cheesecake Factory brand had become so widespread that Overton took the company public. The restaurant's stock opened at $20 and by the end of its first day had gone up to $27.25. Since it's gone public, the company has expanded across the country.

Even though The Cheesecake Factory is now a nationally recognized brand with 153 locations, the company does not franchise its restaurants. In Overton's eyes, a Cheesecake Factory franchise would be just too complicated for the average businessperson. The restaurant is famous for its enormous menu and portions to match. "It takes true restaurant pros to operate one, so we don't feel that franchising will happen," says Overton. "All the complications of having such a large menu make it difficult." So far Overton appears to be making the right move. When the financial crisis hit in 2008, Overton's complete control allowed him to pull the company out of some deals and slow down expansion. At a time when most restaurants were losing business, in 2009 revenues for The Cheesecake Factory had gone up 4 percent.

Just like David Overton, all business owners must decide for themselves which form of business is best for them. Whether you dream of starting a business for yourself, going into business with a partner, forming a corporation, or someday being a leading franchisor, it's important to know that each form of ownership has its advantages and disadvantages. You will learn about them all in this chapter.

Sources: Dinah Eng, "Cheesecake Factory's Winning Formula," *Fortune,* May 9, 2011; Sarah E. Needleman, "Aspiring Drummer Discovers Sweet Success in Restaurants," *The Wall Street Journal,* October 19, 2011; Victoria Thompson, "The Cheesecake Factory: Feeding the 'Common Man,'" *ABC Nightline,* August 31, 2011; and "Our Story," www.thecheesecakefactory.com, accessed March 23, 2012.

Around April 15th every year, we are a very sought out company. With thousands of locations in the United States, we make tax filing much easier. Most people are unaware that we are actually a Canadian franchise even though we have our headquarters in the United States. Who are we? (Find the answer in the chapter.)

Need help understanding Forms of Business Ownership?
www.introbiz.tv/QR5-1

sole proprietorship
A business that is owned, and usually managed, by one person.

partnership
A legal form of business with two or more owners.

corporation
A legal entity with authority to act and have liability apart from its owners.

BASIC FORMS OF BUSINESS OWNERSHIP

Hundreds of thousands of people have started new businesses in the United States. In fact, more than 600,000 are started each year.[1] Chances are, you've thought of owning your own business or know someone who has.

How you form your business can make a tremendous difference in your long-term success. The three major forms of business ownership are (1) sole proprietorships, (2) partnerships, and (3) corporations. Each has advantages and disadvantages that we'll discuss.

It can be easy to get started in your own business. You can begin a lawn mowing service, develop a website, or go about meeting other wants and needs of your community. A business owned, and usually managed, by one person is called a **sole proprietorship.** That is the most common form of business ownership.

Many people do not have the money, time, or desire to run a business on their own. When two or more people legally agree to become co-owners of a business, the organization is called a **partnership.**

Sole proprietorships and partnerships are relatively easy to form, but there are advantages to creating a business that is separate and distinct from the owners. This is a **corporation,** a legal entity with authority to act and have liability apart from its owners. The almost 5 million corporations in the United States make up

figure 5.1

FORMS OF BUSINESS OWNERSHIP

Although corporations make up only 20 percent of the total number of businesses, they make 81 percent of the total receipts. Sole proprietorships are the most common form (72 percent), but they earn only 6 percent of the receipts.

Source: U.S. Internal Revenue Service.

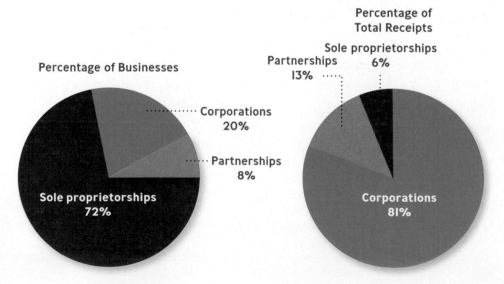

122

only 20 percent of all businesses, but they earn 81 percent of total U.S. business receipts (see Figure 5.1).

Keep in mind that just because a business starts in one form of ownership, it doesn't have to stay in that form.[2] Many companies start out in one form, then add (or drop) a partner or two, and eventually become corporations, limited liability companies, or franchisors.[3] Let's begin our discussion by looking at the most basic form of ownership—the sole proprietorship.

LEARNING goal 1

Compare the advantages and disadvantages of sole proprietorships.

SOLE PROPRIETORSHIPS

Advantages of Sole Proprietorships

Sole proprietorships are the easiest kind of businesses to explore in your quest for an interesting career. Every town has sole proprietors you can visit and talk with about the joys and frustrations of being in business on their own.[4] Most will mention the benefits of being their own boss and setting their own hours. Other advantages include:

1. *Ease of starting and ending the business.* All you have to do to start a sole proprietorship is buy or lease the needed equipment (a saw, a laptop, a tractor, a lawn mower) and put up some announcements saying you are in business. You may have to get a permit or license from the local government, but often that is no problem. It is just as easy to get out of business; you simply stop. There is no one to consult or disagree with about such decisions.

2. *Being your own boss.* Working for others simply does not have the same excitement as working for yourself—at least, that's the way sole proprietors feel. You may make mistakes, but they are your mistakes—and so are the many small victories each day.

3. *Pride of ownership.* People who own and manage their own businesses are rightfully proud of their work. They deserve all the credit for taking the risks and providing needed goods or services.

4. *Leaving a legacy.* Owners can leave an ongoing business for future generations.

5. *Retention of company profits.* Owners not only keep the profits earned but also benefit from the increasing value as the business grows.

6. *No special taxes.* All the profits of a sole proprietorship are taxed as the personal income of the owner, and the owner pays the normal income tax on that money.[5] However, owners do have to pay the self-employment tax (for Social Security and Medicare). They also have to estimate their taxes and make quarterly payments to the government or suffer penalties for nonpayment.

Warren Brown's career is finally "rising." Brown left a promising law career to create Cakelove, a bustling bakery that specializes in making pastries from scratch using natural ingredients. Brown regularly appears on the Food Network. Do you have a passion you would like to pursue as a business?

Disadvantages of Sole Proprietorships

Not everyone is equipped to own and manage a business. Often it is difficult to save enough money to start a business and keep it going. The costs of inventory, supplies, insurance, advertising, rent, computers, utilities, and so on may be too much to cover alone. There are other disadvantages:

1. *Unlimited liability—the risk of personal losses.* When you work for others, it is their problem if the business is not profitable. When you own your own business, you and the business are considered one. You have **unlimited liability;** that is, any debts or damages incurred by the business are your debts and you must pay them, even if it means selling your home, your car, or whatever else you own. This is a serious risk, and undertaking it requires not only thought but also discussion with a lawyer, an insurance agent, an accountant, and others.

2. *Limited financial resources.* Funds available to the business are limited to what the one owner can gather. Since there are serious limits to how much money one person can raise, partnerships and corporations have a greater probability of obtaining the financial backing needed to start and equip a business and keep it going.

3. *Management difficulties.* All businesses need management; someone must keep inventory, accounting, and tax records. Many people skilled at selling things or providing a service are not so skilled at keeping records. Sole proprietors often find it difficult to attract qualified employees to help run the business because often they cannot compete with the salary and benefits offered by larger companies.

4. *Overwhelming time commitment.* Though sole proprietors say they set their own hours, it's hard to own a business, manage it, train people, and have time for anything else in life when there is no one with whom to share the burden. The owner of a store, for example, may put in 12 hours a day at least six days a week—almost twice the hours worked by a nonsupervisory employee in a large company. Imagine how this time commitment affects the sole proprietor's family life. Many sole proprietors will tell you, "It's not a job, it's not a career, it's a way of life."

5. *Few fringe benefits.* If you are your own boss, you lose the fringe benefits that often come with working for others. You have no paid health insurance, no paid disability insurance, no pension plan, no sick leave, and no vacation pay. These and other benefits may add up to 30 percent or more of a worker's compensation.

6. *Limited growth.* Expansion is often slow since a sole proprietorship relies on its owner for most of its creativity, business know-how, and funding.

7. *Limited life span.* If the sole proprietor dies, is incapacitated, or retires, the business no longer exists (unless it is sold or taken over by the sole proprietor's heirs).

Talk with a few local sole proprietors about the problems they've faced in being on their own. They are likely to have many interesting stories about problems getting loans from the bank, problems with theft, and problems simply keeping up with the business. These are reasons why many sole proprietors choose to find partners to share the load.

Being the sole proprietor of a company, like a dog-walking service, means making a major time commitment to run the business, including constantly seeking out new customers and looking for reliable employees when the time comes to grow. If you were a sole proprietor, what would you need to do if you wanted to take a week's vacation?

unlimited liability
The responsibility of business owners for all of the debts of the business.

progress assessment

- Most people who start businesses in the United States are sole proprietors. What are the advantages and disadvantages of sole proprietorships?
- Why would unlimited liability be considered a major drawback to sole proprietorships?

LEARNING goal 2

Describe the differences between general and limited partners, and compare the advantages and disadvantages of partnerships.

PARTNERSHIPS

A partnership is a legal form of business with two or more owners. There are several types: (1) general partnerships, (2) limited partnerships, and (3) master limited partnerships. In a **general partnership** all owners share in operating the business and in assuming liability for the business's debts. A **limited partnership** has one or more general partners and one or more limited partners. A **general partner** is an owner (partner) who has unlimited liability and is active in managing the firm. Every partnership must have at least one general partner. A **limited partner** is an owner who invests money in the business but does not have any management responsibility or liability for losses beyond his or her investment. **Limited liability** means that the limited partners' liability for the debts of the business is *limited* to the amount they put into the company; their personal assets are not at risk.

One form of partnership, the **master limited partnership (MLP),** looks much like a corporation (which we discuss next) in that it acts like a corporation and is traded on the stock exchanges like a corporation, but is taxed like a partnership and thus avoids the corporate income tax.[6] Master limited partnerships are normally found in the oil and gas industry. For example, Sunoco Inc. formed the MLP Sunoco Logistics Partners (SXL) to acquire, own, and operate a group of crude oil and refined-product pipelines and storage facilities. Income received by SXL is not taxed before it is passed on to investors as dividends as it would be if SXL were a corporation.[7]

Another type of partnership was created to limit the disadvantage of unlimited liability. A **limited liability partnership (LLP)** limits partners' risk of losing their personal assets to the outcomes of only their own acts and omissions and those of people under their supervision. If you are a limited partner in an LLP, you can operate without the fear that one of your partners might commit an act of malpractice resulting in a judgment that takes away your house, car, retirement plan, even your collection of vintage Star Wars action figures, as would be the case in a general partnership. However, in many states this personal protection does not extend to contract liabilities such as bank loans, leases, and business debt the partnership takes on; loss of personal assets is still a risk if these are not paid. In states without additional contract liability protections for LLPs, the LLP is in many ways similar to an LLC (discussed later in the chapter).

All states except Louisiana have adopted the Uniform Partnership Act (UPA) to replace earlier laws governing partnerships. The UPA defines the three

general partnership
A partnership in which all owners share in operating the business and in assuming liability for the business's debts.

limited partnership
A partnership with one or more general partners and one or more limited partners.

general partner
An owner (partner) who has unlimited liability and is active in managing the firm.

limited partner
An owner who invests money in the business but does not have any management responsibility or liability for losses beyond the investment.

limited liability
The responsibility of a business's owners for losses only up to the amount they invest; limited partners and shareholders (stockholders) have limited liability.

master limited partnership (MLP)
A partnership that looks much like a corporation (in that it acts like a corporation and is traded on a stock exchange) but is taxed like a partnership and thus avoids the corporate income tax.

limited liability partnership (LLP)
A partnership that limits partners' risk of losing their personal assets to only their own acts and omissions and to the acts and omissions of people under their supervision.

figure 5.2

QUESTIONS TO ASK WHEN
CHOOSING A BUSINESS
PARTNER

There's no such thing as a perfect partner, but you should share some common thoughts on the business. Ask yourself:

Do you share the same goals?

Do you share the same vision for the company's future?

What skills does the person have?

Are those skills the same as yours, or do they complement your skills?

What contacts, resources, or special attributes will the person bring to the business?

What type of decision maker is the person?

Is this someone with whom you could happily share authority for all major business decisions?

Do you trust each other?

How does the person respond to adversity?

Does he or she try to solve the problem or try to defend his or her ego?

Can the person accept constructive criticism without getting defensive?

To what extent can you build fun and excitement into the partnership?

key elements of any general partnership as (1) common ownership, (2) shared profits and losses, and (3) the right to participate in managing the operations of the business.

Advantages of Partnerships

Often, it is much easier to own and manage a business with one or more partners. Your partner may be skilled at inventory control and accounting, while you do the selling or servicing. A partner can also provide additional money, support, and expertise as well as cover for you when you are sick or on vacation. Figure 5.2 suggests several questions to ask yourself when choosing a partner.

Partnerships usually have the following advantages:

1. *More financial resources.* When two or more people pool their money and credit, it is easier to pay the rent, utilities, and other bills incurred by a business. A limited partnership is specially designed to help raise money. As mentioned earlier, a limited partner invests money in the business but cannot legally have management responsibility and has limited liability.

Kate and Andy Spade started a business selling a $155 black nylon handbag in 1993. Their business has grown into a global brand. What makes the pair of Spades such great business partners? It's their differences: Kate is the creative soul who designs the products and Andy is the risk taker who shapes the brand. What problems might partners who share both business and home encounter that other partners might not?

2. *Shared management and pooled/complementary skills and knowledge.* It is simply much easier to manage the day-to-day activities of a business with carefully chosen partners. Partners give each other free time from the business and provide different skills and perspectives. Some people find that the best partner is a spouse. Many husband-and-wife teams manage restaurants, service shops, and other businesses.[8]

3. *Longer survival.* One study that examined 2,000 businesses started since 1960 found that partnerships were four times more likely to succeed than sole proprietorships. Being watched by a partner can help a businessperson become more disciplined.

4. *No special taxes.* As with sole proprietorships, all profits of partnerships are taxed as the personal income of the owners, who pay the normal income tax on that money. Similarly, partners must estimate their taxes and make quarterly payments or suffer penalties for nonpayment.

Disadvantages of Partnerships

Anytime two people must agree, conflict and tension are possible. Partnerships have caused splits between relatives, friends, and spouses. Let's explore the disadvantages of partnerships:

1. *Unlimited liability.* Each *general* partner is liable for the debts of the firm, no matter who was responsible for causing them. You are liable for your partners' mistakes as well as your own. Like sole proprietors, general partners can lose their homes, cars, and everything else they own if the business loses a lawsuit or goes bankrupt.

2. *Division of profits.* Sharing risk means sharing profits, and that can cause conflicts. There is no set system for dividing profits in a partnership, and they are not always divided evenly. For example, if one partner puts in more money and the other puts in more hours, each may feel justified in asking for a bigger share of the profits.

3. *Disagreements among partners.* Disagreements over money are just one example of potential conflict in a partnership. Who has final authority over employees? Who hires and fires employees? Who works what hours? What if one partner wants to buy expensive equipment for the firm and the other partner disagrees? All terms of the partnership should be spelled out in writing to protect all parties and minimize misunderstandings. The Making Ethical Decisions box offers an example of a difference of opinions between partners.

4. *Difficulty of termination.* Once you have committed yourself to a partnership, it is not easy to get out of it. Sure, you can just quit. However, questions about who gets what and what happens next are often difficult to resolve when the partnership ends. Surprisingly, law firms often have faulty partnership agreements and find that breaking up is hard to do. How do you get rid of a partner you don't like? It is best to decide such questions up front in the partnership agreement. Figure 5.3 gives you ideas about what to include in partnership agreements.

The best way to learn about the advantages and disadvantages of partnerships is to interview several people who have experience with them. They will give you insights and hints on how to avoid problems.

MAKING ethical decisions

Good Business, Bad Karma?

Imagine that you and your partner own a construction company. You receive a bid from a subcontractor that you know is 20 percent too low. Such a loss to the subcontractor could put him out of business. Accepting the bid will certainly improve your chances of winning the contract for a big shopping center project. Your partner wants to take the bid and let the subcontractor suffer the consequences of his bad estimate. What do you think you should do? What will be the consequences of your decision?

figure 5.3

HOW TO FORM A PARTNERSHIP

It's not hard to form a partnership, but it's wise for each prospective partner to get the counsel of a lawyer experienced with such agreements. Lawyers' services are usually expensive, so would-be partners should read all about partnerships and reach some basic agreements before calling a lawyer.

For your protection, be sure to put your partnership agreement in writing. The Model Business Corporation Act recommends including the following in a written partnership agreement:

1. The name of the business. Many states require the firm's name to be registered with state and/or county officials if the firm's name is different from the name of any of the partners.

2. The names and addresses of all partners.

3. The purpose and nature of the business, the location of the principal offices, and any other locations where business will be conducted.

4. The date the partnership will start and how long it will last. Will it exist for a specific length of time, or will it stop when one of the partners dies or when the partners agree to discontinue?

5. The contributions made by each partner. Will some partners contribute money, while others provide real estate, personal property, expertise, or labor? When are the contributions due?

6. The management responsibilities. Will all partners have equal voices in management, or will there be senior and junior partners?

7. The duties of each partner.

8. The salaries and drawing accounts of each partner.

9. Provision for sharing of profits or losses.

10. Provision for accounting procedures. Who'll keep the accounts? What bookkeeping and accounting methods will be used? Where will the books be kept?

11. The requirements for taking in new partners.

12. Any special restrictions, rights, or duties of any partner.

13. Provision for a retiring partner.

14. Provision for the purchase of a deceased or retiring partner's share of the business.

15. Provision for how grievances will be handled.

16. Provision for how to dissolve the partnership and distribute the assets to the partners.

One fear of owning your own business or having a partner is the fear of losing everything you own if someone sues the business or it loses a lot of money. Many businesspeople try to avoid this and the other disadvantages of sole proprietorships and partnerships by forming corporations. We discuss this basic form of business ownership in the following section.

conventional (C) corporation
A state-chartered legal entity with authority to act and have liability separate from its owners.

progress assessment

- What is the difference between a limited partner and a general partner?
- What are some of the advantages and disadvantages of partnerships?

LEARNING goal 3

Compare the advantages and disadvantages of corporations, and summarize the differences between C corporations, S corporations, and limited liability companies.

CORPORATIONS

Many corporations—like General Electric, Microsoft, and Walmart—are big and contribute substantially to the U.S. economy. However, it's not necessary to be big to incorporate. Incorporating may be beneficial for small businesses as well.

A **conventional (C) corporation** is a state-chartered legal entity with authority to act and have liability separate from its owners—its *stockholders*. Stockholders are not liable for the debts or other problems of the corporation beyond the money they invest in it by buying ownership shares, or stock, in the company. They don't have to worry about losing their house, car, or other property because of some business problem—a significant benefit. A corporation not only limits the liability of owners but often enables many people to share in the ownership (and profits) of a business without working there or having other commitments to it.[9] Corporations may choose whether to offer ownership to outside investors or remain privately held. (We discuss stock ownership in Chapter 19.) Figure 5.4 describes various types of corporations.

Advantages of Corporations

Most people are not willing to risk everything to go into business. Yet for a business to grow, prosper, and create economic opportunity, many people have to be willing to invest money in it. One way to solve this problem is to create an artificial being, an entity that exists only in the eyes of the law—a corporation. Let's explore some of the advantages of corporations:

1. *Limited liability.* A major advantage of corporations is the limited liability of their owners. Remember, limited liability means that the owners of a business are responsible for its losses only up to the amount they invest in it.

2. *Ability to raise more money for investment.* To raise money, a corporation can sell shares of its stock to anyone who is interested. This means that millions of people can own part of major companies like IBM, Apple, and Coca-Cola, and smaller corporations as well. If a company sells 10 million

Burton Baskin and Irvine Robbins ran their ice cream businesses separately for two years. Once they had succeeded apart, Baskin and Robbins became partners and were able to avoid many of the pitfalls of starting a new business from scratch. They flipped a coin to see whose name would come first. What factors besides the partners' individual success do you think contributed to their long-lasting partnership?

figure 5.4

CORPORATE TYPES

Corporations can fit in more than one category.

You may find some confusing types of corporations when reading about them. Here are a few of the more widely used terms:

An *alien corporation* does business in the United States but is chartered (incorporated) in another country.

A *domestic corporation* does business in the state in which it's chartered (incorporated).

A *foreign corporation* does business in one state but is chartered in another. About one-third of all corporations are chartered in Delaware because of its relatively attractive rules for incorporation. A foreign corporation must register in states where it operates.

A *closed (private) corporation* is one whose stock is held by a few people and isn't available to the general public.

An *open (public) corporation* sells stock to the general public. General Motors and ExxonMobil are examples of public corporations.

A *quasi-public corporation* is a corporation chartered by the government as an approved monopoly to perform services to the general public. Public utilities are examples of quasi-public corporations.

A *professional corporation* is one whose owners offer professional services (doctors, lawyers, etc.). Shares in professional corporations aren't publicly traded.

A *nonprofit (or not-for-profit) corporation* is one that doesn't seek personal profit for its owners.

A *multinational corporation* is a firm that operates in several countries.

shares of stock for $50 a share, it will have $500 million available to build plants, buy materials, hire people, manufacture products, and so on. Such a large amount of money would be difficult to raise any other way.

Corporations can also borrow money by obtaining loans from financial institutions like banks. They can also borrow from individual investors by issuing bonds, which involve paying investors interest until the bonds are repaid sometime in the future.[10] You can read about how corporations raise funds through the sale of stocks and bonds in Chapter 19.

3. *Size.* "Size" summarizes many of the advantages of some corporations. Because they can raise large amounts of money to work with, big corporations can build modern factories or software development facilities with the latest equipment. They can hire experts or specialists in all areas of operation. They can buy other corporations in different fields to diversify their business risks. In short, a large corporation with numerous resources can take advantage of opportunities anywhere in the world.

But corporations do not have to be large to enjoy the benefits of incorporating. Many doctors, lawyers, and individuals, as well as partners in a variety of businesses, have incorporated. The vast majority of corporations in the United States are small businesses.

4. *Perpetual life.* Because corporations are separate from those who own them, the death of one or more owners does not terminate the corporation.

5. *Ease of ownership change.* It is easy to change the owners of a corporation. All that is necessary is to sell the stock to someone else.

6. *Ease of attracting talented employees.* Corporations can attract skilled employees by offering such benefits as stock options (the right to purchase shares of the corporation for a fixed price).

7. *Separation of ownership from management.* Corporations are able to raise money from many different owners/stockholders without getting them

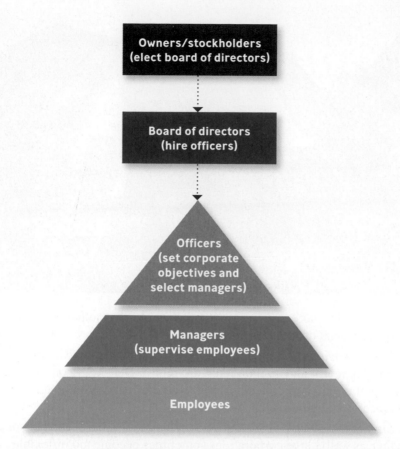

figure 5.5

HOW OWNERS AFFECT MANAGEMENT

Owners have an influence on how a business is managed by electing a board of directors. The board hires the top officers (and fires them if necessary). It also sets the pay for those officers. The officers then select managers and employees with the help of the human resources department.

involved in management. The corporate hierarchy in Figure 5.5 shows how the owners/stockholders are separate from the managers and employees. The owners/stockholders elect a board of directors, who hire the officers of the corporation and oversee major policy issues. The owners/stockholders thus have some say in who runs the corporation but have no real control over the daily operations.[11]

Disadvantages of Corporations

There are so many sole proprietorships and partnerships in the United States that there must be some disadvantages to incorporating. Otherwise, everyone would do it. The following are a few of the disadvantages:

1. *Initial cost.* Incorporation may cost thousands of dollars and require expensive lawyers and accountants. There are less expensive ways of incorporating in certain states (see the following subsection), but many people do not have the time or confidence to go through this procedure without the help of a potentially expensive lawyer.

2. *Extensive paperwork.* The paperwork needed to start a corporation is just the beginning. A sole proprietor or partnership may keep rather broad accounting records. A corporation, in contrast, must keep detailed financial records, the minutes of meetings, and more. As noted in Figure 5.4, many firms incorporate in Delaware or Nevada because these states' business-oriented laws make the process easier than it is in other states.

3. *Double taxation.* Corporate income is taxed twice. First the corporation pays tax on its income before it can distribute any, as *dividends,* to stockholders. Then the stockholders pay income tax on the dividends they receive.[12]

States often tax corporations more heavily than other enterprises, and some special taxes apply only to corporations.

4. *Two tax returns.* An individual who incorporates must file both a corporate tax return and an individual tax return. Depending on the size of the corporation, a corporate return can be quite complex and require the assistance of a certified public accountant (CPA).

5. *Size.* Size may be one advantage of corporations, but it can be a disadvantage as well. Large corporations sometimes become too inflexible and tied down in red tape to respond quickly to market changes, and their profitability can suffer.

6. *Difficulty of termination.* Once a corporation has started, it's relatively hard to end.

7. *Possible conflict with stockholders and board of directors.* Conflict may brew if the stockholders elect a board of directors who disagree with management. Since the board of directors chooses the company's officers, entrepreneurs serving as managers can find themselves forced out of the very company they founded. This happened to Tom Freston, one of the founders of MTV, and Steve Jobs, a founder of Apple Computer (Jobs of course returned to the company later).

Many businesspeople are discouraged by the costs, paperwork, and special taxes corporations must pay. However, many others believe the advantages of incorporation outweigh the hassles.

Individuals Can Incorporate

Not all corporations are large organizations with hundreds of employees and thousands of stockholders. Truckers, doctors, lawyers, plumbers, athletes, and small-business owners of all kinds can also incorporate. Normally, individuals who incorporate do not issue stock to outsiders; therefore, they do not share all the advantages and disadvantages of large corporations (such as size and more money for investment). Their major advantages are limited liability and possible tax benefits. Although you are not required to file for incorporation through a lawyer, it is usually wise to consult one. In addition to lawyers' fees, the secretary of state's office charges a fee for incorporating a business, varying by state from a low of

$50 (in Colorado, Iowa, Kentucky, Mississippi, and Oklahoma) to a high of $300 (in Texas).[13] Like the fee, the length of time it will take to actually have your business incorporated will vary by state. The average time is approximately 30 days from the date of application. Figure 5.6 outlines how to incorporate.

S Corporations

An **S corporation** is a unique government creation that looks like a corporation but is taxed like sole proprietorships and partnerships. (The name comes from the fact that the rules governing them are in Subchapter S of Chapter 1 of the Internal Revenue Code.) The paperwork and details of S corporations are similar to those of conventional (C) corporations. S corporations have shareholders, directors, and employees, and the benefit of limited liability, but their profits are taxed only as the personal income of the shareholders—thus avoiding the double taxation of C corporations.

Avoiding double taxation is reason enough for approximately 3 million U.S. companies to operate as S corporations. Yet not all businesses can become S corporations. In order to qualify, a company must:

1. Have no more than 100 shareholders. (All members of a family count as one shareholder.)

2. Have shareholders that are individuals or estates, and who (as individuals) are citizens or permanent residents of the United States.

3. Have only one class of stock. (You can read more about the various classes of stock in Chapter 19.)

4. Derive no more than 25 percent of income from passive sources (rents, royalties, interest).

An S corporation that loses its S status may not operate under it again for at least five years. The tax structure of S corporations isn't attractive to all businesses. For one thing, the benefits change every time the tax rules change. The best way to learn all the benefits or shortcomings for a specific business is to go over the tax advantages and liability differences with a lawyer, an accountant, or both.

S corporation
A unique government creation that looks like a corporation but is taxed like sole proprietorships and partnerships.

figure 5.6

HOW TO INCORPORATE

The process of forming a corporation varies somewhat from state to state. The articles of incorporation are usually filed with the secretary of state's office in the state in which the company incorporates. The articles contain:

- The corporation's name.
- The names of the people who incorporated it.
- Its purposes.
- Its duration (usually perpetual).
- The number of shares that can be issued, their voting rights, and any other rights the shareholders have.
- The corporation's minimum capital.
- The address of the corporation's office.
- The name and address of the person responsible for the corporation's legal service.
- The names and addresses of the first directors.
- Any other public information the incorporators wish to include.

Before a business can so much as open a bank account or hire employees, it needs a federal tax identification number. To apply for one, get an SS-4 form from the IRS.

In addition to the articles of incorporation listed, a corporation has bylaws. These describe how the firm is to be operated from both legal and managerial points of view. The bylaws include:

- How, when, and where shareholders' and directors' meetings are held, and how long directors are to serve.
- Directors' authority.
- Duties and responsibilities of officers, and the length of their service.
- How stock is issued.
- Other matters, including employment contracts.

Limited Liability Companies

A **limited liability company (LLC)** is similar to an S corporation, but without the special eligibility requirements. LLCs were introduced in Wyoming in 1977 and were recognized by the Internal Revenue Service as a partnership for federal income tax purposes in 1988. By 1996, all 50 states and the District of Columbia recognized LLCs.

The number of LLCs has risen dramatically since 1988, when there were fewer than 100 filings to operate them. Today more than half of new business registrations in some states are LLCs.

Why the drive toward forming LLCs? Advantages include:

1. *Limited liability.* Personal assets are protected. Limited liability was previously available only to limited partners and shareholders of C corporations.
2. *Choice of taxation.* LLCs can choose to be taxed as partnerships or as corporations. Partnership-level taxation was previously a benefit normally reserved for partners or S corporation owners.
3. *Flexible ownership rules.* LLCs do not have to comply with ownership restrictions as S corporations do. Owners can be a person, partnership, or corporation.
4. *Flexible distribution of profits and losses.* Profits and losses don't have to be distributed in proportion to the money each person invests, as in corporations. LLC members agree on the percentage to be distributed to each member.
5. *Operating flexibility.* LLCs do have to submit articles of organization, which are similar to articles of incorporation, but they are not required to keep minutes, file written resolutions, or hold annual meetings. An LLC also submits a written operating agreement, similar to a partnership agreement, describing how the company is to be operated.

Of course, LLCs have their disadvantages as well. These include:

1. *No stock.* LLC ownership is nontransferable. LLC members need the approval of the other members in order to sell their interests in the company. In contrast, regular and S corporation stockholders can sell their shares as they wish.
2. *Limited life span.* LLCs are required to identify dissolution dates in the articles of organization (no more than 30 years in some states). The death of a member can cause LLCs to dissolve automatically. Members may choose to reconstitute the LLC after it dissolves.

PetZen Products LLC offers doggie treadmills to help the nation's overweight pets get back their puppy figures. What are the advantages and disadvantages of LLCs?

3. *Fewer incentives.* Unlike corporations, LLCs can't deduct the cost of fringe benefits for members owning 2 percent or more of the company. And since there's no stock, they can't use stock options as incentives to employees.
4. *Taxes.* LLC members must pay self-employment taxes—the Medicare/Social Security taxes paid by sole proprietors and partnerships—on their profits. In contrast, S corporations pay self-employment tax on owners' salaries but not on the entire profits.
5. *Paperwork.* While the paperwork required of LLCs is not as great as that required of corporations, it is more than required of sole proprietors.

| | SOLE PROPRIETORSHIP | Partnerships | | Corporations | | |
		GENERAL PARTNERSHIP	LIMITED PARTNERSHIP	CONVENTIONAL CORPORATION	S CORPORATION	LIMITED LIABILITY COMPANY
Documents Needed to Start Business	None; may need permit or license	Partnership agreement (oral or written)	Written agreement; must file certificate of limited partnership	Articles of incorporation, bylaws	Articles of incorporation, bylaws, must meet criteria	Articles of organization and operating agreement; no eligibility requirements
Ease of Termination	Easy to terminate: just pay debts and quit	May be hard to terminate, depending on the partnership agreement	Same as general partnership	Hard and expensive to terminate	Same as conventional corporation	May be difficult, depending upon operating agreement
Length of Life	Terminates on the death of owner	Terminates on the death or withdrawal of partner	Same as general partnership	Perpetual life	Same as conventional corporation	Varies according to dissolution dates in articles of organization
Transfer of Ownership	Business can be sold to qualified buyer	Must have other partner(s)' agreement	Same as general partnership	Easy to change owners; just sell stock	Can sell stock, but with restrictions	Can't sell stock
Financial Resources	Limited to owner's capital and loans	Limited to partners' capital and loans	Same as general partnership	More money to start and operate; may sell stocks and bonds	Same as conventional corporation	Same as partnership
Risk of Losses	Unlimited liability	Unlimited liability	Limited liability	Limited liability	Limited liability	Limited liability
Taxes	Taxed as personal income	Taxed as personal income	Same as general partnership	Corporate, double taxation	Taxed as personal income	Varies
Management Responsibilities	Owner manages *all* areas of the business	Partners share management	Can't participate in management	Separate management from ownership	Same as conventional corporation	Varies
Employee Benefits	Usually fewer benefits and lower wages	Often fewer benefits and lower wages; promising employee could become a partner	Same as general partnership	Usually better benefits and wages, advancement opportunities	Same as conventional corporation	Varies, but are not tax deductible

The start-up cost for an LLC varies. Online legal services such as Legal Zoom (www.legalzoom.com) can file the necessary paperwork for as little as $150. Figure 5.7 summarizes the advantages and disadvantages of the major forms of business ownership.

figure 5.7

COMPARISON OF FORMS OF BUSINESS OWNERSHIP

- What are the major advantages and disadvantages of incorporating a business?
- What is the role of owners (stockholders) in the corporate hierarchy?
- If you buy stock in a corporation and someone gets injured by one of the corporation's products, can you be sued? Why or why not?
- Why are so many new businesses choosing a limited liability company (LLC) form of ownership?

merger
The result of two firms forming one company.

acquisition
One company's purchase of the property and obligations of another company.

vertical merger
The joining of two companies involved in different stages of related businesses.

horizontal merger
The joining of two firms in the same industry.

LEARNING goal 4

Define and give examples of three types of corporate mergers, and explain the role of leveraged buyouts and taking a firm private.

CORPORATE EXPANSION: MERGERS AND ACQUISITIONS

The merger mania of the late 1990s reached its peak in 2000, when the total spent on mergers and acquisitions hit a stunning $3.4 trillion and a new deal was being struck every 17 minutes. It seemed as though each deal made was intended to top the one before. Most of the new deals involved companies trying to expand within their own fields to save costs, enter new markets, position for global competition, or adapt to changing technologies or regulations. Those proved to be unattainable goals for many of the merged giants; two-thirds of mergers of the late 1990s failed to meet their goals. By 2009, the bleak U.S. economy caused the volume of mergers and acquisitions to plummet 86 percent. 2010 offered some renewed optimism as mergers increased 14 percent.[14]

What's the difference between mergers and acquisitions? A **merger** is the result of two firms joining to form one company. It is similar to a marriage, joining two individuals as one family. An **acquisition** is one company's purchase of the property and obligations of another company. It is more like buying a house than entering a marriage.

There are three major types of corporate mergers: vertical, horizontal, and conglomerate. A **vertical merger** joins two firms operating in different stages of related businesses. A merger between a soft drink company and an artificial sweetener maker would ensure the merged firm a constant supply of an ingredient the soft drink manufacturer needs. It could also help ensure quality control of the soft drink company's products.

A **horizontal merger** joins two firms in the same industry and allows them to diversify or expand their products. A soft drink company and a mineral water company that merge can now supply a variety of drinking products.

Mars, the maker of M&M's, acquired the Wm. Wrigley Jr. Company for $23 billion. What type of merger is this (vertical, horizontal, or conglomerate)?

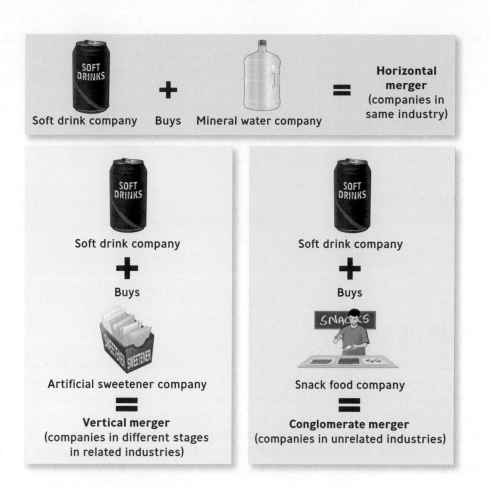

figure 5.8

TYPES OF MERGERS

A **conglomerate merger** unites firms in completely unrelated industries in order to diversify business operations and investments. A soft drink company and a snack food company would form a conglomerate merger. Figure 5.8 illustrates the differences among the three types of mergers.

Rather than merge or sell to another company, some corporations decide to maintain, or in some cases regain, control of a firm internally. By *taking a firm private,* management or a group of stockholders obtain all the firm's stock for themselves by buying it back from the other stockholders.[15] Burger King and Gymboree are firms that have been taken private. Suppose employees believe they may lose their jobs, or managers believe they could improve corporate performance if they owned the company. Does either group have an opportunity of taking ownership of the company? Yes—they might attempt a leveraged buyout.

A **leveraged buyout (LBO)** is an attempt by employees, management, or a group of private investors to buy out the stockholders in a company, primarily by borrowing the necessary funds. The employees, managers, or investors now become the owners of the firm. LBOs have ranged in size from $50 million to $31 billion and have involved everything from small family businesses to giant corporations like Hertz Corporation, Toys "R" Us, Chrysler, and the former RJR Nabisco.[16]

Today, business acquisitions are not limited to U.S. buyers. Foreign companies have found the fastest way to grow is often to buy an established operation that can enhance their technology or expand the number of brands they offer. Swiss drugmaker Roche paid $43 billion to take control of biotechnology giant Genentech.

conglomerate merger
The joining of firms in completely unrelated industries.

leveraged buyout (LBO)
An attempt by employees, management, or a group of investors to purchase an organization primarily through borrowing.

Belgium's InBev purchased the largest U.S. brewer, Anheuser-Busch and its Budweiser and Bud Light brands, for $52 billion. Number two brewer Miller Brewing Company was acquired by London-based SAB.[17] In 2010, foreign investors poured over $300 billion into U.S. companies.

However, such deals are not always welcomed. In 2005, U.S. lawmakers feared the proposed purchase of U.S. oil company Unocal by a Chinese oil company might threaten American economic and national security interests. CNOOC, the Chinese company, eventually withdrew its bid.

LEARNING goal 5

> Outline the advantages and disadvantages of franchises, and discuss the opportunities for diversity in franchising and the challenges of global franchising.

FRANCHISES

In addition to the three basic forms of business ownership, there are two special forms: franchises and cooperatives. Let's look at franchises first. A **franchise agreement** is an arrangement whereby someone with a good idea for a business (the **franchisor**) sells the rights to use the business name and sell a product or service (the **franchise**) to others (the **franchisees**) in a given territory.

Some people, uncomfortable with the idea of starting their own business from scratch, would rather join a business with a proven track record through a franchise agreement. A franchise can be formed as a sole proprietorship, a partnership, or a corporation. The U.S. Census Bureau estimates that one out of every ten businesses in the United States is a franchise.[18] Some of the best-known franchises are McDonald's, Jiffy Lube, 7-Eleven, Weight Watchers, and Holiday Inn.

According to the International Franchise Association, the more than 750,000 franchised businesses operating in the United States create approximately 8 million jobs that produce a direct and indirect economic impact of $782 billion in the U.S. economy.[19] The most popular businesses for franchising are restaurants (fast food and full service) and gas stations with convenience stores.[20] McDonald's, the largest restaurant chain in the United States in terms of sales, is often considered the gold standard of franchising.[21] Retail stores, financial

franchise agreement
An arrangement whereby someone with a good idea for a business sells the rights to use the business name and sell a product or service to others in a given territory.

franchisor
A company that develops a product concept and sells others the rights to make and sell the products.

franchise
The right to use a specific business's name and sell its products or services in a given territory.

franchisee
A person who buys a franchise.

Door-to-Door Dry Cleaning franchises are the brainchild of John Dame and his wife Joey. All franchisees need to get started is a truck to make pickups and deliveries, and a contract with a local dry cleaner. Start-up costs can be as low as $40,000 and profits as high as 26 percent. The Dames provide two weeks of training and plenty of online support. What type of service franchise might appeal to you as a business owner?

services, health clubs, hotels and motels, and automotive parts and service centers are also popular franchised businesses. Today a fast-growing franchise sector is senior care. In fact, *Entrepreneur* magazine's 2011 list of 100 fastest-growing franchises included eight senior care concepts.[22] With roughly 40 million seniors in the United States today and projections the number will double in the next 20 years, it's a market that is not going to disappear. See Figure 5.9 for some tips on evaluating franchises.

figure 5.9

BUYING A FRANCHISE

Since buying a franchise is a major investment, be sure to check out a company's financial strength before you get involved. Watch out for scams too. Scams called *bust-outs* usually involve people coming to town, renting nice offices, taking out ads, and persuading people to invest. Then they disappear with the investors' money. For example, in San Francisco a company called T.B.S. Inc. sold distributorships for in-home AIDS tests. It promised an enormous market and potential profits of $3,000 for an investment of less than $200. The "test" turned out to be nothing more than a mail-order questionnaire about lifestyle.

A good source of information about evaluating a franchise deal is the handbook *Investigate before Investing,* available from International Franchise Association Publications.

Checklist for Evaluating a Franchise

The Franchise

Did your lawyer approve the franchise contract you're considering after he or she studied it paragraph by paragraph?

Does the franchise give you an exclusive territory for the length of the franchise?

Under what circumstances can you terminate the franchise contract and at what cost to you?

If you sell your franchise, will you be compensated for your goodwill (the value of your business's reputation and other intangibles)?

If the franchisor sells the company, will your investment be protected?

The Franchisor

How many years has the firm offering you a franchise been in operation?

Does it have a reputation for honesty and fair dealing among the local firms holding its franchise?

Has the franchisor shown you any certified figures indicating exact net profits of one or more going firms that you personally checked yourself with the franchisee? Ask for the company's disclosure statement.

Will the firm assist you with

A management training program?

An employee training program?

A public relations program?

Capital?

Credit?

Merchandising ideas?

Will the firm help you find a good location for your new business?

Has the franchisor investigated you carefully enough to assure itself that you can successfully operate one of its franchises at a profit both to itself and to you?

You, the Franchisee

How much equity capital will you need to purchase the franchise and operate it until your income equals your expenses?

Does the franchisor offer financing for a portion of the franchising fees? On what terms?

Are you prepared to give up some independence of action to secure the advantages offered by the franchise? Do you have your family's support?

Does the industry appeal to you? Are you ready to spend much or all of the remainder of your business life with this franchisor, offering its product or service to the public?

Your Market

Have you made any study to determine whether the product or service that you propose to sell under the franchise has a market in your territory at the prices you'll have to charge?

Will the population in the territory given to you increase, remain static, or decrease over the next five years?

Will demand for the product or service you're considering be greater, about the same, or less five years from now than it is today?

What competition already exists in your territory for the product or service you contemplate selling?

Sources: U.S. Department of Commerce, *Franchise Opportunities Handbook;* and Steve Adams, "Buying a Brand," *Patriot Ledger* (Quincy, MA), March 1, 2008.

Advantages of Franchises

Franchising has penetrated every aspect of U.S. and global business life by offering products and services that are reliable, convenient, and competitively priced. Franchising clearly has some advantages:

1. *Management and marketing assistance.* Compared with someone who starts a business from scratch, a franchisee usually has a much greater chance of succeeding because he or she has an established product to sell, help choosing a location, and assistance in all phases of promotion and operation. It's like having your own store but with full-time consultants when you need them. Franchisors usually provide intensive training. For example, McDonald's sends all new franchisees and managers to Hamburger University in Oak Brook, Illinois.[23]

    Some franchisors help their franchisees with local marketing efforts rather than having them depend solely on national advertising. Franchisees also have a network of fellow franchisees facing similar problems who can share their experiences. The UPS Store provides its more than 4,500 franchisees with a software program that helps them build customer databases along with quick and personal one-on-one phone and e-mail support.

2. *Personal ownership.* A franchise operation is still your business, and you enjoy as much of the incentives and profit as any sole proprietor would. You are still your own boss, although you must follow more rules, regulations, and procedures than with your own privately owned business.

3. *Nationally recognized name.* It is one thing to open a gift shop or an ice cream store. It is quite another to open a new Hallmark store or a Baskin-Robbins. With an established franchise, you get instant recognition and support from a product group with established customers around the world.

4. *Financial advice and assistance.* Two major problems for small-business owners are arranging financing and learning to keep good records. Franchisees often get valuable assistance and periodic advice from people with expertise in these areas. In fact, some franchisors provide financing to potential franchisees they feel will be valuable parts of the franchise system. For example, Merry Maids, a leader in the maid service business, offers up to 80 percent financial assistance with their franchise fee to promising franchisees.

5. *Lower failure rate.* Historically, the failure rate for franchises has been lower than that of other business ventures. However, franchising has grown so rapidly that many weak franchises have entered the field, so you need to be careful and invest wisely.

Disadvantages of Franchises

There are, however, some potential pitfalls to franchising. Check out any franchise arrangement with present franchisees and discuss the idea with an attorney and an accountant. Disadvantages of franchises include the following:

1. *Large start-up costs.* Most franchises demand a fee for the rights to the franchise. Start-up costs for a Jazzercise franchise range from $3,000, but if it's Dunkin' Donuts you're after, you'd better have a lot more dough— approximately $2 million.[24]

2. *Shared profit.* The franchisor often demands either a large share of the profits in addition to the start-up fees or a percentage commission based on sales, not profit. This share is called a *royalty.* For example, if a franchisor demands a 10 percent royalty on a franchise's net sales, 10 cents of every dollar the franchisee collects (before taxes and other expenses) must be paid to the franchisor.

3. *Management regulation.* Management "assistance" has a way of becoming managerial orders, directives, and limitations. Franchisees feeling burdened by the company's rules and regulations may lose the drive to run their own business. Often franchisees will band together to resolve their grievances with franchisors rather than fighting their battles alone. For example, in 2010 the KFC National Council & Advertising Cooperative, which represents all U.S. franchisees, sued KFC to gain control of advertising strategies. The franchisees were angry over Yum! Brands' (owners of KFC) decision to implement an ad strategy that emphasized a shift to grilled chicken rather than fried chicken. The campaign centered around the slogan "Unthink KFC," which was exactly what customers did. Sales plummeted 7 percent that quarter and franchisees had to throw away up to 50 percent of their grilled chicken supplies.[25] In another case, Burger King franchisees filed suit over whether the franchisor could impose $1 pricing on them for double cheeseburgers they claim lost them money.[26]

4. *Coattail effects.* What happens to your franchise if fellow franchisees fail? The actions of other franchises have an impact on your future growth and profitability. Due to this *coattail effect,* you could be forced out of business even if your particular franchise has been profitable. For example, the customer passion for high-flying franchisor Krispy Kreme in the early 2000s sank as the market became flooded with new stores and the availability of the product at retail locations caused overexposure. McDonald's and Subway franchisees complain that due to the company's relentless growth, some new stores have taken business away from existing locations, squeezing franchisees' profits per outlet.

Judi Sheppard Missett started a dance-fitness program called Jazzercise in 1969. The worldwide franchise company now takes fitness-minded adults and kids in 32 countries through weekly classes blending jazz dance, resistance training, Pilates, yoga and kickboxing moves choreographed to the latest popular music. Jazzercise is consistently listed among Entrepreneur magazine's top 20 franchises. What accounts for its appeal?

Keeping Franchises in the Family

When entrepreneurs operate franchises, they attach their existing business skills to established brand names. In this way, franchises are like big family businesses. The parent company has laid the groundwork for the brand, and every person running a franchise contributes to the company's image.

But what happens when franchises literally become a family affair? With a poor job market and banks still afraid to lend, more people are joining up with family members who are making a good living in franchising. While working with family can be stressful, open communication from all parties usually leads to a more accepting environment than in standard company cultures. In fact, for many people the problem about family franchising isn't what happens while the shop is open. After all, franchises aren't like standard mom-and-pop stores since the franchisor owns many aspects of the business, including the rights to the company name. So while a family can spend their whole lives building a successful franchise, once the franchisee dies it's often up to the franchisor to determine its successor.

However, it's certainly possible for franchisees to pass their businesses down to their kids. They must simply act in advance before the worst happens. For instance, Glenn and Martha Dodd operated a Fastsigns franchise in Houston since 1994. Once their children expressed interest in carrying on the family legacy, the Dodds reached out to the corporate office to enroll the kids in the necessary ownership courses. They easily qualified for ownership since they worked in their parents' copy shop for most of their lives.

The process isn't so easy everywhere, though. Brent Upchurch similarly spent his formative years in his father's McDonald's stores. When he was ready to take the leap into ownership, he had to begin an 11-year apprenticeship where he worked in every imaginable position at McDonald's. Even after he earned approval for ownership, he had to wait another three years before he was granted a majority stake. Such a rigorous vetting process ensures that whoever takes control of the business will actually know what they are doing. This often makes succession in franchises more successful than with pure family operations.

Sources: Jason Daley, "How to Create a Succession Plan for a Franchise Business," *Entrepreneur,* December 2, 2011; and Rob McKinlay, "Keep It in the Family," *Business Franchise,* accessed May 4, 2012.

---

5. *Restrictions on selling.* Unlike owners of private businesses, who can sell their companies to whomever they choose on their own terms, many franchisees face restrictions on the resale of their franchises. To control quality, franchisors often insist on approving the new owner, who must meet their standards. The Connecting with Small Business box discusses the difficulty of passing ownership of a franchise on to family members.

6. *Fraudulent franchisors.* Most franchisors are not large systems like McDonald's and Subway. Many are small, rather obscure companies that prospective franchisees may know little about. Most are honest, but complaints to the Federal Trade Commission have increased about franchisors that delivered little or nothing of what they promised. Before you buy a franchise, make certain you check out the facts fully and remember the old adage "You get what you pay for."

Diversity in Franchising

A lingering issue in franchising is the number of women who own franchises. While women own about half of all U.S. companies and are opening businesses at double the rate of men, their ownership of franchises is about 25 percent.[27] Some think there is not so much a glass ceiling for women as a green ceiling—lack of money. Many experts believe more needs to be done to educate women business owners about the opportunities and forms of financing available for franchise growth. The International Franchise Association has increased its efforts to attract more women into franchising.[28]

Women are getting the message. In fact, women aren't just franchisees anymore; they're becoming franchisors as well. Women are finding if they face difficulty getting financing for growing their business, turning to franchisees to help carry expansion costs can help. For example, top-rated franchise companies Auntie Anne's, Decorating Den, and Jazzercise are owned by women.

Minority-owned businesses are growing at more than six times the national rate. Franchisors are becoming more focused on recruiting minority franchisees. MinorityFran is an initiative by the International Franchise Association to build awareness of franchising opportunities within minority communities. The U.S. Commerce Department's Federal Minority Business Development Agency provides aspiring minority business owners with training in how to run franchises. Domino's Pizza launched a minority franchisee recruitment program called Delivering the Dream. The company provides financial support and a financing partner to help budding franchisees "realize their dream."

Today over 20 percent of franchises are owned by African Americans, Latinos, Asians, and Native Americans. Franchising opportunities seem perfectly attuned to the needs of aspiring minority businesspeople. For example, Junior Bridgeman was a basketball star in college and enjoyed a stellar career with the Milwaukee Bucks and Los Angeles Clippers in the NBA. He transferred his dedication on the court to dedication to building Bridgeman Foods. His company now owns several Wendy's franchises and runs 162 other Wendy's restaurants.[29]

Home-Based Franchises

Home-based businesses offer many obvious advantages, including relief from the stress of commuting, extra time for family activities, and low overhead expenses. One disadvantage is the feeling of isolation. Compared to home-based entrepreneurs, home-based franchisees feel less isolated. Experienced franchisors often share their knowledge of building a profitable enterprise with other franchisees.

Home-based franchises can be started for as little as $5,000. Today you can be a franchisee in areas ranging from cleaning services to tax preparation, child care, pet care, or direct mail services. But don't get the idea working at home is easy. Home-based franchisee Ralph Santisteban was excited by the challenge when he bought his CruiseOne franchise. What he didn't expect was the 12 to 14 hours per day he put in to get the business going.[30] Before investing in a home-based franchise it is helpful to ask yourself the following questions: Are you willing to put in long hours? Can you work in a solitary environment? Are you motivated and well organized? Does your home have the space you need for the business? Can your home also be the place you work? It's also important to check out the franchisor carefully.

E-Commerce in Franchising

The Internet has changed franchising in many ways. Most brick-and-mortar franchises have expanded their businesses online and created virtual storefronts to deliver increased value to customers. Franchisees like Carole Shutts, a Rocky Mountain Chocolate Factory franchisee in Galena, Illinois, increased her sales by setting up her own website. Many franchisors, however, prohibit franchisee-sponsored

Holiday Inn's InterContinental Amstel hotel in Amsterdam has been celebrated as the Netherlands' most beautiful and luxurious hotel. Holiday Inn franchises try to complement the environment of the area they serve. This hotel is on the crossroads of Amsterdam's financial and exclusive shopping districts. What do you think would have been the reaction if Holiday Inn had built the typical U.S.-style Holiday Inn in this area?

websites because conflicts can erupt if the franchisor creates its own website. Sometimes franchisors send "reverse royalties" to franchisees who believe their sales were hurt by the franchisor's Internet sales, but that doesn't always bring about peace. Before buying a franchise, read the small print regarding online sales.

Today potential franchisees can make a choice between starting an online business or a business requiring an office or storefront outside of the home.[31] Quite often the decision comes down to financing. Traditional brick-and-mortar franchises require finding real estate and often require a high franchise fee. Online franchises like Printinginabox.com charge no up-front franchise fee and require little training to start a business. Franchisees pay only a set monthly fee. Online franchises also do not set exclusive territories limiting where the franchisee can compete. An online franchisee can literally compete against the world.[32]

Using Technology in Franchising

Franchisors often use technology, including social media, to extend their brands, to meet the needs of both their customers and their franchisees, and even to expand their businesses.[33] For example, Candy Bouquet International, Inc., of Little Rock, Arkansas, offers franchises that sell candies in flowerlike arrangements. Franchisees have brick-and-mortar locations to serve walk-in customers, but they also are provided leads from the company's main website. All franchisees are kept up-to-date daily on company news via e-mail, and they use a chat room to discuss issues and product ideas with each other. The company has found the Internet a great way of disseminating information that is revolutionizing franchisor support and franchisee communications. Candy Bouquet plans international expansion in the near future.

Some franchisors use social media not only to reach customers and current franchisees, but also to recruit new franchisees. See the Connecting Through Social Media box for an example of a company using a Facebook game to attract potential franchisees.

Franchising in Global Markets

Franchising today is truly a global effort. U.S. franchisors are counting their profits in euros, yuan, pesos, won, krona, baht, yen, and many other currencies. McDonald's has more than 33,000 restaurants in 119 countries serving over 68 million customers each day.[34]

Because of its proximity and shared language, Canada is the most popular target for U.S.-based franchises. Franchisors are finding it surprisingly easier now to move into China, South Africa, the Philippines, and the Middle East. Plus it's not just the large franchises like Subway and Marriott Hotels making the move. Newer, smaller franchises are going global as well. Auntie Anne's sells hand-rolled pretzels in 22 different countries including Indonesia, Malaysia, the Philippines, Singapore, Venezuela, and Thailand. Build-A-Bear Workshops has 63 franchisees in 12 countries including South Africa and the United Arab Emirates.[35] In 2005, 29-year-old Matthew Corrin launched Freshii, a sandwich, salad, and soup restaurant with fresh affordable food in trendy locations. He already has 45 locations in four countries with a new store in India on the horizon.[36]

What makes franchising successful in global markets is what makes it successful in the United States: convenience and a predictable level of service and quality. Franchisors, though, must be careful and do their homework before entering into global franchise agreements. Three questions to ask before forming a global franchise are: Will your intellectual property be protected? Can you give proper support to global partners? Are you able to adapt to franchise regulations in other countries? If the answer is yes to all three questions, global franchising creates great opportunities. It's also important to remember that adapting products and brand names to different countries creates challenges. In France, people thought a furniture-stripping franchise called Dip 'N' Strip was a bar that featured strippers.

Just as McDonald's and Subway have exported golden arches and sub sandwiches worldwide, foreign franchises see the United States as a popular target. Japanese franchises like Kumon Learning Centers and Canadian franchises like tax preparer H&R Block are very active in the United States.[37] H&R Block even has its headquarters in Kansas City, Missouri. Other franchises are hoping to change our tastes here. Ly Qui Trung would like to see his Pho24 noodle bars become a part of the American landscape and Canada's Yogen Früz frozen yogurt wants us to eat healthier desserts.

LEARNING goal 6

Explain the role of cooperatives.

COOPERATIVES

Some people dislike the notion of owners, managers, workers, and buyers being separate individuals with separate goals, so they have formed cooperatives, a different kind of organization to meet their needs for electricity, child care, housing, health

cooperative
A business owned and controlled by the people who use it—producers, consumers, or workers with similar needs who pool their resources for mutual gain.

care, food, and financial services. A **cooperative,** or co-op, is owned and controlled by the people who use it—producers, consumers, or workers with similar needs who pool their resources for mutual gain. In many rural parts of the country, for example, the government sells wholesale power to electric cooperatives at rates 40 to 50 percent below the rates nonfederal utilities charge. Electric cooperatives serve 42 million U.S. consumer-members in 47 states—or 12 percent of the population.

Worldwide, some 750,000 cooperatives serve 730 million members—120 million of them in the United States.[38] Members democratically control these businesses by electing a board of directors that hires professional management. Some co-ops ask members/customers to work for a number of hours a month as part of their membership duties. You may have one of the country's 4,000 food co-ops near you. If so, stop by and chat to learn more about this growing aspect of the U.S. economy. If you are interested in knowing more about cooperatives, contact the National Cooperative Business Association at 202-638-6222 or visit its website at www.ncba.coop.

Another kind of cooperative in the United States is formed to give members more economic power as a group than they have as individuals.[39] The best example is a farm cooperative. The goal at first was for farmers to join together to get better prices for their food products. Eventually the idea expanded, and farm cooperatives now buy and sell fertilizer, farm equipment, seed, and other products in a multibillion-dollar industry. Cooperatives have an advantage in the marketplace because they don't pay the same kind of taxes corporations pay.

Cooperatives are still a major force in agriculture and other industries today. Some top co-ops have familiar names such as Land O' Lakes, Sunkist, Ocean Spray, Blue Diamond, Associated Press, Ace Hardware, True Value Hardware, Riceland Foods, and Welch's.

WHICH FORM OF OWNERSHIP IS FOR YOU?

You can build your own business in a variety of ways. You can start your own sole proprietorship, partnership, corporation, LLC, or cooperative—or you can buy a franchise and be part of a larger corporation. There are advantages and disadvantages to each. Before you decide which form is for you, evaluate all the alternatives carefully.

The miracle of free enterprise is that the freedom and incentives of capitalism make risks acceptable to many people who go on to create the great corporations of America. You know many of their names and companies: James Cash Penney (JCPenney), Steve Jobs (Apple Computer), Sam Walton (Walmart), Levi Strauss (Levi Strauss), Henry Ford (Ford Motor Company), Thomas Edison (General Electric), Bill Gates (Microsoft), and so on. They started small, accumulated capital, grew, and became industrial leaders. Could you do the same?

progress assessment

- What are some of the factors to consider before buying a franchise?
- What opportunities are available for starting a global franchise?
- What is a cooperative?

summary

Learning Goal 1. Compare the advantages and disadvantages of sole proprietorships.

- **What are the advantages and disadvantages of sole proprietorships?**

The advantages of sole proprietorships include ease of starting and ending, ability to be your own boss, pride of ownership, retention of profit, and no special taxes. The disadvantages include unlimited liability, limited financial resources, difficulty in management, overwhelming time commitment, few fringe benefits, limited growth, and limited life span.

Learning Goal 2. Describe the differences between general and limited partners, and compare the advantages and disadvantages of partnerships.

- **What are the three key elements of a general partnership?**

The three key elements of a general partnership are common ownership, shared profits and losses, and the right to participate in managing the operations of the business.

- **What are the main differences between general and limited partners?**

General partners are owners (partners) who have unlimited liability and are active in managing the company. Limited partners are owners (partners) who have limited liability and are not active in the company.

- **What does *unlimited liability* mean?**

Unlimited liability means that sole proprietors and general partners must pay all debts and damages caused by their business. They may have to sell their houses, cars, or other personal possessions to pay business debts.

- **What does *limited liability* mean?**

Limited liability means that corporate owners (stockholders) and limited partners are responsible for losses only up to the amount they invest. Their other personal property is not at risk.

- **What is a master limited partnership?**

A master limited partnership is a partnership that acts like a corporation but is taxed like a partnership.

- **What are the advantages and disadvantages of partnerships?**

The advantages include more financial resources, shared management and pooled knowledge, and longer survival. The disadvantages include unlimited liability, division of profits, disagreements among partners, and difficulty of termination.

Learning Goal 3. Compare the advantages and disadvantages of corporations, and summarize the differences between C corporations, S corporations, and limited liability companies.

- **What is the definition of a corporation?**

A corporation is a state-chartered legal entity with authority to act and have liability separate from its owners.

- **What are the advantages and disadvantages of corporations?**

The advantages include more money for investment, limited liability, size, perpetual life, ease of ownership change, ease of drawing talented employees, and separation of ownership from management. The disadvantages include initial cost, paperwork, size, difficulty in termination, double taxation, and possible conflict with a board of directors.

- **Why do people incorporate?**

Two important reasons for incorporating are special tax advantages and limited liability.

- **What are the advantages of S corporations?**

S corporations have the advantages of limited liability (like a corporation) and simpler taxes (like a partnership). To qualify for S corporation status, a company must have fewer than 100 stockholders (members of a family count as one shareholder), its stockholders must be individuals or estates and U.S. citizens or permanent residents, and the company cannot derive more than 25 percent of its income from passive sources.

- **What are the advantages of limited liability companies?**

Limited liability companies have the advantage of limited liability without the hassles of forming a corporation or the limitations imposed by S corporations. LLCs may choose whether to be taxed as partnerships or corporations.

Learning Goal 4. Define and give examples of three types of corporate mergers, and explain the role of leveraged buyouts and taking a firm private.

- **What is a merger?**

A merger is the result of two firms forming one company. The three major types are vertical mergers, horizontal mergers, and conglomerate mergers.

- **What are leveraged buyouts, and what does it mean to take a company private?**

Leveraged buyouts are attempts by managers and employees to borrow money and purchase the company. Individuals who, together or alone, buy all the stock for themselves are said to take the company private.

Learning Goal 5. Outline the advantages and disadvantages of franchises, and discuss the opportunities for diversity in franchising and the challenges of global franchising.

- **What is a franchise?**

An arrangement to buy the rights to use the business name and sell its products or services in a given territory is called a franchise.

- **What is a franchisee?**

A franchisee is a person who buys a franchise.

- **What are the benefits and drawbacks of being a franchisee?**

The benefits include getting a nationally recognized name and reputation, a proven management system, promotional assistance, and pride of ownership. Drawbacks include high franchise fees, managerial regulation, shared profits, and transfer of adverse effects if other franchisees fail.

- **What is the major challenge to global franchises?**

It is often difficult to transfer an idea or product that worked well in the United States to another culture. It is essential to adapt to the region.

Learning Goal 6. Explain the role of cooperatives.

- **What is the role of a cooperative?**

Cooperatives are organizations owned by members/customers. Some people form cooperatives to acquire more economic power than they would have as individuals. Small businesses often form cooperatives to gain more purchasing, marketing, or product development strength.

key terms

acquisition 136	general partner 125	limited partnership 125
conglomerate merger 137	general partnership 125	master limited partnership (MLP) 125
conventional (C) corporation 129	horizontal merger 136	merger 136
cooperative 146	leveraged buyout (LBO) 137	partnership 122
corporation 122	limited liability 125	S corporation 133
franchise 138	limited liability company (LLC) 134	sole proprietorship 122
franchise agreement 138	limited liability partnership (LLP) 125	unlimited liability 124
franchisee 138	limited partner 125	vertical merger 136
franchisor 138		

critical thinking

Imagine you are considering starting your own business.

1. What kinds of products or services will you offer?
2. What talents or skills do you need to run the business?
3. Do you have all the skills and resources to start the business, or will you need to find one or more partners? If so, what skills would your partners need to have?
4. What form of business ownership would you choose—sole proprietorship, partnership, C corporation, S corporation, or LLC? Why?

developing workplace skills

1. Research businesses in your area and identify sole proprietorships, partnerships, corporations, and franchises. Arrange interviews with managers using each form of ownership and get their impressions, hints, and warnings. (If you are able to work with a team of fellow students, divide the interviews among team members.) How much does it cost to start? How many hours do they work? What are the specific benefits? Share the results with your class.

2. Have you thought about starting your own business? What opportunities seem attractive? Think of a friend or friends whom you might want for a partner or partners in the business. List all the financial resources and personal skills you will need to launch the business. Then make separate lists of the personal skills and the financial resources that you and your friend(s) might bring to your new venture. How much capital and what personal skills will be needed beyond those you already have? Develop an action plan for needed capital.

3. Let's assume you want to open one of the following new businesses. What form of business ownership would you choose for each? Why?

   a. Video game rental store.

   b. Wedding planning service.

    c. Software development firm.

    d. Online bookstore.

4. Successful businesses continually change hands. Methods of change discussed in this chapter include mergers, acquisitions, taking a firm private, and using leveraged buyouts. Search for an article online that illustrates how one of these methods changed an organization. What led to the change? How did this change affect the company's stakeholders? What benefits did the change provide? What new challenges were created?

5. Find information online about a business cooperative (e.g., Welch's, Land O' Lakes, Sunkist). Research how it was formed, who can belong to it, and how it operates.

taking it to the net

Purpose

To explore franchising opportunities and to evaluate the strengths and weaknesses of a selected franchise.

Exercise

Go to Franchise Expo (**www.franchiseexpo.com**).

1. Use the search tool to find a franchise that has the potential of fulfilling your entrepreneurial dreams. Navigate to the profile of the franchise you selected. Explore the franchise's website if a link is available. Refer to the questions listed in Figure 5.9 in this chapter and assess the strengths and weaknesses of your selected franchise. (Hint: The website also contains tips for evaluating a franchise listing.)

2. Did your search give you enough information to answer most of the questions in Figure 5.9? If not, what other information do you need, and where can you obtain it?

casing the web

To access the case "Stopped Cold," visit **www.mhhe.com/P2P2e**

PODS: The Evolution of a Small Business

The moving and storage industry has been revolutionized over the last 10 years by PODS. The company had its origins with firefighters who would create temporary storage units to hold people's personal possessions after a fire partially damaged their home. These units were large containers covered by tarps located in front of the damaged house. Though not very sophisticated, the tarp-covered containers spawned the entrepreneurial creation of the PODS container. The company began as a sole proprietorship, largely funded through venture capital for its development and growth. Bank financing was not possible in the early stages of the PODS business model.

Located in Clearwater, Florida, PODS has serviced over 240 million consumers, facilitated 250,000 long-distance relocations, has made over 1 million deliveries of container units, and currently has over 140,000 containers in service. The PODS container provides people the opportunity to store their possessions for as long as they wish, and when ready to relocate, the container is moved to the new location. In essence, PODS revolutionized moving by introducing flexibility and convenience to consumers to move the way they want and when they want.

PODS began as a sole proprietorship and relied on venture capital for its growth. The company was not favorably viewed as an investment for traditional bank debt financing, given the capital-intensive nature of the business. The collateral (storage containers) did not have a secondary market in case of default. The company evolved to a franchise model with operations in the United States, Canada, and Australia. Smaller cities or markets are franchised, whereas larger cities such as Chicago are reserved for corporate operations.

The company enjoys an innovator advantage in the moving and storage industry. Today, the company has grown to 132 franchise markets. The requirements for a PODS franchise include the $250,000 franchise fee providing exclusivity of the territory and a substantial investment in containers, averaging $2,500 per storage unit.

Thinking It Over

1. *Identify the three forms of business ownership.*

2. *Why did PODS rely on venture capital to fund its expansion to a franchise operation?*

3. *What types of questions does an entrepreneur typically ask before starting a business?*

Entrepreneurship and STARTING A Small Business

LEARNING goals

After you have read and studied this chapter, you should be able to

1 Explain why people take the risks of entrepreneurship; list the attributes of successful entrepreneurs; and describe entrepreneurial teams, intrapreneurs, and home- and web-based businesses.

2 Discuss the importance of small business to the American economy and summarize the major causes of small-business failure.

3 Summarize ways to learn about how small businesses operate.

4 Analyze what it takes to start and run a small business.

5 Outline the advantages and disadvantages small businesses have in entering global markets.

profile

Entrepreneurs often get business ideas from their own day-to-day experiences. For Aviva Weiss, her job as an occupational therapist brought her into contact with many products designed for special needs kids. Although she sometimes noticed design flaws, Weiss didn't start paying close attention to the poor quality of these products until her daughter was diagnosed with a sensory disorder. As a child who was overstimulated by her environment, Weiss's daughter needed a special weighted vest to help her focus. But when Weiss received the vest in the mail she couldn't believe her eyes. "It was superugly," she says. "I thought, 'There's no reason that special-needs products should make kids stand out even more.'"

Soon Weiss started making "humanized" versions of the vest that looked more like something from the Gap instead of a clinical special needs catalog. As she broke into redesigning clothes and other products, she and her husband Haskel, an educator, started to explore the market. The two realized they had found a relatively untapped niche and set out to learn more about business. They attended trade shows, consulted with experts, and took business classes at the nearby Wharton School of the University of Pennsylvania. After tapping into their savings and borrowing funds from family members, the Weisses founded their company, Fun and Function, in 2005.

Initially the company sold all of its products from a 120-page catalog. By 2007, Fun and Function was doing well enough for the Weisses to start selling online and to wholesalers. The expansion put additional stress on the Weisses, however, as the two continued to work full-time jobs while raising five children. With so many things going on in their lives at once, they made rookie mistakes like underpricing items and laying out their catalog's design poorly. In 2008, Aviva Weiss decided to try to limit the stress by leaving her job as an occupational therapist in order to focus solely on running the company from home. Her dedication paid off as Fun and Function grew seven-fold from 2007 to 2010. By 2011, the company's total sales climbed to almost $2 million.

Today Fun and Function sells everything from clothing to games, toys, and other learning tools. One important lesson that Weiss learned is that her company needs to keep branching out into new areas in order to grow. She recently launched an offshoot of Fun and Function called By Kids Only. This online service allows children to submit their own clothing designs and then vote on which designs get chosen for production. While the clothes can be purchased for any child,

CONNECTING WITH

Aviva Weiss

Co-Founder of Fun and Function

Weiss always keeps the needs of children with developmental disabilities at the forefront of her thoughts. By Kids Only's clothing fits snugly since it helps autistic children to feel grounded. The clothes are also tagless, seamless, and made of the softest material possible so they don't aggravate any children with sensory disorders.

Weiss became concerned that Fun and Function's growth might result in the loss of the personal touch that has made her work so successful. In 2010 the Weisses hired a couple of people from outside the family with expertise in the special needs market. One of these employees advised Weiss to focus more on customers at schools and therapy centers, since institutional customers typically place large, reoccurring orders. This went against Weiss's initial business model of making products to express individuality and fun. After careful consideration, though, Weiss knew she had to take the risk. Now Fun and Function's catalog places a special focus on schools, including tools for electronic learning. Although it will take a while to determine if Weiss's risky move worked, her response to such a tough decision shows that she has what it takes to be a successful entrepreneur.

Stories about people who take risks, like Aviva Weiss, are commonplace in this age of the entrepreneur. As you read about such risk takers in this chapter, maybe you'll be inspired to become an entrepreneur yourself.

Sources: Adam Bluestein, "Case Study: Targeting the Right Market," *Inc.*, October 2011; Deborah L. Cohen, "Mother's Care for Special Needs Kids Sparks Business," *Reuters*, September 7, 2011; and Patricia Dove, "Website Gives Kids Chance to Design Their Own Clothes," *Gloucester County Times*, July 18, 2011.

entrepreneurship
Accepting the risk of starting and running a business.

Wacky grocer Jim Bonaminio may put on his wizard suit and roller-skate through his Jungle Jim's International Market, but he's serious when it comes to his business. Instead of competing on price against Walmart, Jungle Jim's competes on product variety. A case holding 1,200 kinds of hot sauce rests beneath an antique fire engine. Why do you think customers might remain loyal to Jungle Jim's?

THE AGE OF THE ENTREPRENEUR

Today most young people know it's unlikely they will get a job in a large corporation and stay 30 years. For those who want more control over their destiny, working in or starting a small business makes sense. **Entrepreneurship** is accepting the risk of starting and running a business. Explore this chapter and think about the possibility of entrepreneurship in your future.

THE JOB-CREATING POWER OF ENTREPRENEURS IN THE UNITED STATES

Well before the recent economic turmoil, one of the major issues in the United States has been the need to create more jobs. With the current high unemployment rate, job creation is even more critical. You can begin to understand the job-creating power of entrepreneurs when you look at some of the great U.S. entrepreneurs from the past and the present. The history of the United States is the history of its entrepreneurs. Consider just a few of the many who have helped shape the U.S. economy:[1]

- DuPont, which manufactures thousands of products under such brand names as Teflon and Lycra, was started in 1802 by French immigrant Éleuthère Irénée du Pont de Nemours. Some 18 shareholders provided $36,000 in start-up money.

- Avon, the familiar beauty products retailer, started in 1886 with $500 David McConnell borrowed from a friend.

- George Eastman launched photographic giant Kodak in 1880 with a $3,000 investment.

- Procter & Gamble, now a multinational marketer of household products, was formed in 1837 by William Procter, James Gamble, and a total of $7,000 in capital.

- Ford Motor Company began with an investment of $28,000 by Henry Ford and 11 associates.

Business Has No Age Limit

Although fortunes are amassed over time, that doesn't mean they are exclusive to older people. Here are just a few examples of young entrepreneurs who found success in their college years:

Derek Johnson came up with the idea for his company, Tatango, during a lunch with a fellow undergrad. As the chair of communications for her sorority, his friend complained that even with Facebook and e-mail she couldn't get important announcements to her entire chapter quickly. Within months Johnson established a mass-texting business that generated more than $500,000 in sales in 2010.

Peter Findley stumbled into the business program of his college after trying a number of different majors. Inspired in an entrepreneurship class, Findley began writing the business plan for Giant Campus. The company organizes summer camps for middle- and high-school age students on college campuses where they learn new media skills like web design. Five years after his initial spark, Giant Campus grew to more than 70 colleges located across the world.

Sam Hogg opened his wallet one day after Christmas and stared at all the plastic gift cards he received. Troubled by the waste of plastic, Hogg was shocked when he learned that 75 million pounds of gift card plastic end up in landfills each year. In 2008 he started GiftZip .com, an electronic gift card aggregator site. With 275 retailers now onboard, use of the site has increased 2,100 percent since the company launched.

John Goscha lived in a dorm for student entrepreneurs in his freshman year at Babson College. He and his friends spent many nights in his room brainstorming on enormous sheets of paper spread across the wall. After a while Goscha wondered if it would be possible simply to write all their ideas directly on the wall. After years of development, he finally devised a paint that can turn any wall into a dry erase board. With help from his friends, he launched IdeaPaint in 2002, and six years later the company won the Innovation Award at NeoCon, one of the design industry's largest showcases.

Sources: Tatango, www.tatango.com, accessed May 2012; Giant Campus, www.giantcampus.com, accessed May 2012; IdeaPaint, www.ideapaint.com, accessed May 2012; Joel Holland, "What's Your Problem?" *Entrepreneur,* May 2010; Jason Daley, "A Charter for New Courses," *Entrepreneur,* April 2010; and Ivy Hughes, "Guilt-Free Gifting," *Entrepreneur,* April 2010.

- Amazon.com began with investments by founder Jeff Bezos's family and friends. Bezos's parents invested $300,000, a huge portion of their retirement account. Today they are billionaires.

These stories have much in common. One or a couple of entrepreneurs had a good idea, borrowed some money from friends and family, and started a business. That business now employs thousands of people and helps the country prosper.

The United States has plenty of entrepreneurial talent. Names such as Mark Zuckerberg (Facebook), Michael Dell (Dell Inc.), Bill Gates (Microsoft), Howard Schultz (Starbucks), Jack Dorsey (Twitter), and Chad Hurley and Steve Chen (YouTube) have become as familiar as those of the great entrepreneurs of the past. The Connecting with Small Business box highlights several young entrepreneurs who started businesses while still in school.

LEARNING goal 1

Explain why people take the risks of entrepreneurship; list the attributes of successful entrepreneurs; and describe entrepreneurial teams, intrapreneurs, and home- and web-based businesses.

WHY PEOPLE TAKE THE ENTREPRENEURIAL CHALLENGE

Taking the risks of starting a business can be scary and thrilling at the same time. One entrepreneur described it as almost like bungee jumping. You might be scared, but if you watch six other people do it and they survive, then you're more likely to do it yourself. Here are some reasons people are willing to take the entrepreneurial risk:

- *Opportunity.* The opportunity to share in the American dream is a tremendous lure. Many people, including those new to this country, may not have the skills for today's complex organizations, but they do have the initiative and drive to work the long hours demanded by entrepreneurship. The same is true of many corporate managers who leave corporate life (by choice or after downsizing) to run businesses of their own. Others, including an increasing number of women, minorities, older people, and people with disabilities, find that starting their own businesses offers them more opportunities than working for others.[2]

- *Profit.* Profit is another important reason to become an entrepreneur. Bill Gates, who co-founded Microsoft, is the richest man in the United States and one of the richest people in the world.[3]

- *Independence.* Many entrepreneurs simply do not enjoy working for someone else. Melissa Harvey, whose company Will n' Rose's LLC produces all-natural nut and whole-grain Kizo bars, says one of the best things about being an entrepreneur is the freedom to pursue your passion: "It's about independence. You can take something that motivates you, that inspires you and act on it without roadblocks."[4]

- *Challenge.* Some people believe that entrepreneurs are excitement junkies who thrive on risk. Entrepreneurs take moderate, calculated risks; they don't just gamble. In general, though, entrepreneurs seek achievement more than power.[5]

What Does It Take to Be an Entrepreneur?

Would you succeed as an entrepreneur? You can learn about the managerial and leadership skills needed to run a firm. However, you may not have the personality to assume the risks, take the initiative, create the vision, and rally others to follow your lead. Such personality traits are harder to learn or acquire than academic skills are. A list of entrepreneurial attributes to look for in yourself includes:[6]

- *Self-directed.* You should be self-disciplined and thoroughly comfortable being your own boss. You alone will be responsible for your success or failure.

- *Self-nurturing.* You must believe in your idea even when no one else does, and be able to replenish your own enthusiasm. When Walt Disney suggested the possibility of a full-length animated feature film, *Snow White,* the industry laughed. His personal commitment and enthusiasm caused the Bank of America to back his venture. The rest is history.

- *Action-oriented.* Great business ideas are not enough. Most important is a burning desire to realize, actualize, and build your dream into reality.

- *Highly energetic.* It's your business, and you must be emotionally, mentally, and physically able to work long and hard. Employees have weekends and vacations; entrepreneurs often work seven days a week and don't take vacations for years. Working 18-hour days in your own business can be exhausting, but most entrepreneurs think it is better than working long hours for someone else.

- *Tolerant of uncertainty.* Successful entrepreneurs take only calculated risks (if they can help it). Still, they must be able to take *some* risks. Remember, entrepreneurship is not for the squeamish or those bent on security. You can't be afraid to fail. Many well-known entrepreneurs failed several times before achieving success. The late football coach Vince Lombardi summarized the entrepreneurial philosophy when he said, "We didn't lose any games this season, we just ran out of time twice." New entrepreneurs must be prepared to run out of time a few times before they succeed.

Paula Deen had a dream that she could grow a business based on her passion for good country cooking. Her home-based catering business grew from a small family operation into multiple television shows, countless cookbooks, several restaurants, a bi-monthly magazine, and an ever-expanding product line. Do you have a passion that you could turn into a profitable business?

Turning Your Passions and Problems into Opportunities

As a young man in Queens, a borough of New York City, Russell Simmons channeled his passion for hip-hop culture into Def Jam Records. Today, his multimillion-dollar empire also includes Phat Farm clothing and Rush Management. Simmons used his time, money, and energy to turn his passion into a sustainable business.[7]

While many entrepreneurs' business ideas are inspired by their passions, many see business opportunities in their problems. For example, Anita Roddick started The Body Shop, which recycles its bottles and jars, because she hated paying for expensive packaging when she bought makeup.[8]

Most entrepreneurs don't get ideas for products and services from some flash of inspiration. The source of innovation is more like a *flashlight.* Imagine a search party walking in the dark, shining lights, looking around, asking questions, and looking some more. "That's how most creativity happens," says business author Dale Dauten. "Calling around, asking questions, saying 'What if?' till you get blisters on your tongue."

To look at problems and/or passions and see opportunities in them, ask yourself these questions: What do I want, but can never find? What product or service would improve my life? What really irritates me, and what product or service would help?

Keep in mind, however, that not all ideas are opportunities. If your idea doesn't meet anyone else's needs, the business won't succeed. You may have a business idea that is a good opportunity if:[9]

- It fills customers' needs.

- You have the skills and resources to start a business.

- You can sell the product or service at a price customers are willing and able to pay—and still make a profit.

- You can get your product or service to customers before your window of opportunity closes (before competitors with similar solutions beat you to the marketplace).
- You can keep the business going.

If you think you may have the entrepreneurial spirit in your blood, complete the Entrepreneurial Readiness Questionnaire below.

Entrepreneurial Teams

entrepreneurial team
A group of experienced people from different areas of business who join together to form a managerial team with the skills needed to develop, make, and market a new product.

An **entrepreneurial team** is a group of experienced people from different areas of business who join to form a managerial team with the skills to develop, make, and market a new product. A team may be better than an individual entrepreneur because team members can combine creative skills with production and marketing skills right from the start. Having a team also can ensure more cooperation and coordination later among functions in the business.

While Steve Jobs was the charismatic folk hero and visionary of Apple Computers, it was Steve Wozniak who invented the first personal computer model and Mike Markkula who offered business expertise and access to venture capital. The key to Apple's early success was that it was built around this "smart team" of entrepreneurs. The team wanted to combine the discipline of a big company with an environment in which people could feel they were participating in a successful venture. The trio of entrepreneurs recruited seasoned managers with similar desires. Everyone worked together to conceive, develop, and market products.[10]

Micropreneurs and Home-Based Businesses

micropreneurs
Entrepreneurs willing to accept the risk of starting and managing the type of business that remains small, lets them do the kind of work they want to do, and offers them a balanced lifestyle.

Not everyone who starts a business wants to grow a mammoth corporation. Some are interested in maintaining a balanced lifestyle while doing the kind of work they want to do. Such business owners are called **micropreneurs.** While other entrepreneurs are committed to the quest for growth, micropreneurs know they can be happy even if their companies never appear on a list of top-ranked businesses.

Many micropreneurs are home-based business owners. More than half of all small businesses are run from owners' homes.[11] Micropreneurs include consultants, video producers, architects, and bookkeepers. Many with professional skills such as graphic design, writing, and translating have found that one way of starting

ENTREPRENEUR READINESS QUESTIONNAIRE

Each of the following items describes something that you may or may not feel represents your personality or other characteristics about you. Read each item and then circle the response (1, 2, 3, 4, or 5) that most nearly reflects the extent to which you agree or disagree that the item seems to fit you.

| | RESPONSE | | | | |
Looking at My Overall Philosophy of Life and Typical Behavior, I Would Say That . . .	AGREE COMPLETELY (1)	MOSTLY AGREE (2)	PARTIALLY AGREE (3)	MOSTLY DISAGREE (4)	DISAGREE COMPLETELY (5)
1. I am generally optimistic.	1	2	3	4	5
2. I enjoy competing and doing things better than someone else.	1	2	3	4	5

(continued)

3. When solving a problem, I try to arrive at the best solution first without worrying about other possibilities.	1	2	3	4	5
4. I enjoy associating with co-workers after working hours.	1	2	3	4	5
5. If betting on a horse race, I would prefer to take a chance on a high-payoff "long shot."	1	2	3	4	5
6. I like setting my own goals and working hard to achieve them.	1	2	3	4	5
7. I am generally casual and easygoing with others.	1	2	3	4	5
8. I like to know what is going on and take action to find out.	1	2	3	4	5
9. I work best when someone else is guiding me along the way.	1	2	3	4	5
10. When I am right I can convince others.					
11. I find that other people frequently waste my valuable time.	1	2	3	4	5
12. I enjoy watching football, baseball, and similar sports events.	1	2	3	4	5
13. I tend to communicate about myself very openly with other people.	1	2	3	4	5
14. I don't mind following orders from superiors who have legitimate authority.	1	2	3	4	5
15. I enjoy planning things more than actually carrying out the plans.	1	2	3	4	5
16. I don't think it's much fun to bet on a "sure thing."	1	2	3	4	5
17. If faced with failure, I would shift quickly to something else rather than sticking to my guns.	1	2	3	4	5
18. Part of being successful in business is reserving adequate time for family.	1	2	3	4	5
19. Once I have earned something, I feel that keeping it secure is important.	1	2	3	4	5
20. Making a lot of money is largely a matter of getting the right breaks.	1	2	3	4	5
21. Problem solving is usually more effective when a number of alternatives are considered.	1	2	3	4	5
22. I enjoy impressing others with the things I can do.	1	2	3	4	5
23. I enjoy playing games like tennis and handball with someone who is slightly better than I am.	1	2	3	4	5
24. Sometimes moral ethics must be bent a little in business dealings.	1	2	3	4	5
25. I think that good friends would make the best subordinates in an organization.	1	2	3	4	5

Scoring:

Give yourself one point for each 1 or 2 response you circled for questions 1, 2, 6, 8, 10, 11, 16, 17, 21, 22, 23.

Give yourself one point for each 4 or 5 response you circled for questions 3, 4, 5, 7, 9, 12, 13, 14, 15, 18, 19, 20, 24, 25.

Add your points and see how you rate in the following categories:

21–25 Your entrepreneurial potential looks great if you have a suitable opportunity to use it. What are you waiting for?

16–20 This is close to the high entrepreneurial range. You could be quite successful if your other talents and resources are right.

11–15 Your score is in the transitional range. With some serious work you can probably develop the outlook you need for running your own business.

6–10 Things look pretty doubtful for you as an entrepreneur. It would take considerable rearranging of your life philosophy and behavior to make it.

0–5 Let's face it. Entrepreneurship isn't really for you. Still, learning what it's all about won't hurt anything.

Source: Kenneth R. Van Voorhis, *Entrepreneurship and Small Business Management* (New York: Allyn & Bacon, 1980).

a freelance business is through websites such as Elance (www.elance.com) and oDesk (www.odesk.com) that link clients and freelancers. The sites post job openings and client feedback and serve as secure intermediaries for clients' payments.

Many home-based businesses are owned by people combining career and family. Don't picture just moms with young children; nearly 60 percent are men. Here are more reasons for the growth of home-based businesses:[12]

- Computer technology has leveled the competitive playing field, allowing home-based businesses to look and act as big as their corporate competitors. Broadband Internet connections, smart phones such as the BlackBerry and the iPhone, and other technologies are so affordable that setting up a business takes a much smaller initial investment than it once did.

- Corporate downsizing has led many to venture out on their own. Meanwhile, the work of the downsized employees still needs to be done, and corporations are outsourcing much of it to smaller companies.

- Social attitudes have changed. Whereas home-based entrepreneurs used to be asked when they were going to get a "real" job, they are now likely to be asked for how-to-do-it advice.

- New tax laws have loosened restrictions on deducting expenses for home offices.

Working at home has its challenges, of course. Here are a few:[13]

- *Getting new customers.* Getting the word out can be difficult because you don't have a retail storefront.

- *Managing time.* You save time by not commuting, but it takes self-discipline to use that time wisely.

- *Keeping work and family tasks separate.* It's great to be able to throw a load of laundry in the washer in the middle of the workday if you need to, but you have to keep such distractions to a minimum. It also takes self-discipline to leave your work at the office if the office is at home.

- *Abiding by city ordinances.* Government ordinances restrict the types of businesses allowed in certain parts of the community and how much traffic a home-based business can attract to the neighborhood.

- *Managing risk.* Home-based entrepreneurs should review their homeowner's insurance policy, since not all policies cover business-related claims. Some even void the coverage if there is a business in the home.

Home-based entrepreneurs should focus on finding opportunity instead of accepting security, getting results instead of following routines, earning a profit instead of earning a paycheck, trying new ideas instead of avoiding mistakes, and creating a long-term vision instead of seeking a short-term payoff. Figure 6.1 lists 10 ideas for potentially successful home-based businesses, and Figure 6.2 highlights clues for avoiding home-based business scams. You can find a wealth of online information about starting a home-based business at *Entrepreneur* magazine's website (www.entrepreneur.com).

Micropreneur Jane Mason, of Virtuous Bread, teaches small bread-making classes in her home kitchen. She also created a network of "Bread Angels," people she taught to start their own home-based bread businesses. Her website contains a blog, a newsletter, and recipes. Mason is more concerned with building positive relationships within communities than with building a huge baking company. Can you see why Mason is considered a micropreneur?

figure 6.1

POTENTIAL HOME-BASED BUSINESSES

Many businesses can be started at home. Listed below are 10 businesses that have low start-up costs, don't require an abundance of administrative tasks, and are in relatively high demand:

1. Cleaning service.
2. Gift-basket business.
3. Web merchant.
4. Mailing list service.
5. Microfarming (small plots of land for such high-value crops as mushrooms, edible flowers, or sprouts).
6. Tutoring.
7. Résumé service.
8. Web design.
9. Medical claims assistance.
10. Personal coaching.

Look for a business that meets these important criteria: (1) The job is something you truly enjoy doing; (2) you know enough to do the job well or you are willing to spend time learning it while you have another job; and (3) you can identify a market for your product or service.

figure 6.1

POTENTIAL HOME-BASED BUSINESSES

figure 6.2

WATCH OUT FOR SCAMS

You've probably read many newspaper and magazine ads selling home-based businesses. You may have even received unsolicited e-mail messages touting the glory of particular work-at-home opportunities. Beware of work-at-home scams! Here are a few clues that tell you a home business opportunity is a scam:

1. The ad promises that you can earn hundreds or even thousands of dollars a week working at home.
2. No experience is needed.
3. You only need to work a few hours a week.
4. There are loads of CAPITAL LETTERS and exclamation points!!!!!
5. You need to call a 900 number for more information.
6. You're asked to send in some money to receive a list of home-based business opportunities.
7. You're pressured to make a decision NOW!!!!

Do your homework before investing in a business opportunity. Call and ask for references. Contact the Better Business Bureau (www.bbb.org), county and state departments of consumer affairs, and the state attorney general's office. Conduct an Internet search and ask people in forums or on social networking sites if they've dealt with the company. Visit websites such as Friends In Business (www.friendsinbusiness.com) to find advice on specific online scams. Most important, don't pay a great deal of money for a business opportunity until you've talked to an attorney.

Web-Based Businesses

The Internet has sprouted a world of small web-based businesses selling everything from staplers to refrigerator magnets to wedding dresses. In 2010, online retail sales reached $172.9 billion, or approximately 7 percent of all retail sales. Online retail sales were up 11 percent in 2010, compared to just 2.5 percent for all retail sales. Forrester Research predicts that online retail sales will reach $250 billion by 2014.[14]

Web-based businesses have to offer more than the same merchandise customers can buy at stores—they must offer unique products or services. For

There are more than 70,000 diamonds for sale on BlueNile.com, a Seattle-based company that took in $11.4 million in net income in 2011. Customers buy directly from the website or through a toll-free number staffed by helpful reps (who don't work on commission). What does Blue Nile offer that other jewelry retailers don't?

affiliate marketing
An Internet-based marketing strategy in which a business rewards individuals or other businesses (affiliates) for each visitor or customer the affiliate sends to its website.

example, Marc Resnik started his web-based distribution company after waking up one morning laughing about his business idea. Now Throw Things.com makes money for him—he's shipped products to more than 44 countries. Although the company's offerings seem like a random collection of unrelated items, everything it sells can be thrown. You can buy promotional products in the "Throw Your Name Around!" section, ventriloquist dummies in the "Throw Your Voice!" section, and sporting equipment in the "Things to Throw!" section. Stranger products include fake vomit ("Throw Up!") and a $3.50 certificate that says you wasted your money ("Throw Your Money Away!"). Resnik doesn't sell very many of those certificates, but he does sell more dummies than anyone else in the United States. About two-thirds of the company's revenue comes from the promotional products section, which allows customers to add a logo to thousands of products. Why is Resnik's business so successful? As one frequent customer said, it's because of Resnik's exceptional service and quick turnaround time.[15]

One of the easiest ways to start a web-based business is through affiliate marketing. **Affiliate marketing** is an Internet-based marketing strategy in which a business rewards individuals or other businesses (affiliates) for each visitor or customer the affiliate sends to its website. For example, imagine you discovered a backpack online made of an extremely lightweight, amazingly strong fabric that holds everything you need for the day, is easy to carry, and looks great. You want to tell all your friends about it, so you register as an affiliate on the seller's website and download to your Facebook page a *widget,* a tiny application that links your page to the seller's site. Whenever anyone clicks on the widget (an image of the product) and buys a backpack, the seller pays you a commission.

If you can make a little money in commissions from sales of a single backpack, imagine setting up an online store with many products you love. Building such a store has become easier with the advent of social commerce services such as Lemonade Inc.'s Lemonade Stand (www.lemonade.com). Once partnered, an online retailer typically provides Lemonade Stand access to product information and images. Lemonade Stand then funnels that information through its website so that users can select which products they would like to appear in their widget product galleries on their websites, Facebook pages, or blogs. Widget users get commissions on sales generated through the widgets. Using social commerce services like Lemonade Stand saves users from the time-consuming task of registering as an affiliate with multiple sellers. Such services are allowing Internet users to become what amounts to peer-to-peer affiliates for e-retailers where the users can make money.

A web-based business isn't always a fast road to success.[16] It can sometimes be a shortcut to failure. Hundreds of high-flying dot-coms crashed after promising to revolutionize the way we shop. That's the bad news. The good news is that you can learn from someone else's failure and spare yourself some pain.

Entrepreneurship within Firms

Entrepreneurship in a large organization is often reflected in the efforts and achievements of **intrapreneurs,** creative people who work as entrepreneurs within corporations. The idea is to use a company's existing resources—human, financial, and physical—to launch new products and generate new profits.[17] At 3M, which produces a wide array of products from adhesives like Scotch tape to nonwoven materials for industrial use, managers are expected to devote 15 percent of their work time to thinking up new products or services.[18] You know those bright-colored Post-it Notes people use to write messages on just about everything? That product was developed by Art Fry, a 3M employee. He needed to mark the pages of his hymnal with something that wouldn't damage the book or fall out. He came up with the idea of the self-stick, repositionable paper slips. The labs at 3M produced a sample, but distributors were unimpressed and market surveys were inconclusive. Nonetheless, 3M kept sending samples to secretaries of top executives. Eventually, after a major sales and marketing program, the orders began pouring in, and Post-it Notes became a big winner. The company continues to update the product; making it from recycled paper is one of many innovations. Post-it Notes have gone international as well—the notepads sent to Japan are long and narrow to accommodate vertical writing. You can even use Post-it Notes electronically—the Post-it Software Notes program allows you to type messages onto brightly colored notes and store them on memo boards, embed them in documents, or send them through e-mail.

A classic intrapreneurial venture is Lockheed Martin Corporation's Skunkworks, a research and development center that turned out such monumental products as the United States' first fighter jet in 1943 and the Stealth fighter in 1991.[19]

When you come up with a winning idea, stick with it. That's certainly been the motto of 3M, the maker of Post-it Notes. The company encourages intrapreneurship among its employees by requiring them to devote at least 15 percent of their time to think about new products. How has this commitment to innovation paid off for 3M and its employees?

Encouraging Entrepreneurship: What Government Can Do

Part of the Immigration Act passed by Congress in 1990 was intended to encourage more entrepreneurs to come to the United States. The act created a category of "investor visas" that allows 10,000 people to come to the United States each year if they invest $1 million in an enterprise that creates or preserves 10 jobs. Some people are promoting the idea of increasing the allowed number of such immigrants. They believe the more entrepreneurs that can be drawn to the United States, the more jobs will be created and the more the economy will grow.[20]

Another way to encourage entrepreneurship is **enterprise zones,** specific geographic areas to which governments attract private business investment by offering lower taxes and other government support. (These are also sometimes called *empowerment zones* or *enterprise communities.*) The government could have a significant effect on entrepreneurship by offering tax breaks to businesses that make investments to create jobs.[21]

States are becoming stronger supporters of entrepreneurs and are creating programs that invest directly in new businesses. Often, state commerce departments serve as clearinghouses for such programs. States are also creating incubators and technology centers to reduce start-up capital needs. **Incubators** offer new businesses in the critical stage of early development low-cost offices with basic services such as accounting, legal advice, and secretarial help. According to a recent

intrapreneurs
Creative people who work as entrepreneurs within corporations.

enterprise zones
Specific geographic areas to which governments try to attract private business investment by offering lower taxes and other government support.

incubators
Centers that offer new businesses low-cost offices with basic business services.

Incubators, such as this one in Alabama, offer new businesses low-cost offices with basic business services such as accounting, legal advice, and secretarial help. Do you have such incubators in your area?

study conducted by the National Business Incubator Association (NBIA), 87 percent of incubator graduates remain in business.[22] To learn more about what incubators offer and to find links to incubators in your area, visit the NBIA's website (www.nbia.org).

There are a few states that offer assistance to qualified candidates under the Self-Employment Assistance (SEA) program. The program allows participants to collect unemployment checks while they build their businesses. Participants often get training and counseling as well. Unemployment checks may not seem like much, but many business owners say they are enough to help them launch their companies without depleting savings to pay for living expenses until their businesses are strong enough to support them. Rose Rios entered the New Jersey SEA program in 2007 when she was laid off from her job in market research. She collected benefits of about $450 while she started a medical communications and market research company. Since then she has brought in over $2.5 million in revenue and hired three full-time employees and several freelancers.[23]

The government can also join with private entities to promote entrepreneurship. For example, Startup America is a White House initiative to "celebrate, inspire, and accelerate high-growth entrepreneurship throughout the nation."[24] It is a public and private effort to bring together the country's most innovative entrepreneurs, corporations, universities, foundations, and other leaders, to work with federal agencies to increase the number and success of U.S. entrepreneurs. One of the core goals is to empower more Americans not just to get a job, but to create jobs. Learn more about the resources offered by Startup America at www.startupamericapartnership.org.[25]

progress assessment

- Why are people willing to take the risks of entrepreneurship?
- What are the advantages of entrepreneurial teams?
- How do micropreneurs differ from other entrepreneurs?
- What are some opportunities and risks of web-based businesses?

LEARNING goal 2

Discuss the importance of small business to the American economy and summarize the major causes of small-business failure.

GETTING STARTED IN SMALL BUSINESS

Let's suppose you have a great idea for a new business, you have the attributes of an entrepreneur, and you're ready to take the leap into business for yourself. How do you start? That's what the rest of this chapter is about.

It may be easier to identify with a small neighborhood business than with a giant global firm, yet the principles of management are similar for each. The management of charities, government agencies, churches, schools, and unions is much the same as the management of small and large businesses. So, as you learn about small-business management, you will take a giant step toward understanding management in general. All organizations demand capital, good ideas, planning, information management, budgets (and financial management in general), accounting, marketing, good employee relations, and good overall managerial know-how. We shall explore these areas as they relate to small businesses and then, later in the book, apply the concepts to large firms and even global organizations.

Small versus Big Business

The Small Business Administration (SBA) defines a **small business** as one that is independently owned and operated, is not dominant in its field of operation, and meets certain standards of size in terms of employees or annual receipts (such as under $2 million a year for service businesses). A small business is considered "small" only in relationship to other businesses in its industry. A wholesaler may sell up to $22 million and still be considered a small business by the SBA. In manufacturing, a plant can have 1,500 employees and still be considered small. Let's look at some interesting statistics about small businesses:[26]

- There are 27.8 million small businesses in the United States.

- Of all nonfarm businesses in the United States, almost 97 percent are considered small by SBA standards.

- Small businesses account for more than 50 percent of the gross domestic product (GDP).

- Nearly 600,000 tax-paying, employee-hiring businesses are started every year.

- Small businesses generate 60–80 percent of the new jobs each year.

- Small businesses employ about half of all private-sector employees.

- About 80 percent of U.S. workers find their first jobs in small businesses.

As you can see, small business is really a big part of the U.S. economy. How big? Let's find out.

Importance of Small Businesses

Since 60–80 percent of the nation's new jobs are in small businesses, there's a very good chance you'll either work in a small business someday or start one. In addition to providing employment opportunities, small firms believe they offer other advantages over larger companies—more personal customer service and the ability to respond quickly to opportunities.

Bigger is not always better. Picture a hole in the ground. If you fill it with boulders, there are many empty spaces between them. If you fill it with sand, there is no space between the grains. That's how it is in business. Big businesses don't serve all the needs of the market. There is plenty of room for small companies to make a profit filling those niches.

small business
A business that is independently owned and operated, is not dominant in its field of operation, and meets certain standards of size (set by the Small Business Administration) in terms of employees or annual receipts.

Thirteen-year-old Madison Waldrop developed her own dress collection called Designs by Malyse, specializing in evening and bridal gowns. One of the young entrepreneur's bridal gowns was featured on the runway at the 2010 Bridal Fashion Week in New York City.

Small-Business Success and Failure

You can't be naïve about business practices, or you'll go broke. It's been reported that half of new businesses don't last five years.[27] Yet a study by economist Bruce Kirchhoff showed that the failure rate is only 18 percent over the first eight years. Kirchhoff contends that other reported failure rates are misinterpretations of Dun & Bradstreet statistics. When small-business owners closed down one business to start another, for instance, they were included in the "failure" category—even though they hadn't failed at all. Similarly, when a business changed its form of ownership or a sole proprietor retired, it was counted as a failure. The good news for entrepreneurs is that business failures are much lower than traditionally reported.[28]

Figure 6.3 lists reasons for small-business failures, among them managerial incompetence and inadequate financial planning. Keep in mind that when a business fails, it is important that the owners learn from their mistakes. Some entrepreneurs who have suffered flops are more realistic than novice entrepreneurs. Because of the lessons they've learned, they may be more successful in their future ventures.[29]

Choosing the right type of business is critical. Many businesses with low failure rates require advanced training to start—veterinary services, dental practices, medical practices, and so on. While training and degrees may buy security, they do not tend to produce much growth—one dentist can fill only so many cavities. If you want to be both independent and rich, you need to go after growth. Often high-growth businesses, such as technology firms, are not easy to start and are even more difficult to keep going.

The easiest businesses to start have the least growth and greatest failure rate (like restaurants). The easiest to keep alive are difficult to get started (like manufacturing). And the ones that can make you rich are both hard to start and hard to keep going (like automobile assembly). See Figure 6.4 to get an idea of the business situations most likely to lead to success.

When you decide to start your own business, think carefully. You're unlikely to find everything you want—easy entry, security, and reward—in one business. Choose those characteristics that matter most to you; accept the absence of the others; plan, plan, plan; and then go for it!

---

figure 6.3

CAUSES OF SMALL-BUSINESS FAILURE

The following are some of the causes of small-business failure:

- Plunging in without first testing the waters on a small scale.
- Underpricing or overpricing goods or services.
- Underestimating how much time it will take to build a market.
- Starting with too little capital.
- Starting with too much capital and being careless in its use.
- Going into business with little or no experience and without first learning something about the industry or market.
- Borrowing money without planning just how and when to pay it back.
- Attempting to do too much business with too little capital.
- Not allowing for setbacks and unexpected expenses.
- Buying too much on credit.
- Extending credit too freely.
- Expanding credit too rapidly.
- Failing to keep complete, accurate records, so that the owners drift into trouble without realizing it.
- Carrying habits of personal extravagance into the business.
- Not understanding business cycles.
- Forgetting about taxes, insurance, and other costs of doing business.
- Mistaking the freedom of being in business for oneself for the liberty to work or not, according to whim.

figure 6.4

SITUATIONS FOR
SMALL-BUSINESS SUCCESS

The following factors increase the chances of small-business success:

- The customer requires a lot of personal attention, as in a beauty parlor.
- The product is not easily made by mass-production techniques (e.g., custom-tailored clothes or custom auto-body work).
- Sales are not large enough to appeal to a large firm (e.g., a novelty shop).
- The neighborhood is not attractive because of crime or poverty. This provides a unique opportunity for small grocery stores and laundries.

- A large business sells a franchise operation to local buyers. (Don't forget franchising as an excellent way to enter the world of small business.)
- The owner pays attention to new competitors.
- The business is in a growth industry (e.g., computer services or web design).

LEARNING goal 3

Summarize ways to learn about how small businesses operate.

LEARNING ABOUT SMALL-BUSINESS OPERATIONS

Hundreds of would-be entrepreneurs ask the same question: "How can I learn to run my own business?" Here are some hints.

Learn from Others

Investigate your local community college for classes on small business and entrepreneurship; there are thousands of such programs throughout the United States. Many bring together entrepreneurs from diverse backgrounds who form helpful support networks. Talk to others who have already done it. They'll tell you that location is critical and caution you not to be undercapitalized, that is, not to start without enough money. They'll warn you about the problems of finding and retaining good workers. And, most of all, they'll tell you to keep good records and hire a good accountant and lawyer before you start. Free advice like this is invaluable.

Get Some Experience

There is no better way to learn small-business management than by becoming an apprentice or working for a successful entrepreneur. Many small-business owners got the idea for their businesses from their prior jobs. The rule of thumb is: Have three years' experience in a comparable business first.[30]

Back in 1818, Cornelius Vanderbilt sold his own sailing vessels and went to work for a steamboat company so that he could learn the rules of the new game of steam. After learning what he needed to know, he quit, started his own steamship company, and became the first U.S. business owner to accumulate $100 million.

Jason White, owner of Crested Butte Angler, turned his love of fishing into a successful guide business. He learned to fish in the Ozarks of Missouri and Arkansas, and now leads fishing excursions in Colorado, Mexico, and Thailand. What experiences have you had that would help you start and run a successful business?

Should You Stay or Should You Go?

Suppose you've worked for two years in a company and you see signs that it is beginning to falter. You and a co-worker have ideas about how to make a company like your boss's succeed. Rather than share your ideas with your boss, you and your friend are considering quitting your jobs and starting your own company together. Should you approach other co-workers about working for your new venture? Will you try to lure your old boss's customers to your own business? What are your alternatives? What are the consequences of each alternative? What's the most ethical choice?

Running a small business part-time, during your off hours or on weekends, can bring the rewards of working for yourself while still enjoying a regular paycheck at another job. It may save you money too, because you're then less likely to make "rookie mistakes" when you start your own business. The Making Ethical Decisions box presents ethical questions about using the knowledge you've gained as an employee to start your own business.

Take Over a Successful Firm

Small-business owners work long hours and rarely take vacations. After many years, they may feel stuck and think they can't get out because they have too much time and effort invested. Thus millions of small-business owners are eager to get away, at least for a long vacation.

This is where you come in. Find a successful businessperson who owns a small business. Tell him or her you are eager to learn the business and would like to serve an apprenticeship, that is, a training period. Say that at the end of the training period (one year or so), you would like to help the owner or manager by becoming assistant manager. Thus you can free the owner to take off weekends and holidays and have a long vacation—a good deal for him or her. For another year or so, work very hard to learn all about the business—suppliers, inventory, bookkeeping, customers, promotion. At the end of two years, make this offer: The owner can retire or work only part-time, and you will take over management of the business. You can establish a profit-sharing plan with the owner plus pay yourself a salary. Be generous with yourself; you'll earn it if you manage the business. You can even ask for 40 percent or more of the profits.

The owner benefits by keeping ownership in the business and making 60 percent of what he or she earned before—without having to work. You benefit by making 40 percent of the profits of a successful firm. This is an excellent deal for an owner about to retire—he or she is able to keep the firm and a healthy profit flow. It is also a clever and successful way to share in the profits of a successful small business without making any personal monetary investment.

If profit sharing doesn't appeal to the owner, you may want to buy the business outright. How do you determine a fair price for a business? Value is based on

(1) what the business owns, (2) what it earns, and (3) what makes it unique. Naturally, an accountant will need to help you determine the business's value.[31]

If you fail at your efforts to take over the business through either profit sharing or buying, you can quit and start your own business fully trained.

LEARNING goal 4

Analyze what it takes to start and run a small business.

MANAGING A SMALL BUSINESS

According to the Small Business Administration, one of the major causes of small business failures is poor management. Keep in mind, though, that *poor management* covers a number of faults. It could mean poor planning, record keeping, inventory control, promotion, or employee relations. Most likely it includes poor capitalization. To help you succeed as a business owner, in the following sections we explore the functions of business in a small-business setting:

- Planning your business.
- Financing your business.
- Knowing your customers (marketing).
- Managing your employees (human resource development).
- Keeping records (accounting).

Although all the functions are important in both the start-up and management phases of the business, the first two—planning and financing—are the primary concerns when you start your business. The others are the heart of your operations once the business is under way.

Begin with Planning

Many people eager to start a small business come up with an idea and begin discussing it with professors, friends, and other businesspeople. At this stage the entrepreneur needs a business plan. A **business plan** is a detailed written statement that describes the nature of the business, the target market, the advantages the business will have over competition, and the resources and qualifications of the owner(s). A business plan forces potential small-business owners to be quite specific about the products or services they intend to offer. They must analyze the competition, calculate how much money they need to start, and cover other details of operation. A business plan is also mandatory for talking with bankers or other investors.

Lenders want to know everything about an aspiring business. First, pick a bank that serves businesses the size of yours. Have a good accountant prepare a complete set of financial statements and a personal balance sheet. Make an appointment before going to the bank, and go to the bank with an accountant and all the necessary financial information. Demonstrate to the banker that you're a person of good character: civic-minded and respected in business and community circles.[32] Finally, ask for *all* the money you need, be specific, and be prepared to personally guarantee the loan.

business plan
A detailed written statement that describes the nature of the business, the target market, the advantages the business will have in relation to competition, and the resources and qualifications of the owner(s).

ModCloth co-founders Susan and Eric Koger started selling vintage clothes when they were in college. They entered a hastily written business plan in a school competition—and lost. While discouraging at first, the loss taught them that they needed to refocus and create a solid business plan if they were going to attract investors. Today their company has 100 full-time employees.

Need help understanding How an Entrepreneur Can Secure Financing for a Small Business? www.introbiz.tv/QR6-1

Writing a Business Plan

A good business plan takes a long time to write, but you've got only five minutes, in the *executive summary,* to convince readers not to throw it away. Since bankers receive many business plans every day, the summary has to catch their interest quickly. There's no such thing as a perfect business plan, but prospective entrepreneurs do think out the smallest details. An outline of a comprehensive business plan is shown below.

Many computer software programs can help you get organized. One highly rated business-plan program is Business Plan Pro by Palo Alto Software. To see samples of successful business plans for a variety of businesses go to www.bplans.com/sample_business_plans. You can also learn more about writing business plans on the Small Business Administration website at www.sba.gov/starting.

Getting the completed business plan into the right hands is almost as important as getting the right information into the plan. Finding funding requires research. Next we discuss sources of money available to new business ventures. All require a comprehensive business plan. The time and effort you invest before starting a business will pay off many times later. The big payoff is survival.

Getting Money to Fund a Small Business

An entrepreneur has several potential sources of capital: personal savings; relatives; former employers; banks; finance companies; venture capitalists; and government agencies such as the Small Business Administration (SBA), the Farmers Home Administration, the Economic Development Authority, and the Minority Business Development Agency. The most common source of funding after personal savings is friends and family.[33]

You may even want to consider borrowing from a potential supplier to your future business. Helping you get started may be in the supplier's interest if there is a chance you will be a big customer later. This is what Ray Kroc did in the early years of McDonald's. When Kroc didn't have the funds available to keep the company going, he asked his suppliers to help him with the necessary funds. These suppliers grew along with McDonald's. It's usually not a good idea to ask such an investor for money at the outset. Begin by asking for advice; if the supplier likes your plan, he or she may be willing to help you with funding too.

OUTLINE OF A COMPREHENSIVE BUSINESS PLAN

A good business plan is between 25 and 50 pages long and takes at least six months to write.

Cover Letter

Only one thing is certain when you go hunting for money to start a business: You won't be the only hunter out there. You need to make potential funders want to read *your* business plan instead of the hundreds of others on their desks. Your cover letter should summarize the most attractive points of your project in as few words as possible. Be sure to

(continued)

address the letter to the potential investor by name. "To whom it may concern" or "Dear Sir" is not the best way to win an investor's support.

Section 1—Executive Summary

Begin with a two-page or three-page management summary of the proposed venture. Include a short description of the business, and discuss major goals and objectives.

Section 2—Company Background

Describe company operations to date (if any), potential legal considerations, and areas of risk and opportunity. Summarize the firm's financial condition, and include past and current balance sheets, income and cash flow statements, and other relevant financial records (you will read about these financial statements in Chapter 17). It is also wise to include a description of insurance coverage. Investors want to be assured that death or other mishaps do not pose major threats to the company.

Section 3—Management Team

Include an organization chart, job descriptions of listed positions, and detailed résumés of the current and proposed executives. A mediocre idea with a proven management team is funded more often than a great idea with an inexperienced team. Managers should have expertise in all disciplines necessary to start and run a business. If not, mention outside consultants who will serve in these roles and describe their qualifications.

Section 4—Financial Plan

Provide five-year projections for income, expenses, and funding sources. Don't assume the business will grow in a straight line. Adjust your planning to allow for funding at various stages of the company's growth. Explain the rationale and assumptions used to determine the estimates. Assumptions should be reasonable and based on industry/historical trends. Make sure all totals add up and are consistent throughout the plan. If necessary, hire a professional accountant or financial analyst to prepare these statements.

Stay clear of excessively ambitious sales projections; rather, offer best-case, expected, and worst-case scenarios. These not only reveal how sensitive the bottom line is to sales fluctuations but also serve as good management guides.

Section 5—Capital Required

Indicate the amount of capital needed to commence or continue operations, and describe how these funds are to be used. Make sure the totals are the same as the ones on the cash-flow statement. This area will receive a great deal of review from potential investors, so it must be clear and concise.

Section 6—Marketing Plan

Don't underestimate the competition. Review industry size, trends, and the target market segment. Sources like *American Demographics* magazine and the *Rand McNally Commercial Atlas and Marketing Guide* can help you put a plan together. Discuss strengths and weaknesses of the product or service. The most important things investors want to know are what makes the product more desirable than what's already available and whether the product can be patented. Compare pricing to the competition's. Forecast sales in dollars and units. Outline sales, advertising, promotion, and public relations programs. Make sure the costs agree with those projected in the financial statements.

Section 7—Location Analysis

In retailing and certain other industries, the location of the business is one of the most important factors. Provide a comprehensive demographic analysis of consumers in the area of the proposed business as well as a traffic-pattern analysis and vehicular and pedestrian counts.

Section 8—Manufacturing Plan

Describe minimum plant size, machinery required, production capacity, inventory and inventory-control methods, quality control, plant personnel requirements, and so on. Estimates of product costs should be based on primary research.

Section 9—Appendix

Include all marketing research on the product or service (off-the-shelf reports, article reprints, etc.) and other information about the product concept or market size. Provide a bibliography of all the reference materials you consulted. This section should demonstrate that the proposed company won't be entering a declining industry or market segment.

If you would like to see sample business plans that successfully secured funding, go to Bplans.com (www.bplans.com). You can also learn more about writing business plans on the Small Business Administration website at www.sba.gov/starting.

The credit crunch spurred by the recent financial crisis made it necessary for small-business owners to do a little extra shopping to find a friendly lender. Many found that smaller community banks were more likely to grant loans than larger regional banks. Since small banks do business in a single town or cluster of towns, they know their customers better. They have more flexibility to make lending decisions based on everything they know about their customers, rather than on a more automated basis as larger banks must.[34]

Community development financial institutions (CDFIs) may be a source of funding for businesses in lower-income communities. Today CDFIs are playing a big role in the economic recovery. CDFIs were first formed in the early 1980s by socially motivated investors such as nuns investing their retirement funds. However, in 2009 more than $1 billion flowed into CDFIs from big investment companies and another $247 million from the government. CDFIs succeeded even after the credit bubble because they maintained the financial discipline other lenders lacked. They have the incentive to make sure their clients succeed because, if borrowers don't repay their loans, the CDFIs take the hit, not investors. Only 1 percent of their loans were not paid back in the last three decades. CDFIs don't just loan money. More importantly, they provide business counseling such as helping owners learn how to develop marketing strategies, manage inventory, and improve cash flow.[35]

Individual investors are also a frequent source of capital for most entrepreneurs. *Angel investors* are private individuals who invest their own money in potentially hot new companies before they go public.[36] A number of websites match people who want money with those willing to lend it; they include Prosper Marketplace, Zopa, Lending Club, Kiva, Virgin Money, CircleLending, and GlobeFunder. Other sites, such as GreenNote and People Capital, specialize in lending to students. This form of individual investing is called peer-to-peer (P2P) lending.[37] A creditworthy borrower often gets such money faster and more easily than going to the bank. And the cost is often less than a bank loan. The Connecting Through Social Media box offers a number of examples of companies that started with P2P loans.

Venture capitalists may finance your project—for a price. Venture capitalists may ask for a hefty stake in your company (as much as 60 percent) in exchange for the cash to start your business. If the venture capitalist takes too large a stake, you could lose control of the business. Since the widespread failure of early web startups, venture capitalists have been willing to invest less and expect more return on their investment if the new company is sold.[38] Therefore, if you're a very small company, you don't have a very good chance of getting venture capital. You'd have a better chance finding an angel investor.

If your proposed venture does require millions of dollars to start, experts recommend that you talk with at least five investment firms and their clients in order to find the right venture capitalist. You may able to connect with potential investors through Angellist.com, a nonprofit service that helps entrepreneurs and venture capitalists get to know each other.[39] To learn more about how to find venture capitalists, visit the National Venture Capital Association's website (www.nvca.org).

Wouldn't it be great if money grew on trees? Unfortunately it doesn't, so prospective entrepreneurs must find other sources of capital such as personal savings, relatives, former employers, banks, finance companies, venture capitalists, and government agencies. What is the most common source of funding after personal savings?

venture capitalists
Individuals or companies that invest in new businesses in exchange for partial ownership of those businesses.

CONNECTING THROUGH
social media

www.kickstarters.com

Peer-to-Peer Lending

For aspiring entrepreneurs, having a good idea is only half the battle. The next hurdle is gathering enough capital to turn a business plan into reality. But bank loans are hard to come by these days. The failed speculation that spurred the financial crisis remains a vivid memory for many investors, making them reluctant to lend funds.

Although traditional avenues of investment may be closed to some, a number of new ventures online can help entrepreneurs acquire cash. Kickstarter.com, for instance, helps potential business owners, as well as musicians and artists, gather funds from a variety of backers. Instead of dealing in interest rates and equity, however, contributors pledge to give as little as $1 in exchange for free products or just a thank-you for helping make the project a reality. Although these may seem like small contributions, a little money from a lot of people can go a long way. Vadim Akimenko posted a $15,000 investment goal on Kickstarter in order to establish a Boston-area butcher shop specializing in meat from local farms. After donations from 201 different people, he surpassed his investment cap by $1,405 and soon opened Akimenko Meats.

For those investors wanting a larger return than a T-bone steak, peer-to-peer lending sites like Lending Club act as a sort of Facebook of money. But instead of collecting online friends, loan-seekers look for people who are willing to lend them money. Individuals set up a profile that outlines their credit history, how much cash they need, and what they intend to do with it. Administrators at Lending Club then assign an interest rate between 6.78 percent and 24.95 percent based on the criteria above. Many users, such as Karla Brazelton of Detroit, use the money to pay down debt. After facing rejection from banks across the board, Brazelton signed up on Lending Club in order to reduce her $7,000 credit card debt. After investment from a small collection of lenders, Brazelton eventually secured a 36-month personal loan at 7.74 percent interest. Not only does the loan help Brazelton, it also provides investors with a much higher rate of return on their money than any standard savings account could offer.

Sources: John Tozzi, "Eight Companies Kick-Started by Fans," *Bloomberg Businessweek,* June 28–July 4, 2010; John Simons, "How to Get a Loan the Web 2.0 Way," *Black Enterprise,* December 1, 2010; and Jeff Hughes, "Lending Club's Challenge: Keeping Up with Rising Demand," *San Francisco Business Times*, May 11, 2012.

The Small Business Administration (SBA)

The **Small Business Administration (SBA)** is a U.S. government agency that advises and assists small businesses by providing management training and financial advice and loans (see Figure 6.5). The SBA started a microloan demonstration program in 1991. The program provides very small loans (up to $50,000) and technical assistance to small-business owners. It is administered through a nationwide network of nonprofit organizations chosen by the SBA. Rather than award loans based on collateral, credit history, or previous business success, the program judges worthiness on belief in the borrowers' integrity and the soundness of their business ideas.[40]

The SBA microloan program helps people like Ted Cooper, who owns Fresh Look Remodeling, a New York–based energy-audit business. Faced with laying off his six workers, Cooper searched for a loan to keep the business going. Before Cooper received a $10,000 SBA microloan, he applied to a few big banks, one of which asked for $15,000 worth of collateral. "If I had that, I wouldn't have needed to borrow it," Cooper said.[41]

Small Business Administration (SBA)
A U.S. government agency that advises and assists small businesses by providing management training and financial advice and loans.

figure 6.5

TYPES OF SBA FINANCIAL
ASSISTANCE

The SBA may provide the following types of financial assistance:

- *Guaranteed loans*—loans made by a financial institution that the government will repay if the borrower stops making payments. The maximum individual loan guarantee is capped at $5 million.
- *Microloans*—amounts ranging from $100 to $50,000 to people such as single mothers and public housing tenants.
- *Export Express*—loans made to small businesses wishing to export. The maximum guaranteed loan amount is $500,000.
- *Community Adjustment and Investment Program (CAIP)*—loans to businesses to create new, sustainable jobs or to preserve existing jobs in eligible communities that have lost jobs due to changing trade patterns with Mexico and Canada following the adoption of NAFTA.
- *Pollution control loans*—loans to eligible small businesses for the financing of the planning, design, or installation of a pollution control facility. This facility must prevent, reduce, abate, or control any form of pollution, including recycling.
- *504 certified development company (CDC) loans*—loans for purchasing major fixed assets, such as land and buildings for businesses in eligible communities, typically rural communities or urban areas needing revitalization. The program's goal is to expand business ownership by minorities, women, and veterans. The maximum guaranteed loan amount is $1.5 million.

Small Business Investment Company (SBIC) Program
A program through which private investment companies licensed by the Small Business Administration lend money to small businesses.

You may also want to consider requesting funds from the **Small Business Investment Company (SBIC) Program.** SBICs are private investment companies licensed by the SBA to lend money to small businesses. An SBIC must have a minimum of $5 million in capital and can borrow up to $2 from the SBA for each $1 of capital it has. It lends to or invests in small businesses that meet its criteria. Often SBICs are able to keep defaults to a minimum by identifying a business's trouble spots early, giving entrepreneurs advice, and in some cases rescheduling loan payments.[42]

Perhaps the best place for young entrepreneurs to start shopping for an SBA loan is a Small Business Development Center (SBDC). SBDCs are funded jointly by the federal government and individual states, and are usually associated with state and community colleges and universities. SBDCs can help you evaluate the feasibility of your idea, develop your business plan, and complete your funding application—all for no charge.

The SBA reduced the size of its application from 150 pages to one page for loans under $50,000. In February 2011, the SBA introduced two new programs called Community Advantage and Small Loan Advantage, which are aimed at providing a simpler and easier way for lenders to make smaller loans to businesses in underserved areas. However, a month later the House Small Business Committee recommended the SBA budget be cut and that no money be used for the new programs.[43] Confused? Since government regulations are constantly changing, you may want to go to the SBA's website (www.sba.gov) for the latest information about SBA programs and other business services.

Obtaining money from banks, venture capitalists, and government sources is very difficult for most small businesses. (You will learn more about financing in Chapter 18.) Those who do survive the planning and financing of their new ventures are eager to get their businesses up and running. Your success in running a business depends on many factors, especially knowing your customers, managing your employees, and keeping good records.

connection

Going Locavore

Over the last few years, more and more people across the country have turned their backs on processed foods to focus on more natural ingredients. But there are some who go even further than filling their shopping carts exclusively with organic foods. Known as "locavores," these particular eaters try to ensure that all the food that goes into their stomachs comes directly from their community.

This isn't exactly a brand-new idea. After all, for thousands of years most people had no other choice but to eat food that grew within a few miles of their homes. In these days of globalization, however, eating locally is a radical choice. Many of the fruits and vegetables that Americans eat either come from far-flung farms across the nation or other countries entirely. Locavores lessen their carbon footprints by buying foods that only have to be shipped short distances. Also, local foods are often organic products made by families and small businesses rather than factory farms.

Still, eating local isn't easy. Foods that are plentiful in some areas can be unavailable in others, potentially leading to a limited diet. Furthermore, restaurant owners often have to make the choice between purchasing a local product or importing a higher quality one. Parmigiano-Reggiano cheese, for instance, is considered the greatest cheese of its type. Should the owner of a gourmet Italian restaurant that uses local ingredients feel forced to buy an inferior product just to support his food community? In the end, the best way for restaurateurs and consumers to cook could be to combine both approaches. Supporting local economies is important in this day and age, but the bounties of the global marketplace should not be ignored either.

Sources: John Mariani, "Locavore, Schmocavore," *Esquire*, May 24, 2011; and John Tierney, "Fresh and Direct from the Garden an Ocean Away," *The New York Times*, August 29, 2011.

Knowing Your Customers

One of the most important elements of small-business success is knowing the **market,** which consists of consumers with unsatisfied wants and needs who have both resources and willingness to buy. Most of our students have the willingness to own a brand-new Maserati sports car. However, few have the resources necessary to satisfy this want. Would they be a good market for a luxury car dealer?

market
People with unsatisfied wants and needs who have both the resources and the willingness to buy.

Once you have identified your market and its needs, you must set out to fill those needs. How? Offer top quality at a fair price with great service. Remember, it isn't enough to get customers—you have to *keep* them. As Victoria Jackson, founder of the $50 million company Victoria Jackson Cosmetics, says of the stars who push her products on television infomercials, "All the glamorous faces in the world wouldn't mean a thing if my customers weren't happy with the product and didn't come back for more." Everything must be geared to bring customers the satisfaction they deserve.

One of the greatest advantages small businesses have is the ability to know their customers better and adapt quickly to their ever-changing needs. The Making the Green Connection box discusses how some restaurants meet their customers' demands for locally produced foods. You will gain more insights about markets in Chapters 13–16. Now let's consider effectively managing the employees who help you serve your market.

Managing Employees

As a business grows, it becomes impossible for an entrepreneur to oversee every detail, even by putting in 60 hours per week. This means that hiring, training, and motivating employees are critical.

It is not easy to find good help when you offer less money, skimpier benefits, and less room for advancement than larger firms do. That's one reason employee relations is important for small-business management. Employees of small companies are often more satisfied with their jobs than are their counterparts in big business. Why? Quite often they find their jobs more challenging, their ideas more accepted, and their bosses more respectful.[44]

Often entrepreneurs are reluctant to recognize that to keep growing, they must delegate authority to others. Who should have this delegated authority, and how much?

This can be a particularly touchy issue in small businesses with long-term employees and in family businesses. As you might expect, entrepreneurs who have built their companies from scratch often feel compelled to promote employees who have been with them from the start—even when they aren't qualified to serve as managers. Common sense tells you this could hurt the business. The idea that you must promote or can't fire people because "they're family" can also hinder growth. Entrepreneurs best serve themselves and the business if they gradually recruit and groom employees for management positions, enhancing trust and support between them. You'll learn more about managing employees in Chapters 7–12.

Not all small businesses stay small; some become business superstars. Take Mattel, for example. Mattel founders Ruth and Elliot Handler started their business in their garage—making picture frames. When they found that the dollhouse furniture they made with the wood scraps sold better than the frames, they changed their business. Today toys like Barbie helped Mattel grow into a $6.4 billion business.

Keeping Records

Small-business owners often say the most important assistance they received in starting and managing their business was in accounting.[45] A businessperson who sets up an effective accounting system early will save much grief later. Computers simplify record keeping and enable a small-business owner to daily follow sales, expenses, and profits. An inexpensive computer system can also help owners with inventory control, customer records, and payroll.

Many business failures are caused by poor accounting practices that lead to costly mistakes. A good accountant can help you decide whether to buy or lease equipment and whether to own or rent a building. He or she may also help you with tax planning, financial forecasting, choosing sources of financing, and writing requests for funds.

Other small-business owners may tell you where to find an accountant experienced in small business. It pays to shop around for advice. You'll learn more about accounting in Chapter 17.

Looking for Help

Small-business owners have learned, sometimes the hard way, that they need outside consulting advice early in the process. This is especially true of legal, tax, and accounting advice but also of marketing, finance, and other areas. Most small and medium-sized firms cannot afford to hire such experts as employees, so they must turn to outside assistance.

A necessary and invaluable aide is a competent, experienced lawyer who knows and understands small businesses. Lawyers can help with leases, contracts, partnership agreements, and protection against liabilities.[46] They don't have to be expensive. In fact, several prepaid legal plans offer services such as drafting legal documents for a low annual rate. Of course, you can find plenty of legal services online. The SBA offers plain-English guides and mini-tutorials that will help you gain a basic understanding of the laws that affect each phase of the life of a small business. FindForms.com offers a search tool that helps you find free legal forms from all over the web as well as advice, links, books, and more. Remember, "free" isn't a bargain if the information isn't correct, so check the sources carefully and double-check any legal actions with an attorney.

Make your marketing decisions long before you introduce a product or open a store. An inexpensive marketing research study may help you determine where to locate, whom to select as your target market, and what is an effective strategy for reaching it. Thus a marketing consultant with small-business experience can be of great help to you, especially one who has had experience with the Internet and social media.

Two other invaluable experts are a commercial loan officer and an insurance agent. The commercial loan officer can help you design an acceptable business plan and give you valuable financial advice as well as lend you money when you need it. An insurance agent will explain all the risks associated with a small business and how to cover them most efficiently with insurance and other means like safety devices and sprinkler systems.

An important source of information for small businesses is the **Service Corps of Retired Executives (SCORE).** This SBA office has more than 13,000 volunteers from industry, trade associations, and education who counsel small businesses at no cost (except for expenses).[47] You can find a SCORE counselor by logging on to www.score.org. The SBA also offers a free, comprehensive online entrepreneurship course for aspiring entrepreneurs.

Often business professors from local colleges will advise small-business owners free or for a small fee. Some universities have clubs or programs that provide consulting services by master of business administration (MBA) candidates for a nominal fee. The University of Maryland and Virginia Tech have internship programs that pair MBA students with budding companies in local incubator programs. The incubator companies pay half the intern's salary, which is around $20 an hour.

It is also wise to seek the counsel of other small-business owners. The website YoungEntrepreneur.com offers experienced entrepreneurs and young startups an open forum to exchange advice and ideas. Visitors have access to articles on marketing, business planning, incorporation, and financial management.

Other sources of counsel include local chambers of commerce, the Better Business Bureau, national and local trade associations, the business reference section of your library, and many small-business-related sites on the Internet. Some can match your consulting needs with the proper consultant, like Company Expert (www.4consulting-services.com).

Their love of bacon inspired Dave Lefkow and Justin Esch to create J&D Bacon Salt, a seasoning that adds the flavor of bacon to anything and everything. With a start-up budget of just $5,000, they promoted their product with strategies like MySpace and Facebook pages, a blog, and free samples. Without food-industry connections, Lefkow and Esch created their own network of support the hard way—by picking up the phone and asking for it. Check out their story at www .baconsalt.com.

Service Corps of Retired Executives (SCORE)
An SBA office with volunteers from industry, trade associations, and education who counsel small businesses at no cost (except for expenses).

progress assessment

- A business plan is probably the most important document a small-business owner will ever create. There are nine sections in the business plan outline in the chapter. Can you describe at least five of those sections now?

LEARNING goal 5

Outline the advantages and disadvantages small businesses have in entering global markets.

GOING GLOBAL: SMALL-BUSINESS PROSPECTS

As we noted in Chapter 3, there are over 313 million people in the United States but more than 7 billion people in the world.[48] Obviously, the world market is a much larger, more lucrative market for small businesses than the United States alone. In spite of that potential, many small businesses still do not think globally. Only 1 percent of small businesses now export, but half are expected to engage in global trade by 2015. Small businesses are well on their way to meeting those expectations; small and medium-sized business accounted for 99 percent of the growth in exporting firms in recent years.[49]

Technological advances have helped increase small business exporting. PayPal makes it possible for small businesses to get paid automatically when they conduct global business online. The Internet also helps small businesses find customers without the expense of international travel. As people acquire more wealth, they often demand specialized products that are not mass-produced and are willing to pay more for niche goods that small businesses offer. Dave Hammond, inventor and founder of Wizard Vending, began to push his gumball machines into the global market via a website. In the site's first year, he sold machines in Austria, Belgium, and Germany.

Still, many small businesses have difficulty getting started in global business. Why are so many missing the boat to the huge global markets? Primarily because the voyage includes a few major hurdles: (1) financing is often difficult to find, (2) would-be exporters don't know how to get started and do not understand the cultural differences between markets, and (3) the bureaucratic paperwork can threaten to bury a small business.

Beside the fact that most of the world's market lies outside the United States, there are other good reasons for going global. Exporting can absorb excess inventory, soften downturns in the domestic market, and extend product lives. It can also spice up dull routines.

Small businesses have several advantages over large businesses in international trade:

- Overseas buyers often enjoy dealing with individuals rather than with large corporate bureaucracies.
- Small companies can usually begin shipping much faster.

- Small companies can provide a wide variety of suppliers.
- Small companies can give customers personal service and undivided attention, because each overseas account is a major source of business to them.

A good place to start finding information about exporting is the Department of Commerce's Bureau of Industry and Security (www.bis.doc.gov). Other sources include the SBA's Office of International Trade. The SBA's Export Express loan program provides export financing opportunities for small businesses. The program is designed to finance a variety of needs of small-business exporters, including participation in foreign trade shows, catalog translations for use in foreign markets, lines of credit for export purposes, and real estate and equipment for the production of goods or services to be exported.

progress assessment

- Why do many small businesses avoid doing business globally?
- What are some of the advantages small businesses have over large businesses in selling in global markets?

summary

Learning Goal 1. Explain why people take the risks of entrepreneurship; list the attributes of successful entrepreneurs; and describe entrepreneurial teams, intrapreneurs, and home- and web-based businesses.

- **What are a few of the reasons people start their own businesses?**

Reasons include profit, independence, opportunity, and challenge.

- **What are the attributes of successful entrepreneurs?**

Successful entrepreneurs are self-directed, self-nurturing, action-oriented, highly energetic, and tolerant of uncertainty.

- **What have modern entrepreneurs done to ensure longer terms of management?**

They have formed entrepreneurial teams with expertise in the many skills needed to start and manage a business.

- **What is a micropreneur?**

Micropreneurs are people willing to accept the risk of starting and managing the type of business that remains small, lets them do the kind of work they want to do, and offers them a balanced lifestyle.

- **What is intrapreneuring?**

Intrapreneuring is the establishment of entrepreneurial centers within a larger firm where people can innovate and develop new product ideas internally.

- **Why has there been such an increase in the number of home-based and web-based businesses in the last few years?**

The increase in power and decrease in price of computer technology have leveled the field and made it possible for small businesses to compete against larger companies—regardless of location.

Learning Goal 2. Discuss the importance of small business to the American economy and summarize the major causes of small-business failure.

- **Why are small businesses important to the U.S. economy?**

Small business accounts for almost 50 percent of gross domestic product (GDP). Perhaps more important to tomorrow's graduates, 80 percent of U.S. workers' first jobs are in small businesses.

- **What does the *small* in small business mean?**

The Small Business Administration defines a small business as one that is independently owned and operated and not dominant in its field of operation, and that meets certain standards of size in terms of employees or sales (depending on the size of others in the industry).

- **Why do many small businesses fail?**

Many small businesses fail because of managerial incompetence and inadequate financial planning. See Figure 6.3 for a list of causes of small-business failure.

Learning Goal 3. Summarize ways to learn about how small businesses operate.

- **What hints would you give someone who wants to learn about starting a small business?**

First, learn from others. Take courses and talk with some small-business owners. Second, get some experience working for others. Third, take over a successful firm. Finally, study the latest in small-business management techniques, including the use of computers for functions like payroll, inventory control, and mailing lists.

Learning Goal 4. Analyze what it takes to start and run a small business.

- **What goes into a business plan?**

See the outline of a business plan in the chapter.

- **What sources of funds should someone wanting to start a new business consider investigating?**

A new entrepreneur has several potential sources of capital: personal savings, relatives, former employers, banks, finance companies, venture capital organizations, government agencies, and more.

- **What are some of the special problems that small-business owners have in dealing with employees?**

Small-business owners often have difficulty finding competent employees and grooming employees for management responsibilities.

- **Where can budding entrepreneurs find help in starting their businesses?**

Help can come from many sources: accountants, lawyers, marketing researchers, loan officers, insurance agents, the SBA, SBDCs, SBICs, and even college professors.

Learning Goal 5. Outline the advantages and disadvantages small businesses have in entering global markets.

- **What are some advantages small businesses have over large businesses in global markets?**

Foreign buyers enjoy dealing with individuals rather than large corporations because (1) small companies provide a wider variety of suppliers and can ship products more quickly and (2) small companies give more personal service.

- **Why don't more small businesses start trading globally?**

There are several reasons: (1) financing is often difficult to find, (2) many people don't know how to get started and do not understand the cultural differences in foreign markets, and (3) the bureaucratic red tape is often overwhelming.

key terms

affiliate marketing 162
business plan 169
enterprise zones 163
entrepreneurial
   team 158
entrepreneurship 154
incubators 163

intrapreneurs 163
market 175
micropreneurs 158
Service Corps of
   Retired Executives
   (SCORE) 177
small business 165

Small Business
   Administration
   (SBA) 173
Small Business
   Investment Company
   (SBIC) Program 174
venture capitalists 172

critical thinking

1. Do you have the entrepreneurial spirit? What makes you think that?
2. Are there any similarities between the characteristics demanded of an entre-preneur and those of a professional athlete? Would an athlete be a good prospect for entrepreneurship? Why or why not? Could teamwork be important in an entrepreneurial effort? Why or why not?
3. Imagine yourself starting a small business. What kind of business would it be? How much competition is there? What could you do to make your business more attractive than those of competitors? Would you be willing to work 60 to 70 hours a week to make the business successful?

developing workplace skills

1. Find issues of *Entrepreneur, Black Enterprise,* and *Inc.* magazines in the library or on the Internet. Read about the entrepreneurs who are heading today's dynamic new businesses. Write a profile about one.
2. Select a small business that looks attractive as a career possibility for you. Talk to at least one person who manages such a business. Ask how he or she started it. Ask about financing; human resource management (hiring, firing, training, scheduling); accounting issues; and other managerial matters. Prepare a summary of your findings, including whether the person's job was rewarding, interesting, and challenging—and why or why not.
3. Contact the Small Business Administration by visiting a local office or the organization's website at www.sba.gov. Write a brief summary of the services the SBA offers.
4. Select a small business in your area or a surrounding area that has failed. List the factors you think led to its failure. Compile a list of actions the business owners might have taken to keep the company in business.
5. Choose a partner from among your classmates and put together a list of factors that might mean the difference between success and failure of a new company entering the business technology industry. Can small startups realistically hope to compete with companies such as Microsoft and Intel? Discuss the list and your conclusions in class.

taking it to the net

Purpose

To assess your potential to succeed as an entrepreneur and to evaluate a sample business plan.

Exercise

1. Go to **www.bizmove.com/other/quiz.htm** and take the interactive entrepreneurial quiz to find out whether you have the qualities to be a successful entrepreneur.

2. If you have entrepreneurial traits and decide you would like to start your own business, you'll need to develop a business plan. Go to **www.bplans.com/ sample_business_plans.cfm** and click on Coffee Shops. Review the sample business plan for Internet Café. Although the plan may not follow the same format as the business plan outline in the chapter, does it contain all the necessary information listed in the outline? If not, what is missing?

casing the web

To access the case "BMOC: Starting a Small Business at School," visit **www.mhhe.com/P2P2e**

video case

Launching a Business: Pillow Pets

"If you like what you do, then life is a whole lot easier for you and for those around you." According to Jennifer and Clint Telfer, this is the key to success as an entrepreneur. Beginning with an idea and using $50,000 from credit cards, the Telfers launched the company CJ Products with the featured line of Pillow Pets. The idea began as Jennifer watched her son patting down his stuffed animal to use it as a pillow. Since that humble beginning, the company has grown tremendously; that growth includes a successful website and licensing agreements with Major League Baseball, the NCAA, and Disney.

Jennifer cites two mistakes they made early on as entrepreneurs: (1) they tried to grow the business too quickly; and (2) they used a less than quality manufacturer. These two errors were costly, and it took the Telfers a year and a half to recover their losses. Since those early setbacks, the Telfers and Pillow Pets have never looked back. Today, the company sells over 15 million units a year.

Part of the Telfers' success stems from their many years as salespeople in retail markets. Success as an entrepreneur requires a passion for what you do, action orientation, self-discipline, and high energy levels.

Small businesses are the backbone of the U.S. economy, with more than 2 million currently operating and over 750,000 new businesses starting up each year. Small businesses are responsible for over 75 percent of all jobs in the United States. In fact, small businesses generate over 50 percent of the U.S. GDP annually. And over 80 percent of all Americans began their first job with a small business. Many of today's large businesses, such as Avon, Ford, DuPont, Walmart, and Amazon.com, all started as small entrepreneurial ventures.

Do you have what it takes to be a successful entrepreneur? While self-discipline and high energy are essential, you must have a passion for what you want to do.

Thinking It Over

1. *How does the notion of taking an existing idea and making it better relate to the successful launch of Pillow Pets?*
2. *There are several types of entrepreneurship. What are they and which type describes CJ Products?*
3. *How did the Telfers finance their startup? Did they rely on bank financing or venture capital?*

Career Outlook
Part 2 Conclusion—Business Ownership

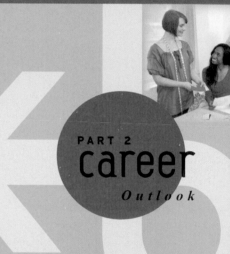

There was a time when it was common for a college graduate to find a job, work at that company for 40 years, climb up the "corporate ladder," and retire. That's not always the case today. Statistically, you are more likely to hop from job to job every few years than to stay in one place, especially at the beginning of your career.

This flexibility provides more opportunities for entrepreneurship or for starting a new business to fill an unmet need in your community. New small businesses are vital to the U.S. economy, especially as the recent economic recession increased unemployment and decreased growth. New business possibilities are as varied as the people who create them.

PART 2
career
Outlook

SKILLS NEEDED

CAREER PATHS

POSSIBLE POSITIONS

PROFILE

COVER LETTER

RESUME

INTERVIEW

Skills Needed

Whether you are applying to buy a franchise or asking the bank for a loan to launch your own business, you'll need to demonstrate on your résumé and cover letter and in your interview that you are:

- **Self-starting**—Have you ever started a club or sports team? Do you propose new ideas to your boss or teacher? Show employers that you don't need others to tell you how and when to do something.

- **Risk-taking**—Are you able to take some risks? Have you ever moved far from home? Or changed careers? Are you the first in your family to attend college? Think back to a time when you took a risk—even if you didn't succeed—and demonstrated your courage.

- **Creative**—What was your last big idea? Have you ever brainstormed a creative solution to a problem? Show you can think outside the box.

- **Ambitious**—Where do you see yourself in 10 years? Share your dreams for yourself—the bigger, the better—and demonstrate that you have the stamina to achieve your goals.

- **Optimistic**—When was the last time you failed at something but chose to see the failure as a temporary setback or, better yet, a new opportunity? Do you see setbacks as lessons you won't have to learn again?

Career Paths

Business owners get started in many ways. Some purchase an existing business. Others buy a franchise. And others create an original idea and develop it from scratch. Whichever starting point you choose, remember the rewards you get from being an entrepreneur are directly related to the time and effort you put into the job. Beyond that, your career path is up to you!

Possible Positions

POSSIBLE POSITIONS FOR WOULD-BE ENTREPRENEURS				
OPPORTUNITY	**MEDIAN SALARY**	**DUTIES**	**REQUIREMENTS**	**GROWTH**
Home-Based, Owner-Run Business	Low at first, but great potential	Launch and run business. Bookkeeping, marketing, customer relations, etc.	Must be self-motivated and ambitious	Fast growth, but lots of risk
Franchise	Considerably higher than nonfranchise operations from the first month of operation	Own and operate part of a larger business organization	Varies. Most franchisors provide considerable training and support	Fast growth
Small Business Consultant	Vary greatly, based on number of contacts and ability to market	Advise businesses in various stages of success or failure	Master's degree in business	Growing
Franchise Director	Depends on the number of franchises and size of the operation	Direct and train franchisees	Varies. Must be able to work with and motivate others	Growing

Source: Bureau of Labor Statistics, *Occupational Outlook Handbook*, 2012–13 Edition.

Profile: Vladim Gamurari, Aspiring Soccer Entrepreneur

Vladim Gamurari moved to the United States in 2002 from Romania knowing very little English. Vladim played soccer all his life, so when the neighborhood middle school was looking for a coach, he volunteered. He loves teaching soccer to kids, so he left his dead-end job and started working at a soccer store. Now he wants to start his own business managing an indoor soccer stadium. Vladim has never owned or operated his own business, so he is applying for a weeklong entrepreneurship program. The program has limited enrollment, and potential participants must submit résumés and participate in an interview process.

Below, you'll find Vladim's application for the program: a cover letter, a résumé, and some sample interview questions. Despite his lack of experience, how did he highlight his leadership skills in his résumé? Does he have the entrepreneurial spirit? Would you accept him if you were in charge of the program? What would you change? What will you apply to your own cover letter, résumé, and interview?

VLADIM'S COVER LETTER

Vladim Gamurari
1532 West Ninth Street
Madison, Wisconsin 26544
423-776-5567
VladimG@hotmail.com

January 8, 2014

Jason Smith
Founder, CEO
Entrepreneurship Excellence Program
394 Jackson Boulevard
Milwaukee, Wisconsin 26593

Dear Mr. Smith,

Thank you for the opportunity to apply to the Entrepreneurship Excellence Program. I have wanted to start my own indoor soccer business since I began volunteering as the soccer coach for Madison North Middle School. Because of my passion for soccer and my experience with it, both here in Wisconsin and in my native country of Romania, working with you seems like a good match. I believe I would be an excellent indoor stadium owner. I have demonstrated a strong work ethic in my sales position and the ability to take the initiative in my volunteer position as a coach.

While I am ambitious and highly motivated, I know that I must develop the skills I need to research, develop, and launch my own indoor soccer league. If I am accepted into your program, I will dedicate my attention and time to learn everything that I need to begin my dream. Without Entrepreneurship Excellence training, I know I will have a much harder time learning how to take my business from an idea to the real thing.

I have experienced how taking new risks can lead to a better life. I left my parents in Romania to come to the United States for a new life. Starting over in a new country was difficult, but it will be worth the work if I can accomplish my business dream. You can count on me to work hard in this program and take advantage of the training that you offer.

Thank you for your consideration, and I look forward to hearing from you.

Sincerely,

Vladim Gamurari
Vladim Gamurari

Tip: Provide results from the experience that you've had to support any claims you make about your abilities.

Tip: Use your cover letter to tell an interesting story about who you are so that an employer will be interested in meeting you.

VLADIM'S RESUME

Vladim Gamurari
1532 West Ninth Street
Madison, Wisconsin 26544
423-776-5567
VladimG@hotmail.com

Education

Madison Community College   Anticipated graduation: May 2014

Associate's Degree, Business

Universitatea de Busines, Braşov, Romania   1998-2001
Economics

Work Experience

Sales Associate, _USA Soccer Outlet_   2008–Present

- Initiate and direct changes in store layout
- Place orders to restock merchandise and handle receiving of products
- Display a helpful attitude that is consistently praised by customers and my supervisor
- Achieved greater responsibility after four promotions in four years

Cashier, _Used Auto Parts_   2003–2008

- Managed register at auto outlet, which averaged 250 customers each month
- Praised for exceptional cash-handling accuracy
- Maintained position and customer relations while learning English

Volunteer Experience

Soccer Coach, _Red Lightning Soccer Team_   2007–Present

- Manage and coach team for neighborhood middle school
- Schedule facilities for practices
- Order and issue equipment and supplies, maintaining accurate inventory
- Help youth develop physical skills and positive attitudes
- Create practice schedules and exercises for the team

Skills

- Skilled at operating computerized cash registers and scanners
- Basic skills in MS Word, Excel, and PowerPoint

Languages

Fluent in Romanian, French, and English

Tip: Start each description with a "power word" verb. For a list, see Figure E.3 in the Epilogue.

Tip: Use details, including numbers when possible, to demonstrate responsibilities.

Tip: Add interesting facts about yourself that make the employer see you as a whole person.

Vladim's Interview

Question: Tell me a little about yourself. What do you do? What are your hobbies?

Poor answer: I sell shoes and uniforms at a soccer store and don't really think that job is going to get me anywhere. It's kind of boring when we don't have customers. I like playing soccer and wish I could do that all the time.

Great answer: I moved here from Romania, where I studied business. I've played soccer since I was a little kid. All the children in the village would run straight to the soccer fields when school was over and play until our mothers called us home. Now I coach the Red Lightning at the middle school near my house. I enjoy helping young people learn more about my favorite sport.

Tip: Honesty is important, but treat the interviewer as a potential employer, not your friend. Use an interview to demonstrate how you would be perfect for the position, not to complain about your life now.

Question: Why should we pick you for this program?

Poor answer: It would really help me out. I need to have a better life. I would appreciate it if you choose me.

Great answer: I am very hard working. I have worked my entire life, and now I have a job and go to school. I have a dream—to open my own indoor soccer stadium—and I will work hard to do it. But I know I need to learn more about business if I want to be a success. I am motivated to work hard at the workshop because I want to accomplish my dream.

Tip: Spend some time thinking about who you are before an interview. What are five words you would use to describe yourself? Choose adjectives that highlight you when you describe yourself.

Question: You have no leadership experience. Why should we accept you?

Poor answer: Yes, I guess you are right. Even though I don't have any experience, I hope you'll give me a chance.

Great answer: While I have never owned or led my own business, I do have experience being a leader. Every week, I coach the soccer team at Madison North Middle School. I decide when and how we practice, I set the lineup for games, and I choose which players will play. I also lead by teaching the team things like good sportsmanship, positive team spirit, and joy of the game. In addition, I organize monthly meetings for parents to set a schedule for snacks and drinks at the games. That was my idea. I am a leader in my community, and I want to be a leader in my own business.

Tip: Get specific. Even if you don't have examples of your entrepreneurial skills in your work experience, find an example in your personal life. Tell your story.

Business Management:
EMPOWERING EMPLOYEES
TO SATISFY CUSTOMERS

The success of any business depends upon the skills and abilities of the people in it – especially the people responsible for managing the business. In the chapters in Part 3, you will begin with an overview of the four functions of management: planning, organizing, leading, and controlling.

LOOKING
Ahead

Look down at your shoes. Who do you think designed and made them? Do you think one person came up with the design, gathered the materials, cut and sewed them, and drove them over to a store near you? Of course not. Many people worked together to get your feet covered. How did they decide who would do what and when? In this section you will learn how managers organize companies to supply the many products and services you want and need.

CHAPTER 7   Management and Leadership

CHAPTER 8   Structuring Organizations for Today's Challenges

CHAPTER 9   Production and Operations Management

7

Management AND Leadership

After you have read and studied this chapter, you should be able to

1 Describe the changes occurring today in the management function.

2 Describe the four functions of management.

3 Relate the planning process and decision making to the accomplishment of company goals.

4 Describe the organizing function of management.

5 Explain the differences between leaders and managers, and describe the various leadership styles.

6 Summarize the five steps of the control function of management.

In today's fame-conscious culture, many celebrities can make money by lending their names to advertise products. The problem with these endorsement deals, though, is that they only last as long as the spokesperson stays famous. For former supermodel Kathy Ireland, such an unsustainable plan simply would not do.

Ireland caught the entrepreneurial bug early in life. As a child she sold painted stones and other crafts door-to-door. By age 11, Ireland was earning $60 a month delivering newspapers. Five years later her income grew even more when a representative for the Elite Modeling Agency discovered her at finishing school. At 20, Ireland appeared in the *Sports Illustrated* Swimsuit Issue (the first of 13 consecutive appearances). When she finally graced the magazine's cover in 1989, it became *Sports Illustrated*'s best-selling issue ever.

Modeling brought Ireland wealth and fame, but she knew that it wouldn't last forever. In 1993, she received an offer to model socks, a gig that most jet-setting supermodels would reject outright. Rather than let herself get down about such an unglamorous job, Ireland turned it into a business opportunity. "I wanted to make it clear to them that I didn't want to just put my name on it," says Ireland. "An endorsement wasn't interesting to me." Instead of acting solely as a spokesperson, she suggested that they brand the socks with her name. Ireland ended up striking a deal with the socks' marketer that gave her a royalty for every product sold. Along with the help of a $50,000 personal loan, Kathy Ireland Worldwide was officially in business.

Once the socks turned out to be a success, Ireland started licensing her name to other types of apparel, like exercise clothes and swimwear. By 1994, she had signed an exclusive deal to sell her products at Kmart. The retailer hoped Ireland would do for clothing what Martha Stewart had done for housewares. However, Ireland's plans for her company stretched out far beyond apparel. The legendary investor and billionaire Warren Buffett once told her that while fashion changes constantly, the home stays relatively the same. Ireland took that advice to heart when her company expanded into furniture by 1998. With this new market, Ireland had finally found a motto for her brand: "Finding solutions for families, especially busy moms." Within a year, Kathy Ireland Worldwide expanded into carpets, flooring, and floor tiles. Kmart, on the other hand, had fallen into bankruptcy around the turn of the millennium. In 2003, Ireland made the bold decision to break off her company's relationship with the retailer as well as apparel altogether.

Although her decision seemed risky at the time, Ireland's gamble paid off handsomely in the long run. By attaching a celebrity name to mundane products like replacement windows and area rugs, Ireland created a recognizable, reliable brand that earns $2 billion in annual retail revenue, more than Martha Stewart.

Ireland has been able to keep the company's overhead amazingly low. Focusing strictly on licensing, Kathy Ireland Worldwide lends its name to items that other businesses produce. This type of company requires a significant amount of legal and financial expertise to stay successful. Although Ireland lacks a higher-level business degree, she closely manages a staff of more than 40 people who take care of the company's technical aspects. Without the hassle of managing production costs or funding marketing campaigns, Ireland could simply sit back and watch the royalties roll in. Instead, she maintains an active role as chief designer. As the head of a global company, Ireland often travels across the world promoting products and gathering inspiration. For instance, in Liverpool, England, a beautiful rusted gate provided the spark for the look of a bed headboard. In fact, the designs for each of her company's 15,000 products started with an idea from Ireland. When she's not traveling, Ireland often holds staff meetings at her home where she fosters the same hospitable atmosphere she tries to put in her products.

Despite her phenomenal success so far, Ireland insists the company still has a long way to go. The future for Ireland includes another foray into retail as well as a line of kitchen products. Given her natural managerial know-how, Ireland will surely see plenty of green in the years to come.

This chapter is all about leadership and management. You will learn that shared leadership is more widespread than you might have imagined. You will also learn about the functions of management and how management differs from leadership. All in all, you should get a better idea of what leaders and managers do and how they do it.

CONNECTING WITH

x Kathy Ireland

CEO of Kathy Ireland Worldwide

Sources: Dorothy Pomerantz, "How Sports Illustrated Swimsuit Model Kathy Ireland Became a $350 Million Mogul," *Forbes,* February 27, 2012; Moira Forbes, "Kathy Ireland: Swimsuit Cover Girl Turned $2 Billion Business Model?" *Forbes,* February 13, 2012; and Marc Snetiker, "Kathy Ireland Is the World's Wealthiest Supermodel-Entrepreneur," *Entertainment Weekly,* February 24, 2012.

LEARNING **goal 1**

Describe the changes occurring today in the management function.

MANAGERS' ROLES ARE EVOLVING

Managers must practice the art of getting things done through organizational resources, which include workers, financial resources, information, and equipment. At one time, managers were called "bosses" and their job consisted of telling people what to do, watching over them to be sure they did it, and reprimanding those who didn't. Many managers still behave that way. Perhaps you've witnessed such behavior; some coaches use this style.

Today, however, most managers tend to be more progressive. For example, they emphasize teams and team building; they create drop-in centers, team spaces, and

Here a Best Buy manager rallies his employees just before opening the store's doors. Rather than telling employees exactly what to do, managers today tend to give their employees enough independence to make their own informed decisions about how best to please customers. How do you think most employees respond to this empowerment on the job?

192

open work areas.[1] They may change the definition of *work* from a task you do for a specified period in a specific place to something you do anywhere, anytime. They tend to guide, train, support, motivate, and coach employees rather than tell them what to do.[2] Managers of high-tech firms, for instance, realize that many workers often know more about technology than they do.[3] Thus most modern managers emphasize teamwork and cooperation rather than discipline and order giving. They may also open their books to employees to share the company's financials.[4]

The years 2008–2012 were particularly hard on managers and workers. The financial crisis forced many leading firms to fire managers and lower-level workers. PepsiCo's CEO Indra Nooyi won praise for rallying employees amid the gloom. But she too announced plans to cut some 3,000 employees. Furthermore, it became more difficult to get financing for new ventures or to modernize existing plants. Managers tended to be cautious in starting new ventures as they waited to see what the economy would do. That hesitancy contributed to the high unemployment the United States experienced in 2010–2012.[5]

The people entering management today are different from those who entered in the past. Leaders of Fortune 100 companies tend to be younger, more of them are female, and fewer of them were educated at elite universities.[6] Managers in the future are more likely to be working in teams and assuming completely new roles in the firm. For one thing, they'll be doing more expansion overseas. Further, they will be taking a leadership role in adapting to climate change. They will also be more concerned with recycling and other "green" issues.[7]

What these changes mean for you is that management will demand a new kind of person: a skilled communicator and team player as well as a planner, organizer, motivator, and leader. Future managers will need to be more globally prepared; that is, they need skills such as adaptability, foreign language skills, and ease in other cultures.[8] We'll address these trends in the next few chapters to help you decide whether management is the kind of career you would like.

Ursula Burns, for example, is the CEO of Xerox.[9] She is a mechanical engineer, and the first African-American woman to run a Fortune 500 company. She was outspoken and blunt in a culture that was probably overly genteel. Burns was just one of the women who inspired an article called "The Year of the Business Woman" in *U.S. News and World Report*.[10] In the following sections, we shall discuss management in general and the functions that Ursula Burns and other new managers are performing.

LEARNING goal 2

Describe the four functions of management.

THE FOUR FUNCTIONS OF MANAGEMENT

The following definition of management provides the outline of this chapter: **Management** is the process used to accomplish organizational goals through planning, organizing, leading, and controlling people and other organizational resources (see Figure 7.1).

Planning includes anticipating trends and determining the best strategies and tactics to achieve organizational goals and objectives. One of the major objectives of organizations is to please customers.[11] The trend today is to have *planning*

management
The process used to accomplish organizational goals through planning, organizing, leading, and controlling people and other organizational resources.

planning
A management function that includes anticipating trends and determining the best strategies and tactics to achieve organizational goals and objectives.

figure 7.1

WHAT MANAGERS DO

Some modern managers perform all of these tasks with the full cooperation and participation of workers. Empowering employees means allowing them to participate more fully in decision making.

Planning	Leading
• Setting organizational goals. • Developing strategies to reach those goals. • Determining resources needed. • Setting precise standards.	• Guiding and motivating employees to work effectively to accomplish organizational goals and objectives. • Giving assignments. • Explaining routines. • Clarifying policies. • Providing feedback on performance.
Organizing	**Controlling**
• Allocating resources, assigning tasks, and establishing procedures for accomplishing goals. • Preparing a structure (organization chart) showing lines of authority and responsibility. • Recruiting, selecting, training, and developing employees. • Placing employees where they'll be most effective.	• Measuring results against corporate objectives. • Monitoring performance relative to standards. • Rewarding outstanding performance. • Taking corrective action when necessary.

organizing
A management function that includes designing the structure of the organization and creating conditions and systems in which everyone and everything work together to achieve the organization's goals and objectives.

leading
Creating a vision for the organization and guiding, training, coaching, and motivating others to work effectively to achieve the organization's goals and objectives.

teams to help monitor the environment, find business opportunities, and watch for challenges. *Planning* is a key management function because accomplishing the other functions depends heavily on having a good plan.

Organizing includes designing the structure of the organization and creating conditions and systems in which everyone and everything work together to achieve the organization's goals and objectives. Many of today's organizations are being designed around pleasing the customer at a profit. Thus they must remain flexible and adaptable, because when customer needs change, firms must change with them. Whole Foods Market, for example, is known for its high-quality, high-priced food items.[12] But it has introduced many lower-cost items to adjust to the financial losses of its customer base. General Motors lost much of its customer base to manufacturers of more fuel-efficient cars. It hopes to win back market share by offering hydrogen-powered or electric vehicles that cost less to run.[13] GM has had some success in doing that.

Leading means creating a vision for the organization and communicating, guiding, training, coaching, and motivating others to achieve goals and objectives in a

Planning is what helps managers understand the environment in which their businesses must operate. When people's tastes and preferences for restaurant meals change, food service managers need to be ready to respond with menu alternatives. What changes have occurred in your own preferences?

timely manner. The trend is to empower employees, giving them as much freedom as possible to become self-directed and self-motivated. This function was once known as *directing;* that is, telling employees exactly what to do. In many smaller firms, that is still the manager's role. In most large firms, however, managers no longer tell people exactly what to do because knowledge workers and others often know how to do their jobs better than the manager does. Nonetheless, leadership is still necessary to keep employees focused on the right tasks at the right time.

Controlling establishes clear standards to determine whether an organization is progressing toward its goals and objectives, rewarding people for doing a good job, and taking corrective action if they are not. Basically, it means measuring whether what actually occurs meets the organization's goals.

Planning, organizing, leading, and controlling are the heart of management, so let's explore them in more detail. The process begins with planning; we'll look at that right after the Progress Assessment.

controlling
A management function that involves establishing clear standards to determine whether or not an organization is progressing toward its goals and objectives, rewarding people for doing a good job, and taking corrective action if they are not.

progress assessment

- What are some of the changes happening in management today?
- What's the definition of *management* used in this chapter?
- What are the four functions of management?

LEARNING goal 3

Relate the planning process and decision making to the accomplishment of company goals.

PLANNING AND DECISION MAKING

Planning, the first managerial function, is setting the organization's vision (including its mission statement), goals, and objectives. Executives find planning to be their most valuable tool. A **vision** is more than a goal; it's a broad explanation of why the organization exists and where it's trying to go. It gives the organization a sense of purpose and a set of values that unite workers in a common destiny. Managing an organization without first establishing a vision is like getting everyone in a rowboat excited about going somewhere, but not telling them exactly where. The boat will just keep changing directions rather than speeding toward an agreed-on goal.[14]

Top management usually sets the vision for the organization and then often works with others in the firm to establish a mission statement. A **mission statement** outlines the organization's fundamental purposes. It should address:

- The organization's self-concept.
- Its philosophy.
- Long-term survival needs.
- Customer needs.
- Social responsibility.
- Nature of the product or service.

The mission statement becomes the foundation for setting specific goals and objectives. **Goals** are the broad, long-term accomplishments an organization wishes to attain. Because workers and management need to agree on them, setting goals is often a team process. **Objectives** are specific, short-term statements detailing

vision
An encompassing explanation of why the organization exists and where it's trying to head.

mission statement
An outline of the fundamental purposes of an organization.

goals
The broad, long-term accomplishments an organization wishes to attain.

objectives
Specific, short-term statements detailing how to achieve the organization's goals.

how to achieve the organization's goals. One of your goals for reading this chapter, for example, may be to learn basic concepts of management. An objective you could use to achieve this goal is to answer the chapter's Progress Assessment questions.

Planning is a continuous process. A plan that worked yesterday may not be successful in today's market.[15] Most planning also follows a pattern. The procedure you'll follow in planning your life and career is basically the same as the one businesses use. It answers several fundamental questions:

1. *What is the situation now?* What are the success factors affecting the industry participants and how do we compare? What is the state of the economy and other environments?[16] What opportunities exist for meeting people's needs? What products and customers are most profitable? Who are our major competitors?[17] What threats are there to our business? These questions are part of **SWOT analysis,** which analyzes the organization's **s**trengths and **w**eaknesses, and the **o**pportunities and **t**hreats it faces, usually in that order. Opportunities and threats are often external to the firm and cannot always be anticipated.[18]

SWOT analysis
A planning tool used to analyze an organization's strengths, weaknesses, opportunities, and threats.

Weaknesses and strengths are more often internal and therefore more within reach of being measured and fixed. Figure 7.2 lists some of the general issues companies consider when conducting a SWOT analysis: What external success factors affect the industry? How does our firm measure up to other firms? What are our social objectives? What are our personal development objectives? What can we do to survive and prosper during a recession? For more on SWOT analysis, see the Taking It to the Net exercise at the end of this chapter.

2. *How can we get to our goal from here?* Answering this question is often the most important part of planning. It takes four forms: strategic, tactical, operational, and contingency (see Figure 7.3).

strategic planning
The process of determining the major goals of the organization and the policies and strategies for obtaining and using resources to achieve those goals.

Strategic planning is done by top management and determines the major goals of the organization and the policies, procedures, strategies, and resources it will need to achieve them. *Policies* are broad guidelines for action, and *strategies* determine the best way to use resources. At the strategic planning stage, top

figure 7.2

SWOT MATRIX

This matrix identifies potential strengths, weaknesses, opportunities, and threats organizations may consider in a SWOT analysis.

Potential Internal STRENGTHS	Potential Internal WEAKNESSES
• Core competencies in key areas • An acknowledged market leader • Well-conceived functional area strategies • Proven management • Cost advantages • Better advertising campaigns	• No clear strategic direction • Obsolete facilities • Subpar profitability • Lack of managerial depth and talent • Weak market image • Too narrow a product line
Potential External OPPORTUNITIES	**Potential External THREATS**
• Ability to serve additional customer groups • Expand product lines • Ability to transfer skills/technology to new products • Falling trade barriers in attractive foreign markets • Complacency among rival firms • Ability to grow due to increases in market demand	• Entry of lower-cost foreign competitors • Rising sales of substitute products • Slower market growth • Costly regulatory requirements • Vulnerability to recession and business cycles • Changing buyer needs and tastes

FORMS OF PLANNING

figure 7.3

PLANNING FUNCTIONS

Very few firms bother to make contingency plans. If something changes the market, such companies may be slow to respond. Most organizations do strategic, tactical, and operational planning.

managers of the company decide which customers to serve, when to serve them, what products or services to sell, and the geographic areas in which to compete.[19] Take Taco Bell, for example. Recognizing the economic slump, the company introduced a "value menu" of items like cheese roll-ups and bean burritos with prices starting at 79 cents. It also went after the "fourth-meal" (late-night) crowd and introduced several low-calorie, low-fat Fresco items. This strategy resulted in an 8 percent increase in sales. Blockbuster was not as successful in fighting off the introduction of new technology, making the company seemingly obsolete.[20]

In today's rapidly changing environment, strategic planning is becoming more difficult because changes are occurring so fast that plans—even those set for just months into the future—may soon be obsolete. Think of how the amusement park company Six Flags had to change its plans when gas went from a couple of dollars per gallon to over four dollars and then dropped back to the three-dollar range again. Think too of how Japanese companies had to respond to the earthquake and tsunami that created such devastation in a short period of time in 2011.[21]

Clearly, some companies are making shorter-term plans that allow for quick responses to customer needs and requests. The goal is to be flexible and responsive to the market.

Tactical planning is the process of developing detailed, short-term statements about what is to be done, who is to do it, and how. Managers or teams of managers at lower levels of the organization normally make tactical plans. Such plans can include setting annual budgets and deciding on other activities necessary to meet strategic objectives. If the strategic plan of a truck manufacturer, for example, is to sell more trucks in the South, the tactical plan might be to fund more research of southern truck drivers' wants and needs, and to plan advertising to reach them.

Operational planning is the process of setting work standards and schedules necessary to implement the company's tactical objectives. Whereas strategic planning looks at the organization as a whole, operational planning focuses on specific supervisors, department managers, and individual employees. The operational plan is the department manager's tool for daily and weekly operations. An operational plan may include, for example, the specific dates for certain truck parts to be completed and the quality specifications they must meet.

Contingency planning is the process of preparing alternative courses of action the firm can use if its primary plans don't work out. The economic and competitive

tactical planning
The process of developing detailed, short-term statements about what is to be done, who is to do it, and how it is to be done.

operational planning
The process of setting work standards and schedules necessary to implement the company's tactical objectives.

contingency planning
The process of preparing alternative courses of action that may be used if the primary plans don't achieve the organization's objectives.

environments change so rapidly that it's wise to have alternative plans of action ready in anticipation of such changes.[22] For example, if an organization doesn't meet its sales goals by a certain date, the contingency plan may call for more advertising or a cut in prices at that time. Crisis planning is a part of contingency planning that anticipates sudden changes in the environment. For example, many cities and businesses have developed plans to respond to terrorist attacks. You can imagine how important such plans would be to hospitals, airlines, the police, and public transportation authorities.

Instead of creating detailed strategic plans, the leaders of market-based companies (companies that respond quickly to changes in competition or to other environmental changes) often simply set direction. They want to stay flexible, listen to customers, and seize opportunities—expected or not. Think of how stores selling to teenagers must adapt to style changes.

The opportunities, however, must fit into the company's overall goals and objectives; if not, the company could lose its focus. Clearly, then, much of management and planning requires decision making.

Decision Making: Finding the Best Alternative

Planning and all the other management functions require decision making. **Decision making** is choosing among two or more alternatives, which sounds easier than it is. In fact, decision making is the heart of all the management functions.

decision making
Choosing among two or more alternatives.

The *rational decision-making model* is a series of steps managers often follow to make logical, intelligent, and well-founded decisions. Think of the steps as the seven Ds of decision making:

1. Define the situation.
2. Describe and collect needed information.
3. Develop alternatives.
4. Develop agreement among those involved.

5. Decide which alternative is best.
6. Do what is indicated (begin implementation).
7. Determine whether the decision was a good one, and follow up.

Managers don't always go through this seven-step process. Sometimes they have to make decisions *on the spot*—with little information available. They still must make good decisions in all such circumstances. **Problem solving** is less formal than decision making and usually calls for quicker action to resolve everyday issues. Both decision making and problem solving call for a lot of judgment.

Problem-solving teams are two or more workers assigned to solve a specific problem (e.g., Why aren't customers buying our service contracts?). Problem-solving techniques include **brainstorming,** that is, coming up with as many solutions as possible in a short period of time with no censoring of ideas. Another technique is called **PMI,** or listing all the **p**luses for a solution in one column, all the **m**inuses in another, and the **i**mplications in a third. The idea is to make sure the pluses exceed the minuses.

You can try using the PMI system on some of your personal decisions to get some practice. For example, should you stay home and study tonight? List all the pluses in one column: better grades, more self-esteem, more responsible behavior, and so on. In the other column, put the minuses: boredom, less fun, and so on. We hope the pluses outweigh the minuses most of the time and that you study often. But sometimes it's best to go out and have some fun, as long as doing so won't hurt your grades or job prospects.

problem solving
The process of solving the everyday problems that occur. Problem solving is less formal than decision making and usually calls for quicker action.

brainstorming
Coming up with as many solutions to a problem as possible in a short period of time with no censoring of ideas.

PMI
Listing all the pluses for a solution in one column, all the minuses in another, and the implications in a third column.

progress assessment

- What's the difference between goals and objectives?
- What does a company analyze when it does a SWOT analysis?
- What are the differences between strategic, tactical, and operational planning?
- What are the seven Ds in decision making?

LEARNING goal 4

Describe the organizing function of management.

ORGANIZING: CREATING A UNIFIED SYSTEM

After managers have planned a course of action, they must organize the firm to accomplish their goals. That means allocating resources (such as funds for various departments), assigning tasks, and establishing procedures. A managerial pyramid shows the levels of management (see Figure 7.4).[23] **Top management,** the highest level, consists of the president and other key company executives who develop strategic plans. Job titles and abbreviations you're likely to see often are chief executive officer (CEO), chief operating officer (COO), chief financial officer (CFO), and chief information officer (CIO) or in some companies chief knowledge

top management
The highest level of management, consisting of the president and other key company executives who develop strategic plans.

figure 7.4

LEVELS OF MANAGEMENT

This figure shows the three levels of management. In many firms, there are several levels of middle management. Recently, however, firms have been eliminating middle-level managers because fewer are needed to oversee self-managed teams of employees.

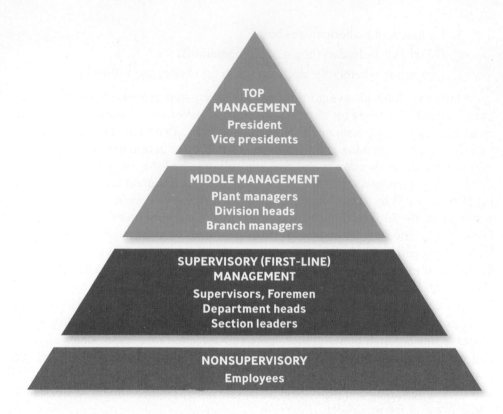

officer (CKO). The CEO is often also the president of the firm and is responsible for all top-level decisions. The CEO and president are the same person in 65 percent of the S&P 500 companies, including big companies like United Parcel Service, John Deere, and General Electric.

CEOs are responsible for introducing change into an organization. The COO is responsible for putting those changes into effect. His or her tasks include structuring work, controlling operations, and rewarding people to ensure that everyone strives to carry out the leader's vision. Many companies today are eliminating the COO function as a cost-cutting measure and assigning that role to the CEO. Often, the CFO participates in the decision to cut the COO position. The CFO is responsible for obtaining funds, planning budgets, collecting funds, and so on. The CIO or CKO is responsible for getting the right information to other managers so they can make correct decisions. CIOs are more important than ever to the success of their companies given the crucial role that information technology has come to play in every aspect of business.[24]

Middle management includes general managers, division managers, and branch and plant managers (in colleges, deans and department heads) who are responsible for tactical planning and controlling. Many firms, as a result of the recession that began in 2008, have eliminated some middle managers through downsizing and have given their remaining managers more employees to supervise.[25] Nonetheless, middle managers are still considered very important to most firms.[26]

Supervisory management includes those directly responsible for supervising workers and evaluating their daily performance; they're often known as first-line managers (or supervisors) because they're the first level above workers. This is the first management position you are most likely to acquire after college.

middle management
The level of management that includes general managers, division managers, and branch and plant managers who are responsible for tactical planning and controlling.

supervisory management
Managers who are directly responsible for supervising workers and evaluating their daily performance.

Tasks and Skills at Different Levels of Management

Few people are trained to be good managers. Usually a person learns how to be a skilled accountant or sales representative or production-line worker, and then—because of her or his skill—is selected to be a manager. Such managers tend to become deeply involved in showing others how to do things, helping them, supervising them, and generally being active in the operating task.

The further up the managerial ladder a person moves, the less important his or her original job skills become. At the top of the ladder, the need is for people who are visionaries, planners, organizers, coordinators, communicators, morale builders, and motivators.[27] Figure 7.5 shows that a manager must have three categories of skills:

1. **Technical skills** are the ability to perform tasks in a specific discipline (such as selling a product or developing software) or department (such as marketing or information systems).

2. **Human relations skills** include communication and motivation; they enable managers to work through and with people. Communication can be especially difficult when managers and employees speak different languages (see the Connecting Across Borders box). Skills associated with leadership—coaching, morale building, delegating, training and development, and supportiveness—are also human relations skills.

3. **Conceptual skills** let the manager picture the organization as a whole and see the relationships among its various parts. They are needed in planning, organizing, controlling, systems development, problem analysis, decision making, coordinating, and delegating.

technical skills
Skills that involve the ability to perform tasks in a specific discipline or department.

human relations skills
Skills that involve communication and motivation; they enable managers to work through and with people.

conceptual skills
Skills that involve the ability to picture the organization as a whole and the relationships among its various parts.

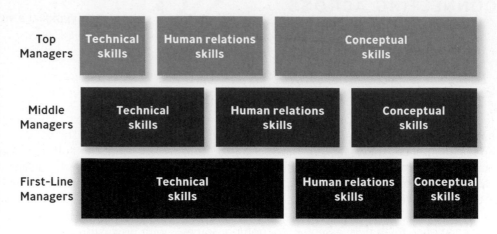

figure 7.5

SKILLS NEEDED AT VARIOUS LEVELS OF MANAGEMENT

All managers need human relations skills. At the top, managers need strong conceptual skills and rely less on technical skills. First-line managers need strong technical skills and rely less on conceptual skills. Middle managers need to have a balance between technical and conceptual skills.

Looking at Figure 7.5, you'll notice that first-line managers need to be skilled in all three areas. However, they spend most of their time on technical and human relations tasks, like assisting operating personnel and giving directions, and less time on conceptual tasks. Top managers, in contrast, need to use few technical skills. Instead, they spend almost all their time on human relations and conceptual tasks. A person who is competent at a low level of management may not be competent at higher levels, and vice versa. Different skills are needed at different levels.

Staffing: Getting and Keeping the Right People

To get the right kind of people to staff an organization, the firm has to offer the right kind of incentives. For example, Google's gourmet chefs cook up free lunches, dinners, and snacks for employees. Would such an incentive appeal to you? How important to you is pay relative to other incentives?

staffing
A management function that includes hiring, motivating, and retaining the best people available to accomplish the company's objectives.

Staffing is recruiting, hiring, motivating, and retaining the best people available to accomplish the company's objectives. Today, staffing is critical, especially in the Internet and high-tech areas. At most high-tech companies, like Google, Sony, and Microsoft, the primary capital equipment is brainpower. A firm with innovative and creative workers can go from startup to major competitor in just a few years.[28]

Many people are not willing to work at companies unless they are treated well and get fair pay. They may leave to find a better balance between work and home. Staffing is becoming a greater part of each manager's assignment, and all managers need to cooperate with human resource management to win and keep good workers. Chapter 11 is devoted to human resource issues, including staffing.

LEARNING goal 5

Explain the differences between leaders and managers, and describe the various leadership styles.

LEADING: PROVIDING CONTINUOUS VISION AND VALUES

One person might be a good manager but not a good leader. Another might be a good leader without being a good manager. Managers strive to produce order and stability, whereas leaders embrace and manage change. Leadership is creating a vision for others to follow, establishing corporate values and ethics, and transforming the way the organization does business in order to improve its effectiveness and efficiency.[29] Good leaders motivate workers and create the environment for them to motivate themselves. Management is carrying out the leader's vision.[30]

Leaders must therefore:

- *Communicate a vision and rally others around that vision.* The leader should be openly sensitive to the concerns of followers, give them responsibility, and win their trust. A successful leader must influence the actions of others. Ellen Kullman took the reins at DuPont in the middle of a crisis. Nonetheless, she set the tone for growth and prosperity in the future.[31]

- *Establish corporate values.* These include concern for employees, for customers, for the environment, and for the quality of the company's products. When companies set their business goals, they're defining the company's values as well. The number one trait that others look for in a leader is honesty. The second requirement is that the leader be forward looking.

- *Promote corporate ethics.* Ethical behavior includes an unfailing demand for honesty and an insistence that everyone in the company gets treated fairly (see the Making Ethical Decisions box). That's why we stress ethical decision making throughout this text. Many businesspeople have made the news by giving away huge amounts to charity, thus setting a model of social concern for their employees and others.[32]

- *Embrace change.* A leader's most important job may be to transform the way the company does business so that it's more effective (does things better) and more efficient (uses fewer resources to accomplish the same objectives).[33]

- *Stress accountability and responsibility.* If there is anything we have learned from the failures of banking managers and other industry and government managers during the recession that began in 2008, it is that leaders need to be held accountable and need to feel responsible for their actions. A key word that has emerged from the crisis is transparency. **Transparency** is the presentation of a company's facts and figures in a way that is clear and apparent to all stakeholders. Clearly it is time to make businessess and the government more transparent so that everyone is more aware of what is happening to the economy and to specific businesses and government agencies.[34]

All organizations need leaders, and all employees can help lead. You don't have to be a manager to perform a leadership function. That is, any employee can motivate others to work well, add to a company's ethical environment, and report ethical lapses when

transparency
The presentation of a company's facts and figures in a way that is clear and apparent to all stakeholders.

When Ellen Kullman took the reins at DuPont, the company was in crisis. Immediately Kullman oversaw two restructurings, dismissed thousands of employees, and asked the remaining employees to take a two- to three-week holiday without pay. Throughout it all Kullman never lost her ready sense of humor and set the tone for the company going forward.

To Share or Not to Share

First-line managers assist in the decisions made by their department heads. The department heads retain full responsibility for the decisions—if a plan succeeds, it's their success; if a plan fails, it's their failure. Now imagine this: As a first-line manager, you have new information that your department head hasn't seen yet. The find-ings in this report indicate that your manager's recent plans are sure to fail. If the plans do fail, the manager will probably be demoted and you're the most likely candidate to fill the vacancy. Will you give your department head the report? What is the ethical thing to do? What might be the consequences of your decision?

Need help understanding Leaders vs. Managers? www.introbiz.tv/QR7-1

autocratic leadership
Leadership style that involves making managerial decisions without consulting others.

participative (democratic) leadership
Leadership style that consists of managers and employees working together to make decisions.

Mike Krzyzewski, coach of Duke University's basketball team, has been successful as an autocratic leader. That makes sense, since you don't want basketball players deciding whether or not to play as a team. On the other hand, can you see why it is not so good to use autocratic leadership with a team of doctors?

they occur. Some employees today are taking a leadership position through the use of social media. (You can read about them in the nearby Connecting Through Social Media box.)

Leadership Styles

Nothing has challenged management researchers more than the search for the best leadership traits, behaviors, or styles. Thousands of studies have tried to identify characteristics that make leaders different from other people. Intuitively, you might conclude the same thing they did: leadership traits are hard to pin down. Some leaders are well groomed and tactful, while others are unkempt and abrasive—yet both may be just as effective.

Just as no one set of traits describes a leader, no one style of leadership works best in all situations. Even so, we can look at a few of the most commonly recognized leadership styles and see how they may be effective (see Figure 7.6):

1. **Autocratic leadership** means making managerial decisions without consulting others. This style is effective in emergencies and when absolute followership is needed—for example, when fighting fires. Autocratic leadership is also effective sometimes with new, relatively unskilled workers who need clear direction and guidance. Coach Phil Jackson used an autocratic leadership style to take the Los Angeles Lakers to three consecutive National Basketball Association championships in his first three seasons. By following his leadership, a group of highly skilled individuals became a winning team. How is the team doing now? What kind of leadership do you see being used most successfully in baseball, football, and other areas?

2. **Participative (democratic) leadership** involves managers and employees working together to make decisions. Research has found that employee participation in decisions may not always increase effectiveness, but it usually does increase job satisfaction.[35] Many large organizations like Google, Apple, IBM, Cisco, and AT&T, and most smaller firms

Boss-centered leadership ◄ ·· ► **Subordinate-centered leadership**

Use of authority by manager						
						Area of freedom for employee
Manager makes decision and announces it it	Manager "sells" decision	Manager presents ideas and invites questions	Manager presents tentative decision subject to change	Manager presents problem, gets suggestions, makes decision	Manager defines limits, asks group to make decision	Manager permits employee to function within limits defined by superior
Autocratic			**Participative/democratic**			**Free rein**

figure 7.6

VARIOUS LEADERSHIP STYLES

Source: Reprinted by permission of the *Harvard Business Review.* An exhibit from "How to Choose a Leadership Pattern" by Robert Tannenbaum and Warren Schmidt (May/June 1973). Copyright © 1973 by the Harvard Business School Publishing Corporation. All rights reserved.

free-rein leadership
Leadership style that involves managers setting objectives and employees being relatively free to do whatever it takes to accomplish those objectives.

have been highly successful using a democratic style of leadership that values traits such as flexibility, good listening skills, and empathy. Employees meet to discuss and resolve management issues by giving everyone some opportunity to contribute to decisions.

3. In **free-rein leadership** managers set objectives and employees are free to do whatever is appropriate to accomplish those objectives. Free-rein leadership is often the most successful leadership style in certain organizations, such as those in which managers supervise doctors, professors, engineers, or other professionals. The traits managers need in such organizations include warmth, friendliness, and understanding. More and more firms are adopting this style of leadership with at least some of their employees.

Individual leaders rarely fit neatly into just one of these categories. We can think of leadership as a continuum along which employee participation varies, from purely boss-centered leadership to subordinate-centered leadership.

Which leadership style is best? Research tells us that it depends largely on what the goals and values of the firm are, who's being led, and in what situations.[36] A manager may be autocratic but friendly with a new trainee, democratic with an experienced employee, and free-rein with a trusted long-term supervisor.

There's no such thing as a leadership trait that is effective in all situations, or a leadership style that always works best. A successful leader in one organization may not be successful in another organization. For example, there was a question about whether or not Meg Whitman, eBay's former CEO, would make a good governor for California

Fast-food restaurant employees often don't have the skill and experience to make empowerment work very well. Instead their managers generally have to supervise and direct them fairly closely. What do you think are some of the consequences for managers of not being able to empower their staff with decision-making authority?

even though she oversaw eBay's growth from $4 million annual revenue and 30 employees to $8 billion and 15,000 employees in her ten-year tenure. Voters of California decided not to elect her, and she went to HP as CEO.[37] A truly successful leader has the ability to adopt the leadership style most appropriate to the situation and the employees.

Empowering Workers

Many leaders in the past gave explicit instructions to workers, telling them what to do to meet the goals and objectives of the organization. The term for this process is *directing.* In traditional organizations, directing includes giving assignments, explaining routines, clarifying policies, and providing feedback on performance. Many organizations still follow this model, especially fast-food restaurants and small retail establishments where the employees don't have the skill and experience needed to work on their own, at least at first.

Progressive leaders, such as those in some high-tech firms and Internet companies, empower employees to make decisions on their own. *Empowerment* means giving employees the authority to make a decision without consulting the manager and the responsibility to respond quickly to customer requests. Managers are often reluctant to give up their decision-making power and often resist empowerment. In firms that implement the concept, however, the manager's role is less that of a boss and director and more that of a coach, assistant, counselor, or team member.[38]

Enabling means giving workers the education and tools they need to make decisions. Clearly, it's the key to the success of empowerment. Without the right education, training, coaching, and tools, workers cannot assume the responsibilities and decision-making roles that make empowerment work.[39]

Managing Knowledge

"Knowledge is power." Empowering employees means giving them knowledge—that is, the information they need to do the best job they can. Finding the right information, keeping it in a readily accessible place, and making it known to everyone in the firm together constitute the tasks of **knowledge management.**

The first step to developing a knowledge management system is determining what knowledge is most important. Do you want to know more about your customers? Do you want to know more about competitors? What kind of information would make your company more effective or more efficient or more responsive to the marketplace? Once you've decided what you need to know, you set out to find answers to those questions.

Knowledge management tries to keep people from reinventing the wheel—that is, duplicating the work of gathering information—every time a decision must be made. A company really progresses when each person continually asks, "What do I still not know?" and "Whom should I be asking?" It's as important to know what's *not* working as it is to know what *is* working. Employees and managers now have texting, tweeting, and other means of keeping in touch with one another, with customers, and with other stakeholders. The key to success is learning how to process information effectively and turn it into knowledge that everyone can use to improve processes and procedures. The benefits are obvious.

enabling
Giving workers the education and tools they need to make decisions.

knowledge management
Finding the right information, keeping the information in a readily accessible place, and making the information known to everyone in the firm.

LEARNING goal 6

Summarize the five steps of the control function of management.

CONTROLLING: MAKING SURE IT WORKS

The control function measures performance relative to the planned objectives and standards, rewards people for work well done, and takes corrective action when necessary. Thus the control process (see Figure 7.7) provides the feedback that lets managers and workers adjust to deviations from plans and to changes in the environment that have affected performance.

Controlling consists of five steps:

1. Establishing clear performance standards. This ties the planning function to the control function. Without clear standards, control is impossible.

2. Monitoring and recording actual performance or results.

3. Comparing results against plans and standards.

One way colleges and universities measure their performance is to track the number of students who complete their degrees or who graduate within a certain number of years. What are some of the factors that could affect the achievement of this performance standard, and how do college administrators take corrective action when necessary?

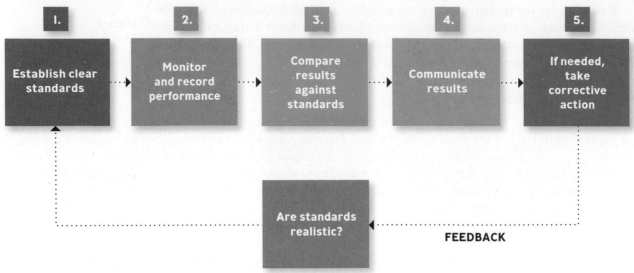

figure 7.7

THE CONTROL PROCESS

The whole control process is based on clear standards. Without such standards, the other steps are difficult, if not impossible. With clear standards, performance measurement is relatively easy and the proper action can be taken.

4. Communicating results and deviations to the appropriate employees.

5. Taking corrective action when needed and providing positive feedback for work well done.

For managers to measure results, the standards must be specific, attainable, and measurable. Setting such clear standards is part of the planning function. Vague goals and standards such as "better quality," "more efficiency," and "improved performance" aren't sufficient because they don't describe in enough detail what you're trying to achieve. For example, let's say you're a runner and you have made the following statement: "My goal is to improve my distance." When you started your improvement plan last year, you ran 2.0 miles a day; now you run 2.1 miles a day. Did you meet your goal? Well, you did increase your distance, but certainly not by very much.

A more appropriate statement would be "My goal is to increase my running distance from two miles a day to four miles a day by January 1." It's important to establish a time period for reaching goals. The following examples of goals and standards meet these criteria:

- Cutting the number of finished product rejects from 10 per 1,000 to 5 per 1,000 by March 31.

- Increasing the number of times managers praise employees from 3 per week to 12 per week by the end of the quarter.

- Increasing sales of product X from 10,000 per month to 12,000 per month by July.

One way to make control systems work is to establish clear procedures for monitoring performance. Accounting and finance are often the foundations for control systems because they provide the numbers management needs to evaluate progress.

A Key Criterion for Measurement: Customer Satisfaction

Traditional measures of success are usually financial; that is, they define success in terms of profits or return on investment. Certainly these measures are still important, but they're not the whole purpose of the firm. Other purposes may include pleasing employees, stakeholders, and customers—including both external and internal customers.

External customers include dealers, who buy products to sell to others, and ultimate customers (also known as end users) such as you and me, who buy products for their own personal use. **Internal customers** are individuals and units within the firm that receive services from other individuals or units. For example, the field salespeople are the internal customers of the marketing research people who prepare market reports for them.

One goal today is to go beyond simply satisfying customers to "delighting" them with unexpectedly good products and services. We'll discuss management in more detail in the next few chapters. Let's pause now, review, and do some exercises. Management is doing, not just reading.

external customers
Dealers, who buy products to sell to others, and ultimate customers (or end users), who buy products for their own personal use.

internal customers
Individuals and units within the firm that receive services from other individuals or units.

progress assessment

- How does enabling help achieve empowerment?
- What are the five steps in the control process?
- What's the difference between internal and external customers?

summary

Learning Goal 1. Describe the changes occurring today in the management function.

- **What does management look like today?**

At one time, managers were called bosses, and their job consisted of telling people what to do, watching over them to be sure they did it, and reprimanding those who didn't. Many, if not most, managers still behave that way. Today, however, some managers tend to be more progressive. For example, they emphasize teams and team building; they create drop-in centers, team spaces, and open work areas. They tend to guide, train, support, motivate, and coach employees rather than tell them what to do.

- **What reasons can you give to account for changes in management?**

Leaders of Fortune 100 companies today tend to be younger, more of them are female, and fewer of them were educated at elite universities. They know that many of their employees know more about technology and other practices than they do. Therefore, they tend to put more emphasis on motivation, teamwork, and cooperation. Managers in the future are likely to be assuming completely new roles in the firm. For one thing, they will be taking a leadership role in adapting to climate change. Further, they'll be doing more expansion overseas.

Learning Goal 2. Describe the four functions of management.

- **What are the primary functions of management?**

The four primary functions are (1) planning, (2) organizing, (3) leading, and (4) controlling.

- **How do you define each of these functions?**

Planning includes anticipating trends and determining the best strategies and tactics to achieve organizational goals and objectives. Organizing includes designing the structure of the organization and creating conditions and systems in which everyone and everything works together to achieve the organization's goals and objectives. Leading means creating a vision for the organization, and communicating, guiding, training, coaching, and motivating others to achieve goals and objectives. Controlling means measuring whether what actually occurs meets the organization's goals.

Learning Goal 3. Relate the planning process and decision making to the accomplishment of company goals.

•   What's the difference between goals and objectives?

Goals are broad, long-term achievements that organizations aim to accomplish, whereas objectives are specific, short-term plans made to help reach the goals.

•   What is a SWOT analysis?

Managers look at the strengths and weaknesses of the firm and the opportunities and threats facing it.

•   What are the four types of planning, and how are they related to the organization's goals and objectives?

Strategic planning is broad, long-range planning that outlines the goals of the organization. *Tactical planning* is specific, short-term planning that lists organizational objectives. *Operational planning* is part of tactical planning and sets specific timetables and standards. *Contingency planning* is developing an alternative set of plans in case the first set doesn't work out.

•   What are the steps involved in decision making?

The seven Ds of decision making are (1) define the situation; (2) describe and collect needed information; (3) develop alternatives; (4) develop agreement among those involved; (5) decide which alternative is best; (6) do what is indicated (begin implementation); and (7) determine whether the decision was a good one, and follow up.

Learning Goal 4. Describe the organizing function of management.

•   What are the three levels of management in the corporate hierarchy?

The three levels of management are (1) top management (highest level consisting of the president and other key company executives who develop strategic plans); (2) middle management (general managers, division managers, and plant managers who are responsible for tactical planning and controlling); and (3) supervisory management (first-line managers/supervisors who evaluate workers' daily performance).

•   What skills do managers need?

Managers must have three categories of skills: (1) technical skills (ability to perform specific tasks such as selling products or developing software), (2) human relations skills (ability to communicate and motivate), and (3) conceptual skills (ability to see organizations as a whole and how all the parts fit together).

•   Are these skills equally important at all management levels?

Managers at different levels need different skills. Top managers rely heavily on human relations and conceptual skills and rarely use technical skills, while first-line supervisors need strong technical and human relations skills but use conceptual skills less often. Middle managers need to have a balance of all three skills (see Figure 7.5).

Learning Goal 5. Explain the differences between leaders and managers, and describe the various leadership styles.

- **What's the difference between a manager and a leader?**

A manager plans, organizes, and controls functions within an organization. A leader has vision and inspires others to grasp that vision, establishes corporate values, emphasizes corporate ethics, and doesn't fear change.

- **Describe the various leadership styles.**

Figure 7.6 shows a continuum of leadership styles ranging from boss-centered to subordinate-centered leadership.

- **Which leadership style is best?**

The most effective leadership style depends on the people being led and the situation. The challenge of the future will be to empower self-managed teams.

- **What does empowerment mean?**

Empowerment means giving employees the authority and responsibility to respond quickly to customer requests. Enabling is giving workers the education and tools they need to assume their new decision-making powers.

- **What is knowledge management?**

Knowledge management is finding the right information, keeping the information in a readily accessible place, and making the information known to everyone in the firm.

Learning Goal 6. Summarize the five steps of the control function of management.

- **What are the five steps of the control function?**

Controlling incorporates (1) setting clear standards, (2) monitoring and recording performance, (3) comparing performance with plans and standards, (4) communicating results and deviations to employees, and (5) providing positive feedback for a job well done and taking corrective action if necessary.

- **What qualities must standards possess to measure performance results?**

Standards must be specific, attainable, and measurable.

key terms

autocratic leadership 204	internal customers 209	planning 193
brainstorming 199	knowledge management 207	PMI 199
conceptual skills 201	leading 194	problem solving 199
contingency planning 199	management 193	staffing 202
controlling 195	middle management 200	strategic planning 196
decision making 198	mission statement 195	supervisory management 200
enabling 207	objectives 195	SWOT analysis 196
external customers 209	operational planning 197	tactical planning 197
free-rein leadership 205	organizing 194	technical skills 201
goals 195	participative (democratic) leadership 204	top management 199
human relations skills 201		transparency 203
		vision 195

critical thinking

Many students say they would like to be a manager someday. Here are some questions to get you started thinking like a manager:

1. Would you like to work for a large firm or a small business? Private or public? In an office or out in the field? Give your reasons for each answer.
2. What kind of leader would you be? Do you have evidence to show that?
3. Do you see any problems with a participative (democratic) leadership style? Can you see a manager getting frustrated when he or she can't control others?
4. Can someone who's trained to give orders (like a military sergeant) be retrained to be a participative leader? How? What problems may emerge?

developing workplace skills

1. Allocate time to do some career planning with a SWOT analysis of your present situation. Choose one career you are interested in and answer the following questions: What does the marketplace for your chosen career look like today? What skills do you have that will make you a winner in that type of career? What weaknesses might you target to correct? What are the threats to your career choice? What are the opportunities? Prepare a two-minute presentation to the class.

2. Bring several decks of cards to class and have the class break up into teams of four or so members. Each team should then elect a leader. Each leader should be assigned a leadership style and learn how to perform that style: autocratic, participative (democratic), or free rein. Have each team try to build a house of cards by stacking them on top of each other. The team with the tallest house wins. Each team member should report his or her experience under the selected style of leadership.

3. In class, discuss the advantages and disadvantages of becoming a manager. Does the size of the business make a difference? What are the advantages of a career in a profit-seeking business versus a career in a nonprofit organization?

4. Review Figure 7.6 and discuss managers you have known, worked for, or read about who have practiced each management style. Students from other countries may have interesting experiences to add. Which managerial style did you like best? Why? Which was or were most effective? Why?

5. Because of the illegal and unethical behavior of a few managers, managers in general are under suspicion for being greedy and dishonest. Discuss the fairness of such charges, and suggest what could be done to improve the opinion of managers among the students in your class.

taking it to the net

Purpose

To perform a simple SWOT analysis.

Exercise

Go to **www.marketingteacher.com**, locate the list of SWOT analyses, and click the link to go to the SWOT for Toys "R" Us.

1. What are Toys "R" Us's strengths, weaknesses, opportunities, and threats?

2. Analyze Toys "R" Us's weaknesses. How do you think the company's strengths might be used to overcome some of its weaknesses?

3. Analyze Toys "R" Us's opportunities and threats. What additional opportunities can you suggest? What additional threats can you identify?

casing the web

To access the case "Leading in a Leaderless Company," visit
www.mhhe.com/P2P2e

video case

Zappos' Team Approach

Located in Las Vegas, Nevada, with its fulfillment center situated next to the UPS hub, Zappos.com has $1 billion in annual revenue. In 2010, Zappos.com was ranked #6 by *Fortune* magazine as one of the best places to work in America. The origin of Zappos was an entrepreneurial effort by Nick Swinmurn called ShoeSite.com. Swinmurn launched this company during the dot-com boom. The concept emerged as a result of Swinmurn's inability to locate shoes that he was looking for in malls. Swinmurn took photos of the shoes from various shoe stores and uploaded them onto his website. He would take orders, go to the shoe store and purchase the shoes for the customer, and ship the shoes the next day. At the time, there was no single place online to purchase shoes in that way.

Today, Zappos is owned by Amazon.com, which purchased the company for $1.2 billion in 2010. Zappos CEO Tony Hsieh remains at the helm of the company, and the culture of the firm remains intact. In short, Amazon.com has allowed Zappos to continue to operate as it had in the past.

The emphasis on customer satisfaction and employee happiness permeates the culture of Zappos. The name "Zappos" is a derivative of the Spanish word for shoes, "zapatos." Its culture is driven by 10 core values, the first being to "wow" the customer.

Two important core values influence the planning, organizing, leading, and controlling functions at the firm. They are (1) pursue growth and learning; and (2) have passion and determination. These and the other core values emphasize teams and employee empowerment, so much so that team leaders (management) are required to spend at least 20 percent of their time off the job with their team members.

Relationship building helps drive a management approach that focuses on the primary goal of the company—that is, to provide the best possible experience for the customer. The four functions of management are discussed in the video, and members of the Zappos team indicate how these functions are practiced at Zappos.

Thinking It Over

1. *What does the vision statement for a company include?*

2. *How does the core value of the pursuit of growth and learning fit with the management functions of planning and organizing?*

3. *Why are team leaders required to spend 20 percent of their time with their teams outside of the work environment?*

Structuring Organizations FOR TODAY'S Challenges

LEARNING goals

After you have read and studied this chapter, you should be able to

1 Outline the basic principles of organization management.

2 Compare the organizational theories of Fayol and Weber.

3 Evaluate the choices managers make in structuring organizations.

4 Contrast the various organizational models.

5 Identify the benefits of interfirm cooperation and coordination.

6 Explain how organizational culture can help businesses adapt to change.

Most people are content to dedicate their lives to just one career. And then there are people like Dave Bing. After playing in the NBA for 12 years, Bing founded a steel company in Detroit that he successfully ran until retiring in 2009. The 65-year-old didn't stop his professional life then, however. That same year, Bing was elected mayor of Detroit in a special election. After a lifetime of accomplishment and hard work, this might be Bing's toughest job yet.

Born in Washington, D.C., Bing showed promise early on as an All-American basketball player in high school. He matched that feat in college at Syracuse University, where he earned a degree in economics. In 1966 the Detroit Pistons picked him second overall in the NBA draft. He spent most of his Hall of Fame career at Detroit, where he was a seven-time All-Star. Even after he was traded to the Washington Bullets in 1975, Bing and his family kept their home in Detroit and stayed there during the off-season. When he finally retired from basketball in 1978, his family moved back to Detroit permanently.

Unfortunately for Bing, NBA players in the 1970s didn't earn the millions that today's basketball stars do. Still, he had big plans for the future. After watching his father struggle for years as a bricklayer, Bing promised himself a long time ago that he would be the boss, not just a worker. Bing found work at a warehouse in a steel mill. There he learned the ins and outs of the business, from shipping to sales. By 1980 he quit the warehouse and started his own steel manufacturing company with $80,000 of his own money and a $250,000 loan. Within six months, Bing Steel had lost all of its money.

Failure didn't get Bing down, though. Instead, he shifted the company's focus to being a middleman supplier rather than a manufacturer. By Bing Steel's second year, contracts with General Motors and other big clients led to revenues of more than $4 million. After five years, revenues had grown to $40 million. Today, Bing Steel is called Bing Group and specializes in a variety of steel-related services. When Bing retired in 2009, annual sales totaled $300 million.

But all that work ended up being a prelude to what Bing sees as his most important task: saving Detroit. As American manufacturing declined over the last few decades, Detroit gradually lost its prominence as the nation's industrial backbone. Years of shuttered factories and urban flight have contributed to its population falling to 900,000 people, down from 2 million in its prime. Approximately 40 square miles of the 139-square-mile metropolis sits almost completely abandoned. And just when matters seemed like they couldn't get worse for the

CONNECTING WITH

X *Dave Bing*

Mayor of Detroit

city, in 2008 Detroit's former mayor Kwame Kilpatrick resigned following an extensive corruption scandal.

Bing was elected mayor in the special election that followed in 2009, and was elected for a full term later that year. In order to save Detroit, Bing wants to do something similar to what GM did when it fell into bankruptcy. The once unstoppable American automobile company eventually collapsed due to the weight of its many brands, factories, and dealerships. To Bing, Detroit has a similar amount of dead weight. So far he has started plans to renovate or raze much of Detroit's degrading blight. In place of the unoccupied land, he wants to put in public parks, new industries, and urban farms, to make use of the real estate and contribute to the economy. But putting his plan into action is the tough part. Many emptied neighborhoods have at least one or two people still living in them, and often they're not willing to leave so easily. Nevertheless, Bing believes that rehabbing the city's land is the only way to deal with the city's other problems, such as its more than $300 million debt and the mere 20 percent graduation rate at Detroit schools. Although he still has a long way to go, Bing hopes he can once again look in the face of failure and pull out a winner.

This chapter is about changing and adapting organizations to today's markets, as Dave Bing is doing in Detroit. Most managers never face challenges that big, but there are plenty of opportunities in every firm to use the principles of organizing to manage—and benefit from—change, especially today as firms adapt to the recent economic crisis.

Sources: Matthew Dolan, "Detroit Struggles for Fiscal Fix," *The Wall Street Journal,* March 18, 2012; Dian Brady, "Hard Choices: Dave Bing," *Bloomberg Businessweek,* May 1, 2011; Michael Rosenberg, "Having Fun Yet, Mr. Mayor?" *Sports Illustrated,* January 18, 2010; Joann Muller, "Detroit Must Shrink to Grow," *Forbes,* October 12, 2010; and Michel Martin, "Detroit Mayor Dave Bing on City's Crisis," *NPR,* January 31, 2012.

This sports equipment company studied the compact-disc industry and learned to use ultraviolet inks to print graphics on skis. It went to the cable television industry to learn how to braid layers of fiberglass and carbon, and adapted that knowledge to make its products. Name that company. (The answer can be found in this chapter.)

LEARNING goal 1

Outline the basic principles of organization management.

EVERYONE'S REORGANIZING

You don't have to look far to find examples of companies reorganizing.[1] A. G. Lafley, former CEO of legendary Procter & Gamble, transformed the company into one of the most innovative firms in the United States. Some entrepreneurial companies are organizing globally from the start and succeeding. Other organizations have been declining, including automobile makers, home builders, and banks. You have been hearing about such failures in the news. Clearly the challenge to reorganize is strong.

Few firms have established as strong an image in the United States as Starbucks, but even that company had to restructure to keep its customer base.[2] As the company expanded its menu to include more sandwiches, one of the unexpected results was a change in the smell of the stores (the odor of burning cheese was overwhelming the smell of coffee). The company restored the stores' aroma by cutting back on sandwiches for a while.[3] Many stores had to be closed and other stores were remodeled to recapture the feel of a Milan coffee bar. In the end, Starbucks regained its market image and is prospering again.[4]

You may be wondering what has happened to U.S. producers—so many seem to be failing. But adjusting to changing markets is a normal function in a capitalist economy. There will be big winners, like Google and Facebook, and big losers as well. The key to success is remaining flexible enough to adapt to the changing times.[5] Often that means going back to basic organizational principles and rebuilding the firm on a sound foundation. This chapter will discuss such basic principles.

The principles of organization apply to businesses of all sizes. Structuring the business, making an appropriate division of labor using job specialization and departmentalization, establishing procedures, and assigning authority are tasks found in most firms. How do these principles operate at your current or most recent job?

Building an Organization from the Bottom Up

No matter the size of the business, the principles of organization are much the same. Let's say you and two friends plan to start a lawn-mowing business. One of the first steps is to organize your business. *Organizing,* or structuring, begins with determining

MAKING ethical decisions

Would You Sacrifice Safety for Profits?

Imagine you have begun a successful lawn-mowing service in your neighborhood. Other lawn-mowing services in the area seem to hire untrained workers, many from other countries. They pay only the minimum wage or slightly more. Most obviously, however, they often provide no safety equipment. Workers don't have ear protection against the loud mowers and blowers. Most don't wear goggles when operating the shredder. Very few wear masks when spraying potentially harmful fertilizers.

You are aware there are many hazards connected with yard work, but safety gear can be expensive and workers often prefer to work without it. You are interested in making as much money as possible, but you also are concerned about the safety and welfare of your workers. You know yard maintenance equipment creates noise pollution, but quiet equipment is expensive.

The corporate culture you create as you begin your service will last a long time. If you emphasize safety and environmental concern from the start, your workers will adopt your values. On the other hand, you can see the potential for making faster profits by ignoring safety rules and paying little attention to the environment as your competitors seem to do. What are the consequences?

what work needs to be done (mowing, edging, trimming) and then dividing up the tasks among the three of you; this is called a *division of labor*. One of you might have a special talent for trimming bushes, while another is better at mowing. The success of a firm often depends on management's ability to identify each worker's strengths and assign the right tasks to the right person. Many jobs can be done quickly and well when each person specializes. Dividing tasks into smaller jobs is called *job specialization*. For example, you might divide the mowing task into mowing, trimming, and raking.

If your business is successful, you'll probably hire more workers to help. You might organize them into teams or departments to do the various tasks. One team might mow while another uses blowers to clean up leaves and debris. If you're really successful over time, you might hire an accountant to keep records, various people to handle advertising, and a crew to maintain the equipment.

You can see how your business might evolve into a company with several departments: production (mowing and everything related to that), marketing, accounting, and maintenance. The process of setting up individual departments to do specialized tasks is called *departmentalization*. Finally, you'll assign authority and responsibility to people so that you can control the whole process. If something went wrong in the accounting department, for example, you would know who was responsible.

Structuring an organization, then, consists of devising a division of labor (sometimes resulting in specialization); setting up teams or departments to do specific tasks (like production and accounting); and assigning responsibility and authority to people. It also includes allocating resources (such as funds for various departments), assigning specific tasks, and establishing procedures for accomplishing the organizational objectives. From the start, you have to make ethical decisions about how you'll treat your workers and how you will benefit the community (see the Making Ethical Decisions box).[6]

You may develop an *organization chart* (discussed later in this chapter) that shows relationships among people: who is accountable for the completion of specific work, and who reports to whom. Finally, you'll monitor the environment to see what competitors are doing and what customers are demanding. Then you must adjust to the new realities. For example, a major lawn care company may begin promoting itself in your area. You might have to make some organizational changes to offer even better service at competitive prices. What would you do first if you began losing business to competitors?

LEARNING goal 2

Compare the organizational theories of Fayol and Weber.

THE CHANGING ORGANIZATION

Never before in the history of business has so much change been introduced so quickly—sometimes too quickly, as we saw with the earthquake and tsunami in Japan in 2011. Think of the effects these disasters have had on the nuclear power industry.[7] As we noted in earlier chapters, much change is due to the evolving business environment—more global competition, a declining economy, faster technological change, and pressure to preserve the natural environment.[8] Equally important to many businesses is the change in customer expectations. Consumers today expect high-quality products and fast, friendly service—at a reasonable cost.[9]

Managing change, then, has become a critical managerial function. That sometimes includes changing the whole organization structure. Such change may occur in nonprofit and government organizations as well as businesses.[10] Many organizations in the past were designed more to facilitate management than to please the customer. Companies designed many rules and regulations to give managers control over employees. As you'll learn later in this chapter, this reliance on rules is called *bureaucracy*. When Hurricane Katrina hit New Orleans in August 2005, the government seemed paralyzed and didn't respond quickly. The victims placed blame on federal, state, and local *bureaucracy*. Meanwhile, more flexible businesses in the area and in other states adjusted to the new conditions, reopened, and waited for the government to catch up. The local, state, and federal responses to the Gulf oil spill in 2010 were not much better. Yes, the government has to wrestle with bureaucracy just as businesses do.

To understand where we are in organization design, it helps to know where we've been. We'll look at that subject next.

The Development of Organization Design

Until the 20th century, most businesses were rather small, the processes for producing goods were relatively simple, and organizing workers was fairly easy. Organizing workers is still not too hard in most small firms, such as a lawn-mowing service or a small shop that produces custom-made boats. Not until the 1900s and the introduction of *mass production* (methods for efficiently producing large quantities of goods) did production processes and business organization become so complex. Usually, the bigger the plant, the more efficient production becomes.

Business growth led to **economies of scale.** This term refers to the fact that companies can reduce their production costs by purchasing raw materials in bulk. The average cost of goods decreases as production levels rise. The cost of building

economies of scale
The situation in which companies can reduce their production costs if they can purchase raw materials in bulk; the average cost of goods goes down as production levels increase.

a car, for example, declined sharply when automobile companies adopted mass production and GM, Ford, and others introduced their huge factories. Over time, such innovations became less meaningful as other companies copied the processes. You may have noticed the benefits of mass production in housing and computers.

During the era of mass production, organization theorists emerged. Two influential thinkers were Henri Fayol and Max Weber. Many of their principles are still being used in businesses throughout the world. Let's explore these principles.

Fayol's Principles of Organization   In France, economic theoretician Henri Fayol published his book *Administration industrielle et générale* in 1919. It was popularized in the United States in 1949 under the title *General and Industrial Management*. Fayol introduced such principles as the following:

- *Unity of command.* Each worker is to report to one, and only one, boss. The benefits of this principle are obvious. What happens if two different bosses give you two different assignments? Which one should you follow? To prevent such confusion, each person should report to only one manager. (Later we'll discuss an organizational plan that seems to violate this principle.)

- *Hierarchy of authority.* All workers should know to whom they report. Managers should have the right to give orders and expect others to follow. (As we discussed in Chapter 7, this concept has changed over time, and empowerment is often more important now.)

- *Division of labor.* Functions are to be divided into areas of specialization such as production, marketing, and finance. (This principle too is being modified, as you'll read later, and cross-functional teamwork is getting more emphasis.)

- *Subordination of individual interests to the general interest.* Workers are to think of themselves as a coordinated team. The goals of the team are more important than the goals of individual workers. (This concept is still very much in use.) Have you heard this concept being applied to football and basketball teams?

- *Authority.* Managers have the right to give orders and the power to enforce obedience. Authority and responsibility are related: whenever authority is exercised, responsibility arises. (This principle is also being modified as managers are beginning to empower employees.)

- *Degree of centralization.* The amount of decision-making power vested in top management should vary by circumstances. In a small organization, it's possible to centralize all decision-making power in the top manager. In a larger organization, however, some decision-making power, for both major and minor issues, should be delegated to lower-level managers and employees.

- *Clear communication channels.* All workers should be able to reach others in the firm quickly and easily.

- *Order.* Materials and people should be placed and maintained in the proper location.

- *Equity.* A manager should treat employees and peers with respect and justice. (That includes, of course, the treatment of women. Note, for example, the Walmart class-action lawsuit where women claimed that the company did not treat them equally.)[11]

- *Esprit de corps.* A spirit of pride and loyalty should be created among people in the firm.

Henri Fayol introduced several management principles still followed today, including the idea that each worker should report to only one manager and that managers, in turn, should have the right to give orders for others to follow and the power to enforce them. Which of Fayol's principles have you observed?

Management courses in colleges throughout the world taught Fayol's principles for years, and they became synonymous with the concept of management. Organizations were designed so that no person had more than one boss, lines of authority were clear, and everyone knew to whom to report. Naturally, these principles tended to be written down as rules, policies, and regulations as organizations grew larger.

That process of rule making has often led to rather rigid organizations that haven't always responded quickly to consumer requests. For example, in various cities, the Department of Motor Vehicles (DMV) and auto repair facilities have been slow to adapt to the needs of their customers. So where did the idea of *bureaucracy* come from? We talk about that next.

Max Weber and Organizational Theory   Max Weber's book *The Theory of Social and Economic Organizations,* like Fayol's, appeared in the United States in the late 1940s. Weber, a German sociologist and economist, promoted the pyramid-shaped organization structure that became popular in large firms. Weber put great trust in managers and felt the firm would do well if employees simply did what they were told. The less decision making they had to do, the better. Clearly, this is a reasonable way to operate if you're dealing with relatively uneducated and untrained workers. Such was generally the case at the time Weber was writing. Most employees today, however, have considerably more education and technical skills.

Weber's principles of organization resembled Fayol's. In addition, Weber emphasized:

- Job descriptions.
- Written rules, decision guidelines, and detailed records.
- Consistent procedures, regulations, and policies.
- Staffing and promotion based on qualifications.

Weber believed that large organizations demanded clearly established rules and guidelines to be followed precisely. In other words, he was in favor of *bureaucracy.* Although his principles made sense at the time, rules and procedures became so rigid in some companies that they grew counterproductive. Some organizations today still thrive on Weber's theories. United Parcel Service (UPS), for example, maintains strict written rules and decision guidelines. Those rules enable the firm to deliver packages quickly because employees don't have to pause to make decisions—procedures are clearly spelled out for them.

Some organizations that follow Weber's principles are less effective than UPS because they don't allow employees to respond quickly to new challenges. That has clearly been the case with disaster relief agencies in many areas. Later, we explore how to make organizations more responsive. First, let's look at some basic terms and concepts.

Turning Principles into Organization Design

Following theories like Fayol's and Weber's, managers in the latter 1900s began designing organizations so that managers could *control* workers. Many companies are still organized that way, with everything set up in a hierarchy. A **hierarchy** is a system in which one person is at the top of the organization and there is a ranked or sequential ordering from the top

---

hierarchy
A system in which one person is at the top of the organization and there is a ranked or sequential ordering from the top down of managers who are responsible to that person.

Max Weber promoted an organizational structure composed of middle managers who implement the orders of top managers. He believed less-educated workers were best managed if managers or supervisors gave them strict rules and regulations to follow and monitored their performance. What industries or businesses today would benefit by using such controls?

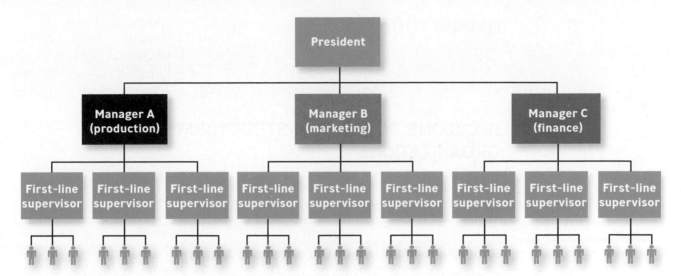

down of managers and others who are responsible to that person. Since one person can't keep track of thousands of workers, the top manager needs many lower-level managers to help. The **chain of command** is the line of authority that moves from the top of the hierarchy to the lowest level. Figure 8.1 shows a typical hierarchy on an organization chart. An **organization chart** is a visual device that shows relationships among people and divides the organization's work; it shows who reports to whom.

Some organizations have a dozen or more layers of management between the chief executive officer (CEO) and the lowest-level employees. If employees want to introduce work changes, they ask a supervisor (the first level of management), who asks his or her manager, who asks a manager at the next level up, and so on. It can take weeks or months for a decision to be made and passed from manager to manager until it reaches employees.

Max Weber used the word *bureaucrat* to describe a middle manager whose function was to implement top management's orders. Thus, **bureaucracy** came to be the term for an organization with many layers of managers.

When employees in a bureaucracy of any size have to ask managers for permission to make a change, the process may take so long that customers become annoyed. Has this happened to you in a department store or other organization? Since customers want efficient service—and they want it *now*—slow service is simply not acceptable in today's competitive firms.[12]

Some companies are therefore reorganizing to let employees make decisions in order to please customers no matter what. Home Depot has adopted this approach to win more customers from competitors. Nordstrom employees can accept a return from a customer without managerial approval, even if the item was not originally sold at that store. As you read earlier in this book, giving employees such authority is called *empowerment*. Remember that empowerment works only when employees are given the proper training and resources to respond. Can you see how such training would help first responders in crisis conditions?

figure 8.1

TYPICAL ORGANIZATION CHART

This is a rather standard chart with managers for major functions and supervisors reporting to the managers. Each supervisor manages three employees.

chain of command
The line of authority that moves from the top of a hierarchy to the lowest level.

organization chart
A visual device that shows relationships among people and divides the organization's work; it shows who reports to whom.

bureaucracy
An organization with many layers of managers who set rules and regulations and oversee all decisions.

progress assessment

- What do the terms *division of labor* and *job specialization* mean?
- What are the principles of management outlined by Fayol?
- What did Weber add to the principles of Fayol?

LEARNING goal 3

Evaluate the choices managers make in structuring organizations.

DECISIONS TO MAKE IN STRUCTURING ORGANIZATIONS

When designing responsive organizations, firms have to make decisions about several organizational issues: (1) centralization versus decentralization, (2) span of control, (3) tall versus flat organization structures, and (4) departmentalization.

Choosing Centralized or Decentralized Authority

centralized authority
An organization structure in which decision-making authority is maintained at the top level of management.

Centralized authority occurs when decision making is concentrated at the top level of management. The retailing giant Target, for example, has a very centralized form of management. *Fortune* magazine commented that Target is so top-down that the CEO personally interviews candidates for the top 600 positions. That doesn't mean Target hasn't adapted to different circumstances, however, as you'll see later in this chapter.

McDonald's believes that purchasing, promotion, and other such decisions are best handled centrally. There's usually little need for each McDonald's restaurant in the United States to carry different food products. McDonald's thus leans toward centralized authority. However, today's rapidly changing markets, added to global differences in consumer tastes, tend to favor some decentralization and thus more delegation of authority, even at McDonald's.[13] Its restaurants in England offer tea, those in France offer a Croque McDo (a hot ham-and-cheese sandwich), those in Japan sell rice, and Chinese McDonald's offer taro and red bean desserts.

decentralized authority
An organization structure in which decision-making authority is delegated to lower-level managers more familiar with local conditions than headquarters management could be.

Decentralized authority occurs when decision making is delegated to lower-level managers and employees more familiar with local conditions than headquarters management could be. JCPenney customers in California, for example,

A broad span of control allows one supervisor to be responsible for many workers whose work tasks are predictable and standardized. In addition to assembly lines, can you think of other management situations that might benefit from a broad span of control? What about in a service industry?

demand clothing styles different from what customers in Minnesota or Maine like. It makes sense to delegate to store managers in various cities the authority to buy, price, and promote merchandise appropriate for each area. In response to the economic crisis that began in 2008, Macy's department store is also shifting to local tastes. The plan, called "My Macy's," proved successful in test markets. Both Home Depot and Lowe's also responded to the financial crisis with similar moves toward catering to local markets. Figure 8.2 lists some advantages and disadvantages of centralized and decentralized authority.

Choosing the Appropriate Span of Control

Span of control describes the optimal number of subordinates a manager supervises or should supervise. What is the "right" span of control? At lower levels, where work is standardized, it's possible to implement a broad span of control (15 to 40 workers). For example, one supervisor can be responsible for 20 or more workers assembling computers or cleaning movie theaters. The appropriate span gradually narrows at higher levels of the organization, because work becomes less standardized and managers need more face-to-face communication.

> **span of control**
> The optimal number of subordinates a manager supervises or should supervise.

The trend today is to expand the span of control as organizations adopt empowerment, reduce the number of middle managers, and hire more talented and better educated lower-level employees. Information technology also allows managers to handle more information, so the span can be broader still.[14]

At Rowe Furniture in Salem, Virginia, the manufacturing chief dismantled the assembly line and empowered the people who had had limited functions—like sewing, gluing, and stapling—with the freedom to make sofas as they saw fit. Productivity and quality soared.

Choosing between Tall and Flat Organization Structures

In the early 20th century, organizations grew even bigger, adding layer after layer of management to create **tall organization structures.** Some had as many as 14 levels, and the span of control was small (few people reported to each manager).

> **tall organization structure**
> An organizational structure in which the pyramidal organization chart would be quite tall because of the various levels of management.

Imagine how a message might be distorted as it moved up the organization and back down through managers, management assistants, secretaries, assistant secretaries, supervisors, trainers, and so on. The cost of all these managers and support people was high, the paperwork they generated was enormous, and the inefficiencies in communication and decision making were often intolerable.

figure 8.2

ADVANTAGES AND DISADVANTAGES OF CENTRALIZED VERSUS DECENTRALIZED AUTHORITY

ADVANTAGES	DISADVANTAGES
Centralized	
• Greater top-management control	• Less responsiveness to customers
• More efficiency	• Less empowerment
• Simpler distribution system	• Interorganizational conflict
• Stronger brand/corporate image	• Lower morale away from headquarters
Decentralized	
• Better adaptation to customer wants	• Less efficiency
• More empowerment of workers	• Complex distribution system
• Faster decision making	• Less top-management control
• Higher morale	• Weakened corporate image

figure 8.3

A FLAT ORGANIZATION STRUCTURE

flat organization structure
An organization structure that has few layers of management and a broad span of control.

More recently, organizations have adopted **flat organization structures** with fewer layers of management (see Figure 8.3) and a broad span of control (many people report to each manager).[15] Flat structures can respond readily to customer demands because lower-level employees have authority and responsibility for making decisions, and managers can be spared some day-to-day tasks. In a bookstore with a flat organization structure, employees may have authority to arrange shelves by category, process special orders for customers, and so on.

Large organizations use flat structures to try to match the friendliness of small firms, whose workers often know customers by name. The flatter organizations become, the broader their spans of control, which means some managers lose their jobs. Figure 8.4 lists advantages and disadvantages of narrow and broad spans of control.

Weighing the Advantages and Disadvantages of Departmentalization

departmentalization
The dividing of organizational functions into separate units.

Departmentalization divides organizations into separate units. The traditional way to departmentalize is by *function*—such as design, production, marketing, and accounting. Departmentalization groups workers according to their skills, expertise, or resource use so that they can specialize and work together more effectively. It may also save costs and thus improve efficiency. Other advantages include the following:

1. Employees can develop skills in depth and progress within a department as they master more skills.

2. The company can achieve economies of scale by centralizing all the resources it needs and locate various experts in that area.

3. Employees can coordinate work within the function, and top management can easily direct and control various departments' activities.

Disadvantages of departmentalization by function include the following:

figure 8.4

ADVANTAGES AND DISADVANTAGES OF A NARROW VERSUS A BROAD SPAN OF CONTROL

The flatter the organization, the broader the span of control.

ADVANTAGES	DISADVANTAGES
Narrow	
• More control by top management	• Less empowerment
• More chances for advancement	• Higher costs
• Greater specialization	• Delayed decision making
• Closer supervision	• Less responsiveness to customers
Broad	
• Reduced costs	• Fewer chances for advancement
• More responsiveness to customers	• Overworked managers
• Faster decision making	• Loss of control
• More empowerment	• Less management expertise

1. Departments may not communicate well. For example, production may be so isolated from marketing that it does not get needed feedback from customers.

2. Employees may identify with their department's goals rather than the organization's. The purchasing department may find a good value somewhere and buy a huge volume of goods. That makes purchasing look good, but the high cost of storing the goods hurts overall profitability.

3. The company's response to external changes may be slow.

4. People may not be trained to take different managerial responsibilities; rather, they tend to become narrow specialists.

5. Department members may engage in groupthink (they think alike) and may need input from outside to become more creative.

Looking at Alternative Ways to Departmentalize Functional separation isn't always the most responsive form of organization. So what are the alternatives? Figure 8.5 shows five ways a firm can departmentalize. One way is by product. A book publisher might have a trade book department (for books sold to the general public), a textbook department, and a technical book department, each with separate development and marketing processes. Such product-focused departmentalization usually results in good customer relations.

Some organizations departmentalize by customer group. A pharmaceutical company might have one department for the consumer market, another that calls on hospitals (the institutional market), and another that targets doctors. You can see how customer groups can benefit from having specialists satisfying their needs.

Some firms group their units by geographic location because customers vary so greatly by region. Japan, Europe, and South America may deserve separate departments, with obvious benefits.

The decision about how to departmentalize depends on the nature of the product and the customers. A few firms find that it's most efficient to separate activities by process. For example, a firm that makes leather coats may have one department

After the material for footballs has been cut and sewn in the Wilson Sporting Goods factory, it moves on to the lacing department where workers like this one open up the deflated balls and prepare them for lacing. What are the advantages and disadvantages of departmentalizing by process like this?

figure 8.5

WAYS TO DEPARTMENTALIZE

A computer company may want to departmentalize by geographic location (countries), a manufacturer by function, a pharmaceutical company by customer group, a leather manufacturer by process, and a publisher by product. In each case the structure must fit the firm's goals.

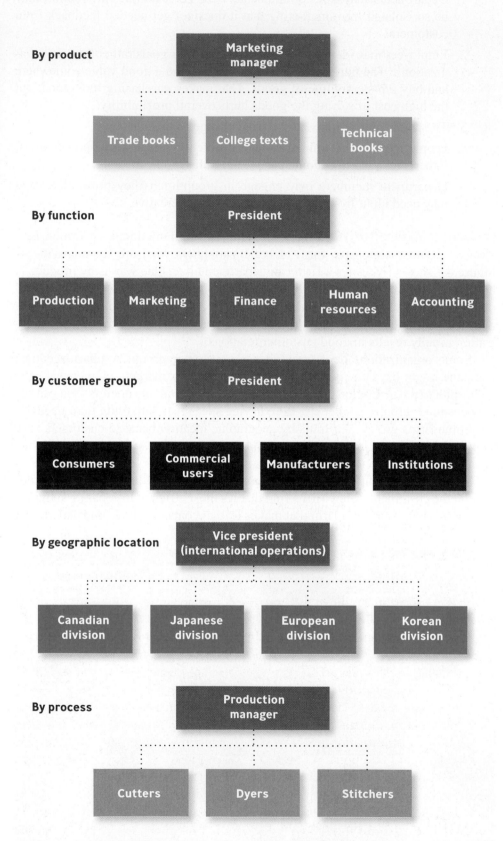

By product

- Marketing manager
  - Trade books
  - College texts
  - Technical books

By function

- President
  - Production
  - Marketing
  - Finance
  - Human resources
  - Accounting

By customer group

- President
  - Consumers
  - Commercial users
  - Manufacturers
  - Institutions

By geographic location

- Vice president (international operations)
  - Canadian division
  - Japanese division
  - European division
  - Korean division

By process

- Production manager
  - Cutters
  - Dyers
  - Stitchers

cut the leather, another dye it, and a third sew the coat together. Such specialization enables employees to do a better job because they can focus on learning a few critical skills.

Some firms use a combination of departmentalization techniques to create *hybrid forms.* For example, a company could departmentalize by function, geographic location, *and* customer groups.

progress assessment

- Why are organizations becoming flatter?
- What are some reasons for having a narrow span of control in an organization?
- What are the advantages and disadvantages of departmentalization?
- What are the various ways a firm can departmentalize?

LEARNING goal 4

Contrast the various organizational models.

ORGANIZATIONAL MODELS

Now that we've explored the basic choices in organization design, let's look in depth at four ways to structure an organization: (1) line organizations, (2) line-and-staff organizations, (3) matrix-style organizations, and (4) cross-functional self-managed teams. You'll see that some of these models violate traditional management principles. The business community is in a period of transition, with some traditional organizational models giving way to new structures. Such transitions can be not only unsettling to employees and managers but also fraught with problems and errors.

Line Organizations

A **line organization** has direct two-way lines of responsibility, authority, and communication running from the top to the bottom of the organization, with everyone reporting to only one supervisor. The military and many small businesses are organized this way. For example, a locally owned pizza parlor might have a general manager and a shift manager. All the general employees report to the shift manager, and he or she reports to the general manager or owner.

A line organization does not have any specialists who provide managerial support. There is no legal department, accounting department, human resources department, or information technology (IT) department. Line organizations follow all of Fayol's traditional management rules. Line managers can issue orders, enforce discipline, and adjust the organization as conditions change.

In large businesses, a line organization may have the disadvantages of being too inflexible, of having few specialists or experts to advise people along the line, and of having lengthy lines of communication.[16] Thus they may be unable to handle complex decisions relating to thousands of products and tons of paperwork. Such organizations usually turn to a line-and-staff form of organization.

line organization
An organization that has direct two-way lines of responsibility, authority, and communication running from the top to the bottom of the organization, with all people reporting to only one supervisor.

Line-and-Staff Organizations

<div class="sidebar">

line personnel
Employees who are part of the chain of command that is responsible for achieving organizational goals.

staff personnel
Employees who advise and assist line personnel in meeting their goals.

</div>

To minimize the disadvantages of simple line organizations, many organizations today have both line and staff personnel. **Line personnel** are responsible for directly achieving organizational goals, and include production workers, distribution people, and marketing personnel. **Staff personnel** advise and assist line personnel in meeting their goals, and include those in marketing research, legal advising, information technology, and human resource management.

See Figure 8.6 for a diagram of a line-and-staff organization. One important difference between line and staff personnel is authority. Line personnel have formal authority to make policy decisions. Staff personnel have authority to advise line personnel and influence their decisions, but they can't make policy changes themselves. The line manager may seek or ignore the advice from staff personnel.

Many organizations benefit from expert staff advice on safety, legal issues, quality control, database management, motivation, and investing. Staff personnel strengthen the line positions and are like well-paid consultants on the organization's payroll.

Matrix-Style Organizations

Both line and line-and-staff organization structures may suffer from inflexibility. Both allow for established lines of authority and communication and work well in organizations with stable environments and slow product development (such as firms selling household appliances). In such firms, clear lines of authority and relatively fixed organization structures are assets that ensure efficient operations.

Need help understanding Line vs. Staff Employees?
www.introbiz.tv/QR8-1

figure 8.6

A SAMPLE LINE-AND-STAFF ORGANIZATION

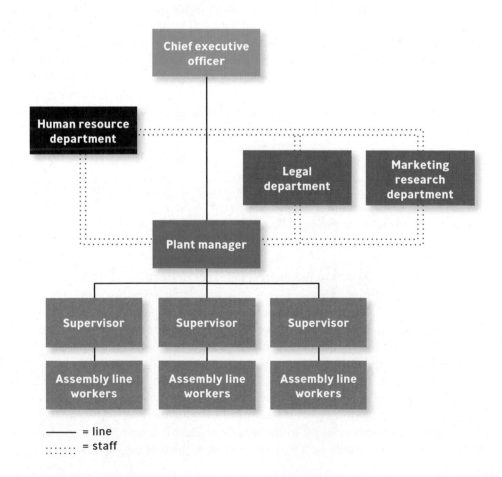

Today's economy, however, is dominated by high-growth industries like telecommunications, nanotechnology, robotics, biotechnology, and aerospace, where competition is stiff and the life cycle of new ideas is short.[17] Emphasis is on product development, creativity, special projects, rapid communication, and interdepartmental teamwork. From those changes grew the popularity of the **matrix organization,** in which specialists from different parts of the organization work together temporarily on specific projects, but still remain part of a line-and-staff structure (see Figure 8.7). In other words, a project manager can borrow people from different departments to help design and market new product ideas.

The matrix structure was developed in the aerospace industry and is now familiar in areas such as banking, management consulting firms, accounting firms, ad agencies, and school systems. Among its advantages:

- It gives managers flexibility in assigning people to projects.
- It encourages interorganizational cooperation and teamwork.
- It can produce creative solutions to product development problems.
- It makes efficient use of organizational resources.

As for disadvantages:

- It's costly and complex.
- It can confuse employees about where their loyalty belongs—with the project manager or with their functional unit.
- It requires good interpersonal skills as well as cooperative employees and managers to avoid communication problems.
- It may be only a temporary solution to a long-term problem.

If you're thinking that matrix organizations violate some traditional managerial principles, you're right. Normally a person can't work effectively for two bosses. Who has the real authority? Whose directive has first priority?

matrix organization
An organization in which specialists from different parts of the organization are brought together to work on specific projects but still remain part of a line-and-staff structure.

figure 8.7

A MATRIX ORGANIZATION

In a matrix organization, project managers are in charge of teams made up of members of several departments. In this case, project manager 2 supervises employees A, B, C, and D. These employees are accountable not only to project manager 2 but also to the head of their individual departments. For example, employee B, a market researcher, reports to project manager 2 *and* to the vice president of marketing.

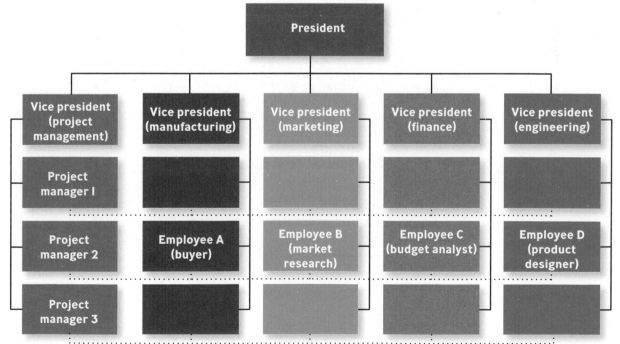

"SEND THIS BACK TO THE LEGAL DEPARTMENT. I THINK THEY COULD MAKE IT MUCH MORE COMPLICATED THAN THIS ..."

Members of a legal department are considered staff personnel in a line-and-staff organization. Staff personnel serve in an advisory role and can work with colleagues and departments at every level in the firm's hierarchy. What are some of the advantages of this type of organization model?

cross-functional self-managed teams
Groups of employees from different departments who work together on a long-term basis.

In reality, however, the system functions more effectively than you might imagine. To develop a new product, a project manager may be given temporary authority to "borrow" line personnel from production, marketing, and other line functions. The employees work together to complete the project and then return to their regular positions. Thus, no one actually reports to more than one manager at a time.

A potential real problem with matrix management, however, is that the project teams are not permanent. They form to solve a problem and then break up. There is little chance for cross-functional learning, because teams work together so briefly.

Decision making in the future will be distributed throughout the organization so that people can respond rapidly to change, says the *Harvard Business Review.* Global teams will collaborate on the Internet for a single project and then disband. Young people who play online games will feel quite comfortable working in such groups.

Cross-Functional Self-Managed Teams

One solution to the temporary nature of matrix teams is to establish long-lived teams and empower them to work closely with suppliers, customers, and others to quickly and efficiently bring out new, high-quality products while giving great service. *BusinessWeek* reports that some 82 percent of white-collar workers partner with co-workers. Over 80 percent say they prefer working in groups of three or more. Most work in groups to learn from others, but 30 percent use groups to accomplish a specific task.

Cross-functional self-managed teams are groups of employees from different departments who work together on a long-term basis (as opposed to the temporary teams established in matrix-style organizations). *Self-managed* means that they are empowered to make decisions without management approval. The barriers among design, engineering, marketing, distribution, and other functions fall when interdepartmental teams are created. Sometimes the teams are interfirm; that is, the members come from two or more companies.

Cross-functional teams work best when leadership is shared. An engineer may lead the design of a new product, but a marketing expert may take the leadership position once it's ready for distribution.

Going Beyond Organizational Boundaries

Cross-functional teams work best when the voice of the customer is brought in, especially in product development tasks. Suppliers and distributors should be on the team as well. A cross-functional team that includes customers, suppliers, and distributors goes beyond organizational boundaries. When suppliers and distributors are in other countries, cross-functional teams may share market information across national boundaries.[18] Government coordinators may assist such projects, letting cross-functional teams break the barriers between government and business.

Cross-functional teams are only one way businesses can interact with other companies. Next we look at others.

progress assessment

- What is the difference between line and staff personnel?
- What management principle does a matrix-style organization challenge?
- What is the main difference between a matrix-style organization's structure and the use of cross-functional teams?

LEARNING goal 5

Identify the benefits of interfirm cooperation and coordination.

MANAGING THE INTERACTIONS AMONG FIRMS

Whether it involves customers, suppliers, distributors, or the government, **networking** uses communications technology and other means to link organizations and allow them to work together on common objectives.[19] Let's explore this concept further.

networking
Using communications technology and other means to link organizations and allow them to work together on common objectives.

Transparency and Virtual Organizations

Networked organizations are so closely linked by the Internet that each can find out what the others are doing in real time. **Real time** simply means the present moment or the actual time in which an event takes place. The Internet has allowed companies to send real-time data to organizational partners as they are developed or collected. The result is transparency (see Chapter 7), which occurs when a company is so open to other companies that electronic information is shared as if the companies were one. With this integration, two companies can work as closely as two departments in traditional firms.

real time
The present moment or the actual time in which something takes place.

You can think of a team of medical specialists in an operating room as a cross-functional, self-managed team. Doctors, nurses, technicians, and anesthesiologists from different departments and areas in the hospital work together to complete successful operations. What kinds of tasks do cross-functional, self-managed teams complete in an office or retail environment?

CONNECTING WITH
small business

Starting Up with a Smaller Staff

Thanks to online services and other advances in technology, new businesses are being launched today with an average of only 4.9 workers, compared to 7.5 in the 1990s. Unfortunately, young companies are subject to the same grim financial realities as their established peers. Since keeping a trim bottom line is the name of the game these days, startups are finding other ways to get essential tasks done without burdening their budget. For instance, in September Sam Rogoway launched his web-based video production company, Near Networks, with a staff of just four people. Rather than hiring a full-time accountant or IT rep, he simply outsources that work to independent agencies.

Over the past 17 years, 65 percent of new Internet jobs came from small employers. With job growth stalled across the board, the steady decline in startup size could account for some of the sluggish labor market. If the economy continues to sputter, as experts anticipate, company launches will likely remain lean. The technological resources available to companies should only improve as time goes on as well. A recent survey found that a small but growing number of businesses are using cloud-computing networks for everything from data storage to customer service and finance. With so many reliable and inexpensive outlets available to them, there's a chance that companies could expand in the long term with even fewer employees than they started out with. For example, one online mattress firm that launched in 2010 with five employees now relies on just two part-time workers to help operate the growing company.

Sources: Angus Loten, "With New Technology, Start-Ups Go Lean," *The Wall Street Journal*, September 15, 2011; and Benjamin F. Kuo, "An Interview with Sam Rogoway, Near Networks," www.socialtech.com, October 14, 2011.

Can you see the implications for organizational design? Most organizations are no longer self-sufficient or self-contained. Rather, they are part of a vast network of global businesses that work closely together. An organization chart showing what people do within any one organization is simply not complete, because the organization is part of a much larger system of firms. A modern chart would show people in different organizations and indicate how they are networked. This is a relatively new concept, however, so few such charts are yet available. The Connecting with Small Business box offers an example of how small businesses outsource work to independent agencies rather than hire full-time workers.

Networked organization structures tend to be flexible. A company may work with a design expert from another company in Italy for a year and then not need that person anymore. It may hire an expert from a company in another country for the next project. Such a temporary network, made of replaceable firms that join and leave as needed, is a **virtual corporation** (see Figure 8.8).[20] This is quite different from a traditional organization structure; in fact, traditional managers sometimes have trouble adapting to the speed of change and the impermanence of relationships in networking. We discuss adaptation to change below; first, we describe how organizations use benchmarking and outsourcing to manage their interactions with other firms.

virtual corporation
A temporary networked organization made up of replaceable firms that join and leave as needed.

Benchmarking and Core Competencies

Organizations historically tried to do all functions themselves. Each had its own department for accounting, finance, marketing, production, and so on. As we've noted, today's organizations look to other organizations for help in areas where they do not generate world-class quality.

benchmarking
Comparing an organization's practices, processes, and products against the world's best.

Benchmarking compares an organization's practices, processes, and products against the world's best. As one example, K2 Skis is a company that makes skis, snowboards, in-line skates, and related products. It studied the compact-disc industry and learned to use ultraviolet inks to print graphics on skis. It went to the aerospace industry to get piezoelectric technology to reduce vibration in its snowboards (the aerospace industry uses the technology for wings on planes). It learned from the cable television industry how to braid layers of fiberglass and carbon, and adapted that knowledge to make skis. As another example, Wyeth, a pharmaceutical company, benchmarked the aerospace industry for project management, the shipping industry for standardization of processes, and computer makers to learn the most efficient way to make prescription drugs.

Benchmarking also has a more directly competitive purpose. In retailing, Target may compare itself to Walmart to see what, if anything, Walmart does better. Target will then try to improve its practices or processes to become even better than Walmart.

If an organization can't do as well as the best in, say, shipping, it will try to outsource the function to an organization like UPS or FedEx that specializes in shipping. Outsourcing, remember, means assigning one or more functions—such as accounting, production, security, maintenance, and legal work—to outside organizations. Even small firms are getting involved in outsourcing. We've already discussed some problems with outsourcing, especially when companies outsource to other countries. Some functions, such as information management and marketing, may be too important to assign to outside firms. In that case, the organization should benchmark the best firms and restructure its departments to try to be equally good. It is important to remember that companies in other countries often outsource their functions to companies in the United States. We call that *insourcing* and it is the source of many jobs.[21]

Nike's core competencies are designing and marketing athletic shoes. The company outsources other functions (i.e., manufacturing) to other companies that assemble shoes better and cheaper than Nike could do on its own. What are the advantages of focusing on the company's core competencies? What are the disadvantages?

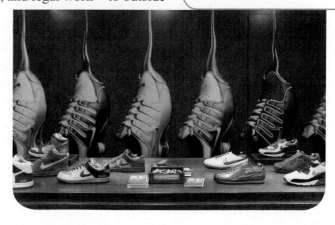

When Twitter and Facebook Are Old School

There was a day when many people were eager to hear about microchips and how they worked. Today, there aren't many people talking about microprocessors or other old high-tech innovations. Today, the focus is on Facebook, Twitter, cloud computing, and the like. People are still debating which eBook reader is the best. But soon people will become so accustomed to having these tools at their fingertips that they will no longer be newsworthy. Matt Ridley writes, "The very notion that we discussed the relative merits of text, email, social network messaging, and tweeting will seem quaint. In the future, my part of the cloud will get a message to a friend's part of the cloud by whichever method works best, and I will not even know which way it went."

There will be dozens of new high-tech gadgets to try. Many of them will be slight improvements on what is available today (just as the iPad 2 was a slight improvement on the original iPad), while others may be revolutionary. What is most relevant to this chapter is how social media will affect organizations in the future. There is likely to be an even greater increase in working from home. There will be closer and better relationships with customers and suppliers and dealers. All in all, social media will continue to have a major influence on how business gets done and where it gets done and who does it. The moral of the story for managers is: Keep up with the latest technology or be left behind.

Sources: Matt Ridley, "Microchips Are Old Hat, Can Tweets Be Far Behind?" *The Wall Street Journal,* March 5–6, 2011; and B. L. Ochman, "3 Things You Need to Know about Social Media," www.mashable.com, accessed April 2011.

core competencies
Those functions that the organization can do as well as or better than any other organization in the world.

When a firm has completed its outsourcing process, the remaining functions are its **core competencies,** those functions it can do as well as or better than any other organization in the world.[22] For example, Nike is great at designing and marketing athletic shoes. Those are its core competencies. It outsources manufacturing, however, to other companies that assemble shoes better and less expensively than Nike can. Similarly, Dell is best at marketing computers and outsources most other functions, including manufacturing and distribution.

After you have structured an organization, you must keep monitoring the environment (including customers) to learn what changes are needed. Dell, for example, recently reversed its practice of outsourcing customer support and now offers a premium service that allows U.S. customers to reach tech support in North America. The following section discusses organizational change in more detail.

ADAPTING TO CHANGE

Once you have formed an organization, you must be prepared to adapt the structure to changes in the market.[23] That's not always easy to do. Over time, an organization can get stuck in its ways. Employees have a tendency to say, "That's the way we've always done things. If it isn't broken, don't fix it." Managers also get complacent. They may say they have 20 years' experience when in fact they've had 1 year's experience 20 times. Do you think that slow adaptation to change was a factor in the decline of the manufacturing sector in the United States?

Introducing change is thus one of the hardest challenges facing any manager. Nonetheless, change is what's happening at General Motors (GM), Ford, Facebook, and other companies eager to become more competitive. If you have old facilities

Traditional Organization   **Inverted Organization**

that are no longer efficient, you have to get rid of them. That's exactly what GM and other companies are doing. In fact, they have asked the government to lend them billions of dollars to help. You may have to cut your labor force to lower costs.

The Internet has created whole new opportunities, not only to sell to customers directly but also to ask them questions and provide them with any information they want. To win market share, companies must coordinate the efforts of their traditional departments and their Internet staff to create friendly, easy-to-manage interactions. Young people today are called **digital natives** because they grew up with the Internet. To reach them, companies are retraining older employees to be more tech-savvy. That means becoming familiar with YouTube, Facebook, Wikis, Skype, Twitter, RSS, and more. The Connecting Through Social Media box explores the future of such high-tech devices.

We've seen that Target is highly centralized. Nonetheless, the company reacts effectively to changes in consumer preferences throughout the country, in part by keeping in touch with an enormous web of people of all ages, interests, and nationalities—its "creative cabinet"—via the Internet. The members of the "cabinet," who never meet so they cannot influence each other, evaluate various new initiatives and recommend new programs to help Target figure out what belongs on store shelves.

Restructuring for Empowerment

To empower employees, firms often must reorganize dramatically to make frontline workers their most important people. **Restructuring** is redesigning an organization so it can more effectively and efficiently serve its customers.[24]

Until recently, department store clerks, bank tellers, and front-desk staff in hotels weren't considered key employees. Instead, managers were considered more important, and they were responsible for directing the work of the frontline people. The organization chart in a typical firm looked much like a pyramid.

A few service-oriented organizations have turned the traditional organization structure upside down. An **inverted organization** has contact people (like nurses) at the top and the chief executive officer at the bottom. Management layers are few, and the manager's job is to *assist and support* frontline people, not boss them around. Figure 8.9 illustrates the difference between an inverted and a traditional organizational structure.

---

figure 8.9

COMPARISON OF AN INVERTED ORGANIZATIONAL STRUCTURE AND A TRADITIONAL ORGANIZATIONAL STRUCTURE

digital natives
Young people who have grown up using the Internet and social networking.

restructuring
Redesigning an organization so that it can more effectively and efficiently serve its customers.

inverted organization
An organization that has contact people at the top and the chief executive officer at the bottom of the organization chart.

Companies based on this organization structure support frontline personnel with internal and external databases, advanced communication systems, and professional assistance. Naturally, this means frontline people have to be better educated, better trained, and better paid than in the past. It takes a lot of trust for top managers to implement such a system—but when they do, the payoff in customer satisfaction and profits is often well worth the effort.[25]

In the past, managers controlled information—and that gave them power. In more progressive organizations today, everyone shares information, often through an elaborate database system, and *among* firms as well as *within* them. No matter what organizational model you choose or how much you empower your employees, the secret to successful organization change is to focus on customers and give them what they want.

LEARNING goal 6

Explain how organizational culture can help businesses adapt to change.

Creating a Change-Oriented Organizational Culture

organizational (or corporate) culture
Widely shared values within an organization that provide unity and cooperation to achieve common goals.

Any organizational change is bound to cause some stress and resistance among members. Firms adapt best when their culture is already change-oriented. **Organizational (or corporate) culture** is the widely shared values within an organization that foster unity and cooperation to achieve common goals. Usually the culture of an organization is reflected in its stories, traditions, and myths.

Each McDonald's restaurant has the same feel, look, and atmosphere; in short, each has a similar organizational culture. It's obvious from visiting almost any McDonald's that the culture emphasizes quality, service, cleanliness, and value.

An organizational culture can also be negative. Have you ever been in an organization where you feel no one cares about service or quality? The clerks may seem uniformly glum, indifferent, and testy. Their mood pervades the atmosphere, and patrons become unhappy or upset. It may be hard to believe an organization, especially a profit-making one, can be run so badly and still survive. Clearly then, when you search for a job, study the organizational culture to see whether you will thrive in it.

Empowering employees who deal directly with customers to solve problems without needing a manager's approval makes a higher level of customer service possible and helps employees grow as well. What kind of guest issues do you think a frontline hotel employee should be allowed to solve on his or her own?

Some of the best organizations have cultures that emphasize service to others, especially customers. The atmosphere reflects friendly, caring people who enjoy working together to provide a good product at a reasonable price. Companies that have such cultures have less need for close supervision of employees. That usually means fewer policy manuals; organization charts; and formal rules, procedures, and controls. The key to a productive culture is mutual trust.[26] You get such trust by giving it. The very best companies stress high moral and ethical values such as honesty, reliability, fairness, environmental protection, and social involvement.

We've been talking as if organizational matters were mostly controllable by management. In fact, the formal structure is just one element of the total organizational system, including its culture. The informal organization is of equal or even greater importance. Let's explore this notion next.

Managing the Informal Organization

All organizations have two organizational systems. The **formal organization** details lines of responsibility, authority, and position. It's the structure shown on organization charts. The other system is the **informal organization,** the system that develops spontaneously as employees meet and form cliques, relationships, and lines of authority outside the formal organization. It's the human side of the organization that doesn't show on any organization chart.

No organization can operate effectively without both types of organization. The formal system is often too slow and bureaucratic to let the organization adapt quickly, although it does provide helpful guides and lines of authority for routine situations.

The informal organization is often too unstructured and emotional to allow careful, reasoned decision making on critical matters. It's extremely effective, however, in generating creative solutions to short-term problems and creating camaraderie and teamwork among employees.[27]

In any organization, it's wise to learn quickly who is important in the informal organization. Following formal rules and procedures can take days. Who in the organization knows how to obtain supplies immediately without the normal procedures? Which administrative assistants should you see if you want your work given first priority? Answers to these questions help people work effectively in many organizations.

The informal organization's nerve center is the *grapevine,* the system through which unofficial information flows between and among managers and employees. Key people in the grapevine usually have considerable influence.

In the old "us-versus-them" system of organizations, where managers and employees were often at odds, the informal system hindered effective management. In more open organizations, managers and employees work together to set

formal organization
The structure that details lines of responsibility, authority, and position; that is, the structure shown on organization charts.

informal organization
The system that develops spontaneously as employees meet and form cliques, relationships, and lines of authority outside the formal organization.

The informal organization is the system that develops as employees meet and form relationships. The grapevine, the unofficial flow of information among employees, is the nerve center of the informal organization. How does the informal organization affect the work environment?

objectives and design procedures. The informal organization is an invaluable managerial asset that can promote harmony among workers and establish the corporate culture.

As effective as the informal organization may be in creating group cooperation, it can still be equally powerful in resisting management directives. Employees may form unions, go on strike together, and generally disrupt operations. Learning to create the right corporate culture and work within the informal organization is thus a key to managerial success.[28]

progress assessment

- What is an inverted organization?
- Why do organizations outsource functions?
- What is organizational culture?

summary

Learning Goal 1. Outline the basic principles of organization management.

- **What is happening today to American businesses?**

They are adjusting to changing markets. That is a normal function in a capitalist economy. There will be big winners, like Google and Facebook, and big losers as well. The key to success is remaining flexible and adapting to the changing times.

- **What are the principles of organization management?**

Structuring an organization means devising a division of labor (sometimes resulting in specialization), setting up teams or departments, and assigning responsibility and authority. It includes allocating resources (such as funds), assigning specific tasks, and establishing procedures for accomplishing the organizational objectives. Managers also have to make ethical decisions about how to treat workers.

Learning Goal 2. Compare the organizational theories of Fayol and Weber.

- **What were Fayol's basic principles?**

Fayol introduced principles such as unity of command, hierarchy of authority, division of labor, subordination of individual interests to the general interest, authority, clear communication channels, order, and equity.

- **What principles did Weber add?**

Weber added principles of bureaucracy such as job descriptions, written rules and decision guidelines, consistent procedures, and staffing and promotions based on qualifications.

Learning Goal 3. Evaluate the choices managers make in structuring organizations.

- **What are the four major choices in structuring organizations?**

Choices to make in structuring and restructuring organizations cover (1) centralization versus decentralization, (2) breadth of span of control, (3) tall versus flat organization structures, and (4) type of departmentalization.

- **What are the latest trends in structuring?**

Departments are often replaced or supplemented by matrix organizations and cross-functional teams that decentralize authority. The span of control becomes larger as employees become self-directed. Another trend is to eliminate managers and flatten organizations.

Learning Goal 4. Contrast the various organizational models.

- **What are the two major organizational models?**

Two traditional forms of organization are (1) line organizations and (2) line-and-staff organizations. A line organization has clearly defined responsibility and authority, is easy to understand, and provides each worker with only one supervisor. The expert advice of staff assistants in a line-and-staff organization helps in areas such as safety, quality control, computer technology, human resource management, and investing.

- **What are the key alternatives to the major organizational models?**

Matrix organizations assign people to projects temporarily and encourage interorganizational cooperation and teamwork. Cross-functional self-managed teams have all the benefits of the matrix style and are long-term.

Learning Goal 5. Identify the benefits of interfirm cooperation and coordination.

- **What are the major concepts involved in interfirm communications?**

Networking uses communications technology and other means to link organizations and allow them to work together on common objectives. A virtual corporation is a networked organization of replaceable firms that join and leave as needed. Benchmarking tells firms how their performance measures up to that of their competitors in specific functions. The company may then *outsource* to companies that perform its weaker functions more effectively and efficiently. The functions that are left are the firm's *core competencies.*

- **What is an inverted organization?**

An inverted organization places employees at the top of the hierarchy; managers are at the bottom to train and assist employees.

Learning Goal 6. Explain how organizational culture can help businesses adapt to change.

- **What is organizational culture?**

Organizational (or corporate) culture consists of the widely shared values within an organization that foster unity and cooperation to achieve common goals.

- **What is the difference between the formal and informal organization of a firm?**

The formal organization details lines of responsibility, authority, and position. It's the structure shown on organization charts. The informal organization is the system that develops spontaneously as employees meet and form cliques, relationships, and lines of authority outside the formal organization. It's the human side of the organization. The informal organization is an invaluable managerial asset that often promotes harmony among workers and establishes the corporate culture. As effective as the informal organization may be in creating group cooperation, it can still be equally powerful in resisting management directives.

key terms

benchmarking 233
bureaucracy 221
centralized
  authority 222
chain of command 221
core competencies 234
cross-functional
  self-managed
  teams 230
decentralized
  authority 222
departmentalization 224

digital natives 235
economies of scale 218
flat organization
  structure 224
formal organization 237
hierarchy 220
informal
  organization 237
inverted
  organization 235
line organization 227
line personnel 228

matrix organization 229
networking 231
organization chart 221
organizational (or
  corporate) culture 236
real time 231
restructuring 235
span of control 223
staff personnel 228
tall organization
  structure 223
virtual corporation 232

critical thinking

Now that you have learned some of the basic principles of organization, pause and think about where you have already applied such concepts yourself or when you have been part of an organization that did.

1. Did you find a division of labor necessary and helpful?
2. Were you assigned specific tasks or left on your own to decide what to do?
3. Were promotions based strictly on qualifications, as Weber suggested? What other factors may have been considered?
4. What problems seem to emerge when an organization gets larger?
5. What organizational changes might you recommend to the auto companies? The airline industry?

developing workplace skills

1. There is no better way to understand the effects of having many layers of management on communication accuracy than the game of Message Relay. Choose seven or more members of the class and have them leave the classroom. Then choose one person to read the following paragraph and another student to listen. Call in one of the students from outside and have the "listener" tell him or her what information was in the paragraph. Then bring in another student and have the new listener repeat the information to him or her. Continue the

process with all those who left the room. Do not allow anyone in the class to offer corrections as each listener becomes the storyteller in turn. In this way, all the students can hear how the facts become distorted over time. The distortions and mistakes are often quite humorous, but they are not so funny in organizations such as Ford, which once had 22 layers of management.

Here's the paragraph:

Dealers in the midwest region have received over 130 complaints about steering on the new Commander and Roadhandler models of our minivans. Apparently, the front suspension system is weak and the ball joints are wearing too fast. This causes slippage in the linkage and results in oversteering. Mr. Berenstein has been notified, but so far only 213 of 4,300 dealers have received repair kits.

2. Describe some informal groups within an organization with which you are familiar at school or work. What have you noticed about how those groups help or hinder progress in the organization?

3. Imagine you are working for Kitchen Magic, an appliance manufacturer that produces dishwashers. A competitor introduces a new dishwasher that uses sound waves not only to clean even the worst burned-on food but also to sterilize dishes and silverware. You need to develop a similar offering fast, or your company will lose market share. Write an e-mail to management outlining the problem and explaining your rationale for recommending use of a cross-functional team to respond quickly.

4. Divide the class into teams of five. Each team should imagine your firm, a producer of athletic shoes, has been asked to join a virtual network. How might you minimize the potential problems of joining? Begin by defining a virtual corporation and listing its advantages and disadvantages. Each team should report its solutions to the class.

5. Many work groups of the future, including management, will be cross-functional and self-managed. To practice working in such an organization, break into groups of five or so students, preferably with different backgrounds and interests. Each group must work together to prepare a report on the advantages and disadvantages of working in teams. Many of the problems and advantages of cross-functional, self-managed teams should emerge in your group as you try to complete this assignment. Each group should report to the class how it handled the problems and benefited from the advantages.

taking it to the net

Purpose

To learn more about the process of organizational change.

Exercise

Xerox is a very familiar corporate name in the United States. There was a time, however, when the company was faltering and needed to adapt to foreign competition. This exercise will help you see how complex such change can be.

1. Do an online search for Xerox Corporation.

2. Read through the history of the company and describe its current strengths, weaknesses, opportunities, and threats (a SWOT analysis; see Chapter 7).

3. Describe Xerox's reasons for success.

casing the web

To access the case "IBM Is Both an Outsourcer and a Major Outsource for Others," visit **www.mhhe.com/P2P2e**

video case

Open-Book Management at New Belgium Brewery

Most Americans define "working" as getting paid to make money for somebody else. As parts of a centralized organization, many employees are directed by a manager who in turn reports to another upper-level boss, which eventually leads up to the top with the CEO. Such a rigid hierarchy can make it difficult for lower-level employees to have a true understanding of how the business is run, let alone any say in the company's overall direction.

That isn't the case, however, for Colorado-based New Belgium Brewery. The company has been an intimate operation ever since founders Jeff Lebesch and Kim Jordan poured their first pint in 1991. Inspired by the local breweries he encountered on a family trip to Belgium, Lebesch began brewing in his own basement with a limited clientele of friends and family. As craft beers grew in popularity through the 1990s and 2000s, New Belgium emerged as one of the biggest brands in the industry,

with its flagship ale Fat Tire finding its way into bars not just in Colorado (or Lebesch's basement), but across the country.

Even as the company has expanded into a nationally recognized brand, New Belgium remains committed first and foremost to the people directly responsible for its success: its employees. From brewmasters to bartenders, the staff at New Belgium enjoys a level of empowerment that other runners in the rat race can only dream of. First of all, several operational divisions are almost completely decentralized. For example, New Belgium's quality assurance section contains no ranking manager to direct the staff. Instead, employees are trusted to make their own decisions if they find an opportunity to improve a product's quality. With less red tape to wade through, quality assurance is given more time to focus on the task at hand, thus improving productivity significantly.

But implementing such an open system is a risky endeavor. Employees need to be self-motivated and possess a legitimate interest in the overall performance of the company, or else productivity can suffer instead of soar. New Belgium keeps its staff tethered to the business's well being by turning them into shareholders. After an employee has worked at the brewery for a year, he or she is given a small slice of the company to own. As New Belgium profits go up, the value of that employee's share goes up as well.

Since employees are not only staff but also shareholders, New Belgium treats them as such with regular updates on the status and future of the company. Called "open-book management," employees are trained in basic financial practices and business lingo, so that Lebesch and Jordan can deliver board of directors-style meetings with their staff that inform them about the company's performance and upcoming plans. Employees are even given a chance to discuss upper management's decisions and to chime in with their own ideas. Keeping staff apprised of the company's daily dealings motivates employees because it teaches staff the importance of how their specific job fits into the overall fabric of the company. Employees are in turn more aware of their own significance in the grand scheme of the brewery, making them more conscious of the decisions they make on the job every day.

The overall environment of the American workplace is changing rapidly. As employees become more educated and managers more open to staff discussion, management structures like New Belgium's could become much more common.

Thinking It Over

1. *What are three major changes that have occurred in the American workplace?*
2. *What is open-book management?*
3. *Briefly identify the elements of organizational culture.*

9 Production AND Operations Management

After you have read and studied this chapter, you should be able to

LEARNING goals

1 Describe the current state of U.S. manufacturing and what manufacturers have done to become more competitive.

2 Describe the evolution from production to operations management.

3 Identify various production processes and describe techniques that improve productivity, including computer-aided design and manufacturing, flexible manufacturing, lean manufacturing, and mass customization.

4 Describe operations management planning issues including facility location, facility layout, materials requirement planning, purchasing, just-in-time inventory control, and quality control.

5 Explain the use of PERT and Gantt charts to control manufacturing processes.

Nothing stays the same for long in today's technology sector. Every day, engineers and computer scientists come up with new ways to perform old tasks, even if those tasks weren't that old to begin with. In this unpredictable industry, any company, large or small, can quickly become obsolete if it does not constantly roll with the changes.

As CEO of IBM, it's Virginia Rometty's job to ensure that her company does exactly that. Rometty has only been in the CEO position since January 2012. Still, as a longtime veteran of the tech giant, Rometty knows better than anybody how important adaptation is to Big Blue. Shortly after graduating from Northwestern University with degrees in computer science and electrical engineering, Rometty joined IBM in 1981 as a systems engineer. First working out of the Detroit office, by 1991 she was overseeing all the company's consulting work in the Great Lakes area.

CONNECTING WITH

Virginia Rometty

President and CEO of IBM

But while Rometty's star was rising, the company itself was collapsing. IBM piled up $16 billion in losses between 1991 and 1993 as sales tanked due to increased competition. A new executive team came on the scene and implemented drastic, companywide changes, including firing 35,000 workers. This wasn't to be the last time IBM had to reinvent itself to fit a changing market, though. By the beginning of the 2000s, Rometty had become one of the company's leading consultants. Her newfound power brought her into the inner circle of then CEO Sam Palmisano, who would oversee IBM's most ambitious retooling yet.

For years IBM had made a fortune producing huge, complicated mainframe systems for companies as well as personal computers. As the millennium rolled around, IBM's machines couldn't compete with new products emerging from competitors like Apple. Seeing no future in hardware, Palmisano made the risky decision to phase out IBM's computer manufacturing arm in favor of a service-based business model focused on consultancy. To accomplish this task, the company bought up many consultancy startups and integrated them into IBM. It was here that Rometty really made a name for herself. Palmisano assigned her to spearhead the $3.9 billion acquisition of the

Pricewaterhouse-Coopers (PwC) consultancy company. At first, PwC's consultants felt uneasy about the big takeover they had just undergone, fearing that IBM would squander the company's talents. Rometty successfully assimilated the new consultants into the IBM fold, however, setting an example for the rest of the company to follow. Today IBM's consultancy and business services unit accounts for more than half of its 427,000 employees.

In 2011, Palmisano announced that he would step down from IBM's top seat after 10 years as CEO. He named Rometty as his successor because of her dedication to finding ways for the company to adapt to constant change. In the years to come, Big Blue is certainly going to need to rely on her expertise. While Rometty plans to keep the consultancy business growing, she is also focused on expanding IBM's role in the software market. Perhaps most important, though, are her plans to establish a greater presence in emerging markets like China and Brazil. Rometty began working closely with these global economies in her previous role as senior vice president of sales and marketing. Soon, sales in these markets will become just as important to the company's bottom line as their domestic efforts.

By playing a key role in IBM's switch from production to service, Virginia Rometty has helped her company achieve record revenues. It has also earned her great respect in the tech industry, as well as a spot on *Fortune* magazine's 50 Most Powerful Women in Business list seven years in a row. In this chapter you'll learn about how other company leaders thrive and survive in the production and operations sector. You'll also find out why the United States, like IBM, is generally moving from a production-based economy to a service economy.

Sources: Carol Hymowitz and Sarah Frier, "Can This IBMer Keep Big Blue's Edge?" *Bloomberg Businessweek*, October 26, 2011; Spencer E. Ante and Joann S. Lublin, "IBM Names Rometty as Next CEO," *The Wall Street Journal*, October 26, 2011; Cade Metz, "IBM Names Virginia Rometty as First Female CEO," *Wired*, October 25, 2011; and Virginia M. Rommety, www.ibm.com, accessed March 2012.

This company's robots manufacture, test, and package motor starters—all untouched by human hands. The machines can fill special orders, even for a single item, without slowing down the process. Name that company. (Find the answer in the chapter.)

LEARNING **goal 1**

Describe the current state of U.S. manufacturing and what manufacturers have done to become more competitive.

MANUFACTURING AND SERVICES IN PERSPECTIVE

Let's begin with a little backstory. In November 2008, *The Washington Post* reported, "Activity in the nation's manufacturing sector . . . declined last month to the lowest level in more than two decades, offering economists more evidence that the country is entering a deep recession."[1] Soon after that, on January 29, 2009, *The Wall Street Journal* reported, "Joblessness was worst in the West and Midwest, indicating that the industries hit first by the recession—housing and manufacturing—continue to lose jobs."[2] Another *Wall Street Journal* article went on to say that unemployment could reach double-digit levels, home values could plunge a total of 36 percent, and stocks could fall a total of 55 percent.[3] Such events led President Obama and Congress to propose a stimulus package that spent about a trillion dollars (including interest) to "create or save" millions of jobs and get the economy moving again—including manufacturing. Much of this chapter is devoted to showing you what manufacturers and service providers can and are doing to revive the U.S. economy to become world-class competitors.[4]

Sure, there has been lots of bad news about the manufacturing sector, but the story may not be as bad as you think.[5] How can we reconcile the fact that so many workers in manufacturing are unemployed while manufacturing output continues to increase? The answer is that today's workers are so productive that the United States needs fewer workers to produce more goods.[6] An article in *The Wall Street Journal* says that we should not go back to a less efficient economy, but should instead retrain the workforce to participate in this dynamic new economy.[7] Many manufacturing jobs are coming back to the United States as wages increase dramatically in other countries.[8]

Some areas of the country are enjoying economic growth from manufacturing while others are experiencing declines. One key to ending such declines is to adapt to the new realities and attract new manufacturers.

Volkswagen is just one of many auto manufacturers that have insourced jobs to the United States like this one in the VW Chattanooga, Tennessee, plant. Why do you suppose so many news reports emphasize outsourcing when thousands of jobs are created by insourcing?

How Germany's Economy Remains Mighty with Manufacturing

Ten years ago, Germany's economy was in a rut. Slow growth and high unemployment made the country seem like a dinosaur in comparison to rapidly expanding neighbors like Spain and Ireland. In reality, though, what looked on the surface like stagnancy was actually Germany sticking to its guns. While other European nations gorged on debt and easy money in the finance world, Germany wisely shored up its industrial might. Now Germany has the most powerful economy on the continent while other countries find themselves deep in debt crises.

So just how did Germany manage such a feat? The work of the power-tool manufacturer Stihl tells part of the story. Although Stihl's chain saws are the priciest on the market today, they're also among the industry's best-selling brands. Stihl ensures its chain saws remain high quality by producing nearly every unit in Germany itself. Most other companies operating today outsource their manufacturing operations to China, where quality is more difficult to control. But Stihl can credit its success to more than just producing locally. When the credit crisis brought the world economy to a halt in 2008, many companies responded by firing workers and cutting costs. Stihl, on the other hand, locked in its staff with employment guarantees until 2015, while simultaneously adding more specialists to its product-development team. As a result, Stihl can continue to command high prices for its top-quality products, allowing it to earn a profit despite the high wages of its workforce.

Germany has hundreds of other companies like Stihl who export their goods to markets across the globe.

The question is, then, can the German model itself be exported to other countries as well? Many nations have certainly tried. Spain's government is attempting to implement a German educational method in its schools that combines hands-on vocational training with standard classroom teaching. Other countries like France and Great Britain have expressed interest in mimicking the model for companies like Stihl. Doing so is easier said than done, however. Stihl, like many other German companies, has been family-owned for generations. To them, the way they do business isn't a radical response to a global economic slowdown—it's the way they've done business since their founding. Teaching such an entrenched system is not an easy thing to do. Nevertheless, the United States and Europe's debt-ridden nations can learn quite a lot from Germany's consistent manufacturing success.

Sources: "What Germany Offers the World," *The Economist,* April 14, 2012; Michael Schuman, "How Germany Became the China of Europe," *Time,* March 7, 2011; and Tom Fairless, "German Industrial Output Rebounds," *The Wall Street Journal,* May 8, 2012.

Operations management is a term that is used in both manufacturing and service organizations. **Operations management** is a specialized area in management that converts or transforms resources, including human resources like technical skills and innovation, into goods and services. It includes inventory management, quality control, production scheduling, follow-up services, and more. In an automobile plant, operations management transforms raw materials, human resources, parts, supplies, paints, tools, and other resources into automobiles. It does this through the processes of fabrication and assembly.

In a college or university, operations management takes inputs such as information, professors, supplies, buildings, offices, and computer systems—and creates services that transform students into educated people. It does this through a process called education. For a more extensive discussion, see the Free Management Library's entry on operations management (www.managementhelp.org/ops_mgnt/ops_mgnt.htm).

operations management
A specialized area in management that converts or transforms resources (including human resources) into goods and services.

Some organizations—such as factories, farms, and mines—produce mostly goods. Others—such as hospitals, schools, and government agencies—produce mostly services. Still others produce a combination of goods and services. For example, an automobile manufacturer not only makes cars but also provides services such as repairs, financing, and insurance. At Wendy's you get goods such as hamburgers and fries, but you also get services such as order taking, order filling, food preparation, and cleanup.

Operations Management in the Service Sector

Operations management in the service industry is all about creating a good experience for those who use the service. In a Ritz-Carlton hotel, for example, operations management includes restaurants that offer the finest in service, elevators that run smoothly, and a front desk that processes people quickly. It may include fresh-cut flowers in the lobbies and dishes of fruit in every room. More important, it may mean spending thousands of dollars to provide training in quality management for every new employee.

Ritz-Carlton's commitment to quality is apparent in the many innovations and changes the company has initiated over the years. These innovations included installation of a sophisticated computerized guest-recognition program and a quality management program designed to ensure that all employees are "certified" in their positions.

Hotel customers today want in-room Internet access and a help center with toll-free telephone service. Executives traveling on business may need video equipment and a host of computer hardware and other aids. At the International House in New Orleans, 16 rooms have Apple TV boxes so that iPod- and iPad-dependent clients can easily stream live video.[16]

Foreign visitors would like multilingual customer-support services. Hotel shops need to carry more than souvenirs, newspapers, and some drugstore and food items to serve today's high-tech travelers: the shops may also carry laptop computer supplies, electrical adapters, and the like. Operations management is responsible for locating and providing such amenities to make customers happy. Ritz-Carlton uses an internal measurement system to assess the performance results of its service delivery system.

In short, delighting customers by anticipating their needs has become the quality standard for luxury hotels, as it has for most other service businesses.[17] But knowing customer needs and satisfying them are two different things. That's why operations management is so important: it is the implementation phase of management. Can you see the need for better operations management in airports, hospitals, government agencies, schools, and nonprofits like the Red Cross? The opportunities seem almost unlimited. Much of the future of U.S. growth is in these service areas, but growth is also needed in manufacturing. Next we'll explore production processes and what companies are doing to keep the United States competitive in that area.

progress assessment

- What have U.S. manufacturers done to regain a competitive edge?
- What must U.S. companies do to continue to strengthen the country's manufacturing base?
- What led companies to focus on operations management rather than production?

Need help understanding the Transformation Process for Goods and Services? www.introbiz.tv/QR9-1

LEARNING goal 3

Identify various production processes and describe techniques that improve productivity, including computer-aided design and manufacturing, flexible manufacturing, lean manufacturing, and mass customization.

PRODUCTION PROCESSES

Common sense and some experience have already taught you much of what you need to know about production processes. You know what it takes to write a term paper or prepare a dinner. You need money to buy the materials, you need a place to work, and you need to be organized to get the task done. The same is true of the production process in industry. It uses basic inputs to produce outputs (see Figure 9.1). Production adds value, or utility, to materials or processes.

Form utility is the value producers add to materials in the creation of finished goods and services, such as by transforming silicon into computer chips or putting services together to create a vacation package. Form utility can exist at the retail level as well. For example, a butcher can produce a specific cut of beef from a whole cow, or a baker can make a specific type of cake from basic ingredients. We'll be discussing utility in more detail in Chapter 15.

Manufacturers use several different processes to produce goods. Andrew S. Grove, the former chairman of computer chip manufacturer Intel, uses this analogy to explain production:

> Imagine that you're a chef . . . and that your task is to serve a breakfast consisting of a three-minute soft-boiled egg, buttered toast, and coffee. Your job is to prepare and deliver the three items simultaneously, each of them fresh and hot.

Grove says this task encompasses the three basic requirements of production: (1) to build and deliver products in response to the demands of the customer at a scheduled delivery time, (2) to provide an acceptable quality level, and (3) to provide everything at the lowest possible cost.

Let's use the breakfast example to understand process and assembly. **Process manufacturing** physically or chemically changes materials. For example, boiling physically changes the egg. Similarly, process manufacturing turns sand into glass or computer chips. The **assembly process** puts together components (eggs, toast, and coffee) to make a product (breakfast). Cars are made through an assembly process that puts together the frame, engine, and other parts.

Production processes are either continuous or intermittent. A **continuous process** is one in which long production runs turn out finished goods over time. As a chef, you could have a conveyor belt that continuously lowers eggs into boiling

form utility
The value producers add to materials in the creation of finished goods and services.

process manufacturing
That part of the production process that physically or chemically changes materials.

assembly process
That part of the production process that puts together components.

continuous process
A production process in which long production runs turn out finished goods over time.

figure 9.1

THE PRODUCTION PROCESS

The production process consists of taking the factors of production (land, etc.) and using those inputs to produce goods, services, and ideas. Planning, routing, scheduling, and the other activities are the means to accomplish the objective—output.

INPUTS	PRODUCTION CONTROL	OUTPUTS
Land	Planning	Goods
Labor	Routing	Services
Capital	Scheduling	Ideas
Entrepreneurship	Dispatching	
Knowledge	Follow-up	

water for three minutes and then lifts them out. A three-minute egg would be available whenever you wanted one. A chemical plant, for example, is run on a continuous process.

It usually makes more sense when responding to specific customer orders to use an **intermittent process.** Here the production run is short (one or two eggs) and the producer adjusts machines frequently to make different products (like the oven in a bakery or the toaster in a diner). Manufacturers of custom-designed furniture would use an intermittent process.

Today many manufacturers use intermittent processes. Computers, robots, and flexible manufacturing processes allow firms to turn out custom-made goods almost as fast as mass-produced goods were once produced.[18] We'll discuss how they do that in more detail in the next few sections as we explore advanced production techniques and technology.

The Need to Improve Production Techniques and Cut Costs

The ultimate goal of operations management is to provide high-quality goods and services instantaneously in response to customer demand. As we stress throughout this book, traditional organizations were simply not designed to be so responsive to the customer. Rather, they were designed to make goods efficiently (inexpensively). The idea behind mass production was to make a large number of a limited variety of products at very low cost.

Over the years, low cost often came at the expense of quality and flexibility. Furthermore, suppliers didn't always deliver when they said they would, so manufacturers had to carry large inventories of raw materials and components to keep producing. Such inefficiencies made U.S. companies vulnerable to foreign competitors who were using more advanced production techniques.

As a result of new global competition, companies have had to make a wide variety of high-quality custom-designed products at very low cost.[19] Clearly, something had to change on the production floor to make that possible. Several major developments have made U.S. companies more competitive: (1) computer-aided design and manufacturing, (2) flexible manufacturing, (3) lean manufacturing, and (4) mass customization.

Computer-Aided Design and Manufacturing

One development that has changed production techniques is the integration of computers into the design and manufacturing of products. The first thing computers did was help in the design of products, in a process called **computer-aided design (CAD).** Today CAD systems allow designers to work in three dimensions.

The next step was to bring computers directly into the production process with **computer-aided manufacturing (CAM).** CAD/CAM, the use of both computer-aided design and computer-aided manufacturing, makes it possible to custom-design products to meet the needs of small markets with very little increase in cost. A manufacturer programs the computer to make a simple design change, and that change is readily incorporated into production. In the clothing industry, a computer

Bakers, like Duff Goldman of Charm City Cakes, add form utility to materials by transforming basic ingredients into special customized cakes. Can you see how the production of such cakes involves both process manufacturing and assembly processes?

intermittent process
A production process in which the production run is short and the machines are changed frequently to make different products.

computer-aided design (CAD)
The use of computers in the design of products.

computer-aided manufacturing (CAM)
The use of computers in the manufacturing of products.

program establishes a pattern and cuts the cloth automatically, even adjusting to a specific person's dimensions to create custom-cut clothing at little additional cost. In food service, CAM supports on-site, small-scale, semiautomated, sensor-controlled baking in fresh-baked cookie shops to make consistent quality easy to achieve.

CAD has doubled productivity in many firms. In the past CAD machines couldn't talk to CAM machines directly. Today, however, software programs unite CAD and CAM: the result is **computer-integrated manufacturing (CIM).** The software is expensive, but it cuts as much as 80 percent of the time needed to program machines to make parts. The printing company JohnsByrne uses CIM in its Niles, Illinois, plant and has noticed decreased overhead, reduced outlay of resources, and fewer errors. Consult the *International Journal of Computer Integrated Manufacturing* for other examples.

Flexible Manufacturing

Flexible manufacturing means designing machines to do multiple tasks so they can produce a variety of products. Allen-Bradley uses flexible manufacturing to build motor starters. Orders come in daily, and within 24 hours the company's 26 machines and robots manufacture, test, and package the starters—which are untouched by human hands. Allen-Bradley's machines are so flexible that managers can include a special order, even a single item, in the assembly without slowing down the process. Did you notice that these products were made without any labor? One way to compete with cheap overseas labor is to have as few workers as possible.

Lean Manufacturing

Lean manufacturing is the production of goods using less of everything than in mass production: less human effort, less manufacturing space, less investment in tools, and less engineering time to develop a new product. Consulting firm RSM McGladrey found that 65 percent of the more than 900 manufacturing and wholesale distribution companies it surveyed nationwide planned to use lean manufacturing.[20] A company becomes lean by continuously increasing its capacity to produce high-quality goods while decreasing its need for resources. Here are some characteristics of lean companies:

- They take half the human effort.
- They have half the defects in the finished product or service.
- They require one-third the engineering effort.
- They use half the floor space for the same output.
- They carry 90 percent less inventory.

Technological improvements are largely responsible for the increase in productivity and efficiency of U.S. plants. That technology made labor more productive and made it possible to pay higher wages. On the other hand, employees can get frustrated by innovations (e.g., they must learn new processes), and companies must constantly train and retrain employees to stay competitive. The need for more

3-D CAD tools allow designers to create cloth prototypes without a pattern's traditional stages: seaming, trying on, alterations, etc. What advantages might this technology offer to smaller manufacturing companies?

computer-integrated manufacturing (CIM)
The uniting of computer-aided design with computer-aided manufacturing.

flexible manufacturing
Designing machines to do multiple tasks so that they can produce a variety of products.

lean manufacturing
The production of goods using less of everything compared to mass production.

Designed by You, Enjoyed by Many

Students today understand the problems that new graduates have with getting a good job in the industry they desire. Eric Heinbockel wanted a career in finance, but an unpaid internship in New York didn't lead to the job he wanted.

He was getting his political science degree at Columbia University when he and two friends decided that entrepreneurship might be the way to go. It seemed that selling chocolate would be a good thing to do. After all, people don't give up their chocolate just because they have less money. Therefore, the three started Chocomize, an online shop that lets chocolate lovers customize their candy bars with ingredients ranging from graham crackers to gold flakes.

Yes, you can mass customize chocolate bars. For example, you can choose between dark, milk, or white chocolate. You can also choose up to five inserts—from 100 different selections.

So, how do you find the money to start such a business? The banks are not lending money to such entrepreneurs. Heinbockel's grandparents offered to help with the funding and one of the owners sold his car. The net proceeds were $100,000, enough to get started.

Chocomize now has three full-time chocolate makers and two who come in when needed. Chocomize is expected to be a success even though it has a European competitor. Big companies are not likely to compete in such a niche market. Sounds like a yummy business, doesn't it?

Sources: Zachary Tracer, "A Sweet Dream for Young Entrepreneurs," *Bloomberg Businessweek,* September 6–September 12, 2010; and www.chocomize.com, accessed May 2012.

---

productivity and efficiency has never been greater. The solution to the economic crisis depends on such innovations. One step in the process is to make products more individualistic. The next section discusses how that happens.

Mass Customization

mass customization
Tailoring products to meet the needs of individual customers.

To *customize* means to make a unique product or provide a specific service to specific individuals. Although it once may have seemed impossible, **mass customization,** which means tailoring products to meet the needs of a large number of individual customers, is now practiced widely. The National Bicycle Industrial Company in Japan makes 18 bicycle models in more than 2 million combinations, each designed to fit the needs of a specific customer. The customer chooses the model, size, color, and design. The retailer takes various measurements from the buyer and faxes the data to the factory, where robots handle the bulk of the assembly.

More and more manufacturers are learning to customize their products. Some colleges, even, are developing promotions for individual students. Some General Nutrition Center (GNC) stores feature machines that enable shoppers to custom-design their own vitamins, shampoo, and lotions. The Custom Foot stores use infrared scanners to precisely measure each foot so that shoes can be made to fit perfectly. Adidas can make each shoe fit perfectly for each customer. Interactive Custom Clothes Company offers a wide variety of options in custom-made jeans, including four different rivet colors. BMW can build a car exactly the way you want it.[21] You can even buy custom-made M&M's in colors of your choice. See the Connecting with Small Business box for a unique way of using mass customization.

Mass customization exists in the service sector as well. Capital Protective Insurance (CPI) uses the latest computer software and hardware to sell customized risk-management plans to companies. Health clubs offer unique fitness programs for individuals, travel agencies provide vacation packages that vary according to individual choices, and some colleges allow students to design their own majors. It is much easier to custom-design service programs than to custom-make goods, because there is no fixed tangible good to adapt. Each customer can specify what he or she wants, within the limits of the service organization—limits that seem to be ever-widening.

As you learned in the opening Profile, manufacturing companies may become service companies over time. As you shall see, operations management concepts are applicable in both situations.

Not only can you customize the colors of your M&Ms, you can also have personal messages and/or images imprinted on them. What other customized products can you think of?

progress assessment

- What is form utility?
- Define and differentiate the following: process manufacturing, assembly process, continuous process, and intermittent process.
- What do you call the integration of CAD and CAM?
- What is mass customization?

LEARNING goal 4

Describe operations management planning issues including facility location, facility layout, materials requirement planning, purchasing, just-in-time inventory control, and quality control.

OPERATIONS MANAGEMENT PLANNING

Operations management planning helps solve many of the problems in the service and manufacturing sectors. These include facility location, facility layout, materials requirement planning, purchasing, inventory control, and quality control. The resources used may be different, but the management issues are similar.

Facility Location

Facility location is the process of selecting a geographic location for a company's operations. In keeping with the need to focus on customers, one strategy is to find a site that makes it easy for consumers to use the company's services and

facility location
The process of selecting a geographic location for a company's operations.

Facility location is a major decision for manufacturing and other companies. The decision involves taking into account the availability of qualified workers; access to suppliers, customers, and transportation; and local regulations including zoning and taxes. How has the growth of commerce on the Internet affected company location decisions?

to communicate about their needs. Flower shops and banks have placed facilities in supermarkets so that their products and services are more accessible than in freestanding facilities. You can find a McDonald's inside some Walmart stores and gas stations. Customers order and pay for their meals at the pumps, and by the time they've filled their tanks, it's time to pick up their food.

The ultimate in convenience is never having to leave home to get services. That's why there is so much interest in Internet banking, Internet shopping, online education, and other services. Internet commerce is now using Facebook and other social media to make transactions even easier.[22] For brick-and-mortar retailers to beat such competition, they have to choose good locations and offer outstanding service.[23] Study the location of service-sector businesses—such as hotels, banks, athletic clubs, and supermarkets—and you'll see that the most successful are conveniently located. Google is building large data centers in the United States where states give out tax breaks and cheap electricity is readily available in large quantities. They are also located near bodies of water for cooling their servers.

Facility Location for Manufacturers

Volkswagen's factory in Bratislava, Slovakia, turns out 250,000 cars a year, including Audi's SUV, which used to be made in Western European plants. Geographic shifts in production sometimes result in pockets of unemployment in some geographic areas and tremendous growth in others. We are witnessing such changes in the United States, as automobile and tractor production has shifted to more southern cities.[24]

Why would companies spend millions of dollars to move their facilities from one location to another? In their decisions they consider labor costs; availability of resources, including labor; access to transportation that can reduce time to market; proximity to suppliers; proximity to customers; crime rates; quality of life for employees; cost of living; and the need to train or retrain the local workforce.

Even though labor is becoming a smaller percentage of total cost in highly automated industries, availability of low-cost labor or the right kind of skilled labor remained a key reason many producers moved their plants to Malaysia, China, India, Mexico, and other countries.[25] In general, however, U.S. manufacturing firms tend to pay more and offer more benefits than local firms elsewhere in the world. One result of the financial crisis that began in 2008 is that U.S. workers now take less pay and receive fewer benefits in order to stay competitive.

Inexpensive resources are another major reason for moving production facilities. Companies usually need water, electricity, wood, coal, and other basic resources. By moving to areas where these are inexpensive and plentiful, firms can significantly lower not only the cost of buying such resources but also the cost of shipping finished products.[26] Often the most important resource is people, so companies tend to cluster where smart and talented people are. Witness Silicon Valley in California and similar areas in Colorado, Massachusetts, Virginia, Texas, Maryland, and other states.

Time-to-market is another decision-making factor. As manufacturers attempt to compete globally, they need sites that allow products to move quickly, at the lowest costs, so they can be delivered to customers fast. Access to highways, rail

lines, waterways, and airports is thus critical.[27] Information technology (IT) is also important to quicken response time, so many firms are seeking countries with the most advanced information systems.

Another way to work closely with suppliers to satisfy customers' needs is to locate production facilities near supplier facilities. That cuts the cost of distribution and makes communication easier.

Many businesses are building factories in foreign countries to get closer to their international customers. That's a major reason the Japanese automaker Honda builds cars in Ohio and the German company Mercedes builds them in Alabama. When U.S. firms select foreign sites, they consider whether they are near airports, waterways, and highways so that raw and finished goods can move quickly and easily.

Businesses also study the quality of life for workers and managers. Are good schools nearby? Is the weather nice? Is the crime rate low? Does the local community welcome new businesses? Do the chief executive and other key managers want to live there? Sometimes a region with a high quality of life is also an expensive one, which complicates the decision. In short, facility location has become a critical issue in operations management. The Making Ethical Decisions box looks at the kinds of decisions companies must make when it comes to locating.

Taking Operations Management to the Internet

Many rapidly growing companies do very little production themselves. Instead, they outsource engineering, design, manufacturing, and other tasks to companies such as Flextronics and Sanmina-SCI that specialize in those functions. They create new relationships with suppliers over the Internet, making operations management an *interfirm* process in which companies work closely together to design, produce, and ship products to customers.

Manufacturing companies are developing Internet-focused strategies that will enable them and others to compete more effectively in the future. These changes are having a dramatic effect on operations managers as they adjust from a one-firm system to an *interfirm* environment and from a relatively stable environment to one that is constantly changing and evolving.

Facility Location in the Future

Information technology (IT)—that is computers, modems, e-mail, voice mail, text messaging, teleconferencing, etc.—is giving firms and employees increased flexibility to choose locations while staying in the competitive mainstream. **Telecommuting,** working from home via computer, is a major trend in business. Companies that no longer need to locate near sources of labor will be able to move to areas where land is less expensive and the quality of life may be higher.[28] Furthermore, more salespeople are keeping in touch with the company and its customers through teleconferencing, using computers to talk with and show images to others.

One big incentive to locate in a particular city or state is the tax situation there and degree of government support. Some states and local governments have higher taxes than others, yet many compete fiercely by offering companies tax reductions and other support, such as zoning changes and financial aid, so they will locate there. Some people would like the federal government to offer financial incentives—beyond what is already being offered by state and local agencies—to various manufacturing companies to build factories in the United States.[29]

Facility Layout

Facility layout is the physical arrangement of resources, including people, to most efficiently produce goods and provide services for customers. Facility layout depends greatly on the processes that are to be performed. For services, the layout is usually designed to help the consumer find and buy things, including on the Internet. Some stores have kiosks that enable customers to search for goods online and place orders or make returns and credit payments in the store. In short, the facilities and Internet capabilities of service organizations are becoming more customer-oriented.

Some service-oriented organizations, such as hospitals, use layouts that improve efficiency, just as manufacturers do. For manufacturing plants, facilities layout has become critical because cost savings of efficient layouts are enormous.

Many companies are moving from an *assembly-line layout,* in which workers do only a few tasks at a time, to a *modular layout,* in which teams of workers combine to produce more complex units of the final product. There may have

At Cisco Systems, work spaces in some offices are fluid and unassigned, so employees with laptops and mobile phones can choose where to sit when they arrive each day. What do you think are some of the advantages of such nontraditional facility layouts? Are there any disadvantages?

been a dozen or more workstations on an assembly line to complete an automobile engine in the past, but all that work might be done in one module today.

When working on a major project, such as a bridge or an airplane, companies use a *fixed-position layout* that allows workers to congregate around the product to be completed.

A *process layout* is one in which similar equipment and functions are grouped together. The order in which the product visits a function depends on the design of the item. This allows for flexibility. The Igus manufacturing plant in Cologne, Germany, can shrink or expand in a flash. Its flexible design keeps it competitive in a fast-changing market. Because the layout of the plant changes so often, some employees use scooters in order to more efficiently provide needed skills, supplies, and services to multiple workstations. A fast-changing plant needs a fast-moving employee base to achieve maximum productivity. Figure 9.2 illustrates typical layout designs.

Materials Requirement Planning

Materials requirement planning (MRP) is a computer-based operations management system that uses sales forecasts to make sure needed parts and materials are available at the right time and place. **Enterprise resource planning (ERP),** a newer version of MRP, combines the computerized functions of all the divisions and subsidiaries of the firm—such as finance, human resources, and order fulfillment—into a single integrated software program that uses a single database. The result is shorter time between orders and payment, less staff needed to do ordering and order processing, reduced inventories, and better customer service. For example, the customer can place an order, either through a customer service representative or online, and immediately see when the order will be filled and how much it will cost. The representative can instantly see the customer's credit rating and order history, the company's inventory, and the shipping schedule. Everyone else in the company can see the new order as well; thus when one department finishes its portion, the order is automatically routed via the ERP system to the next department. The customer can see exactly where the order is at any point by logging into the system.

Purchasing

Purchasing is the function that searches for high-quality material resources, finds the best suppliers, and negotiates the best price for quality goods and services. In the past, manufacturers dealt with many suppliers so that if one couldn't deliver, the firm could get materials from someone else. Today, however, manufacturers rely more heavily on just one or two suppliers, because the relationship between suppliers and manufacturers is much closer than before. Producers share so much information that they don't want too many suppliers knowing their business.

The Internet has transformed the purchasing function. A business looking for supplies can contact an Internet-based purchasing service and find the best items at the best price. Similarly, a company wishing to sell supplies can use the Internet to find all the companies looking for such supplies. The time and dollar cost of purchasing items has thus been reduced tremendously.

Just-in-Time Inventory Control

One major cost of production is the expense of holding parts, motors, and other items in storage for later use. Storage not only subjects items to obsolescence, pilferage, and damage but also requires construction and maintenance of costly

materials requirement planning (MRP)
A computer-based operations management system that uses sales forecasts to make sure that needed parts and materials are available at the right time and place.

enterprise resource planning (ERP)
A newer version of materials requirement planning (MRP) that combines the computerized functions of all the divisions and subsidiaries of the firm—such as finance, human resources, and order fulfillment—into a single integrated software program that uses a single database.

purchasing
The function in a firm that searches for high-quality material resources, finds the best suppliers, and negotiates the best price for goods and services.

figure 9.2

TYPICAL LAYOUT DESIGNS

PRODUCT LAYOUT (also called Assembly Line Layout)
Used to produce large quantities of a few types of products.

PROCESS LAYOUT
Frequently used in operations that serve different customers' different needs.

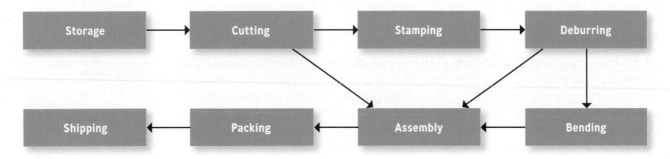

CELLULAR or MODULE LAYOUT
Can accommodate changes in design or customer demand.

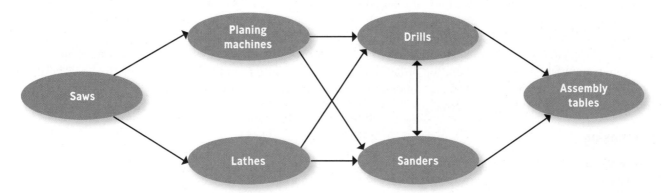

FIXED-POSITION LAYOUT
A major feature of planning is scheduling work operations.

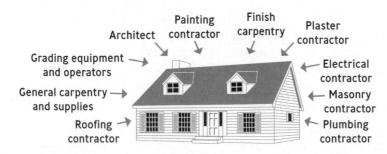

warehouses. To cut such costs, many companies have implemented a concept called **just-in-time (JIT) inventory control.** JIT systems keep a minimum of inventory on the premises—and deliver parts, supplies, and other needs just in time to go on the assembly line. To work effectively, however, the process requires an accurate production schedule (using ERP) and excellent coordination with carefully selected suppliers, who are usually connected electronically so they know what will be needed and when. Sometimes the suppliers build new facilities close to the main producer to minimize distribution time. JIT runs into problems when suppliers are farther away. Weather may delay shipments, for example. You saw the problems that emerged when weather (earthquakes and the resulting tsunami) disrupted the supply chain of materials from Japan to the United States in 2011. JIT systems make sure the right materials are at the right place at the right time at the cheapest cost to meet both customer and production needs. That's a key step in modern production innovation.

Quality Control

Maintaining **quality** means consistently producing what the customer wants while reducing errors before and after delivery. In the past, firms often conducted quality control at the end of the production line. Products were completed first and then tested for quality. This resulted in several problems:

1. The need to inspect work required extra people and resources.

2. If an error was found, someone had to correct the mistake or scrap the product. This, of course, was costly.

3. If the customer found the mistake, he or she might be dissatisfied and might even buy from another firm thereafter.

Such problems led to the realization that quality is not an outcome; it is a never-ending process of continually improving what a company produces. Quality control should thus be part of the operations management planning process rather than simply an end-of-the-line inspection.[30]

Companies have turned to the use of modern quality-control standards such as Six Sigma. **Six Sigma quality,** which sets a benchmark of just 3.4 defects per million opportunities, detects potential problems to prevent their occurrence. That's important to a company that makes 4 million transactions a day, like some banks.

Statistical quality control (SQC) is the process some managers use to continually monitor all phases of the production process and assure quality is being built into the product from the beginning. **Statistical process control (SPC)** is the process of testing statistical samples of product components at each stage of production and plotting the test results on a graph. Managers can thus see and correct any deviation from quality standards. Making sure products meet standards all along the production process reduces the need for a quality-control inspection at the end because mistakes are caught much earlier in the process. SQC and SPC thus save companies much time and money.

Some companies use a quality-control approach called the Deming cycle (after the late W. Edwards Deming, the father of the movement toward quality). Its steps are Plan, Do, Check, Act (PDCA). Again, the idea is to find potential errors *before* they happen.

U.S. businesses are getting serious about providing top customer service, and many are already doing it. Service organizations are finding it difficult to provide outstanding service every time because the process is so labor-intensive. Physical goods (e.g., a gold ring) can be designed and manufactured to near perfection. However, it

just-in-time (JIT) inventory control
A production process in which a minimum of inventory is kept on the premises and parts, supplies, and other needs are delivered just in time to go on the assembly line.

quality
Consistently producing what the customer wants while reducing errors before and after delivery to the customer.

Six Sigma quality
A quality measure that allows only 3.4 defects per million opportunities.

statistical quality control (SQC)
The process some managers use to continually monitor all phases of the production process to assure that quality is being built into the product from the beginning.

statistical process control (SPC)
The process of testing statistical samples of product components at each stage of the production process and plotting those results on a graph. Any variances from quality standards are recognized and can be corrected if beyond the set standards.

The Nestlé Purina PetCare Company, headquartered in St. Louis, received the 2010 Malcolm Baldrige National Quality Award in the manufacturing category. What quality criteria do you think the award was based on?

is hard to reach such perfection when designing and providing a service experience such as a dance on a cruise ship or a cab drive through New York City.

The Baldrige Awards

In the United States in 1987, a standard was set for overall company quality with the introduction of the Malcolm Baldrige National Quality Awards, named in honor of the late U.S. secretary of commerce. Companies can apply for these awards in each of the following areas: manufacturing, services, small businesses, nonprofit/government, education, and health care. The 2011–2012 Criteria for Performance (also called the Business/Nonprofit Criteria) are now available.

To qualify, an organization has to show quality in seven key areas: leadership, strategic planning, customer and market focus, information and analysis, human resources focus, process management, and business results. Major criteria for earning the award include whether customer wants and needs are being met and whether customer satisfaction ratings are better than those of competitors. As you can see, the focus is shifting away from just making quality goods and services to providing top-quality customer service in all respects.

ISO 9000 and ISO 14000 Standards

ISO 9000
The common name given to quality management and assurance standards.

The International Organization for Standardization (ISO) is a worldwide federation of national standards bodies from more than 140 countries that set global measures for the quality of individual products. ISO is a nongovernmental organization established in 1947 to promote the development of world standards to facilitate the international exchange of goods and services. (ISO is not an acronym. It comes from the Greek word *isos,* meaning "oneness.") **ISO 9000** is the common name given to quality management and assurance standards.

The standards require that a company determine what customer needs are, including regulatory and legal requirements, and make communication arrangements to handle issues such as complaints. Other standards cover process control, product testing, storage, and delivery.

What makes ISO 9000 so important is that the European Union (EU) demands that companies that want to do business with the EU be certified by ISO standards. Some major U.S. companies are also demanding that suppliers meet these standards. Several accreditation agencies in Europe and the United States will certify that a company meets the standards for all phases of its operations, from product development through production and testing to installation.

ISO 14000
A collection of the best practices for managing an organization's impact on the environment.

ISO 14000 is a collection of the best practices for managing an organization's impact on the environment. As an environmental management system, it does not prescribe a performance level. Requirements for certification include having an environmental policy, having specific improvement targets, conducting audits of environmental programs, and maintaining top management review of the processes.

Certification in both ISO 9000 and ISO 14000 would show that a firm has a world-class management system in both quality and environmental standards. In the past, firms assigned employees separately to meet each set of standards. Today, ISO 9000 and 14000 standards have been blended so that an organization can work on both at once. ISO is now compiling social responsibility guidelines to go with the other standards.

LEARNING goal 5

Explain the use of PERT and Gantt charts to control manufacturing processes.

CONTROL PROCEDURES: PERT AND GANTT CHARTS

Operations managers must ensure products are manufactured and delivered on time, on budget, and to specifications. How can managers be sure all will go smoothly and be completed by the required time? One popular technique for monitoring the progress of production was developed in the 1950s for constructing nuclear submarines: the **program evaluation and review technique (PERT).** PERT users analyze the tasks to complete a given project, estimate the time needed to complete each, and compute the minimum time needed to complete the whole project.

The steps used in PERT are (1) analyzing and sequencing tasks that need to be done, (2) estimating the time needed to complete each task, (3) drawing a PERT network illustrating the information from steps 1 and 2, and (4) identifying the critical path. The **critical path** is the sequence of tasks that takes the longest time to complete. We use the word *critical* because a delay anywhere along this path will cause the project or production run to be late.

Figure 9.3 illustrates a PERT chart for producing a music video. The squares indicate completed tasks, and the arrows indicate the time needed to complete each. The path from one completed task to another illustrates the relationships among tasks; the arrow from "set designed" to "set materials purchased" indicates

program evaluation and review technique (PERT)
A method for analyzing the tasks involved in completing a given project, estimating the time needed to complete each task, and identifying the minimum time needed to complete the total project.

critical path
In a PERT network, the sequence of tasks that takes the longest time to complete.

figure 9.3

PERT CHART FOR A MUSIC VIDEO

The minimum amount of time it will take to produce this video is 15 weeks. To get that number, you add the week it takes to pick a star and a song to the four weeks to design a set, the two weeks to purchase set materials, the six weeks to construct the set, the week of rehearsals, and the final week when the video is made. That's the critical path. Any delay in that process will delay the final video.

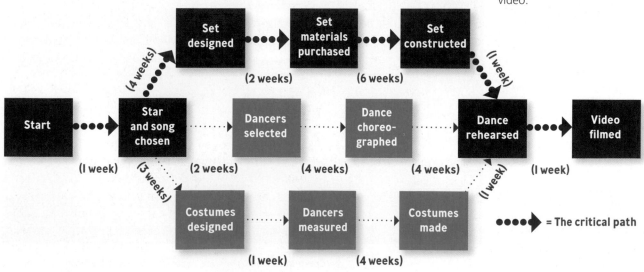

we must design the set before we can purchase the materials. The critical path, indicated by the bold black arrows, shows producing the set takes more time than auditioning dancers, choreographing dances, or designing and making costumes. The project manager now knows it's critical that set construction remain on schedule if the project is to be completed on time, but short delays in dance and costume preparation are unlikely to delay it.

A PERT network can be made up of thousands of events over many months. Today, this complex procedure is done by computer. Another, more basic strategy manufacturers use for measuring production progress is a Gantt chart. A **Gantt chart** (named for its developer, Henry L. Gantt) is a bar graph, now also prepared by computer, that clearly shows what projects are being worked on and how much has been completed at any given time. Figure 9.4, a Gantt chart for a doll manufacturer, shows that the dolls' heads and bodies should be completed before the clothing is sewn. It also shows that at the end of week 3, the dolls' bodies are ready, but the heads are about half a week behind. Using a Gantt-like computer program, a manager can trace the production process minute by minute to determine which tasks are on time and which are behind, so that adjustments can be made to allow the company to stay on schedule.

PREPARING FOR THE FUTURE

The United States remains a major industrial country, but competition grows stronger each year. Tremendous opportunities exist for careers in operations management as both manufacturing and service companies fight to stay competitive. Students who can see future trends and have the skills to own or work in tomorrow's highly automated factories and modern service facilities will benefit.

Gantt chart
Bar graph showing production managers what projects are being worked on and what stage they are in at any given time.

progress assessment

- Draw a PERT chart for making a breakfast of three-minute eggs, buttered toast, and coffee. Define the critical path.
- How could you use a Gantt chart to keep track of production?

figure 9.4

GANTT CHART FOR A DOLL MANUFACTURER

A Gantt chart enables a production manager to see at a glance when projects are scheduled to be completed and what the status is now. For example, the dolls' heads and bodies should be completed before the clothing is sewn, but they could be a little late as long as everything is ready for assembly in week 6. This chart shows that at the end of week 3, the dolls' bodies are ready, but the heads are about half a week behind.

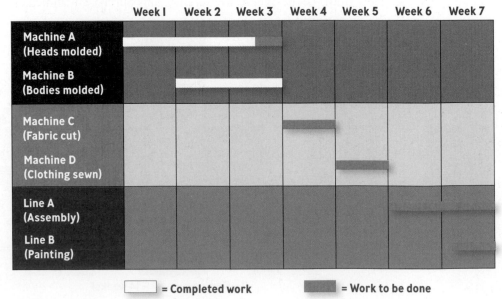

= Completed work   = Work to be done

summary

Learning Goal 1. Describe the current state of U.S. manufacturing and what manufacturers have done to become more competitive.

- **What is the current state of manufacturing in the United States?**

Activity in the nation's manufacturing sector has declined. The result has been an increase in joblessness. One cause of that increase is the fact that companies have become more productive, meaning that they need fewer employees to do the same amount of work. Much of this chapter is devoted to showing you what manufacturers and service providers can do to revive the U.S. economy to become world-class competitors.

- **What have U.S. manufacturers done to achieve increased output?**

U.S. manufacturers have increased output by emphasizing close relationships with suppliers and other companies to satisfy customer needs; continuous improvement; quality; site selection; use of the Internet to unite companies; and production techniques such as enterprise resource planning, computer-integrated manufacturing, flexible manufacturing, and lean manufacturing.

Learning Goal 2. Describe the evolution from production to operations management.

- **What is production management?**

Production management consists of all the activities managers do to help their firms create goods. To reflect the change in importance from manufacturing to services, the term *production* is often replaced by the term *operations*.

- **What is operations management?**

Operations management is the specialized area in management that converts or transforms resources, including human resources, into goods and services.

- **What kind of firms use operations managers?**

Firms in both the manufacturing and service sectors use operations managers.

Learning Goal 3. Identify various production processes and describe techniques that improve productivity, including computer-aided design and manufacturing, flexible manufacturing, lean manufacturing, and mass customization.

- **What is process manufacturing, and how does it differ from assembly processes?**

Process manufacturing physically or chemically changes materials. Assembly processes put together components.

- **How do CAD/CAM systems work?**

Design changes made in computer-aided design (CAD) are instantly incorporated into the computer-aided manufacturing (CAM) process. The linking of CAD and CAM is computer-integrated manufacturing (CIM).

- **What is flexible manufacturing?**

Flexible manufacturing means designing machines to produce a variety of products.

- **What is lean manufacturing?**

Lean manufacturing is the production of goods using less of everything than in mass production: less human effort, less manufacturing space, less investment in tools, and less engineering time to develop a new product.

- **What is mass customization?**

Mass customization means making custom-designed goods and services for a large number of individual customers. Flexible manufacturing makes mass customization possible. Given the exact needs of a customer, flexible machines can produce a customized good as fast as mass-produced goods were once made. Mass customization is also important in service industries.

Learning Goal 4. Describe operations management planning issues including facility location, facility layout, materials requirement planning, purchasing, just-in-time inventory control, and quality control.

- **What is facility location and how does it differ from facility layout?**

Facility location is the process of selecting a geographic location for a company's operations. Facility layout is the physical arrangement of resources, including people, to produce goods and services effectively and efficiently.

- **How do managers evaluate different sites?**

Labor costs and land costs are two major criteria for selecting the right sites. Other criteria include whether resources are plentiful and inexpensive, skilled workers are available or are trainable, taxes are low and the local government offers support, energy and water are available, transportation costs are low, and the quality of life and of education are high.

- **What relationship do materials requirement planning (MRP) and enterprise resource planning (ERP) have with the production process?**

MRP is a computer-based operations management system that uses sales forecasts to make sure the needed parts and materials are available at the right time and place. Enterprise resource planning (ERP), a newer version of MRP, combines the computerized functions of all the divisions and subsidiaries of the firm—such as finance, material requirements planning, human resources, and order fulfillment—into a single integrated software program that uses a single database. The result is shorter time between orders and payment, less staff to do ordering and order processing, reduced inventories, and better customer service for all the firms involved.

- **What is just-in-time (JIT) inventory control?**

JIT requires suppliers to deliver parts and materials just in time to go on the assembly line so they don't have to be stored in warehouses.

- **What is Six Sigma quality?**

Six Sigma quality sets standards at just 3.4 defects per million opportunities and detects potential problems before they occur. Statistical quality control (SQC) is the process some managers use to continually monitor all processes in the production process and ensure quality is being built into the product from the beginning. Statistical process control (SPC) tests statistical samples of product components at each stage of the production process and plots the results on a graph so managers can recognize and correct deviations from quality standards.

- **What quality standards do firms use in the United States?**

To qualify for the Malcolm Baldrige National Quality Award, a company must demonstrate quality in seven key areas: leadership, strategic planning, customer and market focus, information and analysis, human resources focus, process management, and business results. International standards U.S. firms strive to meet include ISO 9000 and ISO 14000. The first is a world standard for quality and the second is a collection of the best practices for managing an organization's impact on the environment.

Learning Goal 5. Explain the use of PERT and Gantt charts to control manufacturing processes.

- **Is there any relationship between a PERT chart and a Gantt chart?**

Figure 9.3 shows a PERT chart. Figure 9.4 shows a Gantt chart. Whereas PERT is a tool used for planning, a Gantt chart is a tool used to measure progress.

key terms

assembly process 251
computer-aided design (CAD) 252
computer-aided manufacturing (CAM) 252
computer-integrated manufacturing (CIM) 253
continuous process 251
critical path 263
enterprise resource planning (ERP) 259
facility layout 258
facility location 255
flexible manufacturing 253

form utility 251
Gantt chart 264
intermittent process 252
ISO 14000 262
ISO 9000 262
just-in-time (JIT) inventory control 261
lean manufacturing 253
mass customization 254
materials requirement planning (MRP) 259
operations management 249
process manufacturing 251

production 248
production management 248
program evaluation and review technique (PERT) 263
purchasing 259
quality 261
Six Sigma quality 261
statistical process control (SPC) 261
statistical quality control (SQC) 261
telecommuting 258

critical thinking

1. Workers on the manufacturing floor are being replaced by robots and other machines. On the one hand, this lets companies compete with cheap labor from other countries. On the other hand, automation eliminates many jobs. Are you concerned that automation may increase unemployment or underemployment in the United States and around the world? Why or why not?

2. Computer-integrated manufacturing (CIM) has revolutionized the production process. What will such changes mean for the clothing industry, the shoe industry, and other fashion-related industries? What will they mean for other consumer and industrial goods industries? How will you benefit as a consumer?

3. One way to create new jobs in the United States is to increase innovation among new graduates from engineering and the sciences. How can the United States motivate more students to major in those areas?

developing workplace skills

1. Choosing the right location for a manufacturing plant or a service organization is often critical to its success. Form small groups and have each group member pick one manufacturing plant or one service organization in town and list at least three reasons why its location helps or hinders its success. If its location is not ideal, what would be a better one?

2. In teams of four or five, discuss the need for better operations management in the airline industry. Have the team develop a report listing (*a*) problems team members have encountered in traveling by air and (*b*) suggestions for improving operations so such problems won't occur in the future.

3. Discuss some of the advantages and disadvantages of producing goods overseas using inexpensive labor. Summarize the moral and ethical dimensions of this practice.

4. Think of any production facility at your school, such as a sandwich shop, library, or copy center, and redesign the layout (make a pencil sketch) to more effectively serve customers and allow employees to be more effective and efficient.

5. Think about recent experiences you have had with service organizations and select one in which you had to wait for an unreasonable length of time to get what you wanted. Describe what happens when customers are inconvenienced, and explain how management could make the operation more efficient and customer-oriented.

taking it to the net

Purpose

To illustrate production processes.

Exercise

Take a virtual tour of the Hershey Foods Corporation's chocolate factory by going to **www.hersheys.com/discover/tour_video.asp**.

1. Does Hershey use process manufacturing or the assembly process? Is the production of Hershey's chocolate an intermittent or continuous production process? Justify your answers.

2. What location factors might go into the selection of a manufacturing site for Hershey's chocolate?

casing the web

To access the case "Griffin Hospital," visit **www.mhhe.com/P2P2e**

 video case

Keeping Your Eye on Ball

It is difficult to read a newspaper, or magazine or listen to a news report without hearing about the downfall of U.S. manufacturing. We are bombarded with facts about the decline of GM and the other auto companies, and how many people are losing their jobs in manufacturing plants. It's all rather depressing, but is the United States really falling that far behind other countries in manufacturing capability? The answer is no, and this video is meant to highlight just one example of a successful manufacturing company. There are thousands of others that could be discussed in a similar manner.

There is no doubt that U.S. manufacturers are being challenged by companies in Mexico, China, India, Brazil, Indonesia, and all over the world—but that is nothing new. The question is whether or not the United States can respond effectively to such challenges today as it has done in the past. Don't forget that much, if not most, of the machinery and equipment being used in foreign plants was produced in the United States. Note, too, that many companies—like Honda and Toyota—have built manufacturing plants in the United States.

This video features Ball metal beverage containers. You've seen them everywhere. But have you given any thought to how those cans came to be? Have you wondered why Ball has been so successful in the United States? Did you read recently that Ball Corporation had expanded operations by buying four U.S. manufacturing plants from brewer Anheuser-Busch InBev NV?

The text mentions several things that U.S. manufacturers are doing to stay competitive in today's global markets. They include focusing on customers; maintaining close relationships with suppliers (e.g., using just-in-time inventory control); practicing continuous improvement; focusing on quality; saving on costs through site selection; utilizing the Internet; and adopting new production processes like computer-integrated manufacturing. Foreign businesses are busy copying what we do, so U.S. producers need to do things better and faster and cheaper, if they can. Speaking of cans, you can see and hear what Ball is doing to stay competitive in the video. Note that Ball is using a continuous process. What other processes might they use?

U.S. companies are using computer-aided design and computer-aided manufacturing, united in computer-integrated manufacturing. They also do flexible manufacturing, which means they can produce a variety of products using the same machinery. It should not surprise you to learn that Ball located its facilities close to its customers. That makes distribution faster, easier, and cheaper.

Of course, quality is a key consideration in any manufacturing plant. Can you imagine trying to open a can and having the opener break off in your fingers or having a can that leaks all over your car? Manufacturers try for zero defects, but often settle for some slightly lower standard such as Six Sigma (only 3.4 defects per million).

Next time you take a cold drink from a can, think about Ball and the other companies that make the United States a major producer of consumer goods. Think, too, of the opportunities that will present themselves to tomorrow's college graduates. Students seem less attracted to manufacturing today, but that means more opportunities tomorrow for those students who see growth in some areas of manufacturing. That includes, of course, companies that produce solar panels, power plants, and more. You only have to look around your home or office to see the many products being made and the many products that will be made using biotechnology, nanotechnology, and so on.

Thinking It Over

1. *Have you given any thought to the future of manufacturing in the United States? What industries might benefit from the government's stimulus package? What evidence have you seen of companies adapting to the new challenges of foreign manufacturers? What is Ball doing to stay competitive?*

2. *The video mentions the loss of U.S. manufacturing to overseas locations. What is this called? What is the opposite trend that has occurred in the United States with companies like Toyota and Honda?*

3. *What is Six Sigma?*

Career Outlook
Part 3 Conclusion—Business Management

Managers are the people who oversee the operations in organizations, such as finance, information, and production. More importantly, they are responsible to the people who work for them. The "people part" of the business is vital to a manager's job. Without managers, there would be no business.

Managers are everywhere; you'll find them in construction, food service, agriculture, education, and in most organizations. Management careers have always been among the most challenging and fulfilling in the field of business, and the roles of and attitudes toward managers shift rapidly.

PART 3
career
Outlook

SKILLS NEEDED

CAREER PATHS

POSSIBLE POSITIONS

PROFILE

COVER LETTER

RESUME

INTERVIEW

Skills Needed

Management styles have changed in the last few decades. Managers are no longer the authoritative, jump-when-I-say-jump-style leaders of the previous generations; rather, they are expected to motivate employees while maintaining production and quality. If you are applying to become a manager, show employers you are:

- **Responsible**—What are you in charge of in your life? Have you been a caregiver for your siblings or parents? Show your leadership potential.

- **Organized**—When is the last time you set and achieved a goal? Or organized a group for a project? Are you good at time management?

- **Empowering**—Can you motivate those around you? Does your input change the way your peers act?

- **A clear communicator**—Have you taken a speech class? Given a Power-Point presentation? Led a training session? Written an editorial?

- **Efficient**—When you start a task, can you finish it quickly? When you set a goal, do you accomplish it completely? If a boss or teacher gives you an assignment, do you meet all of their criteria?

Career Paths

Managers often work within a hierarchy that has a definite bottom and top. Many managers start at the "bottom" as employees or interns and work their way up the ladder. However, progressing to middle and top levels of management is far from automatic. As one gets closer to the top, there are fewer and fewer opportunities. The competitive and competent people are most likely to move ahead.

Possible Positions

POSSIBLE POSITIONS IN MANAGEMENT				
OPPORTUNITY	MEDIAN SALARY	DUTIES	REQUIREMENTS	GROWTH
Health Services Manager	$84,270 per year	Plan, direct, and coordinate medical services, possibly for a hospital or medical practice	Bachelor's degree in health administration, sometimes a state license	Faster than average. As the population ages, demand for health care will increase greatly
Construction Manager	$83,860 per year	Plan, budget, and supervise construction projects	Bachelor's degree and preferably work experience	Slightly faster than average. A substantial number of current managers will be retiring over the next decade
Food Service Manager	$48,130 per year	Manage daily operations of restaurants and dining establishments	Experience in food services. Bachelor's degree holders have a significant edge	Expected to decline, but new opportunities in groceries and recreation are growing
Farmers and Agricultural Managers	$60,750 per year	Run establishments that produce crops, livestock, and dairy products	High school diploma and on-site training	Declining moderately

Source: Bureau of Labor Statistics, *Occupational Outlook Handbook*, 2012–13 Edition.

Profile: Moira Jackson, Fashion Student

Moira is a 21-year-old student at a community college. When Moira turned 15, she had a baby, dropped out of high school, and started working at a local pizza buffet. However, Moira wants more for her life. She's always seen herself as a "diva" and a "fashionista," so after completing her GED and on track to earn an associate's degree in business from a community college, Moira wants to get a bachelor's degree in fashion merchandising from a four-year university. Until then, she is applying to be an assistant manager of a clothing store in the mall near her daughter's day care.

How does Moira use her cover letter, résumé and interview to make herself attractive to the store? What skills does she highlight? Would this résumé work for her college application or for scholarships?

MOIRA'S COVER LETTER

Tip: Often the experiences you have from a different type of job can be transferable to the one you are applying for. For example, if you interact effectively with customers at one type of job, explain that you'd do the same in this position that you'd like to have.

Tip: While you might want to talk about how a job could make your life better, remember to keep your message focused on how you can help the employer.

Tip: Give concrete examples to back up claims about what you are good at.

Moira Jackson
45 Bond Boulevard — Topeka, Kansas 67440
816-578-2235 — Moira.Jackson3@yahoo.com

March 7, 2014
Kathy Johnston
Manager and Owner
Guess Who Fashions
Topeka, Kansas 66845

Dear Ms. Johnston:

My goal is to be the next assistant manager at Guess Who Fashions, and I am writing to tell you why I am the perfect person for the job. I think about fashion trends and topics so much that my friends and family call me "The Fashionista." When not reading textbooks for class, I always have a fashion magazine in my hand. One day, I want to use my passion for clothing design to run my own store. Working as your assistant manager, I would not only serve customers well but also be attentive to learning every detail that goes into making a store successful.

My high-energy, positive personality and dedication to work have resulted in keeping my current job for six years. I enjoy interacting with people and would be a good member of a team. I've worked hard for the things that I have. For example, working many hours at my current job has enabled me to pay for college, and now I'm on track to graduate this semester.

Because I've been financially independent since a young age, I've learned to manage my time and money efficiently to work and attend school. That's why I think I could be an organized assistant manager. Also, even though most of my money goes to living expenses and tuition, I have developed a sense of style and know how to shop wisely for clothing. I buy neutral pieces and accent them with jewelry and up-to-date blouses. My friends say that I know the trends before everyone else. I could use this talent to cultivate regular customers who would return to the store for help. My supervisor at the Pizza Palace has noticed how many customers ask for me when they bring the family in to dine. I make our customers feel like family.

Thank you for considering my strong desire to join your team. Please feel free to contact me with questions. I am eager to speak with you about the position.

Sincerely,

Moira Jackson
Moira Jackson

MOIRA'S RESUME

Moira Jackson
45 Bond Boulevard — Topeka, Kansas 67440
816-578-2235 — Moira.Jackson3@yahoo.com

Objective

To help Guess Who Fashions be successful by assisting customers to find chic outfits for the right price

Education

Allen Community College   Anticipated graduation: May 2014
Associate of Arts

Summary

- Working toward associate's degree in business
- Earned 75 percent of college tuition through current job
- Motivated, energetic personality
- Computer literate: Windows, Word, Excel, and PowerPoint

Work History

Pizza Palace Buffet

2007 – Present

- Provided customers with positive dining experience
- Maintained equipment cleanliness nightly
- Praised for exceptional cash register accuracy
- Mentored new employees on job requirements
- Balanced work schedule with school and family successfully

Child Care Provider

2006 – 2007

- Oversaw health and safety of children
- Recruited new families for business
- Developed schedule of fees and charges for clients
- Created advertising posters for the neighborhood

Relevant Coursework

- Human Relations in Business
- Principles of Management

Tip: If you include an objective, make sure that it explains how you can benefit the employer.

Tip: Employers are impressed by students who fund their own education.

Tip: A "job" doesn't have to be with a company. Demonstrate how you've earned money on your own.

Moira's Interview

Question: Why do you want to work at Guess Who Fashions?

Poor answer: I have a great sense of style and love clothes. Look at my dress—professional but still modern. I could probably do better than some of the employees whom I've seen in this store. Plus I wouldn't mind the discount that store employees receive.

Great answer: With my sense of style and love of fashion, I think I would really shine in your store. I love to be around clothing and to help customers find chic outfits for the right price. This wouldn't even feel like work to me.

Tip: Find a way to promote yourself without insulting the employer's existing business or employees. If you have criticisms, make them constructive—if you mention them at all. And the interview is not the time to talk about what benefits you might receive—emphasize what you can do for them.

Question: What is your biggest weakness?

Poor answer: I can't really think of one right now. I mean I know not everyone is perfect. Maybe I sometimes freak out when things are stressful but everyone does that.

Great answer: I struggled initially in some of my team projects at school. I was so concerned about my grades that I would tend to take over and do most of the work myself. I would get so stressed out. Then a teacher explained to me that the purpose of group projects is to teach people to work together. She said that if I didn't learn to trust other people's work I would never learn to delegate. I still like to lead group projects, but now I think more about how to motivate the team members to contribute their best work. That's what I would try to do as an assistant manager—motivate the sales staff to provide excellent service. I know now that I can't do all of the work myself—you have to work through a team of people.

Tip: Everyone has a weakness, so think critically about what you have worked to improve about yourself. Make sure your answer shows how you are growing as a person and that you are aware of how your behaviors affect your job performance. Tell a story that explains your motivation to change.

Question: How would you manage an employee who was unmotivated and constantly late?

Poor answer: I would just tell them that they'll be fired if they don't come on time and work harder. That should take care of the problem.

Great answer: That's a good question. It would be difficult, because I want employees to enjoy working here, but I also have to think about the success of the store. I would talk to the employee in private to start off. If the problem can be fixed, I'd rather find a solution than a new employee. I think you have to try to understand what motivates people to do their best. We once had a person on our team in my class who was always late to our group meetings. I took her aside and said that she probably didn't realize how unproductive we were in the time that we were waiting for her and that we'd all be so much more efficient as busy students if she could arrive earlier. She did much better after that.

Tip: If you need a second to think, take a deep breath and compliment the question. Interviewers don't mind if you take time to form your answer. They're often interested in the thought that you'd put into solving a difficult problem. And if you can tell a brief story that illustrates when you dealt with a similar problem, you'll increase the credibility of your answer.

Management of Human Resources:

MOTIVATING EMPLOYEES

TO PRODUCE QUALITY GOODS

AND SERVICES

PART 4

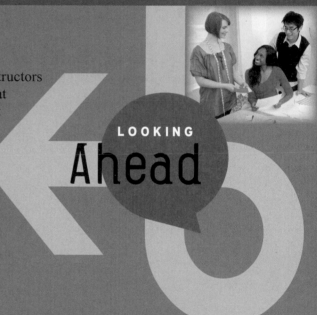

LOOKING Ahead

What motivates you to do well in school? (Believe us, your instructors really want to know.) And managers really want to know what motivates their employees to perform well. After all, if you haven't read it before you'll read it now: Motivated employees are any business's greatest resource. Recruiting, hiring, training, motivating, and compensating competent employees is critical to every company's success.

Of course, managing human resources is a complex task. In this section of the text, you will learn about many issues facing human resource managers in today's workplace.

CHAPTER 10   Motivating Employees

CHAPTER 11   Human Resource Management: Finding and Keeping the Best Employees

CHAPTER 12   Dealing with Union and Employee-Management Issues

10

Motivating
EMPLOYEES

After you have read and studied this chapter, you should be able to

LEARNING goals

1 Explain Taylor's theory of scientific management.

2 Describe the Hawthorne studies and their significance to management.

3 Identify the levels of Maslow's hierarchy of needs and apply them to employee motivation.

4 Distinguish between the motivators and hygiene factors identified by Herzberg.

5 Differentiate among Theory X, Theory Y, and Theory Z.

6 Explain the key principles of goal-setting, expectancy, reinforcement, and equity theories.

7 Show how managers put motivation theories into action through such strategies as job enrichment, open communication, and job recognition.

8 Show how managers personalize motivation strategies to appeal to employees across the globe and across generations.

As the CEO of a major data analytics company, Jim Goodnight is in the business of interpreting information. Every day Goodnight's company SAS (pronounced like *sass*) analyzes huge amounts of data for its big-name clients. Although Goodnight juggles quite a bit of info in his head on any given day, there's one piece of data that's by far the most important to him. "Ninety-five percent of my assets drive out the gate every evening," says Goodnight about his dedicated staff. "It's my job to maintain a work environment that keeps those people coming back every morning."

Goodnight doesn't have too much trouble making that happen. SAS occupies a sprawling campus in Cary, North Carolina, that would make even the flashiest Silicon Valley tech giant blush. Laid across more than 900 acres, the SAS headquarters houses a world-class day care center, an Olympic-sized pool, a hair salon, an army of massage therapists, and a number of athletic fields and courts. The campus also has its own health center staffed with nearly 60 doctors, nurses, physical therapists, nutritionists, and other health professionals. One of its many cafeterias even has an in-house piano player! Suffice it to say, Goodnight likes to keep his more than 12,000 employees across the globe healthy and happy.

On the surface, Goodnight's generosity could seem strange for a man so focused on the power of hard data. A lifelong North Carolinian, Goodnight spent his childhood developing a strong work ethic in his father's hardware store. He eventually went to North Carolina State University, where he earned a doctorate in statistics. After earning his PhD, Goodnight stayed on at the university as a professor from 1972 to 1976. He left teaching and founded SAS with three other colleagues from the university. Goodnight's obsession with computers and dedication to creating cutting-edge analytical software allowed SAS to distinguish itself quickly from the competition. The company has been a force to be reckoned with ever since. SAS brings in $2.4 billion in annual revenue and has never failed to grow with each passing year.

At the core of this whole operation are the employees. To Goodnight, none of the company's advanced software or powerful number-crunching computers can compare to the human beings who keep the whole operation humming. "Right off the bat, we decided we were going to invest in making the work environment as pleasant as possible," says Goodnight. Along with profit-sharing opportunities, the company's first employees received 90 percent health care coverage, including vision and dental. Goodnight also implemented a 35-hour workweek that would ensure people wouldn't be forced to sacrifice their personal lives for work.

It's been the same way at SAS ever since. All the perks and benefits help employees forget about the trouble of their daily lives in order to focus on their work. This creates an efficient office environment that keeps staffers motivated and fulfilled. As a result, people tend to stay with SAS for a long time. Employees spend an average of 10 years at the company; 300 staffers have been on board for more than 25 years. What's more, while the average employee turnover rate for the software industry clocks in at 22 percent, SAS has an average turnover rate of only 2 percent. Ultimately, Goodnight is a practical, statistically minded manager who wants the best for his employees because that's what is best for the company. That attitude has helped SAS stay at the top of numerous "Best Places to Work" lists over the years.

In this chapter, you'll learn about the theories and practices managers like Jim Goodnight use in motivating their employees to focus on goals common to them and the organization.

CONNECTING WITH

X *Jim Goodnight*

CEO of SAS

Sources: Chris Kanaracus, "SAS Institute Eyes the Big Data Market," *PC World*, April 30, 2012; David A. Kaplan, "The Best Company to Work For: SAS," *Fortune*, February 8, 2010; Leigh Buchanan, "How SAS Continues to Grow," *Inc.*, September 2011; and "Jim Goodnight, CEO," www.sas.com, accessed May 2012.

The employees of this company are told exactly how to do their jobs—and we do mean exactly. For instance they are instructed to carry their keys on their ring finger with the teeth up. If they are considered too slow, a supervisor will shadow them with a stopwatch and clipboard and prod them along. Name that company. (Find the answer in the chapter.)

THE VALUE OF MOTIVATION

"If work is such fun, how come the rich don't do it?" quipped comedian Groucho Marx. Well, the rich do work—Bill Gates didn't make his billions playing computer games. And workers can have fun, if managers make the effort to motivate them.

It's difficult to overstate the importance of workers' job satisfaction. Happy workers usually lead to happy customers, and happy customers lead to successful businesses. On the other hand, unhappy workers are likely to leave. When that happens, the company usually loses more than an experienced employee. It can also lose the equivalent of 6 to 18 months' salary to cover the costs of recruiting and training a replacement.[1] The "soft" costs of losing employees are even greater: loss of intellectual capital, decreased morale of remaining workers, increased employee stress, decreased customer service, interrupted product development, and a poor reputation.

While it is costly to recruit and train new workers, it's also expensive to retain those who are disengaged. The word *engagement* is used to describe employees' level of motivation, passion, and commitment. Engaged employees work with passion and feel a connection to their company.[2] Disengaged workers have essentially checked out; they plod through their day putting in time, but not energy. Not only do they act out their unhappiness at work, but disengaged employees undermine the efforts of engaged co-workers. A Gallup survey estimated that the lower productivity of actively disengaged workers costs the U.S. economy about $300 billion a year. This number may increase in the near future considering the effect the recent recession has had on employee loyalty. In 2011, only 47 percent of employees surveyed said that they felt a very strong loyalty to their employer, down from 59 percent just three years earlier. While employers reported increased productivity (doing more with less), this gain came at the expense of employee loyalty. It is important that managers turn the tide around.[3]

Motivating the right people to join the organization and stay with it is a key function of managers. Top-performing managers are usually surrounded by top-performing employees. It is no coincidence that geese fly faster in formation than alone. Although the

One important type of motivator is intrinsic (inner) rewards, which include the personal satisfaction you feel for a job well done. People who respond to such inner promptings often enjoy their work and share their enthusiasm with others. Are you more strongly motivated by your own desire to do well, or by extrinsic rewards like pay and recognition?

desire to perform well ultimately comes from within, good managers stimulate people and bring out their natural drive to do a good job. People are willing to work, and work hard, if they feel their work makes a difference and is appreciated.[4]

People are motivated by a variety of things, such as recognition, accomplishment, and status. An **intrinsic reward** is the personal satisfaction you feel when you perform well and complete goals. The belief that your work makes a significant contribution to the organization or to society is a form of intrinsic reward. An **extrinsic reward** is given to you by someone else as recognition for good work. Pay increases, praise, and promotions are extrinsic rewards.

This chapter will help you understand the concepts, theories, and practice of motivation. We begin with a look at some traditional theories of motivation. Why should you bother to know about these theories? Because sometimes "new" approaches aren't really new; variations of them have been tried in the past. Knowing what has gone before will help you see what has worked and what hasn't. First, we discuss the Hawthorne studies because they created a new interest in worker satisfaction and motivation. Then we look at some assumptions about employees that come from the traditional theorists. You will see the names of these theorists over and over in business literature and future courses: Taylor, Mayo, Maslow, Herzberg, and McGregor. Finally, we'll introduce modern motivation theories and show you how managers apply them.

LEARNING goal 1

Explain Taylor's theory of scientific management.

Frederick Taylor: The Father of Scientific Management

Several 19th-century thinkers presented management principles, but not until the early 20th century did any work with lasting implications appear. *The Principles of Scientific Management* was written by U.S. efficiency engineer Frederick Taylor and published in 1911, earning Taylor the title "father of scientific management." Taylor's goal was to increase worker productivity to benefit both the firm and the worker. The solution, he thought, was to scientifically study the most efficient ways to do things, determine the one "best way" to perform each task, and then teach people those methods. This approach became known as **scientific management.** Three elements were basic to Taylor's approach: time, methods, and rules of work. His most important tools were observation and the stopwatch. Taylor's thinking lies behind today's measures of how many burgers McDonald's expects its cooks to flip.

A classic Taylor story describes his study of men shoveling rice, coal, and iron ore with the same type of shovel. Believing different materials called for different shovels, he proceeded to invent a wide variety of sizes and shapes of shovels and, stopwatch in hand, measured output over time in what were called **time-motion studies.** These were studies of the tasks performed in a job and the time needed for each. Sure enough, an average person could shovel 25 to 35 tons more per day using the most efficient motions and the proper shovel. This finding led to time-motion studies of virtually every factory job. As researchers determined the most efficient ways of doing things, efficiency became the standard for setting goals.

intrinsic reward
The personal satisfaction you feel when you perform well and complete goals.

extrinsic reward
Something given to you by someone else as recognition for good work; extrinsic rewards include pay increases, praise, and promotions.

scientific management
Studying workers to find the most efficient ways of doing things and then teaching people those techniques.

UPS tells drivers how to get out of their trucks, how fast to walk, how many packages to pick up and deliver a day, and even how to hold their keys. Can you see how UPS follows the principles of scientific management by teaching people the one "best way" to perform each task?

time-motion studies
Studies, begun by Frederick Taylor, of which tasks must be performed to complete a job and the time needed to do each task.

principle of motion economy
Theory developed by Frank and Lillian Gilbreth that every job can be broken down into a series of elementary motions.

Taylor's scientific management became the dominant strategy for improving productivity in the early 1900s. One follower of Taylor was Henry L. Gantt, who developed charts by which managers plotted the work of employees a day in advance down to the smallest detail. (See Chapter 9 for a discussion of Gantt charts.) U.S. engineers Frank and Lillian Gilbreth used Taylor's ideas in a three-year study of bricklaying. They developed the **principle of motion economy,** showing how every job could be broken into a series of elementary motions called a *therblig* (*Gilbreth* spelled backward with the *t* and *h* transposed). They then analyzed each motion to make it more efficient.

Scientific management viewed people largely as machines that needed to be properly programmed. There was little concern for the psychological or human aspects of work. Taylor believed that workers would perform at a high level of effectiveness—that is, be motivated—if they received high enough pay.[5]

Some of Taylor's ideas are still in use. Some companies continue to emphasize conformity to work rules rather than creativity, flexibility, and responsiveness. For example, United Parcel Service (UPS) tells drivers how to get out of their trucks (with right foot first), how fast to walk (three feet per second), how many packages to pick up and deliver a day (an average of 400), and how to hold their keys (teeth up, third finger). Drivers wear ring scanners, electronic devices on their index fingers wired to a small computer on their wrists. The devices shoot a pattern of photons at a bar code on a package to let a customer check the Internet and know exactly where a package is at any given moment. If a driver is considered slow, a supervisor rides along, prodding the driver with stopwatches and clipboards. UPS has a training center in Landover, Maryland, with simulators that teach employees how to properly lift and load boxes, drive their trucks proficiently, and even lessen the risk of slipping and falling when carrying a package.

The benefits of relying on workers to come up with solutions to productivity problems have long been recognized, as we shall discover next.

LEARNING goal 2

Describe the Hawthorne studies and their significance to management.

Elton Mayo and the Hawthorne Studies

One study, inspired by Frederick Taylor's research, began at the Western Electric Company's Hawthorne plant in Cicero, Illinois, in 1927 and ended six years later. Let's see why it is one of the major studies in management literature.

Elton Mayo and his colleagues from Harvard University came to the Hawthorne plant to test the degree of lighting associated with optimum productivity. In this respect, their study was a traditional scientific management study. The idea was to keep records of the workers' productivity under different levels of illumination. But the initial experiments revealed what seemed to be a problem. The researchers had expected productivity to fall as the lighting was dimmed. Yet the experimental group's productivity went up regardless of whether the lighting was bright or dim, and even when it was reduced to about the level of moonlight.

In a second series of 13 experiments, a separate test room was set up where researchers could manipulate temperature, humidity, and other environmental factors. Productivity went up each time; in fact, it increased by 50 percent overall.

When the experimenters repeated the original conditions (expecting productivity to fall to original levels), productivity increased yet again. The experiments were considered a total failure at this point. No matter what the experimenters did, productivity went up. What was causing the increase?

In the end, Mayo guessed that some human or psychological factor was at play. He and his colleagues interviewed the workers, asking about their feelings and attitudes toward the experiment. The answers began a profound change in management thinking that still has repercussions today. Here is what the researchers concluded:

- The workers in the test room thought of themselves as a social group. The atmosphere was informal, they could talk freely, and they interacted regularly with their supervisors and the experimenters. They felt special and worked hard to stay in the group. This motivated them.

- The workers were included in planning the experiments. For example, they rejected one kind of pay schedule and recommended another, which was adopted. They believed their ideas were respected and felt engaged in managerial decision making. This, too, motivated them.

- No matter the physical conditions, the workers enjoyed the atmosphere of their special room and the additional pay for being more productive. Job satisfaction increased dramatically.

Researchers now use the term **Hawthorne effect** to refer to people's tendency to behave differently when they know they're being studied. The Hawthorne study's results encouraged researchers to study human motivation and the managerial styles that lead to higher productivity. Research emphasis shifted from Taylor's scientific management toward Mayo's new human-based management.

Mayo's findings led to completely new assumptions about employees. One was that pay is not the only motivator. In fact, money was found to be a relatively ineffective motivator. New assumptions led to many theories about the human side of motivation. One of the best-known motivation theorists was Abraham Maslow, whose work we discuss next.

Little did Elton Mayo and his research team from Harvard University know they would forever change managers' beliefs about employee motivation. Their research at the Hawthorne plant of Western Electric in Cicero, Illinois (pictured here), gave birth to the concept of human-based motivation by showing that employees behaved differently simply because they were involved in planning and executing the experiments.

LEARNING goal 3

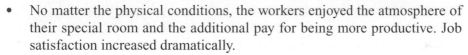

Identify the levels of Maslow's hierarchy of needs and apply them to employee motivation.

Hawthorne effect
The tendency for people to behave differently when they know they are being studied.

MOTIVATION AND MASLOW'S HIERARCHY OF NEEDS

Psychologist Abraham Maslow believed that to understand motivation at work, we must understand human motivation in general. It seemed to him that motivation arises from need. That is, people are motivated to satisfy unmet needs. Needs that have already been satisfied no longer provide motivation.

Figure 10.1 shows **Maslow's hierarchy of needs,** whose levels are:

Physiological needs: Basic survival needs, such as the need for food, water, and shelter.

Safety needs: The need to feel secure at work and at home.

Social needs: The need to feel loved, accepted, and part of the group.

Esteem needs: The need for recognition and acknowledgment from others, as well as self-respect and a sense of status or importance.

Self-actualization needs: The need to develop to one's fullest potential.

When one need is satisfied, another, higher-level need emerges and motivates us to satisfy it. The satisfied need is no longer a motivator. For example, if you just ate a full-course dinner, hunger would not be a motivator (at least for several hours), and your attention may turn to your surroundings (safety needs) or family (social needs). Of course, lower-level needs (perhaps thirst) may reemerge at any time they are not being met and take your attention away from higher-level needs.

To compete successfully, U.S. firms must create a work environment that includes goals such as social contribution, honesty, reliability, service, quality, dependability, and unity—for all levels of employees. Chip Conley of Joie de Vivre, a chain of 30 boutique hotels, thinks about higher-level needs such as meaning (self-actualization) for all employees, including lower-level workers. Half his employees are housekeepers who clean toilets all day. How does he help them feel they're doing meaningful work? One technique is what he calls the George Bailey exercise, based on the main character in the movie *It's a Wonderful Life.* Conley asked small groups of housekeepers what would happen if they weren't there every day. Trash would pile up, bathrooms would be full of wet towels, and let's not even think about the toilets. Then he asked them to come up with some other name for housekeeping. They offered suggestions like "serenity keepers," "clutter busters," or "the peace-of-mind police." In the end, these employees had a sense of how the customer's experience wouldn't be the same without them. This gave meaning to their work that helped satisfy higher-level needs.[6]

Need help understanding Maslow's Hierarchy? www.introbiz.tv/QR10-1

---

figure 10.1

MASLOW'S HIERARCHY OF NEEDS

Maslow's hierarchy of needs is based on the idea that motivation comes from need. If a need is met, it's no longer a motivator, so a higher-level need becomes the motivator. Higher-level needs demand the support of lower-level needs. This chart shows the various levels of need. Do you know where you are on the chart right now?

goal 4

Distinguish between the motivators and hygiene factors identified by Herzberg.

HERZBERG'S MOTIVATING FACTORS

Another direction in managerial theory explores what managers can do with the job itself to motivate employees. In other words, some theorists ask: Of all the factors controllable by managers, which are most effective in generating an enthusiastic work effort?

In the mid-1960s, psychologist Frederick Herzberg conducted the most discussed study in this area. Herzberg asked workers to rank various job-related factors in order of importance relative to motivation. The question was: What creates enthusiasm for workers and makes them work to full potential? The most important factors were:

1. Sense of achievement.
2. Earned recognition.
3. Interest in the work itself.
4. Opportunity for growth.
5. Opportunity for advancement.
6. Importance of responsibility.
7. Peer and group relationships.
8. Pay.
9. Supervisor's fairness.
10. Company policies and rules.
11. Status.
12. Job security.
13. Supervisor's friendliness.
14. Working conditions.

Factors receiving the most votes all clustered around job content. Workers like to feel they contribute to the company (sense of achievement was number 1). They want to earn recognition (number 2) and feel their jobs are important (number 6). They want responsibility (which is why learning is so important) and to earn recognition for that responsibility by having a chance for growth and advancement. Of course, workers also want the job to be interesting. Do you feel the same way about your work?

Workers did not consider factors related to job environment to be motivators. It was interesting to find that one of those factors was pay. Workers felt the *absence* of good pay, job security, and friendly supervisors could cause dissatisfaction, but their presence did not motivate employees to work harder; it just provided satisfaction and contentment. Would you work harder if you were paid more?

Herzberg concluded that certain factors, which he called **motivators,** made employees productive and gave them satisfaction. These factors, as you have seen, mostly related to job content. Herzberg called other elements of the job

motivators
In Herzberg's theory of motivating factors, job factors that cause employees to be productive and that give them satisfaction.

figure 10.2

HERZBERG'S MOTIVATORS AND HYGIENE FACTORS

There's some controversy over Herzberg's results. For example, sales managers often use money as a motivator. Recent studies have shown that money can be a motivator if used as part of a recognition program.

MOTIVATORS	HYGIENE (MAINTENANCE) FACTORS
(These factors can be used to motivate workers.)	(These factors can cause dissatisfaction, but changing them will have little motivational effect.)
Work itself	Company policy and administration
Achievement	Supervision
Recognition	Working conditions
Responsibility	Interpersonal relations (co-workers)
Growth and advancement	Salary, status, and job security

hygiene factors
In Herzberg's theory of motivating factors, job factors that can cause dissatisfaction if missing but that do not necessarily motivate employees if increased.

hygiene factors (or maintenance factors). These related to the job environment and could cause dissatisfaction if missing but would not necessarily motivate employees if increased. See Figure 10.2 for a list of motivators and hygiene factors.

Herzberg's motivating factors led to this conclusion: The best way to motivate employees is to make their jobs interesting, help them achieve their objectives, and recognize their achievement through advancement and added responsibility.[7] A review of Figure 10.3 shows the similarity between Maslow's hierarchy of needs and Herzberg's theory.

Look at Herzberg's motivating factors, identify those that motivate you, and rank them in order of importance to you. Keep them in mind as you consider jobs and careers. What motivators do your job opportunities offer you? Are they the ones you consider important? Evaluating your job offers in terms of what's really important to you will help you make a wise career choice.

figure 10.3

COMPARISON OF MASLOW'S HIERARCHY OF NEEDS AND HERZBERG'S THEORY OF FACTORS

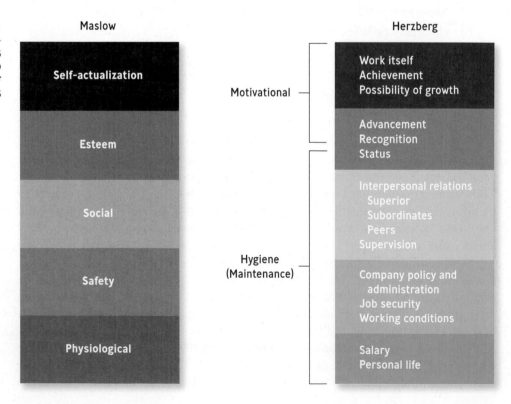

progress assessment

- What are the similarities and differences between Taylor's time-motion studies and Mayo's Hawthorne studies?
- How did Mayo's findings influence scientific management?
- Draw a diagram of Maslow's hierarchy of needs. Label and describe the parts.
- Explain the distinction between what Herzberg called motivators and hygiene factors.

LEARNING goal 5

Differentiate among Theory X, Theory Y, and Theory Z.

MCGREGOR'S THEORY X AND THEORY Y

The way managers go about motivating people at work depends greatly on their attitudes toward workers. Management theorist Douglas McGregor observed that managers' attitudes generally fall into one of two entirely different sets of managerial assumptions, which he called Theory X and Theory Y.

Theory X

The assumptions of Theory X management are:

- The average person dislikes work and will avoid it if possible.
- Because of this dislike, workers must be forced, controlled, directed, or threatened with punishment to make them put forth the effort to achieve the organization's goals.
- The average worker prefers to be directed, wishes to avoid responsibility, has relatively little ambition, and wants security.
- Primary motivators are fear and punishment.

The natural consequence of these assumptions is a manager who is very busy and watches people closely, telling them what to do and how to do it. Motivation is more likely to take the form of punishment for bad work than reward for good work. Theory X managers give workers little responsibility, authority, or flexibility. Taylor and other theorists who preceded him would have agreed with Theory X. Time-motion studies calculated the one best way to perform a task and the optimal time to devote to it. Researchers assumed workers needed to be trained and carefully watched to see that they conformed to standards.

Many managers and entrepreneurs still suspect that employees cannot be fully trusted and need to be closely supervised. No doubt you have seen such managers in action. How did they make you feel? Were these managers' assumptions accurate regarding workers' attitudes?

Theory Y

Theory Y makes entirely different assumptions about people:

- Most people like work; it is as natural as play or rest.
- Most people naturally work toward goals to which they are committed.

Theory X managers do not come in one-size-fits-all packages. Take Salina Lo of Ruckus Wireless, for example. On the job this graduate of University of California at Berkeley is a tough and exacting Theory X manager. Her in-your-face style has earned her a reputation as one of the industry's toughest managers. Would you prefer to work for a Theory X or a Theory Y manager?

- The depth of a person's commitment to goals depends on the perceived rewards for achieving them.

- Under certain conditions, most people not only accept but also seek responsibility.

- People are capable of using a relatively high degree of imagination, creativity, and cleverness to solve problems.

- In industry, the average person's intellectual potential is only partially realized.

- People are motivated by a variety of rewards. Each worker is stimulated by a reward unique to him or her (time off, money, recognition, and so on).

Rather than authority, direction, and close supervision, Theory Y managers emphasize a relaxed managerial atmosphere in which workers are free to set objectives, be creative, be flexible, and go beyond the goals set by management. A key technique here is *empowerment,* giving employees authority to make decisions and tools to implement the decisions they make. For empowerment to be a real motivator, management should follow these three steps:

1. Find out what people think the problems in the organization are.
2. Let them design the solutions.
3. Get out of the way and let them put those solutions into action.

Often employees complain that although they're asked to engage in company decision making, their managers fail to actually empower them to make decisions. Have you ever worked in such an atmosphere? How did that make you feel?

OUCHI'S THEORY Z

One reason many U.S. companies choose a more flexible managerial style is to meet competition from firms in Japan, China, and the European Union. In the 1980s, Japanese companies seemed to be outperforming U.S. businesses. William

Google has its own state-of-the-art gym and resistance swimming pool to help employees work off the extra pounds. Large and colorful exercise balls are everywhere to remind employees to take care of their bodies. Can you think of any other examples of the kind of holistic concern for employees suggested by William Ouchi's Theory Z style of management?

Ouchi, management professor at the University of California–Los Angeles, wondered whether the reason was the way Japanese companies managed their workers. The Japanese approach, which Ouchi called Type J, included lifetime employment, consensual decision making, collective responsibility for the outcomes of decisions, slow evaluation and promotion, implied control mechanisms, nonspecialized career paths, and holistic concern for employees. In contrast, the U.S. management approach, which Ouchi called Type A, relied on short-term employment, individual decision making, individual responsibility for the outcomes of decisions, rapid evaluation and promotion, explicit control mechanisms, specialized career paths, and segmented concern for employees.

Type J firms are based on the culture of Japan, which includes a focus on trust and intimacy within the group and family. Conversely, Type A firms are based on American culture, which includes a focus on individual rights and achievements. Ouchi wanted to help U.S. firms adopt successful Japanese strategies, but he realized it wouldn't be practical to expect U.S. managers to accept an approach based on the culture of another country. Judge for yourself. A job for life may sound good until you think of the implications: no chance to change jobs and no opportunity to move quickly through the ranks.

Ouchi recommended a hybrid approach, Theory Z (see Figure 10.4). Theory Z includes long-term employment, collective decision making, individual responsibility for the outcomes of decisions, slow evaluation and promotion, moderately specialized career paths, and holistic concern for employees (including family). Theory Z views the organization as a family that fosters cooperation and organizational values.

In recent years, demographic and social changes, fierce global competition, and the worst recession in their country's history have forced Japanese managers to reevaluate the way they conduct business. The effects of the 2011 earthquake on Japanese businesses reinforced the need to change. They now need to become both more dynamic and more efficient in order to compete effectively.

Electronics giant Hitachi was the first major Japanese company to quit requiring corporate calisthenics. Having everyone start the day with group exercises had symbolized doing the same thing the same way, and reinforced the cultural belief

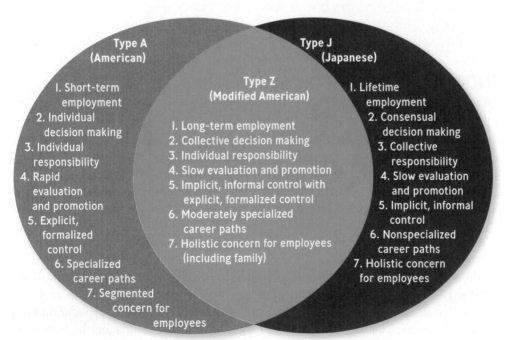

figure 10.4

THEORY Z: A BLEND OF AMERICAN AND JAPANESE MANAGEMENT APPROACHES

figure 10.5

A COMPARISON OF THEORIES
X, Y, AND Z

THEORY X	THEORY Y	THEORY Z
1. Employees dislike work and will try to avoid it.	1. Employees view work as a natural part of life.	1. Employee involvement is the key to increased productivity.
2. Employees prefer to be controlled and directed.	2. Employees prefer limited control and direction.	2. Employee control is implied and informal.
3. Employees seek security, not responsibility.	3. Employees will seek responsibility under proper work conditions.	3. Employees prefer to share responsibility and decision making.
4. Employees must be intimidated by managers to perform.	4. Employees perform better in work environments that are nonintimidating.	4. Employees perform better in environments that foster trust and cooperation.
5. Employees are motivated by financial rewards.	5. Employees are motivated by many different needs.	5. Employees need guaranteed employment and will accept slow evaluations and promotions.

that employees should not take risks or think for themselves. Many managers think such conformity is what hurt Japanese business. Will Japanese managers move toward the hybrid Theory Z in the future? We'll have to wait and see. An appropriate managerial style matches the culture, situation, and specific needs of the organization and its employees. (See Figure 10.5 for a summary of Theories X, Y, and Z.)

LEARNING goal 6

Explain the key principles of goal-setting, expectancy, reinforcement, and equity theories.

goal-setting theory
The idea that setting ambitious but attainable goals can motivate workers and improve performance if the goals are accepted, accompanied by feedback, and facilitated by organizational conditions.

management by objectives (MBO)
A system of goal setting and implementation; it involves a cycle of discussion, review, and evaluation of objectives among top and middle-level managers, supervisors, and employees.

GOAL-SETTING THEORY AND MANAGEMENT BY OBJECTIVES

Goal-setting theory says setting ambitious but attainable goals can motivate workers and improve performance if the goals are accepted and accompanied by feedback, and if conditions in the organization pave the way for achievement. All organization members should have some basic agreement about both overall goals and specific objectives for each department and individual. Thus there should be a system to engage everyone in the organization in goal setting and implementation.

The late management expert Peter Drucker developed such a system in the 1960s. "Managers cannot motivate people; they can only thwart people's motivation because people motivate themselves," he said. Called **management by objectives (MBO),** Drucker's system of goal setting and implementation includes a cycle of discussion, review, and evaluation of objectives among top and middle-level managers, supervisors, and employees. It calls on managers to formulate goals in cooperation with everyone in the organization, to commit employees to those goals, and to monitor results and reward accomplishment. Government agencies like the Department of Defense use MBO.

MBO is most effective in relatively stable situations when managers can make long-range plans and implement them with few changes.[8] Managers must also understand the difference between helping and coaching subordinates. *Helping* means working with the subordinate and doing part of the work if necessary. *Coaching* means acting as a resource—teaching, guiding, and recommending— but not participating actively or doing the task. The central idea of MBO is that employees need to motivate themselves.

Employee input and expectations are important.[9] Problems can arise when management uses MBO as a strategy for forcing managers and workers to commit to goals that are not agreed on together, but are instead set by top management.[10]

Victor Vroom identified the importance of employee expectations and developed a process called expectancy theory. Let's examine this concept next.

MEETING EMPLOYEE EXPECTATIONS: EXPECTANCY THEORY

According to Victor Vroom's **expectancy theory,** employee expectations can affect motivation. That is, the amount of effort employees exert on a specific task depends on their expectations of the outcome. Vroom contends that employees ask three questions before committing their maximum effort to a task: (1) Can I accomplish the task? (2) If I do accomplish it, what's my reward? (3) Is the reward worth the effort? (See Figure 10.6.)

Think of the effort you might exert in class under the following conditions: Suppose your instructor says that to earn an A in the course, you must achieve an average of 90 percent on coursework plus jump eight feet high. Would you exert maximum effort toward earning an A if you knew you could not possibly jump eight feet high? Suppose your instructor said any student can earn an A in the course, but you know this instructor has not awarded an A in 25 years of teaching. If the reward of an A seems unattainable, would you exert significant effort in the course? Better yet, let's say you read online that businesses prefer hiring C-minus students to A-plus students. Does the reward of an A seem worth it? Now think of similar situations that may occur on the job.

Expectancy theory does note that expectation varies from individual to individual. Employees establish their own views of task difficulty and the value of the

expectancy theory
Victor Vroom's theory that the amount of effort employees exert on a specific task depends on their expectations of the outcome.

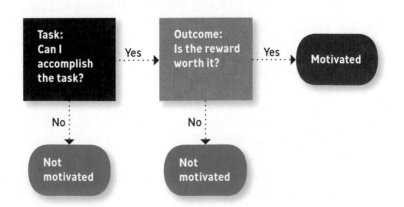

figure 10.6

EXPECTANCY THEORY

The amount of effort employees exert on a task depends on their expectations of the outcome.

reward.[11] Researchers David Nadler and Edward Lawler modified Vroom's theory and suggested that managers follow five steps to improve employee performance:[12]

1. Determine what rewards employees value.
2. Determine each employee's desired performance standard.
3. Ensure that performance standards are attainable.
4. Guarantee rewards tied to performance.
5. Be certain that employees consider the rewards adequate.

REINFORCING EMPLOYEE PERFORMANCE: REINFORCEMENT THEORY

reinforcement theory
Theory that positive and negative reinforcers motivate a person to behave in certain ways.

According to **reinforcement theory,** positive reinforcers, negative reinforcers, and punishers motivate a person to behave in certain ways. In other words, motivation is the result of the carrot-and-stick approach: individuals act to receive rewards and avoid punishment. Positive reinforcements are rewards such as praise, recognition, and a pay raise. Punishment includes reprimands, reduced pay, and layoffs or firing. Negative reinforcement occurs when people work to escape the punishers. Escaping the punishment reinforces or rewards the positive behavior. A manager might also try to stop undesirable behavior by not responding to it. This response is called extinction because managers hope the unwanted behavior will become extinct. Figure 10.7 illustrates how a manager can use reinforcement theory to motivate workers.

TREATING EMPLOYEES FAIRLY: EQUITY THEORY

equity theory
The idea that employees try to maintain equity between inputs and outputs compared to others in similar positions.

Equity theory looks at how employees' perceptions of fairness affect their willingness to perform. It assumes employees ask, "If I do a good job, will it be worth it?" and "What's fair?" Employees try to maintain equity between what they put into the job and what they get out of it, comparing those inputs and outputs to those of others in similar positions. Workers find comparative information through personal relationships, professional organizations, and other sources.

When workers perceive inequity, they will try to reestablish fairness in a number of ways. For example, suppose you compare the grade you earned on a term paper with your classmates' grades. If you think you received a lower grade than

figure 10.7

REINFORCEMENT THEORY

Managers can either add or subtract stimuli (positive reinforcement, negative reinforcement, or punishers) to increase desired behavior or decrease undesired behavior.

Source: Casey Limmer, MSW, LCSW, Washington University.

	ADD STIMULI	SUBTRACT STIMULI
Increase Behavior	Positive Reinforcement: Jill gets praise (the reinforcement added) for turning in her reports on time (target behavior to increase).	Negative Reinforcement: Jack is on probation (punishment that will be removed) until such time as he can turn in 3 reports on time (target behavior to increase).
Decrease Behavior	Punishment: Jack gets written up (the punisher) for turning in his reports late (target behavior to decrease).	Extinction: Jill does not get praise (reinforcement is removed) when her reports are turned in late (target behavior to decrease), no matter how well done they are.

someone who put out the same effort as you, you may (1) reduce your effort on future class projects or (2) rationalize the difference by saying, "Grades are overvalued anyway!" If you think your paper received a higher grade than comparable papers, you will probably (1) increase your effort to justify the higher reward in the future or (2) rationalize by saying, "I'm worth it!"

In the workplace, perceived inequity may lead to lower productivity, reduced quality, increased absenteeism, and voluntary resignation.

Remember that equity judgments are based on perception and are therefore subject to error. When workers overestimate their own contributions—as happens often—they feel *any* rewards given out for performance are inequitable. Sometimes organizations try to deal with this by keeping employee salaries secret, but secrecy may make things worse. Employees are likely to overestimate the salaries of others, in addition to overestimating their own contribution. The best remedy is generally clear and frequent communication. Managers must communicate as clearly as possible both the results they expect and the outcomes that will occur.[13]

progress assessment

- Briefly describe the managerial attitudes behind Theories X, Y, and Z.
- Explain goal-setting theory.
- Evaluate expectancy theory. When could expectancy theory apply to your efforts or lack of effort?
- Explain the principles of equity theory.

LEARNING goal 7

Show how managers put motivation theories into action through such strategies as job enrichment, open communication, and job recognition.

PUTTING THEORY INTO ACTION

Now that you know what a few theorists have to say about motivation, you might be asking yourself "So what? What do all those theories have to do with what really goes on in the workplace today?" Fair question. Let's look at how companies put the theories into action through job enrichment, open communication, and job recognition.

Motivation through Job Enrichment

Managers have extended both Maslow's and Herzberg's theories through **job enrichment,** a strategy that motivates workers through the job itself. Work is assigned so that individuals can complete an identifiable task from beginning to end and are held responsible for successful achievement. Job enrichment is based on Herzberg's higher motivators, such as responsibility, achievement, and recognition. It stands in contrast to *job simplification,* which produces task efficiency by breaking a job into simple steps and assigning people to each. Review Maslow's and Herzberg's work to see how job enrichment grew from those theories.

job enrichment
A motivational strategy that emphasizes motivating the worker through the job itself.

Here a worker in Baccarat's factory puts the finishing touches on a crystal vase. One of the hallmarks of job enrichment is the worker's ability to perform a complete task from beginning to end. Why do you think this might be more motivating than simply adding a few parts to an assembly on a production line?

job enlargement
A job enrichment strategy that involves combining a series of tasks into one challenging and interesting assignment.

job rotation
A job enrichment strategy that involves moving employees from one job to another.

Those who advocate job enrichment believe that five characteristics of work are important in motivation and performance:

1. *Skill variety.* The extent to which a job demands different skills.
2. *Task identity.* The degree to which the job requires doing a task with a visible outcome from beginning to end.
3. *Task significance.* The degree to which the job has a substantial impact on the lives or work of others in the company.
4. *Autonomy.* The degree of freedom, independence, and discretion in scheduling work and determining procedures.
5. *Feedback.* The amount of direct and clear information given about job performance.

Variety, identity, and significance contribute to the meaningfulness of the job. Autonomy gives people a feeling of responsibility; feedback contributes to a feeling of achievement and recognition.[14]

One type of job enrichment is **job enlargement,** which combines a series of tasks into one challenging and interesting assignment. Maytag, the home appliance manufacturer, redesigned its washing machine production process so that employees could assemble an entire water pump instead of just adding one part. **Job rotation** also makes work more interesting and motivating by moving employees from one job to another. One problem, of course, is the need to train employees to do several different operations. However, the resulting increase in motivation and the value of having flexible, cross-trained employees usually offsets the costs.[15]

Motivating through Open Communication

Communication and information must flow freely throughout the organization when employees are empowered to make decisions—they can't make them in a vacuum. Procedures for encouraging open communication include the following:

- *Create an organizational culture that rewards listening.* Top managers must create places to talk and show employees that talking with superiors counts—by providing feedback, adopting employee suggestions, and rewarding upward communication—even if the discussion is negative. Employees must feel free to say anything they deem appropriate and believe their opinions are valued.[16]

- *Train supervisors and managers to listen.* Most people receive no training in how to listen, in school or anywhere else, so organizations must do such training themselves or hire someone to do it.

- *Use effective questioning techniques.* We get information through questioning. Different kinds of questions yield different kinds of information. Closed questions that generate yes/no answers don't encourage the longer, more thoughtful responses that open questions do. Appropriate personal questions can create a sense of camaraderie between employee and manager.

Make the World Your Office

People today are used to using their phones to text, tweet, surf the web, and run apps as they go about their personal lives. They expect to do the same in their business lives. Businesses can no longer limit themselves to traditional intranets (company networks) to communicate *to* employees; they must find ways to communicate *with* them. They must provide truly interactive employee communications systems. It's all about promoting and improving engagement and interaction. The new systems should provide communication features that include collaboration tools, discussion groups, and real-time messaging.

Employees expect real-time communication and online interaction with their fellow workers. They also expect to have 24/7 access to company information such as news, policies, forms, corporate directories and documents, and to have self-service control regardless of their location. They want easy access to personal information like pay stubs, retirement account balances, and health insurance benefits information. Most importantly, they expect this communication to be proactive; that is, that the system automatically reaches out to them. For example, the system should automatically inform them if there are deadlines to be met.

All of this communication must be able to be done from mobile phones and iPads. Imagine a manager notifying his staff that the office will be closed due to flooded roads by sending them messages on their phones via text, e-mail, or an app specific to employee communication. Now that's a message we bet you'd like to get before you head out the door!

Sources: John Lamb, "Interactive Employee Communication," *Employee Benefit Advisor,* January 1, 2011; and Elizabeth Galentine, "The Next Wave in Benefit Communication," *Employee Benefit Advisor,* May 1, 2012.

- *Remove barriers to open communication.* Separate offices, parking areas, bathrooms, and dining rooms for managers only set up barriers. Other barriers are different dress codes and different ways of addressing one another (like calling workers by their first names and managers by their last). Removing such barriers may require imagination and managers' willingness to give up special privileges.

- *Avoid vague and ambiguous communication.* Passive voice appears weak and tentative. Statements such as "Mistakes were made" leave you wondering who made the mistakes. Hedging is another way managers send garbled messages. Terms like *possibly* and *perhaps* sound wishy-washy to employees who need more definitive direction.

- *Make it easy to communicate.* Encouraging organization members to eat together at large lunch tables, allowing employees to gather in conference rooms, having organizational picnics and athletic teams, and so on can help workers at all levels mix with one another.

- *Ask employees what is important to them.* Managers shouldn't wait until the exit interview to ask an employee, "What can I do to keep you?" Then it's too late. Instead they should have frequent *stay interviews* to find out what matters to employees and what they can do to keep them on the job.[17]

The Connecting Through Social Media box offers advice on using open communication strategies in businesses.

Applying Open Communication in Self-Managed Teams

Before the recent economic crisis, the auto companies were often cited for good practices. At Ford Motor Company, for example, a group known as Team Mustang set the guidelines for how production teams should be formed. Given the challenge to create a car that would make people dust off their old "Mustang Sally" records and dance into showrooms, the 400-member team was also given the freedom to make decisions without waiting for approval from headquarters. Everyone worked under one roof in an old warehouse where drafting experts sat next to accountants, engineers next to stylists. Budgetary walls between departments were knocked down too as department managers were persuaded to surrender some control over their subordinates on the team.

In the car business nothing works like the "wow" factor. At Ford, the 400-member Team Mustang group was empowered to create the "wow" response for the company's sleek Mustang convertible. The work team, suppliers, company managers, and even customers worked together to make the Mustang a winner in the very competitive automobile market.

When the resulting Mustang convertible displayed shaking problems, engineers were so motivated to finish on time and under budget that they worked late into the night, sleeping on the floor when necessary. Senior Ford executives were tempted to intervene, but they stuck with their promise not to meddle. Working with suppliers, the team solved the shaking problem and still came in under budget and a couple of months early. The new car was a hit with drivers, and sales soared.[18]

To implement such teams, managers at most companies must reinvent work. This means respecting workers, providing interesting work, developing workers' skills, allowing autonomy, decentralizing authority, and rewarding good work. Next we'll take a look at some of the ways companies recognize and reward good work.

Recognizing a Job Well Done

Letting people know you appreciate their work is usually more powerful than giving a raise or bonus alone.[19] When asked in a recent survey their reason for changing jobs, only 42 percent of the participants listed increased compensation and benefits, while 83 percent said they left for increased responsibilities and/or a more senior role.[20] Clearly, providing advancement opportunity is important in retaining valuable employees.

Promotions aren't the only way to celebrate a job well done. Recognition can be as simple as noticing positive actions out loud, making employees feel their efforts are worthwhile and valued enough to be noticed. For example: "Sarina, you didn't say much in the meeting today. Your ideas are usually so valuable; I missed hearing them." This comment lets Sarina know her ideas are appreciated, and she'll be more apt to participate fully in the next meeting.

Here are just a few examples of ways managers have raised employee spirits without raising paychecks:

- A Los Angeles law firm sent 400 employees and their families to Disneyland for the day. FedEx Office did something similar, but it sent high-achieving employees to Disneyland *and* put the company's top executives in those employees' place while they were gone.

- Accounting firm KPMG gave employees a sundae surprise of gourmet ice cream and toppings.

- Give More Media offers perks like Netflix and XM Satellite Radio memberships. It also encourages participation in its Smile and Give program, which gives employees three paid days off to work for a nonprofit of their choice.

- Lotus Public Relations in New York City has an annual "Lotus Day." One year employees sailed the Hudson, ate in an expensive restaurant, and enjoyed a comedy show and drinks. Other everyday perks include a free snack cabinet, free coffee, and free unlimited city commuting.

- Walt Disney World offers more than 200 employee recognition programs. The Spirit of Fred Award is named after an employee named Fred, who makes each award (a certificate mounted and varnished on a plaque) himself. Fred's name became an acronym for Friendly, Resourceful, Enthusiastic, and Dependable.

- Maritz Inc., in Fenton, Missouri, has a Thanks a Bunch program that gives flowers to a selected employee in appreciation of a job well done. That employee passes the bouquet to someone else who helped. The idea is to see how many people are given the flowers throughout the day. The bouquet comes with thank-you cards that are entered into a drawing for awards like binoculars and jackets.

- Hewlett-Packard (HP) bestows its Golden Banana Award for a job well done. The award started when an engineer burst into his manager's office saying he'd found the solution to a long-standing problem. In his haste to find something to give the employee to show his appreciation, the manager grabbed a banana from his lunch and said, "Well done! Congratulations!" The Golden Banana is now one of the most prestigious honors given to an inventive HP employee.

Travelocity's Gnomie Award, based on the company's mascot, the traveling gnome, is given to employees nominated by their peers for outstanding performance. Winners receive a $750 travel voucher, a paid day off, recognition at the company's quarterly meeting, and a golden gnome. What part do you think these awards play in motivating the winners to continue their outstanding performance?

The Connecting with Small Business box offers examples of what a number of small businesses have done to motivate employees.

Giving valued employees prime parking spots, more vacation days, or more flexible schedules may help them feel their work is appreciated, but sometimes nothing inspires workers like the prospect of a payout down the road. Companies that offer a small equity stake or stock options often have a good chance of developing loyal employees

The same things don't motivate all employees. Next we'll explore how employees from different cultures and generations are motivated in different ways.

LEARNING goal 8

Show how managers personalize motivation strategies to appeal to employees across the globe and across generations.

PERSONALIZING MOTIVATION

Managers cannot use one motivational formula for all employees. They have to get to know each worker personally and tailor the motivational effort to the individual. This is further complicated by the increase in global business and the fact that

A Little Fun Can Be a Big Motivator

How can small businesses motivate their workers to perform their best when they can't offer their employees the financial incentives larger businesses can? Many strive to create an upbeat, relaxed company culture to encourage employees to bond with one another. For example, at Blurb, a San Francisco–based specialty publishing company, at the end of every Friday the conference room is transformed into a concert venue as employees play the video game Rock Band. The manager provides refreshments along with the game, allowing the staff to relax and let the stress of the workweek pass into memory. Sprout Group, a small marketing firm based in Utah, uses a similarly laid-back strategy with weekly company trips to the movie theater where tickets and popcorn are on the boss.

Employee motivation isn't just about morale-boosting leisure activities like video games and movie nights. Besides providing social interaction, management needs to communicate clearly with the staff in order to give purpose and direction. At the small consulting firm Sonoma Partners, veteran employees mentor new hires to acquaint them with the work environment and show them how to excel. Not only does this method help new employees bond with their colleagues; it also sets them on the path to becoming productive workers.

Small businesses have a greater opportunity to motivate with open communication and broad responsibility. Individual workers can have more say in the company and not feel like just another drone in the great corporate beehive. As long as management encourages innovation from employees (and throws an occasional video game party), small businesses should have no trouble motivating their employees.

Sources: Sarah E. Needleman, "Business Owners Try to Motivate Employees," *The Wall Street Journal,* January 14, 2010; Toddi Gutner, "Motivate Employees with Goal-Setting," www .smallbusiness.foxbusiness.com, April 13, 2011; and Camille Tuutti, "Fun, Competition Inspire Better Service and Happier Employees," *Federal Computer Week,* May 18, 2012.

managers now work with employees from a variety of cultural backgrounds. Cultural differences also exist between generations raised in the same country. Let's look at how managers personalize their strategies to appeal to employees across the globe and across generations.

Motivating Employees across the Globe

Different cultures experience motivational approaches differently; therefore, managers study and understand these cultural factors in designing a reward system. In a *high-context culture,* workers build personal relationships and develop group trust before focusing on tasks. In a *low-context culture,* workers often view relationship building as a waste of time that diverts attention from the task. Koreans, Thais, and Saudis tend to be high-context workers who often view their U.S. colleagues as insincere due to their need for data and quick decision making.

Dow Chemical solved a cross-cultural problem with a recognition program for its 52,000 employees in over 37 countries who use a wide variety of languages and currencies. Globoforce Ltd. created a web-based program for Dow called Recognition@Dow that automatically adjusts for differences created by cultural preferences, tax laws, and even local standards of living. Thus a U.S. employee might receive

a gift certificate for Macy's, whereas a Chinese employee receives one for online retailer Dangdang.com. The system even allows employees to nominate colleagues for recognition using an "award wizard" to help determine the appropriate award.[21]

Understanding motivation in global organizations and building effective global teams is still a new task for most companies. Developing group leaders who are culturally astute, flexible, and able to deal with ambiguity is a challenge businesses face in the 21st century. See the Connecting Across Borders box for more about managing culturally diverse employees.

Motivating Employees across Generations

Baby boomers (born between 1946 and 1964), Generation X members (born between 1965 and 1980), and Generation Y members, also known as Millennials or echo boomers (born between 1980 and 2000), are linked through experiences they shared in their formative years—usually the first 10 years of life. The beliefs you accept as a child affect how you view risk, challenge, authority, technology, relationships, and economics. When you're in a management position, they can even affect whom you hire, fire, or promote.

In general, boomers were raised in families that experienced unprecedented economic prosperity, secure jobs, and optimism about the future. Gen Xers were raised in dual-career families with parents who focused on work. As children, they attended day care or became latchkey kids. Their parents' layoffs added to their insecurity about a lifelong job. Millennials were raised by indulgent parents, and most don't remember a time without cell phones, computers, and electronic entertainment.

Millennials tend to be skeptical, outspoken, and image-driven as well as adaptable, tech-savvy employees with a sense of fun and tolerance. It is important for managers of all ages to be aware that employees of different generations communicate differently. How do you think generational differences will affect this manager and employee?

The main constant in the lives of Gen Xers and Millennials is inconstancy. Consider the unprecedented change in the past 10–20 years in every area (i.e., economic, technological, scientific, social, and political). Gen Xers and Millennials expect change. It is the absence of change that they find questionable.[22]

How do generational differences among these groups affect motivation in the workplace? Boomer managers need to be flexible with their Gen X and Millennial employees, or they will lose them. Gen X employees need to use their enthusiasm for change and streamlining to their advantage.[23] Although many are unwilling to pay the same price for success their parents and grandparents did, their concern about undue stress and long hours doesn't mean they lack ambition. They want economic security as much as older workers, but they have a different approach to achieving it. Rather than focusing on job security, Gen Xers tend to focus on career security instead and are willing to change jobs to find it.[24]

Many Gen Xers are now managers themselves, responsible for motivating other employees. What kind of managers are they? In general, they are well equipped to motivate people. They usually understand that there is more to life than work, and they think a big part of motivating is letting people know you recognize that fact. Gen X managers tend to focus more on results than on hours in the workplace. They tend to be flexible and good at collaboration and consensus building. They often think in broader terms than their predecessors because the media have exposed them to problems around the world. They also have a big impact on their team members. They are more likely to give them the goals and outlines of the project and leave them alone to do their work.[25]

Perhaps the best asset of Gen X managers is their ability to give employees feedback, especially positive feedback. One reason might be that they expect more of it themselves. One new employee was frustrated because he hadn't received feedback from his boss since he was hired—two weeks earlier. In short, managers need to realize that young workers demand performance reviews and other forms of feedback more than the traditional one or two times a year.

As Millennials continue to enter the job market, they are creating a workplace four generations deep. As a group, they tend to share a number of characteristics: they're impatient, skeptical, blunt, and expressive; image-driven; and inexperienced. Like any other generation, they can transform their characteristics into unique skills. For example, Millennials tend to be adaptable, tech-savvy, able to grasp new concepts, practiced at multitasking, efficient, and tolerant. Perhaps the most surprising attribute they share is a sense of commitment.[26] Millennials place a higher value on work-life balance, expect their employers to adapt to them (not the other way around), and are more likely to rank fun and stimulation in their top five ideal-job requirements.[27] What do you think are the most effective strategies managers can use to motivate Millennial workers?

Many Millennials aren't rushing to find lifetime careers after graduation. They're "job surfing" and aren't opposed to living with their parents while they test out jobs. Some of this career postponement isn't by choice as much as a result of the state of the economy. The recession hurt younger workers more deeply than other workers. In July 2010, the unemployment rate was 15.3 percent for those aged 20 to 24, while the overall unemployment rate was 9.5 percent. Unemployment for 18- to 29-year-olds was the highest it's been in more than three decades. In fact, today Millennials are less likely to be employed than Gen Xers or boomers were at the same age. The recession has increased the competition for jobs as younger workers struggle to enter the job market, boomers try to make up lost retirement savings, and Gen Xers fight to pay mortgages and raise families.[28]

As Millennials assume more responsibilities in the workplace, they sometimes must manage and lead others far older than themselves. How can young managers lead others who may have more experience than they do? Perhaps the three most important things to keep in mind are to be confident, be open-minded, and solicit feedback regularly. Just remember that asking for input and advice is different from asking for permission or guidance.[29]

It is important for managers of all ages to be aware that employees of different generations communicate differently. The traditionalists, the generation that lived through the Great Depression and World War II, prefer to communicate face-to-face. Their second choice is by phone, but recordings often frustrate them. Boomers prefer to communicate in meetings or conference calls. Gen Xers generally prefer e-mail and will choose meetings only if there are no other options. Millennials most often use technology to communicate, particularly through social media.[30]

In every generational shift, the older generation tends to say the same thing about the new: "They break the rules." The traditionalists said it of the baby boomers. Boomers look at Gen Xers and say, "Why are they breaking the rules?" And now Gen Xers are looking at Millennials and saying, "What's wrong with these kids?"

One thing in business is likely to remain constant: much motivation will come from the job itself rather than from external punishments or rewards. Managers need to give workers what they require to do a good job: the right tools, the right information, and the right amount of cooperation. Motivation doesn't have to be difficult. It begins with acknowledging a job well done—and especially doing so in front of others. After all, as we said earlier, the best motivator is frequently a sincere "Thanks, I really appreciate what you're doing."

progress assessment

- What are several steps firms can take to increase internal communications and thus motivation?
- What problems may emerge when firms try to implement participative management?
- Why is it important to adjust motivational styles to individual employees? Are there any general principles of motivation that today's managers should follow?

summary

Learning Goal 1. Explain Taylor's theory of scientific management.

- **What is Frederick Taylor known for?**

Human efficiency engineer Frederick Taylor was one of the first people to study management and has been called the father of scientific management. He conducted time-motion studies to learn the most efficient way of doing a job and then trained workers in those procedures. He published his book *The Principles of Scientific Management* in 1911. Henry L. Gantt and Frank and Lillian Gilbreth were followers of Taylor.

Learning Goal 2. Describe the Hawthorne studies and their significance to management.

- **What led to the more human-based managerial styles?**

The greatest impact on motivation theory was generated by the Hawthorne studies in the late 1920s and early 1930s. In these studies, Elton Mayo found that human factors such as feelings of involvement and participation led to greater productivity gains than did physical changes in the workplace.

Learning Goal 3. Identify the levels of Maslow's hierarchy of needs and apply them to employee motivation.

- **What did Abraham Maslow find human motivation to be based on?**

Maslow studied basic human motivation and found that motivation was based on needs. He said that a person with an unfilled need would be motivated to satisfy it and that a satisfied need no longer served as motivation.

- **What levels of need did Maslow identify?**

Starting at the bottom of Maslow's hierarchy and going to the top, the levels of need are physiological, safety, social, esteem, and self-actualization.

- **Can managers use Maslow's theory?**

Yes, they can recognize what unmet needs a person has and design work so that it satisfies those needs.

Learning Goal 4. Distinguish between the motivators and hygiene factors identified by Herzberg.

- **What is the difference between Frederick Herzberg's motivator and hygiene factors?**

Herzberg found that while some factors motivate workers (motivators), others cause job dissatisfaction if missing but are not motivators if present (hygiene or maintenance factors).

- **What are the factors called motivators?**

The work itself, achievement, recognition, responsibility, growth, and advancement.

- **What are the hygiene (maintenance) factors?**

Company policies, supervision, working conditions, interpersonal relationships, and salary.

Learning Goal 5. Differentiate among Theory X, Theory Y, and Theory Z.

- **Who developed Theory X and Theory Y?**

Douglas McGregor held that managers have one of two opposing attitudes toward employees. He called them Theory X and Theory Y.

- **What is Theory X?**

Theory X assumes the average person dislikes work and will avoid it if possible. Therefore, people must be forced, controlled, and threatened with punishment to accomplish organizational goals.

- **What is Theory Y?**

Theory Y assumes people like working and will accept responsibility for achieving goals if rewarded for doing so.

- **What is Theory Z?**

William Ouchi based Theory Z on Japanese management styles and stresses long-term employment; collective decision making; individual responsibility; slow evaluation and promotion; implicit, informal control with explicit, formalized control; moderately specialized career paths; and a holistic concern for employees (including family).

Learning Goal 6. Explain the key principles of goal-setting, expectancy, reinforcement, and equity theories.

- **What is goal-setting theory?**

Goal-setting theory is based on the notion that setting ambitious but attainable goals will lead to high levels of motivation and performance if the goals are accepted and accompanied by feedback, and if conditions in the organization make achievement possible.

- **What is management by objectives (MBO)?**

MBO is a system of goal setting and implementation; it includes a cycle of discussion, review, and evaluation of objectives among top and middle-level managers, supervisors, and employees.

- **What is the basis of expectancy theory?**

According to Victor Vroom's expectancy theory, employee expectations can affect an individual's motivation.

- **What are the key elements of expectancy theory?**

Expectancy theory centers on three questions employees often ask about performance on the job: (1) Can I accomplish the task? (2) If I do accomplish it, what's my reward? and (3) Is the reward worth the effort?

- **What are the variables in reinforcement theory?**

Positive reinforcers are rewards like praise, recognition, or raises that a worker might strive to receive after performing well. Negative reinforcers are punishments such as reprimands, pay cuts, or firing that a worker might be expected to try to avoid.

- **According to equity theory, employees try to maintain equity between inputs and outputs compared to other employees in similar positions. What happens when employees perceive that their rewards are not equitable?**

If employees perceive they are under-rewarded, they will either reduce their effort or rationalize that it isn't important. If they perceive that they are over-rewarded, they will either increase their effort to justify the higher reward in the future or rationalize by saying, "I'm worth it!" Inequity leads to lower productivity, reduced quality, increased absenteeism, and voluntary resignation.

Learning Goal 7. Show how managers put motivation theories into action through such strategies as job enrichment, open communication, and job recognition.

- **What characteristics of work affect motivation and performance?**

The job characteristics that influence motivation are skill variety, task identity, task significance, autonomy, and feedback.

- **Name two forms of job enrichment that increase motivation.**

Job enlargement combines a series of tasks into one challenging and interesting assignment. Job rotation makes work more interesting by moving employees from one job to another.

- **How does open communication improve employee motivation?**

Open communication helps both top managers and employees understand the objectives and work together to achieve them.

- **How can managers encourage open communication?**

Managers can create an organizational culture that rewards listening, train supervisors and managers to listen, use effective questioning techniques, remove barriers to open communication, avoid vague and ambiguous communication, and actively make it easier for all to communicate.

Learning Goal 8. Show how managers personalize motivation strategies to appeal to employees across the globe and across generations.

- **What is the difference between high-context and low-context cultures?**

In high-context cultures, people build personal relationships and develop group trust before focusing on tasks. In low-context cultures, people often view relationship building as a waste of time that diverts attention from the task.

- **How are Generation X managers likely to be different from their baby boomer predecessors?**

Baby boomers tend to be willing to work long hours to build their careers and often expect their subordinates to do likewise. Gen Xers may strive for a more balanced lifestyle and are likely to focus on results rather than on how many hours their teams work. Gen Xers tend to be better than previous generations at working in teams and providing frequent feedback. They are not bound by traditions that may constrain those who have been with an organization for a long time and are willing to try new approaches to solving problems.

- **What are some common characteristics of Millennials?**

Millennials tend to be adaptable, tech-savvy, able to grasp new concepts, practiced at multitasking, efficient, and tolerant. They often place a higher value on work-life balance, expect their employers to adapt to them, and are more likely to rank fun and stimulation in their top five ideal-job requirements.

key terms

equity theory 290	job enlargement 292	motivators 283
expectancy theory 289	job enrichment 291	principle of motion economy 280
extrinsic reward 279	job rotation 292	reinforcement theory 290
goal-setting theory 288	management by objectives (MBO) 288	scientific management 279
Hawthorne effect 281		
hygiene factors 284	Maslow's hierarchy of needs 282	time-motion studies 280
intrinsic reward 279		

critical thinking

Your job right now is to finish reading this chapter. How strongly would you be motivated to do that if you were sweating in a room at 105 degrees Fahrenheit? Imagine your roommate has turned on the air-conditioning. Once you are more comfortable, are you more likely to read? Look at Maslow's hierarchy of needs to see what need would be motivating you at both times. Can you see how helpful Maslow's theory is in understanding motivation by applying it to your own life?

developing workplace skills

1. Talk with several of your friends about the subject of motivation. What motivates them to work hard or not work hard in school and on the job? How important to them is self-motivation as opposed to external reward?

2. Look over Maslow's hierarchy of needs and try to determine where you are right now on the hierarchy. What needs of yours are not being met? How could a company go about meeting those needs and thus motivate you to work more effectively?

3. One recent managerial idea is to let employees work in self-managed teams. There is no reason why such teams could not be formed in colleges as well as businesses. Discuss the benefits and drawbacks of dividing your class into self-managed teams for the purpose of studying, doing cases, and so forth.

4. Think of all the groups with which you have been associated over the years—sports groups, friendship groups, and so on—and try to recall how the leaders of those groups motivated the group to action. Did the leaders assume a Theory X or a Theory Y attitude? How often was money a motivator? What other motivational tools were used and to what effect?

5. Herzberg concluded that pay was not a motivator. If you were paid to get better grades, would you be motivated to study harder? In your employment experiences, have you ever worked harder to obtain a raise or as a result of receiving a large raise? Do you agree with Herzberg about the effects of pay?

taking it to the net

Purpose

To assess your personality type using the Jung-Myers-Briggs typology test and to evaluate how well the description of your personality type fits you.

Exercise

Sometimes understanding differences in employees' personalities helps managers understand how to motivate them. Find out about your personality by going to the Human Metrics website **(www.humanmetrics.com)** and take the Jung Typology Test (based on Carl Jung's and Isabel Myers-Briggs's approaches to typology). (Disclaimer: The test, like all other personality tests, is only a rough and preliminary indicator of personality.)

1. After you identify your personality type, read the corresponding personality portrait. How well or how poorly does the identified personality type fit?

2. Sometimes a personality test does not accurately identify your personality, but it may give you a place to start looking for a portrait that fits. After you have read the portraits on the website, ask a good friend or relative which one best describes you.

casing the web

To access the case "Making Teams Work in a Changing Market," visit **www.mhhe.com/P2P2e**

video case

Management Philosophy at The Container Store

In 1978, The Container Store opened in a 1600-square-foot facility in Dallas, Texas. The store was designed to provide containers to help people organize their lives both at home and work. The Container Store's vibrant brand consists of 10,000 products with 50 stores across the country and $650 million in annual sales. For 12 consecutive years, The Container Store has been rated by *Fortune* magazine as one of the top 100 companies to work for.

A motivational environment that puts employees first, customers second, and shareholders third, has helped the company achieve profitability and success. The Container Store management philosophy is: If employees are happy and taken care of, they will treat the customers in the same fashion. The

secret to success, according to company CEO Kip Tindell, is outstanding customer service. The Container Store achieves this core principle through employee teamwork. The management structure is transparent and flat, not hierarchical like many firms. Additionally, the company provides significantly more employee training than the industry norm. The company emphasizes its seven core principles with the focus on building relationships with its customers. According to Tindell, The Container Store cannot compete with Walmart on volume, but it beats them in relationship building.

Employees are dedicated, motivated, and happy at work. In fact, The Container Store emphasizes the importance of employees having fun at work.

According to employees, there are not only strong relationships and support among employees in each store, but also strong and open communication channels throughout the organization.

Continuous improvement and shared responsibility are essential elements in building relationships with employees. Employees perform a wide range of tasks in each store. The video briefly examines each of the major motivational theories beginning with scientific management and Frederick Taylor. Elton Mayo's famous Hawthorne studies in 1937 are also discussed, along with Maslow's hierarchy of needs, Herzberg's motivator factors, McGregor's Theory X and Theory Y, and Ouchi's Theory Z. With each perspective, The Container Store approach illustrates key features of each of the motivational theories, emphasizing that happy employees result in employees providing outstanding customer service.

Thinking It Over

1. *Identify two fundamental differences in the motivational theories of Frederick Taylor's scientific management and in Elton Mayo's human relations perspective as illustrated by the Hawthorne studies.*

2. *Container Store CEO Kip Tindell suggests that employee effort is based on 25 percentage mandatory tasks and 75 percentage voluntary. What does he mean by this?*

3. *Why is relationship building a core principle at The Container Store?*

Human RESOURCE Management

FINDING AND KEEPING THE BEST EMPLOYEES

LEARNING goals

After you have read and studied this chapter, you should be able to

1 Explain the importance of human resource management, and describe current issues in managing human resources.

2 Illustrate the effects of legislation on human resource management.

3 Summarize the five steps in human resource planning.

4 Describe methods that companies use to recruit new employees, and explain some of the issues that make recruitment challenging.

5 Outline the six steps in selecting employees.

6 Illustrate employee training and development methods.

7 Trace the six steps in appraising employee performance.

8 Summarize the objectives of employee compensation programs, and evaluate pay systems and fringe benefits.

9 Demonstrate how managers use scheduling plans to adapt to workers' needs.

10 Describe how employees can move through a company: promotion, reassignment, termination, and retirement.

CONNECTING WITH

X *Kim Jordan*

CEO of New Belgium Brewing Company

Kim Jordan is one of those lucky people who gets to spend her life working with the things she loves. As co-founder and CEO of New Belgium Brewing Company, Jordan was able to combine her passions for beer and bicycling into a successful national business. The bike she rides to work every day looks quite similar to the red bicycle on the label of the company's signature brew, Fat Tire Amber Ale. Employees are awarded the same type of bike on their one-year anniversaries at the company. But it's the other gift they receive that day that's of particular interest. Besides a shiny new bicycle, employees are also awarded an ownership stake in the company.

Employee ownership has been a key part of New Belgium's business model since the beginning. Jordan and her husband Jeff Lebesch founded the company in 1991 when the couple quit their day jobs and started brewing beer in their basement full-time. Lebesch had already been homebrewing for two years, after being inspired by a bicycle trip through the beer-centric nation of Belgium in 1989. Since Lebesch had the beer under control, Jordan took every other responsibility, working as the brewery's first bottler, sales rep, distributor, marketer, and financial planner. As the Fort Collins, Colorado, company became more successful, Lebesch and Jordan realized that they couldn't keep doing everything on their own. So they hired an aspiring brewer and friend named Brian Callahan. Since he would be putting in as much work at the company as they would, the two felt the right thing to do would be to cut Callahan in on the ownership of the company. So that's exactly what they did.

And that's exactly what New Belgium's done ever since. Of course, the brewery has grown quite a bit since then. The company is now the third-largest craft brewer in the United States, and the seventh-biggest of all breweries in the country. New Belgium ships beer to 28 states and earns more than $100 million in revenue annually. It even announced plans in 2012 to open up a new $175 million brewing facility in Asheville, North Carolina, in order to start supplying the East Coast with beer.

Jordan has never forgotten her loyal staff through all that expansion. Along with the one-year anniversary bike and ownership award, employees who stay on for five years get an all-expenses-paid trip to Belgium. Staffers also get their fair share of beer. Each employee is allotted two six-packs a week plus a daily shift beer. It's no wonder that the employee retention rate at New Belgium is a staggering 92 percent. But people don't stay at the company just for the free beer, bikes, and Belgian vacations. Since most of New Belgium's staff also own part of the company, that means they get to have a say in the way the company is run. "I like collaboration," says Jordan. "I like riffing off of other people and that process where you build something that's bigger and better than you can imagine." Important company issues are brought to the attention of employees, and solutions are decided by a vote. For instance, in 1998 employees voted unanimously to convert the brewery to wind power, even though that would mean cutting into raises and benefits as well. Now the company even generates some electricity on-site through a water-treatment plant that converts methane from the brewing process into energy.

The company's free-thinking atmosphere will be essential in the years to come if it is to stay successful. In New Belgium's early days, the company was a bit of an oddity. Now there are more than 1,800 craft breweries in the United States, with more popping up every year. New Belgium also faces stiff competition from larger brewers who are pushing into the craft market as well. In order to continue thriving in this cutthroat landscape, Jordan knows that the most important thing is the beer. "We can be as groovy as we want to be," says Jordan. "But if we can't keep the doors open because our beers lack quality, it won't matter." At New Belgium, though, great beer starts with happy, fulfilled employees, and Jordan aims to keep it that way.

In this chapter, you'll learn how businesses that succeed like New Belgium recruit, manage, and make the most of their employees.

Sources: Steve Raabe, "New Belgium Plans to Build $175 Million Brewery in North Carolina," *The Denver Post,* April 5, 2012; Devin Leonard, "New Belgium and the Battle of the Microbrews," *Bloomberg Businessweek,* December 1, 2011; Jennifer Wang, "Brewing Big (With a Micro Soul)," *Entrepreneur,* October 13, 2009; and "Our Story," www.NewBelgium.com, accessed May 23, 2012.

LEARNING goal 1

Explain the importance of human resource management, and describe current issues in managing human resources.

WORKING WITH PEOPLE IS JUST THE BEGINNING

Students often say they want to go into human resource management because they want to "work with people." Human resource managers do work with people, but they are also deeply involved in planning, record keeping, and other administrative duties. To begin a career in human resource management, you need a better reason than "I want to work with people." This chapter will tell you what else human resource management is all about.

human resource management (HRM)
The process of determining human resource needs and then recruiting, selecting, developing, motivating, evaluating, compensating, and scheduling employees to achieve organizational goals.

Human resource management (HRM) is the process of determining human resource needs and then recruiting, selecting, developing, motivating, evaluating, compensating, and scheduling employees to achieve organizational goals (see Figure 11.1). For many years, human resource management was called "personnel" and involved clerical functions such as screening applications, keeping records, processing the payroll, and finding new employees when necessary. The roles and responsibilities of HRM have evolved primarily because of two key factors: (1) organizations' recognition of employees as their ultimate resource and (2) changes in the law that rewrote many traditional practices. Let's explore both.

Developing the Ultimate Resource

One reason human resource management is receiving increased attention now is that the U.S. economy has experienced a major shift—from traditional manufacturing industries to service and high-tech manufacturing industries that require highly technical job skills. This shift means that many workers must be retrained for new, more challenging jobs. They truly are the ultimate resource. People develop the ideas that eventually become products to satisfy consumers' wants and needs. Take away their creative minds, and leading firms such as Disney, Apple, Procter & Gamble, Google, and General Electric would be nothing.

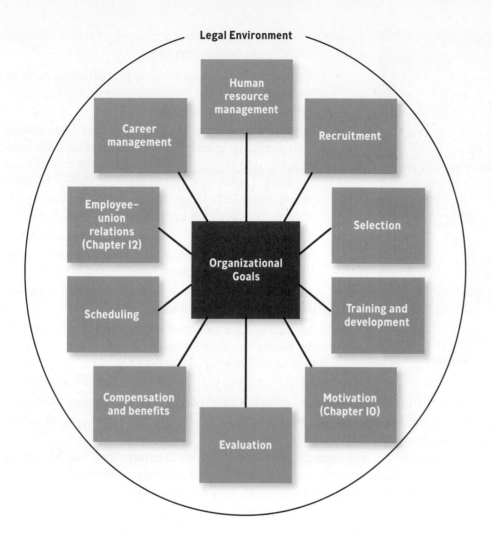

figure 11.1

HUMAN RESOURCE MANAGEMENT

As this figure shows, human resource management is more than hiring and firing personnel. All activities are designed to achieve organizational goals within the laws that affect human resource management. (Note that human resource management includes motivation, as discussed in Chapter 10, and employee-union relations, as discussed in Chapter 12.)

In the past, human resources were plentiful, so there was little need to nurture and develop them. If you needed qualified people, you simply hired them. If they didn't work out, you fired them and found others. Most firms assigned the job of recruiting, selecting, training, evaluating, compensating, motivating, and, yes, firing people to the functional departments that employed them, like accounting, manufacturing, and marketing. Today the job of human resource management has taken on an increased role in the firm since *qualified* employees are much scarcer, which makes recruiting and retaining people more important and more difficult.[1]

In the future, human resource management may become the firm's most critical function, responsible for dealing with all aspects of a business's most critical resource—people. In fact, the human resource function has become so important that it's no longer the job of just one department; it's a responsibility of *all* managers. What are some human resource challenges all managers face? We'll outline a few next.

The Human Resource Challenge

Many of the changes that have had the most dramatic impact on U.S. business are those in the labor force. The ability to compete in global markets depends on new ideas, new products, and new levels of productivity—in other words, on

U.S. firms face a shortage of workers skilled in areas like science, green technology, and the development of clean energy sources like these solar panels. What other job markets do you think will grow as companies focus more on environmentally friendly policies? Which ones appeal to you?

people with good ideas. These are some of the challenges and opportunities in human resources:[2]

- Shortages of trained workers in growth areas, such as computer technology, biotechnology, robotics, green technology, and the sciences.

- An increasing number of skilled and unskilled workers from declining industries, such as steel and automobiles, who are unemployed or underemployed and need retraining. *Underemployed workers* are those who have more skills or knowledge than their current jobs require or those with part-time jobs who want to work full-time.

- A growing percentage of new workers who are under-educated and unprepared for jobs in the contemporary business environment.

- A shortage of workers in skilled trades due to retirement of aging baby boomers.

- An increasing number of baby boomers who, due to the recession, delay retirement (preventing the promotion of younger workers) or move to lower-level jobs (increasing the supply of workers for such jobs).

- An increasing number of both single-parent and two-income families, resulting in a demand for job sharing, maternity leave, and special career advancement programs for women.

- A shift in employee attitudes toward work. Leisure time has become a much higher priority, as have flextime and a shorter workweek.

- A recession that took a toll on employee morale and increased the demand for temporary and part-time workers.

- A challenge from overseas labor pools whose members work for lower wages and are subject to fewer laws and regulations than U.S. workers. This results in many jobs being outsourced overseas.

- An increased demand for benefits tailored to the individual yet cost-effective to the company.

- Growing concerns over health care, elder care, child care, drug testing, workplace violence (all discussed in Chapter 12), and opportunities for people with disabilities.

- Changes in health care laws that have added a large number of new regulations that employers must read, interpret, implement, and track.

- A decreased sense of employee loyalty, which increases employee turnover and the cost of replacing lost workers.

Given these issues, you can see why human resource management has taken a central place in management thinking. However, significant changes in laws covering hiring, safety, unionization, equal pay, and affirmative action have also had a major influence. Let's look at their impact on human resource management.

LEARNING goal 2

Illustrate the effects of legislation on human resource management.

LAWS AFFECTING HUMAN RESOURCE MANAGEMENT

Until the 1930s, the U.S. government had little to do with human resource decisions. Since then, legislation and legal decisions have greatly affected all areas of human resource management, from hiring to training to monitoring working conditions (see Figure 11.2). These laws were passed because many businesses did not exercise fair labor practices voluntarily.

figure 11.2

GOVERNMENT LEGISLATION AFFECTING HUMAN RESOURCE MANAGEMENT

National Labor Relations Act of 1935. Established collective bargaining in labor–management relations and limited management interference in the right of employees to have a collective bargaining agent.

Fair Labor Standards Act of 1938. Established a minimum wage and overtime pay for employees working more than 40 hours a week. Amendments expanded the classes of workers covered, raised the minimum wage, redefined regular-time work, raised overtime payments, and equalized pay scales for men and women.

Manpower Development and Training Act of 1962. Provided for the training and retraining of unemployed workers.

Equal Pay Act of 1963. Specified that men and women doing equal jobs must be paid the same wage.

Civil Rights Act of 1964. For firms with 15 or more employees, outlawed discrimination in employment based on sex, race, color, religion, or national origin.

Age Discrimination in Employment Act of 1967. Outlawed employment practices that discriminate against people 40 and older. An amendment outlaws requiring retirement by a specific age.

Occupational Safety and Health Act of 1970. Regulated the degree to which employees can be exposed to hazardous substances and specified the safety equipment the employer must provide.

Equal Employment Opportunity Act of 1972. Strengthened the Equal Employment Opportunity Commission (EEOC) and authorized the EEOC to set guidelines for human resource management.

Comprehensive Employment and Training Act of 1973 (CETA). Provided funds for training unemployed workers.

Vocational Rehabilitation Act of 1973. Extended protection to people with any physical or mental disability.

Employee Retirement Income Security Act of 1974 (ERISA). Regulated and insured company retirement plans.

Immigration Reform and Control Act of 1986. Required employers to verify employment eligibility of all new hires including U.S. citizens.

Supreme Court ruling against set-aside programs (affirmative action), 1989. Declared that setting aside 30 percent of contracting jobs for minority businesses was reverse discrimination and unconstitutional.

Older Workers Benefit Protection Act, 1990. Protects older people from signing away their rights to pensions and protection from illegal age discrimination.

Civil Rights Act of 1991. For firms with over 15 employees, extends the right to a jury trial and punitive damages to victims of intentional job discrimination.

Americans with Disabilities Act of 1990 (1992 implementation). Prohibits employers from discriminating against qualified individuals with disabilities in hiring, advancement, or compensation and requires them to adapt the workplace if necessary.

Family and Medical Leave Act of 1993. Businesses with 50 or more employees must provide up to 12 weeks of unpaid leave per year upon birth or adoption of an employee's child or upon serious illness of a parent, spouse, or child.

Americans with Disabilities Amendments Act of 2008 (ADA). Provides broader protection for disabled workers and reverses Supreme Court decisions deemed too restrictive. Adds disabilities such as epilepsy and cancer to ADA coverage.

Lilly Ledbetter Fair Pay Act of 2009. Amends the Civil Rights Act of 1964 by changing the start of the 180-day statute of limitations for filing a discrimination suit from the date of the first discriminatory paycheck to the date of the most recent discriminatory paycheck.

affirmative action
Employment activities designed to "right past wrongs" by increasing opportunities for minorities and women.

reverse discrimination
Discrimination against members of a dominant or majority group (e.g., whites or males) usually as a result of policies designed to correct previous discrimination against minority or disadvantaged groups.

The Americans with Disabilities Act guarantees that all U.S. workers have equal opportunity in employment. This legislation requires businesses to make "reasonable accommodations" on the job for people with disabilities. What required accommodations do you think would be reasonable?

One of the more important pieces of social legislation passed by Congress was the Civil Rights Act of 1964. This act generated much debate and was amended 97 times before final passage. Title VII of that act brought the government directly into the operations of human resource management. Title VII prohibits discrimination in hiring, firing, compensation, apprenticeships, training, terms, conditions, or privileges of employment based on race, religion, creed, sex, or national origin. Age was later added to the conditions of the act. The Civil Rights Act of 1964 was expected to stamp out discrimination in the workplace, but specific language in it made enforcement quite difficult. Congress took on the task of amending the law.

In 1972, the Equal Employment Opportunity Act (EEOA) was added as an amendment to Title VII. It strengthened the Equal Employment Opportunity Commission (EEOC), which was created by the Civil Rights Act, by giving it rather broad powers. For example, it permitted the EEOC to issue guidelines for acceptable employer conduct in administering equal employment opportunity. The EEOC also mandated specific record-keeping procedures, and Congress vested it with the power of enforcement to ensure these mandates were carried out. The EEOC became a formidable regulatory force in the administration of human resource management.

Perhaps the most controversial policy enforced by the EEOC was **affirmative action,** designed to "right past wrongs" by increasing opportunities for minorities and women. Interpretation of the affirmative action law led employers to actively recruit, and in some cases give preference to, women and minority group members. Questions persist about the legality of affirmative action and the effect it may have in creating a sort of reverse discrimination in the workplace. **Reverse discrimination** has been defined as discriminating against members of a dominant or majority group (e.g.,whites or males) usually as a result of policies designed to correct previous discrimination against minority or disadvantaged groups. The issue has generated much heated debate as well as many lawsuits.[3]

The Civil Rights Act of 1991 expanded the remedies available to victims of discrimination by amending Title VII of the Civil Rights Act of 1964. Now victims of discrimination have the right to a jury trial and punitive damages. Human resource managers must follow court decisions closely to see how the law is enforced.[4]

The Office of Federal Contract Compliance Programs (OFCCP) ensures that employers comply with nondiscrimination and affirmative action laws and regulations when doing business with the federal government.

Laws Protecting Employees with Disabilities and Older Employees

As you read above, laws prohibit discrimination related to race, sex, or age in hiring, firing, and training. The Vocational Rehabilitation Act of 1973 extended protection to people with any physical or mental disability.

The Americans with Disabilities Act of 1990 (ADA) requires employers to give applicants with physical or mental disabilities the same consideration for employment as people without disabilities. It also requires making "reasonable accommodations" for employees with disabilities, such as modifying equipment or widening doorways. Accommodations are not always expensive; an inexpensive headset can allow someone with cerebral palsy to talk on the phone.[5] The ADA also protects individuals with disabilities from discrimination in public accommodations, transportation, and telecommunications.[6]

Most companies have no trouble making structural changes to be accommodating. Some, however, find cultural changes difficult. Employers used to think that being fair meant treating everyone the same, but *accommodation* in fact means treating people *according to their specific needs.* That can include putting up barriers to isolate people readily distracted by noise, reassigning workers to new tasks, and making changes in supervisors' management styles.

In 2008, Congress passed the Americans with Disabilities Amendments Act, which overturned Supreme Court decisions that had reduced protections for certain people with disabilities such as diabetes, epilepsy, heart disease, autism, major depression, and cancer.[7] In 2011, the EEOC issued new regulations that widened the range of disabilities covered by the ADA and shifted the burden of proof of disability in labor disputes from employees to business owners.[8] Enforcement promises to be a continuing issue for human resource management. [9]

The Age Discrimination in Employment Act of 1967 (ADEA) protects individuals 40 or older from employment and workplace discrimination in hiring, firing, promotion, layoff, compensation, benefits, job assignments, and training. The ADEA is enforced by the EEOC, applies to employers with 20 or more employees, and protects both employees and job applicants. It also outlaws mandatory retirement in most organizations. It does, however, allow age restrictions for certain job categories such as airline pilot or bus driver if evidence shows that the ability to perform significantly diminishes with age or that age imposes a danger to society.

Effects of Legislation

Clearly, laws ranging from the Social Security Act of 1935 to the 2008 Americans with Disabilities Amendments Act require human resource managers to keep abreast of laws and court decisions to effectively perform their jobs. Choosing a career in human resource management offers a challenge to anyone willing to put forth the effort. Remember:

- Employers must know and act in accordance with the legal rights of their employees or risk costly court cases.
- Legislation affects all areas of human resource management, from hiring and training to compensation.
- Court cases demonstrate that it is sometimes legal to go beyond providing equal rights for minorities and women to provide special employment (affirmative action) and training to correct discrimination in the past.
- New court cases and legislation change human resource management almost daily; the only way to keep current is to read the business literature and stay familiar with emerging issues.

progress assessment

- What is human resource management?
- What did Title VII of the Civil Rights Act of 1964 achieve?
- What is the EEOC, and what was the intention of affirmative action?
- What does *accommodations* mean in the Americans with Disabilities Act of 1990?

LEARNING goal 3

Summarize the five steps in human resource planning.

DETERMINING A FIRM'S HUMAN RESOURCE NEEDS

job analysis
A study of what employees do who hold various job titles.

job description
A summary of the objectives of a job, the type of work to be done, the responsibilities and duties, the working conditions, and the relationship of the job to other functions.

job specifications
A written summary of the minimum qualifications required of workers to do a particular job.

All management, including human resource management, begins with planning. The five steps in the human resource planning process are:

1. *Preparing a human resource inventory of the organization's employees.* This inventory should include ages, names, education, capabilities, training, specialized skills, and other relevant information (such as languages spoken). It reveals whether the labor force is technically up-to-date and thoroughly trained.

2. *Preparing a job analysis.* A **job analysis** is a study of what employees do who hold various job titles. It's necessary in order to recruit and train employees with the necessary skills to do the job. The results of job analysis are two written statements: job descriptions and job specifications. A **job description** specifies the objectives of the job, the type of work, the responsibilities and duties, working conditions, and the job's relationship to other functions. **Job specifications** are a written summary of the minimal education and skills to do a particular job. In short, job descriptions are about the job, and job specifications are about the person who does the job. Visit the Occupational Information Network (O*NET) at www.onetcenter.org for detailed information about job analyses and job descriptions. See Figure 11.3 for a hypothetical job description and job specifications.

figure 11.3

JOB ANALYSIS

A job analysis yields two important statements: job descriptions and job specifications. Here you have a job description and job specifications for a sales representative.

JOB ANALYSIS
Observe current sales representatives doing the job. Discuss job with sales managers. Have current sales reps keep a diary of their activities.

JOB DESCRIPTION	JOB SPECIFICATIONS
Primary objective is to sell company's products to stores in Territory Z. Duties include servicing accounts and maintaining positive relationships with clients. Responsibilities include: • Introducing the new products to store managers in the area. • Helping the store managers estimate the volume to order. • Negotiating prime shelf space. • Explaining sales promotion activities to store managers. • Stocking and maintaining shelves in stores that wish such service.	Characteristics of the person qualifying for this job include: • Two years' sales experience. • Positive attitude. • Well-groomed appearance. • Good communication skills. • High school diploma and two years of college credit.

3. *Assessing future human resource demand.* Because technology changes rapidly, effective human resource managers are proactive; that is, they forecast the organization's requirements and train people ahead of time or ensure trained people are available when needed.

4. *Assessing future labor supply.* The labor force is constantly shifting: getting older, becoming more technically oriented, attracting more women. Some workers will be scarcer in the future, like computer and robotic repair workers, and others will be oversupplied, like assembly-line workers.

5. *Establishing a strategic plan.* The human resource strategic plan must address recruiting, selecting, training, developing, appraising, compensating, and scheduling the labor force. Because the first four steps lead up to this one, we'll focus on them in the rest of the chapter.

Some companies use advanced technology to perform the human resource planning process more efficiently. IBM manages its global workforce of about 100,000 employees and 100,000 subcontractors with a database that matches employee skills, experiences, schedules, and references with jobs available. If a client in Quebec, Canada, has a month-long project requiring a consultant who speaks English and French, has an advanced degree in engineering, and is experienced with Linux programming, IBM's database can find the best-suited consultant available and put him or her in touch with the client.

Need help understanding the Five Steps of Human Resource Planning? www.introbiz.tv/QR11-1

LEARNING goal 4

Describe methods that companies use to recruit new employees, and explain some of the issues that make recruitment challenging.

RECRUITING EMPLOYEES FROM A DIVERSE POPULATION

Recruitment is the set of activities for obtaining the right number of qualified people at the right time. Its purpose is to select those who best meet the needs

recruitment
The set of activities used to obtain a sufficient number of the right employees at the right time.

Human resource managers today have the opportunity to recruit people from a wide range of cultural and ethnic backgrounds. What are some of the advantages of a diverse workforce?

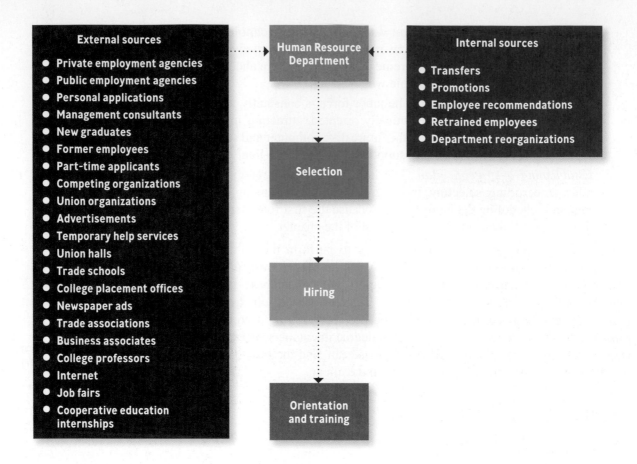

External sources

- Private employment agencies
- Public employment agencies
- Personal applications
- Management consultants
- New graduates
- Former employees
- Part-time applicants
- Competing organizations
- Union organizations
- Advertisements
- Temporary help services
- Union halls
- Trade schools
- College placement offices
- Newspaper ads
- Trade associations
- Business associates
- College professors
- Internet
- Job fairs
- Cooperative education internships

Human Resource Department

Internal sources

- Transfers
- Promotions
- Employee recommendations
- Retrained employees
- Department reorganizations

Selection

Hiring

Orientation and training

figure 11.4

EMPLOYEE SOURCES

Internal sources are often given first consideration, so it's useful to get a recommendation from a current employee of the firm for which you want to work. College placement offices are also an important source. Be sure to learn about such facilities early so that you can plan a strategy throughout your college career.

of the organization. You might think a continuous flow of new people into the workforce makes recruiting easy. On the contrary, it's become very challenging for several reasons:

- Some organizations have policies that demand promotions from within, operate under union regulations, or offer low wages, which makes recruiting and keeping employees difficult or subject to outside influence and restrictions.

- The emphasis on corporate culture, teamwork, and participative management makes it important to hire people who not only are skilled but also fit in with the culture and leadership style of the organization.[10] Wegmans Food Markets (a perennial member of *Fortune* magazine's list of best companies to work for) encourages employees to do whatever they think is necessary to make a customer happy. For example, they don't have to ask a supervisor if they need to cook a Thanksgiving turkey at the store for a customer whose oven is too small or go to a customer's home to check a food order.

- Sometimes people with the necessary skills are not available; then workers must be hired and trained internally.

Human resource managers can turn to many sources for recruiting assistance (see Figure 11.4). *Internal sources* include current employees who can be transferred or promoted or who can recommend others to hire. Using internal sources is

Attracting Big Players to Your Small Business

To survive, it's critical for small businesses to recruit and retain qualified workers. However, competing for top talent is difficult when you can't afford corporate-level benefits or expensive recruiters to hunt down the best people. Despite these hurdles, small-business management consultants say there are many ways to lure desirable workers:

- *Transform ads into promotional tools.* Ecoprint, a small print shop in Maryland, touts the benefits of working for this collegial company in its regular advertisements.

- *Post job openings on the Internet.* Running an ad on an online service like CareerBuilder.com or Monster.com for 30 days costs about one-fourth the price of a comparable ad in the *New York Times* that runs for one week.

- *Let your staff help recruit and select hires.* The more staff is engaged in the search and interview process, the better chance to find recruits with the right personality and skills.

- *Create a dynamic workplace that attracts local, energetic applicants.* Sometimes word-of-mouth is the most effective recruiting tool.

- *Test-drive an employee.* Hiring contingent workers allows you to test candidates for a few months before deciding whether to make an offer of permanent employment.

- *Hire customers.* Loyal customers sometimes make the smartest employees. Build-A-Bear Workshop often hires customers who come into its stores and exhibit a real interest in the company and its products.

- *Check community groups and local government agencies.* Don't forget to check state-run employment agencies. Many nonprofit organizations serve immigrants new to a region or people in need of a job who become excellent candidates you can train.

- *Work hard for publicity in local media.* Publicity is more believable than advertising.

- *Lure candidates with a policy of promotions and raises.* Most employees want to know they can move up. Give employees an incentive for learning the business.

- *Outsource fringe benefit management to a professional employer organization (PEO).* It's tough to build a benefits program equivalent to those offered by large companies, but PEOs may offer lower insurance rates due to economies of scale. Face it, any way you can close the gap may help attract qualified workers.

Sources: "7 Tips for Motivating Employees," *Inc.,* April 20, 2010; Leigh Buchanan, "Opening the Books and Motivating the Workers," *Inc.,* June 8, 2010; and Donna Wells, "5 Social Media Recruiting Tools for Small Business," www.mashable.com, accessed May 2012.

less expensive than recruiting from outside and helps maintain employee morale. However, it isn't always possible to find qualified workers within the company, so human resource managers also use *external sources* such as advertisements, public and private employment agencies, college placement bureaus, management consultants, Internet sites, professional organizations, referrals, and online and walk-in applications.

Recruiting qualified workers may be particularly difficult for small businesses with few staff members and less-than-competitive compensation to attract external sources. CareerBuilder.com and Monster.com have helped such firms. They attract more than 80 million visitors per month.[11] The Connecting with Small Business box offers additional ways small businesses can recruit.

LEARNING goal 5

Outline the six steps in selecting employees.

SELECTING EMPLOYEES WHO WILL BE PRODUCTIVE

Selection is the process of gathering information and deciding who should be hired, under legal guidelines, to serve the best interests of the individual and the organization. Selecting and training employees are extremely expensive processes in some firms. Just think what's involved: advertising or recruiting agency fees, interview time, medical exams, training costs, unproductive time spent learning the job, possible travel and moving expenses, and more. It can cost one and a half times the employee's annual salary to recruit, process, and train even an entry-level worker, and over six figures for a top manager.

A typical selection process has six steps:

1. *Obtaining complete application forms.* Although equal employment laws limit the kinds of questions that can appear, applications help reveal the applicant's educational background, work experience, career objectives, and other qualifications directly related to the job.

   Large retail employers like Winn-Dixie and Finish Line make the application process more efficient by using an automated program called Workforce Acquisition. An applicant sits at a computer and answers questions about job experience, time available to work, and personality. The software e-mails a report to the hiring manager recommending whether to interview the applicant and, if so, suggesting questions to ask. Mike Marchetti, executive vice president of store operations for Finish Line, says his company processed 330,000 applications, eliminating 60,000 interview hours and reducing turnover 24 percent.[12]

2. *Conducting initial and follow-up interviews.* A staff member from the human resource department often screens applicants in a first interview. If the interviewer considers the applicant a potential hire, the manager who will supervise the new employee may interview the applicant as well. It's important that managers prepare adequately for the interview to avoid selection decisions they may regret.[13] No matter how innocent the intention, missteps such as asking about pregnancy or child care could later be evidence if the applicant files discrimination charges.

3. *Giving employment tests.* Organizations often use tests to measure basic competency in specific job skills like welding or firefighting, and to help evaluate applicants' personalities and interests. The tests should always be directly related to the job. Employment tests have been legally challenged as potential means of discrimination.[14] Many companies test potential employees in assessment centers where they perform actual job tasks. Such testing can make the selection process more efficient and will generally satisfy legal requirements.

4. *Conducting background investigations.* Most organizations now investigate a candidate's work record, school record, credit history, and references more carefully than in the past to help identify those most likely to succeed. It is simply too costly to hire, train, and motivate people only to lose them and have to start the process over. Services such as LexisNexis allow prospective employers not only to conduct speedy background checks of criminal records, driving records, and credit histories but also to verify work experience and professional and educational credentials.[15]

5. *Obtaining results from physical exams.* There are obvious benefits to hiring physically and mentally healthy people. However, according to the Americans with Disabilities Act, medical tests cannot be given just to screen out individuals. In some states, physical exams can be given only after an offer of employment has been accepted. In states that allow pre-employment physical exams, they must be given to everyone applying for the same position. Pre-employment testing to detect drug or alcohol abuse has been controversial, as has screening to detect carriers of HIV, the virus that causes AIDS.

6. *Establishing trial (probationary) periods.* Often an organization will hire an employee conditionally to let the person prove his or her value on the job. After a specified probationary period (perhaps six months or a year), the firm can either permanently hire or discharge that employee on the basis of supervisors' evaluations. Although such systems make it easier to fire inefficient or problem employees, they do not eliminate the high cost of turnover.

The selection process is often long and difficult, but it is worth the effort to select new employees carefully because of the high cost of replacing them.[16] Care helps ensure that new employees meet all requirements, including communication skills, education, technical skills, experience, personality, and health.

Hiring Contingent Workers

A company with employment needs that vary—from hour to hour, day to day, week to week, or season to season—may find it cost-effective to hire contingent workers. **Contingent workers** include part-time workers (anyone who works 1 to 34 hours per week), temporary workers (workers paid by temporary employment agencies), seasonal workers, independent contractors, interns, and co-op students.

Companies may also hire contingent workers when full-timers are on some type of leave (such as maternity leave), when there is a peak demand for labor or products (like the holiday shopping season), or when quick service to customers is a priority. Companies also tend to hire more contingent workers in an uncertain economy, particularly when they are available and qualified, and when the jobs require minimal training.

Contingent workers receive few benefits; they are rarely offered health insurance, vacation time, or company pensions. They also tend to earn less than permanent workers do. On the positive side, many on temporary assignments are eventually offered full-time positions. Managers see using temporary workers as a way of weeding out poor workers and finding good hires. Although exact numbers are difficult to gather, the Bureau of Labor Statistics estimates there are approximately

selection
The process of gathering information and deciding who should be hired, under legal guidelines, to serve the best interests of the individual and the organization.

contingent workers
Employees that include part-time workers, temporary workers, seasonal workers, independent contractors, interns, and co-op students.

Seasonal businesses, such as Halloween stores and haunted houses, depend on hiring contingent (temporary) workers to help them through the limited times they are operational. What are the advantages and disadvantages of hiring contingent workers? What are the advantages and disadvantages of being a contingent worker?

5.7 million contingent workers in the United States, with the majority under age 25.[17] Experts say temps are filling openings in an increasingly broad range of jobs, from unskilled manufacturing and distribution positions to middle management. Increasing numbers of contingent workers are educated professionals such as accountants, attorneys, and engineers.

Many companies include college students in their contingent workforce plan. Working with temporary staffing agencies, companies have easier access to workers who have already been screened. Of course, temp agencies benefit college students as well. Once the agencies have assessed the workers, their information is entered into their databases. Then when students are coming back in town for vacations or whatever, they can call the agency and ask them to put their names into the system for work assignments. There is no need to spend time searching for openings or running around town for interviews. Randstad USA, a global staffing services giant with over 350 branches in the United States, welcomes college students primarily because of their computer skills and familiarity with many of the popular software programs companies use.[18]

College interns can be considered temporary workers. However, when these internships are unpaid, ethical questions could arise (see the Making Ethical Decisions box).

In an era of rapid change and economic uncertainty, some contingent workers have even found that temping can be more secure than full-time employment.

progress assessment

- What are the five steps in human resource planning?
- What factors make it difficult to recruit qualified employees?
- What are the six steps in the selection process?
- Who is considered a contingent worker, and why do companies hire such workers?

LEARNING goal 6

Illustrate employee training and development methods.

TRAINING AND DEVELOPING EMPLOYEES FOR OPTIMUM PERFORMANCE

training and development
All attempts to improve productivity by increasing an employee's ability to perform. Training focuses on short-term skills, whereas development focuses on long-term abilities.

As technology and other innovations change the workplace, companies must offer training programs that often are quite sophisticated. The term **training and development** includes all attempts to improve productivity by increasing an employee's ability to perform. A well-designed training program often leads to higher retention rates, increased productivity, and greater job satisfaction. Employers in the United States generally find that money for training is well spent. *Training* focuses on short-term skills, whereas *development* focuses on long-term abilities. Both include three steps: (1) assessing organization needs and employee skills to determine training needs; (2) designing training activities to meet identified needs;

and (3) evaluating the training's effectiveness. Some common training and development activities are employee orientation, on-the-job training, apprenticeships, off-the-job training, vestibule training, job simulation, and management training.

- **Orientation** is the activity that initiates new employees into the organization; to fellow employees; to their immediate supervisors; and to the policies, practices, and objectives of the firm. Orientation programs range from informal talks to formal activities that last a day or more and often include scheduled visits to various departments and required reading of handbooks. For example, at Zappos every new employee in the online retailer's Henderson, Nevada, headquarters must spend two weeks answering customer calls, two weeks learning in a classroom, and a week shipping boxes in the company's Kentucky fulfillment center.[19]

- **On-the-job training** lets the employee learn by doing, or by watching others for a while and then imitating them, right at the workplace. Salespeople, for example, are often trained by watching experienced salespeople perform (often called *shadowing*). Naturally, this can be either quite effective or disastrous, depending on the skills and habits of the person being observed. On-the-job training is the easiest kind of training to implement when the job is relatively simple (such as clerking in a store) or repetitive (such as collecting refuse, cleaning carpets, or mowing lawns). More demanding or intricate jobs require a more intense training effort.

orientation
The activity that introduces new employees to the organization; to fellow employees; to their immediate supervisors; and to the policies, practices, and objectives of the firm.

on-the-job training
Training at the workplace that lets the employee learn by doing or by watching others for a while and then imitating them.

321

At FedEx, time is money. That's why the company spends six times more on employee training than the average firm. Does the added expense pay off? You bet. FedEx enjoys a remarkably low 4 percent employee turnover rate. Should other companies follow FedEx's financial commitment to training? Why?

apprentice programs
Training programs during which a learner works alongside an experienced employee to master the skills and procedures of a craft.

off-the-job training
Internal or external training programs away from the workplace that develop any of a variety of skills or foster personal development.

online training
Training programs in which employees complete classes via the Internet.

vestibule training
Training done in schools where employees are taught on equipment similar to that used on the job.

Intranets and other forms of technology make cost-effective on-the-job training programs available 24 hours a day. Computer systems can monitor workers' input and give them instructions if they become confused about what to do next.

- In **apprentice programs** a learner works alongside an experienced employee to master the skills and procedures of a craft. Some apprentice programs include classroom training. Trade unions in skilled crafts, such as bricklaying and plumbing, require a new worker to serve as an apprentice for several years to ensure excellence as well as to limit entry to the union. Workers who successfully complete an apprenticeship earn the classification *journeyman*. As baby boomers retire from skilled trades such as pipefitting, welding, and carpentry, shortages of trained workers will result. Apprentice programs may be shortened to prepare people for skilled jobs in changing industries such as auto repair and aircraft maintenance that require increased knowledge of computer technology. About 450,000 apprentices are registered with the U.S. Department of Labor.[20]

- **Off-the-job training** occurs away from the workplace and consists of internal or external programs to develop any of a variety of skills or to foster personal development. Training is becoming more sophisticated as jobs become more sophisticated. Furthermore, training is expanding to include education (through the PhD) and personal development. Subjects may include time management, stress management, health and wellness, physical education, nutrition, and even art and languages.

- **Online training** demonstrates how technology is improving the efficiency of many off-the-job training programs. Most colleges and universities now offer a wide variety of online classes, sometimes called *distance learning,* including introductory business courses. Both nonprofit and profit-seeking businesses make extensive use of online training. The Red Cross offers an online tutorial called "Be Red Cross Ready" to help citizens prepare for disasters such as floods, tornadoes, or hurricanes.[21] Technology giants like EMC and large manufacturers like Timken use the online training tool GlobeSmart to teach employees how to operate in different cultures.[22] Online training's key advantage is the ability to provide a large number of employees with consistent content tailored to specific training needs at convenient times.

- **Vestibule training** (or near-the-job training) is done in classrooms with equipment similar to that used on the job so that employees learn proper methods and safety procedures before assuming a specific job assignment. Computer and robotics training is often completed in a vestibule classroom.

- **Job simulation** is the use of equipment that duplicates job conditions and tasks so that trainees can learn skills before attempting them on the job. It differs from vestibule training in that it duplicates the *exact* combination of conditions that occur on the job. This is the kind of training given to astronauts, airline pilots, army tank operators, ship captains, and others who must learn difficult procedures off the job.

NASA's KC-135 aircraft helped astronauts like these train for space missions. After the plane makes a fast and steep ascent, it suddenly free-falls for 20 to 30 seconds enabling the passengers to experience "apparent weightlessness." (For obvious reasons the plane is also known as the Vomit Comet.) Do you think simulation training is effective for jobs like this? Why or why not?

Management Development

Managers often need special training. To be good communicators, they need to learn listening skills and empathy. They also need time management, planning, and human relations skills. **Management development,** then, is the process of training and educating employees to become good managers, and then monitoring the progress of their managerial skills over time. Management development programs are widespread, especially at colleges, universities, and private management development firms. Managers may participate in role-playing exercises, solve various management cases, and attend films and lectures.[23]

Management development is increasingly being used as a tool to accomplish business objectives. General Electric's and Motorola's management teams were built with significant investment in their development. Most management training programs include several of the following:

- *On-the-job coaching.* A senior manager assists a lower-level manager by teaching needed skills and providing direction, advice, and helpful feedback. E-coaching is being developed to coach managers electronically, though it will take time and experimentation before firms figure out how to make coaches come to life online.[24]

- *Understudy positions.* Job titles such as *undersecretary* and *assistant* are part of a relatively successful way of developing managers. Selected employees work as assistants to higher-level managers and participate in planning and other managerial functions until they are ready to assume such positions themselves.

- *Job rotation.* So that they can learn about different functions of the organization, managers are often given assignments in a variety of departments. Such job rotation gives them the broad picture of the organization they need to succeed.[25]

job simulation
The use of equipment that duplicates job conditions and tasks so trainees can learn skills before attempting them on the job.

management development
The process of training and educating employees to become good managers, and then monitoring the progress of their managerial skills over time.

Informal marketing gatherings like this are sponsored by Likemind, an association of creative professionals who meet weekly in 55 cities worldwide. "We just show up over coffee and talk," said one participant in Detroit. Why do you think younger workers prefer such informal gatherings?

networking
The process of establishing and maintaining contacts with key managers in and outside the organization and using those contacts to weave strong relationships that serve as informal development systems.

mentor
An experienced employee who supervises, coaches, and guides lower-level employees by introducing them to the right people and generally being their organizational sponsor.

• *Off-the-job courses and training.* Managers periodically go to classes or seminars for a week or more to hone technical and human relations skills. Major universities like the University of Michigan, MIT, and the University of Chicago offer specialized short courses to assist managers in performing their jobs more efficiently. McDonald's Corporation has its own Hamburger University. Managers and potential franchisees attend six days of classes and complete a course of study equivalent to 36 hours of college business-school credit.[26]

Networking

Networking is the process of establishing and maintaining contacts with key managers in your own and other organizations, and using those contacts to weave strong relationships that serve as informal development systems. Of equal or greater importance may be a **mentor,** a corporate manager who supervises, coaches, and guides selected lower-level employees by introducing them to the right people and generally acting as their organizational sponsor. In most organizations informal mentoring occurs as experienced employees assist less experienced workers. However, many organizations formally assign mentors to employees considered to have strong potential.[27]

It's also important to remember that networking and mentoring go beyond the business environment. For example, college is a perfect place to begin networking. Associations you nurture with professors, with local businesspeople through internships, and especially with your classmates can provide a valuable network to turn to for the rest of your career.

Diversity in Management Development

As more women moved into management, they learned the importance of networking and of having mentors. Unfortunately, women often have more difficulty than men in networking or finding mentors, since most senior managers are male. Women, however, won a major legal victory when the U.S. Supreme Court ruled it illegal to bar women from certain clubs, long open to men only, where business activity flows and contacts are made. This decision allowed more women to enter established networking systems or, in some instances, create their own.

Similarly, African American and Hispanic managers learned the value of networking. Both groups are forming pools of capital and new opportunities helping many individuals overcome traditional barriers to success. *Black Enterprise* magazine sponsors several networking forums each year for African American professionals. The Hispanic Alliance for Career Enhancement (HACE) is committed to building career opportunities and career advancement for Hispanics. Monte Jade is an association that helps Taiwanese and Chinese assimilate in U.S. business. Sulekha is an Indian networking group that unites Indians in the United States and around the world.

Companies that take the initiative to develop female and minority managers understand three crucial principles: (1) grooming women and minorities for management positions isn't about legality, morality, or even morale but rather about bringing more talent in the door, the key to long-term profitability; (2) the best women and minorities will become harder to attract and retain, so companies that commit to development early have an edge; and (3) having more women and minorities at all levels lets businesses serve their increasingly female and minority customers better. If you don't have a diversity of people working in the back room, how are you going to satisfy the diversity of people coming in the front door?

LEARNING **goal 7**

Trace the six steps in appraising employee performance.

APPRAISING EMPLOYEE PERFORMANCE TO GET OPTIMUM RESULTS

Managers must be able to determine whether their workers are doing an effective and efficient job, with a minimum of errors and disruptions. They do so by using a **performance appraisal,** an evaluation that measures employee performance against established standards in order to make decisions about promotions, compensation, training, or termination. Performance appraisals have six steps:

performance appraisal
An evaluation that measures employee performance against established standards in order to make decisions about promotions, compensation, training, or termination.

1. *Establishing performance standards.* This step is crucial. Standards must be understandable, subject to measurement, and reasonable. Both manager and subordinate must accept them.

2. *Communicating those standards.* It's dangerous to assume that employees know what is expected of them. They must be told clearly and precisely what the standards and expectations are, and how to meet them.

3. *Evaluating performance.* If the first two steps are done correctly, performance evaluation is relatively easy. It is a matter of evaluating the employee's behavior to see whether it matches standards.

4. *Discussing results with employees.* Employees often make mistakes and fail to meet expectations at first. It takes time to learn a job and do it well. Discussing an employee's successes and areas that need improvement can provide managers an opportunity to be understanding and helpful and guide the employee to better performance. The performance appraisal can also allow employees to suggest how a task could be done better.

5. *Taking corrective action.* As part of performance appraisal, a manager can take corrective action or provide feedback to help the employee perform better. The key word is *perform.* The primary purpose of an appraisal is to improve employee performance if possible.

6. *Using the results to make decisions.* Decisions about promotions, compensation, additional training, or firing are all based on performance evaluations. An effective performance appraisal system is also a way of satisfying legal requirements about such decisions.

Managing effectively means getting results through top performance. That's what performance appraisals are for at all levels of the organization, including at the top where managers benefit from reviews by their subordinates and peers.

In the *360-degree review,* management gathers opinions from all around the employee, including those under, above, and on the same level, to get an accurate, comprehensive idea of the worker's abilities. Figure 11.5 illustrates how managers can make performance appraisals more meaningful.

figure 11.5

CONDUCTING EFFECTIVE APPRAISALS AND REVIEWS

1. **DON'T** attack the employee personally. Critically evaluate his or her work.
2. **DO** allow sufficient time, without distractions, for appraisal. (Take the phone off the hook or close the office door.)
3. **DON'T** make the employee feel uncomfortable or uneasy. *Never* conduct an appraisal where other employees are present (such as on the shop floor).
4. **DO** include the employee in the process as much as possible. (Let the employee prepare a self-improvement program.)
5. **DON'T** wait until the appraisal to address problems with the employee's work that have been developing for some time.
6. **DO** end the appraisal with positive suggestions for employee improvement.

progress assessment

- Name and describe four training techniques.
- What is the primary purpose of a performance appraisal?
- What are the six steps in a performance appraisal?

LEARNING goal 8

Summarize the objectives of employee compensation programs, and describe various pay systems and fringe benefits.

COMPENSATING EMPLOYEES: ATTRACTING AND KEEPING THE BEST

Companies don't just compete for customers; they also compete for employees. Compensation is one of the main tools companies use to attract qualified employees, and one of their largest operating costs. The long-term success of a firm—perhaps even its survival—may depend on how well it can control employee costs and optimize employee efficiency. Service organizations like hospitals and airlines struggle with high employee costs since these firms are *labor-intensive* (the primary cost of operations is the cost of labor). Manufacturing firms in the auto and steel industries have asked employees to take reductions in wages (called givebacks) to make the firms more competitive. (We discuss this in Chapter 12.) Those are just a few reasons compensation and benefit packages require special attention. In fact, some experts believe determining how best to compensate employees is today's greatest human resources challenge.[28]

A carefully managed and competitive compensation and benefit program can accomplish several objectives:

- Attracting the kinds of people the organization needs, and in sufficient numbers.
- Providing employees with the incentive to work efficiently and productively.
- Keeping valued employees from going to competitors or starting competing firms.

- Maintaining a competitive position in the marketplace by keeping costs low through high productivity from a satisfied workforce.

- Providing employees with some sense of financial security through fringe benefits such as insurance and retirement benefits.

Pay Systems

The way an organization chooses to pay its employees can have a dramatic effect on efficiency and productivity. Managers thus look for a system that compensates employees fairly.

Many companies still use the pay system known as the Hay system, devised by Edward Hay. This plan is based on job tiers, each of which has a strict pay range. The system is set up on a point basis with three key factors considered: know-how, problem solving, and accountability.

Firms like San Francisco–based Skyline Construction let workers pick their own pay system. They can earn a fixed salary or collect a lower salary with potential for a bonus. John Whitney, author of *The Trust Factor,* believes that companies should set pay at the market level or better and then award all employees the same percentage merit raise. Doing so, he says, sends the message that everyone in the company is important. Figure 11.6 outlines some of the most common pay systems. Which do you think is the fairest?

Compensating Teams

Thus far, we've talked about compensating individuals. What about teams? Since you want your teams to be more than simply a group of individuals, would you compensate them like individuals? If you can't answer that question immediately, you're not alone. Most managers believe in using teams, but fewer are sure about how to pay them. Team-based pay programs are not as effective or as fully developed as managers would hope. Measuring and rewarding individual performance on teams, while at the same time rewarding team performance, is tricky—but it can be done. Professional football players, for example, are rewarded as a team when they go to the playoffs and to the Super Bowl, but they are paid individually as well. Companies are now experimenting with and developing similar incentive systems.

Jim Fox, founder and senior partner of compensation and human resource specialist firm Fox Lawson & Associates, insists that setting up the team right in the first place is the key element to designing an appropriate team compensation plan. He believes the pay model to enhance performance will be a natural outcome of the team's development process. Jay Schuster, coauthor of a study of team pay, found that when pay is based strictly on individual performance, it erodes team cohesiveness and makes the team less likely meet its goals as a collaborative effort. Workplace studies indicate over 50 percent of team compensation plans are based on team goals. Skill-based pay and gain-sharing systems are the two most common compensation methods for teams.

Skill-based pay rewards the growth of both the individual and the team. Base pay is raised when team members learn and apply new skills. Baldrige Award winner Eastman Chemical Company rewards its teams for proficiency in technical, social, and business knowledge skills. A cross-functional compensation policy team defines the skills. The drawbacks of skill-based pay are twofold: the system is complex, and it is difficult to relate the acquisition of skills directly to profit gains.

Competitive compensation and benefit programs can have a tremendous impact on employee efficiency and productivity. Sometimes businesses reward exceptional performance by awarding bonuses. Does your instructor ever award bonuses for exceptional performance in class?

figure 11.6

PAY SYSTEMS

Some of the different pay systems are as follows:

- **Salary:** Fixed compensation computed on weekly, biweekly, or monthly pay periods (e.g., $1,600 per month or $400 per week). Salaried employees do not receive additional pay for any extra hours worked.

- **Hourly wage or daywork:** Wage based on number of hours or days worked, used for most blue-collar and clerical workers. Often employees must punch a time clock when they arrive at work and when they leave. Hourly wages vary greatly. The federal minimum wage is $7.25, and top wages go as high as $40 per hour or more for skilled craftspeople. This does not include benefits such as retirement systems, which may add 30 percent or more to the total package.

- **Piecework system:** Wage based on the number of items produced rather than by the hour or day. This type of system creates powerful incentives to work efficiently and productively.

- **Commission plans:** Pay based on some percentage of sales. Often used to compensate salespeople, commission plans resemble piecework systems.

- **Bonus plans:** Extra pay for accomplishing or surpassing certain objectives. There are two types of bonuses: monetary and cashless. Money is always a welcome bonus. Cashless rewards include written thank-you notes, appreciation notes sent to the employee's family, movie tickets, flowers, time off, gift certificates, shopping sprees, and other types of recognition.

- **Profit-sharing plans:** Annual bonuses paid to employees based on the company's profits. The amount paid to each employee is based on a predetermined percentage. Profit sharing is one of the most common forms of performance-based pay.

- **Gain-sharing plans:** Annual bonuses paid to employees based on achieving specific goals such as quality measures, customer satisfaction measures, and production targets.

- **Stock options:** Right to purchase stock in the company at a specific price over a specific period. Often this gives employees the right to buy stock cheaply despite huge increases in the price of the stock. For example, if over the course of his employment a worker received options to buy 10,000 shares of the company stock at $10 each and the price of the stock eventually grows to $100, he can use those options to buy the 10,000 shares (now worth $1 million) for $100,000.

Most *gain-sharing systems* base bonuses on improvements over previous performance. Nucor Steel, one of the largest U.S. steel producers, calculates bonuses on quality—tons of steel that go out the door with no defects. There are no limits on bonuses a team can earn; they usually average around $20,000 per employee each year.[29]

It is important to reward individual team players also. Outstanding team players—who go beyond what is required and make an outstanding individual contribution—should be separately recognized, with cash or noncash rewards. A good way to compensate for uneven team participation is to let the team decide which members get what type of individual award. After all, if you really support the team process, you need to give teams freedom to reward themselves.

Fringe Benefits

fringe benefits
Benefits such as sick-leave pay, vacation pay, pension plans, and health plans that represent additional compensation beyond base wages.

Fringe benefits include sick-leave pay, vacation pay, pension plans, and health plans that provide additional compensation to employees beyond base wages.

Benefits in recent years grew faster than wages and can't really be considered fringe anymore. In 1929, such benefits accounted for less than 2 percent of payroll; today they account for about 30 percent. Health care costs have soared, forcing employees to pay a larger share of their own health insurance bill. Since 2000, the cost to the employee for employee-only coverage has increased 86 percent; the cost of family coverage premiums has increased 80 percent.[30] Employees often request more fringe benefits instead of salary, in order to avoid higher taxes. This has resulted in increased debate and government investigation.

Fringe benefits can include recreation facilities, company cars, country club memberships, discounted massages, special home-mortgage rates, paid and unpaid sabbaticals, day care services, and executive dining rooms. Employees often want dental care, mental health care, elder care, legal counseling, eye care, and even short workweeks.[31]

Understanding that it takes many incentives to attract and retain the best employees, dozens of firms among *Fortune* magazine's "100 Best Companies to Work For" list offer so-called soft benefits. *Soft benefits* help workers maintain the balance between work and family life that is often as important to hardworking employees as the nature of the job itself.[32] These perks include on-site haircuts and shoe repair, concierge services, and free breakfasts.[33] Freeing employees from errands and chores gives them more time for family—and work. Biotechnology firm Genentech even offers doggie day care and an on-site farmer's market.[34]

At one time, most employees sought benefits that were similar. Today, however, some may seek child-care benefits while others prefer attractive pension plans. To address such growing demands, over half of all large firms offer **cafeteria-style fringe benefits,** in which employees can choose the benefits they want up to a certain dollar amount. Such plans let human resource managers equitably and cost-effectively meet employees' individual needs by allowing them choice.

As the cost of administering benefits programs has accelerated, many companies have chosen to outsource this function. Managing benefits can be especially complicated when employees are located in other countries. The Connecting Across Borders box discusses the human resource challenges faced by global businesses. To put it simply, benefits are often as important to recruiting top talent as salary and may even become more important in the future.

The workers at DreamWorks Studios who helped create the popular Shrek movies enjoy perks like free breakfast and lunch, afternoon yoga classes, free movie screenings, on-campus art classes, and monthly parties. How might fringe benefits like these affect employee performance?

cafeteria-style fringe benefits
Fringe benefits plan that allows employees to choose the benefits they want up to a certain dollar amount.

LEARNING **goal 9**

Demonstrate how managers use scheduling plans to adapt to workers' needs.

SCHEDULING EMPLOYEES TO MEET ORGANIZATIONAL AND EMPLOYEE NEEDS

Workplace trends and the increasing costs of transportation have led employees to look for scheduling flexibility. Flextime, in-home employment, and job sharing are becoming important benefits employees seek.

Coping with Cultural Challenges

Human resource management of a global workforce begins with an understanding of the customs, laws, and local business needs of every country in which the organization operates. Country-specific cultural and legal standards can affect a variety of human resource functions:

- *Compensation.* Salaries must be converted to and from foreign currencies. Often employees with international assignments receive special allowances for relocation, children's education, housing, travel, and other business-related expenses.

- *Health and pension standards.* There are different social contexts for benefits in other countries. In the Netherlands, the government provides retirement income and health care.

- *Paid time off.* Four weeks of paid vacation is the standard of many European employers. But many other countries lack the short-term and long-term absence policies offered in the United States, including sick leave, personal leave, and family and medical leave. Global companies need a standard definition of *time off.*

- *Taxation.* Different countries have varying taxation rules, and the payroll department is an important player in managing immigration information.

- *Communication.* When employees leave to work in another country, they often feel disconnected from their home country. Wise companies use their intranet and the Internet to help these faraway employees keep in direct contact.

Human resource policies at home are influenced more and more by conditions and practices in other countries and cultures. Human resource managers need to sensitize themselves and their organizations to overseas cultural and business practices.

Sources: Anne Vo and Pauline Stanton, "The Transfer of HRM Policies and Practices to a Transitional Business System," *The Journal of Human Resource Management,* April 1, 2011; and Liisa Mäkelä and Vesa Suutari, "Coping with Work-Family Conflicts in the Global Career Context," *International Business Review,* April 14, 2011.

Flextime Plans

flextime plan
Work schedule that gives employees some freedom to choose when to work, as long as they work the required number of hours or complete their assigned tasks.

A **flextime plan** gives employees some freedom to choose which hours to work, as long as they work the required number of hours or complete their assigned tasks. The most popular plans allow employees to arrive between 7:00 and 9:00 a.m. and leave between 4:00 and 6:00 p.m. Flextime plans generally incorporate core time. **Core time** is the period when all employees are expected to be at their job stations. An organization may designate core time as 9:00 to 11:00 a.m. and 2:00 to 4:00 p.m. During these hours all employees are required to be at work (see Figure 11.7). Flextime allows employees to adjust to work-life demands. Two-income families find them especially helpful. Companies that use flextime say that it boosts employee productivity and morale.[35]

Flexible hours

Core time   **Core time**

Lunch period

6:30 7:00 7:30 8:00 8:30 9:00 9:30 10:00 10:30 11:00 11:30 12:00 12:30 1:00 1:30 2:00 2:30 3:00 3:30 4:00 4:30 5:00 5:30 6:00 6:30

Sarah's starting time   **Sarah's lunch period**   **Sarah's quitting time**

Flextime is not for all organizations, however. It doesn't suit shift work like fast-food or assembly processes like manufacturing, where everyone on a given shift must be at work at the same time. Another disadvantage is that managers often have to work longer days to assist and supervise in organizations that may operate from 6:00 a.m. to 6:00 p.m. Flextime also makes communication more difficult since certain employees may not be there when others need to talk to them. Furthermore, if not carefully supervised, some employees could abuse the system, causing resentment among others.[36]

Another option that about one in four companies uses is a **compressed workweek.** An employee works the full number of hours, but in fewer than the standard number of days. For example, an employee may work four 10-hour days and then enjoy a long weekend, instead of working five 8-hour days with a traditional weekend. There are obvious advantages of compressed workweeks, but some employees get tired working such long hours, and productivity can decline. Others find the system a great benefit, however, and are enthusiastic about it. Nurses often work compressed weeks.

Home-Based Work

Nearly 10 million U.S. workers now telecommute, working at home at least several days per month. Approximately 12 percent of businesses use some home-based

figure 11.7

A FLEXTIME CHART

At this company, employees can start work anytime between 6:30 and 9:30 a.m. They take a half hour for lunch anytime between 11:00 a.m. and 1:30 p.m. and can leave between 3:00 and 6:30 p.m. Everyone works an eight-hour day. The blue arrows show a typical employee's flextime day.

core time
In a flextime plan, the period when all employees are expected to be at their job stations.

compressed workweek
Work schedule that allows an employee to work a full number of hours per week but in fewer days.

Working from home gives workers the flexibility to choose their own hours and to take time out for personal tasks. It requires self-discipline in order to stay focused on the job and not allow yourself to be distracted. Do you think you have the discipline to be a home-based worker?

work.[37] Home-based workers can choose their own hours, interrupt work for child care or other tasks, and take time out for personal reasons. Working at home isn't for everyone. It requires discipline to stay focused on the job and not be easily distracted.

Home-based work can be a cost saver for employers. For example, Bank of America introduced a program it calls My Work that saves an estimated $5,500 per enrolled employee every year (this adds up to a $100 million a year savings). Employees in the program work remotely about 60 percent of the time. When they do come into the office, they work in communal areas or plug laptops into mobile workstations on a first-come, first-served basis. Bank of America was able to terminate leases and sublease space it no longer needed.[38] Many other large companies offer "hot-desking," or sharing a desk with other employees who work at different times.

Many companies are hiring U.S. home-based call agents rather than using either more expensive in-house operators or less-qualified offshore call centers. Office Depot shifted to home-based call agents and saved 30 or 40 percent on the cost of each call by not providing workspace (or benefits) for its home-based call-center workers. Figure 11.8 outlines the benefits and challenges of home-based work to organizations, individuals, and society.

Job-Sharing Plans

Job sharing lets two or more part-time employees share one full-time job. Students and parents with small children, for instance, may work only during school hours, and older workers can work part-time before fully retiring or after retiring. Benefits of job sharing include:

job sharing
An arrangement whereby two part-time employees share one full-time job.

figure 11.8

BENEFITS AND CHALLENGES OF HOME-BASED WORK

Home-based work (also known as telecommuting) offers many benefits and challenges to organizations, individuals, and society as a whole.

	BENEFITS	CHALLENGES
To Organization	• Increases productivity due to fewer sick days, fewer absences, higher job satisfaction, and higher work performance ratings • Broadens available talent pool • Reduces costs of providing on-site office space	• Makes it more difficult to appraise job performance • Can negatively affect the social network of the workplace and can make it difficult to promote team cohesiveness • Complicates distribution of tasks (should office files, contact lists, and such be allowed to leave the office?)
To Individual	• Makes more time available for work and family by reducing or eliminating commute time • Reduces expenses of buying and maintaining office clothes • Avoids office politics • Helps balance work and family • Expands employment opportunities for disabled individuals	• Can cause feeling of isolation from social network • Can raise concerns regarding promotions and other rewards due to being out of sight, out of mind • May diminish individual's influence within company due to limited opportunity to learn the corporate culture
To Society	• Decreases traffic congestion • Discourages community crime that might otherwise occur in bedroom communities • Increases time available to build community ties	• Increases need to resolve zoning regulations forbidding business deliveries in residential neighborhoods • May reduce ability to interact with other people in a personal, intimate manner

- Employment opportunities for those who cannot or prefer not to work full-time.

- An enthusiastic and productive workforce.

- Reduced absenteeism and tardiness.

- Ability to schedule part-time workers into peak demand periods (e.g., banks on payday).

- Retention of experienced employees who might otherwise have retired.

Disadvantages include the need to hire, train, motivate, and supervise at least twice as many people and perhaps prorate some fringe benefits. But firms are finding that the advantages generally outweigh the disadvantages.

LEARNING goal 10

> Describe how employees can move through a company: promotion, reassignment, termination, and retirement.

MOVING EMPLOYEES UP, OVER, AND OUT

Employees don't always stay in the position they were hired to fill. They may excel and move up the corporate ladder or fail and move out the door. Employees can also be reassigned or retire. Of course, some choose to move themselves by going to another company.

Promoting and Reassigning Employees

Many companies find that promotion from within the company improves employee morale. It's also cost-effective in that the promoted employees are already familiar with the corporate culture and procedures and don't need to spend valuable time on basic orientation.

In the new, flatter corporate structures (see Chapter 8), there are fewer levels for employees to reach than in the past. Thus they often move *over* to a new position rather than *up*. Such lateral transfers allow employees to develop and display new skills and learn more about the company overall. Reassignment is one way of motivating experienced employees to remain in a company with few advancement opportunities.[39]

Terminating Employees

We've seen that the relentless pressure of global competition, shifts in technology, increasing customer demands for greater value, and uncertain economic conditions have human resource managers struggling to manage layoffs and firings. Even if the economy is booming, many companies are hesitant to hire or rehire workers full-time. Why is that the case? One reason is that the cost of terminating employees is prohibitively high in terms of lost training costs and possible damages and legal fees for wrongful discharge suits. That's why many companies are either using temporary employees or outsourcing certain functions.

As the economic crisis grew, managers had to terminate a growing number of employees. Do you think they will rehire full-time employees when the economy recovers? Why or why not? What alternatives do employers have?

HR on the Go

Today, technology allows people to work from wherever they want. Ninety-four percent of remote workers use a smartphone on a daily basis while another 41 percent use a tablet like an iPad. While all these gadgets ensure that people can work from anywhere, keeping in touch with the main office can be more of a challenge than you might think. Without regular face-to-face contact with the boss, some employees can start to lose track of important materials like timesheets or their retirement plans.

Luckily, there's an app for that. A program developed by ADP Mobile Solutions allows employees to check HR, payroll, and benefits information anytime and any place, on their mobile devices. They can also clock in and out, check their timesheets, and manage their 401(k). The app could prove to be indispensible for people who work on the go and can't always make it into the office for a quick checkup. Think of it as human resources without the, you know, human part.

Sources: Jason Ankeny, "ADP's New Payroll On-The-Go HR App," *Entrepreneur,* October 14, 2011; and Marie Larsen, "ADP Launches Mobile HR App," *Recruiter.com,* July 19, 2011.

At one time the prevailing employment doctrine in the United States was "employment at will." This meant managers had as much freedom to fire workers as workers had to leave voluntarily. Most states now limit the at-will doctrine to protect employees from wrongful firing. An employer can no longer fire someone for exposing the company's illegal actions or refusing to violate a law. Employees who are members of a minority or other protected group also may have protections under equal employment law. In some cases, workers fired for using illegal drugs have sued on the grounds that they have an illness (addiction) and are therefore protected by laws barring discrimination under the Americans with Disabilities Act (ADA). Well-intended legislation has in some ways restricted management's ability to terminate employees as it increased workers' rights to their jobs. See Figure 11.9 for advice about how to minimize the chance of wrongful discharge lawsuits.

Retiring Employees

Companies looking to downsize sometimes offer early retirement benefits to entice older (and more expensive) workers to retire. Such benefits can include one-time cash payments, known in some companies as *golden handshakes.* The advantage early retirement benefits have over layoffs or firing is the increased morale of surviving employees. Retiring senior workers earlier also increases promotion opportunities for younger employees.

Losing Valued Employees

In spite of a company's efforts to retain them, some talented employees will choose to pursue opportunities elsewhere. Knowing their reasons for leaving can be invaluable in preventing the loss of other good people in the future. One way to learn the reasons is to have an outside expert conduct an *exit interview.* Outsiders

Consultants offer this advice to minimize the chance of a lawsuit for wrongful discharge:

- Prepare before hiring by requiring recruits to sign a statement that retains management's freedom to terminate at will.
- Don't make unintentional promises by using such terms as *permanent employment.*
- Document reasons before firing and make sure you have an unquestionable business reason for the firing.
- Fire the worst first and be consistent in discipline.
- Buy out bad risk by offering severance pay in exchange for a signed release from any claims.
- Be sure to give employees the true reasons they are being fired. If you do not, you cannot reveal it to a recruiter asking for a reference without risking a defamation lawsuit.
- Disclose the reasons for an employee's dismissal to that person's potential new employers. For example, if you fired an employee for dangerous behavior and you withhold that information from your references, you can be sued if the employee commits a violent act at his or her next job.

figure 11.9

HOW TO AVOID WRONGFUL DISCHARGE LAWSUITS

Sources: "In Economics Old and New, Treatment of Workers Is Paramount," *The Washington Post,* February 11, 2001, p. L1; and U.S. Law, www.uslaw.com.

can provide confidentiality and anonymity that earns more honest feedback than employees are comfortable giving in face-to-face interviews with their bosses. Web-based systems can capture, track, and statistically analyze employee exit interview data to generate reports that identify trouble areas. Such programs can also coordinate exit interview data with employee satisfaction surveys to predict which departments should expect turnover to occur.

Attracting and retaining the best employees is the key to success in the competitive global business environment. Dealing with controversial issues employees have on the job is challenging and never-ending. Chapter 12 discusses such issues.

progress assessment

- Can you name and describe five alternative compensation techniques?
- What advantages do compensation plans such as profit sharing offer an organization?
- What are the benefits and challenges of flextime? Telecommuting? Job sharing?

summary

Learning Goal 1. Explain the importance of human resource management, and describe current issues in managing human resources.

- **What are current challenges and opportunities in the human resource area?**

Many current challenges and opportunities arise from changing demographics: more women, minorities, immigrants, and older workers in the workforce. Others include a shortage of trained workers and an abundance of unskilled workers, skilled workers in declining industries requiring retraining, changing employee work attitudes, and complex laws and regulations.

Learning Goal 2. Illustrate the effects of legislation on human resource management.

* **What are some of the key laws?**

See Figure 11.2 and review the text section on laws.

Learning Goal 3. Summarize the five steps in human resource planning.

* **What are the steps in human resource planning?**

The five steps are (1) preparing a human resource inventory of the organization's employees; (2) preparing a job analysis; (3) assessing future demand; (4) assessing future supply; and (5) establishing a plan for recruiting, hiring, educating, appraising, compensating, and scheduling employees.

Learning Goal 4. Describe methods that companies use to recruit new employees, and explain some of the issues that make recruitment challenging.

* **What methods do human resource managers use to recruit new employees?**

Recruiting sources are classified as either internal or external. Internal sources include those hired from within (transfers, promotions, reassignments) and employees who recommend others to hire. External recruitment sources include advertisements, public and private employment agencies, college placement bureaus, management consultants, professional organizations, referrals, walk-in applications, and the Internet.

* **Why has recruitment become more difficult?**

Legal restrictions complicate hiring and firing practices. Finding suitable employees can be more difficult if companies are considered unattractive workplaces.

Learning Goal 5. Outline the six steps in selecting employees.

* **What are the six steps in the selection process?**

The steps are (1) obtaining complete application forms, (2) conducting initial and follow-up interviews, (3) giving employment tests, (4) conducting background investigations, (5) obtaining results from physical exams, and (6) establishing a trial period of employment.

Learning Goal 6. Illustrate employee training and development methods.

* **What are some training activities?**

Training activities include employee orientation, on- and off-the-job training, apprentice programs, online training, vestibule training, and job simulation.

* **What methods help develop managerial skills?**

Management development methods include on-the-job coaching, understudy positions, job rotation, and off-the-job courses and training.

* **How does networking fit in this process?**

Networking is the process of establishing contacts with key managers within and outside the organization to get additional development assistance.

Learning Goal 7. Trace the six steps in appraising employee performance.

* **How do managers evaluate performance?**

The steps are (1) establish performance standards; (2) communicate those standards; (3) compare performance to standards; (4) discuss results; (5) take corrective action when needed; and (6) use the results for decisions about promotions, compensation, additional training, or firing.

Learning Goal 8. Summarize the objectives of employee compensation programs, and describe various pay systems and fringe benefits.

• **What are common types of compensation systems?**

They include salary systems, hourly wages, piecework, commission plans, bonus plans, profit-sharing plans, and stock options.

• **What types of compensation are appropriate for teams?**

The most common are gain-sharing and skill-based compensation programs. Managers also reward outstanding individual performance within teams.

• **What are fringe benefits?**

Fringe benefits include sick leave, vacation pay, company cars, pension plans, and health plans that provide additional compensation to employees beyond base wages. Cafeteria-style fringe benefits plans let employees choose the benefits they want, up to a certain dollar amount.

Learning Goal 9. Demonstrate how managers use scheduling plans to adapt to workers' needs.

• **What scheduling plans can adjust work to employees' need for flexibility?**

Such plans include job sharing, flextime, compressed workweeks, and working at home.

Learning Goal 10. Describe how employees can move through a company: promotion, reassignment, termination, and retirement.

• **How can employees move within a company?**

Employees can be moved up (promotion), over (reassignment), or out (termination or retirement) of a company. They can also choose to leave a company to pursue opportunities elsewhere.

key terms

affirmative action 312
apprentice programs 322
cafeteria-style fringe benefits 329
compressed workweek 331
contingent workers 319
core time 331
flextime plan 330
fringe benefits 328
human resource management (HRM) 308

job analysis 314
job description 314
job sharing 332
job simulation 323
job specifications 314
management development 323
mentor 324
networking 324
off-the-job training 322
online training 322

on-the-job training 321
orientation 321
performance appraisal 325
recruitment 315
reverse discrimination 312
selection 319
training and development 320
vestibule training 322

critical thinking

1. Does human resource management interest you as a career? What are your experiences working with human resource professionals?
2. What effects have dual-career families had on the human resource function?
3. What problems can arise when family members work together in the same firm?
4. If you were a human resource manager, how would you address the brain drain that occurs as knowledgeable workers retire?
5. Imagine you must fire an employee. What effect might the dismissal have on remaining employees? Explain how you would tell the employee and your other subordinates.

developing workplace skills

1. Look in the classified ads in your local newspaper or on the Internet and find at least two positions you might like to have when you graduate. List the qualifications specified in each of the ads and identify methods the companies might use to determine how well applicants meet them.

2. Read several current business periodicals to find information about the latest court rulings on benefits, affirmative action, and other human resource issues. Summarize your findings. Is there a trend in these decisions? If so, what is it, and what will it mean for tomorrow's college graduates?

3. Recall any on-the-job and off-the-job training sessions you've experienced. Write a brief critique of each. How would you improve them? Share your ideas with the class.

4. Consider the following occupations: doctor, computer salesperson, computer software developer, teacher, and assembly worker. Identify the method of compensation you think is appropriate for each. Explain your answer.

5. Choose one of these positions: a human resource manager notifying employees of mandatory drug testing or an employee representative protesting such testing. Write a memorandum supporting your position.

taking it to the net

Purpose

The two purposes here are to illustrate the types of questions managers typically ask during interviews and practice answering such questions in a safe environment.

Exercise

Go to Monster.com's virtual interview page at **http://resources.monster.com/ tools/quiz_section2.asp.** This page offers links to virtual interviews for jobs in a variety of fields. Select the one in the field that most interests you and then answer the sample interview questions. This interactive section gives you the opportunity to test your answers so that when you do go on an actual interview you are less likely to fumble for an answer.

casing the web

To access the case "Dual-Career Planning," visit **www.mhhe.com/P2P2e**

McGraw Hill connect® |BUSINESS

video case

Human Resource Management at SAS

When a professor and students at North Carolina State University were asked to develop statistical analysis tools for the state's agricultural industry 35 years ago, SAS was born. Over the last 35 years, SAS has experienced both revenue and profit growth each year. Today, SAS has 400 offices with operations in 50 countries and over 12,000 employees. Over 90% of the Fortune 500 companies use SAS in their operations. Recently, SAS has been rated by *Fortune* magazine as the number one company to work for.

Strong relationships among employees, management, and the company are key to developing the culture of innovation and creativity that characterizes SAS. The company's core values include both trust and respect for employees. The hiring process, employee promotions, and employee development opportunities reinforce this culture. Leadership opportunities come primarily from within the company, or as SAS puts it, leaders are grown organically in the company because they know and understand the culture. Over 90 percent of all open positions are filled by internal candidates.

Human resource management, a strategic function at SAS, is responsible for recruiting, hiring, motivating, evaluating, and rewarding employees. The video points out how the legal and regulatory environment in the United States. impacts the HR function through the Civil Rights Act, the Equal Employment Opportunity Commission, Affirmative Action, and the Americans with Disabilities Act.

SAS values diversity, especially in hiring women and minorities. In fact, 50 percent of the workforce and the management team at SAS are women. SAS has well-developed HR policies and sees this function as the keeper of the culture. SAS is also well known for retaining employees long term. The company is viewed as having a strong employment brand and offers competitive salaries and a very progressive set of benefits, including child day care, fitness facilities, dry cleaning services, and a summer camp for employees' children.

Hiring at SAS is overseen by the human resources department but involves a team of individuals in the interview process to ensure that prospective employees have both the technical skills required and are a good "fit" for the company's culture. The company has performance management in place that focuses on shared understanding between employees and managers with ongoing feedback. This approach reduces the amount of formal structure required in the organization. The company operates on a reward system based on a total award philosophy with profit sharing representing a significant portion of overall compensation.

Thinking It Over

1. *SAS provides innovative or nontraditional benefits to employees. Name a few of these benefits. Why does SAS provide these benefits to employees?*

2. *Identify the different types of pay systems that a company may provide.*

3. *HR uses a five-step process to determine its human resource needs for a company. Identify at least three of these.*

12 Dealing with Union
AND EMPLOYEE–MANAGEMENT
Issues

After you have read and studied this chapter, you should be able to

LEARNING goals

1 Trace the history of organized labor in the United States.

2 Discuss the major legislation affecting labor unions.

3 Outline the objectives of labor unions.

4 Describe the tactics used by labor and management during conflicts, and discuss the role of unions in the future.

5 Assess some of today's controversial employee–management issues, such as executive compensation, pay equity, sexual harassment, child care and elder care, drug testing, and violence in the workplace.

The relationship between management and employees is a delicate one. While both have a vested interest in seeing their business thrive, the needs and desires of each party can sometimes be wholly different. Few people understand this better than National Basketball Association Commissioner David Stern. During his nearly three-decade-long leadership of the NBA, Stern has presided over no less than four player lockouts. The most recent one delayed the start of the 2011–2012 season for months.

A native New Yorker with a law degree from Columbia University, Stern has never been the type to shy away from an argument. He first joined the NBA in 1966 as an outside legal counselor before becoming the league's General Counsel in 1978. At the beginning of the 1980s, he was promoted to the role of Executive Vice President. In these early years Stern served as a central participant in several matters that would change the shape of the NBA. He spearheaded settlements between players and coaches that would lead to the implementation of free agency, salary caps, and revenue sharing.

It's that last item that caused so much trouble for Stern and the NBA in 2011. Ever since becoming commissioner in 1984, Stern has led the league to unprecedented growth. Income from ticket sales, TV contracts, video games, and merchandise is more than 15 times larger than the era before he came on the scene. Stern has also transformed the NBA into a global phenomenon, with games televised in 215 countries and in 43 languages. Still, even with this worldwide athletic empire, in 2009 the NBA lost $380 million despite $4 billion in revenues. How could such a powerful brand post such immense losses? According to Stern, one did not need to look further than the players themselves, who get 57 percent of all revenue earned.

This wasn't the first time Stern had gone head-to-head against an angry players' union. The NBA faced similar labor issues in 1998 as a player lockout cancelled all games during October, November, December, and January of 1999. Stalled talks almost axed the rest of the season as well before a last-minute compromise finally ended the standoff. Insiders credit Stern himself with leveraging the deal as he painted the protesting players in the press as a bunch of rich, spoiled athletes.

Stern didn't have the same public relations luck this last go-round, though. The NBA lockout began as soon as the league's collective bargaining agreement with the players expired in the summer of 2011. With NBA revenues so high, some fans had trouble believing that the players were actually the problem within the league. Nevertheless, Stern demanded harsh terms for players in his first

CONNECTING WITH
David Stern
Commissioner of the NBA

proposed agreement. He wanted to reduce players' salaries by as much as 40 percent, passing $750 million to $800 million from the players' union to the league itself. Naturally, the athletes resisted the cuts, and a bitter collective bargaining debate ensued. By September the league had cancelled spring training camps and the first preseason games.

Soon enough the NBA cancelled all regular season games up until the end of November. By then, though, the owners and the players had reached a deal in which players received a pay cut of approximately $300 million. The two parties agreed to split earnings on a 49 to 51 basis, a sliding scale that depends on the league's financial performance. For instance, if a season's revenues are particularly good, players will earn 51 percent of the profits. If a season doesn't bring in a lot of money, players could get as little as 49 percent of the total take. Once the deal was officially signed on December 8, 2011, Stern announced that the 2011–2012 NBA season had been reduced to a 66-game campaign rather than the standard 82 games.

Even though Stern got the pay cuts he wanted, the lockout was not without cost. Owners and players each lost an estimated $400 million. The labor dispute also created bad blood between players and owners that will take a while to heal. Still, it didn't do much to diminish the league's popularity. Game attendance and TV ratings both went up in the abbreviated season that followed the lockout. David Stern and the rest of the NBA certainly hope it stays that way well into the future, after his planned retirement in 2014.

Professional sports, of course, is not the only industry that has problems dealing with labor–management relations, employee compensation, and other work-related issues. This chapter discusses such issues and other employee–management concerns, including executive pay, pay equity, child and elder care, drug testing, and violence in the workplace.

Sources: Sam Mamudi, "NBA Enjoys Post-Lockout Bounce," *MarketWatch*, February 22, 2012; Howard Beck, "N.B.A. Reaches Tentative Deal to Save the Season," *The New York Times*, November 26, 2011; Tommy Craggs, "David Stern vs. Roger Goodell," *The New York Times*, March 25, 2011; Amy Shipley, "NBA Players, Owners Closely Watching NFL Labor Case," *The Washington Post*, April 7, 2011; Mike Bresnahan, "David Stern Says Change Is Needed," *The Los Angeles Times*, February 19, 2011; and Steve Moore, "The Global Basketball Association," *The Wall Street Journal*, October 23, 2010.

As the number of women in the workplace began growing rapidly about 25 years ago, this company recognized that providing child care benefits would be a real advantage for companies. Today it is the largest provider of child care at worksites, operating about 700 child care centers for 400 companies including 90 companies in the Fortune 500. Name that company. (The answer is in the chapter.)

EMPLOYEE–MANAGEMENT ISSUES

union

An employee organization whose main goal is representing its members in employee–management negotiation of job-related issues.

A good starting point in discussing employee–management relations in the United States is a discussion of labor unions. A **union** is an employee organization whose main goal is representing its members in employee–management negotiations over job-related issues. Recently labor unions have been in the news more than they have been for years. The conflicts between management and various sports teams is just one issue making headlines.

Another major issue in the news has to do with public sector labor unions (those employees who work for governments, such as teachers, firefighters, police officers, etc.). With many states facing serious debt problems, state governments are trying to find ways of cutting costs, particularly labor costs. However, states with public sector unions have limited ability to cut labor costs because of prior agreements with the unions that represent public workers. The governor of Wisconsin decided to challenge public sector labor unions on the issue of collective bargaining. We shall discuss collective bargaining in depth later in the chapter. For now, it is enough to say that public sector labor unions have been in the news because of such conflicts between the governments of various states and public sector labor unions. Before we get into such issues, however, let's explore the nature of unions in general and what the issues have been over time.

The relationship between managers and employees isn't always smooth. Management's responsibility to produce a profit by maximizing productivity sometimes necessitates hard decisions, which limit managers' chances to win popularity contests with workers. Labor (the collective term for nonmanagement workers) is interested in fair and competent management, human dignity, and a reasonable share in the wealth its work generates. Like other managerial challenges, employee–management issues require open discussion, goodwill, and compromise.

Workers originally formed unions to protect themselves from intolerable work conditions and unfair treatment. They also secured some say in the operation of their jobs. As the number of private union members grew, workers gained more negotiating power with managers and more political power. For example, labor unions were largely responsible for the establishment of minimum-wage laws, overtime rules, workers' compensation, severance pay, child-labor laws, job safety regulations, and more.[1]

Union strength among private workers, however, has waned as private labor unions have lost the economic and political power they once had, and membership has declined.[2] Economists suggest that increased global competition, shifts from manufacturing to service and high-tech industries that are less heavily unionized, growth in part-time work, and changes in management philosophies are some of the reasons for private labor's decline. Others contend the decline is a result of labor's success in seeing the issues it championed become law.[3]

Many insist that private unions have seen their brightest days; others insist that the role and influence of unions—particularly in selected regions—will continue to arouse emotions and opinions that contrast considerably.[4] Let's briefly look at labor unions and then analyze some key issues affecting employee–management relations.

LEARNING goal 1

Trace the history of organized labor in the United States.

LABOR UNIONS FROM DIFFERENT PERSPECTIVES

Are labor unions necessary in the U.S. economy today? Yes, says a teacher protesting at the state capitol building in Wisconsin, as does a plumber carrying a picket sign in New York City. Both elaborate on the dangers to workers if employers continue to try to weaken or break apart unions.[5] Wisconsin's budget-strapped governor and a small manufacturer in New York would disagree, and complain about being restricted by union wage and benefit obligations in an increasingly competitive global economy.[6]

Historians generally agree that today's unions are an outgrowth of the economic transition caused by the Industrial Revolution of the 19th and early 20th centuries. Workers who once toiled in the fields, dependent on the mercies of nature for survival, found themselves relying on the continuous roll of factory presses and assembly lines for their living. Making the transition from an agricultural economy to an industrial economy was quite difficult.[7] Over time, workers in businesses learned that strength through unity (unions) could lead to improved job conditions, better wages, and job security.

Today's critics of organized labor maintain that few of the inhuman conditions once dominant in U.S. industry exist in the modern workplace. They argue that labor is an industry in itself, and protecting workers has become secondary. Some analysts maintain that the current legal system and changing management philosophies minimize the possibility that sweatshops (workplaces of the late 19th and early 20th centuries with unsatisfactory, unsafe, or oppressive labor conditions) could reappear in the United States.[8] Let's look at the history of labor unions to see how we got to where we are today.

While the technological achievement of the Industrial Revolution brought countless new products to market and reduced the need for physical labor in many industries, it also put pressure on workers to achieve higher productivity in factory jobs that called for long hours and low pay. Can you see how these conditions made it possible for labor unions to take hold by the turn of the 20th century?

The History of Organized Labor

Formal labor organizations in the United States date to the time of the American Revolution. As early as 1792, cordwainers (shoemakers) in Philadelphia met to discuss fundamental work issues of pay, hours, conditions, and job security—pretty much the same issues that dominate labor negotiations today. The cordwainers were a **craft union,** an organization of skilled specialists in a particular craft or trade, typically local or regional.[9] Most craft unions were established to achieve some short-range goal, such as curtailing the use of convict labor as an alternative to available free labor. Often, after attaining their goal, the union disbanded. This situation changed dramatically in the late 19th century with the expansion of the Industrial Revolution in the United States. The Industrial Revolution brought enormous productivity increases, gained through mass production and job specialization, that made the United States an economic world power. This growth, however, created problems for workers in terms of productivity expectations, hours of work, wages, job security, and unemployment.

Workers were faced with the reality that productivity was vital. Those who failed to produce, or who stayed home because they were ill or had family problems, lost their job. Over time, the increased emphasis on production led firms to expand the hours of work. The length of the average workweek in 1900 was 60 hours, compared to 36–40 today, but an 80-hour week was not uncommon for some industries.[10] Wages were low, and child labor was widespread.[11] Minimum-wage laws and unemployment benefits were nonexistent, which made periods of unemployment hard on families who earned subsistence wages. The nearby Connecting with Small Business box highlights the severity of these conditions and the tragedy that resulted.

The first truly national labor organization was the **Knights of Labor,** formed by Uriah Smith Stephens in 1869. The Knights offered membership to all private working people, including employers, and promoted social causes as well as labor and economic issues. By 1886, the organization claimed a membership of 700,000. The Knights' intention was to gain significant *political* power and eventually restructure the U.S. economy. The organization fell from prominence, however, after being blamed for a bomb that killed eight policemen during a labor rally at Haymarket Square in Chicago in 1886.

A rival group, the **American Federation of Labor (AFL),** was formed that same year. By 1890, the AFL, under the dynamic leadership of Samuel Gompers, stood at the forefront of the labor movement. The AFL was never one big union, but rather an organization of craft unions that championed fundamental labor issues. It intentionally limited membership to skilled workers (craftspeople), assuming they would have better bargaining power than unskilled workers in obtaining concessions from employers. As a federation, its many individual unions can become members yet keep their separate union status.

Over time, an unauthorized AFL group called the Committee of Industrial Organizations began to organize **industrial unions,** which consisted of unskilled and semiskilled workers in mass-production industries such as automobile manufacturing and mining. John L. Lewis, president of the United Mine Workers, led this committee. His objective was to organize both craftspeople and unskilled workers under one banner.

When the AFL rejected his proposal in 1935, Lewis broke away to form the **Congress of Industrial Organizations (CIO).** The CIO soon rivaled the AFL in membership, partly because of the passage of the National Labor Relations Act (also called the Wagner Act) that same year (see the next section).[12] For 20 years,

craft union
An organization of skilled specialists in a particular craft or trade.

Knights of Labor
The first national labor union; formed in 1869.

American Federation of Labor (AFL)
An organization of craft unions that championed fundamental labor issues; founded in 1886.

industrial unions
Labor organizations of unskilled and semiskilled workers in mass-production industries such as automobiles and mining.

Congress of Industrial Organizations (CIO)
Union organization of unskilled workers; broke away from the American Federation of Labor (AFL) in 1935 and rejoined it in 1955.

The Triangle Fire

On March 25, 1911, a warm spring day in New York City, hundreds of young women (the youngest 14 years old) were busy at work at the Triangle Shirtwaist Company when the unthinkable happened. A fire raced from the eighth floor to the ninth and then the tenth. As the panic-stricken women tried to race to safety they found that a crucial door was locked, trapping them within the fire. It was suggested at a later trial that the door was kept locked to prevent theft. In the blaze that lasted about 18 minutes, 146 workers were killed. Many of the workers burned to death, while others jumped to their fate holding hands with their clothes burning. The fire became the touchstone for organized labor and raised support for changes in the workplace.

Prior to the tragedy at Triangle Shirtwaist, workers had struck for higher pay, shorter hours (the average workweek was often 60 hours), and safer workplace conditions. Unfortunately public opinion was strongly against them. After the tragedy, the International Ladies' Garment Workers' Union (now called Workers United) grew in numbers and in public support. Today labor leaders say that the Triangle fire is proof of why labor unions are crucial to maintain workplace balance in the United States. At a ceremony in New York City commemorating the 100th anniversary of the fire, labor leaders encouraged workers to not let the modern labor movement die.

The 100th anniversary of the Triangle Shirtwaist fire came at a time when *public* union workers in Wisconsin, Ohio, and other states battled to retain their right to collectively bargain. In Wisconsin, 150,000 people protested the limits placed on collective bargaining rights of state employees, fearing this could spread to union busting across the nation. Several states are also considering becoming right-to-work states, a move that would limit the power of labor unions in general. It's hard to imagine that in the 1950s, unions represented 36 percent of the private sector workers in the United States. compared to just 6.9 percent today. It's uncertain if private labor will be Big Labor again, remain Little Labor, or fall to Mini Labor. What is certain, however, is that *public sector* unions are likely to be in the news for a long time to come—certainly until the debt crisis has subsided, which may be a long time coming.

Sources: Bill Singer, "The Triangle Fire: Remembered a Century Later," *Forbes*, March 9, 2011; "100 Years after Triangle Fire Killed 146 in NYC and Galvanized Labor, the Horror Resonates," *The Washington Post*, March 22, 2011; and Beth Fouhy, "NYC Marks 100th Anniversary of Deadly Factory Fire," *Bloomberg Businessweek*, March 25, 2011.

the two organizations struggled for power. It wasn't until passage of the Taft-Hartley Act in 1947 (see Figure 12.1) that they saw the benefits of a merger. In 1955, 16 million union members united to form the AFL-CIO. Today, the AFL-CIO is trying to regain influence after suffering problems in the early 2000s.

In 2005, seven member unions, including the Service Employees International Union (the AFL-CIO's largest union with 2.2 million members) left the AFL-CIO to form a coalition with six other unions called Change to Win (CtW). By 2010, three of the unions in CtW (Carpenters, UNITE, and Laborers) decided to return to the AFL-CIO.[13] The AFL-CIO today maintains affiliations with 56 national and international labor unions and has about 12.2 million members.[14]

Public Sector Union Membership

Many people today think of union workers as people who work in construction and manufacturing. In other words, they think that union people work in the private sector of the economy. Today, however, for the first time in U.S. history, 7.6 million of the 14.8 million workers in unions work in government, not the private sector.[15] What this means is taxpayers, not stockholders, are paying the cost of union workers' wages and benefits.[16] Unfortunately for the unions, the huge state and local government revenue losses caused by the economic crisis beginning in 2008 have put pressure on governments to reduce wage and benefit costs.[17] Today, at least 17 states are trying to restrict union rights and cut labor costs.[18]

LEARNING goal 2

Discuss the major legislation affecting labor unions.

LABOR LEGISLATION AND COLLECTIVE BARGAINING

Much of the growth and influence of organized labor in the United States has depended primarily on two major factors: the law and public opinion.[19] Figure 12.1 outlines five major federal laws with a significant impact on the rights and operations of labor unions. Take a few moments to read it before going on. Note that such laws govern private workers.

The Norris-LaGuardia Act paved the way for union growth in the United States. This legislation prohibited employers from using contracts that forbid union activities such as a yellow-dog contract.[20] A **yellow-dog contract** required employees to agree, as a condition of employment, not to join a union. The National Labor Relations Act (or Wagner Act) passed three years later provided labor with clear legal justification to pursue key issues that were strongly supported by Samuel Gompers and the AFL. One of these issues, **collective bargaining,** is the process whereby union and management representatives negotiate a contract for workers. Gompers believed collective bargaining was critical to workers obtaining a fairer share of the economic pie and improving work conditions on the job. The Wagner Act expanded labor's right to collectively bargain by obligating employers to meet at reasonable times and bargain in good faith with respect to wages, hours, and other terms and conditions of employment.[21]

It is collective bargaining among *public* union workers that has become the key issue today. Many public employees are not given the privilege of collective bargaining, but many employees at the state level do have such privileges. One of the issues is the fact that public employees are paid by the state (read you and me). Thus we all have an interest in how much such workers are being paid and what privileges they have won in collective bargaining. When it is perceived that public employees are winning more or better health care, more or better hours of work, and so on, some have questioned whether or not such negotiations should be allowed to continue. That was the issue in states like Wisconsin and Ohio where public and private union members joined together to fight any efforts to take away collective bargaining among public employees.

yellow-dog contract
A type of contract that required employees to agree as a condition of employment not to join a union; prohibited by the Norris-LaGuardia Act in 1932.

collective bargaining
The process whereby union and management representatives form a labor–management agreement, or contract, for workers.

figure 12.1

MAJOR LEGISLATION
AFFECTING LABOR–
MANAGEMENT RELATIONS

Norris-LaGuardia Act, 1932	Prohibited courts from issuing injunctions against nonviolent union activities; outlawed contracts forbidding union activities; outlawed the use of yellow-dog contracts by employers. (Yellow-dog contracts were contractual agreements forced on workers by employers whereby the employee agreed not to join a union as a condition of employment.)
National Labor Relations Act (Wagner Act), 1935	Gave employees the right to form or join labor organizations (or to refuse to form or join); the right to collectively bargain with employers through elected union representatives; and the right to engage in labor activities such as strikes, picketing, and boycotts. Prohibited certain unfair labor practices by the employer and the union, and established the National Labor Relations Board to oversee union election campaigns and investigate labor practices. This act gave great impetus to the union movement.
Fair Labor Standards Act, 1938	Set a minimum wage and maximum basic hours for workers in interstate commerce industries. The first minimum wage set was 25 cents an hour, except for farm and retail workers.
Labor–Management Relations Act (Taft-Hartley Act), 1947	Amended the Wagner Act; permitted states to pass laws prohibiting compulsory union membership (right-to-work laws); set up methods to deal with strikes that affect national health and safety; prohibited secondary boycotts, closed shop agreements, and featherbedding (the requiring of wage payments for work not performed) by unions. This act gave more power to management.
Labor–Management Reporting and Disclosure Act (Landrum-Griffin Act), 1959	Amended the Taft-Hartley Act and the Wagner Act; guaranteed individual rights of union members in dealing with their union, such as the right to nominate candidates for union office, vote in union elections, attend and participate in union meetings, vote on union business, and examine union records and accounts; required annual financial reports to be filed with the U.S. Department of Labor. One goal of this act was to clean up union corruption.

Union Organizing Campaigns

The Wagner Act established an administrative agency (discussed in Appendix 1), the National Labor Relations Board (NLRB), to oversee labor–management relations.[22] The NLRB consists of five members appointed by the U.S. president and is authorized to investigate and remedy unfair labor practices. It also provides workplace guidelines and legal protection to workers seeking to vote on organizing a union to represent them. **Certification** is the formal process whereby the NLRB recognizes a labor union as the authorized bargaining agent for a group of employees. Figure 12.2 describes the steps in a union organizing campaign leading to certification. After the election, both the union and company have five days to contest the results with the NLRB. Workers also have a clear process to

certification
Formal process whereby a union is recognized by the National Labor Relations Board (NLRB) as the bargaining agent for a group of employees.

figure 12.2

STEPS IN UNION-ORGANIZING AND DECERTIFICATION CAMPAIGNS

Note that the final vote in each case requires that the union receive over 50 percent of the *votes cast*. Note, too, that the election is secret.

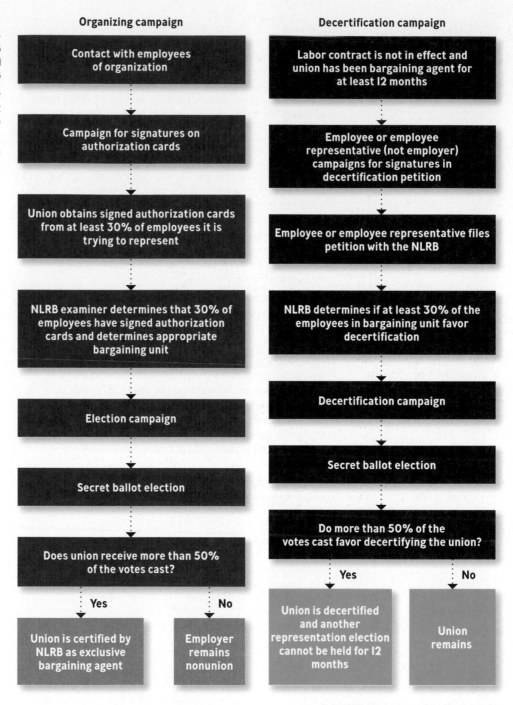

decertification
The process by which workers take away a union's right to represent them.

remove a union as its workplace representative. **Decertification,** also described in Figure 12.2, is the process by which workers can take away a union's right to represent them.

Unions have strongly urged Congress to pass the Employee Free Choice Act (EFCA), which would make it much easier for unions to organize workers. The EFCA would replace the secret ballot now used in union certification with a *card check* whereby workers could openly approve union representation simply by signing a card.[23] If a majority of workers sign the cards, the union would be certified. Unfortunately for unions, this legislation failed to receive the needed support in the U.S. Congress and seems unlikely to pass in the near future.

LEARNING goal 3

Outline the objectives of labor unions.

Objectives of Organized Labor over Time

The objectives of labor unions shift with social and economic trends. In the 1980s, job security and union recognition were the key focus. In the 1990s and into the 2000s, unions again focused on job security mainly due to the growth of global competition and outsourcing. The AFL-CIO, for example, was a major opponent of NAFTA (see Chapter 3) and other free trade agreements, fearing its members would lose jobs to low-wage workers in other nations. Labor unions have strongly opposed the increase in offshore outsourcing for the same reason.

The **negotiated labor–management agreement,** informally referred to as the labor contract, sets the tone and clarifies the terms and conditions under which management and the union will function over a specific period. Unions attempt to address their most pressing concerns in the labor contract. Negotiations cover a wide range of work topics, and it can take a long time to reach an agreement. Figure 12.3 lists topics commonly negotiated by management and labor.

Labor unions generally insist that a contract contain a **union security clause** stipulating that employees who reap union benefits either officially join or at least pay dues to the union. After passage of the Wagner Act, labor unions sought strict security in the form of the **closed shop agreement,** which specified that workers had to be members of a union before being hired for a job. To labor's dismay, the Labor–Management Relations Act (Taft-Hartley Act) outlawed this practice in 1947 (see Figure 12.4).

negotiated labor–management agreement (labor contract) Agreement that sets the tone and clarifies the terms under which management and labor agree to function over a period of time.

union security clause Provision in a negotiated labor–management agreement that stipulates that employees who benefit from a union must either officially join or at least pay dues to the union.

closed shop agreement Clause in a labor–management agreement that specified workers had to be members of a union before being hired (was outlawed by the Taft-Hartley Act in 1947).

1. Management rights
2. Union recognition
3. Union security clause
4. Strikes and lockouts
5. Union activities and responsibilities
   a. Dues checkoff
   b. Union bulletin boards
   c. Work slowdowns
6. Wages
   a. Wage structure
   b. Shift differentials
   c. Wage incentives
   d. Bonuses
   e. Piecework conditions
   f. Tiered wage structures
7. Hours of work and time-off policies
   a. Regular hours of work
   b. Holidays
   c. Vacation policies

   d. Overtime regulations
   e. Leaves of absence
   f. Break periods
   g. Flextime
   h. Mealtime allotments
8. Job rights and seniority principles
   a. Seniority regulations
   b. Transfer policies and bumping
   c. Promotions
   d. Layoffs and recall procedures
   e. Job bidding and posting
9. Discharge and discipline
   a. Suspension
   b. Conditions for discharge
10. Grievance procedures
   a. Arbitration agreement
   b. Mediation procedures
11. Employee benefits, health, and welfare

figure 12.3

ISSUES IN A NEGOTIATED LABOR–MANAGEMENT AGREEMENT

Labor and management often meet to discuss and clarify the terms that specify employees' functions within the company. The topics listed in this figure are typically discussed during these meetings.

figure 12.4

DIFFERENT FORMS OF UNION AGREEMENTS

TYPE OF AGREEMENT	DESCRIPTION
Closed shop	The Taft-Hartley Act made this form of agreement illegal. Under this type of labor agreement, employers could hire only current union members for a job.
Union shop	The majority of labor agreements are of this type. In a union shop, the employer can hire anyone, but as a condition of employment, employees hired must join the union to keep their jobs.
Agency shop	Employers may hire anyone. Employees need not join the union, but are required to pay a union fee. A small percentage of labor agreements are of this type.
Open shop	Union membership is voluntary for new and existing employees. Those who don't join the union don't have to pay union dues. Few union contracts are of this type.

union shop agreement
Clause in a labor–management agreement that says workers do not have to be members of a union to be hired, but must agree to join the union within a prescribed period.

agency shop agreement
Clause in a labor–management agreement that says employers may hire nonunion workers; employees are not required to join the union but must pay a union fee.

right-to-work laws
Legislation that gives workers the right, under an open shop agreement, to join or not join a union if it is present.

Today, unions favor the **union shop agreement,** under which workers do not have to be members of a union to be hired but must agree to join within a prescribed period (usually 30, 60, or 90 days). However, under a contingency called an **agency shop agreement,** employers may hire workers who are not required to join the union but must pay a special union fee or regular union dues. Labor leaders believe that such fees or dues are justified because the union represents all workers in collective bargaining, not just its members.

The Taft-Hartley Act recognized the legality of the union shop but granted individual states the power to outlaw such agreements through **right-to-work laws.**[24] To date, 23 states have passed such legislation (see Figure 12.5).[25] In a right-to-work state, an **open shop agreement** gives workers the option to join or not join a union if one exists. A worker who does not join cannot be forced to pay a fee or dues.[26]

Future contract negotiations will likely focus on evolving workplace issues such as child and elder care, worker retraining, two-tiered wage plans, drug testing, and other such work-related issues. Job security will remain a top union priority due to the threat of job losses from offshore outsourcing and free trade agreements. For public union employees, the major issue may be collective bargaining in general.

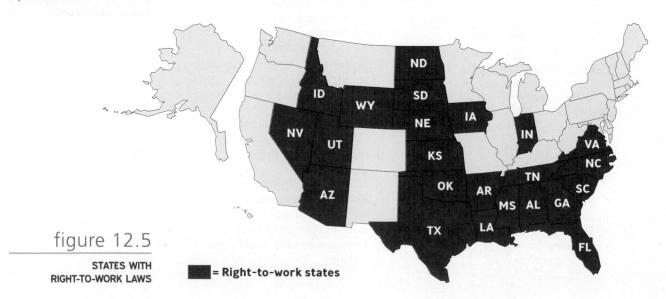

figure 12.5

STATES WITH RIGHT-TO-WORK LAWS

■ = Right-to-work states

Resolving Labor–Management Disagreements

The negotiated labor–management agreement becomes a guide to work relations between management and the union. However, it doesn't necessarily end negotiations between them because there are sometimes differences concerning interpretations of the agreement. For example, managers may interpret a certain clause in the agreement to mean they are free to select who works overtime. Union members may interpret the same clause to mean that managers must select employees for overtime on the basis of seniority. If the parties can't resolve such controversies, employees may file a grievance.

A **grievance** is a charge by employees that management is not abiding by or fulfilling the terms of the negotiated labor–management agreement as they perceive it. Overtime rules, promotions, layoffs, transfers, and job assignments are generally sources of employee grievances. Handling them demands a good deal of contact between union officials and managers. Grievances, however, do not imply that a company has broken the law or the labor agreement. In fact, the vast majority of grievances are negotiated and resolved by **shop stewards** (union officials who work permanently in an organization and represent employee interests on a daily basis) and supervisory-level managers. However, if a grievance is not settled at this level, formal grievance procedures will begin. Figure 12.6 illustrates the steps a formal grievance procedure could follow.

open shop agreement
Agreement in right-to-work states that gives workers the option to join or not join a union, if one exists in their workplace.

grievance
A charge by employees that management is not abiding by the terms of the negotiated labor–management agreement.

shop stewards
Union officials who work permanently in an organization and represent employee interests on a daily basis.

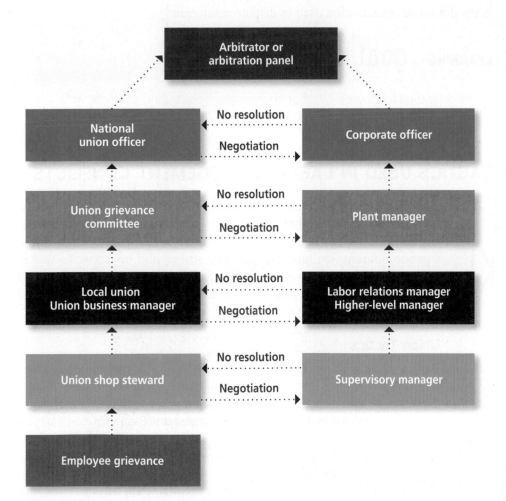

figure 12.6

THE GRIEVANCE RESOLUTION PROCESS

The grievance process may move through several steps before the issue is resolved. At each step, the issue is negotiated between union officials and managers. If no resolution comes internally, an outside arbitrator may be mutually agreed on. If so, the decision by the arbitrator is binding (legally enforceable).

Need help understanding Mediation vs. Arbitration?
www.introbiz.tv/QR12-1

bargaining zone
The range of options between the initial and final offer that each party will consider before negotiations dissolve or reach an impasse.

mediation
The use of a third party, called a mediator, who encourages both sides in a dispute to continue negotiating and often makes suggestions for resolving the dispute.

arbitration
The agreement to bring in an impartial third party (a single arbitrator or a panel of arbitrators) to render a binding decision in a labor dispute.

Writer/actor Tina Fey joined about 12,000 movie and television writers in a strike against the Alliance of Motion Picture and Television Producers in 2007, delaying the production of dozens of new TV episodes and movies.

Mediation and Arbitration

During the negotiation process, there is generally a **bargaining zone,** which is the range of options between the initial and final offers that each party will consider before negotiations dissolve or reach an impasse. If labor and management negotiators aren't able to agree on alternatives within this bargaining zone, mediation may be necessary.

Mediation is the use of a third party, called a *mediator,* who encourages both sides in a dispute to continue negotiating and often makes suggestions for resolving the matter. Keep in mind that mediators evaluate facts in the dispute and then make suggestions, not decisions. Elected officials (both current and past), attorneys, and college professors often serve as mediators in labor disputes. The National Mediation Board provides federal mediators when requested in a labor dispute.[27] In 2011, the National Football League and National Football League Players Association asked for the assistance of a federal mediator in their attempt to forge a new contract between the players and the league.[28]

A more extreme option used to resolve conflicts is **arbitration**—an agreement to bring in an impartial third party—a single arbitrator or arbitration panel—to render a binding decision in a labor dispute.[29] The arbitrator(s) must be acceptable to both labor and management. You may have heard of professional baseball players filing for arbitration to resolve a contract dispute with their teams.[30] Many negotiated labor–management agreements in the United States call for the use of arbitration to end labor disputes. The nonprofit American Arbitration Association is the dominant organization used in dispute resolution.[31]

LEARNING goal 4

Describe the tactics used by labor and management during conflicts, and discuss the role of unions in the future.

TACTICS USED IN LABOR–MANAGEMENT CONFLICTS

If labor and management cannot reach an agreement through collective bargaining, and negotiations break down, either side, or both, may use specific tactics to enhance its negotiating position and perhaps sway public opinion. Unions primarily use strikes and boycotts, as well as pickets and work slowdowns. Management may implement lockouts, injunctions, and even strikebreakers. The following sections explain each tactic briefly.

Union Tactics

A **strike** occurs when workers collectively refuse to go to work. Strikes have been the most potent union tactic. They attract public attention to a labor dispute and can cause operations in a company to slow down or totally cease. Besides refusing to work, strikers may also picket the company, walking around carrying signs and talking with the public and the media about the issues in the dispute. Unions also often use picketing as an informational tool before going on strike. The purpose is to alert the public to an issue stirring labor unrest, even though a strike has not yet been approved by the union's membership. Strikes sometimes lead to the resolution of a labor dispute; however, they also have generated violence and extended bitterness. Often after a strike is finally settled, labor and management remain openly hostile toward each other and mutual complaints of violations of the negotiated labor–management agreement continue.

The public often realizes how important a worker is when he or she goes on strike. Imagine the economic and social disaster if a town's police force or firefighters went on strike. That's why many states prohibit such public safety workers from striking, even though they can be unionized. Employees of the federal government, such as postal workers, can unionize but are also denied the right to strike. When strikes are prohibited, however, workers sometimes display their frustrations by engaging in sickouts (often called the *blue flu*). That is, they arrange as a group to be absent from work and claim illness as the reason. You may have witnessed such a sickout during the Wisconsin union dispute.

Under the Taft-Hartley Act, the U.S. president can ask for a **cooling-off period,** during which workers return to their jobs while negotiations continue, to prevent a strike in a critical industry such as airlines or railroads.[32] The cooling-off period can last up to 80 days.

Today, both labor and management seek to avoid strikes. Still, you may recall the 100-day screenwriters' strike in 2007–2008 that shut down some television shows and moved many famous faces to picket lines. As technological change, offshore outsourcing, and reductions in worker benefits such as health insurance and pensions continue, it's unlikely that strikes will disappear. Strikes in entertainment, health care, transportation, professional sports, and other industries prove the strike is not dead as a labor tactic.

Unions also attempt boycotts as a means to obtain their objectives in a labor dispute. Boycotts can be classified as primary or secondary. A **primary boycott** occurs when labor encourages both its members and the general public not to buy the products or services of a firm engaged in a labor dispute. A **secondary boycott** is an attempt by labor to convince others to stop doing business with a firm that is the subject of a primary boycott. Labor unions can legally authorize primary boycotts, but the Taft-Hartley Act prohibits using secondary boycotts. For example, a union could not initiate a secondary boycott against a retail chain because its stores carry products of a company that's the target of a primary boycott.

Management Tactics

Like labor unions, management also uses specific tactics to achieve its workplace goals. A **lockout** is an attempt by management to put pressure on union workers by temporarily closing the business. When workers don't work, they don't get paid. Though management rarely uses lockouts to achieve its objectives, the high-profile lockout of National Football League players in 2011 shows that this tactic is still used.[33] Management, however, most often uses injunctions and strikebreakers to counter labor demands it sees as excessive.

strike
A union strategy in which workers refuse to go to work; the purpose is to further workers' objectives after an impasse in collective bargaining.

cooling-off period
When workers in a critical industry return to their jobs while the union and management continue negotiations.

primary boycott
When a union encourages both its members and the general public not to buy the products of a firm involved in a labor dispute.

secondary boycott
An attempt by labor to convince others to stop doing business with a firm that is the subject of a primary boycott; prohibited by the Taft-Hartley Act.

lockout
An attempt by management to put pressure on unions by temporarily closing the business.

The 2011 conflict between NFL players and owners resulted in the owners locking the players out of team facilities for many months. How did the lockout affect the 2011–2012 season? What effect did the lockout have on fans?

Would You Cross the Line?

The recent economic slowdown has been very difficult. Your wallet has just three pictures of George Washington staring back at you, and bills for your college expenses, food, and other expenses keep going up. You read last weekend that Shop-Till-You-Drop, a local grocery chain in your town, is looking for workers to replace striking members of United Food and Commercial Workers (UFCW). The workers are striking because of a reduction in health insurance benefits and reduced payment to their pensions.

Several classmates at your college are UFCW members employed at Shop-Till-You-Drop stores, and many other students at your college are supporting the strike. The stores also employ many people from your neighborhood whose families depend on the income and benefits. Shop-Till-You-Drop argues that the company has made a fair offer to the union, but with the increasing cost of health care and other benefits, the workers' demands are excessive and could force the company into bankruptcy.

Shop-Till-You-Drop is offering replacement workers an attractive wage rate and flexible schedules to cross the picket line and work during the strike. The company has suggested the possibility of permanent employment, depending on the results of the strike. As a struggling student, you could use the job and the money for tuition and expenses. Will you cross the picket line and apply? What could be the consequences of your decision? Is your choice ethical?

---

injunction
A court order directing someone to do something or to refrain from doing something.

An **injunction** is a court order directing someone to do something or to refrain from doing something. Management has sought injunctions to order striking workers back to work, limit the number of pickets during a strike, or otherwise deal with any actions that could be detrimental to the public welfare. For a court to issue an injunction, management must show a just cause, such as the possibility of violence or destruction of private property.

Employers have had the right to replace striking workers since a 1938 Supreme Court ruling, but this tactic was used infrequently until the 1980s. The use of strikebreakers since then has been a particular source of hostility and violence in labor relations. **Strikebreakers** (called scabs by unions) are workers hired to do the jobs of striking employees until the labor dispute is resolved. The National Football League, for example, used strikebreakers to replace striking players in 1987.[34] Be sure to read the nearby Making Ethical Decisions box, which deals with this issue.

strikebreakers
Workers hired to do the jobs of striking workers until the labor dispute is resolved.

The Future of Unions and Labor–Management Relations

givebacks
Concessions made by union members to management; gains from labor negotiations are given back to management to help employers remain competitive and thereby save jobs.

Organized labor is at a crossroads. As noted earlier, only about 7 percent of workers in the private sector are unionized and more than half of all union members work in the public sector, with union membership varying considerably by state (see Figure 12.7).[35] Once-powerful unions like the United Auto Workers (UAW) have lost three-fourths of their membership since 1979.[36] This loss has occurred despite unions like the UAW granting management concessions, or **givebacks,** of

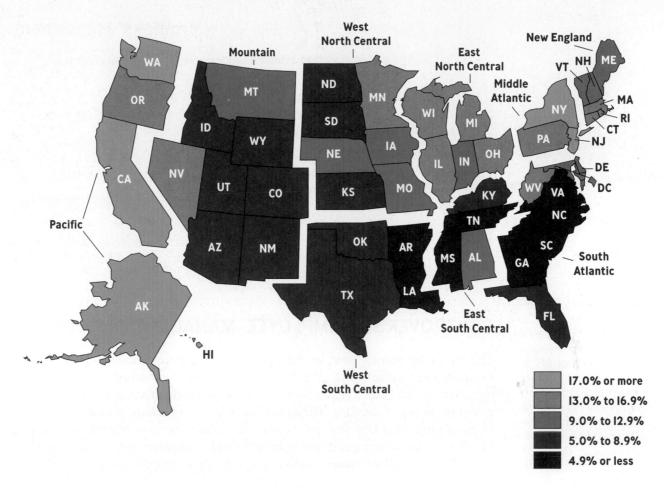

17.0% or more
13.0% to 16.9%
9.0% to 12.9%
5.0% to 8.9%
4.9% or less

figure 12.7

UNION MEMBERSHIP BY STATE

Source: Bureau of Labor Statistics, www.bls.gov, accessed November 2011.

previous gains in attempts to save jobs.[37] Both public and private sector union members now face challenges as they try to maintain remaining wage and fringe benefit gains achieved in past negotiations. Perhaps what's even more concerning to labor unions is that union membership is highest among workers 55–64 years old and lowest among workers 18–25 years old.[38]

Unions in the future will undoubtedly be quite different from those in the past. Today the largest union in the United States is the Service Employees International Union (SEIU) with 2.2 million members. Notice the emphasis is on services. To grow, unions will have to include more white-collar, female, and foreign-born workers than they have traditionally included. The traditional manufacturing base that unions depended on for growth needs to give way to organizing efforts in industries like health care (over 12 million workers) and information technology (over 3 million workers).[39] Unions will also need to take on a new role in assisting management in training workers, redesigning jobs, and assimilating the changing workforce to the job requirements of the new service and knowledge-work economy. How organized labor and management handle these challenges may well define the future for labor unions. After the Progress Assessment, we will look at other issues facing employees and managers in the 21st century.

- What are the major laws that affected union growth, and what does each one cover?
- How do changes in the economy affect the objectives of unions?
- What are the major tactics used by unions and by management to assert their power in contract negotiations?
- What types of workers do unions need to organize in the future?

LEARNING goal 5

Assess some of today's controversial employee–management issues, such as executive compensation, pay equity, sexual harassment, child care and elder care, drug testing, and violence in the workplace.

Disney's CEO Robert Iger enjoyed a salary plus bonus of $17.5 million in 2012. He also received additional stock awards making his total compensation for the year a hefty $40 million. Corporate boards of directors determine executive compensation. Do you think this is a fair system of compensation for CEOs? Do you think workers should have input?

CONTROVERSIAL EMPLOYEE–MANAGEMENT ISSUES

This is an interesting time in the history of employee–management relations. Organizations are active in global expansion, offshore outsourcing, and technology change. The United States economy is on the road to recovery from the worst recession in many decades. The government has been taking a more active role in mandating what benefits and assurances businesses must provide to workers. Employees are raising questions of fairness and workplace security. Let's look at several key workplace issues, starting with executive compensation.

Executive Compensation

LeBron James dribbles his way to $48 million a year, Johnny Depp acts his way to $75 million a year, Beyoncé Knowles sings her way to $35 million a year, and Oprah Winfrey still talks her way to over $290 million a year.[40] Is it out of line, then, for Lawrence Ellison, CEO of Oracle, to make $67 million a year?[41] Chapter 2 explained that the U.S. free-market system is built on incentives that allow top executives to make such large amounts—or more. Today, however, the government, boards of directors, stockholders, unions, and employees are challenging this principle and arguing that executive compensation has gotten out of line. In fact, the average total CEO compensation (salary, bonuses, and incentives) at a major company was $9.2 million, compared to just over $40,000 for the average worker.[42]

In theory, CEO compensation and bonuses were determined by the firm's profitability or an increase in its stock price. The logic of this assumption was that as the fortunes of a company and its stockholders grew, so would the rewards of the CEO. Today, however, executives generally receive stock options (the ability to buy company stock at a set price at a later date) and restricted stock (stock issued directly to the CEO that can't be sold usually for three or four years) as part of their compensation.[43] Stock options account for over 50 percent of a CEO's compensation, and restricted stock makes up almost 25 percent. The decline in the stock prices during the financial

Executive Compensation around the World

Huge salaries awarded to executives have been controversial since well before the Great Recession reared its ugly head in 2008. But the credit crisis really put many executive pay packages into perspective. Even as the economy crumbled around them, the leaders of some of the country's largest financial institutions walked away with millions of dollars in bonuses and stock options. In 2011, the CEOs of the nation's 500 biggest companies enjoyed a pay raise of 16 percent, averaging $10.5 million each and amounting to a total of $5.2 billion.

However, just because this is how U.S. companies compensate their people at the top doesn't mean it's the same around the world. For instance, Jiang Jianqing is chairman of the Industrial and Commercial Bank of China, the largest bank on the planet. In 2008, he earned just a bit more than $234,000. In Japan, a 2010 initiative required all companies that pay their executives more than $1.1 million annually to disclose their salaries to the government. Surprisingly, fewer than 300 people working at Japan's 3,813 public companies earned enough to disclose their incomes. The study found that executive pay averages approximately $580,000 in Japan, compared to $3.5 million in the United States.

So what explains this global gulf in executive compensation? Ultimately, it's a matter of culture. In China many companies are owned by the state. In order to keep costs low, the government often imposes salary caps on all their workers, including executives. For Japanese businessmen, the country's traditional values make extravagant wealth appear improper and unseemly. People are expected to work hard and earn a good living, but owning a limitless fortune is considered socially unacceptable. The story's different for countries with cultures similar to the United States. In 2010, CEO pay in Canada jumped 27 percent as executives collected an average of $8.38 million. In the end, in order for executive compensation practices to change, the United States. needs to undergo a significant cultural change as well.

Sources: Scott DeCarlo, "America's Highest Paid CEOs," *Forbes,* April 4, 2012; Jason Clenfield, "In Japan, Underpaid—and Loving It," *Bloomberg Businessweek,* July 1, 2010; and Rachel Mendleson, "CEO Compensation in Canada Jumped 27 Percent in 2010, CCPA Says," *The Huffington Post,* January 2, 2012.

crisis in 2008–2009 allowed executives to obtain stock options at very low prices. The market's recovery in 2010–2011 made the options very lucrative, causing executive pay to skyrocket 27 percent in 2010 compared to 2.1 percent for average workers.[44]

What's even more frustrating to those who question how much executives are paid, is that CEOs are often rewarded richly even if their company does not meet expectations, or they leave under pressure. Regulators approved a combined $17 million to the CEOs of taxpayer-backed mortgage giants Fannie Mae and Freddie Mac even though the companies required $153 billion in taxpayer subsidies to keep operating.[45] Mark Hurd walked away with a $40 million severance package after he resigned as CEO at Hewlett-Packard following a sexual harassment violation.[46] Many CEOs are also awarded fat retainers, consulting contracts, and lavish perks when they retire.

Management consultant Peter Drucker (1909–2005) long criticized executive pay levels. He suggested CEOs should not earn more than 20 times the salary of the company's lowest-paid employee.[47] Not many companies have placed such limits on executive compensation. Today the average CEO makes over 400 times what the lowest-paid employee earns.[48] Some numbers can be staggering. For example, a custodian earning just over minimum wage at Liberty Media would have to work approximately 4,400 years to make what CEO Gregory Maffei earned in 2010 ($87 million).[49]

As global competition intensifies, executive paychecks in Europe have increased, but European CEOs typically earn less than 50 percent what U.S. CEOs make. In some European countries, such as Germany, by law workers have a say in company management and are entitled to seats on the board of directors of major firms. Since boards set executive pay, this could be a reason why pay imbalances are less in Germany. This process, called *co-determination,* calls for cooperation between management and workers in decision making. In Japan, few Japanese CEOs take home super-sized paychecks like in the United States.[50] See the Connecting Across Borders box for further discussion about how CEO compensation in the United States compares to other countries.

Today, government and shareholder pressure for full disclosure of executive compensation is putting U.S. boards of directors on notice that they are not there simply to enrich CEOs. The recent financial crisis strengthened shareholders' desire to overhaul executive compensation. The passage of the Dodd-Frank Wall Street Reform and Consumer Protection Act was intended to give shareholders more say in compensation decisions.

Still, it's important to remember that most U.S. executives are responsible for multibillion-dollar corporations, work 70-plus hours a week, and often travel excessively. Many have turned potential problems at companies into successes and reaped huge benefits for employees and stockholders as well as themselves. Furthermore, there are few seasoned, skilled professionals who can manage large companies, especially troubled companies looking for the right CEO to accomplish a turnaround. There's no easy answer to the question of what is fair compensation for executives, but it's a safe bet the controversy will not go away.

Pay Equity

The Equal Pay Act of 1963 requires companies to give equal pay to men and women who do the same job. For example, it's illegal to pay a female nurse less than a male nurse unless factors such as seniority, merit pay, or performance incentives are involved.[51] But *pay equity* goes beyond the concept of equal pay for equal work; it says people in jobs that require similar levels of education, training, or skills should receive equal pay. Pay equity compares the value of a job like a hair stylist or librarian (traditionally women's jobs) with jobs like a plumber or truck driver (traditionally men's jobs). Such a comparison shows that "women's" jobs tend to pay less—sometimes much less. This disparity caused a brief reconsideration of a 1980s concept called *comparable worth* that suggested people in jobs requiring similar levels of education, training, or skills should receive equal pay. Evidence did not support that comparable worth would lead to better market equilibrium, only more chaos and inequity.

In the United States today, women earn 81 percent of what men earn, although the disparity varies by profession, job experience and tenure, and level of education.[52] In the past, the primary explanation for this disparity was that women worked only 50 to 60 percent of their available years once they left school, whereas men normally worked all those years. This explanation doesn't have much substance today because fewer women leave the workforce for an extended time. Other explanations suggest many women devote more time to their families than men do and thus accept lower-paying jobs with more flexible hours.

Today women are competing financially with men in fields such as health care, biotechnology, information technology, and other knowledge-based jobs. Younger women seem to be faring better than older women financially. Recent

Women have made important strides in business, politics, and sports. They still, however, are behind when it comes to getting paid. Today women earn only 81 percent of what men earn. Such disparities cause many to support the case for comparable worth and a more equitable workplace. What's your opinion concerning this issue?

WE NEED TO GET AN EQUAL PAY EXPERT IN...

LET'S GET A GIRL—IT'LL BE CHEAPER!

JOHN BYRNE

reports suggest that young urban women actually earn 8 percent more than their male counterparts due to their higher college graduation rates. Today women earn almost 60 percent of the bachelor's and master's degrees awarded.[53] With more women earning business degrees, the number of women in management and high-paying finance jobs has also increased considerably over the past 10 years.[54] Still, Heather Boushey, a senior economist at the Center for American Progress, believes that the government puts too much faith in the idea that education will automatically close the pay gap. She and other critics claim that women, especially women with children, still earn less, are less likely to go into business, and are more likely to live in poverty than men.[55] There is no question that pay equity promises to remain a challenging employee–management issue.

Sexual Harassment

Sexual harassment refers to unwelcome sexual advances, requests for sexual favors, and other verbal or physical conduct of a sexual nature that creates a hostile work environment.[56] Conduct on the job can be considered illegal under specific conditions:

- An employee's submission to such conduct is explicitly or implicitly made a term or condition of employment, or an employee's submission to or rejection of such conduct is used as the basis for employment decisions affecting the worker's status. A threat like "Go out with me or you're fired" or "Go out with me or you'll never be promoted here" constitutes *quid pro quo sexual harassment.*

- The conduct unreasonably interferes with a worker's job performance or creates an intimidating, hostile, or offensive work environment. This type of harassment is *hostile work environment sexual harassment.*

The Civil Rights Act of 1991 governs sexual harassment of both men and women.[57] In 1997, the Supreme Court reinforced this fact when it said same-sex harassment also falls within the purview of sexual harassment law. Managers and workers are now much more sensitive to sexual comments and behavior than they were in the past. The number of complaints filed with the Equal Employment Opportunity Commission (EEOC) declined to its lowest number since 1993. Still, EEOC statistics show sexual harassment remains a persistent employee complaint.

The Supreme Court in 1996 broadened the scope of what can be considered a hostile work environment; the key word seemed to be *unwelcome,* a term for behavior that would offend a reasonable person. Companies have found that the U.S. justice system means business in enforcing sexual harassment laws. In a highly publicized case, Madison Square Garden lost a judgment of $11.6 million to a former executive who sued New York Knicks' basketball coach Isiah Thomas and other team executives for sexual harassment. The Ivy League's Yale University has been the subject of an ongoing investigation of sexual harassment by the Department of Education's Civil Rights Office.[58] Foreign companies doing business in the United States are also not immune to sexual harassment charges as both Toyota and Nissan discovered.

A key problem is that workers and managers often know a policy concerning sexual harassment exists, but have no idea what it says. To remedy this, some states have taken the lead. California

sexual harassment
Unwelcome sexual advances, requests for sexual favors, and other conduct (verbal or physical) of a sexual nature that creates a hostile work environment.

Unwelcome sexual advances, requests for sexual favors, and other verbal or physical conduct are prohibited under the Civil Rights Act of 1991. While most employees are aware of sexual harassment policies in the workplace, they are often not certain what sexual harassment actually means. Should companies train employees about the dos and don'ts of acceptable sexual conduct on the job?

and Connecticut require all companies with 50 employees or more to provide sexual harassment prevention training to supervisors. Maine requires such training for companies with 15 or more employees. Many companies have set up rapid, effective grievance procedures and react promptly to allegations of harassment. Such efforts may save businesses millions of dollars in lawsuits and make the workplace more productive and harmonious. Nonetheless, there is a long way to go before sexual harassment as a key employee–management issue disappears.

Child Care

Today for the first time in U.S. history women outnumber men in the workforce.[59] Approximately three-fourths of women with children under 18 (including over 60 percent of mothers with children under age 3) are in the workforce. Such statistics concern employers for two reasons: (1) absences related to child care cost U.S. businesses billions of dollars annually, and (2) the issue of who should pay for employee child care raises a question that often divides employees. Many co-workers oppose child care benefits for parents or single parents, arguing that single workers and single-income families should not subsidize child care. Others contend that employers and the government have the responsibility to create child care systems to assist employees. Unfortunately federal assistance has not increased since passage of the Welfare Reform Act many years ago, and few expect new government spending for child care due to the current federal deficit problems. Thus, child care remains an important workplace issue.

A number of large companies offer child care as an employee benefit. *Working Mother* magazine compiles an annual list of the 100 best companies for working mothers. IBM and Johnson & Johnson have made the list every year for the past 25 years.[60] Both companies are praised as particularly sympathetic and cooperative with working mothers. Other large firms with extensive child care programs include American Express, Bristol-Myers Squibb, and Intel, which provides online homework assistance for employees' children.[61] Some additional child care benefits provided by employers include:

- Discount arrangements with national child care chains.
- Vouchers that offer payments toward child care the employee selects.
- Referral services that help identify high-quality child care facilities to employees.
- On-site child care centers at which parents can visit children at lunch or during lag times throughout the workday.
- Sick-child centers to care for moderately ill children.

Unfortunately, small businesses with fewer than 100 employees cannot compete with big companies in providing assistance with child care. Some small companies, however, have found that implementing creative child care programs can help them compete with larger organizations in hiring and retaining qualified employees. Haemonetics, located in Braintree, Massachusetts, is a leading company in blood processing technology that believes creating

On-site day care is still a relatively uncommon employee benefit in the United States today. Although it is often expensive to operate, it can pay big dividends in employee satisfaction and productivity. Who should pay for employee benefits like child care and elder care, the employee or the company?

a work-life balance is the key to keeping valued workers. The company operates "Kid's Space" at its corporate headquarters staffed by highly qualified early childhood educators who develop planned and spontaneous daily activities. Kid's Space also provides emergency child care services for employees whose children are ill or whose regular child care arrangements are disrupted.[62]

Twenty-five years ago, entrepreneurs Roger Brown and Linda Mason recognized the emerging need for child care as a benefit in the workplace. The husband-and-wife team started Bright Horizons Family Solutions Inc. to provide child care at worksites for employers. Today, their company is the leading provider in the corporate-sponsored child care market and runs nearly 700 child care centers for about 400 companies including 90 Fortune 500 companies. Increasing numbers of two-income households and the over 13 million single-parent households in the United States ensure that child care will remain a key employee–management issue even as businesses face the growing challenge of elder care.

Elder Care

Currently, there are approximately 40 million Americans over the age of 65.[63] Over the next 20 years, the number of Americans over 65 is expected to grow to over 70 million; that will be approximately 20 percent of the U.S. population in 2030. The likelihood that an American age 65 will live to age 90 has also increased significantly. What this means is that many workers will be confronted with how to care for older parents and other relatives. Today in the United States, 65.7 million caregivers (constituting 29 percent of the adult population) are providing some care to an elderly person.[64] According to the National Alliance for Caregiving, such caregiving obligations cause employees to miss approximately 15 million days of work per year. Companies are losing an estimated $35 billion a year in reduced productivity, absenteeism, and turnover from employees responsible for aging relatives. Elder care is becoming a key workplace issue.

The U.S. Office of Personnel Management (OPM) found that employees with elder care responsibilities need information about medical, legal, and insurance issues, as well as the full support of their supervisors and company. The OPM also suggests such caregivers may require flextime, telecommuting, part-time employment, or job sharing. Some firms offer employee assistance programs. DuPont and JPMorgan Chase provide elder care management services that include a needs assessment program for the employee. AAA and UPS offer health-spending accounts in which employees can put aside pretax income for elder care expenses. The number of companies offering an elder care benefit program are small, however, compared to child care. A Hewitt Associates survey found that only 49 percent of companies either currently had an elder care program or planned to introduce one in the near future. Unfortunately, the government does not provide much relief since both Medicare and Medicaid place heavy financial burdens for care on family caregivers.

According to the American Association of Retired Persons (AARP), as more experienced and high-ranking employees care for older parents and relatives, the costs to companies will rise even higher. This argument makes sense, since older, more experienced workers often hold jobs more critical to a company than those held by younger workers (who are most affected by child care issues). Many firms now face the fact that transfers and promotions are often out of the question for employees whose elderly parents need ongoing care. Unfortunately, as the nation gets older, the elder care situation will grow considerably worse, meaning this employee–management issue will persist well into the future.

Drug abuse costs the U.S. economy hundreds of billions of dollars in lost work, health care costs, crime, traffic accidents, and productivity. It is estimated that each drug abuser can cost an employer approximately $10,000 a year. Today, over 80 percent of major companies drug test new employees and 40 percent conduct random drug testing. Do you think these efforts are successful in reducing drug abuse in the workplace? Why or why not?

Drug Testing

Not long ago, acquired immunodeficiency syndrome (AIDS) caused great concern in the workplace. Many companies called for pre-employment testing for AIDS. Thankfully, the spread of AIDS has declined in the United States—good news for all citizens and for business. However, alcohol and drug abuse are serious workplace issues that touch far more workers and stretch from factory floors to construction sites to the locker rooms of professional sports teams.

Alcohol is the most widely used drug in the workplace, with an estimated 6.5 percent of full-time U.S. employees believed to be heavy drinkers.[65] Approximately 40 percent of industrial injuries and fatalities can be linked to alcohol consumption. According to the Department of Health and Human Services' Substance Abuse & Mental Health Services Association, more than 8 percent of full-time workers ages 18–49 use illegal drugs. In some industries, such as food services and construction, the percentage of workers using illegal drugs is much higher.

Individuals who use illegal drugs are three and a half times more likely to be in workplace accidents and five times more likely to file a workers' compensation claim than other employees.[66] According to the National Institute on Drug Abuse, employed drug users cost their employers about twice as much in medical and workers' compensation claims as do their drug-free co-workers. The U.S. Department of Labor projects that over a one-year period, drug abuse costs the U.S. economy $414 billion in lost work, health care costs, crime, traffic accidents, and other expenses, and over $150 billion in lost productivity. The National Institutes of Health estimates each drug abuser can cost an employer approximately $10,000 annually. Drug abusers are associated with 50 percent on-the-job accident rates, 10 percent higher absenteeism, 30 percent more turnover, and more frequent workplace violence incidents. Today, over 80 percent of major companies drug test new employees and 40 percent conduct random drug testing.[67]

Violence in the Workplace

Even though workplace violence has declined since the 1990s, the threat has in no way disappeared.[68] Employers must be vigilant about potential violence in the workplace. The Bureau of Labor Statistics reports that more than 2 million Americans are impacted by workplace violence annually.[69] The Occupational Safety and Health Administration (OSHA) reports that homicides account for 16 percent of all workplace deaths and are the number one cause of death for women in the workplace. In fact, one in six violent crimes in the United States occurs at work.

Many companies have taken action to prevent problems before they occur. They have held focus groups that invite employee input, hired managers with strong interpersonal skills, and employed skilled consultants to deal with any growing potential for workplace violence. State Farm Insurance and Verizon Wireless are among companies that have initiated policies to deal with this growing threat. At software firm Mindbridge, based in Worcester, Pennsylvania, two company officials must be present whenever an employee is disciplined or fired. In many states employers can seek a temporary restraining order on behalf of workers experiencing threats or harassment.

Some companies believe that the media exaggerates reports of workplace violence. According to the Bureau of Labor Statistics, 70 percent of U.S. workplaces neither provide any formal training for dealing with prevention of violence at work nor have a policy that addresses workplace violence.[70] Unfortunately, organizations such as the U.S. Postal Service and Xerox can attest that workplace violence is all too real and is likely to be an issue for the foreseeable future.

Firms that have healthy employee–management relations have a better chance to prosper than those that don't. Taking a proactive approach is the best way to ensure positive employee–management work environments. The proactive manager anticipates potential issues and works toward resolving them before they get out of hand—a good lesson for any manager.

progress assessment

- How does top-executive pay in the United States compare with top-executive pay in other countries?
- What's the difference between pay equity and equal pay for equal work?
- How is the term *sexual harassment* defined, and when does sexual behavior become illegal?
- What are some of the issues related to child care and elder care, and how are companies addressing those issues?

summary

Learning Goal 1. Trace the history of organized labor in the United States.

- **What was the first union?**

The cordwainers (shoemakers) organized a craft union of skilled specialists in 1792. The Knights of Labor, formed in 1869, was the first national labor organization.

- **How did the AFL-CIO evolve?**

The American Federation of Labor (AFL), formed in 1886, was an organization of craft unions. The Congress of Industrial Organizations (CIO), a group of unskilled and semiskilled workers, broke off from the AFL in 1935. Over time, the two organizations saw the benefits of joining and became the AFL-CIO in 1955. The AFL-CIO is a federation of labor unions, not a national union.

Learning Goal 2. Discuss the major legislation affecting labor unions.

- **What are the provisions of the major legislation affecting labor unions?**

See Figure 12.1.

Learning Goal 3. Outline the objectives of labor unions.

- **What topics typically appear in labor–management agreements?**

See Figure 12.3.

Learning Goal 4. Describe the tactics used by labor and management during conflicts, and discuss the role of unions in the future.

- **What are the tactics used by unions and management in conflicts?**

Unions can use strikes and boycotts. Management can use strikebreakers, injunctions, and lockouts.

- **What will unions have to do to cope with declining membership?**

Unions are facing a changing workplace. The Service Employees International Union (SEIU), with 2.2 million members, is the now the largest union. Going forward, unions must adapt to an increasingly white-collar, female, and culturally diverse workforce. To help keep U.S. businesses competitive in global markets, many have taken on a new role in assisting management in training workers, redesigning jobs, and assimilating the changing workforce.

Learning Goal 5. Assess some of today's controversial employee–management issues, such as executive compensation, pay equity, sexual harassment, child care and elder care, drug testing, and violence in the workplace.

- **What is a fair wage for managers?**

The market and the businesses in it set managers' salaries. What is fair is open to debate.

- **How are equal pay and pay equity different?**

The Equal Pay Act of 1963 provides that workers receive equal pay for equal work (with exceptions for seniority, merit, or performance). Pay equity is the demand for equivalent pay for jobs requiring similar levels of education, training, and skills.

- **How are some companies addressing the child care issue?**

Responsive companies are providing child care on the premises, emergency care when scheduled care is interrupted, discounts with child care chains, vouchers to be used at the employee's chosen care center, and referral services.

- **What is elder care, and what problems do companies face with regard to this growing problem?**

Workers who need to provide elder care for dependent parents or others are generally more experienced and vital to the mission of the organization than younger workers are. The cost to business is very large and growing.

- **Why are more and more companies now testing workers and job applicants for substance abuse?**

Drug abuse costs the U.S. economy $414 billion in lost work, health care costs, crime, traffic accidents, and other expenses, and over $150 billion in lost productivity. Individuals who use drugs are three and a half times more likely to be in workplace accidents and five times more likely to file a workers' compensation claim than those who do not use drugs.

key terms

agency shop
   agreement 350
American Federation of
   Labor (AFL) 344
arbitration 353

bargaining zone 352
certification 347
closed shop
   agreement 349
collective bargaining 346

Congress of Industrial
   Organizations (CIO) 344
cooling-off period 353
craft union 344
decertification 348

givebacks 355

grievance 351

industrial unions 344

injunction 354

Knights of Labor 344

lockout 354

mediation 353

negotiated
labor–management

agreement (labor
contract) 349

open shop
agreement 351

primary boycott 353

right-to-work laws 350

secondary boycott 354

sexual harassment 359

shop stewards 351

strike 353

strikebreakers 355

union 342

union security
clause 349

union shop
agreement 350

yellow-dog
contract 346

critical thinking

1. Do you believe that union shop agreements are violations of a worker's freedom of choice in the workplace? Do you think open shop agreements unfairly penalize workers who pay dues to unions they have elected to represent them in the workplace?

2. Some college football and basketball coaches earn huge incomes. Should college volleyball and swimming coaches be paid comparably? Should players in the Women's National Basketball Association (WNBA) be paid the same as their male counterparts in the National Basketball Association (NBA)? What role should market forces and government play in determining such wages?

3. If a company provides employer-paid child care services to workers with children, should those who don't have children or don't need child care services be paid extra?

developing workplace skills

1. Check whether your state supports the right of public employees (police, firefighters, teachers) to unionize and collectively bargain. If not, should it? Should such workers be allowed to strike?

2. Evaluate the following statement: "Labor unions are dinosaurs that have outlived their usefulness in today's knowledge-based economy." After your evaluation, take the position on this statement that differs from your own point of view and defend that position. Be sure to consider such questions as: Do unions serve a purpose in some industries? Do unions make the United States less competitive in global markets?

3. Research federal and state legislation related to child care, parental leave, and elder care benefits for employees. Are specific trends emerging? Should companies be responsible for providing such workplace benefits, or should the government share some responsibility? Why?

4. Compile a list of two or three employee–management issues not covered in the chapter. Compare your list with those of several classmates and see which issues you selected in common and which are unique to each individual. Pick an issue you all agree will be important in the future and discuss its likely effects and outcomes.

5. Do businesses and government agencies have a duty to provide additional benefits to employees beyond fair pay and good working conditions? Should benefits like health care be mandatory? Propose a system you consider fair and equitable for employees and employers.

taking it to the net

Purpose

To understand why workers choose to join unions and how unions have made differences in certain industries.

Exercise

Visit the AFL-CIO website (**www.aflcio.org**) and find information about why workers join unions and what the benefits have been.

1. What percentage of workers in your state are members of a union? If it is higher or lower than the national average, explain why unions do or do not have strength in your state.

2. Explain how union membership has affected minorities, women, older workers, and part-time workers.

3. The AFL-CIO site presents the union's perspective on labor issues. Look at the key issues and check sources such as the National Association of Manufacturers (**www.nam.org**) and the National Right to Work Legal Defense Foundation (**www.righttowork.org**) that support management's perspectives and compare their positions on these issues.

casing the web

To access the case "The Unions versus Walmart," visit
www.mhhe.com/P2P2e

video case

United We Stand

After reading this chapter, you are familiar with the history of labor unions. You have learned the tactics that labor uses to demand new benefits from management, and you have learned the tactics that management uses to respond to labor demands. You are also familiar with the various laws that are involved in labor–management disputes. You may get the impression from the media that labor unions are in decline and don't have much clout anymore. In fact, the number of people in labor unions has declined dramatically, but that doesn't mean that labor unions are not important today or that they have lost their passion for seeking fair treatment by companies.

We are so accustomed to thinking about labor unions in the auto, steel, and other related industries that we tend to overlook some truly key industries where labor unions are very important. No doubt you have heard in passing of the Screen Actors Guild (SAG), the American Federation of Television and Radio Artists, and the Writers Guild of America. But do you have any idea what issues the membership faces in such unions? Are they the same issues that unions have always had—seniority, pay, benefits, etc.—or are they somehow different?

Many young people dream of becoming a "movie star." They see the glamour, the excitement, the adulation of the fans, and the huge paychecks. What they don't see behind the scenes is the constant fight going on to win and keep certain privileges that past actors have won. Back in the 1930s, actors worked unrestricted hours, had no required meal breaks, and had unbreakable seven-year contracts. The producers tried to control who you could marry, what political views to express, and what your morals should be. The Screen Actors Guild won some concessions for the actors in 1937, but the studios pretty much still "owned" their stars. Eventually the stars won the right to better contracts, to the point where independent studios were formed and actors could control their own careers, even demanding a percentage of the gross for their pay (Jimmy Stewart, 1950).

Other issues concerned residuals for films shown on TV and in reruns. Contracts had to do with things like commercials and how the actors would be paid for them. Today's contracts deal with issues like diversity, salary and work conditions, financial assurances, safety considerations, and so on. Stipulations are constantly changing for actors. For example, independent film producers in the United States and around the world have different rules and requirements. TV commercials now appear on cell phones. The Screen Actors Guild keeps up with such changes to assure fair treatment of its members.

While SAG is for movie actors, the American Federation of Television and Radio Artists is a performer's union for actors, radio and TV announcers, and newspersons, singers, and others who perform on radio and/or TV. It negotiates wages and working conditions much like SAG, including health care and pensions. You can imagine negotiating an issue like equal pay for equal work when dealing with highly paid actors and actresses with huge egos.

The Writers Guild of America (WGA) represents writers in the motion picture, broadcast, and news media industries. Like actors, writers have issues dealing with pay, benefits, retirement, etc. The more you think about it, the more it will become clear to you that actors and others in the entertainment industry need unions or some other kind of organization to protect them from unfair practices. You can only imagine what treatment actors and others get from independent companies in other countries if they don't have representation.

Unions today are gathering momentum in industries where the pay is traditionally relatively low and the work is hard. That includes nursing, teaching (including college teachers), and other professions (profit, nonprofit, and government).

Thinking It Over

1 *What is the general attitude in your class toward labor unions? Are there many union workers in your town? Where do you see labor unions gaining strength in the future?*

2. *One of the primary concerns of traditional labor unions is the treatment of outsourcing. Could the entertainment industry outsource operations? How would this affect SAG and the other unions?*

3. *The video touches on the era of Senator Joe McCarthy and the House Un-American Activities Committee. Do you think there is ever a reason for government to intervene in the entertainment industry and its unions to influence its message? Why or why not?*

Career Outlook
PART 4 CONCLUSION—MANAGEMENT OF HUMAN RESOURCES

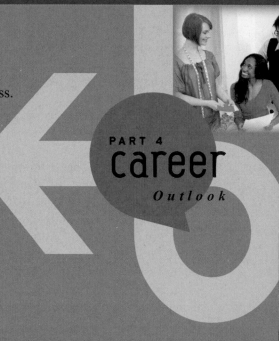

Managing human resources is an increasingly important part of business and is growing much faster than other fields in business. Human resource specialists recruit, select, interview, recommend, train, and inform employees and managers. They are the link between management and employees, especially in large organizations, and they are responsible for keeping the company informed and compliant with current and new laws. Increasingly, they are moving from being behind the scenes to joining management in shaping policy and procedure.

Job satisfaction and employee retention are markers of how successful a human resources department is. For example, if employees dislike their jobs and leave for new ones often, that is a sign that the human resource managers are not being effective.

PART 4
career
Outlook

SKILLS NEEDED

CAREER PATHS

POSSIBLE POSITIONS

PROFILE

COVER LETTER

RESUME

INTERVIEW

Skills Needed to Succeed in Management of Human Resources

In order to be hired as a human resources professional, you should demonstrate on your cover letter and résumé that you are:

- **A good communicator**—Can you write? Can you speak? Have you ever given a speech? Did you take a class in communications?

- **A motivator**—Can you change people's minds? Are you encouraging? Do friends come to you when they need a boost?

- **Organized**—Is your life in order? Are you in charge of important documents for yourself or your family? Do you keep a planner?

- **A planner**—Have you ever planned a short- or long-term project? For example, refinished your bathroom? Traveled on a small budget? Saved for your child's tuition?

- **A good researcher**—Do you like to read? Are you good at remembering rules and regulations?

Career Paths

The educational backgrounds of human resource managers vary considerably, and their duties and responsibilities vary from job to job. That means the skills you've learned as a teacher, volunteer, or parent may be just as valuable as technical training. College graduates or those who have earned certification have the best chance for finding a job or advancing in a current job.

Possible Positions

POSSIBLE POSITIONS IN HUMAN RESOURCES

OPPORTUNITY	MEDIAN SALARY	DUTIES	REQUIREMENTS	GROWTH
Human Resources Manager	$99,180 per year	Oversee recruiting, interviewing, hiring, and employee planning for an organization	Bachelor's degree and management experience	Average growth
Human Resources Specialist	$52,690 per year	Recruit, screen, interview, and place employees; also work in payroll, benefits and training	Most positions require a bachelor's degree, but work experience can be substituted for higher education	Faster than average
Compensation and Benefits Managers	$89,270 per year	Direct how and how much an organization pays employees	Bachelor's degree and work experience	Slower than average growth
Training and Development Managers	$89,170 per year	Plan and direct programs to enhance employee knowledge and skills	Bachelor's degree	Slightly faster than average growth

Source: Bureau of Labor Statistics, *Occupational Outlook Handbook,* 2012–13 Edition.

Profile: Aini Batak, Recruiter and Trainer

Aini Batak never wanted to be an accountant, but in her strictly religious household, she was expected to honor the wishes of her father, who wanted her to go into accounting. She left the workforce after five years in accounting to take care of her three children. Fifteen years later, her sons are grown, and she wants to start the job she dreamed of: helping young people find quality jobs. Her friends in human resources at her old company always impressed Aini, and now she is in school to learn more about working with people instead of numbers.

Aini is about to graduate from college and is applying to be an intern in a human resources department. How does she use her résumé, cover letter, and interview to get the job for which she has prepared? How does she turn her experience as a mom into a selling point for a company? Would you hire her?

AINI'S COVER LETTER

Aini Batak

April 27, 2014
Michela Maddox
Human Relations Manager
Fast-As-Lightning Deliveries
Orlando, Florida 32828

Dear Ms. Maddox:

I'd like to be your Fast-As-Lightning Deliveries summer intern this year. Alyssa Hudson, one of your staff members, alerted me to the position, and I'd like to explain why I could make a real contribution to your firm.

As a human resource student at Valencia Community College, I admire Fast-As-Lightning's effective business model and could recruit and motivate your biggest employee demographic: teenagers and young men. I've raised three of the kind of upstanding young men who you want to hire as deliverers at Fast-As-Lightning and I know what characteristics to look for when recruiting. As a human resource student, I've learned that I have the skills to recruit, hire, and manage a staff of delivery professionals. Recently, I trained 100+ parents for band fundraising activities and ran a workshop to train the band students to sell our annual coupon books. We increased our revenues by five percent each year because I motivated students and parents, recruited effective parents to our activities, and kept accurate records.

My lifetime of lessons learned will set me apart from many of your applicants. My passion to work with people propelled me to return to school to study human resource management rather than continue as an accountant. However, I learned in my recent human resource course project that my training as an accountant will serve me well; the small businesses that we worked with praised my attention to detail.

While new to human resources, I am not new to the challenges of developing young people, running business endeavors with accuracy, and motivating people to achieve. I'm eager to talk with you about how I can contribute and will contact you in two weeks to check the status of my application.

Thank you for the opportunity,

Aini Batak
Aini Batak

4 Set Street, Orlando, Florida 32828 • 407-366-3479 • Abatak@mail.com

Tip: If you know someone connected to the organization, use that person's name.

Tip: Emphasize what you have to offer rather than your time off from employment.

Tip: Put yourself in the shoes of the people hiring and demonstrate that you have abilities you think they would value in an employee.

AINI'S RESUME

Aini Batak
Human Resources Trainer and Recruiter

Summary of Qualifications

I am a former accountant transitioning into human resources by undergoing a two-year training program at Valencia Community College. I am applying for a student internship to complete my training requirements and learn about my new field.

My skills include:

- Employee coaching
- Recruitment
- Training and development

I am a:

- Fast learner
- Dedicated worker ←
- Motivator

Tip: If you don't have enough professional experience to fill a résumé, include personality traits attractive to the company.

Education

Human Resources Certification Program: Training and Recruitment
Anticipated Graduation: May 2014
Valencia Community College

Bachelor's Degree in Business
Emphasis in Accounting
Graduated Cum Laude
University of Florida ←

Tip: If you have more training than experience, highlight your education.

Experience

Recruitment Liaison

Recruiting for Small Businesses Class at Valencia Community College, Fall 2013

- Identified staff vacancies for participating local businesses
- Created job descriptions and profiles for positions
- Developed interview and selection models for businesses

Fundraiser
Sunny Shores High School Band Booster Club, 2008–2011 ←

Tip: Fill in any gaps in your experience with personal experience or volunteer work.

- Trained 100+ parents on fundraising ventures for band booster club
- Recruited and mentored president, vice president, and treasurer
- Served as link between school officials and parents
- Increased fundraising revenues by at least five percent each year

Bookkeeper
Hedgewell Locksmiths, Inc., 1994–1999

- Verified invoices and maintained daily records
- Prepared reports and financial statements for managers
- Monitored loans and accounts

4 Set Street, Orlando, Florida 32828 • 407-366-3479 • Abatak@mail.com

Aini's Interview

Question: What would you bring to our human resources team?

Poor answer: I'm terrific with kids, and I know you hire a lot of them. I'm sure I can figure out human resources if you'll give me a chance. I'm just a little rusty because I'm reentering the job market.

Great answer: I have a passion for motivating others. I am leaving my training as an accountant because I want to help people find their dream jobs. My whole heart is in this work, and I think your employees will feel that. As a bonus, you'll find that my accounting background makes me very accurate, and I know that's important when keeping employee records.

Tip: Stay positive. Don't outline your weaknesses for the employer. Everyone has obstacles to overcome, but your job is to show your interviewer how lucky they would be to hire you. Think ahead of time about your strengths and realize that skills from your previous field of work may be transferable.

Question: Describe a challenge in your life and how you overcame it.

Poor answer: *Laughs.* Well, I'll tell you—raising three teenage boys is a challenge. If it's not one thing it's another. I just take one day at a time.

Great answer: It's been a challenge to get to where I am today. I became an accountant to honor my father's wishes, but what I've always wanted to do is work with people. I've grown in my determination and faith in myself and realize that one can always change directions and fulfill one's dreams. That's why I could be so good in human resources. Not only do I know that I'm now doing what I love, but I can also inspire employees to love their work. I've found myself mentoring the younger students in my Human Resources program and realize how much skill I can bring to managing others.

Tip: This is a common interview question, so be prepared with a response. You can share as much about your personal life as you feel comfortable sharing but also plan to tie your answer back to the job you are interviewing for. Interviewers are checking to see how you handle adversity.

Question: As a recruiter and trainer, how would you work with trainees, especially if they are from different cultures or backgrounds than you?

Poor answer: Well I am Indonesian, so almost everyone in this city is from a different culture than me. I'm used to it. I just pretend like I'm the same as everybody else so no one thinks I'm different or weird.

Great answer: I'm a very open person, and I love to learn about new cultures and new people. When running the band fundraisers, I was working with parents and students from many backgrounds. One thing that helped unite us was that we all had the same goal to support the band. On the job, I'd also find ways to unite us as a team. Also, I would check in with my trainees regularly to make sure they understand and are comfortable with the skills they are learning and that they feel valued. I've learned that little things make people feel included. Just calling people by name—and pronouncing their names correctly—makes people feel important.

Tip: If you have a gap in your work history—like taking time off to raise children—turn it into an advantage. Share the skills you learned during your time away from the workforce and show how you are unique to candidates who have never left their jobs.

Marketing:
DEVELOPING AND IMPLEMENTING CUSTOMER-ORIENTED MARKETING PLANS

Marketing used to be limited to one-way communication: businesses made things and then told people about them in an effort to convince them to buy. Today, marketing managers must listen more than talk. They must listen to customers in order to learn what they truly want. They must listen to suppliers in order to learn what is available and how quickly they can get it. They must even listen to special interest groups (i.e., environmental groups, etc.) in order to make sure their products and services meet their standards.

In the chapters in this Part you will learn about the marketing process including how businesses develop new products, determine their prices, build efficient distribution systems, and promote their products to potential buyers.

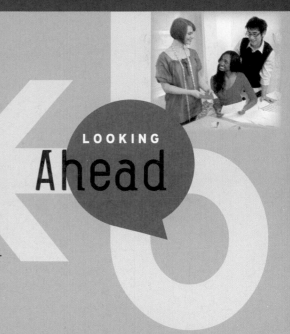

LOOKING
Ahead

CHAPTER 13   Marketing: Helping Buyers Buy

CHAPTER 14   Developing and Pricing Goods and Services

CHAPTER 15   Distributing Products

CHAPTER 16   Using Effective Promotions

13

MARKETING: HELPING
BUYERS Buy

LEARNING goals

After you have read and studied this chapter, you should be able to

1 Define *marketing,* and apply the marketing concept to both for-profit and nonprofit organizations.

2 Describe the four Ps of marketing.

3 Summarize the marketing research process.

4 Show how marketers use environmental scanning to learn about the changing marketing environment.

5 Explain how marketers apply the tools of market segmentation, relationship marketing, and the study of consumer behavior.

6 Compare the business-to-business market and the consumer market.

profile

CONNECTING WITH

Cesar Conde

President of Univision

The United States has long been a melting pot where people from many cultures live together and prosper. America's Latino community especially thrived over the last few decades. As this demographic grew, many new companies were started that provide products and services for the Hispanic population.

Of all these enterprises, few are more successful than the Spanish-language television network Univision. Led by company president Cesar Conde, Univision offers news, sporting events, and soap operas (called telenovelas) to its viewership. Founded as a small station in San Antonio, Univision is now the nation's fastest-growing television network by far. Sometimes it attracts even more viewers than major networks like CBS, ABC, and NBC. "We feel it's important that we step up and provide that type of programming our community is asking for," Conde says.

As the child of immigrants, Conde represents the younger generation of Latinos born in the United States that Univision is targeting. Growing up in Florida, Conde was inspired early in life by the success and intelligence of his parents. His father came from Peru and worked as a cardiologist while his mother, who hails from Cuba, taught at the University of Miami. Conde followed in their academic footsteps by earning a bachelor's degree from Harvard University and then an MBA from the prestigious Wharton School of the University of Pennsylvania. After college, Conde began his career in mergers and acquisitions. He soon left the financial sector, though, to pursue a path more in sync with his Hispanic upbringing. In the 1990s he became a business development executive at StarMedia, the first online company that focused primarily on Spanish- and Portuguese-speaking audiences.

His job at StarMedia eventually led him to Univision. He worked in almost every department at the network, from sales and business development to interactive media. In the early 2000s, however, he took a brief detour from his Univision career to work in Washington, D.C. President George W. Bush appointed him as one of 12 White House fellows, where he worked closely with Secretary of State Colin Powell. After his year of service to the federal government, Conde returned to Univision. By the time he turned 35 in 2009, he was named president of the company.

As leader of Univision, Conde excels at using clever marketing strategies to give his audience the content that they want to see. For instance, telenovelas are extremely popular with viewers and operate differently from traditional American soap operas. Telenovelas air in prime time rather than during the day, and the stars of the show can become as famous in their communities as celebrities like George Clooney or Angelina Jolie. In order to ensure a consistent availability of original programming, Conde founded Univision Studios when he assumed the presidency of the company. The expanded production facilities allow Univision to produce more than 4,000 hours of original content every year. Univision's news coverage often takes detailed looks at the state of Latin America. Although outsiders might mistake this for international journalism, many viewers hold a deeply personal connection to that part of the world. "A lot of our audience is coming to us because they want to know what's going on in their country of origin," Conde says. "That gives us a little bit of a different perspective, I think."

Still, Conde doesn't see the future of Hispanic broadcasting as a strictly Spanish-speaking operation. In 2012 he announced plans to launch an English-language network aimed at multilingual viewers in conjunction with ABC. After all, like Conde, many Latinos were born in the United States, giving them an intimate understanding of English as well as Spanish. By 2013, Conde hopes to add a 24-hour news network to Univision's portfolio as well. "The key to success is providing culturally relevant content and programming," Conde says. "At the end of the day, we want to make sure that we're connecting in a unique way."

That's really what marketing is all about. In this chapter you'll learn how master marketers like Cesar Conde identify their audience and figure out how to reach them. Whether through distribution, advertising, or publicity, successful marketing makes a connection with a customer that they won't soon forget.

Sources: NPR Staff, "What's the Fastest-Growing TV Network in America?" *NPR*, May 22, 2011; Scott Hiassen, "Univision, ABC News to Team Up on English-Language Network Targeting Hispanics," *The Miami Herald*, May 7, 2012; "Cesar Conde," corporate.univision.com, accessed May 18, 2012; and "Cesar Conde Breakfast," *The Paley Center for Media*, Video, February 22, 2012.

Where's the beef? Many people don't care about the answer to that question anymore. As the trend toward vegetarianism grows, this well-known company in Canada offers a vegan version of its chicken sandwich in 500 of its 750 stores. What is the name of this company? (Find the answer in the chapter.)

LEARNING goal 1

Define *marketing,* and apply the marketing concept to both for-profit and nonprofit organizations.

WHAT IS MARKETING?

marketing
The activity, set of institutions, and processes for creating, communicating, delivering, and exchanging offerings that have value for customers, clients, partners, and society at large.

The term marketing means different things to different people. Many think of marketing as simply "selling" or "advertising."[1] Yes, selling and advertising are part of marketing, but it's much more. The American Marketing Association has defined **marketing** as the activity, set of institutions, and processes for creating, communicating, delivering, and exchanging offerings that have value for customers, clients, partners, and society at large. We can also think of marketing, more simply, as the activities buyers and sellers perform to facilitate mutually satisfying exchanges.

In the past marketing focused almost entirely on helping the seller sell. That's why many people still think of it as mostly selling, advertising, and distribution *from the seller to the buyer.* Today, much of marketing is instead about *helping the buyer buy.* One author calls it "The Power of Pull."[2] Let's examine a couple of examples.

Today, when people want to buy a new or used car, they often turn to the Internet first. They go to a website like Vehix (www.vehix.com) to search for the vehicle they want and even take a virtual ride.[3] At other websites they compare prices and features. By the time they go to the dealer, they may know exactly which car they want and the best price available.

The websites have *helped the buyer buy.* Not only are customers spared searching one dealership after another to find the best price, but manufacturers and dealers are eager to participate so that they don't lose customers. The future of marketing is doing everything you can to help the buyer buy.[4]

Let's look at another case. In the past, one of the few ways students and parents could find the college with the right "fit" was to travel from campus to campus, a grueling and expensive process. Today, colleges use podcasts, virtual tours, live chats, and other interactive technologies to make on-campus visits less necessary. Such virtual tours help students and their parents buy.

Of course, helping the buyer buy also helps the seller sell. Think about that for a minute.

Here's an example from *The Wall Street Journal:* In the vacation market, many people find the holiday they want themselves. They use the Internet to find the right spot, and then make choices, sometimes questioning potential sellers online. In industries like this, the role of marketing is to make sure that a company's products or services are easily found online, and that the company responds effectively to potential customers.[5]

These are only a few examples of the marketing trend toward helping buyers buy. Consumers today spend hours searching the Internet for good deals. Wise marketers provide a wealth of information online and even cultivate customer relationships using blogs and social networking sites such as Facebook and Twitter.[6]

Online communities provide an opportunity to observe people (customers and others) interacting with one another, expressing their own opinions, forming relationships, and commenting on various goods and services.[7] It is important for marketers to track what relevant bloggers are writing by doing blog searches using key terms that define their market. Vendors who have text-mining tools can help companies measure conversations about their products and their personnel. Much of the future of marketing lies in mining such online conversations and responding appropriately.[8] Retailers and other marketers who rely solely on *traditional* advertising and selling are losing out to the new ways of marketing.[9]

The Evolution of Marketing

What marketers do at any particular time depends on what they need to do to fill customers' needs and wants, which continually change. Let's take a brief look at how those changes have influenced the evolution of marketing. Marketing in the United States has passed through four eras: (1) production, (2) selling, (3) marketing concept, and (4) customer relationship (see Figure 13.1).

The Production Era   From the time the first European settlers began their struggle to survive in America until the early 1900s, the general philosophy of business was "Produce as much as you can, because there is a limitless market for it." Given the limited production capability and vast demand for products in those days, that production philosophy was both logical and profitable. Business owners were mostly farmers, carpenters, and trade workers. They needed to produce more and more, so their goals centered on *production*. You can see this same process occurring in

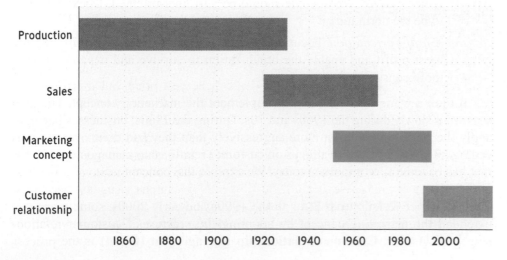

figure 13.1

MARKETING ERAS

The evolution of marketing in the United States involved four eras: (1) production, (2) selling, (3) marketing concept, and (4) customer relationship.

The history of the Ford Motor Company is written in ever-increasing motoring values. The Mercury 8, an entirely new car, is a new chapter in that history. Priced between the Ford V-8 and the Lincoln-Zephyr V-12, the Mercury brings to its price field many advantages of both these Ford-built cars . . . advantages that are best expressed in the phrase "top value."

THE NEW

MERCURY 8

A PRODUCT OF THE FORD MOTOR COMPANY

The size of the Mercury is not an illusion. This is a big, wide car, exceptionally roomy, with large luggage compartment. Note these generous dimensions—wheelbase 116 inches; over-all length 16 feet, 2 inches. The front compartment in sedan body types is 54 inches wide, and the rear compartment measures 56 inches from side to side. A new 95-horsepower V-type 8-cylinder engine assures brilliant, economical performance.

• Mercury interiors combine convenience and comfort with luxury. Brakes are hydraulic. • See, drive this new quality car.

A REMARKABLY QUIET, RESTFUL CAR

The Mercury 8 offers you remarkable freedom from noise and vibration—thanks to thorough soundproofing. All the resources of modern technology have been used by Ford research engineers to track down and eliminate engine, body and chassis noises. New materials and many rubber mountings also contribute to making the Mercury "silent as the night," restful and relaxing.

FORD-BUILT MEANS TOP VALUE

FORD MOTOR COMPANY NOW OFFERS FORD, MERCURY, LINCOLN-ZEPHYR AND LINCOLN MOTOR CARS

In the selling era, the focus of marketing was on selling, with little service afterward and less customization. What economic and social factors made this approach appropriate for the time?

marketing concept
A three-part business philosophy: (1) a customer orientation, (2) a service orientation, and (3) a profit orientation.

the oil industry today, where producers can often sell as much oil as they can produce. For a long time, GE thought that they would sell all the products they produced. Now they know better, of course.[10] The greatest marketing need today is for more production and less expensive distribution and storage.

The Selling Era By the 1920s, businesses had developed mass-production techniques (such as automobile assembly lines), and production capacity often exceeded the immediate market demand. Therefore, the business philosophy turned from producing to *selling*.[11] Most companies emphasized selling and advertising in an effort to persuade consumers to buy existing products; few offered extensive service after the sale.

The Marketing Concept Era After World War II ended in 1945, returning soldiers starting new careers and beginning families sparked a tremendous demand for goods and services. The postwar years launched the sudden increase in the birthrate that we now call the baby boom, and also a boom in consumer spending. Competition for the consumer's dollar was fierce. Businesses recognized that they needed to be responsive to consumers if they wanted to get their business, and a philosophy emerged in the 1950s called the marketing concept.

The **marketing concept** had three parts:

1. *A customer orientation.* Find out what consumers want and provide it for them. (Note the emphasis on meeting consumer needs rather than on promotion or sales.)
2. *A service orientation.* Make sure everyone in the organization has the same objective: customer satisfaction. This should be a total and integrated organizational effort. That is, everyone from the president of the firm to the delivery people should be customer-oriented. Does that seem to be the norm today?
3. *A profit orientation.* Focus on those goods and services that will earn the most profit and enable the organization to survive and expand to serve more consumer wants and needs.

It took a while for businesses to implement the marketing concept. The process went slowly during the 1960s and 70s. During the 1980s, businesses began to apply the marketing concept more aggressively than they had done over the preceding 30 years. That led to a focus on customer relationship management (CRM) that has become very important today. We explore that concept next.

The Customer Relationship Era In the 1990s and early 2000s, some managers extended the marketing concept by adopting the practice of customer relationship management. **Customer relationship management (CRM)** is the process of learning as much as possible about present customers and doing everything you can over time to satisfy them—or even to exceed their expectations—with goods and services. The idea is to enhance customer satisfaction and stimulate long-term customer loyalty.[12] For example, most airlines offer frequent-flier programs that reward loyal customers with free flights. The newest in customer relationship building, as mentioned earlier, involves social networks, online communities, tweets, and blogs.[13]

3 out of 4
car seats aren't
used correctly.
Surprised?

The LATCH system makes it easier to be sure your child's car seat is installed correctly every time. Just clip it to the lower anchors, attach the top tether, and pull the straps tight. To find out more, **visit safercar.gov.**

U.S. Department of Transportation   LATCH

Clearly, the degree of consumer dissatisfaction that exists, especially with services such as airlines and phone companies, shows that marketers have a long way to go to create customer satisfaction and loyalty. According to a recent study, only 6.8 percent of marketers said they have excellent knowledge of their customers when it comes to demographic, behavioral, and psychographic (how they think) data.

customer relationship management (CRM)
The process of learning as much as possible about customers and doing everything you can to satisfy them—or even exceed their expectations—with goods and services.

The newest in CRM efforts is customer-managed relationships (CMR). The idea is to give the customer the power to build relationships with suppliers and consumers. Websites like Expedia, Travelocity, and Priceline allow customers to find the best price or set their own.[14] Since consumers are interested in green marketing today, relationship building also means responding to that desire. The Making the Green Connection box explores "going green" in the apparel industry.

Nonprofit Organizations and Marketing

Even though the marketing concept emphasizes a profit orientation, marketing is a critical part of almost all organizations, including nonprofits. Charities use marketing to raise funds for combating world hunger, for instance, or to obtain other resources.[15] The Red Cross uses promotion to encourage people to donate blood when local or national supplies run low. Greenpeace uses marketing to promote ecologically safe technologies. Environmental groups use marketing to try to cut carbon emissions. Churches use marketing to attract new members and raise funds. Politicians use marketing to get votes.

States use marketing to attract new businesses and tourists. Many states, for example, have competed to get automobile companies from other countries to locate plants in their area.[16] Schools use marketing to attract new students. Other organizations, such as arts groups, unions, and social groups, also use marketing.[17] The Ad Council, for example, uses public service ads to create awareness and change attitudes on such issues as drunk driving and fire prevention.

Organizations use marketing, in fact, to promote everything from environmentalism and crime prevention ("Take A Bite Out Of Crime") to social issues ("Choose Life").

connection

www.levi.com

Are Your Blue Jeans "Green" Jeans?

How far will companies go with relationship building through green marketing? Well, the clothing industry is developing a software tool to help them measure the environmental impact of their apparel and footwear, from raw material to garbage dump. You may be surprised by how "dirty" the apparel industry can be. For example, tanning leather often involves toxic chemicals. Making polyester uses large amounts of crude oil and other materials that release volatile compounds.

A series of questions is used to determine just how "green" some products are. The questions cover every step in the life of a product from raw-material production to manufacturing, shipping, and even disposal. Levi's gets points for having a recycling program that lets consumers drop off their old jeans at Goodwill.

Would you look at a label to determine whether or not you would buy tennis shoes or a garment based on its eco-friendliness? The apparel industry is counting on you to do so. And it is preparing for that choice by changing fabrics, distribution procedures, and more, all with the goal of establishing and maintaining good relationships with their customers.

Sources: "Levi's New Jeans Design Cuts Water Use by 96 Percent," www.greenbiz.com, accessed June 2011; and Maggie Fazeli Fard, "Green Graduations at Washington Area Universities," *The Washington Post*, May 21, 2012.

LEARNING goal 2

Describe the four Ps of marketing.

THE MARKETING MIX

Need help understanding the Marketing Mix?
www.introbiz.tv/QR13-1

marketing mix
The ingredients that go into a marketing program: product, price, place, and promotion.

We can divide much of what marketing people do into four factors, called the four Ps to make them easy to remember. They are:

1. Product
2. Price
3. Place
4. Promotion

Managing the controllable parts of the marketing process means (1) designing a want-satisfying *product*, (2) setting a *price* for the product, (3) putting the product in a *place* where people will buy it, and (4) *promoting* the product, including how "green" it is. These four factors are called the **marketing mix** because businesses blend them together in a well-designed marketing program (see Figure 13.2).

Applying the Marketing Process

The four Ps are a convenient way to remember the basics of marketing, but they don't necessarily include everything that goes into the marketing process for all

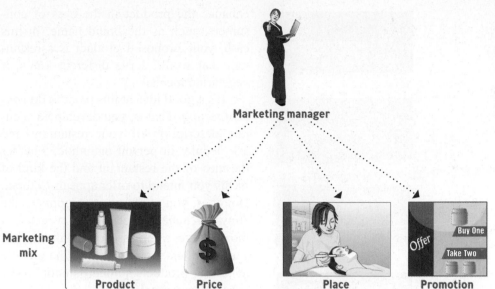

Marketing manager

Marketing mix

Product   Price   Place   Promotion

figure 13.2

MARKETING MANAGERS AND THE MARKETING MIX

Marketing managers must choose how to implement the four Ps of the marketing mix: product, price, place, and promotion. The goals are to please customers and make a profit.

products. One of the best ways to understand the entire marketing process is to take a product or a group of products and follow the process that led to their development and sale (see Figure 13.3).

Imagine, for example, that you and your friends want to start a moneymaking business near your college. You've noticed a lot of vegetarians among your acquaintances. You do a quick survey in a few dorms, sororities, and fraternities and find many vegetarians—and other students who like to eat vegetarian meals once in a while.[18] Your preliminary research indicates some demand for a vegetarian restaurant nearby. You check the fast-food stores in the area and find that none offer more than one or two vegetarian meals. In fact, most don't have any, except salads and some soups.

Further research identifies a number of different kinds of vegetarians. Lacto-ovo vegetarians eat dairy products and eggs. Lacto-vegetarians eat dairy products but no eggs. Fruitarians eat mostly raw fruits, grains, and nuts. Vegans eat neither eggs nor dairy products. Flexitarians eat the occasional cheesecake, hamburger, or whatever.

Your research identifies vegan farmers who don't use any synthetic chemical fertilizers, pesticides, herbicides, or genetically modified ingredients. You also find that KFC Canada offers a vegan version of its chicken sandwich in 500 of its 750 outlets. Is the Colonel on to something? He may be, since there are successful vegetarian restaurants even in Argentina, where the per-capita consumption of beef is the highest in the world. You conclude that a vegetarian restaurant would have to appeal to all kinds of vegetarians to be a success.

You've just performed the first few steps in the marketing process. You noticed an opportunity (a need for vegetarian food near campus). You conducted some preliminary research to see whether your idea had any merit. And then you identified groups of people who might be interested in your product. They will be your *target market* (the people you will try to persuade to come to your restaurant).

Designing a Product to Meet Consumer Needs

Once you've researched consumer needs and found a target market (which we'll discuss in more detail later) for your product, the four Ps of marketing come into play. You start by developing a product or products. A **product** is any physical good, service, or idea that satisfies a want or need, plus anything that would

product
Any physical good, service, or idea that satisfies a want or need plus anything that would enhance the product in the eyes of consumers, such as the brand.

figure 13.3

THE MARKETING PROCESS WITH THE FOUR PS

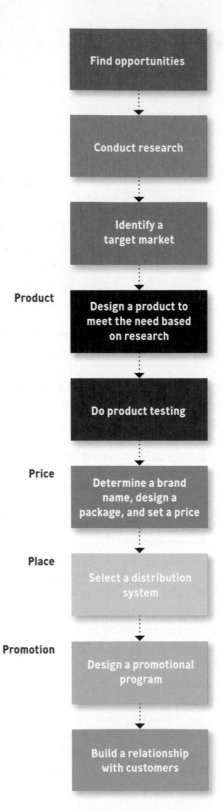

test marketing
The process of testing products among potential users.

brand name
A word, letter, or group of words or letters that differentiates one seller's goods and services from those of competitors.

enhance the product in the eyes of consumers, such as the brand name. In this case, your proposed product is a restaurant that would serve different kinds of vegetarian meals.

It's a good idea at this point to do *concept testing*. That is, you develop an accurate description of your restaurant and ask people, in person or online, whether the idea of the restaurant and the kind of meals you intend to offer appeals to them. If it does, you might go to a supplier, like Amy's Kitchen, that makes vegetarian meals, to get samples you can take to consumers to test their reactions. The process of testing products among potential users is called **test marketing.**

If consumers like the products and agree they would buy them, you have the information you need to find investors and look for a convenient location to open a restaurant. You'll have to think of a catchy name. (For practice, stop for a minute and try to think of one.) We'll use Very Vegetarian in this text, although we're sure you can think of a better name. Meanwhile, let's continue with the discussion of product development.

You may want to offer some well-known brand names to attract people right away. A **brand name** is a word, letter, or group of words or letters that differentiates one seller's goods and services from those of competitors. Brand names of vegetarian products include Tofurky, Mori-Nu, and Yves Veggie Cuisine. We'll discuss the product development process in detail in Chapter 14, and follow the Very Vegetarian case to show you how all marketing and other business decisions tie together. For now, we're simply sketching the whole marketing process to give you an overall picture. So far, we've covered the first P of the marketing mix: product. Next comes price.

Setting an Appropriate Price

After you've decided what products and services you want to offer consumers, you have to set appropriate prices.[19] Those depend on a number of factors. In the restaurant business, the price could be close to what other restaurants charge to stay competitive. Or you might charge less to attract business, especially at the beginning. Or you may offer high-quality products for which customers are willing to pay a little more (as Starbucks does). You also have to consider the costs of producing, distributing, and promoting the product, which all influence your price. We'll discuss pricing issues in more detail in Chapter 14.

A vegetarian restaurant might fill a popular need in the neighborhood of many college campuses today. Is there one near your school? What can you tell about its manager's application of the four Ps of marketing – product, price, place, and promotion?

Getting the Product to the Right Place

There are several ways you can serve the market for vegetarian meals. You can have people come in, sit down, and eat at the restaurant, but that's not the only alternative—think of pizza. You could deliver the food to customers' dorms, apartments, and student unions. You may want to sell your products in supermarkets or health-food stores, or through organizations that specialize in distributing food products. Such *intermediaries* are the middle links in a series of organizations that distribute goods from producers to consumers. (The more traditional word for them is *middlemen*.) Getting the product to consumers when and where they want it is critical to market success.[20] Don't forget to consider the Internet as a way to reach consumers. We'll discuss the importance of marketing intermediaries and distribution in detail in Chapter 15.

Developing an Effective Promotional Strategy

The last of the four Ps of marketing is promotion. **Promotion** consists of all the techniques sellers use to inform people about and motivate them to buy their products or services. Promotion includes advertising; personal selling; public relations; publicity; word of mouth (viral marketing); and various sales promotion efforts, such as coupons, rebates, samples, and cents-off deals.[21] We'll discuss promotion in detail in Chapter 16.

Promotion often includes relationship building with customers. Among other activities, that means responding to suggestions consumers make to improve the products or their marketing, including price and packaging. For Very Vegetarian, postpurchase, or after-sale, service may include refusing payment for meals that weren't satisfactory and stocking additional vegetarian products customers say they would like. Listening to customers and responding to their needs is the key to the ongoing process that is marketing. The Connecting Through Social Media box discusses how businesses can use social media and smartphones to build relationships with customers.

promotion
All the techniques sellers use to inform people about and motivate them to buy their products or services.

progress assessment

- What does it mean to "help the buyer buy"?
- What are the three parts of the marketing concept?
- What are the four Ps of the marketing mix?

Getting Attention through Mobile Marketing

You don't have to try very hard these days to find people with their eyes fixated on smartphones. These devices are more and more common, and marketers have taken notice. But using smartphones as promotional tools can be a tricky business. After all, most people use their mobile device to interact in some way. Therefore, a successful mobile marketing campaign should aim to connect meaningfully with a person, rather than just throw an ad in their face.

An app called WeReward, for instance, engages with users on this all-important personal level. WeReward combines the most basic elements of social media sites like Facebook, Twitter, and Foursquare into one easy package. The idea is for users to earn points by either "checking in" to a business, taking a picture of a product, or actually buying a product through a WeReward sponsorship. The points can then be redeemed for cash and other discounts at participating retailers. Also, whenever users earn points, their username and the name of the company they are patronizing get posted on the WeReward website. That way marketers get their due by having their business mentioned online while other users get to see where their friends are shopping.

In the lightning quick world of new media, it's difficult to say which ideas will stick and which will disappear like so many MySpaces. No one knows if a service like WeReward has the legs to be a big success. Still, that's what makes mobile marketing such an exciting area of business. Since it's so young that no one really knows the perfect method yet, people can really do anything they want with it. So keep a lookout for new ways to reach out to people through your own social networks. Who knows, what you find out could lead to the "Next Big Thing."

Sources: Carmine Gallo, "Why Your Mobile Marketing Campaign Won't Work," *Forbes,* April 16, 2012; and Dan O'Shea, "An All-in-One Mobile Marketing Tool," *Entrepreneur,* October 2011.

LEARNING goal 3

Summarize the marketing research process.

PROVIDING MARKETERS WITH INFORMATION

marketing research
The analysis of markets to determine opportunities and challenges, and to find the information needed to make good decisions.

Every decision in the marketing process depends on information. When they conduct **marketing research,** marketers analyze markets to determine opportunities and challenges, and to find the information they need to make good decisions.

Marketing research helps identify what products customers have purchased in the past, and what changes have occurred to alter what they want now and what they're likely to want in the future. Marketers also conduct research on business trends, the ecological impact of their decisions, global trends, and more. Businesses need information to compete effectively, and marketing research is the activity that gathers it. Besides listening to customers, marketing researchers also pay attention to what employees, shareholders, dealers, consumer advocates, media representatives, and other stakeholders have to say. As noted earlier, some of that research is now being gathered online through blogs and social networks.

The Marketing Research Process

A simplified marketing research process consists of at least four key steps:

1. Defining the question (the problem or opportunity) and determining the present situation.
2. Collecting research data.
3. Analyzing the research data.
4. Choosing the best solution and implementing it.

The following sections look at each of these steps.

Defining the Question and Determining the Present Situation   Marketing researchers need the freedom to discover what the present situation is, what the problems or opportunities are, what the alternatives are, what information they need, and how to go about gathering and analyzing data.

Collecting Data   Usable information is vital to the marketing research process. Research can become quite expensive, however, so marketers must often make a trade-off between the need for information and the cost of obtaining it. Normally the least expensive method is to gather information already compiled by others and published in journals and books or made available online.

Such existing data are called **secondary data,** since you aren't the first one to gather them. Figure 13.4 lists the principal sources of secondary marketing research information. Despite its name, *secondary* data is what marketers should gather *first* to avoid incurring unnecessary expense. To find secondary data about vegetarians, go to the website for *Vegetarian Times* (www.vegetariantimes.com) or search other websites on vegetarianism.

Often, secondary data don't provide all the information managers need for important business decisions. To gather additional in-depth information, marketers must do their own research. The results of such *new studies* are called **primary data.** One way to gather primary data is to conduct a survey.

Telephone surveys, online surveys, mail surveys, and personal interviews are the most common forms of primary data collection. Focus groups (defined below) are another popular method of surveying individuals. What do you think would be the best way to survey students about your potential new restaurant? Would you do a different kind of survey after it had been open a few months? How could you help vegetarians find your restaurant? That is, how could you help your buyers buy? One question researchers pay close attention to is: "Would you recommend this product to a friend?"

A **focus group** is a group of people who meet under the direction of a discussion leader to communicate their opinions about an organization, its products, or other given issues. This textbook is updated periodically using many focus groups made up of faculty and students. They tell us, the authors, what subjects and examples they like and dislike, and the authors follow their suggestions for changes.

Marketers can now gather both secondary and primary data online. The authors of this text, for example, do much research online, but they also gather data from books, articles, interviews, and other sources.

Personal interviews are one way of collecting primary research data about customers' needs, wants, and buying habits. Perhaps someone has stopped you in a shopping mall recently to ask you some questions about a product or product category you use. What might contribute to the difficulty of collecting information through such interviews, and how can marketers improve the process?

secondary data
Information that has already been compiled by others and published in journals and books or made available online.

primary data
Data that you gather yourself (not from secondary sources such as books and magazines).

focus group
A small group of people who meet under the direction of a discussion leader to communicate their opinions about an organization, its products, or other given issues.

PRIMARY SOURCES	SECONDARY SOURCES
Interviews Surveys Observation Focus groups Online surveys Questionnaires Customer comments Letters from customers	**Government Publications** *Statistical Abstract of the United States* *Census of Transportation* *Survey of Current Business* *Annual Survey of Manufacturers* *Census of Retail Trade* **Commercial Publications** ACNielsen Company studies on retailing and media Marketing Research Corporation of America studies on consumer purchases Selling Areas—Marketing Inc. reports on food sales **Magazines** *Entrepreneur* *Journal of Retailing* *Journal of Advertising Research* *Bloomberg Businessweek* *Journal of Consumer Research* *Fortune* Trade magazines appropriate to your industry such as *Progressive Grocer* *Inc.* *Journal of Advertising* *Advertising Age* *Journal of Marketing Research* *Forbes* *Marketing News* Reports from various chambers of commerce *Harvard Business Review* *Hispanic Business* *Journal of Marketing* *Black Enterprise* **Newspapers** *The Wall Street Journal, Barron's,* your local newspapers **Internal Sources** Company records Income statements Balance sheets Prior research reports **General Sources** Internet searches Commercial databases Google-type searches

figure 13.4

SELECTED SOURCES OF PRIMARY AND SECONDARY INFORMATION

You should spend a day or two at the library becoming familiar with these sources. You can read about primary research in any marketing research text from the library.

Analyzing the Research Data   Marketers must turn the data they collect in the research process into useful information. Careful, honest interpretation of the data can help a company find useful alternatives to specific marketing challenges. For example, by doing primary research, Fresh Italy, a small Italian pizzeria, found that its pizza's taste was rated superior to that of the larger pizza chains. However, the company's sales lagged behind the competition. Secondary research on the industry revealed that free delivery (which Fresh Italy did not offer) was more important to customers than taste. Fresh Italy now delivers—and has increased its market share.

Choosing the Best Solution and Implementing It   After collecting and analyzing data, market researchers determine alternative strategies and make recommendations about which may be best and why. This final step in a research effort also includes following up on actions taken to see whether the results were what was expected. If not, the company can take corrective action and conduct new studies in its ongoing attempt to provide consumer satisfaction at the lowest cost. You can see, then, that marketing research is a *continuous process* of responding to changes in the marketplace and in consumer preferences.

The authors of this text enjoy the benefits of using focus groups. College faculty and students come to these meetings and tell us how to improve this book and its support material. We listen carefully and make as many changes as we can in response. Suggestions have included adding more descriptive captions to the photos in the book and making the text as user-friendly as possible. How are we doing so far?

LEARNING **goal 4**

Show how marketers use environmental scanning to learn about the changing marketing environment.

THE MARKETING ENVIRONMENT

Marketing managers must be aware of the surrounding environment when making marketing mix decisions. **Environmental scanning** is the process of identifying factors that can affect marketing success. As you can see in Figure 13.5, they include global, technological, sociocultural, competitive, and economic influences. We discussed these factors in some detail in Chapter 1, but now let's review them from a strictly marketing perspective.

environmental scanning
The process of identifying the factors that can affect marketing success.

Global Factors

Using the Internet, businesses can reach many of the world's consumers relatively easily and carry on a dialogue with them about the goods and services they want. By 2018, half of all small businesses will be engaged in global trade.

The globalization process puts more pressure on those whose responsibility it is to deliver products. Many marketers outsource delivery to companies like FedEx, UPS, and DHL, which have a solid reputation for shipping goods quickly.[22]

Technological Factors

The most important technological changes also relate to the Internet. Using consumer databases, blogs, social networking, and the like, companies can develop products and services that closely match consumers' needs. As you read in Chapter 9,

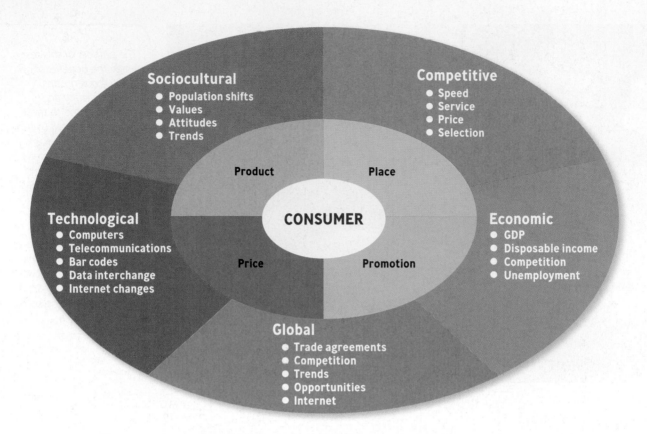

figure 13.5

THE MARKETING ENVIRONMENT

firms can now produce customized goods and services for about the same price as mass-produced goods. Thus flexible manufacturing and mass customization are also major influences on marketers. You can imagine, for example, using databases to help you devise custom-made fruit mixes and various salads for your customers at Very Vegetarian.

Sociocultural Factors

Marketers must monitor social trends to maintain their close relationship with customers, since population growth and changing demographics can have an effect on sales. One of the fastest-growing segments of the U.S. population in the 21st century is people over 65. The increase in the number of older adults creates growing demand for nursing homes, health care, prescription drugs, recreation, continuing education, and more.

Other shifts in the U.S. population are creating new challenges for marketers as they adjust their products to meet the tastes and preferences of Hispanic, Asian, and other growing ethnic groups (see the Connecting Across Borders box).[23] To appeal to diverse groups, marketers must listen better and be more responsive to unique ethnic needs. What might you do to appeal to specific ethnic groups with Very Vegetarian?

Competitive Factors

Of course, marketers must pay attention to the dynamic competitive environment. Many brick-and-mortar companies must be aware of new competition from the Internet, including firms that sell automobiles, insurance, music, and clothes.

As Population Booms, Marketers Target Hispanics

From 2000 to 2010, Hispanics accounted for more than half of the population growth in the United States. This huge new market represents a gold mine for companies hoping to shore up poor domestic sales in the wake of the recession. Procter & Gamble, for instance, is planning to feature more Spanish on its products and hire Hispanic spokespeople to advertise them. According to industry analysts, Latino households tend to buy more beauty and cleaning products than other American shoppers. Experts also claim that Hispanics are more loyal to brands, making them a perfect demographic for a personal care company like Procter & Gamble.

If Latinos end up buying as many products as companies hope, the boost those purchases would give to the economy will be significant. Consumer spending fell steadily after the recession, and many retailers and suppliers haven't recovered. Growing communities like the Hispanic population could be just who many companies need to attract.

Still, marketers have to be careful not to pander to their audience. Glenn Llopis, the founder of the Center for Hispanic Leadership, said that Latinos respond to brands that are relevant to their culture and not simply interested in taking their money. "Now that we have confirmed that cultural sustainability matters to U.S. Hispanics, companies must become more educated about the Latino community not just as consumers—but more importantly, as people, and the identity we represent as a diverse community," said Llopis. Only time will tell if companies like Procter & Gamble will be able to market discreetly to Hispanics or if their efforts will be viewed as little more than tactless grabs for cash.

Sources: Glenn Llopis, "U.S. Economy at Risk if Corporations Ignore the Impact of Hispanics in America," *The Huffington Post,* May 20, 2012; and Ellen Byron, "Hola: P&G Seeks Latino Shoppers," *The Wall Street Journal,* September 15, 2011.

In the book business, Barnes & Noble is still adjusting to the new reality of Amazon.com's huge selection of books at good prices. Borders Books went out of business.[24] What will the challenge from Kindle and other eReaders provide? Now that consumers can literally search the world for the best buys through the Internet, marketers must adjust their pricing, delivery, and services accordingly. Can you see any opportunities for Very Vegetarian to make use of the Internet and social media?

Economic Factors

Marketers must pay close attention to the economic environment. As we began the new millennium, the United States was experiencing unparalleled growth, and customers were eager to buy even the most expensive automobiles, watches, and vacations. But as the economy slowed, marketers had to adapt by offering products that were less expensive and more tailored to consumers with modest incomes.[25]

The economic collapse beginning in 2008 really slowed sales and became global in scope. You can see why environmental scanning is critical to a company's success during rapidly changing economic times. What economic changes are occurring around your school that might affect a new restaurant? How have the economic crisis, the wars in Iraq and Afghanistan, or natural disasters affected your area?

TWO DIFFERENT MARKETS: CONSUMER AND BUSINESS-TO-BUSINESS (B2B)

Marketers must know as much as possible about the market they wish to serve. As we defined it in Chapter 6, a *market* consists of people with unsatisfied wants and needs who have both the resources and the willingness to buy. There are two major markets in business: the *consumer market* and the *business-to-business market*. The **consumer market** consists of all the individuals or households that want goods and services for personal consumption or use and have the resources to buy them.

The **business-to-business (B2B) market** consists of all the individuals and organizations that want goods and services to use in producing other goods and services or to sell, rent, or supply goods to others. Oil-drilling bits, cash registers, display cases, office desks, public accounting audits, and business software are B2B goods and services. Traditionally, they have been known as *industrial* goods and services because they are used in industry.

The important thing to remember is that the buyer's reason for buying—that is, the end use of the product—determines whether a product is a consumer product or a B2B product. A cup of yogurt that a student buys for breakfast is a consumer product. However, when Very Vegetarian purchases the same cup of yogurt to sell to its breakfast customers, it has purchased a B2B product. The following sections outline consumer and B2B markets.

The business-to-business (B2B) market consists of individuals and organizations that sell goods and services to other businesses. A manufacturer, for instance, buys its parts and supplies in the B2B market.

consumer market
All the individuals or households that want goods and services for personal consumption or use.

business-to-business (B2B) market
All the individuals and organizations that want goods and services to use in producing other goods and services or to sell, rent, or supply goods to others.

market segmentation
The process of dividing the total market into groups whose members have similar characteristics.

target marketing
Marketing directed toward those groups (market segments) an organization decides it can serve profitably.

progress assessment

- What are the four steps in the marketing research process?
- What is environmental scanning?
- What factors are included in environmental scanning?

LEARNING goal 5

Explain how marketers apply the tools of market segmentation, relationship marketing, and the study of consumer behavior.

THE CONSUMER MARKET

The total potential consumer market consists of the 7 billion people in global markets. Because consumer groups differ greatly by age, education level, income, and taste, a business usually can't fill the needs of every group. It must decide which groups to serve, and then develop products and services specially tailored to their needs.

Take the Campbell Soup Company, for example. You know Campbell for its traditional soups such as chicken noodle and tomato. You may also have noticed that Campbell has expanded its U.S. product line to appeal to a number of different tastes. Aware of population growth in the South and in Latino communities in cities across the nation, it introduced a Creole soup for the southern market and a red bean soup for the Latino market. In Texas and California, where people like their food with a bit of kick, Campbell makes its nacho cheese soup spicier than in other parts of the country. It's just one company that has had some success studying the consumer market, breaking it down into categories, and developing products for separate groups.

The process of dividing the total market into groups with similar characteristics is called **market segmentation.** Selecting which groups or segments an organization can serve profitably is **target marketing.** For example, a shoe store may choose to sell only women's shoes, only children's shoes, or only athletic shoes. The issue is finding the right *target market*—the most profitable segment—to serve.

Segmenting the Consumer Market

A firm can segment the consumer market several ways (see Figure 13.6). Rather than selling your product throughout the United States, you might focus on just one or two regions where you can be most successful, say southern states such as Florida, Texas, and South Carolina. Dividing a market by cities, counties, states, or regions is **geographic segmentation.**

Alternatively, you could aim your product's promotions toward people ages 25 to 45 who have some college education and above-average incomes. Automobiles such as Lexus are often targeted to this audience. Age, income, and education level are criteria for **demographic segmentation.** So are religion, race, and occupation. Demographics are the most widely used segmentation variable, but not necessarily the best.

You may want your ads to portray a target group's lifestyle. To do that, you would study the group's values, attitudes, and interests in a strategy called **psychographic segmentation.** If you decide to target Generation Y, you would do an in-depth study of members' values and interests, like which TV shows they watch and which personalities they like best. With that information you would develop advertisements for those TV shows using those stars.

In marketing for Very Vegetarian, what benefits of vegetarianism might you talk about? Should you emphasize freshness, heart-healthiness, taste, or something else? Determining which product benefits your target market prefers and using those benefits to promote a product is **benefit segmentation.**

You can also determine who are the big eaters of vegetarian food. Does your restaurant seem to attract more men or more women? More students or more faculty members? Are your repeat customers from the local community or are they commuters? Separating the market by volume of product use is called **volume (or usage) segmentation.** Once you know who your customer base is, you can design your promotions to better appeal to that specific group or groups.

geographic segmentation
Dividing a market by cities, counties, states, or regions.

demographic segmentation
Dividing the market by age, income, and education level.

psychographic segmentation
Dividing the market using groups' values, attitudes, and interests.

benefit segmentation
Dividing the market by determining which benefits of the product to talk about.

The Internet has dramatically increased the ways in which companies can reach out to customers and conduct relationship marketing. For example, it can assist marketers in customizing products like the photo books and calendars shown here.

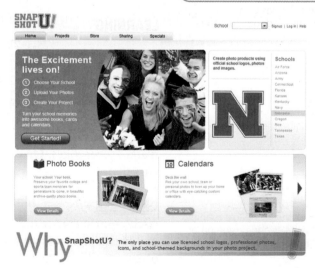

figure 13.6

MARKET SEGMENTATION

This table shows some of the methods marketers use to divide the market. The aim of segmentation is to break the market into smaller units.

MAIN DIMENSION	SAMPLE VARIABLES	TYPICAL SEGMENTS
Geographic segmentation	Region	Northeast, Midwest, South, West
	City or county size	Under 5,000; 5,000–10,999; 11,000–19,999; 20,000–49,000; 50,000 and up
	Density	Urban, suburban, rural
Demographic segmentation	Gender	Male, female
	Age	Under 5; 5–10; 11–18; 19–34; 35–49; 50–64; 65 and over
	Education	Some high school or less, high school graduate, some college, college graduate, postgraduate
	Race	Caucasian, African American, Indian, Asian, Hispanic
	Nationality	American, Asian, Eastern European, Japanese
	Life stage	Infant, preschool, child, teenager, collegiate, adult, senior
	Income	Under $15,000; $15,000–$24,999; $25,000–$44,999; $45,000–$74,999; $75,000 and over
	Household size	1; 2; 3–4; 5 or more
	Occupation	Professional, technical, clerical, sales supervisors, farmers, students, home-based business owners, retired, unemployed
Psychographic segmentation	Personality	Gregarious, compulsive, extroverted, aggressive, ambitious
	Values	Actualizers, fulfillers, achievers, experiencers, believers, strivers, makers, strugglers
	Lifestyle	Upscale, moderate
Benefit segmentation	Comfort	(Benefit segmentation divides an already established market into smaller, more homogeneous segments. Those people who desire economy in a car would be an example. The benefit desired varies by product.)
	Convenience	
	Durability	
	Economy	
	Health	
	Luxury	
	Safety	
	Status	
Volume segmentation	Usage	Heavy users, light users, nonusers
	Loyalty status	None, medium, strong

volume (or usage) segmentation
Dividing the market by usage (volume of use).

niche marketing
The process of finding small but profitable market segments and designing or finding products for them.

The best segmentation strategy is to use all the variables to come up with a consumer profile that represents a sizable, reachable, and profitable target market. That may mean not segmenting the market at all and instead going after the total market (everyone). Or it may mean going after ever-smaller segments. We'll discuss that strategy next.

Reaching Smaller Market Segments

Niche marketing is identifying small but profitable market segments and designing or finding products for them. Because it so easily offers an unlimited choice of goods, the Internet is transforming a consumer culture once based on big hits and best-sellers into one that supports more specialized niche products.[26] Just how small such a segment can be is illustrated by FridgeDoor.com. This company sells refrigerator magnets on the Internet. It keeps some 1,500 different magnets in stock and sells as many as 400 a week.

One-to-one marketing means developing a unique mix of goods and services for *each individual customer.* Travel agencies often develop such packages, including airline reservations, hotel reservations, rental cars, restaurants, and admission to museums and other attractions for individual customers. This is relatively easy to do in B2B markets where each customer may buy in huge volume. But one-to-one marketing is now becoming possible in consumer markets as well. Dell produces a unique computer system for each customer. Can you envision designing special Very Vegetarian menu items for individual customers?

Moving toward Relationship Marketing

In the world of mass production following the Industrial Revolution, marketers responded by practicing mass marketing. **Mass marketing** means developing products and promotions to please large groups of people. That is, there is little market segmentation. The mass marketer tries to sell the same products to as many people as possible. That means using mass media such as TV, radio, and newspapers to reach them. Although mass marketing led many firms to success, marketing managers often got so caught up with their products and competition that they became less responsive to the market. Airlines, for example, are so intent on meeting competition that they often annoy their customers.

Relationship marketing tends to lead away from mass production and toward custom-made goods and services. The goal is to keep individual customers over time by offering them new products that exactly meet their requirements. The latest in technology enables sellers to work with individual buyers to determine their wants and needs and to develop goods and services specifically designed for them, like hand-tailored shirts and unique vacations.

Understanding consumers is so important to marketing that a whole area of marketing emerged called consumer behavior. We explore that area next.

The Consumer Decision-Making Process

Figure 13.7 shows the consumer decision-making process and some outside factors that influence it. The five steps in the process are often studied in courses on consumer behavior.

The first step is *problem recognition,* which may occur when your washing machine breaks down and you realize you need a new one. This leads to an *information search*—you look for ads and brochures about washing machines. You may consult a secondary data source like *Consumer Reports* or other information, perhaps online. And you'll likely seek advice from other people who have purchased washing machines.

After compiling all this information, you *evaluate alternatives* and make a *purchase decision.* But your buying process doesn't end here. After the purchase, you may ask the people you spoke to previously how their machines perform and then do other comparisons to your new washer.

Consumer behavior researchers investigate people's buying decisions and the factors that influence their choices. Social, psychological, and marketing mix factors are important when we decide what to buy. So are the store environment and our previous buying experiences. What influences the choices you make in your local supermarket?

one-to-one marketing
Developing a unique mix of goods and services for each individual customer.

mass marketing
Developing products and promotions to please large groups of people.

relationship marketing
Marketing strategy with the goal of keeping individual customers over time by offering them products that exactly meet their requirements.

Marketing researchers investigate these consumer thought processes and behavior at each stage in a purchase to determine the best way to help the buyer buy. This area of study is called *consumer behavior.*

Consumer behavior researchers also study the influences that affect consumer behavior. Figure 13.7 shows several: marketing mix variables (the four Ps); psychological influences, such as perception and attitudes; situational influences, such as the type of purchase and the physical surroundings; and sociocultural influences, such as reference groups and culture. Other important factors include these:

Need help understanding
Marketers Segment
Target Market?
www.introbiz.tv/QR13-2

- *Learning* creates changes in an individual's behavior resulting from previous experiences and information. If you've tried a particular brand of shampoo and don't like it, you've learned not to buy it again.

- *Reference group* is the group an individual uses as a reference point in forming beliefs, attitudes, values, or behavior. A college student who carries a briefcase instead of a backpack may see businesspeople as his or her reference group.

- *Culture* is the set of values, attitudes, and ways of doing things transmitted from one generation to another in a given society. The U.S. culture emphasizes and transmits the values of education, freedom, and diversity.

- *Subculture* is the set of values, attitudes, and ways of doing things that results from belonging to a certain ethnic group, racial group, or other group with which one closely identifies (e.g., teenagers).

figure 13.7

THE CONSUMER DECISION-MAKING PROCESS AND OUTSIDE INFLUENCES

There are many influences on consumers as they decide which goods and services to buy. Marketers have some influence, but it's not usually as strong as sociocultural influences. Helping consumers in their information search and their evaluation of alternatives is a major function of marketing.

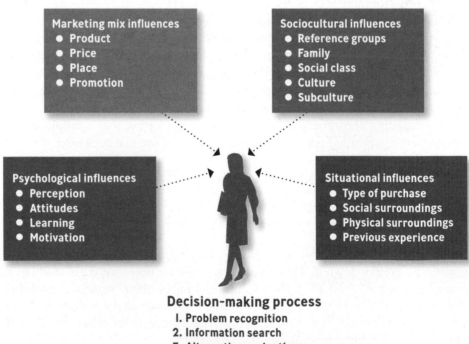

Marketing mix influences
- Product
- Price
- Place
- Promotion

Sociocultural influences
- Reference groups
- Family
- Social class
- Culture
- Subculture

Psychological influences
- Perception
- Attitudes
- Learning
- Motivation

Situational influences
- Type of purchase
- Social surroundings
- Physical surroundings
- Previous experience

Decision-making process
1. Problem recognition
2. Information search
3. Alternative evaluation
4. Purchase decision or no purchase
5. Postpurchase evaluation (cognitive dissonance)

- *Cognitive dissonance* is a type of psychological conflict that can occur after a purchase. Consumers who make a major purchase may have doubts about whether they got the best product at the best price. Marketers must reassure such consumers after the sale that they made a good decision. An auto dealer, for example, may send positive press articles about the particular car a consumer purchased, offer product guarantees, and provide certain free services.

Many universities have expanded the marketing curriculum to include courses in business-to-business marketing. As you'll learn below, that market is huge.

LEARNING goal 6

Compare the business-to-business market and the consumer market.

THE BUSINESS-TO-BUSINESS MARKET

Business-to-business (B2B) marketers include manufacturers; intermediaries such as retailers; institutions like hospitals, schools, and charities; and the government. The B2B market is larger than the consumer market because items are often sold and resold several times in the B2B process before they reach the final consumer. B2B marketing strategies also differ from consumer marketing because business buyers have their own decision-making process. Several factors make B2B marketing different, including these:

1. Customers in the B2B market are relatively few; there are just a few construction firms or mining operations compared to the 70 million or so households in the U.S. consumer market.

2. Business customers are relatively large; that is, big organizations account for most of the employment and production of various goods and services. Nonetheless, there are many small- to medium-sized firms in the United States that together make an attractive market.

3. B2B markets tend to be geographically concentrated. For example, oilfields are found in the Southwest and Alaska. Thus B2B marketers can concentrate their efforts on a particular area and minimize distribution problems by locating warehouses near industrial centers.

4. Business buyers are generally more rational and less emotional than ultimate consumers; they use product specifications to guide buying choices and often more carefully weigh the total product offer, including quality, price, and service.

5. B2B sales tend to be direct, but not always. Tire manufacturers sell directly to auto manufacturers but use intermediaries, such as wholesalers and retailers, to sell to ultimate consumers.

6. Whereas consumer promotions are based more on *advertising,* B2B sales are based on *personal selling.* There are fewer customers and they usually demand more personal service.

	BUSINESS-TO-BUSINESS MARKET	CONSUMER MARKET
Market Structure	Relatively few potential customers Larger purchases Geographically concentrated	Many potential customers Smaller purchases Geographically dispersed
Products	Require technical, complex products Frequently require customization Frequently require technical advice, delivery, and after-sale service	Require less technical products Sometimes require customization Sometimes require technical advice, delivery, and after-sale service
Buying Procedures	Buyers are trained Negotiate details of most purchases Follow objective standards Formal process involving specific employees Closer relationships between marketers and buyers Often buy from multiple sources	No special training Accept standard terms for most purchases Use personal judgment Informal process involving household members Impersonal relationships between marketers and consumers Rarely buy from multiple sources

figure 13.8

COMPARING BUSINESS-TO-BUSINESS AND CONSUMER BUYING BEHAVIOR

Figure 13.8 shows some of the differences between buying behavior in the B2B and consumer markets. B2B buyers also use the Internet to make purchases. You'll learn more about the business-to-business market in advanced marketing courses.

YOUR PROSPECTS IN MARKETING

There is a wider variety of careers in marketing than in most business disciplines. If you major in marketing, an array of career options will be available to you. You could become a manager in a retail store like Saks or Target. You could do marketing research or work in product management. You could go into selling, advertising, sales promotion, or public relations. You could work in transportation, storage, or international distribution. You could design interactive websites to implement CRM. These are just a few of the possibilities. Think, for example, of the many ways to use Facebook, Google, and other new technologies in marketing. As you read through the following marketing chapters, consider whether a marketing career would interest you.

progress assessment

- Can you define the terms *consumer market* and *business-to-business market?*
- Can you name and describe five ways to segment the consumer market?
- What is niche marketing, and how does it differ from one-to-one marketing?
- What are four key factors that make B2B markets different from consumer markets?

summary

Learning Goal 1. Define *marketing,* and apply the marketing concept to both for-profit and nonprofit organizations.

- **What is marketing?**

Marketing is the activity, set of institutions, and processes for creating, communicating, delivering, and exchanging offerings that have value for customers, clients, partners, and society at large.

- **How has marketing changed over time?**

During the *production era,* marketing was largely a distribution function. Emphasis was on producing as many goods as possible and getting them to markets. By the early 1920s, during the *selling era,* the emphasis turned to selling and advertising to persuade customers to buy the existing goods produced by mass production. After World War II, the tremendous demand for goods and services led to the *marketing concept era,* when businesses recognized the need to be responsive to customers' needs. During the 1990s, marketing entered the *customer relationship era,* focusing on enhancing customer satisfaction and stimulating long-term customer loyalty. The newest in customer relationship building involves social networks, online communities, and blogs.

- **What are the three parts of the marketing concept?**

The three parts of the marketing concept are (1) a customer orientation, (2) a service orientation, and (3) a profit orientation (that is, marketing goods and services that will earn a profit and enable the firm to survive and expand).

- **What kinds of organizations are involved in marketing?**

All kinds of organizations use marketing, including for-profit and nonprofit organizations like states, charities, churches, politicians, and schools.

Learning Goal 2. Describe the four Ps of marketing.

- **How do marketers implement the four Ps?**

The idea behind the four Ps is to design a *product* people want, *price* it competitively, *place* it where consumers can find it easily, and *promote* it so consumers know it exists.

Learning Goal 3. Summarize the marketing research process.

- **What are the steps in conducting marketing research?**

(1) Define the problem or opportunity and determine the present situation, (2) collect data, (3) analyze the data, and (4) choose the best solution.

Learning Goal 4. Show how marketers use environmental scanning to learn about the changing marketing environment.

- **What is environmental scanning?**

Environmental scanning is the process of identifying factors that can affect marketing success. Marketers pay attention to all the environmental factors that create opportunities and threats.

- **What are some of the more important environmental trends in marketing?**

The most important global and technological change is probably the growth of the Internet. Another is the growth of consumer databases, with which companies can develop products and services that closely match consumers' needs. Marketers must monitor social trends like population growth and shifts to maintain their close relationship with customers. They must also monitor the dynamic competitive and economic environments.

Learning Goal 5. Explain how marketers apply the tools of market segmentation, relationship marketing, and the study of consumer behavior.

• **What are some of the ways marketers segment the consumer market?**

Geographic segmentation means dividing the market into different regions. Segmentation by age, income, and education level is *demographic segmentation*. We study a group's values, attitudes, and interests using *psychographic segmentation*. Determining which benefits customers prefer and using them to promote a product is *benefit segmentation*. Separating the market by usage is called *volume segmentation*. The best segmentation strategy is to use all the variables to come up with a consumer profile for a target market that's sizable, reachable, and profitable.

• **What is the difference between mass marketing and relationship marketing?**

Mass marketing means developing products and promotions to please large groups of people. Relationship marketing tends to lead away from mass production and toward custom-made goods and services. Its goal is to keep individual customers over time by offering them products or services that meet their needs.

• **What are some of the factors that influence the consumer decision-making process?**

See Figure 13.7 for some of the major influences on consumer decision making. Other factors are learning, reference group, culture, subculture, and cognitive dissonance.

Learning Goal 6. Compare the business-to-business market and the consumer market.

• **What makes the business-to-business market different from the consumer market?**

Customers in the B2B market are relatively few and large. B2B markets tend to be geographically concentrated, and industrial buyers generally are more rational than ultimate consumers in their selection of goods and services. B2B sales tend to be direct, and there is much more emphasis on personal selling than in consumer markets.

key terms

benefit
  segmentation 391
brand name 382
business-to-business
  (B2B) market 390
consumer market 390
customer relationship
  management (CRM) 379

demographic
  segmentation 391
environmental
  scanning 387
focus group 385
geographic
  segmentation 391
marketing 376

marketing concept 378
marketing mix 380
marketing
  research 384
market
  segmentation 390
mass marketing 393
niche marketing 392

one-to-one
 marketing 393
primary data 385
product 381
promotion 383

psychographic
 segmentation 391
relationship
 marketing 393
secondary data 385

target marketing 390
test marketing 382
volume
 (or usage)
 segmentation 392

critical thinking

1. When businesses buy goods and services from other businesses, they usually buy in large volume. Salespeople in the business-to-business area usually are paid on a commission basis; that is, they earn a certain percentage of each sale they make. Why might B2B sales be a more financially rewarding career area than consumer sales?

2. Industrial companies sell goods such as steel, lumber, computers, engines, parts, and supplies. Name three such companies in your region.

3. What environmental changes are occurring in your community? What has been the impact of the recent economic crisis? What environmental changes in marketing are most likely to change your career prospects in the future? How can you learn more about those changes? What might you do to prepare for them?

4. Which of your needs are not being met by businesses and/or nonprofit organizations in your area? Are there enough people with similar needs to attract an organization that would meet those needs? How would you find out?

developing workplace skills

1. Think of an effective marketing mix for a new electric car or a brushless car wash for your neighborhood. Be prepared to discuss your ideas in class.

2. Working in teams of five (or on your own), think of a product or service your friends want but cannot get on or near campus. You might ask your friends at other schools what's available there. What kind of product would fill that need? Discuss your results in class and how you might go about marketing that new product or service.

3. Business has fallen off greatly at your upscale restaurant because of the economic crisis. List four things you can do to win back the loyalty of your past customers.

4. Working in teams of four or five (or on your own), list as many brand names of pizza as you can, including from pizza shops, restaurants, supermarkets, and so on. Merge your list with the lists from other groups or classmates. Then try to identify the target market for each brand. Do they all seem to be after the same market, or are there different brands for different markets? What are the separate appeals?

5. Take a little time to review the concepts in this chapter as they apply to Very Vegetarian, the restaurant we used as an example throughout. Have an open discussion in class about (*a*) a different name for the restaurant, (*b*) a location for the restaurant, (*c*) a promotional program, and (*d*) a way to establish a long-term relationship with customers.

taking it to the net

Purpose

To demonstrate how the Internet can be used to enhance marketing relationships.

Exercise

Nike wants to help its customers add soul to their soles and express their individuality by customizing their own shoes. See for yourself at **www.nike.com**. Enter "customize" in the search box and build a shoe that fits your style.

1. What if you're in the middle of your shoe design and have questions about what to do next? Where can you go for help?

2. How does Nike's website help the company strengthen its relationships with its stakeholders? Give examples to support your answer.

3. How do the elements of the website reflect Nike's target market?

4. Does Nike invite comments from visitors to its website? If so, how does this affect its attempt to build positive relationships with its customers?

casing the web

To access the case "Measuring Marketing Effectiveness," visit
www.mhhe.com/P2P2e

video case

Using the 4 Ps at Energizer

The Energizer Bunny is a marketing icon. How many people are not familiar with this marketing campaign? The precursor to the company known today as Energizer was founded by two inventors: the inventor of the battery and the inventor of the flashlight. The synergy should be obvious. This partnership grew into the leading manufacturer and seller of batteries in the world today. Energizer is truly a global company operating across the globe. Energizer has developed and implemented an outstanding marketing approach to its product lines. In fact, Energizer demonstrates the full range of marketing concepts, including the use of social media and market research in successfully promoting and sustaining a brand.

Advertising Age magazine ranks the brand icon Energizer Bunny as the number five brand icon of

the twentieth century. This provides Energizer a competitive advantage in many of its markets. The company is continually involved in new product development through the identification and understanding of consumer needs, including how a person intends to use a battery, in what devices, and the types of users for various products where Energizer batteries can be used.

Energizer has a well-developed and highly effective marketing division that is responsible for helping to ensure the success of current and new products. The video walks the viewer through the four Ps of marketing—product, price, place, and promotion—and shows how Energizer utilizes marketing concepts effectively.

The company views its approach to marketing and selling its product lines as one that is focused on developing, cultivating, and expanding customer relationships. Energizer is a company that has been significantly impacted by the growth of technology and uses this and the growth of the Internet as parts of its overall marketing communications approach to develop strong and lasting relationships with its customers.

The video demonstrates the importance of relationship marketing as a key to Energizer's success. The complexities involved in the marketing mix, marketing research, and new product development are highlighted through specific examples, such as the new product introduced by the company each summer. We see how the company uses qualitative data such as focus groups and secondary data to test-market its product, elicit customer feedback, collect demographic and other data, and match its marketing strategy to be consistent with the appropriate segmentation factors.

Thinking It Over

1. *Identify the elements that must be considered in the marketing environment.*
2. *Briefly discuss the evolution of marketing as described in the video.*
3. *The Energizer Bunny is considered a marketing icon. What does this mean?*

14

Developing and Pricing
GOODS AND Services

LEARNING goals

After you have read and studied this chapter, you should be able to

1 Describe a total product offer.

2 Identify the various kinds of consumer and industrial goods.

3 Summarize the functions of packaging.

4 Contrast *brand, brand name,* and *trademark,* and show the value of brand equity.

5 Explain the steps in the new-product development process.

6 Describe the product life cycle.

7 Identify various pricing objectives and strategies.

Some of the best business ideas are born out of necessity. Savvy entrepreneurs know that if they have a need the market can't fill, they had better look for a way to fill it themselves. No matter how much technology streamlines our lives, there will always be problems that only old-fashioned ingenuity can solve.

Randy Hetrick found himself in that position during his time as a Navy Seal. These elite commandos keep their bodies in the same type of peak physical condition as professional athletes. But maintaining that level of fitness in the field can be difficult. During a training mission in Southeast Asia, Hetrick and his team had to remain undercover in a warehouse for weeks.

CONNECTING WITH

X *Randy Hetrick*

CEO of Fitness Anywhere

Although he had plenty of room for pushups and situps, Hetrick needed more intensive exercise to stay in shape. He remembered a workout that used his body weight as resistance rather than barbells. In order to suspend his body, he created a "gizmo" out of spare parachute harnesses and nylon webbing and attached it to the end of a door. It worked great and quickly became a hit with his whole squadron. As the years went by, the contraption became Hetrick's passion, as he developed and improved the product along with the help of his fellow Seals.

Still, Hetrick knew that if he really wanted to get the device off the ground he'd need more education about the business world. After 14 years in the Navy, Hetrick left to earn his MBA at Stanford University. At first he had a tough time convincing people that his product was worth anything. "I thought he was nuts, to be completely honest," says Stanford's Business School Dean Garth Saloner. "It looked like an old belt with stirrups." Despite the challenges he faced, Hetrick worked on the product with conditioning coaches at the school's gym and turned it into a refined prototype. His old belt had evolved into a sophisticated piece of equipment featuring three adjustable straps attached to a metal ring. It allowed users to perform hundreds of different exercises by suspending their legs in the air or simply leaning forward.

By the time he earned his MBA in 2004, Hetrick had raised $350,000 in capital from military friends and Stanford investors to launch Fitness Anywhere in a cramped San Francisco office space. His beloved "gizmo"

changed into the TRX Suspension Trainer and sold for about $150 to $200. The company grew quickly as the TRX became popular in military circles as well as with civilian consumers. As Fitness Anywhere picked up steam, Hetrick wondered if it was time to reevaluate his business model. After all, since interest in the TRX had grown so quickly, there had to be other ways to take advantage of its success. Also, most other exercise companies made their money from exclusively selling gear. This was Hetrick's chance to stand out from the pack by branching out. Fitness Anywhere started providing classes, instructional DVDs, and online videos about suspension training. These added services launched the company into profitability. By 2011, Hetrick and his 120 employees saw revenues hit $50 million.

Fitness Anywhere relocated into an office worthy of such a successful startup. Occupying four floors of a San Francisco office building, staffers work while sitting on exercise balls or at stand-up desks. The top floor is a 2,500-square-foot gym overlooking the city, while kitchens throughout the office offer an array of energy bars and protein shakes. Employees are expected to live a healthy lifestyle both at work and at home. "Working out is not only sanctioned, it almost is required," says Hetrick. In the end Hetrick figures if you're selling a healthier lifestyle, you ought to live that way yourself. That "walk the talk" attitude has served him well in the past and should continue to as Fitness Anywhere sprints into the future.

Like Randy Hetrick, the companies that command the business world are innovative pioneers. In this chapter you'll learn all about how entrepreneurs develop and price new products and services. You will also learn about packaging, branding, and other elements of a total product offer.

Sources: Leigh Buchanan, "Walking the Walk (Running the Run, Etc.)" *Inc.*, June 2011; "Business Unusual: Operation Muffintop," *Entrepreneur*, January 14, 2010; "Who's Laughing Now?" *Stanford Business Magazine*, Winter 2009; and Antone Gonsalves, "Former Navy SEAL Sells TRX Fitness Gear to 'Enable' Content Sales," *Bloomberg*, March 8, 2011.

It's no secret that the airline industry is extremely competitive and many airlines have cut basic services like free baggage and food. In order to set itself apart from its competitors, this company takes a different path by offering door-to-door limousine service and in-flight massages. What is the name of this company? (Find the answer in the chapter.)

LEARNING goal 1

Describe a total product offer.

PRODUCT DEVELOPMENT AND THE TOTAL PRODUCT OFFER

value
Good quality at a fair price. When consumers calculate the value of a product, they look at the benefits and then subtract the cost to see if the benefits exceed the costs.

Global managers will be challenging U.S. managers with new products at low prices.[1] The best way to compete is to design and promote better products, meaning products that customers perceive to have the best **value**—good quality at a fair price.[2] You may have noticed that many restaurants were pushing "value meals" when the economy slowed from 2008 to 2012. Have you tried, for example, the new, smaller Blizzard from Dairy Queen?[3]

One of the American Marketing Association's definitions of marketing says it's "a set of processes for creating, communicating, and delivering *value* to customers." When consumers calculate the value of a product, they look at the benefits and then subtract the cost (price) to see whether the benefits exceed the costs, including the cost of driving to the store (or shipping fees if they buy the product online). Note that L.L. Bean eliminated shipping charges. That lowers the cost for consumers and makes their products more desirable (valuable).[4]

Whether consumers perceive a product as the best value depends on many factors, including the benefits they seek and the service they receive. To satisfy consumers, marketers must learn to listen better and constantly adapt to changing market demands. For example, traditional phone companies must now compete with Voice over Internet Protocol (VoIP)—a system that allows people to make very inexpensive phone calls through the Internet. And U.S. automobile companies must adapt to foreign producers by offering more competitive cars, or face extinction.[5]

Marketers have learned that adapting products to new competition and new markets is an ongoing need. We're sure you've noticed menu changes at your local fast-food restaurants over time. An organization can't do a one-time survey of consumer wants and needs, design a group of products to meet those needs, put them in the stores, and then just relax. It must constantly monitor changing consumer wants and needs, and adapt products, policies, and services accordingly. Did you know that McDonald's sells as much chicken as beef these days?[6] Some is being sold as a Chicken Biscuit for breakfast. Those double cheeseburgers fast-food

CONNECTING THROUGH
social media

www.bocktown.com

Settling Up Simply through Social Media

The social media world is in a state of constant change. So why shouldn't businesses follow suit? That's at least how the owner of Bocktown Beer and Grill sees business today. The Pittsburgh gastropub rotates its beer taps on a daily basis, meaning what was there yesterday might not be back the next. They hold polls on Facebook and Twitter to let customers decide which craft beer appears next on the tap. Bocktown also optimized their website for mobile phones, making it easier for customers to engage with the brand on the go.

But their next experiment might prove to be the most radical one yet. Bocktown recently introduced Tabbedout, a mobile payment app that allows customers to pay straight from their smartphones. Developed by a startup in Austin, Texas, customers can get started with the service by entering their credit card information on the app. The data is stored on their device and remains encrypted, ensuring that it's even safer than dropping off your card

with a server. Users can then enter an establishment like Bocktown that uses Tabbedout and immediately open a tab through the app. Tabbedout creates a unique five-digit code that tallies the total bill. Once they've finished, all the customers need to do is settle their tab by pressing a button in the app and then walk out the door.

So far Bocktown says that the app is a blessing to both servers and customers alike. In 2011 the app was being used in approximately 350 establishments across the country. In a few years, restaurants that don't carry a similar app may seem backward. In the meantime, bars like Bocktown will continue to blaze the trails that others may eventually follow.

Sources: Scott Reitz "Tabbedout: The iPhone App That Lets You Close Your Tab without Really Opening One," *The Dallas Observer*, April 9, 2012; and Jason Ankeny, "Tabbedout: A Mobile Payment App for Restaurants and Bars," *Entrepreneur*, December 15, 2011.

---

restaurants were serving for $1.00 turned out to be a money loser, even though they were popular with consumers. You can't give consumers *too* good a deal or you can go out of business.

McDonald's and other restaurants are constantly trying new ideas. McDonald's added smoothies, oatmeal with fruit, and McBaguettes.[7] In Kokomo, Indiana, McDonald's tried waiter service and a more varied menu. In New York, it offered McDonuts to compete with Krispy Kreme. In Atlanta and other cities, McDonald's had computer stations linked to the Internet. In Hawaii, it tried a Spam breakfast platter, and in Columbus, Ohio, a mega-McDonald's had a karaoke booth. McDonald's has a McCafé in Chicago's Loop that sells premium coffee, pastries, and wrapped sandwiches. It has more than 300 such cafés in other countries, and most McDonald's in the United States are putting in something similar. Watch out Starbucks. Some McDonald's even have digital-media kiosks that allow customers to burn custom CDs from a catalog of 70,000 songs, print digital photos, and download ringtones for mobile phones. See the Connecting Through Social Media box for an example of how one bar uses Facebook and Twitter to let customers decide which craft beers to have on tap.

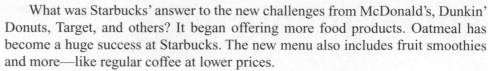

distributed product development
Handing off various parts of your innovation process—often to companies in other countries.

total product offer
Everything that consumers evaluate when deciding whether to buy something; also called a value package.

What was Starbucks' answer to the new challenges from McDonald's, Dunkin' Donuts, Target, and others? It began offering more food products. Oatmeal has become a huge success at Starbucks. The new menu also includes fruit smoothies and more—like regular coffee at lower prices.

All fast-food organizations must constantly monitor all sources of information for new-product ideas. McDonald's isn't alone in that. Look at those baguettes and cream cheese croissants at 7-Eleven—they're right next to the cappuccino machine. KFC put in a line of chicken sandwiches. Burger King tried an X-treme Double Cheeseburger. Wendy's is trying a major coffee program in Mississippi, including iced coffee, and introducing a whole new lineup of other products.

Offerings may differ in various locations according to the wants of the local community. In Iowa pork tenderloin is big, but in Oklahoma City it's tortilla scramblers. Globally, companies must adapt to local tastes. At Bob's Big Boy in Thailand, you can get Tropical Shrimp; at Carl's Jr. in Mexico, you can order the Machaca Burrito; and at Shakey's Pizza in the Philippines, you can get Cali Shandy, a Filipino beer. Product development, then, is a key activity in any modern business, anywhere in the world.

You can imagine what can happen when your product loses some of its appeal. Zippo lighters, for example, may lose some market as people turn away from smoking. Zippo, therefore, tried offering products such as key holders, tape measures, and belt buckles. They are no longer being sold, but Zippo has recently introduced a new men's fragrance and a clothing line that includes hoodies, ball caps, and jeans.[8]

Distributed Product Development

The increase in outsourcing and alliance building has resulted in innovation efforts that often require using multiple organizations separated by cultural, geographic, and legal boundaries. **Distributed product development** is the term used to describe handing off various parts of your innovation process—often to companies in other countries. It is difficult enough to coordinate processes within a firm; it becomes substantially more difficult when trying to coordinate multifirm processes.[9] Great care must be taken to establish goals and procedures and standards before any such commitment is made.[10] One company that has collaborated with many other firms to make innovative products is 3M Company. It has developed some 55,000 products from Scotch tape to Thinsulate, and many of those products are embedded in other products such as the iPhone.[11]

Apple's iPhone offers a range of features and functions, including the ability to make video calls, take photos, check e-mail, browse websites, get directions, tell time, keep a shopping list, record appointments in your calendar, download songs, sync with your other devices, and even make and receive phone calls. The product will likely continue to evolve and improve. What would you like Apple to add to the iPhone's total product offer?

Developing a Total Product Offer

From a strategic marketing viewpoint, a product is more than just the physical good or service. A **total product offer** consists of everything consumers evaluate when deciding whether to buy something. Thus, the basic product or service may be a washing machine, an insurance policy, or a beer, but the total product offer includes some or all of the *value* enhancers in Figure 14.1. You may hear some people call the basic product the "core product" and the total product offer the "augmented product." Can you see how sustainability can be part of the augmented product?

When people buy a product, they may evaluate and compare total product offers on many dimensions. Some are tangible (the product itself and its package); others are intangible (the producer's reputation and the image created by advertising). A successful

figure 14.1

POTENTIAL COMPONENTS OF A
TOTAL PRODUCT OFFER

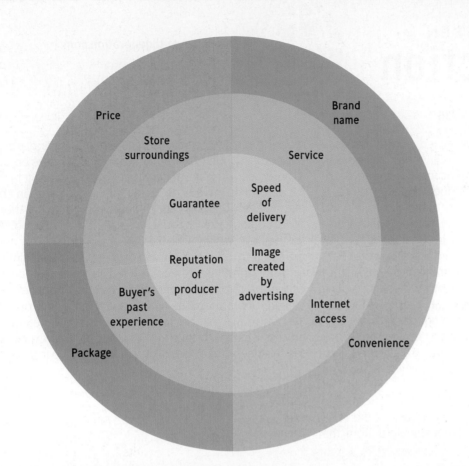

marketer must begin to think like a consumer and evaluate the total product offer as a collection of impressions created by all the factors listed in Figure 14.1. It is wise to talk with consumers to see which features and benefits are most important to them and which value enhancers they want or don't want in the final offering. Frito-Lay, for example, had to drop biodegradable bags because they were "too noisy." The Making the Green Connection box discusses how one company successfully uses recyclable materials in its packaging.

What questions might you ask consumers when developing the total product offer for Very Vegetarian? (Recall the business idea we introduced in Chapter 13.) Remember, store surroundings are important in the restaurant business, as are the parking lot and the condition of bathrooms. When designing services, some have even suggested the importance of things like feelings in general.[12]

Sometimes an organization can use low prices to create an attractive total product offer. For example, outlet stores offer brand-name goods for less. Shoppers like getting high-quality goods and low prices, but they must be careful. Outlets also carry lower-quality products with similar but not exactly the same features as goods carried in regular stores. Different consumers may want different total product offers, so a company must develop a variety of offerings.

Product Lines and the Product Mix

Companies usually don't sell just one product. A **product line** is a group of products that are physically similar or intended for a similar market. They usually face similar competition. In one product line, there may be several competing brands. Notice, for example, Diet Coke, Diet Coke with Splenda, Coke Zero, Diet Coke with Lemon, Diet Coke with Lime, Diet Vanilla Coke, and Diet Cherry Coke. Makes it

product line
A group of products that are physically similar or are intended for a similar market.

Thinking Outside the Bottle

With more people today concerned about the environment than ever before, recycling has become an established ritual for many Americans. But all recyclable items are not made equal. Cardboard, for instance, is much easier to process and reuse than plastic. It's also more likely to be sorted into the recycling bin. While most of the country's plastic bottles only make it as far as the dump, 81 percent of all cardboard is recycled.

For Seventh Generation, a green products manufacturer, this plastic problem frustrated the company for years. After all, why bother to make sustainable products if most of them will end up in the dump anyway? In 2012, though, the company figured out a way to turn their trouble into an opportunity. In the fall of that year, the company released a new line of laundry detergent packaged in cardboard.

The environmental impact of the switch from plastic to cardboard is apparent at every step in the recycling process. While cardboard goes straight from the recycling bin to the Seventh Generation bottling plant, plastic must undergo a number of additional steps before it becomes a usable material. In that process, it takes 51 percent less water to treat the cardboard than the plastic. Even the shipping benefits are obvious. About 161,000 folded cardboard shells can fit in a truck bound for the filling facility. Only 25,000 empty bottles can fit in the same truck, making most of the truck's load simply air. Although the detergent is filled into plastic pouches within the cardboard, three times as many pouches can be made from the same amount of plastic used for bottles. Only time will tell, however, if Seventh Generation's process is cost effective and efficient. If it is, expect to see this new kind of packaging a lot in the near future!

Sources: Jill Ettinger, "Seventh Generation 'Greenest' American Brand, According to New Research," *Organic Authority,* June 18, 2011; and Emma Haak, "Package Ripple," *Fast Company,* December 2011/January 2012.

---

kind of hard to choose, doesn't it? Even Coke commercials have product managers who can't tell the difference between Coke and Coke Zero. Have you seen the new aluminum Coke bottle? It's recyclable, resealable, less costly to make than a plastic or glass bottle, and feels cooler to the touch. Both Coke and Pepsi have added water and sports drinks to their product lines to meet new consumer tastes.

Procter & Gamble (P&G) has many brands in its laundry detergent product line, including Tide, Era, Downy, and Bold. P&G's product lines together make up its **product mix,** the combination of all product lines offered by a manufacturer. Have you noticed that there are some 352 distinct types of toothpastes available in stores?[13] Do you think that is too many or not?

Service providers have product lines and product mixes as well. A bank or credit union may offer a variety of services from savings accounts, automated teller machines, and computer banking to money market funds, safety deposit boxes, car loans, mortgages, traveler's checks, online banking, and insurance. AT&T combines services (communications) with goods (phones) in its product mix, with special emphasis on wireless.

product mix
The combination of product lines offered by a manufacturer.

product differentiation
The creation of real or perceived product differences.

convenience goods and services
Products that the consumer wants to purchase frequently and with a minimum of effort.

LEARNING goal 2

Identify the various kinds of consumer and industrial goods.

PRODUCT DIFFERENTIATION

Product differentiation is the creation of real or perceived product differences. Actual product differences are sometimes quite small, so marketers must use a creative mix of pricing, advertising, and packaging (value enhancers) to create a unique, attractive image. Various bottled water companies, for example, have successfully attempted product differentiation. The companies made their bottled waters so attractive through pricing and promotion that now restaurant customers often order water by brand name.

There's no reason why you couldn't create a similar attractive image for Very Vegetarian, your vegetarian restaurant. Small businesses can often win market share with creative product differentiation. Yearbook photographer Charlie Clark competes by offering multiple clothing changes, backgrounds, and poses along with special allowances, discounts, and guarantees. His small business has the advantage of being more flexible in adapting to customer needs and wants, and he's able to offer attractive product options. Clark has been so successful that companies use him as a speaker at photography conventions. How could you respond creatively to the consumer wants of vegetarians?

Marketing Different Classes of Consumer Goods and Services

One popular classification of consumer goods and services has four general categories—convenience, shopping, specialty, and unsought.

1. **Convenience goods and services** are products the consumer wants to purchase frequently and with a minimum of effort, like candy, gum, milk, snacks, gas, and banking services. One store that sells mostly convenience goods is 7-Eleven. Location, brand awareness, and image are important for marketers of convenience goods and services. The Internet has taken convenience to a whole new level, especially for banks and other service companies. Companies that don't offer such services are likely to lose market share to those that do unless they offer outstanding service to customers who visit in person.

2. **Shopping goods and services** are products the consumer buys only after comparing value, quality, price, and style from a variety of sellers. Shopping goods and services are sold largely through *shopping centers* where consumers can make comparisons of products like clothes, shoes, appliances, and auto repair services. Target is one store that sells mostly shopping goods. Because many consumers carefully compare such products, marketers can emphasize price differences, quality differences, or some combination of the two. Think of how the Internet has helped you find the right shopping goods.

3. **Specialty goods and services** are consumer products with unique characteristics and brand identity. Because consumers perceive that specialty goods have no reasonable substitute, they put forth a special effort to purchase them. Examples include fine watches, expensive wine, fur coats, jewelry, imported chocolates, and services provided by medical specialists or business consultants.

shopping goods and services
Those products that the consumer buys only after comparing value, quality, price, and style from a variety of sellers.

specialty goods and services
Consumer products with unique characteristics and brand identity. Because these products are perceived as having no reasonable substitute, the consumer puts forth a special effort to purchase them.

Tap the "Gift a Drink" button on Pepsi's new Social Vending Machine, enter your info, choose a drink, record an optional video message, enter your friends' info, and instantly they'll receive a text message with a code to redeem their drink at another sociable machine. Do you think this new machine will be popular?

Specialty goods are often marketed through specialty magazines. Specialty skis may be sold through sports magazines and specialty foods through gourmet magazines. Again, the Internet helps buyers find specialty goods. In fact, some specialty goods can be sold exclusively on the Internet.

4. **Unsought goods and services** are products consumers are unaware of, haven't necessarily thought of buying, or suddenly find they need to solve an unexpected problem. They include emergency car-towing services, burial services, and insurance.

The marketing task varies according to the category of product; convenience goods are marketed differently from specialty goods. The best way to promote convenience goods is to make them readily available and create the proper image. Some combination of price, quality, and service is the best appeal for shopping goods. Specialty goods rely on reaching special market segments through advertising. Unsought goods such as life insurance often rely on personal selling. Car towing relies heavily on Yellow Pages advertising.

Whether a good or service falls into a particular class depends on the individual consumer. Coffee can be a shopping good for one consumer, while flavored gourmet roast is a specialty good for another. Some people shop around to compare different dry cleaners, so dry cleaning is a shopping service for them. Others go to the closest store, making it a convenience service. Marketers must carefully monitor their customer base to determine how consumers perceive their products.[14]

Marketing Industrial Goods and Services

Many goods could be classified as consumer goods or industrial goods, based on their uses. A computer kept at home for personal use is clearly a consumer good. But in a commercial setting, such as an accounting firm or manufacturing plant, the same computer is an industrial good.

Industrial goods (sometimes called business goods or B2B goods) are products used in the production of other products. They are sold in the business-to-business (B2B) market. Some products can be both consumer and industrial goods. We've just mentioned how personal computers fit in both categories. As a consumer good, a computer might be sold through electronics stores or computer magazines. Most of the promotion would be advertising. As an industrial good, personal computers are more likely to be sold through salespeople or on

Many goods could be classified as consumer goods or industrial goods, based on their uses. For example, a computer that a person uses at home for personal use would clearly be a consumer good. But that same computer used in a commercial setting, such as a hospital, would be classified as an industrial good. What difference does it make how a good is classified?

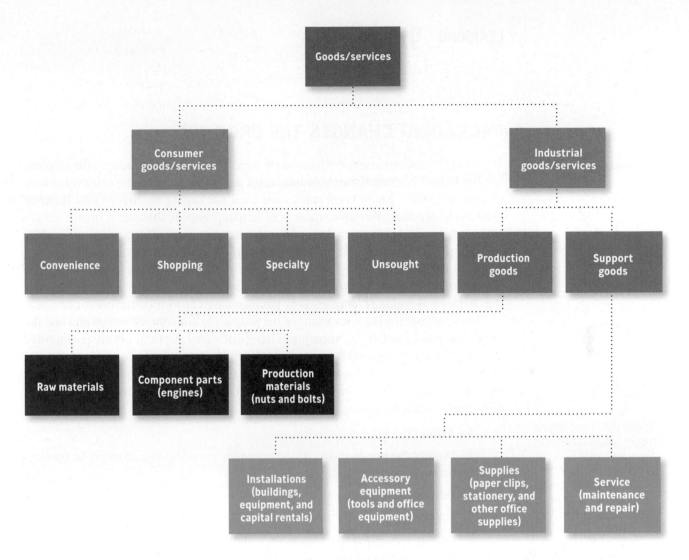

figure 14.2

VARIOUS CATEGORIES OF
CONSUMER AND INDUSTRIAL
GOODS AND SERVICES

the Internet. Advertising is less of a factor when selling industrial goods. Thus, you can see that classifying goods by user category helps marketers determine the proper marketing mix strategy.

Figure 14.2 shows some categories of both consumer goods and industrial goods and services. *Installations* consist of major capital equipment such as new factories and heavy machinery. *Capital items* are expensive products that last a long time. A new factory building is both a capital item and an installation. *Accessory equipment* consists of capital items that are not quite as long-lasting or expensive as installations—like computers, copy machines, and various tools. Various categories of industrial goods are shown in the figure.

progress assessment

- What value enhancers may be included in a total product offer?
- What's the difference between a product line and a product mix?
- Name the four classes of consumer goods and services, and give examples of each.
- Describe three different types of industrial goods.

LEARNING **goal 3**

Summarize the functions of packaging.

PACKAGING CHANGES THE PRODUCT

We've said that consumers evaluate many aspects of the total product offer, including the brand. It's surprising how important packaging can be in such evaluations of various goods. Many companies have used packaging to change and improve their basic product. We have squeezable ketchup bottles that stand upside down; square paint cans with screw tops and integrated handles; plastic bottles for motor oil that eliminate the need for funnels; toothpaste pumps; packaged dinners and other foods, like popcorn, that can be cooked in a microwave oven; single-use packets of spices; and so forth. Another interesting innovation is aromatic packaging. Arizona Beverage Company now has aromatic caps on its flavored iced teas.

In each case, the package changed the product in consumers' minds and opened large new markets. Do you sometimes have difficulty opening plastic packaging? Which packaging innovations do you like best? Can you see some market potential in developing better packaging? Packaging has even become a profession. Check out the Michigan State University School of Packaging, for example. Packages must perform the following functions:

1. Attract the buyer's attention.
2. Protect the goods inside, stand up under handling and storage, be tamper-proof, and deter theft.
3. Be easy to open and use.
4. Describe and give information about the contents.
5. Explain the benefits of the good inside.
6. Provide information on warranties, warnings, and other consumer matters.
7. Give some indication of price, value, and uses.

Packaging can also make a product more attractive to retailers. The Universal Product Codes (UPCs) on many packages help stores control inventory. They combine a bar code and a preset number that gives the retailer information about the product's price, size, color, and other attributes. In short, packaging changes the product by changing its visibility, usefulness, or attractiveness.

One relatively new packaging technology for tracking products is the radio frequency identification (RFID) chip, especially the ones made with nanoparticle powder. When attached to a product, the chip sends out signals telling a company where the product is at all times. RFID chips carry more information than bar codes, don't have to be read one at a time (whole pallets can be read in an instant), and can be read at a distance. Walmart has been a leader in using RFID technology.

The Growing Importance of Packaging

Packaging has always been an important aspect of the product offer, but today it's carrying more of the promotional burden than in the past. Many products once sold by salespersons are now sold in self-service outlets, and

Even industrial products can benefit from innovative packaging. This foot-tall High-Tech CFO. Action Figure is a talking doll created by a design consulting firm in response to a client's request for a written report for business analysts. Long after a report would have been filed, the Chief Financial Officer doll is still sitting on executives' desks. Can you think of other packaging innovations for office products?

High-Tech
CFO
Action
Figure

SERVICESOURCE

the package has acquired more sales responsibility. The Fair Packaging and Labeling Act was passed to give consumers much more quantity and value information on product packaging.

Packaging may make use of a strategy called **bundling,** which combines goods and/or services for a single price. Virgin Airlines has bundled door-to-door limousine service and in-flight massages in its total product offer. Financial institutions are offering everything from financial advice to help in purchasing insurance, stocks, bonds, mutual funds, and more. When combining goods or services into one package, marketers must not include so much that the price gets too high. It's best to work with customers to develop value enhancers that meet their individual needs.[15]

bundling
Grouping two or more products together and pricing them as a unit.

LEARNING goal 4

Contrast *brand, brand name,* and *trademark,* and show the value of brand equity.

brand
A name, symbol, or design (or combination thereof) that identifies the goods or services of one seller or group of sellers and distinguishes them from the goods and services of competitors.

trademark
A brand that has exclusive legal protection for both its brand name and its design.

BRANDING AND BRAND EQUITY

A **brand** is a name, symbol, or design (or combination thereof) that identifies the goods or services of one seller or group of sellers and distinguishes them from the goods and services of competitors. The word *brand* includes practically all means of identifying a product. As we noted in Chapter 13, a *brand name* consists of a word, letter, or group of words or letters that differentiates one seller's goods and services from those of competitors. Brand names you may be familiar with include Red Bull, Sony, Del Monte, Campbell, Levi's, Google, Borden, Michelob, and of course many more. Brand names give products a distinction that tends to make them attractive to consumers. The Connecting Across Borders box discusses product names in more depth.

A **trademark** is a brand that has exclusive legal protection for both its brand name and its design. Trademarks like McDonald's golden arches are widely recognized and help represent the company's reputation and image. McDonald's might sue to prevent a company from selling, say, McDonnel hamburgers. Did you know there are Starsbuck coffee shops in China? (Look closely at that name.)

People are often impressed by certain brand names, even though they say there's no difference between brands in a given product category. For example, even when people say that all aspirin is alike, if you put two aspirin bottles in front of them—one with the Bayer label and one with an unknown name—most choose the one with the well-known brand name. Gasoline buyers often choose a brand name (e.g., Exxon) over price.

For the buyer, a brand name ensures quality, reduces search time, and adds prestige to purchases. For the seller, brand names facilitate new-product introductions, help promotional efforts, add to repeat purchases, and differentiate products so that prices can be set higher. What brand-name products do you prefer?

The new Heinz Dip & Squeeze ketchup package allows restaurant owners to offer their customers a choice of peeling off the lid for dipping or tearing off the top for squeezing. The new package contains three times the ketchup of traditional sachets and uses less packaging. Shaped like the iconic bottles, the packets reinforce the Heinz Ketchup brand.

CONNECTING ACROSS
borders

www.nabisco.com

What's in a Name?

So, you've developed a product and you're ready to take it on the market. What should you call it? America's favorite cookie, Oreo, is said to be a great name because the two O's nicely mirror the shape of the cookie itself. Could the name be part of the charm? Twitter has become the most-used word in the English language according to Global Language Monitor data. Think of the names that come to your mind when you think of American products: Coke, Pepsi, Häagen-Dazs (yes, an American product), and so on.

At one time, finding a name for a product was relatively simple. Now, with a couple hundred countries on the cyber-platform, choosing the right name is a global issue. For example, a web development company in New Zealand chose the name hairyLemon. It has been estimated that at least a third of hairyLemon's business came from its name. Not all do-it-yourself names have been successful. For example, when Russian gas company Gazprom formed a joint venture with Nigeria's NNPC, the company was called NiGaz. Not a great name, we'd say.

Every once in a while, a successful name is created by accident. For example, the popular search engine was supposed to be called Googol (a scientific name for 1 followed by one hundred zeros). However, the founders made a typo when registering the domain name. The error resulted in a warm, catchy, human-sounding name.

In the marketing chapter, we chose the name Very Vegetarian for our new vegetarian restaurant. Have you come up with a better name? Would it help to brainstorm names with others? Would it be worthwhile to bring in an expert?

What if you wanted to build vegetarian restaurants at schools around the world? Would that make a difference? Can you see why names are critical to the long-run success of many firms?

Sources: Susan Purcell and Jay Jurisich, "Enter the Lexicon," *Bloomberg Businessweek*, October 25–October 31, 2010; Igor International Naming and Branding Agency, www.igorinternational.com, accessed May 2012; and Elizabeth Sile, "How to Pick a Name for Your Business," *OPEN Forum*, May 11, 2012.

Brand Categories

manufacturers' brands
The brand names of manufacturers that distribute products nationally.

dealer (private-label) brands
Products that don't carry the manufacturer's name but carry a distributor or retailer's name instead.

Several categories of brands are familiar to you. **Manufacturers' brands** represent manufacturers that distribute products nationally—Xerox, Kodak, Sony, and Dell, for example.

Dealer (private-label) brands are products that don't carry the manufacturer's name but carry a distributor or retailer's name instead. Kenmore and DieHard are dealer brands sold by Sears. These brands are also known as *house brands* or *distributor brands*.

Many manufacturers fear having their brand names become generic names. A *generic name* is the name for a whole product category. Did you know that aspirin and linoleum were once brand names? So were nylon, escalator, kerosene, and zipper. All those names became so popular, so identified with the product, that they lost their brand status and became generic. (Such issues are decided in the courts.)

Their producers then had to come up with new names. The original Aspirin, for example, became Bayer aspirin. Companies working hard to protect their brand names today include Xerox and Rollerblade (in-line skates).

Generic goods are nonbranded products that usually sell at a sizable discount compared to national or private-label brands. They feature basic packaging and are backed with little or no advertising. Some are of poor quality, but many come close to the same quality as the national brand-name goods they copy. There are generic tissues, generic cigarettes, generic drugs, and so on. Consumers today are buying large amounts of generic products because their overall quality has improved so much in recent years. What has been your experience trying generic products?

Knockoff brands are illegal copies of national brand-name goods. If you see an expensive brand-name item such as a Polo shirt or a Rolex watch for sale at a ridiculously low price, you can be pretty sure it's a knockoff. Often the brand name is just a little off, too, like Palo (Polo) or Bolex (Rolex). Look carefully. Zippo has taken to calling counterfeit copies "Rippos."[16]

Generating Brand Equity and Loyalty

A major goal of marketers in the future will be to reestablish the notion of brand equity. **Brand equity** is the value of the brand name and associated symbols. Usually, a company cannot know the value of its brand until it sells it to another company. Brand names with high reported brand equity ratings include Reynolds Wrap aluminum foil and Ziploc food bags. What's the most valuable brand name today? It's Apple. Microsoft is not far behind.[17]

The core of brand equity is **brand loyalty,** the degree to which customers are satisfied, like the brand, and are committed to further purchases. A loyal group of customers represents substantial value to a firm, and that value can be calculated. One way manufacturers are trying to create more brand loyalty is by lowering the carbon footprint of their products.

In the past, companies tried to boost their short-term performance by offering coupons and price discounts to move goods quickly. This eroded consumers' commitment to brand names, especially of grocery products. Many consumers complain when companies drop brand names like Astro Pops or Flex shampoo.[18] Such complaints show the power of brand names.[19] Now companies realize the value of brand equity and are trying harder to measure the earning power of strong brand names.

Brand awareness refers to how quickly or easily a given brand name comes to mind when someone mentions a product category. Advertising helps build strong brand awareness. Established brands, such as Coca-Cola and Pepsi, are usually among the highest in brand awareness. Sponsorship of events, like football's Orange Bowl and NASCAR's Cup Series, helps improve brand awareness. Simply being there over and over also increases brand awareness. That's one way Google became such a popular brand.

Perceived quality is an important part of brand equity. A product that's perceived as having better quality than its competitors can be priced accordingly. The key to creating a perception of quality is to identify what consumers look for in a high-quality product, and then to use that information in every message the company sends out. Factors influencing the perception of quality include price, appearance, and reputation.

Consumers often develop *brand preference*—that is, they prefer one brand over another—because of such cues. When consumers reach the point of *brand insistence,* the product becomes a specialty good. For example, a consumer may insist on Goodyear tires for his or her car.

generic goods
Nonbranded products that usually sell at a sizable discount compared to national or private-label brands.

knockoff brands
Illegal copies of national brand-name goods.

brand equity
The value of the brand name and associated symbols.

brand loyalty
The degree to which customers are satisfied, like the brand, and are committed to further purchases.

brand awareness
How quickly or easily a given brand name comes to mind when a product category is mentioned.

It's now so easy to copy a product's benefits that off-brand products can draw consumers away from brand-name goods. Brand-name manufacturers like Intel Corporation have to develop new products and new markets faster and promote their names better than ever before to hold off challenges from competitors.

Creating Brand Associations

brand association
The linking of a brand to other favorable images.

The name, symbol, and slogan a company uses can assist greatly in brand recognition for that company's products. **Brand association** is the linking of a brand to other favorable images, like famous product users, a popular celebrity, or a particular geographic area. Note, for example, how ads for Mercedes-Benz associate its company's cars with successful people who live luxurious lives. The person responsible for building brands is known as a brand manager or product manager. We'll discuss that position next.

Brand Management

brand manager
A manager who has direct responsibility for one brand or one product line; called a *product manager* in some firms.

A **brand manager** (known as a *product manager* in some firms) has direct responsibility for one brand or product line, and manages all the elements of its marketing mix: product, price, place, and promotion. Thus, you might think of the brand manager as the president of a one-product firm.

One reason many large consumer-product companies created this position was to have greater control over new-product development and product promotion. Some companies have brand-management *teams* to bolster the overall effort. In B2B companies, brand managers are often known as product managers.

progress assessment

- What seven functions does packaging now perform?
- What's the difference between a brand name and a trademark?
- Can you explain the difference between a manufacturer's brand, a dealer brand, and a generic brand?
- What are the key components of brand equity?

LEARNING goal 5

Explain the steps in the new-product development process.

THE NEW-PRODUCT DEVELOPMENT PROCESS

The odds a new product will fail are high.[20] Over 80 percent of products introduced in any year fail to reach their business objectives. Not delivering what is promised is a leading cause of new-product failure. Other causes include getting ready for marketing too late, poor positioning, too few differences from competitors, and poor packaging. Small firms especially may experience a low success rate unless they do proper product planning and new-product development. As Figure 14.3 shows, new-product development for producers consists of six stages.

New products continue to pour into the market every year, and their profit potential looks tremendous. Think, for example, of the potential of home videoconferencing, interactive TV, Wii games and products, smartphones, iPads, and other innovations.[21] Where do these ideas come from? How are they tested? What's the life span for an innovation? Let's look at these issues.

Generating New-Product Ideas

It now takes about seven ideas to generate one commercial product. Most ideas for new industrial products come from employee suggestions rather than research and development. Research and development, nonetheless, is a major source of new products. Employees are a major source for new consumer-goods ideas. Firms should also listen to their suppliers for new-product ideas because suppliers are often exposed to new ideas. Present customers are also a good source for new-product ideas.[22]

Product Screening

Product screening reduces the number of new-product ideas a firm is working on at any one time so it can focus on the most promising. *Screening* applies criteria to determine whether the product fits well with present products, has good profit potential, and is marketable. The company may assign each of these factors a weight and compute a total score for each new product so that it can compare their potentials.

figure 14.3

THE NEW-PRODUCT DEVELOPMENT PROCESS

Product development is a six-stage process. Which stage do you believe to be the most important?

Idea generation (based on consumer wants and needs)

↓

Product screening

↓

Product analysis

↓

Development (including building prototypes)

↓

Testing

↓

Commercialization (bringing the product to the market)

product screening
A process designed to reduce the number of new-product ideas being worked on at any one time.

Tom Szaky of TerraCycle makes new products such as plant food, planters, pencil cases, and tote bags from discarded products made by other companies. (To see his bags made from drink pouches and Oreo cookie wrappers, go to www.terracycle.net.) What products do you own that are made of recycled material?

Keep on Food Truckin'

In many cities, street vendors hawking hot dogs and other traditional fare are part of Americana. They are American icons. But that icon is changing. Not only is their menu changing from greasy hot dogs and salty pretzels to crème brûlée and organic drinks, but also how customers find them is becoming more high tech. Some vendors now use Twitter and other social media to reveal their current locations and build customer relationships.

There are some cities, like Chicago, where legislation restricts food trucks for health and sanitary reasons. But in cities like New York, Portland, and Austin, you can find these mobile units selling hot dogs and, often, more gourmet offerings. French rotisserie RoliRoti in San Francisco, Vietnamese banh mi at Nom Nom in L.A., and Gruyère grilled cheese in Austin are offering gourmet food items not usually found in standard street vendor carts. Here are just a few of the mobile units you can find online:

- Clover Food Truck in Boston/Cambridge offers a rotating menu of local organic materials.
- Sugar Philly Truck in Philadelphia offers crème brûlée hot off the truck.
- Dim and Den Sum in Cleveland has some of the best food truck art in America.
- KOi Fusion PDX in Portland is one of the few mobile eateries in that town.

You may enjoy looking online for a mobile unit near you. Such exploring may give you an idea about how you may start your own small business on a truck. The possibilities seem endless. You should be able to put into practice all of the product concepts you learned in this chapter. Say, how about a vegetarian truck?

Sources: Leslie Robarge, "Gourmet Food Truck Smackdown," *Bloomberg Businessweek*, March 14–March 20, 2011; Matt Vilano, "The Secret Sauce Part 11," *Entrepreneur*, April 2011; and Cloverfoodlab.com, DimandDenSum.com, accessed April 2012.

Product Analysis

product analysis
Making cost estimates and sales forecasts to get a feeling for profitability of new-product ideas.

After product screening comes **product analysis,** or making cost estimates and sales forecasts to get a feeling for the profitability of new-product ideas. Products that don't meet the established criteria are withdrawn from consideration.

Product Development and Testing

If a product passes the screening and analysis phase, the firm begins to develop it further, testing many different product concepts or alternatives. A firm that makes packaged meat products may develop the concept of a chicken dog—a hot dog made of chicken that tastes like an all-beef hot dog. It will develop a prototype, or sample, so that consumers can try the taste. The Connecting with Small Business box discusses some new ideas for products.

concept testing
Taking a product idea to consumers to test their reactions.

Concept testing takes a product idea to consumers to test their reactions. Do they see the benefits of this new product? How frequently would they buy it? At what price? What features do they like and dislike? What changes in it would they make? The firm tests samples using different packaging, branding, and ingredients until a product emerges that's desirable from both production and marketing perspectives. Some new hotels are being built to match the trendy W chain. They are said to have "hipness." Such innovations must be tried on consumers to see if they indeed recognize and appreciate the new "hip" design.[23] As you plan for Very Vegetarian, can you see the importance of concept testing for new vegetarian dishes?

Commercialization

Even if a product tests well, it may take quite a while to achieve success in the market. Take the zipper, for example, the result of one of the longest development efforts on record for a consumer product. After Whitcomb Judson received the first patents for his clothing fastener in the early 1890s, it took more than 15 years to perfect the product—and even then consumers weren't interested. Judson's company suffered numerous financial setbacks, name changes, and relocations before settling in Meadville, Pennsylvania. Finally, the U.S. Navy started using zippers during World War I. Today, Talon Inc. is the leading U.S. maker of zippers, producing some 500 million of them a year.

The example of the zipper shows why the marketing effort must include **commercialization,** which includes (1) promoting the product to distributors and retailers to get wide distribution, and (2) developing strong advertising and sales campaigns to generate and maintain interest in the product among distributors and consumers. New products are now getting rapid exposure to global markets through commercialization on the Internet and social media. Websites enable consumers to view new products, ask questions, and make purchases easily and quickly.[24]

commercialization
Promoting a product to distributors and retailers to get wide distribution, and developing strong advertising and sales campaigns to generate and maintain interest in the product among distributors and consumers.

LEARNING goal 6

Describe the product life cycle.

THE PRODUCT LIFE CYCLE

Once a product has been developed and tested, it goes to market. There it may pass through a **product life cycle** of four stages: introduction, growth, maturity, and decline (see Figure 14.4). This cycle is a *theoretical* model of what happens to sales and profits for a *product class* over time. However, not all individual products follow the life cycle, and particular brands may act differently. For example, while frozen foods as a generic class may go through the entire cycle, one brand may never get beyond the introduction stage. Some product classes, such as microwave ovens, stay in the introductory stage for years. Some products, like catsup, become classics and never experience decline. Others, such as fad clothing, may go through the entire cycle in a few months. Still others may be withdrawn from the market altogether. Nonetheless, the product life cycle may provide some basis for anticipating future market developments and for planning marketing strategies.

product life cycle
A theoretical model of what happens to sales and profits for a product class over time; the four stages of the cycle are introduction, growth, maturity, and decline.

Example of the Product Life Cycle

The product life cycle can give marketers valuable clues to successfully promoting a product over time. Some products, like crayons and sidewalk chalk, have very

figure 14.4

SALES AND PROFITS DURING THE PRODUCT LIFE CYCLE

Note that profit levels start to fall *before* sales reach their peak. This is due to increasing price competition. When profits and sales start to decline, it's time to come out with a new product or to remodel the old one to maintain interest and profits.

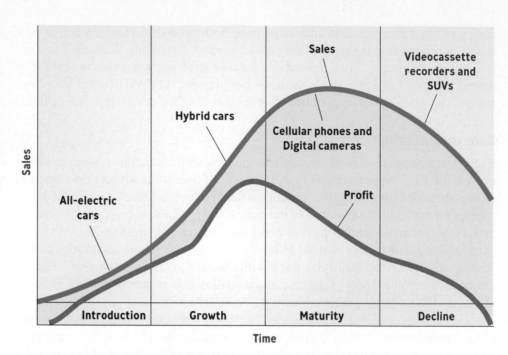

long product life cycles, change very little, and never seem to go into decline. Crayola has been successfully selling crayons for 100 years! How long do you think the new virtual video games will last?[25]

You can see how the theory works by looking at the product life cycle of instant coffee. When it was introduced, most people didn't like it as well as "regular" coffee, and it took several years for instant coffee to gain general acceptance (introduction stage). At one point, though, instant coffee grew rapidly in popularity, and many brands were introduced (growth stage). After a while, people became attached to one brand and sales leveled off (maturity stage). Sales then went into a slight decline when freeze-dried coffees were introduced (decline stage). Now freeze-dried coffee is, in turn, at the decline stage as consumers are buying bags of coffee from Starbucks and brewing them at home. It's extremely important for marketers to recognize what stage a product is in so that they can make intelligent and efficient marketing decisions about it.

Using the Product Life Cycle

Different stages in the product life cycle call for different marketing strategies. Figure 14.5 outlines the marketing mix decisions you might make. As you go through the figure, you'll see that each stage calls for multiple marketing mix changes. Remember, these concepts are largely theoretical and you should use them only as guidelines. We'll discuss the price strategies mentioned in the figure later in this chapter.

Figure 14.6 shows in theory what happens to sales volume, profits, and competition during the product life cycle. Compare it to Figure 14.4. Both figures show that a product at the mature stage may reach the top in sales growth while profit is decreasing. At that stage, a marketing manager may decide to create a new image for the product to start a new growth cycle. You may have noticed how Arm & Hammer baking soda gets a new image every few years to generate new sales. One year it's positioned as a deodorant for refrigerators and the next as a substitute for harsh chemicals in swimming pools. Knowing what stage in the cycle a product has reached helps marketing managers decide when such strategic changes are needed.

Need help understanding Product Life Cycle? www.introbiz.tv/QR14-1

figure 14.5

SAMPLE STRATEGIES FOLLOWED DURING THE PRODUCT LIFE CYCLE

LIFE CYCLE STAGE	MARKETING MIX ELEMENTS			
	PRODUCT	PRICE	PLACE	PROMOTION
Introduction	Offer market-tested product; keep mix small	Go after innovators with high introductory price (skimming strategy) or use penetration pricing	Use wholesalers, selective distribution	Dealer promotion and heavy investment in primary demand advertising and sales promotion to get stores to carry the product and consumers to try it
Growth	Improve product; keep product mix limited	Adjust price to meet competition	Increase distribution	Heavy competitive advertising
Maturity	Differentiate product to satisfy different market segments	Further reduce price	Take over wholesaling function and intensify distribution	Emphasize brand name as well as product benefits and differences
Decline	Cut product mix; develop new-product ideas	Consider price increase	Consolidate distribution; drop some outlets	Reduce advertising to only loyal customers

LIFE CYCLE STAGE	SALES	PROFITS	COMPETITORS
Introduction	Low sales	Losses may occur	Few
Growth	Rapidly rising sales	Very high profits	Growing number
Maturity	Peak sales	Declining profits	Stable number, then declining
Decline	Falling sales	Profits may fall to become losses	Declining number

figure 14.6

HOW SALES, PROFITS, AND COMPETITION VARY OVER THE PRODUCT LIFE CYCLE

Theoretically, all products go through these stages at various times in their life cycle. What happens to sales as a product matures?

progress assessment

- What are the six steps in the new-product development process?
- What is the difference between product screening and product analysis?
- What are the two steps in commercialization?
- What is the theory of the product life cycle?

LEARNING goal 7

Identify various pricing objectives and strategies.

COMPETITIVE PRICING

Pricing is so important to marketing and the development of total product offers that it has been singled out as one of the four Ps in the marketing mix, along with product, place, and promotion. It's one of the most difficult of the four Ps for a manager to control, however, because price is such a critical ingredient in consumer evaluations of the product. In this section, we'll explore price both as an ingredient of the total product offer and as a strategic marketing tool.

Pricing Objectives

A firm may have several objectives in mind when setting a pricing strategy. When pricing a new vegetarian offering, we may want to promote the product's image. If we price it *high* and use the right promotion, maybe we can make it the Evian of vegetarian meals. We also might price it high to achieve a certain profit objective or return on investment. We could also price our product *lower* than its competitors, because we want low-income people to afford this healthy meal. That is, we could have some social or ethical goal in mind. Low pricing may also discourage competition because it reduces the profit potential, but it may help us capture a larger share of the market.

Thus a firm may have several pricing objectives over time, and it must formulate these objectives clearly before developing an overall pricing strategy. Popular objectives include the following:

1. *Achieving a target return on investment or profit.* Ultimately, the goal of marketing is to make a profit by providing goods and services to others. Naturally, one long-run pricing objective of almost all firms is to optimize profit. One way companies have tried to increase profit is by reducing the amount provided to customers. Thus cereal companies have cut the amount of cereal in a box, toilet paper companies are making their products smaller, and so on.[26] Have you noticed this happening for products you buy?

2. *Building traffic.* Supermarkets often advertise certain products at or below cost to attract people to the store. These products are called *loss leaders*. The long-run objective is to make profits by following the short-run objective of building a customer base. The Internet portal Yahoo once provided a free auction service to compete with eBay. Why give such a service away? To increase advertising revenue on the Yahoo site and attract more people to Yahoo's other services.

3. *Achieving greater market share.* One way to capture a larger part of the market is to offer lower prices, low finance rates (like 0 percent financing), low lease rates, or rebates.

4. *Creating an image.* Certain watches, perfumes, and other socially visible products are priced high to give them an image of exclusivity and status.

5. *Furthering social objectives.* A firm may want to price a product low so people with little money can afford it. The government often subsidizes the price of farm products to keep basic necessities like milk and bread easily affordable.

A firm may have short-run objectives that differ greatly from its long-run objectives. Managers should understand both types at the beginning and put both into their strategic marketing plan. They should also set pricing objectives in the context of other marketing decisions about product design, packaging, branding, distribution, and promotion. All these marketing decisions are interrelated.

Intuition tells us the price charged for a product must bear some relationship to the cost of producing it. Prices usually *are* set somewhere above cost. But as we'll see, price and cost aren't always related. In fact, there are three major approaches to pricing strategy: cost-based, demand-based (target costing), and competition-based.

Cost-Based Pricing

Producers often use cost as a primary basis for setting price. They develop elaborate cost accounting systems to measure production costs (including materials, labor, and overhead), add in a margin of profit, and come up with a price. Picture the process in terms of producing a car. You add up all the various components—engine parts, body, tires, radio, door locks and windows, paint, and labor—add a profit margin, and come up with a price. The question is whether the price will be satisfactory to the market as well. How has the market responded to the prices of U.S. cars lately? In the long run, the market—not the producer—determines what the price will be (see Chapter 2). Pricing should take into account costs, but it should also include the expected costs of product updates, the marketing objectives for each product, and competitor prices.

Demand-Based Pricing

Unlike cost-based pricing, **target costing** is demand-based. That means we design a product so it not only satisfies customers but also meets the profit margins we've set. Target costing makes the final price an *input* to the product development process, not an outcome of it. You first estimate the selling price people would be willing to pay for a product and then subtract your desired profit margin. The result is your target cost of production, or what you can spend to profitably produce the item. Imagine how you would use this process to make custom-made jewelry.

Competition-Based Pricing

Competition-based pricing is a strategy based on what all the other competitors are doing. The price can be at, above, or below competitors' prices. Pricing depends on customer loyalty, perceived differences, and the competitive climate. **Price leadership** is the strategy by which one or more dominant firms set pricing practices all competitors in an industry follow. You may have noticed that practice among oil companies.

target costing
Designing a product so that it satisfies customers and meets the profit margins desired by the firm.

competition-based pricing
A pricing strategy based on what all the other competitors are doing. The price can be set at, above, or below competitors' prices.

price leadership
The strategy by which one or more dominant firms set the pricing practices that all competitors in an industry follow.

Some products are priced high to create a high-status image of exclusivity and desirability. Salvatore Ferragamo shoes fall into this category. What is the total product offer for a product like this?

Break-Even Analysis

Before you begin selling a new vegetarian sandwich, it may be wise to determine how many sandwiches you'd have to sell before making a profit. You'd then determine whether you could reach such a sales goal. **Break-even analysis** is the process used to determine profitability at various levels of sales. The break-even point is the point where revenues from sales equal all costs. The formula for calculating the break-even point is as follows:

$$\text{Break-even point (BEP)} = \frac{\text{Total fixed costs (FC)}}{\text{Price of one unit (P)} - \text{Variable costs (VC) of one unit}}$$

break-even analysis
The process used to determine profitability at various levels of sales.

Total fixed costs are all the expenses that remain the same no matter how many products are made or sold. Among the expenses that make up fixed costs are the amount paid to own or rent a factory or warehouse and the amount paid for business insurance. **Variable costs** change according to the level of production. Included are the expenses for the materials used in making products and the direct costs of labor used in making those goods. For producing a specific product, let's say you have a fixed cost of $200,000 (for mortgage interest, real estate taxes, equipment, and so on). Your variable cost (e.g., labor and materials) per item is $2. If you sold the products for $4 each, the break-even point would be 100,000 items. In other words, you wouldn't make any money selling this product unless you sold more than 100,000 of them:

total fixed costs
All the expenses that remain the same no matter how many products are made or sold.

variable costs
Costs that change according to the level of production.

$$\text{BEP} = \frac{\text{FC}}{\text{P-VC}} = \frac{\$200,000}{\$4.00-\$2.00} = \frac{\$200,000}{\$2.00} = 100,000 \text{ boxes}$$

Other Pricing Strategies

Let's say a firm has just developed a new line of products, such as Blu-ray players. The firm has to decide how to price these sets at the introductory stage of the product life cycle. A **skimming price strategy** prices a new product high to recover research and development costs and make as much profit as possible while there's little competition. Of course, those large profits will eventually attract new competitors.

skimming price strategy
Strategy in which a new product is priced high to make optimum profit while there's little competition.

A second strategy is to price the new players low. Low prices will attract more buyers and discourage other companies from making sets because profits are slim. This **penetration strategy** enables the firm to penetrate or capture a large share of the market quickly.

penetration strategy
Strategy in which a product is priced low to attract many customers and discourage competition.

Shoppers around the world look for bargains, as these consumers in Seoul, South Korea, are doing. How many different ways can marketers appeal to shoppers' desires to find the lowest price? Do online retailers adopt different pricing strategies?

Retailers use several pricing strategies. **Everyday low pricing (EDLP)** is the choice of Home Depot and Walmart. They set prices lower than competitors and don't usually have special sales. The idea is to bring consumers to the store whenever they want a bargain rather than having them wait until there is a sale.

Department stores and some other retailers most often use a **high–low pricing strategy.** Regular prices are higher than at stores using EDLP, but during special sales they're lower. The problem with such pricing is that it encourages consumers to wait for sales, thus cutting into profits. As online shopping continues to grow, you may see fewer stores with a high–low strategy because consumers will be able to find better prices on the Internet.

Retailers can use price as a major determinant of the goods they carry. Some promote goods that sell for only 99 cents, or for only $10. Some of those 99-cent stores have raised their prices to over a dollar because of rising costs.

You learned earlier in this chapter that bundling means grouping two or more products together and pricing them as a unit. For example, a store might price washers and dryers as a unit. Jiffy Lube offers an oil change and lube, checks your car's fluid levels and air pressure, and bundles all these services into one price. Research suggests that a discount will increase sales more effectively if it's offered on an attractive, pleasurable item.[27]

Psychological pricing means pricing goods and services at price points that make the product appear less expensive than it is. A house might be priced at $299,000 because that sounds like a lot less than $300,000. Gas stations almost always use psychological pricing.

everyday low pricing (EDLP)
Setting prices lower than competitors and then not having any special sales.

high–low pricing strategy
Setting prices that are higher than EDLP stores, but having many special sales where the prices are lower than competitors'.

psychological pricing
Pricing goods and services at price points that make the product appear less expensive than it is.

How Market Forces Affect Pricing

Recognizing that different consumers may be willing to pay different prices, marketers sometimes price on the basis of consumer demand rather than cost or some other calculation. That's called *demand-oriented pricing,* and you can observe it at movie theaters with low rates for children and drugstores with discounts for senior citizens. The Washington Opera Company in Washington, DC, raised prices on prime seating and lowered them on less-attractive seats. This strategy raised the company's revenues 9 percent.

Marketers are facing a new pricing problem: Customers can now compare prices of many goods and services on the Internet, at websites like DealTime.com and MySimon.com. Priceline.com introduced consumers to a "demand collection system," in which buyers post the prices they are willing to pay and invite sellers to accept or decline the price. Consumers can get great prices on airlines, hotels, and other products by naming their price. They can also buy used goods online. Clearly, price competition is going to heat up as consumers have more access to price information from all around the world.[28] As a result, nonprice competition is likely to increase.

NONPRICE COMPETITION

Marketers often compete on product attributes other than price. You may have noted that price differences are small for products like gasoline, candy bars, and even major products such as compact cars and private colleges.

You won't typically see price as a major promotional appeal on television. Instead, marketers tend to stress product images and consumer benefits such as comfort, style, convenience, and durability.

Many small organizations promote the services that accompany basic products rather than price in order to compete with bigger firms. Good service will enhance a relatively homogeneous product. Danny O'Neill, for example, is a small wholesaler who sells gourmet coffee to upscale restaurants. He has to watch competitors' prices *and* the services they offer so that he can charge the premium prices he wants. To charge high prices, he has to offer and then provide superior service. Larger companies often do the same thing. Some airlines stress friendliness, large "sleeping" seats, promptness, abundant flights, and other such services. Many hotels stress "no surprises," business services, health clubs, and other extras.

progress assessment

- Can you list two short-term and two long-term pricing objectives? Can the two be compatible?
- What are the limitations of a cost-based pricing strategy?
- What is psychological pricing?

summary

Learning Goal 1. Describe a total product offer.

- **What's included in a total product offer?**

A total product offer consists of everything consumers evaluate when deciding whether to buy something. It includes price, brand name, and satisfaction in use.

- **What's the difference between a product line and a product mix?**

A product line is a group of physically similar products with similar competitors. A product line of gum may include bubble gum and sugarless gum. A product mix is a company's combination of product lines. A manufacturer may offer lines of gum, candy bars, and breath mints in its product mix.

- **How do marketers create product differentiation for their goods and services?**

Marketers use a combination of pricing, advertising, and packaging to make their products seem unique and attractive.

Learning Goal 2. Identify the various kinds of consumer and industrial goods.

- **What are consumer goods?**

Consumer goods are sold to ultimate consumers like you and me for personal use.

- **What are the four classifications of consumer goods and services, and how are they marketed?**

There are convenience goods and services (requiring minimum shopping effort); shopping goods and services (for which people search and compare price and quality); specialty goods and services (which consumers go out of their way to get, and for which they often demand specific brands); and unsought goods and services (products consumers are unaware of, haven't thought of buying, or need to solve an unexpected problem). Convenience goods and services are best promoted by location, shopping goods and services by some price/quality appeal, and specialty goods and services by specialty magazines and interactive websites.

- **What are industrial goods, and how are they marketed differently from consumer goods?**

Industrial goods are products sold in the business-to-business (B2B) market and used in the production of other products. They're sold largely through salespeople and rely less on advertising.

Learning Goal 3. Summarize the functions of packaging.

- **What are the seven functions of packaging?**

Packaging must (1) attract the buyer's attention; (2) protect the goods inside, stand up under handling and storage, be tamperproof, and deter theft; (3) be easy to open and use; (4) describe the contents; (5) explain the benefits of the good inside; (6) provide information about warranties, warnings, and other consumer matters; and (7) indicate price, value, and uses. Bundling means grouping two or more products into a unit, through packaging, and charging one price for them.

Learning Goal 4. Contrast *brand, brand name,* and *trademark,* and show the value of brand equity.

- **Can you define brand, brand name, and trademark?**

A *brand* is a name, symbol, or design (or combination thereof) that identifies the goods or services of one seller or group of sellers and distinguishes them from the goods and services of competitors. The word *brand* includes all means of identifying a product. A *brand name* consists of a word, letter, or group of words or letters that differentiates one seller's goods and services from those of competitors. A *trademark* is a brand that has exclusive legal protection for both its brand name and design.

- **What is brand equity, and how do managers create brand associations?**

Brand equity is the value of a brand name and associated symbols. Brand association is the linking of a brand to other favorable images such as product users, a popular celebrity, or a geographic area.

- **What do brand managers do?**

Brand managers coordinate product, price, place, and promotion decisions for a particular product.

Learning Goal 5. Explain the steps in the new-product development process.

- **What are the six steps of the product development process?**

The steps of product development are (1) generation of new-product ideas, (2) product screening, (3) product analysis, (4) development, (5) testing, and (6) commercialization.

Learning Goal 6. Describe the product life cycle.

- **What is the product life cycle?**

The product life cycle is a theoretical model of what happens to sales and profits for a product class over time.

- **What are the four stages in the product life cycle?**

The four product life cycle stages are introduction, growth, maturity, and decline.

Learning Goal 7. Identify various pricing objectives and strategies.

- **What are pricing objectives?**

Pricing objectives include achieving a target profit, building traffic, increasing market share, creating an image, and meeting social goals.

- **What strategies can marketers use to determine a product's price?**

A skimming strategy prices the product high to make big profits while there's little competition. A penetration strategy uses low price to attract more customers and discourage competitors. Demand-oriented pricing starts with consumer demand rather than cost. Competition-oriented pricing is based on all competitors' prices. Price leadership occurs when all competitors follow the pricing practice of one or more dominant companies.

- **What is break-even analysis?**

Break-even analysis is the process used to determine profitability at various levels of sales. The break-even point is the point where revenues from sales equal all costs.

- **Why do companies use nonprice strategies?**

Pricing is one of the easiest marketing strategies to copy. It's often not a good long-run competitive tool.

key terms

brand 413
brand association 416
brand awareness 415
brand equity 415
brand loyalty 415
brand manager 416
break-even analysis 424
bundling 413
commercialization 419
competition-based pricing 423
concept testing 418
convenience goods and services 408
dealer (private-label) brands 414
distributed product development 406

everyday low pricing (EDLP) 425
generic goods 415
high–low pricing strategy 425
industrial goods 410
knockoff brands 415
manufacturers' brands 414
penetration strategy 424
price leadership 423
product analysis 418
product differentiation 408
product life cycle 419
product line 407
product mix 408

product screening 417
psychological pricing 425
shopping goods and services 409
skimming price strategy 424
specialty goods and services 409
target costing 423
total fixed costs 424
total product offer 406
trademark 413
unsought goods and services 410
value 404
variable costs 424

critical thinking

1. What value enhancers affected your choice of the school you attend? Did you consider size, location, price, reputation, WiFi services, library and research services, sports, and courses offered? What factors were most important? Why? What schools were your alternatives? Why didn't you choose them?

2. What could you do to enhance the product offer of Very Vegetarian, other than changing the menu from time to time?

3. How could you use psychological pricing when making up the menu at Very Vegetarian?

4. Are you impressed by the use of celebrities in product advertisements? What celebrity could you use to promote Very Vegetarian?

developing workplace skills

1. Look around your classroom and notice the different types of shoes students are wearing. What product qualities were they looking for when they chose their shoes? How important were price, style, brand name, and color? Describe the product offerings you would feature in a new shoe store designed to appeal to college students.

2. A total product offer consists of everything consumers evaluate when choosing among products, including price, package, service, and reputation. Working in teams, compose a list of factors consumers might consider when evaluating the total product offer of a vacation resort, a cell phone, and a rental apartment.

3. How important is price to you when buying the following: clothes, milk, computers, haircuts, rental cars? What nonprice factors, if any, are more important than price? How much time do you spend evaluating factors other than price when making such purchases?

4. Go through several local stores of different types and note how often they use psychological pricing. Discuss the practice with the class to see whether students recognize the influence psychological pricing has upon them.

taking it to the net

Purpose

To assess how consumers can use the Internet to shop for various goods.

Exercise

Shopbots are Internet sites for finding the best prices on goods you need. No shopbot searches the entire Internet, so it's a good idea to use more than one to get the best deals. Furthermore, not all shopbots quote shipping and handling costs. Here are some to try: MySimon.com, PriceGrabber.com, PriceSCAN.com, and YahooShopping.com.

1. Which of the shopbots offers the most goods and the most information? How helpful are the consumer reviews? The product descriptions?

2. Which shopbot is easiest to use? The hardest? Why?

3. Write down some of the prices you find on the Internet and then go to a local store, such as Walmart or Target, and compare prices. Does either source (online or brick-and-mortar) consistently offer the best price?

4. Compare shopping on the Internet to shopping in stores. What are the advantages and disadvantages of each? Which has the best total product offer?

casing the web

To access the case, "Everyday Low Pricing," visit
www.mhhe.com/P2P2e

video case

Dream Dinners Food-to-Go

Dream Dinners is a Washington-based, innovative food-to-go concept. The company is franchised around the country and collectively sells over 700,000 servings each month. At Dream Dinners, customers are able to put together a variety of meals that can be taken home and prepared in minutes. This approach provides a nutritious meal, saves customers time, and is convenient, while also helping families reestablish "dinner time" as an important social event. The value proposition that is presented includes time savings and convenient, nutritional family meals for customers. The Dream Dinners concept demonstrates the process of the total product offering and each of the steps in the process.

This business concept evolved from the experiences of a group of women friends who met monthly to cook dinners to place in freezers to help each other out. The group did this for about seven years before launching the business model. The driving force behind the concept is to reemphasize the value of family time at dinner. Providing customers the ability to assemble a month's worth of dinners would save tremendous time at home and would allow for more quality time to be spent with family members. The company describes its core demographic as women with school-age children.

Dream Dinners seeks to influence how its customers value their product. The company discovered that their best marketing promotion comes from social media and word of mouth of customers who are in their stores. A satisfied customer tells her friends and so on. Customers perceive value from a product by weighing the benefits they expect from the product and the cost of receiving those goods. The importance of listening to the customer is critical to success in today's competitive marketplace. The video explains how Dream Dinners engages in the product development process through growing its markets by offering environmentally friendly products. To this end, Dream Dinners provides 3–4 new dinner options each month. The company gauges its business success through a pricing model that is based on a cost-plus margin.

Success is defined as an average dollar ticket that consists of a customer spending a minimum of $150 per month by assembling 6 full-size dinners or 12 small-size dinners. The company has four key principles that it uses to assess its overall effectiveness. These principles are: (1) that the meals are easy, wonderful, and delicious; (2) that customers have a great experience in the store assembling meals; (3) that the menu items are easy for the store owner to provide; and (4) that the menu items are acceptable to the home office. The key differentiator for Dream Dinners is the quality of the food when compared with competitors.

Thinking It Over

1. *Briefly define a "brand."*
2. *What are the steps in the new-product development process?*
3. *What is the principle promotion strategy used by Dream Dinners?*

Distributing
PRODUCTS

LEARNING
goals

After you have read and studied this chapter, you should be able to

1 Explain the concept of marketing channels and their value.

2 Demonstrate how intermediaries perform the six marketing utilities.

3 Identify the types of wholesale intermediaries in the distribution system.

4 Compare the distribution strategies retailers use.

5 Explain the various kinds of nonstore retailing.

6 Explain the various ways to build cooperation in channel systems.

7 Describe logistics and outline how intermediaries manage the transportation and storage of goods.

For Charlie Chanaratsopon, running a business came naturally. In his youth he gained a strong work ethic and an entrepreneurial mind working in his parents' jewelry manufacturing business in Houston, Texas. From there he went on to Loyola Marymount University where he earned a degree in finance with a minor in economics. His business pedigree helped him get a job right out of college as an analyst for a major bank. Despite his success, though, Chanaratsopon was not happy.

It turned out that crunching numbers all day was not fulfilling for him. After two years in the banking industry, he quit and returned to his parents' company. But he didn't head back to the nest just to coast in a cushy job. While he was in college Chanaratsopon liked to wander around shopping malls and observe what people bought. During one of these trips, Chanaratsopon discovered that people were more likely to buy accessories at retail outlets rather than buy entirely new outfits. After all, accessories are an inexpensive way to alter an ensemble's look, while clothes can be expensive. So when he came back home after his experience in the corporate world, he asked his parents if he could attach a retail space to their jewelry factory. Armed with his parents' permission and $800,000 in startup cash, Chanaratsopon founded his boutique, Charming Charlie, in 2004.

From the beginning, Chanaratsopon's solid business plan ensured that Charming Charlie would stay afloat. Still, he felt he needed more business knowledge in order to grow the store into a national success. Two years after founding Charming Charlie, Chanaratsopon enrolled in the MBA program at Columbia University to learn more about retail. He bounced his ideas off the faculty and used his classmates as a sounding board for his future plans. By the time he earned his MBA, Chanaratsopon had opened several new stores. For every year afterward, he managed to double the number of stores open from the previous year. As of 2012, Chanaratsopon operated more than 180 locations in 33 states, employing more than 6,000 people.

At graduate school Chanaratsopon learned that he could turn his concept into a smash hit with a clever distribution plan. First of all, the jewelry needed to be cheap. Using his parents' connections, he found suppliers from whom he could buy stock in bulk to keep prices low. Every item at Charming Charlie costs between $4.97 and $49.97, providing an item for every budget. He knew that low prices wouldn't do all the work, though. To make his products really pop, Chanaratsopon decided to organize them all by color rather than type. He figured out that customers responded more to what would match their outfits rather than what specific accessories were available. The color-coded shelves made shopping in a Charming Charlie store a unique experience that customers were sure to tell their friends about.

As his brand continues to pick up steam, Chanaratsopon keeps a close eye on the company's growth. In fact, the stagnant real estate market played a key role in Charming Charlie's expansion. The price of property became so reasonable as the company was growing that Chanaratsopon was able to move the brand into many locations quickly. His ultimate plan is to have more than 1,000 stores in the United States, with other locations set to open in the Middle East within five years. Still only in his 30s, the only thing holding Charlie Chanaratsopon back is his own ambition, which he fortunately has in abundance.

The four Ps of marketing are product, place, promotion, and price. This chapter is all about place. The place function goes by many other names as well, including shipping, warehousing, distribution, logistics, and supply-chain management. We'll explore all these concepts in this chapter. At the end, you will have a much better understanding of the many steps required to get products from the producer to the consumer.

CONNECTING WITH

x *Charlie Chanaratsopon*

Founder of Charming Charlie

Sources: Alexandra Wolfe, "A Former Bank Analyst's Thing for Bling," *Bloomberg Businessweek,* February 16, 2012; Tanya Rutledge, "Charming Charlie: A Jewel of a Chain," *The Houston Chronicle,* December 2, 2011; Lauren Parker, "2011 Rising Retail Star: Charming Charlie," *Accessories Magazine,* March 1, 2011; and Tanya Mannes, "Red Gown? Black Suit? Mall Store Sorts Accessories by Color," *The San Diego Union-Tribune,* May 17, 2012.

Although this automobile manufacturer builds its cars in South Korea, the 30,000 components come from all over the world. For example, the airbags come from a Swedish company that makes them in Utah. Its supply chain is truly interfirm and international. What is the name of this company? (Find the answer in the chapter.)

marketing intermediaries
Organizations that assist in moving goods and services from producers to businesses (B2B) and from businesses to consumers (B2C).

channel of distribution
A whole set of marketing intermediaries, such as agents, brokers, wholesalers, and retailers, that join together to transport and store goods in their path (or channel) from producers to consumers.

LEARNING **goal 1**

Explain the concept of marketing channels and their value.

THE EMERGENCE OF MARKETING INTERMEDIARIES

It's easy to overlook distribution and storage in marketing, where the focus is often on advertising, selling, marketing research, and other functions. But it doesn't take much to realize how important distribution is. Imagine the challenge Timberland faces of getting raw materials together, making 12 million pairs of shoes, and then distributing those shoes to stores throughout the world. That's what thousands of manufacturing firms—making everything from automobiles to toys—have to deal with every day. Imagine further that there has been a major volcano eruption or tsunami that has caused a disruption in the supply of goods. Such issues are commonplace for distribution managers.[1]

Fortunately there are hundreds of thousands of companies and individuals whose job it is to help move goods from the raw-material state to producers and then on to consumers. Then, as is often the case, the products are sent from consumers to recyclers and back to manufacturers or assemblers. Did you know that only 20 percent of plastic water bottles are recycled? See the Making the Green Connection box for more on sustainability and the distribution process.[2]

Managing the flow of goods has become one of the most important managerial functions for many organizations. Let's look at how this function is carried out.

Distribution warehouses store goods until they are needed. Have you ever thought about the benefits of having food, furniture, clothing, and other needed goods close at hand?

Marketing intermediaries (once called *middlemen*) are organizations that assist in moving goods and services from producers to businesses (B2B) and from businesses to consumers (B2C). They're called intermediaries because they're in the middle of a series of organizations that join together to help distribute goods from producers to consumers. A **channel of distribution** consists of a whole set of marketing intermediaries, such as agents, brokers, wholesalers, and retailers, that join together to transport and store goods in their path (or channel) from producers to

consumers. **Agents/brokers** are marketing intermediaries who bring buyers and sellers together and assist in negotiating an exchange but don't take title to the goods—that is, at no point do they own the goods. Think of real estate agents as an example.

A **wholesaler** is a marketing intermediary that sells to other organizations, such as retailers, manufacturers, and hospitals. Wholesalers are part of the B2B system. Because of high distribution costs, Walmart has been trying to eliminate independent wholesalers from its system and do the job itself.[3] That is, Walmart provides its own warehouses and has its own trucks. It has over 120 distribution centers and 53,000 trailers to distribute goods to its stores. Finally, a **retailer** is an organization that sells to ultimate consumers (people like you and me).

Channels of distribution help ensure communication flows *and* the flow of money and title to goods. They also help ensure that the right quantity and assortment of goods will be available when and where needed. Figure 15.1 shows selected channels of distribution for both consumer and industrial goods.

You can see the distribution system in the United States at work when you drive down any highway and see the thousands of trucks and trains moving goods from here to there. Less visible, however, are the many distribution warehouses that store goods until they are needed. Have you ever thought about the benefits of having food, furniture, and other needed goods close at hand? Have you seen distribution warehouses along the road as you drive from town to town?

Why Marketing Needs Intermediaries

Figure 15.1 shows that some manufacturers sell directly to consumers. So why have marketing intermediaries at all? The answer is that intermediaries perform certain

agents/brokers
Marketing intermediaries who bring buyers and sellers together and assist in negotiating an exchange but don't take title to the goods.

wholesaler
A marketing intermediary that sells to other organizations.

retailer
An organization that sells to ultimate consumers.

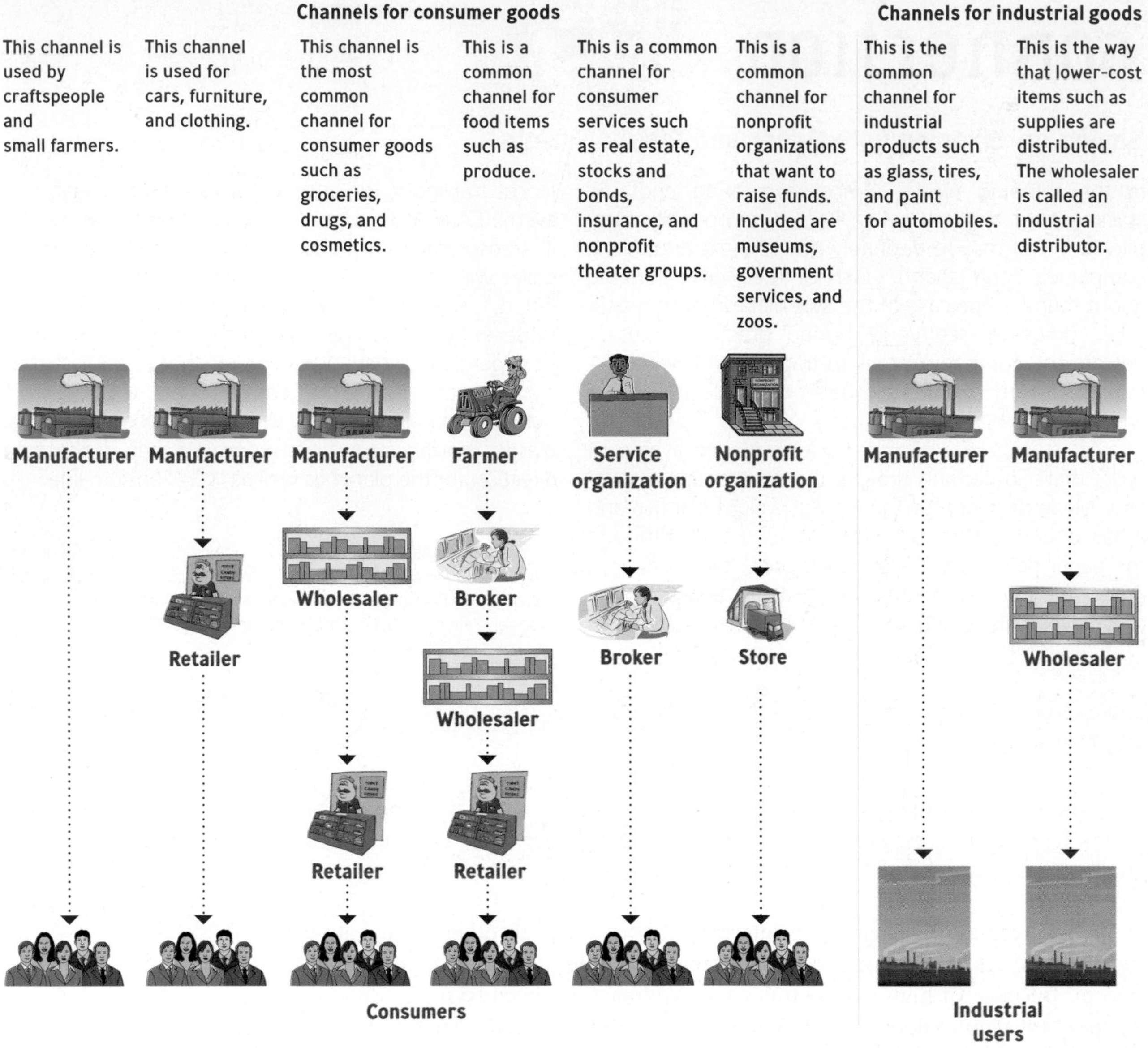

Channels for consumer goods

This channel is used by craftspeople and small farmers.

This channel is used for cars, furniture, and clothing.

This channel is the most common channel for consumer goods such as groceries, drugs, and cosmetics.

This is a common channel for food items such as produce.

This is a common channel for consumer services such as real estate, stocks and bonds, insurance, and nonprofit theater groups.

This is a common channel for nonprofit organizations that want to raise funds. Included are museums, government services, and zoos.

Channels for industrial goods

This is the common channel for industrial products such as glass, tires, and paint for automobiles.

This is the way that lower-cost items such as supplies are distributed. The wholesaler is called an industrial distributor.

| Manufacturer | Manufacturer | Manufacturer | Farmer | Service organization | Nonprofit organization | Manufacturer | Manufacturer |

Retailer · Wholesaler · Broker · Broker · Store · Wholesaler

Wholesaler

Retailer · Retailer

Consumers

Industrial users

figure 15.1

SELECTED CHANNELS OF DISTRIBUTION FOR CONSUMER AND INDUSTRIAL GOODS AND SERVICES

marketing tasks—such as transporting, storing, selling, advertising, and relationship building—faster and more cheaply than most manufacturers could.[4] Here's a simple analogy: You could personally deliver packages to people anywhere in the world, but usually you don't. Why not? Because it's generally cheaper and faster to have them delivered by the U.S. Postal Service or a private firm such as UPS.[5]

Similarly, you could sell your home by yourself or buy stock directly from individual companies, but you probably wouldn't. Why? Again, because agents and brokers are marketing intermediaries who make the exchange process easier and more efficient and profitable.[6] In the next section, we'll explore how intermediaries improve the efficiency of various exchanges.

How Intermediaries Create Exchange Efficiency

Here is an easy way to see the benefits of using marketing intermediaries. Suppose five manufacturers of various food products each tried to sell directly to five retailers. The number of exchange relationships needed to create this market is 5 times 5, or 25.

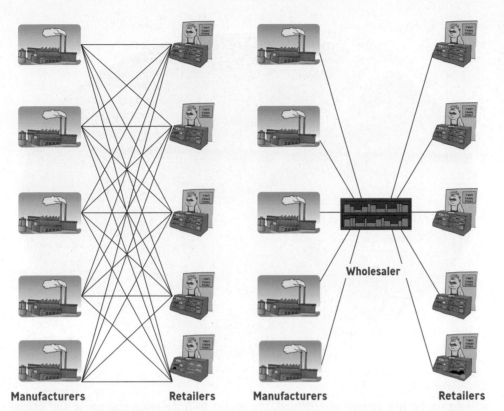

figure 15.2

HOW INTERMEDIARIES CREATE EXCHANGE EFFICIENCY

This figure shows that adding a wholesaler to the channel of distribution cuts the number of contacts from 25 to 10. This improves the efficiency of distribution.

Manufacturers   **Retailers**   **Manufacturers**   **Retailers**

Wholesaler

But picture what happens when a wholesaler enters the system. The five manufacturers each contact the wholesaler, establishing five exchange relationships. The wholesaler then establishes contact with the five retailers, creating five more exchange relationships. The wholesaler's existence reduces the number of exchanges from 25 to only 10. Figure 15.2 shows this process.

Some economists have said that intermediaries add *costs* and should be eliminated. Marketers say intermediaries add *value,* and that the *value greatly exceeds the cost.* Let's explore this debate and see what value intermediaries provide.[7]

The Value versus the Cost of Intermediaries

The public has often viewed marketing intermediaries with a degree of suspicion. Some surveys show about half the cost of what we buy is marketing costs that go largely to pay for the work of intermediaries. If we could only get rid of intermediaries, people reason, we could greatly reduce the cost of everything we buy. Sounds good, but is the solution really that simple?

Take a box of cereal that sells for $4. How could we, as consumers, get the cereal for less? Well, we could all drive to Michigan, where some cereal is produced, and save shipping costs. But imagine millions of people getting in their cars and driving to Michigan just to buy cereal. No, it doesn't make sense. It's much cheaper to have intermediaries bring the cereal to major cities. That might make transportation and warehousing by wholesalers necessary. These steps add cost, don't they? Yes, but they add value as well—the value of not having to drive to Michigan.

The cereal is now in a warehouse somewhere on the outskirts of the city. We could all drive down to the wholesaler and pick it up. But that still isn't the most economical way to buy cereal. If we figure in the cost of gas and time, the cereal

figure 15.3

DISTRIBUTION'S EFFECT ON YOUR FOOD DOLLAR

Note that the farmer gets only 25 cents of your food dollar. The bulk of your money goes to intermediaries to pay distribution costs. Their biggest cost is labor (truck drivers, clerks), followed by warehouses and storage.

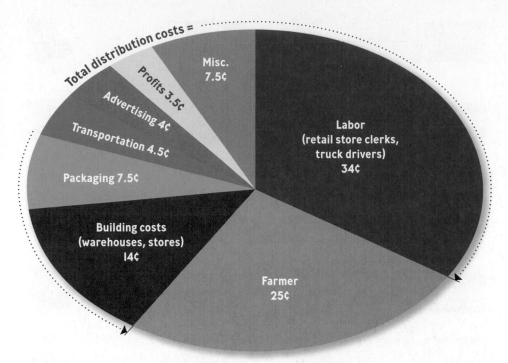

Total distribution costs =

Misc. 7.5¢

Profits 3.5¢

Advertising 4¢

Transportation 4.5¢

Packaging 7.5¢

Building costs (warehouses, stores) 14¢

Labor (retail store clerks, truck drivers) 34¢

Farmer 25¢

will again be too expensive. Instead, we prefer to have someone move the cereal from the warehouse to a truck, drive it to the corner supermarket, unload it, unpack it, price it, shelve it, and wait for us to come in to buy it. To make it even more convenient, the supermarket may stay open for 24 hours a day, seven days a week. Think of the costs. But think also of the value! For $4, we can get a box of cereal *when* we want it, and with little effort.

If we were to get rid of the retailer, we could buy a box of cereal for slightly less, but we'd have to drive farther and spend time in the warehouse looking through rows of cereals. If we got rid of the wholesaler, we could save a little more money, not counting our drive to Michigan. But a few cents here and there add up—to the point where distribution (marketing) may add up to 75 cents for every 25 cents in manufacturing costs. Figure 15.3 shows where your money goes in the distribution process. The largest percentage goes to people who drive trucks and work in wholesale and retail organizations. Note that only 3.5 cents goes to profit.

Here are three basic points about intermediaries:

1. Marketing intermediaries can be eliminated, but their activities can't; that is, you can eliminate some wholesalers and retailers, but then consumers or someone else would have to perform the intermediaries' tasks, including transporting and storing goods, finding suppliers, and establishing communication with suppliers.

2. Intermediary organizations have survived because they perform marketing functions faster and more cheaply than others can. To maintain their competitive position in the channel, they now must adopt the latest technology. That includes search engine optimization, social networking (on sites like Facebook), and analyzing website statistics to understand their customers better.

3. Intermediaries add costs to products, but these costs are usually more than offset by the values they create.

LEARNING goal 2

Demonstrate how intermediaries perform the six marketing utilities.

THE UTILITIES CREATED BY INTERMEDIARIES

Utility, in economics, is the want-satisfying ability, or value, that organizations add to goods or services by making them more useful or accessible to consumers than they were before. The six kinds of utility are form, time, place, possession, information, and service. Although producers provide some utilities, marketing intermediaries provide most. Let's look at how.

Form Utility

Traditionally, producers rather than intermediaries have provided form utility (see Chapter 9) by changing raw materials into useful products. Thus, a farmer who separates the wheat from the chaff and the processor who turns the wheat into flour are creating form utility. Retailers and other marketers sometimes provide form utility as well. For example, retail butchers cut pork chops from a larger piece of meat and trim off the fat. The servers at Starbucks make coffee just the way you want it. Dell assembles computers according to customers' wishes.

Time Utility

Intermediaries, such as retailers, add **time utility** to products by making them available when consumers need them. Devar Tennent lives in Boston. One winter evening while watching TV with his brother, Tennent suddenly got the urge for a hot dog and a Coke. The problem was there were no hot dogs or Cokes in the house.

Devar ran down to the corner delicatessen and bought some hot dogs, buns, Cokes, and potato chips. He also bought some frozen strawberries and ice cream. Devar was able to get these groceries at midnight because the local deli was open 24 hours a day. That's time utility. You can buy goods at any time on the Internet, but you can't beat having them available right around the corner *when you want them.* On the other hand, note the value an Internet company provides by staying accessible 24 hours a day.

Place Utility

Intermediaries add **place utility** to products by placing them *where* people want them. While traveling through the badlands of South Dakota, Juanita Ruiz got hungry and thirsty. There are no stores for miles in this part of the country, but Juanita saw signs along the road saying a 7-Eleven was ahead. Following the signs, she stopped at the store for refreshments. She also bought some sunglasses and souvenir items there. The goods and services provided by 7-Eleven are in a convenient place for vacationers. Throughout the United States, 7-Eleven stores remain popular because they are usually in easy-to-reach locations. They provide place utility. As more and more sales become global, place utility will grow in importance.

utility
In economics, the want-satisfying ability, or value, that organizations add to goods or services.

time utility
Adding value to products by making them available when they're needed.

place utility
Adding value to products by having them where people want them.

Think of how many stores provide time utility by making goods and services available to you 24 hours a day, seven days a week. Have you ever needed to renew a prescription late at night or needed a late-night snack? Can you see how time utility offers added value?

Possession Utility

possession utility
Doing whatever is necessary to transfer ownership from one party to another, including providing credit, delivery, installation, guarantees, and follow-up service.

Intermediaries add **possession utility** by doing whatever is necessary to transfer ownership from one party to another, including providing credit. Activities associated with possession utility include delivery, installation, guarantees, and follow-up service. Larry Rosenberg wanted to buy a nice home in the suburbs. He found just what he wanted, but he didn't have the money he needed. So he went with the real estate broker to a local savings and loan and borrowed money to buy the home. Both the real estate broker and the savings and loan are marketing intermediaries that provide possession utility. For those who don't want to own goods, possession utility makes it possible for them to use goods through renting or leasing.

Information Utility

information utility
Adding value to products by opening two-way flows of information between marketing participants.

Intermediaries add **information utility** by opening two-way flows of information between marketing participants. Jerome Washington couldn't decide what kind of TV set to buy. He looked at various ads in the newspaper, talked to salespeople at several stores, read material at the library and on the Internet, and tweeted his friends. Newspapers, salespeople, libraries, websites, and government publications are all information sources made available by intermediaries. They provide information utility.

Service Utility

service utility
Adding value by providing fast, friendly service during and after the sale and by teaching customers how to best use products over time.

Intermediaries add **service utility** by providing fast, friendly service during and after the sale and by teaching customers how to best use products over time. Sze Leung bought a personal computer for his home office. Both the computer manufacturer and the retailer Leung used continue to offer help whenever he needs it. He also gets software updates for a small fee to keep his computer up-to-date. What attracted Leung to the retailer in the first place was the helpful, friendly service he received from the salesperson in the store. Service utility is rapidly becoming the most important utility for many retailers, because without it they would lose business to direct marketing (e.g., marketing by catalog or on the Internet). Can you see how the Internet can provide some forms of service utility?

Service after the sale is one of the contributing factors to Apple's success. Customers can call to make an appointment with an Apple Genius who will help them learn how to use their computers, iPhones, or iPads. How does this service add value to Apple's products?

progress assessment

- What is a channel of distribution, and what intermediaries participate in it?
- Why do we need intermediaries? Illustrate how intermediaries create exchange efficiency.
- How would you defend intermediaries to someone who said getting rid of them would save consumers millions of dollars?
- Can you give examples of the utilities intermediaries create and how they provide them?

LEARNING goal 3

Identify the types of wholesale intermediaries in the distribution system.

WHOLESALE INTERMEDIARIES

Let's distinguish wholesaling from retailing and clearly define the functions of each. Some producers deal only with wholesalers and won't sell directly to retailers or to end users (consumers). Some producers deal with both wholesalers and retailers, but give wholesalers a bigger discount. In turn, some wholesalers sell to both retailers and consumers. The office superstore Staples is a good example. It sells office supplies to small businesses and to consumers as well. Warehouse clubs such as Sam's Club and Costco are other companies with both wholesale and retail functions.

The difference is this: A *retail sale* is the sale of goods and services to consumers *for their own use.* A *wholesale sale* is the sale of goods and services to businesses and institutions, like schools or hospitals, *for use in the business,* or to wholesalers or retailers *for resale.*

Wholesalers make business-to-business sales. Most people are not as familiar with the various kinds of wholesalers as they are with retailers. Let's explore some of these helpful wholesale intermediaries. Most of them provide a lot of marketing jobs and offer you a good opportunity.

Merchant Wholesalers

Merchant wholesalers are independently owned firms that take title to the goods they handle. About 80 percent of wholesalers fall in this category. There are two types of merchant wholesalers: full-service and limited-function. *Full-service wholesalers* perform all the distribution functions (see Figure 15.4). *Limited-function wholesalers* perform only selected functions, but try to do them especially well. Three common types of limited-function wholesalers are rack jobbers, cash-and-carry wholesalers, and drop shippers.

Rack jobbers furnish racks or shelves full of merchandise, like music, toys, hosiery, and health and beauty aids, to retailers. They display the products and sell them on consignment, meaning they keep title to the goods until they're sold and then share the profits with the retailer. Have you seen shelves at the supermarket full of CDs and related items? Rack jobbers likely put them there.

Cash-and-carry wholesalers serve mostly smaller retailers with a limited assortment of products. Traditionally, retailers went to such wholesalers, paid cash, and carried the goods back to their stores—thus the term *cash-and-carry.* Today, stores such as Staples allow retailers and others to use credit cards for wholesale purchases. Thus the term *cash-and-carry* is becoming obsolete for wholesalers.

Drop shippers solicit orders from retailers and other wholesalers and have the merchandise shipped directly from a producer to a buyer. They own the merchandise but don't handle, stock, or deliver it. That's done by the producer. Drop shippers tend to handle bulky products such as coal, lumber, and chemicals.

merchant wholesalers
Independently owned firms that take title to the goods they handle.

rack jobbers
Wholesalers that furnish racks or shelves full of merchandise to retailers, display products, and sell on consignment.

cash-and-carry wholesalers
Wholesalers that serve mostly smaller retailers with a limited assortment of products.

drop shippers
Wholesalers that solicit orders from retailers and other wholesalers and have the merchandise shipped directly from a producer to a buyer.

figure 15.4

A FULL-SERVICE WHOLESALER

A FULL-SERVICE WHOLESALER WILL:	THE WHOLESALER MAY PERFORM THE FOLLOWING SERVICES FOR CUSTOMERS:
1. Provide a sales force to sell the goods to retailers and other buyers.	1. Buy goods the end market will desire and make them available to customers.
2. Communicate manufacturers' advertising deals and plans.	2. Maintain inventory, thus reducing customers' costs.
3. Maintain inventory, thus reducing the level of the inventory suppliers have to carry.	3. Transport goods to customers quickly.
4. Arrange or undertake transportation.	4. Provide market information and business consulting services.
5. Provide capital by paying cash or making quick payments for goods.	5. Provide financing through granting credit, which is especially critical to small retailers.
6. Provide suppliers with market information they can't afford or can't obtain themselves.	6. Order goods in the types and quantities customers desire.
7. Undertake credit risk by granting credit to customers and absorbing any bad debts, thus relieving the supplier of this burden.	
8. Assume the risk for the product by taking title.	

Source: Thomas C. Kinnear, *Principles of Marketing*, 4th ed., © 1995, p. 394. Reprinted by permission of Pearson Education, Inc., Upper Saddle River, NJ.

Agents and brokers are a familiar type of intermediary. Typically they don't take possession of the goods they sell. A real estate broker, for instance, facilitates the transaction between seller and buyer but never holds title to the house. What functions does a realtor provide in a home sale?

Agents and Brokers

Agents and brokers bring buyers and sellers together and assist in negotiating an exchange. However, unlike merchant wholesalers, agents and brokers never own the products they distribute. Usually they do not carry inventory, provide credit, or assume risks. While merchant wholesalers earn a profit from the sale of goods, agents and brokers earn commissions or fees based on a percentage of the sales revenues. Agents maintain long-term relationships with the people they represent, whereas brokers are usually hired on a temporary basis.

Agents who represent producers are either *manufacturer's agents* or *sales agents*. As long as they do not carry competing products, manufacturer's agents may represent several manufacturers in a specific territory. They often work in the automotive supply, footwear, and fabricated steel industries. Sales agents represent a single producer in a typically larger territory.

Brokers have no continuous relationship with the buyer or seller. Once they negotiate a contract between the parties, their relationship ends. Producers of seasonal products like fruits and vegetables often use brokers, as does the real estate industry.

progress assessment

- Describe the activities of rack jobbers and drop shippers.
- What kinds of products would call for each of the different distribution strategies: intensive, selective, and exclusive?

exclusive distribution
Distribution that sends products to only one retail outlet in a given geographic area.

LEARNING goal 5

Explain the various kinds of nonstore retailing.

NONSTORE RETAILING

Nothing else in retailing has received more attention recently than electronic retailing. Internet retailing is just one form of nonstore retailing. Other categories are telemarketing; vending machines, kiosks, and carts; direct selling; multilevel marketing; and direct marketing. Small businesses can use nonstore retailing to open up new channels of distribution for their products.

electronic retailing
Selling goods and services to ultimate customers (e.g., you and me) over the Internet.

Electronic Retailing

Electronic retailing consists of selling goods and services to ultimate consumers over the Internet. Thanks to website improvements and discounting, online retail sales have risen dramatically over the last few years.[9] But getting customers is only half the battle. The other half is delivering the goods, providing helpful service, and keeping your customers. When electronic retailers lack sufficient inventory or fail to deliver goods on time (especially at holidays and other busy periods), customers often give up and go back to brick-and-mortar stores.

Most Internet retailers offer e-mail order confirmation. But sometimes they are less good at handling complaints, accepting returns, and providing personal help. Some are improving customer service by adding help buttons that lead customers to real-time online assistance from a human employee.

Many brick-and-mortar stores have added Internet services for the added convenience of their customers. Some people shop online and then go to the store to buy the merchandise. Others both shop and buy on the Internet. What are the advantages and disadvantages of shopping and buying online?

Old brick-and-mortar stores that add online outlets are sometimes called brick-and-click stores. They allow customers to choose which shopping technique suits them best. Most companies that want to compete in the future will probably need both a real store and an online presence to provide consumers with all the options they want. Walmart has added same-day in-store pickup of online purchases to its services.[10]

Traditional retailers like Sears have learned that selling on the Internet calls for a new kind of distribution. Sears's warehouses were accustomed to delivering truckloads of goods to the company's retail outlets. But they were not prepared to deliver to individual consumers, except for large orders like furniture and appliances. It turns out, therefore, that both traditional and Internet retailers have to develop new distribution systems to meet the demands of today's Internet-savvy shoppers. It's often easy to sell goods and services on eBay, but there is always the need to distribute those goods. Most people outsource that function to FedEx or UPS, which have the needed expertise.

Telemarketing

telemarketing
The sale of goods and services by telephone.

Telemarketing is the sale of goods and services by telephone. Some 80,000 companies use it to supplement or replace in-store selling and complement online selling. Many send a catalog to consumers, who order by calling a toll-free number. Many electronic retailers provide a help feature online that serves the same function.

Vending Machines, Kiosks, and Carts

direct selling
Selling to consumers in their homes or where they work.

Vending machines dispense convenience goods when consumers deposit sufficient money. They carry the benefit of location—they're found in airports, office buildings, schools, service stations, and other areas where people want convenience items. In Japan, they sell everything from bandages and face cloths to salads and spiced seafood. Vending by machine will be an interesting area to watch as more innovations are introduced in the United States. U.S. vending machines are already selling iPods, Bose headphones, sneakers, digital cameras, and DVD movies. You can even find earthworms, medical marijuana, and Chardonnay in vending machines.[11] An ATM machine in Abu Dhabi dispenses gold.[12]

Vending machines and kiosks are convenient and easy for customers to use. They also have lower overhead than stores do. What do stores provide that kiosks and vending machines don't?

Carts and kiosks have lower overhead costs than stores do, so they can offer lower prices on items such as T-shirts, purses, watches, and cell phones. You often see vending carts outside stores or along walkways in malls. Many mall owners love them because they're colorful and create a marketplace atmosphere. Kiosk workers often dispense coupons and helpful product information. You may have noticed airlines are using kiosks to speed the process of getting on the plane. Most provide a boarding pass and allow you to change your seat. Many kiosks serve as gateways to the Internet, so in one place consumers can shop at a store and still have access to all the products available on the Internet. What's your reaction to such kiosks?

Direct Selling

Direct selling reaches consumers in their homes or workplaces. Because so many men and women work outside the home and aren't in during the day, companies that use direct selling are sponsoring parties at workplaces or evenings and weekends. Major users of this sales category include cosmetics producers and vacuum cleaner manufacturers. Trying to copy their success, other businesses are venturing into direct selling with lingerie, artwork, and candles sold at house parties they sponsor. Some companies, however, such as those in encyclopedia sales, have dropped most of their direct selling efforts in favor of Internet selling.

Multilevel Marketing

Over 1,000 U.S. companies have had success using multilevel marketing (MLM) and salespeople who work as independent contractors. One of the most successful MLM firms today is called Team. It sells MonaVie, a fruit juice in a wine bottle for $39. Salespeople earn commissions on their own sales, create commissions for the "upliners" who recruited them, and receive commissions from any "downliners" they recruit to sell. When you have hundreds of downliners—people recruited by the people you recruit—your commissions can be sizable. Some people make tens of thousands of dollars a month this way. That doesn't mean you should get involved with such schemes. More often than not, people at the bottom buy the products themselves and sell a bare minimum to others.

The main attraction of multilevel marketing for employees, other than the potential for making money, is the low cost of entry. For a small investment, the average person can start up a business and begin recruiting others. Many people question MLM because some companies using it have acted unethically. Potential employees must be very careful to examine the practices of such firms. Nonetheless, MLM's sales of $30 billion a year demonstrate the potential for success in this form of marketing.

Direct Marketing

Direct marketing includes any activity that directly links manufacturers or intermediaries with the ultimate consumer. One of the fastest-growing types of retailing, it includes direct mail, catalog sales, and telemarketing as well as online marketing. Popular consumer catalog companies that use direct marketing include Coldwater Creek, L.L. Bean, and Lands' End (now owned by Sears). Direct marketing has created tremendous competition in some high-tech areas as well.

Direct marketing has become popular because shopping from home or work is more convenient for consumers than going to stores. Instead of driving to a mall, people can shop in catalogs and advertising supplements in the newspaper and then buy by phone, mail, or computer. Interactive online selling is expected to provide increasing competition for retail stores. Recently, L.L. Bean put pressure on rivals by eliminating shipping charges. That made L.L. Bean even more attractive to people who like to shop by catalog or online.[13]

Direct marketing took on a new dimension with *interactive video*. Producers now provide all kinds of information on websites. Consumers can ask questions, seek the best price, and order goods and services—all online. Companies that use interactive video have become major competitors for those who market through paper catalogs.

To offer consumers the maximum benefit, marketing intermediaries must work together to ensure a smooth flow of goods and services. There hasn't always been total harmony in the channel of distribution. As a result, channel members have created systems to make the flows more efficient. We'll discuss those next.

direct marketing
Any activity that directly links manufacturers or intermediaries with the ultimate consumer.

LEARNING **goal 6**

Explain the various ways to build cooperation in channel systems.

BUILDING COOPERATION IN CHANNEL SYSTEMS

corporate distribution system
A distribution system in which all of the organizations in the channel of distribution are owned by one firm.

One way traditional retailers can compete with online retailers is to be so efficient that online retailers can't beat them on cost—given the need for customers to pay for delivery. That means manufacturers, wholesalers, and retailers must work closely to form a unified system. How can manufacturers get wholesalers and retailers to cooperate in such a system? One way is to link the firms in a formal relationship. Four systems have emerged to tie firms together: corporate systems, contractual systems, administered systems, and supply chains.

Corporate Distribution Systems

In a **corporate distribution system** one firm owns all the organizations in the channel of distribution. If the manufacturer owns the retail firm, clearly it can maintain a great deal of control over its operations. Sherwin Williams, for example, owns its own retail stores and coordinates everything: display, pricing, promotion, inventory control, and so on.

contractual distribution system
A distribution system in which members are bound to cooperate through contractual agreements.

Contractual Distribution Systems

If a manufacturer can't buy retail stores, it can try to get retailers to sign a contract to cooperate with it. In a **contractual distribution system** members are bound to cooperate through contractual agreements. There are three forms of contractual systems:

Franchisors like Chocolate Chocolate Chocolate Company use a contractual distribution system that requires franchisees to follow the franchisors' rules and procedures. How does such a system ensure consistent quality and level of service?

1. *Franchise systems* such as McDonald's, KFC, Baskin-Robbins, and AAMCO. The franchisee agrees to all the rules, regulations, and procedures established by the franchisor. This results in the consistent quality and level of service you find in most franchised organizations.
2. *Wholesaler-sponsored chains* such as Ace Hardware and IGA food stores. Each store signs an agreement to use the same name, participate in chain promotions, and cooperate as a unified system of stores, even though each is independently owned and managed.
3. *Retail cooperatives* such as Associated Grocers. This arrangement is much like a wholesaler-sponsored chain except it is initiated by the retailers. The same degree of cooperation exists, and the stores remain independent. Normally in such a system, retailers agree to focus their purchases on one wholesaler, but cooperative retailers could also purchase a wholesale organization to ensure better service.

Administered Distribution Systems

If you were a producer, what would you do if you couldn't get retailers to sign an agreement to cooperate? You might manage all the marketing functions yourself, including display, inventory control, pricing, and promotion. A system in which producers manage all the marketing functions at the retail level is called an **administered distribution system.** Kraft does that for its cheeses. Scott does it for its seed and other lawn care products. Retailers cooperate with producers in such systems because they get a great deal of free help. All the retailer has to do is ring up the sale.

Supply Chains

A **supply chain (or value chain)** consists of all the linked activities various organizations must perform to move goods and services from the sources of raw materials to ultimate consumers. A supply chain is longer than a channel of distribution because it includes links from suppliers to manufacturers, whereas the channel of distribution begins with manufacturers.[14] Channels of distribution are part of the overall supply chain (see Figure 15.6).

Included in the supply chain are farmers, miners, suppliers of all kinds (parts, equipment, supplies), manufacturers, wholesalers, and retailers. **Supply-chain management** is the process of managing the movement of raw materials, parts, work in progress, finished goods, and related information through all the organizations in the supply chain; managing the return of such goods if necessary; and recycling materials when appropriate.[15]

One complex supply chain is that for the automaker Kia's Sorento model. The Sorento is assembled in South Korea and made of over 30,000 components from all over the world. The shock and front-loading system is from AF Sachs AG, the front-wheel drive is from BorgWarner, and the tires are from Michelin. Air bags are sometimes flown in from Swedish company Autoliv Inc., which makes them in Utah. As you can see, supply-chain management is interfirm and international.[16] Increasingly, it also involves services. To learn about supply chains and services, see the nearby Connecting Across Borders box.

Companies like SAP, i2, and Oracle have developed software to coordinate the movement of goods and information so that producers can translate consumer wants into products with the least amount of materials, inventory, and time. Firms can move parts and information so smoothly, they look like one firm.

Computers make such links possible. Naturally, the systems are quite complex and expensive, but they can pay for themselves in the long run because of inventory savings, customer service improvement, and responsiveness to market changes. Because such systems are so effective and efficient, they are sometimes called *value chains* instead of supply chains.[17]

Not all supply chains are as efficient as they can be. Some companies have struggled with high distribution costs, including the cost of disruptions, inefficient truck routes, and excess inventory.[18] The complexity of supply-chain

administered distribution system
A distribution system in which producers manage all of the marketing functions at the retail level.

supply chain (value chain)
The sequence of linked activities that must be performed by various organizations to move goods from the sources of raw materials to ultimate consumers.

supply-chain management
The process of managing the movement of raw materials, parts, work in progress, finished goods, and related information through all the organizations involved in the supply chain; managing the return of such goods, if necessary; and recycling materials when appropriate.

figure 15.6

THE SUPPLY CHAIN

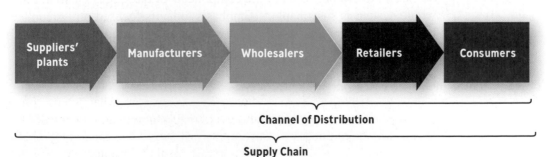

The Globe's Growing Service Supply Chain

It is easy to imagine the supply chain for parts and materials that go into goods. For example, you can easily imagine components traveling from Thailand, the Philippines, Malaysia, and Taiwan to a factory in China where they are assembled before being sold as iPhones or iPads in an Apple store in New York. In the future, it may be more important to study and understand the supply chain for services. Imagine call centers as part of the service supply chain. They are relatively easy to establish and most of us have experienced talking to someone on the phone from Asia when we've had technology problems. Now imagine outsourcing other services such as the programming of software, reviewing legal documents, and processing expense reports and the like.

Much movie animation is now taking place in the Philippines, and companies in China are providing research and development services. One article stated, "We're heading for a day when a Malaysian architect will sketch out a new office tower for London, a Philippine architect will prepare detailed renderings, and a Chinese engineer will assess the structural soundness of the design. Or a specialist firm in Bangalore will administer health benefits for a Kansas company." The competition among foreign suppliers is intense, including the need to find workers with strong language skills. Those countries that excel in providing supply chains for goods (e.g., China) may not be the same as those providing expertise in services (e.g., India). Of course, one of the countries that could become a leader in supplying supply-chain services is the United States. One important step is to make supply chains secure. The 2011 disasters in Japan showed people that the supply chain is only as good as the weakest link.

Sources: Joseph Sternberg, "Now Comes the Global Revolution in Services," *The Wall Street Journal,* February 10, 2011; Janet Napolitano, "How to Secure the Global Supply Chain," *The Wall Street Journal,* January 6, 2011; and Bruce Einhorn, Tim Culpan and Alan Ohnsman, "Now, A Weak Link in the Supply Chain," *Bloomberg Businessweek,* March 21–March 27, 2011.

management often leads firms to outsource the whole process to experts that know how to integrate it. Richardson Electronics of La Fox, Illinois, does business in 125 countries with 37 different currencies. It relies on Oracle's PeopleSoft Supply Chain Management and Financial Management solutions. Oracle's PeopleSoft also provides financial help, making it easier and less expensive to ship goods anywhere in the world and be sure of payment. Outsourcing is on the rise as more firms realize how complex distribution is.

Outsourcing this function can have serious consequences, as companies learned when they found lead paint in toys and contaminants in the drug heparin.[19] Cardinal Health, the nation's second-largest drug distributor, became much more successful when the CEO reorganized the supply chain.[20] All companies must be careful to evaluate each of the components of the supply chain to make sure the whole system is sustainable.[21] Emphasis today is focused on "green" technology because so much of what affects the environment is caused by distribution.[22]

LEARNING goal 7

Describe logistics and outline how intermediaries manage the transportation and storage of goods.

LOGISTICS: GETTING GOODS TO CONSUMERS EFFICIENTLY

Shipping costs have risen dramatically in recent years. When shipping from country to country, it is often impossible to use trucks or trains because the goods have to travel over water. Shipping by air is often prohibitively expensive, which sometimes narrows the choice to moving goods by ship. But how do you get the goods to the ship—and from the ship to the buyer? How do you keep costs low enough to make exchanges beneficial for you and your customers? And how do you handle foreign trade duties and taxes? Distributing goods globally is complicated. As transportation and distribution have grown more complex, marketers have responded by developing more sophisticated systems.

To better manage customs problems, for instance, many turn to web-based trade compliance systems. Firms like TradePoint and Xporta determine what paperwork is needed, cross-checking their databases for information about foreign trade duties and taxes, U.S. labor law restrictions, and federal regulations from the Food and Drug Administration or the Bureau of Alcohol, Tobacco, and Firearms. In other words, they manage logistics.[23]

Logistics is the planning, implementing, and controlling of the physical flow of materials, final goods, and related information from points of origin to points of consumption to meet customer requirements at a profit. **Inbound logistics** brings raw materials, packaging, other goods and services, and information from suppliers to producers.

Materials handling is the movement of goods within a warehouse, from warehouses to the factory floor, and from the factory floor to various workstations. *Factory processes* change raw materials and parts and other inputs into outputs, such as finished goods like shoes, cars, and clothes.

Outbound logistics manages the flow of finished products and information to business buyers and ultimately to consumers like you and me. **Reverse logistics** brings goods back to the manufacturer because of defects or for recycling materials.[24]

Logistics is as much about the movement of *information* as it is about the movement of goods. Customer wants and needs must flow through the system all the way to suppliers and must do so in real time. Information must also flow

logistics
The marketing activity that involves planning, implementing, and controlling the physical flow of materials, final goods, and related information from points of origin to points of consumption to meet customer requirements at a profit.

inbound logistics
The area of logistics that involves bringing raw materials, packaging, other goods and services, and information from suppliers to producers.

materials handling
The movement of goods within a warehouse, from warehouses to the factory floor, and from the factory floor to various workstations.

outbound logistics
The area of logistics that involves managing the flow of finished products and information to business buyers and ultimate consumers (people like you and me).

How do you move heavy raw materials like timber from one country to another? This photo shows some of the firms engaged in the logistics process. A trucking firm brings the logs to a dock where huge cranes lift them into the hold of a ship. The ship must be unloaded and the logs put on another truck to travel to a processing plant. Why is managing the logistics process a key to survival in some industries?

reverse logistics
The area of logistics that involves bringing goods back to the manufacturer because of defects or for recycling materials.

down through the system with no delay. That, of course, demands sophisticated hardware and software. One company in India, Fabindia (a seller of hand-woven garments and home furnishings), ensures close relationships with its suppliers by having its suppliers become shareholders.

Third-party logistics is the use of outside firms to help move goods from here to there. It is part of the trend to outsource functions your firm cannot do more efficiently than outside firms.[25] The 3PLs (third-party logistics providers) that have superior capability in business intelligence and are proactively sharing that knowledge are the ones who will grow in the future.[26] Greatwide Logistics Services, for example, does business with six of the top 10 grocery retailers and wholesalers in the United States.[27]

Texas Instruments (TI) is one of the world's largest makers of silicon chips. About 75 percent of its semiconductor products move through its distribution network. The company uses a regional distribution center in Singapore to serve customers in Asia; one in Dallas to serve North America; one in Utrecht, the Netherlands, to serve Europe; and one in Tsubuka, Japan, to serve markets in that country. TI uses a 3PL service to handle the day-to-day operations of those warehouses. Moving goods from one place to another is a major part of logistics.

How do you get products to people around the world after the sale? What are your options? You could send goods by truck, train, ship, or pipeline. You could use a shipping specialist, such as UPS, FedEx, or the U.S. Postal Service, but often that is expensive, especially for large items. Nonetheless, some of the most sophisticated marketers outsource the distribution process to such specialists.[28] All transportation modes can be evaluated on basic service criteria: cost, speed, dependability, flexibility, frequency, and reach. Figure 15.7 compares the various transportation modes on these criteria.

figure 15.7

COMPARING TRANSPORTATION MODES

Combining trucks with railroads lowers cost and increases the number of locations reached. The same is true when combining trucks with ships. Combining trucks with airlines speeds goods over long distances and gets them to almost any location.

Trains Are Great for Large Shipments

The largest percentage of goods in the United States (by volume) is shipped by rail. As a whole, the rail industry carries about 43 percent of all freight (as measured in ton miles), but uses only 7 percent of the total energy used to move freight.[29] Railroad shipment is best for bulky items such as coal, wheat, automobiles, and heavy equipment. In *piggyback* shipping, a truck trailer is detached from the cab, loaded onto a railroad flatcar, and taken to a destination where it will be offloaded, attached to a truck, and driven to the customer's plant. Railroads should continue to hold their own in competition with other modes of transportation. They offer a relatively energy-efficient way to move goods and could experience significant gains if fuel prices climb.

MODE	COST	SPEED	ON-TIME DEPENDABILITY	FLEXIBILITY HANDLING PRODUCTS	FREQUENCY OF SHIPMENTS	REACH
Railroad	Medium	Slow	Medium	High	Low	High
Trucks	High	Fast	High	Medium	High	Highest
Pipeline	Low	Medium	Highest	Lowest	Highest	Lowest
Ships (water)	Lowest	Slowest	Lowest	Highest	Lowest	Low
Airplane	Highest	Fastest	Low	Low	Medium	Medium

Railroads carry over a third of all goods shipped within the United States,. and are expected to remain a dominant transportation mode. What are some of the advantages of shipping by rail, for both large and small producers?

A company may not ship enough goods to think of using a railroad. Such smaller manufacturers or marketers can get good rates and service by using a **freight forwarder,** which puts many small shipments together to create a single large one that can be transported cost-effectively by truck or train. Some freight forwarders also offer warehousing, customs assistance, and other services along with pickup and delivery. You can see the benefits of such a company to a smaller seller. A freight forwarder is just one of many distribution specialists that have emerged to help marketers move goods from one place to another.

freight forwarder
An organization that puts many small shipments together to create a single large shipment that can be transported cost-effectively to the final destination.

Trucks Are Good for Small Shipments to Remote Locations

The second-largest surface transportation mode is motor vehicles (trucks and vans). As Figure 15.7 shows, trucks reach more locations than trains and can deliver almost any commodity door-to-door.

You could buy your own truck to make deliveries, but for widespread delivery you can't beat trucking specialists. Like freight forwarders, they have emerged to supply one important marketing function—transporting goods. Railroads have joined with trucking firms to further the process of piggybacking with 20-foot-high railroad cars, called double stacks, that carry two truck trailers, one on top of the other.

When fuel prices rise, trucking companies look for ways to cut costs. The newest measure of transportation from farm to consumer is the *carbon cost.* Some argue that the fewer miles food travels, the better for the environment, but that may not always be true.

Water Transportation Is Inexpensive but Slow

When sending goods overseas, often the least expensive way is by ship. Obviously, ships are slower than ground or air transportation, so water transportation isn't appropriate for goods that need to be delivered quickly. There was a huge dropoff in shipping when oil prices skyrocketed, improved somewhat when oil prices came down, and dropped off again when oil prices rose again. Water transport is local as well as international. If you live near the Mississippi River, you've likely seen towboats hauling as many as 30 barges at a time, with a cargo of up to 35,000 tons. On smaller rivers, towboats can haul about eight barges, carrying up to 20,000 tons—that's the equivalent of four 100-car railroad trains. Add to that Great Lakes shipping, shipping from coast to coast and along the coasts, and international shipments, and water transportation takes on a new dimension as a key transportation mode. When truck trailers are placed on ships to travel long distances at lower rates, it's called *fishyback* (see the explanation of piggyback above). When they are placed in airplanes, by the way, that's *birdyback*.

Pipelines Are Fast and Efficient

One transportation mode we don't often observe is pipeline. Pipelines primarily transport water, petroleum, and petroleum products—but a lot more products than you may imagine are shipped by pipelines. For example, coal can be sent by pipeline by first crushing it and mixing it with water.

Air Transportation Is Fast but Expensive

Today, only a small proportion of shipping goes by air. Nonetheless, air transportation is a critical factor in many industries, carrying everything from small packages to luxury cars and elephants. Its primary benefit is speed. No firms know this better than FedEx and UPS. As just two of several competitors vying for the fast-delivery market, FedEx and UPS have used air transport to expand into global markets.

The air freight industry is starting to focus on global distribution. Emery, now part of UPS, has been an industry pioneer in establishing specialized sales and operations teams aimed at serving the distribution needs of specific industries. KLM Royal Dutch Airlines has cargo/passenger planes that handle high-profit items such as diplomatic pouches and medical supplies. Specializing in such cargo has enabled KLM to compete with FedEx, TNT, and DHL.

Intermodal Shipping

intermodal shipping
The use of multiple modes of transportation to complete a single long-distance movement of freight.

Intermodal shipping uses multiple modes of transportation—highway, air, water, rail—to complete a single long-distance movement of freight. Services that specialize in intermodal shipping are known as intermodal marketing companies. Today, railroads are merging with each other and with other transportation companies to offer intermodal distribution.

Picture an automobile made in Japan for sale in the United States. It's shipped by truck to a loading dock, and from there moved by ship to a port in the United States. It may be placed on another truck and then taken to a railroad station for loading on a train that will take it across the country, to again be loaded on a truck for delivery to a local dealer. No doubt you've seen automobiles being hauled across the country by train and by truck. Now imagine that one integrated shipping firm handled all that movement. That's what intermodal shipping is all about.

The Storage Function

The preceding sections detailed the various ways of shipping goods once the company has sold them. But that's only the first step in understanding the system that moves goods from one point to another. Another important part of a complex logistics system is storage.

Buyers want goods delivered quickly. That means marketers must have goods available in various parts of the country ready to be shipped locally when ordered. A good percentage of the total cost of logistics is for storage. This includes the cost of the storage warehouse (distribution facility) and its operation, plus movement of goods within the warehouse.

There are two major kinds of warehouses: storage and distribution. A *storage warehouse* holds products for a relatively long time. Seasonal goods such as lawn mowers are kept in such a warehouse. *Distribution warehouses* are facilities used to gather and redistribute products. You can picture a distribution warehouse for FedEx or UPS handling thousands of packages in a very short time. The packages are picked up at places throughout the country and then processed for reshipment at these centers. General Electric's combination storage and distribution facility in San Gabriel Valley, California, gives you a feel for how large such buildings can be. It is nearly half a mile long and 465 feet wide—that's enough to hold almost 27 football fields.

RFID tags are being used in all kinds of situations, from the movement of goods to the tracking of livestock. RFID tags in products like these jeans helps retailers and producers track products from the suppliers' docks through the retailers' doors. How can RFID tags help you avoid losing your luggage, car keys, and other things?

Tracking Goods

How do producers keep track of where their goods are at any given time? As we noted in Chapter 14, companies use Universal Product Codes—the familiar black-and-white bar codes and a preset number—to keep track of inventory. Bar codes got a big lift when camera phone apps made it possible to compare prices and read reviews about products from different suppliers.[30]

Radio frequency identification (RFID), which we also mentioned earlier, is newer technology that tags merchandise so that it can be tracked from its arrival on the supplier's docks to its exit through the retailer's door. Walmart, Target, and other organizations all plan to require suppliers to use RFID. Currently, RFID tags cost about 10 cents each, but the goal is to get the cost down to about 1 cent.

Few companies are more interested in tracking items than UPS, which now uses a mix of Bluetooth's short-range radio capability and wireless receivers to track merchandise. It claims the system is even better than RFID. The U.S. State Department is producing an electronic passport card as a substitute for booklet passports to be used by U.S. citizens who travel often to Canada, Mexico, and the Caribbean. It uses an RFID chip to provide data about the user. The card is very controversial, however, because some people believe it can be easily altered.

WHAT ALL THIS MEANS TO YOU

The life or death of a firm often depends on its ability to take orders, process orders, keep customers informed about the progress of their orders, get the goods out to customers quickly, handle returns, and manage any recycling issues. Some of the most exciting firms in the marketplace are those that assist in some aspect of supply-chain management.

What all this means to you is that many new jobs are becoming available in the exciting area of supply-chain management. These include jobs in distribution: trains, airplanes, trucks, ships, and pipelines. It also means jobs handling information flows between and among companies, including website development. Other jobs include processing orders, keeping track of inventory, following the path of products as they move from seller to buyer and back, recycling goods, and much more.

progress assessment

- What four systems have evolved to tie together members of the channel of distribution?
- How does logistics differ from distribution?
- What are inbound logistics, outbound logistics, and reverse logistics?

summary

Learning Goal 1. Explain the concept of marketing channels and their value.

• What is a channel of distribution?

A channel of distribution consists of a whole set of marketing intermediaries, such as agents, brokers, wholesalers, and retailers, that join together to transport and store goods in their path (or channel) from producers to consumers.

• How do marketing intermediaries add value?

Intermediaries perform certain marketing tasks—such as transporting, storing, selling, advertising, and relationship building—faster and more cheaply than most manufacturers could. Channels of distribution ensure communication flows and the flow of money and title to goods. They also help ensure that the right quantity and assortment of goods will be available when and where needed.

• What are the principles behind the use of such intermediaries?

Marketing intermediaries can be eliminated, but their activities can't. Without wholesalers and retailers, consumers would have to perform the tasks of transporting and storing goods, finding suppliers, and establishing communication with them. Intermediaries add costs to products, but these costs are usually more than offset by the values they create.

Learning Goal 2. Demonstrate how intermediaries perform the six marketing utilities.

• How do intermediaries perform the six marketing utilities?

A retail grocer may cut or trim meat, providing some form utility. But marketers are more often responsible for the five other utilities. They provide time utility by having goods available *when* people want them, and place utility by having goods *where* people want them. Possession utility makes it possible for people to own things and includes credit, delivery, installation, guarantees, and anything else that completes the sale. Marketers also inform consumers of the availability of goods and services with advertising, publicity, and other means. That provides information utility. Finally, marketers provide fast, friendly, and efficient service during and after the sale (service utility).

Learning Goal 3. Identify the types of wholesale intermediaries in the distribution system.

- **What is a wholesaler?**

A wholesaler is a marketing intermediary that sells to organizations and individuals, but not to final consumers.

- **What are some wholesale organizations that assist in the movement of goods from manufacturers to consumers?**

Merchant wholesalers are independently owned firms that take title to the goods they handle. *Rack jobbers* furnish racks or shelves full of merchandise to retailers, display products, and sell on consignment. *Cash-and-carry wholesalers* serve mostly small retailers with a limited assortment of products. *Drop shippers* solicit orders from retailers and other wholesalers and have the merchandise shipped directly from a producer to a buyer.

Learning Goal 4. Compare the distribution strategies retailers use.

- **What is a retailer?**

A retailer is an organization that sells to ultimate consumers. Marketers develop several strategies based on retailing.

- **What are three distribution strategies marketers use?**

Marketers use three basic distribution strategies: intensive (putting products in as many places as possible), selective (choosing only a few stores in a chosen market), and exclusive (using only one store in each market area).

Learning Goal 5. Explain the various kinds of nonstore retailing.

- **What are some of the forms of nonstore retailing?**

Nonstore retailing includes online marketing; telemarketing (marketing by phone); vending machines, kiosks, and carts (marketing by putting products in convenient locations, such as in the halls of shopping centers); direct selling (marketing by approaching consumers in their homes or places of work); multilevel marketing (marketing by setting up a system of salespeople who recruit other salespeople and help them to sell directly to customers); and direct marketing (direct mail and catalog sales). Telemarketing and online marketing are also forms of direct marketing.

Learning Goal 6. Explain the various ways to build cooperation in channel systems.

- **What are the four types of distribution systems?**

The four distribution systems that tie firms together are (1) *corporate systems,* in which all organizations in the channel are owned by one firm; (2) *contractual systems,* in which members are bound to cooperate through contractual agreements; (3) *administered systems,* in which all marketing functions at the retail level are managed by manufacturers; and (4) *supply chains,* in which the various firms in the supply chain are linked electronically to provide the most efficient movement of information and goods possible.

Learning Goal 7. Describe logistics and outline how intermediaries manage the transportation and storage of goods.

- **What is logistics?**

Logistics includes planning, implementing, and controlling the physical flow of materials, final goods, and related information from points of origin to points of consumption to meet customer requirements at a profit.

- **What is the difference between logistics and distribution?**

Distribution generally means transportation. Logistics is more complex. *Inbound logistics* brings raw materials, packaging, other goods and services, and information from suppliers to producers. *Materials handling* is the moving of goods from warehouses to the factory floor and to various workstations. *Outbound logistics* manages the flow of finished products and information to business buyers and ultimate consumers (people like you and me). *Reverse logistics* brings goods back to the manufacturer because of defects or for recycling materials.

- **What are the various transportation modes?**

Transportation modes include rail (for heavy shipments within the country or between bordering countries); trucks (for getting goods directly to consumers); ships (for slow, inexpensive movement of goods, often internationally); pipelines (for moving water, oil, and other such goods); and airplanes (for shipping goods quickly).

- **What is intermodal shipping?**

Intermodal shipping uses multiple modes of transportation—highway, air, water, rail—to complete a single long-distance movement of freight.

- **What are the different kinds of warehouses?**

A storage warehouse stores products for a relatively long time. Distribution warehouses are used to gather and redistribute products.

key terms

administered
 distribution
 system 449
agents/brokers 435
cash-and-carry
 wholesalers 441
channel of
 distribution 434
contractual distribution
 system 448
corporate distribution
 system 448
direct marketing 447
direct selling 446
drop shippers 441
electronic retailing 445

exclusive
 distribution 445
freight forwarder 453
inbound logistics 451
information utility 440
intensive distribution 444
intermodal shipping 454
logistics 451
marketing
 intermediaries 434
materials handling 451
merchant
 wholesalers 441
outbound logistics 451
place utility 439

possession utility 440
rack jobbers 441
retailer 435
reverse logistics 452
selective
 distribution 444
service utility 440
supply chain (value
 chain) 449
supply-chain
 management 449
telemarketing 446
time utility 439
utility 439
wholesaler 435

critical thinking

1. Imagine that we have eliminated marketing intermediaries, and you need groceries and shoes. How would you find out where the shoes and groceries are? How far would you have to travel to get them? How much money do you think you'd save for your time and effort?
2. Which intermediary do you think is most important today and why? What changes are happening to companies in that area?
3. One scarce item in the future will be water. If you could think of an inexpensive way to get water from places of abundance to places where it is needed for drinking, farming, and other uses, you could become a wealthy marketing intermediary. Pipelines are an alternative, but could you also freeze the water and ship it by train or truck? Could you use ships to tow icebergs to warmer climates? What other means of transporting water might there be?

developing workplace skills

1. The six utilities of marketing are form, time, place, possession, information, and service. Give examples of organizations in your area that perform each of these functions.

2. Form small groups and diagram how Dole might get pineapples from a field in Thailand to a canning plant in California to a store near your college. Include the intermediaries and the forms of transportation each one might use.

3. Compare the merits of buying and selling goods in stores and over the Internet. What advantages do stores have? Has anyone in the class tried to sell anything on the Internet? How did he or she ship the product?

4. In class, discuss the differences between wholesaling and retailing and why retailing has more appeal for students considering jobs. Since fewer students seek jobs in wholesaling than in retailing, do you think wholesaling jobs may be easier to get?

5. One part of retailing is using auction sites like eBay to sell new and used merchandise. Form small groups and discuss group members' experiences using eBay. What tips have they learned? How do eBay users minimize the problems associated with shipping?

taking it to the net

Purpose

To examine how small businesses can learn to use the Internet to distribute their products directly to customers.

Exercise

Many small-business owners have no idea how to begin selling goods over the Internet. Several free websites have been developed to help them get started with tasks from setting up their site to doing online marketing, handling credit purchases, and more. Go to **Homestead.com** or **BlueVoda.com** and listen to the presentations they make. Search the web to find other sources of help in designing your own website. Then answer the following questions:

1. How long do the websites say that it takes to get started?

2. Does the process seem easier or harder than you imagined?

3. Do you have questions that the websites did not answer?

4. What help are you given, if any, in planning how to ship your goods?

casing the web

To access the case "Multilevel Marketing," visit
www.mhhe.com/P2P2e.

video case

Making Life Easier

The way we watch movies has changed dramatically over time. In the beginning, people had to go to a movie theater to see a movie. Later we could rent or buy a movie from a video store to watch at home. Movie watching got easier because some intermediary (movie theaters, rental firms, etc.) made the process easier.

It was not too surprising, therefore, when a new intermediary called Netflix came along to make the process even easier. All you have to do is select a film on the Netflix website and wait for the movie to show up in your mailbox. Of course, this made the U.S. Postal Service another helpful intermediary. What could be easier?

It would be easier for consumers if movies could be streamed electronically (on demand) to your computer or TV or even to your cell phones or other portable viewers. Today Netflix subscribers can do just that.

Intermediaries may add a little cost to the price we pay for goods, but the benefits we receive are usually much greater than the small cost. Intermediaries add time value by making goods available *when* we want them. For Netflix that means providing movies at any time. Intermediaries also provide place utility. Thus Netflix movies are available in any *place*. Netflix provides possession utility through easy online payment.

None of these movie-providing services is of much value unless we learn about them somehow. Thus information utility—provided by the various media—is invaluable. Can you see why newspapers, radio, TV, websites, and other media might be called intermediaries that provide information utility?

Whether or not Netflix remains dominant in providing movies on demand depends greatly on how well it provides service utility. Will the company continue to be the easiest, fastest, and most comprehensive source of movies? Time will tell.

Netflix is an example of how quickly new ways of distribution can affect both consumers and businesses. We are all familiar with wholesalers and retailers and their use of warehouses to store goods. We are also aware of how these traditional ways of distributing goods are being replaced by online buying and selling and alternative distribution agencies such as FedEx, UPS, and the U.S. Postal Service.

Can you envision a day when airplanes, trucks, ships, and trains are replaced by other modes of transportation? Can you picture pipelines being used to ship products such as coal and packages of all kinds? Change comes quickly in the area of distribution, and those who lead are often quite profitable. Netflix is just one example.

Thinking It Over

1. *List several ways you may view movies today. Which way is the most popular for you and your friends?*

2. *What changes have you seen occurring in retail distribution? Do you anticipate more changes? Do these changes make your life easier or harder? Why?*

3. *What is the major difference between wholesale and retail?*

16

USING Effective Promotions

LEARNING goals

After you have read and studied this chapter, you should be able to

1 Identify the new and traditional tools that make up the promotion mix.

2 Contrast the advantages and disadvantages of various advertising media, including the Internet and social media.

3 Illustrate the steps of the B2B and B2C selling processes.

4 Describe the role of the public relations department, and show how publicity fits in that role.

5 Assess the effectiveness of various forms of sales promotion, including sampling.

6 Show how word of mouth, e-mail marketing, viral marketing, blogging, podcasting, and mobile marketing work.

profile

Some people believe that social media is too new to be understood completely. It's all the more appropriate then that one of social media's foremost experts happens to be quite young herself. Although Shama Kabani is still in her twenties, her accomplishments far exceed her age. As founder of The Marketing Zen Group, she is redefining the role that social media plays at companies around the world.

Born in India, Kabani moved to Texas at age nine with her parents. She grew up as a self-described constant learner who always explored a subject down to its finest details. Kabani used that natural curiosity at the University of Texas at Austin where she earned a graduate degree in Organizational Communication. She chose Twitter as the subject of her graduate thesis when the fledgling social network only had around 2,000 active users. "What I found in my research was that this was more than people being in social networks, and people connecting. It was a dramatic shift, a changing in society," says Kabani. "We were going from a culture of press doing media—which of course is huge—to people being the media." After graduating in 2009, the 24-year-old Kabani founded Marketing Zen in Dallas with $1,500 of her own money.

Although Kabani originally started Marketing Zen as a general consulting company, the firm's focus quickly shifted to online media as social networking grew more popular. According to Kabani, every day she asks herself the same question: "What can I do today to increase value for our trusted audience (blog readers, TV watchers, Twitter followers, etc.), for our team and for our clients?" The answer to that question differs from client to client. For an online dog food retailer, for instance, Marketing Zen established a blog and a Twitter presence so the company could interact closely with pet-food bloggers. For a Boston dance studio, the company built a website that focused on generating more targeted sales leads. Not only can Marketing Zen advise companies about how to better harness the power of the web, it can implement those ideas as well. More often than not, Kabani and her staff use their expertise to come up with something that is easy to use and appealing to the customer.

In fact, Marketing Zen's staff acts as a great example of the power of online communication. Most of the company's 30 employees were hired virtually and do all their work online. Kabani hasn't even met some of Marketing Zen's most important staffers face-to-face. As she's shown time and again, though, people don't need to be physically connected in order to interact meaningfully and professionally.

CONNECTING WITH

Shama Kabani

President of The Marketing Zen Group

In 2010 Kabani laid out all her ideas in a best-selling book called *The Zen of Social Media Marketing: An Easier Way to Build Credibility*. In it, she describes how the best companies integrate social networking into their bigger marketing picture rather than relying on it entirely. "You don't get anything for tweets, you don't get anything for your Facebook page," says Kabani. "But you do get something when, for example, you do an event, and PR works with social media to leverage those platforms." She also explains that social networking should be about the individual receiving the information, not the company itself. "The biggest mistake I see companies making is mistaking the medium for the message," says Kabani. "Great, you're on Twitter, but what do you have to say?"

To her credit, Shama Kabani appears to have a great deal to say. Along with her work at Marketing Zen and her writing, she hosts a number of television programs that air both online and on television. She also speaks at events across the world about subjects like social networking and marketing. She even mentored a group of Egyptian women about entrepreneurship and starting an online community from scratch. Not bad for someone who has yet to turn 30.

In this chapter we explore all the traditional and new elements of promotion. We'll explain how marketers use different media for promotion and the advantages and disadvantages of each. We'll also take a look at the role of public relations as well as the differences between B2C and B2B promotions. Finally, throughout the chapter we'll pay particular attention to the promotional uses of Shama Kabani's areas of expertise: electronic media like blogging, social networking, and podcasts.

Sources: Matt Villano, "From Grad Student to Social Media Millionaire," *Entrepreneur,* September 5, 2011; Michael J. Chin, "Interview: Shama Kabani," *Color Magazine,* December 2011–January 2012; "Best Advice I Ever Got: Shama Kabani," *Inc.,* March 16, 2012; and www.marketingzen .com, "Shama Kabani: President of The Marketing Zen Group," accessed May 2012.

This beverage company has 8.5 million Facebook fans. It posts two daily messages and then monitors how many times each message is reviewed, how many times it is shared, and what the fan response to the message is. It also uses Facebook to test potential ads before airing them on traditional media like TV. What is the name of this company? (Find the answer in the chapter.)

LEARNING goal 1

Identify the new and traditional tools that make up the promotion mix.

PROMOTION AND THE PROMOTION MIX

Promotion is one of the four Ps of marketing. As noted in Chapter 13, promotion consists of all the techniques sellers use to motivate people to buy their products or services. Both profit-making and nonprofit organizations use promotional techniques to communicate with people in their target market about goods and services, and to persuade them to participate in a marketing exchange.[1] Marketers use many different tools to promote their products.[2] Traditionally, those tools were advertising, personal selling, public relations, and sales promotion. Today they also include e-mail promotions, mobile promotions (those that use cell phones), social networking, blogging, podcasting, tweets, and more.[3] The Connecting with Small Business box explores what happens when a business uses customers to promote its products online.

promotion mix
The combination of promotional tools an organization uses.

The combination of promotional tools an organization uses is called its **promotion mix;** see Figure 16.1. We show the product in the middle of the figure to illustrate that the product itself can also be a promotional tool, such as when marketers give away free samples.

figure 16.1

THE TRADITIONAL PROMOTION MIX

Turning Customers into Spokepeople

Celebrity endorsements can give some products an element of glamour that consumers hadn't noticed before. However, a celebrity's stamp of approval doesn't always translate into a sales slam dunk. Not only are endorsements expensive, they can also strike consumers as dishonest. After all, why would someone who pulls in seven figures a year care about a sale at Macy's?

For as much authority as celebrities are granted, the word of the common shopper has become more and more powerful over the last few years. Social media allows consumers to praise or punish companies on a mass scale. To that end, many small companies attempt to interact with their customers online to get them talking positively about their products. But perhaps no one does it better than online footwear retailer ShoeDazzle. Even though the company is part-owned by Kim Kardashian, ShoeDazzle relies on video testimonials from real customers to expand its brand.

ShoeDazzle doesn't operate like most web retailers. A team of stylists selects shoes, handbags, and other accessories for customers based on their own style preferences. Given its unorthodox business model, the site relies heavily on word-of-mouth promotion. After a few years in operation, ShoeDazzle took its organic approach to another level when it began soliciting its best customers for video testimonials about the company. Customers simply go to the ShoeDazzle site, press "record" on the page, and automatically upload their testimonial to the company. Other customers immediately responded to these relatable, honest judgments of ShoeDazzle's service. Company executives credit the testimonials with the site's growing monthly visit count of more than 2.4 million hits. With such an affordable gimmick, it might just be a matter of time until real people become the new celebrities in marketing.

Sources: Jennifer Alsever, "Video Testimonials Turn Customers Into Spokepeople," *Inc.*, December 2011; and E.B. Boyd, "ShoeDazzle Ditches Monthly Subscriptions for Boutique-Style Pampering," *Fast Company*, March 29, 2012.

Integrated marketing communication (IMC) combines the promotional tools into one comprehensive, unified promotional strategy. With IMC, marketers can create a positive brand image, meet the needs of the consumer, and meet the strategic marketing and promotional goals of the firm. Emphasis today is on integrating traditional media, like TV, with social media[4] or integrating print media with online sites.[5]

Figure 16.2 shows the six steps in a typical promotional campaign. Let's begin exploring promotional tools by looking at advertising—the most visible tool.

integrated marketing communication (IMC)
A technique that combines all the promotional tools into one comprehensive, unified promotional strategy.

LEARNING goal 2

Contrast the advantages and disadvantages of various advertising media, including the Internet and social media.

Need help understanding Integrated Marketing Communication?
www.introbiz.tv/QR16-1

ADVERTISING: INFORMING, PERSUADING, AND REMINDING

Advertising is paid, nonpersonal communication through various media by organizations and individuals who are in some way *identified in the message*. Identification of the sender separates advertising from *propaganda*, which is nonpersonal

figure 16.2

STEPS IN A PROMOTIONAL CAMPAIGN

1. Identify a target market. (Refer back to Chapter 13 for a discussion of segmentation and target marketing.)
2. Define the objectives for each element of the promotion mix. Goals should be clear and measurable.
3. Determine a promotional budget. The budgeting process will clarify how much can be spent on advertising, personal selling, and other promotional efforts.
4. Develop a unifying message. The goal of an integrated promotional program is to have one clear message communicated by advertising, public relations, sales, and every other promotional effort.
5. Implement the plan. Advertisements, blogs, and other promotional efforts must be scheduled to complement efforts being made by public relations and sales promotion. Salespeople should have access to all materials to optimize the total effort.
6. Evaluate effectiveness. Measuring results depends greatly on clear objectives. Each element of the promotional mix should be evaluated separately, and an overall measure should be taken as well. It is important to learn what is working and what is not.

advertising
Paid, nonpersonal communication through various media by organizations and individuals who are in some way identified in the advertising message.

communication that *does not have an identified sponsor*. Propaganda is often distributed by the government in various countries. Figure 16.3 lists various categories of advertising. Take a minute to look it over; you'll see there's a lot more to advertising than just television commercials.

It's also easy to appreciate the impact of advertising spending on the U.S. economy; see Figure 16.4. Total ad volume exceeds $241 billion yearly. Note that direct mail is the number one medium, with expenditures over $52 billion. Would you have guessed that direct mail is number one? Broadcast TV is number two,

figure 16.3

MAJOR CATEGORIES OF ADVERTISING

Different kinds of advertising are used by various organizations to reach different market targets.

- *Retail advertising*—advertising to consumers by various retail stores such as supermarkets and shoe stores.
- *Trade advertising*—advertising to wholesalers and retailers by manufacturers to encourage them to carry their products.
- *Business-to-business advertising*—advertising from manufacturers to other manufacturers. A firm selling motors to auto companies would use business-to-business advertising.
- *Institutional advertising*—advertising designed to create an attractive image for an organization rather than for a product. "We Care about You" at Giant Food is an example. "Virginia Is for Lovers" and "I ❤ New York" were two institutional campaigns by government agencies.
- *Product advertising*—advertising for a good or service to create interest among consumer, commercial, and industrial buyers.
- *Advocacy advertising*—advertising that supports a particular view of an issue (e.g., an ad in support of gun control or against nuclear power plants). Such advertising is also known as cause advertising.
- *Comparison advertising*—advertising that compares competitive products. For example, an ad that compares two different cold care products' speed and benefits is a comparative ad.
- *Interactive advertising*—customer-oriented communication that enables customers to choose the information they receive, such as interactive video catalogs that let customers select which items to view.
- *Online advertising*—advertising messages that appear on computers as people visit different websites.
- *Mobile advertising*—advertising that reaches people on their cell phones.

with expenditures of over $36 billion. Cable networks bring in another $27 billion. Note that the Internet is at $25 billion. That's double what it was in 2005. The leading advertising agencies still take the bulk of promotional dollars and still have a major impact on consumers.[6]

How do we, as consumers, benefit from these advertising expenditures? First, ads are informative. Direct mail is full of information about products, prices, features, store policies, and more; so is newspaper advertising. Newspaper advertising is down because more and more people are getting their news on mobile devices.[7]

Second, not only does advertising inform us, but the money advertisers spend for commercial time pays the production costs of TV and radio programs. Advertising also covers the major costs of producing newspapers and magazines. Subscriptions and newsstand revenues cover only mailing and promotional costs. Figure 16.5 compares the advantages and disadvantages for marketers of various

figure 16.4

ESTIMATED U.S. ADVERTISING SPENDING BY MEDIUM (IN BILLIONS OF DOLLARS)

RANK	MEDIUM	PROJECTED ADVERTISING SPENDING
1	Direct mail	52.3
2	Broadcast TV (network, spot, synd.)	36.8
3	Newspaper	23.4
4	Cable TV networks	27.0
5	Radio	15.9
6	Yellow Pages	11.9
7	Consumer magazine	9.1
8	Internet	25.3
9	All other	39.7
Total		241.4 billion

Source: www.businessinsider.com, 2011.

MEDIUM	ADVANTAGES	DISADVANTAGES
Newspapers	Good coverage of local markets; ads can be placed quickly; high consumer acceptance; ads can be clipped and saved.	Ads compete with other features in paper; poor color; ads get thrown away with paper (short life span).
Television	Uses sight, sound, and motion; reaches all audiences; high attention with no competition from other material.	High cost; short exposure time; takes time to prepare ads. Digital video recorders skip over ads.
Radio	Low cost; can target specific audiences; very flexible; good for local marketing.	People may not listen to ad; depends on one sense (hearing); short exposure time; audience can't keep ad.
Magazines	Can target specific audiences; good use of color; long life of ad; ads can be clipped and saved.	Inflexible; ads often must be placed weeks before publication; cost is relatively high.
Outdoor	High visibility and repeat exposures; low cost; local market focus.	Limited message; low selectivity of audience.
Direct mail	Best for targeting specific markets; very flexible; ad can be saved.	High cost; consumers may reject ad as junk mail; must conform to post office regulations.
Yellow Pages–type advertising	Great coverage of local markets; widely used by consumers.	Competition with other ads; cost may be too high for very small businesses.
Internet	Inexpensive global coverage; available at any time; interactive.	Customers may leave the site before buying.
Mobile advertising	Great reach among younger shoppers.	Easy to ignore, avoid.
Social media	Wonderful communication tools.	Time drain.

figure 16.5

ADVANTAGES AND DISADVANTAGES OF VARIOUS ADVERTISING MEDIA

The most effective media are often very expensive. The inexpensive media may not reach your market. The goal is to use the medium that can reach your desired market most effectively and efficiently.

advertising media. Notice that newspapers, radio, and the Yellow Pages are especially attractive to local advertisers.

Marketers must choose which media will best reach the audience they desire. Radio advertising, for example, is less expensive than TV advertising and often reaches people when they have few other distractions, such as while they're driving. Radio is thus especially effective at selling *services* people don't usually read about in print media—banking, mortgages, continuing education, and brokerage services, to name a few. On the other hand, radio has become so commercial-ridden that many people are paying to switch to commercial-free satellite radio. Marketers also search for other places to put advertising, such as on video screens mounted in elevators. Have you noticed ads on park benches and grocery carts? You've certainly seen them on websites you visit.

Mobile marketing via cell phones started out mostly as text messages, but now Starbucks can send signals to your phone as you approach the store, reminding you to stop in for a latte. Kraft Foods developed the iPhone Assistant, an iPhone application that serves up recipes for users—recipes made with Kraft products. Other retailers use e-mail advertisements to build brand awareness and drive people to their stores or websites.[8] Social media in general is growing so fast that marketers can hardly keep up.[9] Take the restaurant industry for example. Starbucks is number one in social media with 12 million Twitter followers. It registers 19.3 million "likes" on Facebook. McDonald's has over 80,000 followers with Twitter and 7 million friends on Facebook.[10]

Another way to get more impact from advertising is to appeal to the interest in green marketing among consumers and businesses.[11] A brief glance through magazines and the business press reveals all kinds of new appeals to sustainability and carbon-cutting measures. In the next sections, we'll look in more depth at some other popular advertising media.

Television Advertising

Television offers many advantages to national advertisers, but it's expensive. Thirty seconds of advertising during the Super Bowl telecast cost about $3 million.[12] How many bottles of beer or automobiles must a company sell to pay for such commercials? A lot, but few media besides television allow advertisers to reach so many people with such impact, although not all ads are equally effective.[13]

Despite what you may read about the growth of alternative promotional tools, TV advertising is still a dominant medium.[14] Digital video recorders (DVRs) enable consumers to skip the ads on TV. This may make TV less attractive to advertisers unless commercials get so much better that people *want* to watch them. New program delivery systems, such as video on demand, make it even more difficult for TV advertisers to catch consumers' eyes. Thus marketers are demanding better and more accurate measures of TV advertising's effectiveness, and many are switching to social media as a result.[15]

Product Placement

TV advertising isn't limited to traditional commercials; sometimes the products appear in the programs themselves. With **product placement,** advertisers pay to put their products into TV shows and movies where the audience will see them.[16] One classic example of product placement is the trail of Reese's Pieces in the movie *E.T.* Did you ever notice the Coca-Cola cups on the judges' table on *American Idol?* Many placements are more subtle, like the wheeled luggage from ZÜCA Inc. that appeared on the TV show *CSI.*

The latest wrinkle in product placement puts virtual products into video games. If you're a gamer, you've seen in-game ads, like ads around the court in basketball

product placement
Putting products into TV shows and movies where they will be seen.

Product placement is often subtle. You can see it in the products used in movies like the ones shown on the table in this one. The goal is to influence you to want that product yourself. What product placements have you noticed in your favorite TV shows and movies?

games. Technology allows vending machines in racing games to be branded and rebranded over time, depending on whether Coke, Pepsi, Exxon, or Shell has purchased ad time.[17]

Infomercials

An **infomercial** is a full-length TV program devoted exclusively to promoting a particular good or service. Infomercials have been successful because they show the product and how it works in great detail. They are the equivalent of sending your very best salespeople to a person's home and having them use all of their techniques to make the sale: drama, demonstration, testimonials, graphics, and more. Because of their success, infomercials are expected to rise to over $170 billion in 2014.[18]

Products that have earned over $1 billion in sales through infomercials include Proactiv (acne cream), Soloflex, Total Gym, Bowflex (exercise machines), the George Foreman Grill, and Ron Popeil's Rotisserie and Grill. Some products, such as personal development seminars, real estate programs, and workout tapes, are hard to sell without showing people a sample of their contents and using testimonials. Have you purchased any products that you saw in an infomercial?

Online Advertising

When marketers advertise on an online search engine such as Google or Bing, they can reach the people they most want to reach—consumers researching vacations, exploring the car market, or checking stocks. One goal of online advertising is to get potential customers to a website where they can learn more about the company and its products—and the company can learn more about them.[19] If users click through an ad to get to the website, the company has an opportunity to gather their names, addresses, opinions, and preferences.[20] Online advertising thus brings customers and companies together. Another advantage is that it enables advertisers to see just how many people have clicked on a commercial and how much of it each potential customer has read or watched. It has been one of the fastest-growing parts of advertising. Spending on online advertising and social media is expected to increase greatly in the next three years.[21]

E-mail marketing has become a big component of online advertising. However, advertisers have to be careful not to overuse it because customers don't like to see too many promotional e-mails in their in-boxes. Thus some companies use e-mail as an alert to send users to other social media such as Facebook and Twitter. The Making Ethical Decisions box discusses how some businesses pay celebrities to tweet pre-written ads.[22]

Interactive promotion allows marketers to go beyond a *monologue,* in which sellers try to persuade buyers to buy things, to a *dialogue,* in which buyers and sellers work together to create mutually beneficial exchange relationships. Garden .com is an online retailer of garden products and services.[23] Dionn Schaffner, the company's vice president of marketing, once said that gardening is an information-intensive activity. Customers obviously want to learn about gardening, but they also seek inspiration by communicating with fellow gardeners and experts. Garden .com's answer to such customers has been to include a forum on its website where people can chat with each other and ask gardening questions.

Technology has greatly improved customer communications.[24] Many companies provide online videos, chat rooms, and other services in a *virtual store* where customers are able to talk to each other, ask questions of salespeople, examine

Pay-Per-Tweet

In the world of Twitter, not all tweets are created equal. Anyone can join the social network for free, leading to a user base ranging from students to celebrities. It's these high-profile personalities, however, that can really make the most of their 140-character statements.

By teaming up with special marketing companies, people like Charlie Sheen and Kim Kardashian earn thousands of dollars simply by mentioning a product in their tweets. Sheen, for instance, incited a flood of traffic for Internships.com when he namechecked the website in one of his first tweets. Celebrities get paid on a sliding scale depending on how many users "follow" their Twitter account. That means a celebrity like Snoop Dogg, who boasts more than 9 million followers, can earn as much as $8,000 per endorsement. In some cases celebrities don't even need to worry about writing the tweets themselves. Media marketers like Ad.ly or IZEA will compose the spots themselves in order to maximize the message's effectiveness.

Of course, celebrities don't want their followers to know that. Many users love how Twitter allows them to interact with their favorite actors and musicians. That personal touch could be lost if more people discover that the famous figures they admire are only using the service to shill for other companies. On the other hand, it's not like the idea of a celebrity spokesperson is a brand-new concept developed by Twitter. People in the public eye will always leverage their fame to make money. In the end, fans will need to be wary about what to believe in their Twitter feeds. Do you think it is ethical for celebrities to get paid to tweet pre-written ads that appear to be their own personal comments?

Sources: Joe Piazza, "How Much Can a Celebrity Make for Tweeting?" *Vulture*, January 28, 2012; WSJ Staff, "How Charlie Sheen and Other Stars Get Paid to Tweet," *The Wall Street Journal*, March 6, 2011; Jane Bolden, "Tweets for Sales: Getting Paid in 140 Characters or Less," *Black Enterprise*, April 1, 2011.

goods and services, and buy products. The Internet is fundamentally changing the way marketers are working with customers. Notice we said *working with* rather than *promoting to*. Marketers now want to *build relationships* with customers over time. That means carefully listening to what consumers want, tracking their purchases, providing them with excellent service, and giving them access to a full range of information.[25]

Here's how online interactive promotion helped one traditional marketer stay competitive. Vita-Mix Corporation makes expensive food blenders. In the beginning, when there was little competition, the company relied mostly on 140

Online advertising is the fastest-growing type of advertising and can offer more than just a list of products and their features. For example, Tissot introduced a new 3-D reality application on its website that allows customers to try on a 3-D virtual watch and interact with its features. Do you think some types of products or services are promoted more effectively online than others?

independent contractors to sell the blenders at state fairs, food events, and stores. Eventually Vita-Mix began using infomercials, and sales passed $100 million. Then commercial blender maker K-Tec in Orem, Utah, began going after Vita-Mix's consumer market. K-Tec promoted its new product on a website that showed the CEO blending things like golf balls, a rotisserie chicken, and, believe it or not, an Apple iPhone. The video eventually got on YouTube, and sales of this new competitor took off. Vita-Mix successfully responded by creating its own site called Vita-Village, showing how to create healthy meals and snacks, and a social network that enables blender fans to share recipes.[26] Online marketers should strive to make sure that their efforts fit into an overall multimedia strategy.

Using Social Media to Monitor Ad Effectiveness

Dr Pepper has an over 8.5 million fan base on Facebook. Now the company can track and test users who say they "like" the soft drink. The company posts two messages daily on a Facebook fan page and then monitors the results. The company can thus measure how many times a message is reviewed, how many times it is shared, and what the fan response is. The company believes that if it is to engage in social media, it has to listen and understand the nature of the conversation, the volume, and the topics being discussed. In short, social media, such as Facebook and Twitter, have made it possible for organizations to test ads before airing them on traditional media like TV and to listen to the reasons why people like and dislike some messages.

It is best, if a company wants to establish a base with customers, to include top managers in the dialogue. For example, Richard Branson of Virgin Group Ltd. and Tony Hsieh of Zappos tweet their customers.[27] Sherry Chris of Better Homes & Gardens Real Estate LLC spends two hours each day reading and contributing to Twitter, Facebook, LinkedIn, and Foursquare. Such involvement with customers has become a major part of many companies' listening strategy. It may take time, but there is not a better way to learn about what customers are thinking and saying about your firm.

Many firms are allowing employees to use their personal phones for business purposes. That includes, of course, using Facebook, Twitter, and other social media.

Global Advertising

Global advertising requires the marketer to develop a single product and promotional strategy it can implement worldwide, like MasterCard's "Price-less" campaign. Certainly global advertising that's the same everywhere can save companies money in research and design. In some cases, however, promotions tailored to specific countries or regions may be more successful since each country or region has its own culture, language, and buying habits.

Some problems do arise when marketers use one campaign in all countries. When a Japanese company tried to use English words to name a popular drink, it came up with Pocari Sweat, not a good image for most English-speaking people.[28] In England, the Ford Probe didn't go over too well because the word *probe* made people think of doctors' waiting rooms and medical examinations.[29] People in the United States may have difficulty with Krapp toilet paper from Sweden. But perhaps worse was the translation of Coors' slogan "Turn it loose," which became "Suffer from diarrhea." Clairol introduced its curling iron, the Mist Stick, to the German market, not realizing *mist* in German can mean "manure." A T-shirt promoting the Pope's visit to Miami read *la papa,* which in Spanish means "the potato." (It should have said *el Papa.*) As you can see, getting the words right in international advertising is tricky and critical. So is understanding the culture, which calls for researching each country, designing appropriate ads, and testing them.

In the United States, some groups are large enough and different enough to call for specially designed promotions. Masterfoods USA, for example, tried to promote dulce de leche (caramel) M&M's to the Hispanic market in cities like Los Angeles, Miami, and San Antonio. The promotion was not successful, however. Knowing the market had potential, Masterfoods changed course and bought a candy company called the Lucas Group, which has had success selling such candies as Felix Sour Fruit and Lucas Hot and Spicy in Mexico. Masterfoods had much more success selling those candies in the United States.[30] The Connecting Across Borders box discusses how another well-known company promotes products in foreign markets.

Many marketers today are moving from globalism (one ad for everyone in the world) to regionalism (specific ads for each country or for specific groups within a country). In the future, marketers will prepare more custom-designed promotions to reach even smaller audiences—audiences as small as one person.[31]

This Maybelline ad is designed for African-American women. There are many ads directed toward the Latina and Asian markets as well. What other groups are attractive candidates for targeted ads?

What's in Your Oreo?

To most Americans, an Oreo is just an Oreo: two layers of crunchy cookie sandwiching a creamy vanilla center. It's been that same way for more than 100 years, after all. With such a successful brand on its hands, Kraft Foods knew it had to take Oreo global to maximize its full potential. With global expansion came a number of variations on Oreo's original cookie-and-creme formula. China, for instance, prefers green tea–flavored Oreos. In Argentina they like their Oreos stuffed with banana and *dulce de*

leche, a type of candied milk. Remember: tastes vary across the globe, and what some people consider normal in one place can be wildly different somewhere else. So be careful if you buy some Oreos in another country. They might not taste good dipped in milk.

Sources: Bruce Einhorn, "There's More to Oreo Than Black and White," *Bloomberg Businessweek,* May 3, 2012; and Laurie Burkitt, "Kraft Craves More of China's Snacks Market," *The Wall Street Journal,* May 29, 2012.

LEARNING **goal 3**

Illustrate the steps of the B2B and B2C selling processes.

PERSONAL SELLING: PROVIDING PERSONAL ATTENTION

personal selling
The face-to-face presentation and promotion of goods and services

Personal selling is the face-to-face presentation and promotion of goods and services, including the salesperson's search for new prospects and follow-up service after the sale. Effective selling isn't simply a matter of persuading others to buy. In fact, it's more accurately described today as helping others satisfy their wants and needs (again, helping the buyer buy).

Given that perspective, you can see why salespeople use the Internet, laptop computers, iPads, and other technology to help customers search for information, design custom-made products, look over prices, and generally do everything it takes to complete the order. The benefit of personal selling is having a person help you complete a transaction. The salesperson should listen to your needs, help you reach a solution, and do everything possible to make accomplishing it smoother and easier.

It's costly for firms to provide customers with personal attention, so those companies that retain salespeople must train them to be especially effective, efficient, and helpful. To attract new salespeople, companies are paying them quite well. The average cost of a single sales call to a potential business-to-business (B2B) buyer is about $400. Surely no firm would pay that much to send anyone but a skillful and highly trained professional salesperson and consultant.

Steps in the Selling Process

The best way to understand personal selling is to go through the selling process. Imagine you are a software salesperson whose job is to show business users the advantages of various programs your firm markets. One product critically important to establishing long-term relationships with customers is customer relationship management (CRM) software, particularly social CRM that integrates social media to create a community-based relationship with customers.[32] Let's go through the seven steps of the selling process to see what you can do to sell social CRM software.

Although this is a business-to-business (B2B) example, the process in consumer selling is similar but less complex. In both cases the salesperson must have deep *product* knowledge—that is, he or she must know the product—and competitors' products—thoroughly.

1. Prospect and Qualify The first step in the selling process is **prospecting,** researching potential buyers and choosing those most likely to buy. The selection process is called **qualifying.** To qualify people means to make sure they have a need for the product, the authority to buy, and the willingness to listen to a sales message. Some people call prospecting and qualifying the process of *lead generation.*

A person who meets the qualifying criteria is called a **prospect.** You often meet prospects at trade shows, where they come to booths sponsored by manufacturers and ask questions. Others may visit your website seeking information. But often the best prospects are people recommended to you by others who use or know about your product. Salespeople often e-mail prospects with proposals to see whether there is any interest before making a formal visit.

You're familiar with all kinds of situations in which people do personal selling. They work in local department stores and sell all kinds of goods and services like automobiles, insurance, and real estate. What could they do to be more helpful to you, the customer?

2. Preapproach The selling process may take a long time, and gathering information before you approach the customer is critical. Before making a sales call, you must do some further research. In the preapproach phase, you learn as much as possible about customers and their wants and needs.[33] Before you try to sell the social CRM software, you'll want to know which people in the company are most likely to buy or use it. What kind of customers do they deal with? What kind of relationship strategies are they using now? How is their system set up, and what kind of improvements are they looking for? All that information should be in a database so that, if one representative leaves the firm, the company can carry information about customers to the new salesperson.

3. Approach "You don't have a second chance to make a good first impression." That's why the approach is so important. When you call on a customer for the first time, you want to give an impression of friendly professionalism, create rapport, build credibility, and start a business relationship.[34] Often a company's decision to use a new software package is based on the buyer's perception of reliable service from the salesperson. In selling social CRM products, you can make it known from the start that you'll be available to help your customer train its employees and to upgrade the package when necessary.

prospecting
Researching potential buyers and choosing those most likely to buy.

qualifying
In the selling process, making sure that people have a need for the product, the authority to buy, and the willingness to listen to a sales message.

prospect
A person with the means to buy a product, the authority to buy, and the willingness to listen to a sales message.

4. Make a Presentation   In your actual presentation of the software, you'll match the benefits of your value package to the client's needs. Companies such as Ventaso Inc. and the Sant Group now provide sales proposal software that includes everything from PowerPoint presentations to competitive analysis. Since you've done your homework and know the prospect's wants and needs, you can tailor your sales presentation accordingly.[35] The presentation is a great time to use testimonials showing potential buyers that they're joining leaders in other firms who are using the product.

5. Answer Objections   You should anticipate any objections the prospect may raise and determine the proper responses. Think of questions as opportunities for creating better relationships, not as challenges to what you're saying. Customers may have legitimate doubts, and you are there to resolve them. Successfully and honestly working with others helps you build relationships based on trust. Often you can introduce the customer to others in your firm who can answer their questions and provide them with anything they need. Using a laptop computer, you may set up a virtual meeting in which the customer can chat with your colleagues and begin building a relationship.

6. Close the Sale   After you've answered questions and objections, you may present a **trial close,** a question or statement that moves the selling process toward the actual purchase. You might ask, "When would be the best time to train your staff to use the new software?" The final step is to ask for the order and show the client where to sign. Once you've established a relationship, the goal of your sales call may be to get a testimonial from the customer.

7. Follow Up   The selling process isn't over until the order is approved and the customer is happy. Salespeople need to be providers of solutions for their customers and to think about what happens after the sale. The follow-up step includes handling customer complaints, making sure the customer's questions are answered, and quickly supplying what the customer wants. Often, customer service is as important to the sale as the product itself. That's why most manufacturers have websites where customers can find information and get questions answered. You can see why we describe selling as a process of *establishing relationships,* not just exchanging goods or services. The sales relationship may continue for years as you respond to new requests for information and provide new services.

The selling process varies somewhat among different goods and services, but the general idea stays the same. Your goals as a salesperson are to help the buyer buy and make sure the buyer is satisfied after the sale. Sales force automation (SFA) includes hundreds of software programs that help salespeople design products, close deals, tap into company intranets, and more. Some salespeople use it to conduct virtual

---

Making the sale isn't the end of the salesperson's relationship with the customer. The salesperson should follow up on the sale to make sure the customer is happy and perhaps suggest something to complement what the customer purchased. Have salespeople been able to sell you more because they used effective follow-up procedures? How did they do it?

trial close
A step in the selling process that consists of a question or statement that moves the selling process toward the actual close.

reality tours of the manufacturing plant for the customer. An IBM salesperson may rely on everything from a BlackBerry and sales management software to wikis (collaborative websites that users can edit), blogs, podcasts, IBM's intranet, and more.

The Business-to-Consumer Sales Process

Most sales to consumers take place in retail stores, where the role of the salesperson differs somewhat from that in B2B selling. In both cases, knowing the product comes first.[36] However, in business-to-consumer (B2C) sales, the salesperson does not have to do much prospecting or qualifying. The seller assumes most people who come to the store are qualified to buy the merchandise (except in sales of expensive products such as automobiles and furniture, during which salespeople may have to ask a few questions to qualify prospective customers before spending too much time with them).

Similarly, retail salespeople don't usually have to go through a preapproach step, although they should understand as much as possible about the type of people who shop at a given store. The salesperson does need to focus on the customer and refrain from talking to fellow salespeople, however—or, worse, to friends on the phone. Have you ever experienced such rude behavior from salespeople? What did you think?

The first formal step in the B2C sales process is the approach. Too many salespeople begin with a line like "May I help you?" but the answer too often is "No." A better approach is "How can I help you?" or, simply, "Welcome to our store." The idea is to show the customer you are there to help and are friendly and knowledgeable.

Discover what the customer wants first, and then make a presentation. Show customers how your products meet their needs and answer questions that help them choose the right products for them.

As in B2B selling, it is important to make a trial close, like "Would you like me to put that on hold?" or "Will you be paying for that with your store credit card?" Selling is an art, and a salesperson must learn how to walk the fine line between being helpful and being pushy. Often individual buyers need some time alone to think about the purchase. The salesperson must respect that need but still be clearly available when needed.

After-sale follow-up is an important but often neglected step in B2C sales. If the product is to be delivered, the salesperson should follow up to be sure it is delivered on time. The same is true if the product has to be installed. There is often a chance to sell more merchandise when a salesperson follows up on a sale. Figure 16.6 shows the whole B2C selling process. Compare it to the seven-step process we outlined earlier for B2B selling.

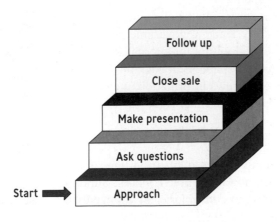

figure 16.6

STEPS IN THE BUSINESS-TO-CONSUMER (B2C) SELLING PROCESS

progress assessment

- What are the four traditional elements of the promotion mix?
- What are the three most important advertising media in order of dollars spent?
- What are the seven steps in the B2B selling process?

LEARNING goal 4

Describe the role of the public relations department, and show how publicity fits in that role.

PUBLIC RELATIONS: BUILDING RELATIONSHIPS

public relations (PR)
The management function that evaluates public attitudes, changes policies and procedures in response to the public's requests, and executes a program of action and information to earn public understanding and acceptance.

Public relations (PR) is the management function that evaluates public attitudes, changes policies and procedures in response to the public's requests, and executes a program of action and information to earn public understanding and acceptance. In other words, a good public relations program has three steps:

1. *Listen to the public.* Public relations starts with good marketing research to evaluate public attitudes.

2. *Change policies and procedures.* Businesses earn understanding not by bombarding the public with propaganda but by creating programs and practices in the public interest. The best way to learn what the public wants is to listen to people often—in different forums, including on the Internet. That includes being able to handle a crisis by communicating online.

3. *Inform people you're responsive to their needs.* It's not enough to simply have programs in the public interest. You have to *tell* the public about those programs. Public relations has more power to influence consumers than other corporate communications because the message comes via the media, a source usually perceived as trustworthy.

Recent events have emphasized the need for good public relations. Such events include Toyota Motor's safety problems, Apple's iPhone antenna problems, BP's oil spill, Japan's nuclear power problems, and the issues surrounding some key actors and sports personalities.

The PR department maintains close ties with company stakeholders (customers, media, community leaders, government officials, and other corporate stakeholders). Marketers are looking for alternatives to advertising. Public relations is a good alternative. As newspapers cut back on their reporting staff, people are looking for other sources of news information, including publicity releases. Linking up with bloggers has become an important way to keep company names in the news.

Publicity: The Talking Arm of PR

Publicity is the talking arm of public relations and one of the major functions of almost all organizations. Here's how it works: Suppose you want to introduce your store, Very Vegetarian, to consumers, but you have little money to promote it. You need to get some initial sales to generate funds. One effective way to reach the public is through publicity.

Publicity is any information about an individual, product, or organization that's distributed to the public through the media and is not paid for or controlled by the seller. It takes skill to write interesting or newsworthy press releases that the media will want to publish. You may need to write different stories for different media. One may introduce the new owners. Another may describe the unusual product offerings. If the stories are published, news about your store will reach many potential consumers (and investors, distributors, and dealers), and you may be on your way to becoming a successful marketer. John D. Rockefeller once remarked, "Next to doing the right thing, the most important thing is to *let people know* that you are doing the right thing." What might Very Vegetarian do to help the community and thus create more publicity?

Besides being free, publicity has several further advantages over other promotional tools like advertising. It may reach people who wouldn't read an ad. It may appear on the front page of a newspaper or in some other prominent position, or be given air time on a television news show. Perhaps the greatest advantage of publicity is its believability. When a newspaper or magazine publishes a story as news, the reader treats that story as news—and news is more believable than advertising.

Publicity has several disadvantages as well. For example, marketers have no control over whether, how, and when the media will use the story. The media aren't obligated to use a publicity release, most of which are thrown away. Furthermore, the media may alter the story so that it's not positive. There's good publicity (iPod sales are taking off) and bad publicity (GM is going bankrupt). Also, once a story has run, it's not likely to be repeated. Advertising, in contrast, can be repeated as often as needed. One way to see that the media handle your publicity well is to establish a friendly relationship with media representatives and be open with them. Then, when you want their support, they're more likely to cooperate.

Some companies will race to extremes to generate publicity. This streaker avoided Super Bowl XXXVIII security to show off a tattooed message for Internet casino GoldenPalace .com. Which do you think attracts more attention for a firm, an appealing news story or a paid ad?

LEARNING goal 5

Assess the effectiveness of various forms of sales promotion, including sampling.

SALES PROMOTION: GIVING BUYERS INCENTIVES

Sales promotion is the promotional tool that stimulates consumer purchasing and dealer interest by means of short-term activities. These activities include such things as displays, trade shows and exhibitions, event sponsorships, and contests. Figure 16.7 lists some B2B sales promotion techniques.

publicity
Any information about an individual, product, or organization that's distributed to the public through the media and that's not paid for or controlled by the seller.

sales promotion
The promotional tool that stimulates consumer purchasing and dealer interest by means of short-term activities.

Trade shows
Portfolios for salespeople
Deals (price reductions)
Catalogs
Conventions

figure 16.7
BUSINESS-TO-BUSINESS SALES PROMOTION TECHNIQUES

figure 16.8

**CONSUMER SALES
PROMOTION TECHNIQUES**

Coupons	Bonuses (buy one, get one free)
Cents-off promotions	Catalogs
Sampling	Demonstrations
Premiums	Special events
Sweepstakes	Lotteries
Contests	In-store displays

For consumer sales promotion activities, think of those free samples you get in the mail, cents-off coupons you clip from newspapers, contests that various retail stores sponsor, and prizes in cereal boxes (see Figure 16.8). You can stimulate sales at Very Vegetarian by putting half-off coupons in the school paper and home mailers. Do you see any problems that might emerge by using Groupon to bring in customers?

Sales promotion programs are designed to supplement personal selling, advertising, public relations, and other promotional efforts by creating enthusiasm for the overall promotional program. There was a big increase in such promotions as the 21st century began, especially online. The recent financial crisis has people looking more closely for coupons and other promotional deals.

Sales promotion can take place both within and outside the company. The most important internal sales promotion efforts are directed at salespeople and other customer-contact people, such as customer service representatives and clerks. Internal sales promotion efforts include (1) sales training; (2) the development of sales aids such as flip charts, portable audiovisual displays, and videos; and (3) participation in trade shows where salespeople can get leads. Other employees who deal with the public may also receive special training to improve their awareness of the company's offerings and make them an integral part of the total promotional effort.

After generating enthusiasm internally, marketers want to make distributors and dealers eager to help promote the product. Trade shows allow marketing intermediaries to see products from many different sellers and make comparisons among them. Today, virtual trade shows on the Internet, called webinars, enable

The International Manufacturing Trade Show in Chicago featured 4,000 booths, giving buyers for other businesses thousands of new products to explore and purchase. Can you see why trade shows in many industries are an efficient and necessary way to stay abreast of the latest developments, competitors, and consumer reactions and needs?

buyers to see many products without leaving the office. Such promotions are usually interactive, so buyers can ask questions, and the information is available 24 hours a day, seven days a week.

After the company's employees and intermediaries have been motivated with sales promotion efforts, the next step is to promote to final consumers using samples, coupons, cents-off deals, displays, store demonstrations, premiums, contests, rebates, and so on. Sales promotion is an ongoing effort to maintain enthusiasm, so sellers use different strategies over time to keep the ideas fresh. You could put food displays in your Very Vegetarian store to show customers how attractive the products look. You could also sponsor in-store cooking demonstrations to attract new vegetarians. You can imagine the success of a promotion using Groupon or LivingSocial.

One popular sales promotion tool is **sampling**—letting consumers have a small sample of the product for no charge. Because many consumers won't buy a new product unless they've had a chance to see it or try it, grocery stores often have people standing in the aisles handing out small portions of food and beverage products. Sampling is a quick, effective way of demonstrating a product's superiority when consumers are making a purchase decision. Standing outside Very Vegetarian and giving out samples would surely attract attention.

Pepsi introduced its SoBe (herbal fortified drinks) product line with a combination of sampling, event marketing, and a new website. *Event marketing* means sponsoring events such as rock concerts or being at various events to promote your products. In the case of SoBe, Pepsi first sent samples to beach cities during spring break where students got samples of the drinks. Similar sampling and event marketing efforts had been successful with Snapple (fruit drinks and iced teas).

Everyone likes a free sample. Sampling is a promotional strategy that lets people try a new product, often in a situation when they can buy it right away if they like it. What are some advantages of sampling food products that advertising can't duplicate?

progress assessment

- What are the three steps in setting up a public relations program?
- What are the sales promotion techniques used to reach consumers?
- What sales promotion techniques are used to reach businesses?

sampling
A promotional tool in which a company lets consumers have a small sample of a product for no charge.

LEARNING goal 6

Show how word of mouth, e-mail marketing, viral marketing, blogging, podcasting, and mobile marketing work.

WORD OF MOUTH AND OTHER PROMOTIONAL TOOLS

Although word of mouth was not traditionally listed as one of the major promotional efforts (it was not considered to be manageable), it is now one of the most effective, especially on the Internet. In **word-of-mouth promotion,** people tell other people about products they've purchased.

When James and Ann Scaggs started a company that repairs iPods, customers were hesitant to part with their units without assurance they would be fixed properly. The Scaggs went to RatePoint, a Web 2.0 system for collecting and displaying word of

word-of-mouth promotion
A promotional tool that involves people telling other people about products they've purchased.

The Dark Side of Yelp

These days many companies manage a website or at least a Facebook page in order to maintain a positive Internet presence. This allows them to control their image on the web and get people talking about their companies.

But there are some places online where businesses can't change how the public sees them. At review sites like Yelp.com, users can log on and write a review about everything from a barbershop to a bakery. Oftentimes it's a good thing. Happy customers who want to spread some love about a favorite spot can show their support with a good review. Occasionally, though, an unsatisfied or just downright mean customer can distract from all those good words with a single cruel post.

Journalists who review restaurants or stores generally give companies the benefit of the doubt on some points. That's not the case with many Yelp users. Unfounded claims, like saying there are rats in the kitchen, can appear factual once they end up in a company's collection of Yelp reviews. And the worst part is that there's nothing business owners can do about it. Since they don't control their Yelp page, anything can be posted on the site, no matter how negative. The best thing they can do is "claim" their Yelp page once they receive several reviews. This allows them to comment on their own page and address the critics but not to remove hateful reviews. In the end, the most a company can do is ensure that every customer that walks in the door leaves satisfied. But as the saying goes, you can't please everyone. You just hope those people don't have Yelp accounts.

Sources: David Sax, 'Yelp's Online Reviewing Mafia," *Bloomberg Businessweek,* June 2, 2011; Max Chafkin, "You've Been Yelped," *Inc.,* February 1, 2010; and Heather Knight, "Yelp Likes City Hall, but What about Yelpers Themselves?" *San Francisco Chronicle,* May 12, 2012.

mouth in the form of customer feedback. Sales immediately went up. Of course, word of mouth can be negative as you can see in the Connecting Through Social Media box.

Anything that encourages people to talk favorably about an organization can be effective word of mouth. Notice, for example, how stores use clowns, banners, music, fairs, and other attention-getting devices to create word of mouth. Clever commercials can also generate word of mouth. The more that people talk about your products and your brand name, the more easily customers remember them when they shop. You might enjoy brainstorming strategies for creating word of mouth about Very Vegetarian.

Viral Marketing

viral marketing
The term now used to describe everything from paying customers to say positive things on the Internet to setting up multilevel selling schemes whereby consumers get commissions for directing friends to specific websites.

A number of companies have begun creating word of mouth by rewarding customers for promoting their products to others. One such strategy encourages people to go into Internet chat rooms and hype bands, movies, video games, and sports teams. People who agree to promote products in this way may get what the industry calls *swag*—free tickets, backstage passes, T-shirts, and other such merchandise. What do you think of the ethics of rewarding people to promote goods and services? What do you think of people sending messages to friends on Facebook and Twitter talking about products?

Viral marketing describes everything from paying customers to say positive things on the Internet (e.g., using Twitter) to setting up multilevel selling schemes whereby consumers get commissions for directing friends to specific websites.

One especially effective strategy for spreading positive word of mouth is to send testimonials to current customers. Most companies use these only in promoting to new customers, but testimonials are also effective in confirming customers' belief that they chose the right company. Therefore, some companies make it a habit to ask customers for referrals.

Word of mouth is so powerful that negative word of mouth can hurt a firm badly. Criticism of a product or company can spread through online forums, social media, and websites. Addressing consumer complaints quickly and effectively is one of the best ways to reduce the effects of negative word of mouth.

Blogging

A **blog**—short for web log—is an online diary that looks like a web page but is easier to create and update by posting text, photos, or links to other sites. There are millions of blogs on the Internet, and thousands of new ones are added each day. How do blogs affect marketing? When a book called *Freakonomics* was about to be released, the publisher sent advance copies to 100 bloggers. These bloggers sent reviews to other bloggers (word of mouth), and soon *Freakonomics* was number three on Amazon.com's list of most-ordered books. You can imagine what blogging can do to promote movies, TV shows, and more.

Podcasting

Podcasting is a means of distributing audio and video programs via the Internet. It lets users subscribe to a number of files, also known as feeds, and then hear or view the material when they choose. Podcasting allows you to become your own newscaster, since—besides giving broadcast radio and TV a new distribution medium—it enables independent producers to create self-published, syndicated "radio shows." Many companies have also found success in creating video for YouTube.

E-Mail Promotions

Armstrong, the flooring manufacturer, has an e-mail marketing program designed to increase brand awareness among commercial suppliers. At one time it sent out monthly e-mails to announce new products and product updates and to keep people loyal to the brand. Over time, however, those e-mails lost their power. Armstrong then turned to an e-mail service provider that completely revamped the program. The provider divided the market into four separate segments and tracked the success of the e-mails much more closely.

E-mail promotions are gaining in popularity. Most marketers make sure their e-newsletters are also viewable on mobile devices like BlackBerrys or iPhones. One key to success, therefore, is to keep the message brief, because mobile users don't want to go through much text.

Mobile Media

With mobile media, marketers make use of the cell phone, using text messaging to promote sweepstakes, send customers news or sports alerts, and give them company information. We've seen that companies can now determine where you are and send you messages about restaurants and other services in your vicinity. Despite some technological glitches to work through, mobile marketing is catching on, including the use of quick response codes.[37]

blog
An online diary (web log) that looks like a web page but is easier to create and update by posting text, photos, or links to other sites.

podcasting
A means of distributing audio and video programs via the Internet that lets users subscribe to a number of files, also known as feeds, and then hear or view the material at the time they choose.

Mobile media allow marketers to reach customers through text messaging. Have you received such promotional messages? For which products are they most effective?

push strategy
Promotional strategy in which the producer uses advertising, personal selling, sales promotion, and all other promotional tools to convince wholesalers and retailers to stock and sell merchandise.

Are you getting the idea that traditional promotional methods are slowly but surely being replaced by new technology? If so, you're getting the right idea. By keeping up with the latest trends, you may be able to grab a good job in promotion while traditionalists are still wondering what happened.[38]

MANAGING THE PROMOTION MIX: PUTTING IT ALL TOGETHER

Each target group calls for a separate promotion mix. Advertising is most efficient for reaching large groups of consumers whose members share similar traits. Personal selling is best for selling to large organizations. To motivate people to buy now rather than later, marketers use sales promotions like sampling, coupons, discounts, special displays, and premiums. Publicity supports other efforts and can create a good impression among all consumers. Word of mouth is often the most powerful promotional tool. Generate it by listening, being responsive, and creating an impression worth passing on to others that you spread through blogging, podcasting, and tweeting.

Promotional Strategies

How do producers move products to consumers? In a **push strategy,** the producer uses advertising, personal selling, sales promotion, and all other promotional tools to convince wholesalers and retailers to stock and sell merchandise, *pushing* it through the distribution system to the stores. If the push strategy works, consumers will walk into a store, see the product, and buy it.

Ads in bus shelters are nothing new, but Kraft recently pumped hot air into 10 Chicago bus stops to promote its Stove Top stuffing mix. The idea was to remind consumers of the warm feeling they get when eating the product. Do you think giving consumers experiences (like warmth on a cold day) is an effective way to remind them of a product?

A **pull strategy** directs heavy advertising and sales promotion efforts toward *consumers.* If the pull strategy works, consumers will go to the store and ask for the products. The store owner will order them from the wholesaler, who in turn will order them from the producer. Products are thus *pulled* through the distribution system.

Dr Pepper has used TV advertising in a pull strategy to increase distribution. Tripledge, a maker of windshield wipers, also tried to capture the interest of retail stores through a pull strategy. Of course, a company could use both strategies in a major promotional effort. The latest pull and push strategies are being conducted on the Internet, with companies sending messages to both consumers and businesses.

It has been important to make promotion part of a total systems approach to marketing. That is, promotion was part of supply-chain management. In such cases, retailers would work with producers and distributors to make the supply chain as efficient as possible. Then a promotional plan would be developed for the whole system. The idea would be to develop a total product offer that would appeal to everyone: manufacturers, distributors, retailers, and consumers.

Today push and pull strategies have lost some of their effectiveness. Still, customers are interested in searching online outlets like Drugstore.com or Zappos and doing online comparison shopping as they pick the products that appeal to them. Some leading marketers sell directly to consumers with products that really stand out because of their design, packaging, price, or color, like the Dyson vacuum. The idea is to help the consumer distinguish your product from the competitors. The term **pick economy** refers to those consumers who pick out their products from online outlets or who do online comparison shopping.

pull strategy
Promotional strategy in which heavy advertising and sales promotion efforts are directed toward consumers so that they'll request the products from retailers.

pick economy
Customers who pick out their products from online outlets or who do online comparison shopping.

progress assessment

- What is viral marketing?
- What are blogging and podcasting?
- Describe a push strategy, a pull strategy, and the pick economy.

summary

Learning Goal 1. Identify the new and traditional tools that make up the promotion mix.

- **What is promotion?**

Promotion is an effort by marketers to inform and remind people in the target market about products and to persuade them to participate in an exchange.

- **What are the four traditional promotional tools that make up the promotion mix?**

The four traditional promotional tools are advertising, personal selling, public relations, and sales promotion. The product itself can also be a promotional tool—that's why it is shown in the middle of Figure 16.1.

- **What are some of the newer tools used in promotion?**

Today's promotional tools include e-mail promotions, mobile promotions (those that use cell phones), social networks. blogging, podcasts, and YouTube.

Learning Goal 2. Contrast the advantages and disadvantages of various advertising media, including the Internet and social media.

- **What is advertising?**

Advertising is limited to paid, nonpersonal (not face-to-face) communication through various media by organizations and individuals who are in some way identified in the advertising message.

- **What are the advantages of using the various media?**

Review the advantages and disadvantages of the various advertising media in Figure 16.5.

- **Why the growing use of infomercials?**

Infomercials are growing in importance because they show products in use and present testimonials to help sell goods and services.

Learning Goal 3. Illustrate the steps of the B2B and B2C selling processes.

- **What is personal selling?**

Personal selling is the face-to-face presentation and promotion of products and services. It includes the search for new prospects and follow-up service after the sale.

- **What are the seven steps of the B2B selling process?**

The steps of the selling process are (1) prospect and qualify, (2) preapproach, (3) approach, (4) make presentation, (5) answer objections, (6) close sale, and (7) follow up.

- **What are the steps in the B2C selling process?**

The steps are the approach, which includes asking questions; the presentation, which includes answering questions; the close; and the follow-up.

Learning Goal 4. Describe the role of the public relations department, and show how publicity fits in that role.

- **What is public relations?**

Public relations (PR) is the function that evaluates public attitudes, changes policies and procedures in response to the public's requests, and executes a program of action and information to earn public understanding and acceptance.

- **What are the three major steps in a good public relations program?**

(1) Listen to the public; (2) develop policies and procedures in the public interest; and (3) tell people you're being responsive to their needs.

- **What is publicity?**

Publicity is the talking part of sales promotion; it is information distributed by the media that's not paid for, or controlled by, the seller. Publicity's greatest advantage is its believability.

Learning Goal 5. Assess the effectiveness of various forms of sales promotion, including sampling.

- **How are sales promotion activities used both within and outside the organization?**

Internal sales promotion efforts are directed at salespeople and other customer-contact people to keep them enthusiastic about the company. Internal sales promotion activities include sales training, sales aids, audiovisual displays, and trade shows. External sales promotions to consumers rely on samples, coupons, cents-off deals, displays, store demonstrators, premiums, and other incentives.

Learning Goal 6. Show how word of mouth, e-mail marketing, viral marketing, blogging, podcasting, and mobile marketing work.

- **Is word of mouth a major promotional tool?**

Word of mouth was not one of the traditional forms of promotion because it was not considered to be manageable, but it has always been an effective way of promoting goods and services.

- **How is word of mouth used in promotion today?**

Some companies reward people to blog or go into Internet chat rooms and talk enthusiastically about bands, movies, video games, and sports teams. People who agree to hype products in this way get *swag*—free tickets, backstage passes, T-shirts, and other merchandise. *Viral marketing* is everything from paying people to say positive things on the Internet to setting up multilevel selling schemes whereby consumers get commissions for directing friends to specific websites. Podcasting is like blogging with an audiovisual focus.

• **What are the major promotional strategies?**

In a *push strategy,* the producer uses advertising, personal selling, sales promotion, and all other promotional tools to convince wholesalers and retailers to stock and sell merchandise. In a *pull strategy,* heavy advertising and sales promotion efforts are directed toward consumers so they'll request the products from retailers. The term *pick economy* refers to those consumers who pick out their products from online outlets such as Drugstore.com or Zappos or who do online comparison shopping.

key terms

advertising 465

blog 483

infomercial 470

integrated marketing
  communication
  (IMC) 465

interactive
  promotion 470

personal selling 474

pick economy 485

podcasting 483

product placement 469

promotion mix 464

prospect 475

prospecting 475

publicity 479

public relations (PR) 478

pull strategy 485

push strategy 484

qualifying 475

sales promotion 479

sampling 481

trial close 476

viral marketing 482

word-of-mouth
  promotion 481

critical thinking

1. What kinds of problems can emerge if a firm doesn't communicate with environmentalists, the news media, and the local community? Do you know of any firms that aren't responsive to your community? What are the consequences?

2. How often do you buy online? If you don't actually buy, do you use the Internet to compare goods and prices? Do you or your friends take advantage of low prices on used goods at eBay or other online sites like Craig's List? Do you look at ads on the Internet? Do they seem to be effective? Do you think you will use the Internet for more purchases over time?

3. As interactive communications between companies and customers grow, do you think traditional advertising will grow or decline? What will be the effect of growth or decline on the price we pay for TV programs, newspapers, and magazines?

4. How have blogging, podcasting, and social media affected other media you use, like news sites, newspapers, or television? Do you think blogging is an influential word-of-mouth promotional tool? Do you read newspapers now or do you get your news some other way?

developing workplace skills

1. Using at least two different media—a newspaper, magazine, television, radio, the Internet—choose two ads you consider effective and two you find ineffective. Be prepared to rationalize your choices.

2. Scan your local newspaper for examples of publicity (stories about new products) and sales promotion (coupons, contests, sweepstakes). Share your examples and discuss the effectiveness of such promotional efforts with the class.

3. Many students shy away from careers in selling, often because they think they are not outgoing enough or that salespeople are dishonest or pushy. Prepare a one-page document about your experience with salespeople and what you think of selling as a career.

4. In small groups, discuss whether you are purchasing more goods using catalogs and/or the Internet and why. Do you look up information on the Internet before buying goods and services? How helpful are such searches? Present your findings to the class.

5. In small groups or individually, list six goods and services most students own or use and discuss promotional techniques that prompt you to buy them: advertising, personal selling, social media, publicity, sales promotion, or word of mouth. Which seems most effective for your group? Why?

taking it to the net

Purpose
To learn about business blogs.

Exercise
Go to **www.google.com/blogger** to learn how easy it is to start your own blog. Then go to the following business-oriented blogs: VentureBlog.com (**www.ventureblog .com**) and PatentPending.blogs.com (**http://patentpending.blogs.com**).

1. What kind of subjects are covered in each blog?

2. What are the advantages and disadvantages of reading such blogs?

3. Would you like to see a blog for this course? For your school?

casing the web

To access the case "Developing a Promotional Strategy for Biltmore Estate," visit **www.mhhe.com/P2P2e**

Integrated Marketing Communications at Groupon

Groupon is a Chicago company that uses social media as its primary marketing tool. The company began as The Point, which was a web-based gathering place where people came together to solve social problems in communities. The Point had about 400 subscribers at its height. When it evolved to its new form, Groupon, its subscriber base grew to over 60 million worldwide.

Groupon is a social-media-based business model that delivers high value to consumers in a new way. Groupon operates in many cities across the United States and in 40 countries. According to company spokesperson, Groupon has saved consumers over $2 billion in two years. The benefit to merchants is primarily direct advertising to potential new customers.

The company offers one deal each day to customers through social media, the Internet, and mobile devices. Until recently, the only promotions used by Groupon were sales promotions based on word of mouth among friends and its presence on Facebook and Twitter.

The video explores the four elements of the promotion mix and discusses each of the elements in detail. The resources dedicated to the four elements in the promotion mix determine the overall success or failure of the marketing effort. Companies need to determine the level of resources to be dedicated to advertising, public relations, personal selling, and sales promotion.

Different forms of advertising and the outlets for advertising are discussed. As we see in the case of Groupon, word of mouth is a very powerful form of promotion.

Thinking It Over

1. *What are the critical differences between publicity and advertising ?*
2. *Identify the four elements of the promotion mix.*
3. *On which of the four elements of the promotion mix does Groupon rely most?*

Career Outlook
Part 5 Conclusion—Marketing

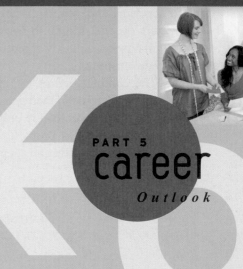

PART 5
career
Outlook

Marketing is a challenging and dynamic part of business. The field is so varied that it can attract people with a tremendous variety of talents, skills, and interests. For example, a number-crunching person can choose marketing research, artistic individuals might be attracted to advertising, and entrepreneurial types might choose wholesaling or retailing. There are dozens of other combinations.

Being successful in marketing means being able to change with the times, especially as international and online markets grow. Tastes for new products and services change rapidly, and new markets quickly replace old ones. Marketing is an area that remains wide open.

SKILLS NEEDED

CAREER PATHS

POSSIBLE POSITIONS

PROFILE

COVER LETTER

RESUME

INTERVIEW

Skills Needed to Succeed in Marketing

To be hired as a marketer, show employers that you are:

- **People-oriented**—Are you the type who has conversations with strangers? Do you like working with others?

- **Trend-setting**—Are you the first to hear about new ideas or products? Do people come to you to find out what's going on?

- **Tuned in**—Do you read books, watch television, and read news online a lot? Are you in touch with what people are saying?

- **A good communicator**—Do people listen when you speak? Are you good at listening to others' needs?

- **Flexible**—Are you comfortable with change? Can you handle an ever-changing job description?

Career Paths

Many marketing careers start out in sales positions, advertising, or retailing. Not all positions in marketing require a four-year degree, although a degree is usually a formally stated prerequisite. In many companies, your skill level is the important factor. Marketing skills can often be developed in two-year business programs and in real-world experience. On-campus clubs such as Future Business Leaders of America (FBLA) and Distributive Education Clubs of America (DECA) can help you learn to compete in the world of marketing while still in school.

Possible Positions

POSSIBLE POSITIONS IN MARKETING

OPPORTUNITY	MEDIAN SALARY	DUTIES	REQUIREMENTS	GROWTH
Advertising and Marketing Managers	$108,260 per year	Plan programs to generate interest in a product or service	Bachelor's degree and 1–5 years work experience	Average growth
Advertising Sales Agent	$45,350 per year	Sell advertising space to businesses and people	Sales experience and communication ability; a high school diploma is sufficient for entry-level positions	Average growth
Buyer	$58,360 per year	Buy products for organizations to use or resell	High school diploma and on-the-job training	Slower than average growth
Public Relations Specialist	$52,090 per year	Handle an organization's communication with consumers, investors and the media	Bachelor's degree in public relations, journalism, English, or business and on-the-job training	Very fast growth, especially in social media

Source: Bureau of Labor Statistics, *Occupational Outlook Handbook,* 2012–13 Edition.

Profile: Brian Weems, Social Media Marketer

When Brian graduated from high school last year and started college, he didn't know what he should do with his life. He spent most of his time on his phone posting songs on Facebook, pinning album covers on Pinterest, checking YouTube for new music, and sharing it all on Twitter. Brian wanted to get his degree eventually, but all he really wanted was to hang out online.

When Brian's business professor caught him on his phone during class, she told him about social media marketing, or using social media to connect customers to products and services. Brian has never had a job, but now he is applying to local businesses offering to bring their social media presence up to date. How does Brian fill his résumé despite his total lack of work experience? How does he use his cover letter and résumé to share his story with business owners?

BRIAN'S COVER LETTER

Brian Weems
873 Jackson Street, Saint Ann, Missouri 63992
314-468-3364, BrianW@gmail.com

March 4, 2014

Leslie Olson
Owner
Chouteau Music and Records
394 Chouteau Street
Saint Louis, Missouri 63115

Dear Ms. Olson,

As a music lover and social media nerd, I know the value of connecting a business like Chouteau Music and Records with its online fans. Like many of your customers, I live my life online. Even when I get away from my computer and go to your store, I still check in, share pictures, and chat with friends on my phone. I think Chouteau Music and Records should have a person dedicated to social media marketing, and I'd like to be that person.

Being active online would help your store connect with customers in a way that it isn't now. I am excited about the possibilities this idea could have for you and Chouteau Music shoppers. Some of your competitors maintain active Facebook, Twitter, and Pinterest accounts—their online presence reminds customers of the value of owning master recordings. Because of the explosion of digitally downloaded music, independent stores like yours can cultivate not only a brick-and-mortar haven for music lovers but an online community as well. With social media, you can attract new customers, keep people "in the know" about local artists, quickly advertise specials, and establish yourself as the local music expert.

As an early adopter and geek for new technology, I've achieved a high Klout score, which means that those measuring social media influence have determined me to be effective. I have 3,000 Twitter followers and a blog that averages 100 daily hits.

I hope you'll give me the opportunity to demonstrate that I have the talent to create connections between Chouteau Music and today's online generation of music lovers.

I would be happy to answer questions about how to launch and manage your store's social media profiles at any time.

I look forward to meeting you,

Brian Weems
Brian Weems

Tip: Letting an employer know that you are a customer helps them know that you understand the business.

Tip: Mention any comparison to the competition in a respectful manner.

Tip: If you use technical jargon, define it for the reader.

BRIAN'S RESUME

Brian Weems

Tip: Even if you aren't looking for a social media job, employers will check you out online. Make sure that anything you post about yourself (including photos) is appropriate for a future employer to see.

Find me here...

facebook.com/brianw
@brianweems
blogger.com/lifeofbrian
foursquare.com/brianw
youtube.com/users/brianw

pinterest.com/brianspicks
flickr.com/photos/brianw
digg.com/users/brianweems
delicious.com/bweems
technorati.com/brianw

Education

Associate in Arts Degree
Business Administration
Saint Louis Community College
Anticipated Graduation: May 2015
GPA: 3.02/4.00

Tip: Only share your GPA if it is higher than a 3.0. Never round up.

Social Media Experience

Introduction to Business Tweeter

- Alert classmates to assignments and due dates via Twitter
- Monitor and respond on account @STLCCBiz

Life of Brian Blogger

- Produce and share posts, stories and photos
- Average over 100 hits per day
- Engage readers and other bloggers via Blogger, Twitter, Facebook, etc.
- Network to build readership; @brianweems has over 3,000 followers

Big Brothers Big Sisters Social-Media Guru

- Create, maintain, and promote Facebook account for youth
- Educate youth on how to be safe and responsible online
- Volunteer web expertise to charitable organization

Tip: If you don't have a title, use a phrase that explains your position. If the job is creative, your title can be creative.

Music Interests

Fierce Music Lover

- Listen to rap, local indie music, jazz, rock, punk, blues
- Play guitar, self-taught
- Help with setup every year at the Big Muddy Blues Festival and LouFest

Brian's Interview

Question: We never thought about having a social media marketer until you submitted your résumé. What made you do that?

Poor answer: You need one. I mean, anyone who knows what they are doing has a social media marketer. I can't believe you don't. Don't you guys use the Internet? If you aren't on Twitter, you are stuck in the past.

Great answer: I know people usually wait until you announce a job opening to apply to your store, but I think I could really help improve your sales. I could connect you to customers before they even get here. I'll attract new customers and remind old ones that they should come by.

Tip: Stay positive and share how you can be good for profits. If you criticize or put down the business, no one will want to work with you.

Question: Your résumé has an interesting layout. I've never seen a QRC on one before! Why design it that way?

Poor answer: Oh, I searched for creative résumés online, and this is what came up. I just copied it. You can find anything online. It's really easy.

Great answer: I'm a creative person, and I wanted you to remember me. Plus, I wanted you to be able to access my web page instantly. I have a unique perspective, and I wanted to show you that on my résumé. I could share that expertise with your customers online, too, and help increase sales.

Tip: If you make a nontraditional résumé, be prepared to explain why. If your résumé is hard to read or is just weird, you'll stand out for the wrong reasons.

Question: You are so young, and you've never had a job before. Why should we hire you?

Poor answer: Some people don't get it. They think the Internet is a fad. I am tired of people telling me that Facebook is a waste of time. You have to hire me because young people are the only ones who really understand this.

Great answer: I am young, but I have the skills and experience to interact with your customers in a way that will get them buying music, instead of just downloading it. I am willing to learn and find ways to improve what I'm doing. Plus, since I'm new to the working world, you'll get to train me exactly the way you want. You'll find that I have a strong work ethic.

Tip: Don't be afraid to say that you are willing to learn. Employers don't expect you to be perfect, but they do expect you to learn how they do business.

Managing Financial Resources

PART 6

As the old song goes, "Money makes the world go around." Well, it may not make the planet spin on its axis, but money certainly keeps businesses and the economy running. In the chapters in this Part, you will learn about where businesses find the money to finance their operations (long-term and short-term financing), how they keep track of the money flowing in and out of the business (accounting), and how they use the securities markets to raise capital (selling stocks and bonds.) You will also learn how you might be able to make a little money yourself (buying stocks and bonds).

LOOKING Ahead

CHAPTER 17   Understanding Accounting and Financial Information

CHAPTER 18   Financial Management

CHAPTER 19   Using Securities Markets for Financing and Investing Opportunities

CHAPTER 20   Money, Financial Institutions, and the Federal Reserve

17

Understanding
ACCOUNTING & FINANCIAL
Information

LEARNING
goals

After you have read and studied this chapter, you should be able to

1 Demonstrate the role that accounting and financial information play for a business and for its stakeholders.

2 Identify the different disciplines within the accounting profession.

3 List the steps in the accounting cycle, distinguish between accounting and bookkeeping, and explain how computers are used in accounting.

4 Explain how the major financial statements differ.

5 Demonstrate the application of ratio analysis in reporting financial information.

When Roxanne Coady first contemplated changing careers and starting her own business, she looked forward to a change of pace. She hoped for a less demanding job than the one she held as the national tax director at BDO Seidman, a New York–based international accounting firm. After 20 years as a certified public accountant (CPA), Coady knew all there was to know about tracking the finances of the nation's biggest companies. When she left the corporate world to live her dream of running a bookstore, her colleagues figured that her new business would be in sound financial hands. She almost proved them wrong.

In its first five years, R.J. Julia Booksellers (named after Coady's grandmother, who died in a concentration camp in World War II) enjoyed strong growth of 30 to 75 percent a year. The company published a first-class newsletter, had free wine and food at author events, provided stylish extra-strength bags for customers, and had a large, well-compensated staff who received regular bonuses. Thanks to all this free-wheeling spending, however, the financial condition of the company quickly deteriorated. Inventory turnover was unacceptable, and business costs were running too high. As a result, the company was failing to turn a profit. The irony was that after Coady's successful accounting career, bookkeeping seemed to be her weakest area in the operation of R.J. Julia Booksellers.

While Coady had always used her head as an accountant, her passion was doing most of the thinking at the bookstore. She treated the company as a personal mission outside the rules of business. Financial standards were lax, cash flow was poor, and return on investment was never thoroughly analyzed. Instead of committing herself to solving the company's problems, she just threw more money at them. In no time Coady had misspent approximately $250,000 of the money she and her husband had saved. Finally, she had to face the fact that the firm had no goal-setting procedures and her staff had never been briefed on meeting financial objectives. The company sorely needed a business overhaul, and Coady, the accountant, was ready to implement it.

She gathered her staff and announced major changes at the store, starting with the preparation of monthly profit-and-loss statements and cash flow analyses that monitored all aspects of the business. She knew the company needed to focus intensely on costs, since profit margins in the book business are slim. She also decided to implement a company training manual and to structure evaluations more carefully. Employees were encouraged to become more efficient. All the changes paid off, and within a few years R.J. Julia had become an institution in the community. It hosts more than 300 events every year and has won a number of local and national awards. Her success eventually allowed her to open another location in a neighboring town.

Today Coady has a new set of challenges before her. After 22 years in the book business, she is currently looking for someone to take over R.J. Julia from her. E-books and other forms of electronic media have changed the publishing world in profound ways. Although Coady would love to keep running the store, she just doesn't think she's the right person for the job anymore. "We think it's time for R.J. Julia to grow in new ways, in the care of new hands that will guide the store to take its proper place in a new world," says Coady. In her time at the store, Coady recognized that the financial principles she had expected from larger businesses she worked with as a CPA were no less relevant to small-business owners. Hopefully whoever succeeds her at R.J. Julia will take that idea to heart as well.

Controlling costs, managing cash flows, understanding profit margins and taxes, and reporting finances accurately are keys to survival for both large and small organizations. This chapter will introduce you to the accounting fundamentals and financial information critical to business success. The chapter also briefly explores the financial ratios that are essential in measuring business performance in a large or small business.

CONNECTING WITH

Roxanne Coady

Founder of R.J. Julia Booksellers

Sources: Pem McNerney, "Roxanne Coady Seeks New Owner for R.J. Julia Booksellers," *Patch.com,* February 6, 2012; Patty Chang Anker, "How Roxanne Coady Quit Her Job and Created the Bookstore of Her Dreams," *Blogher .com,* November 1, 2011; and Sally Allen, "Independent Bookstores to Thrive, I Hope!" *Salon.com* October 13, 2011.

LEARNING goal 1

Demonstrate the role that accounting and financial information play for a business and for its stakeholders.

THE ROLE OF ACCOUNTING INFORMATION

Stories like R.J. Julia's are repeated every day throughout the business community. Small and large businesses often survive or fail according to how well they handle financial procedures. Financial management is the heartbeat of competitive businesses, and accounting information helps keep the heartbeat stable.

Accounting reports and financial statements reveal as much about a business's health as pulse and blood pressure readings tell us about a person's health. Thus, you have to know something about accounting if you want to succeed in business. It's almost impossible to understand business operations without being able to read, understand, and analyze accounting reports and financial statements.

By the end of the chapter, you should have a good idea what accounting is, how it works, and the value it offers businesses. You should also know some accounting terms and understand the purpose of accounting statements. Your new understanding will pay off as you become more active in business or will help you in simply understanding what's going on in the world of business and finance.

What Is Accounting?

accounting
The recording, classifying, summarizing, and interpreting of financial events and transactions to provide management and other interested parties the information they need to make good decisions.

Accounting is the recording, classifying, summarizing, and interpreting of financial events and transactions in an organization to provide management and other interested parties the financial information they need to make good decisions about its operation. Financial transactions include buying and selling goods and services, acquiring insurance, paying employees, and using supplies. Usually we group all purchases together, and all sales transactions together. The method we use to record and summarize accounting data into reports is an *accounting system* (see Figure 17.1).

A major purpose of accounting is to help managers make well-informed decisions. Another is to report financial information about the firm to interested stakeholders, such as employees, owners, creditors, suppliers, unions, community activists, investors, and the government (for tax purposes) (see Figure 17.2). Accounting is divided into several major disciplines. Let's look at those next.

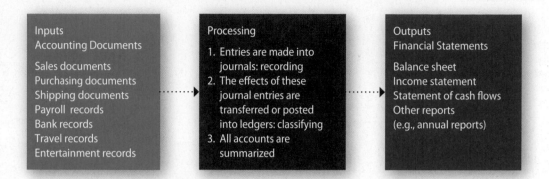

Inputs	Processing	Outputs
Accounting Documents	1. Entries are made into journals: recording	Financial Statements
Sales documents	2. The effects of these journal entries are transferred or posted into ledgers: classifying	Balance sheet
Purchasing documents		Income statement
Shipping documents		Statement of cash flows
Payroll records	3. All accounts are summarized	Other reports
Bank records		(e.g., annual reports)
Travel records		
Entertainment records		

figure 17.1

THE ACCOUNTING SYSTEM

The inputs to an accounting system include sales documents and other documents. The data are recorded, classified, and summarized. They're then put into summary financial statements such as the income statement and balance sheet and statement of cash flows.

LEARNING goal 2

Identify the different disciplines within the accounting profession.

ACCOUNTING DISCIPLINES

You may think accounting is only for profit-seeking firms. Nothing could be further from the truth. Accounting, often called the language of business, allows us to report financial information about nonprofit organizations such as churches, schools, hospitals, fraternities, and government agencies.[1] The accounting profession is divided into five key working areas: managerial accounting, financial accounting, auditing, tax accounting, and governmental and not-for-profit accounting.[2] All five are important, and all create career opportunities.[3] Let's explore each.

Managerial Accounting

Managerial accounting provides information and analysis to managers *inside* the organization to assist them in decision making. Managerial accounting is concerned with measuring and reporting costs of production, marketing, and other functions; preparing budgets (planning); checking whether or not units are staying within their budgets (controlling); and designing strategies to minimize taxes.

If you are a business major, you'll probably take a course in managerial accounting. You may even pursue a career as a certified management accountant.[4] A **certified management accountant (CMA)** is a professional accountant who has met certain educational and experience requirements, passed a qualifying

managerial accounting
Accounting used to provide information and analyses to managers inside the organization to assist them in decision making.

USERS	TYPE OF REPORT
Government taxing authorities (e.g., the Internal Revenue Service)	Tax returns
Government regulatory agencies	Required reports
People interested in the organization's income and financial position (e.g., owners, creditors, financial analysts, suppliers)	Financial statements found in annual reports (e.g., income statement, balance sheet, statement of cash flows)
Managers of the firm	Financial statements and various internally distributed financial reports

figure 17.2

USERS OF ACCOUNTING INFORMATION AND THE REQUIRED REPORTS

Many types of organizations use accounting information to make business decisions. The reports need to vary according to the information each user requires. An accountant must prepare the appropriate forms.

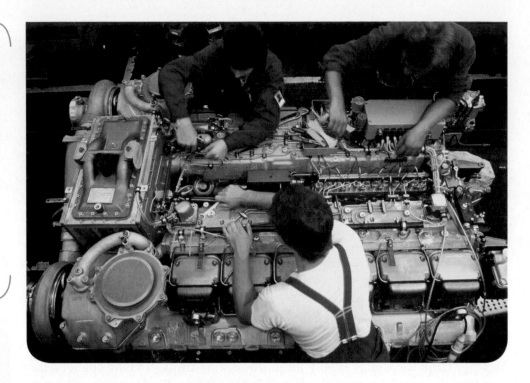

Assembling a marine diesel engine requires many tools, parts, raw materials, and other components as well as labor costs. Keeping these costs at a minimum and setting realistic production schedules is critical to a business's survival. What other internal departments must management accountants team with to ensure company competitiveness?

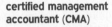

certified management accountant (CMA)
A professional accountant who has met certain educational and experience requirements, passed a qualifying exam, and been certified by the Institute of Certified Management Accountants.

financial accounting
Accounting information and analyses prepared for people outside the organization.

annual report
A yearly statement of the financial condition, progress, and expectations of an organization.

private accountant
An accountant who works for a single firm, government agency, or nonprofit organization.

public accountant
An accountant who provides accounting services to individuals or businesses on a fee basis.

exam, and been certified by the Institute of Certified Management Accountants.[5] With the growing emphasis on global competition, outsourcing, and organizational cost-cutting, managerial accounting is one of the most important areas you may study in your college career.

Financial Accounting

Financial accounting differs from managerial accounting in that the financial information and analyses it generates are for people primarily *outside* the organization. The information goes not only to company owners, managers, and employees, but also to creditors and lenders, employee unions, customers, suppliers, government agencies, and the general public. External users are interested in questions like: Is the organization profitable? Is it able to pay its bills? How much debt does it owe? These questions and others are often answered in the company's **annual report,** a yearly statement of the financial condition, progress, and expectations of an organization. As pressure from stakeholders for detailed financial information has grown, companies have poured more information than ever into their annual reports.

It's critical for firms to keep accurate financial information. Therefore, many organizations employ a **private accountant** who works for a single firm, government agency, or nonprofit organization. However, not all firms or nonprofit organizations want or need a full-time accountant. Fortunately, thousands of accounting firms in the United States provide the accounting services an organization needs through public accountants.[6]

For a fee, a **public accountant** provides accounting services to individuals or businesses. Such services can include designing an accounting system, helping select the correct software to run the system, and analyzing an organization's financial performance. An accountant who passes a series of examinations established by the American Institute of Certified Public Accountants (AICPA) and meets the state's requirement for education and experience is recognized as a **certified public accountant (CPA).** CPAs find careers as private or public accountants and are often sought to fill other financial positions within organizations.[7] Today, there are over 650,000 CPAs in the United States, 370,000 of whom are members of the AICPA.[8]

Accountants know it's vital for users of a firm's accounting information to be assured the information is accurate. The independent Financial Accounting Standards Board (FASB) defines the *generally accepted accounting principles (GAAP)* that accountants must follow. If accounting reports are prepared in accordance with GAAP, users can expect the information to meet standards upon which accounting professionals have agreed.

The accounting profession suffered a dark period in the early 2000s when accounting scandals at WorldCom, Enron, and Tyco raised public suspicions about the profession and corporate integrity in general. Arthur Andersen, one of the nation's leading accounting firms, was forced out of business after being convicted of obstruction of justice for shredding records in the Enron case (the conviction was later overturned by the U.S. Supreme Court).

Scrutiny of the accounting industry intensified, and resulted in the U.S. Congress's passage of the Sarbanes-Oxley Act (called Sarbox). This legislation created new government reporting standards for publicly traded companies. It also created the Public Company Accounting Oversight Board (PCAOB), which is charged with overseeing the AICPA.[9] Prior to the passage of Sarbox, the accounting profession was self-regulated.[10] Figure 17.3 lists some of the major provisions of Sarbanes-Oxley.

The financial crisis beginning in 2008 led Congress to pass the Dodd-Frank Wall Street Reform and Consumer Protection Act. The Dodd-Frank Act increased financial regulation affecting accounting by increasing the power of the PCAOB to oversee auditors of brokers and dealers in securities markets.[11] We'll discuss the Dodd-Frank Act in more depth in Chapter 19.

The accounting profession understands that to be effective, accountants must be considered as professional as doctors or lawyers. Besides completing more than 150 hours of intense training and a rigorous exam, CPAs on average take 40 hours of continuing education training a year, are subject to recertification, undergo ethics training requirements, and must pass an ethics exam.

Auditing

Reviewing and evaluating the information used to prepare a company's financial statements is referred to as **auditing.** Private accountants within an organization often perform internal audits to guarantee that it is carrying out proper accounting

certified public accountant (CPA)
An accountant who passes a series of examinations established by the American Institute of Certified Public Accountants (AICPA).

auditing
The job of reviewing and evaluating the information used to prepare a company's financial statements.

- Prohibits accounting firms from providing certain non-auditing work (such as consulting services) to companies they audit.
- Strengthens the protection for whistleblowers who report wrongful actions of company officers.
- Requires company CEOs and CFOs to certify the accuracy of financial reports and imparts strict penalties for any violation of securities reporting (e.g., earnings misstatements).
- Prohibits corporate loans to directors and executives of the company.
- Establishes the five-member Public Company Accounting Oversight Board (PCAOB) under the Securities and Exchange Commission (SEC) to oversee the accounting industry.
- Stipulates that altering or destroying key audit documents will result in felony charges and significant criminal penalties.

figure 17.3

KEY PROVISIONS OF THE SARBANES-OXLEY ACT

independent audit
An evaluation and unbiased opinion about the accuracy of a company's financial statements.

certified internal auditor (CIA)
An accountant who has a bachelor's degree and two years of experience in internal auditing, and who has passed an exam administered by the Institute of Internal Auditors.

tax accountant
An accountant trained in tax law and responsible for preparing tax returns or developing tax strategies.

procedures and financial reporting.[12] Public accountants also conduct independent audits of accounting information and related records. An **independent audit** is an evaluation and unbiased opinion about the accuracy of a company's financial statements. Annual reports often include an auditor's unbiased written opinion.

After the accounting scandals of the early 2000s, questions surfaced about the ethics of allowing an accounting firm to do both auditing and consulting work for the same company. In response, the Sarbanes-Oxley Act put in place new rules about auditing and consulting to ensure the integrity of the auditing process. Auditing procedures again came under fire in 2011.[13] Many called for stricter controls over auditing procedures after analyzing the failure of Lehman Brothers in 2008 and the financial crisis that followed.[14]

In doing their job, auditors not only examine the financial health of an organization but also its operational efficiencies and effectiveness.[15] Accountants who have a bachelor's degree and two years of experience in internal auditing, and who pass an exam administered by the Institute of Internal Auditors, can earn professional accreditation as a **certified internal auditor (CIA).**[16]

Tax Accounting

Taxes enable governments to fund roads, parks, schools, police protection, the military, and other functions. Federal, state, and local governments require individuals and organizations to file tax returns at specific times and in a precise format. A **tax accountant** is trained in tax law and is responsible for preparing tax returns or developing tax strategies. Since governments often change tax policies according to specific needs or objectives, the job of the tax accountant is always challenging.[17] And as the burden of taxes grows in the economy, the role of the tax accountant becomes increasingly valuable to the organization, individual, or entrepreneur.[18]

Government and Not-for-Profit Accounting

Government and not-for-profit accounting supports organizations whose purpose is not generating a profit, but serving ratepayers, taxpayers, and others according to a duly approved budget. Federal, state, and local governments require an accounting system that helps taxpayers, special interest groups, legislative bodies, and creditors ensure that the government is fulfilling its obligations and making proper use of taxpayers' money. Government accounting standards are set by an organization called the Governmental Accounting Standards Board (GASB).[19] The Federal Bureau of Investigation, the Internal Revenue Service, the Missouri Department of Natural Resources, and the Cook County Department of Revenue are just a few of the many government agencies that offer career possibilities to accountants seeking to work in government accounting.

Not-for-profit organizations also require accounting professionals. Charities like the Salvation Army, Red Cross, museums, and hospitals all hire accountants to show contributors how their money is spent. In fact, their need for trained accountants is growing since donors to nonprofits want to see exactly how and where the funds they contribute are being spent.

The National Park Service, with its workforce of over 26,000 employees, maintains and protects places special to the people of the United States, like the faces on Mount Rushmore. Such government organizations employ accountants, auditors, and financial managers.

During the deep recession beginning in 2008, many businesses and individuals cut back on donations, making it more important than ever to account for every dollar contributed.[20]

As you can see, managerial and financial accounting, auditing, tax accounting, and governmental and not-for-profit accounting each require specific training and skill. After the Progress Assessment, we will clarify the difference between accounting and bookkeeping.

government and not-for-profit accounting
Accounting system for organizations whose purpose is not generating a profit but serving ratepayers, taxpayers, and others according to a duly approved budget.

progress assessment

- What is the key difference between managerial and financial accounting?
- How is the job of a private accountant different from that of a public accountant?
- What is the job of an auditor? What's an independent audit?

LEARNING goal 3

List the steps in the accounting cycle, distinguish between accounting and bookkeeping, and explain how computers are used in accounting.

Need help understanding the Accounting Cycle?
www.introbiz.tv/QR17-1

THE ACCOUNTING CYCLE

The **accounting cycle** is a six-step procedure that results in the preparation and analysis of the major financial statements (see Figure 17.4). It relies on the work of both a bookkeeper and an accountant. **Bookkeeping,** the recording of business transactions, is a basic part of financial reporting. Accounting, however, goes far beyond the mere recording of financial information. Accountants classify and summarize financial data provided by bookkeepers, and then interpret the data and report the information to management. They also suggest strategies for improving the firm's financial condition and prepare financial analyses and income tax returns.

A bookkeeper's first task is to divide all the firm's transactions into meaningful categories such as sales documents, purchasing receipts, and shipping documents, being very careful to keep the information organized and manageable. Bookkeepers then record financial data from the original transaction documents (sales slips

accounting cycle
A six-step procedure that results in the preparation and analysis of the major financial statements.

bookkeeping
The recording of business transactions.

figure 17.4

STEPS IN THE ACCOUNTING CYCLE

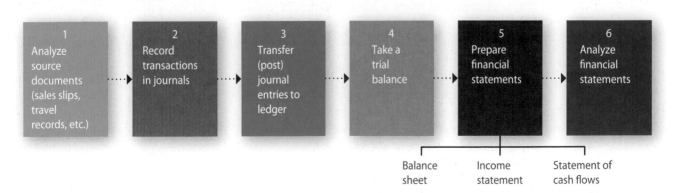

| 1 Analyze source documents (sales slips, travel records, etc.) | 2 Record transactions in journals | 3 Transfer (post) journal entries to ledger | 4 Take a trial balance | 5 Prepare financial statements | 6 Analyze financial statements |

Balance sheet   Income statement   Statement of cash flows

journal
The record book or computer program where accounting data are first entered.

double-entry bookkeeping
The practice of writing every business transaction in two places.

ledger
A specialized accounting book or computer program in which information from accounting journals is accumulated into specific categories and posted so that managers can find all the information about one account in the same place.

trial balance
A summary of all the financial data in the account ledgers that ensures the figures are correct and balanced.

and so forth) into a record book or computer program called a **journal.** The word *journal* comes from the French word *jour,* which means "day." Therefore, a journal is where the day's transactions are kept.

It's quite possible to make a mistake when recording financial transactions, like entering $10.98 as $10.89. That's why bookkeepers record all transactions in two places so they can check one list of transactions against the other to make sure both add up to the same amount. If the amounts are not equal, the bookkeeper knows there is a mistake. The practice of writing every transaction in two places is called **double-entry bookkeeping.** It requires two entries in the journal and in the ledgers (discussed next) for each transaction.

Suppose a business wanted to determine how much it paid for office supplies in the first quarter of the year. Without a specific bookkeeping tool, that would be difficult—even with accurate accounting journals. Therefore, bookkeepers use a specialized accounting book or computer program called a **ledger.** In the ledger, they transfer (or post) information from accounting journals into specific categories so managers can find all the information about a single account, like office supplies or cash, in one place.

The next step in the accounting cycle is to prepare a **trial balance,** a summary of all the financial data in the account ledgers that ensures the figures are correct and balanced. If the information in the account ledgers is not accurate, the accountant must correct it before preparing the firm's financial statements. Using the correct information, the accountant then prepares the firm's financial statements—including a balance sheet, an income statement, and a statement of cash flows—according to generally accepted accounting principles.

Accounting Technology

Not long ago, accountants and bookkeepers needed to enter all of a firm's financial information by hand. Today, technology has simplified the accounting process considerably.[21] Computerized accounting programs post information from journals instantaneously, even from remote locations, so that financial information is readily available whenever the organization needs it. Such assistance frees accountants' time for more important tasks such as financial analysis. Computerized accounting programs are particularly helpful to small-business owners, who often lack the strong accounting support within their companies that larger firms enjoy. Accounting software—such as Intuit's QuickBooks and Sage's Peachtree—addresses the specific needs of small businesses, often significantly different from the needs of a major corporation.[22] Small-business owners, however, need to understand exactly which computer systems and programs are best suited for their particular company needs.[23] That's one reason why entrepreneurs planning to start a business should either hire or consult with an accountant to identify the particular needs of their firm. They can then develop a specific computer accounting system that works with the accounting software they've chosen.

With sophisticated accounting software available, you might wonder why you need to study and understand accounting. Without question a computer is a wonderful tool for businesspeople and certainly helps ease the monotony of bookkeeping and accounting work. Unfortunately the work of an accountant requires training and very specific competencies that computers are not programmed to handle. It's the partnership of technology and an accountant's knowledge that helps a firm make the right financial decisions. After the Progress Assessment, we'll explore the balance sheet, income statement, and statement of cash flows. It's from the information contained in these financial statements that the accountant analyzes and evaluates the financial condition of the firm.

progress assessment

- How is the job of the bookkeeper different from that of an accountant?
- What's the purpose of accounting journals and of a ledger?
- Why does a bookkeeper prepare a trial balance?
- How has computer software helped businesses in maintaining and compiling accounting information?

LEARNING goal 4

Explain how the major financial statements differ.

UNDERSTANDING KEY FINANCIAL STATEMENTS

An accounting year is either a calendar or fiscal year. A calendar year begins January 1st and ends December 31st. A fiscal year can begin at any date designated by the business. A **financial statement** is a summary of all the financial transactions that have occurred over a particular period. Financial statements indicate a firm's financial health and stability and are key factors in management decision making.[24] That's why stockholders (the owners of the firm), bondholders and banks (people and institutions that lend money to the firm), labor unions, employees, and the Internal Revenue Service are all interested in a firm's financial statements. The key financial statements of a business are:

financial statement
A summary of all the transactions that have occurred over a particular period.

1. The *balance sheet,* which reports the firm's financial condition *on a specific date.*

2. The *income statement,* which summarizes revenues, cost of goods, and expenses (including taxes), for a specific period and highlights the total profit or loss the firm experienced *during that period.*

3. The *statement of cash flows,* which provides a summary of money coming into and going out of the firm. It tracks a company's cash receipts and cash payments.

The differences among the financial statements can best be summarized this way: The balance sheet details what the company owns and owes on a certain day; the income statement shows the revenue a firm earned selling its products compared to its selling costs (profit or loss) over a specific period of time; and the statement of cash flows highlights the difference between cash coming in and cash going out of a business. To fully understand this important financial information, you need to know the purpose of an organization's financial statements.[25] To help with this task, we'll explain each statement in more detail next.

The Fundamental Accounting Equation

Imagine you don't owe anybody money. That is, you have no liabilities (debts). In this case, your assets (cash and so forth) are equal to what you *own* (your equity). However, if you borrow some money from a friend, you have incurred a liability. Your assets are now equal to what you *owe* plus what you own. Translated into business terms, Assets = Liabilities + Owners' equity.

In accounting, this equation must always be balanced. For example, suppose you have $50,000 in cash and decide to use that money to open a small coffee shop. Your business has assets of $50,000 and no debts. The accounting equation would look like this:

$$\text{Assets} = \text{Liabilities} + \text{Owners' equity}$$
$$\$50{,}000 = \$0 \qquad + \$50{,}000$$

You have $50,000 cash and $50,000 owners' equity (the amount of your investment in the business—sometimes referred to as net worth). However, before opening the business, you borrow $30,000 from a local bank; now the equation changes. You have $30,000 of additional cash, but you also have a debt (liability) of $30,000. (Remember, in double-entry bookkeeping we record each business transaction in two places.)

Your financial position within the business has changed. The equation is still balanced, but we change it to reflect the borrowing transaction:

$$\text{Assets} = \text{Liabilities} + \text{Owners' equity}$$
$$\$80{,}000 = \$30{,}000 \quad + \$50{,}000$$

This **fundamental accounting equation** is the basis for the balance sheet.

The Balance Sheet

A **balance sheet** is the financial statement that reports a firm's financial condition at a specific time. As highlighted in the sample balance sheet in Figure 17.5 (for our hypothetical vegetarian restaurant, Very Vegetarian, introduced in Chapter 13), assets are listed in a separate column from liabilities and owners' (or stockholders') equity. The assets are equal to, or *balanced* with, the liabilities and owners' (or stockholders') equity. The balance sheet is that simple.

Let's say you want to know what your financial condition is at a given time. Maybe you want to buy a house or car and therefore need to calculate your available resources. One of the best measuring sticks is your balance sheet. First, add up everything you own—cash, property, and money owed you. These are your assets. Subtract from that the money you owe others—credit card debt, IOUs, car loan, and student loan. These are your liabilities. The resulting figure is your net worth, or equity. This is fundamentally what companies do in preparing a balance sheet: they follow the procedures set in the fundamental accounting equation. In that preparation, it's important to follow generally accepted accounting principles (GAAP).

Since it's critical that you understand the financial information on the balance sheet, let's take a closer look at what is in a business's asset account and what is in its liabilities and owners' equity accounts.

Classifying Assets

Assets are economic resources (things of value) owned by a firm. Assets include productive, tangible items such as equipment, buildings, land, furniture, and motor vehicles that help generate income, as well as intangible items with value like

fundamental accounting equation

Assets = Liabilities + Owners' equity; this is the basis for the balance sheet.

balance sheet

Financial statement that reports a firm's financial condition at a specific time and is composed of three major accounts: assets, liabilities, and owners' equity.

assets

Economic resources (things of value) owned by a firm.

Service businesses like dog groomers rely on the same set of financial statements as manufacturers like Ford and retail sales firms like Macy's. What are some of the assets and liabilities a typical service business like this one would carry on its balance sheet?

GROOMING

VERY VEGETARIAN
Balance Sheet
December 31, 2014

Assets

① Current assets

Cash	$ 15,000	
Accounts receivable	200,000	
Notes receivable	50,000	
Inventory	335,000	
Total current assets		$ 600,000

② Fixed assets

Land		$ 40,000
Building and improvements	$ 200,000	
Less: Accumulated depreciation	−90,000	
	110,000	
Equipment and vehicles	$ 120,000	
Less: Accumulated depreciation	−80,000	
	40,000	
Furniture and fixtures	$ 26,000	
Less: Accumulated depreciation	−10,000	
	16,000	
Total fixed assets		206,000

③ Intangible assets

Goodwill		$ 20,000
Total intangible assets		20,000
Total assets		$ 826,000

Liabilities and Owners' Equity

④ Current liabilities

Accounts payable		$ 40,000
Notes payable (due June 2015)		8,000
Accrued taxes		150,000
Accrued salaries		90,000
Total current liabilities		$ 288,000

⑤ Long-term liabilities

Notes payable (due Mar. 2018)		$ 35,000
Bonds payable (due Dec. 2020)		290,000
Total long-term liabilities		325,000
Total liabilities		$ 613,000

⑥ Owners' equity

Common stock (1,000,000 shares)		$ 100,000
Retained earnings		113,000
Total owners' equity		213,000
Total liabilities & owners' equity		$ 826,000

figure 17.5

SAMPLE VERY VEGETARIAN BALANCE SHEET

① Current assets: Items that can be converted to cash within one year.

② Fixed assets: Items such as land, buildings, and equipment that are relatively permanent.

③ Intangible assets: Items of value such as patents and copyrights that don't have a physical form.

④ Current liabilities: Payments that are due in one year or less.

⑤ Long-term liabilities: Payments that are not due for one year or longer.

⑥ Owners' equity: The value of what stockholders own in a firm (also called stockholders' equity).

patents, trademarks, copyrights, and goodwill. Goodwill represents the value attached to factors such as a firm's reputation, location, and superior products. Goodwill is included on a balance sheet when one firm acquires another and pays more for it than the value of its tangible assets. Intangible assets like brand names can be among the firm's most valuable resources. Think of the value of brand names such as Starbucks, Coca-Cola, McDonald's, and Apple. Not all companies, however, list intangible assets on their balance sheets.

liquidity
The ease with which an asset can be converted into cash.

current assets
Items that can or will be converted into cash within one year.

fixed assets
Assets that are relatively permanent, such as land, buildings, and equipment.

intangible assets
Long-term assets (e.g., patents, trademarks, copyrights) that have no real physical form but do have value.

liabilities
What the business owes to others (debts).

accounts payable
Current liabilities are bills the company owes to others for merchandise or services purchased on credit but not yet paid for.

notes payable
Short-term or long-term liabilities that a business promises to repay by a certain date.

bonds payable
Long-term liabilities that represent money lent to the firm that must be paid back.

owners' equity
The amount of the business that belongs to the owners minus any liabilities owed by the business.

Accountants list assets on the firm's balance sheet in order of their **liquidity,** or the ease with which they can convert them to cash. Speedier conversion means higher liquidity. For example, an *account receivable* is an amount of money owed to the firm that it expects to receive within one year. It is considered a liquid asset because it can be quickly converted to cash. Land, however, is not considered a liquid asset because it takes time, effort, and paperwork to sell. It is considered as a fixed or long-term asset. Assets are thus divided into three categories, according to how quickly they can be turned into cash:

1. **Current assets** are items that can or will be converted into cash within one year. They include cash, accounts receivable, and inventory.

2. **Fixed assets** are long-term assets that are relatively permanent such as land, buildings, and equipment. (On the balance sheet we also refer to these as property, plant, and equipment.)

3. **Intangible assets** are long-term assets that have no physical form but do have value. Patents, trademarks, copyrights, and goodwill are intangible assets.

Liabilities and Owners' Equity Accounts

Liabilities are what the business owes to others—its debts. *Current liabilities* are debts due in one year or less. *Long-term liabilities* are debts not due for one year or more. The following are common liability accounts recorded on a balance sheet (look at Figure 17.5 again):

1. **Accounts payable** are current liabilities or bills the company owes others for merchandise or services it purchased on credit but has not yet paid for.

2. **Notes payable** can be short-term or long-term liabilities (like loans from banks) that a business promises to repay by a certain date.

3. **Bonds payable** are long-term liabilities; money lent to the firm that it must pay back. (We discuss bonds in depth in Chapters 18 and 19.)

As you saw in the fundamental accounting equation, the value of things you own (assets) minus the amount of money you owe others (liabilities) is called *equity.* The value of what stockholders own in a firm (minus liabilities) is called *stockholders' equity* or *shareholders' equity.* Because stockholders are the owners of a firm, we also call stockholders' equity **owners' equity,** or the amount of the business that belongs to the owners, minus any liabilities the business owes. The formula for owners' equity, then, is assets minus liabilities.

The owners' equity account will differ according to the type of organization. For sole proprietors and partners, owners' equity means the value of everything owned by the business minus any liabilities of the owner(s), such as bank loans. Owners' equity in these firms is called the *capital account.*

For corporations, the owners' equity account records the owners' claims to funds they have invested in the firm (such as stock), as well as retained earnings. **Retained earnings** are accumulated earnings from the firm's profitable operations that are reinvested in the business and not paid out to stockholders in distributions of company profits. (Distributions of profits, called dividends, are discussed in Chapter 19.) Take a few moments to look again at Figure 17.5 and see what facts you can determine about the vegetarian restaurant, Very Vegetarian, from its balance sheet. After the Progress Assessment, have some fun and estimate your own personal net worth, following the directions in Figure 17.6.

Assets		Liabilities	
Cash	$ _____	Installment loans & interest	$ _____
Savings account	_____	Other loans & interest	_____
Checking account	_____	Credit card accounts	_____
Home	_____	Mortgage	_____
Stocks & bonds	_____	Taxes	_____
Automobile	_____	Cell phone service	_____
IRA or Keogh	_____		
Personal property	_____		
Other assets	_____		
Total assets	$ _____	Total liabilities	$ _____

Determine your net worth:

Total assets	$ _____
Total liabilities	— _____
Net worth	$ _____

figure 17.6

YOU INCORPORATED

How do you think You Inc. stacks up financially? Let's take a little time to find out. You may be pleasantly surprised, or you may realize that you need to think hard about planning your financial future. Remember, your net worth is nothing more than the difference between what you own (assets) and what you owe (liabilities). Be honest, and do your best to give a fair evaluation of your private property's value.

progress assessment

- What do we call the formula for the balance sheet? What three accounts does it include?
- What does it mean to list assets according to liquidity?
- What's the difference between long-term and short-term liabilities on the balance sheet?
- What is owners' equity and how do we determine it?

retained earnings
The accumulated earnings from a firm's profitable operations that were reinvested in the business and not paid out to stockholders in dividends.

income statement
The financial statement that shows a firm's profit after costs, expenses, and taxes; it summarizes all of the resources that have come into the firm (revenue), all the resources that have left the firm (expenses), and the resulting net income or net loss.

net income or net loss
Revenue left over or depleted after all costs and expenses, including taxes, are paid.

The Income Statement

The financial statement that shows a firm's bottom line—that is, its profit after costs, expenses, and taxes—is the **income statement.** The income statement summarizes all the resources, called *revenue,* that have come into the firm from operating activities, money resources the firm used up, expenses it incurred in doing business, and resources it has left after paying all costs and expenses, including taxes. The resources (revenue) left over or depleted are referred to as **net income or net loss** (see Figure 17.7).

The income statement reports the firm's financial operations over a particular period of time, usually a year, a quarter of a year, or a month. It's the financial statement that reveals whether the business is actually earning a profit or losing money. The income statement includes valuable financial information for stockholders, lenders, potential investors, employees, and of course the government. Because it's so valuable, let's take a quick look at how to compile the income statement. Then we will discuss what each element in it means.

	Revenue
–	Cost of goods sold
=	Gross profit (gross margin)
–	Operating expenses
=	Net income before taxes
–	Taxes
=	Net income or loss

figure 17.7

SAMPLE VERY VEGETARIAN INCOME STATEMENT

① Revenue: Value of what's received from goods sold, services rendered, and other financial sources.

② Cost of goods sold: Cost of merchandise sold or cost of raw materials or parts used for producing items for resale.

③ Gross profit: How much the firm earned by buying or selling merchandise.

④ Operating expenses: Cost incurred in operating a business.

⑤ Net income after taxes: Profit or loss over a specific period after subtracting all costs and expenses, including taxes.

VERY VEGETARIAN
Income Statement
For the Year Ended December 31, 2014

①	Revenues			
	Gross sales		$ 720,000	
	Less: Sales returns and allowances	$ 12,000		
	Sales discounts	8,000	−20,000	
	Net sales			$700,000
②	Cost of goods sold			
	Beginning inventory, Jan. 1		$ 200,000	
	Merchandise purchases	$400,000		
	Freight	40,000		
	Net purchases		440,000	
	Cost of goods available for sale	$640,000		
	Less ending inventory, Dec. 31		−230,000	
	Cost of goods sold			−410,000
③	Gross profit			$290,000
④	Operating expenses			
	Selling expenses			
	Salaries for salespeople	$ 90,000		
	Advertising	18,000		
	Supplies	2,000		
	Total selling expenses		$ 110,000	
	General expenses			
	Office salaries	$ 67,000		
	Depreciation	1,500		
	Insurance	1,500		
	Rent	28,000		
	Light, heat, and power	12,000		
	Miscellaneous	2,000		
			112,000	
	Total operating expenses			222,000
	Net income before taxes			$ 68,000
	Less: Income tax expense			19,000
⑤	Net income after taxes			$ 49,000

Revenue

cost of goods sold (or cost of goods manufactured) A measure of the cost of merchandise sold or cost of raw materials and supplies used for producing items for resale.

Revenue is the monetary value of what a firm received for goods sold, services rendered, and other payments (such as rents received, money paid to the firm for use of its patents, interest earned, etc.). Be sure not to confuse the terms *revenue* and *sales;* they are not the same thing. True, most revenue the firm earns does come from sales, but companies can also have other sources of revenue. Also, a quick glance at the income statement shows you that *gross sales* refers to the total of all sales the firm completed. *Net sales* are gross sales minus returns, discounts, and allowances.

Cost of Goods Sold

gross profit (or gross margin) How much a firm earned by buying (or making) and selling merchandise.

The **cost of goods sold (or cost of goods manufactured)** measures the cost of merchandise the firm sells or the cost of raw materials and supplies it used in producing items for resale. It makes sense to compare how much a business earned by selling merchandise and how much it spent to make or buy the merchandise. The cost of goods sold includes the purchase price plus any freight charges paid to transport goods, plus any costs associated with storing the goods.

In financial reporting, it doesn't matter when a firm places a particular item in its inventory, but it does matter how an accountant records the cost of the item when the firm sells it. To find out why, read the Connecting with Small Business box about two different inventory valuation methods.

When we subtract the cost of goods sold from net sales, we get gross profit or gross margin. **Gross profit (or gross margin)** is how much a firm earned by buying (or making) and selling merchandise. In a service firm, there may be no cost of goods sold; therefore, gross profit could *equal* net sales. Gross profit does not tell you everything you need to know about the firm's financial performance. To get that, you must also subtract the business's expenses.

Operating Expenses

In selling goods or services, a business incurs certain **operating expenses** such as rent, salaries, supplies, utilities, and insurance. Other operating expenses that appear on an income statement, like depreciation, are a bit more complex. For example, have you ever heard that a new car depreciates in market value as soon as you drive it off the dealer's lot? The same principle holds true for assets such as equipment and machinery. **Depreciation** is the systematic write-off of the cost of a tangible asset over its estimated useful life. Under accounting rules set by GAAP and the Internal Revenue Service (which are beyond the scope of this chapter), companies are permitted to recapture the cost of these assets over time by using depreciation as an operating expense.

We can classify operating expenses as either selling or general expenses. *Selling expenses* are related to the marketing and distribution of the firm's goods or services, such as advertising, salespeople's salaries, and supplies. *General expenses* are administrative expenses of the firm such as office salaries, depreciation, insurance, and rent. Accountants are trained to help you record all applicable expenses and find other relevant expenses you can deduct from your taxable income as a part of doing business.

Net Profit or Loss

After deducting all expenses, we can determine the firm's net income before taxes, also referred to as net earnings or net profit (see Figure 17.7 again). After allocating for taxes, we get to the *bottom line,* which is the net income (or perhaps net loss) the firm incurred from revenue minus sales returns, costs, expenses, and taxes over a period of time. We can now answer the question "Did the business earn or lose money in the specific reporting period?"

As you can see, the basic principles of the balance sheet and income statement are already familiar to you. You know how to keep track of costs and expenses when you prepare your own budget. If your rent and utilities exceed your earnings, you know you're in trouble. If you need more money, you may need to sell some of the things you own to meet your expenses. The same is true in business. Companies need to keep track of how much money they earn and spend, and how much cash they have on hand. The only difference is that they tend to have more complex problems and a good deal more information to record than you do.

Jennifer Behar runs a small bakery that sells products like chocolate biscotti and rosemary flatbread to high-end retailers like Whole Foods Market and Dean & DeLuca. Behar began her business with borrowed funds and doubled revenues in one year. What is the difference between revenue and sales?

operating expenses
Costs involved in operating a business, such as rent, utilities, and salaries.

depreciation
The systematic write-off of the cost of a tangible asset over its estimated useful life.

LIFO or FIFO?

Generally accepted accounting principles (GAAP) sometimes permit an accountant to use different methods of accounting for a firm's inventory. Let's look at two possible treatments—-FIFO and LIFO.

Say a college bookstore buys 100 copies of a particular textbook in July at $100 a copy. When classes begin, the bookstore sells 50 copies of the text to students at $120 each. Since the book will be used again next term, the store places the 50 copies it did not sell in its inventory until then.

In late December, when the bookstore orders 50 additional copies of the text to sell for the coming term, the publisher's price has increased to $110 a copy due to inflation and other production and distribution costs. The bookstore now has in its inventory 100 copies of the same textbook from different purchase cycles. If it sells 50 copies to students at $120 each at the beginning of the new term, what's the bookstore's cost of the book for accounting purposes? Actually, it depends.

The books are identical, but the accounting treatment could be different. If the bookstore uses a method called first in, first out (FIFO), the cost of goods sold is $100 for each textbook, because the textbook the store bought first—the *first in*—cost $100. The bookstore could use another method, however. Under last in, first out (LIFO), its *last* purchase of the textbooks, at $110 each, determines the cost of each of the 50 textbooks sold.

If the book sells for $120, what is the difference in gross profit (margin) between using FIFO and using LIFO? As you can see, the inventory valuation method used makes a difference.

Users of financial statements are interested in how a firm handles the flow of cash coming into a business and the cash flowing out of the business. Cash flow problems can plague both businesses and individuals. Keep this in mind as we look at the statement of cash flows next.

The Statement of Cash Flows

statement of cash flows
Financial statement that reports cash receipts and disbursements related to a firm's three major activities: operations, investments, and financing.

The **statement of cash flows** reports cash receipts and cash disbursements related to the three major activities of a firm:

- *Operations* are cash transactions associated with running the business.
- *Investments* are cash used in or provided by the firm's investment activities.
- *Financing* is cash raised by taking on new debt, or equity capital or cash used to pay business expenses, past debts, or company dividends.

Accountants analyze all changes in the firm's cash that have occurred from operating, investing, and financing in order to determine the firm's net cash position. The statement of cash flows also gives the firm some insight into how to handle cash better so that no cash flow problems occur—such as having no cash on hand for immediate expenses.[26]

Most businesses incur operating expenses including rent, salaries, utilities, supplies, and insurance. What are some of the likely operating expenses for this firm?

Figure 17.8 shows a sample statement of cash flows, again using the example of Very Vegetarian. As you can see, the statement of cash flows answers such questions as: How much cash came into the business from current operations, such as buying and selling goods and services? Did the firm use cash to buy stocks, bonds, or other investments? Did it sell some investments that brought in cash? How much money did the firm take in from issuing stock?

VERY VEGETARIAN
Statement of Cash Flows
For the Year Ended December 31, 2014

① Cash flows from operating activities		
Cash received from customers	$ 700,000	
Cash paid to suppliers and employees	(567,000)	
Interest paid	(64,000)	
Income tax paid	(19,000)	
Interest and dividends received	2,000	
Net cash provided by operating activities		$52,000
② Cash flows from investing activities		
Proceeds from sale of plant assets	$ 4,000	
Payments for purchase of equipment	(23,000)	
Net cash provided by investing activities		(19,000)
③ Cash flows from financing activities		
Proceeds from issuance of short-term debt	$ 2,000	
Payment of long-term debt	(8,000)	
Payment of dividends	(15,000)	
Net cash inflow from financing activities		(21,000)
Net change in cash and equivalents		$ 12,000
Cash balance (beginning of year)		3,000
Cash balance (end of year)		$ 15,000

figure 17.8

SAMPLE VERY VEGETARIAN STATEMENT OF CASH FLOWS

① Cash receipts from sales, commissions, fees, interest, and dividends. Cash payments for salaries, inventories, operating expenses, interest, and taxes.

② Includes cash flows that are generated through a company's purchase or sale of long-term operational assets, investments in other companies, and its lending activities.

③ Cash inflows and outflows associated with the company's own equity transactions or its borrowing activities.

Cash flow is the difference between money coming into and going out of a business. Careful cash flow management is a must for a business of any size, but it's particularly important for small businesses and for seasonal businesses like ski resorts. Have you read of any firms that were forced into bankruptcy because of cash flow problems?

cash flow
The difference between cash coming in and cash going out of a business.

We analyze these and other financial transactions to see their effect on the firm's cash position. Managing cash flow can mean success or failure of any business, which is why we analyze it in more depth in the next section.

The Need for Cash Flow Analysis

Cash flow, if not properly managed, can cause a business much concern. Understanding cash flow analysis is important and not difficult to understand.[27] Let's say you borrow $100 from a friend to buy a used bike and agree to pay her back at the end of the week. You then sell the bike for $150 to someone else, who also agrees to pay you by the end of the week. Unfortunately, by the weekend your buyer does not have the money as promised, and says he will have to pay you next month. Meanwhile, your friend wants the $100 you agreed to pay her by the end of the week!

What seemed a great opportunity to make an easy $50 profit is now a cause for concern. You owe $100 and have no cash. What do you do? If you were a business, you might default on the loan and possibly go bankrupt, even though you had the potential for profit.

It's possible for a business to increase its sales and profits yet still suffer cash flow problems.[28] **Cash flow** is simply the difference between cash coming in and cash going out of a business. Poor cash flow constitutes a major operating problem for many companies and is particularly difficult for small and seasonal businesses.[29] Accountants sometimes face tough ethical challenges in reporting the flow of funds into a business. Read the Making Ethical Decisions box to see how such an ethical dilemma can arise.

How do cash flow problems start? Often in order to meet the growing demands of customers, a business buys goods on credit (using no cash). If it then sells a large number of goods on credit (getting no cash), the company needs more credit from a lender (usually a bank) to pay its immediate bills. If a firm has reached its credit limit and can borrow no more, it has a severe cash flow problem. It has cash coming in at a later date, but no cash to pay current expenses. That problem could, unfortunately, force the firm into bankruptcy, even though sales may be strong—all because no cash was available when it was most needed. Cash flow analysis shows that a business's relationship with its lenders is critical to preventing cash flow problems. Accountants can provide valuable insight and advice to businesses in managing cash flow, suggesting whether they need cash and how much.[30] After the Progress Assessment, we will see how accountants analyze financial statements using ratios.

progress assessment

- What are the key steps in preparing an income statement?
- What's the difference between revenue and income on the income statement?
- Why is the statement of cash flows important in evaluating a firm's operations?

LEARNING goal 5

Demonstrate the application of ratio analysis in reporting financial information.

ANALYZING FINANCIAL PERFORMANCE USING RATIOS

The firm's financial statements—its balance sheet, income statement, and statement of cash flows—form the basis for financial analyses performed by accountants inside and outside the firm. **Ratio analysis** is the assessment of a firm's financial condition, using calculations and financial ratios developed from the firm's financial statements. Financial ratios are especially useful in comparing the company's performance to its financial objectives and to the performance of other firms in its industry. You probably are already familiar with the use of ratios. For example, in basketball, we express the number of shots made from the foul line with a ratio: shots made to shots attempted. A player who shoots 85 percent from the foul line is considered an outstanding foul shooter; you don't want to foul this player in a close game.

Whether ratios measure an athlete's performance or the financial health of a business, they provide valuable information. Financial ratios provide key insights into how a firm compares to other firms in its industry on liquidity, amount of debt, profitability, and overall business activity. Understanding and interpreting business ratios is important to sound financial analysis. Let's look briefly at four key types of ratios businesses use to measure financial performance.

ratio analysis
The assessment of a firm's financial condition using calculations and interpretations of financial ratios developed from the firm's financial statements.

515

Liquidity Ratios

We've discussed that *liquidity* refers to how fast an asset can be converted to cash. Liquidity ratios measure a company's ability to turn assets into cash to pay its short-term debts (liabilities that must be repaid within one year). These short-term debts are of particular importance to the firm's lenders who expect to be paid on time. Two key liquidity ratios are the current ratio and the acid-test ratio.[31]

The *current ratio* is the ratio of a firm's current assets to its current liabilities. This information appears on the firm's balance sheet. Look back at Figure 17.5, which details Very Vegetarian's balance sheet. The company lists current assets of $600,000 and current liabilities of $288,000, yielding a current ratio of 2.08, which means Very Vegetarian has $2.08 of current assets for every $1 of current liabilities. See the following calculation:

$$\text{Current ratio} = \frac{\text{Current assets}}{\text{Current liabilities}} = \frac{\$600,000}{\$288,000} = \$2.08$$

The question the current ratio attempts to answer is: Is Very Vegetarian financially secure for the short term (less than one year)? It depends! Usually a company with a current ratio of 2 or better is considered a safe risk for lenders granting short-term credit, since it appears to be performing in line with market expectations. However, lenders will also compare Very Vegetarian's current ratio to that of competing firms in its industry and to its current ratio from the previous year to note any significant changes.

Another key liquidity ratio, called the *acid-test* or *quick ratio,* measures the cash, marketable securities (such as stocks and bonds), and receivables of a firm, compared to its current liabilities. Again, this information is on a firm's balance sheet.

$$\text{Acid-test ratio} = \frac{\text{Cash} + \text{Accounts receivable} + \text{Marketable securities}}{\text{Current liabilities}}$$

$$= \frac{\$265,000}{\$288,000} = 0.92$$

This ratio is particularly important to firms with difficulty converting inventory into quick cash. It helps answer such questions as: What if sales drop off and we can't sell our inventory? Can we still pay our short-term debt? Though ratios vary among industries, an acid-test ratio between 0.50 and 1.0 is usually considered satisfactory, but bordering on cash flow problems. Therefore, Very Vegetarian's acid-test ratio of 0.92 could raise concerns that perhaps the firm may not meet its short-term debt and may have to go to a high-cost lender for financial assistance.

Leverage (Debt) Ratios

Leverage (debt) ratios measure the degree to which a firm relies on borrowed funds in its operations. A firm that takes on too much debt could experience problems repaying lenders or meeting promises made to stockholders. The *debt to owners' equity ratio* measures the degree to which the company is financed by borrowed funds that it must repay. Again, let's use Figure 17.5 to measure Very Vegetarian's level of debt:

$$\text{Debt to owners' equity ratio} = \frac{\text{Total liabilities}}{\text{Owners' equity}} = \frac{\$613,000}{\$213,000} = 288\%$$

Anything above 100 percent shows a firm has more debt than equity. With a ratio of 288 percent, Very Vegetarian has a rather high degree of debt compared to its equity, which implies that lenders and investors may perceive the firm to be quite risky. However, again *it's important to compare a firm's debt ratios to those of other firms in its industry,* because debt financing is more acceptable in some industries than in others. Comparisons with the same firm's past debt ratios can also identify possible trends within the firm or industry.

Profitability (Performance) Ratios

Profitability (performance) ratios measure how effectively a firm's managers are using its various resources to achieve profits. Three of the more important ratios are earnings per share (EPS), return on sales, and return on equity.

EPS is a revealing ratio because earnings help stimulate the firm's growth and provide for stockholders' dividends. The Financial Accounting Standards Board requires companies to report their quarterly EPS in two ways: basic and diluted. The *basic earnings per share (basic EPS) ratio* helps determine the amount of profit a company earned for each share of outstanding common stock.[32] The *diluted earnings per share (diluted EPS) ratio* measures the amount of profit earned for each share of outstanding common stock, but also considers stock options, warrants, preferred stock, and convertible debt securities the firm can convert into common stock. For simplicity's sake, we will compute only the basic EPS for Very Vegetarian:

Building luxury hotels, like the Vdara at City Center in Las Vegas, generally requires taking on a high degree of debt before the hotel ever earns its first dollar. Once opened, the company incurs heavy expenses daily just to keep the business functioning efficiently. Would monitoring the four key accounting ratios be a major part of the accountant's job at the Vdara?

$$\text{Basic earnings per share} = \frac{\text{Net income after taxes}}{\text{Number of common stock shares outstanding}}$$

$$= \frac{\$49,000}{1,000,000 \text{ shares}} = \$.049 \text{ per share}$$

Another reliable indicator of performance is *return on sales,* which tells us whether the firm is doing as well as its competitors in generating income from sales. We calculate it by comparing net income to total sales. Very Vegetarian's return on sales is 7 percent, a figure we must measure against similar numbers for competing firms to judge Very Vegetarian's performance:

$$\text{Return on sales} = \frac{\text{Net income}}{\text{Net sales}} = \frac{\$49,000}{\$700,000} = 7\%$$

The higher the risk of failure or loss in an industry, the higher the return investors expect on their investment; they expect to be well compensated for shouldering such odds. *Return on equity* indirectly measures risk by telling us how much a firm earned for each dollar invested by its owners. We calculate it by comparing a company's net income to its total owners' equity. Very Vegetarian's return on

Inventory turnover is critical to just about any business, particularly restaurants that serve perishable items and that must turn over tables to keep the flow of food moving and profits up. Can you think of other businesses that need to watch their inventory turnover closely?

equity looks reasonably sound since some believe anything over 15 percent is considered a reasonable return:

$$\text{Return on equity} = \frac{\text{Net income after tax}}{\text{Total owners' equity}} = \frac{\$49,000}{\$213,000} = 23\%$$

Remember that profits help companies like Very Vegetarian grow. That's why profitability ratios are such closely watched measurements of company growth and management performance.

Activity Ratios

Converting the firm's inventory to profits is a key function of management. Activity ratios tell us how effectively management is turning over inventory.

The *inventory turnover ratio* measures the speed with which inventory moves through the firm and gets converted into sales. Idle inventory sitting in a warehouse earns nothing and costs money. The more efficiently a firm sells or turns over its inventory, the higher its revenue. We can measure the inventory turnover ratio for Very Vegetarian as follows:

figure 17.9

ACCOUNTS IN THE BALANCE
SHEET AND INCOME STATEMENT

Balance Sheet Accounts			Income Statement Accounts			
ASSETS	LIABILITIES	OWNERS' EQUITY	REVENUES	COST OF GOODS SOLD		EXPENSES
Cash	Accounts payable	Capital stock	Sales revenue	Cost of buying goods	Wages	Interest
Accounts receivable	Notes payable	Retained earnings	Rental revenue	Cost of storing goods	Rent	Donations
Inventory	Bonds payable	Common stock	Commissions revenue		Repairs	Licenses
Investments	Taxes payable	Treasury stock	Royalty revenue		Travel	Fees
Equipment					Insurance	Supplies
Land					Utilities	Advertising
Buildings					Entertainment	Taxes
Motor vehicles					Storage	
Goodwill						

Speaking a Universal Accounting Language

Throughout this text you've read about the tremendous impact the global market has on business. U.S. companies like Coca-Cola earn the majority of their revenues from global markets, which helps their profitability but creates considerable accounting headaches. Since no global accounting system exists, multinationals like Coca-Cola must adapt their accounting procedures to different countries' rules. However, if the Financial Accounting Standards Board (FASB) in the United States and the London-based International Accounting Standards Board (IASB) get their way, that situation could change.

The governing bodies of the accounting profession have made significant progress toward integrating the U.S. accounting code with the International Financial Reporting Standards (IFRS) used around the world. The U.S. Securities and Exchange Commission (SEC) seems to support such a change and has suggested the IFRS replace the long-standing generally accepted accounting principles (GAAP) in the near future. However, moving to one accounting standard is not likely to happen before 2015 in order to allow companies and auditors in the United States ample time to prepare for the change. Many accountants also question if the international standards under IFRS would provide the same quality of financial reporting as the GAAP.

James Quigley, chief executive officer of Deloitte Touche Tohmatsu, one of the Big Four accounting firms in the United States, favors the move to IFRS. He believes that since we have global capital markets, we need global standards for accounting. Colleges and accounting firms across the country are waiting to see if they need to get ready for implementation of IFRS. Like it or not, it appears that IFRS is coming sooner or later to an accounting department near you.

Sources: Doug DeLoach, "IFRS: International Methods on Convergent Path," *Atlanta Business Chronicle,* January 14, 2011; "Global Accounting Standards Move Forward," *South Florida Business Journal,* April 21, 2011; and Adam Jones, "IASB Optimistic on U.S. Rules Timing, *The Financial Times,* April 22, 2011.

$$\text{Inventory turnover} = \frac{\text{Costs of goods sold}}{\text{Average inventory}} = \frac{\$410,000}{\$215,000} = 1.19 \text{ times}$$

A lower-than-average inventory turnover ratio often indicates obsolete merchandise on hand or poor buying practices. Managers need to be aware of proper inventory control and anticipated inventory turnover to ensure proper performance. For example, have you ever worked as a food server in a restaurant like Very Vegetarian? How many times did your employer expect you to *turn over* a table (keep changing customers at the table) in an evening? The more times a table turns, the higher the return to the owner. Of course, like other ratios, rates of inventory turnover vary from industry to industry.

Accountants and other finance professionals use several other specific ratios, in addition to the ones we've discussed. To review where the accounting information in ratio analysis comes from, see Figure 17.9 for a quick reference. Remember, financial analysis begins where the accounting financial statements end.

Like other business disciplines, accounting is subject to change. Currently, the accounting profession is feeling the impact of the global market. The Connecting Across Borders box discusses a movement taking hold to globalize accounting procedures. It's something that accountants will be following closely. Before leaving this chapter, it's worth saying once more that, as the language of business, accounting is a worthwhile language to learn.

- What is the primary purpose of performing ratio analysis using the firm's financial statements?
- What are the four main categories of financial ratios?

summary

Learning Goal 1. Demonstrate the role that accounting and financial information play for a business and for its stakeholders.

- **What is accounting?**

Accounting is the recording, classifying, summarizing, and interpreting of financial events and transactions that affect an organization. The methods we use to record and summarize accounting data into reports are called an accounting system.

Learning Goal 2. Identify the different disciplines within the accounting profession.

- **How does managerial accounting differ from financial accounting?**

Managerial accounting provides information and analyses to managers within the firm to assist them in decision making. Financial accounting provides information and analyses to external users of data such as creditors and lenders.

- **What is the job of an auditor?**

Auditors review and evaluate the standards used to prepare a company's financial statements. An independent audit is conducted by a public accountant and is an evaluation and unbiased opinion about the accuracy of a company's financial statements.

- **What is the difference between a private accountant and a public accountant?**

A public accountant provides services for a fee to a variety of companies, whereas a private accountant works for a single company. Private and public accountants do essentially the same things with the exception of independent audits. Private accountants do perform internal audits, but only public accountants supply independent audits.

Learning Goal 3. List the steps in the accounting cycle, distinguish between accounting and bookkeeping, and explain how computers are used in accounting.

- **What are the six steps of the accounting cycle?**

The six steps of the accounting cycle are (1) analyzing documents; (2) recording information into journals; (3) posting that information into ledgers; (4) developing a trial balance; (5) preparing financial statements—the balance sheet, income statement, and statement of cash flows; and (6) analyzing financial statements.

- **What is the difference between bookkeeping and accounting?**

Bookkeeping is part of accounting and includes the systematic recording of data. Accounting includes classifying, summarizing, interpreting, and reporting data to management.

- **What are journals and ledgers?**

Journals are the first place bookkeepers record transactions. Bookkeepers then summarize journal entries by posting them to ledgers. Ledgers are specialized accounting books that arrange the transactions by homogeneous groups (accounts).

- **How do computers help accountants?**

Computers can record and analyze data and provide financial reports. Software can continuously analyze and test accounting systems to be sure they are functioning correctly. Computers can help decision making by providing appropriate information, but they cannot themselves make good financial decisions. Accounting applications and creativity are still human functions.

Learning Goal 4. Explain how the major financial statements differ.

- **What is a balance sheet?**

A balance sheet reports the financial position of a firm on a particular day. The fundamental accounting equation used to prepare the balance sheet is Assets = Liabilities + Owners' equity.

- **What are the major accounts of the balance sheet?**

Assets are economic resources owned by the firm, such as buildings and machinery. Liabilities are amounts the firm owes to creditors, bondholders, and others. Owners' equity is the value of everything the firm owns—its assets—minus any liabilities; thus, Owners' equity = Assets − Liabilities.

- **What is an income statement?**

An income statement reports revenues, costs, and expenses for a specific period of time (say, the year ended December 31, 2014). The formulas we use in preparing the income statement are:

- **Revenue − Cost of goods sold = Gross margin**

- **Gross margin − Operating expenses = Net income before taxes**

- **Net income before taxes − Taxes = Net income (or net loss)**

Net income or loss is also called the bottom line.

- **What is a statement of cash flows?**

Cash flow is the difference between cash receipts (money coming in) and cash disbursements (money going out). The statement of cash flows reports cash receipts and disbursements related to the firm's major activities: operations, investments, and financing.

Learning Goal 5. Demonstrate the application of ratio analysis in reporting financial information.

- **What are the four key categories of ratios?**

The four key categories of ratios are liquidity ratios, leverage (debt) ratios, profitability (performance) ratios, and activity ratios.

- **What is the major value of ratio analysis to the firm?**

Ratio analysis provides the firm with information about its financial position in key areas *for comparison to other firms in its industry and its own past performance.*

key terms

accounting 498	current assets 508	liabilities 508
accounting cycle 503	depreciation 511	liquidity 508
accounts payable 508	double-entry bookkeeping 504	managerial accounting 499
annual report 500	financial accounting 500	net income or net loss 509
assets 506	financial statement 505	notes payable 508
auditing 501	fixed assets 508	operating expenses 511
balance sheet 506	fundamental accounting equation 506	owners' equity 508
bonds payable 508	government and not-for-profit accounting 503	private accountant 500
bookkeeping 503		public accountant 500
cash flow 514	gross profit (or gross margin) 510	ratio analysis 515
certified internal auditor (CIA) 502	income statement 509	retained earnings 509
certified management accountant (CMA) 500	independent audit 502	statement of cash flows 512
certified public accountant (CPA) 501	intangible assets 508	tax accountant 502
cost of goods sold (or cost of goods manufactured) 510	journal 504	trial balance 504
	ledger 504	

critical thinking

1. As a potential investor in a firm or perhaps the buyer of a particular business, would it be advisable to evaluate the company's financial statements? Why or why not? What key information would you seek from a firm's financial statements?

2. Why must accounting reports be prepared according to specific procedures (GAAP)? Should we allow businesses some flexibility or creativity in preparing financial statements? Why or why not?

3. What value do financial ratios offer investors in reviewing the financial performance of a firm?

4. Why is it important to remember financial ratios can differ from industry to industry?

developing workplace skills

1. Contact a CPA at a firm in your area, or talk with a CPA in your college's business department. Ask what challenges, changes, and opportunities he or she foresees in the accounting profession in the next five years. List the CPA's forecasts on a sheet of paper and then compare them with the information in this chapter.

2. Go to the websites of the American Institute of Certified Public Accountants (www.aicpa.org) and the Institute of Management Accountants (www.imanet .org). Browse the sites and find the requirements for becoming a certified public accountant (CPA) and a certified management accountant (CMA). Compare the requirements of the programs and decide which program is more appealing to you.

3. Suppose you are a new board member for an emerging not-for-profit organization hoping to attract new donors. Contributors want to know how efficiently not-for-profit organizations use their donations. Unfortunately, your fellow board members see little value in financial reporting and analysis and believe the good works of the organization speak for themselves. Prepare a fact sheet convincing the board of the need for effective financial reporting with arguments about why it helps the organization's fund-raising goals.

4. Obtain a recent annual report for a company of your choice. (Hints: *The Wall Street Journal* has a free annual reports service, and virtually all major companies post their annual reports on their websites.) Look over the firm's financial statements and see whether they match the information in this chapter. Read the auditor's opinion (usually at the end of the report) and evaluate what you think are the most important conclusions of the auditors.

5. Obtain a recent annual report for a company of your choice (see the hints just above in exercise 4) and try your hand at computing financial ratios. Compute the current ratio, debt to owners' equity ratio, and basic earnings per share ratio. Then request an annual report from one of the firm's major competitors and compute the same ratios for that company. What did you find?

taking it to the net

Purpose

To calculate and analyze the current and quick (acid-test) ratios of different businesses.

Exercise

Potz and Pans, a small gift shop, has current assets of $45,000 (including inventory valued at $30,000) and $9,000 in current liabilities. WannaBees, a specialty clothing store, has current assets of $150,000 (including inventory valued at $125,000) and $85,000 in current liabilities. Both businesses have applied for loans. Click the Calculators box on the toolbar at **www.bankrate.com** and then click on Small Business to answer the following questions:

1. Calculate the current ratio for each company. Which company is more likely to get the loan? Why?

2. The acid-test ratio subtracts the value of the firm's inventory from its total current assets. Because inventory is often difficult to sell, this ratio is considered an even more reliable measure of a business's ability to repay loans than the current ratio. Calculate the acid-test ratio for each business and decide whether you would give either the loan. Why or why not?

casing the web

To access the case "Between a Rock and a Hard Rock," visit
www.mhhe.com/P2P2e

video case

The Accounting Function at Goodwill Industries

Goodwill Industries is a major charitable organization that relies primarily on financial and nonfinancial donations and grants. It has retail operations that help sustain its financial operations so as to fulfill its mission to help train, support, and employ disadvantaged individuals and those with disabilities.

The video introduces the accounting function and the specific steps involved in the accounting cycle. The similarities and differences between for-profit and not-for-profit entities are discussed in detail. The importance of accounting in providing financial information and analysis is featured.

Emphasis is placed on financial statements as well as ratio analysis in helping gauge the financial health of the organization.

Accounting is crucial for all organizations, whether they are a small business, large corporation, or a governmental or not-for-profit organization. The different types of accounting are discussed, including managerial, financial, tax, auditing, governmental, and not-for-profit. Balance sheets, income statements, and statements of cash flows provide important information for managers and others in the organization, helping to demonstrate whether the organization is on budget or whether there are variances between projected and actual revenues. Costs and expenses have to be kept in line and are carefully monitored and analyzed by the accounting function.

Sufficient cash flow is critical to the sustainability of any organization, particularly the not-for-profit organization; in this case, Goodwill. Not-for-profit organizations utilize performance ratio analysis to gauge their overall financial performance. The results of these analyses help management assess the organization's performance against its plan or budget. They also help to develop strategic plans for the future as well as to benchmark against other similar companies.

Thinking It Over

1. *What are some of the key differences between assets and liabilities? Which of the three financial statements features these categories prominently?*

2 *Identify the six steps in the accounting cycle.*

3. *Identify the different types of accounting. Which approaches are used by Goodwill?*

18

Financial
MANAGEMENT

After you have read and studied this chapter, you should be able to

1 Explain the role and responsibilities of financial managers.

2 Outline the financial planning process, and explain the three key budgets in the financial plan.

3 Explain why firms need operating funds.

4 Identify and describe different sources of short-term financing.

5 Identify and describe different sources of long-term financing.

Having a great idea is only the first step in starting a business. In fact, coming up with the concept is the cheapest part of the process. Entrepreneurs need money to turn their ideas into reality. Luckily, a number of investment groups are more than willing to open their wallets for what they think is going to be the next big thing. But in order to attract these "angel investors," entrepreneurs need to be sure that their business concepts have reached their full potential.

James Reinhart knows this about as well as anyone. As CEO of the clothing exchange website thredUp, Reinhart had trouble getting the attention of investors with his company's original concept. While Reinhart was getting his MBA at Harvard Business School, he and his classmate Oliver Lubin discovered that they owned too many clothes. Both estimated that they only wore about 25 percent of their entire wardrobe while the rest just took up space. So along with Reinhart's former college roommate Chris Homer, they explored the idea for a hand-me-down clothing site. Reinhart's concept was to create an online community where people could buy and sell used clothing cheaply. After gathering start-up funds of $70,000 from family, friends, and personal savings, Reinhart and company launched thredUp in September 2009.

Within three months the site drew in more than 10,000 members. Despite the initial interest, though, Reinhart knew that the company would need to grow faster to compete with other hungry startups. That's when he received a bit of inspiration from home. With his wife pregnant, Reinhart suddenly realized there could be an untapped online market for children's clothing. Research revealed that children grew out of their clothes every three to six months and that parents would ultimately go through 1,400 articles of clothing during a child's growth. Some parents spent as much as $20,000 on their kids' clothes throughout childhood. That's when thredUp's true potential became apparent to Reinhart: instead of reaching out to adults, the site could target parents looking to "trade up" their kids' wardrobes.

By April 2010, thredUp's new service was in operation with an unusual exchange system. The site's stock of used clothing is exclusively provided by community members. People send in clothes after receiving empty shipping bags from the site in the mail.

Professional buyers assess each article of clothing, its quality, and the company's ability to resell it. The higher the quality, the more money the company pays the sender. There are no price negotiations, and once the company receives the bag of clothes, it will not send it back if the seller isn't happy with the price the buyers say the items are worth. The company then resells the clothing on its website.

CONNECTING WITH

James Reinhart

CEO of thredUp

Although the process may seem strange, it instantly became a hit with parents wanting to offload heaps of outgrown clothes as well as others looking for new outfits. Reinhart managed to implement the exchange plan thanks to a $250,000 angel investment from a group that loved thredUp's new strategy. As the community continued to thrive, thredUp attracted $1.4 million more in investment in April 2010. Reinhart used that money to phase out the site's original service entirely in order to focus solely on the children's clothing venture. By May 2011, the company secured a round of venture capital, this time topping out at a whopping $7 million. With that amount of cash on hand, Reinhart could be tempted to expand thredUp into other areas. But instead he's more focused on spending the money improving the current business model. "As an entrepreneur, you're always thinking about the adjacent things to do, but we have the opportunity to build a really big, important business in the market," Reinhart said. "That's what we're going to do."

Risk and uncertainty clearly define the role of financial management. In this chapter, you'll explore the role of finance in business. We'll discuss the challenges and the tools top managers like James Reinhart use to attain financial stability and growth.

Sources: Gwen Moran, "How a Used Clothing Site Raised $8.4 Million in Venture Capital," *Entrepreneur,* September 11, 2011; Geoffrey A. Fowler, "thredUp: Making Hand-Me-Downs Go Viral," *The Wall Street Journal,* April 9, 2010; Ellen Lee, "thredUp Lets Parents Swap Kids' Used Clothes, Toys," *The San Francisco Chronicle,* February 12, 2011; and Philip Levinson, "thredUp's HBS Founders Master the Art of the Pivot," *The Harbus,* March 7, 2012.

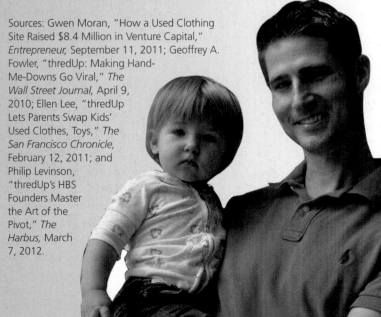

At one time this company was the largest automobile maker in the world. Due to severe financial problems in 2009, the company came very close to extinction. A $7 billion government-backed loan and an additional $43 billion government investment in the company helped it survive. It is now attempting a comeback as a much smaller company. What is the name of this company? (Find the answer in the chapter.)

LEARNING goal 1

Explain the role and responsibilities of financial managers.

THE ROLE OF FINANCE AND FINANCIAL MANAGERS

finance
The function in a business that acquires funds for the firm and manages those funds within the firm.

financial management
The job of managing a firm's resources so it can meet its goals and objectives.

financial managers
Managers who examine financial data prepared by accountants and recommend strategies for improving the financial performance of the firm.

The goal of this chapter is to answer two major questions: "What is finance?" and "What do financial managers do?" **Finance** is the function in a business that acquires funds for the firm and manages them within the firm. Finance activities include preparing budgets; doing cash flow analysis; and planning for the expenditure of funds on such assets as plant, equipment, and machinery. **Financial management** is the job of managing a firm's resources to meet its goals and objectives. Without a carefully calculated financial plan, a firm has little chance for survival, regardless of its product or marketing effectiveness. Let's briefly review the roles of accountants and financial managers.

We can compare an accountant to a skilled laboratory technician who takes blood samples and other measures of a person's health and writes the findings on a health report (in business, this process is the preparation of financial statements). A financial manager is like the doctor who interprets the report and makes recommendations that will improve the patient's health. In short, **financial managers** examine financial data prepared by accountants and recommend strategies for improving the financial performance of the firm.

Clearly financial managers can make sound financial decisions only if they understand accounting information. That's why we examined accounting in Chapter 17. Similarly, a good accountant needs to understand finance. Accounting and finance go together like peanut butter and jelly. In large and medium-sized organizations, both the accounting and finance functions are generally under the control of a chief financial officer (CFO).[1] However, financial management could also be in the hands of a person who serves as company treasurer or vice president of finance. A comptroller is the chief *accounting* officer.

Figure 18.1 highlights a financial manager's tasks. As you can see, two key responsibilities are to obtain funds and to effectively control the use of those funds. Controlling funds includes managing the firm's cash, credit accounts (accounts receivable), and inventory. Finance is a critical activity in both profit-seeking and nonprofit organizations.

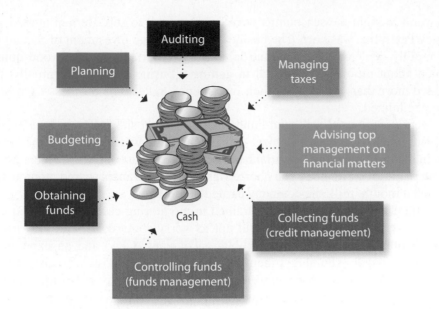

figure 18.1

WHAT FINANCIAL
MANAGERS DO

Michael Miller overhauled the underperforming Goodwill Industries operation in Portland, Oregon, by treating the nonprofit like a for-profit business. He trimmed operating expenses 30 percent by comparing sales by store, closing weak outlets and opening new ones in better locations, and cutting distribution costs. Sales soared from $4 million to over $50 million.

Finance is important, no matter what the firm's size. As you may remember from Chapter 6, financing a small business is essential if the firm expects to survive its important first five years. But the need for careful financial management remains a challenge that any business, large or small, must face throughout its existence.[2] This is a lesson many U.S. businesses learned the hard way in the late 2000s when a financial crisis threatened the economy.[3]

General Motors, once the world's dominant automaker, faced extinction in 2009 because of severe financial problems. The company survived due to a direct government loan of $7 billion and an additional $43 billion in bailout funds provided by the U.S. Treasury.[4] (The $43 billion gave the government a 60 percent ownership stake in the company.) That same year, the government also approved an $85 billion loan to save insurance giant American International Group (AIG) and passed the $700 billion Troubled Assets Relief Program (TARP) to help restore confidence in the financial system.[5]

The Value of Understanding Finance

Three of the most common reasons a firm fails financially are:

1. Undercapitalization (insufficient funds to start the business).
2. Poor control over cash flow.
3. Inadequate expense control.

You can see all three in the following classic story:

Two friends, Elizabeth Bertani and Pat Sherwood, started a company called Parsley Patch on what can best be described as a shoestring budget. It began when Bertani prepared salt-free seasonings for her husband, who was on a no-salt diet. Her friend

Sherwood thought the seasonings were good enough to sell. Bertani agreed, and Parsley Patch Inc. was born. The business began with an investment of $5,000 that was rapidly depleted on a logo and label design. Bertani and Sherwood quickly learned about the need for capital in getting a business going. Eventually, they invested more than $100,000 of their own money to keep the business from being undercapitalized.

Everything started well, and hundreds of gourmet shops adopted the product line. But when sales failed to meet expectations, the women decided the health-food market offered more potential because salt-free seasonings were a natural for people with restricted diets. The choice was a good one. Sales soared, approaching $30,000 a month. Still, the company earned no profits.

Bertani and Sherwood weren't trained in monitoring cash flow or in controlling expenses. In fact, they were told not to worry about costs, and they hadn't. They eventually hired a certified public accountant (CPA) and an experienced financial manager, who taught them how to compute the costs of their products, and how to control expenses as well as cash moving in and out of the company (cash flow). Soon Parsley Patch was earning a comfortable margin on operations that ran close to $1 million a year. Luckily, the owners were able to turn things around before it was too late. Eventually, they sold the firm to spice and seasonings giant McCormick.[6]

If Bertani and Sherwood had understood finance before starting their business, they might have been able to avoid the problems they encountered. The key word here is *understood.* You do not have to pursue finance as a career to understand it. Financial understanding is important to anyone who wants to start a small business, invest in stocks and bonds, or plan a retirement fund. In short, finance and accounting are two areas everyone in business should study. Since we discussed accounting in Chapter 17, let's look more closely at what financial management is all about.

What Is Financial Management?

Financial managers are responsible for paying the company's bills at the appropriate time, and for collecting overdue payments to make sure the company does not lose too much money to bad debts (people or firms that don't pay their bills). Therefore, finance functions, such as buying merchandise on credit (accounts payable) and collecting payment from customers (accounts receivable), are key components of the financial manager's job.[7] While these functions are vital to all types of businesses, they are particularly critical to small and medium-sized businesses, which typically have smaller cash or credit cushions than large corporations.

It's essential that financial managers stay abreast of changes or opportunities in finance, such as changes in tax law, since taxes represent an outflow of cash from the business.[8] Financial managers must also analyze the tax implications of managerial decisions to minimize the taxes the business must pay. Usually a member of the firm's finance department, the internal auditor, also checks the journals, ledgers, and financial statements the accounting department prepares, to make sure all transactions are in accordance with generally accepted accounting principles

Most businesses have predictable day-to-day needs, like the need to buy supplies, pay for fuel and utilities, and pay employees. Financial management is the function that helps ensure firms have the funds they need when they need them. What would happen to the company providing the work in this photo if it couldn't buy fuel for its trucks?

(GAAP). Without such audits, accounting statements would be less reliable. Therefore, it is important that internal auditors be objective and critical of any improprieties or deficiencies noted in their evaluation.[9] Thorough internal audits assist the firm in financial planning, which we'll look at next.[10]

LEARNING goal 2

Outline the financial planning process, and explain the three key budgets in the financial plan.

FINANCIAL PLANNING

Financial planning means analyzing short-term and long-term money flows to and from the firm.[11] Its overall objective is to optimize the firm's profitability and make the best use of its money. It has three steps: (1) forecasting the firm's short-term and long-term financial needs, (2) developing budgets to meet those needs, and (3) establishing financial controls to see whether the company is achieving its goals (see Figure 18.2). Let's look at each step and the role it plays in improving the organization's financial health.

Forecasting Financial Needs

Forecasting is an important part of any firm's financial plan.[12] A **short-term forecast** predicts revenues, costs, and expenses for a period of one year or less. Part of the short-term forecast may be a **cash flow forecast,** which predicts the cash

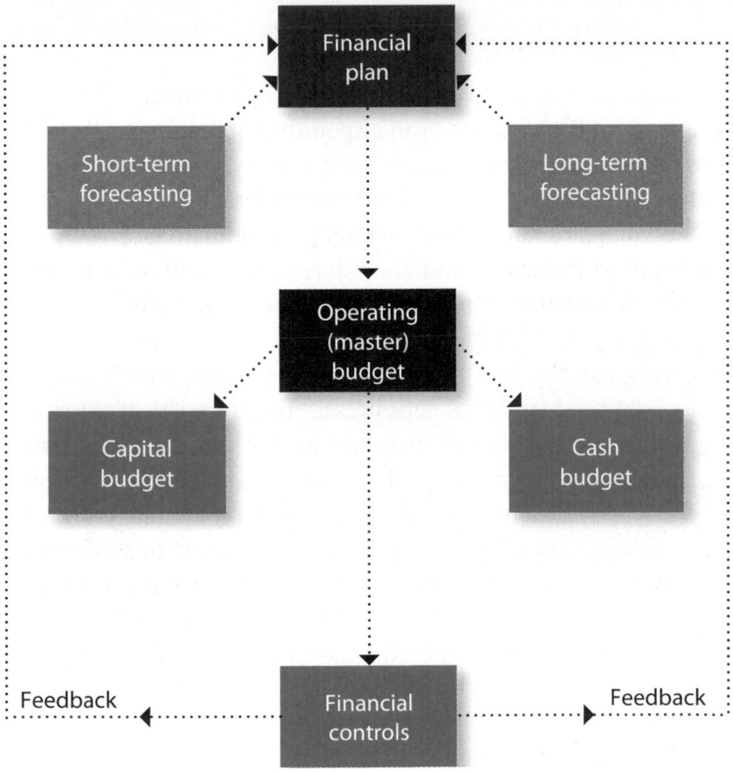

short-term forecast
Forecast that predicts revenues, costs, and expenses for a period of one year or less.

cash flow forecast
Forecast that predicts the cash inflows and outflows in future periods, usually months or quarters.

figure 18.2

FINANCIAL PLANNING

Note the close link between financial planning and budgeting.

inflows and outflows in future periods, usually months or quarters. The inflows and outflows of cash recorded in the cash flow forecast are based on expected sales revenues and various costs and expenses incurred, as well as when they are due for payment. The company's sales forecast estimates projected sales for a particular period. A business often uses its past financial statements as a basis for projecting expected sales and various costs and expenses.

A **long-term forecast** predicts revenues, costs, and expenses for a period longer than 1 year, sometimes as long as 5 or 10 years. This forecast plays a crucial part in the company's long-term strategic plan, which asks questions such as: What business are we in? Should we be in it five years from now? How much money should we invest in technology and new plant and equipment over the next decade? Will we have cash available to meet long-term obligations? Innovations in web-based software help financial managers address these long-term forecasting questions.

The long-term financial forecast gives top management, as well as operations managers, some sense of the income or profit potential of different strategic plans.[13] It also helps in preparing company budgets.

Working with the Budget Process

A **budget** sets forth management's expectations for revenues and, on the basis of those expectations, allocates the use of specific resources throughout the firm. As a financial plan, it depends heavily on the accuracy of the firm's balance sheet, income statement, statement of cash flows, and short-term and long-term financial forecasts, which all need to be as accurate as possible. To prepare budgets, financial managers must therefore take their forecasting responsibilities seriously.[14] A budget becomes the primary guide for the firm's financial operations and expected financial needs.

There are usually several types of budgets in a firm's financial plan:

- A capital budget.
- A cash budget.
- An operating or master budget.

Let's look at each.

A **capital budget** highlights a firm's spending plans for major asset purchases that often require large sums of money, like property, buildings, and equipment.

A **cash budget** estimates cash inflows and outflows during a particular period, like a month or a quarter. It helps managers anticipate borrowing needs, debt repayment, operating expenses, and short-term investments, and is often the last budget prepared. A sample cash budget for our example company, Very Vegetarian, is provided in Figure 18.3.

The **operating (or master) budget** ties together the firm's other budgets and summarizes its proposed financial activities. More formally, it estimates costs and expenses needed to run a business, given projected revenues. The firm's spending on supplies, travel, rent, technology, advertising, and salaries is determined in the operating budget, generally the most detailed a firm prepares.

Financial planning obviously plays an important role in the firm's operations and often determines what long-term investments it makes, when it will need specific funds, and how it will generate them. Once a company forecasts its short-term and long-term financial needs and compiles budgets to show how it will allocate funds, the final step in financial planning is to establish financial controls. Before we talk about those, however, Figure 18.4 challenges you to check your personal financial planning skill by developing a monthly budget for "You Incorporated."

long-term forecast
Forecast that predicts revenues, costs, and expenses for a period longer than 1 year, and sometimes as far as 5 or 10 years into the future.

budget
A financial plan that sets forth management's expectations and, on the basis of those expectations, allocates the use of specific resources throughout the firm.

capital budget
A budget that highlights a firm's spending plans for major asset purchases that often require large sums of money.

cash budget
A budget that estimates cash inflows and outflows during a particular period like a month or a quarter.

operating (or master) budget
The budget that ties together the firm's other budgets and summarizes its proposed financial activities.

VERY VEGETARIAN
Monthly Cash Budget

figure 18.3

A SAMPLE CASH BUDGET FOR VERY VEGETARIAN

	January	February	March
Sales forecast	$50,000	$45,000	$40,000
Collections			
Cash sales (20%)		$ 9,000	$ 8,000
Credit sales (80% of past month)		$40,000	$36,000
Monthly cash collection		$49,000	$44,000
Payments schedule			
Supplies and material		$11,000	$10,000
Salaries		12,000	12,000
Direct labor		9,000	9,000
Taxes		3,000	3,000
Other expenses		7,000	6,000
Monthly cash payments		$42,000	$39,000
Cash budget			
Cash flow		$ 7,000	$ 5,000
Beginning cash		−1,000	6,000
Total cash		$ 6,000	$11,000
Less minimum cash balance		−6,000	−6,000
Excess cash to market securities		$ 0	$ 5,000
Loans needed for minimum balance		0	0

Establishing Financial Controls

Financial control is a process in which a firm periodically compares its actual revenues, costs, and expenses with its budget. Most companies hold at least monthly financial reviews as a way to ensure financial control. Such control procedures help managers identify variances to the financial plan and allow them to take corrective action if necessary. Financial controls also help reveal which specific accounts, departments, and people are varying from the financial plan. Finance managers can judge whether these variances are legitimate and thereby merit adjustments to the plan. Shifts in the economy or unexpected global events can also alter financial plans. For example, unrest in the Middle East and the spike in oil prices in 2011 caused many companies to consider adjusting their financial plans.[15] After the Progress Assessment, we'll see why firms need readily available funds.

financial control
A process in which a firm periodically compares its actual revenues, costs, and expenses with its budget.

progress assessment

- Name three finance functions important to the firm's overall operations and performance.
- What three primary financial problems cause firms to fail?
- How do short-term and long-term financial forecasts differ?
- What is the purpose of preparing budgets in an organization? Can you identify three different types of budgets?

	EXPECTED	ACTUAL	DIFFERENCE
Monthly income			
Wages (net pay after taxes)	_____	_____	_____
Savings account withdrawal	_____	_____	_____
Family support	_____	_____	_____
Loans	_____	_____	_____
Other sources	_____	_____	_____
Total monthly income	_____	_____	_____
Monthly expenses			
Fixed expenses			
Rent or mortgage	_____	_____	_____
Car payment	_____	_____	_____
Health insurance	_____	_____	_____
Life insurance	_____	_____	_____
Tuition or fees	_____	_____	_____
Other fixed expenses	_____	_____	_____
Subtotal of fixed expenses	_____	_____	_____
Variable expenses			
Food	_____	_____	_____
Clothing	_____	_____	_____
Entertainment	_____	_____	_____
Transportation	_____	_____	_____
Phone	_____	_____	_____
Utilities	_____	_____	_____
Publications	_____	_____	_____
Internet connection	_____	_____	_____
Cable television	_____	_____	_____
Other expenses	_____	_____	_____
Subtotal of variable expenses	_____	_____	_____
Total expenses	_____	_____	_____
Total income − Total expenses = Cash on hand/(Cash deficit)	_____	_____	_____

figure 18.4

YOU INCORPORATED MONTHLY BUDGET

In Chapter 17, you compiled a sample balance sheet for You Inc. Now, let's develop a monthly budget for You Inc. Be honest and think of everything that needs to be included for an accurate monthly budget for You!

LEARNING goal 3

Explain why firms need operating funds.

THE NEED FOR OPERATING FUNDS

In business, the need for operating funds never seems to end. That's why sound financial management is essential to all businesses. And like our personal financial needs, the capital needs of a business change over time. Remember the example of Parsley Patch to see why a small business's financial requirements can shift considerably. The same is true for large corporations such as Apple, Johnson & Johnson, and Nike when they venture into new-product areas or new markets. Virtually all organizations have operational needs for which they need funds. Key areas include:

- Managing day-by-day needs of the business.
- Controlling credit operations.

- Acquiring needed inventory.
- Making capital expenditures.

Let's look carefully at the financial needs of these key areas, which affect both the smallest and the largest of businesses.

Managing Day-by-Day Needs of the Business

If workers expect to be paid on Friday, they don't want to wait until Monday for their paychecks. If tax payments are due on the 15th of the month, the government expects the money on time. If the interest payment on a business loan is due on the 30th of this month, the lender doesn't mean the 1st of next month. As you can see, funds have to be available to meet the daily operational costs of the business.

Financial managers must ensure that funds are available to meet daily cash needs without compromising the firm's opportunities to invest money for its future.[16] Money has a *time value*. In other words, if someone offered to give you $200 either today or one year from today, you would benefit by taking the $200 today. Why? It's very simple. You could invest the $200 you receive today and over a year's time it would grow. The same is true in business; the interest a firm gains on its investments is important in maximizing the profit it will gain. That's why financial managers often try to minimize cash expenditures to free up funds for investment in interest-bearing accounts. They suggest the company pay its bills as late as possible (unless a cash discount is available for early payment). They also advise companies to try to collect what's owed them as fast as possible, to maximize the investment potential of the firm's funds.[17] Efficient cash management is particularly important to small firms since their access to capital is much more limited than larger businesses. Software from companies like Peachtree can assist small firms in handling day-to-day cash management.

Controlling Credit Operations

Financial managers know that in today's highly competitive business environment, making credit available helps keep current customers happy and helps attract new ones. Credit for customers can be especially important during tough financial times like the recession that began in 2008 when lenders were hesitant to make loans.

The problem with selling on credit is that as much as 25 percent of the business's assets could be tied up in its credit accounts (accounts receivable). This forces the firm to use its own funds to pay for goods or services sold to customers who bought on credit. Financial managers in such firms often develop efficient collection procedures, like offering cash or quantity discounts to buyers who pay their accounts by a certain time. They also scrutinize old and new credit customers to see whether they have a history of meeting credit obligations on time.

One convenient way to decrease the time and expense of collecting accounts receivable is to accept bank credit cards such as MasterCard or Visa. The banks that issue these cards have already established the customer's creditworthiness, which reduces the business's risk. Businesses must pay a fee to accept credit cards, but the costs are usually offset by the benefits.[18]

It's difficult to think of a business that doesn't make credit available to its customers. However, collecting accounts receivable can be time-consuming and expensive. Accepting credit cards such as Visa, MasterCard, and American Express can simplify transactions for sellers and guarantee payment. What types of products do you regularly purchase with a credit card?

Good Finance or Bad Medicine?

Imagine that you have just earned your business degree and have been hired as a hospital administrator at a small hospital that, like many others, is experiencing financial problems. Having studied finance, you know that efficient cash management is important to all firms in all industries to meet the day-by-day operations of the firm. One way to ensure such efficiency is to use a carefully planned and managed inventory control system that can reduce the amount of cash an organization has tied up in inventory. Being familiar with just-in-time inventory, you know it is a proven system that helps reduce the costs of managing inventory.

At a meeting of the hospital's executive committee, you recommend that the hospital save money by using a just-in-time inventory system to manage its drug supply. You suggest discontinuing the hospital's large stockpile of drugs, especially expensive cancer treatment drugs that tie up a great deal of the hospital's cash, and shift to ordering them just when they are needed. Several members seem to like the idea, but the doctors in charge of practicing medicine and oncology are outraged, claiming you are sacrificing patients' well-being for cash. After debate, the committee says the decision is up to you. What will you do? What could result from your decision?

Acquiring Needed Inventory

As we saw in Chapter 13, effective marketing requires focusing on the customer and providing high-quality service and readily available goods. A carefully constructed inventory policy helps manage the firm's available funds and maximize profitability. Doozle's, an ice cream parlor in St. Louis, Missouri, deliberately ties up fewer funds in its inventory of ice cream in winter. It's obvious why: demand for ice cream is lower in winter.

Just-in-time inventory control (see Chapter 9) and other such methods can reduce the funds a firm must tie up in inventory. Carefully evaluating its inventory turnover ratio (see Chapter 17) can also help a firm control the outflow of cash for inventory. A business of any size must understand that poorly managed inventory can seriously affect cash flow and drain its finances dry.[19] The nearby Making Ethical Decisions box raises an interesting question about sound financial management and inventory control in a critical industry.

Making Capital Expenditures

capital expenditures
Major investments in either tangible long-term assets such as land, buildings, and equipment or intangible assets such as patents, trademarks, and copyrights.

Capital expenditures are major investments in either tangible long-term assets such as land, buildings, and equipment, or intangible assets such as patents, trademarks, and copyrights. In many organizations the purchase of major assets—such as land for future expansion, manufacturing plants to increase production capabilities, research to develop new-product ideas, and equipment to maintain or exceed current levels of output—is essential. Expanding into new markets can be expensive with no guarantee of success. Therefore, it's critical that companies weigh all possible options before committing a large portion of available resources.

Consider a firm that needs to expand its production capabilities due to increased customer demand. It could buy land and build a new plant, purchase an existing plant, or rent space. Can you think of financial and accounting considerations at play in this decision?

SHORT-TERM FUNDS	LONG-TERM FUNDS
Monthly expenses	New-product development
Unanticipated emergencies	Replacement of capital equipment
Cash flow problems	Mergers or acquisitions
Expansion of current inventory	Expansion into new markets (domestic or global)
Temporary promotional programs	New facilities

figure 18.5

WHY FIRMS NEED FUNDS

The need for operating funds raises several questions for financial managers: How does the firm obtain funds to finance operations and other business needs? Will it require specific funds in the long or the short term? How much will it cost (i.e., interest) to obtain these funds? Will they come from internal or external sources? We address these questions next.

Alternative Sources of Funds

We described finance earlier as the function in a business responsible for acquiring and managing funds. Sound financial management determines the amount of money needed and the most appropriate sources from which to obtain it. A firm can raise needed capital by borrowing money (debt), selling ownership (equity), or earning profits (retained earnings).[20] **Debt financing** refers to funds raised through various forms of borrowing that must be repaid. **Equity financing** is money raised from within the firm, from operations or through the sale of ownership in the firm (stock). Firms can borrow funds either short-term or long-term. **Short-term financing** refers to funds needed for a year or less. **Long-term financing** covers funds needed for more than a year (usually 2 to 10 years). Figure 18.5 highlights why firms may need short-term and long-term funds.

We'll explore the different sources of short- and long-term financing next. Let's first pause to check your understanding by doing the Progress Assessment.

debt financing
Funds raised through various forms of borrowing that must be repaid.

equity financing
Money raised from within the firm, from operations or through the sale of ownership in the firm (stock or venture capital).

short-term financing
Funds needed for a year or less.

long-term financing
Funds needed for more than a year (usually 2 to 10 years).

progress assessment

- Money has time value. What does this mean?
- Why is accounts receivable a financial concern to the firm?
- What's the primary reason an organization spends a good deal of its available funds on inventory and capital expenditures?
- What's the difference between debt and equity financing?

Need help understanding Equity Financing and Debt Financing? www.introbiz.tv/QR18-1

LEARNING **goal 4**

Identify and describe different sources of short-term financing.

OBTAINING SHORT-TERM FINANCING

The bulk of a finance manager's job does not relate to obtaining *long-term* funds. In small businesses, for example, long-term financing is often out of the question. Instead, day-to-day operations call for the careful management of *short-term* financial needs. Firms may need to borrow short-term funds for purchasing additional inventory or for meeting bills that come due unexpectedly. Like an individual, a business, especially a small business, sometimes needs to secure short-term funds when its cash reserves are low. Let's see how it does so.

Trade Credit

trade credit
The practice of buying goods and services now and paying for them later.

Trade credit is the practice of buying goods or services now and paying for them later. It is the most widely used source of short-term funding, the least expensive, and the most convenient.[21] Small businesses rely heavily on trade credit from firms such as United Parcel Service, as do large firms such as Kmart or Macy's. When a firm buys merchandise, it receives an invoice (a bill) much like the one you receive when you buy something with a credit card. As you'll see, however, the terms businesses receive are often different from those on your monthly statement.

Business invoices often contain terms such as *2/10, net 30*. This means the buyer can take a 2 percent discount for paying the invoice within 10 days. Otherwise the total bill (net) is due in 30 days. Finance managers pay close attention to such discounts because they create opportunities to reduce the firm's costs. Think about it for a moment: If the terms are 2/10, net 30, the customer will pay 2 percent more by waiting an extra 20 days to pay the invoice. If the firm *can* pay its bill within 10 days, it is needlessly increasing its costs by not doing so.

promissory note
A written contract with a promise to pay a supplier a specific sum of money at a definite time.

Some suppliers hesitate to give trade credit to an organization with a poor credit rating, no credit history, or a history of slow payment. They may insist the customer sign a **promissory note,** a written contract with a promise to pay a supplier a specific sum of money at a definite time. Promissory notes are negotiable. The supplier can sell them to a bank at a discount (the amount of the promissory note less a fee for the bank's services in collecting the amount due), and the business is then responsible for paying the bank.

One thing you can never have too much of is cash. Financial managers must make certain there is enough cash available to meet daily financial needs and still have funds to invest in its future. What does it mean when we say cash has a time value?

Family and Friends

As we discussed in Chapter 17, firms often have several bills coming due at the same time with no sources of funds to pay them. Many small firms obtain short-term funds by borrowing money from family and friends. Such loans can create problems, however, if all parties do not understand cash flow. That's why it's sometimes better, when possible, to go to a commercial bank that fully understands the business's risk and can help analyze its future financial needs rather than borrow from friends or relatives.

Entrepreneurs appear to be listening to this advice. According to the National Federation of Independent Business, entrepreneurs today are relying less on family and friends as a source of borrowed funds than they have in the past.[22] If an entrepreneur decides to ask family or friends for financial assistance, it's important that both parties (1) agree to specific loan terms, (2) put the agreement in writing, and (3) arrange for repayment in the same way they would for a bank loan. Such actions help keep family relationships and friendships intact.[23]

Commercial Banks

Banks, being sensitive to risk, generally prefer to lend short-term money to larger, established businesses. Imagine the different types of businesspeople who go to banks for a loan, and you'll get a better idea

of the requests bankers evaluate. Picture, for example, a farmer going to the bank in spring to borrow funds for seed, fertilizer, equipment, and other needs that will be repaid after the fall harvest. Or consider a local toy store buying merchandise for Christmas sales. The store borrows the money for such purchases in the summer and plans to pay it back after Christmas. Restaurants often borrow funds at the beginning of the month and pay at the end of the month.

How much a business borrows and for how long depends on the kind of business it is, and how quickly it can resell the merchandise it purchases with a bank loan or use it to generate funds. In a large business, specialists in a company's finance and accounting departments do a cash flow forecast.[24] Small-business owners generally lack such specialists and must monitor cash flow themselves.

The financial crisis beginning in 2008 severely curtailed bank lending to small businesses. It was difficult for even a promising and well-organized small business to obtain a bank loan. Fortunately, the situation seems to be changing.[25] What's important for a small firm to remember is if it gets a bank loan, the owner or person in charge of finance should keep in close touch with the bank and send regular financial statements to keep the bank up-to-date on its operations. The bank may spot cash flow problems early or be more willing to lend money in a crisis if the business has established a strong relationship built on trust and sound management. The Connecting Through Social Media box highlights the problems and opportunities small businesses face in attempting to secure financing.

Different Forms of Short-Term Loans

Commercial banks offer different types of short-term loans. A **secured loan** is backed by *collateral,* something valuable such as property. If the borrower fails to pay the loan, the lender may take possession of the collateral. An automobile loan is a secured loan. If the borrower doesn't repay it, the lender will repossess the car. Inventory of raw materials like coal and steel often serves as collateral for business loans. Collateral removes some of the bank's risk in lending the money.

secured loan
A loan backed by collateral, something valuable such as property.

unsecured loan
A loan that doesn't require any collateral.

line of credit
A given amount of unsecured short-term funds a bank will lend to a business, provided the funds are readily available.

revolving credit agreement
A line of credit that's guaranteed but usually comes with a fee.

Accounts receivable are company assets often used as collateral for a loan; this process is called *pledging* and works as follows: A percentage of the value of a firm's accounts receivable pledged (usually about 75 percent) is advanced to the borrowing firm.[26] As customers pay off their accounts, the funds received are forwarded to the lender in repayment of the funds that were advanced.

An **unsecured loan** is more difficult to obtain because it doesn't require any collateral. Normally, lenders give unsecured loans only to highly regarded customers—long-standing businesses or those considered financially stable.

If a business develops a strong relationship with a bank, the bank may open a **line of credit** for the firm, a given amount of unsecured short-term funds a bank will lend to a business, provided the funds are readily available. A line of credit is *not* guaranteed to a business. However, it speeds up the borrowing process since a firm does not have to apply for a new loan every time it needs funds. As businesses mature and become more financially secure, banks will often increase their line of credit. Some even offer a **revolving credit agreement,** a line of credit that's guaranteed but usually comes with a fee. Both lines of credit and revolving credit agreements are particularly good sources of funds for unexpected cash needs.[27]

If a business is unable to secure a short-term loan from a bank, the financial manager may seek short-term funds from **commercial finance companies.** These non-deposit-type organizations make short-term loans to borrowers who offer tangible assets like property, plant, and equipment as collateral. Commercial finance companies will often make loans to businesses that cannot get short-term funds elsewhere. Since commercial finance companies assume higher degrees of risk than commercial banks, they usually charge higher interest rates. General Electric Capital is one of the world's largest commercial finance companies, with $584 billion in assets and operations in over 50 countries around the world.[28]

commercial finance companies
Organizations that make short-term loans to borrowers who offer tangible assets as collateral.

Factoring Accounts Receivable

One relatively expensive source of short-term funds for a firm is **factoring,** the process of selling accounts receivable for cash. Factoring dates as far back as 4,000 years, during the days of ancient Babylon. Here's how it works: Let's say a firm sells many of its products on credit to consumers and other businesses, creating a number of accounts receivable. Some buyers may be slow in paying their bills, so a large amount of money is due the firm. A *factor* is a market intermediary (usually a financial institution or a commercial bank) that agrees to buy the firm's accounts receivable, at a discount, for cash.[29] The discount depends on the age of the accounts receivable, the nature of the business, and the condition of the economy. When it collects the accounts receivable that were originally owed to the firm, the factor keeps them.

factoring
The process of selling accounts receivable for cash.

While factors charge more than banks' loan rates, remember many small businesses cannot qualify for a loan. So even though factoring is an expensive way of raising short-term funds, it is popular among small businesses.[30] A company can often reduce its factoring cost if it agrees to reimburse the factor for slow-paying accounts, or to assume the risk for customers who don't pay at all. Remember factoring is not a loan; it is the sale of a firm's asset (accounts receivable). Factoring is common in the clothing and furniture businesses, and in growing numbers of global trade ventures.[31]

Commercial Paper

commercial paper
Unsecured promissory notes of $100,000 and up that mature (come due) in 270 days or less.

Often a corporation needs funds for just a few months and prefers not to have to negotiate with a commercial bank. One strategy available to larger firms is to sell commercial paper. **Commercial paper** consists of *unsecured* promissory notes, in amounts of $100,000 and up, that mature or come due in 270 days or less. Commercial paper states a fixed amount of money the business agrees to repay to the lender (investor) on a specific date at a specified rate of interest.

Because commercial paper is unsecured, only financially stable firms (mainly large corporations with excellent credit reputations) are able to sell it. Commercial paper can be a quick path to short-term funds at lower interest than charged by commercial banks. Even very stable firms, however, had trouble selling commercial paper during the financial crisis. The Federal Reserve stepped in and assisted many companies with their short-term financing by purchasing their short-term commercial paper. Since most commercial paper matures in 30 to 90 days, it can be an investment opportunity for buyers who can afford to put up cash for short periods to earn some interest on their money.

Credit Cards

According to the National Small Business Association (NSBA), nearly half of all small firms now use credit cards to finance their businesses. Even though more businesses are turning to credit cards for financing, two-thirds believe the terms of their cards are getting worse and it's very likely they are correct. When the Credit Card Responsibility Accountability and Disclosure Act of 2009 was passed, it reduced consumer interest rates and approved many protections for consumers against card-company abuses. Unfortunately rates for small-business credit cards increased almost 30 percent since small businesses did not fall under the protection of the law.[32] Still, with many traditional financing options closed to them, entrepreneurs are being forced to finance their firms with credit cards.

Credit cards provide a readily available line of credit that can save time and the likely embarrassment of being rejected for a bank loan. Of course, in contrast to the convenience they offer, credit cards are extremely risky and costly. Interest rates can be exorbitant, and there can be considerable penalties if users fail to make their payments on time. Savvy businesspersons study the perks that are offered with many cards and determine which might be the most beneficial to their companies. Joe Speiser, of pet-food distributor Petflow.com, found a cash-back card that helped put additional dollars back into his business.[33] Still, when dealing with credit cards, remember it's an expensive way to borrow money and credit cards are probably best used as a last resort.

After checking your progress below, we'll look into long-term financing options.

progress assessment

- What does an invoice containing the terms *2/10, net 30* mean?
- What's the difference between trade credit and a line of credit?
- What's the key difference between a secured and an unsecured loan?
- What is factoring? What are some of the considerations factors consider in establishing their discount rate?

LEARNING goal 5

Identify and describe different sources of long-term financing.

OBTAINING LONG-TERM FINANCING

In a financial plan, forecasting determines the amount of funding the firm will need over various periods and the most appropriate sources for obtaining those funds. In setting long-term financing objectives, financial managers generally ask three questions:

1. What are our organization's long-term goals and objectives?
2. What funds do we need to achieve the firm's long-term goals and objectives?
3. What sources of long-term funding (capital) are available, and which will best fit our needs?

Firms need long-term capital to purchase expensive assets such as plant and equipment, to develop new products, or perhaps finance their expansion. In major corporations, the board of directors and top management usually make decisions about long-term financing, along with finance and accounting executives. Pfizer, one of the world's largest research-based biomedical and pharmaceutical companies, spends over $9 billion a year researching and developing new products. The development of a single new drug could take 10 years and cost the firm close to $1.3 billion before it brings in any profit.[34] It's easy to see why high-level managers make the long-term financing decisions at Pfizer. Owners of small and medium-sized businesses are almost always actively engaged in analyzing their long-term financing decisions.

As we noted earlier, long-term funding comes from two major sources, debt financing and equity financing. Let's look at these sources next. But first check out the Connecting Across Borders box to learn why a source of long-term funding is raising eyebrows in the financial community.

Debt Financing

Debt financing is borrowing money the company has a legal obligation to repay. Firms can borrow by either getting a loan from a lending institution or issuing bonds.

Debt Financing by Borrowing from Lending Institutions Long-term loans are usually due within 3 to 7 years but may extend to 15 or 20 years. A **term-loan agreement** is a promissory note that requires the borrower to repay the loan with interest in specified monthly or annual installments. A major advantage is that the interest is tax-deductible.

Long-term loans are both larger and more expensive to the firm than short-term loans. Since the repayment period can be quite long, lenders assume more risk and usually require collateral, which may be real estate, machinery, equipment, company stock, or other items of value. Lenders may also require certain restrictions to force the firm to act responsibly. The interest rate is based on the

term-loan agreement
A promissory note that requires the borrower to repay the loan in specified installments.

adequacy of collateral, the firm's credit rating, and the general level of market interest rates. The greater the risk a lender takes in making a loan, the higher the rate of interest. This principle is known as the **risk/return trade-off.**

risk/return trade-off
The principle that the greater the risk a lender takes in making a loan, the higher the interest rate required.

indenture terms
The terms of agreement in a bond issue.

Debt Financing by Issuing Bonds If an organization is unable to obtain its long-term financing needs by getting a loan from a lending institution, it may try to issue bonds. To put it simply, a bond is like an IOU with a promise to repay the amount borrowed, with interest, on a certain date. The terms of the agreement in a bond issue are the **indenture terms.** The types of organizations that can issue bonds include federal, state, and local governments; federal government agencies; foreign governments; and corporations.

You may already be familiar with bonds. You may own investments like U.S. government savings bonds, or perhaps you volunteered your time to help a local school district pass a bond issue. If your community is building a new stadium or cultural center, it may sell bonds to finance the project. Businesses and

Major League Baseball is a big business, and building a new stadium requires big dollars. When the St. Louis Cardinals needed financing to replace their old stadium with a new state-of-the-art facility, St. Louis County issued bonds that helped finance the construction of the Cardinals' new home. What organizations in your community have issued bonds, and for what purpose?

governments compete when issuing bonds. Potential investors (individuals and institutions) measure the risk of purchasing a bond against the return the bond promises to pay—the interest—and the issuer's ability to repay when promised.

Like other forms of long-term debt, bonds can be secured or unsecured. A **secured bond** is issued with some form of collateral, such as real estate, equipment, or other pledged assets. If the bond's indenture terms are violated (e.g., not paying interest payments), the bondholder can issue a claim on the collateral. An **unsecured bond,** called a debenture bond, is backed only by the reputation of the issuer. Investors in such bonds simply trust that the organization issuing the bond will make good on its financial commitments.

Bonds are a key means of long-term financing for many organizations. They can also be valuable investments for private individuals or institutions. Given this importance, we will discuss bonds in depth in Chapter 19.

secured bond
A bond issued with some form of collateral.

unsecured bond
A bond backed only by the reputation of the issuer; also called a debenture bond.

Equity Financing

If a firm cannot obtain a long-term loan from a lending institution or is unable to sell bonds to investors, it may seek equity financing. Equity financing makes funds available when the owners of the firm sell shares of ownership to outside investors in the form of stock, when they reinvest company earnings in the business, or when they obtain funds from venture capitalists.

Equity Financing by Selling Stock   The key thing to remember about stock is that stockholders become owners in the organization. Generally, the corporation's board of directors decides the number of shares of stock that will be offered to investors for purchase. The first time a company offers to sell its stock to the general public is called an *initial public offering (IPO).*[35] Selling stock to the public to obtain funds is by no means easy or automatic. U.S. companies can issue stock for public purchase only if they meet requirements set by the U.S. Securities and Exchange Commission (SEC) and various state agencies. They can offer different types of stock such as common and preferred. We'll discuss IPOs and common and preferred stock in depth in Chapter 19.

Equity Financing from Retained Earnings   You probably remember from Chapter 17 that the profits the company keeps and reinvests in the firm are called *retained earnings*. Retained earnings often are a major source of long-term funds, especially for small businesses. They often have fewer financing alternatives, such as selling stock or bonds, than large businesses do. However, large corporations also depend on retained earnings for needed long-term funding. In fact, retained earnings are usually the most favored source of meeting long-term capital needs. A company that uses them saves interest payments, dividends (payments for investing in stock), and any possible underwriting fees for issuing bonds or stock. Retained earnings also create no new ownership in the firm, as stock does.

Suppose you wanted to buy an expensive personal asset such as a new car. Ideally you would go to your personal savings account and take out the necessary cash. No hassle! No interest! Unfortunately, few people have such large amounts of cash available. Most businesses are no different. Even though they would like to finance long-term needs from operations (retained earnings), few have the resources available to accomplish this.

Equity Financing from Venture Capital   The hardest time for a business to raise money is when it is starting up or just beginning to expand. A startup business typically has few assets and no market track record, so the chances of borrowing significant amounts of money from a bank are slim. **Venture capital** is money invested in new or emerging companies that some investors—venture capitalists—believe have great profit potential. Venture capital helped firms like Intel, Apple, and Cisco Systems get started and let Facebook and Google expand and grow. Venture capitalists invest in a business in return for part ownership of the business. They expect higher-than-average returns and competent management performance for their investment.

The venture capital industry originally began as an alternative investment vehicle for wealthy families. The Rockefeller family, for example (whose vast fortune came from John D. Rockefeller's Standard Oil Company, started in the

venture capital
Money that is invested in new or emerging companies that are perceived as having great profit potential.

19th century), financed Sanford McDonnell when he was operating his company from an airplane hangar. That small venture eventually grew into McDonnell Douglas, a large aerospace and defense contractor that merged with Boeing Corporation in 1997. The venture capital industry grew significantly in the 1990s, especially in high-tech centers like California's Silicon Valley, where venture capitalists concentrated on Internet-related companies. In the early 2000s, problems in the technology industry and a slowdown in the overall economy reduced venture capital expenditures. The recent financial crisis caused venture capital spending to drop to new lows. However, as the economy began to grow in 2011, venture capital again returned to the market.[36]

Comparing Debt and Equity Financing

Figure 18.6 compares debt and equity financing options. Raising funds through borrowing to increase the firm's rate of return is referred to as **leverage.** Though debt increases risk because it creates a financial obligation that must be repaid, it also enhances the firm's ability to increase profits. Recall that two key jobs of the financial manager or CFO are forecasting the firm's need for borrowed funds and planning how to manage these funds once they are obtained.

Firms are very concerned with the cost of capital. **Cost of capital** is the rate of return a company must earn in order to meet the demands of its lenders and expectations of its equity holders (stockholders or venture capitalists). If the firm's earnings are larger than the interest payments on borrowed funds, business owners can realize a higher rate of return than if they used equity financing. Figure 18.7 describes an example, again involving our vegetarian restaurant, Very Vegetarian (introduced in Chapter 13). If Very Vegetarian needed $200,000 in new financing, it could consider debt by selling bonds or equity through offering stock. Comparing the two options in this situation, you can see that Very Vegetarian would benefit by selling bonds since the company's earnings are greater than the interest paid on borrowed funds (bonds). However, if the firm's earnings were less than the interest paid on borrowed funds (bonds), Very Vegetarian could lose money. It's also important to remember that bonds, like all debt, have to be repaid at a specific time.

leverage
Raising needed funds through borrowing to increase a firm's rate of return.

cost of capital
The rate of return a company must earn in order to meet the demands of its lenders and expectations of its equity holders.

	Type of Financing	
CONDITIONS	**DEBT**	**EQUITY**
Management influence	There's usually none unless special conditions have been agreed on.	Common stockholders have voting rights.
Repayment	Debt has a maturity date. Principal must be repaid.	Stock has no maturity date. The company is never required to repay equity.
Yearly obligations	Payment of interest is a contractual obligation.	The firm isn't legally liable to pay dividends.
Tax benefits	Interest is tax-deductible.	Dividends are paid from after-tax income and aren't deductible.

figure 18.6

DIFFERENCES BETWEEN DEBT AND EQUITY FINANCING

figure 18.7

USING LEVERAGE (DEBT) VERSUS EQUITY FINANCING

Very Vegetarian wants to raise $200,000 in new capital. Compare the firm's debt and equity options.

ADDITIONAL DEBT		ADDITIONAL EQUITY	
Stockholders' equity	$500,000	Stockholders' equity	$500,000
Additional equity	—	Additional equity	$200,000
Total equity	$500,000	Total equity	$700,000
Bond @ 8% interest	200,000	Bond interest	—
Total shareholder equity	$700,000	Total shareholder equity	$700,000

YEAR-END EARNINGS			
Gross profit	$100,000	Gross profit	$100,000
Less bond interest	−16,000	Less interest	—
Operating profit	$ 84,000	Operating profit	$100,000
Return on equity	16.6%	Return on equity	14.2%
($84,000 ÷ $500,000 = 16.6%)		($100,000 ÷ $700,000 = 14.2%)	

Individual firms must determine exactly how to balance debt and equity financing by comparing the costs and benefits of each. Leverage ratios (discussed in Chapter 17) can also give companies an industry standard for this balance, to which they can compare themselves. Still debt varies considerably among major companies and industries. For example, automaker Ford Motor Company has almost $130 billion of debt on its balance sheet. This seems mild compared to General Electric, which has over $480 billion of debt on its balance sheet.[37] Leisure industry giants Sands and Trump Hotels and Casinos carry billions of dollars of debt to finance their hotels, condos, and golf courses. In contrast, tech leaders Apple and Microsoft have no long-term debt and both have had more than $50 billion in cash available at times. According to Standard & Poor's and Moody's Investors Service (firms that provide corporate and financial research), the debt of a large industrial corporation typically ranges between 33 and 40 percent of its total assets. The amount of small-business debt obviously varies considerably from firm to firm.

Lessons from the Financial Crisis

The financial crisis that started in 2008 caused financial markets to suffer their worst fall since the Great Depression of the 1920s and 1930s. The collapse of financial markets could be laid at the feet of financial managers for failing to do their job effectively. Poor investment decisions and risky financial dealings (especially in real estate) caused long-standing financial firms such as Lehman Brothers to close their doors.[38] The multibillion-dollar Ponzi scheme of once respected financial manager Bernie Madoff further caused the public's trust in financial managers to disappear.[39] Unfortunately, it also caused many investors' funds to disappear as well.

The financial meltdown of the late 2000s led the U.S. Congress to pass sweeping financial regulatory reform. The Dodd-Frank Wall Street Reform and Consumer Protection Act affects almost every aspect of the U.S. financial services industry.[40] As the government increases its involvement and intervention in financial markets, the requirements of financial institutions and financial managers have become more stringent. This means that the job of the financial manager promises to become even more challenging. The events in the late 2000s questioned the integrity and good judgment of financial managers much like events in the early 2000s questioned the integrity and judgment of the accounting industry (see Chapter 17). Without a doubt, financial managers have a long road back to earning the trust of the public.

Chapter 19 takes a close look at securities markets as a source of securing long-term financing for businesses and as a base for investment options for private investors. You will learn how securities exchanges work, how firms issue stocks and bonds, how to choose the right investment strategy, how to buy and sell stock, where to find up-to-date information about stocks and bonds, and more. Finance takes on a new dimension when you see how you can participate in financial markets yourself.

progress assessment

- What are the two major forms of debt financing available to a firm?
- How does debt financing differ from equity financing?
- What are the three major forms of equity financing available to a firm?
- What is leverage, and why do firms choose to use it?

summary

Learning Goal 1. Explain the role and responsibilities of financial managers.

- **What are the most common ways firms fail financially?**

The most common financial problems are (1) undercapitalization, (2) poor control over cash flow, and (3) inadequate expense control.

- **What do financial managers do?**

Financial managers plan, budget, control funds, obtain funds, collect funds, conduct audits, manage taxes, and advise top management on financial matters.

Learning Goal 2. Outline the financial planning process, and explain the three key budgets in the financial plan.

- **What are the three budgets in a financial plan?**

The capital budget is the spending plan for expensive assets such as property, plant, and equipment. The cash budget is the projected cash balance at the end of a given period. The operating (master) budget summarizes the information in the other two budgets. It projects dollar allocations to various costs and expenses given various revenues.

Learning Goal 3. Explain why firms need operating funds.

- **What are firms' major financial needs?**

Businesses need financing for four major tasks: (1) managing day-by-day operations, (2) controlling credit operations, (3) acquiring needed inventory, and (4) making capital expenditures.

- **What's the difference between debt financing and equity financing?**

Debt financing raises funds by borrowing. Equity financing raises funds from within the firm through investment of retained earnings, sale of stock to investors, or sale of part ownership to venture capitalists.

- **What's the difference between short-term and long-term financing?**

Short-term financing raises funds to be repaid in less than a year, whereas long-term financing raises funds to be repaid over a longer period.

Learning Goal 4. Identify and describe different sources of short-term financing.

- **Why should businesses use trade credit?**

Trade credit is the least expensive and most convenient form of short-term financing. Businesses can buy goods today and pay for them sometime in the future.

- **What is meant by a line of credit and a revolving credit agreement?**

A line of credit is an agreement by a bank to lend a specified amount of money to the business at any time, if the money is available. A revolving credit agreement is a line of credit that guarantees a loan will be available—for a fee.

- **What's the difference between a secured loan and an unsecured loan?**

An unsecured loan has no collateral backing it. Secured loans have collateral backed by assets such as accounts receivable, inventory, or other property of value.

- **Is factoring a form of secured loan?**

No, factoring means selling accounts receivable at a discounted rate to a factor (an intermediary that pays cash for those accounts and keeps the funds it collects on them).

- **What's commercial paper?**

Commercial paper is a corporation's unsecured promissory note maturing in 270 days or less.

Learning Goal 5. Identify and describe different sources of long-term financing.

- **What are the major sources of long-term financing?**

Debt financing is the sale of bonds to investors and long-term loans from banks and other financial institutions. Equity financing is obtained through the sale of company stock, from the firm's retained earnings, or from venture capital firms.

- **What are the two major forms of debt financing?**

Debt financing comes from two sources: selling bonds and borrowing from individuals, banks, and other financial institutions. Bonds can be secured by some form of collateral or unsecured. The same is true of loans.

- **What's leverage, and how do firms use it?**

Leverage is borrowing funds to invest in expansion, major asset purchases, or research and development. Firms measure the risk of borrowing against the potential for higher profits.

key terms

budget 532
capital budget 532
capital expenditures 536
cash budget 532
cash flow forecast 531
commercial finance
  companies 541
commercial paper 542
cost of capital 547
debt financing 537
equity financing 537
factoring 541
finance 528

financial control 533
financial
  management 528
financial managers 528
indenture terms 544
leverage 547
line of credit 540
long-term
  financing 537
long-term forecast 532
operating (or master)
  budget 532
promissory note 538

revolving credit
  agreement 540
risk/return trade-off 544
secured bond 545
secured loan 539
short-term financing 537
short-term forecast 541
term-loan
  agreement 543
trade credit 538
unsecured bond 545
unsecured loan 540
venture capital 546

critical thinking

1. What are the primary sources of short-term funds for new business owners? What are their sources of long-term funds?
2. Why does a finance manager need to understand accounting information if the firm has a trained accountant on its staff?
3. Why do firms generally prefer to borrow funds to obtain long-term financing rather than issue shares of stock?

developing workplace skills

1. Go to your college's website and see whether its operating budget is online. If not, go to the campus library and see whether the reference librarian has a copy of your college's operating budget for the current year. Try to identify major capital expenditures your college has planned for the future.

2. One of the most difficult concepts to get across to small-business owners is the need to take all the trade credit they can get. For example, the credit terms 2/10, net 30 can save businesses money if they pay their bills in the first 10 days. Work with a group of classmates to build a convincing argument for using trade credit.

3. Go online and check the capitalization required to open a franchise of your choice, like Subway or McDonald's. Does the franchisor offer financial assistance to prospective franchisees? Evaluate the cost of the franchise versus its business potential using the risk/return trade-off discussed in the chapter.

4. Contact a lending officer at a local bank in your community, or visit the bank's website, to check the bank's policies on providing a business a line of credit and a revolving line of credit. Evaluate the chances that this bank will give a small business either form of short-term loan.

5. Factoring accounts receivable is a form of financing used since the days of Babylonian King Hammurabi 4,000 years ago. Today it's still a source of short-term funds used by small businesses. Visit www.21stfinancialsolutions.com to get more in-depth information about factoring and be prepared to discuss the pros and cons of factoring.

taking it to the net

Purpose

To identify which types of companies qualify for financing through the Small Business Administration.

Exercise

Many small-business owners have a difficult time finding financing to start or expand their business. The Small Business Administration is one potential source of financing for many types of small businesses, but there are also some businesses that do not qualify for SBA loans. Go to **www.sba.gov/content/businesses -eligible-ineligible-sba-assistance** and see whether the following businesses are eligible to apply for SBA financing:

1. Growing Like a Weed is a lawn care business that needs funding to buy additional equipment in order to expand. Does it meet SBA criteria? Why or why not?

2. Glamour Galore is a cosmetic company that pays sales commissions based on a system that depends upon salespeople recruiting additional salespeople. It needs funding to build a marketing campaign. Does it meet SBA criteria? Why or why not?

3. Bells'n'Whistles is a pinball refurbishing company. Its founding partners need funding to buy inventory. Do they meet SBA criteria? Why or why not?

4. Lettuce Entertain You is a company needing funding to remodel an old warehouse to house its latest restaurant. Does it meet SBA criteria? Why or why not?

casing the web

To access the case "Surviving Financially in the Nonprofit World," visit **www.mhhe.com/P2P2e**

Starting Up: Tom and Eddie's

This video features the startup company called Tom and Eddie's, an upscale hamburger restaurant in the Chicago area. Started in 2009 at the height of the recession, the partners had a difficult time securing bank financing. As a result, they financed the operation themselves with the help of a third partner, Vince Nocarando. The partners both had long and successful careers as executives with McDonald's. Tom was Executive Vice President for New Locations and Eddie was the President and CEO of North American operations.

Both partners, as a result of their experience at McDonald's, are well suited for the restaurant business. One of the most challenging and important elements of a successful startup, like Tom and Eddie's, is a talented financial manager. Recognizing the importance of the financial function, they hired another former McDonald's executive, Brian Gordon, as CFO. Gordon explains that cash flow is the most important element in starting up a restaurant. In fact, cash flow is more important than profits in the first and perhaps second year of operation. Second to cash flow in terms of importance for sustainability is the management and control of inventory.

Cash flow is important, according to the CFO, because of the "known" costs, such as rent, payroll, inventory, taxes, and utilities. These are "known" costs because they are recurring and the relative costs are known on a weekly or monthly basis. CFO Gordon explains that cash flow is important in managing these known costs because of the significant "unknown" factor, which is sales.

Tom and Eddie's uses a very technology-intensive inventory management and control system because of the perishable nature of foodstuffs associated with the restaurant business. According to CFO Gordon, the restaurant has "net 14" terms with their food vendors. This means that the invoice is paid 14 days after the receipt of the goods. This is a form of financing, according to the CFO, that allows the company to turn that inventory once or twice during the 14-day period.

At the time of the video, Tom and Eddie's was in its fifteenth month of operation with three restaurants in the Chicago area. According to one of the partners, Eddie, the goal is to grow to 10 stores and then look at franchising the operation. When considering where to open a new operation, Eddie indicates that careful consideration is given to the demographics of the area, including the average income level of those working and living in the area to be served, the age of the population, the square footage of the surrounding commercial space, and ease of access to the location. Equipment is purchased rather than financed by the partners.

According to the partners, entrepreneurs think in terms of opportunities, not in terms of potential failure. With 15 months of successful operation, capital will be easier to raise from traditional sources of financing, such as banks, to expand the operation. Who knows, maybe a franchised Tom and Eddie's will be opening soon in a location near you.

Thinking It Over

1. *What are the three factors associated with operating funds, according to the video?*

2. *What is meant by the term "front of the house"?*

3. *Why, according to the video, was bank financing unavailable for Tom and Eddie's startup?*

19

Using Securities
MARKETS FOR Financing
& INVESTING
Opportunities

LEARNING goals

After you have read and studied this chapter, you should be able to

1. Describe the role of securities markets and of investment bankers.

2. Identify the stock exchanges where securities are traded.

3. Compare the advantages and disadvantages of equity financing by issuing stock, and detail the differences between common and preferred stock.

4. Compare the advantages and disadvantages of obtaining debt financing by issuing bonds, and identify the classes and features of bonds.

5. Explain how to invest in securities markets and set investment objectives such as long-term growth, income, cash, and protection from inflation.

6. Analyze the opportunities stocks offer as investments.

7. Analyze the opportunities bonds offer as investments.

8. Explain the investment opportunities in mutual funds and exchange-traded funds (ETFs).

9. Describe how indicators like the Dow Jones Industrial Average affect the market.

In some ways, investing has become almost too easy. Anybody with an e-mail address and a bank account can open an account with an online brokerage like E*Trade or Schwab and instantly start trading stocks from around the world. At the same time, though, the tangle of toxic investments that fueled the economic meltdown beginning in 2008 taught many investors just how complicated the financial world can be.

Many people, hoping to find ways to better understand investing, have turned to media such as CNBC to help guide them through the sea of easily available information. CNBC's multiple Emmy-Award-winning Maria Bartiromo's accessible analysis of the day-to-day intricacies of Wall Street has made her the face of investing for millions of Americans. A recent study of Bartiromo's CNBC peers, both men and women, found that many are inclined to stir up media stunts that cause investors to sell their stocks. Bartiromo, on the other hand, uses her well-earned "street cred" wisely and incites far fewer sells than her colleagues. And in a 24-hour news cycle that sometimes resembles a circus more than actual journalism, Bartiromo's integrity is all the more valuable.

Born and raised in Brooklyn, Bartiromo spent her youth working in the coat checkroom of her family's Italian restaurant. Eventually she made it to the kitchen, where she closely observed her father's dogged work ethic as head chef. "Every day, I witnessed my father dedicate himself and his life to his family," said Bartiromo. "He'd regularly work long hours, day after day and he never complained." After graduating from New York University, Bartiromo brought that same dedication to her work as an overnight producer at CNN. Although her responsibilities were limited strictly to behind the camera, she quietly began gathering taped segments of herself as anchor in her off-hours. None of these pieces ever made it to air, but they were promising enough to land her a job at CNBC.

After working for two years at the network, Bartiromo distinguished herself by becoming the first journalist to broadcast directly from the hectic floor of the New York Stock Exchange. By the late 1990s, she was a CNBC fixture, earning the nickname the "Money Honey." But Bartiromo is far more than a pretty face in an anchor's chair. Her dislike for sensationalism and her

CONNECTING WITH
X · Maria Bartiromo
of CNBC

candid interviews with everyone from former General Electric CEO Jack Welch to U2 lead singer Bono made her a top draw at the station. By the 2000s, she was lead anchor at two of the network's biggest shows, *Closing Bell* and *The Wall Street Journal Report with Maria Bartiromo.* The latter was recently rated the most watched financial news program in the country. She has written several books and numerous columns and articles in publications such as *BusinessWeek, Milano Finanza, Individual Investor, Ticker, Financial Times, Newsweek,* and the *New York Post.* In 2009, the *Financial Times* named her one of the "50 Who Shaped the Decade." In 2011 she was the first journalist to be inducted into the Cable Hall of Fame.

When the stock market tanked in 2008, Bartiromo provided frontline insight on the extent of the crisis. Her lengthy relationship with the NYSE gave her a unique perspective on events. Also, her years of experience helped translate the complicated technical language and concepts of the financial sector into more digestible terms. As she watched Wall Street collapse around her, Bartiromo felt saddened for her investment friends who were losing their jobs in droves. Still, she did not fail to recognize those unethical individuals who managed to profit from the crisis. "At the heart of everything on Wall Street has to be integrity," said Bartiromo. "I am outraged to see some of these executives walk away with giant pay packages . . . however, I also believe that an across-the-board, blanket statement that all business is 'bad' is just not true."

To be a successful investor, you need a little education. In this chapter you'll learn about the many ways that money can be invested in securities markets.

Sources: Lily Altavena, "Know Your Trustees: Maria Bartiromo," *NYU Local,* February 8, 2012; Kristina Peterson "CNBC CEO Chats Seldom Break News: Study," *The Wall Street Journal,* February 17, 2011; Michael Martin, "How Maria Bartiromo May Become the Best Teacher You've Ever Had," *The Huffington Post,* April 15, 2010; and "Maria Bartiromo" CNBC TV Profiles, http://www.cnbc.com/id/15838253, accessed May 2012.

LEARNING goal 1

Describe the role of securities markets and of investment bankers.

THE FUNCTION OF SECURITIES MARKETS

Securities markets—financial marketplaces for stocks, bonds, and other investments—serve two major functions. First, they assist businesses in finding long-term funding to finance capital needs, such as expanding operations, developing new products, or buying major goods and services. Second, they provide private investors a place to buy and sell securities (investments) such as stocks and bonds that can help them build their financial future. In this chapter, we look at securities markets first from the perspective of funding for businesses and second as markets for private investors to buy and trade investments.

Securities markets are divided into primary and secondary markets. *Primary markets* handle the sale of *new* securities. This is an important point to understand. Corporations make money on the sale of their securities (stock) only once—when they sell it on the primary market. The first public offering of a corporation's stock is called an **initial public offering (IPO).** After that, the *secondary market* handles the trading of these securities between investors, with the proceeds of the sale going to the investor selling the stock, not to the corporation whose stock is sold. For example, imagine your vegetarian restaurant, Very Vegetarian, has grown into a chain and your products are available in many retail stores throughout the country. You want to raise additional funds to expand further. If you offer 1 million shares of stock in your company at $10 a share, you can raise $10 million at this initial offering. However, after the initial sale, if Shareholder Jones decides to sell 100 shares of her Very Vegetarian stock to Investor Smith, Very Vegetarian collects nothing from that transaction. Smith buys the stock from Jones, not from Very Vegetarian. It is possible, however, for companies like Very Vegetarian to offer additional shares of stock for sale to raise additional capital.

As mentioned in Chapter 18, we can't overemphasize the importance of long-term funding to businesses. Given a choice, businesses normally prefer to meet their long-term financial needs by using retained earnings or borrowing funds either from a lending institution (bank, pension fund, insurance company) or corporate bond issue. However, if long-term funds are not available from retained earnings or lenders, a company may be able to raise capital by issuing corporate stock. (Recall from Chapter 18 that selling stock in the corporation is a form of *equity financing* and issuing corporate bonds is a form of *debt financing*.) Social networking giant Facebook's IPO in 2012 raised $16 billion for the company.[1] Visa, the world's largest processor of debit and credit cards, raised $18 billion from its IPO in 2008.[2] These sources of equity and bond financing are not available to all companies, especially small businesses.

Let's imagine you need further long-term financing to *expand* operations at Very Vegetarian. Your chief financial officer (CFO) says the company lacks sufficient retained earnings and she doesn't think it can secure the needed funds from a lending institution. She suggests that you offer shares of stock or issue corporate bonds to private investors to secure the funding. She warns, however, that issuing shares of stock or corporate bonds is not simple or automatic. To get approval for stock or bond issues you must make extensive financial disclosures and undergo detailed scrutiny by the U.S. Securities and Exchange Commission (SEC). Because of these requirements, your CFO recommends that the company turn to an investment banker for assistance. Let's see why.

initial public offering (IPO)
The first public offering of a corporation's stock.

The Role of Investment Bankers

Investment bankers are specialists who assist in the issue and sale of new securities. These large financial firms can help companies like Very Vegetarian prepare the extensive financial analyses necessary to gain SEC approval for bond or stock issues. Investment bankers can also *underwrite* new issues of stocks or bonds. That is, the investment banking firm buys the entire stock or bond issue at an agreed-on discount, which can be quite sizable, and then sells the issue to private or institutional investors at full price.[3]

Institutional investors are large organizations—such as pension funds, mutual funds, and insurance companies—that invest their own funds or the funds of others. Because of their vast buying power, institutional investors are a powerful force in securities markets.

Before we look at stocks and bonds as long-term financing and investment opportunities in more depth, it's important to understand stock exchanges—the places where stocks and bonds are traded.

investment bankers
Specialists who assist in the issue and sale of new securities.

institutional investors
Large organizations—such as pension funds, mutual funds, and insurance companies—that invest their own funds or the funds of others.

LEARNING **goal 2**

Identify the stock exchanges where securities are traded.

STOCK EXCHANGES

As the name implies, a **stock exchange** is an organization whose members can buy and sell (exchange) securities on behalf of companies and individual investors. The New York Stock Exchange (NYSE) was founded in 1792 and was primarily

stock exchange
An organization whose members can buy and sell (exchange) securities for companies and individual investors.

The NYSE Euronext was the largest floor-based exchange, where stock trades were made on the crowded floor of the exchange. Today stocks are bought and sold primarily on electronic networks. The illustration (on the right) of the exchange floor today seems deserted compared to the old days.

over-the-counter (OTC) market
Exchange that provides a means to trade stocks not listed on the national exchanges.

NASDAQ
A nationwide electronic system that links dealers across the nation so that they can buy and sell securities electronically.

a floor-based exchange, which means trades physically took place on the floor of the stock exchange. Things changed in 2005 when the NYSE merged with Archipelago, a securities trading company that specialized in electronic trades. Two years later, it merged with Europe's Euronext exchange, and became the NYSE Euronext. In 2011, the NYSE Euronext agreed to be acquired by Deutsche Börse AG of Germany in a deal valued at approximately $10 billion.[4]

Today, the floor of the NYSE Euronext is now largely symbolic.[5] Most trading takes place on computers that can transact thousands of stock trades within seconds.[6] In fact, trading stocks has become a very small part of the exchange's revenue. The bulk of the company's revenue comes from selling complex financial contracts and market information to companies like Yahoo and Google that offer stock quotes as a service on their websites.[7] They also earn revenue from fees paid by over 8,000 companies listed on the NYSE Euronext.[8]

Not all securities are traded on registered stock exchanges. The **over-the-counter (OTC) market** provides companies and investors with a means to trade stocks not listed on the large securities exchanges. The OTC market is a network of several thousand brokers who maintain contact with one another and buy and sell securities through a nationwide electronic system. Trading is conducted between two parties directly, instead of through an exchange like the NYSE Euronext.

The **NASDAQ** (originally known as the National Association of Securities Dealers Automated Quotations) was the world's first electronic stock market. It evolved from the OTC market but is no longer part of it. The NASDAQ is an electronic-based network that links dealers so they can buy and sell securities electronically rather than in person. In 2007, the NASDAQ purchased the Swedish OMX Group and is now the NASDAQ OMX Group.[9] It is the largest U.S. electronic stock trading market and has more trading volume than any electronic exchange in the world. The NASDAQ originally dealt mostly with smaller firms, but today well-known companies such as Microsoft, Intel, Google, Starbucks, Cisco, and Dell trade their stock on the NASDAQ. The NASDAQ also handles federal, state, and city government bonds and lists approximately 3,000 companies.

Adding a company to an exchange is a highly competitive undertaking, and the battle between the stock exchanges for a stock listing is often fierce.[10] If a company fails to meet the requirements of an exchange, the stock can be delisted from the exchange.[11] You can find the requirements for registering (listing) stocks on the NYSE Euronext and NASDAQ on their websites at www.nyse.com and www.nasdaq.com. The Connecting with Small Business box presents an interesting idea of adding a new exchange for smaller businesses to the securities landscape.

You Are Not Too Small to Trade

Since the beginning of the financial crisis in 2008, small businesses have found it difficult, if not impossible, to secure financing from banks. Even the old "air-ball loans" that banks would grant to businesses they had a personal relationship with disappeared. David Weild, former vice-chairman of NASDAQ, thinks he has a solution to this problem. He would like to see the creation of a new stock exchange where small companies can raise needed capital.

Weild's suggested exchange would move slower than the large exchanges that rely on electronic trading, and it would cost more to buy and sell a stock. It would also involve a larger role for stockbrokers, who would go back to the old days of calling clients about new companies they have discovered that offer investment potential. To lure stockbrokers into the exchange, he would consider setting minimum and maximum brokerage commissions to make their efforts worthwhile. He also feels the exchange would be a source for attracting venture capitalists.

While Weild's proposed exchange is a new idea in the United States, it's important to note that China established the ChiNext stock exchange that is designed for start-up companies. The ChiNext was created as part of the Shenzhen exchange with the purpose of making it easier for "strategically important emerging companies" to gain access to capital. Liu Zehui, executive director of Legend Capital, feels the ChiNext exchange is doing exactly what it's intended to do. "The ChiNext market has released the pent-up passion for innovation and entrepreneurship in China," he says. "It tells everyone that you don't have to have a powerful dad to get rich."

Sources: Kevin Hamlin, Eva Woo, Dexter Roberts, and Frances Liu, "In China, a Stock Market Where Start-Ups Thrive," *Bloomberg Businessweek*, November 28, 2010; Reinhardt Krause, "China, Emerging-Market Stocks Rising, but Experts Still Cautious," *Investor's Business Daily*, April 7, 2011; and Emily Lambert, "Trading Places," *Forbes*, April 11, 2011.

Securities Regulations and the Securities and Exchange Commission

The **Securities and Exchange Commission (SEC)** is the federal agency responsible for regulating the various stock exchanges. The Securities Act of 1933 helps protect investors by requiring full disclosure of financial information by firms selling bonds or stock. The U.S. Congress passed this legislation to deal with the free-for-all atmosphere that existed in the securities markets during the 1920s and the early 1930s that helped cause the Great Depression. The Securities and Exchange Act of 1934 created the SEC.

Companies trading on the national exchanges must register with the SEC and provide it with annual updates. The 1934 act also established specific guidelines that companies must follow when issuing financial securities such as stocks or bonds. For example, before issuing either stocks or bonds for sale to the public, a company must file a detailed registration statement with the SEC that includes extensive economic and financial information. The condensed version of that registration document—called a **prospectus**—must be sent to prospective investors.

Securities and Exchange Commission (SEC)
The federal agency that has responsibility for regulating the various stock exchanges.

prospectus
A condensed version of economic and financial information that a company must file with the SEC before issuing stock; the prospectus must be sent to prospective investors.

figure 19.1

IS IT INSIDER TRADING
OR NOT?

Insider trading involves buying or selling a stock on the basis of company information not available to the investing public. It's sometimes difficult to identify insider trading. The following hypothetical examples will give you an idea of what's legal and what's illegal. See how many of the questions you can answer. The answers are at the end of this box.

1. You work in research and development at a large company and have been involved in a major effort that should lead to a blockbuster new product coming to the market. News about the product is not public, and very few other workers even know about it. Can you purchase stock in the company?

2. Pertaining to the above situation, you are in a local coffee bar and mention to a friend about what's going on at the company. Another customer seated at an adjoining table overhears your discussion. Can this person legally buy stock in the company before the public announcement?

3. You work as an executive secretary at a major investment banking firm. You are asked to copy documents that detail a major merger about to happen that will keenly benefit the company being taken over. Can you buy stock in the company before the announcement is made public?

4. Your stockbroker recommends that you buy shares in a little-known company. The broker seems to have some inside information, but you don't ask any questions about his source. Can you buy stock in this company?

5. You work as a cleaning person at a major securities firm. At your job you come across information from the trash cans and computer printers of employees of the firm that provide detailed information about several upcoming deals the firm will be handling. Can you buy stock in the companies involved?

Answers: 1. No; 2. Yes; 3. No; 4. Yes; 5. No.

The 1934 act also established guidelines to prevent insiders within the company from taking advantage of privileged information they may have. *Insider trading* is using knowledge or information that individuals gain through their position that allows them to benefit unfairly from fluctuations in security prices. The key words here are *benefit unfairly*. Insiders within a firm are permitted to buy and sell stock in the company they work for, so long as they do not take unfair advantage of information unknown to the public.

Originally, the SEC defined the term *insider* rather narrowly as covering a company's directors and employees and their relatives. Today the term has been broadened to include just about anyone with securities information not available to the general public. Let's say the CFO of Very Vegetarian tells her next-door neighbor she is finalizing paperwork to sell the company to a large corporation, and the neighbor buys the stock based on this information. A court may well consider the purchase an insider trade. Penalties for insider trading can include fines or imprisonment. For example, billionaire hedge fund manager Raj Rajaratnam was convicted of insider trading in a high-profile case in 2011. Rajaratnam faces 11 years in prison along with fines and forfeitures of $156.6 million.[12] Look at Figure 19.1 and test your skill in identifying insider trading.

Foreign Stock Exchanges

Thanks to expanded communications and the relaxation of many legal barriers, investors can buy securities from companies almost anywhere in the world. If you uncover a foreign company you feel has great potential for growth, you can purchase shares of its stock with little difficulty from U.S. brokers who have access to foreign stock exchanges. Foreign investors can also invest in U.S. securities, and large foreign stock exchanges, like those in London and Tokyo, trade large amounts of U.S. securities daily. The number of U.S. companies listed on foreign stock exchanges is growing. In addition to the London and Tokyo exchanges, other major stock exchanges are located in Shanghai, Sydney, Hong Kong, São Paolo, and Toronto. There are stock exchanges in Africa as well.[13]

Raising long-term funds using equity financing by issuing stock is an option many companies pursue. After the Progress Assessment, let's look in more depth at how firms raise capital by issuing stock.

progress assessment

- What is the primary purpose of a securities exchange?
- What does NASDAQ stand for? How does this exchange work?

LEARNING goal 3

Compare the advantages and disadvantages of equity financing by issuing stock, and detail the differences between common and preferred stock.

HOW BUSINESSES RAISE CAPITAL BY SELLING STOCK

Stocks are shares of ownership in a company. A **stock certificate** represents stock ownership. It specifies the name of the company, the number of shares owned, and the type of stock it represents. Today, companies are not required to issue paper stock certificates to owners since stock is generally held electronically.

Stock certificates sometimes indicate a stock's *par value,* which is a dollar amount assigned to each share of stock by the corporation's charter. Today, since par values do not reflect the market value of the stock (what the stock is actually worth), most companies issue *no-par* stock. **Dividends** are part of a firm's profits that the firm may (but is not required to) distribute to stockholders as either cash payments or additional shares of stock. Dividends are declared by a corporation's board of directors and are generally paid quarterly.

Advantages and Disadvantages of Issuing Stock

Some advantages to a firm of issuing stock include:

- As owners of the business, stockholders never have to be repaid their investment.
- There's no legal obligation to pay dividends to stockholders; therefore, the firm can reinvest income (retained earnings) to finance future needs.
- Selling stock can improve the condition of a firm's balance sheet since issuing stock creates no debt. (A corporation may also buy back its stock to improve its balance sheet and make the company appear stronger financially.)

stocks
Shares of ownership in a company.

stock certificate
Evidence of stock ownership that specifies the name of the company, the number of shares it represents, and the type of stock being issued.

dividends
Part of a firm's profits that the firm may distribute to stockholders as either cash payments or additional shares of stock.

When LinkedIn issued its initial public offering (IPO), the company gained more than $4 billion from the sale. Can you see why issuing stock can be an appealing option for financing a company's growth?

common stock
The most basic form of ownership in a firm; it confers voting rights and the right to share in the firm's profits through dividends, if approved by the firm's board of directors.

Disadvantages of issuing stock include:

- As owners, stockholders (usually only common stockholders) have the right to vote for the company's board of directors. (Typically, one vote is granted for each share of stock.) Issuing new shares of stock can thus alter the control of the firm.

- Dividends are paid from profit after taxes and are not tax-deductible.

- The need to keep stockholders happy can affect managers' decisions.

Companies can issue two classes of stock: common and preferred. Let's see how these two forms of equity financing differ.

Issuing Shares of Common Stock

Common stock is the most basic form of ownership in a firm. In fact, if a company issues only one type of stock, by law it must be common stock. Holders of common stock have the right to (1) elect members of the company's board of directors and vote on important issues affecting the company and (2) share in the firm's profits through dividends, if approved by the firm's board of directors. Having voting rights in a corporation allows common stockholders to influence corporate policy because the board members they elect choose the firm's top management and make major policy decisions. Common stockholders also have a *preemptive right* to purchase new shares of common stock before anyone else. This allows common stockholders to maintain their proportional share of ownership in the company.

Issuing Shares of Preferred Stock

Owners of **preferred stock** are given preference in the payment of company dividends and must be paid their dividends in full before any common stock dividends can be distributed (hence the term *preferred*). They also have a prior claim on company assets if the firm is forced out of business and its assets sold.[14] Normally, however, preferred stockholders do not get voting rights in the firm.

Preferred stock may be issued with a par value that becomes the base for a fixed dividend the firm is willing to pay. For example, if a preferred stock's par value is $50 a share and its dividend rate is 4 percent, the dividend is $2 a share. An owner of 100 preferred shares receives a fixed yearly dividend of $200 if dividends are declared by the board of directors.

Preferred stock can have other special features that common stock doesn't have. For example it can be *callable,* which means preferred stockholders could be required to sell their shares back to the corporation. Preferred stock can also be converted to shares of common stock (but not the other way around), and it can be *cumulative.* That is, if one or more dividends are not paid when promised, they accumulate and the corporation must pay them in full at a later date before it can distribute any common stock dividends.

Companies often prefer to raise capital by debt financing. One debt funding option frequently used by larger firms is issuing corporate bonds. Let's look at what's involved with issuing corporate bonds and how they differ from issuing stock.

progress assessment

- Name at least two advantages and two disadvantages of a company's issuing stock as a form of equity financing.
- What are the major differences between common stock and preferred stock?

preferred stock
Stock that gives its owners preference in the payment of dividends and an earlier claim on assets than common stockholders if the company is forced out of business and its assets sold.

LEARNING goal 4

Compare the advantages and disadvantages of obtaining debt financing by issuing bonds, and identify the classes and features of bonds.

HOW BUSINESSES RAISE CAPITAL BY ISSUING BONDS

A **bond** is a corporate certificate indicating that an investor has lent money to a firm (or a government). An organization that issues bonds has a legal obligation to make regular interest payments to investors and to repay the entire bond principal amount at a prescribed time.[15] Let's further explore the language of bonds so you understand exactly how they work.

bond
A corporate certificate indicating that a person has lent money to a firm (or a government).

Learning the Language of Bonds

Corporate bonds are usually issued in units of $1,000 (government bonds can be in much larger amounts). The *principal* is the face value (dollar value) of a bond, which the issuing company is legally bound to repay in full to the bondholder on the **maturity date. Interest** is the payment the bond issuer makes to the bondholders to compensate them for the use of their money. If Very Vegetarian issues a $1,000 bond with an interest rate of 5 percent and a maturity date of 2022, it is agreeing to pay the bondholder a total of $50 interest each year until a specified date in 2022, when it must repay the full $1,000. Maturity dates can vary. Firms such as Disney, IBM, and Coca-Cola have issued bonds with 100-year maturity dates.[16]

Bond interest is sometimes called the *coupon rate,* a term that dates back to when bonds were issued as *bearer* bonds. The holder, or bearer, was considered the bond's owner. Back then, the company issuing the bond kept no record of changes in ownership. Bond interest was paid to whoever clipped coupons attached to the bond and sent them to the issuing company for payment. Today, bonds are registered to specific owners and changes in ownership are recorded electronically.

The interest rate paid by U.S. government bonds influences the bond interest rate businesses must pay. U.S. government bonds are considered safe investments, so they can pay lower interest. Figure 19.2 describes several types of government bonds that compete with U.S. corporate bonds in securities markets. Bond interest rates also vary according to the state of the economy, the reputation of the issuing company, and the interest rate for bonds of similar companies. Though bond interest is quoted for an entire year, it is usually paid in two installments, and the rate generally cannot be changed.

maturity date
The exact date the issuer of a bond must pay the principal to the bondholder.

interest
The payment the issuer of the bond makes to the bondholders for use of the borrowed money.

BOND	DESCRIPTION
U.S. government bond	Issued by the federal government; considered the safest type of bond investment
Treasury bill (T-bill)	Matures in less than a year; issued with a minimum denomination of $1,000
Treasury note	Matures in 10 years or less; sold in denominations of $1,000 and $5,000
Treasury bond	Matures in 25 years or more; sold in denominations of $1,000 and $5,000
Municipal bond	Issued by states, cities, counties, and other state and local government agencies; usually exempt from federal taxes
Yankee bond	Issued by a foreign government; payable in U.S. dollars

Bond rating organizations assess the creditworthiness of a corporation's bond issues. Independent rating firms such as Standard & Poor's, Moody's Investors Service, and Fitch Ratings rate bonds according to their degree of risk. Bonds can range from the highest quality to junk bonds (which we discuss later in this chapter).[17] Figure 19.3 gives an example of the range of bond ratings.

Advantages and Disadvantages of Issuing Bonds

Bonds offer long-term financing advantages to an organization:

- Bondholders are creditors of the firm, not owners. They seldom vote on corporate matters; thus, management maintains control over the firm's operations.

- Bond interest is a business expense and tax-deductible to the firm (see Chapter 17).

- Bonds are a temporary source of funding. They're eventually repaid and the debt obligation is eliminated.

- Bonds can be repaid before the maturity date if they contain a *call provision.* They can also be converted to common stock. (We discuss both features below.)

Bonds also have drawbacks:

- Bonds increase debt (long-term liabilities) and may adversely affect the market's perception of the firm.

- Paying interest on bonds is a legal obligation. If interest is not paid, bondholders can take legal action to force payment.

- The face value of the bond must be repaid on the maturity date. Without careful planning, this obligation can cause cash flow problems when the repayment comes due.

debenture bonds
Bonds that are unsecured
(i.e., not backed by
any collateral such as
equipment).

Different Classes of Bonds

Corporations can issue two different classes of corporate bonds. *Unsecured bonds,* usually called **debenture bonds,** are not backed by any specific collateral (such as land or equipment). Only firms with excellent reputations and credit ratings can

| BOND RATING AGENCIES | | | |
MOODY'S	STANDARD & POOR'S	FITCH RATINGS	DESCRIPTIONS
Aaa	AAA	AAA	Highest quality (lowest default risk)
Aa	AA	AA	High quality
A	A	A	Upper medium grade
Baa	BBB	BBB	Medium grade
Ba	BB	BB	Lower medium grade
B	B	B	Speculative
Caa	CCC, CC	CCC	Poor (high default risk)
Ca	C	DDD	Highly speculative
C	D	D	Lowest grade

figure 19.3

BOND RATINGS: MOODY'S INVESTORS SERVICE, STANDARD & POOR'S INVESTOR SERVICE, AND FITCH RATINGS

issue debenture bonds, due to the lack of security they provide investors. *Secured bonds,* sometimes called mortgage bonds, are backed by collateral such as land or buildings that is pledged to bondholders if interest or principal isn't paid when promised. A corporate bond issuer can choose to include different bond features. Let's look at some special features.

Special Bond Features

By now you should understand that bonds are issued with an interest rate, are unsecured or secured by some type of collateral, and must be repaid at their maturity date. This repayment requirement often leads companies to establish a reserve account called a **sinking fund.** Its primary purpose is to ensure that enough money will be available to repay bondholders on the bond's maturity date. Firms issuing sinking-fund bonds periodically *retire* (set aside) some part of the principal prior to maturity so that enough funds will accumulate by the maturity date to pay off the bond. Sinking funds are generally attractive to both issuing firms and investors for several reasons:

sinking fund
A reserve account in which the issuer of a bond periodically retires some part of the bond principal prior to maturity so that enough capital will be accumulated by the maturity date to pay off the bond.

- They provide for an orderly retirement (repayment) of a bond issue.
- They reduce the risk the bond will not be repaid.
- They support the market price of the bond because they reduce the risk the bond will not be repaid.

A *callable bond* permits the bond issuer to pay off the principal before its maturity date. This gives companies some discretion in their long-term forecasting. Suppose Very Vegetarian issued $10 million in 20-year bonds at 10 percent interest. Its yearly interest expense is $1 million ($10 million times 10 percent). If market conditions change and bonds of the same quality now pay only 7 percent, Very Vegetarian will be paying 3 percent, or $300,000 ($10 million times 3 percent), in excess interest yearly. The company could benefit by calling in (paying off) the old bonds and issuing new bonds at the lower rate. If a company calls a bond before maturity, it often pays investors a price above the bond's face value.

Investors can convert *convertible bonds* into shares of common stock in the issuing company.[18] This can be an incentive for an investor because common stock value tends to grow faster than a bond. Therefore, if the value of the firm's common stock grows sizably over time, bondholders can compare the value of continued bond interest earned with the potential profit of a specified number of shares of common stock.[19]

Now that you understand the advantages and disadvantages of stocks and bonds as a financing tool from a company's perspective, let's explore the opportunities stocks and bonds provide for *investors*. First, though, let's check your progress.

progress assessment

- Why are bonds considered a form of debt financing?
- What does it mean if a firm issues a 9 percent debenture bond due in 2025?
- Explain the difference between an unsecured and a secured bond.
- Why are convertible bonds attractive to investors?

LEARNING goal 5

Explain how to invest in securities markets and set investment objectives such as long-term growth, income, cash, and protection from inflation.

stockbroker
A registered representative who works as a market intermediary to buy and sell securities for clients.

HOW INVESTORS BUY SECURITIES

Investing in stocks and bonds is not difficult. First, you decide what stock or bond you want to buy. After that, you find a brokerage firm authorized to trade securities to execute your order. A **stockbroker** is a registered representative who works for a brokerage firm as a market intermediary to buy and sell securities for clients. Stockbrokers place an order and negotiate a price. After the transaction is completed, the trade is reported to your broker, who notifies you. Today, large brokerage firms maintain automated order systems that allow brokers to enter your order the instant you make it. The order can be confirmed in seconds.

A stockbroker can also be a source of information about what stocks or bonds would best meet your financial objectives, but it's still important to learn about stocks and bonds on your own.[20] Investment analysts' advice may not always meet your specific expectations and needs.

*Online brokers like Scottrade and E*Trade specialize in providing information for investors. What are some of the features of this website that are designed to provide investment information?*

Investing through Online Brokers

Today, investors can choose from multiple online trading services to buy and sell stocks and bonds. Ameritrade, E*Trade, Scottrade, and Fidelity are among the leaders.[21] Investors who trade online are willing to do their own research and make investment decisions without the direct assistance of a broker. This allows online brokers the ability to charge much lower trading fees than traditional stockbrokers. The leading online services do provide important market information, such as company financial data, price histories of a stock, and analysts' reports. Often the level of information services you receive depends on the size of your account and your level of trading.

Money Going Up in Smoke

You recently received news that your Uncle Alex passed away after a long battle with lung cancer. To your surprise, he left you $25,000 in his will, saying you were his favorite nephew. You remember your uncle as a hardworking man who loved baseball and liked nothing better than to watch you pitch for your college team. Unfortunately, your uncle started smoking as a young man and eventually became a heavy chain-smoker. His doctors said that smoking was the primary cause of his lung cancer.

After receiving the inheritance, you wonder where to invest the money. Your old teammate Jack, who is now a financial advisor, recommends that you buy stock in a well-known multinational firm that offers a good dividend and has solid growth potential. He tells you the firm's primary product is tobacco, but assures you it produces many other products as well. You know Jack has your best interests at heart. You also believe Uncle Alex would like to see the money he left you grow. However, you wonder if a company that markets tobacco is an appropriate place to invest your inheritance. What are the ethical alternatives in this situation? What are the consequences of the alternatives? What will you do?

Whether you decide to use an online broker or to invest through a traditional stockbroker, remember that investing means committing your money with the hope of making a profit. The dot-com bubble in the early 2000s and the financial crisis beginning in 2008 proved again that investing is a risky business. Therefore, the first step in any investment program is to analyze your level of risk tolerance. Other factors to consider include your desired income, cash requirements, and need to hedge against inflation, along with the investment's growth prospects. The Making Ethical Decisions box describes an interesting stock investment decision.

You are never too young or too old to invest, but you should first ask questions and consider investment alternatives. Let's take a look at several strategies.

Choosing the Right Investment Strategy

Investment objectives change over the course of a person's life. A young person can better afford to invest in high-risk investment options such as stocks than a person nearing retirement. Younger investors generally look for significant growth in the value of their investments over time. If stocks go into a tailspin and decrease in value, as they did in 2008, a younger person has time to wait for stock values to rise again. Older people, perhaps on a fixed income, lack the luxury of waiting and may be more inclined to invest in bonds that offer a steady return as a protection against inflation.

Consider five key criteria when selecting investment options:

1. *Investment risk.* The chance that an investment will be worth less at some future time than it's worth now.
2. *Yield.* The expected return on an investment, such as interest or dividends, usually over a period of one year.
3. *Duration.* The length of time your money is committed to an investment.

CONNECTING ACROSS
borders

www.schwab.com

Investment Opportunities Home and Away

Reading about the ups and downs of U.S. stocks may frighten you out of even thinking about investing in global stocks. Add in the news about unstable governments under attack in Middle East countries, European debt problems, and natural disasters in Japan and Indonesia and the thought of investing in global stocks may seem even less attractive. Recalling the risk/return trade-off, your inclination may be to forget about global stocks and stick with safe U.S. securities like IBM, Apple, and Procter and Gamble. Financial analysts disagree and argue that investing in some global stocks can be a good idea.

Consider some statistics that support their suggestion. The growth rate in the United States from 2002 to 2010 was 37 percent. This pales compared with the growth rate in the BRIC (Brazil, Russia, India, and China) nations (see Chapter 3). China experienced growth of 628 percent, Brazil 1,171 percent, India 1,229 percent, and Russia 1,512 percent. The risk/return trade-off still applies, but given the potential returns, we would be remiss to not at least explore the opportunities that exist in global markets. The following suggestions may help build your financial future:

- Invest in global companies you are familiar with and that have a solid record of performance. Names like Honda (Japan), Shell Oil (Netherlands), Nestlé (Switzerland), Samsung (South Korea), and Siemens (Germany) come to mind.

- Invest in global stocks listed on U.S. stock exchanges since they must comply with U.S. accounting standards and rules of the Securities and Exchange Commission.

- Contact U.S. brokers about American depository receipts (ADRs) that you can purchase that represent a set number of shares in a foreign company that are held on deposit at a foreign branch of a U.S. bank.

- Countless mutual and exchange-traded funds offer a bevy of global opportunities that focus on countries such as China and Brazil or entire regions such as Africa, Asia, Europe, or Latin America.

- Use extreme caution or completely avoid investing in stocks from countries that have a history of currency problems or political instability.

Keep your long-term financial goals in mind when considering any investments, and stay abreast of the news daily, especially when risking your capital in global markets.

Sources: "Global Stock Markets," *Charles Schwab On Investing,* Spring 2011; Anna Prior, "Investing in Smaller Emerging Markets," *Smart Money,* April 4, 2011; Jason Raznick, "Dividends, Emerging Markets . . . Oh My," *Forbes,* May 9, 2011; and Andrew Tanzer, "The World's Best Stocks," *Kiplinger's Personal Finance,* February 2011.

4. *Liquidity.* How quickly you can get back your invested funds in cash if you want or need them.

5. *Tax consequences.* How the investment will affect your tax situation.

What's important in any investment strategy is the risk/return trade-off. Setting investment objectives such as *growth* (choosing stocks you believe will increase in price) or *income* (choosing bonds that pay consistent interest) should set the tone for your investment strategy.

diversification
Buying several different investment alternatives to spread the risk of investing.

Reducing Risk by Diversifying Investments

Diversification involves buying several different types of investments to spread the risk of investing. An investor may put 25 percent of his or her money into U.S. stocks that have relatively high risk but strong growth potential, another 25 percent in conservative government bonds, 25 percent in dividend-paying stocks that provide income, 10 percent in an international mutual fund (discussed later), and the rest in the bank for emergencies and other possible investment opportunities. By diversifying with such a *portfolio strategy* or *allocation model,* investors decrease the chance of losing everything they have invested.[22]

Both stockbrokers and certified financial planners (CFPs) are trained to give advice about the investment portfolio that would best fit each client's financial objectives. However, the more investors themselves read and study the market, the higher their potential for gain.[23] A short course in investments can also be useful. Stocks and bonds are investment opportunities individuals can use to enhance their financial future. The Connecting Across Borders box discusses growing opportunities investors can find in global stocks. Before we look at stocks and bonds in depth, let's check your understanding with the Progress Assessment.

Securities markets are like financial supermarkets—there are lots of investment options to choose from. That's why it's important to determine what investment strategy is right for you. Watching investment programs like CNBC's Mad Money with Jim Cramer could be a good starting point. How do you think your investment objectives will change over your lifetime?

progress assessment

- What is the key advantage of investing through online brokers? What is the key disadvantage?
- What is the primary purpose of diversifying investments?

LEARNING goal 6

Analyze the opportunities stocks offer as investments.

INVESTING IN STOCKS

Buying stock makes investors part owners of a company. This means that as stockholders they can participate in its success. Unfortunately, they can also lose money if a company does not do well or the overall stock market declines. The stock market fall beginning in 2008 was proof of that.

Stock investors are often called bulls or bears according to their perceptions of the market. *Bulls* believe that stock prices are going to rise; they buy stock in anticipation of the increase. A bull market is when overall stock prices are rising. *Bears* expect stock prices to decline and sell their stocks in anticipation of falling prices. That's why when stock prices are declining steadily, the market is called a bear market.

The market price and growth potential of most stock depends heavily on how well the corporation is meeting its business objectives. A company that achieves its objectives offers great potential for **capital gains,** the positive difference between the price at which you bought a stock and what you sell it for.[24] For example, an investment of $2,250 in 100 shares of McDonald's when the company first offered

capital gains
The positive difference between the purchase price of a stock and its sale price.

stock splits
An action by a company that gives stockholders two or more shares of stock for each one they own.

If you stroll through Times Square in New York City, you never have to wonder how stocks on the NASDAQ exchange are performing. The NASDAQ price wall continuously updates prices and the number of shares being traded. Originally, the NASDAQ dealt primarily with small companies; today, it competes with the NYSE Euronext for new stock listings.

its stock to the public in 1965 would have grown to 74,360 shares (after the company's 12 stock splits) worth approximately $5.7 million as of year-end market close on December 31, 2010.[25] Now that's a lot of Big Macs!

Investors often select stocks depending on their investment strategy. Stocks issued by higher-quality companies such as Coca-Cola, Johnson & Johnson, and Procter & Gamble are referred to as *blue-chip stocks* (a term derived from poker where the highest value chip was the blue chip). These stocks generally pay regular dividends and experience consistent price appreciation.

Stocks of corporations in emerging fields such as technology, biotechnology, or Internet-related firms, whose earnings are expected to grow at a faster rate than other stocks, are referred to as *growth stocks*. While riskier, growth stocks offer the potential for higher returns. Stocks of public utilities are considered *income stocks* because they usually offer investors a high dividend yield that generally keeps pace with inflation. There are even *penny stocks*, representing ownership in companies that compete in high-risk industries like oil exploration. Penny stocks sell for less than $2 (some analysts say less than $5) and are considered risky investments.

When purchasing stock, investors have choices when placing buy orders. A *market order* tells a broker to buy or sell a stock immediately at the best price available. A *limit order* tells the broker to buy or sell a stock at a specific price, if that price becomes available. Let's say a stock is selling for $40 a share. You believe the price will eventually go higher but could drop to $36 first. You can place a limit order at $36, so your broker will buy the stock at $36 if it drops to that price. If the stock never falls to $36, the broker will not purchase it for you.

Stock Splits

Brokers prefer stock purchases in *round lots* of 100 shares at a time. Investors, however, often cannot afford to buy 100 shares, which may sell for as much as $100 each, and therefore often buy in *odd lots*, or fewer than 100 shares at a time. High per-share prices can induce companies to declare **stock splits,** in which they issue two or more shares for every one that's outstanding. If Very Vegetarian stock were selling for $100 a share, the firm could declare a two-for-one stock split. Investors who owned one share of Very Vegetarian would now own two, each worth only $50 (half as much as before the split).

Stock splits cause no change in the firm's ownership structure and no immediate change in the investment's value. Investors generally approve of stock splits, however, because demand for a stock may be greater at $50 than at $100, and the price may then go up in the near future. A company cannot be forced to split its stock, and today stock splits are becoming less common.[26] Legendary American investor Warren Buffett's firm, Berkshire Hathaway, has never split its Class A stock even when its per-share price surpassed $150,000.[27]

Buying Stock on Margin

Buying stock on margin means borrowing some of the stocks' purchase cost from the brokerage firm. The margin is the portion of the stocks' purchase price that investors must pay with their own money. The board of governors of the Federal Reserve System sets *margin rates* in the U.S. market. Briefly, if the margin rate is 50 percent, an investor who qualifies for a margin account may borrow up to 50 percent of the stock's purchase price from the broker.

Although buying on margin sounds like an easy way to buy more stocks, the downside is that investors must repay the credit extended by the broker, plus interest. If the investor's account goes down in value, the broker may issue a *margin call,* requiring the investor to come up with funds to cover the losses the account has suffered.[28] If the investor is unable to fulfill the margin call, the broker can legally sell off shares of the investor's stock to reduce the broker's chance of loss. Margin calls can force an investor to repay a significant portion of his or her account's loss within days or even hours. Buying on margin is thus a risky way to invest in stocks.

> **buying stock on margin**
> Purchasing stocks by borrowing some of the purchase cost from the brokerage firm.

Understanding Stock Quotations

Publications like *The Wall Street Journal, Barron's,* and *Investor's Business Daily* carry a wealth of information concerning stocks and other investments. Your local newspaper may carry similar information as well. Financial websites like MSN Money, Yahoo! Finance, and CNBC carry up-to-the-minute information about companies that is much more detailed and only a click away. Take a look at Figure 19.4 to see an example of a stock quote from MSN Money for Microsoft. Microsoft trades on the NASDAQ exchange under the symbol MSFT. Preferred stock is identified by the letters *pf* following the company symbol. Remember, corporations can have several different preferred stock issues.

The information provided in the quote is easy to understand. It includes the highest and lowest price the stock traded for that day, the stock's high and low over the past 52 weeks, the dividend paid (if any), the stock's dividend yield (annual dividend as a percentage of the stock's price per share), important ratios like the price/earnings (P/E) ratio (the price of the stock divided by the firm's per-share earnings), and the return on equity. Investors can also see the number of shares outstanding and the total market capitalization of the firm. More technical features, such as the stock's beta (which measures the degree of the stock's risk), may also appear. Figure 19.4 illustrates the stock's intraday trading (trading throughout

figure 19.4

UNDERSTANDING STOCK QUOTATIONS

the current day), but you can also click to see charts for different time periods. Similar information about bonds, mutual funds, and other investments is also available online.

You might want to follow the market behavior of specific stocks that catch your interest, even if you lack the money to invest in them. Many successful investors started in college by building hypothetical portfolios of stocks and tracking their performance. The more you know about investing before you actually risk your money, the better. (The Developing Workplace Skills and Taking It to the Net exercises at the end of this chapter have exercises you can use for practice.)

LEARNING goal 7

Analyze the opportunities bonds offer as investments.

INVESTING IN BONDS

Investors looking for guaranteed income and limited risk often turn to U.S. government bonds for a secure investment. These bonds have the financial backing and full faith and credit of the federal government. Municipal bonds are offered by local governments and often have advantages such as tax-free interest.[29] Some may even be insured. Corporate bonds are a bit more risky and challenging.

First-time corporate bond investors often ask two questions. The first is, "If I purchase a corporate bond, do I have to hold it until the maturity date?" No, you do not. Bonds are bought and sold daily on major securities exchanges (the secondary market we discussed earlier). However, if you decide to sell your bond to another investor before its maturity date, you may not get its face value (usually $1,000). If your bond does not have features that make it attractive to other investors, like a high interest rate or early maturity, you may have to sell at a *discount*, that is, a price less than the bond's face value. But if other investors do highly value it, you may be able to sell your bond at a *premium*, a price above its face value. Bond prices generally fluctuate inversely with current market interest rates. This means *as interest rates go up, bond prices fall, and vice versa.* Like all investments, however, bonds have a degree of risk.

The second question is, "How can I evaluate the investment risk of a particular bond issue?" Standard & Poor's, Moody's Investors Service, and Fitch Ratings rate the risk of many corporate and government bonds (look back at Figure 19.3). In evaluating the ratings, recall the risk/return trade-off: The higher the risk of a bond, the higher the interest rate the issuer must offer. Investors will invest in a bond considered risky only if the potential return (interest) is high enough. In fact, some will invest in bonds considered junk.

Investing in High-Risk (Junk) Bonds

junk bonds
High-risk, high-interest bonds.

Although bonds are considered relatively safe investments, some investors look for higher returns through riskier bonds called **junk bonds.** Standard & Poor's, Moody's Investors Service, and Fitch Ratings define junk bonds as those with high risk *and* high default rates. Junk bonds pay investors interest as long as the value of the company's assets remains high and its cash flow stays strong.[30] Although

GOLDMAN SACHS GROUP INC

OVERVIEW	
Price:	104.32
Coupon (%):	7.350
Maturity Date:	1-Oct-2012
Yield to Maturity (%):	-3.289
Current Yield (%):	7.045
Fitch Ratings:	A
Coupon Payment Frequency:	Semi-Annual
First Coupon Date:	1-Apr-2000
Type:	Corporate
Callable:	No

figure 19.5

UNDERSTANDING BOND
QUOTATIONS

the interest rates are attractive and often tempting, if the company can't pay off the bond, the investor is left with an investment that isn't worth more than the paper it's written on—in other words, junk.

Understanding Bond Quotations

Bond prices are quoted as a percentage of $1,000, and their interest rate is often followed by an *s* for easier pronunciation. For example, 9 percent bonds due in 2022 are called 9s of 22. Figure 19.5 is an example of a bond quote for Goldman Sachs from Yahoo! Finance. The quote highlights the bond's interest rate (coupon rate), maturity date, rating, current price, and whether it's callable. The more you know about bonds, the better prepared you will be to discuss your financial objectives with investment advisors and brokers and be sure their advice is consistent with your best interests and objectives.

LEARNING goal 8

Explain the investment opportunities in mutual funds and exchange-traded funds (ETFs).

INVESTING IN MUTUAL FUNDS AND EXCHANGE-TRADED FUNDS

A **mutual fund** buys stocks, bonds, and other investments and then sells shares in those securities to the public. A mutual fund is like an investment company that pools investors' money and then buys stocks or bonds (for example) in many companies in accordance with the fund's specific purpose.[31] Mutual fund managers are specialists who pick what they consider to be the best stocks and bonds available and help investors diversify their investments.

Mutual funds range from very conservative funds that invest only in government securities to others that specialize in emerging biotechnology firms, Internet companies, foreign companies, precious metals, and other investments with greater risk. Some funds will have a mix of investments like stocks and bonds. The number of mutual funds available today is staggering. For example, there were 4,613 stock mutual funds investing in U.S. stocks in 2012.[32] Investors have invested over $12 trillion in mutual funds. Figure 19.6 gives you a list of some mutual fund investment options.

mutual fund
An organization that buys stocks and bonds and then sells shares in those securities to the public.

figure 19.6

MUTUAL FUND OBJECTIVES

Mutual funds have a wide array of investment categories. They range from low-risk, conservative funds to others that invest in high-risk industries. Listed here are abbreviations of funds and what these abbreviations stand for.

AB	Investment-grade corporate bonds	MP	Stock and bond fund
AU	Gold oriented	MT	Mortgage securities
BL	Balanced	MV	Mid-cap value
EI	Equity income	NM	Insured municipal bonds
EM	Emerging markets	NR	Natural resources
EU	European region	PR	Pacific region
GL	Global	SB	Short-term corporate bonds
GM	General municipal bond	SC	Small-cap core
GT	General taxable bonds	SE	Sector funds
HB	Health/biotech	SG	Small-cap growth
HC	High-yield bonds	SM	Short-term municipal bonds
HM	High-yield municipal bonds	SP	S&P 500
IB	Intermediate-term corporate bonds	SQ	Specialty
IG	Intermediate-term government bonds	SS	Single-state municipal bonds
IL	International	SU	Short-term government bonds
IM	Intermediate-term municipal bonds	SV	Small-cap value
LC	Large-cap core	TK	Science & technology
LG	Large-cap growth	UN	Unassigned
LT	Latin America	UT	Utility
LU	Long-term U.S. bonds	WB	World bonds
LV	Large-cap value	XC	Multi-cap core
MC	Mid-cap core	XG	Multi-cap growth
MG	Mid-cap growth	XV	Multi-cap value

Sources: *The Wall Street Journal* and *Investor's Business Daily.*

Young or new investors are often advised to buy shares in *index funds* that invest in a certain kind of stocks or bonds or in the market as a whole. An index fund may focus on large companies, small companies, emerging countries, or real estate (real estate investment trusts, or REITs). One way to diversify your investments is by investing in a variety of index funds. A stockbroker, certified financial planner (CFP), or banker can help you find the option that best fits your investment objectives. The *Morningstar Investor* newsletter is an excellent resource for evaluating mutual funds, as are business publications such as *Bloomberg Businessweek, The Wall Street Journal, Money, Forbes, Investor's Business Daily,* and many others.

With mutual funds it's simple to change your investment objectives if your financial objectives change. For example, moving your money from a bond fund to a stock fund is no more difficult than making a phone call or clicking a mouse. Another advantage of mutual funds is that you can generally buy directly from the fund and avoid broker fees or commissions. However, check for fees and charges of the mutual fund because they can differ significantly. A *load fund,* for example, charges investors a commission to buy or sell its shares; a *no-load fund* charges no commission.[33]

exchange-traded funds (ETFs)
Collections of stocks, bonds, and other investments that are traded on exchanges but are traded more like individual stocks than like mutual funds.

It's important to check the long-term performance of the fund's managers; the more consistent the performance of the fund's management, the better.[34] Mutual funds called *open-end funds* will accept the investments of any interested investors. *Closed-end funds,* however, limit the number of shares; once the fund reaches its target number, no new investors can buy into the fund.

Exchange-traded funds (ETFs) resemble both stocks and mutual funds. They are collections of stocks, bonds, and other investments that are traded on securities exchanges but are traded more like individual stocks than like mutual funds.

Mutual funds, for example, permit investors to buy and sell shares only at the close of the trading day. ETFs can be purchased or sold at any time during the trading day just like individual stocks.

The key points to remember about mutual funds and ETFs is that they offer small investors a way to spread the risk of stock and bond ownership and have their investments managed by a financial specialist for a fee. Financial advisors put mutual funds and ETFs high on the list of recommended investments, particularly for small or first-time investors.[35]

Understanding Mutual Fund Quotations

You can investigate the specifics of various mutual funds by contacting a broker or contacting the fund directly by phone or through its website. Business publications and online sources also provide information about mutual funds.

Look at the example of the T. Rowe Price Blue Chip Growth fund from Yahoo! Finance in Figure 19.7. The fund's name is listed in large letters. The net asset value (NAV) is the price per share of the mutual fund. The NAV is calculated by dividing the market value of the mutual fund's portfolio by the number of shares it has outstanding. The chart also shows the fund's year-to-date (YTD) return, the change in the NAV from the previous day's trading, and the fund's net assets.

Figure 19.8 evaluates bonds, stocks, mutual funds, and ETFs according to risk, income, and possible investment growth (capital gain).

figure 19.7
UNDERSTANDING MUTUAL FUND QUOTATIONS

figure 19.8
COMPARING INVESTMENTS

Investment	Degree of risk	Expected income	Possible growth (capital gain)
Bonds	Low	Secure	Little
Preferred stock	Medium	Steady	Little
Common stock	High	Variable	Good
Mutual funds	Medium	Variable	Good
ETFs	Medium	Variable	Good

- What is a stock split? Why do companies sometimes split their stock?
- What does buying stock on margin mean?
- What are mutual funds and ETFs?
- What is the key benefit to investors in investing in a mutual fund or ETF?

LEARNING goal 9

Describe how indicators like the Dow Jones Industrial Average affect the market.

UNDERSTANDING STOCK MARKET INDICATORS

Investors today have an enormous wealth of investment information available to them. Newspapers like *The Wall Street Journal, Barron's, Investor's Business Daily,* and *USA Today* provide vast amounts of information about companies and global markets. Television networks like MSNBC and CNBC offer daily investment analysis and different viewpoints to assist investors. Websites like MSN Money and Yahoo! Finance offer financial information to investors free of charge that not long ago was only available to brokers for a hefty fee. But keep in mind that investing is an inexact science. Every time someone sells a stock, believing it will fall, someone else is buying it, believing its price will go higher.

You often hear news reports end with a comment like, "The Dow was up 190 points today in active trading." Ever wonder what that's all about? The **Dow Jones Industrial Average (the Dow)** is the average cost of 30 selected industrial stocks. The financial industry uses it to give an indication of the direction (up or down) of the stock market over time. Charles Dow began the practice of measuring stock averages in 1884, using the prices of 12 key stocks. In 1982, the Dow was broadened to include 30 stocks. The 12 original and the 30 current stocks in the Dow are illustrated in Figure 19.9. Do you recognize any of the 12 original companies?

Today, Dow Jones & Company substitutes new stocks in the Dow when it's deemed appropriate. In 1991, Disney was added to reflect the increased economic importance of the service sector. In 1999, the Dow added Home Depot and SBC Communications along with its first NASDAQ stocks, Intel and Microsoft. In 2004, American International Group (AIG), Pfizer, and Verizon replaced AT&T, International Paper, and Eastman Kodak. (In 2005, AT&T rejoined the Dow when it merged with SBC.) In 2008, Chevron, Bank of America, and Kraft Foods replaced Altria Group, Honeywell, and AIG. In 2009, Travelers and Cisco replaced Citigroup and General Motors.

Critics argue that the 30-company Dow sample is too small to get a good statistical representation of the direction of the market over time. Many investors and analysts prefer to follow stock indexes like the Standard & Poor's 500 (S&P 500), which tracks the performance of 400 industrial, 40 financial, 40 public utility, and 20 transportation stocks. Investors also closely follow the NASDAQ average, which is quoted each trading day to show trends in this important exchange.

Dow Jones Industrial Average (the Dow)
The average cost of 30 selected industrial stocks, used to give an indication of the direction (up or down) of the stock market over time.

figure 19.9

THE ORIGINAL DOW AND
CURRENT DOW

THE ORIGINAL DOW 12	THE 30 CURRENT DOW COMPANIES	
American Cotton Oil	Alcoa	Intel
American Sugar Refining Co.	American Express	Johnson & Johnson
American Tobacco	AT&T	JPMorgan Chase
Chicago Gas	Bank of America	McDonald's
Distilling & Cattle Feeding Co.	Boeing	Merck
General Electric Co.	Caterpillar	Microsoft
Laclede Gas Light Co.	Chevron	Pfizer
National Lead	Cisco	Procter & Gamble
North American Co.	Coca-Cola	3M
Tennessee Coal, Iron & Railroad Co.	DuPont	Travelers
U.S. Leather	ExxonMobil	United Health Group
U.S. Rubber Co.	General Electric	United Technologies
	Hewlett-Packard	Verizon
	Home Depot	Wal-Mart Stores
	IBM	Walt Disney

Staying abreast of the market will help you decide what investments seem most appropriate to your needs and objectives. Remember two key investment realities: Your personal financial objectives and needs change over time, and markets can be volatile. Let's look at market volatility and the challenges that present investors with new risks and opportunities.

Riding the Market's Roller Coaster

Throughout the 1900s, the stock market had its ups and downs, spiced with several major tremors. The first major crash occurred on Tuesday, October 29, 1929 (called Black Tuesday), when the stock market lost almost 13 percent of its value in a single day. This day, and the deep depression that followed, reinforced the reality of market volatility, especially to those who bought stocks heavily on margin. On October 19, 1987, the stock market suffered the largest one-day drop in its history,

Investing in the stock market has never been for the faint of heart. The market seems to have continuous steep climbs and sharp falls. Do you have the risk tolerance to survive the wild market swings?

losing over 22 percent of its value. On October 27, 1997, investors again felt the market's fury. Fears of an impending economic crisis in Asia caused panic and widespread losses. Luckily, the market regained its strength after a short downturn.

After regaining strength in the late 1990s, the market again suffered misfortune in the early 2000s. All told, investors lost $7 trillion in market value from 2000 through 2002. A recovery that started in the mid-2000s was cut short in 2008, when the financial crisis fueled a massive exodus from the stock market, resulting in record losses.

What caused the market turmoil of 1987, 1997, 2000–2002, and 2008? In 1987, analysts agreed it was **program trading,** in which investors give their computers instructions to sell automatically to avoid potential losses if the price of their stock dips to a certain point. On October 19, 1987, computers' sell orders caused many stocks to fall to unbelievable depths. The crash prompted the U.S. exchanges to create mechanisms called *curbs* and *circuit breakers* to restrict program trading whenever the market moves up or down by a large number of points in a trading day. A key computer is turned off and program trading is halted. If you watch programming on CNBC or MSNBC, you'll see the phrase *curbs in* appear on the screen.

Circuit breakers are more drastic than curbs and are triggered when the Dow falls 10, 20, or 30 percent in a day. That happened on October 27, 1997, when the market suffered an approximate 7 percent decline and the market closed for the day at 3:30 p.m. instead of 4:00. Many believe the 1997 market drop (caused by the financial crisis in Asia) could have been much worse without the trading restrictions. Depending on the rate of decline and the time of day, circuit breakers will halt trading for half an hour to two hours so traders have time to assess the situation.

In the late 1990s the stock market reached unparalleled heights only to collapse into a deep decline in 2000–2002. The bursting of the dot-com bubble was the primary reason. A bubble is caused when too many investors drive the price of something (in this case dot-com stocks) unrealistically high.

The dot-com crash was, unfortunately, accompanied by disclosures of financial fraud at companies such as WorldCom, Enron, Global Crossing, and Tyco. Investors had trusted that the real value of these companies was fairly reflected in their financial statements. This trust was shattered when they found investment analysts often provided clients with wildly optimistic evaluations and recommendations about companies they knew were not worth their current prices.

After the financial downturn caused by the dot-com bubble, the stock market surged in the mid-2000s with the Dow setting a record high in October 2007. The market's growth was dramatic, especially in the real estate sector. From 2000 to 2006 prices of existing homes rose 50 percent; however, between 2006 and 2011, housing values fell $6.3 trillion.[36] The real estate bubble was like the dot-com bubble before it: Investors believed that home prices would increase forever. Financial institutions reduced their lending requirements for buyers, home builders overbuilt, and buyers overspent, all sharing blame for the crisis. The government also contributed to the problem by requiring more mortgages be given to low- and moderate-income buyers, many with weak credit scores or no verification of income or assets. These *subprime*

program trading
Giving instructions to computers to automatically sell if the price of a stock dips to a certain point to avoid potential losses.

The economic crisis that began in 2008 caused much anguish among Wall Street workers and people in general. How effective has the government's response been thus far?

loans were pooled together and repackaged as mortgage-backed securities that were sold to investors (discussed in Chapter 20). What followed were huge numbers of foreclosures, the failure of government-sponsored mortgage giants Fannie Mae and Freddie Mac, and more than 350 bank failures.[37]

The collapse of the real estate market caused the economy a combined loss of $8 trillion in housing and commercial property (more than the GDP of China).[38] Financial institutions, like Lehman Brothers, went out of business and Wall Street icon Merrill Lynch was purchased by Bank of America. With financial markets in the worst condition since the Great Depression and the economy in a deep recession, the federal government took action. Congress passed a $700 billion financial package called the Troubled Asset Relief Program (TARP) that allowed the Treasury Department to purchase or insure "troubled assets" to bolster banks and bail out the automotive industry and insurer American International Group (AIG). Unfortunately, in 2009 the economy continued to decline and unemployment grew to double digits, causing President Obama to encourage passage of an $800 billion economic stimulus package—a blend of tax cuts and increased government spending—that was intended to reduce unemployment and provide a "significant boost" to the crippled economy.

As the economy slowly moves to recovery today from the financial crisis beginning in 2008, a few positive economic signs have surfaced. The amount of TARP funds spent did not approximate the $700 billion Congress allocated. Plus troubled banks have repaid most of the money they received through TARP, and AIG and General Motors expect to repay the government in full. However, unemployment and slow economic growth continue to be major causes for concern. It's very likely the financial crisis will affect the economy for a long time.[39]

Investing Challenges in the 21st-Century Market

As you can see from the previous section, in the stock market, what goes up also goes down. Financial markets will likely experience changes in the future that will only heighten investor risk. The financial crisis also reinforced that the world's economies are closely linked. The United States was not the only nation affected by the financial crisis; financial markets in Europe, Asia, and South America felt the pain as well. Persistent challenges and even political and social change promise to make securities markets exciting but not stable places to be in the 21st century. Figure 19.10 highlights new government regulations designed to address some of these challenges.

Diversify your investments, and be mindful of the risks of investing. Taking a long-term perspective is also a wise idea. There's no such thing as easy money or a sure thing. If you carefully research companies and industries, keep up with the news, and make use of investment resources—such as newspapers, magazines, newsletters, the Internet, and TV programs—the payoff can be rewarding over time.

- Gave the government power to seize and shutter large financial institutions on the verge of collapse.
- Put derivatives and complicated financial deals (including those that packaged subprime mortgages) under strict governmental oversight.
- Required hedge funds to register with the SEC and provide information about trades and portfolio holdings.
- Created the Consumer Financial Protection Bureau to watch over the interests of American consumers by reviewing and enforcing federal financial laws.

figure 19.10

CLEANING UP THE STREET

Key Provisions of the Dodd-Frank Wall Street Reform and Consumer Protection Act

- What does the Dow Jones Industrial Average measure? Why is it important?
- Why do the 30 companies comprising the Dow change periodically?
- Explain program trading and the problems it can create.

summary

Learning Goal 1. Describe the role of securities markets and of investment bankers.

- **What opportunities do securities markets provide businesses and individual investors?**

By issuing securities businesses are able to raise much-needed funding to help finance their major expenses. Individual investors can share in the success and growth of emerging or established firms by investing in them.

- **What role do investment bankers play in securities markets?**

Investment bankers are specialists who assist in the issue and sale of new securities.

Learning Goal 2. Identify the stock exchanges where securities are traded.

- **What are stock exchanges?**

Stock exchanges are securities markets whose members are engaged in buying and selling securities such as stocks and bonds.

- **What are the different exchanges?**

The NYSE Euronext lists the stock of over 8,000 companies. The NASDAQ is a telecommunications network that links dealers across the nation so that they can buy and sell securities electronically rather than in person. It is the largest U.S. electronic stock trading market. There are stock exchanges all over the world.

- **What is the over-the-counter (OTC) market?**

The OTC market is a system for exchanging stocks not listed on the national exchanges.

- **How are securities exchanges regulated?**

The Securities and Exchange Commission (SEC) regulates securities exchanges and requires companies that intend to sell bonds or stock to provide a prospectus to potential investors.

- **What is insider trading?**

Insider trading is the use of information or knowledge individuals gain that allows them to benefit unfairly from fluctuations in security prices.

Learning Goal 3. Compare the advantages and disadvantages of equity financing by issuing stock, and detail the differences between common and preferred stock.

- **What are the advantages and disadvantages to a firm of selling stock?**

The advantages of selling stock include the following: (1) the stock price never has to be repaid to stockholders, since they become owners in the company;

(2) there is no legal obligation to pay stock dividends; and (3) the company incurs no debt, so it may appear financially stronger. Disadvantages of selling stock include the following: (1) stockholders become owners of the firm and can affect its management by voting for the board of directors; (2) it is more costly to pay dividends since they are paid in after-tax profits; and (3) managers may be tempted to make stockholders happy in the short term rather than plan for long-term needs.

- **What are the differences between common and preferred stock?**

Holders of common stock have voting rights in the company. In exchange for having no voting rights, preferred stockholders receive a fixed dividend that must be paid in full before common stockholders receive a dividend. Preferred stockholders are also paid back their investment before common stockholders if the company is forced out of business.

Learning Goal 4. Compare the advantages and disadvantages of obtaining debt financing by issuing bonds, and identify the classes and features of bonds.

- **What are the advantages and disadvantages of issuing bonds?**

The advantages of issuing bonds include the following: (1) management retains control since bondholders cannot vote; (2) interest paid on bonds is tax-deductible; (3) bonds are only a temporary source of financing, and after they are paid off the debt is eliminated; (4) bonds can be paid back early if they are issued with a call provision; and (5) sometimes bonds can be converted to common stock. The disadvantages of bonds include the following: (1) because bonds are an increase in debt, they may adversely affect the market's perception of the company; (2) the firm must pay interest on its bonds; and (3) the firm must repay the bond's face value on the maturity date.

- **What are the different types of bonds?**

Unsecured (debenture) bonds are not supported by collateral, whereas secured bonds are backed by tangible assets such as mortgages, buildings, and equipment.

Learning Goal 5. Explain how to invest in securities markets and set investment objectives such as long-term growth, income, cash, and protection from inflation.

- **How do investors normally make purchases in securities markets?**

Investors purchase investments through market intermediaries called stockbrokers, who provide many different services. Online investing has become increasingly popular.

- **What are the criteria for selecting investments?**

Investors should determine their overall financial objectives and evaluate investments according to (1) risk, (2) yield, (3) duration, (4) liquidity, and (5) tax consequences.

- **What is diversification?**

Diversification means buying several different types of investments (government bonds, corporate bonds, preferred stock, common stock, global stock) with different degrees of risk. The purpose is to reduce the overall risk an investor would assume by investing in just one type of security.

Learning Goal 6. Analyze the opportunities stocks offer as investments.

- **What is a market order?**

A market order tells a broker to buy or sell a security immediately at the best price available.

- **A limit order?**

A limit order tells the broker to buy or sell if the stock reaches a specific price.

- **What does it mean when a stock splits?**

When a stock splits, stockholders receive two (or more) shares of stock for each share they own. Each is worth half (or less) of the original share, so while the number of the shares increases, the total value of stockholders' holdings stays the same. The lower per-share price that results may increase demand for the stock.

- **What does buying on margin mean?**

An investor buying on margin borrows part (the percentage allowed to be borrowed is set by the Federal Reserve) of the cost of a stock from the broker to get shares of stock without immediately paying the full price.

- **What type of information do stock quotations give you?**

Stock quotations provide the highest and lowest price in the last 52 weeks; the dividend yield; the price/earnings ratio; the total shares traded that day; and the closing price and net change in price from the previous day.

Learning Goal 7. Analyze the opportunities bonds offer as investments.

- **What is the difference between a bond selling at a discount and a bond selling at a premium?**

In the secondary market a bond selling at a premium is priced above its face value. A bond selling at a discount sells below its face value.

- **What is a junk bond?**

Junk bonds are high-risk (rated BB or below), high-interest debenture bonds that speculative investors often find attractive.

- **What information does a bond quotation give you?**

A bond quotation gives the bond's interest rate (coupon rate), maturity date, rating, current price, and whether it's callable.

Learning Goal 8. Explain the investment opportunities in mutual funds and exchange-traded funds (ETFs).

- **How can mutual funds help individuals diversify their investments?**

A mutual fund is an organization that buys stocks and bonds and then sells shares in those securities to the public, enabling individuals to invest in many more companies than they could otherwise afford.

- **What are ETFs?**

Like mutual funds, ETFs are collections of stocks that are traded on securities exchanges, but they are traded more like individual stocks.

Learning Goal 9. Describe how indicators like the Dow Jones Industrial Average affect the market.

- **What is the Dow Jones Industrial Average?**

The Dow Jones Industrial Average is the average price of 30 specific stocks that analysts use to track the direction (up or down) of the stock market.

key terms

bond 563
buying stock on margin 571
capital gains 569
common stock 562
debenture bonds 564
diversification 568
dividends 561
Dow Jones Industrial Average (the Dow) 576
exchange-traded funds (ETFs) 574

initial public offering (IPO) 557
institutional investors 557
interest 563
investment bankers 557
junk bonds 572
maturity date 563
mutual fund 573
NASDAQ 558
over-the-counter (OTC) market 558

preferred stock 563
program trading 578
prospectus 559
Securities and Exchange Commission (SEC) 559
sinking fund 565
stockbroker 566
stock certificate 561
stock exchange 557
stocks 561
stock splits 570

critical thinking

1. Imagine you inherited $50,000 and you want to invest it to meet two financial goals: (*a*) to save for your wedding, which you plan to have in two years, and (*b*) to save for your retirement a few decades from now. How would you invest the money? Explain your answer.

2. If you are considering investing in the bond market, how could information provided by Standard & Poor's, Moody's Investors Service, and Fitch Ratings help you?

3. Why do companies like callable bonds? Why are investors generally not very fond of them?

4. If you were thinking about investing in the securities market, would you prefer individual stocks, mutual funds, or ETFs? Explain your choice by comparing the advantages and disadvantages of each.

5. Consider the companies added and subtracted from the Dow Jones Industrial Average over the past five years. (Go to www.djaverages.com to learn more about these companies.) What types of companies were added and deleted? Why do you think the changes were made? Do you think new changes will be made in the next five years? Why?

developing workplace skills

1. Go to the websites of Charles Schwab (www.schwab.com), E*Trade (www.etrade.com), and Ameritrade (www.ameritrade.com). Investigate each of these brokerage companies to compare their fees and what they offer in terms of research and advice. Which firm seems most appropriate to your investment objectives? Be prepared to defend your choice to the class.

2. Visit MSN Money or Yahoo! Finance and select six stocks for your portfolio—three from the NYSE and three from the NASDAQ. Track the stocks daily for three weeks using the graphs provided on the websites to see how market trends and information affected your stock's performance. Report your observations.

3. U.S. government bonds compete with corporations for investors' dollars. Check out the different types of bonds the federal government offers and list the types most appealing to you. Be sure to check out TIPs.

4. See whether anyone in class is interested in forming an investment group. If so, each member should choose one stock and one mutual fund or ETF. Record each student's selections and the corresponding prices. In two weeks measure the percentage of change in the investments and discuss the results.

5. Go to the websites of Charles Schwab (www.schwab.com), E*Trade (www .etrade.com), or Ameritrade (www.ameritrade.com) and find two IPOs offered in the past year or so. Track the performance of each from its introduction to its present market price. Report your observations.

taking it to the net

Purpose

To evaluate and understand the advantages and disadvantages of ETFs.

Exercise

Exchange-traded funds (ETFs) are a low-cost, flexible way to diversify a portfolio. To learn more, go to Yahoo! Finance (**www.finance.yahoo.com**) and click on investing, then on the ETFs tab.

1. What are the pros and cons of investing in ETFs?

2. What are the five most actively traded ETFs?

3. Which ETFs grew the most in the last three years?

4. In which industry sectors or countries do these high-growth ETFs specialize?

casing the web

To access the case "Making Dreams Come True," visit **www.mhhe .com/P2P2e**

video case

Where Did All My Money Go?

Many people have lost lots of money recently through investing. Some people reacted by diversifying their remaining investments: putting some money under the mattress, some in a jar in the kitchen, and burying some in the backyard. But this is not the time to avoid investing. The idea is to buy when the market is low and sell when the market is high. If the market is relatively low, it may be the time to invest.

But how do you know what the best investments are? Is there an objective source you can use to get investment advice? The answer is, yes, you can get much helpful and unbiased information from Morningstar.

Most people choose between stocks and bonds. When you buy stocks, you buy part ownership of a firm. You can choose from large firms like AT&T and Microsoft or smaller firms. Morningstar can help you choose from the thousands of firms available.

One way to spread the risk of investing in stock is to diversify. That is, you can buy stock in a variety of firms in a variety of sectors. For example, you can buy stock in firms from other countries, in service firms, manufacturing firms, healthcare firms, and so on. One easy way to diversify is to buy mutual funds. Such funds buy a whole range of stocks and then sell you a portion of that fund. ETFs, or exchange-traded funds, are much like mutual funds, but you buy and sell them through stock exchanges much like you would buy individual shares of stock.

In the long run, most investment advisors recommend investing in stock. Yes, the stock market goes up and down, but they say, in the long run, stocks usually go up. Since young people can wait for years to sell their stock, investment advisors like Morningstar would usually recommend stock (or mutual funds) to them.

Would Morningstar also recommend bonds? Sure. When you buy a bond, you lend a company (or the government, if you buy government bonds) money. The company (or the government) promises to return the money to you, plus interest. If the interest is high enough, such an investment makes sense. Of course, some companies are riskier than others, so the interest paid on bonds varies. Morningstar will help you choose bonds that are appropriate for you and your situation.

As you have learned from the recent fall in stock prices, investing is not easy. Almost everyone needs some advice. Morningstar has earned a reputation for being objective and helpful.

This video is meant to reveal the benefits and drawbacks of investing. But stocks and bonds can earn you a nice return on your investment if you know what you are doing. If you don't know what you are doing, you can lose your savings rather quickly. Morningstar is just one source of information. You should explore as many sources as possible to learn about investing. Such sources include your textbook, your local newspaper, magazines such as *Money* and *Personal Finance,* and TV shows featuring financial news.

Everyone should have some money set aside (e.g., in a bank) for emergencies. Everyone should diversify their investments among stocks, bonds, real estate, and other investments, depending on their income and their willingness to assume risk.

Morningstar and other sources of advice are very important to your financial health. You have seen how some people believed that real estate could do nothing but go up. The recent real estate crash proved them wrong. The same is true of stocks, bonds, gold, oil, and other investments. They all involve risk, and expert advice is often wrong so it pays to have the best, unbiased advice, like that you get from Morningstar. It also helps to have several sources of advice, including your own knowledge gathered carefully over time.

Thinking It Over

1. *What do you know about investing in stocks, bonds, mutual funds, ETFs, and other investments? What sources of information have you used in the past for making investments?*

2. *Should you totally rely on Morningstar or any other investment advice service or should you search out several sources of advice? How can you know what advice is best?*

3. *Given what you've read in this text and from other sources, would you recommend that your fellow students invest in stocks, bonds, mutual funds, ETFs, real estate, or some other investments? Why?*

Money, Financial INSTITUTIONS, and the Federal Reserve

LEARNING goals

After you have read and studied this chapter, you should be able to

1 Explain what money is and what makes money useful.

2 Describe how the Federal Reserve controls the money supply.

3 Trace the history of banking and the Federal Reserve System.

4 Classify the various institutions in the U.S. banking system.

5 Briefly trace the causes of the banking crisis starting in 2008 and explain how the government protects your funds during such crises.

6 Describe how technology helps make banking more efficient.

7 Evaluate the role and importance of international banking, the World Bank, and the International Monetary Fund.

profile

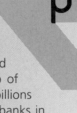

Ben Bernanke (pronounced ber-*nan'*-kee) is the head of the Federal Reserve, the agency in charge of the nation's monetary policy. At the Fed, Bernanke manages the money supply and interest rates, which keeps him under close examination by the media. Lately the Fed has flooded the world with dollars, which many believe caused stock and other asset prices to rise, eliminated the risk of deflation, and prevented a double-dip recession. Many other critics, however, believe that the Fed's actions created more inflation and put the United States deeper into a debt crisis that may never be resolved. In short, Ben Bernanke is the center of much attention when it comes to the economy. No doubt it was this attention that led *Time* magazine to name Bernanke as "Person of the Year" in 2010.

Born in Augusta, Georgia, Bernanke taught himself calculus in high school and scored 1590 of a possible 1600 on his SAT. He graduated from Harvard University summa cum laude with a bachelor's degree in economics. After earning a PhD from MIT, he became an economics professor and department chair at Princeton University. He then served as chair of the President's Council of Economic Advisors in 2005 and was a member of the Board of Governors at the Federal Reserve from 2002 to 2005.

President George W. Bush appointed Bernanke to the Fed in 2006, instantly making him one of the most powerful people in the United States. The Senate approved a second term for Bernanke as Fed chief under President Obama. It was Bernanke, along with former Treasury Secretary Henry Paulson, who convinced Congress to commit more than $700 billion to try to end the banking collapse. Bernanke lowered interest rates for banks to near zero

and kept them there for a few years, and was among the group of advisors who made billions of dollars available to banks in an effort to ease the credit crisis.

With nearly every decision he makes, Bernanke affects the economy in some way. Bernanke's challenges today include keeping inflation in check, increasing the value of the dollar, and getting the economy moving upward again. Part of that plan includes credit easing and buying more than a trillion dollars in debt and mortgage-backed securities. Although his aggressive monetary policy has made him the focus of criticism in the past, he no doubt played a key role in lessening the impact of the 2008 credit crisis. Hopefully his actions in the future will prevent such a catastrophe of that magnitude from ever occurring again.

You will learn more about the Federal Reserve and the banking system in general in this chapter. Using that information, you can better understand Bernanke's decisions. Keep up with what he is doing by reading the business press and listening to business reports. His successes and failures will be making headlines for a long time.

CONNECTING WITH

Ben Bernanke

X Chairman of the Federal Reserve

Sources: Roger Lowenstein, "The Villain," *The Atlantic,* April 2012; Peter Coy, "Ben Bernanke Is a Dove Because Congress Isn't," *Bloomberg Businessweek,* February 29, 2012; "Bernanke's Inflation Paradox," *The Wall Street Journal,* April 26, 2011; J. Alex Tarquinio, Sean Fieler, and Jeffrey Bell, "Our Unaccountable Fed," *The Wall Street Journal,* April 6, 2011; and Agustino Fontevecchia, "No Hassle for Bernanke: New Fed Governors Won't Limit the Chairman," *Forbes,* May 17, 2012.

NAME THAT company

This banklike store in Austin, Texas, was designed to serve low-income clients who don't have traditional bank accounts. Customers pay a one-time $10 fee that allows them to cash checks and put the money onto debit cards. What is the name of this company? (The answer can be found in the chapter.)

LEARNING **goal 1**

Explain what money is and what makes money useful.

WHY MONEY IS IMPORTANT

The Federal Reserve, or the Fed, is the organization in charge of money in the United States. You will be hearing a lot about it and its head, Ben Bernanke, in the coming years. That is why we chose him to be the subject of the Profile for this chapter. The banking crisis and the moves being made globally by the Fed and other banks to halt a global financial crisis are too complex to discuss in detail here. Our goal in this chapter is simply to introduce you to the world of banking and the role of the Federal Reserve.

Two of the most critical issues in the United States today, economic growth and the creation of jobs, depend on the ready availability of money. Money is so important to the economy that many institutions have evolved to manage it and make it available when you need it. Today you can get cash from an automated teller machine (ATM) almost anywhere in the world, and most organizations will also accept a check, credit card, debit card, or smart card for purchases.[1] Behind the scenes is a complex system of banking that makes the free flow of money possible. Each day, about $4 trillion is exchanged in the world's currency markets. Therefore, what happens to any major country's economy has an effect on the U.S. economy and vice versa. That's why the financial crisis in the United States affected economies throughout the world.

New engraved bills make counterfeiting much more difficult than in the past. The bills look a little different from older ones and are different colors. If you owned a store, what would you do to make sure employees wouldn't accept counterfeit bills?

There's no way to understand the U.S. economy without understanding global money exchanges and the institutions involved in the creation and management of money. Let's start at the beginning by discussing exactly what the word *money* means and how the supply of money affects the prices you pay for goods and services.

What Is Money?

Money is anything people generally accept as payment for goods and services. In the past, objects as diverse as salt, feathers, fur pelts, stones, rare shells, tea, and horses have served as money. In fact, until the 1880s, cowrie shells were one of the world's most popular currencies.

Barter is the direct trading of goods or services for other goods or services. Though barter may sound like something from the past, many people have discovered the benefits of bartering online.[2] Others barter goods and services the old-fashioned way—face-to-face. In Siberia people have bought movie tickets with two eggs, and in Ukraine people have paid their energy bills with sausages and milk. Today you can go to a *barter exchange* where you can put goods or services into the system and get trade credits for other goods and services that you need. The barter exchange makes it easier to barter because you don't have to find people with whom to barter. The exchange does that for you.

The problem with traditional barter is that eggs and milk are difficult to carry around. Most people need some object that's portable, divisible, durable, and stable so that they can trade goods and services without carrying the actual goods around with them. One solution is coins and paper bills. The five standards for a useful form of money are:

- *Portability.* Coins and paper money are a lot easier to take to market than pigs or other heavy products.

- *Divisibility.* Different-sized coins and bills can represent different values. Prior to 1963, a U.S. quarter had half as much silver content as a half-dollar coin, and a dollar had four times the silver of a quarter. Because silver is now too expensive, today's coins are made of other metals, but the accepted values remain.

- *Stability.* When everybody agrees on the value of coins, the value of money is relatively stable. In fact, U.S. money has become so stable that much of the world has used the U.S. dollar as the measure of value. If the value of the dollar fluctuates too rapidly, the world may turn to some other form of money, such as the euro, for the measure of value.

- *Durability.* Coins last for thousands of years, even when they've sunk to the bottom of the ocean, as you've seen when divers find old coins in sunken ships.

- *Uniqueness.* It's hard to counterfeit, or copy, elaborately designed and minted coins. With the latest color copiers, people are able to duplicate the look of paper money relatively easily. Thus, the government has had to go to extra lengths to make sure *real* dollars are readily identifiable. That's why you have newer paper money with the picture slightly off center and with invisible lines that quickly show up when reviewed by banks and stores. The new $100 bill has features such as a three dimensional ribbon as well as ink that contains microscopic flakes that shift color with

Although people have long used barter to exchange goods without money, one problem is that objects like chickens and eggs are harder to carry around than a ten-dollar bill. What other drawbacks does bartering have?

money
Anything that people generally accept as payment for goods and services.

barter
The direct trading of goods or services for other goods or services.

movement.[3] The new bill had its problems, however, and the Bureau of Engraving and Printing had to sort through millions of bills to eliminate faulty ones.[4]

Coins and paper money simplified exchanges. Most countries have their own currencies, and they're all about equally portable, divisible, and durable. However, they're not always equally stable.[5]

Electronic cash (e-cash) is one of the newest forms of money. You can make online payments using Quicken or Microsoft Money or e-mail e-cash using Pay-Pal. Recipients can choose automatic deposit to their bank, e-dollars for spending online, or a traditional check in the mail. Bitcoin is a digital version of money that is tougher to forge, cuts across international boundaries, and can be stored on your hard drive instead of in a bank. However, the Bitcoin is not yet generally accepted and some of the transactions may be illegal.[6] Nonetheless, efforts will be made in the future to create a cashless society using some other form of currency than the bills and coins we now use.[7]

LEARNING goal 2

Describe how the Federal Reserve controls the money supply.

What Is the Money Supply?

As Fed chairman, Ben Bernanke is in control of the U.S. money supply. Two questions emerge from that sentence. What is the money supply? Why does it need to be controlled?

The **money supply** is the amount of money the Federal Reserve makes available for people to buy goods and services. And, yes, the Federal Reserve, in tandem with the U.S. Treasury, can print more money if it is needed. For example, some of the trillions of dollars that are being spent over the next few years to get the economy moving again were printed with authorization from the Federal Reserve. The terms QE 1 and QE 2 literally meant quantitative easing one and two, but the real meaning was that the Fed was creating more money because it believed that money was needed to get the economy moving again.[8]

There are several ways of referring to the U.S. money supply. They're called M-1, M-2, and M-3. The M stands for money, and the 1, 2, and 3 stand for different definitions of the money supply.

M-1 includes coins and paper bills, money that's available by writing checks (demand deposits and share drafts), and money held in traveler's checks—that is, money that can be accessed quickly and easily. **M-2** includes everything in M-1 plus money in savings accounts, and money in money market accounts, mutual funds, certificates of deposit, and the like—that is, money that may take a little more time to obtain than coins and paper bills. M-2 is the most commonly used definition of money.[9] **M-3** is M-2 plus big deposits like institutional money market funds.

Managing Inflation and the Money Supply

Imagine what would happen if governments (or in the case of the United States, the Federal Reserve, a nongovernmental organization) were to generate twice as much money as exists now.[10] There would be twice as much money available, but

money supply
The amount of money the Federal Reserve Bank makes available for people to buy goods and services.

M-1
Money that can be accessed quickly and easily (coins and paper money, checks, traveler's checks, etc.)

M-2
Money included in M-1 plus money that may take a little more time to obtain (savings accounts, money market accounts, mutual funds, certificates of deposit, etc.).

M-3
M-2 plus big deposits like institutional money market funds.

still the same amount of goods and services. What would happen to prices? (Hint: Remember the laws of supply and demand from Chapter 2.) Prices would go up, because more people would try to buy goods and services with their money and bid up the price to get what they wanted. This rise in price is called *inflation,* which some people call "too much money chasing too few goods."

Now think about the opposite: What would happen if the Fed took money out of the economy? Prices would go down because there would be an oversupply of goods and services compared to the money available to buy them; this decrease in prices is called *deflation.*

Now we come to our second question about the money supply: Why does it need to be controlled? The reason is that doing so allows us to manage, somewhat, the prices of goods and services. The size of the money supply also affects employment and economic growth or decline. That's why the Fed and Ben Bernanke are so important.[11]

The Global Exchange of Money

A *falling dollar value* means that the amount of goods and services you can buy with a dollar decreases. A *rising dollar value* means that the amount of goods and services you can buy with a dollar goes up. Thus, the price in euros you pay for a German car will be lower if the U.S. dollar rises relative to the euro.[12] However, if the euro rises relative to the dollar, the cost of cars from Germany will go up and U.S. consumers may buy fewer German cars.

What makes the dollar weak (falling value) or strong (rising value) is the position of the U.S. economy relative to other economies. When the economy is strong, the demand for dollars is high and the value of the dollar rises. When the economy is perceived as weakening, however, the demand for dollars declines and the value of the dollar falls. The value of the dollar thus depends on a relatively strong economy. (See Chapter 3 for further discussion of effects of changes in currency values or exchange rates.) In the following section, we'll discuss in more detail the money supply and how it's managed. Then we'll explore the U.S. banking system and how it lends money to businesses and individuals, like you and me.

CONTROL OF THE MONEY SUPPLY

Theoretically, with the proper monetary policy in place to control the money supply, one can keep the economy growing without causing inflation. (See Chapter 2 to review monetary policy.) Again, the organization in charge of monetary policy is the Federal Reserve.

Basics about the Federal Reserve

The Federal Reserve System consists of five major parts: (1) the board of governors; (2) the Federal Open Market Committee (FOMC); (3) 12 Federal Reserve banks; (4) three advisory councils; and (5) the member banks of the system. Figure 20.1 shows where the 12 Federal Reserve banks are located.[13]

The board of governors administers and supervises the 12 Federal Reserve banks. The seven members of the board are appointed by the president and

The Federal Reserve System includes 12 member banks (see Figure 20.1). This is the Federal Reserve Bank in New York City. What special role in the Fed does the president of this particular bank play?

figure 20.1

THE 12 FEDERAL RESERVE
DISTRICT BANKS

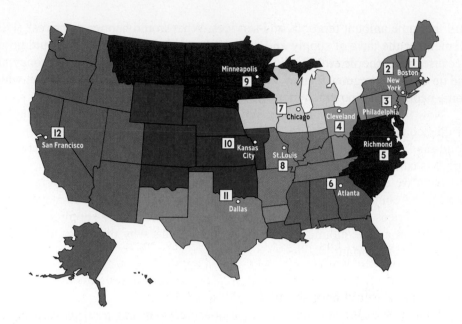

confirmed by the senate. The board's primary function is to set monetary policy. The Federal Open Market Committee (FOMC) has 12 voting members and is the policy-making body. The committee is made up of the seven-member board of governors plus the president of the New York reserve bank and four members who rotate in from the other reserve banks. The advisory councils represent the various banking districts, consumers, and member institutions, including banks, savings and loan institutions, and credit unions. They offer suggestions to the board and to the FOMC.

The Fed buys and sells foreign currencies, regulates various types of credit, supervises banks, and collects data on the money supply and other economic activity. As part of monetary policy, the Fed determines the reserve requirement, that is, the level of reserve funds all financial institutions must keep at one of the 12 Federal Reserve banks.[14] It buys and sells government securities in *open-market*

figure 20.2

HOW THE FEDERAL RESERVE
CONTROLS THE MONEY SUPPLY

CONTROL METHOD	IMMEDIATE RESULT	LONG-TERM EFFECT
Reserve Requirements		
A. Increase.	Banks put more money into the Fed, *reducing* money supply; thus, there is less money available to lend to customers.	Economy slows.
B. Decrease.	Banks put less money into the Fed, *increasing* the money supply; thus, there is more money available to lend to customers.	Economy speeds up.
Open-Market Operations		
A. Fed sells bonds.	Money flows from the economy to the Fed.	Economy slows.
B. Fed buys bonds.	Money flows into the economy from the Fed.	Economy speeds up.
Managing the Discount Rate		
A. Rate increases.	Banks borrow less from the Fed; thus, there is less money to lend.	Economy slows.
B. Rate decreases.	Banks borrow more from the Fed; thus, there is more money to lend.	Economy speeds up.

operations. Finally, it lends money to member banks at an interest rate called the *discount rate.*

As noted, the three basic tools the Fed uses to manage the money supply are reserve requirements, open-market operations, and the discount rate (see Figure 20.2). Let's explore how it administers each.

The Reserve Requirement

The **reserve requirement** is a percentage of commercial banks' checking and savings accounts they must keep in the bank (as cash in the vault) or in a non-interest-bearing deposit at the local Federal Reserve district bank.[15] The reserve requirement is one of the Fed's most powerful tools. When it increases the reserve requirement, money becomes scarcer, which in the long run tends to reduce inflation. For instance, if Omaha Security Bank holds deposits of $100 million and the reserve requirement is, say, 10 percent, then the bank must keep $10 million on reserve. If the Fed were to increase the reserve requirement to 11 percent, then the bank would have to put an additional $1 million on reserve, reducing the amount it could lend out. Since this increase in the reserve requirement would affect all banks, the money supply would be reduced and prices would likely fall.

A decrease of the reserve requirement, in contrast, *increases* the funds available to banks for loans, so they make more loans and money becomes more readily available. An increase in the money supply can *stimulate the economy* to achieve higher growth rates, but it can also create inflationary pressures. That is, the prices of goods and services may go up. Can you see why the Fed may want to decrease the reserve requirement when the economy is in a recession?

reserve requirement
A percentage of commercial banks' checking and savings accounts that must be physically kept in the bank.

Need help understanding How the Federal Reserve Tries to Stablize the Economy? www.introbiz.tv/QR20-1

Open-Market Operations

Open-market operations consist of the buying and selling of government bonds. To decrease the money supply, the federal government sells U.S. government bonds to the public. The money it gets as payment is no longer in circulation, decreasing the money supply. If the Fed wants to increase the money supply, it buys government bonds back from individuals, corporations, or organizations that are willing to sell. The money the Fed pays for these securities enters circulation, increasing the money supply. That's why the Fed's Bernanke bought bonds during the recent recession. The idea was to get the economy growing again.[16]

open-market operations
The buying and selling of U.S. government bonds by the Fed with the goal of regulating the money supply.

The Discount Rate

The Fed has often been called the bankers' bank, because member banks can borrow money from the Fed and pass it on to their customers in the form of loans. The **discount rate** is the interest rate the Fed charges for loans to member banks. An increase in the discount rate discourages banks from borrowing and reduces the number of available loans, decreasing the money supply. In contrast, lowering the discount rate encourages member banks to borrow money and increases the funds they have available for loans, which increases the money supply. For many months, the Fed lowered the discount rate to almost zero, hoping to increase bank lending. Nonetheless, many banks still seemed reluctant to make loans.[17]

The discount rate is one of two interest rates the Fed controls. The other is the rate banks charge each other, called the *federal funds rate.*

discount rate
The interest rate that the Fed charges for loans to member banks.

The Federal Reserve's Check-Clearing Role

If you write a check to a local retailer that uses the same bank you do, it is a simple matter to reduce your account by the amount of the check and increase the amount in the retailer's account. But what happens if you write a check to a retailer in another state? That's where the Fed's check-clearing function comes into play.

That retailer will take the check to its bank. That bank will deposit the check for credit in the closest Federal Reserve bank. That bank will send the check to your local Federal Reserve bank for collection. The check will then be sent to your bank and the amount of the check will be withdrawn. Your bank will authorize the Federal Reserve bank in your area to deduct the amount of the check. That bank will pay the Federal Reserve bank that began the process in the first place. It will then credit the deposit account in the bank where the retailer has its account. That bank will then credit the account of the retailer. (See Figure 20.3 for a diagram of such

Suppose Mr. Brown, a farmer from Quince Orchard, Maryland, purchases a tractor from a dealer in Austin, Texas.

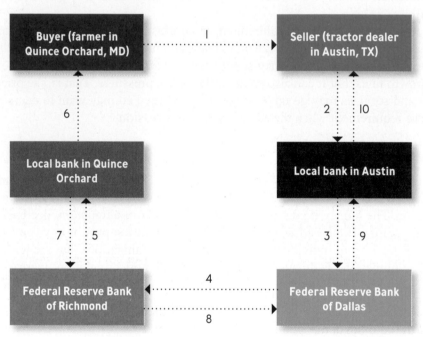

1. Mr. Brown sends his check to the tractor dealer.
2. The dealer deposits the check in his account at a local bank in Austin.
3. The Austin bank deposits the check for credit in its account at the Federal Reserve Bank of Dallas.
4. The Federal Reserve Bank of Dallas sends the check to the Federal Reserve Bank of Richmond for collection.
5. The Federal Reserve Bank of Richmond forwards the check to the local bank in Quince Orchard, where Mr. Brown has his account.
6. The local bank in Quince Orchard deducts the check amount from Mr. Brown's account.
7. The Quince Orchard bank authorizes the Federal Reserve Bank of Richmond to deduct the check amount from its deposit account with the Federal Reserve Bank.
8. The Federal Reserve Bank of Richmond pays the Federal Reserve Bank of Dallas.
9. The Federal Reserve Bank of Dallas credits the Austin bank's deposit account.
10. The Austin bank credits the tractor dealer's account.

figure 20.3

CHECK-CLEARING PROCESS
THROUGH THE FEDERAL
RESERVE BANK SYSTEM

an interstate transaction.) This long and involved process is a costly one; therefore, banks take many measures to lessen the use of checks. Such efforts include the use of credit cards, debit cards, and other electronic transfers of money.[18]

As you can see, the whole economy is affected by the Federal Reserve System's actions. Next we'll briefly discuss the history of banking to give you some background about why the Fed came into existence. Then we'll explore what's happening in banking today.

progress assessment

- What is money?
- What are the five characteristics of useful money?
- What is the money supply, and why is it important?
- How does the Federal Reserve control the money supply?
- What are the major functions of the Federal Reserve? What other functions does it perform?

LEARNING goal 3

Trace the history of banking and the Federal Reserve System.

THE HISTORY OF BANKING AND THE NEED FOR THE FED

At first, there were no banks in the United States. Strict laws in Europe limited the number of coins people could bring to the colonies in the New World. Thus, colonists were forced to barter for goods; for example, they might trade cotton and tobacco for shoes and lumber.

The demand for money was so great that Massachusetts issued its own paper money in 1690, and other colonies soon followed suit. But continental money, the first paper money printed in the United States, became worthless after a few years because people didn't trust its value.

Land banks were established to lend money to farmers. But Great Britain, still in charge of the colonies at that point, ended land banks by 1741. The colonies rebelled against these and other restrictions on their freedom, and a new bank was formed in Pennsylvania during the American Revolution to finance the war against England.

In 1791, after the United States gained independence, Alexander Hamilton persuaded Congress to form a *central bank* (a bank at which other banks could keep their funds and borrow funds if needed). This first version of a federal bank closed in 1811, only to be replaced in 1816 because state-chartered banks couldn't support the War of 1812. The battle between the Second (Central) Bank of the United States and state banks got hot in the 1830s. Several banks in Tennessee were hurt by pressure from the Central Bank. The fight ended when the Central Bank was closed in 1836. You can see that there was great resistance to a central bank, like the Federal Reserve, through much of U.S. history.

By the time of the Civil War, the U.S. banking system was a mess. Different banks issued different kinds of currencies. People hoarded gold and silver coins because they were worth more as precious metal than as money. That may be happening again today. In any case, the chaos continued long after the war ended, reaching something of a climax in 1907, when many banks failed. People got nervous about the safety of banks and in a run on the banks attempted to withdraw their funds. Soon the cash was depleted and some banks had to refuse money to depositors. This caused people to distrust the banking system in general.

Despite the long history of opposition to a central bank, the cash shortage problems of 1907 led to the formation of an organization that could lend money to banks—the Federal Reserve System. It was to be a "lender of last resort" in such emergencies. Under the Federal Reserve Act of 1913, all federally chartered banks had to join the Federal Reserve. State banks could also join. The Federal Reserve became the bankers' bank. If banks had excess funds, they could deposit them in the Fed; if they needed extra money, they could borrow from the Fed. The Federal Reserve System has been intimately related to banking ever since, but never more than now.

Banking and the Great Depression

The Federal Reserve System was designed to prevent a repeat of the 1907 panic. Nevertheless, the stock market crash of 1929 led to bank failures in the early 1930s. When the stock market began tumbling, people hurried to banks to withdraw cash. In spite of the Federal Reserve System, the banks ran out of money and states were forced to close them. President Franklin D. Roosevelt extended the period of bank closings in 1933 to gain time to come up with a solution to the problem. In 1933 and 1935, Congress passed legislation to strengthen the banking system. The most important move was to establish federal deposit insurance to further protect the public from bank failures. As you can see, bank crises are nothing new; they often occur during a recession. From 1945 to 2007, the United States experienced 10 recessions. The average duration was 10 months.

The Federal Reserve System was designed in 1913 to prevent the kind of run on banks that had occurred in 1907. Yet the stock market crash of 1929 caused depositors to make another run on their banks and take big withdrawals. Federal deposit insurance was established in 1933 to protect depositors' money. Do you think these protections are enough?

LEARNING **goal 4**

Classify the various institutions in the U.S. banking system.

THE U.S. BANKING SYSTEM

The U.S. banking system consists of commercial banks, savings and loan associations, and credit unions. In addition, there are various financial organizations, or nonbanks, that accept no deposits but offer many of the services of regular banks. Let's discuss the activities and services of each, starting with commercial banks.

Commercial Banks

A **commercial bank** is a profit-seeking organization that receives deposits from individuals and corporations in the form of checking and savings accounts and uses these funds to make loans. It has two types of customers—depositors and borrowers—and is equally responsible to both. A commercial bank makes a profit by efficiently using depositors' funds as inputs (on which it pays interest) to invest in interest-bearing loans to other customers.[19] If the revenue generated by loans exceeds the interest paid to depositors plus operating expenses, the bank makes a profit.

Services Provided by Commercial Banks

Individuals and corporations that deposit money in a checking account can write personal checks to pay for almost any purchase or transaction. The technical name for a checking account is a **demand deposit** because the money is available on demand from the depositor. Typically, banks impose a service charge for check-writing privileges or demand a minimum deposit. They might also charge a small handling fee for each check written. For corporate depositors, the amount of the service charge depends on the average daily balance in the checking account, the number of checks written, and the firm's credit rating and credit history.

In the past, checking accounts paid no interest to depositors, but interest-bearing checking accounts have experienced phenomenal growth in recent years. Commercial banks also offer a variety of savings account options. A savings account is technically a **time deposit** because the bank can require a prior notice before you make a withdrawal. Compare online and neighborhood banks to find where your money can earn the most interest.

A **certificate of deposit (CD)** is a time-deposit (savings) account that earns interest, to be delivered on the certificate's maturity date. The depositor agrees not to withdraw any of the funds until then. CDs are now available for periods of months to years; usually the longer the period, the higher the interest rate. The interest rates also depend on economic conditions. At the present time, interest rates are very low because the economy is not robust.

Commercial banks also offer credit cards to creditworthy customers, life insurance, inexpensive brokerage services, financial counseling, automatic payment of bills, safe-deposit boxes, individual retirement accounts (IRAs), traveler's checks, trust departments, automated teller machines, and overdraft checking account privileges. The latter means preferred customers can automatically get loans when they've written checks exceeding their account balance. The Connecting Through Social Media box discusses how banks are using social media to reach new market segments.

commercial bank
A profit-seeking organization that receives deposits from individuals and corporations in the form of checking and savings accounts and then uses some of these funds to make loans.

demand deposit
The technical name for a checking account; the money in a demand deposit can be withdrawn anytime on demand from the depositor.

time deposit
The technical name for a savings account; the bank can require prior notice before the owner withdraws money from a time deposit.

certificate of deposit (CD)
A time-deposit (savings) account that earns interest to be delivered at the end of the certificate's maturity date.

ATMs can dispense maps and directions, phone cards, and postage stamps. They can sell tickets to movies, concerts, and sporting events and show movie trailers, news tickers, and video ads. Some can take orders for flowers and DVDs and download music and games.

Services to Borrowers

Commercial banks offer a variety of services to individuals and corporations in need of a loan. Generally, loans are given on the basis of the recipient's creditworthiness, although the real estate collapse beginning in 2008 was partially due to banks ignoring that rule. Banks want to manage their funds effectively and are supposed to screen loan applicants carefully to ensure that the loan plus interest will be paid back on time. Clearly banks failed to do that in the period leading up to the banking crisis. We will discuss why that happened later in the chapter. The Making Ethical Decisions box explores a more minor issue that could occur in your banking efforts.

savings and loan association (S&L)
A financial institution that accepts both savings and checking deposits and provides home mortgage loans.

Savings and Loan Associations (S&Ls)

A **savings and loan association (S&L)** is a financial institution that accepts both savings and checking deposits and provides home mortgage loans. S&Ls are often known as thrift institutions because their original purpose (starting in 1831) was to promote consumer thrift and home ownership. To help them encourage home ownership, thrifts were permitted for many years to offer slightly higher interest rates on savings deposits

than banks. Those rates attracted a large pool of funds, which S&Ls used to offer long-term fixed-rate mortgages. They no longer offer better rates than banks, however.

Between 1979 and 1983, about 20 percent of the nation's S&Ls failed. Perhaps the biggest reason is that capital gains taxes were raised, making it less attractive to invest in real estate (because the added tax reduced profits). Investors therefore walked away from their real estate loans, leaving S&Ls with lots of properties worth less than the outstanding loans on them. When they sold those properties, the S&Ls lost money. The recent drop in real estate prices has caused similar problems for banks and S&Ls.

In the 1980s, the government stepped in to strengthen S&Ls, permitting them to offer higher interest rates, allocate up to 10 percent of their funds to commercial loans, and offer mortgages with adjustable interest rates based on market conditions. You can learn more about this by looking up the Glass-Steagall Act.[20] In addition, S&Ls were permitted to offer a variety of new banking services, such as financial counseling to small businesses and credit cards. As a result, they became much more similar to commercial banks.

Credit Unions

Credit unions are nonprofit, member-owned financial cooperatives that offer the full variety of banking services to their members—interest-bearing checking accounts at relatively high rates, short-term loans at relatively low rates, financial counseling, life insurance policies, and a limited number of home mortgage loans. They are organized by government agencies, corporations, unions, and professional associations.

As nonprofit institutions, credit unions enjoy an exemption from federal income taxes. You might want to visit a local credit union to see whether you are eligible to belong, and then compare the rates to those at local banks. Ed Mierzwinski, a consumer program director for the U.S. Public Interest Research Group, says, "The average consumer does much better at a credit union than a bank. Credit unions have lower requirements for waiving fees, offer better deals on car loans, and are generally more flexible in responding to customers' problems."[21] Credit unions often have fewer

credit unions
Nonprofit, member-owned financial cooperatives that offer the full variety of banking services to their members.

Credit unions are member-owned financial cooperatives that offer their members a wide range of banking services and, because they are nonprofits, are exempt from federal income tax. Do you belong to a credit union?

branches than banks and less access to ATMs. It's best to determine what services you need and then compare those services to the same services offered by banks.

Other Financial Institutions (Nonbanks)

nonbanks
Financial organizations that accept no deposits but offer many of the services provided by regular banks (pension funds, insurance companies, commercial finance companies, consumer finance companies, and brokerage houses).

Nonbanks are financial organizations that accept no deposits but offer many of the services provided by regular banks. Nonbanks include life insurance companies, pension funds, brokerage firms, commercial finance companies, and corporate financial services (like GE Capital). Nonbanks cut back their lending considerably during the banking crisis beginning in 2008. Such a drop-off in lending contributed to slowing the economy greatly.

As competition between banks and nonbanks has increased, the dividing line between them has become less apparent. This is equally true in Europe, where U.S. companies compete with European banks. The diversity of financial services and investment alternatives nonbanks offer has led banks to expand their own services. In fact, many banks have merged with brokerage firms to offer full-service financial assistance.

Life insurance companies provide financial protection for policyholders, who periodically pay premiums. In addition, insurers invest the funds they receive from policyholders in corporate and government bonds. In recent years, more insurance companies have begun to provide long-term financing for real estate development projects. Do you think that was a wise decision?

pension funds
Amounts of money put aside by corporations, nonprofit organizations, or unions to cover part of the financial needs of members when they retire.

Pension funds are monies put aside by corporations, nonprofit organizations, or unions to help fund their members' financial needs when they retire. Contributions to pension funds are made by employees, employers, or both. To generate additional income, pension funds typically invest in low-return but safe corporate stocks or other conservative investments such as government securities and corporate bonds.

Many financial services organizations that provide retirement and health benefits, such as TIAA-CREF, are becoming a major force in U.S. financial markets. They also lend money directly to corporations.

Brokerage firms have traditionally offered investment services in stock exchanges in the United States and abroad. They have also made serious inroads into regular banks' domain by offering high-yield combination savings and checking accounts. In addition, they offer money market accounts with check-writing privileges and allow investors to borrow, using their securities as collateral.

Commercial and consumer finance companies offer short-term loans to those who cannot meet the credit requirements of regular banks, such as new businesses, or who have exceeded their credit limit and need more funds. College students with no credit history often turn to consumer finance companies for education loans. Be careful when borrowing from such institutions because their interest rates can be quite high. The Connecting with Small Business box offers an example of a newer type of nonbank that offers services to people who do not have traditional checking accounts.

progress assessment

- Why did the United States need a Federal Reserve Bank?
- What's the difference between a bank, a savings and loan association, and a credit union?
- What is a consumer finance company?

The Rise of the Nonbank

About a fourth of American households don't have a bank account. That creates a huge market for alternative banking such as that provided by Mango Store. It is a banklike facility in Austin, Texas. Clients pay a one-time $10 fee that lets them cash as many checks as they want by putting the money onto debit cards. More sophisticated services cost extra. Nonetheless, Mango's fees are much lower than a typical local bank.

Mango hopes its customers will increase their earning power and remain customers over time. First, however, the company must get customers through the door and onto its system. Because the majority of Mango's cash is stored in the outside ATM, the interior can emphasize open spaces and security cameras. Customers can use self-serve kiosks to check card balances and transfer funds. Bilingual counselors help customers understand the system. To help customers better

understand the services available and the costs, the store has banners clearly displaying fees.

Sources: Dan Macsai, "The Mango Store Lets You Bank without Commitment," *Fast Company,* July 1, 2010; "Mango Financial, Inc., Debuts First U.S. Store in Austin," PR Newswire.com, accessed May 2011; and mangomoney.com, accessed May 2012.

LEARNING goal 5

Briefly trace the causes of the banking crisis starting in 2008 and explain how the government protects your funds during such crises.

THE RECENT BANKING CRISIS AND HOW THE GOVERNMENT PROTECTS YOUR MONEY

What led to the recent banking crisis? There is no simple answer. Some people believe the Federal Reserve is partly responsible because it kept the cost of borrowing so low that people were tempted to borrow more than they could afford to pay back. Congress, very interested in creating more "affordable housing," prodded banks to lend to people with minimal assets. The Community Reinvestment Act further encouraged loans to families with questionable ability to repay.

Other organizations pressured banks, normally quite risk-averse, to make risky loans. Banks learned they could avoid much of the risk by dividing their portfolios of mortgages up and selling the mortgage-backed securities (MBSs) to other banks and other organizations all over the world. These securities seemed quite safe because they were backed by the homes that were mortgaged. Fannie Mae and Freddie Mac are both quasi-government agencies that seemed to guarantee the value of MBSs. Banks sold more and more of such seemingly

safe securities, hoping to make lots of money. Bankers were also accused of pushing loans onto naive consumers.

Meanwhile, the Federal Reserve and the Securities and Exchange Commission failed to issue sufficient warnings. That is, they failed in their regulatory duties. When the value of homes began to decline, people began defaulting on their loans (not paying them) and turned the properties back over to the banks. Since the banks owned the mortgages on those homes, their profits declined dramatically, leading to the recent banking crisis—and the need for the government to help the banks out. Not doing so was considered too risky because the whole economy might fail. The long-term effects of that process are not yet known.

So whom do we blame for the banking crisis? The answer is that we could blame the Fed for suppressing interest rates, Congress for promoting questionable loans, the banks for making such loans and creating mortgage-backed securities that were not nearly as safe as promoted, government regulatory agencies for not doing their job, and people who took advantage of low interest rates to borrow money they couldn't reasonably hope to repay. No matter who was to blame, the crisis still needed to be solved.

Toward the end of George W. Bush's presidency, the Treasury Department proposed a $700 billion "bailout" package, known as the Troubled Asset Relief Program (TARP). The program was enacted in October 2008. President Barack Obama, who took office in January 2009, proposed over $800 billion in additional government spending plus a stimulus package. The economy responded, but very slowly.

The bursting of the housing bubble forced a sharp decline in home values. When homeowners discovered they owed more on their mortgages than their homes were worth, many stopped paying off their loans, and the banks foreclosed on their homes. This forced home prices to fall lower still and put even more people in jeopardy of losing their homes. What can the government do to help homeowners?

Protecting Your Funds

The recent banking crisis is nothing new. The government had seen similar problems during the Great Depression of the 1930s. To prevent investors from ever again being completely wiped out during an economic downturn, it created three major organizations to protect your money: the Federal Deposit Insurance Corporation (FDIC); the Savings Association Insurance Fund (SAIF); and the National Credit Union Administration (NCUA). All three insure deposits in individual accounts up to a certain amount. Because these organizations are so important to the safety of your money, let's explore them individually in more depth.

The Federal Deposit Insurance Corporation (FDIC)

Federal Deposit Insurance Corporation (FDIC)
An independent agency of the U.S. government that insures bank deposits.

The **Federal Deposit Insurance Corporation (FDIC)** is an independent agency of the U.S. government that insures bank deposits. If a bank were to fail, the FDIC would arrange to have that bank's accounts transferred to another bank or reimburse depositors up to $250,000. The FDIC covers about 13,000 institutions, mostly commercial banks.

The Savings Association Insurance Fund (SAIF)

The **Savings Association Insurance Fund (SAIF)** insures holders of accounts in savings and loan associations. A brief history will show why it was created. Some 1,700 bank and thrift institutions had failed during the early 1930s, and people were losing confidence in them. The FDIC and the Federal Savings and Loan Insurance Corporation (FSLIC) were designed (in 1933 and 1934, respectively) to create more confidence in banking institutions by protecting people's savings from loss. In the 1980s, to get more control over the banking system in general, the government placed the FSLIC under the FDIC and gave it a new name: the Savings Association Insurance Fund (SAIF).

The National Credit Union Administration (NCUA)

The National Credit Union Administration (NCUA) provides up to $250,000 coverage per individual depositor per institution. This coverage includes all accounts—checking accounts, savings accounts, money market accounts, and certificates of deposit. Depositors qualify for additional protection by holding accounts jointly or in trust. Individual retirement accounts (IRAs) are also separately insured up to $250,000. Credit unions, like banks, suffered from the banking crisis beginning in 2008 and got money from the federal government to make more loans.

Savings Association Insurance Fund (SAIF)
The part of the FDIC that insures holders of accounts in savings and loan associations.

electronic funds transfer (EFT) system
A computerized system that electronically performs financial transactions such as making purchases, paying bills, and receiving paychecks.

LEARNING goal 6

Describe how technology helps make banking more efficient.

Smartphone apps, such as FaceCash, allow users to pay for purchases with their phones. What problems could there be with such capabilities?

USING TECHNOLOGY TO MAKE BANKING MORE EFFICIENT

Imagine the cost to a bank of approving a written check, physically processing it through the banking system, and mailing it back to you. It's expensive. Bankers have long looked for ways to make the system more efficient.

One solution was to issue credit cards to reduce the flow of checks, but they too have their costs: there's still paper to process. Accepting Visa and MasterCard costs retailers about $2 per $100 purchase; Amex costs them about $2.50. In the future we'll see much more electronic rather than physical exchange of money, because it is the most efficient way to transfer funds.

If you must use a credit card, be sure to search for one that offers the best deal for you. Some offer cash back, others offer free travel, and so forth. Don't just sign up for whatever card is offering free T-shirts on campus. Do your research.

In an **electronic funds transfer (EFT) system,** messages about a transaction are sent from one computer to another. Thus, organizations can transfer funds more quickly and economically than with paper

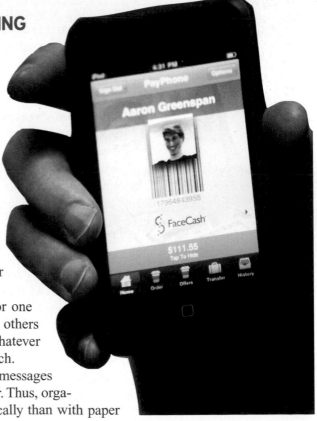

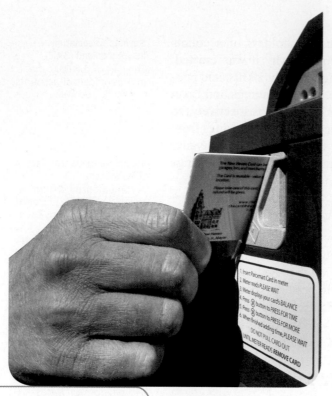

checks. EFT tools include electronic check conversion, debit cards, smart cards, direct deposits, and direct payments. The latest technology, developed by information commerce company First Data, is the GO-Tag, a pea-shaped chip with a radio transmitter inside that can stick to a cell phone or ID badge to make payments fast and easy. It takes only a second to complete a transaction with a GO-Tag, much faster than even a credit card.

A **debit card** serves the same function as a check—it withdraws funds from a checking account. It looks like a credit card but withdraws (debits) money that is already in your account. When the sale is recorded, the debit card sends an electronic signal to the bank, automatically transferring funds from your account to the store's. A record of transactions immediately appears online. Debit transactions surpassed credit years ago and continue to grow twice as fast.[22]

Payroll debit cards are an efficient way for some firms to pay their workers and an alternative to cash for those who don't qualify for a credit or debit card—the so-called unbanked. Employees can access funds in their accounts immediately after they are posted, withdraw them from an ATM, pay bills online, or transfer funds to another cardholder. The system is much cheaper for companies than issuing checks and more convenient for employees. On the other hand, debit cards don't offer the same protection as credit cards. If someone steals your credit card, you are liable only for a certain amount. You are liable for everything when someone steals your debit card.

A **smart card** is an electronic funds transfer tool that combines a credit card, debit card, phone card, driver's license card, and more. Smart cards replace the typical magnetic strip on a credit or debit card with a microprocessor. The card can then store a variety of information, including the holder's bank balance. Merchants can use this information to check the card's validity and spending limits, and transactions can debit up to the amount on the card.

Some smart cards have embedded radio frequency identification (RFID) chips that make it possible to enter buildings and secure areas and to buy gas and other items with a swipe of the card. A biometric function lets you use your fingerprint to boot up your computer. Students are using smart cards to open locked doors to dorms and identify themselves to retailers near campus and online. The cards also serve as ATM cards.

For many, the ultimate convenience in banking is automatic transactions such as direct deposit and direct payments. A *direct deposit* is a credit made directly to a checking or savings account in place of a paycheck. The employer contacts the bank and orders it to transfer funds from the employer's account to the worker's account. Individuals can use direct deposits to transfer funds to other accounts, such as from a checking account to a savings or retirement account.

A *direct payment* is a preauthorized electronic payment. Customers sign a separate form for each company whose bill they would like to automatically pay from their checking or savings account on a specified date. The customer's bank completes each transaction and records it on the customer's monthly statement.

Need to pass the security check in your office building, put gas in your car, and get cash at the ATM? No problem. Smart cards with embedded RFID chips can take care of these tasks and then some. Has cash become a thing of the past?

debit card

An electronic funds transfer tool that serves the same function as checks: it withdraws funds from a checking account.

smart card

An electronic funds transfer tool that is a combination credit card, debit card, phone card, driver's license card, and more.

Online Banking

All top U.S. retail banks now allow customers to access their accounts online, and most have bill-paying capacity. Thus, you can complete all your financial transactions from home, using your telephone or your computer to transfer funds from one account to another, pay your bills, and check the balance in each of your accounts. You can apply for a car loan or mortgage and get a response while you wait. Buying and selling stocks and bonds is equally easy.

Internet banks such as E*Trade Bank offer online banking only, not physical branches. They can offer customers higher interest rates and lower fees because they do not have the overhead costs traditional banks have. While many consumers are pleased with the savings and convenience, not all are happy with the service. Why? Some are nervous about security. People fear putting their financial information into cyberspace, where others may see it despite all the assurances of privacy. Further, some people want to be able to talk to a knowledgeable person one-on-one when they have banking problems.

The future thus seems to be with traditional banks that offer both online services and brick-and-mortar facilities. Even small, local banks offer online services now.

LEARNING goal 7

> Evaluate the role and importance of international banking, the World Bank, and the International Monetary Fund.

INTERNATIONAL BANKING AND BANKING SERVICES

Banks help companies conduct business in other countries by providing three services: letters of credit, banker's acceptances, and money exchange. If a U.S. company wants to buy a product from Germany, the company could pay a bank to issue a letter of credit. A **letter of credit** is a promise by the bank to pay the seller a given amount if certain conditions are met. For example, the German company may not be paid until the goods have arrived at the U.S. company's warehouse. A **banker's acceptance** promises that the bank will pay some specified amount at a particular time. No conditions are imposed. Finally, a company can go to a bank and exchange U.S. dollars for euros to use in Germany; that's called *currency* or *money exchange*.

Banks are making it easier than ever for travelers and businesspeople to buy goods and services overseas. Automated teller machines now provide yen, euros, and other foreign currencies through your personal Visa, MasterCard, Cirrus, or American Express card.

letter of credit
A promise by the bank to pay the seller a given amount if certain conditions are met.

banker's acceptance
A promise that the bank will pay some specified amount at a particular time.

Leaders in International Banking

It would be shortsighted to discuss the U.S. economy apart from the world economy. If the Federal Reserve decides to lower interest rates, within minutes foreign investors can withdraw their money from the United States and put it in countries with higher rates. Of course, the Fed's increasing of interest rates can draw money to the United States equally quickly.

Today's money markets thus form a global market system of which the United States is just a part. International bankers make investments in any country where they can get a maximum return for their money at a reasonable risk. That's how about $4 trillion is traded daily! The net result of international banking and finance has been to link the economies of the world into one interrelated system with no regulatory control. U.S. firms must compete for funds with firms all over the world. An efficient firm in London or Tokyo is more likely to get international financing than a less efficient firm in Detroit or Chicago. Global markets mean that banks do not necessarily keep their money in their own countries. They make investments where they get the maximum return.

What this means for you is that banking is no longer a domestic issue; it's a global one. To understand the U.S. financial system, you must learn about the global financial system. To understand the state of the U.S. economy, you need to learn about the economic condition of countries throughout the world. In the new world economy financed by international banks, the United States is just one player. To be a winner, it must stay financially secure and its businesses must stay competitive in world markets. Is that happening today?

The World Bank and the International Monetary Fund (IMF)

The bank primarily responsible for financing economic development is the International Bank for Reconstruction and Development, or the **World Bank**.[23] After World War II, it lent money to countries in Western Europe so they could rebuild. Today, it lends most of its money to developing nations to improve their productivity and help raise standards of living and quality of life. That includes working to eliminate diseases that kill millions of people each year.

The World Bank has faced considerable criticism and protests around the world. Environmentalists charge that it finances projects damaging to the ecosystem. Human rights activists and unionists say the bank supports countries that restrict religious freedoms and tolerate sweatshops. AIDS activists complain that it does not do enough to get low-cost AIDS drugs to developing nations.

Despite its efforts to improve, the World Bank still has many critics. Some want it to forgive the debts of developing countries and others want it to stop making such loans until the countries institute free markets and the right to own property. Some changes in World Bank policy may lie ahead.[24]

In contrast to the World Bank, the **International Monetary Fund (IMF)** was established to foster cooperative monetary policies that stabilize the exchange of one national currency for another.[25] About 185 countries are voluntary members of the IMF and allow their money to be freely exchanged for foreign money, keep the IMF informed about changes in monetary policy, and modify those policies on the advice of the IMF to accommodate the needs of the entire membership.

The IMF is designed to oversee member countries' monetary and exchange rate policies. Its goal is to maintain a global monetary system that works best for all nations and enhances world trade. While it is not primarily a lending institution like the World Bank, its members do contribute funds according to

World Bank
The bank primarily responsible for financing economic development; also known as the International Bank for Reconstruction and Development.

International Monetary Fund (IMF)
Organization that assists the smooth flow of money among nations.

The World Bank and the International Monetary Fund (IMF) are intergovernmental organizations that help support the global banking community. Both draw protests for their actions. Why?

CONNECTING ACROSS
borders

www.imf.org

Troubles Facing the World's Financial Watchdogs

In the past, the World Bank and the IMF have had to face major crises throughout the world. Today, the issues seem to be as great as ever. For example, the United States has very high unemployment and a debt crisis that exceeds anything in the past. A similar debt crisis is occurring in many European countries. Japan is trying to recover from its earthquake and tsunami and other disasters (e.g., the nuclear problems). There are major disruptions occurring In the Middle East, and the United States is uncertain as to what to do. Emerging nations such as China and Brazil are having problems with high inflation, and food prices are rising all over the planet. Poorer nations are having a particularly hard time because of the high food prices.

The Chair of the IMF's governing body says, "There are significant vulnerabilities still in the global financial and economic systems. That reflects the legacy of an international monetary system that is still not in what we consider satisfactory shape."

The IMF and the World Bank are both trying to come up with answers to the global issues that have become very serious. The United States is a major contributor to those organizations, but there is not enough money to pay down the U.S. debt, much less solve the problems of the rest of the world.

Sources: Neil Irwin, "World Bank, IMF Leaders: Recovery Still a Shaky One," *The Washington Post,* April 17, 2011; and Howard Schneider, "IMF Pushes Europe to Do More to Fight Debt Crisis," *The Washington Post,* January 19, 2012.

their ability, and those funds are available to countries in financial difficulty.[26] The IMF saw a slowing in the global economy in 2010 and was prepared to give certain countries a boost if necessary.[27] The IMF is usually in favor of free capital inflows, but recently it has allowed countries to put up barriers to protect their economies from inflation or bubbles in their stock markets. Countries included in this effort included Italy, Spain, and Turkey.[28] The Connecting Across Borders box discusses what is happening today at the World Bank and the IMF.

progress assessment

- What are some of the causes for the banking crisis that began in 2008?
- What is the role of the FDIC?
- How does a debit card differ from a credit card?
- What is the World Bank and what does it do?
- What is the IMF and what does it do?

summary

Learning Goal 1. Explain what money is and what makes money useful.

- **What is money?**

Money is anything people generally accept as payment for goods and services.

- **What are the five standards for a useful form of money?**

The five standards for a useful form of money are portability, divisibility, stability, durability, and uniqueness.

Learning Goal 2. Describe how the Federal Reserve controls the money supply.

- **How does the Federal Reserve control the money supply?**

The Federal Reserve makes financial institutions keep funds in the Federal Reserve System (reserve requirement), buys and sells government securities (open-market operations), and lends money to banks (the discount rate). To increase the money supply, the Fed can cut the reserve requirement, buy government bonds, and lower the discount rate.

Learning Goal 3. Trace the history of banking and the Federal Reserve System.

- **How did banking evolve in the United States?**

Massachusetts issued its own paper money in 1690; other colonies followed suit. British land banks lent money to farmers but ended such loans by 1741. After the American Revolution, there was much debate about the role of banking, and heated battles between the Central Bank of the United States and state banks. Eventually, a federally chartered and state-chartered system was established, but chaos continued until many banks failed in 1907. The system was revived by the Federal Reserve only to fail again during the Great Depression. There have been 10 recessions since then, including the recession starting in 2008. The Federal Reserve is doing all it can to solve the current banking crisis.

Learning Goal 4. Classify the various institutions in the U.S. banking system.

- **What institutions make up the banking system?**

Savings and loans, commercial banks, and credit unions are all part of the banking system.

- **How do they differ from one another?**

Before deregulation in 1980, commercial banks were unique in that they handled both deposits and checking accounts. At that time, savings and loans couldn't offer checking services; their main function was to encourage thrift and home ownership by offering high interest rates on savings accounts and providing home mortgages. Deregulation closed the gaps between banks and S&Ls, and they now offer similar services.

- **What kinds of services do they offer?**

Banks and thrifts offer such services as savings accounts, checking accounts, certificates of deposit, loans, individual retirement accounts (IRAs), safe-deposit boxes, online banking, life insurance, brokerage services, and traveler's checks.

- **What is a credit union?**

A credit union is a member-owned cooperative that offers everything a bank does—it takes deposits, allows you to write checks, and makes loans. It also may sell life insurance and offer mortgages. Credit union interest rates are sometimes higher than those from banks, and loan rates are often lower.

- **What are some of the other financial institutions that make loans and perform banklike operations?**

Nonbanks include life insurance companies that lend out their funds, pension funds that invest in stocks and bonds and make loans, brokerage firms that offer investment services, and commercial finance companies.

Learning Goal 5. Briefly trace the causes of the banking crisis starting in 2008 and explain how the government protects your funds during such crises.

- **What caused the banking crisis that began in 2008?**

The goal was to have affordable housing, so the government urged banks to make loans to some who could not afford to repay. The banks wanted to minimize the risk of such loans, so they created mortgage-backed securities and sold them to other banks and organizations throughout the world. The government did not regulate these transactions well, and many banks failed because housing values fell and people defaulted on their loans. Many have been blamed for the loss: the Fed, Congress, bank managers, Fannie Mae, and Freddie Mac among them.

- **What agencies insure the money you put into a bank, S&L, or credit union?**

Money deposited in banks is insured by the Federal Deposit Insurance Corporation (FDIC). Money in S&Ls is insured by another agency connected to the FDIC, the Savings Association Insurance Fund (SAIF). Money in credit unions is insured by the National Credit Union Administration (NCUA). Accounts are now insured to $250,000.

Learning Goal 6. Describe how technology helps make banking more efficient.

- **What are debit cards and smart cards?**

A debit card looks like a credit card but withdraws money that is already in your account. When the sale is recorded, the debit card sends an electronic signal to the bank, automatically transferring funds from your account to the store's. A smart card is an electronic funds transfer tool that combines a credit card, debit card, phone card, driver's license card, and more. Smart cards replace the typical magnetic strip on a credit or debit card with a microprocessor.

- **What is the benefit of automatic transactions and online banking?**

A *direct deposit* is a credit made directly to a checking or savings account in place of a paycheck. A *direct payment* is a preauthorized electronic payment. Customers sign a separate form for each company whose bill they would like to automatically pay from their checking or savings account on a specified date. The customer's bank completes each transaction and records it on the customer's monthly statement. All top U.S. retail banks now allow customers to access their accounts online, and most have bill-paying capacity.

Learning Goal 7. Evaluate the role and importance of international banking, the World Bank, and the International Monetary Fund.

- **What do we mean by global markets?**

Global markets mean that banks do not necessarily keep their money in their own countries. They make investments where they get the maximum return. What this means for you is that banking is no longer a domestic issue; it's a global one.

• **What roles do the World Bank and the IMF play?**

The World Bank (also called the International Bank for Reconstruction and Development) is primarily responsible for financing economic development. The International Monetary Fund (IMF), in contrast, was established to assist the smooth flow of money among nations. It requires members (who join voluntarily) to allow their own money to be exchanged for foreign money freely, to keep the IMF informed about changes in monetary policy, and to modify those policies on the advice of the IMF to accommodate the needs of the entire membership. Lately the IMF has been lending money to countries affected by the U.S. banking crisis, and the United States has promised more money to the IMF.

key terms

banker's acceptance 605
barter 589
certificate of deposit (CD) 597
commercial bank 597
credit unions 599
debit card 604
demand deposit 597
discount rate 593
electronic funds transfer (EFT) system 603

Federal Deposit Insurance Corporation (FDIC) 602
International Monetary Fund (IMF) 606
letter of credit 605
M-1 590
M-2 590
M-3 590
money 589
money supply 590
nonbanks 600

open-market operations 593
pension funds 600
reserve requirement 593
savings and loan association (S&L) 598
Savings Association Insurance Fund (SAIF) 603
smart card 604
time deposit 597
World Bank 606

critical thinking

1. If you were Ben Bernanke, chairman of the Federal Reserve, what economic figures might you use to determine how well you were doing? What role did Bernanke play in the recent banking crisis?
2. How much cash do you usually carry with you? What other means do you use to pay for items at the store or on the Internet? What trends do you see in such payments? How might those trends make your purchase experience more satisfactory?
3. If the value of the dollar declines relative to the euro, what will happen to the price of French wine sold in U.S. stores? Will people in France be more or less likely to buy a U.S.-made car? Why or why not?
4. Do you keep your savings in a bank, an S&L, a credit union, or some combination? Have you compared the benefits you could receive from each? Where would you expect to find the best loan values?

developing workplace skills

1. In a small group, discuss the following: What services do you use from banks and S&Ls? Does anyone use online banking? What seem to be its pluses and minuses? Use this opportunity to compare the rates and services of various local banks and S&Ls.

2. Poll the class to see who uses a bank and who uses a credit union. Have class members compare the services at each (interest rates on savings accounts, services available, loan rates). If anyone uses an online service, see how those rates compare. If no one uses a credit union or online bank, discuss the reasons.

3. One role of the Federal Reserve is to help process your checks. In small groups discuss when and where you use checks, credit cards, debit cards, and cash. Do you often write checks for small amounts? Would you stop if you calculated how much it costs to process such checks? Have you switched to debit cards as a result? Discuss your findings with the class.

4. Form several smaller groups and discuss the recent banking crisis. How has it affected the people in the class? What has happened to banks and the economy in general since the start of the banking crisis? What have been the political implications of recent economic changes?

5. Write a one-page paper on the role of the World Bank and the International Monetary Fund in providing loans to countries. Is it important for U.S. citizens to lend money to people in other countries through such organizations? Why or why not? Be prepared to debate the value of these organizations in class.

taking it to the net

Purpose

To learn more about the banking crisis that began in 2008 and what has happened since.

Exercise

1. Do an Internet search to find the latest articles on the global financial crisis. What has happened to banking in the United States and around the world since 2009? What role has the Fed played in trying to end the crisis in the United States?

2. How many search items have appeared covering this issue? What does the number of articles tell you about the importance of this issue?

3. Develop your own story about the causes of the banking crisis. Talk to others in the class and compare stories. What organizations share the blame for the crisis?

casing the web

To access the case "Learning about the Federal Reserve System," visit
www.mhhe.com/P2P2e

video case

The Financial Crisis

By the year 2011, millions had lost homes, businesses had failed, foreclosures were at an all-time record high, and unemployment remained very high at 9 percent. These outcomes were due, in large part, to the financial crisis of 2006–2010.

In the year 2000, the tech stock bubble burst, which sent markets plummeting around the globe. Around the same time, ethics violations surfaced for major companies including Enron, WorldCom, Global Crossing, and Tyco. With the economy in a slump, the government wanted to stimulate consumer spending and business investment. To do this, the Federal Reserve lowered the prime interest rate from 6.5 percent to 1 percent. This ease of credit made mortgages, credit cards, and other consumer loans easy to get. In fact, the average household debt to disposable income in 2007 was 127 percent.

The U.S. Congress, through the 2010 financial crisis investigating committee, determined that the crisis was avoidable. Some of the factors identified as leading to the crisis included the proliferation of subprime mortgages that, in the period between 2004 and 2006, comprised about 20 percent of all mortgages. This was a twofold increase in subprime loans.

The SEC lowered the leverage requirements for investment banks, leading banks to borrow significantly more than they had in reserves. During this period of time, mortgage-backed securities (MBS) were bundled and sold to investors. These MBS products included subprime mortgages, as well. During this same period of time, the major financial rating agencies such as Moody's and Standard and Poor's continued to provide AAA ratings (the highest rating) for MBS products, assuring investors of their value.

In 2007, the housing bubble burst, with housing prices tumbling and the value of MBS products falling, in some cases, to worthless status. Many people found themselves "underwater," meaning that they owed more on their houses than they were worth. These folks and many who had subprime mortgages defaulted on their obligations. As the MBS declined in value, investment banks and other financial firms begin to fail, as their debt was higher than the value of their assets.

This financial crisis had global consequences. The failure of very large (or too big to fail) investment banks could not be allowed to stand; thus the federal government intervened with a $700 billion bailout for banks called the Troubled Asset Relief Program (TARP), designed to bail out troubled banks and prevent further failures. In 2009, the president signed an $800 billion stimulus designed to help stimulate the economy, help businesses borrow and invest, and as a result, create jobs.

The global crisis of confidence described in the video represents the largest economic failure since the Great Depression of the 1930s. The long-term effects of the financial crisis are yet to be determined.

Thinking It Over

1. *Describe how the Federal Reserve can attempt to stimulate the economy.*
2. *What is meant by the term "housing bubble"?*
3. *Identify two of the reasons the Congressional committee identified for the recent financial crisis.*

Career Outlook
Part 6 Conclusion—Financial Management

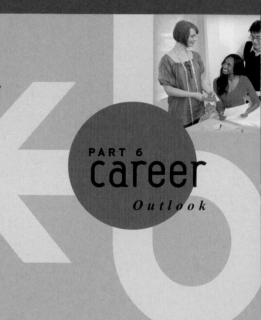

PART 6
career
Outlook

Careers in accounting and finance have existed for centuries. Archaeologists discovered financial records dating back to 300 BC in the ruins of ancient Babylon. European monarchs in the 18th and 19th centuries relied on bankers and professional financiers to recover from wars and to build the new industrial revolution.

Today, accountants and financial managers are as much in demand as ever. Computerization has enriched both career areas immensely. Because of changing laws and regulations, a company's accurate reporting of financial data is a top priority. Nearly every business uses the services of financial professionals, whether they are accountants, bookkeepers, or financial consultants.

SKILLS NEEDED

CAREER PATHS

POSSIBLE POSITIONS

PROFILE

COVER LETTER

RESUME

INTERVIEW

Skills Needed to Succeed in Financial Management

In order to find a job in financial management, you must prove to your employer that you are:

- **Good at math**—Do you like numbers? Are you a good math student?
- **Patient**—Are you comfortable working on long-term projects? Are you willing to invest time in your work?
- **Good at managing data**—Can you see trends and relationships in numbers and data? Can you look at a spreadsheet or graph and understand the main points? Are you a detail-oriented person?
- **A communicator**—Can you explain complicated mathematical concepts? Can you write and speak well?
- **Ethical**—Can you follow rules and guidelines? Are you honest? Can you find the moral answer in a world of gray areas?

Career Paths

In the wake of corporate scandals and the recent financial crisis, the business world has increased its focus on accounting. In addition, as the population ages, more and more baby boomers are seeking financial advice for their retirement. That means this career field is wide open for those with the right background, especially a bachelor's degree.

Continuing education is becoming increasingly important because of the growing complexity of global commerce, changing federal and state laws, and the constant introduction of new, complex financial instruments. A well-trained, experienced financial manager who can stay up-to-date with the latest regulations is a prime candidate for promotion into top management.

Possible Positions

POSSIBLE POSITIONS IN FINANCE

OPPORTUNITY	MEDIAN SALARY	DUTIES	REQUIREMENTS	GROWTH
Financial Analysts	$74,350 per year	Guide businesses and individuals making investment decisions	Bachelor's degree	Faster than average
Financial Examiners	$74,940 per year	Ensure compliance with laws governing financial institutions	Bachelor's degree	Faster than average
Personal Financial Advisors	$64,750 per year	Advise people about taxes, investments, and insurance	Bachelor's degree	Much faster than average
Accountants and Auditors	$61,690 per year	Prepare and examine financial records	Bachelor's degree	Average

Source: Bureau of Labor Statistics, *Occupational Outlook Handbook*, 2012–13 Edition.

Profile: Hector Gonzales, Personal Financial Advisor

Always good with numbers, Hector planned to find a career working in finance, but when his mother was diagnosed with cancer, Hector left college without a degree in order to take care of her. He worked nights in a casino, where his natural abilities at math made him a quick and talented blackjack dealer. Hector took care of his mother until she died three years later.

Part of caring for his mother included managing her finances. Hector learned he enjoyed making decisions about investments and managing her accounts. When she died, his mother left Hector enough money to go back to school and earn a bachelor's degree in finance. Now, Hector has the education he needs to work as a personal financial advisor, where he can help adults with ill parents manage their finances the way he did for his own mother.

How does Hector portray himself in his cover letter, résumé, and interview? Does he highlight the skills and education he has? Would you hire him?

HECTOR'S COVER LETTER

Hector Trone-Gonzales

248 Juniata Street   Cell: 555-263-6788
Brooklyn, New York 11249   HectorTG@gmail.com

April 8, 2014

Eliza Toler
New York Financial Planners
394 Broadway
New York, New York 10001

Dear Ms. Toler:

When my mother was dying of cancer, she felt comforted that she had me to manage her investments and accounts. I pored over books and websites to find the best ways to pay for my mother's therapy, all while caring for her every day. I know how stressful and how vital financial health is to a family, especially one with medical problems. My personal experiences paired with my newly obtained degree in finance make me the perfect candidate to join your financial-planning business.

> Tip: Telling a true and relevant story can bring you to life in the eyes of the recruiter.

I learned about this position from one of your current financial planners, Jackson Green, who lectured at my business school a few months ago. I have the qualities that he said top financial planners possess: I'm naturally good with numbers, I'm very organized, and I can work within rules and regulations to find the best ways to turn a client's money into security. Volunteering for an elder day care organization, I enjoyed working with families to help them make wise financial decisions.

> Tip: Make sure that the recruiter sees that your skills match the skills that the company is looking for.

I'm excited for the opportunity to interview with someone at New York Financial Planners regarding your new opening, and I plan on following up with your office next week to see when we can arrange a convenient appointment time. My contact information is on this letter and my résumé, and I hope you will feel free to contact me anytime.

> Tip: If appropriate, describe your follow-up plans—and then carry through with them.

Thank you for your consideration, and I look forward to hearing from you.

Sincerely,

Hector Trone-Gonzales
Hector Trone-Gonzales

616

Hector Trone-Gonzales

248 Juniata Street
Brooklyn, New York 11249

Cell: 555-263-6788
HectorTG@gmail.com

Summary

New graduate with outstanding analytical skills and experience with
end-of-life financial management

Qualifications

- Cutting-edge knowledge of financial rules and regulations
- Training in math, finance, and business
- Proven organizational, multitasking, and problem-solving skills
- Willing to travel or relocate if necessary

Education

Bachelor's of Science in Business Administration - Finance
Anticipated Graduation: May 2014
New York University

Experience

Financial Planning Volunteer

Rosanna's Elder Day Care, Queens, New York   2010–2014

- Volunteered three hours per week during the school year
- Advised elder day care clients and families about finances

Blackjack Dealer

Opus Casinos, Long Island, New York   2005–2009

- Managed blackjack games with more than 100 players each night
- Entertained guests with calculations of odds during game

Financial Manager and Planner

Queens, New York   2005–2008

- Coordinated my mother's finances to pay for health care
- Invested and managed accounts to sustain portfolio

Tip: Willingness to relocate could be the difference between you and your competition. Highlight it, but only if it's true.

Tip: Details like numbers help support the extent of your experience.

Tip: Include relevant personal experiences if they help prove that you have skills related to the job.

Hector's Interview

Question: Why do you want to work for us?

Poor answer: Well, my mother wanted me to work for you. She always talked about how good a math student I was, and she wanted me to have a steady job in finance somewhere. She left me the money to get a degree when she died, so I felt like I had to do it. That's why I'm here.

Great answer: I've spent years in school preparing to do something I'm passionate about: helping families with aging parents keep their finances in order. Now that I'm ready to graduate, I'm looking for a place to put my skills and interests to work. I want to work for you because I know you serve the kinds of clients whom I know I could help.

Tip: Employers want to hear about your dreams and goals, not someone else's dreams and goals for you. Tell an interviewer what you want, what you like, what gets you excited.

Question: Why should we hire you?

Poor answer: I'm a new college graduate, so I'm pretty cheap. I figure you are looking to pay around $40,000 a year for this entry-level position, but I'd be willing to take it for 10 percent less as long as I can look forward to twice-annual bonuses. That's a bargain!

Great answer: I'm a new graduate, so I have the most up-to-date training possible. I'm naturally organized and analytical, so I'm well equipped to do the job you want me to do. Plus, I have the experience. I've effectively planned the finances for my own family, and now I volunteer at an elder-care facility helping families in my neighborhood. I'm looking for a new opportunity to continue doing this work and help even more people.

Tip: Don't talk salary until after you've been offered the job. It's rude and presumptive. Instead, focus on selling yourself, highlighting your best qualities.

Question: Do you have any questions for us?

Poor answer: No. I just want the job!

Great answer: Of course. I'd like to know more about your company's management style. What will my relationship with my direct boss be like? Is your office climate casual and collaborative or is it quiet and professional? How do you ensure that your employees have the most up-to-date training? What on my résumé best prepares me for the job you are hiring for?

Tip: Always have questions. Research the company online or in your local library. Questions show interest and curiosity.

APPENDIX 1

WORKING within the Legal ENVIRONMENT

LEARNING goals

1 Define *business law,* distinguish between statutory and common law, and explain the role of administrative agencies.

2 Define *tort law* and explain the role of product liability in tort law.

3 Identify the purposes and conditions of patents, copyrights, and trademarks.

4 Describe warranties and negotiable instruments as covered in the Uniform Commercial Code.

5 List and describe the conditions necessary to make a legally enforceable contract, and describe the possible consequences if such a contract is violated.

6 Summarize several laws that regulate competition and protect consumers in the United States.

7 Explain the role of tax laws in generating income for the government and as a method of discouraging or encouraging certain behaviors among taxpayers.

8 Distinguish among the various types of bankruptcy as outlined by the Bankruptcy Code.

9 Explain the role of deregulation as a tool to encourage competition.

The pharmaceutical companies rely on big, risky investments in new drugs in order to grow. Although a successful drug can bring in as much as $5 billion a year, the cost of research required to bring the drug to market in the first place often doubles that. Even after medicine hits the pharmacy counters, there's still a risk that all those studies could have missed an unforeseen side effect, inevitably leading to lawsuits. As former general counsel for the pharmaceutical giant Merck, Kenneth Frazier knows the defendant's position well and uses that experience in his new role as the company's CEO.

CONNECTING WITH

X   *Kenneth C. Frazier*

CEO of Merck

Hailing from a tough area of Philadelphia, the death of Frazier's mother when he was 12 left him in the care of his exacting father, a janitor who "demanded excellence" from his son. Heeding his father's guidance, Frazier graduated from high school at 16 and attended Pennsylvania State University. After college his admiration of legal pioneers like Supreme Court Justice Thurgood Marshall and civil rights leaders led Frazier to law school. Despite receiving acceptance letters from other elite schools like Stanford, Cornell, and Columbia, Frazier only had eyes for Harvard University.

After he earned his law degree, Frazier took a job at the Philadelphia firm Drinker Biddle & Reath. He soon gained a reputation as a ferocious litigator. In 1991 Frazier and two colleagues were able to secure a new trial for Willie "Bo" Cochran, a man who spent nearly 20 years on death row for murder. Although a court eventually acquitted Cochran in 1997, by that time Frazier had moved on to Merck, defending the company in liability suits. His work caught the attention of executives who promoted Frazier to Merck's general counsel in 1999.

Frazier's greatest challenge appeared in 2004, after Merck discovered that its blockbuster drug Vioxx actually doubled the risk of heart attack and stroke. A surge of lawsuits against Merck surfaced when the company pulled the pill off the market. With annual sales for Vioxx at $2.5 billion, Frazier was faced with a monumental decision. Either he could follow the industry standard and settle all complaints out of court, or he could take the risky route and fight each case in front of a judge. Frazier opted for the latter. He ended up winning 11 of 16 lawsuits at trial before agreeing to set up a $4.85 billion settlement fund in 2007. Although the final legal bill totaled $7.7 billion, Frazier nevertheless managed to greatly reduce the $18 billion that analysts estimated Merck would lose.

Frazier's success in the Vioxx case earned him a promotion to the head of human health business, Merck's largest unit. Three years later he was appointed CEO. As Merck's leader, Frazier has made in-depth drug research a top priority. Perhaps dreading another Vioxx situation, Frazier allocated $8.5 billion to research in 2011 alone. Although Merck's stock tumbled the day Frazier announced his plan, the long-term payoff of that research could be huge. Still, that reward may lie quite far down the line. In 2012 Frazier announced that the ailing world economy, along with the growing generic prescriptions market, will hurt Merck's growth for the next couple of years. While Frazier is confident the company can get past these lean times, who knows if Merck's board will feel the same way. One thing is for sure, though: there'll always be a spot in the courtroom for Frazier should he need to leave business behind.

Legal issues affect almost every area of our lives and of business, too. The United States has more lawyers than any other developed nation in the world and is clearly the world's most litigious society. In this chapter, we will briefly discuss the history and structure of the U.S. legal system. Then we will take a look at key areas of business law such as torts, patents, copyrights, and trademarks as well as sales law, contract law, laws to protect competition and consumers, tax law, and bankruptcy law. We will also discuss the controversial topic of deregulation. You probably won't be ready to go head-to-head with Kenneth Frazier after reading this chapter, but if you use it as a foundation to the study of law, who knows what your future may be?

Sources: Tom Randall, "Merck's Risky Bet on Research," *Bloomberg Businessweek,* April 21, 2011; Christopher K. Hepp, "New Merck CEO Kenneth C. Frazier Has Philadelphia Roots," *The Philadelphia Inquirer,* December 1, 2010; and Linda A. Johnson, "Merck CEO: Generics, Economy to Make 2012–13 Tough," *Associated Press,* May 22, 2012.

NAME THAT company

This automaker sold more cars in the United States than any other auto producer. In 2010–2011, however, the company was forced to recall 3 million cars due to sudden acceleration incidents. It's likely the company will face years of litigation from customers who were affected by the product problem. Name that company. (Find the answer in the appendix.)

LEARNING **goal 1**

Define *business law,* distinguish between statutory and common law, and explain the role of administrative agencies.

THE CASE FOR LAWS

Imagine a society without laws. Just think: no speed limits, no age restrictions on the consumption of alcohol, no limitations on who can practice law or medicine— a society where people are free to do whatever they choose, with no interference. Obviously, the more we consider this possibility, the more unrealistic we realize it is. Laws are an essential part of a civilized nation. Over time, though, the depth and scope of the body of laws must change to continue reflecting the needs of society. The **judiciary** is the branch of government chosen to oversee the legal system through a system of courts.

The U.S. court system is organized at the federal, state, and local levels. At both the federal and state levels, trial courts hear cases involving criminal and civil law. *Criminal law* defines crimes, establishes punishments, and regulates the investigation and prosecution of people accused of committing crimes. *Civil law* proceedings cover noncriminal acts—marriage, personal injury suits, and so on. Both federal and state systems have appellate courts that hear appeals from the losing party about decisions made at the trial-court level. Appellate courts can review and overturn these decisions.

The judiciary also governs the activities and operations of business, including hiring and firing practices, unpaid leave for family emergencies, environmental protection, worker safety, freedom from sexual harassment at work, and more. As you may suspect, businesspeople prefer to set their own standards of behavior and often complain that the government is overstepping its bounds in governing business. Unfortunately, as was evident in the economic crisis that began in 2008, the U.S. business community did not implement acceptable standards—particularly in financial markets—causing government to expand its control and enforcement procedures. This chapter will look at specific laws and regulations and how they affect businesses.

Business law refers to the rules, statutes, codes, and regulations that provide a legal framework for the conduct of business and that are enforceable by court action. A businessperson must be familiar with laws regarding product liability,

judiciary
The branch of government chosen to oversee the legal system through a system of courts.

business law
The rules, statutes, codes, and regulations that provide a legal framework for the conduct of business and that are enforceable by court action.

statutory law
State and federal constitutions, legislative enactments, treaties of the federal government, and ordinances—in short, written law.

common law
The body of law that comes from decisions handed down by courts; also referred to as unwritten law.

sales, contracts, fair competition, consumer protection, taxes, and bankruptcy. Let's start by discussing the foundations of law and what the legal system is all about.

Statutory and Common Law

Two major fields of law are important to business-people: statutory law and common law.

Statutory law includes state and federal constitutions, legislative enactments, treaties of the federal government, and ordinances—in short, written law. You can read the statutes that make up this body of law, but they are often written in language whose meaning must be determined in court. With almost 1.4 million lawyers, the United States has more lawyers per citizen than any country in the world.[1]

Common law is the body of law that comes from decisions handed down by courts. We often call it *unwritten law* because it does not appear in any legislative enactment, treaty, or other written document. Under common law principles, what judges have decided in previous cases is very important in deciding today's cases. Such decisions are called **precedent,** and they guide judges in the handling of new cases. Common law evolves through decisions made in trial courts, appellate courts, and special courts (e.g., probate courts or bankruptcy courts). Lower courts (trial courts) must abide by the precedents set by higher courts (e.g., appellate courts) such as the U.S. Supreme Court.

In the U.S. judicial system, judges are guided in their decisions by the precepts of common law (often called unwritten law because it is based on previous court decisions). Such decisions become precedent and assist other judges in making legal rulings. What are some practical benefits of this process?

Administrative Agencies

Administrative agencies are federal or state institutions and other government organizations created by Congress or state legislatures with delegated power to create rules and regulations within their given area of authority.

Legislative bodies can create administrative agencies and also terminate them. Some administrative agencies hold quasi-legislative, quasi-executive, and quasi-judicial powers. This means that an agency is allowed to pass rules and regulations within its area of authority, conduct investigations in cases of suspected rules violations, and hold hearings if it feels rules and regulations have been violated.

Administrative agencies issue more rulings affecting business and settle more business disputes than courts do. Such agencies include the Securities and Exchange Commission (SEC), the Federal Communications Commission, and the Equal Employment Opportunity Commission (EEOC). Figure A1.1 lists and describes the powers and functions of several administrative agencies at the federal, state, and local levels of government.

precedent
Decisions judges have made in earlier cases that guide the handling of new cases.

administrative agencies
Federal or state institutions and other government organizations created by Congress or state legislatures with delegated power to create rules and regulations within their mandated area of authority.

progress assessment

- What is business law?
- What's the difference between statutory and common law?
- What is an administrative agency?

EXAMPLES OF FEDERAL, STATE, AND LOCAL ADMINISTRATIVE AGENCIES

EXAMPLES	POWERS AND FUNCTIONS
Federal Agencies	
Federal Trade Commission	Enforces laws and guidelines regarding unfair business practices and acts to stop false and deceptive advertising and labeling.
Food and Drug Administration	Enforces laws and regulations to prevent distribution of adulterated or misbranded foods, drugs, medical devices, cosmetics, and veterinary products, as well as any hazardous consumer products.
State Agencies	
Public utility commissions	Set rates that can be charged by various public utilities to prevent unfair pricing by regulated monopolies (e.g., natural gas, electric power companies).
State licensing boards	License various trades and professions within a state (e.g., state cosmetology board, state real estate commission).
Local Agencies	
Maricopa County Planning Commission	Oversees land-use proposals, long-term development objectives, and other long-range issues in Maricopa County, Arizona.
City of Chesterfield Zoning Board	Sets policy regarding zoning of commercial and residential property in the city of Chesterfield, Missouri.

LEARNING goal 2

Define *tort law* and explain the role of product liability in tort law.

TORT LAW

tort
A wrongful act that causes injury to another person's body, property, or reputation.

A **tort** is a wrongful act that causes injury to another person's body, property, or reputation. Although torts often are noncriminal acts, courts can award victims compensation if the conduct that caused the harm is considered intentional. Legally, an *intentional* tort is a willful act that results in injury. The question of intent was a major factor in the lawsuits against the U.S. tobacco industry. Courts had to decide whether tobacco makers intentionally withheld information from the public about the harmful effects of their products.

negligence
In tort law, behavior that causes unintentional harm or injury.

Negligence, in tort law, describes behavior that causes *unintentional* harm or injury. A court's finding of negligence can lead to huge judgments against businesses. In a classic case, McDonald's lost a lawsuit to an elderly woman severely burned by hot coffee bought at a drive-through window. The jury felt that McDonald's failed to provide an adequate warning on the cup. Product liability is a controversial area of tort law, so let's take a closer look at this issue.

Product Liability

product liability
Part of tort law that holds businesses liable for harm that results from the production, design, or use of products they market.

Few issues in business law raise as much debate as product liability.[2] Critics believe product liability laws have gone too far; others feel these laws should be expanded. **Product liability** holds businesses liable for harm that results from the production, design, or inadequate warnings of products they market. The average product liability case costs businesses $5 million, including defense costs, out-of-court settlements, and jury awards.

At one time the legal standard for measuring product liability was whether a producer knowingly placed a hazardous product on the market. Today, many states have extended product liability to the level of **strict product liability**—legally meaning liability without regard to fault. That is, a company that places a defective product on the market can be held liable for damages—a monetary settlement awarded to a person injured by another's actions—even if the company did not know of the defect at the time of sale.[3]

Strict product liability is a major concern for businesses. More than 70 companies have been forced into bankruptcy due to asbestos litigation and the issue is not yet closed. About 3,000 new cases of mesothelioma (a cancer linked to asbestos exposure) are diagnosed every year, keeping the legal docket busy.[4] Lead-based paint producers continue to face expensive lawsuits even though lead-based paint has been banned in the United States since 1978.[5] Mattel was forced to recall 500,000 toy cars produced in China due to lead paint concerns. Toyota Motors recalled 3 million cars in 2010 and 2011 due to sudden acceleration incidents.[6] The company now faces years of litigation from consumers affected by the problem.[7]

Kenneth Frazier, the CEO of Merck and the subject of the Profile of this chapter, knows all too well that manufacturers of chemicals and drugs are vulnerable to lawsuits under strict product liability.[8] Even if a product has gone through the lengthy testing and evaluation process and has been approved by the Food and Drug Administration (FDA), the product's manufacturer is still subject to strict product liability if a side effect or other health problem emerges.[9]

strict product liability
Legal responsibility for harm or injury caused by a product regardless of fault.

figure A1.2

MAJOR PRODUCT LIABILITY CASES

COMPANY	YEAR	SETTLEMENT
Ford Motor Company	1978	$125 million in punitive damages awarded in the case of a 13-year-old boy severely burned in a rear-end collision involving a Ford Pinto
A. H. Robins	1987	Dalkon Shield intrauterine birth-control devices recalled after eight separate punitive-damage awards
Playtex Company	1988	Considered liable and suffered a $10 million damage award in the case of a toxic shock syndrome fatality in Kansas; removed certain types of tampons from the market
Jack in the Box	1993	Assessed large damages after a two-year-old child who ate at Jack in the Box died of *E. coli* poisoning and others became ill
Sara Lee Corporation	1998	Costly company recall necessitated when tainted hot dogs caused food-poisoning death of 15 people
General Motors	1999	Suffered $4.8 billion punitive award in a faulty fuel-tank case
Major Tobacco Firms	2004	$130 billion sought by the federal government for smoking cessation programs (settled for $10 billion)

Sources: U.S. Department of Justice and American Trial Lawyers Association.

Some product liability cases have raised intriguing questions about responsibility.[10] Handgun manufacturers were unsuccessfully sued by cities including Chicago and Miami for the costs of police work and medical care necessitated by gun violence. McDonald's faced a product liability suit (later dismissed) claiming that its food caused obesity, diabetes, and other health problems in children.[11] Some communities, however, have reacted by banning trans fats in food, regulating menu information, and eliminating toys in children's products like McDonald's Happy Meals. Many schools are replacing soft drinks in vending machines with fruit juice and water.

Tort and product liability reform has been a key objective of business for many years. Congress took action with passage of the Class Action Fairness Act in 2005, which expanded federal jurisdiction over many large class-action lawsuits.[12] Businesses and insurance companies argue that more needs to be done to assist companies with product liability. Consumer protection groups disagree and feel not enough is being done to protect consumers. Figure A1.2 highlights several major product liability awards that have cost companies dearly.

LEARNING goal 3

Identify the purposes and conditions of patents, copyrights, and trademarks.

LEGALLY PROTECTING IDEAS: PATENTS, COPYRIGHTS, AND TRADEMARKS

Have you ever invented a product you think may have commercial value? Many people have, and to protect their ideas they took the next step and applied for a patent. A **patent** is a document that gives inventors exclusive rights to their inventions for 20 years from the date they file the patent applications.[13]

The 6,200 examiners in the U.S. Patent and Trademark Office (USPTO) review over 535,000 patent requests each year and grant almost 250,000. The agency has a current backlog of 1,200,000 patents that are pending and 700,000 awaiting initial review; the approval process generally takes almost three years.[14] To reduce the backlog, the U.S. Supreme Court imposed stricter standards of "obviousness" on the process, which means that a patent cannot be granted for an invention that is an obvious extension of an existing product. The court, however, has not offered legal clarity on exactly what can be patented.[15]

Patent applicants must make sure a product is truly unique and should seek the advice of an attorney; in fact, fewer than 2 percent of product inventors file on their own. How good are your chances of receiving a patent if you file for one? About 50 percent of patent applications are approved, with fees that vary according to the complexity of the patent. A patent dealing with complex technology can cost anywhere from $10,000 to $30,000.[16] A patent dealing with simpler concepts will cost the inventor about $7,000 to $10,000.

Patent owners have the right to sell or license the use of their patent to others. Foreign companies are also eligible to file for U.S. patents. They account for nearly half the U.S. patents issued. Penalties for violating a patent (patent infringement) can be costly.[17] Dr. Gary Michelson received a settlement of $1.35 billion from Medtronic Inc. to end litigation and license patents covering

patent
A document that gives inventors exclusive rights to their inventions for 20 years.

a range of back-surgery products. The USPTO does not take action on behalf of patent holders if patent infringement occurs. The defense of patent rights is solely the job of the patent holder and can be quite expensive.[18]

The American Inventors Protection Act requires that patent applications be made public after 18 months regardless of whether a patent has been awarded. This law was passed in part to address critics who argued that some inventors intentionally delayed or dragged out a patent application because they expected others to eventually develop similar products or technology. Then when someone (usually a large company) filed for a similar patent, the inventor surfaced to claim the patent—referred to as a *submarine patent*—and demanded large royalties (fees) for its use. The late engineer Jerome Lemelson, for example, reportedly collected more than $1.3 billion in patent royalties for a series of long-delayed patents—including forerunners of the fax machine, the Walkman, and the bar-code scanner—from auto, computer, retail, and electronics companies.

Technology companies like Verizon, Google, and Cisco have taken action to defend themselves against patent infringement suits by joining Allied Security Trust, a not-for-profit firm that acquires intellectual property of interest to its members. The idea is to buy up patents that could impact their companies before they fall into the hands of others (mainly law firms and venture capitalists) looking to pursue settlements or legal damages against the tech firms.

Just as a patent protects an inventor's right to a product or process, a **copyright** protects a creator's rights to materials such as books, articles, photos, paintings, and cartoons. Copyrights are filed with the Library of Congress and require a minimum of paperwork. They last for the lifetime of the author or artist plus 70 years and can be passed on to the creator's heirs. The Copyright Act of 1978, however, gives a special term of 75 years from publication to works published before January 1, 1978, whose copyrights had not expired by that date. The holder of a copyright can either prevent anyone from using the copyrighted material or charge a fee for using it. Author J. K. Rowling won a copyright violation suit against a fan who wanted to publish an unauthorized Harry Potter encyclopedia. If a work is created by an employee in the normal course of a job, the copyright belongs to the employer and lasts 95 years from publication or 120 years from creation, whichever comes first.

A *trademark* is a legally protected name, symbol, or design (or combination of these) that identifies the goods or services of one seller and distinguishes them from those of competitors. Trademarks generally belong to the owner forever, as long as they are properly registered and renewed every 10 years. Some well-known trademarks include the Aflac duck, Disney's Mickey Mouse, the Nike swoosh, and the golden arches of McDonald's. Like a patent, a trademark is protected against infringement. Businesses fight hard to protect trademarks, especially in global markets where trademark pirating can be extensive.[19] (Chapter 14 discusses trademarks in more detail.)

Media companies have sued YouTube for carrying videos of their popular television shows on its web-site. YouTube says that it makes every effort to remove any copyrighted video that users download to the site. Do you think YouTube should be held liable for copyrighted video downloaded by others? Why or why not?

copyright
A document that protects a creator's rights to materials such as books, articles, photos, paintings, and cartoons.

Uniform Commercial Code (UCC)
A comprehensive commercial law adopted by every state in the United States that covers sales laws and other commercial laws.

progress assessment

- What is tort law?
- What is product liability? What is strict product liability?
- How many years is a patent protected from infringement?
- What is a copyright?

Would you buy a new car if the dealer offered no warranty? How about an iPhone or a major kitchen appliance with no guarantee of performance? Warranties are an important part of a product and are generally of major concern to purchasers. It's important to check whether a product's warranty is full or limited. Should colleges offer students warranties with their degree programs?

LEARNING goal 4

Describe warranties and negotiable instruments as covered in the Uniform Commercial Code.

SALES LAW: THE UNIFORM COMMERCIAL CODE

At one time, laws governing businesses varied from state to state, making interstate trade extremely complicated. Today, all states have adopted the same commercial law. The **Uniform Commercial Code (UCC)** is a comprehensive commercial law that covers sales laws and other commercial laws. Since all 50 states have adopted the law (although it does not apply in certain sections of Louisiana), the UCC simplifies commercial transactions across state lines.

The UCC has 11 articles, which contain laws covering sales; commercial paper such as promissory notes and checks; bank deposits and collections; letters of credit; bulk transfers; warehouse receipts, bills of lading, and other documents of title; investment securities; and secured transactions. We do not have space in this text to discuss all 11 articles, but we will discuss two: Article 2, which regulates warranties, and Article 3, which covers negotiable instruments.

Warranties

A *warranty* guarantees that the product sold will be acceptable for the purpose for which the buyer intends to use it. There are two types of warranties. **Express warranties** are specific representations by sellers that buyers rely on regarding the goods they purchase. The warranty you receive in the box with an iPad or a toaster is an express warranty.

Implied warranties are legally imposed on the seller, who implies that a product will conform to the customary standards of the trade or industry in which it competes. An implied warranty entitles you to expect that a toaster will toast your bread to your desired degree (light, medium, dark) or that food you buy for consumption off an establishment's premises is fit to eat.[20]

Warranties can be either full or limited. A full warranty requires a seller to replace or repair a product at no charge if the product is defective, whereas a limited warranty typically limits the defects or mechanical problems the seller covers. Companies often offer extended warranties that provide more coverage, but for a price, of course.[21] Many of the rights of buyers, including the right to accept or reject goods, are spelled out in Article 2 of the UCC.

Negotiable Instruments

Negotiable instruments are forms of commercial paper (such as checks) that are transferable among businesses and individuals; they represent a promise to pay a specified amount. Article 3 of the Uniform Commercial Code requires negotiable instruments to follow four conditions. They must (1) be written and signed by the maker or drawer, (2) be made payable on demand or at a certain time, (3) be made payable to the bearer (the person holding the instrument) or to specific order, and (4) contain an unconditional promise to pay a specified amount of money. Checks or other forms of negotiable instruments are transferred (negotiated for payment) when the payee signs the back. The payee's signature is called an *endorsement*.

LEARNING goal 5

> List and describe the conditions necessary to make a legally enforceable contract, and describe the possible consequences if such a contract is violated.

CONTRACT LAW

If I offer to sell you my bike for $50 and later change my mind, can you force me to sell the bike by saying we had a contract? If I lose $120 to you in a poker game, can you sue in court to get your money? If I agree to sing at your wedding for free and back out at the last minute, can you claim I violated a contract? These are the kinds of questions contract law answers.

A **contract** is a legally enforceable agreement between two or more parties. **Contract law** specifies what constitutes a legally enforceable agreement. Basically, a contract is legally binding if the following conditions are met:

1. *An offer is made.* An offer to do something or sell something can be oral or written. If I agree to sell you my bike for $50, I have made an offer. That offer is not legally binding, however, until the following other conditions are met.

2. *There is a voluntary acceptance of the offer.* The principle of *mutual acceptance* means that both parties to a contract must agree on the terms. If I use duress—coercion through force or threat of force—in getting you to agree to buy my bike, the contract will not be legal. You couldn't use duress to get me to sell my bike, either. Even if we both agree, though, the contract is still not legally binding without the next four conditions.

3. *Both parties give consideration.* **Consideration** means something of value. If I agree to sell you my bike for $50, the bike and the $50 are consideration, and we have a legally binding contract. If I agree to sing at your wedding and you do not give me anything in return (consideration), we have no contract.

---

express warranties
Specific representations by the seller that buyers rely on regarding the goods they purchase.

implied warranties
Guarantees concerning products legally imposed on the seller.

negotiable instruments
Forms of commercial paper (such as checks) that are transferable among businesses and individuals and represent a promise to pay a specified amount.

contract
A legally enforceable agreement between two or more parties.

contract law
Set of laws that specify what constitutes a legally enforceable agreement.

consideration
Something of value; consideration is one of the requirements of a legal contract.

4. *Both parties are competent.* A person under the influence of alcohol or drugs, or a person of unsound mind (one who has been legally declared incompetent), cannot be held to a contract. In many cases, a minor may not be held to a contract either. If a 15-year-old agrees to pay $10,000 for a car, the seller will not be able to enforce the contract due to the buyer's lack of competence.

5. *The contract covers a legal act.* A contract covering the sale of illegal drugs or stolen merchandise is unenforceable since such sales are violations of criminal law. (If gambling is prohibited by state law in your state, you cannot sue to collect the poker debt.)

6. *The contract is in proper form.* An agreement for the sale of goods worth $500 or more must be in writing. Contracts that cannot be fulfilled within one year also must be put in writing. Contracts regarding real property (land and everything attached to it) must be in writing.

Breach of Contract

breach of contract
When one party fails to follow the terms of a contract.

Both parties in a contract may voluntarily choose to end the agreement. **Breach of contract** occurs when one party fails to follow the terms of a contract. If that happens the following may occur:

1. *Specific performance.* The party who violated the contract may be required to live up to the agreement if money damages would not be adequate. If I legally offered to sell you a rare painting, I would have to sell you that painting.

damages
The monetary settlement awarded to a person who is injured by a breach of contract.

2. *Payment of damages.* If I fail to live up to a contract, you can sue me for **damages,** usually the amount you would lose from my nonperformance. If we had a legally binding contract for me to sing at your wedding, for example, and I failed to come, you could sue me for the cost of hiring a new singer.

3. *Discharge of obligation.* If I fail to live up to my end of a contract, you can agree to drop the matter. Generally you would not have to live up to your end of the agreement either.

Lawyers would not be paid so handsomely if contract law were as simple as implied in these rules. That's why it's always best to put a contract in writing even though oral contracts can be enforceable under contract law. The contract should clearly specify the offer and consideration, and the parties to the contract should sign and date it. A contract does not have to be complicated as long as (1) it is in writing, (2) it specifies mutual consideration, and (3) it contains a clear offer and agreement.

progress assessment

- What is the purpose of the Universal Commercial Code (UCC)?
- Compare express and implied warranties.
- What are the four elements of a negotiable instrument specified in the UCC?
- What are the six conditions for a legally binding contract? What can happen if a contract is breached?

LEARNING goal 6

Summarize several laws that regulate competition and protect consumers in the United States.

PROMOTING FAIR AND COMPETITIVE BUSINESS PRACTICES

Competition is a cornerstone of the free-market system (see Chapter 2). A key responsibility of legislators is to pass laws that ensure a competitive atmosphere among businesses and promote fair business practices. The U.S. Justice Department's antitrust division and other government agencies serve as watchdogs to guarantee competition in markets flows freely and new competitors have open access to the market. The government's power here is broad. The Justice Department's antitrust division has investigated the competitive practices of market giants such as Microsoft, Apple, Visa, and Google. Figure A1.3 highlights several high-profile antitrust cases.

Antitrust oversight was not always the rule, however. Big businesses were once able to force smaller competitors out of business with little government resistance. The following brief history details how government responded to past problems. We'll also look at new challenges government regulators face today.

The History of Antitrust Legislation

In the late 19th century, big oil companies, railroads, steel companies, and other industrial firms dominated the U.S. economy. Some feared that such large and powerful companies would be able to crush any competitors and then charge high prices. In that atmosphere, Congress passed the Sherman Antitrust Act in 1890 to prevent large organizations from stifling the competition of smaller or newer firms. The Sherman Act forbids (1) contracts, combinations, or conspiracies in restraint of trade, and (2) the creation of actual monopolies or attempts to monopolize any part of trade or commerce.

figure A1.3
HISTORY OF HIGH-PROFILE ANTITRUST CASES

CASE	OUTCOME
United States v. *Standard Oil* 1911	Standard Oil broken up into 34 companies; Amoco, Chevron, and ExxonMobil are results of the breakup
United States v. *American Tobacco* 1911	American Tobacco split into 16 companies; British Tobacco and R. J. Reynolds are results of the breakup
United States v. *E. I. du Pont de Nemours* 1961	DuPont ordered to divest its 23 percent ownership stake in General Motors
United States v. *AT&T* 1982	Settled after Ma Bell agreed to spin off its local telephone operations into seven regional operating companies
United States v. *Microsoft* 2000	Microsoft ordered to halt prior anticompetitive practices

Source: U.S. Department of Justice.

Because some of the language in the Sherman Act was vague, there was doubt about just what practices it prohibited. To clarify its intentions Congress enacted the following laws.

- *The Clayton Act of 1914.* The Clayton Act prohibits exclusive dealing, tying contracts, and interlocking directorates. It also prohibits buying large amounts of stock in competing corporations. *Exclusive dealing* is selling goods with the condition that the buyer will not buy from a competitor (when the effect lessens competition). A *tying contract* requires a buyer to purchase unwanted items in order to purchase desired ones. Let's say I wanted to purchase 20 cases of Pepsi-Cola per week to sell in my restaurant. Pepsi, however, says it will sell me the 20 cases only if I also agree to buy 10 cases each of its Mountain Dew and Diet Pepsi products. My purchase of Pepsi-Cola would be *tied* to the purchase of the other two products. An *interlocking directorate* occurs when a company's board of directors includes members of the boards of competing corporations.

- *The Federal Trade Commission Act of 1914.* The Federal Trade Commission Act prohibits unfair methods of competition in commerce. This legislation set up the five-member Federal Trade Commission (FTC) to enforce compliance with the act. The FTC deals with a wide range of competitive issues—everything from preventing companies from making misleading "Made in the USA" claims to insisting funeral providers give consumers accurate, itemized price information about funeral goods and services.[22] The activity level of the FTC typically depends on its commission members at the time. It has the added responsibility for overseeing mergers and acquisitions (Chapter 5) in the health care, energy, computer hardware, automotive, and biotechnology industries. The Wheeler-Lea Amendment of 1938 gave the FTC additional jurisdiction over false or misleading advertising, along with the power to increase fines if its requirements are not met within 60 days.

- *The Robinson-Patman Act of 1936.* The Robinson-Patman Act prohibits price discrimination and applies to both sellers and buyers who knowingly induce or receive price discrimination. Certain types of price-cutting are criminal offenses punishable by fine and imprisonment. That includes price differences that "substantially" weaken competition unless they can be justified by lower selling costs associated with larger purchases. The law also prohibits advertising and promotional allowances unless they are offered to all retailers, large and small. Remember that this legislation applies to business-to-business transactions and not to business-to-consumer transactions.

The change in U.S. business from manufacturing to knowledge-based technology has created new regulatory challenges for federal agencies. In the early 2000s, Microsoft's competitive practices were the focus of an intense antitrust investigation by the Justice Department. The government charged that Microsoft hindered competition by refusing to sell its Windows operating system to computer manufacturers that refused to sell Windows-based computers exclusively.[23] The case ended with a settlement between the Justice Department and Microsoft that expired in 2011. Many antitrust advocates believe the case broadened the definition of anticompetitive behavior and proved the government's resolve in enforcing antitrust laws.[24] The NASDAQ OMX and Intercontinental Exchange Inc., for example, withdrew their bid for the NYSE Euronext when the Justice Department threatened an antitrust lawsuit in 2011.[25] Google and Yahoo dropped a proposed agreement whereby Google would have provided some search advertising for Yahoo when the Justice Department promised legal action. It's safe to conclude antitrust issues will persist in the future.

LAWS TO PROTECT CONSUMERS

Consumerism is a social movement that seeks to increase and strengthen the rights and powers of buyers in relationship to sellers. It is the people's way of getting a fair share and equitable treatment in marketing exchanges. The Public Company Accounting Reform and Investor Protection Act (better known as the Sarbanes-Oxley Act) was passed to allay concerns about falsified financial statements from companies like Enron and WorldCom in the early 2000s. The financial crisis beginning in 2008 again fueled consumer anger, this time against the Treasury Department, Federal Reserve, and Securities and Exchange Commission (SEC) for their lack of oversight of the financial markets. The collapse of the real estate market, crisis in the banking industry, and failure of quasi-governmental mortgage

consumerism
A social movement that seeks to increase and strengthen the rights and powers of buyers in relation to sellers.

figure A1.4

CONSUMER PROTECTION LAWS

Fair Packaging and Labeling Act (1966)	Makes unfair or deceptive packaging or labeling of certain consumer commodities illegal.
Child Protection Act (1966)	Removes from sale potentially harmful toys and allows the FDA to pull dangerous products from the market.
Truth-in-Lending Act (1968)	Requires full disclosure of all finance charges on consumer credit agreements and in advertisements of credit plans.
Child Protection and Toy Safety Act (1969)	Protects children from toys and other products that contain thermal, electrical, or mechanical hazards.
Fair Credit Reporting Act (1970)	Requires that consumer credit reports contain only accurate, relevant, and recent information and are confidential unless a proper party requests them for an appropriate reason.
Consumer Product Safety Act (1972)	Created an independent agency to protect consumers from unreasonable risk of injury arising from consumer products and to set safety standards.
Magnuson-Moss Warranty–Federal Trade Commission Improvement Act (1975)	Provides for minimum disclosure standards for written consumer product warranties and allows the FTC to prescribe interpretive rules and policy statements regarding unfair or deceptive practices.
Alcohol Labeling Legislation (1988)	Provides for warning labels on liquor saying that women shouldn't drink when pregnant and that alcohol impairs a person's abilities.
Nutrition Labeling and Education Act (1990)	Requires truthful and uniform nutritional labeling on every food the FDA regulates.
Consumer Credit Reporting Reform Act (1997)	Increases responsibility of credit issuers for accurate credit data and requires creditors to verify that disputed data are accurate. Consumer notification is necessary before reinstating the data.
Children's Online Privacy Protection Act (2000)	Gives parents control over what information is collected online from their children under age 13; requires website operators to maintain the confidentiality, security, and integrity of the personal information collected from children.
Country of Origin Labeling Law (2009)	Requires that the product label on most food products sold in U.S. supermarkets gives the product's country of origin.
Credit Card Accountability, Responsibility, and Disclosure (CARD) Act (2009)	Designed to protect consumers from unfair credit card practices.

agencies such as Fannie Mae and Freddie Mac led to passage of the Dodd-Frank Wall Street Reform and Consumer Protection Act.[26] This legislation created the Consumer Financial Protection Bureau that provides government oversight involving consumers in areas such as online banking, home mortgage loans, and high-interest payday loans.[27] Figure A1.4 lists other major consumer protection laws.

LEARNING goal 7

Explain the role of tax laws in generating income for the government and as a method of discouraging or encouraging certain behaviors among taxpayers.

TAX LAWS

taxes
How the government (federal, state, and local) raises money.

Mention taxes and most people frown. **Taxes** are the way federal, state, and local governments raise money. They affect almost every individual and business in the United States.

Governments primarily use taxes as a source of funding for their operations and programs. Taxes can also help discourage or encourage certain behaviors among taxpayers. If the government wishes to reduce consumer use of certain classes of products like cigarettes or liquor, it can pass *sin taxes* on them to raise their cost. Since the financial crisis began in 2008, increasing sin taxes (i.e., taxes on things like liquor and cigarettes) has also become a popular way for cash-starved states to raise revenue.[28] In other situations, the government may encourage businesses to hire new employees or purchase new equipment by offering a *tax credit,* an amount firms can deduct from their tax bill.

Taxes are levied from a variety of sources. Income taxes (personal and business), sales taxes, and property taxes are the major bases of tax revenue. The federal government receives its largest share of taxes from income.[29] States and local communities make extensive use of sales taxes. School districts generally depend on property taxes.

figure A1.5

TYPES OF TAXES

TYPE	PURPOSE
Income taxes	Taxes paid on the income received by businesses and individuals. Income taxes are the largest source of tax income received by the federal government.
Property taxes	Taxes paid on real and personal property. *Real property* is real estate owned by individuals and businesses. *Personal property* is a broader category that includes any movable property such as tangible items (wedding rings, equipment, etc.) or intangible items (stocks, checks, mortgages, etc.). Taxes are based on their assessed value.
Sales taxes	Taxes paid on merchandise sold at the retail level.
Excise taxes	Taxes paid on selected items such as tobacco, alcoholic beverages, airline travel, gasoline, and firearms. These are often referred to as *sin taxes*. Income generated from the tax goes toward a specifically designated purpose. For example, gasoline taxes often help the federal government and state governments pay for highway construction or improvements.

The tax policies of states and cities are important considerations when businesses seek to locate operations. They also affect personal decisions such as retirement. As government revenues at all levels dwindle, new tax issues are sure to be debated. States claim they are losing billions in sales taxes by not collecting from Internet sales transactions.[30] States like Illinois, Arkansas, Connecticut, and New York have already taken action.[31] New York, for example, passed a law that requires out-of-state online companies to collect sales taxes from New York shoppers. Other states are petitioning Congress to pass a law permitting them to collect sales taxes from e-commerce transactions.[32] The European Union levies certain Internet taxes, so expect the U.S. debate to intensify. Figure A1.5 highlights the primary types of taxes levied on individuals and businesses.

LEARNING goal 8

Distinguish among the various types of bankruptcy as outlined by the Bankruptcy Code.

BANKRUPTCY LAWS

Bankruptcy is the legal process by which a person, business, or government entity, unable to meet financial obligations, is relieved of those debts by a court. Courts divide any of the debtor's assets among creditors, allowing them to recover at least part of their money and freeing the debtor to begin anew. The U.S. Constitution gives Congress the power to establish bankruptcy laws, and legislation has existed since the 1890s. Major amendments to the bankruptcy code include the Bankruptcy Amendments and Federal Judgeship Act of 1984, the Bankruptcy Reform Act of 1994, and the Bankruptcy Abuse Prevention and Consumer Protection Act of 2005.

The 1984 law allows a person who is bankrupt to keep part of the equity (ownership) in a house and car, and some other personal property. The 1994 Act amended more than 45 sections of the bankruptcy code and created reforms to speed up and simplify the process. The Bankruptcy Abuse Prevention and Consumer Protection Act of 2005 was passed to reduce the total number of bankruptcy filings and to eliminate the perceived ease of filing. The legislation increased the cost of filing and made it difficult for people (especially those with high incomes) to escape overwhelming debt from credit cards, medical bills, student loans, or other loans not secured through a home or other asset. It also requires debtors to receive credit counseling.

Bankruptcies started growing in the late 1980s and have increased tremendously since. Many attribute the increase to a lessening of the stigma of bankruptcy, an increase in understanding of bankruptcy law and its protections, and increased advertising by bankruptcy attorneys. Some suggest that the ease with which certain consumers could get credit contributed to the number of filings by allowing people to readily overspend. The 2005 reform helped reduce the annual number of bankruptcy filings to 600,000 from an average of 1.5 million between 2001 and 2004. However, the financial crisis beginning in 2008 pushed the number of bankruptcies again to over a million. As the economy continues to come back slowly, bankruptcies reached approximately 1.3 million in 2012. Although high-profile bankruptcies of businesses—such as Blockbuster, Circuit City, Borders, and General Motors—tend to dominate the news, over 90 percent of bankruptcy filings each year are by individuals.

bankruptcy
The legal process by which a person, business, or government entity unable to meet financial obligations is relieved of those obligations by a court that divides any assets among creditors, allowing creditors to get at least part of their money and freeing the debtor to begin anew.

voluntary bankruptcy
Legal procedures initiated by a debtor.

involuntary bankruptcy
Bankruptcy procedures filed by a debtor's creditors.

Bankruptcy can be either voluntary or involuntary. In **voluntary bankruptcy,** the debtor applies for bankruptcy; in **involuntary bankruptcy,** the creditors start legal action against the debtor. Most bankruptcies are voluntary, since creditors usually wait in hopes they will be paid all the money due them rather than settle for only part of it.

Bankruptcy procedures begin when a petition is filed with the court under one of the following sections of the Bankruptcy Code:

Chapter 7—"straight bankruptcy" or liquidation (used by businesses and individuals).

Chapter 11—reorganization (used almost exclusively by businesses).

Chapter 13—repayment (used by individuals).

Chapter 7 is the most popular form of bankruptcy among individuals; it requires the sale of nonexempt assets.[33] Under federal exemption statutes, a debtor may be able to retain (exempt) up to $21,625 of equity in a home; up to $3,225 of equity in an automobile; up to $11,525 in household furnishings, apparel, and musical instruments; and up to $1,450 in jewelry.[34] States can choose different exemption statutes. When the sale of assets is over, creditors, including the government if taxes are owed, divide the remaining cash as stipulated by law. First, creditors with secured claims receive the collateral for their claims or repossess the claimed asset (such as an automobile or home); then unsecured claims (backed by no asset) are paid in this order:

1. Costs of the bankruptcy case.

2. Any business costs incurred after bankruptcy was filed.

3. Wages, salaries, or commissions owed (limited to $2,000 per creditor).

4. Contributions to employee benefit plans.

5. Refunds to consumers who paid for products that weren't delivered (limited to $900 per claimant).

6. Federal and state taxes.

Figure A1.6 outlines the steps used in liquidating assets under Chapter 7.

Under Chapter 11 bankruptcy law, the mighty can fall. Borders, the second largest U.S. bookstore chain, filed for bankruptcy after management changes, job cuts, and debt restructuring failed to make up for declining book sales. Do you know of other companies forced into bankruptcy due to the recent recession?

In Chapter 11 bankruptcy, a company sued by creditors continues to operate under court protection while it tries to work out a plan for paying off its debts. Under certain conditions it may sell assets, borrow money, and change company officers to strengthen its market position. A court-appointed trustee supervises the proceedings and protects the creditors' interests.

A company does not have to be insolvent to file for relief under Chapter 11. In theory, it is a way for sick companies to recover, designed to help both debtors and creditors find the best solution. In reality, however, less than one-third of Chapter

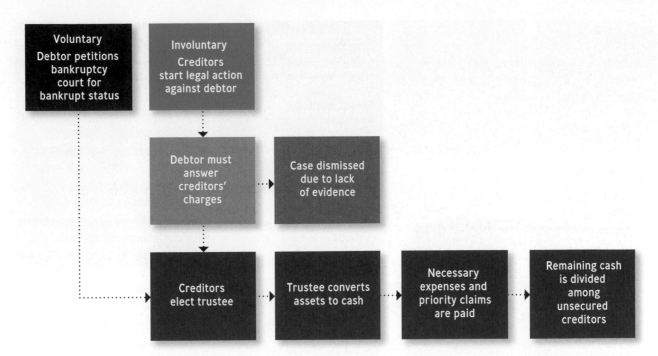

figure A1.6

HOW ASSETS ARE DIVIDED IN BANKRUPTCY

This figure shows that the creditor (the person owed money) selects the trustee (the person or organization that handles the sale of assets). Note that the process may be started by the debtor or the creditors.

11 companies survive—usually those with lots of cash available. The Bankruptcy Reform Act of 1994 provides a fast-track procedure for small businesses filing under Chapter 11. Individuals can also file under Chapter 11, but it's uncommon.

Chapter 13 permits individuals, including small-business owners, to pay back creditors over three to five years. Chapter 13 proceedings are less complicated and less expensive than Chapter 7 proceedings. The debtor files a proposed plan with the court for paying off debts. If the plan is approved, the debtor pays a court-appointed trustee in monthly installments as agreed on in the repayment plan. The trustee then pays each creditor.

LEARNING goal 9

Explain the role of deregulation as a tool to encourage competition.

DEREGULATION VERSUS REGULATION

Under article 1, section 8, clause 3 of the U.S. Constitution, the Commerce Clause gives Congress the right "to regulate commerce." The debate concerning the degree of regulation, however, has been a source of disagreement for many years.[35] At one time, the United States had laws and regulations covering almost every aspect of business. Some felt there were too many laws and regulations, costing the public too much money (see Figure A1.7). A movement toward deregulation took hold. **Deregulation** means that the government withdraws certain laws and regulations that seem to hinder competition. The most publicized examples of deregulation first occurred in the airline and telecommunications industries.

Consumers clearly benefited from the Airline Deregulation Act of 1978 that ended federal control of commercial airlines. Before passage of the act, the government restricted where airlines could land and fly. When the restrictions were

deregulation
Government withdrawal of certain laws and regulations that seem to hinder competition.

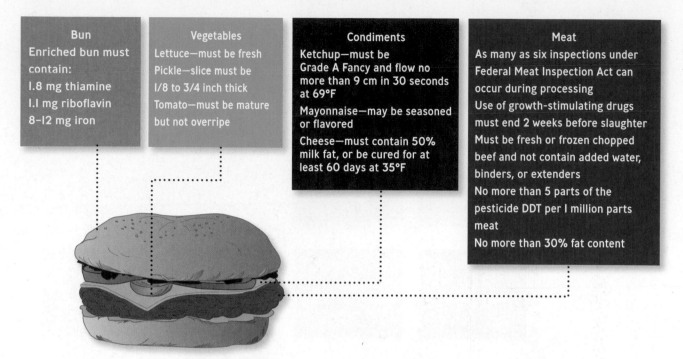

Bun
Enriched bun must contain:
1.8 mg thiamine
1.1 mg riboflavin
8–12 mg iron

Vegetables
Lettuce—must be fresh
Pickle—slice must be 1/8 to 3/4 inch thick
Tomato—must be mature but not overripe

Condiments
Ketchup—must be Grade A Fancy and flow no more than 9 cm in 30 seconds at 69°F
Mayonnaise—may be seasoned or flavored
Cheese—must contain 50% milk fat, or be cured for at least 60 days at 35°F

Meat
As many as six inspections under Federal Meat Inspection Act can occur during processing
Use of growth-stimulating drugs must end 2 weeks before slaughter
Must be fresh or frozen chopped beef and not contain added water, binders, or extenders
No more than 5 parts of the pesticide DDT per 1 million parts meat
No more than 30% fat content

figure A1.7

HAMBURGER REGULATIONS

Does this amount of regulation seem just right, too little, or too much for you?

lifted, airlines began competing for different routes and charging lower prices. The skies were also opened to new competitors, such as Southwest, to take advantage of new opportunities.[36] Today some believe the airline industry could use more government intervention since passenger services have decreased, delays and flight cancellations have increased, and charges, such as bag fees, have become common.

Passage of the Telecommunications Act in 1996 brought similar deregulation to telecommunications and gave consumers a flood of options in local telephone service markets. There was also a significant increase in retail video competition. In the past, most households received only four TV channels (the three major networks—NBC, CBS, and ABC—and public broadcasting). Today most households receive a dozen or more over-the-air stations and hundreds more on cable, satellite, and the Internet.

Deregulation efforts have also been attempted in the electric power industry. Twenty-two states have passed utility deregulation laws intended to increase competition and provide consumers with lower price options. California became the first state to deregulate electric power in the late 1990s and experienced significant problems, especially with large-scale blackouts (loss of power). Blackouts also occurred on the East Coast. Still, some utility deregulation programs have been somewhat successful. Time will tell whether utility deregulation will survive and prosper.

Unfortunately, deregulation has not always worked as desired. The financial market crisis beginning in 2008 reopened the question of how much deregulation is too much. New regulations in the banking and investments industries changed the nature of financial and mortgage markets and created huge problems. For example, the Federal Reserve System's reluctance to toughen mortgage regulations and the government's insistence on providing more home loans to high-risk borrowers contributed to the collapse in the real estate market.[37] The financial crisis that followed led to passage of the most sweeping regulation of financial markets since the Great Depression.[38]

In 2010, the U.S. Congress passed the Patient Protection and Affordable Care Act (PPACA), also known as Obamacare, that introduced a comprehensive system of mandated health insurance for 32 million Americans not covered under an insurance plan.[39] The bill also provides for increased government regulation of the insurance industry. While the bill is to be phased in over a four-year period, proposed adjustments to the legislation promise to keep the PPACA in the news.[40]

Most agree some regulation of business seems necessary to ensure fair and honest dealings with the public. Corporate scandals in the early 2000s and the financial crisis led consumers and investors to call for increased government regulation in the financial sector. While the final resolution of the government's health care bill remains to be seen, most agree that businesses will need to deal with some form of health care regulation. With increasing global competition, U.S. business will need to work with government to create a competitive environment that is fair and open and accept responsibilities to all stakeholders.

progress assessment

- What is the primary purpose of antitrust law?
- Describe the different bankruptcy provisions under Chapters 7, 11, and 13.
- What is deregulation? Give examples of successful and unsuccessful deregulation.

summary

Learning Goal 1. Define *business law,* distinguish between statutory and common law, and explain the role of administrative agencies.

- **What is the difference between statutory law and common law?**

Statutory law includes state and federal constitutions, legislative enactments, treaties of the federal government, and ordinances—in short, written law. Common law is the body of unwritten law that comes from decisions handed down by judges.

- **What are administrative agencies?**

Administrative agencies are federal or state institutions and other government organizations created by Congress or state legislatures with power to create rules and regulations within their area of authority.

Learning Goal 2. Define *tort law* and explain the role of product liability in tort law.

- **What is an intentional tort?**

An intentional tort is a willful act that results in injury.

- **What is negligence?**

Negligence, in tort law, is behavior that causes *unintentional* harm or injury. Findings of negligence can lead to huge judgments against businesses.

Learning Goal 3. Identify the purposes and conditions of patents, copyrights, and trademarks.

- **What are patents and copyrights?**

A patent is a document that gives inventors exclusive rights to their inventions for 20 years from the date they file the patent applications. A copyright protects a creator's rights to materials such as books, articles, photos, paintings, and cartoons.

- **What is a trademark?**

A trademark is a legally protected name, symbol, or design (or combination of these) that identifies the goods or services of one seller and distinguishes them from those of competitors.

Learning Goal 4. Describe warranties and negotiable instruments as covered in the Uniform Commercial Code.

- **What does Article 2 of the UCC cover?**

Article 2 contains laws regarding warranties. Express warranties are guarantees made by the seller, whereas implied warranties are guarantees imposed on the seller by law.

- **What does Article 3 of the UCC cover?**

Article 3 covers negotiable instruments such as checks. A negotiable instrument must (1) be written and signed by the maker or drawer, (2) be made payable on demand or at a certain time, (3) be made payable to the bearer (the person holding the instrument) or to specific order, and (4) contain an unconditional promise to pay a specified amount of money.

Learning Goal 5. List and describe the conditions necessary to make a legally enforceable contract, and describe the possible consequences if such a contract is violated.

- **What makes a contract enforceable under the law?**

An enforceable contract must meet six conditions: (1) an offer must be made, (2) the offer must be voluntarily accepted, (3) both parties must give consideration, (4) both parties must be competent, (5) the contract must be legal, and (6) the contract must be in proper form.

- **What are the possible consequences if a contract is violated?**

If a contract is violated, one of the following may be required: (1) specific performance, (2) payment of damages, or (3) discharge of obligation.

Learning Goal 6. Summarize several laws that regulate competition and protect consumers in the United States.

- **What does the Sherman Act cover?**

The Sherman Act forbids contracts, combinations, or conspiracies in restraint of trade and actual monopolies or attempts to monopolize any part of trade or commerce.

- **What does the Clayton Act add?**

The Clayton Act prohibits exclusive dealing, tying contracts, interlocking directorates, and buying large amounts of stock in competing corporations.

- **Which act regulates false and deceptive advertising?**

The Federal Trade Commission Act prohibits unfair methods of competition in commerce, including deceptive advertising.

- **Which act prohibits price discrimination and demands proportional promotional allowances?**

The Robinson-Patman Act applies to both sellers and buyers who knowingly induce or receive an unlawful discrimination in price.

Learning Goal 7. Explain the role of tax laws in generating income for the government and as a method of discouraging or encouraging certain behaviors among taxpayers.

- **How does the government use taxes to encourage or discourage certain behavior among taxpayers?**

If the government wishes to change citizens' behavior, it can reduce their use of certain classes of products (cigarettes, liquor) by passing *sin taxes* to raise their cost. In other situations, the government may offer tax credits to encourage businesses to hire new employees or purchase new equipment.

Learning Goal 8. Distinguish among the various types of bankruptcy as outlined by the Bankruptcy Code.

- **What are the bankruptcy laws?**

Chapter 7 calls for straight bankruptcy, in which all assets are divided among creditors after exemptions. Chapter 11 allows a firm to reorganize and continue operation after paying only a limited portion of its debts. Chapter 13 allows individuals to pay their creditors over an extended period of time.

Learning Goal 9. Explain the role of deregulation as a tool to encourage competition.

- **What are a few of the most publicized examples of deregulation?**

Perhaps the most publicized examples of deregulation have been those in the airline and telecommunications industries.

key terms

administrative agencies A1-3

bankruptcy A1-15

breach of contract A1-10

business law A1-2

common law A1-2

consideration A1-9

consumerism A1-13

contract A1-9

contract law A1-9

copyright A1-7

damages A1-10

deregulation A1-17

express warranties A1-9

implied warranties A1-9

involuntary bankruptcy A1-16

judiciary A1-2

negligence A1-4

negotiable instruments A1-9

patent A1-6

precedent A1-3

product liability A1-4

statutory law A1-2

strict product liability A1-5

taxes A1-14

tort A1-4

Uniform Commercial Code (UCC) A1-8

voluntary bankruptcy A1-16

critical thinking

1. Supporters of tort reform say it's unfair that plaintiffs (the parties bringing lawsuits) don't have to pay damages to the defendants (the parties subject to the lawsuits) if they lose the case. Should plaintiffs pay damages if they lose a case? Why or why not?

2. Go to the website of the U.S. Patent and Trademark Office (www.uspto.gov) and view the information about obtaining a patent. See whether you can estimate how long the process will take and what your cost will be.

3. Call your local real estate board or visit a realtor and obtain a copy of a real estate contract. Read it carefully to see how it meets the six requirements stated in the chapter for a contract to be legal and binding.

4. Twenty-two states have implemented utility deregulation. Has your state or a neighboring state implemented utility deregulation? How does it seem to be working?

developing workplace skills

1. Do you think the laws that promote fair and competitive practices are effective in the United States? Why or why not? Provide evidence for your view.

2. Increasing numbers of individuals file for bankruptcy each year. Do you think the U.S. Congress was correct in toughening the bankruptcy laws?

3. Pick a side: Should government action to deal with deceptive business practices increase, or should we count on business to regulate itself to prevent deceptive practices? Which solution is better for society and business in the long run?

4. Does your state have an income tax? What percentage of your income do you have to pay in state income tax? What about property taxes and sales taxes? How do these taxes in your area compare to those in three other states and communities of your choice?

5. In 2005, Congress passed bankruptcy reform legislation that makes it more difficult for individuals to file for bankruptcy under Chapter 7 and limits certain debts that cannot now be eliminated. Research the law and offer reasons why you support or oppose it. You might want to go to www.bankruptcyaction .com for help.

taking it to the net

You and several of your musician friends decide to start a band you want to call the Subprimes. You want to protect the band name and the new songs you've written so that other groups can't use them. Go to the U.S. Patent and Trademark Office's website (**www.uspto.gov**) to find out how to get the protection you seek.

1. Do you need to apply for patents, copyrights, or trademarks, or some combination of these to protect your band name and songs?

2. When can you use the trademark symbols™ and ®?

3. How can you secure a copyright for your songs?

4. What are the advantages of registering copyrights?

APPENDIX 2

Managing Personal
FINANCES

After you have read and studied this appendix, you should be able to

1 Outline the six steps for controlling your assets.

2 Explain how to build a financial base, including investing in real estate, saving money, and managing credit.

3 Explain how buying the appropriate insurance can protect your financial base.

4 Outline a strategy for retiring with enough money to last a lifetime.

Understanding the ins and outs of finances in the business world can be difficult for many people. But there's one type of business in which you must be an expert: the business of *you*. All of us need to understand the importance of keeping our personal finances in order. After all, the recent credit crisis showed just how volatile the economy can be. Those who don't save and spend responsibly in the better times could find themselves in trouble when the good times turn bad.

Few people know this better than Carmen Wong Ulrich. In her roles as a writer, television host, and businesswoman, Ulrich has taught thousands about the importance of prudent personal finance. The daughter of a Dominican mother and a Chinese father, Ulrich learned her first lessons on the subject from her parents. In fact, at age 12 she opened her first bank account with the help of her dad. He made sure that she knew early on how to keep a close eye on her money and not to be afraid of banks. His most important lesson, though, was letting her know that anyone could take responsibility for his or her own finances, no matter their age, color, or gender. "Here I was, a girl, opening her own bank account at 12 years old," says Ulrich. "I didn't realize for years just how powerful that was until I'd tell that story to female audiences and I'd hear from them that, gender-wise, it was amazing that my dad took his daughter to do something so powerful for her independence so early."

Although her parents taught her well about personal finance, Ulrich's adolescence was rather turbulent otherwise. Upon her parents' divorce, she discovered that her dad was not actually her biological father. Her mother's remarriage to an Italian American man added to her already culturally confused upbringing. "We had culture clash upon culture clash," says Ulrich. "And not just of nationalities. We moved from an urban setting, New York City, to a town in rural New Hampshire where nobody understood my mother's accent." Despite her stormy family life, Ulrich managed to excel at school. She graduated from Fairfield University with a degree in psychology and art history. Later, she went on to Columbia University, where she earned a master's degree in psychology.

All that education came with a price tag, though, and upon graduation Ulrich found herself drowning in student loan debt. Luckily, she had experience dealing with her own finances since childhood.

CONNECTING WITH

x *Carmen Wong Ulrich*

Personal Finance Expert

She eventually pulled herself out of debt through wise spending and regular saving. As she began to rise through the ranks as a journalist, Ulrich wrote extensively on the subject of personal finance. Drawing from her own experience as well as her background in psychology, Ulrich informed people about how they could manage their money responsibly. In 2006 she wrote a book entitled *Generation Debt: Take Control of Your Money*, in which she detailed multiple ways for college grads to reduce their student loan and consumer debt. The book's success eventually led her to a hosting gig at CNBC's *On the Money*, a show focused on personal financial advice. Although the show was canceled in 2009, Ulrich used her exposure to land regular spots on other programs, like *The Today Show* on NBC and *The Dr. Oz Show*. By 2010 she had published her second book, *The Real Cost of Living: Making the Best Decisions for You, Your Life, and Your Money*.

Carmen Wong Ulrich's passion for personal finance goes far beyond the success she has enjoyed as a result of her expertise. "I believe—passionately believe—that the ability to manage your personal finances determines what kind of life you're able to lead," says Ulrich. "It is an advantage so great and life-changing that to not have the correct information and motivation can be the difference between scrambling to pay your bills and not having to make note of the price of everything in your grocery cart." We think she's 100 percent right on that. Your personal financial choices will be some of the biggest decisions of your life. From paying for a degree to buying a house, personal finance requires that you pay close attention to your money and how you spend (and save) it. In this chapter we'll take a look at all the ways that will help you keep your finances in order so you can be prepared for all the curveballs that life will inevitably throw you.

Sources: Carmen Wong Ulrich, "The Financial Wisdom of Our Fathers: A Father's Day Tribute," *The Huffington Post*, June 17, 2012; Carmen Wong Ulrich, "Mission Accepted," *CNBC.com*, May 30, 2008; "Carmen Wong Ulrich: How a How-to Writer Learned How," *SCPS Newsletter*, Winter 2009; and "Biography: Carmen Wong Ulrich," *Carmenwongulrich.com*, accessed July 2012.

NAME THAT company

One way to save money is to use your credit cards wisely. There are organizations that can help you compare credit cards to get the most out of them. What is the name of one of those organizations? (You can find the answer in this appendix.)

LEARNING goal 1

Outline the six steps for controlling your assets.

THE NEED FOR PERSONAL FINANCIAL PLANNING

The United States is largely a capitalist country. It follows, then, that the secret to success in such a country is to have capital, or money. With capital, you can take nice vacations, raise a family, invest in stocks and bonds, buy the goods and services you want, give generously to others, and retire with enough money to see you through. Money management, however, is not easy. You have to earn the money in the first place. Your chances of becoming wealthy are much greater if you choose to become an entrepreneur. That's one of the reasons why we have put so much emphasis on entrepreneurship throughout the text, including a whole chapter on the subject. Of course, there are risks in starting a business, but the best time to take risks is when you are young. Would it help you to be more motivated if you knew that there are over a thousand billionaires in the world and they average some $4.5 billion in wealth?[1]

After you earn the money, you have to learn to spend some wisely, save the rest, and insure yourself against the risks of serious accidents, illness, or death. With a little bit of luck, you may be one of the millionaires discussed in this book.[2]

You'll likely need some help. Recently high school seniors averaged a grade of 48.3 percent on questions having to do with financial concepts. Another report found that college students are also poorly educated about financial matters such as IRAs and 401(k) plans. Even people who are retired are finding that they don't know enough about such plans.[3] This appendix will give you the basics so that you'll be ahead of the game. Financial management is so important to your fiscal health that you may enjoy taking an entire class on it.

Financial Planning Begins with Making Money

You already know one of the secrets to finding a good-paying job is having a good education. Throughout history, an investment in education has paid off regardless of the state of the economy or political ups and downs. Benjamin Franklin said, "If a man empties his purse into his head, no one can take it away from him. An investment in knowledge always pays the best interest." Education has become even more important since we entered the information age. A typical full-time worker in the United States with a four-year college degree can earn about $50,000—about

62 percent more than one with only a high school diploma. The lifetime income of families headed by individuals with a bachelor's degree can be about $1.6 million more than the incomes of families headed by those with a high school diploma. One way to start to become a millionaire, therefore, is to finish college. The government is eager for you to go to college and is willing to help you with tax breaks like tax-free education savings accounts. Make sure you investigate all the financial help available to you.

Making money is one thing; saving, investing, and spending it wisely is something else.[4] Following the advice in the next section will help you become one of those with enough to live in comfort throughout your life.

Six Steps to Controlling Your Assets

The only way to save enough money to do all the things you want to do in life is to spend less than you make.[5] Although you may find it hard to save today, it is not only possible but imperative if you want to accumulate enough to be financially secure.[6] Fewer than 1 in 10 U.S. adults has accumulated enough money by retirement age to live comfortably, and 36 percent of U.S. households don't have a retirement account. Don't become one of them. The following are six steps you can take today to get control of your finances.

Step 1: Take an Inventory of Your Financial Assets To take inventory, you need to develop a balance sheet for yourself, like the one in Chapter 17. Remember, a balance sheet starts with the fundamental accounting equation: Assets = Liabilities + Owners' equity. List your tangible assets (such as TV, DVR player, iPod, iPad, computer, cell phone, bicycle, car, jewelry, clothes, and savings account) on one side, and your liabilities (including mortgage, credit card debt, and auto and education loans) on the other.

Assign a dollar figure to each of your assets, based on its current value, not what you originally paid for it. If you have debts, subtract them from your assets to get your net worth. If you have no debts, your assets equal your net worth. If your liabilities exceed the value of your assets, you aren't on the path to financial security. You may need more financial discipline in your life.

Let's also create an income statement for you. At the top of the statement is revenue (all the money you take in from your job, investments, and so on). Subtract all your costs and expenses (rent or mortgage, credit card and other loan payments, utilities, commuting costs, and so on) to get your net income or profit. Software programs like Quicken and websites like Dinkytown.net have a variety of tools that can easily help you with these calculations.

Now is also an excellent time to think about how much money you will need to accomplish all your goals. The more clearly you can visualize your goals, the easier it is to begin saving for them.

Step 2: Keep Track of All Your Expenses Do you occasionally find yourself running out of cash? If you experience a cash flow problem, the only way to trace where the money is going is to keep track of every cent you spend. Keeping records of your expenses can be tedious, but it's a necessary step if you want to learn discipline. Actually, it could turn out to be enjoyable because it gives you such a feeling of control.

Here's what to do: List *everything* you spend as you go through the day. That list is your journal. At the end of the week, transfer your journal entries into a record book or computerized accounting program.

Develop spending categories (accounts) to make your task easier and more informative. You can have a category called "Food" for all food you bought from the grocery or convenience store during the week. You might want a separate account for meals eaten away from home, because you can dramatically cut these costs if you make your meals at home.

Other accounts could include rent, insurance, automobile repairs and gasoline, clothing, utilities, toiletries, entertainment, and donations to charity. Most people also like to have a category called "Miscellaneous" for impulse items like latte and candy. You won't believe how much you fritter away on miscellaneous items unless you keep a *detailed* record for at least a couple of months.

Develop your accounts on the basis of what's most important to you or where you spend the most money.[7] Once you have recorded all your expenses for a few months, you'll easily see where you are spending too much and what you have to do to save more. A venti mocha frappuccino at a coffee specialty shop costs about $4.25. If you cut back from five to one a week, you'll save $17 a week, or over $850 a year. Over 10 years, that could mean an extra $12,000 for retirement, if you invest the money wisely.

Step 3: Prepare a Budget   Once you know your financial situation and your sources of revenue and expenses, you're ready to make a personal budget. Remember, budgets are financial plans. A household budget includes mortgage or rent, utilities, food, clothing, vehicles, furniture, life insurance, car insurance, medical care, and taxes.[8]

You'll need to choose how much to allow for such expenses as eating out, entertainment, cell phone use, and so on. Keep in mind that what you spend now reduces what you can save later. Spending $3.50 or more a day for cigarettes or coffee adds up to about $25 a week, $100 a month, $1,200 a year. If you can save $4 or $5 a day, you'll have almost $1,800 saved by the end of the year. Keep this up during four years of college and you'll have saved more than $7,000 by graduation. And that's before adding any interest your money will earn. Cost-saving choices you might consider to reach this goal are listed in Figure A2.1.

figure A2.1

POSSIBLE COST-SAVING CHOICES

The choices you make today can have a dramatic impact on your financial future. Compare the differences these few choices you can make now would mean to your future net worth. If you would make the lower-cost choices every month during your four years of college, and invest the savings in a mutual fund earning 6 percent compounded annually, you would double your money every 12 years.

FIRST CHOICE COST PER MONTH	ALTERNATE CHOICE COST PER MONTH	SAVINGS PER MONTH
Starbucks caffè latte	Quick Trip's Cappuccino	
$3.00 for 20 days = $60.00	$0.60 for 20 days = $12.00	$48.00
Fast-food lunch of burger, fries, and soft drink	Lunch brought from home	
$4.00 for 20 days = $80.00	$2 for 20 days = $40.00	40.00
Evian bottled water	Generic bottled water	
$1.50 for 20 days = $30.00	$.50 for 20 days = $10.00	20.00
CD = $15.00	Listen to your old CDs = $0.00	15.00
Banana Republic T-shirt = $34.00	Old Navy T-shirt = $10.00	24.00
	Total savings per month	$147.00
		× 48 months
	Total savings through 4 years of college	$7,056.00

Running a household is similar to running a small business. It takes the same careful record keeping, the same budget processes and forecasting, and the same control procedures. Sometimes it also creates the same need to borrow funds or rely on a credit card and become familiar with interest rates. The time you spend practicing budgeting techniques will benefit you throughout your life. You might start by going online to Mint.com. It will help you with your budgeting needs.

Step 4: Pay Off Your Debts The first thing to do with the money remaining after you pay your monthly bills is to pay off your debts, starting with those carrying the highest interest rates. Credit card debt may be costing you 18 percent or more a year. A survey of 100 campuses found 26 percent of college students said they had been charged a fee for a late payment. It's better to pay off a debt that costs 18 percent than put the money in a bank account that earns, say, 2 percent or less. Check credit card statements and other mailings carefully to make certain the charges are accurate.

It might take a little time to balance your income with your expenses to make sure you have money left to save and invest, but the effort is worth it. People who don't take this step can reach retirement without enough funds to live on. How could you cut back your expenses?

Step 5: Start a Savings Plan It's important to save some money each month in a separate account for large purchases you're likely to make (such as a car or house). Then, when it comes time to make that purchase, you'll have the needed cash. Save at least enough for a significant down payment so that you can reduce the finance charges you'll pay to borrow the rest.

The best way to save money is to *pay yourself first.* When you get your paycheck, first take out money for savings and then plan what to do with the rest. You can arrange with your bank or mutual fund to deduct a certain amount for savings every month. You'll be pleasantly surprised when the money starts accumulating and earning interest over time. With some discipline, you can eventually reach your goal of becoming a millionaire. It's not as difficult as you may think. Figure A2.2 shows how $5,000 grows over various periods at different rates of return. If you start saving at age 40, you'll have 25 years in by the time you reach 65.

Step 6: Borrow Only to Buy Assets That Increase in Value or Generate Income Don't borrow money for ordinary expenses; you'll only get into more debt that way. If you have budgeted for emergencies, such as car repairs and health care costs, you should be able to stay financially secure. Most financial experts advise saving about six months of earnings for contingencies. Keep this money in highly liquid accounts, such as a bank account or money market fund.

	Annual Rate of Return			
TIME	**2%**	**5%**	**8%**	**11%**
5 years	$5,520	$ 6,381	$ 7,347	$ 8,425
10 years	6,095	8,144	10,795	14,197
15 years	6,729	10,395	15,861	23,923
20 years	7,430	13,266	23,305	40,312
25 years	8,203	16,932	34,242	67,927

figure A2.2

HOW MONEY GROWS

This chart illustrates how $5,000 would grow at various rates of return. Recent savings account interest rates were very low (less than 2 percent), but in earlier years they've been over 5 percent.

Only the most unexpected of expenses should cause you to borrow. It is hard to wait until you have enough money to buy what you want, but learning to wait is a critical part of self-discipline. Of course, you can always try to produce more income by working overtime or by working on the side for extra revenue.

If you follow these six steps, not only will you have money for investment but you'll have developed most of the financial techniques needed to become financially secure. If you find it hard to live within a budget at first, remember the payoff is well worth the effort.

LEARNING goal 2

Explain how to build a financial base, including investing in real estate, saving money, and managing credit.

BUILDING YOUR FINANCIAL BASE

The path to success in a capitalist system is to have capital to invest, yet many students today graduate with debt.[9] As you've read, accumulating capital takes discipline and careful planning. With the money you save, however, you can become an entrepreneur, one of the fastest ways to wealth. As you read in this appendix's opening Profile, that often means living frugally.

Living frugally is extremely difficult for the average person. Most people are eager to spend their money on a new car, furniture, electronics, clothes, entertainment, and the like. They look for a fancy apartment with all the amenities. A capital-generating strategy may require forgoing most (though not all) of these purchases to accumulate investment money. It might mean living like a frugal college student, in a relatively inexpensive apartment furnished in hand-me-downs from parents, friends, Craigslist, and resale shops.

For five or six years, you can manage with the old sound system, a used car, and a few nice clothes. The strategy is sacrifice, not luxury. It's important not to feel burdened by this plan; instead, feel happy knowing your financial future will be more secure. That's the way the majority of millionaires got their money. If living frugally seems too restrictive for you, you can still save at least a little. It's better to save a smaller amount than not to save at all.

It's wise to plan your financial future with the same excitement and dedication you bring to other aspects of your life. If you get married, for example, it is important to discuss financial issues with your spouse. Conflicts over money are a major cause of divorce, so agreeing on a financial strategy before marriage is very important.[10]

A great strategy for couples is to try to live on one income and to save the other. The longer you wait to marry, the more likely it will be that one of you can be earning enough to do that—as a college graduate. If the second spouse makes $25,000 a year after taxes, saving that income for five years quickly adds up to $125,000 (plus interest).

What do you do with the money you accumulate? Your first investment might be a low-priced home.[11] Why? The purpose of this investment is to lock in payments for your shelter at a fixed amount. Through the years, home ownership has been a wise investment, unlike renting, but that may be changing.[12] Many people take huge risks by buying too much home for their income. Furthermore, people sometimes take out interest-only or other loans that are very risky, as recent headlines have shown. The rule of thumb "Don't buy a home that costs more than two and a half times your annual income" still stands. Buy for the long term and stay within your means. What has happened to housing prices in your area over the last couple of years? Lower prices mean opportunity if the market gains strength.[13]

Real Estate: Historically, a Relatively Secure Investment

The real estate bust beginning in 2008 was a relatively uncommon occurrence. House prices had risen dramatically, causing a bubble that burst.

Prices have fallen sharply, but history shows that home prices are likely to rise again and will continue to provide several investment benefits. First, a home is the one investment that you can live in. Second, once you buy a home, your mortgage payments are relatively fixed (though taxes and utilities may go up). As your income rises, mortgage payments get easier to make, but renters often find that rents go up at least as fast as income. On the other hand, the recent fall in home prices has made it more important than ever for you to check whether it is better to own or rent. How deeply particular cities were affected by the falling housing prices varies greatly from region to region.[14]

Buying a home has usually been a very good and safe investment. But sometimes housing prices can rise fast, as they did between 2000 and 2007, and then fall, as they've done since 2008. What has happened to housing prices in your area over the last few years?

Paying for a home has historically been a good way of forcing yourself to save. You must make the payments every month. Those payments are an investment that proves very rewarding over time for most people. A home is also a good asset to use when applying for a business loan.

Some couples have used the seed money accumulated from saving one income (in the strategy outlined above) to buy two attached homes so that they can live in one part and rent out the other. The rent they earn covers a good part of the payments for both homes, so the couple can live comfortably, yet inexpensively, while their investment in a home appreciates. In this way they accumulate capital, and as they grow older, they pull far ahead of their peers in terms of financial security. As capital accumulates and values rise, they can sell and buy an even larger apartment building or a single-family home. Many have made fortunes in real estate in just this way.

Once you understand the benefits of home ownership versus renting, you can decide whether those same principles apply to owning the premises where you set up your own business—or owning your own equipment, vehicles, and the like. Figure A2.3 will give you some idea of how expensive a house you can afford, given your income. You can find current mortgage interest rates and mortgage calculators at Interest.com.

Tax Deductions and Home Ownership

Buying a home is likely to be the largest and perhaps the most important investment you'll make. It's nice to know that the federal government is willing to help you with it. Here's how: Interest on your home mortgage payments is tax-deductible. So are your real estate taxes. Since virtually all your mortgage payments during the first few years are applied to the interest on your loan, almost all the early payments are tax-deductible—a tremendous benefit. If your payments are $1,000

figure A2.3

HOW MUCH HOUSE CAN YOU AFFORD?

Monthly mortgage payments—including interest, principal, real estate taxes, and insurance—generally shouldn't amount to more than 28 percent of monthly income. Here's how much people in various income categories can afford to pay for a home if they use a 30-year mortgage and make a 10 percent down payment. How do you think the changes in mortgage interest rates affect the average price of homes?

INCOME	MONTHLY PAYMENT	Interest Rates			
		5%	6%	7%	15%
$ 30,000	$ 700	$106,263	$ 98,303	$ 91,252	$ 56,870
50,000	1,167	180,291	167,081	155,376	98,606
80,000	1,867	287,213	266,056	247,308	155,916
100,000	2,333	361,240	334,832	311,433	198,013

Source: Federal Housing Finance Board.

a month and your income is in a 25 percent tax bracket, during the early years of your mortgage the government will, in effect, give you credit for about $250 of your payment, lowering your real cost. This makes home ownership much more competitive with renting than it may appear.

There are three keys to getting the optimal return on a home or any real estate investment: location, location, and location. A home in the best part of town, near good schools, shopping, and work, is usually a sound financial investment. Less expensive homes may appreciate in value more slowly than homes in the city or town center. It's usually better, from a financial viewpoint, to buy a smaller home in a great location than a large home in a not-so-great setting.

Where to Put Your Savings

Where are some other good places to save your money? For a young person, one of the worst places to keep long-term investments is a bank or savings and loan. It is important to have savings equivalent to about six months of living expenses in the bank for emergencies, but the bank is not the best place to invest. Internet banks pay higher interest than your local bank, but even their rates are relatively low.

One of the best places to invest over time has been the stock market. The stock market does tend to go up and down, but over a longer period of time it has proved to be one of the best investments. About half of U.S. households own stock and mutual funds. Most financial experts believe the stock market will grow more slowly in the future than it has over the last 50 years, but the U.S. economy has always managed to rise up after a crisis like the stock market fall of recent years.

The future always looks gloomy during a financial crisis, but that doesn't mean you shouldn't take risks. Remember, the greater the risk, usually the greater the return. When stock prices are low, that's the time to *buy*. When stocks collapse, it's an opportunity to get into the stock market, not avoid it. The average investor buys when the market is high and sells when it's low. Clearly, that's not a good idea. It takes courage to buy when everyone else is selling. In the long run, however, this **contrarian approach** to investing is the way the rich get richer.

contrarian approach
Buying stock when everyone else is selling or vice versa.

Chapter 19 gave you a foundation for starting an investment program. That chapter also talked about bonds, but bonds have traditionally lagged behind stocks as a long-term investment.

Learning to Manage Credit

Credit cards are an important element in your personal financial system, even if you rarely use them.[15] First, you may have to own a credit card to buy certain goods or even rent a car, because some businesses require one for identification and to ensure payment. Second, you can use a credit card to keep track of purchases. A gasoline credit card gives you records of purchases over time for your income tax returns (if you drive for work) and financial planning purposes. Third, a credit card is more convenient than cash or checks. You can carry less cash and easily cancel a stolen card to protect your account. Not all credit cards are alike, however. You can decide which card is best for you by comparing them at CardRatings.com or CreditCards.com.[16]

College credit card debt is on the rise. Half of college students have four or more cards and only 17 percent report regularly paying off their balance.[17] If you do use a credit card, pay the balance in full during the period when no interest is charged. Finance charges on credit card purchases usually amount to 12 to 26 percent annually. Some credit card companies will reward you for paying on time.[18] If you finance a TV, home appliances, or other purchases with a credit card, you may end up spending much more than if you pay with cash. Not having to pay 18 percent or more in interest is as good as earning 18 percent tax-free. You may want to choose a card that pays you back in cash or offers credits toward the purchase of a car or frequent-flier miles. The value of these "givebacks" can be as high as 5 percent. Some cards have no annual fees; others have lower interest rates.

Credit card companies like First USA often encourage young people to apply for credit cards by giving away gifts for signing up. Why are such companies so willing to give you a credit card?

The danger of a credit card is the flip side of its convenience. It's too easy to buy things you wouldn't buy if you had to pay cash, or to pile up debts you can't repay. If you aren't the type who can stick to a financial plan or household budget, *it may be better not to have a credit card at all.*[19] Imagine a customer who has a $10,000 balance on his or her credit card with a 16 percent interest rate and pays the minimum 4 percent monthly payment. How long will it take to pay off the debt, and what would the cost for interest be? The answers: 14 years and nearly $5,000—and that's without using the card again to purchase so much as a candy bar. Prior to 2006, the minimum payment was 2 percent. The lower minimum payment may have been enticing for the short term, but over time that same $10,000 balance would have taken over 30 years to repay and cost over $18,000 in interest if only the 2 percent minimum was paid.

Some people would be better off with a *debit* card only. Debit cards can be set up so that you cannot spend more than you have in the bank, a great benefit for those who are not as careful with their spending as they should be.[20] Furthermore, there are no interest payments or annual fees.

Of the debtors seeking help at the National Consumer Counseling Service, more than half were between 18 and 32. The Credit CARD Act of 2009 created new consumer credit card protections and went into effect February 2010. The new law allows card issuers to increase interest rates for only a limited number of reasons and restricts increasing rates at all during the first year of a new card account. People must be at least 21 years old or get an adult to co-sign with them if they want new credit cards on their own.[21] The Consumer Financial Protection Bureau regulates financial products and services, including mortgages, credit cards, student loans, and debt collection. You would be wise to explore what is available to you.

- What are the six steps you can take to control your finances?
- What steps should a person follow to build capital?
- Why is real estate a good investment?

LEARNING **goal 3**

Explain how buying the appropriate insurance can protect your financial base.

PROTECTING YOUR FINANCIAL BASE: BUYING INSURANCE

One of the last things young people think about is the idea that they may become sick, get injured, or die. It is not a pleasant thought, but the unexpected does happen every day. To protect your loved ones from the loss of your income, you should buy life insurance. Nearly a third of U.S. households have no life insurance coverage. This is one sign of how the financial pressures of today have affected families.

The simplest and least expensive form of life insurance is **term insurance.** It is pure insurance protection for a given number of years that typically costs less the younger you buy it (see Figure A2.4). Every few years, you might have to renew the policy, and the premium can then rise. Check prices through a service like InsWeb.com or use one of Quicken's personal finance software packages.

How much insurance do you need? *Newsweek* posed this question: We just had our first baby; how much life insurance should we have? Answer: Seven times your family income plus $100,000 for college. Apportion your coverage so that a spouse earning 60 percent of the income carries 60 percent of the insurance.

Multiyear level-premium insurance guarantees that you'll pay the same premium for the life of the policy. Recently, 40 percent of new term policies guaranteed a set rate for 20 years or more. Some companies allow you to switch your term policy for a more expensive whole or universal life policy.

Whole life insurance combines pure insurance and savings, so you are buying both insurance and a savings plan. This may be a good idea for those people who

term insurance
Pure insurance protection for a given number of years.

whole life insurance
Life insurance that combines pure insurance and savings.

figure A2.4

WHY BUY TERM INSURANCE?

INSURANCE NEEDS IN EARLY YEARS ARE HIGH	INSURANCE NEEDS DECLINE AS YOU GROW OLDER
1. Children are young and need money for education.	1. Children are grown.
2. Mortgage is high relative to income.	2. Mortgage is low or completely paid off.
3. Often there are auto payments and other bills to pay.	3. Debts are paid off.
4. Loss of income would be disastrous.	4. Insurance needs are few.
	5. Retirement income is needed.

have trouble saving money. A universal life policy lets you choose how much of your payment should go to insurance and how much to investments. The investments in such plans traditionally are very conservative but pay a steady interest rate.[22]

Variable life insurance is a form of whole life insurance that invests the cash value of the policy in stocks or other high-yielding securities. Death benefits may thus vary, reflecting the performance of the investments.

Life insurance companies recognized people's desire to earn higher returns on their insurance (and to protect themselves against running out of money before they die) and began selling annuities. An **annuity** is a contract to make regular payments to a person for life or for a fixed period. With an annuity, you are guaranteed to have an income until you die.

There are two kinds of annuities: fixed and variable. *Fixed annuities* are investments that pay the policyholder a specified interest rate. They are not as popular as *variable annuities,* which provide investment choices identical to mutual funds. Such annuities are becoming more popular than term or whole life insurance. But buyers must be careful in selecting an insurance company and choosing the investments made with their money.

Consult a financial adviser who is not an insurance agent and who can help you make the wisest decision about insurance. You can also check out the insurance company through a rating service such as A.M. Best (www.ambest.com) or Moody's Investors Service (www.moodys.com).

Health Insurance

The 2010 law called the Patient Protection and Affordable Care Act (PPACA) requires nonexempted individuals to maintain a minimum level of health insurance or pay a tax penalty. On June 28, 2012, the Supreme Court announced its ruling that this highly controversial law (often called Obamacare) was constitutional in that it was within Congress's power to tax. It is important that you follow the changes as the new law is implemented because almost everything to do with your health care could be affected.

You may already have health insurance coverage through your employer. If not, you can buy health insurance from providers like Blue Cross/Blue Shield, a health maintenance organization (HMO), or a preferred provider organization (PPO). For quick online help in choosing a health insurance provider, eHealthInsurance.com can help you get affordable health insurance quotes and compare individual health insurance plans side by side so that you can find the best medical insurance plans for your needs and budget. You may be able to buy health insurance for less through a professional organization. One of the more popular health insurance alternatives is a health savings account (HSA), a tax-deferred savings account linked to a low-cost, high-deductible health insurance policy. The idea is to use the money that would have been spent on high-cost, low-deductible health insurance and deposit it in a health savings account. You can use the money in the HSA only for needed health care services. One major benefit to you is that the money grows tax-free until you take it out.

Your chances of becoming disabled at an early age are much higher than your chances of dying in an accident. It's dangerous financially not to have any health insurance. Hospital costs are simply too high to risk financial ruin by going uninsured. It is often a good idea to supplement health insurance policies with **disability insurance** that pays part of the cost of a long-term sickness or an accident. Call an insurance agent or check online for possible costs of such insurance. The cost is relatively low to protect yourself from losing your income for an extended period.

variable life insurance
Whole life insurance that invests the cash value of the policy in stocks or other high-yielding securities.

annuity
A contract to make regular payments to a person for life or for a fixed period.

disability insurance
Insurance that pays part of the cost of a long-term sickness or an accident.

Homeowner's or Renter's Insurance

You may be surprised how much it would cost to replace all the things you own. As you begin to accumulate possessions, you may want to have apartment or home-owner's insurance that covers their loss. Specify that you want *guaranteed replacement cost*. That means the insurance company will give you whatever it costs to buy all those things *new*. It costs a little more than a policy without guaranteed replacement, but you will get a lot more if you have a loss.

The other option is insurance that covers the *depreciated cost* of the items. A sofa you bought five years ago for $600 may be worth only $150 now. That current value is what your insurance would pay you, not the $700 or more to buy a brand-new sofa. If your computer is stolen, you might get only a couple hundred dollars rather than its replacement cost.

Most policies don't cover expensive items like engagement and wedding rings. You can buy a *rider* to your policy to cover them at a reasonable cost.

Other Insurance

Most states require drivers to have automobile insurance; if your state doesn't, it's a good idea to buy it anyway. Be sure to insure against losses from uninsured motorists. Consider accepting a large deductible to keep the premiums low, and pay for small damages yourself.

You'll also need liability insurance to protect yourself against being sued by someone you accidentally injure. Often you can get a discount by buying all your insurance (life, health, homeowner's, automobile) with one company. This is called an **umbrella policy.** Look for other discounts such as for safe driving, good grades, and more.

umbrella policy
A broadly based insurance policy that saves you money because you buy all your insurance from one company.

LEARNING goal 4

> Outline a strategy for retiring with enough money to last a lifetime.

PLANNING YOUR RETIREMENT

It may seem a bit early to be planning your retirement; however, not doing so would be a big mistake.[23] Successful financial planning means long-range planning, and retirement is a critical phase of life.[24] What you do now could make a world of difference in your quality of life after age 65, or whenever you retire.

Social Security

Social Security is the Old-Age, Survivors, and Disability Insurance Program established by the Social Security Act of 1935. It consists not of a fund of money but of a continuous flow of contributions in and payments out. The Social Security money you'll begin to receive when you retire will come directly from the Social Security taxes being paid by workers at that time. However, the number of people retiring and living longer is increasing dramatically, while the number paying into Social Security is declining.[25] Maintaining Social Security may thus require reducing benefits, encouraging people to retire later, limiting cost-of-living adjustments (COLAs) made to benefits over time, and increasing Social Security taxes.

Social Security
The term used to describe the Old-Age, Survivors, and Disability Insurance Program established by the Social Security Act of 1935.

One purpose of planning your personal finances is to have enough money for retirement. If you plan to relax and travel when you retire, you need to begin saving now. What are your retirement goals, and what resources will you need to accomplish them?

Social Security will likely not provide you with ample funds for retirement.[26] Plan now to save your own funds for your nonworking years. The government has established incentives to encourage you. Here are some specifics.

Individual Retirement Accounts (IRAs)

Traditionally, an **individual retirement account (IRA)** has been a tax-deferred investment plan that enables you (and your spouse, if you are married) to save part of your income for retirement. A traditional IRA allows people who qualify to deduct from their reported income the money they put into an account. **Tax-deferred contributions** are those for which you pay no current taxes, but the earnings gained in the IRA are taxed as income when they are withdrawn from your IRA after retirement.

Let's see why a traditional IRA is a good deal for an investor. The tremendous benefit is the fact that the invested money is not taxed. That means faster and higher returns for you. Say you put $5,000 into an IRA each year. (The maximum IRA contribution was $5,000 in 2012 and can increase each year in line with inflation. If you're 50 or older, you can make an additional $1,000 "catch-up" contribution.) Normally you'd pay taxes on that $5,000 when you receive it as income. But because you put it into an IRA, you won't. If you're in the 25 percent tax bracket, that means you'll save $1,250 in taxes! Put another way, the $5,000 you save costs you only $3,750—a huge bargain.

The earlier you start saving, the better—because your money has a chance to double and double again. If you save $5,000 a year for 35 years in an IRA and earn 10 percent a year, you'll accumulate savings of more than $1.5 million. If you start when you're just out of school, you'll be a millionaire by the time you're 55. All you have to do is save $5,000 a year and earn 10 percent. You may be wise to use a Roth IRA instead (see following).

If you increase your contribution to the maximum allowable each time it is raised, you can reach your million-dollar goal even earlier. The actual rate of return depends on the type of investments you choose. No one can predict future

individual retirement account (IRA)
A tax-deferred investment plan that enables you (and your spouse, if you are married) to save part of your income for retirement; a traditional IRA allows people who qualify to deduct from their reported income the money they put into an account.

tax-deferred contributions
Retirement account deposits for which you pay no current taxes, but the earnings gained are taxed as regular income when they are withdrawn at retirement.

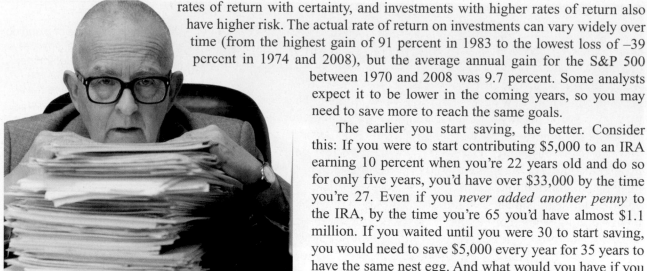

rates of return with certainty, and investments with higher rates of return also have higher risk. The actual rate of return on investments can vary widely over time (from the highest gain of 91 percent in 1983 to the lowest loss of –39 percent in 1974 and 2008), but the average annual gain for the S&P 500 between 1970 and 2008 was 9.7 percent. Some analysts expect it to be lower in the coming years, so you may need to save more to reach the same goals.

The earlier you start saving, the better. Consider this: If you were to start contributing $5,000 to an IRA earning 10 percent when you're 22 years old and do so for only five years, you'd have over $33,000 by the time you're 27. Even if you *never added another penny* to the IRA, by the time you're 65 you'd have almost $1.1 million. If you waited until you were 30 to start saving, you would need to save $5,000 every year for 35 years to have the same nest egg. And what would you have if you started saving at 22 *and* continued nonstop every year until 65? More than $3 million! Can you see why investment advisers often say that an IRA is the best way to invest in your retirement?

If the value of your retirement account plunges, you may have to defer your dream of an early retirement. If you have already started to save for your retirement, is your portfolio well diversified?

A second kind of IRA is the **Roth IRA.** You don't get up-front deductions from your taxes as with a traditional IRA, but earnings grow tax-free and are tax-free when withdrawn. *This is usually the best deal for college-age students.* You can transfer money from a traditional IRA into a Roth IRA. You will have to pay taxes first, but the long-term benefits often make this exchange worthwhile if you believe your tax rate will be higher when you retire than it is now.

Both types of IRA have advantages and disadvantages, so ask a financial adviser which is best for you. You may decide to have both.

You can't take money from either type of IRA until you are 59½ years old without paying a 10 percent penalty. That's a benefit for you, because it can keep you from tapping into your IRA in an emergency or when you're tempted to make a large impulse purchase. But the money is there if a real need or emergency arises. The government now allows you to take out some funds to invest in an education or a first home. But check the rules; they change over time.

Your local bank, savings and loan, and credit union all have different types of IRAs. Insurance companies offer them too. If you're looking for a higher return (and more risk), you can put your IRA funds into U.S. and international stocks, bonds, mutual funds, exchange-traded funds, or precious metals. You can switch from fund to fund or from investment to investment. You can even open several different IRAs as long as the total doesn't exceed the government's limit. Consider contributing to an IRA through payroll deductions to ensure that you invest the money before you're tempted to spend it.[27]

Roth IRA
An IRA where you don't get up-front deductions on your taxes as you would with a traditional IRA, but the earnings grow tax-free and are also tax-free when they are withdrawn.

Simple IRAs

Companies with 100 or fewer workers can provide them with a simple IRA. Employees can contribute a larger part of their income annually than with a regular IRA (up to $11,500 versus $5,000), and the company matches their contribution. This plan enables people to save much more money over time and can help small companies compete for available workers.

401(k) Plans

A **401(k) plan** is an employer-sponsored savings plan that allows you to deposit a set amount of pretax dollars and collect compounded earnings tax-free until withdrawal, when the money is taxed at ordinary income tax rates. Such plans account for about half the private pension savings in the United States; 401(k)s at more than 220,000 companies now cover some 55 million workers. These or similar plans are the only pension many people have, but only about 70 percent of eligible employees make any contributions, and many companies are discontinuing their benefits.

The plans have three benefits: (1) your contributions reduce your present taxable income, (2) tax is deferred on the earnings, and (3) many employers will match your contributions, sometimes 50 cents on a dollar. No investment will give you a better deal than an instant 50 percent return on your money. Not all companies have equally good programs, so be sure to check out what is available to you.[28]

You should deposit at least as much as your employer matches, often up to 15 percent of your salary.[29] You can usually select how the money in a 401(k) plan is invested: stocks, bonds, and in some cases real estate. Be careful not to invest all your money in the company where you work. It's always best to diversify your funds among different companies and among stocks, bonds, and real estate investment trusts.

Like the simple IRA, there is a simple 401(k) plan for those firms that employ 100 or fewer employees. Employees again are allowed to invest an amount (maximum of $16,500 in 2011) that is matched by the employer. This is a rather new program, but it should also prove popular among small businesses in attracting new workers.

401(k) plan
A savings plan that allows you to deposit pretax dollars and whose earnings compound tax-free until withdrawal, when the money is taxed at ordinary income tax rates.

Keogh Plans

Millions of small-business owners don't have the benefit of a corporate retirement system. Such people can contribute to an IRA, but the amount they can invest is limited. The alternative for all those doctors, lawyers, real estate agents, artists, writers, and other self-employed people is to establish their own Keogh plan. It's like an IRA for entrepreneurs. You can also look into simplified employee pension (SEP) plans, the best types of IRAs for sole proprietors.

The advantage of Keogh plans is that participants can invest up to $40,000 per year. Like traditional IRAs, Keogh funds aren't taxed until they are withdrawn, nor are the returns the funds earn. Thus, a person in the 25 percent tax bracket who invests $10,000 yearly in a Keogh saves $2,500 in taxes. That means, in essence, that the government is financing 25 percent of his or her retirement fund. As with an IRA, this is an excellent deal.

As with an IRA, there's a 10 percent penalty for early withdrawal. Also like an IRA, funds may be withdrawn in a lump sum or spread out over the years. However, the key decision is the one you make now—to begin early to put funds into an IRA, a Keogh plan, or both so that the "magic" of compounding can turn that money into a sizable retirement fund.

Your financial assets can protect your children and even your grandchildren far into the future, if you have taken the right steps through estate planning. What can you do now in order to make sure your assets are divided the way you would like them to be when you're gone?

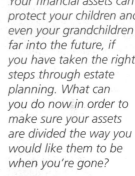

Financial Planners

If the idea of developing a comprehensive financial plan for yourself or your business seems overwhelming, relax; help is available from financial planners.[30]

Be careful, though—anybody can claim to be a financial planner today. It's often best to find a certified financial planner (CFP), that is, a professional who has completed a curriculum on 106 financial topics and a 10-hour examination. In the United States today there are about 36,000 CFPs. Unfortunately, many so-called financial planners are simply insurance salespeople.

In the past few years, there has been an explosion in the number of companies offering other businesses financial services, sometimes called one-stop financial centers or financial supermarkets because they provide a variety of financial services, ranging from banking service to mutual funds, insurance, tax assistance, stocks, bonds, and real estate. It pays to shop around for financial advice. Find someone who understands your business and is willing to spend some time with you.

Financial planning covers all aspects of investing, from life and health insurance all the way to retirement and death. Financial planners can advise you on the proper mix of IRAs, stocks, bonds, real estate, and so on.

Estate Planning

Your retirement may be far away, but it is never too early to begin thinking about estate planning, or making financial arrangements for those who will inherit from you. You may even help your parents or others to do such planning. An important first step is to select a guardian for your minor children. That person should have a genuine concern for your children as well as a parental style and moral beliefs you endorse.

Also ensure that you leave sufficient resources to rear your children, not only for living expenses but also for medical bills, college, and other major expenses. Often life insurance is a good way to ensure such a fund. Be sure to discuss all these issues with the guardian, and choose a contingent guardian in case the first choice is unable to perform the needed functions.

will
A document that names the guardian for your children, states how you want your assets distributed, and names the executor for your estate.

A second step is to prepare a **will,** a document that names the guardian for your children, states how you want your assets distributed, and names the executor for your estate. An **executor** assembles and values your estate, files income and other taxes, and distributes assets.

A third step is to prepare a durable power of attorney. This document gives an individual you name the power to take over your finances if you become incapacitated. A *durable power of attorney for health care* delegates power to a person you name to make health care decisions for you if you are unable to make such decisions yourself.

executor
A person who assembles and values your estate, files income and other taxes, and distributes assets.

Other steps to follow are beyond the scope of this text. You may need to contact a financial planner/attorney to help you do the paperwork and planning to preserve and protect your investments for your children and spouse and others.[31] But it all begins with a strong financial base.

progress assessment

- What are three advantages of using a credit card?
- What kind of life insurance is recommended for most people?
- What are the advantages of investing through an IRA? A Keogh account? A 401(k) account?
- What are the main steps in estate planning?

summary

Learning Goal 1. Outline the six steps for controlling your assets.

- **What are the six steps to managing personal assets?**

(1) Take an inventory of your financial assets by developing a balance sheet for yourself with the fundamental accounting equation: Assets = Liabilities + Owners' equity; (2) keep track of all your expenses; (3) prepare a budget; (4) pay off your debts; (5) start a savings plan (the best way is to pay yourself first); and (6) if you must borrow, borrow only for assets that can increase in value or generate income.

Learning Goal 2. Explain how to build a financial base, including investing in real estate, saving money, and managing credit.

- **How can I accumulate funds?**

First, find a job. Try to live as frugally as possible. Invest your savings to generate even more capital. One such investment is a duplex home where the renter helps the owner pay the mortgage.

- **Why is real estate such a good investment?**

First, a home is the one investment you can live in. Second, once you buy a home, the payments are relatively fixed (though taxes and utilities may go up). As your income rises, the house payments get easier to make, while rents tend to go up at least as fast as income.

- **How does the government help you buy real estate?**

The government allows you to deduct interest payments on the mortgage, which lets you buy more home for the money.

- **Where is the best place to keep savings?**

It is best, in the long run, to invest in stocks. Although they go up and down in value, in the long run stocks earn more than most other investments. Diversify among mutual funds and other investments.

- **What is a good way to handle credit cards?**

Pay the balance in full during the period when no interest is charged. Not having to pay 16 percent interest is as good as earning 16 percent tax-free. Often a debit card is better than a credit card because it limits your spending to the amount you have in the bank.

Learning Goal 3. Explain how buying the appropriate insurance can protect your financial base.

- **What is the role of insurance in protecting capital?**

Insurance protects you from loss. If you were to die, your heirs would lose the income you would have earned. You can buy life insurance to make up for some or all of that loss.

- **Why is term insurance preferred?**

Term insurance is pure insurance protection for a given number of years. You can buy much more term insurance than whole life insurance for the same amount of money.

- **Do I need other insurance?**

It is important to have health insurance to protect against large medical bills. You also need car insurance (get a high deductible) and liability insurance in case you injure someone. You should also have homeowner's or renter's insurance. Often an umbrella policy will provide all your insurance protection for a lower cost.

Learning Goal 4. Outline a strategy for retiring with enough money to last a lifetime.

• Can I rely on Social Security to cover my retirement expenses?

Social Security depends on payments from current workers to cover the needs of retired people. Fewer workers are paying into the system, so you cannot rely on it to cover all your retirement expenses.

• What are the basics of saving for retirement?

Supplement Social Security with savings plans of your own. Everyone should have an IRA or some other retirement account. A Roth IRA is especially good for young people because your money grows tax-free and is tax-free when you withdraw it. For entrepreneurs, a Keogh plan or simplified employee pension (SEP) plan is wise. If you work for someone else, check out the 401(k) plan. Find a financial adviser who can recommend the best savings plan and help you make other investments.

• What are the basics of estate planning?

You need to choose a guardian for your children, prepare a will, and assign an executor for your estate. Sign a durable power of attorney to enable someone else to handle your finances if you are not capable. The same applies to a health durable power of attorney. Estate planning is complex and often calls for the aid of a financial planner/attorney, but the money is well spent to protect your assets.

key terms

401(k) plan A2-15
annuity A2-11
contrarian approach A2-8
disability insurance A2-11
executor A2-16

individual retirement account (IRA) A2-13
Roth IRA A2-14
Social Security A2-12
tax-deferred contributions A2-13
term insurance A2-10

umbrella policy A2-12
variable life insurance A2-11
whole life insurance A2-10
will A2-16

critical thinking

1. Have you given any thought to becoming an entrepreneur? Do the statistics about millionaires in this appendix give you some courage to pursue such a venture?
2. Housing prices in many parts of the United States are falling. What is the situation where you live? Would you encourage a college graduate in your area to buy a home or rent?
3. What kinds of questions must a person ask before considering the purchase of a home?
4. What insurance coverage do you have? What type of insurance do you need to buy next?

developing workplace skills

1. Check your local paper or use an online realtor to gather information regarding the cost to rent a two-bedroom apartment and to buy a two-bedroom condominium in your area. Go to Dinkytown.net and use the site's "rent-versus-buy calculator" to compare these costs. Discuss your findings in small groups.

2. Talk with someone you know who has invested in a family home. What appreciation have they gained on the purchase price? (Or, conversely, how has the value depreciated?) What other benefits has the home brought? Draw up a list of the benefits and drawbacks of owning a home and real estate in general as an investment. Be prepared to give a one-minute presentation on what you learned.

3. Find out the cost of major medical/hospital treatments in your area. Ask some older friends or acquaintances about medical insurance and whether they have ever gone without any. What types of insurance do they recommend? Discuss your results with the class.

4. The best time to start saving for the future is *now*. To prove this point to yourself, calculate how much you will have at age 65 if you begin saving $100 a month now, and $100 a month 10 years from now. Type "compound interest calculator" in a search engine and find an appropriate site to help you with the calculations.

5. Check out the benefits and drawbacks of both traditional and Roth IRAs. Be prepared to make a two-minute presentation about each and to discuss your findings in class.

taking it to the net

Purpose

To use online resources to make smart personal finance decisions.

Exercise

Use the calculators at **Dinkytown.net** to answer the following questions:

1. You need $5,000 for a trip to Europe in two years. How much would you have to deposit monthly in a savings account paying 1 percent in order to meet your goal?

2. Investing $1,000 at 6 percent for five years, what is the difference in purchasing power of your savings if inflation increases by 2 percent annually during that time? By 4 percent?

3. Starting today, how much would you need to save each month in order to become a millionaire before you retire?

4. You need a new car. What car can you afford if you have $1,500 for a down payment, can make monthly payments of $300, and get $1,000 for trading in your old clunker?

5. How much house can you afford if you earn $36,000 a year and have $10,000 savings for a down payment, a $6,000 car loan balance, and no credit card debts?

getting the job
YOU want

We hope that as you've read the text (particularly the Career Outlook sections at the end of each part), you've developed an idea of the type of career you'd like to build for yourself. If so, how will you go about getting a job you want in your chosen field? That is what this Epilogue is all about. In this section, you'll read more about some of the job search suggestions described earlier in the Career Outlook sections. Good luck—we hope you find a job doing something you love!

- Job Search Strategy

- Search for Jobs Online

- Job Search Resources

- Writing Your Résumé

- Putting Your Résumé Online

- Writing a Cover Letter

- Preparing for Job Interviews

One of the most important goals of this book is to help you get the job you want. First, you have to decide what you want to do. So far we've helped you explore this decision by explaining what people do in the various business functions: human resource management, marketing, accounting, finance, and so on. There are many good books about finding the job you want, so we can only introduce the subject here.

If you are a returning student, you have both blessings and handicaps that younger students do not have. First, you may have had a full-time job already. Second, you are more likely to know what kind of job you don't want. That is a real advantage. By exploring the various business careers in depth, you should be able to choose a career path that will meet your objectives.

If you have a full-time job right now, you already know that working while going to school requires juggling school and work responsibilities. Many older students must also balance family responsibilities in addition to those of school and work. But take heart. You have also acquired many skills from these experiences. Even if they were acquired in unrelated fields, these skills will be invaluable as you enter your new career. You can compete with younger students because you have the focus that comes with experience. Instructors enjoy having both kinds of students in class because they have different perspectives.

So, whether you're beginning your first career or your latest career, it's time to develop a strategy for finding and getting a personally satisfying job.

Do you look forward to saying, "I got the job!" after your years of college study? Job fairs are among the many resources that can help you find the right job for you. Is it ever too early to start thinking about your career?

JOB SEARCH STRATEGY

It is never too early to begin thinking about a future career or careers. The following strategies will give you some guidance in that pursuit:

1. **Begin with self-analysis.** You might begin your career quest by completing a self-analysis inventory. You can refer to Figure E.1 for a sample of a simple assessment.

2. **Search for jobs you would enjoy.** Begin at your college's career planning office or website, if your school has one. Talk to people in various careers, even after you've found a job. Career progress demands continuous research.

3. **Begin the networking process.** Networking remains the number one way for new job seekers to get their foot in the door. You can start with your fellow students, family, relatives, neighbors, friends, professors, and local businesspeople. Be sure to keep a record of names, addresses, and phone numbers of contacts, including where they work, the person who recommended them to you, and the relationship between the source person and the contact. A great way to build contacts and make a good impression on employers is to do part-time work and summer internships for firms you find interesting.

4. **Use social media for help.** Many professionals use online social networking sites, like Facebook, Twitter, and LinkedIn, to expand their networks and share industry news. If you haven't already, start profiles with these sites and start making connections. Don't sign up for a profile if you won't use it; employers will only think you don't finish what you start. When posting to these websites, be careful to include only information you would want a potential hiring agent to see and not something that might hurt your chances for landing a job.

Interests
1. How do I like to spend my time?
2. Do I enjoy being with people?
3. Do I like working with mechanical things?
4. Do I enjoy working with numbers?
5. Am I a member of many organizations?
6. Do I enjoy physical activities?
7. Do I like to read?

Abilities
1. Am I adept at working with numbers?
2. Am I adept at working with mechanical things?
3. Do I have good verbal and written communication skills?
4. What special talents do I have?
5. In which abilities do I wish I were more adept?

Education
1. Have I taken certain courses that have prepared me for a particular job?
2. In which subjects did I perform the best? The worst?
3. Which subjects did I enjoy the most? The least?
4. How have my extracurricular activities prepared me for a particular job?
5. Is my GPA an accurate picture of my academic ability? Why?
6. Do I want a graduate degree? Do I want to earn it before beginning my job?
7. Why did I choose my major?

Experience
1. What previous jobs have I held? What were my responsibilities in each?
2. Were any of my jobs applicable to positions I may be seeking? How?
3. What did I like the most about my previous jobs? Like the least?
4. Why did I work in the jobs I did?
5. If I had to do it over again, would I work in these jobs? Why?

Personality
1. What are my good and bad traits?
2. Am I competitive?
3. Do I work well with others?
4. Am I outspoken?
5. Am I a leader or a follower?
6. Do I work well under pressure?
7. Do I work quickly, or am I methodical?
8. Do I get along well with others?
9. Am I ambitious?
10. Do I work well independently of others?

Desired job environment
1. Am I willing to relocate? Why?
2. Do I have a geographic preference? Why?
3. Would I mind traveling in my job?
4. Do I have to work for a large, nationally known firm to be satisfied?
5. Must I have a job that initially offers a high salary?
6. Must the job I assume offer rapid promotion opportunities?
7. In what kind of job environment would I feel most comfortable?
8. If I could design my own job, what characteristics would it have?

Personal goals
1. What are my short- and long-term goals? Why?
2. Am I career-oriented, or do I have broader interests?
3. What are my career goals?
4. What jobs are likely to help me achieve my goals?
5. What do I hope to be doing in 5 years? In 10 years?
6. What do I want out of life?

figure E.1

A PERSONAL ASSESSMENT

5. **Prepare a good cover letter and résumé.** Once you know what you want to do and where you would like to work, you need to develop a good résumé and cover letter. Your résumé lists your education, work experience, and activities. We'll talk about these key job search tools in more detail. We'll also give you a list of resources you can use.

6. **Develop interviewing skills.** Interviewers will be checking your appearance (clothes, haircut, fingernails, shoes); your attitude (friendly, engaged); your verbal ability (speaking clearly); and your motivation (enthusiasm, passion). Note also that interviewers want you to have been active outside of school and to have set goals. Have someone evaluate you on these qualities now to see if you have any weak points. You can then work on those weaknesses before you have any actual job interviews. We'll give you some clues on how to do this later.

7. **Follow up.** Write a thank-you e-mail after interviews, even if you think they didn't go well. You have a chance to make a lasting impression with a follow-up note. If you are interviewed by a group of people, ask for their

business cards at the interview and e-mail them each separately. Let the company know you are still interested and indicate your willingness to travel to be interviewed. Get to know people in the company and learn from them whom to contact and what qualifications to emphasize.

SEARCHING FOR JOBS ONLINE

Social networking has become a powerful force in the job search. This should be no surprise; networking has always been the best way to hear about job leads, and networking online only makes it easier to connect and communicate with the people who could one day hire you.

Professional interview behavior includes writing a follow-up letter to thank the person or persons you met. What are your goals in writing such a letter?

Employers can use your online profiles to find your previous employers, learn more about your personality and interests, and gauge if you'd match the company's needs. Employers can also find red flags that can keep you from being hired, such as provocative photos, evidence of excessive drinking or drug use, bad-mouthing previous employers, or discriminatory comments about race, age, gender, or other topics. The key is to build a professional yet genuine personality online, one you won't mind showing to your future boss.

You can be sure that a future employer will check out your social media personality before hiring you. Here are a few social media sites you should be on:

- Facebook—"Like" the company's page on Facebook and look through its posts, photos, and comments to get a sense for what the company does.

- Twitter—Follow people who work in the industries and positions you are applying for. Share links to interesting articles or updates, and "re-tweet," or repeat, interesting stories from other professionals.

- LinkedIn—Companies have always relied on current employees to find their best new employees, and LinkedIn makes finding those connections easier. Using LinkedIn, you may find out that your high school friend's old college roommate is hiring, and that connection could be enough to get you the job.

- Google+: Organize your business contacts into "circles" and consider reaching out to them in "hangouts" to discuss industry news and find job openings.

- Pinterest: Share photos or videos that showcase your skills, especially if your experiences are creative or visual. Or, just show employers your personality by sharing images you enjoy.

- YouTube: Show off your communication skills and personality by posting videos. If you don't have videos from your previous work experiences, consider starting a video blog where you share your opinions on topics relevant to your business.

- Blog/Personal Website: While you should be careful about posting any personal information that could lead to identity theft on a public website, consider the value of writing regularly about a topic related to your career interests. A well-written blog can attract the attention of employers. However, if you create a blog, remember to proofread everything you post. Be sure to call attention to your blog posts by using Twitter and LinkedIn updates with links to what you write.

JOB SEARCH RESOURCES

Your school placement bureau's office and website are good places to begin learning about potential employers. On-campus interviewing is often a great source of jobs (see Figure E.2). Your library and the Internet may have annual reports that will give you even more information about your selected companies.

Other good sources of jobs include the want ads, job fairs, summer and other internship programs, placement bureaus, and sometimes walking into firms that appeal to you and asking for an interview. The *Occupational Outlook Quarterly*, produced by the U.S. Department of Labor, says this about job hunting:

> *The skills that make a person employable are not so much the ones needed on the job as the ones needed to get the job, skills like the ability to find a job opening, complete an application, prepare the résumé, and survive an interview.*

Here are a few printed sources you can use for finding out about jobs, writing résumés and cover letters, and other career information:

1. U.S. Department of Labor, "Occupational Outlook Handbook," 2012–2013.
2. Lauren Berger, *All Work, No Pay: Finding an Internship, Building Your Resume, Making Connections, and Gaining Job Experience* (Ten Speed Press, 2012).
3. Jenny Blake, *Life After College: The Complete Guide to Getting What You Want* (Running Press, 2011).
4. Steve Dalton, *The 2-Hour Job Search: Using Technology to Get the Right Job Faster* (Ten Speed Press, 2012).
5. Richard N. Bolles, *What Color Is Your Parachute? 2013: A Practical Manual for Job-Hunters and Career-Changers* (Ten Speed Press, 2012).
6. Nancy Schuman and Burton Jay Nadler, *1,001 Phrases You Need to Get a Job: The "Hire Me" Words That Set Your Cover Letter, Resume, and Job Interview Apart* (Adams Media, 2012).
7. Yana Parker, *The Damn Good Resume Guide, Fifth Edition: A Crash Course in Resume Writing* (Ten Speed Press, 2012).
8. Lindsey Pollak, *Getting from College to Career, Revised Edition: Your Essential Guide to Succeeding in the Real World* (HarperBusiness, 2012).

figure E.2

WHERE COLLEGE STUDENTS FIND JOBS

SOURCE OF JOB	
Online searches	College faculty/staff referrals
On-campus interviewing	Internship programs
Write-ins	High-demand major programs
Current employee referrals	Minority career programs
Job listings with placement office	Part-time employment
Responses from want ads	Unsolicited referrals from placement
Walk-ins	Women's career programs
Cooperative education programs	Job listings with employment agencies
Summer employment	Referrals from campus organizations

9. Brian D. Krueger, *The College Grad Job Hunter, Sixth Edition* (FW Media, 2011).

To find information about careers or internships online, try these sites (though keep in mind that addresses on the Internet are subject to sudden and frequent change):

- www.CareerBuilder.com
- www.Monster.com
- www.JobSearch.about.com
- www.Indeed.com
- www.GlassDoor.com
- www.TweetMyJobs.com

It's never too early in your career to begin designing a résumé and thinking of cover letters. A quality résumé is both deep and wide: deep, meaning you had a deep commitment to your activities (leadership roles, responsibilities, long-term commitments), and wide, meaning you were active in several, varied areas (jobs, internships, clubs, volunteering).

By preparing a résumé now, you may find gaps that need to be filled before you can land the job you want. For example, if you discover that you haven't been involved in enough outside activities to impress an employer, join a club or volunteer your time. If you are weak on job experience, seek an internship or part-time job to fill in that gap.

It's never too soon to prepare a résumé, so let's discuss how.

WRITING YOUR RÉSUMÉ

A résumé is a one-page document that lists information an employer would need to evaluate whether you qualify for that company's job opening. A résumé explains your immediate goals and career objectives as well as your educational background, experience, interests, and other relevant data. For example, experience working with teams is important to many companies. If you don't show an employer you have experience working with teams on your résumé, how can that employer decide if you should get an interview? Employers don't *read* résumés—they *scan* them, so use action words like those listed in Figure E.3 to grab an employer's attention quickly. You must be comprehensive and clear in your résumé if you are to communicate all your attributes.

Your résumé is an advertisement for yourself. If your ad is better than the other person's ad, you're more likely to get the interview. In this case, *better* means that your ad highlights your attributes more attractively. In discussing your education, for example, be sure to highlight your extracurricular activities such as part-time jobs, sports, and clubs. If you did well in school, include your grades. Be sure

Administered	Directed	Investigated	Scheduled
Budgeted	Established	Managed	Served
Conducted	Handled	Operated	Supervised
Coordinated	Implemented	Organized	Teamed
Designed	Improved	Planned	Trained
Developed	Increased	Produced	Wrote

figure E.3

SAMPLE ACTION WORDS

to describe your previous jobs, including your responsibilities, achievements, and special projects. If you include an interests section, don't just list your hobbies, but describe how deeply you are involved. If you organized the club, volunteered your time, or participated in an organization, make sure to say so in the résumé. The idea is to make yourself look as good on paper as you are in reality.

Here are some hints on preparing your résumé:

- Keep it simple. Put a summary of your skills and your objective at the top so that the reader can capture as much as possible in the first 30 seconds.

- If you e-mail your résumé, send it in the text of the message; don't just send it as an attachment. It takes too long for the receiver to open an attachment.

- Customize each mailing to that specific company. You may use a standard résumé, but add data to customize it and to introduce it.

- Use any advertised job title as the subject of your e-mail message, including any relevant job numbers.

See Figure E.4 for a sample résumé. Most companies prefer that you keep your résumé to one page unless you have many years of experience.

PUTTING YOUR RÉSUMÉ ONLINE

Many larger firms seek candidates on the Internet, and online tools can help you expand your résumé into a portfolio complete with links, work samples, and even video. An online résumé can thus allow you to reach the greatest number of potential employers with the least amount of effort.

But remember, thousands of other eager job hunters send résumés online, and the volume can overwhelm recruiters. That doesn't mean you shouldn't post your résumé online, but you can't just send a few hundred résumés into cyberspace and then sit back and wait for the phone to ring. Include online résumés as a tool in your job search process, but continue to use the more traditional tools, such as networking.

If you are sending a résumé through a career listing site like Monster.com, the company may be using a computer program to scan your résumé for keywords before actual humans get their hands on it. Computer programs look at résumés much differently than people do, so some people's perfectly executed, beautifully worded résumés don't pass the computer's test. If you are submitting a résumé online, you must understand what the computer is programmed to look for. While scannable resumes are on their way out, you may still find value in creating an online resume that will pass the computer scan with flying colors. Here are five ways to write an online résumé that will get you past the computer evaluation stage:

- Include as many of the keywords in the company's job description as possible. If you are applying for a sales management position, use the words "sales," "managed," and "manager" often in your résumé.

- Visit the employer's website. Are there any words they use to describe their corporate culture? If so, include those adjectives in your résumé as well.

- Keep your formatting simple and streamlined. Avoid underlining, italics, and boxes. You don't want to confuse the computer with fancy designs. Keep it simple and save your formatted résumé for the next stages in the process.

- List all the universities or colleges you've attended, even if it was just for a class or a semester. Some computer programs assign higher point values to prestigious universities.

figure E.4

SAMPLE RÉSUMÉ

Yann Ng
345 Big Bend Boulevard
Kirkwood, MO, 63122
314-555-5385
yng@stilnet.com

Job objective: Sales representative in business-to-business marketing

Education: Earned 100 percent of college expenses working 35 hours per week

A.A. in Business, May 2011
St. Louis Community College at Meramec
Grade Point Average: 3.6

B.S. in Business, Marketing Major, expected May 2013
University of Missouri, St. Louis
Grade Point Average: 3.2 overall, 3.5 in major
Dean's List for two semesters

Experience

Schnuck's Supermarket, Des Peres, MO, 5/09 – present

- Responded to customer requests quickly as evening and weekend checkout cashier
- Trained new hires to build customer retention, loyalty, and service
- Learned on-the-job principles behind brand management, retail sales, and consumer product marketing

Mary Tuttle's Flowers, Kirkwood, MO, Summer 2007 and Summer 2008

- Created flower arrangements to customer specifications, managed sales transactions, and acted as an assistant to the manager
- Developed skills in customer relationship management
- Created window displays to enhance visual merchandising and retail marketing to consumers

Student Leadership

SLCC Student Representative Board: Created action plan for fundraising drive, which resulted in our largest donations ever to Habitat for Humanity

UMSL Student American Marketing Association: Ran team-building and recruitment activities, which resulted in a 10 percent increase in membership

UMSL Student Government Association: Ran focus groups to help prioritize goals, helping us target changes in the way we allocate student fees

Language Skills: Fluent in English, Vietnamese, and French

Computer Skills: Microsoft Office, Photoshop, and HTML/Web Publishing

- Developed own website (www.yng@stilnet.com)
- Created effective PowerPoint slides using Photoshop for Consumer Behavior class

- Don't ever lie, exaggerate, or cheat the system. You'll get caught, and you won't get the job.

Figure E.5 offers a sample online résumé, but you should consult the latest résumé handbook to see what the newer résumés should look like.

Posting résumés to online job sites can cause privacy nightmares for job seekers, who fear everything from identity theft to losing their current job when employers find out that they are looking for new jobs. Sometimes posted résumés are sold to other sites or individuals willing to pay for them. Scam artists posing as

Yann Ng
345 Big Bend Boulevard
Kirkwood, MO, 63122
314-555-5385
yng@stilnet.com

Job objective: Sales representative in business-to-business marketing

Education:
A.A. in Business, May 2011
St. Louis Community College at Meramec
Grade point average: 3.6

B.S. in Business, Marketing major, expected May 2013
University of Missouri, St. Louis
Grade point average: 3.2 overall, 3.5 in major)
Dean's List for two semesters

Experience:
Schnuck's Supermarket, Des Peres, MO, 5/09 – present Responded to customer requests quickly as evening and weekend checkout cashier. Trained new hires to build customer retention, loyalty, and service. Learned on-the-job principles behind brand management, retail sales, and consumer product marketing.

Mary Tuttle's Flowers, Kirkwood, MO, Summer 2007 and Summer 2008 Created flower arrangements to customer specifications, managed sales transactions, and acted as an assistant to the manager. Developed skills in customer relationship management. Created window displays to enhance visual merchandising and retail marketing to consumers.

Student Leadership
SLCC Student Representative Board: Created action plan for fundraising drive
UMSL Student American Marketing Association: Ran team-building and recruitment activities UMSL Student Government Association: Ran focus groups to help prioritize goals

Language Skills
English
Vietnamese
French

Computer Skills
Microsoft Office
Photoshop
HTML/Web Publishing

recruiters can download all the résumés they want and do virtually whatever they want with them. At worst, online résumés can give identity thieves a starting point to steal personal information.

Here are tips to protect your résumé and your identity:

- *Never* include highly private information, such as Social Security numbers and birthdays.
- Check job boards' privacy policies to see how information is used and resold.
- Post résumés directly to employers if possible.
- Date résumés and remove them promptly after finding a job.
- If possible, withhold confidential information such as telephone numbers and your name and use temporary e-mail addresses for contacts.

Some companies take résumés via Twitter before accepting full-page résumés by e-mail. Find a creative way to shorten your career objectives, experience, and interests to under 140 characters and share it with your connections.

WRITING A COVER LETTER

A cover letter is used to announce your availability and to introduce the résumé, but it also showcases your personality to an employer, often for the first time. The cover letter is probably one of the most important advertisements anyone will write in a lifetime—so it should be done right.

First, the cover letter should indicate that you've researched the organization and are interested in a job there. Let the organization know what sources you used and what you know in the first paragraph to get the attention of the reader and show your interest.

You may have heard people say, "What counts is not what you know, but whom you know." If you don't know anyone, *get* to know someone. You can do this by calling the organization, visiting the offices, or reaching out on social media to talk to people who already have the kind of job you're hoping to get. Then, at the beginning of your cover letter, mention that you've talked with some of the firm's employees, showing the letter reader that you "know someone," if only casually, and that you're interested enough to actively pursue the organization. This is all part of networking.

Describe yourself in the next paragraph of your cover letter. Be sure to show how your experiences will benefit the organization. For example, don't just say, "I will be graduating with a degree in marketing." Say, "You will find that my college training in marketing and marketing research has prepared me to learn your marketing system quickly and begin making a contribution right away." The sample cover letter in Figure E.6 will give you a better feel for how this looks.

Use the last paragraph of your cover letter to say you are available for an interview at a time and place convenient for the interviewer. Offer to follow up with a phone call or e-mail if you don't hear from the employer after some time. Again, see the sample cover letter in Figure E.6 for guidance. Notice in this letter how the writer subtly shows that she reads business publications and draws attention to her résumé.

Principles to follow in writing a cover letter and preparing your résumé include:

- Be confident. List all your good qualities and attributes.
- Don't be apologetic or negative. Write as one professional to another, not as a humble student begging for a job.
- Describe how your experience and education can add value to the organization.
- Research every prospective employer thoroughly before writing anything. Use a rifle approach rather than a shotgun approach. That is, write effective marketing-oriented letters to a few select companies rather than general letters to a long list.
- Have your materials prepared by an experienced keyboarder if you are not highly skilled yourself. Use printing services like FedEx Office if you do not have access to a good-quality printer.
- Have someone edit your materials for spelling, grammar, and style. Don't be like the student who sent out a second résumé to correct "some mixtakes." Or another who said, "I am acurite with numbers."
- Don't send the names of references until asked.

figure E.6

SAMPLE COVER LETTER

345 Big Bend Blvd.
Kirkwood, MO 63122
October 10, 2013

Mr. Carl Karlinski
Premier Designs
45 Apple Court
Chicago, IL 60536

Dear Mr. Karlinski: (Address the letter to a real person whenever possible.)

Recent articles in *Inc.* and *Success* praised your company for its innovative products and strong customer orientation. Having used your creative display materials at Mary Tuttle's Flowers, I'm familiar with your visually stimulating designs. Christie Bouchard, your local sales representative, told me all about your products and your sales training program at Premier Designs. Having talked with her about the kind of salespeople you are seeking, I believe I have the motivation and people skills to be successful.

Proven Sales Ability: For two summers, I created and sold flower arrangements at Mary Tuttle's Flowers, developing a loyal customer base. Also, for four years, I've practiced personable customer relations, based on the excellent customer-oriented training program that Schnuck's Supermarket delivers in the St. Louis region. I know our regular customers by name; they've told me that they first look for my station when they are checking out. I would bring this same attention to developing relationships in a business-to-business sales position.

Self-Motivation: I've worked 35 hours per week and every summer during my college years and have paid for 100 percent of my expenses. In addition, I've paid for trips to Asia, Europe, and the Americas.

Leadership: I've served actively in student governance both on the Student Representative Board at St. Louis Community College and as a part of the student government at the University of Missouri. I've always gotten to know other students to find out how I could make a difference through my student government work. I would take the initiative to not only serve customers well but also to help other new salespeople.

I will be in the Chicago area the week of January 4–9 and would appreciate the opportunity to meet with you to learn more about Premier's sales opportunities. I will phone your administrative assistant to check on your availability. Thank you for considering my application. I would work hard to maintain and expand the business-to-business relationships that have made Premier Designs so successful.

Sincerely,

Yann Ng

PREPARING FOR JOB INTERVIEWS

Companies use interviews to decide which qualified candidates are the best match for the job, so be prepared for your interviews. There are five stages of interview preparation:

1. **Do research about the prospective employers.** Learn what industry the firm is in, its competitors, the products or services it produces and their acceptance in the market, and the title of your desired position. You can find such information in the firm's annual reports, in Standard & Poor's, Hoover's, Moody's manuals, and various business publications such as

Fortune, Bloomberg Businessweek, and *Forbes.* Ask your librarian for help or search the Internet. You can look in the *Reader's Guide to Business Literature* to locate the company name and to look for articles about it. This important first step shows you have initiative and interest in the firm.

2. **Practice the interview.** Figure E.7 lists some of the more frequently asked questions in an interview. Practice answering these questions at the placement office and with your roommate, parents, or friends. Don't memorize your answers, but do be prepared—know what you're going to say. Interviewers will be impressed if you prepare questions for them about the products, job, company culture, and so on. Figure E.8 shows sample questions you might ask. Be sure you know whom to contact, and write down the names of everyone you meet. Review the action words in Figure E.3 and try to fit them into your answers.

3. **Be professional during the interview.** You should look and sound professional throughout the interview. Dress appropriately. When you meet the interviewers, greet them by name, smile, and maintain good eye contact. Sit up straight in your chair and be alert and enthusiastic. If you have practiced, you should be able to relax and be confident. Other than that, be yourself, answer questions, and be friendly and responsive. (You will learn more about what types of questions job interviewers are legally allowed to ask you in Chapter 11.) Remember, the interview is not one-way communication; don't forget to ask the questions you've prepared before the interview. Do *not* ask about salary, however, until you've been offered a job. When

figure E.7

FREQUENTLY ASKED QUESTIONS

- How would you describe yourself?
- What are your greatest strengths and weaknesses?
- How did you choose this company?
- What do you know about the company?
- What are your long-range career goals?
- What courses did you like best? Least?
- What are your hobbies?
- Do you prefer a specific geographic location?

- Are you willing to travel (or move)?
- Which accomplishments have given you the most satisfaction?
- What things are most important to you in a job?
- Why should I hire you?
- What experience have you had in this type of work?
- How much do you expect to earn?

figure E.8

SAMPLE QUESTIONS TO ASK THE INTERVIEWER

- Who are your major competitors, and how would you rate their products and marketing relative to yours?
- How long does the training program last, and what is included?
- How soon after school would I be expected to start?
- What are the advantages of working for this firm?
- How much travel is normally expected?
- What managerial style should I expect in my area?
- How would you describe the working environment in my area?

- How would I be evaluated?
- What is the company's promotion policy?
- What is the corporate culture?
- What is the next step in the selection procedures?
- How soon should I expect to hear from you?
- What other information would you like about my background, experience, or education?
- What is your highest priority in the next six months and how could someone like me help?

you leave, thank the interviewers and, if you're still interested in the job, tell them so. If they don't tell you, ask them what the next step is. Maintain a positive attitude. Figures E.9 and E.10 outline what the interviewers will be evaluating.

4. **Follow up on the interview.** First, write down what you can remember from the interview: names of the interviewers and their titles, dates for training, etc., so you can send a follow-up letter, a letter of recommendation, or some other information to keep their interest. Your enthusiasm for working for the company could be a major factor in them hiring you.

5. **Be prepared to act.** Know what you want to say if you do get a job offer. You may not want the job once you know all the information. Don't expect to receive a job offer from everyone you meet, but do expect to learn something from every interview. With some practice and persistence, you should find a rewarding and challenging job.

figure E.9

TRAITS RECRUITERS SEEK IN JOB PROSPECTS

1. **Ability to communicate.** Do you have the ability to organize your thoughts and ideas effectively? Can you express them clearly when speaking or writing? Can you present your ideas to others in a persuasive way?
2. **Intelligence.** Do you have the ability to understand the job assignment? Learn the details of operation? Contribute original ideas to your work?
3. **Self-confidence.** Do you demonstrate a sense of maturity that enables you to deal positively and effectively with situations and people?
4. **Willingness to accept responsibility.** Are you someone who recognizes what needs to be done and is willing to do it?
5. **Initiative.** Do you have the ability to identify the purpose of work and to take action?
6. **Leadership.** Can you guide and direct others to obtain the recognized objectives?
7. **Energy level.** Do you demonstrate a forcefulness and capacity to make things move ahead? Can you maintain your work effort at an above-average rate?
8. **Imagination.** Can you confront and deal with problems that may not have standard solutions?
9. **Flexibility.** Are you capable of changing and being receptive to new situations and ideas?
10. **Interpersonal skills.** Can you bring out the best efforts of individuals so they become effective, enthusiastic members of a team?
11. **Self-knowledge.** Can you realistically assess your own capabilities? See yourself as others see you? Clearly recognize your strengths and weaknesses?
12. **Ability to handle conflict.** Can you successfully contend with stress situations and antagonism?
13. **Competitiveness.** Do you have the capacity to compete with others and the willingness to be measured by your performance in relation to that of others?
14. **Goal achievement.** Do you have the ability to identify and work toward specific goals? Do such goals challenge your abilities?
15. **Vocational skills.** Do you possess the positive combination of education and skills required for the position you are seeking?
16. **Direction.** Have you defined your basic personal needs? Have you determined what type of position will satisfy your knowledge, skills, and goals?

Source: "So You're Looking for a Job?" The College Placement Council.

Candidate: "For each characteristic listed below there is a rating scale of 1 through 7, where '1' is generally the most unfavorable rating of the characteristic and '7' the most favorable. Rate each characteristic by *circling* just one number to represent the impression you gave in the interview that you have just completed."

Name of Candidate _____

1. Appearance

| Sloppy | 1 | 2 | 3 | 4 | 5 | 6 | 7 | Neat |

2. Attitude

| Unfriendly | 1 | 2 | 3 | 4 | 5 | 6 | 7 | Friendly |

3. Assertiveness/Verbal Ability

a. Responded completely to questions asked

| Poor | 1 | 2 | 3 | 4 | 5 | 6 | 7 | Excellent |

b. Clarified personal background and related it to job opening and description

| Poor | 1 | 2 | 3 | 4 | 5 | 6 | 7 | Excellent |

c. Able to explain and sell job abilities

| Poor | 1 | 2 | 3 | 4 | 5 | 6 | 7 | Excellent |

d. Initiated questions regarding position and firm

| Poor | 1 | 2 | 3 | 4 | 5 | 6 | 7 | Excellent |

e. Expressed thorough knowledge of personal goals and abilities

| Poor | 1 | 2 | 3 | 4 | 5 | 6 | 7 | Excellent |

4. Motivation

| Poor | 1 | 2 | 3 | 4 | 5 | 6 | 7 | High |

5. Subject/Academic Knowledge

| Poor | 1 | 2 | 3 | 4 | 5 | 6 | 7 | Good |

6. Stability

| Poor | 1 | 2 | 3 | 4 | 5 | 6 | 7 | Good |

7. Composure

| Ill at ease | 1 | 2 | 3 | 4 | 5 | 6 | 7 | Relaxed |

8. Personal Involvement/Activities, Clubs, Etc.

| Low | 1 | 2 | 3 | 4 | 5 | 6 | 7 | Very high |

9. Mental Impression

| Dull | 1 | 2 | 3 | 4 | 5 | 6 | 7 | Alert |

10. Adaptability

| Poor | 1 | 2 | 3 | 4 | 5 | 6 | 7 | Good |

11. Speech Pronunciation

| Poor | 1 | 2 | 3 | 4 | 5 | 6 | 7 | Good |

12. Overall Impression

| Unsatisfactory | 1 | 2 | 3 | 4 | 5 | 6 | 7 | Highly satisfactory |

13. Would you hire this individual if you were permitted to make a decision right now?

| | Yes | No | |

All your efforts pay off when you land the job you want and take the first big step in your career. Go for it!

BE PREPARED TO CHANGE CAREERS

If you're like most people, you'll follow several different career paths over your lifetime. This enables you to try different jobs and to stay fresh and enthusiastic. The key to moving forward and finding personal satisfaction in your career is a willingness to change and grow. This means that you'll have to write many cover letters and résumés and go through many interviews. Each time you change jobs, go through the steps in this section of the Epilogue to be sure you're fully prepared. Good luck!

chapter notes

PROLOGUE

1. U.S. Department of Education Institute for Education Science, http://nces.ed.gov, accessed June 2011.
2. U.S. Census Bureau, www.census.gov, accessed June 2011.
3. Anne Kates Smith, "New Jobs, New Skills," *Kiplinger's Personal Finance,* November 2010.
4. Robert Rodriguez, "How Rude! Poor Etiquette on the Rise, Workplace Experts Say," *Sun-Journal* (Lewiston, ME), January 13, 2008.
5. Robert Half International, "Tech Etiquette," www.careerbuilder.com, accessed June 2011.
6. Rachel Farrell, "Social Media Can Kill Your Career—But Not the Way You Think," www.careerbuilder.com, accessed June 2011.

CHAPTER 1

1. Ed Nash, "Is Your Company Late to the Mobile Party?," *The Wall Street Journal,* April 12, 2012.
2. Lewis D'Vorkin, "The Wealth List in a New Era," *Forbes,* March 28, 2011.
3. "Billionaire Box Score," *Forbes,* March 26, 2012.
4. John B. Taylor, "A Two-Track Plan to Restore Growth," *The Wall Street Journal,* January 28, 2011.
5. A.G. Lafley, "I Think of My Failures as a Gift," *Harvard Business Review,* April 2011.
6. Keith Naughton, "The Happiest Man in Detroit," *Bloomberg Businessweek,* February 7–February 13, 2011.
7. Daniel Burke, "The Happiness Business," *The Washington Post,* December 4, 2010.
8. Robert Frick, "What Price Happiness?," *Kiplinger's Personal Finance,* January 2012.
9. N. Craig Smith, Sean Ansett, and Lior Erez, "How Gap Inc. Engaged with Its Stakeholders," *MIT Sloan Management Review,* Summer 2011.
10. Jennifer Kho, "World Leaders in Clean Capitalism," *Corporate Knights,* Winter 2012.
11. David Ryan, "Help for Unemployment: Insourcing," *The Washington Times,* April 26, 2012.
12. John Bussey, "U.S. Manufacturing, Defying Naysayers," *The Wall Street Journal,* April 20, 2012.
13. Steven Prokesch, "The Reluctant Social Entrepreneur," *Harvard Business Review,* June 2011.
14. Bruce Einhorn and Ruth David, "An IPO for India's Top Lender to the Poor," *Bloomberg Businessweek,* May 10–May 16, 2010.
15. John Cuneo, "10 Perks We Love," *Inc.,* June 2010.
16. Joann S. Lubin and Kelly Eggers, "More Women Are Primed to Land CEO Roles," *The Wall Street Journal,* April 30, 2012.
17. Mike Cosgrove, "Debt, Tax Burdens Holding Back Growth," *Investor's Business Daily,* February 3, 2011.
18. "Stimulus Packages Helped Economy, Study Says," *Los Angeles Times,* May 3, 2012.
19. Max H. Bazerman and Ann E. Tenbrunsel, "Ethical Breakdowns," *Harvard Business Review,* April 2011.

20. David J. Lynch, "Did That Robot Take My Job?" *Bloomberg Businessweek,* January 9–January 15, 2012.
21. John Jannarone, "Retailers Struggle in Amazon Jungle," *The Wall Street Journal,* February 22, 2011.
22. Robert Hsu, "450 Million Chinese Internet Users Are a Big 2011 Trend," *Investors Place Asia,* January 3, 2011.
23. Freescoreonline.com, accessed May 12, 2012.
24. "Senior Services," *Entrepreneur,* January 2011.
25. "John Tozzi," "Home-Care Companies Brace for Regulation," *Bloomberg Businessweek,* March 21–March 27, 2011.
26. Matt Villano, "Selling Green," *Entrepreneur,* November 2011.
27. Neil Irwin and Todd Lindeman, "Why the Job Hunt Is So Hard," *The Washington Post,* September 14, 2011.

CHAPTER 2

1. Edwin J. Feulner, "A Step Backward for Economic Freedom in 2012," *The Wall Street Journal,* January 12, 2012.
2. Terry Miller, "The U.S. Loses Ground on Economic Freedom," *The Wall Street Journal,* January 12, 2011.
3. Warren Stephens, "Business Regulation vs. Growth: The View from Middle America," *The Wall Street Journal,* August 25, 2011.
4. David Malpass, "The U.S. Needs a New Debt Limit," *Forbes,* February 27, 2012.
5. Bryan Walsh, "Down and Dirty," *Time,* March 21, 2011.
6. Bryan Walsh, "The End of the Line," *Time,* July 18, 2011.
7. Jason Daley, "Green Fallout," *Entrepreneur,* August 2010.
8. Megan McArole, "Europe's Real Crisis," *The Atlantic,* April 2012.
9. Jonathan R. Laing, "Beyond Laissez-Faire," *Barron's,* February 28, 2011.
10. Ibid.
11. Margaret Tavev, "Millionaires Who Dream of Giving More to the IRS," *Bloomberg Businessweek,* April 23–April 29, 2012.
12. Amy C. Cosper, "Trash Talk," *Entrepreneur,* April 2011.
13. Henry R. Nav, "Lesson from the Great Expansion," *The Wall Street Journal,* January 26, 2012.
14. Dominic Barton, "Capitalism for the Long Term," *Harvard Business Review,* March 2011.
15. Gordon G. Chang, "Perils of State Capitalism," *National Review,* July 19, 2011.
16. Ibid.
17. Hernando de Soto, "Egypt's Economic Apartheid," *The Wall Street Journal,* February 3, 2011.
18. Stuart F. Brown and Anne Vanermey, "New Ways to Solve the Energy Challenge," *Fortune,* January 16, 2012.
19. "McDonald's: A Healthier Happy Meal?," *The Week,* August 12, 2012.
20. Duane Stanford, "Nature's Gatorade," *Bloomberg Businessweek,* March 14–March 20, 2011.
21. John Cassidy, "The Jobs Numbers and the Real Threat to Obama," *Fortune,* April 30, 2012.
22. Geoffrey A. Fowler, "Billionaire Families Join Pledge on Giving," *The Wall Street Journal,* April 20, 2012.

23. Caroline Winter, David Glovin, and Jennifer Daniel, "The Great Hedge Fund Takedown," *Bloomberg Businessweek,* March 14–March 20, 2011.
24. Michael Porter and Mark R. Kramer, "Creating Shared Value," *Harvard Business Review,* January–February 2011.
25. Todd Ganos, "Why Socialism Doesn't Work," *Forbes,* February 17, 2012.
26. Linda Darling-Hammond, "They're Number One," *neatoday,* October/November 2010.
27. "The Keynesian Dead End," *The Wall Street Journal,* June 26–27, 2010.
28. "The Vanishing Worker," *The Wall Street Journal,* May 5–6, 2012.
29. Gene Epstein, "Deflation Demystified," *Barron's,* August 30, 2010.
30. Ronald McKinnon, "The Return of Stagflation," *The Wall Street Journal,* May 24, 2011.
31. Mark J. Perry, "The Truth about U.S. Manufacturing," *The Wall Street Journal,* February 25, 2011.
32. Richard H. K. Vietor and Matthew Weinzierl, "Macroeconomic Policy and U.S. Competitiveness," *Harvard Business Review,* March 2012.
33. Benjamin Bower, "Keynes Was a Better Economist Than His Disciples Are," *The Wall Street Journal,* July 2, 2010.
34. Susan Lund and Richard Dobbs, "Myths about Interest Rates," *The Washington Post,* January 23, 2011.
35. Neil Irwin, "Bernanke Defends U.S. Policies," *The Washington Post,* February 19, 2011.

CHAPTER 3

1. Michael Bekins, "Taking Your Career on the Road," *The Wall Street Journal,* June 14, 2010.
2. "World Population Clock," U.S. Census Bureau, www.census.gov/ipc/www/popclockworld.html, accessed May 2012; and WorldAtlas.com, accessed May 2012.
3. "U.S. Trade Deficit Expands Even as Exports Accelerate,"*The New York Times,* February 11, 2011.
4. UPS.com, accessed March 11, 2011; Walmart.com, accessed March 11, 2011; and "The Beast in the Bush," *The Economist,* February 19, 2011.
5. NBA.com, accessed May 2012.
6. "Bigger Abroad," *The Economist,* February 19, 2011.
7. World Bank, www.worldbank.org, accessed May 2012; and World Trade Organization, www.wto.org, accessed May 2012.
8. Andrew Malcolm, "Australia's Prime Minister Julia Gillard: 'There's a Reason the World Always Looks to America," *Los Angeles Times,* March 10, 2011.
9. "Time to Act on Free Trade," *The Washington Post,* March 14, 2011.
10. Jack Markowitz, "China's Idea of Free Trade Hardly Fair," *Pittsburgh Tribune-Review,* January 20, 2011; and Bill Lambrecht, "U.S. Accused of Letting China Flout Trade Law," *St. Louis Post-Dispatch,* March 17, 2011.
11. Matthew J. Slaughter, "Comparative Advantage and American Jobs, *The Wall Street Journal,* January 26, 2011; and www.NetMBA.com, accessed May 2012.
12. Steven Pearlstein and Dana Rodrik, "The Globalization Paradox," *The Washington Post,* March 13, 2011; and Clyde Prestowitz, "Why Isn't the iPhone Made in America?" *Foreign Policy,* March 8, 2011.
13. Cyndia Zwahlen, "Exporting Presents Opportunities and Challenges for Small Businesses," *Los Angeles Times,* February 21, 2011; and Matt Glynn, "A Helping Hand for Small Businesses Wanting to Export; Ex-Im Bank Works to Support Deals," *The Buffalo News,* February 2, 2012.
14. Courtney Rubin, "Obama Encourages Small Firms to Go Global," *Inc.,* March 15, 2010; Martha White, "Thinking Small," *Slate,* December 6, 2010; and John Tozzi, "Small Business Exports Edge Up," *Bloomberg Businessweek,* February 2, 2012.
15. www.zeromillion.com, accessed May 2012; and www.myprimetime.com, accessed May 2012.
16. Fredrick Balfour and Michael Wei, "Selling Skin Cream to China's 'City Jade Men,'" *Bloomberg Businessweek,* January 9, 2011.
17. C. Fred Bergston, "How Best to Boost U.S. Exports," *The Washington Post,* February 3, 2010.
18. "U.S. Trade Deficit Expands Even as Exports Accelerate," *The New York Times,* February 11, 2011; and Robert J. Samuelson, "The Economy's Uncharted Path," *The Washington Post,* February 6, 2012.
19. Keith Bradsher, "Inflation in China May Limit U.S. Trade Deficit," *The New York Times,* January 30, 2011.
20. Michelle Jarboe, "President Obama to Hear about Tight Budgets, Taxes, and Trade from Cleveland-Area Small Businesses," *The Plain Dealer,* February 11, 2011.
21. Mark Drajem, "Chinese Steel Drill-Pipe Exporters to Face U.S. Dumping Duties," *Bloomberg Businessweek,* February 7, 2011; and John Bussey, "U.S. Attacks China Inc.," *The Wall Street Journal,* February 3, 2012.
22. www.goldmarks.com, accessed May 2012.
23. "Frederick's of Hollywood Announces International Expansion," *PR Newswire,* March 15, 2011.
24. Adam Wooten, "Local Export Assistance Remedies International Headaches," *Deseret News* (Salt Lake City), January 28, 2011; www.buyusa.gov, accessed May 2012; www.export.gov, accessed May 2012; and Linda Goodspeed, "How to Evaluate and Enter Foreign Markets Successfully," *The Business Journals,* January 25, 2012.
25. www.rockymountainchocolatefactory.com, accessed May 2012.
26. Lan Ann Nguyen, "Home Cooking," *Forbes,* February 28, 2011; and Mike Eckel, "Living Loud in Hanoi," *The Seattle Times,* February 28, 2011.
27. www.yum.com, accessed May 2012; Vincent Mao, "China Demand Boosts Yum's Sales, Earnings," *Investor's Business Daily,* February 4, 2011; and Stephanie Clouser, "Yum to Trim Ownership of Taco Bell, Other U.S. Units," *Los Angeles Business,* February 8, 2012.
28. www.yum.com, accessed May 2012; and Celia Hatton, "KFC's Finger-Lickin' Success in China," CBS News, March 6, 2011.
29. Alan R. Elliott "Jabil and TTM in Early Stage Chart Patterns," *Investor's Business Daily,* March 2, 2011.
30. www.flextronics.com, accessed May 2012.
31. Jessica Beaton, "Shanghai Disneyland Budget: The Numbers Are In," CNN International, March 7, 2011; and "Shanghai Reveals New Disneyland Blueprints for First Time," *Forbes,* March 9, 2011.
32. "Marriott Joint-Venture a Sign of Things to Come," *Travelweekly,* March 15, 2011.
33. www.pepsico.com, accessed March 15, 2011.
34. Sean D. Hamill, "How UPMC's Overseas Operation Blossomed in 14 Years," *Pittsburgh Post-Gazette,* May 30, 2010; and University of Pittsburgh Medical Center, www.upmc.com, accessed May 2012.
35. www.nestle.com, accessed May 2012.
36. Veera Pandiyan, "Time to Ace the Race Card for Better Unity," *The Malaysian Star,* March 10, 2011; and Adam Wooten, "Watch the Calendar for Good Times in International Business," *Deseret News* (Salt Lake City), January 6, 2012.

37. Chrissie Thompson, "Lincoln Number 1 in Long-Term Quality, but Foreign Brands Still Better Overall," *Detroit Free Press,* March 17, 2011; and Chris Woodyard, "Auto Exports from U.S. on Rise," *USA Today,* March 7, 2011.

38. Adam Wooten, "Wrong Flowers Can Mean Death for Global Business," *Deseret News* (Salt Lake City), February 4, 2011.

39. Jennifer Reingold, "Can P&G Make Money in Places Where People Earn $2 a Day?" *Fortune,* January 17, 2011; and www.procter&gamble.com, accessed May 2012.

40. Hao Li, "Marc Chandler: In Defense of the Dollar," *International Business Times,* March 4, 2011.

41. Chris Isidore, "European Leaders Scramble to Contain Greek Debt Crisis," *CNN Money,* May 16, 2012.

42. "Cuba Cuts Hard Currency Peso to Par with Dollar," Associated Press, March 14, 2011; and Paul Abelsky, "Belarus Central Bank Says No Plans to Devalue Domestic Currency," *Bloomberg,* March 15, 2011.

43. www.wto.org, accessed May 2012; and www.worldbank.org, accessed May 2012.

44. Dionne Searcey, "Former Enforcer Sees Looming Fights," *The Wall Street Journal,* March 17, 2011; and "IBM to Pay $10M to Settle Foreign Bribery Case," *Accounting Today,* March 18, 2011.

45. "Bribery/Anti-Corruption: Introduction," *The Lawyer,* March 19, 2011; and www.oecd.org, accessed May 2012.

46. Ian Fletcher, "In Praise of Mercantilism (or Why Economic History Isn't Boring)," *The Huffington Post,* March 19, 2011; and www.referenceforbusiness.com, accessed March 19, 2011.

47. Sarah Stephens, "Like Oil and Water in the Gulf," *Los Angeles Times,* March 14, 2011.

48. Jennifer Liberto, "Newest Trade War: Obama vs. Congress," CNN Money.com, March 19, 2011; and David Shepardson, "Obama Administration Urges Speedy Approval of Korea Trade Deal," *The Detroit News,* March 10, 2011.

49. www.wto.org, accessed May 2012.

50. "WTO Rules in China's Favor in U.S. Trade Dispute," *Los Angeles Times,* March 11, 2011; "A Win for China," *The Wall Street Journal,* March 17, 2011; and Tom Barkley, "China Loses Trade Appeal Over Its Curbs on Exports," *The Wall Street Journal,* January, 31, 2012.

51. "Doha Round: U.S. Presses China, India, and Brazil," BBC Mobile, March 1, 2011; and "A Deadline for Doha," *The Economist,* January 27, 2011.

52. Riva Froymovich, "EU: Euro-Zone GDP Slows in H2 2010 as Expected," *The Wall Street Journal,* March 1, 2011; and http://europa.eu./, accessed May 2012.

53. Reinhardt Krause, "Euro Debt Too High; 'Haircuts' Inevitable?" *Investor's Business Daily,* March 10, 2011.

54. Ian Talley, Charles Forelle, and Riva Froymovich, "IMF: EU Crisis Pact Important Step, Awaiting More Progress," *The Wall Street Journal,* March 17, 2011.

55. Matthew Dalton, "EU Agrees on Economic Overhaul," *The Wall Street Journal,* March 15, 2011.

56. "Unasur Fearful of Overlapping with the Andean Pack and Mercosur," *Merco Press,* June 16, 2010.

57. www.aseansec.org, accessed May 2012.

58. www.ustr.gov/trade-agreements, accessed May 2012.

59. Bill Ong Hing, "Mexico's Economy Is the Problem That Anti-Immigration Laws Won't Solve," *The Huffington Post,* February 28, 2011.

60. Sewell Chan, "U.S. Plans for Trade Are Stalled," *The New York Times,* February 28, 2011.

61. Tom Barkley, "U.S. Seeks Major Progress on Trans Pacific Trade Deal by November," *The Wall Street Journal,* March 14, 2011.

62. "The 9 Billion-People Question," *The Economist,* February 26, 2011; and "World Population Clock," U.S. Census Bureau, www.census.gov/ipc/www/popclockworld.html, accessed May 2012.

63. Owen Fletcher, "Foreign Direct Investment in China Rises 17%," *The Wall Street Journal,* January 19, 2011.

64. Chinmei Sung and Jay Wang, "Foreign Investment in China Climbs for 13th Straight Month to $7.6 Billion," *Bloomberg,* September 14, 2010; and "Now No. 2, Could China Become No. 1?" *Time,* February 28, 2011.

65. www.mckinsey.com/mgi, accessed May 2012.

66. "Daniel Tencer, "Number of Cars Worldwide Surpasses 1 Billion," *The Huffington Post Canada,* October 24, 2011.

67. Peter Coy, "If Demography Is Destiny, Then India Has the Edge," *Bloomberg Businessweek,* January 23, 2011.

68. Tim Gosling, "Multinationals Sensing Business Opportunities in Russia," *Business New Europe,* February 25, 2011.

69. Rachel Morarjee, "Foreign Investment in Russian Car Market Moves Up a Gear," *Business New Europe,* March 18, 2011; and Tim Higgins and Tommaso Ebhardt, "Deal Means Ford Will Build Cars in Russia," *Bloomberg News,* February 19, 2011.

70. Lyubov Pronina, "Dreams of an iPad Economy for Russia," *Bloomberg Businessweek,* February 13, 2011; and Tom Barkley, "China Loses Trade Appeal Over Its Curbs on Exports," *The Wall Street Journal,* January, 31, 2012.

CHAPTER 4

1. Gary Weiss, "Enron 10 Years After: From Bad to Worse," *MSN Money,* April 18, 2012.

2. Zachary Karabell, "The Big Bad Bankers, and Their Bonuses, Are Back," *Time,* January 22, 2011.

3. Joy Fitzgerald, "Seek Financial Disclosure," *The Boston Herald,* January 12, 2011; and Timothy R. Homan, "Economics Professors Will Consider Code of Ethics," *Bloomberg Businessweek,* January 1, 2011.

4. "Versions of the Golden Rule in 21 World Religions," Religious Tolerance, www.religioustolerance.org, accessed March 14, 2011.

5. P. M. Pursey, A. R. Heugens, Muel Kaptein, and J. (Hans) van Oosterhout, "Contracts to Communities: A Processual Model of Organizational Virtue," *Journal of Management Studies,* January 2008; Martha Perego, "Focus on the Fundamentals," *Public Management,* January 1, 2009; and Holly Rosenkrantz, "Workers Report Pressure on Ethics Rules as Retaliation Rises," *Bloomberg Businessweek*, January 9, 2012.

6. U.S. Census Bureau.

7. "David Nagel, "Cognite 3.5 Moves to Android, Integrates Plagiarism Detection," *THE Journal,* February 15, 2011; Turnitin, www.turnitin.com, accessed May 2012; Kellie B. Gormly, "Internet Creates a Rise in Cut-and-Paste Plagiarism," *Pittsburgh Tribune-Review,* January 23, 2012; and "Turnitin Joins Forces with ProQuest to Add Dissertations to Turnitin," *Manufacturing Close-Up,* March 13, 2012.

8. Kathy Gurchiek, "Ethics, Schmethics, U.S. Teens Say," *HR News,* February 1, 2008; and Cheating Culture, www.cheatingculture.com/academic-dishonesty, accessed May 2012.

9. Kenneth Blanchard and Norman Vincent Peale, *The Power of Ethical Management* (New York: William Morrow, 1996).

10. Richard F. Stolz, "Taking the Lead," *Human Resource Executive,* May 16, 2007; Jeff Waller, "Creating Ethical Business Standards: Adopt a Modern Ethics Policy and Make It Public," *Alaska Business Monthly,* April 1, 2010; and John Allen, "Nature vs. Nurture: Company Culture Can Be Defined and Refined." *Houston Business Journal,* February 25, 2011.

11. Peter R. Kensicki, "Code-Dependent: Creating a Company-wide Ethics Policy Will Spur Professionalism and Success," *Best's Review,* January 1, 2010; and Jessica D. Squazzo, "Ethical Challenges and Responsibilities of Leaders," *Healthcare Executive,* January 1, 2012.

12. Michael Quint, "Cuomo Orders Ethics Training for Staff, Top Officials," *Bloomberg Businessweek,* January 3, 2011; Steve Karnowski, "New Food Safety Law Protects Whistleblowers," *Bloomberg Businessweek,* February 11, 2011; Ryan J. Donmoyer, "IRS Alters Rules to Pay Informants in More Cases," *Bloomberg Businessweek,* January 14, 2011; David S. Hilzenrath, "IRS Reverses Position, Which Could Benefit Whistleblowers," *The Washington Post,* January 15, 2011; Ben Sutherly, "Incentive Missing to Report Fraud," *Dayton Daily News,* February 6, 2011; Joe Davidson, "A Victory for Chambers Might Not Be a Victory for Whistleblowers," *The Washington Post,* January 13, 2011; "In Fired Park Police Chief's Saga, a Happy Ending and a Warning," *The Washington Post,* January 20, 2011; David S. Hilzenrath, "SEC Names Head of New Whistleblower Office," *The Washington Post,* February 19, 2011; Joanne S. Barry, "Dodd-Frank Sleeper Leaves Confusion in Its Wake," *The CPA Journal,* January 1, 2011; "Guidelines Stress Whistleblower Protection," *Healthcare Risk Management,* January 1, 2011; Paul Sweeney, "Will New Regulations Deter Corporate Fraud?" *Financial Executive,* January 1, 2011; Robert Schmidt, "U.S. Regulators Struggle to Keep Up with Dodd-Frank," *Bloomberg Businessweek,* February 10, 2011; and Kay Bell, "Enron Whistleblower Gets $1 Million from the IRS," MSN, www.msn.com, March 18, 2011.

13. Miranda S. Spivack, "Corruption Probe of Johnsons Renews Ethics Reform Debate in Prince George's," *The Washington Post,* February 16, 2011.

14. "German Ex-Judge Becomes Daimler Integrity Chief," *Forbes,* February 15, 2011.

15. James R. Rubin, "How to Build Support for a Corporate Conscience," *The Washington Post,* January 22, 2012.

16. Kent Byus, Donald Deis, and Bo Ouyang, "Doing Well by Doing Good: Corporate Social Responsibility and Profitability," *SAM Advanced Management Journal,* January 1, 2010; "Juniper Networks Earns Ethics Inside Certification from the Ethisphere Institute," *Politics & Government Week,* February 17, 2011; and "Corporate Social Responsibility Can Enhance Customer Value," *States News Service,* February 15, 2011.

17. Gates Foundation, www.gatesfoundation.org, accessed May 2012.

18. TNT, www.tnt.com, accessed May 2012.

19. Patagonia, www.patagonia.com, accessed May 2012.

20. Xerox, www.xerox.com, accessed March 17, 2011; and Suzanne Stevens, "Xerox Lends Exec to Hacienda CDC," *Portland Business Journal,* March 4, 2011.

21. Joshua Kucera, "Bottom Line on Corporate Giving," *U.S. News & World Report,* November 2010; and Committee Encouraging Corporate Philanthropy, www.corporatephilanthropy.org, accessed February 2012.

22. Samantha Marshall, "Incorporating the Cause; Gen Y Entrepreneurs Pair Profits with Philanthropy," *Crain's New York Business,* January 14, 2008; and "Generation Y: A Snapshot of People in Their Twenties," *The Chronicle of Philanthropy,* May 3, 2010.

23. "Juniper Networks Earns Ethics Inside Certification from the Ethisphere Institute."

24. "Executives Say Crowdsourcing Is Valuable to Corporate Social Responsibility Efforts," *Telecommunications Weekly,* February 23, 2011.

25. "Donna Gehrke-White, "Weston Company Invests in Bonds for the Good," *Sun Sentinel,* May 18, 2012.

26. Elliot Smith, "SAC's Trading Mimics Insider Dealings Identified by Prosecutors," *Bloomberg Businessweek,* February 11, 2011; Caroline Winter, David Glovin, and Jennifer Daniel, "A Guide to the Galleon Case," *Bloomberg Businessweek,* March 10, 2011; Paul M. Barrett, Katherine Burton, and Saijel Kishan, "The Rajaratnam Conviction," *Bloomberg Businessweek,* May 11, 2011; and Bob Van Voris and Patricia Hurtado, "Whitman Capital Founder Indicted on Insider-Trading Charges," Bloomberg Businessweek, February 12, 2012.

27. David Saxby, "What Makes a Satisfied Employee?" *Rural Telecommunications,* January 1, 2008; and Dennis Huspeni, "Human Resource Personnel Balance Process, Compassion," *Denver Business Journal,* March 19, 2010.

28. Bill Catlette and Richard Hadden, *Contented Cows Still Give Better Milk* (Contented Cow Partners, 2012); Bill Catlette and Richard Hadden, *Contented Cows Moove Faster* (R. Brent & Company, 2007); and Contented Cow Partners, www.contentedcows.com, accessed May 2012.

29. Costco, www.costco, accessed May 2012.

30. Association of Certified Fraud Examiners, www.acfe.com, accessed May 2012; and Douglas M. Boyle, Brian W. Carpenter, and Dana R. Hermanson, "CEOs, CFOs, and Accounting Fraud," *The CPA Journal,* January 1, 2012.

31. American Solar Energy Society, www.ases.org, accessed May 2012.

32. Tim Grant, "'Socially Responsible' Investing Joins Your Money with Your Ideals," *Pittsburgh Post-Gazette,* March 16, 2010; Social Funds, www.socialfunds.com, accessed May 2012; and Social Investment Forum, www.socialinvest.org, accessed May 2012.

33. www.ethisphere.com, accessed May 2012.

34. Rainforest Action Network, www.ran.org, accessed May 2012.

35. Price Waterhouse Coopers' 2011 Global CEO Survey, www.pwc.com, accessed May 2012; and Chris Gay, "Are Bank Stocks 'Responsible'?" *The Wall Street Journal,* February 6, 2012.

36. Ibid.

37. Eugenia Levenson, "Citizen Nike," *Fortune,* November 17, 2008.

38. Ibid; and Charles Duhigg and Nick Wingfield, "Apple Opens Factory Doors to Inspection of Conditions," *International Herald Tribune,* February 15, 2012.

39. Andrew Bast, "Going After Graft," *Newsweek,* November 1, 2010; Ben Stier, "Too Big to Be Nailed," *Fortune,* April 19, 2010; and Daniel Gilbert, "Ego, Alcohol to Blame, Says KBR's Ex-Chief," *The Wall Street Journal,* February 24, 2012.

40. Organization of American States, www.oas.org, accessed May 2012.

CHAPTER 5

1. www.sba.gov, accessed May 2012; and www.score.org, accessed May 2012.

2. Deborah McSweeney, "How to Decide Which Business Structure Fits Your Business Idea Best," *Business Insider,* March 25, 2011; and Sara Schafer, "Partner Up for Success: Best Business Structures for Young Producers," *Top Producer,* January 1, 2012.

3. www.taxes.about.com, accessed May 2012; and www.myownbusiness.org, accessed May 2012.

4. Richard Gibson, "Help from the Inside," *The Wall Street Journal,* February 14, 2011.

5. Donald Marron, "Six Things to Remember about Taxes and Small Business," *Christian Science Monitor,* March 3, 2011.

6. Dimitra DeFotis, "Master Limited Partnerships: A Good Place to Get 6% Payouts," *Barron's,* March 7, 2011; and Gail Liberman, "Master Limited Partnerships May Be Fruitful but Risky," *Palm Beach Daily News,* March 4, 2012.

7. www.sunoco.com, accessed May 2012.
8. Colleen Dibaise, Sarah E. Needleman, and Emily Maltby, "Married to the Job (And Each Other)," *The Wall Street Journal,* February 14, 2011.
9. Robert Weisman, "Biotechs Strike Partnerships to Spread Their Costs and Risks," *The Boston Globe,* January 15, 2012.
10. Jonnelle Marte, "A New Haven in Corporate Bonds," *Smart Money Magazine,* March 4, 2011.
11. "WomenCorporateDirectors Launches Global Nominating Commission to Increase Diversity in Directory Slates," *The Wall Street Journal,* May 2, 2012.
12. Derek Thompson, "What's Mitt Romney's Real Tax Rate: 15 Percent or 50 Percent?" *National Journal,* January 31, 2012; and Uwe E. Reinhardt, "Capital Gains vs. Ordinary Income," *The New York Times,* March 16, 2012.
13. www.incorporate101.com, accessed May 2012.
14. Michael J. De La Merced and Jeffrey Cane, "Confident Deal Makers Pulled Out Checkbooks in 2010," *The New York Times,* January 3, 2011; and Melanie Grayce West, "M&A: Not Just for the Corporate Set," *The Wall Street Journal,* February 28, 2012.
15. Patrick Seitz, "Shifting from Public to Private," *Investor's Business Daily,* March 14, 2011.
16. Andrea Murphy, "From LBO to IPO," *Forbes Magazine,* February 9, 2011.
17. www.sabmiller.com, accessed May 2012.
18. U.S. Census Bureau, www.census.gov, accessed May 2012.
19. www.franchise.org, accessed May 2012.
20. Ned Smith, "Franchises Play Vital Role in U.S. Economy," *Business News Daily,* September 15, 2010; and Rachel Reynolds, "Attorneys Offer Tips on Successfully Starting a Franchise, an Increasingly Popular Business Plan in Recent Years," *Business First,* March 16, 2012.
21. Julie Jargon, "Subway Runs Past McDonald's Chain," *The Wall Street Journal,* March 8, 2011.
22. Jason Daily, "A Senior Moment," *Entrepreneur,* January 25, 2011.
23. www.aboutmcdonald's.com, accessed May 2012.
24. www.franchisetimes.com, accessed May 2012.
25. Rosemary Black, "KFC Is Hot on Grilled Chicken but Customers Aren't Buying It," *The New York Daily News,* August 17, 2010; and Burt Helm, "At KFC, a Battle among the Chicken-Hearted," *Bloomberg Businessweek,* August 29, 2010.
26. Richard Gibson, "Franchisee v. Franchisor," *The Wall Street Journal,* February 4, 2011.
27. www.smallbiztrends.com, accessed May 2012.
28. www.franchise.org, accessed May 2012.
29. Nancy Weingartner, "Junior Executives," *Franchise Times,* March 28, 2011.
30. Issie Lapowsky, "How to Start a Home-Based Franchise," *Inc.,* May 13, 2010.
31. Mark Henricks, "Sponsored Section: Bricks or Clicks?" *Inc.,* February 1, 2010.
32. Ibid.
33. Jason Ankeny, "Social Climbers," *Entrepreneur,* January 2011.
34. www.franchisedirect.com, accessed May 2012; www.franchise.org, accessed May 2012; and www.mcdonalds.com, accessed May 2012.
35. Kavita Kumar, "Build-A-Bear Stirs to New Life after the Long, Cold Recession," *St. Louis Post-Dispatch,* March 20, 2011.
36. Eric Markowitz, "A Fresh Take on a Franchise Start-Up," *Inc.,* March 16, 2011.
37. www.franchisedirect.com, accessed May 2012; and www.hrblock.com, accessed May 2012.
38. www.usda.gov, accessed May, 2012.
39. Mark Day, "Can Worker-Owned Cooperatives Offer a Solution to Our Economic Woes?" *La Prensa San Diego,* February 11, 2011; and K. Charles Ling, "The Nature of Cooperatives: Roles in Economizing Transaction Cost Is a New Dimension for Understanding Value of Co-Ops," *Rural Cooperatives,* January 1, 2012.

CHAPTER 6

1. Philipp Harper, "History's 10 Greatest Entrepreneurs," www.msnbc.com, accessed May 2012; and Andrew Beattie, "The 10 Greatest Entrepreneurs," www.investopedia.com, accessed May 2012.
2. Stefan Theil, "Golden Age," *Newsweek,* September 6, 2010; and Rebecca U. Cho, "The Time for Entrepreneurship Is Now," *Inland Valley Daily Bulletin,* February 20, 2011.
3. "The Forbes 400 Richest People in America," www.Forbes.com, accessed March 2012; and Edwin Durgy, "Forbes Billionaires Hall Of Fame," *Forbes,* March 26, 2012.
4. www.willnroses.com, accessed May 2012.
5. Jennifer, Wilson, "Four Myths of Entrepreneurship," *PT in Motion,* February 1, 2011.
6. Paul Davis, "Requirements for Business Success," *National Driller,* January 1, 2011; Erik Calonius, "How to Think Like Steve Jobs," *Fortune,* March 15, 2011; and Jay Goltz, "Six Attributes of Successful Entrepreneurs," *The New York Times,* February 23, 2012.
7. www.rushcommunications.com, accessed May 2012.
8. www.anitaroddick.com, accessed May 2012.
9. Robert Celaschi, "Startup Savvy: A Little Planning Can See the Smallest Businesses through the Rough Times," *Boston Business Journal,* July 2, 2010; and Jennifer Wang, "Be Disruptive," *Entrepreneur,* January 2011.
10. Long Cheng, Zhong-Ming Wang, and Wei Zhang, "The Effects of Conflict on Team Decision Making," *Social Behavior and Personality,* March 1, 2011.
11. "Thinking Small," *The Kiplinger Letter,* July 20, 2010.
12. Starting a Profitable Home Business Made Easy by Internet Marketing Consult Michael Bashi's New Training Website," *San Francisco Chronicle,* May 19, 2012.
13. Lesley Spencer Pyle, "Working from Home Doesn't Have to Be a Stigma," *Entrepreneur,* March 5, 2010; Bianca Male, "Working from Home Is Hard Work," *Entrepreneur,* February 26, 2010; and Jennifer Wang, "9 Pitfalls of Working from Home," www.entrepreneur.com, accessed May 2012.
14. Erick Schonfeld, "Forrester Forecast: Online Sales Will Grow to $250 Billion by 2014," www.techcrunch.com, accessed May 2012.
15. Kyle Swenson, "Sales for Dummies," *All Business,* www.allbusiness.com, accessed May 2012; and www.throwthings.com, accessed May 2012.
16. Gwen Moran, "The Sins of Website Design," *Entrepreneur,* January 2011.
17. Allison Proffitt, "Driving Innovation from Within," *Bio-IT World,* May 17, 2012.
18. www.3m.com, accessed May 2012.
19. www.lockheedmartin.com, accessed May 2012.
20. James R. Edwards, Jr., "Securing the Blessings of Liberty," *Center for Immigration Studies,* March 2011.
21. Andrew Hanson and Shawn Rohlin, "The Effect of Location-Based Tax Incentives on Establishment Location and Employment across Industry Sectors," *Public Finance Review,* March 2011.
22. National Business Incubator Association, www.nbia.org, accessed May 2012.

23. Barbara Haislip, "Laid Off and Launching," *The Wall Street Journal,* February 14, 2011.
24. www.whitehouse.gov/issues/startup-america.
25. "White House Names Network for Teaching Entrepreneurship to Startup America Partnership," *U.S. Newswire,* January 31, 2011; and Jim Kuhnhenn, "Startups Get Lift from White House," *The Seattle Times,* February 1, 2011.
26. "Small Business Administration, www.sba.gov, accessed May 2012; U.S. Census Bureau, www.census.gov, accessed May 2012; Vivien Lou Chen and Timothy R. Homan, "Small Business Is Hiring, but Very Carefully," *Bloomberg Businessweek,* January 6, 2011; and "Uncorking Enterprise," *The Economist,* February 26, 2011.
27. National Business Incubator Association, www.nbia.org, accessed March 2012; and Jim Cipriani Jr. and Alan Weinstein, "Do You Have What It Takes to Run Your Own Biz?" *Business First,* March 2, 2012.
28. Scott Shane, "The Silver Lining to the Drop in Startups," *Bloomberg Businessweek,* May 8, 2012.
29. Deniz Ucbasaran, Paul Westhead, and Mike Wright, "Why Serial Entrepreneurs Don't Learn from Failure," *Harvard Business Review,* April 2011.
30. Emmett Dulaney, "Don't Underestimate Experience When Starting a Business," *The Herald Bulletin,* March 28, 2011.
31. "How to Buy a Business," *Entrepreneur,* www.entrpreneur.com, accessed May 2012.
32. Ivy Hughes, "A Simple Plan," *Entrepreneur,* August 2010; and James D. Rosenblatt, "Now Is the Time for Small Businesses to Plan Ahead," *San Antonio Business Journal,* January 27, 2012.
33. "How to Raise Money for Your Business," *Entrepreneur,* www.entrepreneur.com, accessed May 2012.
34. Ibid.
35. "Milwaukee Bank to Leverage Grant to Grow Business Lending," *Northwestern Financial Review,* March 1, 2012.
36. Brock Blake, "The Right Financing: How to Choose between Investor Capital and a Business Loan," *Utah Business,* January 1, 2012; and Carol Tice, "Angels, Equity and a Shark of One's Own," *Entrepreneur,* www.entrepreneur.com, May 18, 2012.
37. Jeff Hughes, "Lending Club's Challenge: Keeping Up with Rising Demand" *San Francisco Business Times,* May 11, 2012.
38. Pui-Wing Tam, "Casing Out Start-Ups Gets More Complicated," *The Wall Street Journal,* February 16, 2011.
39. Dan Primack, "Venture Capital Gets Disrupted (in a Good Way)," *Fortune,* March 7, 2011.
40. Marshall Eckblad, "The SBA Has a Deal for You," *The Wall Street Journal,* June 21, 2010; and U.S. Small Business Administration, www.sba.gov, accessed May 2012.
41. April H. Lee, "Loan Program Helps Some Small U.S. Businesses Survive," *The Wall Street Journal,* April 11, 2011.
42. Small Business Investor Association, www.nasbic.org, accessed March 2012; and Small Business Administration, www.sba.gov, accessed March 2012.
43. Karen E. Klein, "The SBA's New Small Business Loan Program," *Bloomberg Businessweek,* February 17, 2011; and Kent Hoover, "House Panel Proposes $100M Cut to SBA Budget," *The Business Journal,* March 21, 2011.
44. David Beisel, "How to Find the Perfect Startup Job," *Fortune,* February 7, 2011.
45. Jonathan Blum, "The Financial Times, They Are A'Changing," *Entrepreneur,* February 2011.
46. Benjamin K. Riley, "Three Legal Lessons for Startups," *Fortune,* February 17, 2011.
47. www.score.org, accessed May 2012; and Small Business Administration, www.sba.gov, accessed May 2012.
48. "World Population Clock," U.S. Census Bureau, www.census.gov/ipc/www/popclockworld.html, accessed May 2012; and WorldAtlas.com, accessed May 2012.
49. Courtney Rubin, "Obama Encourages Small Firms to Go Global," *Inc.,* March 15, 2010; Martha White, "Thinking Small," *Slate,* December 6, 2010; and "Atlanta Small Businesses Gain Competitive Edge with Invest Atlanta Partnership with Ex-Im Bank," *The Wall Street Journal,* May 16, 2012.

CHAPTER 7

1. Anita Wooley and Thomas Malone, "What Makes a Team Smarter? More Women," *Harvard Business Review,* June 2011.
2. Gary Hamel, "First, Let's Fire All the Managers," *Harvard Business Review,* March 2012.
3. Liz Wiseman, "Intelligence Multipliers," *Leader to Leader,* Winter 2011.
4. Leigh Buchanan, "Learning from the Best," *Inc.,* June 2010.
5. Rich Karlgaard, "The 4% Solution: America Needs Growth," *Forbes,* May 7, 2012.
6. Joan S. Lublin and Kelly Eggers, "More Women Are Primed to Land CEO Roles," *The Wall Street Journal,* April 30, 2012.
7. Daniel C. Esty and Steve Charnovitz, "Green Rules to Drive Innovation," *Harvard Business Review,* March 2012.
8. Mac Margolis, "Executives Wanted," *Newsweek,* June 14, 2010.
9. Ken Fisher, "Portfolio Juice from Hero CEOs," *Forbes,* May 9, 2011.
10. Johanna Neuman, "The Year of the (Business) Woman," *U.S. News and World Report,* Summer 2010.
11. "It Takes More Than Lip Service to Improve Your Company's Customer Service," an ad for BMO Harris Bank, *Forbes,* May 7, 2012.
12. John Mackey, "What Is It That Only I Can Do?" *Harvard Business Review,* January–February 2011.
13. Monica Langley and Sharon Terlep, "'I'm Not a Car Guy': On the Road with the New Man at GM's Wheel," *The Wall Street Journal,* January 8–9, 2011.
14. Robert H. Schaffer, "Mistakes Leaders Keep Making," *Harvard Business Review,* September 2010.
15. A. G. Lafley, "I Think of My Failures as a Gift," *Harvard Business Review,* April 2011.
16. Mark Whitehouse, "Elusive Economic Indicator: Quality of Life Gauge," *The Wall Street Journal,* January 10, 2011.
17. Jason Dean and Aaron Back, "China Growth Shows Contrast with U.S.," *The Wall Street Journal,* January 21, 2011.
18. Elie Ofek and Luc Wathieu, "Trends That Could Shake Up Your Business," *Harvard Business Review,* July–August 2010.
19. Stephen Bungay, "How to Make the Most of Your Company's Strategy," *Harvard Business Review,* January–February 2011.
20. Carl Icahn, "Why Blockbuster Failed," *Harvard Business Review,* April, 2011.
21. "Lessons from a Killer Quake," *Newsweek,* March 21, 2011.
22. William Pesek, "The Cataclysm This Time," *Bloomberg Businessweek,* March 21–March 27, 2011.
23. Jennifer Wang, "Business Models Illustrated," *Entrepreneur,* April 2010.
24. Peter S. Delisi, Dennis Moberg, and Ronald Danielson, "Why CIOs Are Last among Equals," *The Wall Street Journal,* May 24, 2010.
25. Lynda Gratton, "The End of the Middle Manager," *Harvard Business Review,* January–February 2011.

26. David Gann, Ammon Salter, Mark Dodgson, and Nelson Phillips, "Inside the World of the Project Baron," *MIT Sloan Management Review,* Spring 2012.
27. Boris Groysberg, L. Kevin Kelly, and Bryan MacDonald, "The New Path to the C-Suite," *Harvard Business Review,* March 2011.
28. Lee Smith, "A Leadership Playbook," *Fortune,* March 21, 2011.
29. Rich Karlgaard, "Ten Tips: Great Restructuring Winners," *Forbes,* February 28, 2011.
30. Christopher Hann, "The Masters," *Entrepreneur,* March 2012.
31. Martin Schoeller, "Can Ellen Kullman Make Dupont Great Again?" *Fortune,* May 3, 2010.
32. Geoffrey A. Fowler, "Billionaire Families Join Pledge on Giving," *The Wall Street Journal,* April 20, 2012.
33. Lawrence C. Strauss, "A Prescription for Success," *Barron's,* April 9, 2012.
34. Amy C. Casper, "The Zen Zone," *Entrepreneur,* March 2012.
35. Tim O'Shaughnessy, "The Way 2 Work," *Inc.,* March 2012.
36. Beth Kowitt, "Why McDonald's Wins in Any Economy," *Fortune,* September 5, 2011.
37. "HP Executive Team," HP.com, accessed May 2012.
38. Fred Hassan, "The Frontline Advantage," *Harvard Business Review,* May 2011.
39. Ronald Riggio, "Not Enough Indians," *Inc.,* February 2012.

CHAPTER 8

1. Howard Schultz, "How Starbucks Got Its Mojo Back," *Newsweek,* March 21, 2011.
2. Adi Ignatius, "We Had to Own the Mistakes," *Harvard Business Review,* July–August 2010.
3. Howard Schultz, "When Latte Lost Its Luster," *The Wall Street Journal,* March 29, 2011.
4. Schultz, "How Starbucks Got Its Mojo Back."
5. Anthony Welcher, "Tweeting to Victory," *The Washington Times,* May 14, 2012.
6. Jason L. Riley, "Was the $5 Billion Worth It?" *The Wall Street Journal,* July 23-24, 2011.
7. Alan Abelson, "Nuclear Nightmare," *Barron's,* March 21, 2011.
8. Daniel C. Esty and Steve Charnovitz, "Green Rules to Drive Innovation," *Harvard Business Review,* March 2012.
9. Virginia Postrel, "Love and Money," *Entrepreneur,* February 2011.
10. Dan Balz, "Obama's Team Moving Ahead Quickly to Prepare for 2012," *The Washington Post,* March 6, 2011.
11. Mark Sherman, "Walmart Faces Class-Action Lawsuit," *The Washington Times,* March 28, 2011.
12. "Love and Money," *Entrepreneur,* February 2011.
13. Tim Devaney, "Lovin' It? Brands' Facebook Face-Lift," *The Washington Times,* February 21, 2012.
14. Gary L. Neilson and Julie Wulf, "How Many Direct Reports?" *Harvard Business Review,* April 2012.
15. Ibid.
16. Roger L. Martin, "How Hierarchy Can Hurt Strategy Execution," *Harvard Business Review,* July–August 2010.
17. Yun-Hee Kim, "New iPad Is Two-Edged Sword for Suppliers," *The Wall Street Journal,* March 4, 2011.
18. "How to Build Business Alliances," *Inc.,* June 2010.
19. Margaret Schweer, Dimitris Assimakopolous, Rob Cross, and Robert J. Thomas, "Building a Well-Networked Organization," *MIT Sloan Management Review,* Winter 2012.
20. Jessica McKimmie, "Virtual Reality," *Inc.,* June 2010.
21. David Ryan, "Help for Unemployment: Insourcing," *The Washington Times,* April 26, 2012.

22. Paul Leinwand and Cesare Mainardi, "The Coherence Premium," *Harvard Business Review,* June 2010.
23. Gerry Johnson, George S. Yip, and Manuel Hensmans, "Achieving Successful Strategic Transformation," *MIT Sloan Management Review,* Spring 2012.
24. Rich Karlgaard, "Ten Tips: Great Restructuring Winners," *Forbes,* February 28, 2011.
25. Michael S. Hopkins, "Putting the Science in Management Science," *MIT Sloan Management Review,* Summer 2010.
26. Pamela S. Shockley-Zalabak and Sherwyn P. Morreale, "Building High-Trust Organizations," *Leader to Leader,* Spring 2011.
27. Alex (Sandy) Pentland, "The New Science of Building Great Teams," *Harvard Business Review,* April 2012.
28. Eoin Whelan, Salvatore Parise, Jasper de Valk, and Rick Aalbers, "Creating Employee Networks That Deliver Open Innovation," *MIT Sloan Management Review,* Fall 2011.

CHAPTER 9

1. Michael S. Rosenwald, "Manufacturing Falls to 26-Year Low," *The Washington Post,* November 4, 2008.
2. Conor Dougherty, "Unemployment Rises in Every State," *The Wall Street Journal,* January 28, 2009.
3. Carmen M. Reinhart and Kenneth S. Rogoff, "What Other Financial Crises Tell Us," *The Wall Street Journal,* February 3, 2009.
4. Ben Casselman, "American Manufacturers Pick Up the Pace," *The Wall Street Journal,* April 3, 2012.
5. John Bussey, "U.S. Manufacturing, Defying Naysayers," *The Wall Street Journal,* April 20, 2012.
6. Thomas G. Donlan, "Manufacturing Jobs," *Barron's,* March 28, 2011.
7. Ibid.
8. Bill Saporito, "Made (Again) in the U.S.A.," *Time,* October 10, 2011.
9. Thomas A. Kochan, "A Jobs Compact for America's Future," *Harvard Business Review,* March 2012.
10. Ylan Q. Mui, "Manufacturing Continues Growth Streak, Bolstering Recovery," *The Washington Post,* April 3, 2012.
11. Justin Lahart, "Building a Case for Producers' Relevance," *The Wall Street Journal,* January 18, 2012.
12. Keith Naughton, "The Happiest Man in Detroit," *Bloomberg Businessweek,* February 7–February 13, 2011.
13. Daniel C. Esty and Steve Charnovitz, "Green Rules to Drive Innovation," *Harvard Business Review,* March 2012.
14. J. Bradford Jensen, "Think Services, Not Manufacturing," *The Washington Post,* February 12, 2012.
15. Greg Bernas, "We're Listening and We Hear the Future," *Forbes,* March 28, 2011.
16. Nancy Trejos, "The Sewing Kit Checks Out, the Future Checks In," *The Washington Post,* March 20, 2011.
17. Yun Mi Antorini, Albert M. Muñiz, Jr., and Tormod Askildsen," Collaborating with Customer Communities," *MIT Sloan Management Review,* Spring 2012.
18. Brian Bremner, "Rise of the Machines (Again)," *Bloomberg Businessweek,* March 7–March 13, 2011.
19. Tom Mulier, "Nestlé's Recipe for Juggling Volatile Commodity Costs," *Bloomberg Businessweek,* March 21–March 27, 2011.
20. Lisa Brown, "Going Lean, but Not Mean," *St. Louis Post-Dispatch,* August 15, 2010.
21. Joan Muller, "The Bespoke Auto," *Forbes,* September 27, 2010.
22. Marilyn Much, "The Changing Face(book) of Internet Commerce," *Investor's Business Daily,* February 2, 2011.

23. John Jannarone, "Retailers Struggle in Amazon Jungle," *The Wall Street Journal,* February 22, 2011.
24. "Time to Head Home for Some Manufacturers," an editorial in *Bloomberg Businessweek,* February 6–February 12, 2012.
25. Sudeep Reddy and Brian Blackstone, "Global Manufacturing Picks Up Pace," *The Wall Street Journal,* March 2, 2011.
26. Jim Efstathiou, Jr., and Kim Chapman, "The Great Shale Gas Rush," *Bloomberg Businessweek,* March 7–March 13, 2011.
27. David Simchi-Levi, James Paul Peruvankal, Narenda Mulani, Bill Read, and John Ferreira, "Is It Time to Rethink Your Manufacturing Strategy?" *MIT Sloan Management Review,* Winter 2012.
28. Joe Gose, "Are Office Buildings Becoming Obsolete?" *Investor's Business Daily,* January 21, 2011.
29. James R. Hagerty, "Assembled Elsewhere," *The Wall Street Journal,* January 25, 2011.
30. Michael Schuman, "How Germany Became the China of Europe," *Time,* March 7, 2011.

CHAPTER 10

1. Rick Brimeyer, "Motivating Employees So That They Give a Rip," *Telegraph-Herald* (Dubuque), March 15, 2010; and F. John Reh, "New Employee Training—Is It Worth the Investment?" About.com *Management,* www.about.com, accessed May 2012.
2. Vineet Nayar, "Employee Happiness: Zappos vs. HCL" *Bloomberg Businessweek,* January 4, 2011; and Victor Lipman, "Think Small. Small Things Make a Big Difference in Employee Engagement," *Forbes,* May 18, 2012.
3. Grace M. Endres, "The Human Resource Craze," *Organization Development Journal,* April 1, 2008; "MetLife Study: Employee Loyalty Not Recession-Proof," *BusinessWire,* March 28, 2011; Jim Harter, Nikki Blacksmith, "Engaged Workers Immune to Stress from Long Commutes; For Disengaged Workers, Long Commutes Linked to Higher Stress Levels," *Gallup Poll News Service,* February 7, 2012; and Steve Schumacher, "Engage and Encourage High-Potential Employees—Or Risk Losing Them," *Engineering and Mining Journal,* February 1, 2012.
4. Susan Adams, "In Praise of Praise," *Forbes,* www.forbes.com, accessed May 2012; and Patricia Sellers, "How Dreamworks' CEO Builds a Happy Workforce," *Fortune,* March 15, 2011.
5. Michael Barone, "Message to Unions: Taylorism Died Long Ago," *Washington Examiner,* March 6, 2011.
6. Mike Hofman, "The Idea That Saved My Company," *Inc.,* October 2007; and Joie de Vivre Hotels, www.jdvhotels.com, accessed May 2012.
7. Luke Haywood, "Watch Your Workers Win," *Management Revue,* January 1, 2011; and "Motivation in Their Work Reduces Stress among IT Consultants," *Information Technology Newsweekly,* March 15, 2011; and Laurel Clark, "Effective Learning and Development Programs Are Crucial: Future-Proof Your Workforce with an Effective Learning and Development Strategy," *Strategic Finance,* March 1, 2012.
8. Amanda Shantz and Gary Latham, "The Effect of Primed Goals on Employee Performance," *Human Resource Management,* March/April 2011.
9. Steve Schumacher, "Employee Evaluation," *Rock Products,* May 1, 2010.
10. Rachel Remley, "Retaining Top Talent," *Collector,* February 1, 2011; and Steve Schumacher, "Engage and Encourage High-Potential Employees—Or Risk Losing Them," *Engineering and Mining Journal,* February 1, 2012.
11. Glenn G. Kautt, "Deep Rewards: If You Want to Motivate Your Clients and Staff, You Need to Develop the Framework for Moving Them in the Right Direction," *Financial Planning,* March 1, 2011; and Joseph S. Eastern, "Employee Rewards," *Internal Medicine News,* January 1, 2012.
12. David Nadler and Edward Lawler, "Motivation—a Diagnostic Approach," *Perspectives on Behavior in Organizations* (New York: McGraw-Hill, 1977).
13. Mohamed Hossam el-Din Hassan Khalifa and Quang Truong, "The Effects of Internal and External Equity on Components of Organizational Commitment," *International Journal of Management,* March 1, 2011; and Rick Wartzman, "Yes, You Can Make Performance Reviews Worthwhile," *Bloomberg Businessweek,* April 8, 2011.
14. "Give Employees a Break and Keep Them Loyal," *The Dominion Post* (Morgantown, WV), March 12, 2011; and Dave Zielinski, "Bring Your Own Device: More Employers Are Allowing Employees to Use Their Own Technology in the Workplace," *HRMagazine,* February 1, 2012.
15. Wenzel Matiaske and Cerd Grozinger, "Introduction: Job Satisfaction Revisited," *Management Revue,* January 1, 2011.
16. Cameron Kauffman, "Employee Involvement: A New Blueprint for Success," *Journal of Accountancy,* May 1, 2010; and Victor Lipman, "Think Small. Small Things Make a Big Difference in Employee Engagement," *Forbes,* May 18, 2012.
17. Sherri May, "Employees Disengaged? Try Out These Practices," *American Banker,* April 27, 2010; and Adrienne Fox, "Make A 'Deal': A Well-Conceived and Well-Communicated Employee Value Proposition Can Re-Recruit Your Employees Every Day," *HRMagazine,* January 1, 2012.
18. "Mustang Sales Strong in March with More Than 130% Increase over February," www.mustangdaily.com, accessed May 2012.
19. "Motivation: 4-to-1 Praise Ratio Works Wonders," *Capital,* February 27, 2011.
20. "The Global Star Search," *Fortune,* February 4, 2008; and Brian W. Swider, Wendy R. Boswell, and Ryan D. Zimmerman, "Examining the Job Search–Turnover Relationship," *Journal of Applied Psychology,* March 2011.
21. Dow Chemical Company, www.dow.com, accessed May 2012.
22. Michelle Kerr, "Champions for Change," *Risk & Insurance,* February 1, 2011.
23. Trish Chandler, "Employee Education, Development Prove Valuable to Businesses," *Business First,* January 14, 2011.
24. Lee Barney, "Speaking the Language of Generations X and Y," *Money Management Executive,* February 14, 2011; and Ronald J. Alsop, "Youth and Consequences," *Workforce Management,* February 1, 2011.
25. "Working with Millennials," *The Futurist,* March 1, 2011; and Leonard Klie, "Gen X: Stuck in the Middle," *CRM Magazine,* February 1, 2012.
26. Patricia Quinn, "A Multigenerational Perspective on Employee Communications," *Risk Management,* January 1, 2010; and Ryan Scott, "Millennials + Cause = Employee Retention," *Huffington Post,* May 16, 2012.
27. David Javitch, "Motivating Gen X, Gen Y Workers," *Entrepreneur,* www.entrepreneur.com, accessed July 12, 2010; Lynnee C. Lancaster, "Are You Ready for 76 Million Echo Boomers?" *Bottom Line Secrets,* September 15, 2010; and Ryan Scott, "Millennials + Cause = Employee Retention," *Huffington Post,* May 16, 2012.
28. Megan L. Thomas, "Gen Y: No Jobs, Lots of Loans, Grim Future," www.msnbc.com, July 29, 2010; Mark Scott, with Suzanne Woollery, Chris Prentice, Moira Herbst, and Matt Robinson, "Gen Y's Empty Piggy Bank," *Bloomberg Businessweek,* July 19–July 25, 2010; and Ethan Rouen, "Gen-Y Looks to Developing Economies for Biz Training," money.cnn.com, February 6, 2012, accessed March 2012.

29. Jodi Glickman, "Leading Older Employees," *Bloomberg Businessweek,* April 5, 2011.

30. Rachel Reynolds, "Corporate Champions See Many Advantages in Diverse Work Force," *Business First,* February 2, 2011; and Rick Birdsall, " Are You a Boomer? Understanding Gen X and Gen Y Is a Challenge," *Alaska Business Monthly,* January 1, 2012.

CHAPTER 11

1. Bill Taylor, "Why We (Shouldn't) Hate HR," *Harvard Business Review,* www.hbr.org, accessed June 2010; and "Not Having Enough High-Potential Leaders in Their Organization Is the Most Pressing Human Resource Challenge," *New Hampshire Business Review,* February 24, 2012.

2. Elisabeth Boone, "Human Resources Consulting," *Rough Notes,* February 1, 2011; Edward E. Lawler, III, Jay Jamrog, and John Boudreau, "Shining Light on HR Profession," *HRMagazine,* February 1, 2011; Benjamin Schneider and Karen B. Paul, "In the Company We Trust," *HRMagazine,* January 1, 2011; Leigh Buchanan, "Meet the Millennials," *Inc.,* September 2010; Joe Light, "Help Wanted," *The Wall Street Journal,* February 26, 2011; Robert Powell, "Working in Retirement," *The Wall Street Journal,* March 21, 2011; Corrinne Hess, "Study: Women Hurt Most by Economic Downturn," *The Business Journal* (Milwaukee), April 28, 2011; and Sonya M. Latta, "Save Your Staff, Improve Your Business: Here's How an HR Professional in an Ohio Social Services Agency Dramatically Reduced Turnover," *HRMagazine,* January 1, 2012.

3. Roger Clegg, "At Age 50, Affirmative Action Looks Tired," *The Washington Times,* March 4, 2011.

4. Richard Thompson Ford, "Everyday Discrimination," *Slate,* March 28, 2011; "Wal-Mart Sex Bias Case Hits Possible Court Block," *Boston Herald,* March 29, 2011; and Greg Stohr, "Wal-Mart Faces the Big Box of Class Actions," *Bloomberg Businessweek,* March 28–April 3, 2011.

5. "Myths and Stereotypes about Mental Disabilities Greatest Barrier to Employment," *States News Service,* March 15, 2011.

6. "ADA Violations at Hilton Hotels," *Paraplegia News,* March 1, 2011.

7. "AARP Lauds New Regulations That Will Help Protect Millions of Americans with Disabilities from Discrimination," *States News Service,* March 24, 2011; Pat Murphy, "Employee with 'Episodic' Disability Can Sue, Rules 7th Circuit," *Lawyers USA,* January 4, 2011; and Roger S. Achille, "Unmedicated Employee 'Disabled' under ADA," *HRMagazine,* February 1, 2012.

8. "Who's Disabled? Feds Expand the Definition," *The Wall Street Journal,* March 25, 2011; Stephanie Armour, "Workers with Epilepsy, Diabetes Gain under Obama Disability Rule," *Bloomberg Businessweek,* March 24, 2011; Karen E. Klein, "Employers Gird for Disabilities Act Changes," *Bloomberg Businessweek,* April 27, 2011; and Monica Mendoza, "New Rules on Business Accessibility Go into Effect March 15," *Colorado Springs Business Journal,* March 8, 2012.

9. Susan M. Schaecher, "Nondisabled People Can't Pursue Claims That Testing Screens Out People with Disabilities," *HRMagazine,* January 1, 2011; Todd Shields, "Jewel-Osco Settles $3.2 Million Lawsuit Involving Employees with Disabilities," *Oak Leaves* (Oak Park, IL), January 20, 2011; and "Job Bias Claims Set New Record on Disability Surge," *Capital* (Annapolis), January 11, 2011.

10. James Dowd, "Experts Share Hiring Strategies—Finding, Keeping Best Workers Takes Effort," *The Commercial Appeal* (Memphis), April 6, 2011; and Sougata Mukherjee, "It's Time to Invest in Employees, Again," *Triangle Business Journal,* February 10, 2012.

11. Steven E. F. Brown, "Survey: Social Networks Top Hiring Tool," *San Francisco Business Times,* June 30, 2010; and Susan Adams, "Expert Tips for Using LinkedIn," *Forbes,* www.forbes.com, accessed May 2012.

12. Kronos, www.kronos.com/hiring-software, accessed May 2012; and Lauren Weber, "Your Résumé vs. Oblivion," *The Wall Street Journal,* January 24, 2012.

13. Jennifer Wang, "Unbeatable," *Entrepreneur,* February 2011; and Eric Herrenkohl, "Searching for Hires in All the Wrong places," *Philadelphia Business Journal,* February 10, 2012.

14. Jim Rendon, "10 Things Human Resources Won't Say," *SmartMoney,* April 22, 2010; and Equal Employment Opportunity Commission, http://www.eeoc.gov/policy/docs/factemployment_procedures.html, accessed May 2012.

15. "LexisNexis, www.lexisnexis.com, accessed March 2012; and Diana Samuels, "Facebook Background Checks Raise Worries," *Silicon Valley / San Jose Business Journal,* March 9, 2012.

16. Rachel Farrell, "6 Cardinal Sins of Management," www.MSN.Careerbuilder.com, accessed May 2012.

17. Nancy Miller, "Temps, the New Normal?" *Barron's,* October 18, 2010; and Nancy Lublin, "In Defense of Millennials," *Fast Company,* October 2010.

18. Randstad, www.us.randstad.com, accessed May 2012.

19. Matt Quinn, "Creative Employee Training Ideas," www.Inc.com, accessed May 2012.

20. U.S. Department of Labor, www.doleta.gov, accessed May 2012.

21. Red Cross, www.redcross.org, accessed May 2012.

22. GlobeSmart, www.globesmart.com, accessed May 2012.

23. Kasthuri V. Henry, "Grooming the Next Generation," *Strategic Finance,* January 1, 2011.

24. Diana Middleton, "Want to Know Which Training Works? Take This Course," *The Wall Street Journal,* www.wsj.com, accessed May 2012.

25. Alix Stuart, "Blazing Their Own Trails," *CFO,* September 2010; and Polly Labarre, "What Does Fulfillment at Work Really Look Like?, *Forbes,* May 1, 2012.

26. McDonald's, www.mcdonalds.com, accessed May 2012.

27. Ivy Hughes, "Meet Your Mentor," *Entrepreneur,* September 2010; Gwen Moran, "Meet Your Mentor," *Entrepreneur,* December 2010; and "Need for More Mentors in Accounting and Finance," *Business Credit,* January 1, 2012.

28. Dave Willmer, "8 Ways to Keep Your Best Workers on Board," *Computerworld,* June 21, 2010; and Vicki Neal and Naomi Cossack, "Emerging Market Salaries, HR Staff Size, Commission-Only Pay," *HRMagazine,* February 1, 2012.

29. Motley Fool Staff, "Q-and-A with Nucor CEO Dan DiMicco," *The Motley Fool,* www.fool.com, January 10, 2011.

30. Josh Heck, "Study: Health Insurance Accounts for 8 Percent of Total Employee Compensation," *Wichita Business Journal,* June 9, 2010; and "Employee Compensation Averages $29.39 an Hour," *Charlotte Business Journal,* June 12, 2010.

31. Jessica Flint, "Analyze This," *Bloomberg Businessweek,* February 21–February 27, 2011; and Joe Mullich, "2011 Benefits Trends," *The Wall Street Journal,* April 5, 2011.

32. "100 Best Companies to Work For," *Fortune,* May 2011.

33. Sarah E. Needleman, "Should a Business Offer Paid Maternity Leave?" *The Wall Street Journal,* July 6, 2010; and Paul Spiegelman, "10 Steps to Make Your Employees Smile," *Inc.,* March 21, 2012.

34. B. Checket-Hanks, "Employee Needs Comes First," *Air Conditioning, Heating & Refrigeration News,* January 31, 2011.

35. "Moving Work Forward," *States News Service,* February 1, 2011; and Katherin Reynolds Lewis, "Flexible Jobs = Happy Worker Bees?" *Fortune,* April 20, 2011.

36. Alix Stuart, "The Perils of Flextime," *CFO,* July/August 2010. "Flex Time Doesn't Mean Flexible Discipline," *Joan Lloyd and Associates,* www.joanlloyd.com, accessed May 2012.

37. Rachel Kenshalo, "Evolving Office Technologies: Telecommuting, Conserving Energy and Resources," *Alaska Business Monthly,* February 1, 2010; and Nathaniel Borenstein and Ben Waber, "Forget the Office: Let Employees Work from Home," *Bloomberg Businessweek,* www.bloomberg.com, accessed March 2012.

38. Shane Kite, "No Dress Code Required," *US Banker,* January 1, 2011.

39. Ben Horowitz, "Why Even Your Ultra-Hip Startup Team Needs Job Titles," *Fortune,* March 16, 2011.

CHAPTER 12

1. James Estrin, "Answers about the Nation's Labor Laws," *The New York Times,* April 4, 2011; and James Sullivan, "Lawrence Recalls Labor Struggles," *The Boston Globe,* January 11, 2012.

2. Sam Hananel, "Membership in Labor Unions Continues to Decline,"*The Washington Times,* January 23, 2011; and Lance Murray, "American Airlines Tells Employees It Will Seek to End Labor Contracts," *Orlando Business Journal,* March 23, 2012.

3. Peter Whoriskey and Amy Gardner, "As Unions' Dynamic Shifts, So Does Fight," *The Washington Post,* February 28, 2011.

4. Drake Bennett, "Dispatch from a Divided State," *Bloomberg Businessweek,* March 20, 2011; and Jim Waters, "Include Right-to-Work Arrow in State's Economic Quiver," *Business First,* March 16, 2012.

5. "Wisconsin and Wider," *The Economist,* February 26, 2011; and "Wisconsin Public Employee Unions File Unfair Labor Complaints," *The Business Journal,* March 21, 2012.

6. Mark Mix, "The Real Issue in Labor Battle," *Investor's Business Daily,* March 8, 2011.

7. Nick Keppler, "Business Leaders Bristle at the Honoring of Labor History," *New Haven Advocate,* March 31, 2011.

8. Nadia Sussman, "Triangle Fire: In Search of Sweatshops," *The New York Times,* March 25, 2011.

9. Jon Healey, "How Hard Should It Be to Form a Union?" *Los Angeles Times,* March 30, 2011.

10. Valerie Van Kooten, "The Fire That Changed History," *The Des Moines Register,* March 23, 2011.

11. Joe DeMarco, "Unions Were Responsible for Child Labor Laws, 40-Hour Work Week," www.madison.com, March 22, 2011.

12. James Estrin, "Answers about the Nation's Labor Laws," *The New York Times,* March 24, 2011.

13. Sam Hananel, "Laborer's Move Boosts Hope for Unified Unions," *Associated Press,* August 14, 2010.

14. www.aflcio.org, accessed May 2012.

15. Mark Niquette, "Workers' Rights Battle Goes National at Pivotal Time for Labor," *Bloomberg Businessweek,* February 22, 2011; and Bureau of Labor Statistics, "Union Members Summary," www.bls.gov, January 27, 2012.

16. Nina Easton, "Labor Unions: Flailing in D.C. and Making Enemies on Main Street," *Fortune,* March 21, 2011.

17. Robert Samuelson, "Is Organized Labor Obsolete?" *The Buffalo News,* March 4, 2011.

18. Mark Niquette, "Workers' Rights Battle Goes National at Pivotal Time for Labor," *Bloomberg Businessweek,* February 22, 2011; and U.S. Department of Labor, www.dol.gov, accessed March 2012.

19. Joanna Weiss, "Unions Are Losing the PR Battle," *The Boston Globe,* February 27, 2011.

20. Ron Borgas, "NFL Talks Take a Backward Step," *The Boston Herald,* March 22, 2011.

21. "Barb Kocera, "'Labor Law Still Matters,' NLRB Chair Says," *Workday Minnesota,* April 4, 2011; Kent Hoover, "NLRB Can Make Companies Promote Union Rights, Judge Says," *The Business Journals,* March 9, 2012; and www.nlrb.gov, accessed March 2012.

22. Antoinette Oliver, "Facebook Comments and the NLRB," *Pittsburgh Post Gazette,* April 4, 2011.

23. David Montgomery, "Feds May Sue Over Secret Ballot Vote," *Rapid City Journal,* March 18, 2011.

24. Robert Barro, "Unions vs. the Right-to-Work," *The Wall Street Journal,* February 28, 2011.

25. Susan Redden, "Debate Heats Up in State Capitol on Right-to-Work Issue," *The Joplin (Missouri) Times,* March 19, 2011; and U.S. Department of Labor, www.dol.gov, accessed March 2012.

26. Grant Schulte, "Anti-Union Mood Moves to Nebraska's Modest Unions," *The Seattle Times,* March 30, 2011; and Thomas Gnau, "Ohio Voters May Get Say on 'Right to Work'; After Indiana Oks Law, a Group Is Working to Get the Issue on Ohio Ballot," *Dayton Daily News,* February 21, 2012.

27. www.dol.gov, accessed March 2012; Christopher Hinton, "American Flight Attendants Forbidden to Strike," *The Wall Street Journal,* March 25, 2011; and National Mediation Board, www.nmb.gov, accessed March 2012.

28. Sam Farmer, "NFL Labor Negotiations Mark 15th Day of Mediation,"*Los Angeles Times,* March 11, 2011.

29. "Entertainment Events Wins Arbitration Relating to Late Night Catechism," *BroadwayWorld.Com,* March 17, 2011.

30. "Wade Davis' $12.6 Million Pre-Arbitration Contract with the Tampa Bay Rays," *Business Insider,* April 4, 2011; and Colin Fly, "Hart Secure with Brewers after Big Season," *USA Today,* March 29, 2011.

31. www.adr.org, accessed May 2012.

32. Terry Maxon, "APFA: American Airlines Is Losing Money, the Economy Is Bad and We're Not Going to Get a Release," *The Dallas Morning News,* March 24, 2011.

33. Ashby Jones, "A Season on the Brink? Judge Declines to Halt NFL Lockout," *The Wall Street Journal,* April 7, 2011.

34. Bill Saporito, "The Life of a $725,000 Scab," *Fortune,* March 20, 2011.

35. "A Union Education," *The Wall Street Journal,* March 1, 2011.

36. David Shephardson, "UAW Membership Up 6 Percent," *The Detroit News,* April 1, 2011.

37. Tom Krisher, "Auto Union Must Look Out for Companies Too," *Bloomberg Businessweek,* February 18, 2011; and LAUSD to Look at Worst-Case Scenario Budget: Proposal Would Cut Adult Education and Potentially Thousands of Jobs, Including Librarians, *Daily News* (Los Angeles, CA), March 9, 2012.

38. Ezra Klein, "Does Big Labor Have Any Big Ideas?" *The Washington Post,* February 27, 2011; and www.aflcio.org, accessed May 2012.

39. www.dol.gov, accessed May 2012; and www.bea.gov, accessed May 2012.

40. "Celebrity 100," *Forbes,* accessed May 2012.

41. Joann S. Lublin, "A Closer Look at Three Big Paydays," *The Wall Street Journal,* November 16, 2011; and Adam Satariano, "Apple CEO's Stock Options Lift 2011 Compensation to $378 Million," *Bloomberg Businessweek,* January 11, 2012.

42. Stephen Gandel, "CEO Pay Up, Average Worker Not So Much," *Time,* March 18, 2011.

43. Gary Strauss and Matt Krantz, "Stock Options Swell CEO Pay," *USA Today,* April 4, 2011.

44. Ibid.

45. Gretchen Morgenson, "Report Criticizes High Pay at Fannie and Freddie," *The New York Times,* March 31, 2011; and Jordan Robertson, "Yahoo's New CEO May Have Compensation as High as $27 Million," *Bloomberg Businessweek,* January 10, 2012.

46. Connie Guglielmo, "HP Chief Executive Hurd Resigns after Sexual Harassment Probe," *Bloomberg Businessweek,* August 7, 2010.

47. Rana Foroohab, "Stuffing Their Pockets," *Newsweek,* September 13, 2010.

48. Todd Frankel, "Do Today's Rich Deserve What They Get? Maybe Not," *St. Louis Post-Dispatch,* March 6, 2011.

49. "25 Highest Paid CEOs with MBAs," *Bloomberg Businessweek,* April 11, 2011; and 25 Highest-Paid Men," *Fortune,* http://money.cnn.com, accessed March 2012.

50. Jason Clenfield and Ian Katz, "In Japan, Underpaid—And Loving It," *Bloomberg Businessweek,* July 11, 2010.

51. Elizabeth G. Olsen, "Wal-Mart's Gender Bias Case: What's at Stake?" *Fortune,* April 4, 2011.

52. Jenna Goudreau, "The 15 Jobs Where Women Earn More Than Men," *Forbes,* March 14, 2011.

53. Lisa Quast, "Good News for Younger Women: There's a Smaller Wage Gap," *Forbes,* November 29, 2010.

54. Stephen Miller, "Despite Strides by U.S. Women, Wage Gap Remains," *Society for Human Resource Management Journal,* March 4, 2011.

55. www.americanprogress.org, accessed May 2012.

56. Katie Kiernan, "Responding to a Sex Harassment Claim," *New Hampshire Business Review,* January 28, 2011; and Karen Ott Mayer, "How to Eliminate Workplace Harassment," *The Business Journals,* January 25, 2012.

57. www.eeoc.gov/law, accessed May 2012; and Alissa Figueroa, "Workplace Harassment: Same Sex Sexual Harassment Cases Are on the Rise," *The Christian Science Monitor,* July 21, 2010.

58. Oliver Staley, "Yale Probed by Education Department over Sex Harassment Claim," *Bloomberg Businessweek,* April 1, 2011.

59. Jessica Bennett, "Everything I Learned about Women I Learned from Reality TV," *Newsweek,* November 11, 2010.

60. www.workingmother.com, accessed May 2012.

61. Selena Maranjian, "The Companies Doing Best by Their Employees," *The Motley Fool,* April 7, 2011.

62. www.haemonetics.com, accessed May 2012.

63. Jason Daley, "A Senior Moment," *Entrepreneur,* January 25, 2011; and U.S. Census Bureau, www.census.gov, accessed March 2012.

64. Pamela Vip, "Caring for an Elderly Loved One Can Take a Financial Toll," *St. Louis Post-Dispatch,* April 3, 2011.

65. www.nih.gov, accessed May 2012.

66. www.dol.gov, accessed May 2012.

67. Jonathan Martin, "Medical-Pot Users Await High Court Decision on Workplace," *The Seattle Times,* February 28, 2011.

68. Andrew Denney, "Workplace Violence Decline," *Columbia Daily Tribune,* March 29, 2011.

69. Rich Cordivari, "Warning Signs of Workplace Violence," *The West Hartford News,* April 3, 2011; and "Workplace Violence," www.osha.gov, accessed March 2012.

70. Lisa Quast, "Workplace Violence—the 5 Most Important Tips Women Need to Know to Protect Themselves," *Forbes,* January 10, 2011.

CHAPTER 13

1. Emily Steel, "At Super Bowl, Many Ads Fail to Score," *The Wall Street Journal,* February 7, 2011.

2. Alden M. Hayashı, "Are You 'Pushing' in a 'Pull' World?" *MIT Sloan Management Review,* Spring 2010.

3. www.vehix.com, accessed April 2011.

4. Amy Chen, "How to Find Hidden Airfare Deals," *Money,* April 2011.

5. Gwen Morgan, "Belly Up to the Widget Buffet," *Entrepreneur,* January 2012.

6. Marilyn Much, "The Changing Face(book) of Internet Commerce," *Investor's Business Daily,* February 2, 2011.

7. Mikal E. Belicove, "A Community of One's Own," *Entrepreneur,* March 2010.

8. David Talbot, "A Social-Media Decoder," *Technology Review,* November–December, 2011.

9. Lauren A. E. Schuker, "Double Feature: Dinner and a Movie," *The Wall Street Journal,* January 5, 2011.

10. Kate Limbauch, "GE Reverses a Crisis Legacy," *The Wall Street Journal,* May 17, 2012.

11. Pamela Oldham, "Selling the Sales Team," *Deliver Magazine,* July 2010.

12. Ed Nash, "Is Your Company Late to the Mobile Party?," *The Wall Street Journal,* April 12, 2012.

13. Amy C. Cosper, "Go Gaga," *Entrepreneur,* February 2011.

14. Douglas MacMillan, "Capitalizing on Travel Misery," *Bloomberg Businessweek,* May 9–May 15, 2011.

15. www.pharpro.com, accessed April 2011.

16. Michael E. Porter and Jan W. Rivkin," Choose the United States" *Harvard Business Review,* March 2012.

17. Sharon Terlep, "UAW Puts Preserving Jobs at Top of Agenda," *The Wall Street Journal,* March 30, 2011.

18. Jennie Yabroff, "No More Sacred Cows," *Newsweek,* January 11, 2010.

19. Uzma Khan and Ravi Dhar, "Making the Price of Indulgence Right," *MIT Sloan Management Review,* Spring 2011.

20. Dana Mattioli, "Macy's Regroups in Warehouse Wars," *The Wall Street Journal,* May 15, 2012.

21. Suzanne Vranica, "*%@#! and Other Ad Trends for 2012," *The Wall Street Journal,* January 4, 2012.

22. Joseph Sternberg, "Now Comes the Global Revolution in Services," *The Wall Street Journal,* February 10, 2011.

23. Mikal E. Belicove, "Gentle Reminders," *Entrepreneur,* April 2011.

24. Joseph Checkler and Jeffrey A. Trachtenberg, "Bookseller Borders Begins a New Chapter . . . 11," *The Wall Street Journal,* February 17, 2011.

25. Yuval Levin, "The Debt Dilemma," *Time,* April 4, 2011.

26. Ellen Byron, "Whitens, Brightens and Confuses," *The Wall Street Journal,* February 23, 2011.

CHAPTER 14

1. Lisa Lin, Tian Ling, and Li Yanping, "Foreign Carmakers Try Brands Just for China," *Bloomberg Businessweek,* March 7–March 13, 2011.

2. "Don't Ruin Your Reputation," *Deliver Magazine,* July 2010.

3. Michelle Locke, "Minidesserts Provide Quick Fix for Snack Lovers," *The Washington Times,* March 25, 2011.

4. David Sharp, "L.L. Bean Puts Pressure on Rivals by Eliminating Shipping Charges," *The Washington Times,* March 25, 2011.

5. Ylan Q. Mui, "Manufacturing Continues Growth Streak, Bolstering Recovery," *The Washington Post,* April 5, 2012.

6. Matthew Barakat, "Better Burgers Are Sizzling," *St. Louis Post-Dispatch,* July 18, 2010.

7. Mathilde Visseyrias, "Are We Ready for McBaguette?," *The Week,* August 12, 2011.
8. James R. Hagerty, "Zippo Preps for a Post-Smoker World," *The Wall Street Journal,* March 8, 2011.
9. Catherine Bolgar, "A Giant Leap for the World of Business and Industry," *The Wall Street Journal,* March 21, 2011.
10. Jason Amaral, Edward G. Anderson Jr., and Geofrey G. Parker, "Putting It Together: How to Succeed in Distributed Product Development," *MIT Sloan Management Review,* Winter 2011.
11. Marc Gunther, "3 M's Innovation Revival," *Fortune,* September 27, 2010.
12. Alina Dizik, "Why All the Locals Are Lounging in the Hotel Lobby," *The Wall Street Journal,* April 19, 2012.
13. Ellen Byron, "Whitens, Brightens and Confuses," *The Wall Street Journal,* February 23, 2011.
14. Matt Vilano, "The Secret Sauce Part II," *Entrepreneur,* April 2011.
15. Shira Ovide, "Perfect Fit: To Some Outfits, Nothing Speaks Like 'Bespoke'," *The Wall Street Journal,* May 4, 2012.
16. Barry Newman, "The Lighter Side of Counterfeiting Puts Zippo in a Fix," *The Wall Street Journal,* March 25, 2011.
17. Kurt Badenhausen, "The World's Most Valuable Brands," *Forbes,* August 30, 2010.
18. Angus Loten and Emily Maltby, "Old Brands Get a Second Shot," *The Wall Street Journal,* April 19, 2012.
19. Kris Hudson and Alexandra Berzon, "Hoteliers Build on the Hipness Factor," *The Wall Street Journal,* February 22, 2011.
20. Joan Schneider and Julie Hall, "Why Most Product Launches Fail," *Harvard Business Review,* April 2011.
21. Walter S. Mosberg, "In and Out of Office: Putting iPads to Work," *The Wall Street Journal,* March 17, 2011.
22. John Donahoe, "How eBay Developed a Culture of Experimentation," *Harvard Business Review,* March 2011.
23. Kris Hudson and Alexandra Berzon, "Hoteliers Build on the Hipness Factor," *The Wall Street Journal,* February 22, 2011.
24. Matt Villano, "The Secret Sauce: Part II," *Entrepreneur,* April 2011.
25. Ari Levy and Joseph Galante, "Who Wants to Buy a Digital Elephant?" *Bloomberg Businessweek,* March 8, 2010.
26. Joe Queenan, "The Incredible Shrinking Everything," *The Wall Street Journal,* April 9–10, 2011.
27. Uzma Khan and Ravi Dhar, "Making the Price of Indulgence Right," *MIT Sloan Management Review,* Spring 2011.
28. Jay Palmer, "Pricing Power in the Grocery Aisle," *Barron's,* February 21, 2011.

2010; Marilyn Alva, "The Retaking of the Retail Trade," *Investor's Business Daily,* February 28, 2011; and "Suburban Renewal," *Barron's,* February 21, 2011.
9. Marilyn Much, "The Changing Face (Book) of Internet Commerce," *Investor's Business Daily,* February 2, 2011.
10. Jonathan Birchall, "Walmart Launches Same-Day Pickup," *Financial Times,* October 7, 2010.
11. Marisa Taylor, "Treasure Hunt," *Smart Money,* April 2011.
12. "An ATM That Dispenses Gold," *The Wall Street Journal,* May 14, 2010.
13. David Sharp, "L.L. Bean Puts Pressure on Rivals by Eliminating Shipping Charges," *The Washington Times,* March 25, 2011.
14. Joe Mullich, "The Resilient Supply Chain," *The Wall Street Journal,* September 22, 2011.
15. Hau L. Lee, "Don't Tweak Your Supply Chain—Rethink It End to End," *Harvard Business Review,* October 2010.
16. Maxwell Murphy, "Reinforcing the Supply Chain," *The Wall Street Journal,* January 11, 2012.
17. Charles H. Fine, "Collaborate or Race? How to Design the Value Chain You Need," *MIT Sloan Management Review,* Winter 2010.
18. Neal E. Boudette, "Quake Throws Auto Nation into a Spin," *The Wall Street Journal,* May 16, 2011.
19. Mark Vandenbosch and Stephen Sapp, "Opportunism Knocks," *MIT Sloan Management Review,* Fall 2010.
20. Kathleen Kingsbury, "Prescription for a Turnaround," *Time,* February 15, 2010.
21. Peter Senge, "The Sustainable Supply Chain," *Harvard Business Review,* October 2010.
22. Todd W. Price, "Making Resource Management Work: Sustainability and the Supply Chain," *Harvard Business Review,* March 2011.
23. "XPorta," *Bloomberg Businessweek,* accessed online, April 12, 2011.
24. "Reverse Logic," an ad in *Bloomberg Businessweek,* March 28–April 3, 2011.
25. "All the Right Moves," an ad in *Fortune,* May 2, 2011.
26. Jennifer Lawler, "The Logic of Thirds," *Entrepreneur,* March 2010.
27. Ibid.
28. Michael Gaynor, "Stand and Deliver," *Washingtonian,* December 2010.
29. Mima Kimes, "Showdown on the Railroad," *Fortune,* September 26, 2011.
30. "A Scantastic App Goes Mainstream," *Entrepreneur,* May 2010.

CHAPTER 15

1. Robert Wright and John Reed, "Pressure Grows on Supply Chains," *Financial Times,* April 21, 2010; and William Pesek, "The Cataclysm This Time," *Bloomberg Businessweek,* March 21–March 27, 2011.
2. "Chain Reaction," an ad in *Fortune,* September 5, 2011.
3. Miguel Bustillo, "Walmart Tests Home Delivery," *The Wall Street Journal,* April 25, 2011.
4. Matthew Boyle, "Who's Really Stocking Your Grocer's Shelf," *Bloomberg Businessweek,* March 28–April 3, 2011.
5. "Transforming the Supply Chain," an ad for UPS in *Fortune,* February 6, 2012.
6. David M. Katz, "The Shortest Distance to Cash," *CFO,* March 2010.
7. Ann Zimmerman, "Check Out the Future of Shopping," *The Wall Street Journal,* May 18, 2011.
8. Cotton Timberlake, "With Stores Nationwide, Macy's Goes Local," *Bloomberg Businessweek,* October 4–October 10,

CHAPTER 16

1. Steven Prokesch, "The Reluctant Social Entrepreneur," *Harvard Business Review,* June 2011.
2. Walter S. Mossberg, "iPad 2: Thin, Not Picture Perfect," *The Wall Street Journal,* March 10, 2011.
3. Brian Quinton, "Multiple Marketing Personalities," *Entrepreneur,* January 2011.
4. Leslie Dance, "It's All about Me," advertisement in *BtoB,* January 17, 2011.
5. Kate Maddox, "Motorola's New Solution," *BtoB,* January 17, 2011.
6. Sam Schechner and Emily Steel, "Demand Builds for TV Ad Time," *The Wall Street Journal,* April 25, 2011.
7. Sharon Begley, "I Can't Think," *Newsweek,* March 7, 2011.
8. Marilyn Much, "The Changing Face(book) of Internet Commerce," *Investor's Business Daily,* February 2, 2011.
9. Scott Cendrowski, "Nike's New Marketing Mojo," *Fortune,* February 27, 2012.

10. Peter Romeo, "Social Media 50," *Restaurant Business,* April 2011.
11. Gregory Unruh and Richard Ettenson, "Growing Green," *Harvard Business Review,* June 2010; and Jason Ankeny, "Green Idols," *Entrepreneur,* April 2011.
12. Sam Schechner and Emily Steel, "Super Bowl Promises Extra Kick for Ads," *The Wall Street Journal,* January 31, 2011.
13. Emily Steel, "At Super Bowl, Many Ads Fail to Score," *The Wall Street Journal,* February 7, 2011.
14. Sam Schechner and Emily Steel, "Demand Builds for TV Ad Time," *The Wall Street Journal,* April 25, 2011.
15. Edmund Lee, "Major Marketers Shift More Dollars toward Social Marketing," *Advertising Age,* April 11, 2011.
16. Peter Burrows, Andy Fixmer, and Aaron Recadela, "The Other Cult in Hollywood," *Bloomberg Businessweek,* May 14–20, 2012.
17. J. Turner, A. Scheller-Wolf, and S. Tayur, "Scheduling of Dynamic In-Game Advertising," *Operations Research,* January–February 2011.
18. Matt Robinson, "As Seen on TV—And Sold at Your Local Store," *Bloomberg Businessweek,* July 26–August 1, 2010.
19. Elizabeth Woyke, "Serendipity Shopping," *Forbes,* August 22, 2011.
20. Ellen Byron, "In-Store Sales Begin at Home," *The Wall Street Journal,* April 25, 2011.
21. Reggie Bradford and David Rollo, "Marketing Flourishes via Social Media," *Advertising Age,* February 14, 2011.
22. "Does Return on Social Media Justify the Spending?" *Deliver Magazine,* July 2010.
23. www.garden.com, accessed April 2011.
24. Brian Truitt, "37 Ways Social Media Can Make Your Life Just a Little Easier," *USA Weekend,* March 25–27, 2011.
25. Christopher Hosford, "Direct in Reverse," *BtoB,* February 14, 2011.
26. www.vitamix.com, accessed April 2011.
27. Geoffrey A. Fowler, "Are You Talking to Me?" *The Wall Street Journal,* April 25, 2011.
28. www.pocarisweat.com, accessed March 2011.
29. www.performanceprobe.com, accessed April 2011.
30. www.masterfoods.com, accessed April 2011.
31. Joann Muller, "The Bespoke Auto," *Forbes,* September 27, 2010.
32. Neil Woodcock, Andrew Green, and Michael Starkey, "Social CRM as a Business Strategy," *Journal of Database Marketing & Customer Strategy Management,* March 2011; and Michael Bush, "What Is Social CRM?" *Advertising Age,* February 28, 2011.
33. Pamela Oldham, "Selling the Sales Team," *Deliver Magazine,* July 2010.
34. David H. Freedman, "On the Road with a Salesperson," *Inc.,* April 2010.
35. Kasey Welrum, "Sales Tips from the World's Toughest Customers," *Inc.,* April 2010.
36. Christopher Hosford, "Content Drives Sales Enablement," *BtoB,* May 2, 2011.
37. Emily Glazer, "Target: Customers on the Go," *The Wall Street Journal,* May 16, 2011.
38. Lauren Coleman-Lochner, "Social Networking Takes Center Stage at P&G," *Bloomberg Businessweek,* April 2–8, 2012.

CHAPTER 17

1. Bill Saporito, "Where the Jobs Are: The Right Spots in the Recovery," *Time,* January 14, 2011; and Bill Carlino, "The Greening of Corporate Accounting: Demand Is Climbing for Sustainability Reporting Services," *Accounting Today,* March 1, 2012.
2. www.bls.gov/oco, accessed May 2012.
3. Ali Velshi, "Today's 'It' Jobs: Accounting and IT," *Money,* February 2011; and Kathleen Mitchell, "Careers in the Making," *BusinessWest,* January 2, 2012.
4. Jeffrey C. Thomson, "Let's Talk about the CPA," *Strategic Finance,* January 1, 2011.
5. www.imanet.org/certification, accessed May 2012.
6. Teresa Odie, "Hot Jobs: Accountants," *Philadelphia Inquirer Digital,* April 19, 2011; and Jeff Zbar, "Accounting Firms Staffing Up to Meet Specialized Needs," *South Florida Business Journal,* March 23, 2012.
7. Lynn Ducey, "How to Choose the Right Accountant for Your Business," *Phoenix Business Journal,* April 13, 2012.
8. www.aicpa.org, accessed May 2012.
9. Francine McKenna, "Why No Warnings? Investors Press Audit Regulator," *Forbes,* March 28, 2011; and "An Assessment of the PCAOB's Enforcement Program to Date under Sarbanes-Oxley," *Mondaq Business Briefing,* January 12, 2012.
10. Roger Parloff, "Sarbanes-Oxley Struck Down? Not Even Close," *Fortune Magazine,* June 28, 2010; and www.pacobus.org, accessed May 2012.
11. Joshua Zumbrun, "Fed Requests Comments on Proposals for Dodd-Frank Law," *Bloomberg Businessweek,* February 8, 2011; and Joshua Gallu, "Dodd-Frank May Cost $6.5 Billion and 5,000 Workers," *Bloomberg Businessweek,* February 14, 2011.
12. Matthew Furman, "Auditing Your Auditor," *CFO,* April 2010; and Julian E. Jacoby and Neal B. Hitzig, "Auditing Internal Controls in Small Populations," *The CPA Journal,* December 1, 2011.
13. Brenden Sheehan, "Senate Questions Auditors' and SEC's Role in Financial Crisis," *Business Insider,* April 13, 2011.
14. Steve Eder, "Lehman Auditor May Bear the Brunt," *The Wall Street Journal,* March 14, 2011.
15. Jim McTague, "Auditors in the Doghouse," *Barron's,* March 21, 2011.
16. www.theiia.org/certification, accessed March 2012; and C.O. Hollis, "CIA Designation Good Goal for Internal Auditors," *Atlanta Business Chronicle,* February 10, 2012.
17. Henry Unger, "How Would You Change Our Tax System?" *The Atlanta Journal-Constitution,* April 18, 2011.
18. "Super Rich See Super Savings on Taxes," *Detroit Free Press,* April 17, 2011.
19. www.gasb.org, accessed May 2012; and "Factbox: Top Budgetary Threats to State, Local Governments," *Reuters,* April 21, 2011.
20. Elizabeth Heubeck, "Nonprofits Face Fierce Funding Climate," *Baltimore Business Journal,* March 11, 2011.
21. Ted Needleman, "Making the Next Step: Mid-Range Accounting Packages Offer More Capabilities for More Users," *Accounting Today,* February 1, 2011; and Tim Mills-Groninger, "Accounting Software: Audits and Lawsuits and Floods, Oh My!" *The NonProfit Times,* January 1, 2012.
22. Jeffrey L. Wilson, "The Best Small Business Accounting Software," *PC Magazine,* May 13, 2010; and Ted Needleman, "Many Points of Entry; Entry-Level Accounting Software Is Getting Harder to Define," *Accounting Today,* February 1, 2012.
23. Dave McClure, "Changing with the Times: Entry-Level Accounting Packages in the Midst of Three Revolutions," *Accounting Today,* January 1, 2011.

24. Joseph M. Langmead and Jalai Soroosh, "Accounting for Financial Instruments: More Turmoil Ahead," *The CPA Journal*, February 1, 2011.
25. Tom Omberg, "Making Financial Reports More Effective and Useful," *Financial Executive*, January 1, 2012.
26. Ken King, "Financial Goals by the Numbers," *Sheboygan Press*, April 30, 2011; and "How to Manage Cash Flow," *Commercial Carrier Journal*, January 1, 2012.
27. Chris James, "Controlling Your Business Cash," *Dallas Business Journal*, July 28, 2010; and Jack G. Hardy, "Get Serious about Cash Flow," *The Miami Herald*, April 25, 2011.
28. Rich Smith, "Under Armour Fouls Out," *The Motley Fool*, April 26, 2011.
29. Sanjiv Mahajan, "Economy Up or Down—'Cash Is Always King,'" *Supply & Demand Chain Executive*, March 1, 2011.
30. Julie Briggs, Tracy Higginbotham, and Theresa Slater, "Here Are Some Tips for Trimming Expenses," *The Post-Standard* (Syracuse, NY), March 1, 2011.
31. www.bizfinance@about.com, accessed May 2012; Mitchell Eichen, "Not All Cash Is Created Equal," *Forbes*, March 25, 2011; and John Adams, "Banks Play Comeback in Business Cash Management," *American Banker*, January 25, 2012.
32. Anand Chokkavelu, "How Cheap Is Nordstrom by the Numbers?" *The Motley Fool*, May 2, 2011.

CHAPTER 18

1. Diane Richey, "Security and the CFO: Show Me the Money," *Security Magazine*, February 1, 2011; and "How to Do It . . . Finance," *McKnight's Long-Term Care News*, January 1, 2012.
2. David Skok, "Cash Is King: 8 Tips for Optimizing Your Startup Financial Strategy," *Fortune*, April 26, 2011.
3. Sewell Chan, "Financial Crisis Was Avoidable, Inquiry Finds," *The New York Times*, January 25, 2011; and Zeke Faux and Phil Mattingly, "MF Global Told S&P 'Never Been Stronger' as Failure Loomed," *Bloomberg Businessweek*, February 8, 2012.
4. Mark Modica, "'Government Motors' Is Still a Lemon," *The New York Post*, April 17, 2011; David Welch, "For Investors the Shine Is Off the New GM," *Bloomberg Businessweek*, April 14, 2011; and Shikha Dalmia, "Despite GM's $8 Billion in Profits, Taxpayers Are Still on the Hook," *The Buffalo News*, March 18, 2012.
5. Robert Samuelson, "Why TARP Has Been a Success Story," *The Washington Post*, March 27, 2011; and Jim Hammerand, "Some Banks Depend Upon TARP Funds," *Minneapolis / St. Paul Business Journal*, March 2, 2012.
6. www.mccormick.com, accessed May 2012.
7. Jonathan Blum, "Smart Money," *Entrepreneur*, February 2011.
8. Kevin Garcia, "How to Undertake a Financial Restructuring," *Inc.*, April 30, 2011.
9. Trevor Clawson, "Are CFOs Getting It Right on Internal Auditing?" *CFO World*, April 21, 2011.
10. Peter Millar, "Making FCPA Compliance Sustainable," *Business Finance Magazine*, May 2, 2011.
11. Martin Zwilling, "How to Predict Your Start-up's Financial Future," *Inc.*, April 8, 2011.
12. David M. Katz, "Luke Skywalker, Supply-Chain Hero," *CFO*, June 11, 2010; and James Lea, "Flawed Decision-Making a Downfall of Many Concerns," *Triangle Business Journal*, March 23, 2012.
13. Joe Keohane, "That Guy Who Called the Big One? Don't Listen to Him. Inside the Paradox of Forecasting," *The Boston Globe*, January 9, 2011.
14. Morey Stettner, "Accurate Budget Forecasts Rely on Full Team Efforts," *Investor's Business Daily*, April 11, 2011.
15. Martin Shenk, "Oil-Price Estimate for 2011 Increased by 8.5% by U.S. on Growing Fuel Demand," *Bloomberg Businessweek*, January 11, 2011; and "The 2011 Oil Shock," *The Economist*, March 3, 2011.
16. Lauren Cannon, "How to Pay Employees When You Can't Make Payroll," *Inc.*, April 1, 2011.
17. Robert Bovarnick, "Make Them Pay," *Forbes*, November 23, 2010; and Jane Meinhardt, "Accounts Receivable Crucial to a Business' Cash Flow," *Tampa Bay Business Journal*, January 20, 2012.
18. Jason Notte, "MasterCard May Best Giant Visa on Swipe Fees," *TheStreet.com*, May 4, 2011; and "MasterCard 1Q Tops Forecasts on Consumer Spending," *The Wall Street Journal*, April 3, 2011.
19. Kishore S. Swaminathan, "Taming the Data That Dominates Our Work Lives," *Fortune Magazine*, April 14, 2011.
20. Bea Quirk, "Find Financing Alternatives to Banks," *Atlanta Business Chronicle*, April 29, 2011; and Emily Maltby, "How to Finance Your Start-Up without Tapping Home Equity," *The Wall Street Journal*, January 31, 2012.
21. "Paying Your Suppliers. What Kind of Payment Methods Will Your Suppliers Prefer?" *Entrepreneur*, May 6, 2011.
22. www.nifb.com/webinars/alternative-funding-sources, accessed May 2012.
23. Pamela Ostermiller, "Borrowing from the Family: Get It in Writing, Even from Mom," *Utah Business*, January 1, 2011; and Caron Beesley, "6 Tips for Borrowing Startup Funds from Friends or Family," Minority Business Development Agency, www.mbda.gov, accessed March 2012.
24. "CFOs Say Cash Flow Is Top Concern and Financial Priority for 2011," *The Secured Lender*, January 1, 2011.
25. Bridget Riley, "Lending Picks Up," *San Francisco Business Times*, May 6, 2011; and Robb Mandelbaum, "Survey Says Small-Business Lending Is Surging," *The New York Times*, April 30, 2011.
26. Vincent Ryan, "Lien on Me," *CFO*, April 2010.
27. www.businessfinance.com/revolving-line-of-credit/htm, accessed May 2012; and Vincent Ryan, "Revolvers Return, with Some Twists," *CFO*, May 1, 2011.
28. www.gecapital.com, accessed May 2012.
29. Dyan Machan, "Borrowers Say They Get Good Deals When Investors Buy Their Receivables," *Smart Money*, March 2011; and Christopher Sheffield, "Factoring Opens Door to Alternative Financing," *Memphis Business Journal*, March 9, 2012.
30. Neil Berdiev, "The Post-Banking Loan," *Entrepreneur*, May 2010; and Kathy Bergstrom, "How to Use Factoring to Increase Cash Flow," *The Business Journals*, January 20, 2012.
31. Karen E. Kline, "A Menu of Finance Options for Exporters," *Bloomberg Businessweek*, March 15, 2011.
33. Ibid.
33. Annamaria Andriotis, "The Return of Small-Business Credit Cards," *The Wall Street Journal*, January 16, 2012.
34. www.pfizer.com, accessed May 2012; and "Power of Incentives," *Investors Business Daily*, April 8, 2011.
35. Tim Mullaney, "Is Help on the Way for the Tech IPO Market?" *USA Today*, May 5, 2011.
36. Ben Worthen, "For Silicon Valley Start-Ups, Funding Boom Is Lopsided," *The Wall Street Journal*, May 6, 2011.
37. "Most Debt-Laden Companies in the S&P 500," www.cnbc.com, accessed May 2012.
38. Matthew Vincent, "Sales Soaring High Despite Regulatory Concerns," *Financial Times*, May 6, 2011; and Rory Lancman, "Wall Street's Sheriff Needs Many More Deputies," *Bloomberg Businessweek*, May 3, 2011.

39. Brooke Masters, "How Madoff Cast His Spell," *Financial Times,* May 4, 2011.
40. Sebastian Walsh, "Is Dodd-Frank Already Doomed to Fail?" *Financial News,* May 6, 2011; and Ben Protess, "Treasury Urges Small Banks to Embrace Dodd-Frank," *The New York Times,* May 2, 2011.

CHAPTER 19

1. Nina Mehta, "Trade Disorder Plagues Nasdaq Handling $16 Billion Facebook IPO," *Bloomberg Businessweek,* May 18, 2012.
2. Roben Farzad, "Initial Private Offering," *Bloomberg Businessweek,* January 16, 2011.
3. Halah Touryalai, "Profit Shakes Up Goldman Sachs," *Forbes,* January 19, 2011.
4. Aaron Lucchetti, Gina Chon, and Jacob Bunge, "Nasdaq Looking for a Partner," *The Wall Street Journal,* February 26, 2011; and Chris Redman, "Are Bigger Stock Exchanges Better?" *Fortune Magazine,* March 21, 2011; and Jacob Bunge, "NYSE Won't Join Deutsche Börse in Fighting EU," *The Wall Street Journal,* March 22, 2011.
5. "Exchange Undergoes a Face-Lift," *The Washington Times,* April 11, 2011; and Michael Santoli, "Nasdaq and ICE Make Their Move," *Barron's,* April 4, 2011.
6. Nina Mehta, Lynn Thomasson, and Paul M. Barrett, "The Machines That Ate the Market," *Bloomberg Businessweek,* May 30, 2010; and David K. Randall, "New York Stock Exchange Sold," *Associated Press,* February 16, 2011.
7. Ibid.
8. www.nyse.com, accessed May 15, 2012.
9. Jonathan Weil, "NASDAQ Eating Machine Starving for NYSE Deal," *Bloomberg Businessweek,* April 27, 2011; and Jonathan Cheng, "A Coming of Age for NASDAQ," *The Wall Street Journal,* March 12, 2012.
10. Nicole Perlroth, "NYSE: You Are Witnessing a 'Complete Crushing' of the NASDAQ," *Forbes,* May 10, 2011.
11. "Metalink's Shares to Be Delisted from NASDAQ," *PR Newswire,* April 18, 2011; and Emily Chasan, "Will Stock Split Really Change Citi's Shareholder Base?" *The Wall Street Journal,* May 10, 2011.
12. Nathaniel Popper, "Galleon Billionaire Raj Rajaratnam Convicted in Insider Trading Case," *Los Angeles Times,* May 11, 2011; Susan Pulliam and Chad Bray, "Trader Draws Record Sentence," *The Wall Street Journal,* October 14, 2011; and Peter Lattman, "Rajaratnam Is Ordered to Pay $92.8 Million Penalty in Trading Case," *The New York Times,* November 9, 2011.
13. Aude Lagorce, "Africa Offers New Investment Opportunities," *St. Louis Post-Dispatch,* July 11, 2011; and Richard (Rick) Mills, "Looking into Africa," *Resource Investor,* May 11, 2011.
14. Jennifer Schonberger, "Preferred Stocks," *Kiplinger's Personal Finance,* April 2011; and Gail Liberman, "Ideas to Boost Yields in Tough Times; Preferred Stock, REITs, Corporate Bonds Are Options," *Palm Beach Daily News,* February 19, 2012.
15. Carla Fried, "Bonds 101," *Money Magazine,* June 2010; and www.investopedia.com, accessed May 2011.
16. "Companies Considering Issuing 100-Year Bonds; Investors Should Steer Clear," *The Wall Street Journal,* August 23, 2010; and Katy Burne, "MIT Offers Century Bond," *The Wall Street Journal,* May 11, 2011.
17. "About Bond Ratings," *Charles Schwab On Investing,* Winter 2010; and Rob Williams, "How to Use Bond Ratings Today," www.schwab.com, accessed May 2012.
18. Robert Frick, "Convertible Bonds," *Kiplinger's Personal Finance,* April 2011.
19. William Baldwin, "Six Ways to Inflation-Proof Your Bonds," *Forbes,* March 2, 2011; and 4 Ways Bonds Can Fit Into Your Portfolio," *Forbes,* February 9, 2012.
20. Kevin Harlan, "The Changing Broker Scene Offers Options for Traders," *Investor's Business Daily,* April 25, 2011; and Eve Kaplan, "The Difference between a Stockbroker, Financial Advisor and Planner Explained," *Forbes,* March 15, 2012.
21. Elizabeth Ody, "The Best of the Online Brokers," *Kiplinger's Personal Finance,* February 2011.
22. David Futrelle, "How Well Do You Know Risk?" *Money Magazine,* January–February 2011; and Elizabeth Ody, "5 Strategies to Lower Risk," *Kiplinger's Personal Finance,* January 2011.
23. "Yale May Not Have the Key: When Diversification Does Not Work," *The Economist,* March 12, 2011.
24. William Baldwin, "Capital Gains and Capital Losses: Rules for Investors," *Forbes,* March 25, 2011.
25. www.aboutmcdonalds/mcd/investors.html, accessed May 2012.
26. Dan Caplinger, "Why This Stock Is Not Doomed," *The Motley Fool,* May 10, 2011; and Eric Savitz, "Apple: CEO Cook Sees No Reason to Split Stock," *Forbes,* March 19, 2012.
27. www.finance.yahoo.com, accessed May 2012.
28. Karen Gullo, "Goldman Sachs Accused by Marvell Founder of Margin Call Fraud," *Bloomberg Businessweek,* April 12, 2011; and Gretchen Morgenson, "Anger at Goldman Still Simmers," *The New York Times,* March 25, 2012.
29. James B. Stewart, "Municipal Bond Investors Can Collect Their Interest and Sleep Peacefully," *Smart Money,* April 2011.
30. "Why Junk Bond Rally Should Be Cheered—and Jeered," *Associated Press,* May 9, 2011; and Nicole Bullock, "Junk Bond Yields Hit Record Lows," *Financial Times,* May 10, 2011.
31. Mark Jewell, "Three Experts Debunk Mutual Fund Myths," *St. Louis Post-Dispatch,* April 3, 2011.
32. John Waggoner, "USA Today's Fund All-Stars: 20 Top Performers," *USA Today,* May 13, 2011; and Investment Company Institute, www.ici.org, accessed May 2012.
33. Elizabeth Ody, "Now You Can Buy Load Funds Commission-Free," *Kiplinger's Personal Finance,* May 2010; Chris Barth, "How a Family Shopping Spree Can Help Your Mutual Fund Performance," *Forbes,* May 4, 2011; and Yahoo Finance, www.finance.yahoo.com, accessed May 2012.
34. Mark Jewell, "Investors Flee Managed Funds," *St. Louis Post-Dispatch,* April 17, 2011; and Hung Tran, "Mutual Funds: Born Here, Moving Where?" *Money Management Executive,* March 26, 2012.
35. Mark Jewell, "ETFs Are Coming of Age with Their Low-Cost Appeal," *St. Louis Post-Dispatch,* January 2, 2011; and Jeremy Vohlwinkle, "How to Start Investing with Small Amounts of Money" *About Financial Planning,* www.financialplan.about.com, accessed May 2012.
36. Robert Samuelson, "For the Young, There's a Silver Lining in the Housing Bust," *The Washington Post,* May 14, 2011.
37. Alex J. Pollock, "On Housing, There Will Be More Lean Years Ahead," *The Wall Street Journal,* May 12, 2011; and Nick Timiraos, "Home Prices Fall, but at a Slower Pace," *The Wall Street Journal,* March 27, 2012.
38. Ibid.
39. Gillian Tett, "TARP Shows That U.S. Can Break Political Deadlock," *Financial Times,* May 12, 2011.

CHAPTER 20

1. Ryan Derousseau, "Cashing In on Mastercard," *Fortune,* May 21, 2012.
2. Eric Spitznagel, "Rise of the Barter Economy," *Bloomberg Businessweek,* April 30–May 6, 2012.
3. Judy Holland, "Face Value," *Washingtonian,* October 2010.
4. Brady Dennis, "New $100 Bills Delayed by Errors In Production," *The Washington Post,* December 7, 2010.
5. Steve Forbes, "Memo to Merkel: Stop Killing the Euro," *Forbes,* April 25, 2011.
6. Andy Greenberg, "Crypto Currency," *Forbes,* May 9, 2011.
7. David Wolman, "Time for Cash Out?," *The Wall Street Journal,* February 11–12, 2012.
8. J. Alex Tarquinis, "When QE2 Weighs Anchor," *Smart Money,* May 2011.
9. Kelly Evans, "Overlooked Inflation Cue: Follow the Money," *The Wall Street Journal,* April 12, 2011.
10. David Von Drehle, "The Many Who Said No to Easy Money," *Time,* February 14, 2011.
11. Paul Krugman, "Earth to Ben Bernanke," *The New York Times Magazine,* April 29, 2012.
12. Forbes, "Memo to Merkel."
13. www.federalreserveonline.gov, accessed April 2011.
14. "How the Fed Works," *Time,* January 4, 2010.
15. www.federalreserve.gov/monetarypolicy/reservereq, accessed April 2011.
16. Michael J. Casey, "The Fed's Four-Trillion Dollar Man," *The Wall Street Journal,* April 12, 2012.
17. Rich Miller, "Raise 'Em or Hold 'Em? Bernanke's Bind," *Bloomberg Businessweek,* May 8, 2011.
18. "Cash Out," *Entrepreneur,* March 2012.
19. www.investorwords.com/955/commercial_bank, accessed April 2011.
20. http://legal-dictionary.thefreedictionary.com/Glass-Steagall1Act, accessed April, 2011.
21. Joan Goldwasser, "Credit Unions Anyone Can Join," *Kiplinger's Personal Finance,* June 2012.
22. Bill Saporito, "The Swipe-Fee Free-for-All," *Time,* April 4, 2011.
23. www.data.worldbank.org/, accessed April 2011.
24. Neil Irwin, "World Bank, IMF Leaders: Recovery Still a Shaky One," *The Washington Post,* April 17, 2011.
25. Howard Schneider, "IMF Chief Sees Recovery as a Work In Progress," *The Washington Post,* April 12, 2011.
26. Howard Schneider, "IMF Pushes Euro-Zone Nations to Do More to Fight Debt Crisis," *The Washington Post,* January 19, 2012.
27. Christopher Dickey, "The Truth Talker," *Newsweek,* January 30, 2012.
28. Ian Talley and Sudeep Reddy, "IMF Shifts Stance on Capital Controls," *The Wall Street Journal,* April 6, 2011.

APPENDIX 1

1. American Bar Association, www.americanbar.org, accessed June 2012.
2. Michael Virtanen, "New York Court Reinstates Restaurant Worker's Product Liability Suit," *Insurance Journal,* May 13, 2011; "NY Top Court Reinstates Product Liability Suit," *The Wall Street Journal,* May 10, 2011; and W. Kip Viscusi, "Does Product Liability Make Us Safer?" *Regulation,* Spring 2012.
3. Carl Schramm, "Are We Thwarting Medical Innovations?" *Forbes,* March 8, 2011; and S.Y. Tan, "Products Liability," *Internal Medicine News,* January 1, 2012.
4. Robert Kelly, "Five Questions: Partner Says Fighting for the Little Guy Drives Law Firm," *St. Louis Post-Dispatch,* May 13, 2011; and Ashby Jones, "Mississippi Jury Returns Largest Asbestos Verdict in U.S. History," *The Wall Street Journal,* May 6, 2011; and Daniel Fisher, "BP Settles with Plaintiff Lawyers, Pegs Cost at $7.8 Billion," *Forbes,* March 3, 2012.
5. Jack Elliott Jr., "Sherwin Williams Appeals Mississippi Lead Paint Verdict," *Bloomberg Businessweek,* April 19, 2011.
6. Jeffrey Liker, "Toyota Recall Crisis: What Have We Learned?" *Harvard Business Review,* February 11, 2011; and Makiko Kitamura, Alan Ohneman, and Yuki Hagiwara, "Why Lexus Doesn't Lead the Pack in China," *Bloomberg Businessweek,* March 24, 2011.
7. Daniel Fisher, "NASA Report Makes Life Tougher for Lawyers Suing Toyota," *Forbes,* February 8, 2011; and Joann Muller, "Toyota Recall: How a Hiccup Became a Big Headache," *Forbes,* March 8, 2012.
8. Tom Randall, "Merck's Risky Bet on Research," *Bloomberg Businessweek,* May 1, 2011.
9. Sophia Pearson and Jeff Feeley, "Merck Vioxx Accord Spawns Pay-Day Scrap among Lawyers," *Bloomberg,* February 18, 2011.
10. Scott James, "Long Battle against Guns Began with Son's Death," *The New York Times,* May 12, 2011.
11. Andrew M. Harris, "McDonald's Obesity Case Can't Proceed as Group Suit," *Bloomberg,* October 27, 2010.
12. Quentin Fottrell, "Will High Court Ruling Hurt Consumers?" *Smart Money,* May 18, 2011.
13. Reuven Brenner, "Google's Conundrum: Buy the Patents or Pay the Lawyers," *Forbes,* April 7, 2011.
14. John Tozzi and Susan Decker, "Patent Reform: High Stakes for Small Biz," *Bloomberg Businessweek,* October 3, 2010; Toby Kusner, "The Patent Office Dilemma: How Congress Robs Peter to Pay Paul," *Forbes,* May 6, 2011; and www.uspto.gov, accessed May 2012.
15. Abigail Field, "The Supreme Court's 'Landmark' Ruling Didn't Really Change Much," *Daily Finance,* June 29, 2011.
16. www.islandpatent.com, accessed May 2012.
17. Brian Deagon, "Big Patent-Infringement Awards More Exception Than Rule: Study," *Investor's Business Daily,* March 24, 2011; and Ben Dobbin, "New Look at Kodak Infringement Claim," *St. Louis Post-Dispatch,* March 26, 2011.
18. Gregg Keizer, "Microsoft Downplays Impact of Possible Supreme Court Ruling," *Computerworld,* April 19, 2011.
19. Stephanie Bodoni, "Microsoft, Nokia, Challenge Apple's 'App Store' EU Trademark," *Bloomberg Businessweek,* May 13, 2011; and Ian Sherr and Spencer E. Ante, "Fight Over iPad Name Spills into U.S. Court," *The Wall Street Journal,* February 23, 2012.
20. Alina Tugend, "Buyer, Be Aware the Law Is on Your Side," *The New York Times,* May 6, 2011; and Mitch Lipka, "'Implied Warranty' Provides an Extra Level of Protection," *The Boston Globe,* February 12, 2012.
21. Patricia Mertz Esswein, "What You Need to Know about Warranties," *Kiplinger's Personal Finance,* January 2011.
22. David J. Popeo, "The SEC's Misguided New Mission: Foreign Government Change Agent," *Forbes,* May 18, 2011; and Dina El Boghdady, "FTC Hard Pressed to Secure Refunds in Job-Scam Cases," *The Washington Post,* January 3, 2012.
23. "Did the Microsoft Case Change the World?" *The New York Times,* May 14, 2011; and Nick Eaton, "DOJ Will Let Microsoft Antitrust Oversight Expire in May," *Seattle Post Intelligencer,* April 28, 2011.
24. David Sarno, "Justice Department's Landmark Judgment against Microsoft Will Expire," *Los Angeles Times,* May 11, 2011; and Thomas Catan, "FTC Attorney to Join Microsoft," *The Wall Street Journal,* February 29, 2012.
25. Nina Mehta, "NYSE-NASDAQ Deal Seen as Producing Multiple Monopolies by Justice Lawyers," *Bloomberg,* May 18, 2011.

26. Ben Protess, "Treasury Urges Small Banks to Embrace Dodd-Frank," *The New York Times,* May 2, 2011; Phil Mattingly, "Dodd-Frank Consumer Bureau Changes Approval by U.S. House Panel," *Bloomberg Businessweek,* May 22, 2011; and Ashby Jones, "Fine Print on Dodd-Frank, 'Sox on Steroids,' Slow to Arrive," *The Wall Street Journal,* May 2, 2011.

27. Michelle Singletary, "Bureau Drafts New Forms to Make Adjustable-Rate Mortgages 'True Costs' Clearer," *The Washington Post,* May 21, 2011; and "Too Big Not to Fail: The Dodd-Frank Act," *The Economist,* February 18, 2012.

28. Douglas A. McIntyre, Ashley C. Allen, Charles B. Stockdale, Michael B. Sauter, and Jonathan Berr, "The 10 States That Profit Most from Sin," *The Atlantic Monthly,* May 16, 2011.

29. John Merline, "Rich Pay Growing Share of Tax," *Investor's Business Daily,* April 27, 2011; and Peter Coy, "Taxation without Complication," *Bloomberg Businessweek,* February 20, 2011.

30. Penelope Lemov, "States Look to Collect Internet Sales Taxes," *Governing,* May 19, 2011; and Janet Novack, "24 States Moving towards Decision on Taxing Groupon, Living-Social Deals," *Forbes,* March 26, 2012.

31. Janet Novack, "Has Amazon Lost the South and Tea Party in Internet Tax War?" *Forbes,* April 29, 2011.

32. Kyung M. Song, "Battle over Internet Sales Taxes Rekindles in Congress," *The Seattle Times,* May 21, 2011.

33. Angie Mohr, "5 Myths about Personal Bankruptcy," *San Francisco Chronicle,* May 5, 2011; and Ian Mount, "Adviser to Businesses Laments Changes to Bankruptcy Law," *The New York Times,* February 29, 2012.

34. www.bankruptcyaction.com, accessed May 2012.

35. Paul M. Barrett, "A New Assault on Regulation Is Gathering Force—and It's Deploying a Constitutional Weapon," *Bloomberg Businessweek,* February 20, 2011; and Wayne Crews, "Why Regulations Aren't Good–Again," Forbes, March 21, 2012.

36. Stephen Breyer, "Airline Deregulation Revisited," *Bloomberg Businessweek,* January 20, 2011; and Joel Millman, "Tiny Airline Cashes In on Small Cities," *The Wall Street Journal,* January 24, 2012.

37. Robert Samuelson, "Stuck in a Post-Crisis Gloom," *The Washington Post,* May 22, 2011; and Charles Gasparino, "More Useless Govt," *The New York Post,* May 22, 2011.

38. Paul Sperry, "Dodd-Frank Red Tape Will Kill 1,000 Small Banks," *Investor's Business Daily,* May 20, 2011; and Sam Batkins, "The Costs of Dodd-Frank? Even the Feds Don't Know," *The Hill,* May 18, 2011.

39. Robert Pear and David M. Herszenhorn, "Obama Hails Vote on Health Care as Answering 'the Call of History,'" *The New York Times,* March 21, 2010; and David Goldstein, "Sebelius Takes the Heat in Debate over Health Care Reform," *The Kansas City Star,* May 21, 2011.

40. "U.S. House of Representatives Votes to Repeal President Obama's Health Care Bill," *The Herald Sun,* January 20, 2011; and Adam Liptak, "On Day 3, Justices Weigh What-Ifs of Health Ruling," *The New York Times,* March 28, 2012.

APPENDIX 2

1. "The Billionaire Issue," *Forbes,* March 28, 2011.

2. "Thinking Your Way to Wealth," *AAA World,* July/August 2010.

3. E. S. Browning, "Retiring Boomers Find 401(K) Plans Fall Short," *The Wall Street Journal,* February 19–20, 2011.

4. "Summoning Reinforcement: Outside Help," *Smart Money,* April 2012.

5. Glenn Townes, "Thrifty Family Living," *Black Enterprise,* March 2011.

6. Paul J. Lim and George Mannes, "How to Reach $1 Million," *Money,* April 2011.

7. Eric C. Meyers, "Trick Yourself into Saving," *Let's Talk Money,* May 2011.

8. Glenn Townes, "Thrifty Family Living," *Black Enterprise,* March 2011.

9. Janet Bodnar, "The College Debt Trap," *Kiplinger's Personal Finance,* December 2010.

10. Kimberly Lankford, "Tying the Knot," *Kiplinger's Personal Finance,* June 2010.

11. James B. Stewart, "Does the Sacred Cow of Home Ownership Make Sense Financially?," *Smart Money,* May 2011.

12. Robert Bridges, "A Home Is a Lousy Investment," *The Wall Street Journal,* July 11, 2011.

13. Marcy Jackson, "Dark Clouds, Silver Lining," *World,* June 16, 2012.

14. Mary Jackson, "Rent or Buy?," *World,* June 16, 2012.

15. J. D. Roth, "Credit Care," *Entrepreneur,* March 2011.

16. "Most Rewarding Cards If . . ." *Money,* May 2011.

17. Angela Wu, "College Credit," *Newsweek,* September 10, 2010.

18. Joan Goldwasser, "Win Rewards for Paying Off Debt," *Kiplinger's Personal Finance,* February 2011.

19. Glenn Townes, "Ingredients for Success," *Black Enterprise,* January 2011.

20. Jeff Wuorio, "Debit Cards Are Great, But Not for Everything," *USA Weekend,* February 18, 2011.

21. Connie Prater, "What the New Credit Card Law Means to You," www.creditcard.com, accessed May 2011.

22. Kimberly Lankford, "Life (Insurance) Begins at 50," *Kiplinger's Personal Finance,* June 2011.

23. Mary Beth Franklin, "The New Look of Retirement," *Kiplinger's Personal Finance,* February 2011.

24. Dallas Salisbury, "Workers Are Waking Up to the New Normal," *The Wall Street Journal,* April 5, 2011.

25. Donna Rosato, "Don't Be Bummed Out, Boomer," *Money,* March 2011.

26. Robert J. Samuelson, "Social Security Is Middle-Class Welfare," *Newsweek,* March 14, 2011.

27. Katherine Boyle, "The Case for Investing Early," *The Washington Post,* May 20, 2012.

28. Ian Salisbury, "Fix Your 401(K)," *Smart Money,* April 2012.

29. "Expanding Your Choices: The 401K-Plus," *Smart Money,* April 2012.

30. Christopher Condon, "The Quiet Force in Personal Finance," *Bloomberg Businessweek,* March 7–13, 2011.

31. Paul Sullivan, "More Money for the Kids," *Fortune,* February 7, 2011.

BONUS CHAPTER A

1. Steve Lohr, "Harnessing the Deluge of Information," *International Herald Tribune,* April 25, 2011.

2. Doug Henschen, "SAP's Blockbuster BusinessObjects Upgrade," *InformationWeek,* March 14, 2011; David Raths, "Business Intelligence Efforts Get a Boost," *Healthcare Informatics,* January 1, 2011; and "Deloitte Announces Alliance Agreement with MicroStrategy to Deliver Business Intelligence and Analytic Solutions, *Computer Weekly News,* March 24, 2011.

3. "CEOs Give Technology Executives Power Tips," *The Wall Street Journal,* May 19, 2011; Shawn Banerji, "The Next Phase of CIO Leadership," *Baseline,* January 1, 2011; Susan Nunziata, "Executive Briefing: Analysis & Insights for the Busy

CIO," *CIO Insight,* March 1, 2011; Robert L. Bailey, "Planning Your Information Career," *Information Management Journal,* January 1, 2011; Chris Murphy, "Create," *InformationWeek,* March 14, 2011; and Ben Kerschberg, "Today's CIO: Where Business Strategy Meets Information Technology," *Forbes,* February 20, 2012.

4. Maryanne MacDonald, "Put an End to Electronic Clutter," *The Commercial Appeal,* March 4, 2011.

5. "Data Mining for Business Intelligence," *Journal of Mathematics,* March 22, 2011; Doug Henschen, "HP's Murky Move Back into Data Warehousing," *InformationWeek,* February 28, 2011; Chris Murphy, "Is Data Mining Free Speech?" *InformationWeek,* May 16, 2011; and Jeremy Quittner, "Big Data or Big Hassle? New SAS Tool Offers Simplicity," *American Banker,* March 30, 2012.

6. Yahoo Pipes, pipes.yahoo.com, accessed May 2012.

7. "IT Service Management Going Social," *CIO,* May 21, 2012.

8. Ed Arnold, "A Second Knock—Sposto Interactive CEO Hears Opportunity Calling Again with Idea for Extranet System," *The Commercial Appeal,* March 14, 2011.

9. Kurt Marko, "How Secure Is Your iPad?" *InformationWeek,* May 12, 2011.

10. Olga Kharif, "Brownnosing for Google Broadband," *Bloomberg Businessweek,* March 11, 2010.

11. Amy Schatz, "Obama Broadband Plan Faces Uncertain Future," *The Wall Street Journal,* February 10, 2011; and Todd Shields, "Airwaves Sharing Proposed between U.S., Wireless Industry," *Bloomberg Businessweek,* March 27, 2012.

12. Stacey Higginbotham, "Broadband Caps: Maybe It's Not Just about TV," *Bloomberg Businessweek,* March 18, 2011; Amy Schatz and Thomas Catan, "AT&T Deal Is Key Test for Obama," *The Wall Street Journal,* March 22, 2011; and Shalini Ramachandran, "Pricing Broadband Appetites," *The Wall Street Journal,* February 28, 2012.

13. Paul Korzeniowski, "Medical Robots Bring Docs to Patients," *Investor's Business Daily,* March 30, 2011.

14. Internet2, www.internet2.edu, accessed May 2012.

15. Douglas MacMillan, "With Friends Like This, Who Needs Facebook?" *Bloomberg Businessweek,* September 13–September 19, 2010; Ben Paynter, "Happy Hour," *Fast Company,* March 2010; and Victoria Barret "The Web's Big Upstart," *Forbes,* September 6, 2010.

16. Jason Daley, "Tearing Down the Walls," *Entrepreneur,* December 2010; and William Wei, "This Interactive Burger Joint May Be the Future of Fast Food," *Business Insider,* May 23, 2012.

17. Sheila Riley, "Social Media Complicating Tech Field's Ethical Issues," *Investor's Business Daily,* March 31, 2011; Jon Newberry "Social Media Create Regulatory Worries for Businesses," *Courier,* February 4, 2011; and Sonia Kolesnikov-Jessop, "Banks Slow to Embrace Social Media," *The New York Times,* March 26, 2012.

18. Doug Henschen, "IT Meets Marketing," *InformationWeek,* April 11, 2011; and Charles Duhigg, "How Companies Learn Your Secrets," *The New York Times,* February 16, 2012.

19. Tony Shaw, "Web 2.0 for Smarter Business," *Baseline,* March 1, 2011.

20. Reinhardt Krauss, "Mobile Pay Spurs Rush to Control Systems," *Investor's Business Daily,* March 30, 2011; Douglas MacMillan, "Turning Smartphones into Cash Registers," *Bloomberg Businessweek,* February 14–February 20, 2011; Pete Barlas, "Mobile Payments Draw a Crowd," *Investor's Business Daily,* March 29, 2011; and David Wolman, "Time for Cash to Cash Out?" *The Wall Street Journal,* February 10, 2012.

21. Michael Green, "Better, Smarter, Faster: Web 3.0 and the Future of Learning," *American Society for Training and Development,* April 1, 2011.

22. K. Rupp and S. Selberherr, " The Economic Limit to Moore's Law," *Semiconductor Manufacturing,* February 2011.

23. Chris Murphy, "Innovation Atrophy," *InformationWeek,* May 30, 2011.

24. Doug Henschen, "They're Ready," *InformationWeek,* February 14, 2011.

25. Bob Evans, "Why CIOs Must Have a Tablet Strategy," *InformationWeek,* March 14, 2011; Robert Cini, "Corporate Technology Experts May Have Some Issues with iPads," *South Florida Business Journal,* January 14, 2011; and Nick Wingfield, "A Vision of a World Dominated by Tablets," *International Herald Tribune,* March 7, 2012.

26. Katie Hoffmann, "IBM Mainframes: Boring but Profitable," *Bloomberg Businessweek,* July 28–August 1, 2010.

27. John Agsalud, "Virtual Desktops Provide Lower Cost, Less Upkeep," *Honolulu Star,* February 22, 2011; and David Stodder, "APM for Virtualization," *InformationWeek,* March 14, 2011.

28. Kurt Eisele-Dyrli, "Expanding Computing with Virtual Desktops," *District Administration,* February 1, 2011; and Quentin Hardy, "A Start-Up Has Plans to Displace the Giants of Networking," *The New York Times,* February 7, 2012.

29. Thomas Claburn, "Google Slows App Rollouts for Businesses," *InformationWeek,* March 28, 2011; Charles Babcock, "What's a Cloud Operating System?" *InformationWeek,* March 28, 2011; and Charles Babcock, "Lessons from FarmVille," *InformationWeek,* May 16, 2011.

30. April Wortham, "Cloud Experts Simplify a Complex Idea," *Houston Business Journal,* January 7, 2011; and Quentin Hardy, "Here Come the Cloud Cartels," *The New York Times,* January 30, 2012.

31. Andrew Binstock, "Cloud Programming? Ready, Set . . . Yow," *InformationWeek,* March 26, 2011; and Charles Babcock, "VMware Tries Integrated Approach to Hybrid Cloud Management," *InformationWeek,* March 28, 2011.

32. Jon Newberry, "A Down-to-Earth Look at Cloud Computing," *Business Courier* (Cincinnati), February 4, 2011; M. O'Bannon, "Three Buzzwords That Really Changed the Profession," *CPA Practice Advisor,* April 1, 2011; Ashlee Vance, "The Power of the Cloud," *Bloomberg Businessweek,* March 7–March 13, 2011; Michal Lev-Ram, "Intel's Sunny Vision for the Cloud," *Fortune,* January 17, 2011; Mickey McManus, "The Madness of the Clouds," *Bloomberg Businessweek,* March 28, 2011; Joseph Galante, "Amazon.com Service Aims to Simplify Cloud Computing," *Bloomberg,* January 19, 2011; and Ashlee Vance, "The Cloud: Battle of the Tech Titans," *Bloomberg Businessweek,* March 3, 2011.

33. Thomas Claburn, "Google Gambles on Chromebooks as a Service," *InformationWeek,* May 30, 2011.

34. Mathew J. Schwartz, "Dropbox Accused of Misleading on Security," *InformationWeek,* May 30, 2011.

35. Gina Smith, "VMware Service Manages Cloud Apps," *InformationWeek,* May 30, 2011; Charles Babcock, "VMware Platform Takes It Deeper into Cloud," *InformationWeek,* April 25, 2011; and Charles Babcock, "VMware's Hybrid Cloud Plan: All in the Family," *InformationWeek,* February 28, 2011.

36. Victoria Barret, "Free Software for Suits," *Forbes,* February 2011; Aaron Ricadela and Cliff Edwards, "Apotheker Pushes HP into Cloud, Software," *Bloomberg Businessweek,* March 15, 2011; Kenneth J. Richard, "Enterprise Software," *InformationWeek,* March 28, 2011; Alexander Wolfe, "IT Pro Ranking," *InformationWeek,* April 11, 2011; and Doug Henschen, "Chatter.com," *InformationWeek,* February 14, 2011.

37. Andrew Conry-Murray, "Your Health? There's an App for That," *InformationWeek,* September 13, 2010; Christianna McCausland, "There's an App Maker for That," *Fast Company,* September 2010; "Top 10 Mobile Apps for Business Collaboration," *InformationWeek,* April 19, 2011; and John Letzing, "Zynga Buys Mobile-Game Sensation 'Draw Something'," *The Wall Street Journal,* March 22, 2012.

38. Marianne Kolbasuk McGee, "Ford Driving Health, Safety with Mobile Apps," *InformationWeek,* May 18, 2011; and Peter Wayner, "Monitoring Your Health with Mobile Devices," *The New York Times,* February 22, 2012.

39. Grant Moerschel, "4 Ways to Lower Mobility Risk," *InformationWeek,* January 31, 2011.

40. Christine Hall, "Dos and Don'ts of IT Security from Houston Experts," *Houston Business Journal,* January 7, 2011; Erik Bataller, "Risk Avengers," *InformationWeek,* January 31, 2011; and Diana Barr, "Passwords, Antivirals Offer Basic Network Protection," *St. Louis Business Journal,* February 24, 2012.

41. Mike Smith, "Information Security," *Mortgage Technology,* March 1, 2011; and Will Daley, "FTC Settles with Game Site for Exposing Users Information," *Bloomberg Businessweek,* March 27, 2012.

42. Mathew J. Schwartz, "Sony Reels from Massive Customer Data Breach," *InformationWeek,* May 16, 2011; Daisuke Wakabayashi, "Accounts Hacked at Small Sony Unit," *The Wall Street Journal,* May 21, 2011; and Devlin Barrett, "U.S. Outgunned in Hacker War," *The Wall Street Journal,* March 28, 2012.

43. "Study Reveals There Is a 'Golden Hour' for Phishing," *Credit Union Journal,* February 7, 2011; and Peter Svensson, "Banks, Card Issuers Warn of E-Mail Breach—Companies Expect Wave of Spam, 'Spear Phishing,'" *The Commerical Appeal,* April 5, 2011.

44. Matt Liebowitz, "Cybercrime Blotter: High Profile Hacks of 2011," *Security News Daily,* February 24, 2011; and Kelly Jackson Higgins, "Hack Highlights Vulnerability," *InformationWeek,* April 11, 2011.

45. Erik Bataller, "Cyber Partnerships," *InformationWeek,* March 28, 2011; and Eric Lichtblau, "Police Are Using Phone Tracking as a Routine Tool," *The New York Times,* March 31, 2012.

46. Platform for Privacy Preferences, www.w3.org/P3P, accessed May 2012.

47. Natasha Singer, "Drawing Some Boundaries around Data Mining," *International Herald Tribune,* May 2, 2011; and Geoffrey A. Fowler, "Tech Giants Agree to Deal on Privacy Policies for Apps," *The Wall Street Journal,* February 22, 2012.

48. Alisa Gumbs, "How Tweet It Is," *Black Enterprise,* December 2010.

BONUS CHAPTER B

1. Leslie P. Norton, "In Japan's Turmoil, There's Fresh Logic in a Logistics Provider," *Barron's,* March 28, 2011.

2. Timothy W. Martin, Thomas M. Burton and Stephanie Simon, "Tornadoes Leave a Trail of Devastation," *The Wall Street Journal,* April 29, 2011.

3. Scott Steinberg, "Protecting Your Business from Identity Theft," *The Costco Connection,* August 2010; and Joan Goldwasser, "Top Gripe: ID Theft," *Kiplinger's Personal Finance,* June 2011.

4. Adrian Sainz and Matt Sedensky, "Memphis Nearing Flood Record," *The Washington Post,* May 10, 2011.

5. "Expecting the Unexpected," advertisement in *Bloomberg Businessweek,* March 7–March 13, 2011.

6. Karan Girotra and Serguei Netessine, "How to Build Risk into Your Business Model," *Harvard Business Review,* May 2011.

7. David Gould, "Running the Risks," *Bloomberg Businessweek,* March 5–March 11, 2012.

8. Andy Pasztor and Peter Sanders, "Boeing Miscalculated Risks," *The Wall Street Journal,* April 6, 2011.

9. Figures are from *GEICO Direct,* Spring/Summer 2010.

10. Dinah Wisenberg Brin, "More Firms Insuring Selves," *The Wall Street Journal,* March 23, 2011.

11. M. P. McQueen, "Disaster Insurance: How Well Are You Covered?" *The Wall Street Journal,* March 26–27, 2011.

12. Joe Mullich, "Sustainability's Third Wave," *The Wall Street Journal,* April 22, 2011.

glossary

401(k) plan (p. A2-15) A savings plan that allows you to deposit pretax dollars and whose earnings compound tax-free until withdrawal, when the money is taxed at ordinary income tax rates.

absolute advantage (p. 62) The advantage that exists when a country has a monopoly on producing a specific product or is able to produce it more efficiently than all other countries.

accounting (p. 498) The recording, classifying, summarizing, and interpreting of financial events and transactions to provide management and other interested parties the information they need to make good decisions.

accounting cycle (p. 503) A six-step procedure that results in the preparation and analysis of the major financial statements.

accounts payable (p. 508) Current liabilities involving money owed to others for merchandise or services purchased on credit but not yet paid for.

acquisition (p. 136) One company's purchase of the property and obligations of another company.

administered distribution system (p. 449) A distribution system in which producers manage all of the marketing functions at the retail level.

administrative agencies (p. A1-3) Federal or state institutions and other government organizations created by Congress or state legislatures with delegated power to pass rules and regulations within their mandated area of authority.

advertising (p. 465) Paid, nonpersonal communication through various media by organizations and individuals who are in some way identified in the advertising message.

affiliate marketing (p. 162) An Internet-based marketing strategy in which a business rewards individuals or other businesses (affiliates) for each visitor or customer the affiliate sends to its website.

affirmative action (p. 312) Employment activities designed to "right past wrongs" by increasing opportunities for minorities and women.

agency shop agreement (p. 350) Clause in a labor–management agreement that says employers may hire nonunion workers; employees are not required to join the union but must pay a union fee.

agents/brokers (p. 435) Marketing intermediaries who bring buyers and sellers together and assist in negotiating an exchange but don't take title to the goods.

American Federation of Labor (AFL) (p. 344) An organization of craft unions that championed fundamental labor issues; founded in 1886.

annual report (p. 500) A yearly statement of the financial condition, progress, and expectations of an organization.

annuity (p. A2-11) A contract to make regular payments to a person for life or for a fixed period.

apprentice programs (p. 322) Training programs involving a period during which a learner works alongside an experienced employee to master the skills and procedures of a craft.

arbitration (p. 353) The agreement to bring in an impartial third party (a single arbitrator or a panel of arbitrators) to render a binding decision in a labor dispute.

assembly process (p. 251) That part of the production process that puts together components.

assets (p. 506) Economic resources (things of value) owned by a firm.

auditing (p. 501) The job of reviewing and evaluating the information used to prepare a company's financial statements.

autocratic leadership (p. 204) Leadership style that involves making managerial decisions without consulting others.

balance of payments (p. 65) The difference between money coming into a country (from exports) and money leaving the country (for imports) plus money flows from other factors such as tourism, foreign aid, military expenditures, and foreign investment.

balance of trade (p. 64) The total value of a nation's exports compared to its imports over a particular period.

balance sheet (p. 506) Financial statement that reports a firm's financial condition at a specific time and is composed of three major accounts: assets, liabilities, and owners' equity.

Note: Terms and definitions printed in italics are considered business slang, or jargon.

ballyhooed   *Talked about in an exaggerated way.*

banker's acceptance (p. 605)   A promise that the bank will pay some specified amount at a particular time.

bankruptcy (p. A1-15)   The legal process by which a person, business, or government entity unable to meet financial obligations is relieved of those obligations by a court that divides any assets among creditors, allowing creditors to get at least part of their money and freeing the debtor to begin anew.

bargaining zone (p. 352)   The range of options between the initial and final offer that each party will consider before negotiations dissolve or reach an impasse.

barter (p. 589)   The direct trading of goods or services for other goods or services.

bear market   *Situation where the stock market is declining in value and investors feel it will continue to decline.*

been there, done that   *Prior experience.*

benchmarking (p. 233)   Comparing an organization's practices, processes, and products against the world's best.

benefit segmentation (p. 391)   Dividing the market by determining which benefits of the product to talk about.

blog (p. 483)   An online diary (weblog) that looks like a web page but is easier to create and update by posting text, photos, or links to other sites.

bond (p. 563)   A corporate certificate indicating that a person has lent money to a firm.

bonds payable (p. 508)   Long-term liabilities that represent money lent to the firm that must be paid back.

bookkeeping (p. 503)   The recording of business transactions.

bottom line   *The last line in a profit and loss statement; it refers to net profit or loss.*

brain drain (p. 42)   The loss of the best and brightest people to other countries.

brainstorming (p. 199)   Coming up with as many solutions to a problem as possible in a short period of time with no censoring of ideas.

brand (p. 413)   A name, symbol, or design (or combination thereof) that identifies the goods or services of one seller or group of sellers and distinguishes them from the goods and services of competitors.

brand association (p. 416)   The linking of a brand to other favorable images.

brand awareness (p. 415)   How quickly or easily a given brand name comes to mind when a product category is mentioned.

brand equity (p. 415)   The value of the brand name and associated symbols.

brand loyalty (p. 415)   The degree to which customers are satisfied, like the brand, and are committed to further purchases.

brand manager (p. 416)   A manager who has direct responsibility for one brand or one product line; called a product manager in some firms.

brand name (p. 382)   A word, letter, or group of words or letters that differentiates one seller's goods and services from those of competitors.

breach of contract (p. A1-10)   When one party fails to follow the terms of a contract.

break-even analysis (p. 424)   The process used to determine profitability at various levels of sales.

brightest days   *The best of times for a person or organization.*

broadband technology (p. A-10)   Technology that offers users a continuous connection to the Internet and allows them to send and receive mammoth files that include voice, video, and data much faster than ever before.

budget (p. 532)   A financial plan that sets forth management's expectations, and, on the basis of those expectations, allocates the use of specific resources throughout the firm.

bull market   *Situation where the stock market is increasing in value and investors feel it will continue to grow.*

bundling (p. 413)   Grouping two or more products together and pricing them as a unit.

bureaucracy (p. 221)   An organization with many layers of managers who set rules and regulations and oversee all decisions.

business (p. 4)   Any activity that seeks to provide goods and services to others while operating at a profit.

business cycles (p. 49)   The periodic rises and falls that occur in economies over time.

business environment (p. 11)   The surrounding factors that either help or hinder the development of businesses.

business intelligence (BI) (p. A-3)   Any of a variety of software applications that analyze an organization's raw data and take out useful insights from it.

business law (p. A1-2)   Rules, statutes, codes, and regulations that are established to provide a legal framework within which business may be conducted and that are enforceable by court action.

business plan (p. 169) A detailed written statement that describes the nature of the business, the target market, the advantages the business will have in relation to competition, and the resources and qualifications of the owner(s).

business-to-business (B2B) market (p. 390) All the individuals and organizations that want goods and services to use in producing other goods and services or to sell, rent, or supply goods to others.

buying stock on margin (p. 571) Purchasing stocks by borrowing some of the purchase cost from the brokerage firm.

cafeteria-style fringe benefits (p. 329) Fringe benefits plan that allows employees to choose the benefits they want up to a certain dollar amount.

cannibalize a business *One franchise pulls business away from another franchise, for example.*

capital budget (p. 532) A budget that highlights a firm's spending plans for major asset purchases that often require large sums of money.

capital expenditures (p. 536) Major investments in either tangible long-term assets such as land, buildings, and equipment or intangible assets such as patents, trademarks, and copyrights.

capital gains (p. 569) The positive difference between the purchase price of a stock and its sale price.

capitalism (p. 35) An economic system in which all or most of the factors of production and distribution are privately owned and operated for profit.

cash-and-carry wholesalers (p. 441) Wholesalers that serve mostly smaller retailers with a limited assortment of products.

cash budget (p. 532) A budget that estimates cash inflows and outflows during a particular period like a month or a quarter.

cash flow (p. 514) The difference between cash coming in and cash going out of a business.

cash flow forecast (p. 531) Forecast that predicts the cash inflows and outflows in future periods, usually months or quarters.

center stage *A very important position.*

centralized authority (p. 222) An organization structure in which decision-making authority is maintained at the top level of management at the company's headquarters.

certificate of deposit (CD) (p. 597) A time-deposit (savings) account that earns interest to be delivered at the end of the certificate's maturity date.

certification (p. 347) Formal process whereby a union is recognized by the National Labor Relations Board (NLRB) as the bargaining agent for a group of employees.

certified internal auditor (CIA) (p. 502) An accountant who has a bachelor's degree and two years of experience in internal auditing, and who has passed an exam administered by the Institute of Internal Auditors.

certified management accountant (CMA) (p. 500) A professional accountant who has met certain educational and experience requirements, passed a qualifying exam in the field, and been certified by the Institute of Certified Management Accountants.

certified public accountant (CPA) (p. 501) An accountant who passes a series of examinations established by the American Institute of Certified Public Accountants (AICPA).

chain of command (p. 221) The line of authority that moves from the top of a hierarchy to the lowest level.

channel of distribution (p. 434) A whole set of marketing intermediaries, such as agents, brokers, wholesalers, and retailers, that join together to transport and store goods in their path (or channel) from producers to consumers.

claim (p. B-6) A statement of loss that the insured sends to the insurance company to request payment.

climate change (p. 19) The movement of the temperature of the planet up or down over time.

climbed the ladder *Promoted to higher-level jobs.*

closed shop agreement (p. 349) Clause in a labor–management agreement that specified workers had to be members of a union before being hired (was outlawed by the Taft-Hartley Act in 1947).

cloud computing (p. A-14) A form of virtualization in which a company's data and applications are stored at offsite data centers that are accessed over the Internet (the cloud).

collective bargaining (p. 346) The process whereby union and management representatives form a labor–management agreement, or contract, for workers.

command economies (p. 43) Economic systems in which the government largely decides what goods and services will be produced, who will get them, and how the economy will grow.

commercial bank (p. 597) A profit-seeking organization that receives deposits from individuals and corporations in the form of checking and savings accounts and then uses some of these funds to make loans.

commercial finance companies (p. 541) Organizations that make short-term loans to borrowers who offer tangible assets as collateral.

commercialization (p. 419) Promoting a product to distributors and retailers to get wide distribution, and developing strong advertising and sales campaigns to generate and maintain interest in the product among distributors and consumers.

commercial paper (p. 542) Unsecured promissory notes of $100,000 and up that mature (come due) in 270 days or less.

common law (p. A1-2) The body of law that comes from decisions handed down by judges; also referred to as unwritten law.

common market (p. 78) A regional group of countries that have a common external tariff, no internal tariffs, and a coordination of laws to facilitate exchange; also called a *trading bloc*. An example is the European Union.

common stock (p. 562) The most basic form of ownership in a firm; it confers voting rights and the right to share in the firm's profits through dividends, if offered by the firm's board of directors.

communism (p. 42) An economic and political system in which the government makes almost all economic decisions and owns almost all the major factors of production.

comparative advantage theory (p. 62) Theory that states that a country should sell to other countries those products that it produces most effectively and efficiently, and buy from other countries those products that it cannot produce as effectively or efficiently.

competition-based pricing (p. 423) A pricing strategy based on what all the other competitors are doing. The price can be set at, above, or below competitors' prices.

compliance-based ethics codes (p. 96) Ethical standards that emphasize preventing unlawful behavior by increasing control and by penalizing wrongdoers.

compressed workweek (p. 331) Work schedule that allows an employee to work a full number of hours per week but in fewer days.

computer-aided design (CAD) (p. 252) The use of computers in the design of products.

computer-aided manufacturing (CAM) (p. 252) The use of computers in the manufacturing of products.

computer-integrated manufacturing (CIM) (p. 253) The uniting of computer-aided design with computer-aided manufacturing.

concept testing (p. 418) Taking a product idea to consumers to test their reactions.

conceptual skills (p. 201) Skills that involve the ability to picture the organization as a whole and the relationship among its various parts.

conglomerate merger (p. 137) The joining of firms in completely unrelated industries.

Congress of Industrial Organizations (CIO) (p. 344) Union organization of unskilled workers; broke away from the American Federation of Labor (AFL) in 1935 and rejoined it in 1955.

consideration (p. A1-9) Something of value; consideration is one of the requirements of a legal contract.

consumerism (p. A1-13) A social movement that seeks to increase and strengthen the rights and powers of buyers in relation to sellers.

consumer market (p. 390) All the individuals or households that want goods and services for personal consumption or use.

consumer price index (CPI) (p. 48) Monthly statistics that measure the pace of inflation or deflation.

contingency planning (p. 199) The process of preparing alternative courses of action that may be used if the primary plans don't achieve the organization's objectives.

contingent workers (p. 319) Workers who do not have the expectation of regular, full-time employment.

continuous process (p. 251) A production process in which long production runs turn out finished goods over time.

contract (p. A1-9) A legally enforceable agreement between two or more parties.

contract law (p. A1-9) Set of laws that specify what constitutes a legally enforceable agreement.

contract manufacturing (p. 68) A foreign country's production of private-label goods to which a domestic company then attaches its brand name or trademark; part of the broad category of *outsourcing*.

contractual distribution system (p. 448) A distribution system in which members are bound to cooperate through contractual agreements.

contrarian approach (p. A2-8) Buying stock when everyone else is selling or vice versa.

controlling (p. 195) A management function that involves establishing clear standards to determine whether or not an organization is progressing toward its goals and objectives, rewarding people for doing a good job, and taking corrective action if they are not.

convenience goods and services (p. 408) Products that the consumer wants to purchase frequently and with a minimum of effort.

conventional (C) corporation (p. 129) A state-chartered legal entity with authority to act and have liability separate from its owners.

cookies (p. A-21)   Pieces of information, such as registration data or user preferences, sent by a website over the Internet to a web browser that the browser software is expected to save and send back to the server whenever the user returns to that website.

cooking the books   *Making accounting information look better than it actually is to outside observers and users of financial information of a company.*

cooling-off period (p. 353)   When workers in a critical industry return to their jobs while the union and management continue negotiations.

cooperative (p. 146)   A business owned and controlled by the people who use it—producers, consumers, or workers with similar needs who pool their resources for mutual gain.

copyright (p. A1-7)   A document that protects a creator's rights to materials such as books, articles, photos, paintings and cartoons.

core competencies (p. 234)   Those functions that the organization can do as well as or better than any other organization in the world.

core time (p. 331)   In a flextime plan, the period when all employees are expected to be at their job stations.

corporate distribution system (p. 448)   A distribution system in which all of the organizations in the channel of distribution are owned by one firm.

corporate philanthropy (p. 99)   The dimension of social responsibility that includes charitable donations.

corporate policy (p. 99)   The dimension of social responsibility that refers to the position a firm takes on social and political issues.

corporate responsibility (p. 99)   The dimension of social responsibility that includes everything from hiring minority workers to making safe products.

corporate social initiatives (p. 99)   Enhanced forms of corporate philanthropy directly related to the company's competencies.

corporate social responsibility (CSR) (p. 98)   A business's concern for the welfare of society.

corporation (p. 122)   A legal entity with authority to act and have liability separate from its owners.

cost of capital (p. 547)   The rate of return a company must earn in order to meet the demands of its lenders and expectations of its equity holders.

cost of goods sold (or cost of goods manufactured) (p. 510)   A measure of the cost of merchandise sold or cost of raw materials and supplies used for producing items for resale.

couch potatoes   *People who sit and watch TV for hours at a time.*

countertrading (p. 74)   A complex form of bartering in which several countries may be involved, each trading goods for goods or services for services.

counting on it   *Expecting it.*

craft union (p. 344)   An organization of skilled specialists in a particular craft or trade.

credit unions (p. 599)   Nonprofit, member-owned financial cooperatives that offer the full variety of banking services to their members.

critical path (p. 263)   In a PERT network, the sequence of tasks that takes the longest time to complete.

cross-functional self-managed teams (p. 230)   Groups of employees from different departments who work together on a long-term basis.

current assets (p. 508)   Items that can or will be converted into cash within one year.

customer relationship management (CRM) (p. 379)   The process of learning as much as possible about customers and doing everything you can over time to satisfy them—or even exceed their expectations—with goods and services.

damages (p. A1-10)   The monetary settlement awarded to a person who is injured by a breach of contract.

database (p. 16)   An electronic storage file for information.

data processing (DP) (p. A-2)   Name for business technology in the 1970s; included technology that supported an existing business and was primarily used to improve the flow of financial information.

dealer (private-label) brands (p. 414)   Products that don't carry the manufacturer's name but carry a distributor or retailer's name instead.

debenture bonds (p. 564)   Bonds that are unsecured (i.e., not backed by any collateral such as equipment).

debit card (p. 604)   An electronic funds transfer tool that serves the same function as checks: it withdraws funds from a checking account.

debt financing (p. 537)   Funds raised through various forms of borrowing that must be repaid.

decentralized authority (p. 222)   An organization structure in which decision-making authority is delegated to lower-level managers more familiar with local conditions than headquarters management could be.

decertification (p. 348)   The process by which workers take away a union's right to represent them.

decision making (p. 198)   Choosing among two or more alternatives.

deflation (p. 47)   A situation in which prices are declining.

demand (p. 37)   The quantity of products that people are willing to buy at different prices at a specific time.

demand deposit (p. 597)   The technical name for a checking account; the money in a demand deposit can be withdrawn anytime on demand from the depositor.

demographic segmentation (p. 391)   Dividing the market by age, income, and education level.

demography (p. 17)   The statistical study of the human population with regard to its size, density, and other characteristics such as age, race, gender, and income.

departmentalization (p. 224)   The dividing of organizational functions into separate units.

depreciation (p. 511)   The systematic write-off of the cost of a tangible asset over its estimated useful life.

depression (p. 49)   A severe recession, usually accompanied by deflation.

deregulation (p. A1-17)   Government withdrawal of certain laws and regulations that seem to hinder competition.

devaluation (p. 74)   Lowering the value of a nation's currency relative to other currencies.

digital natives (p. 235)   Young people who have grown up using the Internet and social networking.

direct marketing (p. 447)   Any activity that directly links manufacturers or intermediaries with the ultimate consumer.

direct selling (p. 446)   Selling to consumers in their homes or where they work.

disability insurance (p. A2-11)   Insurance that pays part of the cost of a long-term sickness or an accident.

discount rate (p. 593)   The interest rate that the Fed charges for loans to member banks.

disinflation (p. 47)   A situation in which price increases are slowing (the inflation rate is declining).

distributed product development (p. 406)   Handing off various parts of your innovation process—often to companies in other countries.

diversification (p. 568)   Buying several different investment alternatives to spread the risk of investing.

dividends (p. 561)   Part of a firm's profits that the firm may distribute to stockholders as either cash payments or additional shares of stock.

double-entry bookkeeping (p. 504)   The practice of writing every business transaction in two places.

Dow Jones Industrial Average (the Dow) (p. 576)   The average cost of 30 selected industrial stocks, used to give an indication of the direction (up or down) of the stock market over time.

drop shippers (p. 441)   Wholesalers that solicit orders from retailers and other wholesalers and have the merchandise shipped directly from a producer to a buyer.

dumping (p. 66)   Selling products in a foreign country at lower prices than those charged in the producing country.

e-commerce (p. 15)   The buying and selling of goods over the Internet.

economic pie   The money available in the economy.

economics (p. 30)   The study of how society chooses to employ resources to produce goods and services and distribute them for consumption among various competing groups and individuals.

economies of scale (p. 218)   The situation in which companies can reduce their production costs if they can purchase raw materials in bulk; the average cost of goods goes down as production levels increase.

electronic funds transfer (EFT) system (p. 603)   A computerized system that electronically performs financial transactions such as making purchases, paying bills, and receiving paychecks.

electronic retailing (p. 445)   Selling goods and services to ultimate customers (e.g., you and me) over the Internet.

e-mail snooped   When someone other than the addressee reads e-mail messages.

embargo (p. 77)   A complete ban on the import or export of a certain product, or the stopping of all trade with a particular country.

empowerment (p. 17)   Giving frontline workers the responsibility, authority, freedom, training, and equipment they need to respond quickly to customer requests.

enabling (p. 207)   Giving workers the education and tools they need to make decisions.

enterprise resource planning (ERP) (p. 259)   A newer version of materials requirement planning (MRP) that combines the computerized functions of all the divisions and subsidiaries of the firm—such as finance, human resources, and order fulfillment—into a single integrated software program that uses a single database.

enterprise zones (p. 163)   Specific geographic areas to which governments try to attract private business investment by offering lower taxes and other government support.

entrepreneur (p. 4)   A person who risks time and money to start and manage a business.

entrepreneurial team (p. 158)   A group of experienced people from different areas of business who join together to form a managerial team with the skills needed to develop, make, and market a new product.

entrepreneurship (p. 154)   Accepting the risk of starting and running a business.

environmental scanning (p. 387)   The process of identifying the factors that can affect marketing success.

equity financing (p. 537)   Money raised from within the firm, from operations or through the sale of ownership in the firm (stock or venture capital).

equity theory (p. 290)   The idea that employees try to maintain equity between inputs and outputs compared to others in similar positions.

ethics (p. 92)   Standards of moral behavior, that is, behavior accepted by society as right versus wrong.

everyday low pricing (EDLP) (p. 425)   Setting prices lower than competitors and then not having any special sales.

exchange rate (p. 74)   The value of one nation's currency relative to the currencies of other countries.

exchange-traded funds (ETFs) (p. 574)   Collections of stocks that are traded on exchanges but are traded more like individual stocks than like mutual funds.

exclusive distribution (p. 445)   Distribution that sends products to only one retail outlet in a given geographic area.

executor (p. A2-16)   A person who assembles and values your estate, files income and other taxes, and distributes assets.

expectancy theory (p. 289)   Victor Vroom's theory that the amount of effort employees exert on a specific task depends on their expectations of the outcome.

exporting (p. 61)   Selling products to another country.

express warranties (p. A1-9)   Specific representations by the seller that buyers rely on regarding the goods they purchase.

external customers (p. 209)   Dealers, who buy products to sell to others, and ultimate customers (or end users), who buy products for their own personal use.

extranet (p. A-9)   A semiprivate network that uses Internet technology and allows more than one company to access the same information or allows people on different servers to collaborate.

extrinsic reward (p. 279)   Something given to you by someone else as recognition for good work; extrinsic rewards include pay increases, praise, and promotions.

facility layout (p. 258)   The physical arrangement of resources (including people) in the production process.

facility location (p. 255)   The process of selecting a geographic location for a company's operations.

factoring (p. 541)   The process of selling accounts receivable for cash.

factors of production (p. 9)   The resources used to create wealth: land, labor, capital, entrepreneurship, and knowledge.

Federal Deposit Insurance Corporation (FDIC) (p. 602)   An independent agency of the U.S. government that insures bank deposits.

finance (p. 528)   The function in a business that acquires funds for the firm and manages those funds within the firm.

financial accounting (p. 500)   Accounting information and analyses prepared for people outside the organization.

financial control (p. 533)   A process in which a firm periodically compares its actual revenues, costs, and expenses with its budget.

financial management (p. 528)   The job of managing a firm's resources so it can meet its goals and objectives.

financial managers (p. 528)   Managers who examine financial data prepared by accountants and recommend strategies for improving the financial performance of the firm.

financial statement (p. 505)   A summary of all the transactions that have occurred over a particular period.

fiscal policy (p. 50)   The federal government's efforts to keep the economy stable by increasing or decreasing taxes or government spending.

fixed assets (p. 508)   Assets that are relatively permanent, such as land, buildings, and equipment.

flat organization structure (p. 224)   An organization structure that has few layers of management and a broad span of control.

flexible manufacturing (p. 243)   Designing machines to do multiple tasks so that they can produce a variety of products.

flextime plan (p. 330)   Work schedule that gives employees some freedom to choose when to work, as long as they work the required number of hours.

focus group (p. 385) A small group of people who meet under the direction of a discussion leader to communicate their opinions about an organization, its products, or other given issues.

foreign direct investment (FDI) (p. 70) The buying of permanent property and businesses in foreign nations.

foreign subsidiary (p. 70) A company owned in a foreign country by another company, called the *parent company.*

formal organization (p. 237) The structure that details lines of responsibility, authority, and position; that is, the structure shown on organization charts.

form utility (p. 251) The value producers add to materials in the creation of finished goods and services.

franchise (p. 138) The right to use a specific business's name and sell its products or services in a given territory.

franchise agreement (p. 138) An arrangement whereby someone with a good idea for a business sells the rights to use the business name and sell a product or service to others in a given territory.

franchisee (p. 138) A person who buys a franchise.

franchisor (p. 138) A company that develops a product concept and sells others the rights to make and sell the products.

free-for-all atmosphere *A situation where all order seems to be lost in conducting business.*

free-market economies (p. 43) Economic systems in which the market largely determines what goods and services get produced, who gets them, and how the economy grows.

free-rein leadership (p. 205) Leadership style that involves managers setting objectives and employees being relatively free to do whatever it takes to accomplish those objectives.

free trade (p. 62) The movement of goods and services among nations without political or economic barriers.

freight forwarder (p. 453) An organization that puts many small shipments together to create a single large shipment that can be transported cost-effectively to the final destination.

fringe benefits (p. 328) Benefits such as sick-leave pay, vacation pay, pension plans, and health plans that represent additional compensation to employees beyond base wages.

from scratch *From the beginning.*

fundamental accounting equation (p. 506) Assets = Liabilities + Owners' equity; this is the basis for the balance sheet.

Gantt chart (p. 264) Bar graph showing production managers what projects are being worked on and what stage they are in at any given time.

General Agreement on Tariffs and Trade (GATT) (p. 77) A 1948 agreement that established an international forum for negotiating mutual reductions in trade restrictions.

general partner (p. 125) An owner (partner) who has unlimited liability and is active in managing the firm.

general partnership (p. 125) A partnership in which all owners share in operating the business and in assuming liability for the business's debts.

generic goods (p. 415) Nonbranded products that usually sell at a sizable discount compared to national or private-label brands.

geographic segmentation (p. 391) Dividing the market by cities, counties, states, or regions.

get in on the dough *Take the opportunity to make some money.*

givebacks (p. 355) Concessions made by union members to management; gains from labor negotiations are given back to management to help employers remain competitive and thereby save jobs.

go for the gold *To work to be the very best (figuratively winning a gold medal).*

go out with me *Go with me to dinner or to a movie or some other entertainment.*

goals (p. 195) The broad, long-term accomplishments an organization wishes to attain.

goal-setting theory (p. 288) The idea that setting ambitious but attainable goals can motivate workers and improve performance if the goals are accepted, accompanied by feedback, and facilitated by organizational conditions.

gone off the deep end *Doing something risky, almost crazy—like jumping into the deep end of a swimming pool when you can't swim.*

goods (p. 4) Tangible products such as computers, food, clothing, cars, and appliances.

goofing off *Doing things at work not associated with the job, such as talking with others at the drinking fountain.*

government and not-for-profit accounting (p. 503) Accounting system for organizations whose purpose is not generating a profit but serving ratepayers, taxpayers, and others according to a duly approved budget.

greening (p. 19) The trend toward saving energy and producing products that cause less harm to the environment.

grievance (p. 351) A charge by employees that management is not abiding by the terms of the negotiated labor–management agreement.

gross domestic product (GDP) (p. 46) The total value of final goods and services produced in a country in a given year.

gross profit (or gross margin) (p. 510) How much a firm earned by buying (or making) and selling merchandise.

hand over the keys *Give access to others.*

hard copy *Copy printed on paper.*

Hawthorne effect (p. 281) The tendency for people to behave differently when they know they are being studied.

health maintenance organizations (HMOs) (p. B-9) Health care organizations that require members to choose from a restricted list of doctors.

health savings accounts (HSAs) (p. B-10) Tax-deferred savings accounts linked to low-cost, high-deductible health insurance policies.

heart *The most important part of something; the central force or idea.*

hierarchy (p. 220) A system in which one person is at the top of the organization and there is a ranked or sequential ordering from the top down of managers who are responsible to that person.

high–low pricing strategy (p. 425) Setting prices that are higher than EDLP stores, but having many special sales where the prices are lower than competitors'.

horizontal merger (p. 136) The joining of two firms in the same industry.

hot second *Immediately.*

human relations skills (p. 201) Skills that involve communication and motivation; they enable managers to work through and with people.

human resource management (HRM) (p. 308) The process of determining human resource needs and then recruiting, selecting, developing, motivating, evaluating, compensating, and scheduling employees to achieve organizational goals.

hygiene factors (p. 284) In Herzberg's theory of motivating factors, job factors that can cause dissatisfaction if missing but that do not necessarily motivate employees if increased.

identity theft (p. 16) The obtaining of individuals' personal information, such as Social Security and credit card numbers, for illegal purposes.

If it isn't broken, don't fix it *Don't risk making things worse by changing things that don't need to be changed.*

implied warranties (p. A1-9) Guarantees legally imposed on the seller.

importing (p. 61) Buying products from another country.

import quota (p. 77) A limit on the number of products in certain categories that a nation can import.

inbound logistics (p. 451) The area of logistics that involves bringing raw materials, packaging, other goods and services, and information from suppliers to producers.

income statement (p. 509) The financial statement that shows a firm's profit after costs, expenses, and taxes; it summarizes all of the resources that have come into the firm (revenue), all the resources that have left the firm (expenses), and the resulting net income or net loss.

incubators (p. 163) Centers that offer new businesses low-cost offices with basic business services.

indenture terms (p. 544) The terms of agreement in a bond issue.

independent audit (p. 502) An evaluation and unbiased opinion about the accuracy of a company's financial statements.

individual retirement account (IRA) (p. A2-13) A tax-deferred investment plan that enables you (and your spouse, if you are married) to save part of your income for retirement; a traditional IRA allows people who qualify to deduct from their reported income the money they put into an account.

industrial goods (p. 410) Products used in the production of other products. Sometimes called business goods or B2B goods.

industrial unions (p. 344) Labor organizations of unskilled and semiskilled workers in mass-production industries such as automobiles and mining.

inflation (p. 47) A general rise in the prices of goods and services over time.

infomercial (p. 470) A full-length TV program devoted exclusively to promoting goods or services.

informal organization (p. 237) The system that develops spontaneously as employees meet and form cliques, relationships, and lines of authority outside the formal organization; that is, the human side of the organization that does not appear on any organization chart.

information systems (IS) (p. A-2) Technology that helps companies do business; includes such tools as automated teller machines (ATMs) and voice mail.

information technology (IT) (p. A-2) Technology that helps companies change business by allowing them to use new methods.

information utility (p. 440) Adding value to products by opening two-way flows of information between marketing participants.

initial public offering (IPO) (p. 557) The first public offering of a corporation's stock.

injunction (p. 354) A court order directing someone to do something or to refrain from doing something.

insider trading (p. 101) An unethical activity in which insiders use private company information to further their own fortunes or those of their family and friends.

institutional investors (p. 557) Large organizations— such as pension funds, mutual funds, and insurance companies—that invest their own funds or the funds of others.

insurable interest (p. B-6) The possibility of the policyholder to suffer a loss.

insurable risk (p. B-5) A risk that the typical insurance company will cover.

insurance policy (p. B-6) A written contract between the insured and an insurance company that promises to pay for all or part of a loss.

intangible assets (p. 508) Long-term assets (e.g., patents, trademarks, copyrights) that have no real physical form but do have value.

integrated marketing communication (IMC) (p. 465) A technique that combines all the promotional tools into one comprehensive and unified promotional strategy.

integrity-based ethics codes (p. 96) Ethical standards that define the organization's guiding values, create an environment that supports ethically sound behavior, and stress a shared accountability among employees.

intensive distribution (p. 444) Distribution that puts products into as many retail outlets as possible.

interactive promotion (p. 470) Promotion process that allows marketers to go beyond a monologue, where sellers try to persuade buyers to buy things, to a dialogue in which buyers and sellers work together to create mutually beneficial exchange relationships.

interest (p. 563) The payment the issuer of the bond makes to the bondholders for use of the borrowed money.

intermittent process (p. 252) A production process in which the production run is short and the machines are changed frequently to make different products.

intermodal shipping (p. 454) The use of multiple modes of transportation to complete a single long-distance movement of freight.

internal customers (p. 209) Individuals and units within the firm that receive services from other individuals or units.

International Monetary Fund (IMF) (p. 606) Organization that assists the smooth flow of money among nations.

Internet2 (p. A-10) The private Internet system that links government supercomputer centers and a select group of universities; it runs more than 22,000 times faster than today's public infrastructure and supports heavy-duty applications.

intranet (p. A-9) A companywide network, closed to public access, that uses Internet-type technology.

intrapreneurs (p. 163) Creative people who work as entrepreneurs within corporations.

intrinsic reward (p. 279) The personal satisfaction you feel when you perform well and complete goals.

inverted organization (p. 235) An organization that has contact people at the top and the chief executive officer at the bottom of the organization chart.

investment bankers (p. 557) Specialists who assist in the issue and sale of new securities.

invisible hand (p. 33) A phrase coined by Adam Smith to describe the process that turns self-directed gain into social and economic benefits for all.

involuntary bankruptcy (p. A1-16) Bankruptcy procedures filed by a debtor's creditors.

IOUs *Debt; abbreviation for "I owe you."*

ISO 14000 (p. 262) A collection of the best practices for managing an organization's impact on the environment.

ISO 9000 (p. 262) The common name given to quality management and assurance standards.

job analysis (p. 314) A study of what is done by employees who hold various job titles.

job description (p. 314) A summary of the objectives of a job, the type of work to be done, the responsibilities and duties, the working conditions, and the relationship of the job to other functions.

job enlargement (p. 292) A job enrichment strategy that involves combining a series of tasks into one challenging and interesting assignment.

job enrichment (p. 291) A motivational strategy that emphasizes motivating the worker through the job itself.

job rotation (p. 292) A job enrichment strategy that involves moving employees from one job to another.

job sharing (p. 332) An arrangement whereby two part-time employees share one full-time job.

job simulation (p. 323) The use of equipment that duplicates job conditions and tasks so that trainees can learn skills before attempting them on the job.

job specifications (p. 314) A written summary of the minimum qualifications required of workers to do a particular job.

joint venture (p. 70) A partnership in which two or more companies (often from different countries) join to undertake a major project.

journal (p. 504) The record book or computer program where accounting data are first entered.

judiciary (p. A1-2) The branch of government chosen to oversee the legal system through a system of courts.

jumped headfirst *Began quickly and eagerly without hesitation.*

junk bonds (p. 572) High-risk, high-interest bonds.

just-in-time (JIT) inventory control (p. 261) A production process in which a minimum of inventory is kept on the premises and parts, supplies, and other needs are delivered just in time to go on the assembly line.

Keynesian economic theory (p. 51) The theory that a government policy of increasing spending and cutting taxes could stimulate the economy in a recession.

key player *Important participant.*

kick back and relax *To take a rest.*

Knights of Labor (p. 344) The first national labor union; formed in 1869.

knockoff brands (p. 415) Illegal copies of national brand-name goods.

know-how *A level of specific expertise.*

knowledge management (p. 207) Finding the right information, keeping the information in a readily accessible place, and making the information known to everyone in the firm.

latchkey kids *School-age children who come home to empty houses since all of the adults are at work.*

law of large numbers (p. B-6) Principle that if a large number of people are exposed to the same risk, a predictable number of losses will occur during a given period of time.

leading (p. 194) Creating a vision for the organization and guiding, training, coaching, and motivating others to work effectively to achieve the organization's goals and objectives.

lean manufacturing (p. 253) The production of goods using less of everything compared to mass production.

ledger (p. 504) A specialized accounting book or computer program in which information from accounting journals is accumulated into specific categories and posted so that managers can find all the information about one account in the same place.

letter of credit (p. 605) A promise by the bank to pay the seller a given amount if certain conditions are met.

level playing field *Treating everyone equally.*

leverage (p. 547) Raising needed funds through borrowing to increase a firm's rate of return.

leveraged buyout (LBO) (p. 137) An attempt by employees, management, or a group of investors to purchase an organization primarily through borrowing.

liabilities (p. 508) What the business owes to others (debts).

licensing (p. 66) A global strategy in which a firm (the licensor) allows a foreign company (the licensee) to produce its product in exchange for a fee (a royalty).

limited liability (p. 125) The responsibility of a business's owners for losses only up to the amount they invest; limited partners and shareholders (stockholders) have limited liability.

limited liability company (LLC) (p. 134) A company similar to an S corporation but without the special eligibility requirements.

limited liability partnership (LLP) (p. 125) A partnership that limits partners' risk of losing their personal assets to only their own acts and omissions and to the acts and omissions of people under their supervision.

limited partner (p. 125) An owner who invests money in the business but does not have any management responsibility or liability for losses beyond the investment.

limited partnership (p. 125) A partnership with one or more general partners and one or more limited partners.

line of credit (p. 540) A given amount of unsecured short-term funds a bank will lend to a business, provided the funds are readily available.

line organization (p. 227) An organization that has direct two-way lines of responsibility, authority, and communication running from the top to the bottom of the organization, with all people reporting to only one supervisor.

line personnel (p. 228) Employees who are part of the chain of command that is responsible for achieving organizational goals.

liquidity (p. 508) The ease with which an asset can be converted into cash.

lockout (p. 354) An attempt by management to put pressure on unions by temporarily closing the business.

logistics (p. 451) The marketing activity that involves planning, implementing, and controlling the physical flow of materials, final goods, and related information from points of origin to points of consumption to meet customer requirements at a profit.

long-term financing (p. 537) Funds needed for more than a year (usually 2 to 10 years).

long-term forecast (p. 532) Forecast that predicts revenues, costs, and expenses for a period longer than 1 year, and sometimes as far as 5 or 10 years into the future.

loss (p. 4) When a business's expenses are more than its revenues.

M-1 (p. 590) Money that can be accessed quickly and easily (coins and paper money, checks, traveler's checks, etc.).

M-2 (p. 590) Money included in M-1 plus money that may take a little more time to obtain (savings accounts, money market accounts, mutual funds, certificates of deposit, etc.).

M-3 (p. 590) M-2 plus big deposits like institutional money market funds.

Ma Bell *Telecommunication giant, AT&T.*

macroeconomics (p. 30) The part of economics study that looks at the operation of a nation's economy as a whole.

management (p. 193) The process used to accomplish organizational goals through planning, organizing, leading, and controlling people and other organizational resources.

management by objectives (MBO) (p. 288) Peter Drucker's system of goal setting and implementation; it involves a cycle of discussion, review, and evaluation of objectives among top and middle-level managers, supervisors, and employees.

management development (p. 323) The process of training and educating employees to become good managers and then monitoring the progress of their managerial skills over time.

managerial accounting (p. 499) Accounting used to provide information and analyses to managers within the organization to assist them in decision making.

manufacturers' brands (p. 414) The brand names of manufacturers that distribute products nationally.

market (p. 175) People with unsatisfied wants and needs who have both the resources and the willingness to buy.

marketing (p. 376) The activity, set of institutions, and processes for creating, communicating, delivering, and exchanging offerings that have value for customers, clients, partners, and society at large.

marketing concept (p. 378) A three-part business philosophy: (1) a customer orientation, (2) a service orientation, and (3) a profit orientation.

marketing intermediaries (p. 434) Organizations that assist in moving goods and services from producers to businesses (B2B) and from businesses to consumers (B2C).

marketing mix (p. 380) The ingredients that go into a marketing program: product, price, place, and promotion.

marketing research (p. 384) The analysis of markets to determine opportunities and challenges, and to find the information needed to make good decisions.

market price (p. 38) The price determined by supply and demand.

market segmentation (p. 390) The process of dividing the total market into groups whose members have similar characteristics.

marriage of software, hardware, etc. *Combination of various technologies.*

Maslow's hierarchy of needs (p. 282) Theory of motivation based on unmet human needs from basic physiological needs to safety, social, and esteem needs to self-actualization needs.

mass customization (p. 254) Tailoring products to meet the needs of individual customers.

mass marketing (p. 393) Developing products and promotions to please large groups of people.

master limited partnership (MLP) (p. 125) A partnership that looks much like a corporation (in that it acts like a corporation and is traded on a stock exchange) but is taxed like a partnership and thus avoids the corporate income tax.

materials handling (p. 451) The movement of goods within a warehouse, from warehouses to the factory floor, and from the factory floor to various workstations.

materials requirement planning (MRP) (p. 259) A computer-based operations management system that uses sales forecasts to make sure that needed parts and materials are available at the right time and place.

matrix organization (p. 229) An organization in which specialists from different parts of the organization are brought together to work on specific projects but still remain part of a line-and-staff structure.

maturity date (p. 563) The exact date the issuer of a bond must pay the principal to the bondholder.

measuring stick *Tool used to evaluate or compare something.*

mediation (p. 353) The use of a third party, called a mediator, who encourages both sides in a dispute to continue negotiating and often makes suggestions for resolving the dispute.

mentor (p. 324) An experienced employee who supervises, coaches, and guides lower-level employees by introducing them to the right people and generally being their organizational sponsor.

merchant wholesalers (p. 441) Independently owned firms that take title to the goods they handle.

merger (p. 136) The result of two firms forming one company.

Mickey D's *Nickname for McDonald's.*

microeconomics (p. 30) The part of economics study that looks at the behavior of people and organizations in particular markets.

micropreneurs (p. 158) Entrepreneurs willing to accept the risk of starting and managing the type of business that remains small, lets them do the kind of work they want to do, and offers them a balanced lifestyle.

middle management (p. 200) The level of management that includes general managers, division managers, and branch and plant managers who are responsible for tactical planning and controlling.

mine the knowledge *Make maximum use of the knowledge employees have.*

mission statement (p. 195) An outline of the fundamental purposes of an organization.

mixed economies (p. 43) Economic systems in which some allocation of resources is made by the market and some by the government.

monetary policy (p. 51) The management of the money supply and interest rates by the Federal Reserve Bank.

money (p. 589) Anything that people generally accept as payment for goods and services.

money supply (p. 590) The amount of money the Federal Reserve Bank makes available for people to buy goods and services.

monopolistic competition (p. 39) The degree of competition in which a large number of sellers produce very similar products that buyers nevertheless perceive as different.

monopoly (p. 40) A degree of competition in which only one seller controls the total supply of a product or service, and sets the price.

more than meets the eye *More than one can see with his or her own eyes; much is happening that is not visible.*

motivators (p. 283) In Herzberg's theory of motivating factors, job factors that cause employees to be productive and that give them satisfaction.

mouse-click away *Ease of doing something by using the computer or Internet.*

muddy the water *Making things even more difficult than they currently are.*

multinational corporation (p. 71) An organization that manufactures and markets products in many different countries and has multinational stock ownership and multinational management.

mutual fund (p. 573) An organization that buys stocks and bonds and then sells shares in those securities to the public.

mutual insurance company (p. B-7) A type of insurance company owned by its policyholders.

NASDAQ (p. 558) A nationwide electronic system that communicates over-the-counter trades to brokers.

national debt (p. 50) The sum of government deficits over time.

negligence (p. A1-4) In tort law, behavior that causes unintentional harm or injury.

negotiable instruments (p. A1-9) Forms of commercial paper (such as checks) that are transferable among businesses and individuals and represent a promise to pay a specified amount.

negotiated labor–management agreement (labor contract) (p. 349) Agreement that sets the tone and clarifies the terms under which management and labor agree to function over a period of time.

net income or net loss (p. 509) Revenue left over after all costs and expenses, including taxes, are paid.

network computing system (or client/server computing) (p. A-14) Computer systems that allow personal computers (clients) to obtain needed information from huge databases in a central computer (the server).

networking (pp. 231, 324) The process of establishing and maintaining contacts with key managers in one's own organization and other organizations and using those contacts to weave strong relationships that serve as informal development systems.

niche marketing (p. 392) The process of finding small but profitable market segments and designing or finding products for them.

nonbanks (p. 600) Financial organizations that accept no deposits but offer many of the services provided by regular banks (pension funds, insurance companies, commercial finance companies, consumer finance companies, and brokerage houses).

nonprofit organization (p. 7) An organization whose goals do not include making a personal profit for its owners or organizers.

North American Free Trade Agreement (NAFTA) (p. 79) Agreement that created a free-trade area among the United States, Canada, and Mexico.

notes payable (p. 508) Short-term or long-term liabilities that a business promises to repay by a certain date.

objectives (p. 195) Specific, short-term statements detailing how to achieve the organization's goals.

off-the-job training (p. 322) Training that occurs away from the workplace and consists of internal or external programs to develop any of a variety of skills or to foster personal development.

oligopoly (p. 39) A degree of competition in which just a few sellers dominate the market.

one-to-one marketing (p. 393) Developing a unique mix of goods and services for each individual customer.

online training (p. 322) Training programs in which employees complete classes via the Internet.

on-the-job training (p. 321) Training at the workplace that lets the employee learn by doing or by watching others for a while and then imitating them.

open-market operations (p. 593) The buying and selling of U.S. government bonds by the Fed with the goal of regulating the money supply.

open shop agreement (p. 351) Agreement in right-to-work states that gives workers the option to join or not join a union, if one exists in their workplace.

operating (or master) budget (p. 532) The budget that ties together the firm's other budgets and summarizes its proposed financial activities.

operating expenses (p. 511) Costs involved in operating a business, such as rent, utilities, and salaries.

operational planning (p. 197) The process of setting work standards and schedules necessary to implement the company's tactical objectives.

operations management (p. 249) A specialized area in management that converts or transforms resources (including human resources) into goods and services.

organizational (or corporate) culture (p. 236) Widely shared values within an organization that provide unity and cooperation to achieve common goals.

organization chart (p. 221) A visual device that shows relationships among people and divides the organization's work; it shows who is accountable for the completion of specific work and who reports to whom.

organizing (p. 194) A management function that includes designing the structure of the organization and creating conditions and systems in which everyone and everything work together to achieve the organization's goals and objectives.

orientation (p. 321) The activity that introduces new employees to the organization; to fellow employees; to their immediate supervisors; and to the policies, practices, and objectives of the firm.

other side of the tracks *The area where people with less money live.*

out of the office loop *Out of the line of communication that occurs in the workplace.*

outbound logistics (p. 451) The area of logistics that involves managing the flow of finished products and information to business buyers and ultimate consumers (people like you and me).

outsourcing (p. 6) Contracting with other companies (often in other countries) to do some or all of the functions of a firm, like its production or accounting tasks.

over-the-counter (OTC) market (p. 558) Exchange that provides a means to trade stocks not listed on the national exchanges.

owners' equity (p. 508) The amount of the business that belongs to the owners minus any liabilities owed by the business.

participative (democratic) leadership (p. 204) Leadership style that consists of managers and employees working together to make decisions.

partnership (p. 122) A legal form of business with two or more owners.

patent (p. A1-6) A document that gives inventors exclusive rights to their inventions for 20 years.

pave the way *Process of making a task easier.*

peanut butter and jelly *Popular combination for a sandwich; the two are seen as perfect complementary products.*

penetration strategy (p. 424) Strategy in which a product is priced low to attract many customers and discourage competition.

pension funds (p. 600) Amounts of money put aside by corporations, nonprofit organizations, or unions to cover part of the financial needs of members when they retire.

perfect competition (p. 39) The degree of competition in which there are many sellers in a market and none is large enough to dictate the price of a product.

performance appraisal (p. 325) An evaluation that measures employee performance against established standards in order to make decisions about promotions, compensation, training, or termination.

perks *Short for* perquisites; *compensation in addition to salary, such as day care or a company car.*

personal selling (p. 474) The face-to-face presentation and promotion of goods and services.

pick economy (p. 485) Customers who pick out their products from online outlets or who do online comparison shopping.

piece of the action *A share in the opportunity.*

pink slip *A notice that you've lost your job.*

pitch in *To help as needed.*

place utility (p. 439) Adding value to products by having them where people want them.

planning (p. 193) A management function that includes anticipating trends and determining the best strategies and tactics to achieve organizational goals and objectives.

PMI (p. 199) Listing all the pluses for a solution in one column, all the minuses in another, and the implications in a third column.

podcasting (p. 483) A means of distributing audio and video programs via the Internet that lets users subscribe to a number of files, also known as feeds, and then hear or view the material at the time they choose.

possession utility (p. 440) Doing whatever is necessary to transfer ownership from one party to another, including providing credit, delivery, installation, guarantees, and follow-up service.

poster child *Best example.*

precedent (p. A1-3) Decisions judges have made in earlier cases that guide the handling of new cases.

preferred provider organizations (PPOs) (p. B-10) Health care organizations similar to HMOs except that they allow members to choose their own physicians (for a fee).

preferred stock (p. 563) Stock that gives its owners preference in the payment of dividends and an earlier claim on assets than common stockholders if the company is forced out of business and its assets sold.

premium (p. B-6) The fee charged by an insurance company for an insurance policy.

price leadership (p. 423) The strategy by which one or more dominant firms set the pricing practices that all competitors in an industry follow.

primary boycott (p. 353) When a union encourages both its members and the general public not to buy the products of a firm involved in a labor dispute.

primary data (p. 385) Data that you gather yourself (not from secondary sources such as books and magazines).

principle of motion economy (p. 280) Theory developed by Frank and Lillian Gilbreth that every job can be broken down into a series of elementary motions.

private accountant (p. 500) An accountant who works for a single firm, government agency, or nonprofit organization.

problem solving (p. 199) The process of solving the everyday problems that occur. Problem solving is less formal than decision making and usually calls for quicker action.

process manufacturing (p. 251) That part of the production process that physically or chemically changes materials.

producer price index (PPI) (p. 48) An index that measures prices at the wholesale level.

product (p. 381) Any physical good, service, or idea that satisfies a want or need plus anything that would enhance the product in the eyes of consumers, such as the brand name.

product analysis (p. 418) Making cost estimates and sales forecasts to get a feeling for profitability of new-product ideas.

product differentiation (p. 408) The creation of real or perceived product differences.

production (p. 248) The creation of finished goods and services using the factors of production: land, labor, capital, entrepreneurship, and knowledge.

production management (p. 248) The term used to describe all the activities managers do to help their firms create goods.

productivity (p. 15) The amount of output you generate given the amount of input (e.g., hours worked).

product liability (p. A1-4) Part of tort law that holds businesses liable for harm that results from the production, design, sale, or use of products they market.

product life cycle (p. 419) A theoretical model of what happens to sales and profits for a product class over time; the four stages of the cycle are introduction, growth, maturity, and decline.

product line (p. 407) A group of products that are physically similar or are intended for a similar market.

product mix (p. 408) The combination of product lines offered by a manufacturer.

product placement (p. 469) Putting products into TV shows and movies where they will be seen.

product screening (p. 417) A process designed to reduce the number of new-product ideas being worked on at any one time.

profit (p. 4) The amount of money a business earns above and beyond what it spends for salaries and other expenses.

program evaluation and review technique (PERT) (p. 263) A method for analyzing the tasks involved in completing a given project, estimating the time needed to complete each task, and identifying the minimum time needed to complete the total project.

program trading (p. 578) Giving instructions to computers to automatically sell if the price of a stock dips to a certain point to avoid potential losses.

promissory note (p. 538) A written contract with a promise to pay a supplier a specific sum of money at a definite time.

promotion (p. 383) All the techniques sellers use to inform people about and motivate them to buy their products or services.

promotion mix (p. 464) The combination of promotional tools an organization uses.

pros and cons *Arguments for and against something.*

prospect (p. 475) A person with the means to buy a product, the authority to buy, and the willingness to listen to a sales message.

prospecting (p. 475) Researching potential buyers and choosing those most likely to buy.

prospectus (p. 559) A condensed version of economic and financial information that a company must file with the SEC before issuing stock; the prospectus must be sent to prospective investors.

psychographic segmentation (p. 391) Dividing the market using the group's values, attitudes, and interests.

psychological pricing (p. 425) Pricing goods and services at price points that make the product appear less expensive than it is.

public accountant (p. 500) An accountant who provides accounting services to individuals or businesses on a fee basis.

public domain software (or freeware) (p. A-16) Software that is free for the taking.

publicity (p. 479) Any information about an individual, product, or organization that's distributed to the public through the media and that's not paid for or controlled by the seller.

public relations (PR) (p. 478) The management function that evaluates public attitudes, changes policies and procedures in response to the public's requests, and executes a program of action and information to earn public understanding and acceptance.

pull strategy (p. 485) Promotional strategy in which heavy advertising and sales promotion efforts are directed toward consumers so that they'll request the products from retailers.

pump up the profits *Making profits in a company appear larger than they actually are under recognized accounting rules.*

purchasing (p. 259) The function in a firm that searches for quality material resources, finds the best suppliers, and negotiates the best price for goods and services.

pure risk (p. B-3) The threat of loss with no chance for profit.

push strategy (p. 484) Promotional strategy in which the producer uses advertising, personal selling, sales promotion, and all other promotional tools to convince wholesalers and retailers to stock and sell merchandise.

qualifying (p. 475) In the selling process, making sure that people have a need for the product, the authority to buy, and the willingness to listen to a sales message.

quality (p. 261) Consistently producing what the customer wants while reducing errors before and after delivery to the customer.

quality of life (p. 6) The general well-being of a society in terms of its political freedom, natural environment, education, health care, safety, amount of leisure, and rewards that add to the satisfaction and joy that other goods and services provide.

quid pro quo *Latin phrase meaning "something given in return for something else."*

quite a stir *Something that causes a feeling of concern.*

rack jobbers (p. 441) Wholesalers that furnish racks or shelves full of merchandise to retailers, display products, and sell on consignment.

ratio analysis (p. 515) The assessment of a firm's financial condition using calculations and interpretations of financial ratios developed from the firm's financial statements.

real time (p. 231) The present moment or the actual time in which something takes place.

recession (p. 49) Two or more consecutive quarters of decline in the GDP.

recruitment (p. 315) The set of activities used to obtain a sufficient number of the right people at the right time.

reinforcement theory (p. 290) Theory that positive and negative reinforcers motivate a person to behave in certain ways.

relationship marketing (p. 393) Marketing strategy with the goal of keeping individual customers over time by offering them products that exactly meet their requirements.

reserve requirement (p. 593) A percentage of commercial banks' checking and savings accounts that must be physically kept in the bank.

resource development (p. 31) The study of how to increase resources and to create the conditions that will make better use of those resources.

restructuring (p. 235) Redesigning an organization so that it can more effectively and efficiently serve its customers.

retailer (p. 435) An organization that sells to ultimate consumers.

retained earnings (p. 509) The accumulated earnings from a firm's profitable operations that were reinvested in the business and not paid out to stockholders in dividends.

revenue (p. 4) The total amount of money a business takes in during a given period by selling goods and services.

reverse discrimination (p. 312) Discrimination against whites or males in hiring or promoting.

reverse logistics (p. 452) The area of logistics that involves bringing goods back to the manufacturer because of defects or for recycling materials.

revolving credit agreement (p. 540) A line of credit that is guaranteed but usually comes with a fee.

right-to-work laws (p. 350) Legislation that gives workers the right, under an open shop, to join or not join a union if it is present.

risk (p. 5) The chance an entrepreneur takes of losing time and money on a business that may not prove profitable.

risk (p. B-3) The chance of loss, the degree of probability of loss, and the amount of possible loss.

risk/return trade-off (p. 544) The principle that the greater the risk a lender takes in making a loan, the higher the interest rate required.

Roth IRA (p. A2-14) An IRA where you don't get up-front deductions on your taxes as you would with a traditional IRA, but the earnings grow tax-free and are also tax-free when they are withdrawn.

rule of indemnity (p. B-7) Rule saying that an insured person or organization cannot collect more than the actual loss from an insurable risk.

rules-of-the-road orientation *Introduction to the proper procedures within an organization.*

sales promotion (p. 479) The promotional tool that stimulates consumer purchasing and dealer interest by means of short-term activities.

sampling (p. 481) A promotional tool in which a company lets consumers have a small sample of a product for no charge.

savings and loan association (S&L) (p. 598) A financial institution that accepts both savings and checking deposits and provides home mortgage loans.

Savings Association Insurance Fund (SAIF) (p. 603) The part of the FDIC that insures holders of accounts in savings and loan associations.

scientific management (p. 279) Studying workers to find the most efficient ways of doing things and then teaching people those techniques.

S corporation (p. 133) A unique government creation that looks like a corporation but is taxed like sole proprietorships and partnerships.

sea of information *Lots of information, often too much to process.*

secondary boycott (p. 354) An attempt by labor to convince others to stop doing business with a firm that is the subject of a primary boycott; prohibited by the Taft-Hartley Act.

222222

secondary data (p. 385) Information that has already been compiled by others and published in journals and books or made available online.

secured bond (p. 545) A bond issued with some form of collateral.

secured loan (p. 539) A loan backed by collateral, something valuable such as property.

Securities and Exchange Commission (SEC) (p. 559) Federal agency that has responsibility for regulating the various exchanges.

selection (p. 319) The process of gathering information and deciding who should be hired, under legal guidelines, for the best interests of the individual and the organization.

selective distribution (p. 444) Distribution that sends products to only a preferred group of retailers in an area.

self-insurance (p. B-4) The practice of setting aside money to cover routine claims and buying only "catastrophe" policies to cover big losses.

Service Corps of Retired Executives (SCORE) (p. 177) An SBA office with volunteers from industry, trade associations, and education who counsel small businesses at no cost (except for expenses).

services (p. 4) Intangible products (i.e., products that can't be held in your hand) such as education, health care, insurance, recreation, and travel and tourism.

service utility (p. 440) Adding value by providing fast, friendly service during and after the sale and by teaching customers how to best use products over time.

sexual harassment (p. 359) Unwelcome sexual advances, requests for sexual favors, and other conduct (verbal or physical) of a sexual nature that creates a hostile work environment.

shaky ground *Idea that possible problems lie ahead.*

shareware (p. A-16) Software that is copyrighted but distributed to potential customers free of charge.

Sherlock Holmes *A famous fictional detective who was particularly adept at uncovering information to solve very difficult mysteries.*

shoestring budget *A budget that implies the company is short on funds and only includes a minimal amount of financial expenditures (i.e., it's as thin as a shoestring).*

shopping goods and services (p. 409) Those products that the consumer buys only after comparing value, quality, price, and style from a variety of sellers.

shop stewards (p. 351) Union officials who work permanently in an organization and represent employee interests on a daily basis.

short-term financing (p. 537) Funds needed for a year or less.

short-term forecast (p. 531) Forecast that predicts revenues, costs, and expenses for a period of one year or less.

sift through mountains of information *Sort through large volumes of information.*

sin taxes *Taxes used to discourage the use of goods like liquor or cigarettes.*

sinking fund (p. 565) A reserve account in which the issuer of a bond periodically retires some part of the bond principal prior to maturity so that enough capital will be accumulated by the maturity date to pay off the bond.

Six Sigma quality (p. 261) A quality measure that allows only 3.4 defects per million opportunities.

skimming price strategy (p. 424) Strategy in which a new product is priced high to make optimum profit while there's little competition.

small business (p. 165) A business that is independently owned and operated, is not dominant in its field of operation, and meets certain standards of size (set by the Small Business Administration) in terms of employees or annual receipts.

Small Business Administration (SBA) (p. 173) A U.S. government agency that advises and assists small businesses by providing management training and financial advice and loans.

Small Business Investment Company (SBIC) Program (p. 174) A program through which private investment companies licensed by the Small Business Administration lend money to small businesses.

smart card (p. 604) An electronic funds transfer tool that is a combination credit card, debit card, phone card, driver's license card, and more.

smoking gun *An issue or other disclosure that could prove a person or organization has done something wrong.*

social audit (p. 104) A systematic evaluation of an organization's progress toward implementing socially responsible and responsive programs.

Social Security (p. A2-12) The term used to describe the Old-Age, Survivors, and Disability Insurance Program established by the Social Security Act of 1935.

socialism (p. 41) An economic system based on the premise that some, if not most, basic businesses should be owned by the government so that profits can be more evenly distributed among the people.

sole proprietorship (p. 122) A business that is owned, and usually managed, by one person.

sovereign wealth funds (SWFs) (p. 72) Investment funds controlled by governments holding large stakes in foreign companies.

span of control (p. 223) The optimum number of subordinates a manager supervises or should supervise.

specialty goods and services (p. 409) Consumer products with unique characteristics and brand identity. Because these products are perceived as having no reasonable substitute, the consumer puts forth a special effort to purchase them.

speculative risk (p. B-3) A chance of either profit or loss.

squeezing franchisees' profits *Tightening or reducing profits.*

staffing (p. 202) A management function that includes hiring, motivating, and retaining the best people available to accomplish the company's objectives.

staff personnel (p. 228) Employees who advise and assist line personnel in meeting their goals.

stagflation (p. 48) A situation when the economy is slowing but prices are going up anyhow.

stakeholders (p. 6) All the people who stand to gain or lose by the policies and activities of a business and whose concerns the business needs to address.

standard of living (p. 5) The amount of goods and services people can buy with the money they have.

state-of-the-art *The most modern type available.*

statement of cash flows (p. 512) Financial statement that reports cash receipts and disbursements related to a firm's three major activities: operations, investments, and financing.

statistical process control (SPC) (p. 261) The process of taking statistical samples of product components at each stage of the production process and plotting those results on a graph. Any variances from quality standards are recognized and can be corrected if beyond the set standards.

statistical quality control (SQC) (p. 261) The process some managers use to continually monitor all phases of the production process to assure that quality is being built into the product from the beginning.

statutory law (p. A1-2) State and federal constitutions, legislative enactments, treaties of the federal government, and ordinances—in short, written law.

staying afloat *Staying in business during tough times.*

stockbroker (p. 566) A registered representative who works as a market intermediary to buy and sell securities for clients.

stock certificate (p. 561) Evidence of stock ownership that specifies the name of the company, the number of shares it represents, and the type of stock being issued.

stock exchange (p. 557) An organization whose members can buy and sell (exchange) securities for companies and investors.

stock insurance company (p. B-7) A type of insurance company owned by stockholders.

stocks (p. 561) Shares of ownership in a company.

stock splits (p. 570) An action by a company that gives stockholders two or more shares of stock for each one they own.

strategic alliance (p. 70) A long-term partnership between two or more companies established to help each company build competitive market advantages.

strategic planning (p. 196) The process of determining the major goals of the organization and the policies and strategies for obtaining and using resources to achieve those goals.

strict product liability (p. A1-5) Legal responsibility for harm or injury caused by a product regardless of fault.

strike (p. 353) A union strategy in which workers refuse to go to work; the purpose is to further workers' objectives after an impasse in collective bargaining.

strikebreakers (p. 355) Workers hired to do the jobs of striking workers until the labor dispute is resolved.

supervisory management (p. 200) Managers who are directly responsible for supervising workers and evaluating their daily performance.

supply (p. 37) The quantity of products that manufacturers or owners are willing to sell at different prices at a specific time.

supply chain (or value chain) (p. 449) The sequence of linked activities that must be performed by various organizations to move goods from the sources of raw materials to ultimate consumers.

supply-chain management (p. 449) The process of managing the movement of raw materials, parts, work in progress, finished goods, and related information through all the organizations involved in the supply chain; managing the return of such goods, if necessary; and recycling materials when appropriate.

SWOT analysis (p. 196) A planning tool used to analyze an organization's strengths, weaknesses, opportunities, and threats.

tactical planning (p. 197) The process of developing detailed, short-term statements about what is to be done, who is to do it, and how it is to be done.

take a break   *To slow down and do something besides work.*

tall organization structure (p. 223)   An organizational structure in which the pyramidal organization chart would be quite tall because of the various levels of management.

target costing (p. 423)   Designing a product so that it satisfies customers and meets the profit margins desired by the firm.

target marketing (p. 390)   Marketing directed toward those groups (market segments) an organization decides it can serve profitably.

tariff (p. 76)   A tax imposed on imports.

tax accountant (p. 502)   An accountant trained in tax law and responsible for preparing tax returns or developing tax strategies.

tax-deferred contributions (p. A2-13)   Retirement account deposits for which you pay no current taxes, but the earnings gained are taxed as regular income when they are withdrawn at retirement.

taxes (p. A1-14)   How the government (federal, state, and local) raises money.

technical skills (p. 201)   Skills that involve the ability to perform tasks in a specific discipline or department.

technology (p. 14)   Everything from phones and copiers to computers, medical imaging devices, personal digital assistants, and the various software programs that make business processes more effective, efficient, and productive.

telecom   *Short for telecommunications.*

telecommuting (p. 258)   Working from home via computer and modem.

telemarketing (p. 446)   The sale of goods and services by telephone.

telephone tag   *To leave a telephone message when you attempt to return a message left for you.*

term insurance (p. A2-10)   Pure insurance protection for a given number of years.

term-loan agreement (p. 543)   A promissory note that requires the borrower to repay the loan in specified installments.

test marketing (p. 382)   The process of testing products among potential users.

thorny issue   *An issue that can cause pain or difficulty (as a thorn on a rose bush may).*

through the grapevine   *Informal information communication; stories told by one person to the next.*

time deposit (p. 597)   The technical name for a savings account; the bank can require prior notice before the owner withdraws money from a time deposit.

time in the trenches   *Working with the other employees and experiencing what they contend with as opposed to managing from an office and relying solely on reports about what is happening in the workplace.*

time-motion studies (p. 280)   Studies, begun by Frederick Taylor, of which tasks must be performed to complete a job and the time needed to do each task.

time utility (p. 439)   Adding value to products by making them available when they're needed.

top management (p. 199)   The highest level of management, consisting of the president and other key company executives who develop strategic plans.

tort (p. A1-4)   A wrongful act that causes injury to another person's body, property, or reputation.

total fixed costs (p. 424)   All the expenses that remain the same no matter how many products are made or sold.

total product offer (p. 406)   Everything that consumers evaluate when deciding whether to buy something; also called a *value package.*

trade credit (p. 538)   The practice of buying goods and services now and paying for them later.

trade deficit (p. 64)   An unfavorable balance of trade; occurs when the value of a country's imports exceeds that of its exports.

trademark (p. 413)   A brand that has exclusive legal protection for both its brand name and its design.

trade protectionism (p. 76)   The use of government regulations to limit the import of goods and services.

trade surplus (p. 64)   A favorable balance of trade; occurs when the value of a country's exports exceeds that of its imports.

training and development (p. 320)   All attempts to improve productivity by increasing an employee's ability to perform. Training focuses on short-term skills, whereas development focuses on long-term abilities.

transparency (p. 203)   The presentation of a company's facts and figures in a way that is clear and apparent to all stakeholders.

trial balance (p. 504)   A summary of all the financial data in the account ledgers that ensures the figures are correct and balanced.

trial close (p. 476)   A step in the selling process that consists of a question or statement that moves the selling process toward the actual close.

trigger-happy *Term that refers to people reacting too fast to the circumstances facing them in a difficult situation.*

turn a blind eye *Ignore something of importance.*

turn the work off *Stop working.*

umbrella policy (p. A2-12) A broadly based insurance policy that saves you money because you buy all your insurance from one company.

unemployment rate (p. 46) The number of civilians at least 16 years old who are unemployed and tried to find a job within the prior four weeks.

Uniform Commercial Code (UCC) (p. A1-8) A comprehensive commercial law, adopted by every state in the United States, that covers sales laws and other commercial laws.

uninsurable risk (p. B-5) A risk that no insurance company will cover.

union (p. 342) An employee organization that has the main goal of representing members in employee–management bargaining over job-related issues.

union security clause (p. 349) Provision in a negotiated labor–management agreement that stipulates that employees who benefit from a union must either officially join or at least pay dues to the union.

union shop agreement (p. 350) Clause in a labor–management agreement that says workers do not have to be members of a union to be hired, but must agree to join the union within a prescribed period.

unlimited liability (p. 124) The responsibility of business owners for all of the debts of the business.

unsecured bond (p. 545) A bond backed only by the reputation of the issuer; also called a debenture bond.

unsecured loan (p. 540) A loan that doesn't require any collateral.

unsought goods and services (p. 410) Products that consumers are unaware of, haven't necessarily thought of buying, or find that they need to solve an unexpected problem.

utility (p. 439) In economics, the want-satisfying ability, or value, that organizations add to goods or services when the products are made more useful or accessible to consumers than they were before.

value (p. 404) Good quality at a fair price. When consumers calculate the value of a product, they look at the benefits and then subtract the cost to see if the benefits exceed the costs.

variable costs (p. 424) Costs that change according to the level of production.

variable life insurance (p. A2-11) Whole life insurance that invests the cash value of the policy in stocks or other high-yielding securities.

venture capital (p. 546) Money that is invested in new or emerging companies that are perceived as having great profit potential.

venture capitalists (p. 172) Individuals or companies that invest in new businesses in exchange for partial ownership of those businesses.

vertical merger (p. 136) The joining of two companies involved in different stages of related businesses.

vestibule training (p. 322) Training done in schools where employees are taught on equipment similar to that used on the job.

viral marketing (p. 482) The term now used to describe everything from paying customers to say positive things on the Internet to setting up multilevel selling schemes whereby consumers get commissions for directing friends to specific websites.

virtual corporation (p. 232) A temporary networked organization made up of replaceable firms that join and leave as needed.

virtualization (p. A-14) A process that allows networked computers to run multiple operating systems and programs through one central computer at the same time.

virtual private network (VPN) (p. A-9) A private data network that creates secure connections, or "tunnels," over regular Internet lines.

virus (p. A-19) A piece of programming code inserted into other programming to cause some unexpected and, for the victim, usually undesirable event.

vision (p. 195) An encompassing explanation of why the organization exists and where it's trying to head.

volume (or usage) segmentation (p. 392) Dividing the market by usage (volume of use).

voluntary bankruptcy (p. A1-16) Legal procedures initiated by a debtor.

walk out the door *Leave the company; quit your job.*

watching over your shoulder *Looking at everything you do.*

Web 2.0 (p. A-12) The set of tools that allow people to build social and business connections, share information, and collaborate on projects online (including blogs, wikis, social networking sites and other online communities, and virtual worlds).

Web 3.0 (p. A-12) A combination of technologies that adds intelligence and changes how people interact with the web, and vice versa (consists of the semantic web, mobile web, and immersive Internet).

whistleblowers (p. 97) Insiders who report illegal or unethical behavior.

whole life insurance (p. A2-10) Life insurance that combines pure insurance and savings.

wholesaler (p. 435) A marketing intermediary that sells to other organizations.

will (p. A2-16) A document that names the guardian for your children, states how you want your assets distributed, and names the executor for your estate.

word-of-mouth promotion (p. 481) A promotional tool that involves people telling other people about products they've purchased.

World Bank (p. 606) The bank primarily responsible for financing economic development; also known as the International Bank for Reconstruction and Development.

World Trade Organization (WTO) (p. 77) The international organization that replaced the General Agreement on Tariffs and Trade and was assigned the duty to mediate trade disputes among nations.

yellow-dog contract (p. 346) A type of contract that required employees to agree as a condition of employment not to join a union; prohibited by the Norris-LaGuardia Act in 1932.

photo credits

Corbis; p.353: © CSM/Landov Images; p.356: © Photo by Eric Charbonneau/WireImage/Getty Images; p.358: © John Byrne,CartoonStock.com; p.359: © Image Source/Corbis RF; p.360: © BananaStock/PunchStock RF; p.362: © Tony Freeman/PhotoEdit.

CHAPTER 13

Page 375: © AP Photo/Lynne Sladky; p.378: © Bettmann/Corbis; p.379: Courtesy of the National Highway Traffic Safety Administration and Ad Council; p.380: © Redfx/Alamy RF; p.383: © Burke/Triolo/Brand X Pictures RF; p.385: © Janine Wiedel Photolibrary/Alamy; p.387: © David Sacks/Getty Images RF; p.390: © Torsten Silz/AFP/Getty Images; p.391: © PRNewsFoto/SnapShotU!/AP Photos; p.393: © Noel Hendrickson/Getty Images RF.

CHAPTER 14

Page 403: From *San Francisco Business Times*, by Spencer Brown, "Fitness Firm TRX Raises Private Equity Bonanza," September 23, 2011; p.405: Courtesy of Bocktown Beer and Grill; p.406: Courtesy of Apple; p.409: Courtesy of Pepsi; p.410(left): © BananaStock/Jupiterimages RF; p.410(right): © Bambu Productions/Iconica/Getty Images RF; p.412: Courtesy of C2Group; p.413: H.J. Heinz Company and Multivac Company-USA; p.414: © Daniel Acker/Bloomberg/Getty Images; p.417: © Tony Kurdzuk/Star Ledger/Corbis; p.418: Edsel Little/Flickr; p.423: © PRNewsFoto/Salvatore Ferragamo, Mark Loader/AP Photos; p.424: © AP Wide World Photos.

CHAPTER 15

Page 433: © Jeff Wilson Photography; p.434: © AP Wide World Photos; p.439: © Zig Urbanski/Alamy; p.440: © Andy Kropa 2006/Redux Pictures; p.442: © Fuse/Getty Images RF; p.444: © Richard B. Levine/Newscom; p.445: © The McGraw-Hill Companies, Inc./Andrew Resek, photographer; p.446: © Photo by Randy Pench/Sacramento Bee/MCT via Getty Images; p.448: Courtesy Chocolate Chocolate Chocolate Company; p.451: © RF/Corbis; p.453: © PhotoLibrary/Getty Images; p.455: © Mark F. Henning/Alamy.

CHAPTER 16

Page 463: Courtesy of Shama Kabani; p.467: © PRNewsFoto/AP Photos; p.469: © Sony Pictures Entertainment/PhotoFest; p.471: © Corbis RF; p.472: © PRNewsFoto/Tissot/AP Photos; p.473: Copyright © 2000-2009 bwgreyscale.com. All rights reserved; p.474: © Flickr/jpellgen; p.475: © Blend Images/Getty Images RF; p.476: © Tim McGuire/Corbis; p.479: © Photo by Elsa/Getty Images; p.480: International Manufacturing Technology Show; p.481: © Jeff Greenberg/PhotoEdit; p.483: © Laurence Mouton/age fotostock RF; p.484: © Kevin Zolkiewicz.

CHAPTER 17

Page 497: Courtesy of RJ Julia Booksellers; p.500: © Michael Rosenfeld/Getty Images; p.502: © AP Photo/Charlie Riedel; p.506: © AP Photo/Jacquelyn Martin; p.511: © Chip Litherland/The New York Times/Redux Pictures; p.512: © The McGraw-Hill Companies, Inc./Jill Braaten, photographer; p.513: © Glen Stubbe/ZUMA Press/Corbis; p.514: © AP Wide World Photos; p.517: © Scott Frances/City Center/Sipa Press/Newscom; p.518: © age fotostock.

CHAPTER 18

Page 527: Courtesy of James Reinhart and thredUp; p.529: © AP Wide World Photos; p.530: © Don Mason/Blend Images/Getty Images RF; p.535:

© ICP/age fotostock; p.538: © Piet Mall/Getty Images; p.539: © Mike Segar/Reuters/Corbis; p.541: © SuperStock; p.545: © AP Photo/James A. Finley; p.546: © Steve Kagan/The New York Times/Redux Pictures.

CHAPTER 19

Page 555: © Fred Prouser/Reuters/Landov; p.556: © Deborah Feingold/Corbis; p.558(left): © AFP Photo/Stan Honda/Getty Images; p.558(right): © AP Photo/New York Stock Exchange; p.559: © STR/AFP/Getty Images/Newscom; p.562: © AP Photo/Mark Lennihan; p.566: © Newscom Photos; p.569: © CNBC/Photofest; p.570: © Dinodia/age fotostock RF; Fig. 19.4: Microsoft, MSN, and Windows Vista are trademarks of the Microsoft group of companies; Fig. 19.5: © Copyright 2011 Goldman Sachs, All Rights Reserved; Fig. 19.7: © T.Rowe Price; p.577: © Shenval/Alamy Images RF; p.578: © Scott Olson/Getty Images.

CHAPTER 20

Page 587: © Tami Chappell/Reuters/Landov Images; p.588: The U.S. Department of the Treasury Bureau of Engraving and Printing; p.589: © Photodisc/Getty Images RF; p.591: © AP Wide World Photos; p.596: © Bettmann/Corbis; p.599: © Tannen Maury/Bloomberg News/Getty Images; p.601: © Misty Keasler; p.602: © Photo by Jacob Kepler/Bloomberg via Getty Images; p.603: © Kirstina Sangsahachart/Palo Alto Daily News/MCT/Newscom; p.604: © George Ruhe/The New York Times/Redux; p.606: © AP Wide World Photos.

APPENDIX 1

Page A1-1: © AP Photo/Alex Brandon; p.A1-3: © Image Source/Getty Images RF; p.A1-7: Newscom Photos; p.A1-8: © BananaStock/Masterfile RF; p.A1-16: © Tripplaar Kristoffler/SIPA/Newscom.

APPENDIX 2

Page A2-1: Hearst Magazine/Philip Friedman/Studio D; p.A2-5: © Image Source/Jupiterimages RF; p.A2-7: © Justin Sullivan/Getty Images; p.A2-9: © Keith Meyers/The New York Times/Redux Pictures; p.A2-13: © Fuse/Getty Images RF; p.A2-14: © Andersen Ross/Getty Images RF; p.A2-15: © Image Source/Getty Images RF.

EPILOGUE

Page E-1: © Julie Toy/Getty Images; p.E-3: © Ryan McVay/Getty Images RF; p.E-13: © Winston Davidian/Getty Images RF.

BONUS A

Page A-1: © Peter Yang/August Images: p.A-3: © Giovanni Mereghetti/age fotostock; p.A-6: © Photographer's Choice/GSO Images/Getty Images; p.A-11: © Photo Illustration by Justin Sullivan/Getty Images; p.A-12: © Brian Sumway/Redux Pictures; p.A-14: © AP Photo/Amy Sancetta; p.A-15: © Casanova/MCRT/Landov; p.A-16: Courtesy of Cisco; p.A-19: © Digital Vision/Getty Images RF; p. A-20(top): © Newscom Photos; p.A-20(bottom): © Scott J. Ferrell/Congressional Quarterly/Newscom.

BONUS B

Page B-1: Courtesy of Joachim Oechslin; p.B-2: © Photo by Dan Kitwood/Getty Images; p.B-4: © Reuters/Chris Keane/Landov; p.B-7: © Yellow Dog Productions/Getty Images; p.B-9: © ERProductions Ltd/Getty Images RF.

A

Aalbers, Rick, N-6
Abelsky, Paul, N-2
Abelson, Alan, N-6
Achille, Roger S., N-8
Adams, John, N-13
Adams, Steve, 139
Adams, Susan, N-7, N-8
Agsalud, John, N-17
Akimenko, Vadim, 173
Allen, Ashley C., N-16
Allen, John, N-2
Allen, Sally, 497
Alsever, Jennifer, 465
Alsop, Ronald J., N-7
Altavena, Lily, 555
Alva, Marilyn, N-11
Amaral, Jason, N-11
Anderson, Edward G., Jr., N-11
Andriotis, Annamaria, N-13
Ankeny, Jason, 145, 334, 405, N-4, N-12
Anker, Patty Chang, 497
Ansett, Sean, N
Ante, Spencer E., 245, N-15
Antorini, Yun Mi, N-6
Aristotle, 92
Armour, Stephanie, N-8
Arnold, Ed, N-17
Askildsen, Tormod, N-6
Assange, Julian, BB-2
Assimakopolous, Dimitris, N-6

B

Babcock, Charles, N-17
Back, Aaron, N-5
Badenhausen, Kurt, N-11
Bailey, Robert L., N-17
Baldwin, William, N-14
Balfour, Frederick, N-1
Balz, Dan, N-6
Banerji, Shawn, N-16
Barakat, Matthew, N-10
Barkley, Tom, N-2
Barlas, Pete, N-17
Barney, Lee, N-7
Barone, Michael, N-7
Barr, Diana, N-18
Barret, Victoria, N-17
Barrett, Devlin, N-18
Barrett, Paul M., N-3, N-14, N-16
Barro, Robert, N-9
Barry, Joanne S., N-3
Bartiromo, Maria, 555
Barton, Dominic, N
Baskin, Burton, 129
Bast, Andrew, N-3
Bataller, Erik, N-18
Batkins, Sam, N-16
Bazerman, Max H., 34, N
Beaton, Jessica, N-1
Beattie, Andrew, N-4

Beesley, Caron, N-13
Begley, Sharon, N-11
Behar, Jennifer, 511
Beisel, David, N-5
Bekins, Michael, N-1
Belicove, Mikal E., N-10
Bell, Jeffrey, 587
Bell, Kay, N-3
Bennett, Drake, N-9
Bennett, Jessica, N-10
Berdiev, Neil, N-13
Berger, Lauren, E-4
Bergsten, C. Fred, 64, N-1
Bergstrom, Kathy, N-13
Bernanke, Ben S., 587, 588, 590, 593, 610
Bernas, Greg, N-6
Berners-Lee, Tim, BA-21
Bernoff, Josh, 206
Berr, Jonathan, N-16
Bertani, Elizabeth, 529–530
Berzon, Alexander, N-11
Bezos, Jeff, 155
Bing, Dave, 215
Binstock, Andrew, N-17
Birchall, Jonathan, N-11
Birdsall, Rick, N-8
Black, Rosemary, N-4
Blacksmith, Nikki, N-7
Blackstone, Brian, N-7
Blake, Brock, N-5
Blake, Janet Cappiello, 93
Blake, Jenny, E-4
Blanchard, Kenneth, 93, N-2
Bluestein, Adam, 153
Blum, Jonathan, N-5, N-13
Bo Ouyang, N-3
Bock, Jessica, 93
Bodnar, Janet, N-16
Bodoni, Stephanie, N-15
Bolden, Jane, 471
Bolgar, Catherine, N-11
Bolles, Richard Nelson, E-4
Bonaminio, Jim, 154
Bono, 555
Boone, Elizabeth, N-8
Borenstein, Nathaniel, N-9
Borgas, Ron, N-9
Boswell, Wendy R., N-7
Boudette, Neal E., N-11
Boudreau, John, N-8
Boushey, Heather, 359
Bovarnick, Robert, N-13
Bower, Benjamin, N-1
Boyd, E. B., 465
Boyle, Douglas M., N-3
Boyle, Katherine, N-16
Boyle, Matthew, N-11
Bradford, Reggie, N-12
Bradsher, Keith, N-1
Brady, Dian, 215
Branson, Richard, 472
Bray, Chad, N-14
Bray, Hiawatha, 14

Brazelton, Karla, 173
Bremner, Brian, N-6
Brenner, Reuven, N-15
Bresnahan, Mike, 341
Breyer, Stephen, N-16
Bridgeman, Junior, 143
Bridges, Robert, N-16
Briggs, Julie, N-13
Brimeyer, Rick, N-7
Brin, Dinah Wisenberg, N-18
Brown, Lisa, 598, N-6
Brown, Roger, 361
Brown, Steven E. F., N-8
Brown, Stuart F., N
Brown, Warren, 123
Browning, E. S., N-16
Buchanan, Leigh, 89, 317, 403, N-5, N-8
Buffett, Warren, 113, 191, 570
Bullock, Nicole, N-14
Bungay, Stephen, N-5
Bunge, Jacob, N-14
Burke, Daniel, N
Burkitt, Laurie, 474
Burne, Katy, N-14
Burns, Ursula, 193
Burrows, Peter, N-12
Burton, Katherine, N-3
Burton, Thomas M., N-18
Bush, George W., 51, 375, 587, 602
Bush, Michael, N-12
Bussey, John, N, N-1, N-6
Bustillo, Miguel, N-11
Byron, Ellen, 389, N-10, N-11, N-12
Byus, Kent, N-3

C

Callahan, Brian, 307
Callender, Heather, 435
Calonius, Erik, N-4
Cane, Jeffrey, N-4
Canli, Turhan, 318
Cannon, Lauren, N-13
Caplinger, Dan, N-14
Carlyle, Thomas, 32
Carpenter, Brian W., N-3
Carroll, Cynthia, 9
Casey, Michael J., N-15
Casper, Amy C., N-6
Casselman, Ben, N-6
Cassidy, John, N
Catan, Thomas, N-15, N-17
Catlette, Bill, 102, N-3
Causey, Richard, 91
Celaschi, Robert, N-4
Cendrowski, Scott, N-11
Chafkin, Max, 482, BA-11
Chan, Sewell, N-2, N-13
Chanaratsopon, Charlie, 433
Chandler, Trish, N-7
Chang, Gordon G., N
Chapman, Kim, N-7
Charnowitz, Steve, N-5, N-6

Chasan, Emily, N-14
Checket-Hanks, B., N-9
Checkler, Joseph, N-10
Chen, Amy, N-10
Chen, Steve, 155
Chen, Vivien Lou, N-5
Cheng, Jonathan, N-14
Cheng, Long, N-4
Chin, Michael J., 463
Cho, Rebecca U., N-4
Chokkavelu, Anand, N-13
Chon, Gina, N-14
Chris, Sherry, 472
Cini, Robert, N-17
Cipriani, Jim, Jr., N-5
Claburn, Thomas, N-17
Clark, Laurel, N-7
Clawson, Trevor, N-13
Clegg, Roger, N-8
Clenfield, Jason, 357, N-10
Clifford, Stephanie, 444
Clooney, George, 375
Clouser, Stephanie, N-1
Coady, Roxanne, 497
Cochran, Willie "Bo," A1-1
Cohen, Deborah L., 153
Cohen, Gary, 26
Coleman-Lochner, Lauren, N-12
Conde, Cesar, 375
Condon, Christopher, N-16
Confucius, 92
Conry-Murray, Andrew, N-18
Cooper, Ted, 173
Cordivan, Rich, N-10
Corrin, Matthew, 145
Cosgrove, Mike, N
Cosper, Amy C., N, N-10
Cossack, Naomi, N-8
Coster, Helen, 64, 540
Coy, Peter, 587, N-2, N-16
Craggs, Tommy, 341
Cramer, Jim, 569, P-5
Crews, Wayne, N-16
Cross, Rob, N-6
Culpan, Tim, 450
Cuneo, John, N

D

Daily, Jason, N-4
Daley, Jason, 64, 142, 155, N, N-10,
   N-17
Daley, Will, N-18
Dalmia, Shikha, N-13
Dalton, Matthew, N-2
Dalton, Steve, E-4
Dame, Joey, 138
Dame, John, 138
Dance, Leslie, N-11
Daniel, Jennifer, N-1, N-3
Danielson, Ronald, N-5
Darling-Hammond, Linda, N-1
Dauten, Dale, 157
David, Ruth, 36, N
Davidson, Joe, N-3
Davis, Paul, N-4
Day, Mark, N-4
De George, Richard T., 108
De La Merced, Michael J., N-4
De Soto, Hernando, N
De Valk, Jasper, N-6
Deagon, Brian, N-15
Dean, Jason, N-5

DeCarlo, Scott, 357
Decker, Susan, N-15
Deen, Paula, 157
DeFotis, Dimitra, N-3
Deis, Donald, N-3
Delisi, Peter S., N-5
Dell, Michael, 155
DeLoach, Doug, 519
DeMarco, Joe, N-9
Deming, W. Edwards, 261
Denney, Andrew, N-10
Dennis, Brady, N-15
Depp, Johnny, 61, 356
Derousseau, Ryan, N-15
Devaney, Tim, N-6
Dhar, Ravi, N-10, N-11
Dibaise, Colleen, N-4
Dickey, Christopher, N-15
Disney, Walt, 156–157
Dizik, Alina, 34, N-11
Dobbin, Ben, N-15
Dobbs, Richard, N-1
Dodd, Glenn, 142
Dodd, Martha, 142
Dodgson, Mark, N-6
Dolan, Kerry A., BA-1
Dolan, Matthew, 215
Donahoe, John, N-11
Donaldson, Sonya A., 206
Donlan, Thomas G., N-6
Donmoyer, Ryan J., N-3
Dorsey, Jack, 155
Dougherty, Conor, N-6
Dove, Patricia, 153
Dow, Charles, 576
Dowd, James, N-8
Drajem, Mark, N-1
Drucker, Peter, 10, 288–289, 357
Du Pont de Nemours, Éleuthère Irénée,
   154
Dubner, Stephen, 29
Ducey, Lynn, N-12
Duhigg, Charles, N-3, N-17
Dulaney, Emmett, N-5
Durgy, Edwin, N-4
D'Vorkin, Lewis, N

E

Eastern, Joseph S., N-7
Eastman, George, 154
Easton, Nina, N-9
Eaton, Nick, N-15
Ebbers, Bernard, 91
Ebhardt, Tommaso, N-2
Eckblad, Marshall, N-5
Eckel, Mike, N-1
Eder, Steve, N-12
Edison, Thomas, 146
Edwards, Cliff, N-17
Edwards, James R., Jr., N-4
Efstathiou, Jim, Jr., N-7
Eggers, Kelly, N, N-5
Eichen, Mitchell, N-13
Einhorn, Bruce, 450, 474, N
Eisele-Dyrli, Kurt, N-17
El Boghdady, Dina, N-15
Elliott, Alan R., N-1
Elliott, Jack, Jr., N-15
Ellos, William J., 108
Endres, Grace M., N-7
Eng, Dinah, 121
Epstein, Gene, N-1

Erez, Lior, N
Esch, Justin, 177
Esswein, Patricia Mertz, N-15
Esterl, Mike, BB-1
Estrin, James, N-9
Esty, Daniel C., 247, N-5, N-6
Ettenson, Richard, N-12
Ettinger, Jill, 408
Evans, Bob, N-17
Evans, Kelly, N-15

F

Fairless, Tom, 249
Farmer, Sam, N-9
Farrell, Rachel, N, N-8
Farzad, Roben, N-14
Faux, Zeke, N-13
Fayol, Henri, 219–220, 238
Feeley, Jeff, N-15
Ferenstein, Greg, BA-1
Ferreira, John, N-7
Feulner, Edwin J., N
Fey, Tina, 352
Field, Abigail, N-15
Fieler, Sean, 587
Figueroa, Alissa, N-10
Findley, Peter, 155
Fine, Charles H., N-11
Fisher, Daniel, 36, N-15
Fisher, Ken, N-5
Fisher, Lucy, 145
Fitzgerald, Joy, N-2
Fixmer, Andy, N-12
Fletcher, Ian, N-2
Fletcher, Owen, N-2
Flint, Jessica, N-8
Fly, Colin, N-9
Fontevecchia, Agustino, 587
Forbes, Moira, 191
Forbes, Steve, N-15
Ford, Henry, 146, 154
Ford, Maggie Fazeli, 380
Forelle, Charles, N-2
Foroohab, Rana, N-10
Fottrell, Quentin, N-15
Fouhy, Beth, 345
Fowler, Geoffrey A., 527, N, N-6, N-12,
   N-18
Fox, Adrienne, N-7
Fox, Jim, 327
Frankel, Todd, N-10
Franklin, Benjamin, A2-2
Franklin, Mary Beth, N-16
Frazier, Kenneth C., A1-1, A1-5
Freedman, David H., N-12
Freston, Tom, 132
Frick, Robert, N, N-14
Fried, Carla, N-14
Friedman, Milton, 98
Frier, Sarah, 245
Froymovich, Riva, N-2
Fry, Art, 163
Furman, Matthew, N-12
Futrelle, David, 29, N-14

G

Galante, Joseph, N-11, N-17
Galentine, Elizabeth, 293
Gallo, Carmine, 384
Gallu, Joshua, N-12
Gamble, James, 154

Gandel, Stephen, N-10
Gann, David, N-6
Ganos, Todd, N-1
Gantt, Henry L., 264, 280, 300
Garcia, Kevin, N-13
Gardner, Amy, N-9
Gardner, David, 556
Gardner, Tom, 556
Gasol, Paul, 61
Gasparino, Charles, N-16
Gates, Bill, 5, 40, 113, 146, 155, 278
Gates, Melinda, 40
Gay, Chris, N-3
Gaynor, Michael, N-11
Gehrke-White, Donna, N-3
Gelin, Marie, 9
Gibson, Richard, N-3, N-4
Gies, Erica, 247
Gilbert, Daniel, N-3
Gilbreth, Frank, 280, 300
Gilbreth, Lillian, 280, 300
Girotra, Karan, N-18
Glazer, Emily, N-12
Glenn, Don, 15
Glickman, Jodi, N-8
Glovin, David, N-1, N-3
Glynn, Matt, N-1
Gnau, Thomas, N-9
Goldman, Duff, 252
Goldstein, David, N-16
Goldwasser, Joan, N-15, N-16, N-18
Goltz, Jay, N-4
Gompers, Samuel, 344, 346
Gonsalves, Antone, 403
Goodnight, Jim, 277
Goodspeed, Linda, N-1
Gordon, Brian, 553
Gormly, Kellie B., N-2
Goscha, John, 155
Gose, Joe, N-7
Gosling, Tim, N-2
Goudreau, Jenna, N-10
Gould, David, N-18
Grant, Tim, N-3
Gratton, Lynda, N-5
Green, Andrew, N-12
Green, Michael, N-17
Greenberg, Andy, N-15
Gregg, Gabi, BA-22
Grove, Andrew S., 251
Groysberg, Boris, N-6
Grozinger, Cerd, N-7
Guglielmo, Connie, N-10
Gullo, Eric, N-14
Gumbs, Alisa, N-18
Gunther, Marc, N-11
Gurchiek, Kathy, N-2
Gutierrez, Karen, 598
Gutner, Toddi, 296

H

Haak, Emma, 408
Hadden, Richard, 102, N-3
Hagerty, James R., N-7, N-11
Hagiwara, Yuki, N-15
Haislip, Barbara, N-5
Hall, Christine, N-18
Hall, Julie, N-11
Hamdan, Sara, 544
Hamel, Gary, N-5
Hamill, Sean D., N-1
Hamilton, Alexander, 595

Hamlin, Kevin, 559
Hammerand, Jim, N-13
Hammond, Dave, 178
Hananel, Sam, N-9
Handler, Elliot, 176
Handler, Ruth, 176
Hann, Christopher, N-6
Hannaford, Kat, 201
Hanson, Andrew, N-4
Hardy, Quentin, N-17
Harlan, Kevin, N-14
Harper, Philipp, N-4
Harris, Andrew M., N-15
Harter, Jim, N-7
Harvey, Melissa, 156
Hassan, Fred, N-6
Hatton, Celia, N-1
Hay, Edward, 327
Hayashi, Alden M., N-10
Haywood, Luke, N-7
Healey, Jon, N-9
Heck, Josh, N-8
Heinbockel, Eric, 254
Helm, Burt, N-4
Henricks, Mark, N-4
Henriques, Diana B., 91
Henry, Kasthuri V., N-8
Henschen, Doug, N-16, N-17
Hensmans, Manuel, N-6
Hepp, Christopher K., A1-1
Herbst, Moira, N-7
Hermanson, Dana R., N-3
Herrenkohl, Eric, N-8
Herszenhorn, David M., N-16
Herzberg, Frederick, 283–284, 291, 300, 304
Hess, Corinne, N-8
Hetrick, Randy, 403
Heubeck, Elizabeth, N-12
Heugens, A. R., N-2
Hiassen, Scott, 375
Higginbotham, Stacey, N-17
Higginbotham, Tracy, N-13
Higgins, Kelly Jackson, N-18
Higgins, Tim, N-2
Hilzenrath, David S., N-3
Hing, Bill Ong, N-2
Hinton, Christopher, N-9
Hitzig, Neal B., N-12
Ho Ching, 9
Hoffmann, Katie, N-17
Hofman, Mike, N-7
Hogg, Sam, 155
Holland, Joel, 155
Holland, Judy, N-15
Hollis, C. O., N-12
Homan, Timothy R., N-2, N-5
Homer, Chris, 527
Hoover, Kent, N-5, N-9
Hopkins, Michael S., N-6
Horowitz, Ben, N-9
Hosford, Christopher, N-12
Hsieh, Tony, 213, 472
Hsu, Robert, N
Hudson, Kris, N-11
Hughes, Chris, BA-1
Hughes, Ivy, 155, N-5, N-8
Hughes, Jeff, N-5
Hurd, Mark, 357
Hurley, Chad, 155
Hurtado, Patricia, N-3
Huspeni, Dennis, N-3
Hymowitz, Carol, 245

I

Icahn, Carl, N-5
Iger, Robert, 356
Ignatius, Adi, N-6
Ihejirika, Maudlyne, 89
Ireland, Kathy, 191
Irwin, Nell, 607, N, N-1, N-15
Isidore, Chris, N-2

J

Jackson, Marcy, N-16
Jackson, Mary, N-16
Jackson, Phil, 204
Jackson, Victoria, 175
Jacoby, Julian E., N-12
James, Chris, N-13
James, LeBron, 356
James, Scott, N-15
Jamrog, Jay, N-8
Jannarone, John, N, N-7
Jarboe, Michelle, N-1
Jargon, Julie, N-4
Javitch, David, N-7
Jefferson, Thomas, 92
Jensen, J. Bradford, N-6
Jewell, Mark, N-14
Jiang Jianqing, 357
Jobs, Steve, 132, 146, 158
Johnson, Derek, 155
Johnson, Gerry, N-6
Johnson, Linda, A1-1
Johnson, Robert Wood, 97
Johnson, William R., 59
Jolie, Angelina, 375
Jonelle, Marte, N-4
Jones, Adam, 519
Jones, Ashby, N-9, N-15, N-16
Jordan, Kim, 242, 243, 307
Judson, Whitcomb, 419
Juergen, Michelle, 9
Julius Sextus Frontinus, BA-4
Jung, Carl, 304

K

Kabani, Shama, 463
Kanaracus, Chris, 277
Kaplan, David A., 277
Kaplan, Eve, N-14
Kaptein, Muel, N-2
Karabell, Zachary, N-2
Karan, Donna, 9
Kardashian, Kim, 465, 471
Karlgaard, Rich, N-5, N-6
Karnowski, Steve, N-3
Karpinski, Rich, 3
Kassalow, Jordan, 64
Katz, David M., N-11, N-13
Katz, Ian, N-10
Kauffman, Cameron, N-7
Kautt, Glenn G., N-7
Keizer, Gregg, N-15
Kelly, Gary, 298
Kelly, L. Kevin, N-6
Kelly, Robert, N-15
Kennedy, John F., 100
Kenshalo, Rachel, N-9
Kensicki, Peter R., N-3
Keohane, Joe, N-13
Keppler, Nick, N-9
Kerr, Michelle, N-7

Kerschberg, Ben, N-17
Keynes, John Maynard, 51
Khalifa, Mohamed Hossam el-Din Hassan, N-7
Khan, Uzma, N-10, N-11
Kharif, Olga, N-17
Kho, Jennifer, N
Kidron, Adam, BA-11
Kiernan, Katie, N-10
Kilman, Scott, BB-1
Kilpatrick, Kwame, 215
Kim, Yun-Hee, N-6
Kimes, Mima, N-11
King, Ken, N-13
Kingsbury, Kathleen, N-11
Kinnander, Ola, 435
Kinnear, Thomas C., 442
Kiplinger, Knight, 321
Kirchhoff, Bruce, 166
Kishan, Saijel, N-3
Kitamura, Makiko, N-15
Kite, Shane, N-9
Klein, Ezra, N-9
Klein, Karen E., N-5, N-8, N-13
Klie, Leonard, N-7
Knight, Heather, 482
Knight, Phil, 106
Knowles, Beyonce, 356
Kocera, Barb, N-9
Kochan, Thomas A., N-6
Koegel, Kathryn, N-12
Koger, Eric, 170
Koger, Susan, 170
Kolesnikov-Jessop, Sonia, N-17
Korzeniowski, Paul, N-17
Kothari, Maghna, 598
Kowitt, Beth, N-6
Kramer, Mark R., N-1
Krantz, Matt, N-10
Krause, Reinhardt, 559, N-2, N-17
Krisher, Tom, N-9
Kroc, Ray, 170
Krueger, Brian D., E-5
Krugman, Paul, N-15
Krzyzewski, Mike, 204
Kucera, Joshua, N-3
Kuhnhenn, Jim, N-5
Kullman, Ellen, 203
Kumar, Kavita, N-4
Kuo, Benjamin K., 232
Kusner, Toby, N-15

L

Labarre, Polly, N-8
Lafley, A. G., 216, N, N-5
Lagorce, Aude, N-14
Lahart, Justin, N-6
Laing, Jonathan R., N
Lamb, John, 293
Lambert, Emily, 559
Lambrecht, Bill, N-1
Lancaster, Lynne C., N-7
Lancman, Rory, N-13
Langley, Monica, N-5
Langmead, Joseph M., N-13
Lankford, Kimberly, N-16
Lapowsky, Issie, N-4
Larsen, Marie, 334
Latham, Gary, N-7
Latta, Sonya M., N-8
Lattman, Peter, N-14
Lattonan, Peter, 444

Lau, Joyce Hor-Chung, 69
Lawler, Edward, 290, N-7, N-8
Lawler, Jennifer, N-11
Lay, Kenneth, 91
Lea, James, N-13
Lebesch, Jeff, 242, 243, 307
Lee, April H., N-5
Lee, Edmund, N-12
Lee, Ellen, 527
Lee, Hau L., N-11
Lefkow, Dave, 177
Leinwand, Paul, N-6
Lemelson, Jerome, A1-7
Lemov, Penelope, N-16
Leonard, Devin, 307
Letzing, John, N-18
Leung, Sze, 440
Levenson, Eugenia, N-3
Levin, Yuval, N-10
Levinson, Philip, 527
Levitt, Steven, 29
Lev-Ram, Michal, N-17
Levy, Ari, N-11
Lewis, John L., 344
Lewis, Katherine Reynolds, N-9
Li, Hao, N-2
Li, Yanping, N-10
Liberman, Gail, N-3, N-14
Liberto, Jennifer, N-2
Lichtblau, Eric, N-18
Liebowitz, Matt, 93, N-18
Light, Joe, N-8
Liker, Jeffrey, N-15
Lim, Paul J., N-16
Limbauch, Kate, N-10
Limmer, Casey, 290
Lin, Lisa, N-10
Lindeman, Todd, N
Ling, K. Charles, N-4
Ling, Tian, N-10
Lipka, Mitch, N-15
Lipman, Victor, N-7
Liptak, Adam, N-16
Liu, Frances, 559
Liu Zehui, 559
Llopis, Glenn, 389
Lo, Selina, 285
Locke, Michelle, N-10
Lohr, Steve, N-16
Lombardi, Candace, 104
Lombardi, Vince, 157
Loomis, Carol, 34
Loten, Angus, 232, N-11
Lowenstein, Roger, 587
Lubin, David A., 247
Lubin, Oliver, 527
Lublin, Joann S., 245, N, N-5, N-9
Lucchetti, Aaron, N-14
Lund, Susan, N-1
Lynch, David J., N

M

Ma, Jason, 201
MacDonald, Bryan, N-6
MacDonald, Maryanne, N-17
Machan, Dyan, N-13
Mackey, John, N-5
MacMillan, Douglas, N-10, N-17
Macsai, Dan, 601
Maddox, Kate, N-11
Madoff, Bernard, 90, 91, 548
Maffei, Gregory, 357

Magaga, Pros, 36
Mahajan, Sanjiv, N-13
Mainardi, Cesare, N-6
Mäkelä, Liisa, 330
Malcolm, Andrew, N-1
Male, Bianca, N-4
Malone, Thomas, N-5
Malpass, David, N
Maltby, Emily, 540, N-4, N-11, N-13
Malthus, Thomas, 31–32, 33
Mamudi, Sam, 341
Mandelbaum, Robb, N-13
Mannes, George, N-16
Mannes, Tanya, 433
Mao, Vincent, N-1
Maranjian, Selena, N-10
Marchetti, Mike, 318
Margolis, Mac, N-5
Mariani, John, 175
Markkula, Mike, 158
Marko, Kurt, N-17
Markowitz, Eric, N-4
Markowitz, Jack, N-1
Marlack, Carol, BB-1
Marron, Donald, N-3
Marshall, Samantha, N-3
Marshall, Thurgood, A1-1
Martin, Jonathan, N-10
Martin, Michael, 555
Martin, Michel, 215
Martin, Roger L., N-6
Martin, Timothy W., N-18
Martinez, Andres R., 44
Marx, Groucho, 278
Maslow, Abraham, 281–282, 284, 291, 300, 304
Mason, Jane, 160
Mason, Linda, 361
Masters, Brooke, N-14
Matiaske, Wenzel, N-7
Mattingly, Phil, N-13, N-16
Mattioli, Dana, 14, N-10
Maxon, Terry, N-9
May, Sherri, N-7
Mayer, Karen Ott, N-10
Mayo, Elton, 280–281, 300, 304
McArdle, Megan, N
McCausland, Christianna, N-18
McClure, Dave, N-12
McConnell, David, 154
McCormick, Cyrus, 20
McDonald, Bob, 105
McDonnell, Sanford, 547
McGee, Marianne Kolbasuk, N-18
McGirt, Ellen, BA-1, BA-11
McGregor, Douglas, 285, 301
McIntyre, Douglas A., N-16
McKenna, Francine, N-12
McKimmie, Jessica, N-6
McKinley, Rob, 142
McKinnon, Ronald, N-1
McManus, Mickey, N-17
McNerney, Pam, 497
McQueen, M. P., N-18
McSweeney, Deborah, N-3
McTague, Jim, N-12
McWhirter, Cameron, BB-1
Mehta, Nina, N-14, N-15
Meinhardt, Jane, N-13
Mellman, Ira, 83
Mendleson, Rachel, 357
Mendoza, Monica, N-8
Merline, John, N-16

Metcalfe, Robert, BA-4
Metz, Cade, 245
Meyers, Eric C., N-16
Michelson, Gary, A1-6 to A1-7
Mickey, John, 546
Middleton, Diana, N-8
Mierzwinski, Ed, 599
Millar, Peter, N-13
Miller, Michael, 529
Miller, Nancy, N-8
Miller, Rich, N-15
Miller, Stephen, N-10
Miller, Terry, N
Millman, Joel, N-16
Mills, Richard, N-14
Mills-Groninger, Tim, N-12
Missett, Judi Sheppard, 141
Mitchell, Kathleen, N-12
Mix, Mark, N-9
Moberg, Dennis, N-5
Modica, Mark, N-13
Moerschel, Grant, N-18
Mohr, Angie, N-16
Montgomery, David, N-9
Moore, Gordon E., BA-13
Moore, Steve, 341
Moorthy, R. S., 108
Moran, Gwen, 527, N-4, N-8
Morarjee, Rachel, N-2
Morgan, Gwen, N-10
Morgenson, Gretchen, N-10, N-14
Morreale, Sherwyn P., N-6
Mossberg, Walter S., N-11
Mount, Ian, N-16
Much, Marilyn, N-6, N-10, N-11
Mui, Ylan Q., N-6, N-10
Mukherjee, Sougata, N-8
Mulani, Narenda, N-7
Mullaney, Tim, N-13
Muller, Joann, 215, N-6, N-12, N-15
Muller, Tom, N-6
Mullich, Joe, N-8, N-11, N-18
Muñiz, Albert M., Jr., N-6
Murphy, Andrea, N-4
Murphy, Chris, N-17
Murphy, Maxwell, N-11
Murphy, Pat, N-8
Murray, Lance, N-9
Myers-Briggs, Isabel, 304

N

Nadler, Burton Jay, E-4
Nadler, David, 290, N-7
Nagel, David, N-2
Napolitano, Janet, 450
Nash, Ed, N, N-10
Naughton, Keith, N, N-6
Nav, Henry R., N
Nayar, Vineet, N-7
Neal, Vicki, N-8
Needleman, Sarah E., 121, 296, N-4, N-8
Needleman, Ted, N-12
Neilson, Gary L., N-6
Netessine, Serguei, N-18
Neuman, Johanna, N-5
Newberry, Jon, N-17
Newman, Barry, N-11
Nguyen, Lan Ann, N-1
Niquette, Mark, N-9
Nocarando, Vince, 553
Nooyi, Indra, 9, 193
Norton, Leslie P., N-18

Notte, Jason, N-13
Novack, Janet, N-16
Nunziata, Susan, N-16

O

Obama, Barack, 12, 51, 63, 246, 579, 602, BA-1, BA-10, BA-11
O'Bannon, M., N-17
O'Brien, Denis, 5
Ochman, B. L., 234
Odie, Teresa, N-12
Ody, Elizabeth, N-14
Oechslin, Joachim, BB-1, BB-2
Ofek, Elie, N-5
Ohnsman, Alan, 450, N-15
Oldham, Pamela, N-10, N-12
Oliver, Antoinette, N-9
Olsen, Elizabeth G., N-10
Olsen, Ken, BA-4
Olson, Ashley, 5
Olson, Mary Kate, 5
Omidi, Maryann, 598
O'Neill, Danny, 426
O'Neill, Jim, 80
O'Reilly, Tim, BA-12
Ornberg, Tom, N-13
O'Shaughnessy, Tim, N-6
O'Shea, Dan, 384
Ostermiller, Pamela, N-13
Ouchi, William, 286–287, 301, 304
Ouyang, Bo, N-3
Overton, David, 121
Ovide, Shira, N-11

P

Palmer, Jay, N-11
Palmisano, Sam, 245
Palms Barber, Brenda, 89
Pandiyan, Veera, N-1
Parise, Salvatore, N-6
Park, Irene, 32
Parker, Geoffrey G., N-11
Parker, Lauren, 433
Parker, Yana, E-4
Parloff, Roger, N-12
Pasztor, Andy, N-18
Patton, Leslie, 69
Paul, Karen B., N-8
Paulson, Henry, 587
Paynter, Ben, N-17
Peale, Norman Vincent, 93, N-2
Pear, Robert, N-16
Pearlstein, Steve, N-1
Pearson, Sophia, N-15
Penney, J. C., 146
Pentland, Alex (Sandy), N-6
Pepper, John Henry, BA-4
Perego, Martha, N-2
Perlroth, Nicole, N-14
Perry, Mark J., N-1
Peruvankal, James Paul, N-7
Pesek, William, N-5, N-11
Peterson, Kristina, 555
Petracca, Laura, 540
Pham, Terry, 3
Phillips, Nelson, N-6
Piazza, Joe, 471
Pollak, Lindsey, E-4
Pollock, Alex J., N-14
Pomerantz, Dorothy, 191
Popeil, Ron, 470

Popeo, David J., N-15
Popper, Nathaniel, N-14
Porter, Michael, N-1, N-10
Postrel, Virginia, N-6
Powell, Colin, 375
Powell, Robert, N-8
Prater, Connie, N-16
Prentice, Chris, N-7
Prestowitz, Clyde, N-1
Price, Todd W., N-11
Primack, Dan, N-5
Prior, Anna, 568
Procter, William, 154
Proffitt, Allison, N-4
Prokesch, Steven, N, N-11
Pronina, Lyubov, N-2
Protess, Ben, N-14, N-16
Pulliam, Susan, N-14
Purcell, Susan, 414
Pursey, P. M., N-2
Pyle, Lesley Spencer, N-4

Q

Quast, Lisa, N-10
Queenan, Joe, N-11
Quigley, James, 519
Quinn, Matt, N-8
Quinn, Patricia, N-7
Quint, Michael, N-3
Quinton, Brian, N-11
Quirk, Bea, N-13
Quittner, Jeremy, N-17

R

Raabe, Steve, 307
Rajaratnam, Raj, 101, 560
Ramachandran, Shalini, N-17
Randall, Tom, A1-1, N-15
Raths, David, N-16
Raznick, Jason, 568
Read, Bill, N-7
Redden, Susan, N-9
Reddy, Sudeep, N-7, N-15
Redman, Chris, N-14
Reed, John, N-11
Reh, F. John, N-7
Reingold, Jennifer, N-2
Reinhardt, Uwe E., N-4
Reinhart, Carmen M., N-6
Reinhart, James, 527
Reitz, Scott, 405
Remley, Rachel, N-7
Rendon, Jim, N-8
Resnik, Marc, 162
Reynolds, Rachel, 297, N-4, N-8
Ricadela, Aaron, N-12, N-17
Ricardo, David, 62
Richard, Kenneth J., N-17
Richey, Dana, N-13
Ridley, Matt, 234
Riggio, Ronald, N-6
Riley, Benjamin K., N-5
Riley, Bridget, N-13
Riley, Jason L., N-6
Riley, Sheila, N-17
Rivkin, Jan W., N-10
Robarge, Leslie, 418
Robbins, Irvine, 129
Roberts, Dexter, 559
Roberts, Julia, 61
Robertson, Jordan, N-10

Robinson, Joe, BA-7
Robinson, Matt, N-7, N-12
Rockefeller, John D., 479, 546–547
Roddick, Anita, 157
Rodriguez, Robert, N
Rodrik, Dana, N-1
Rogoff, Kenneth S., N-6
Rogoway, Sam, 232
Rohlin, Shawn, N-4
Rollo, David, N-12
Romeo, Peter, N-12
Rometty, Virginia, 245
Roos, Richard, 111–112
Roosevelt, Franklin D., 36, 53, 596
Rosato, Donna, N-16
Rosenberg, Larry, 440
Rosenberg, Michael, 215
Rosenblatt, James D., N-5
Rosenkrantz, Holly, N-2
Rosenwald, Michael S., N-6
Roth, J. D., N-16
Rouen, Ethan, N-7
Rowling, J. K., A1-7
Rubin, Courtney, N-1, N-5
Rubin, James R., N-3
Ruiz, Juanita, 439
Rupp, K., N-17
Rutledge, Tanya, 433
Ryan, David, N, N-6
Ryan, Vincent, N-13

S

Sainz, Adrian, N-18
Salisbury, Dallas, N-16
Salisbury, Ian, N-16
Saloner, Garth, 403
Salter, Ammon, N-6
Samuels, Diana, N-8
Samuelson, Robert J., N-1, N-9, N-13, N-14, N-16
Sanders, Peter, N-18
Santisteban, Ralph, 143
Santoli, Michael, N-14
Saporito, Bill, N-6, N-9, N-12, N-15
Sapp, Stephen, N-11
Sarno, David, N-15
Satariano, Adam, N-9
Sauter, Michael B., N-16
Savitz, Eric, N-14
Sax, David, 482
Saxby, David, N-3
Scaggs, Ann, 481–482
Scaggs, James, 481–482
Schadler, Ted, 206
Schaecher, Susan M., N-8
Schafer, Sara, N-3
Schaffer, Robert H., N-5
Schaffner, Dionn, 470
Schatz, Amy, N-17
Schechner, Sam, N-11, N-12
Scheller-Wolf, A., N-12
Schmidt, Robert, N-3
Schmidt, Warren, 205
Schneider, Benjamin, N-8
Schneider, Howard, 607, N-15
Schneider, Joan, N-11
Schoeller, Martin, N-6
Schonberger, Jennifer, N-14
Schonfeld, Erick, N-4
Schramm, Carl, N-15
Schreiner, Bruce, 93
Schuker, Lauren A. E., N-10

Schulte, Grant, N-9
Schultz, Howard, 63, 155, N-6
Schumacher, Steve, N-7
Schuman, Michael, 249, N-7
Schuman, Nancy, E-4
Schumpeter, Joseph, 49
Schuster, Jay, 327
Schwabel, Don, 29
Schwartz, Mathew J., N-17, N-18
Schweer, Margaret, N-6
Scott, Mark, N-7
Scott, Ryan, N-7
Searcey, Dionne, N-2
Sedensky, Matt, N-18
Seitz, Patrick, N-4
Selberherr, S., N-17
Sellers, Patricia, N-7
Senge, Peter, N-11
Shane, Scott, N-5
Shantz, Amanda, N-7
Sharp, David, N-10, N-11
Shaw, Tony, N-17
Sheehan, Brendan, N-12
Sheen, Charlie, 471
Sheffield, Christopher, N-13
Shenk, Martin, N-13
Shepardson, David, N-2, N-9
Sherman, Mark, N-6
Sherr, Ian, N-15
Sherwood, Pat, 529–530
Shields, Todd, N-8, N-17
Shipley, Amy, 341
Shockley-Zalabak, Pamela S., N-6
Shread, Paul, 206
Shutts, Carole, 143–144
Sile, Elizabeth, 414
Simchi-Levi, David, N-7
Simmons, Russell, 157
Simon, Stephanie, BB-1, N-18
Simons, John, 173
Singer, Bill, 345
Singer, Natasha, N-18
Singletary, Michelle, N-16
Skilling, Jeffrey, 91
Skjelmose, Jeanette, 435
Skok, David, N-13
Slater, Theresa, N-13
Slaughter, Matthew J., N-1
Smith, Adam, 33, 34, 57, 98
Smith, Anne Kates, 83, N
Smith, Elliot, N-3
Smith, Gina, N-17
Smith, Lee, N-6
Smith, Mike, N-18
Smith, N. Craig, N
Smith, Ned, N-4
Smith, Rich, N-13
Smith, Will, 61
Snetiker, Marc, 191
Snoop Dogg, 471
Solomon, Robert C., 108
Song, Kyung M., N-16
Soroosh, Jalai, N-13
Spade, Andy, 126
Spade, Kate, 126
Speiser, Joe, 542
Sperry, Paul, N-16
Spiegelman, Paul, N-8
Spitznagel, Eric, N-15
Spivack, Miranda S., N-3
Squazzo, Jessica D., N-3
Staley, Oliver, N-10
Stanford, Duane, N

Stanton, Pauline, 330
Starkey, Michael, N-12
Steel, Emily, N-10, N-11, N-12
Steinberg, Scott, N-18
Steinke, H. Dean, 96
Stephens, Sarah, N-2
Stephens, Warren, N
Stern, David, 341
Sternberg, Joseph, 450, N-10
Stettner, Morey, N-13
Stevens, Suzanne, N-3
Stewart, James B., N-14, N-16
Stewart, Martha, 191
Stier, Ben, N-3
Stockdale, Charles B., N-16
Stodder, David, N-17
Stohr, Greg, N-8
Stolz, Richard F., N-2
Strauss, Gary, N-10
Strauss, Lawrence C., N-6
Strauss, Levi, 146
Strohmeyer, Robert, BA-7
Stuart, Alix, N-8, N-9
Sullivan, James, N-9
Sullivan, Paul, N-16
Sung, Chinmei, N-2
Sussman, Nadia, N-9
Sutherly, Ben, N-3
Suutari, Vesa, 330
Svensson, Peter, N-18
Swaminathan, Kishore S., N-13
Sweeney, Paul, N-3
Swenson, Kyle, N-4
Swider, Brian W., N-7
Swindberg, Nick, 213
Szaky, Tom, 417

T

Talbot, David, N-10
Talley, Ian, N-2, N-15
Tam, Pui-Wing, N-5
Tan, S. Y., N-15
Tannenbaum, Robert, 205
Tanzer, Andrew, 568
Tarquinio, J. Alex, 587, N-15
Tavev, Margaret, N
Taylor, Bill, N-8
Taylor, Frederick, 279–280, 300, 304
Taylor, John B., N
Taylor, Marisa, N-11
Tayur, S., N-12
Telfer, Clint, 182
Telfer, Jennifer, 182
Tenbrunsel, Ann E., 34, N
Tencer, Daniel, N-2
Tennent, Devar, 439
Terlep, Sharon, N-5, N-10
Tett, Gillian, N-14
Theil, Stefan, N-4
Thelli, Joe, 201
Thomas, Isiah, 359
Thomas, Megan L., N-7
Thomas, Robert J., N-6
Thomasson, Lynn, N-14
Thompson, Chrissie, N-2
Thompson, Derek, N-4
Thompson, Victoria, 121
Thomson, Jeffrey C., N-12
Tice, Carol, N-5
Tierney, John, 175
Timberlake, Cotton, N-11
Timiraos, Nick, N-14

Tindell, Kip, 304
Toman, Emily, 3
Toral, Ruben, 83
Touryalai, Halah, N-14
Townes, Glenn, N-16
Townsend, Matt, 444
Tozzi, John, 173, N, N-1, N-15
Tracer, Zachary, 254
Trachtenberg, Jeffrey A., N-10
Tran, Hung, N-14
Trejos, Nancy, N-6
Trudeau, Garry, 106
Truitt, Brian, N-12
Trung, Ly Qui, 68, 145
Truong, Quang, N-7
Tugend, Alina, N-15
Turner, J., N-12
Tuuti, Camille, 296

U

Ucbasaran, Deniz, N-5
Ulrich, Carmen Wong, A2-1
Unger, Henry, N-12
Unruh, Gregory, N-12
Upchurch, Brent, 142

V

Van Kooten, Valerie, N-9
Van Oosterhout, J. (Hans), N-2
Van Voorhis, Kenneth R., 159
Van Voris, Bob, N-3
Vance, Ashlee, N-17
Vandenbosch, Mark, N-11
Vanderbilt, Cornelius, 167
Vandewater, Cathy, 321
Vanermey, Anne, N
Velshi, Ali, N-12
Vernon, Lillian, 9
Vietor, Richard H. K., N-1
Villano, Matt, 418, 463, N, N-11
Vincent, Matthew, N-13
Vip, Pamela, N-10
Virtanen, Michael, N-15
Viscusi, W. Kip, N-15
Visseyrias, Mathilde, N-11
Vo, Anne, 330
Vohlwinkle, Jeremy, N-14
Von Drehle, David, N-15

Vranica, Suzanne, N-10
Vroom, Victor, 289

W

Waber, Ben, N-9
Wakabayashi, Daisuke, N-18
Waldrop, Madison, 165
Waller, Jeff, N-2
Walsh, Bryan, N
Walsh, Sebastian, N-14
Walton, Sam, 4, 5, 146
Wang, Jay, N-2
Wang, Jennifer, 307, N-4, N-5, N-8
Wang, Zhong-Ming, N-4
Warner, H. M., BA-4
Wartzman, Rick, N-7
Washington, Jerome, 440
Waters. Jim, N-9
Wathieu, Luc, N-5
Watson, Thomas, BA-4
Wayner, Peter, N-18
Weber, Lauren, N-8
Weber, Max, 220, 221, 238
Wei, Michael, N-1
Wei, William, N-17
Weil, Jonathan, N-14
Weild, David, 559
Weingartner, Nancy, N-4
Weinstein, Alan, N-5
Weinstein, Bruce, 321
Weise, Karen, 104
Weisman, Robert, N-4
Weiss, Aviva, 153
Weiss, Gary, N-2
Weiss, Haskel, 153
Weiss, Joanna, N-9
Welch, David, N-13
Welch, Jack, 555
Welcher, Anthony, N-6
Wells, Donna, 317
Welrum, Kasey, N-12
West, Melanie Grayce, N-4
Westhead, Paul, N-5
Whelan, Eoin, N-6
White, Jason, 167
White, Martha, N-1, N-5
Whitehouse, Mark, N-5
Whitman, Meg, 205–206
Whitney, Eli, 20

Whitney, John, 327
Whoriskey, Peter, N-9
Wienzierl, Matthew, N-1
Willard, Cody, BA-4
Williams, Rob, N-14
Willmer, Dave, N-8
Wilson, Jeffrey L., N-12
Wilson, Jennifer, N-4
Winfrey, Oprah, 9, 356
Wingfield, Nick, N-3, N-17
Winter, Caroline, N-1, N-3
Wiseman, Liz, N-5
Wolfe, Alexandra, 433, N-17
Wolman, David, N-15, N-17
Woo, Eva, 559
Woodcock, Neil, N-12
Wooley, Anita, N-5
Woollery, Suzanne, N-7
Wooten, Adam, N-1, N-2
Wortham, April, N-17
Wortham, Jenna, BA-1
Worthen, Ben, N-13
Woyke, Elizabeth, N-12
Wozniack, Steve, 158
Wright, Mike, N-5
Wright, Robert, N-11
Wu, Angela, N-16
Wulf, Julie, N-6
Wuorio, Jeff, N-16

Y

Yabroff, Jennie, N-10
Yao Ming, 61
Yip, George S., N-6
Yunus, Muhammad, 7

Z

Zanuck, Darryl, BA-4
Zbar, Jeff, N-12
Zhang, Wei, N-4
Zielinski, Dave, N-7
Zimmerman, Ann, N-11
Zimmerman, Ryan D., N-7
Zuckerberg, Mark, 155, BA-1
Zumbrun, Joshua, N-12
Zupek, Rachel, P-4
Zwahlen, Cynthia, N-1
Zwilling, Martin, N-13

organization index

A

A. H. Robins, A1-5
A. M. Best, A2-11
AAA, 361
AAMCO, 448
AARP, 361
ABC, A1-18
Abu Dhabi Investment Authority, 544
AC Hotels, 70
Ace Hardware, 146, 448
Adidas, 254, 598
ADP Mobile Solutions, 334
Advertising Council, 379
AF Sachs AG, 449
Aflac, A1-7
AFL-CIO, 345, 349, 363, 366
AICPA; see American Institute of Certified
    Public Accountants
AIG; see American International Group
Akimenko Meats, 173
Al Muhairy Group, 68
Alcoa, 577
Allen-Bradley, 253
Alliance of Motion Picture and Television
    Producers, 352
Allied Security Trust, A1-7
Altria Group, 576
Amazon.com, 155, 183, 213, 388, 444,
    BA-12, BA-15, BA-16
Amdocs, BA-12 to BA-13
American Arbitration Association, 352
American Cotton Oil, 577
American Eagle, 21
American Express, 360, 535, 577, 603, 605
American Federation of TV and Radio Artists,
    366–367
American Institute of Certified Public
    Accountants (AICPA), 500, 501
American International Group (AIG), 529,
    576, 579
American Marketing Association, 376, 404
American Solar Energy Society, 104
American Sugar Refining Co., 577
American Tobacco, 577, A1-11
Ameritrade, 566, 583, 584
Amtrak, 198
Anglo-American, 9
Anheuser-Busch, 137–138
Apple Computer, 73, 132, 158, 204, 245, 250,
    308, 406, 415, 440, 450, 472, 478, 507,
    534, 546, 548, 568, A1-11, BA-15
Archipelago, 558
Arista Records, 29
Arizona Beverage Company, 412
Arm & Hammer, 420
Armstrong, 483
Arthur Andersen, 501
Associated Grocers, 448
Associated Press, 146
Association of Certified Fraud Examiners, 102
AT&T, 204, 408, 576, 577, 585, A1-11
Auntie Anne's Pretzels, 143, 144
Autoliv Inc., 449

Avon, 154, 183
AXA Group, BB-1

B

Babson College, 155
Baccarat, 292
Bagel Works, 101
Ball Corporation, 269
Bank of America, 157, 331, 576, 577, 579, 598
Barnes & Noble, 388
Baskin-Robbins, 129, 140, 448
Bayer, 413, 415
BDO Seidman, 497
Berkshire Hathaway, 570
Best Buy, 192, 206
Better Business Bureau, 177
Better Homes & Gardens Real Estate LLC, 472
Bill and Melinda Gates Foundation; see Gates
    Foundation
Bing Group, 215
Blockbuster, 197, A1-15
BLS; see Bureau of Labor Statistics
Blue Cross/Blue Shield, A2-11, BB-9
Blue Diamond, 146
BlueNile.com, 162
Blurb, 296
BMW, 255
Bob's Big Boy, 406
Bocktown Beer and Grill, 405
Body Shop, 157
Boeing, 63, 90, 547, 577, BB-3
Boise Cascade, 105
Borden, 413
Borders Books, 389, A1-15, A1-16
BorgWarner, 449
BP, 71, 81, 478
Bridgeman Foods, 143
Bright Horizons Family Solutions, Inc., 361
Bristol-Myers Squibb, 360
British Airways, 19
Build-A-Bear Workshop Inc., 144, 317
Bumrungrad International Hospital, 83
Bureau of Alcohol, Tobacco, and Firearms, 451
Bureau of Export Administration, 64
Bureau of Labor Statistics (BLS), 319–320,
    362, 363
Burger King, 137, 406

C

Cakelove, 123
Campbell Soup Company, 391, 413
Candy Bouquet International, 144
Capital Protective Insurance (CPI), 255
Cardinal Health, 450
Careerbuilder.com, 317, E-5
Carl's Junior, 406
Caterpillar, 63, 577
CBS, A1-18
Celestial Seasonings, 100
Cell Phones for Soldiers, 112
Census Bureau, 92, 138
Center for American Progress, 359
Center for Hispanic Leadership, 389

CH2M Hill, 87
Change to Win, 345
Charles Schwab, 555, 583, 584
Charm City Cakes, 252
Charming Charlie, 433
Cheesecake Factory, 121
Chef America, 71
Chevron, 71, 81, 247, 576, 577
Chicago Gas, 577
China National Petroleum, 71
ChiNext, 559
Chocolate Chocolate Chocolate Company, 448
Chocomize, 254
Chrysler, 137
Ciba Specialty Chemicals, 103
CircleLending, 172
Circuit City, A1-15
Cirrus, 605
Cisco Systems, 204, 258, 546, 558, 576, 577,
    A1-7, BA-16
Citibank, BA-20
Citigroup, 71, 105, 576
City of Chesterfield Zoning Board, A1-4
CJ Products, 182
Clairol, 473
Clover Food Truck, 418
CNBC, 555, 569, 571, 576, 578, A2-1
CNN, 555
CNOOC, 138
Coca-Cola, 12, 19, 66, 70, 73, 407–408, 413,
    414, 415, 469, 470, 507, 519, 563, 570,
    577
Coinstar, 27
Coldwater Creek, 447
Committee Encouraging Corporate
    Philanthropy, 100
Consumer Reports, 32
Container Store, 304–305
Cook County Department of Revenue, 502
Coors Brewing Company, 73, 473
Costco, 102, 441
Council of Economic Advisers, 587
CPI; see Capital Protective Insurance
Craigslist, 15
Crayola Crayons, 420
Crested Butte Angler, 167
Critical Infrastructure Protection Board, BA-21
CruiseOne, 143
Custom Foot, 254

D

Dairy Queen, 404
Dangdang.com, 297
Dealtime.com, 425
Dean & DeLuca, 511
Decorating Den, 143
Def Jam Records, 157
Del Monte, 413
Dell Computer, 69, 155, 234, 393, 414, 439, 558
Deloitte Touche Tomatsu, 519
Designs by Malyse, 165
Detroit Pistons, 215
Deutsche Börse AG, 558
DHL, 387, 454

Digicel, 5
Digital Equipment Corporation, BA-4
Dim and Den Sum, 418
Disney Company, 12, 70, 156–157, 182, 295, 308, 356, 563, 576, 577, A1-7, BA-13 to BA-14
Distilling & Cattle Feeding Co., 577
Domino's Pizza, 143
Door-to-Door Dry Cleaning, 138
Doozle's, 536
Dow Chemical, 106, 296–297
Dow Jones & Company, 576
Dr Pepper, 472, 484
Dream Dinners, 430–431
Dreamworks, 329
Dreyer's Ice Cream, 71
Drinker Biddle & Reath, A1-1
Dropbox, BA-16
Drugstore.com, 485
Dualstar, 5
Duke University, 204
Dun & Bradstreet, 166
Dunkin' Donuts, 68, 140, 141, 406
Dupont, 19, 154, 183, 203, 247, 577, A1-11
Dyson, 485

E

E*Trade, 555, 566, 583, 584
E*Trade Bank, 605
Eastman Chemical Company, 327
Eastman Kodak, 154, 414, 576
eBay, 101, 205–206, 422, BA-20
Economic Development Authority, 170
Ecoprint, 317
eHealthInsurance.com, A2-11
Elance.com, 160
Electrolux, 73
Elite Modeling Agency, 191
EMC, 322
Emirates Associated Business Group, 67
Energizer, 400–401
Enron, 90, 91, 97, 98, 501, 578, 612, A1-13
Ethisphere, 105
Euronext, 558
E-Vault, BA-8
Expedia, 379
Exxon Mobil, 71, 81, 413, 470, 577

F

Fabindia, 452
Facebook, 4, 13, 93, 145, 155, 162, 206, 234, 235, 256, 377, 384, 396, 405, 463, 468, 472, 473, 482, 489, 546, 557, BA-1, BA-11, BA-12, E-1, E-3, P-7
Fannie Mae; see Federal National Mortgage Association
Fastsigns, 142
Fat Straws, 3
Federal Home Loan Mortgage Corporation (Freddie Mac), 357, 579, 601, A1-14
Federal National Mortgage Association (Fannie Mae), 357, 579, 601, A1-14
FedEx, 233, 322, 387, 446, 452, 454, 455, 461
FedEx Office, 294
Fidelity, 566
FINCA; see Foundation for International Community Assistance
Finish Line, 318
Firestone, BB-4
First Data, 604
FirstUSA, A2-9
Fitch Ratings, 564, 565, 572
Fitness Anywhere, 403

Flextronics, 257
Florida Power and Light, 40
Florida Public Service Commission, 40
FNMA; see Federal National Mortgage Association
Food and Drug Administration, 451
Ford Motor Company, 46, 74–75, 81, 154, 183, 219, 234, 294, 473, 548, A1-5, BA-17, BB-4
Foundation for International Community Assistance (FINCA), 36
4Food, BA-11
Foursquare, 384, 472
Fox Lawson & Associates, 327
Freddie Mac; see Federal Home Loan Mortgage Corporation
Frederick's of Hollywood, 67
Free Management Library, 250
Fresh Italy, 386
Fresh Look Remodeling, 173
Freshii, 145
FridgeDoor.com, 393
Fun and Function, 153

G

Galleon Group, 101
Gap, 153
Garden.com, 470
Gates Foundation, 40, 99
Gazprom, 414
GE; see General Electric
Genentech, 137, 329
General Electric Capital Corporation, 541, 600
General Electric (GE), 19, 129, 200, 308, 323, 455, 548, 555, 577
General Motors (GM), 81, 194, 215, 219, 234, 269, 529, 576, 579, A1-5, A1-15
General Nutrition Center (GNC), 254
Giant Campus, 155
GiftZip.com, 155
Give More Media, 295
Global Crossing, 578, 612
GlobeFunder, 172
GM; see General Motors
GNC; see General Nutrition Center
Goldman Sachs, 80, 105, 573
Goodwill Industries, 524–525, 529
Goodyear, 415
Google, 15, 201, 202, 204, 256, 286, 308, 396, 413, 414, 415, 546, 558, A1-7, A1-11, A1-13, BA-8, BA-12, BA-15, E-3
Grameen Bank, 7
Greatest Good, 29
Greatwide Logistics Services, 452
Green Marketing International Inc., BB-11
Green Mountain Coffee Roasters, 102
GreenNote, 172
Greenpeace, 379
Groupon, 480, 481, 489
Gymboree, 137

H

H. B. Fuller Company, 74
H&R Block, 145
Häagen-Dazs, 145
HACE; see Hispanic Alliance for Career Enhancement
Haemonetics, 360–361
hairyLemon, 414
Hallmark, 140
Harvard University, 280
HealthSouth, 90

Heinz, 59
Hershey Foods Corporation, 268, BA-22
Hertz Corporation, 137
Hewlett-Packard (HP), 70, 295, 357, 577
Hilton, 101
Hispanic Alliance for Career Enhancement (HACE), 324
Hitachi, 70, 287–288
H.J. Heinz Company, 413
Holiday Inn, 68, 138, 144
Home Depot, 105, 221, 223, 425, 576, 577
Honda, 7, 46, 71, 73, 257, 269, 568
Honeywell, 576
Hoover's, E-10
Houston Rockets, 60, 61
HP; see Hewlett-Packard
Hyundai, 7

I

i2, 449
IASB; see International Accounting Standards Board
IBM, 15, 19, 63, 69, 82, 100, 101, 204, 242, 245, 248, 315, 360, 476–477, 563, 568, 577, BA-4, BA-14, BA-15
IdeaPaint, 155
IGA, 448
Igus, 259
Ikea, 435
Illinois Department of Corrections, 89
Imax Corporation, 80
ImClone, 90
InBev, 137–138
Industrial and Commercial Bank of China, 357
Institute of Certified Management Accountants, 500
Insurance Information Institute, BB-14
Intel, 101, 104, 251, 360, 546, 558, 576, 577, BA-13
InterActive Custom Clothes, 254–255
Intercontinental Exchange Inc., A1-12 to A1-13
International Accounting Standards Board (IASB), 519
International Franchise Association, 138
International Franchise Association Education Foundation, 143
International House, 250
International Ladies' Garment Workers' Union, 345
International Paper, 576
Internships.com, 471
Intuit, 504
Iron Mountain, BA-8

J

Jack in the Box, A1-5
Japan Post Holdings, 71
Jazzercise, 140, 143
JCPenney, 222–223
Jenny Craig, 71
Jiffy Lube, 138, 425
John Deere, 200
Johnson & Johnson, 19, 96, 97, 98, 360, 534, 570, 577
Joie de Vivre, 282
JPMorgan Chase, 105, 361, 577
Jumo, BA-1
Jungle Jim's International Market, 154

K

K2 Skis, 233
Kaiser Permanente, BB-9

Kathy Ireland Worldwide, 191
KB Toys, 444
KFC, 68, 73, 141, 381, 406, 448
Kia, 449
Kickstarter.com, 173
Kiva, 172
KLM Royal Dutch Airlines, 454
Kmart, 191, 538
Kodak; *see* Eastman Kodak
KOi Fusion PDX, 418
KPMG, 295
Kraft Foods, 449, 468, 474, 484, 576
Krispy Kreme, 141, 405
K-Tec, 472
Kumon Learning Centers, 145

L

L. L. Bean, 404, 447
Laclede Gas Light Co., 577
Land O'Lakes, 146
Lands' End, 447
LegalZoom, 135
Legend Capital, 559
Lehman Brothers, 502, 548, 579
Lemonade Inc., 162
Lending Club, 172, 173, 540
Lendio, 540
Lenovo Group Ltd., 19
Levi-Strauss, 81, 380, 413
LexisNexis, 319
Liberty Media, 357
Library of Congress, A1-7
LinkedIn, 472, 562, E-1, E-3
Living Social, 481
Lockheed Martin Corporation, 163
Los Angeles Lakers, 61, 204
Lotus Development, 101
Lotus Public Relations, 295
Lowe's, 223, BB-4
Lucas Group, 473

M

Macy's, 223, 297, 465, 506, 538
Madison Square Garden, 359
Major League Baseball (MLB), 61, 182, 545
Mango Store, 601
Maricopa County Planning Commission, A1-4
Maritz, Inc., 295
Marketing Zen Group, 463
Marriott International, 70, 144
Mars, 136
MasterCard, 473, 535, 603, 605
Masterfoods USA, 473
Mattel, 176, A1-5
Maybelline, 473
Maytag, 206
McCormick, 530
McDonald's, 26–27, 68, 69, 73, 99, 106,
    138–139, 140, 141, 142, 145, 170, 222,
    236, 256, 279, 324, 404–405, 406, 413,
    448, 468, 507, 553, 569–570, 577, A1-4,
    A1-6, A1-7
McDonnell Douglas, 547
MCI Inc., 91
McKinsey & Company, BB-1
Medtronic Inc., 82, A1-6 to A1-7
Mercedes, 71, 257, 416
Merck, 96, 577, A1-1, A1-5
Meridan Group, 63
Merrill Lynch, 579
Merry Maids, 140
Michelin, 247, 449
Michelob, 413
Michigan State University School of
    Packaging, 412

Microsoft, 5, 40, 129, 155, 202, 415, 548,
    558, 571, 576, 577, 585, 590, A1-11,
    A1-12, BA-16
Miller Brewing Company, 138
Mindbridge, 362
Minority Business Development Agency, 170
Missouri Department of Natural Resources, 502
Mitsubishi, BA-6
MLB; *see* Major League Baseball
ModCloth, 170
Monster.com, 317, E-5
Monte Jade, 324
Moody's Investors Service, 548, 564, 565,
    572, 612, E-10
Morningstar, 585
Motley Fool, 556
Motorola, 108, 323
Mozy, BA-8
MSNBC, 576, 578
MTV, 132, BA-22
Munich American Reinsurance Company, BB-1
Munich Re, BB-1, BB-2
MySimon.com, 425, 430

N

NASA, 323
NASCAR, 415
NASDAQ OMX Group, 558, 559, A1-12 to
    A1-13
National Alliance for Caregiving, 361
National Basketball Association (NBA), 60,
    61, 143, 204, 215, 341
National Bicycle Industrial Company, 254
National Business Group on Health, 83
National Business Incubator Association
    (NBIA), 164
National Collegiate Athletic Association
    (NCAA), 182
National Consumer Counseling Service, A2-9
National Cooperative Business Association, 146
National Federation of Independent Business,
    538
National Football League (NFL), 61, 352,
    353, 354
National Football League Players Association
    (NFLPA), 352
National Institute of Health, 362
National Institute on Drug Abuse, 362
National Lead, 577
National Mediation Board, 352
National Park Service, 502
National Small Business Association, 542
National Venture Capital Association, 172
NBA; *see* National Basketball Association
NBC, A1-18, A2-1
NBIA; *see* National Business Incubator
    Association
NCAA; *see* National Collegiate Athletic
    Association
Near Networks, 232
Nestlé, 19, 70, 71, 262, 568
Netflix, 460–461, BA-10
NetworkforGood.org, 100
New Belgium Brewery, 242–243, 307
New Jersey Nets, 60
New York Knicks, 359
NFL; *see* National Football League
NiGaz, 414
Nike, 69, 81, 106–107, 233, 234, 400, 534, A1-7
Nissan, 359
NNPC, 414
Nokia, 247
Nom Nom, 418
Nordstrom, 221
North American Co., 577

North Lawndale Employment Network, 89
Norton, BA-19
Nucor Steel, 328
NYSE Euronext, 558, A1-13

O

Occupational Safety and Health
    Administration (OSHA), 362
Ocean Spray, 146
oDesk.com, 160
OECD; *see* Organization for Economic
    Cooperation and Development
Office Depot, 331
Office of Federal Contract Compliance
    Programs, 312
Office of Personnel Management (OPM), 361
OMX Group, 558
OPM; *see* Office of Personnel Management
Opportunity International, 56–57
Oracle Corporation, 449, 450
Organization for Economic Cooperation and
    Development (OECD), 75, 107
Organization of American States, 107
OSHA; *see* Occupational Safety and Health
    Administration

P

Packard Bell, BA-3
Palo Alto Software, 170
Pandora, BA-10
Parsley Patch, 529–530, 534
Patagonia, 99
PayPal, 178, 590, BA-20
People Capital, 172
PepsiCo, 9, 70, 73, 74, 103, 193, 247, 408,
    409, 414, 415, 470, 481, A1-12
Perdue Chicken, 73
Perrier, 71
Peterson Institute for International
    Economics, 64
Petflow.com, 542
PetZen Products LLC, 134
Pfizer, 543, 576, 577
Phat Farm, 157
Phillips-Van Heusen, 106
Pho24, 68, 145
Pinterest, E-3
Pizza Hut, 68
Playtex Company, A1-5
PODS, 151
Priceline.com, 379, 425
PricewaterhouseCoopers, 245
Printinginabox.com, 144
Procter & Gamble, 74, 105, 154, 216, 247,
    308, 389, 408, 444, 568, 570, 577
Prosper Marketplace, 172

R

R. J. Julia Booksellers, 497, 498
Rainforest Action Network (RAN), 105
Ralston Purina, 71
RAN; *see* Rainforest Action Network
Randstad USA, 320
RatePoint, 481–482
RCA, BA-3
Red Bull, 413
Red Cross, 7, 322, 379, 502
Redbox, 26–27
Rhino Records, 111–112
Riceland Foods, 146
Richardson Electronics, 450
Ritz-Carlton Hotel Company, 250
RJR Nabisco, 137
Roche, 137

Rocky Mountain Chocolate Factory, 68, 143–144
Rolex, 415
RoliRoti, 418
Rollerblade, 415
Rowe Furniture, 223
RSM McGladrey, 253
Ruckus Wireless, 285
Rush Management, 157

S

S&P; *see* Standard & Poor's
SAB, 138
Sage, 504
St. Louis Cardinals, 545
Saks Fifth Avenue, 396
Salvation Army, 7, 502
Salvatore Ferragamo, 423
Sam's Club, 441
Samsung, 70, 568
Samuel Adams, 63
Sands Hotels, 548
Sanmina-SCI, 257
SAP, 449, BA-16
Sara Lee Corporation, A1-5
SAS, 277, 339
SBC Communications Inc., 576
Scott, 449
Scottrade, 566
Screen Actors Guild, 366–367
Sears, Roebuck & Company, 106, 107, 414, 446
Second Bank of the United States, 595
Service Employees International Union (SEIU), 345, 355, 364
7-Eleven, 3, 27, 138, 406, 409, 439
Seventh Generation, 408
Shakey's Pizza, 406
Shanghai Electric, 19
Shanghai Shendi Group, 70
Shell Oil, 19, 71, 470, 568
Sherwin-Williams, 448
ShoeDazzle, 465
Siemens, 82, 568
Sinopac, 71
Six Flags, 197
Skyline Construction, 327
Skype, 235
Small Business Exporters Association, 64
Snapple, 481
Sonoma Partners, 296
Sony, 202, 413, BA-19
Southwest Airlines, 298, A1-18
Sprout Group, 296
Standard & Poor's, 548, 564, 565, 572, 576, 612, E-10
Standard Oil, 546–547, A1-11
Staples, 441
Starbucks, 63, 155, 216, 383, 405, 406, 420, 439, 468, 507, 558, 598, BA-13
StarKist, 103
StarMedia, 375
State Farm Insurance, 362
State Grid, 71
Stihl, 249
Stop & Shop, 14
Students for Responsible Business, 100
Substance Abuse & Mental Health Services Association, 362
Subway, 68, 141, 142, 144, 145
SuccessFactor, BA-16
Sugar Philly Truck, 418
Sulekha, 324
Sunkist, 146
Sunoco, Inc., 125
Sunoco Logistics Partners (SXL), 125

Sustainability Consortium, 104
Sweet Beginnings, 89

T

T. Rowe Price, 575
Taco Bell, 68, 197
Talon, Inc., 419
Target, 222, 235, 396, 406, 409, 430, 455
Tata Global Beverages, 70
Tatango, 155
Team, 447
Temasek Holdings, 9
Tennessee Coal, Iron & Railroad Co., 577
TerraCycle, 417
Texas Instruments (TI), 452
thredUp, 527
3Com, BA-4
3M, 163, 406, 577
ThrowThings.com, 162
TIAA-CREF, 600
Timberland, 99, 434
Timken, 322
Tissot, 472
TNT, 99, 454
Tom and Eddie's, 553
Toyota Motor, 7, 71, 81, 269, 359, 478, A1-5
Toys "R" Us, 137, 444
TradePoint, 451
Transparency International, 75
Transportation Security Administration, 198
Travelers, 576, 577
Travelocity, 295, 379
Triangle Shirtwaist Company, 345
Tripledge, 484
True Value Hardware, 146
Trump Hotels and Casinos, 548
20th Century Fox, BA-4
Twitter, 14, 155, 206, 234, 235, 377, 384, 405, 414, 418, 463, 468, 471, 472, 473, 482, 489, BA-12, BA-22, E-1, E-3, E-9
Tyco International, 90, 501, 578, 612
Tyson Foods, BB-4

U

Ugly Dolls, 63
United Auto Workers, 354
United Health Group, 577
United Mine Workers, 344
United Parcel Service (UPS), 61, 200, 220, 233, 279, 280, 297, 361, 387, 436, 446, 452, 454, 455, 461, 538
U.S. Department of Commerce, 63, 64, 68, 143, 179
U.S. Department of Defense, 289
U.S. Department of Education, 359
U.S. Department of Health and Human Services, 362
U.S. Department of Homeland Security, BA-21
U.S. Department of Justice, A1-11, A1-12 to A1-13
U.S. Department of Labor, 102, 322, 362, E-4
U.S. Department of State, 455, BB-2
U.S. Department of Treasury, A1-13
U.S. Government Printing Office, 64
U.S. Navy, 419
U.S. Patent and Trademark Office (USPTO), A1-6, A1-7, A1-22, A1-23
U.S. Postal Service, 363, 436, 452, 460, 461
U.S. Public Interest Research Group, 599
U.S. Supreme Court, 311, 324, 359, 501, A1-3, A1-6, A2-11
United Technologies, 577
United Way, 7
University of California–Los Angeles, 287
University of Maryland, 177

University of Oregon, 32
University of Pittsburgh, 70
Univision, 375
Unocal, 138
UPS; *see* United Parcel Service
UPS Store, 140
US Bank, 598
U.S. Leather, 577
U.S. Rubber Co., 577

V

Vehix, 376
VeriSign, BA-21
Verizon, 576, 577, A1-7
Victoria Jackson Cosmetics Company, 175
Victoria's Secret, 598
Virgin Airlines, 413
Virgin Group Ltd., 472
Virgin Money, 172
Virginia Tech, 177
Virtuous Bread, 160
Visa, 535, 603, 605, A1-11
VisionSpring, 64
Vita-Mix, 471–472
VMware, BA-16
Volkswagen, 81, 246, 256
VolunteerMatch.org, 100

W

Walmart, 4, 5, 19, 61, 71, 73, 80, 102, 104, 129, 154, 183, 233, 256, 412, 425, 430, 435, 446, 455, 577, BA-8
Walt Disney Company; *see* Disney Company
Warner Bros., 67, BA-4
Washington Opera Company, 425
Wegman's Food Markets, 316
Weight Watchers, 138
Welch's, 146
Wells Fargo Bank, 100
Wendy's, 143, 250, 406
Western Electric, 280–281
Western Union, BA-4
Whole Foods Market, 194, 511
WikiLeaks, BB-2
Will n' Rose's LLC, 156
Wilson Sporting Goods, 225
Winn-Dixie, 318
Winterthur Life & Pensions, BB-1
Wizard Vending, 178
WorldCom, 90, 91, 102, 501, 578, 612, A1-13
Wrigley Company, 136
Writers Guild of America, 367
Wyeth, 233

X

Xerox Corporation, 69, 100, 193, 242, 363, 414, 415
Xporta, 451
XSAg.com, 15

Y

Yahoo, 422, 430, 558, 571, 573, 575, 576, A1-13, BA-8
Yale University, 359
Yelp, 482
Yogen Früz, 145
YoungEntrepreneur.com, 177
YouTube, 155, 206, 235, A1-7, BA-11, E-3
Yum! Brands, 68, 141

Z

Zappos, 213, 321, 472, 485
Zippo, 406, 415
Zopa, 172

subject index

A

Absolute advantage, 62
Accessory equipment, 411
Accountability, 203
Accountants
  certified management, 499–500
  certified public, 500–501
  private, 500
  public, 500–501
Accounting
  areas
    auditing, 501–502, 530–531
    financial, 500–501
    government and not-for-profit, 502–503
    managerial, 499–500
    tax, 502
  defined, 498
  distinction from bookkeeping, 503
  ethical issues, 515
  fundamental equation, 506
  journals, 503–504
  ledgers, 504
  oversight of profession, 501, 502
  purposes, 498
  relationship to finance, 528
  reports, 498, 499
  scandals, 501
  in small businesses, 176, 504
  technology used in, 504
  users of information, 498, 499
Accounting cycle, 503–504
Accounting firms
  consulting work, 502
  scandals, 501
Accounting standards
  generally accepted principles, 501, 511, 519
  international, 519
Accounting system, 498, 499
Accounts payable, 508
Accounts receivable
  collecting, 535
  as current asset, 508
  factoring, 541
Acid-test (quick) ratio, 516
Acquisitions, 136; *see also* Mergers and
  acquisitions
Activity ratios, 518–519
ADA; *see* Americans with Disabilities Act
Administered distribution systems, 448–449
Administrative agencies, A1-3, A1-4
ADRs; *see* American depository receipts
Advantage
  absolute, 62
  comparative, 62
Advertising
  categories, 466–467
  celebrity endorsements, 465, 471
  defined, 465–466
  direct mail, 447, 466, 468
  expenditures, 466–467
  in foreign countries, 73
  global, 473
  greenwashing, 32

  infomercials, 470
  Internet, 467, 468, 470–472
  magazine, 468
  media, 467–468
  mobile, 468, 483–484
  newspaper, 467, 468
  outdoor, 468
  product placement, 469–470
  public benefits of, 467
  public service, 379
  radio, 468
  on social media, 468, 471, 472
  television, 466–467, 468, 469, 470
  testimonials, 483
  Yellow Pages, 468
Affiliate marketing, 162
Affirmative action, 312
Afghanistan, 19
AFL; *see* American Federation of Labor
AFL-CIO, 345, 349, 363, 366
Africa
  common markets, 78–79
  economic growth, 44
  as market, 81
African Americans; *see also* Minorities
  affirmative action, 312
  franchising opportunities, 143
  managers, 193, 324–325
Age; *see* Aging of population; Demography
Age Discrimination in Employment Act of
  1967, 311, 313
Agency shop agreements, 350
Agents/brokers, 434–435, 442
Aging of population
  baby boomers, 17–18
  of consumers, 17–18, 388
  discrimination issues, 313
  elder care, 361
  in United States, 17–18, 388
  of workforce, 313
Agriculture; *see also* Food industry
  cooperatives, 146
  history, 20–21
  number of farmers, 20
  technology used in, 15, 20
Air transportation, 454
Airlines
  costs of increased security, 19
  deregulation, A1-17 to A1-18
Alcohol abuse, 362
Alcohol Labeling Legislation (1988), A1-13
Alliances, strategic, 70
Allocation model, 569
American depository receipts (ADRs), 568
American Federation of Labor (AFL), 344
American Indians; *see* Minorities
American Inventors Protection Act, A1-7
Americans with Disabilities Act (ADA) of
  1990, 311, 312–313, 319, 334
Americans with Disabilities Amendments Act
  of 2008, 311, 313
Angel investors, 172, 527
Annual reports, 500, E-10
Annuities, A2-11

Antitrust laws, 40, A1-11 to A1-13
Application forms, 318
Application service providers (ASPs), BA-14
Application software; *see* Apps; Software
Apprentice programs, 322
Apps
  functions, BA-16 to BA-17
  human resource management, 334
  marketing, 384
  payment, 405
  retail, 14, BA-13 to BA-14
  translation, 201
Arbitration, 352, 353
Argentina, 78
Articles of incorporation, 133
ASEAN Economic Community, 78
Asia; *see also individual countries*
  common markets, 78
  franchises, 144
  manufacturing in, 18–19
  markets, 80–81
  sweatshop labor, 106
Asian Americans, 324; *see also* Minorities
ASPs; *see* Application service providers
Assembly line layouts, 259, 260
Assembly process, 251
Assets
  accounts receivable, 540
  on balance sheet, 506–508
  capital expenditures, 536
  as collateral for loans, 539–540
  current, 508
  defined, 506
  depreciation, 511
  division of in bankruptcies, A1-16, A1-17
  fixed, 508
  goodwill, 507
  intangible, 506–507, 508
  liquidity, 508
  personal, A2-3
ATMs; *see* Automated teller machines
Auditing, 501–502, 530–531
Audits, social, 104–105
Authority
  centralized, 219, 222, 223
  chain of command, 221
  decentralized, 222–224
  line versus staff, 228
  managerial, 219
Autocratic leadership, 204
Automated teller machines (ATMs), 598, 605
Automation; *see* Technology
Automobile industry
  mass production, 218–219
  non-U.S. manufacturers, 7, 71, 72, 257
  supply chain management, 449
Automobile insurance, A2-12

B

B2B; *see* Business-to-business (B2B)
  market
B2C; *see* Business-to-consumer (B2C)
  transactions

Baby boomers
    aging of, 17–18
    births of, 377
    differences from other generations, 297,
        298, 299
Balance of payments, 65
Balance of trade, 64
Balance sheets; *see also* Ratio analysis
    accounts, 518
    assets, 506–508
    defined, 505, 506
    liabilities and owners' equity, 508
    personal, 506, 509, A2-3
    sample, 507
Baldrige Awards, 262, 327
Bangladesh, Grameen Bank, 7
Banker's acceptances, 605
Bankruptcies; *see also* Business failures
    corporate, A1-15 to A1-17
    defined, A1-15
    division of assets, A1-16, A1-17
    in economic crisis of 2008–2011, 579,
        A1-15
    involuntary, A1-16
    laws, A1-15 to A1-17
    number of, A1-15
    personal, A1-15
    procedures, A1-16 to A1-17
    voluntary, A1-16
Bankruptcy Abuse Prevention and Consumer
        Protection Act of 2005, A1-15
Bankruptcy Amendments and Federal
        Judgeships Act of 1984, A1-15
Bankruptcy Reform Act of 1994, A1-15, A1-17
Bankruptcy Reform Act of 2005, A1-15
Banks; *see also* Central banks; Economic
        crisis of 2008–; Investment bankers
    automated teller machines (ATMs), 598, 604
    banker's acceptances, 605
    certificates of deposit (CDs), 597
    check clearing, 594–595
    commercial, 597–598
    community development financial
        institutions, 172
    credit cards; *see* Credit cards
    debit cards, 604, A2-9
    demand deposits, 597
    deregulation, A1-18
    factoring, 541
    failures, 596
    federal deposit insurance, 596, 602–603
    future of, 605
    history in United States, 595–596
    international, 605–606
    IRAs, A2-14
    letters of credit, 605
    loans; *see* Loans
    microcredit, 7, 36
    online banking, 605
    regulation of, 548, 579
    relationships with, 538–539
    reserve requirements, 592, 593
    short-term financing, 538–540
    small businesses and, 170, 172, 177
    technology used in, 603–605
    time deposits, 597
    trade financing, 605
    Troubled Assets Relief Program, 529, 579,
        602
Bar codes, 412, 455
Bargaining zone, 352
Barriers to trade; *see* Trade barriers
Barron's, 576

Barter, 74–75, 589
Baseball
    major league, 61, 545
    stadiums, 545
Basic earnings per share, 517
"Basic Guide to Exporting," 64
Bears, 569
Benchmarking, 232–233
Benefit segmentation, 391, 392
Benefits; *see* Fringe benefits
BI; *see* Business intelligence
Bible, 92
Billboards, 468
Biometric devices, BA-6
Bitcoin, 590
Black Enterprise magazine, 324
Blogs, 206, 483
Bloomberg Businessweek, 574
Blue-chip stocks, 570
Boards of directors, 131, BB-4
Bolivia, 78
Bonds
    advantages and disadvantages, 564
    debenture, 564–565
    defined, 544, 563
    features
        call provisions, 565
        convertible, 565–566
        sinking funds, 565
    government, 563–564, 592–593
    indenture terms, 544
    interest, 563, 572
    investing in, 572–573
    issuing, 544–545, 557
    junk, 572–573
    maturity dates, 563
    prices, 573
    quotations, 573
    ratings, 564, 565, 572
    secured, 545, 565
    unsecured, 545, 564–565
Bonds payable, 508
Bonus plans, 328
Bookkeeping, 503–504
Booms, 49
Borrowing; *see* Credit; Debt; Loans
Boycotts, 353
Brain drain, 42
Brainstorming, 199
Brand associations, 416
Brand awareness, 415
Brand equity, 415
Brand insistence, 415
Brand loyalty, 415–416
Brand managers, 416
Brand names, 382, 413–415, 507
Brand preferences, 415–416
Brands; *see also* Trademarks
    categories, 414–415
    defined, 413
    knockoff, 415
Brazil, 66, 78, 81, 106
Breach of contract, A1-10
Break-even analysis, 424
Breweries, 63
Bribery, 34, 75, 106, 107; *see also* Corruption
BRIC economies, 81, 568; *see also* Brazil;
        China; India; Russia
Broadband technology, BA-10
Brokerage firms
    online, 566–567
    services, 600
    stockbrokers, 566, 570

Brokers; *see* Agents/brokers; Stockbrokers
Brunei, 78
Bubbles
    real estate, 578, 612, A2-7
    in securities markets, 578
Budget deficits, 50
Budgets
    capital, 532
    cash, 532
    defined, 532
    developing, 532
    operating (master), 532
    personal, 532, 534, A2-4 to A2-5
    sample, 533
Bulls, 569
Bundling, 413, 425
Bureaucracy, 218, 220, 221
Business
    benefits to community, 33–34
    defined, 4
    evolution in United States, 20–21
    future careers in, 21
Business cycle, 49; *see also* Recessions
Business environment; *see also* Legal
        environment
    competitive, 16–17
    defined, 11
    ecological, 19
    economic and legal, 12–13, 73–75, 389
    elements of, 11
    global, 18–19
    importance, 11
    social, 17–18, 72–73, 388
    technological, 14–16
Business ethics; *see* Ethics
Business failures; *see also* Bankruptcies
    banks, 596
    causes, 166, 169, 529
    Internet companies, 162
    number of, 4, 166
    savings and loan associations, 599
    small businesses, 166, 169
Business information systems; *see*
        Information technology
Business intelligence (BI), BA-3
Business law, A1-2 to A1-3; *see also* Legal
        environment
Business leaders, successful, 146; *see also*
        Entrepreneurs
Business ownership forms
    comparison, 135
    cooperatives, 146
    corporations, 122–123; *see also*
        Corporations
    franchises, 138–142; *see also* Franchises
    numbers of and total receipts, 122
    partnerships, 122, 125–128
    selecting, 146
    sole proprietorships, 122, 123–124
Business Plan Pro, 170
Business plans, 170–171
Business process information, BA-5
Businesses, starting; *see also* Business
        ownership forms; Entrepreneurship
    business plans, 170–171
    ethical issues, 168
    government assistance, 163–164
    number of new businesses, 122
    small businesses, 164–167, 232
    web-based, 161–162
Business-to-business (B2B) companies,
        15, 259; *see also* Marketing
        intermediaries

Business-to-business (B2B) market
    channels of distribution, 435, 436
    comparison to consumer market, 395–396
    defined, 390
    industrial goods and services, 410–411, 436
    personal selling, 393, 395, 474–477
    sales promotion techniques, 479
Business-to-business (B2B) transactions, 15
Business-to-consumer (B2C) transactions, 15, 477; *see also* Consumer market
Buying behavior; *see* Consumer behavior
Buying stock on margin, 571

C

C corporations, 129
CAD; *see* Computer-aided design
Cafeteria-style fringe benefits, 329
CAFTA; *see* Central American Free Trade Agreement
California
    Silicon Valley, 256, 547
    utility deregulation, A1-18
Callable bonds, 565
CAM; *see* Computer-aided manufacturing
Cambodia, 78
Canada; *see also* North American Free Trade Agreement
    executive compensation, 357
    franchises, 144, 145
Capital; *see also* Equity financing
    cost of, 547
    as factor of production, 9–10
Capital budgets, 532
Capital expenditures, 536
Capital gains, 569–570
Capital items, 411
Capitalism; *see also* Markets
    compared to other systems, 45
    defined, 35, 43
    foundations of, 35–36
    rights in, 35–36
    in United States, 34–35
    wealth creation, 33, 34–35, 40
Carbon footprints, 103
Card checks, 348
Careers
    changing, E-13
    in future, 21, P-3 to P-4
    information sources, E-4 to E-5
    in marketing, 396
    in operations management, 264
    self-assessments, E-1, E-2, P-4 to P-5
    in supply chain management, 455–456
    working for large businesses, 8
Cars; *see* Automobile industry
Carts and kiosks, 446
Cash budgets, 532
Cash flow
    defined, 514
    personal, A2-3
    problems with, 535
Cash flow analysis, 514
Cash flow forecasts, 531–532
Cash flow statement; *see* Statement of cash flows
Cash-and-carry wholesalers, 441
Catalog sales, 447
Category killer stores, 443
CDFIs; *see* Community development financial institutions
CDs; *see* Certificates of deposit
Celebrity endorsements, 465, 471
Cell phones, 468, 483–484, 598, P-7; *see also* Mobile technology; Smartphones

Cellular layouts; *see* Modular layouts
Central American Free Trade Agreement (CAFTA), 79
Central banks; *see also* Federal Reserve System
    history, 595–596
    influence on interest rates, 51, 592, 593
Centralized authority, 219, 222, 223
CEOs; *see* Chief executive officers; Managers
Certificates of deposit (CDs), 597
Certification, 347–348
Certified financial planners (CFPs), 569, A2-16
Certified internal auditors (CIAs), 502
Certified management accountants (CMAs), 499–500
Certified public accountants (CPAs), 500–501
CFOs; *see* Chief financial officers
CFPs; *see* Certified financial planners
Chain of command, 221
Change
    adapting to, 216, 234–238
    management of, 218
    risk management and, BB-2 to BB-3
Channels of distribution, 434–435, 436; *see also* Distribution; Supply chain management
Chapter 7 bankruptcies, A1-16, A1-17
Chapter 11 bankruptcies, A1-16 to A1-17
Chapter 13 bankruptcies, A1-16, A1-17
Charitable giving, 99, 100; *see also* Nonprofit organizations
Check clearing, 594–595
Chief executive officers (CEOs), 199–200, 356–358; *see also* Managers
Chief financial officers (CFOs), 199–200, 528
Chief information officers (CIOs), 199–200, BA-3
Chief operating officers (COOs), 199–200
Child care benefits, 360–361
Child Protection Act (1966), A1-13
Child Protection and Toy Safety Act (1969), A1-13
Children
    child care benefits, 360–361
    guardians, A2-16
Children's Online Privacy Protection Act (2000), A1-13
Chile, 78
China
    automobile industry, 80
    bribery in, 106
    competition with United States, 18–19
    dumping disputes, 66
    economic reforms, 42
    executive compensation, 357
    exports, 61, 65, 80
    foreign investment, 80
    franchises, 68, 69
    Internet use, 15
    joint ventures in, 70
    manufacturing in, 18–19, 65, 82
    as market, 74, 80–81
    nontariff barriers, 77
    oil companies, 138
    prison labor, 106
    stock exchanges, 559
    WTO membership, 81
CIAs; *see* Certified internal auditors
CIM; *see* Computer-integrated manufacturing
CIO; *see* Congress of Industrial Organizations
CIOs; *see* Chief information officers
Circuit breakers, 578
Civil law, A1-2
Civil Rights Act of 1964, 311, 312
Civil Rights Act of 1991, 311, 312, 359

Claims, insurance, BB-6
Class Action Fairness Act, A1-6
Clayton Act of 1914, A1-12
Client/server computing; *see* Network computing systems
Climate change, 19
Closed shop agreements, 349, 350
Closed-end mutual funds, 574
Clothing, environmental impact, 380
Cloud computing, BA-14 to BA-16
CMAs; *see* Certified management accountants
Coaching, 289, 323
Coattail effect, 141
Codes of ethics, 96–98
Cognitive dissonance, 395
Collection procedures, 535
Collective bargaining, 345, 346
Colleges and universities; *see also* Education; Students
    value of education, A2-2 to A2-3, P-3
    virtual tours, 376
Colombia, 78
COMESA, 78–79
Command economies, 43; *see also* Communism; Socialism
Commercial banks, 597–598; *see also* Banks
Commercial finance companies, 541, 600
Commercial law, A1-8 to A1-9; *see also* Legal environment
Commercial paper, 542
Commercialization, 419
Commissions, 328
Common law, A1-2, A1-3
Common markets, 77–79; *see also* European Union
Common stock, 562; *see also* Stocks
Communication, open, 292–294
Communications technology; *see* Cell phones; Internet; Networks; Technology
Communism, 42, 43, 45
Community development financial institutions (CDFIs), 172
Community service, 99–100
Comparable worth, 358
Comparative advantage theory, 62
Compensation; *see also* Fringe benefits
    comparable worth, 358
    employee retention and, 102
    executive, 356–358
    in foreign countries, 330
    as motivator, 281
    objectives, 326–327
    pay equity, 358–359
    pay systems, 327, 328
    of teams, 327–328
    wages, 328
Competition
    antitrust laws, 40, A1-11 to A1-13
    effects on marketing, 388–389
    empowerment and, 16–17
    in free markets, 39
    global, 18–19
    monopolistic, 39
    nonprice, 425–426
    perfect, 39
Competition-based pricing, 423
Competitive environment, 16–17
Compliance-based ethics codes, 96
Comprehensive Employment and Training Act of 1973, 311
Compressed workweek, 331
Comptrollers, 528
Computer viruses, BA-19
Computer-aided design (CAD), 252

Computer-aided manufacturing (CAM), 252–253
Computer-integrated manufacturing (CIM), 253
Computers; *see* Information technology
Concept testing, 382, 418–419
Conceptual skills, 201
Conglomerate mergers, 137
Congress of Industrial Organizations (CIO), 344–345
Consideration, A1-9
Constitution, U.S., A1-15, A1-17
Consultants, 502
Consumer behavior, 393–395
Consumer credit; *see* Credit cards; Personal financial planning
Consumer Credit Reporting Reform Act (1997), A1-13
Consumer finance companies, 600
Consumer Financial Protection Bureau, A1-14, A2-9
Consumer market; *see also* Green products; Retail industry
    brand preferences, 415–416
    channels of distribution, 434–435, 436
    comparison to business-to-business market, 395–396
    defined, 390
    goods and services classification, 409–410, 411
    mass marketing, 393
    niche marketing, 392–393
    one-to-one marketing, 393
    relationship marketing, 393
    sales promotion techniques, 480, 481
    segmentation, 390–392
Consumer price index (CPI), 48
Consumer Product Safety Act (1972), A1-13
Consumer protection, A1-13 to A1-14
Consumerism, A1-13
Consumers; *see* Consumer market; Customers
Contingency planning, 197–198
Contingent workers, 319–320; *see also* Temporary employees
Continuous process, 251–252
Contract law, A1-9 to A1-10
Contract manufacturing, 68–70, 106
Contracts
    breach of, A1-10
    conditions for legal enforcement, A1-9 to A1-10
    defined, A1-9
Contractual distribution systems, 448
Contrarian approach, A2-8
Control procedures
    Gantt charts, 264
    PERT charts, 263–264
Controlling
    defined, 195
    performance standards, 208–209
    steps, 207–208
Convenience goods and services, 408, 409, 410
Convenience stores, 443
Conventional (C) corporations, 129
Convertible bonds, 565–566
Convertible preferred stock, 562
Cookies, BA-21
Cooling-off periods, 353
Cooperatives
    agricultural, 146
    defined, 146
    food, 146, 448
    retail, 448
COOs; *see* Chief operating officers
Copyright Act of 1978, A1-7

Copyrights, A1-7, BA-20; *see also* Intellectual property protection
Core competencies, 234
Core time, 330, 331
Corporate and Criminal Fraud Accountability (Sarbanes-Oxley) Act, 96, 501, 502, A1-13
Corporate bonds; *see* Bonds
Corporate distribution systems, 448
Corporate income taxes, 131–132, A1-14
Corporate philanthropy, 99, 100
Corporate policy, 99
Corporate responsibility, 99; *see also* Corporate social responsibility
Corporate scandals
    accounting-related, 91, 501, 502
    motives for misconduct, 40
    recent, 90, 91, 102
Corporate social initiatives, 99
Corporate social responsibility (CSR)
    community service by employees, 99–100
    debates on, 98–99
    defined, 98
    elements of, 99–100
    environmental issues, 103–104, 105
    international standards, 107–109
    investors and, 105
    reports, 105
    responsibilities to stakeholders
        customers, 100, 105
        employees, 102
        investors, 101–102
        society and environment, 103–104
    social audits, 104–105
    watchdogs, 105
Corporations
    advantages, 129–130
    articles of incorporation, 133
    boards of directors, 131, BB-4
    bylaws, 133
    conventional (C), 129
    defined, 122–123
    disadvantages, 131–132
    financing sources, 129–130
    incorporation process, 131, 133
    individuals as, 132–133
    limited liability companies, 134–135
    S, 132, 133
    separation of ownership and management, 130–131
    sizes, 129, 130
    taking private, 137
    taxes, 131–132, A1-14
    types, 130
    virtual, 231–232, 233
Corruption; *see also* Corporate scandals
    bribery, 34, 75, 106
    in business, 12–13, 34, 40
    in developing countries, 34, 75
    in foreign countries, 106
    international agreements on, 107–109
    laws against, 12–13, 75, 107
Cost accounting, 423
Cost of capital, 547
Cost of goods sold (cost of goods manufactured), 510–511
Cost-based pricing, 423
Costs; *see also* Expenses
    cutting, 252
    forecasting, 531–532
    operating, 511
    total fixed, 424
    transportation, 435
    variable, 424

Counterfeiting, 589–590
Countertrading, 74–75
Country of Origin Labeling Law (2009), A1-13
Coupons, bond, 563
Coupons, promotional, 480
Court system, A1-2, A1-3; *see also* Legal environment
Cover letters, E-2, E-9 to E-10
CPAs; *see* Certified public accountants
CPI; *see* Consumer price index
Craft unions, 344
Credit; *see also* Debt; Loans; Short-term financing
    managing, A2-8 to A2-9
    microlending firms, 36, 56–57
    peer-to-peer, 172, 173, 540
    for small businesses, 170–172
    trade, 538
Credit Card Responsibility Accountability and Disclosure (CARD) Act of 2009, 542, A1-13, A2-9
Credit cards
    accepting, 535, 603
    financing small businesses, 542
    interest rates, 542, A2-5, A2-9
    managing, A2-8 to A2-9
    processing costs, 603
Credit lines, 540
Credit operations, 535
Credit unions, 599–600, 603, A2-14
Crime; *see also* Corruption
    cyber-, 93, BA-20
    employee fraud, 102
    identity theft, 16, E-8
    insider trading, 101–102, 560
Criminal law, A1-2
Crisis planning, 198
Critical Infrastructure Information Act, BA-21
Critical path, 263
CRM; *see* Customer relationship management
Cross-functional teams; *see* Self-managed cross-functional teams
Crowdfunding, 540
CSR; *see* Corporate social responsibility
Cuba
    economy, 42
    embargo on, 76
Cultural competency, 297
Cultural diversity; *see also* Diversity
    ethical issues, 108
    in global markets, 72–73
    motivational approaches, 296–297
    in United States, 17, 72, 388, 389, 473
Culture; *see also* Organizational culture
    high- or low-context, 296
    influences on buying decisions, 394
    meaning, 72
    sub-, 394
Cumulative preferred stock, 562
Curbs, 578
Currencies
    convertible, 12
    devaluations, 73
    euro, 78, 591
    exchange rates, 74, 591
    exchanging, 605
    trading, 74, 588
    U.S. dollar, 74, 591
Current assets, 508
Current liabilities, 508
Current ratio, 516
Customer databases, 16, 387
Customer group departmentalization, 225, 226
Customer relationship era, 377–378

Customer relationship management (CRM)
  activities, 383
  defined, 377–378
  software, 475
Customer service
  in corporate cultures, 236
  improving, 221
Customers
  aging of population, 17–18, 388
  buying decisions, 105, 393–395, BB-11
  complaints, 206, 482
  consumer protection, A1-13 to A1-14
  corporate responsibility to, 100
  diverse population, 17, 388, 389
  expectations, 16
  external, 209
  focus on, 236
  internal, 209
  involvement in product development, 230
  knowing, 175
  marketing to, 376–377
  online dialogues with, 470–471
  prospects, 475
  qualifying, 475
  responsiveness to, 16
  satisfaction, 208–209
  of small businesses, 175
Customization, 254–255
Cybercrime, 93, BA-20
Cyberspace; see Internet
Cyberterrorism, BA-20
Cyclical unemployment, 47

D

Damages, A1-10
Data
  defined, BA-2
  managing, BA-7 to BA-8
  for marketing research, 385–386
  primary, 385–386
  secondary, 385
Data mining, BA-8
Data processing (DP), BA-2; see also
    Information technology
Data warehouses, BA-8
Databases, 16; see also Customer databases
Day care; see Child care benefits
Dealer (private-label) brands, 414
Debenture bonds, 564–565
Debit cards, 604, A2-9
Debt; see also Bonds; Credit cards; Loans;
    Mortgages
  leverage ratios, 516–517, 548
  personal, A2-5 to A2-6
Debt financing
  balancing with equity, 547–548
  bonds, 544–545, 557
  compared to equity financing, 547–548
  defined, 537
  loans, 543–544
Debt to owners' equity ratio, 516–517
Decentralized authority, 222–224
Decertification, 348
Decision making
  centralized or decentralized, 219,
    222–224
  defined, 198
  empowering employees, 206–207, 221; see
    also Empowerment
  ethical, 93–94, 204
  rational model, 198–199
Defense industry, 19

Deficits
  budget, 50
  trade, 64, 65
Defined-contribution plans, A2-15
Deflation, 47–48
Demand, 37
Demand curve, 37–38
Demand deposits, 597
Demand-based pricing, 423
Deming cycle, 261
Democratic leadership, 204–205
Demographic segmentation, 391, 392
Demography; see also Aging of population;
    Diversity
  defined, 17
  population growth, 32
  single parents, 18
  world population by continent, 61
Department of Motor Vehicles (DMV), 220
Department stores, 443
Departmentalization, 217, 224–227
Depreciation, 511
Depressions, 49; see also Great Depression
Deregulation, 40, A1-17 to A1-19
Devaluations, 74
Developing countries
  corruption, 34, 75
  countertrading, 74–75
  microlending, 36, 56–57
  obstacles to trade with, 75
  population growth, 32
  transportation and storage systems, 75
Digital natives, 235
Digital video recorders, 469
Diluted earnings per share, 517
Direct deposits, 604
Direct mail, 447, 466, 468
Direct marketing, 447
Direct payments, 604
Direct selling, 446–447
Directing, 206
Directors, corporate, 131, BB-4
Disability insurance, A2-11, BB-10
Disabled individuals; see also Diversity
  accommodations, 312–313
  laws protecting, 311, 312–313, 334
  telecommuting, BA-17
Disaster aid, 99
Discount rate, 592, 593
Discount stores, 443
Discrimination
  age-related, 313
  in employment tests, 318
  gender-based, 312, 358
  laws prohibiting, 311–313, 334
  price, A1-12
  reverse, 312
Disinflation, 47
Distance learning, 322
Distributed product development, 406
Distribution; see also Marketing intermediaries;
    Supply chain management
  administered systems, 448–449
  channels of, 434–435
  contractual systems, 448
  cooperation in, 448–450
  corporate systems, 448
  for e-commerce transactions, 446
  of new products, 383
  outsourcing, 452
  physical, 451
  retail strategies, 443–444
  sustainability issues, 435

Distributor brands, 414
Distributors, 230; see also Marketing
    intermediaries
Diversification, 568–569
Diversity; see also Cultural diversity
  of customers, 17, 388, 389
  in franchising, 142 143
  generational differences, 17–18, 297–299
  groups, 17
  in management development, 324–325
  of U.S. population, 17
  of workforce, 17
Dividends
  common stock, 561, 570
  preferred stock, 562
Division of labor, 216–217, 219
DMV; see Department of Motor Vehicles
Dodd-Frank Wall Street Reform and
    Consumer Protection Act, 97, 358, 501,
    548, 579, A1-14
Doha Round, 77
Dollar, U.S., 74, 591; see also Currencies
Dot-coms; see Internet companies
Double-entry bookkeeping, 504
Dow Jones Industrial Average, 576, 577
DP; see Data processing
Drop shippers, 441
Drug companies; see Pharmaceutical
    companies
Drug testing, 362
Dumping, 66
Durable power of attorney, A2-16

E

EAC; see East Africa Community
EACs; see Export Assistance Centers
Earnings; see also Compensation; Income
  of college graduates, A2-2 to A2-3, P-3
  gender differences, 358–359
  retained, 508, 509, 546
Earnings per share (EPS), 517
  basic, 517
  diluted, 517
  price/earnings ratios, 571
Earnings statement; see Income statement
East Africa Community (EAC), 79
Ecological environment, 19; see also
    Environmental issues
E-commerce; see also Internet
  affiliate marketing, 162
  combined with traditional retail stores
    (click-and-brick), 446, 447
  customer relationships, 445, 470–471
  defined, 15
  distribution systems, 446
  in franchising, 143–144
  global opportunities, 178
  growth, 15, 256
  interactive features, 447, 465, 470–471
  mobile access, 384
  niche marketing, 393
  pick economy, 485
  price comparisons, 425
  setting up, 161–162
  taxation of, A1-15
Economic and legal environment, 12–13,
    73–75, 389; see also Legal environment
Economic crisis of 2008–
  bankruptcies, 579, A1-15
  causes, 13, 578–579, 601–602, 612
  credit crunch, 172, 542
  effects in retail, 223, 388

effects on small businesses, 539
effects on workers, 256, 299
executive compensation and, 356, 358
federal bailout, 51, 529, 579, 602
federal stimulus package, 51, 246, 579, 602
fiscal policy responses, 51
global effects, 607
monetary policy, 587
regulatory shortcomings, 602, A1-13, A1-18
stock market decline, 567, 579
subprime mortgages, 13, 578–579, 601
unemployment, 193, 246, 299
Economic systems; *see also* Capitalism;
    Markets
  command economies, 43
  communism, 42, 43, 45
  comparison, 45
  free-market, 43
  mixed economies, 43–44, 45
  socialism, 41–42, 43, 45
Economics
  allocation of resources, 31
  defined, 30
  as "dismal science," 31–32
  Keynesian, 51
  macro-, 30–31
  micro-, 30
Economies of scale, 218–219
Ecuador, 78
EDI; *see* Electronic data interchange
EDLP; *see* Everyday low pricing
Education; *see also* Students; Training and
    development
  economic development and, 32
  value of, A2-2 to A2-3, P-3
EEOA; *see* Equal Employment Opportunity Act
EEOC; *see* Equal Employment Opportunity
    Commission
EFCA; *see* Employee Free Choice Act
Efficiency, 15
EFT; *see* Electronic funds transfer (EFT)
    systems
Elder care, 361
Elderly; *see* Senior citizens
Electric utilities, 40; *see also* Utilities
Electronic cash, 590
Electronic data interchange (EDI), BA-9
Electronic funds transfer (EFT) systems,
    603–604
Electronic retailing, 445–446; *see also*
    E-commerce
E-mail; *see also* Internet
  advertising, 470
  managing, BA-7
  netiquette, P-6 to P-7
  phishing scams, BA-20
  privacy issues, BA-21 to BA-22
  promotion via, 483
Embargoes, 76, 77
Emerging markets; *see* BRIC economies;
    Developing countries; Global markets
Employee benefits; *see* Fringe benefits
Employee Free Choice Act (EFCA), 348
Employee Retirement Income Security Act
    (ERISA) of 1974, 311
Employee–management relations; *see also*
    Unions
  arbitration, 352, 353
  bargaining zone, 352
  ethical values in, 94–96, 108, 217
  fairness in, 102
  future of, 354–356
  grievances, 351

helping vs. coaching, 289
impact of technology, BA-18
issues, 342
  child care, 360–361
  drug testing, 362
  elder care, 361
  e-mail privacy, BA-21
  executive compensation, 356–358
  pay equity, 358–359
  sexual harassment, 359–360
  violence in workplace, 362–363
language differences, 201
lockouts, 353, 354
mediation, 352, 353
resolving disagreements, 351
in small businesses, 176
tactics used in conflicts, 352–354
Employees; *see also* Compensation;
    Diversity; Empowerment; Human
    resource management; Labor;
    Recruitment; Staffing; Teams; Training
    and development
  aging of, 313
  community service, 99–100
  corporate responsibility to, 102
  e-mail use, BA-21
  enabling, 207
  engagement, 278
  fraud by, 102
  line personnel, 228
  losing, 334–335
  orientation, 321
  part-time, 319, 332
  performance appraisals, 325–326
  promotions, 313, 333
  retention, 102, 334–335
  retirements, 334
  safety issues, 217
  scheduling, 329–332
  staff personnel, 228
  terminating, 333–334
  transfers, 333
Employment; *see* Careers; Jobs; Recruitment
Empowerment
  as competitive advantage, 16–17
  decision making, 206–207, 221
  defined, 17
  effects on managerial authority, 219
  increased span of control, 223
  knowledge needed for, 207
  as motivator, 286
  restructuring for, 235–236
  role of managers in, 194–195, 206–207
  of self-managed teams, 230
  Theory Y management and, 285–286
Enabling, 207
Endorsements, celebrity, 465, 471
Energy use; *see* Greening
Engagement, employee, 278
Enterprise portals, BA-10
Enterprise resource planning (ERP), 259
Enterprise risk management (ERM), BB-2
Enterprise zones, 163
Entertainment industry; *see* Movies; Television
Entrepreneurial teams, 158
Entrepreneurs
  charitable giving, 40
  defined, 4
  microloans, 36, 56–57
  micropreneurs, 158–160
  minority group members, 8
  opportunities for, 8–9
  personality traits, 156–157

readiness questionnaire, 158–159
retirement planning, A2-15
social, 7–8
successful, 4, 146, 154–155, 156–157
wealth creation by, 9–10
women, 9, 142–143
young, 155
Entrepreneurship; *see also* Businesses, starting;
    Home-based businesses; Small businesses
  advantages, 8
  compared to working in large businesses, 8
  defined, 154
  as factor of production, 9–10
  within firms, 163
  government support of, 12–13, 163–164
  history, 154
  laws encouraging, 12–13, 163–164
  motivations, 156
  opportunities, 157–158, 167–168
Environment; *see* Business environment
Environmental issues; *see also* Greening
  climate change, 19
  corporate responsibility and, 103–104, 105
  fishing, 103
  ISO 14000 standards, 262
  personal decisions, 20
  risks, BB-11
  sustainability, 104, 247, 408, 435
Environmental scanning, 387–389
EPS; *see* Earnings per share
Equal Employment Opportunity Act (EEOA),
    311, 312
Equal Employment Opportunity Commission
    (EEOC), 312, 313, 359, A1-3
Equal Pay Act of 1963, 311, 358
Equilibrium prices, 37–38
Equipment, 411
Equity, owners'; *see* Owners' equity
Equity financing, 545; *see also* Stocks
  balancing with debt, 548
  compared to debt financing, 547–548
  defined, 537
  retained earnings, 546
  selling stock, 545, 556–557
  for small businesses, 559
  venture capital, 172, 546–547
Equity theory, 290–291
ERISA; *see* Employee Retirement Income
    Security Act
ERM; *see* Enterprise risk management
ERP; *see* Enterprise resource planning
Estate planning, A2-16
ETFs; *see* Exchange-traded funds
Ethics; *see also* Corporate scandals; Corporate
    social responsibility; Corruption
  in accounting, 515
  in banks, 599
  cheating by students, 92–93
  cultural differences and, 108
  defined, 92
  dilemmas, 93–94, 204, 321
  enforcement, 97–98
  failures, 13
  in financial management, 536
  formal policies, 96–98
  in global markets, 75, 106–109
  individual responsibility, 13, 92–94, P-8
  insider trading, 101–102, 560
  investment decisions, 567
  legality and, 90, 94, 112–113
  organizational, 94–96, 203–204
  orientation questionnaire, 95
  outsourcing, 257

Ethics—*Cont.*
  personal dilemmas, 13
  promoting, 203–204
  safety issues, 217
  standards, 92
  starting businesses, 168
  strikebreakers, 354
  values in organizational cultures, 217, 236
Ethics codes, 96–98
Ethics offices, 96, 98
Ethnic groups, marketing to, 388; *see also*
  Cultural diversity; Minorities
Ethnocentricity, 72
Etiquette, P-5 to P-8
Euro, 78, 591; *see also* Currencies
Europe; *see also individual countries*
  codetermination, 358
  executive compensation, 358
  financial institutions, 600
European Economic Community, 78
European Union (EU); *see also* Euro
  anti-corruption statements, 107
  history, 78
  Internet taxation, A1-15
  members, 78
  quality standards, 262
Everyday low pricing (EDLP), 425
Exchange efficiency, 436–437
Exchange rates, 74, 591
Exchanges; *see* Stock exchanges
Exchange-traded funds (ETFs), 568, 574–575
Exclusive dealing, A1-12
Exclusive distribution, 444, 445
Executive compensation, 356–358
Executives; *see* Managers
Executors, A2-16
Exit interviews, 334–335
Expectancy theory, 289–290
Expenses; *see also* Costs
  forecasting, 531–532
  general, 511
  operating, 511
  personal, A2-3 to A2-4, A2-6
  selling, 511
Export Administration Act of 1979, 76
Export Assistance Centers (EACs), 68
Exporting; *see also* Global markets; Trade
  challenges, 178
  defined, 61
  financing, 179
  government assistance, 64, 68, 179
  information on, 64, 179
  jobs created by, 64
  letters of credit and, 605
  obstacles, 75
  opportunities, 63–64
  by small businesses, 68, 178–179
Export-trading companies, 68
Express warranties, A1-8
External customers, 209
Extranets, BA-9
Extrinsic rewards, 279

F

Facility layout, 258–259, 260
Facility location
  defined, 255
  factors, 256–257
  in foreign countries, 256
  in future, 258
  for manufacturers, 256–257
  for service businesses, 255–256
Factoring, 541

Factors of production, 9–10
Failures; *see* Business failures
Fair Credit Reporting Act (1970), A1-13
Fair Labor Standards Act of 1938, 311, 347
Fair Packaging and Labeling Act (1966), 413,
  A1-13
Families; *see also* Children
  elder care, 361
  financing from, 538
  franchises run by, 142
  single parents, 18
Family and Medical Leave Act of 1993, 311
Family-friendly fringe benefits, 18
Farming; *see* Agriculture
FASB; *see* Financial Accounting Standards
  Board
FBI; *see* Federal Bureau of Investigation
FDA; *see* Food and Drug Administration
FDIC; *see* Federal Deposit Insurance
  Corporation
Federal budget deficit, 50
Federal Bureau of Investigation (FBI), 502
Federal Communications Commission, A1-3
Federal Deposit Insurance Corporation
  (FDIC), 602
Federal funds rate, 593
Federal government; *see* U.S. government
Federal Housing Administration (FHA), BB-5
Federal Open Market Committee (FOMC),
  591, 592
Federal Reserve Act of 1913, 596
Federal Reserve System
  banking crisis of 2008–2009 and, 601, 602,
    A1-13, A1-18
  banks, 591, 592
  Bernanke as chairman, 587, 590
  check-clearing role, 594–595
  Consumer Financial Protection Bureau,
    A1-14, A2-9
  control of money supply, 590–591
  discount rate, 592, 593
  financial crisis responses, 542
  formation, 596
  functions, 592–593, 596
  interest rates, 592, 593, 601
  margin rates, 571
  monetary policy, 51–52, 592–593
  need for, 595–596
  open-market operations, 592–593
  organization of, 591–592
  quantitative easing, 590
  reserve requirements, 592
Federal Savings and Loan Insurance
  Corporation (FSLIC), 603
Federal Trade Commission Act of 1914, A1-12
Federal Trade Commission (FTC), 16, 142,
  A1-4, A1-12, A1-13
FHA; *see* Federal Housing Administration
FIFO (first in, first out), 512
Films; *see* Movies
Finance; *see also* Financial management
  defined, 528
  importance, 529–530
  relationship to accounting, 528
Financial accounting, 500–501; *see also*
  Accounting
Financial Accounting Standards Board
  (FASB), 501, 515, 519
Financial control, 533
Financial crises; *see* Economic crisis of 2008–
Financial institutions; *see* Banks; Credit
  unions; Nonbanks; Savings and loan
  associations
Financial leverage, 547–548

Financial management; *see also* Financial
  planning; Short-term financing
  debt financing, 537, 543–545
  defined, 528
  equity financing, 537, 545–547
  ethical issues, 536
  leverage, 547
  long-term financing, 537, 543
  operating funds, 534–537
  reasons for business failures, 529
  in recessions, 535, 539, 548–549
  in small businesses, 170–172, 529–530
  sources of funds, 537
  tax management, 530
Financial managers
  defined, 528
  tasks, 529, 530–531
  titles, 528
Financial markets; *see* Securities markets
Financial planning
  budgets, 532
  controls, 533
  forecasts, 531–532
  importance, 532
  personal; *see* Personal financial planning
  steps, 531
Financial ratios; *see* Ratio analysis
Financial services; *see* Banks
Financial statements
  annual reports, 500, E-10
  auditing, 502, 530–531
  balance sheet
    accounts, 518
    assets, 506–508
    defined, 505, 506
    liabilities and owners' equity, 508
    personal, 506, 509, A2-3
  defined, 505
  income statement, 518
    accounts, 518
    defined, 505
    net income, 511
    operating expenses, 511
    personal, A2-3
  statement of cash flows, 505, 512–514
Firewalls, BA-9
Firing employees, 333–334
Firms; *see* Corporations
First in, first out (FIFO), 512
First-line managers, 200, 204
Fiscal policy, 50–51
Fixed assets, 508
Fixed-position layouts, 259, 260
Flat organization structures, 224
Flexible manufacturing, 253
Flextime plans, 330–331
Floating exchange rates, 74
Focus groups, 385
FOMC; *see* Federal Open Market Committee
Food and Drug Administration (FDA), A1-4,
  A1-5, A1-13
Food industry; *see also* Agriculture
  cooperatives, 146, 448
  food trucks, 418
  local sources, 175
  marketing intermediaries, 437–438
  regulation of, A1-13, A1-18
  supermarkets, 316, 443, 481
Forecasts, 531–532
Foreign Corrupt Practices Act of 1978, 75, 107
Foreign currencies; *see* Currencies
Foreign direct investment, 70–71, 80
Foreign exchange; *see* Currencies
Foreign markets; *see* Global markets; Trade

Foreign stock exchanges, 560–561, 568
Foreign subsidiaries, 70–71
Form utility, 251, 439
Formal organization, 237
Forms of business ownership; *see* Business
      ownership forms
Fortune, Best Places to Work, 304, 329, 339
Four Ps of marketing, 380–383
401(k) plans, A2-15
Franchise agreements, 138
Franchisees, 138
Franchises
   advantages, 140
   defined, 138
   disadvantages, 141–142
   as distribution system, 448
   diversity in, 142–143
   e-commerce use, 143–144
   evaluation checklist, 139
   family businesses, 142
   fast-growing, 139
   home-based, 143
   international, 68, 144–145
   scams, 142
   start-up costs, 140
   success rates, 140
   technology used in, 143–144
   websites, 143–144
Franchisors, 138
Fraud; *see also* Corporate scandals
   by employees, 102
   by franchisors, 142
   home-based business scams, 161
   online, 93
   phishing scams, BA-20
   Ponzi schemes, 91
Freakonomics, 29, 483
Free markets; *see* Capitalism; Markets
Free trade; *see also* Trade
   defined, 62
   laws to ensure fairness, 66
   pros and cons, 62
Free trade agreements; *see* Central American
      Free Trade Agreement; Common
      markets; North American Free Trade
      Agreement
Freedom, 36
Freedom of Information Act, BA-21
Free-market economies, 43; *see also*
      Capitalism; Markets
Free-rein leadership, 205
Freight forwarders, 453
Frictional unemployment, 47
Fringe benefits
   cafeteria-style, 329
   child care, 360–361
   defined, 328
   employee retention and, 102
   family-friendly, 18
   in foreign countries, 330
   401(k) plans, A2-15
   health insurance, 329, BB-9 to BB-10
   objectives, 326–327
   outsourcing, 317, 329
   pensions, 600
   vacation time, 328, 330
FSLIC; *see* Federal Savings and Loan
      Insurance Corporation
FTC; *see* Federal Trade Commission
Full-service wholesalers, 441, 442
Functional departmentalization, 224–225, 226
Fundamental accounting equation, 506
Funds; *see* Financial management; Mutual
      funds

G

GAAP; *see* Generally accepted accounting
      principles
Gain-sharing plans, 328
Gantt charts, 264
GASB; *see* Governmental Accounting
      Standards Board
GATT; *see* General Agreement on Tariffs and
      Trade
GDP (gross domestic product), 46
Gender discrimination, 312, 358; *see also*
      Women
General Agreement on Tariffs and Trade
      (GATT), 77
General expenses, 511
General partners, 125
General partnerships, 125
Generally accepted accounting principles
      (GAAP), 501, 511, 519
Generation X, 297–298, 299
Generation Y (Millennials), 297–299, 391, 598
Generational differences, 17–18, 297–299
Generic goods, 415
Generic names, 414–415
Geographic departmentalization, 225, 226
Geographical segmentation, 391, 392
Germany
   codetermination, 358
   imported beer, 63
   manufacturing in, 249
   standard of living, 5
Givebacks, 354, 355
Global business; *see also* Multinational
      corporations
   accounting standards, 519
   opportunities, 63–64
Global environment, 18–19
Global markets; *see also* Exporting;
      Importing; Trade
   adapting products for, 406, 474
   adapting to other cultures, 69, 72–73, 473
   advertising, 473
   banking, 605–606
   business etiquette, P-7
   countertrading, 74–75
   currency markets, 74, 588
   distribution, 450
   effects on marketing process, 387
   ethical concerns in, 75, 106–109
   forces affecting
      economic, 73–75
      legal and regulatory, 75
      physical and environmental, 75
      sociocultural, 72–73
   foreign direct investment, 70–71, 80
   large businesses, 63
   local contacts, 75
   logistics companies, 451
   marketing strategies, 73
   measuring, 64–65
   securities markets, 560–561, 568
   size of, 60–61
   small businesses, 63, 178–179
   stock exchanges, 560–561, 568
   strategies for reaching, 66, 72
      contract manufacturing, 68–70, 106
      direct investment, 70–71, 80
      franchises, 68
      joint ventures, 70
      licensing, 66–67
      strategic alliances, 70
Global Reporting Initiative (GRI), 104
Global warming, 19

Globalization, 18–19
Goals, 195–196
Goal-setting theory, 288
Going public; *see* Initial public offerings; Stocks
Golden handshakes, 334
Golden Rule, 92
Goods; *see also* Products
   defined, 4
   industrial, 410–411, 436
Goodwill, 507
Government and not-for-profit accounting,
      502–503
Government bonds, 563–564, 592–593
Governmental Accounting Standards Board
      (GASB), 502
Governments; *see also* Local governments;
      State governments; U.S. government
   accounting, 502
   bribery of officials, 75, 106
   economic policies, 50–52
   entrepreneurship encouraged by, 12–13,
      163–164
   fiscal policy, 50–51
   monetary policy, 51–52, 592–593
   regulations; *see* Regulations
   relations with businesses, 12–13
   sovereign wealth funds, 71, 72, 544
   spending policies, 50–51
   taxes; *see* Taxes
Grapevine, 237
Great Depression, 49, 596, 602
Green products
   carbon footprints, 103
   consumer preferences, BB-11
   defining, 103
   false claims, 32
   measuring impact, 380
   packaging, 408
   purchasing, 20
Greening; *see also* Environmental issues
   defined, 19
   jobs created by, 103–104
   local foods, 175
   marketing, 468–469
   measuring, 104
   personal decisions, 20
   of suppliers, 247
Greenwashing, 32
GRI; *see* Global Reporting Initiative
Grievances, 351
Grocery stores; *see* Supermarkets
Gross domestic product (GDP), 46
Gross profit, 510, 511
Growth stocks, 570

H

Hackers, BA-19, BA-20
Hamburger University (McDonald's), 140, 324
Hardware, BA-13 to BA-16
Hawthorne effect, 280–281
Hawthorne studies, 280–281
Health care, offshore outsourcing, 83; *see
      also* Pharmaceutical companies
Health insurance
   buying, A2-11
   for employees, 329, BB-9 to BB-10
   reforms, A1-19, A2-11, BB-9
   types, BB-8
Health maintenance organizations (HMOs),
      A2-11, BB-9 to BB-10
Health savings accounts (HSAs), A2-11, BB-10
Health threats, BB-4
Hedge funds, 101

Herzberg's motivating factors, 283–284
Hierarchy, 199–200, 219, 220–221
Hierarchy of needs, 281–282, 284
High-context cultures, 296
Higher education; *see* Colleges and
    universities; Education
High-low pricing strategy, 425
High-tech companies; *see* Internet companies;
    Technology
Hiring; *see* Recruitment
Hispanic Americans, 8, 324, 375, 389, 473
HMOs; *see* Health maintenance organizations
Home countries, 71
Home-based businesses; *see also* Small
    businesses
    challenges, 160
    franchises, 143
    insurance coverage, BB-11
    potential areas, 161
    reasons for growth of, 160
    scams, 161
    technology used in, 160
Home-based work; *see* Telecommuting
Homeowners insurance, A2-12, BB-8, BB-11
Homes, buying, A2-6 to A2-8
Homosexuals; *see* Diversity
Hong Kong, franchises, 69; *see also* China
Horizontal mergers, 136
Hotels, 250, 282
House brands, 414
Housing; *see* Mortgages; Real estate
HRM; *see* Human resource management
HSAs; *see* Health savings accounts
Human relations skills, 201
Human resource management; *see also*
    Recruitment; Training and development
    activities, 308, 309
    challenges, 309–310
    cultural differences, 73, 330
    defined, 308
    ethical issues, 321
    global workforce and, 330
    laws affecting, 311–313, 334
    performance appraisals, 325–326
    planning, 314–315
    promotions and transfers, 333
    technology-related issues, BA-17 to BA-18
    terminations, 333–334
    trends, 308–309
Hurricane Katrina, 218
Hygiene factors, 283–284

I

Identity theft, 16, E-8
IFRS; *see* International Financial Reporting
    Standards
IMC; *see* Integrated marketing communication
IMF; *see* International Monetary Fund
Immersive Internet, BA-13
Immigrants, 163, 375; *see also* Cultural
    diversity; Minorities
Immigration Act of 1990, 163
Immigration Reform and Control Act of
    1986, 311
Implied warranties, A1-8
Import quotas, 76, 77
Importing; *see also* Global markets; Tariffs; Trade
    defined, 61
    letters of credit and, 605
    logistics companies and, 451
    opportunities, 63
Inbound logistics, 451
Income; *see also* Compensation; Earnings

    net, 509, 511
    retained earnings, 508, 509, 546
Income statement
    accounts, 518
    cost of goods sold, 510–511
    defined, 505, 509
    net income, 511
    operating expenses, 511
    personal, A2-3
    revenue, 509, 510
    sample, 510
Income stocks, 570
Income taxes; *see* Taxes
Incorporation; *see also* Corporations
    articles of, 133
    of individuals, 132–133
    process, 131, 133
Incubators, 163–164
Indenture terms, 544
Independent audits, 502
Index funds, 574
India
    competition with United States, 18
    joint ventures in, 70
    as market, 74, 81
    nontariff barriers, 77
    outsourcing to, 82
    service industries, 82
Individual retirement accounts (IRAs)
    deposit insurance, 603
    Roth, A2-14
    SEP plans, A2-15
    simple, A2-14
    traditional, 597, A2-13 to A2-14
Indonesia, 78, 81
Industrial goods, 410–411, 436
Industrial Revolution, 343, 344
Industrial unions, 344
Infant industries, 76
Inflation, 47–48, 590–591
Infoglut, BA-6
Infomercials, 470
Informal organization, 237–238
Information
    managing, BA-6 to BA-8
    public, BA-6, BA-21
    storing and mining, BA-8
    types, BA-5 to BA-6
Information systems (IS), BA-2
Information technology (IT); *see also* Internet;
    Networks; Software; Technology
    computer-aided design and manufacturing,
        252–253
    defined, BA-2
    effects on management, BA-17 to BA-22
    for employee training and development, 322
    file management, BA-7 to BA-8
    hardware, BA-13 to BA-16
    outsourcing, BA-14
    privacy issues, BA-21 to BA-22
    role in business, BA-2 to BA-5
    security issues, BA-18 to BA-21
    skills needed, BA-17, BA-22
    stability issues, BA-22
    training, 235, BA-17
    use in manufacturing, 252–253, 259
Information utility, 440
Initial public offerings (IPOs), 545, 556, 557
Injunctions, 353–354
Innovation, by entrepreneurs, 157–158; *see*
    also Product development
Insider trading, 101–102, 560
Insourcing, 7, 233, 246
Installations, 411

Institutional investors, 557
Insurable interest, BB-6
Insurable risk, BB-5 to BB-6
Insurance; *see also* Health insurance
    annuities, A2-11
    automobile, A2-12
    for boards of directors, BB-4
    business ownership policies, BB-5
    buying, BB-5 to BB-6
    claims, BB-6
    disability, A2-11, BB-10
    government programs, BB-5
    for home-based businesses, BB-11
    homeowners, A2-12, BB-8, BB-11
    liability, A2-12, BB-8, BB-10 to BB-11
    life, A2-10 to A2-11, BB-8, BB-11
    premiums, BB-6
    property, BB-8
    reinsurance, BB-1
    renter's, A2-12
    rule of indemnity, BB-7
    self-, BB-4 to BB-5
    for small businesses, 177
    types, BB-7 to BB-9
    umbrella policies, A2-12
    uninsurable risks, BB-5
    workers' compensation, BB-10
Insurance companies
    IRAs with, A2-14
    life, 600
    mutual, BB-7
    ratings, A2-11
    stock, BB-7
Insurance policies, BB-6 to BB-7
Intangible assets, 506–507, 508
Integrated marketing communication (IMC), 465
Integrity-based ethics codes, 96
Intellectual property protection
    copyrights, 92, A1-7, BA-20
    Internet issues, BA-20
    patents, A1-6 to A1-7
    plagiarism from Internet, 92
    trademarks, 413, A1-7
Intensive distribution, 444
Interactive promotion, 470–471
Inter-American Convention Against
    Corruption, 107
Interest, on bonds, 563
Interest rates
    on bonds, 563, 572
    central bank influence on, 51, 592, 593
    on credit cards, 542, A2-5, A2-9
    discount rate, 592, 593
    federal funds rate, 593
    on loans, 543–544
    risk/return trade-off, 544
Intermediaries; *see* Marketing intermediaries
Intermittent process, 252
Intermodal shipping, 454
Internal customers, 209
Internal Revenue Service (IRS), 133, 502, 511
International Bank for Reconstruction and
    Development; *see* World Bank
International banking, 605–606; *see also* Banks
International business; *see* Global business;
    Multinational corporations
International Financial Reporting Standards
    (IFRS), 519
International Manufacturing Trade Show, 480
International markets; *see* Global markets
International Monetary Fund (IMF), 44,
    606–607
International Organization for Standardization
    (ISO), 107–109, 262

International trade; *see* Global markets; Trade
Internet; *see also* E-commerce; Social media
  advertising on, 467, 470–472
  agriculture-related websites, 15
  application service providers, BA-14
  backup services, BA-8
  banking, 605
  blogs, 206, 483
  connections to, BA-10
  consumer use for research, 377, 425, 485
  cookies, BA-21
  cybercrime, 93, BA-20
  dialogues with customers, 470–471
  e-mail; *see* E-mail
  employee familiarity with, 235
  financial sites, 571
  financing websites, 172, 173, 540
  future uses, BA-12 to BA-13
  intellectual property violations, 92, BA-20
  interactions among firms, 231–232, 257
  investment information, 571, 576
  job search resources, E-3, E-5
  mobile access, 384, BA-13
  netiquette, P-6 to P-7
  online brokers, 566–567
  operations management using, 257
  phishing scams, BA-20
  podcasting, 483
  privacy issues, 16, BA-21 to BA-22, E-7 to E-8
  recruiting employees, 317
  résumés posted on, E-6 to E-9
  review sites, 482
  security issues, BA-9, BA to 18–BA-21
  training programs, 322
  viral marketing, 482–483
  virtual trade shows, 480–481
  viruses, BA-19
Internet companies, 161–162, 546; *see also* E-commerce
Internet2, BA-10
Internships, 177, 320, 321
Interviews
  conducting, 318
  exit, 334–335
  following up, E-3, E-12
  preparing for, E-10 to E-11
  questions, 318, E-11
  skills, E-2 to E-3
Intranets, BA-9
Intrapreneurs, 163
Intrinsic rewards, 279
Inventory
  acquiring, 536
  as collateral for loans, 539
  just-in-time, 260–261, 536
  valuation, 512
Inventory turnover ratio, 518–519
Inverted organizations, 235–236
Investing; *see also* Mutual funds; Securities markets
  in bonds, 572–573
  buying securities, 566–567
  capital gains, 569–570
  comparing investments, 575
  contrarian approach, A2-8
  diversification, 568–569
  ethical issues, 567
  401(k) plans, A2-15
  in global markets, 568
  information sources, 571, 576
  IRAs, 597, 603, A2-13 to A2-14
  in real estate, A2-6 to A2-8

  risks, 567–568
  selling securities, 566–567
  in stocks, 569–570, A2-8
  strategies, 567–568, 570
  in 21st century, 579
Investment
  foreign direct, 70–71, 80
  sovereign wealth funds, 71, 72, 544
Investment bankers, 557
Investors; *see also* Owners' equity; Venture capitalists
  angels, 172, 527
  corporate responsibility to, 101–102
  institutional, 557
  socially conscious, 105
Investor's Business Daily, 574, 576
Invisible hand, 33–34
Involuntary bankruptcy, A1-16
IPOs; *see* Initial public offerings
Iraq war, 19
IRAs; *see* Individual retirement accounts
IRS; *see* Internal Revenue Service
IS; *see* Information systems
Islam, 73
ISO 9000 standards, 262
ISO 14000 standards, 262
Israel, 69
IT; *see* Information technology
Italy, 70, 106

J

Jamaica, 74–75
Japan
  bribery scandal, 106
  earthquake and tsunami, 218, 261
  executive compensation, 357, 358
  franchises, 68
  management approach, 286–287
  mass customization, 254
  standard of living, 5
  vending machines, 446
JIT; *see* Just-in-time inventory control
Job analysis, 314
Job descriptions, 314
Job enlargement, 292
Job enrichment, 291–292
Job interviews, 318
Job rotation, 292, 323
Job searches; *see also* Interviews; Recruitment; Résumés
  Internet resources, E-3, E-5
  self-assessments, E-1, E-2, P-4 to P-5
  sources of jobs, E-4
  strategies, E-1 to E-3
  traits sought by recruiters, E-12
Job simplification, 291
Job simulation, 322, 323
Job specialization, 217
Job specifications, 314
Jobs; *see also* Careers; Outsourcing; Recruitment
  created by small businesses, 165
  displaced by technology, 21
  in green industries, 103–104
  insourcing, 7, 233, 246
  lost due to free-trade agreements, 79
  in service industries, 21, 247
Job-sharing plans, 332
Joint ventures, international, 70
Journals, 503–504
Journeymen, 322
Judiciary, A1-2, A1-3; *see also* Legal environment

Junk bonds, 572–573
Just-in-time (JIT) inventory control, 260–261, 536

K

Keogh plans, A2-15
Key economic indicators, 46–49
Keynesian economic theory, 51
Knights of Labor, 344
Knockoff brands, 415
Knowledge
  distinction from information, BA-3
  as factor of production, 9–10
  retention, P-5
Knowledge management, 207
Koran, 73, 92
Korea; *see* North Korea; South Korea
Kuwait, 544

L

Labor; *see also* Employee–management relations; Employees; Unions
  as factor of production, 9–10
  international standards, 107
  legislation related to, 346–348, 353
  productivity, 15
  sweatshop conditions, 106–107, 343
Labor-Management Relations Act (Taft-Hartley Act), 345, 347, 350, 353
Labor-Management Reporting and Disclosure Act (Landrum-Griffin Act), 347
Land, as factor of production, 9–10
Land banks, 595
Landrum-Griffin Act, 347
Lao People's Democratic Republic, 78
Last in, first out (LIFO), 512
Latin America; *see also individual countries*
  common markets, 78
  immigrants from, 375
  relations between managers and workers, 73, 108
Latinos; *see* Hispanic Americans
Law of large numbers, BB-6
Laws; *see* Legal environment
Lawsuits
  product liability, A1-4 to A1-5, BB-11
  threat of, BB-4
  wrongful discharge, 334, 335
Lawyers, 177
Layoffs; *see* Terminating employees
Layout, facility, 258–259, 260
LBOs; *see* Leveraged buyouts
Leadership
  autocratic, 204
  free-rein, 205
  need for, 203
  participative (democratic), 204–205
  styles, 204–206
Leading
  defined, 194–195
  empowering workers, 206–207
  knowledge management, 207
  need for, 203
  roles, 203–204
  styles, 204–206
Lean manufacturing, 253–254
Ledgers, 504
Legal environment; *see also* Intellectual property protection; Lawsuits; Regulations; Taxes
  administrative agencies, A1-3, A1-4
  antitrust laws, 40, A1-11 to A1-13

Legal environment—*Cont.*
  bankruptcy laws, A1-15 to A1-17
  business law, 12, A1-2 to A1-3
  consumer protection, A1-13 to A1-14
  contract law, A1-9 to A1-10
  corporate accountability, 90
  credit cards, 542
  cybercrime, 93, BA-20
  deregulation, 40, A1-17 to A1-19
  effects on global markets, 75
  ethical decisions, 90, 94, 112–113
  human resource management, 311–313, 334
  labor laws, 346–348, 353
  need for laws, A1-2
  negotiable instruments, A1-9
  partnership laws, 125–126, 128
  product liability, A1-4 to A1-6
  punishment for corporate wrongdoing, 91
  sales law, A1-8 to A1-9
  tort law, A1-4 to A1-6
  trade-related laws, 66
  types of laws, A1-3
  warranties, A1-8 to A1-9
Legislation; *see* Legal environment
Less-developed countries; *see* Developing countries
Letters of credit, 605
Leverage, 547
Leverage ratios, 516–517, 548
Leveraged buyouts (LBOs), 137
Liabilities, 508; *see also* Debt
Liability
  limited, 125, 129
  unlimited, 124, 127
Liability insurance, A2-12, BB-8, BB-10 to BB-11
Licensing, 66–67
Life cycle, product, 419–421
Life insurance, A2-10 to A2-11, BB-8, BB-11
Life insurance companies, 600
LIFO (last in, first out), 512
Lilly Ledbetter Fair Pay Act of 2009, 311
Limit orders, 570
Limited liability, 125, 129
Limited liability companies (LLCs), 134–135
Limited liability partnerships (LLPs), 125
Limited partners, 125
Limited partnerships, 125
Limited-function wholesalers, 441
Line organizations, 227
Line personnel, 228
Line-and-staff organizations, 228
Lines of credit, 540
Liquidity, 508
Liquidity ratios, 516
LLCs; *see* Limited liability companies
LLPs; *see* Limited liability partnerships
Load mutual funds, 574
Loans; *see also* Credit; Debt; Mortgages
  bank, 538–540, 598
  from commercial finance companies, 541, 600
  long-term, 543–544
  microlending firms, 36, 56–57
  peer-to-peer, 172, 173, 540
  secured, 539–540
  short-term, 538–541
  unsecured, 540
Local governments
  administrative agencies, A1-4
  municipal bonds, 564, 572
  taxes, A1-14
Location, facility; *see* Facility location

Location-based services, BA-13
Locavores, 175
Lockouts, 353, 354
Logistics
  defined, 451
  inbound, 451
  information flows, 451–452
  international, 451
  need for, 451
  outbound, 451
  reverse, 451
  storage, 454–455
  third-party, 452
Logistics companies, 451, 452
Long-term financing
  balancing debt and equity, 548
  debt, 537, 543–545
  defined, 537
  equity, 537, 545–547
  objectives, 543
Long-term forecasts, 532
Long-term liabilities, 508
Loss leaders, 422
Losses
  defined, 4
  net, 509, 511
Low-context cultures, 296

M

M-1, 590
M-2, 590
M-3, 590
M&A; *see* Mergers and acquisitions
Macroeconomics, 30–31
Magazine advertising, 468
Magnuson-Moss Warranty-Federal Trade Commission Improvement Act (1975), A1-13
Mail; *see* Direct mail; E-mail
Mail-order firms; *see* Catalog sales
Malaysia, 78, 81
Malcolm Baldrige National Quality Awards, 262, 327
Malpractice insurance, BB-11
Managed security services providers (MSSPs), BA-19
Management; *see also* Employee–management relations; Empowerment; Motivation; Small business management
  boards of directors, 131, BB-4
  challenges, 193
  of change, 218
  contrast between American and Japanese styles, 286–287
  controlling, 195, 207–209
  decision making, 198–199
  defined, 193
  directing, 206
  effects of information technology, BA to 17–BA-22
  ethics in, 94–96, 203
  functions, 193–195
  leading
    defined, 194–195
    empowering workers, 206–207
    knowledge management, 207
    need for, 203
    styles, 204–206
  levels
    bureaucracies, 221
    middle, 200, 221
    number of, 223–224
    supervisory, 200, 204

    tasks and skills, 201–202
    top, 199–200
  organizing; *see* Organizing
  planning
    contingency, 197–198
    defined, 193–194
    forms, 196–197
    goals and objectives, 195–196
    importance, 195, 198
    mission statements, 195
    operational, 197
    performance standards, 208–209
    questions answered by, 196
    strategic, 196–197
    SWOT analysis, 196
    tactical, 197
    vision creation, 195
  problem solving, 199
  scientific, 279–281
  separation from ownership, 130–131
  tactics used in conflicts with labor, 353–354
Management by objectives (MBO), 288–289
Management development, 323–325
Managerial accounting, 499–500
Managers
  authority, 219
  changing roles, 192–193
  compensation, 356–358
  differences from leaders, 203
  generational differences, 298
  in Latin America, 73
  mentors, 324
  progressive, 192–193, 206
  roles, 17
  span of control, 223–224
  supervisory, 200, 204
Managing diversity; *see* Diversity
Manpower Development and Training Act of 1962, 311
Manufacturer's agents, 442
Manufacturers' brands, 414–415
Manufacturing; *see also* Automobile industry; Operations management
  competitiveness, 248
  contract, 68–70, 106
  costs, 252
  environmental impact, 380
  facility layout, 258–259, 260
  facility location, 256–257
  foreign companies in United States, 248, 257
  jobs replaced by technology, 21
  mass production, 218
  operations management, 249
  output, 246
  outsourcing, 81–82
  production techniques
    computer-aided design and manufacturing, 252–253
    flexible manufacturing, 253
    improving, 252–253
    Internet purchasing, 259
    just-in-time inventory control, 260–261
    lean manufacturing, 253–254
    mass customization, 254–255
  productivity improvements, 21, 48
  technology used in, 21, 259
  in United States, 246–247, 269
Margin, buying stock on, 571
Market indices, 576–578
Market orders, 570
Market prices, 37–38, 39, 425
Market segmentation, 390–392
Marketable securities; *see* Securities markets

Marketing; *see also* Personal selling; Promotion
  careers in, 396
  consultants, 177
  consumer decision-making process, 393–395
  defined, 376
  eras, 377–379
  evolution of, 377–379
  four Ps, 380–383
  greenwashing, 32
  helping buyers buy, 376–377
  mass, 393
  by nonprofit organizations, 379
  one-to-one, 393
  by small businesses, 175, 177
  test, 382
  value in, 404
Marketing concept, 377
Marketing concept era, 377
Marketing environment, 387–389
Marketing intermediaries; *see also* Business-to-business (B2B) companies; Retail industry; Wholesalers
  cooperation among, 448–450
  defined, 434
  exchange efficiency created by, 436–437
  in food industry, 437–438
  need for, 435–436, 437–438
  roles, 383
  sales promotion to, 480–481
  types, 434–435
  utilities created by, 439–440
  value versus cost of, 437–438
Marketing mix, 380–383, 420–421
Marketing research
  data analysis, 386
  data collection, 385
  data sources, 385–386
  defined, 384
  focus groups, 385
  process, 385–386
  by small businesses, 177
  strategy implementation, 386
  surveys, 385
Markets; *see also* Business-to-business (B2B) market; Capitalism; Consumer market; Global markets; Securities markets
  competition in, 39
  defined, 175
  demand, 37
  free, 40, 43
  functioning of, 36–39
  inequality in, 40
  price determination, 37–38
  supply, 37
Maslow's hierarchy of needs, 281–282, 284
Mass customization, 254–255
Mass marketing, 393
Mass production, 218
Master limited partnerships (MLPs), 125
Materials handling, 451
Materials requirement planning (MRP), 259
Matrix organizations, 228–230
Maturity dates, 563
MBO; *see* Management by objectives
Media, 479; *see also* Advertising; Newspapers; Social media; Television
Mediation, 352
Medical tourism, 83
Medicine; *see* Health care
Mentors, 324
Mercantilism, 76
Merchant wholesalers, 441

Mercosur, 78
Mergers and acquisitions
  conglomerate mergers, 137
  defined, 136
  foreign companies involved in, 137–138
  horizontal mergers, 136
  leveraged buyouts, 137
  types, 136–137
  vertical mergers, 136
Mexico, 10, 79; *see also* North American Free Trade Agreement
Microeconomics, 30; *see also* Prices
Microlending firms, 36, 56–57
Micropreneurs, 158–160
Middle management, 200, 221
Middlemen; *see* Marketing intermediaries
Millennial generation (Gen Y), 297–299, 391, 598
Minorities; *see also* African Americans; Discrimination; Diversity
  entrepreneurs, 8
  franchisees, 143
  Hispanic Americans, 8, 324, 375, 389, 473
  managers, 193, 324–325
Mission statements, 195
Mississippi River, 454
Mixed economies, 43–44, 45
MLM; *see* Multilevel marketing
MLPs; *see* Master limited partnerships
MNCs; *see* Multinational corporations
Mobile advertising, 468, 483–484
Mobile technology; *see also* Apps; Smartphones
  banking with, 598
  Internet access, 384, BA-13
  location-based services, BA-13
  payments, 405
Model Business Corporation Act, 128
Modular layouts, 259, 260
Monetary policy, 51–52, 591
Money; *see also* Currencies
  coins, 589
  counterfeiting, 589–590
  defined, 589
  electronic cash, 590
  history, 589, 595–596
  importance, 588–589
  time value of, 535
Money magazine, 574
Money management; *see* Personal financial planning
Money supply, 51–52, 590–591
Monopolies
  absolute advantage, 62
  antitrust laws, 40, A1-11 to A1-13
  defined, 40
Monopolistic competition, 39
Moral values, 92; *see also* Ethics
Morningstar Investor, 574
Mortgage bonds, 565
Mortgages
  FHA, BB-5
  payments, A2-7 to A2-8
  securitization, 578–579, 601–602, 612
  subprime, 13, 578–579, 601
  tax deduction for interest payments, A2-7 to A2-8
Motion pictures; *see* Movies
Motivation
  cultural differences and, 296–297
  equity theory, 290–291
  expectancy theory, 289–290
  extrinsic rewards, 279

  generational differences, 297–299
  goal-setting theory, 288
  Herzberg's factors, 283–284
  importance, 278–279
  intrinsic rewards, 279
  job enrichment and, 291–292
  management by objectives, 288–289
  Maslow's hierarchy of needs, 281–282, 284
  by money, 281
  personalizing, 295–299
  recognition, 294–295
  reinforcement theory, 290
  in small businesses, 296
  Theory X and Theory Y, 285–286, 288
  Theory Z, 286–288
Motivators, 283–284
Motor vehicles; *see* Automobile industry
Movies
  global market, 61
  product placement, 469
  unions, 366–367
MRP; *see* Materials requirement planning
MSSPs; *see* Managed security services providers
Multicultural population, 388; *see also* Cultural diversity
Multilevel marketing (MLM), 447
Multinational corporations; *see also* Global markets
  accounting standards, 519
  defined, 71
  ethical issues, 106–109
  foreign direct investment, 80
  foreign subsidiaries, 70–71
  largest, 71
Municipal bonds, 564, 572
Muslims, 73
Mutual funds
  closed-end, 574
  defined, 573
  fees, 574
  index funds, 574
  international stocks, 568
  investing in, 573–574
  net asset values, 575
  no-load, 574
  objectives, 574
  quotations, 575
  socially responsible, 105
Mutual insurance companies, BB-7
Myanmar, 78

N

NAFTA; *see* North American Free Trade Agreement
Nanobots, BA-17 to BA-18
NASDAQ
  average, 576
  defined, 558
  as electronic stock exchange, 558, BA-4
  stock quotations, 571–572
  stocks and bonds traded on, 558
  Times Square price wall, 570
National Association of Securities Dealers Automated Quotations; *see* NASDAQ
National banks, 595
National Credit Union Administration (NCUA), 602, 603
National debt, 50
National Flood Insurance Association, BB-5
National Labor Relations Act of 1935 (Wagner Act), 311, 344, 346, 347, 349, BA-12

National Labor Relations Board (NLRB), 347
Natural disasters, 218, BB-2
NCUA; *see* National Credit Union Administration
Needs, hierarchy of, 281–282, 284
Negligence, A1-4
Negotiable instruments, A1-9
Negotiated labor-management agreements (labor contracts), 349
Neo-Malthusians, 32
Net; *see* Internet
Net income or net loss, 509, 511
Netiquette, P-6 to P-7
Network computing systems (client/server computing), BA-14
Networking; *see also* Social media
  among firms, 231–232, 257
  in job searches, E-1
  by managers, 324
  online, BA-11
  by students, P-5
Networks; *see also* Internet
  broadband, BA-10
  extranets, BA-9
  firewalls, BA-9
  intranets, BA-9
  portals, BA-10
  virtual private, BA-9
  virtualization, BA-14 to BA-15
New businesses; *see* Businesses, starting; Entrepreneurs
New Jersey state government, 164
New product development; *see* Product development
New York Stock Exchange (NYSE)
  crashes, 577–578
  Dow Jones Industrial Average, 576, 577
  electronic trading, 558
  history, 557–558
  listing requirements, 558
  news coverage, 555
  stock quotations, 571–572
News releases, 479
Newspapers
  advertising, 467, 468
  publicity in, 479
  stock quotations, 571–572
Niche marketing, 392–393
NLRB; *see* National Labor Relations Board
No-load mutual funds, 574
Nonbanks, 541, 597, 600, 601
Nonprice competition, 425–426
Nonprofit organizations; *see also* Charitable giving
  accounting, 502–503
  defined, 7
  marketing, 379
  objectives, 7
  social media and, BA-1
  using business principles in, 7–8
  volunteering for, 99–100
Nonstore retailing, 445–447
Nontariff barriers, 77
Norris-LaGuardia Act, 346, 347
North American Free Trade Agreement (NAFTA), 79, 349
North Korea, 31, 42
Notes payable, 508
Not-for-profit organizations; *see* Nonprofit organizations
Nutrition Labeling and Education Act (1990), A1-13
NYSE; *see* New York Stock Exchange

O
Objectives, 195–196
Occupational Safety and Health Act of 1970, 311
Occupations; *see* Careers; Jobs
Odd lots, 570
Off-the-job training, 322
Old-Age, Survivors, and Disability Insurance Program; *see* Social Security
Older customers, 17–18, 388
Older employees, 313
Older Workers Benefit Protection Act, 311
Oligopolies, 39–40
One-to-one marketing, 393
Online banking, 605
Online brokers, 566–567
Online business; *see* E-commerce; Internet
Online training, 322
On-the-job training, 321–322
Open communication, 292–294
Open shop agreements, 350, 351
Open-end mutual funds, 574
Open-market operations, 592–593
Operating (master) budgets, 532
Operating expenses, 511
Operating funds
  for capital expenditures, 536
  credit operations, 535
  day-to-day needs, 535
  for inventory, 536
  need for, 534–537
  sources, 537
Operational planning, 197
Operations management
  careers in, 264
  control procedures, 263–264
  defined, 249
  in manufacturing, 249, 251–252
  in service industries, 250
  use of Internet, 257
Operations management planning, 255
  enterprise resource planning, 259
  facility layout, 258–259, 260
  facility location, 255–257
  materials requirement planning, 259
  quality control, 261–262
Opportunities; *see* SWOT analysis
Options, stock, 328, 356
Organization charts, 199–200, 218, 221
Organizational (or corporate) culture
  defined, 236
  informal organization, 237–238
  negative, 236
  open communication in, 292–294
  values, 217
Organizational design; *see also* Teams
  bureaucracy, 218, 220, 221
  centralization, 219, 222, 223
  chain of command, 221
  decentralization, 222–224
  departmentalization, 217, 224–227
  division of labor, 216–217, 219
  Fayol's principles, 219–220
  functional structures, 224–225
  hierarchy, 199–200, 219, 220–221
  historical development, 218–220
  hybrid forms, 227
  informal organization, 237–238
  inverted structures, 235–236
  line organizations, 227
  line-and-staff organizations, 228
  matrix organizations, 228–230

  pyramid structures, 220–221, 223
  restructuring, 16–17, 235–236
  span of control, 223–224
  tall versus flat structures, 223–224
  traditional principles, 218–220
  Weber's principles, 220
Organized labor; *see* Unions
Organizing
  change in, 218, 234–238
  defined, 194
  interactions among firms, 231–232
  levels of management, 199–200, 220–221
Orientation, 321
OTC markets; *see* Over-the-counter markets
Outbound logistics, 451
Outdoor advertising, 468
Outlet stores, 443
Outsourcing; *see also* Suppliers
  contract manufacturing, 68–70, 106
  defined, 6
  distribution, 452
  employee benefits, 317, 329
  ethical issues, 257
  to home-based businesses, 160
  information technology services, BA-14
  logistics, 452
  offshore, 81–82
  problems with, 233
  production, 81–82, 233
  pros and cons, 82
  reversing decisions, 233
  of service jobs, 81–82, 450
  by small businesses, 232
  supply chain management, 450
  sweatshop labor issue, 106–107
  training, BA-17
Over-the-counter (OTC) markets, 558
Owners' equity; *see also* Stocks
  defined, 508
  ratio of debt to, 516–517
  return on, 517–518
Ownership, separation from management, 130–131; *see also* Business ownership forms

P
Packaging, 408, 412–413
Pakistan, 73, 106
Par value, of stock, 561
Paraguay, 78
Parent companies, 70
Parents, single, 18; *see also* Children; Families
Participative (democratic) leadership, 204–205
Partnerships
  advantages, 126–127
  agreements, 128
  choosing partners, 126
  defined, 122
  disadvantages, 127
  general, 125
  limited, 125
  limited liability, 125
  master limited, 125
Part-time employees, 319, 332
Patient Protection and Affordable Care Act (PPACA), A1-19, A2-11
Patents, A1-6 to A1-7; *see also* Intellectual property protection
Pay equity, 358–359
Pay systems, 327, 328; *see also* Compensation
Payroll debit cards, 604

PCAOB; *see* Public Company Accounting Oversight Board
P/E; *see* Price/earnings ratio
Peer-to-peer lending, 172, 173, 540
Penetration pricing strategy, 424
Penny stocks, 570
Pension Benefit Guaranty Corporation, BB-5
Pension funds, 600
People's Republic of China; *see* China
PEOs; *see* Professional employer organizations
Perfect competition, 39
Performance appraisals, 325–326
Performance ratios, 517–518
Performance standards, 208–209
Personal financial planning
  advisers, A2-15 to A2-16
  balance sheets, 506, 509, A2-3
  budgets, 532, 534, A2-4 to A2-5
  building financial base, A2-6 to A2-7
  debts, A2-5 to A2-6, A2-8 to A2-9
  estate planning, A2-16
  expenditures, A2-3 to A2-4, A2-6
  income statements, A2-3
  insurance, A2-10 to A2-12
  investments; *see* Investing
  need for, A2-2
  real estate, A2-6 to A2-8
  retirement planning, A2-12
    401(k) plans, A2-15
    IRAs, 597, 603, A2-13 to A2-14
    Keogh plans, A2-15
    Social Security, 18, A2-12 to A2-13, BB-5
  savings, A2-5, A2-8
  steps, A2-3 to A2-6
Personal selling; *see also* Sales representatives
  benefits, 474
  in business-to-business market, 393, 395, 474–477
  costs, 474
  defined, 474
  relationships with customers, 476–477
  steps, 475–476
Personnel; *see* Human resource management
PERT (program evaluation and review technique) charts, 263–264
Peru, 73, 78
Pharmaceutical companies, 543, A1-1, A1-5
Philanthropy, 99, 100
Philippines, 78, 81, 144
Phishing, BA-20
Physical distribution; *see* Distribution
Physically challenged; *see* Disabled individuals
Pick economy, 485
Piecework pay systems, 328
Pipelines, 454
Place utility, 439
Planning; *see also* Financial planning; Operations management planning
  business plans, 170–171
  contingency, 197–198
  defined, 193–194
  forms, 196–197
  goals and objectives, 195–196
  human resources, 314–315
  importance, 195, 198
  mission statements, 195
  operational, 197
  performance standards, 208–209
  questions answered by, 196
  in small businesses, 169–170
  strategic, 196–197

SWOT analysis, 196
  tactical, 197
  vision creation, 195
Plastic money; *see* Credit cards
PMI (pluses, minuses, implications), 199
Podcasting, 483
Political economy, 76
Pollution; *see* Environmental issues
Population growth, 32; *see also* Demography
Pop-up stores, 444
Portfolio strategy, 569
Possession utility, 440
Post-it Notes, 163
PPACA; *see* Patient Protection and Affordable Care Act
PPI; *see* Producer price index
PPOs; *see* Preferred provider organizations
PR; *see* Public relations
Preapproach, 475
Precedents, A1-3
Preemptive rights, 562
Preferred provider organizations (PPOs), A2-11, BB-10
Preferred stock, 562–563
Premiums, BB-6
Press releases, 479
Price discrimination, A1-12
Price indexes, 47–48
Price leadership, 423
Price/earnings ratio (P/E), 571
Prices
  comparing on Internet, 425
  determination of, 37–38
  equilibrium, 37–38
  inflation and deflation, 47–48, 590–591
  market, 37–38, 39, 425
  market forces and, 37–38, 425
  of new products, 382–383, 422–425
Pricing strategies
  break-even analysis, 424
  bundling, 413, 425
  competition-based pricing, 423
  cost-based pricing, 423
  demand-based pricing, 423
  everyday low pricing, 425
  high-low, 425
  objectives, 422–423
  penetration, 424
  psychological pricing, 425
  in retail, 425
  skimming, 424
Primary boycotts, 353
Primary data, 385–386
Primary markets, 556
Principle of motion economy, 280
Privacy, on Internet, 16, BA-21 to BA-22, E-7 to E-8
Private accountants, 500
Private enterprise system; *see* Capitalism
Private property, 35
Private-label brands, 414
Problem solving, 199
Process departmentalization, 225–227
Process layouts, 259, 260
Process manufacturing, 251
Processes, production, 251–252
Producer price index (PPI), 48
Product analysis, 418
Product departmentalization, 225, 226
Product development
  commercialization, 419
  concept testing, 382, 418–419
  design, 382

  distributed, 406
  process, 382, 416–419
  prototypes, 418
  test marketing, 382
  total product offer, 406–407
  value enhancers, 406
Product differentiation, 39, 408, 409
Product liability
  defined, A1-4 to A1-5
  insurance, BB-11
  major awards, A1-5, A1-6
  strict, A1-5
Product life cycle, 419–421
Product lines, 407–408
Product managers, 416
Product mix, 408
Product placement, 469–470
Product screening, 417
Production; *see also* Manufacturing; Quality
  computer-aided design and manufacturing, 252–253
  control procedures, 263–264
  costs, 424
  defined, 248
  factors of, 9–10
  flexible manufacturing, 253
  just-in-time inventory control, 260–261, 536
  lean manufacturing, 253–254
  mass, 218
  mass customization, 254–255
  outsourcing of, 81–82, 233
  processes, 251–252
Production era, 377–378
Production management, 248, 251–252
Productivity
  agricultural, 20
  benefits of flextime plans, 330
  defined, 15
  Hawthorne effect, 280–281
  impact of training, 320
  increases in
    in manufacturing, 21, 48
    in United States, 48–49
    use of technology, 15, 48, 252–253
  labor, 15
  scientific management and, 279–280
  in service sector, 48–49
  in United States, 48–49
Products
  adapting, 404–405, 406, 474
  brands, 413–415; *see also* Brand names
  complaints about, 206, 482
  consumer goods and services, 409–410, 411
  customized, 254–255
  defined, 381–382
  development; *see* Product development
  distribution; *see* Distribution
  environmental impact, 380
  failures, 416
  generic goods, 415
  green
    carbon footprints, 103
    consumer preferences, BB-11
    defining, 103
    false claims, 32
    measuring impact, 380
    packaging, 408
    purchasing, 20
  industrial goods and services, 410–411, 436
  naming, 414
  packaging, 408, 412–413
  pricing, 382–383
  tracking technology, 412, 455, BA-5

Professional behavior, P-5 to P-8
Professional business strategies, P-5
Professional employer organizations (PEOs),
    317
Profit and loss statement; *see* Income
    statement
Profitability ratios, 517–518
Profits
   defined, 4
   gross, 510, 511
   matching risk and, 5
   net, 511
Profit-sharing plans, 328
Program evaluation and review technique
    (PERT) charts, 263–264
Program trading, 578
Project management
   Gantt charts, 264
   PERT charts, 263–264
Project managers, 230
Promissory notes, 538
Promotion; *see also* Advertising; Personal
    selling
   campaign steps, 466
   defined, 383
   integrated marketing communication, 465
   interactive, 470–471
   on Internet, 470–472
   sales, 479–481
   strategies, 484–485
   techniques, 383, 464–465
   word-of-mouth, 481–483
Promotion mix, 464–465, 484
Promotions, of employees, 313, 333
Property, private ownership, 35
Property insurance, A2-12, BB-8, BB-11
Property taxes, A1-14, A2-7
Prospecting, 475
Prospects, 475
Prospectuses, 559–560
Protectionism, 76–77
Protective tariffs, 76
Prototypes, 418
Psychographic segmentation, 391, 392
Psychological pricing, 425
Public, business responsibility to; *see*
    Corporate social responsibility
Public accountants, 500–501
Public Company Accounting Oversight Board
    (PCAOB), 501
Public domain software (freeware), BA-16
Public information, BA-6, BA-21
Public insurance, BB-5
Public relations (PR), 478
Public sector; *see* Governments
Public sector unions, 342, 345, 346
Public utilities; *see* Utilities
Publicity, 478–479
Pull strategy, 484–485
Purchasing, 259; *see also* Suppliers; Supply
    chain management
Pure risk, BB-3
Push strategy, 484, 485

Q

Qualifying, 475
Quality
   Baldrige Awards, 262, 327
   defined, 261
   ISO 9000 standards, 262
   perceived, 415
   six sigma, 261

Quality control
   continuous improvement process, 261
   at end of production, 261
   in service industries, 261–262
Quality Digest, BB-2
Quality of life, 6, 257
Quick ratio, 516

R

Race; *see* Diversity; Minorities
Rack jobbers, 441
Radio advertising, 468
Radio frequency identification (RFID), 412,
    455, 604, BA-5
Railroads, 452–453
Ratio analysis
   activity ratios, 518–519
   defined, 515
   leverage ratios, 516–517, 548
   liquidity ratios
     acid-test (quick) ratio, 516
     current ratio, 516
     purpose, 516
   profitability ratios, 517–518
     basic earnings per share, 517
     diluted earnings per share, 517
     return on equity, 517–518
     return on sales, 517
Real estate; *see also* Mortgages
   bubbles, 578, 612, A2-7
   investing in, A2-6 to A2-8
   property taxes, A1-14, A2-7
Real time, 231
Realtors, 440
Recessions; *see also* Economic crisis of 2008–
   definition, 49
   duration, 596
   effects in retail, 223, 388
   financial management, 535, 539, 548–549
Recognizing employees, 294–295
Recruitment, employee; *see also* Interviews;
    Job searches
   affirmative action and, 311
   application forms, 318
   background investigations, 319
   challenges, 316
   of contingent workers, 319–320
   defined, 315–316
   employment tests, 318
   online services, 317
   physical exams, 319
   selecting employees, 318–320
   by small businesses, 317
   sources, 316–317
   traits sought, E-12
   trial periods, 319
Recycling, 408
Reference groups, 394
Regulations; *see also* Legal environment
   consumer protection, A1-13 to A1-14
   deregulation, 40, A1-17 to A1-19
   effects on global markets, 75
   financial services, 548, 579, A1-13, A1-18
   on hamburgers, A1-18
   health care system, A1-19
   packaging, 413
   securities markets, 545, 559–560
   support for, A1-18, A1-19
Reinforcement theory, 290
Reinsurance, BB-1
Relationship marketing, 393
Religious differences, 72–73

Renter's insurance, A2-12
Research; *see* Marketing research; Product
    development
Reserve requirements, 592, 593
Resignations, 334–335
Resource development, 31
Resource files, P-5
Resources; *see* Factors of production
Restrictions on trade; *see* Trade barriers
Restructuring
   competing with, 16–17
   for empowerment, 235–236
Résumés
   cover letters, E-2, E-9 to E-10
   key words, E-5, E-6
   posting on Internet, E-6 to E-9
   sample, E-7, E-8
   writing, E-2, E-5 to E-6
Retail industry; *see also* E-commerce
   authority structures, 222–223
   catalog companies, 447
   cooperatives, 448
   decentralized authority, 221
   distribution strategies, 443–444
   jobs in, 21
   nonstore retailing, 445–447
   number of stores in United States, 443
   pop-up stores, 444
   pricing strategies, 425
   in recessions, 388
   salespersons, 477
   supermarkets, 316, 443, 481
   technology used in, 14, BA-13 to BA-14
   types of stores, 443
Retailers, 435, 441
Retained earnings, 508, 509, 546
Retirement planning, A2-12
   defined-contribution plans, A2-15
   401(k) plans, A2-15
   IRAs, 597, 603, A2-13 to A2-14
   Keogh plans, A2-15
   Social Security, 18, A2-12 to A2-13, BB-5
Retirements, 334
Return on equity (ROE), 517–518
Return on investment (ROI), 422
Return on sales, 517
Returns, risk and, 544, 572–573
Revenue tariffs, 76
Revenues
   defined, 4, 509
   forecasting, 531–532
   on income statement, 509, 510
Reverse discrimination, 312
Reverse logistics, 451
Revolving credit agreements, 540
RFID; *see* Radio frequency identification
Right-to-work laws, 350
Risk
   avoidance, BB-4
   defined, 5, BB-3
   insurable, BB-5 to BB-6
   investment, 567–568, 572–573
   matching profits and, 5
   pure, BB-3
   reduction, BB-3 to BB-4
   return on equity, 517–518
   speculative, BB-3
   uninsurable, BB-5
Risk management; *see also* Insurance
   environmental risks, BB-11
   importance, BB-2
   options, BB-3 to BB-5
   rapid change and, BB-2 to BB-3

Risk/return trade-off, 544, 572–573
Robinson-Patman Act of 1936, A1-12
Rockefeller family, 546–547
ROE; *see* Return on equity
ROI; *see* Return on investment
Ronald McDonald Houses, 99
Roth IRAs, A2-14
Round lots, 570
Royalties, 66
Rule of indemnity, BB-7
Russia
    barter trade, 589
    dumping disputes, 66
    factors of production, 10
    income tax rates, 42
    as market, 81
Rwanda, 44

S

S corporations, 132, 133
S&Ls; *see* Savings and loan associations
SADC; *see* Southern African Development
    Community
Safety, 217
SAIF; *see* Savings Association Insurance
    Fund
Salaries, 328; *see also* Compensation
Sales; *see also* Personal selling
    difference from revenues, 510
    gross, 510
    net, 510
    return on, 517
Sales agents, 442
Sales law, A1-8 to A1-9
Sales promotion; *see also* Promotion
    defined, 479
    internal, 480
    to marketing intermediaries, 480–481
    sampling, 481
    techniques, 479–481
Sales representatives; *see also* Personal selling
    compensation, 474
    in retail stores, 477
    sales promotion to, 480
Sales taxes, 41, A1-14
Sampling, 481
Sarbanes-Oxley Act, 96, 501, 502, A1-13
Saudi Arabia, 63, 73
Savings; *see also* Retirement planning
    personal, A2-5, A2-8
    rates of return, A2-5
Savings accounts
    in banks, 597
    deposit insurance, 602–603
    in savings and loans, 598–599
Savings and loan associations (S&Ls)
    defined, 598
    failures, 599
    federal deposit insurance, 602–603
    IRAs, A2-14
    as marketing intermediaries, 440
    services, 598–599
Savings Association Insurance Fund (SAIF),
    602, 603
SBA; *see* Small Business Administration
SBDCs; *see* Small Business Development
    Centers
SBIC; *see* Small Business Investment
    Company
Scandals; *see* Corporate scandals; Corruption
Scientific management, 279–281
SCM; *see* Supply chain management

SCORE; *see* Service Corps of Retired
    Executives
Seasonal unemployment, 47
Seasonal workers; *see* Temporary employees
SEC; *see* Securities and Exchange Commission
Secondary boycotts, 353, 354
Secondary data, 385
Secondary markets, 556
Secured bonds, 545, 565
Secured loans, 539–540
Securities; *see* Bonds; Securities markets;
    Stocks
Securities Act of 1933, 559
Securities and Exchange Act of 1934, 559–560
Securities and Exchange Commission (SEC)
    accounting standards, 519
    banking crisis of 2008–2009 and, 602, A1-13
    criticism of, A1-13
    defined, 559
    establishment, 559
    fair disclosure regulation, 101–102
    influence on business, A1-3
    insider trading regulations, 101–102, 560
    investment bank regulations, 612
    Public Company Accounting Oversight
        Board, 501
    regulation of markets, 559–560, 568
    regulation of stock and bond issuance, 545,
        557, 559–560
Securities markets; *see also* Investing; Stock
    exchanges
    bubbles, 578
    functions, 556–557
    insider trading, 101–102, 560
    over-the-counter, 558
    primary, 556
    quotations, 571–572
    regulation of, 545, 559–560
    secondary, 556
    volatility, 577–579
Security, information technology, BA-18 to
    BA-21
Selection of employees, 318–320
Selective distribution, 444
Self-insurance, BB-4 to BB-5
Self-managed cross-functional teams, 230, 294
Selling; *see* Personal selling; Retail industry;
    Sales promotion
Selling era, 377
Selling expenses, 511
Semantic web, BA-12 to BA-13
Senior citizens; *see also* Aging of population
    as consumers, 17–18, 388
    elder care, 361
    employees, 313
Service Corps of Retired Executives
    (SCORE), 177
Service industries
    competitiveness, 248
    facility location, 255–256
    home-based businesses, 161
    inverted organizations, 235–236
    jobs in, 21, 247
    operations management, 250
    outsourcing jobs, 81–82, 450
    packaging, 413
    product lines and product mixes, 408
    productivity, 48–49
    quality control, 261–262
    supply chain management, 450
    types of organizations, 22
    unions, 345, 355
    in United States, 247, 248

Service utility, 440
Services, defined, 4
Sexual harassment, 359–360
Sexual orientation; *see* Diversity
Shadowing, 321
Shareholders; *see* Stockholders
Shareware, BA-16
Sherman Antitrust Act, A1-11 to A1-12
Shipping; *see* Logistics; Transportation
Ships, 453–454
Shop stewards, 351
Shopping goods and services, 409, 410
Short-term financing
    banks, 538–540
    commercial paper, 542
    defined, 537–538
    factoring, 541
    family and friends, 538
    lines of credit, 540
    loans, 538–541
    promissory notes, 538
    revolving credit agreements, 540
    for small businesses, 538, 540
    trade credit, 538
Short-term forecasts, 531–532
Simple IRAs, A2-14
Sin taxes, A1-14
Singapore, 78, 81
Single parents, 18
Sinking funds, 565
Site selection; *see* Facility location
Six Sigma quality, 261
Skill-based pay, 327
Skills; *see also* Training and development
    conceptual, 201
    human relations, 201
    management, 201
    technical, 201, BA-17, BA-22
Skimming price strategy, 424
Small Business Administration (SBA)
    business financing from, 170, 173–174, 552
    defined, 173
    definition of small business, 165
    export financing, 179
    information on exporting, 64, 179
    reasons for business failures, 169
    Service Corps of Retired Executives, 177
    website, 170, 174, 177
Small Business Development Centers
    (SBDCs), 174
Small Business Investment Company (SBIC)
    Program, 174
Small-business management
    accounting systems, 176, 504
    employee management, 176
    financial management, 170–172,
        529–530
    financing
        bank loans, 172
        credit cards, 542
        retained earnings, 546
        short-term, 538, 540
        sources, 170–172, 540
        venture capital, 172, 546–547
    functions, 169
    importance, 169
    insurance, 177
    learning about, 167–168, 177
    legal environment, 12–13
    marketing, 175, 177
    MBA students as interns, 177
    motivating employees, 296
    planning, 169–170

Small-business management—*Cont.*
  promotion, 465
  recruiting employees, 317
  retirement plans, A2-14
Small businesses; *see also* Businesses, starting;
      Entrepreneurship; Home-based businesses
  banks and, 170, 172, 177
  defined, 165
  e-commerce, 384
  exporting, 68, 178–179
  failures, 166, 169
  family-run, 176
  global markets, 63, 178–179
  importance, 165
  jobs created by, 165
  legal help, 177
  markets, 175
  nonprice competition, 426
  number of, 165
  outside help, 177, 232
  outsourcing by, 232
  product differentiation, 409
  stock exchange for, 559
  success factors, 167
  taking over existing firms, 168–169
Smart cards, 604
Smartphones, 384, 598; *see also* Apps; Cell
      phones; Mobile technology
Social audits, 104–105
Social entrepreneurs, 7–8
Social environment, 17–18, 72–73, 388
Social justice, 103
Social media
  advertising on, 468, 471, 472
  business use of, 463, BA-11
  celebrity use of, 471
  communication with customers, 206, 405,
      465, 598
  consumer complaints, 206
  employee communications using, 293
  employee use, BA-11 to BA-12, P-7
  franchise use, 145
  future of, 234
  lending sites, 172
  mobile access, 384, 598
  monitoring ad effectiveness, 472
  networking on, E-1 to E-2, E-3
  political use, BA-1
  professional behavior, P-7
  promotional strategies, 465, 471
  review sites, 482
  scams, 93
  selling through, 384
Social responsibility; *see* Corporate social
      responsibility
Social Security, 18, A2-12 to A2-13
Social Security Act of 1935, A2-12
Social/collaboration software, BA-16
Socialism
  benefits, 41–42
  command economies, 43
  compared to other systems, 45
  defined, 41
  government functions, 41, 43
  income redistribution, 41
  negative consequences, 42, 43
Socially responsible investing (SRI), 105
Society, responsibility to; *see* Corporate
      social responsibility
Software; *see also* Apps; Information
      technology
  accounting, 504
  antivirus, BA-19

business intelligence, BA-3
business plan, 170
cookies, BA-21
customer relationship management, 475
employee application screening, 318
functions, BA-16
Microsoft's competitive practices, A1-12
public domain, BA-16
shareware, BA-16
supply chain management, 449, 450
Sole proprietorships
  advantages, 123
  defined, 122
  disadvantages, 124
  owners' equity, 508
South Africa, 44, 62, 81, 144
South Korea, 31, 77, 81, 106
Southern African Development Community
      (SADC), 79
Sovereign wealth funds (SWFs), 71, 72, 544
Soviet Union (former); *see* Russia
Span of control, 223–224
SPC; *see* Statistical process control
Specialty goods and services, 409–410
Specialty stores, 443
Speculative risk, BB-3
Spending; *see* Expenses
Spyware, BA-21
SQC; *see* Statistical quality control
SRI; *see* Socially responsible investing
Staff personnel, 228
Staffing; *see also* Employees; Recruitment
  defined, 202
  importance, 202
  retention, 102, 334–335
  small businesses, 232
Stagflation, 48
Stakeholders
  defined, 6
  relationships with, 478
  responding to, 6
  responsibilities to, 100–102
Standard & Poor's 500, 576
Standard of living, 5–6
Standards; *see also* Regulations
  accounting, 501, 511, 519
  ISO, 262
Startup America, 164
Start-up companies; *see* Businesses, starting
State governments; *see also* Governments
  administrative agencies, A1-4
  competition to attract businesses, 379
  public sector unions and, 342, 345, 346
  right-to-work laws, 350
  support for entrepreneurs, 163–164
  taxes, A1-14 to A1-15
Statement of cash flows, 505, 512–514
Statement of financial position; *see* Balance
      sheets
Statement of income and expenses; *see*
      Income statement
Statistical process control (SPC), 261
Statistical quality control (SQC), 261
Statutory law, A1-2, A1-3; *see also* Legal
      environment
Stock certificates, 561
Stock exchanges; *see also* NASDAQ; New
      York Stock Exchange; Securities
      markets
  crash of 1929, 596
  defined, 557
  electronic, 558, BA-4
  global, 560–561, 568

indicators, 576–578
listing requirements, 558
program trading, 578
for small businesses, 559
U.S., 557–558
volatility, 577–579
Stock insurance companies, BB-7
Stock options, 328, 356
Stock splits, 570
Stockbrokers, 566, 570; *see also* Brokerage
      firms
Stockholders, 131, 508, 562; *see also*
      Owners' equity
Stocks
  advantages and disadvantages, 561–562
  American depository receipts, 568
  buying on margin, 571
  defined, 561
  dividends, 561, 570
  in 401(k) plans, A2-15
  initial public offerings, 545, 556, 557
  investing in, 569–570, A2-8
  issuing, 545, 556–557, 562
  par value, 561
  preferred, 562–563
  price/earnings ratios, 571
  quotations, 571–572
Storage, 454–455
Stores; *see* Retail industry; Supermarkets
Strategic alliances, 70
Strategic planning, 196–197
Strengths; *see* SWOT analysis
Strict product liability, A1-5
Strikebreakers, 354, 355
Strikes, 352–353
Structural unemployment, 47
Students
  cheating, 92–93
  course resources, P-12 to P-14
  employment, 320
  internships, 177, 320, 321
  knowledge retention, P-5
  networking, P-5
  professional behavior, P-5 to P-8
  resource files, P-5
  study hints, P-8 to P-10
  test-taking hints, P-10
  time management, P-10 to P-11
Study hints, P-8 to P-10
Subcontracting; *see* Outsourcing
Subcultures, 394
Submarine patents, A1-7
Subprime mortgage crisis, 13, 578–579, 601
Subsidiaries, foreign, 70–71
Substance abuse, 362
Supermarkets, 316, 443, 481
Supervisory management, 200, 204
Suppliers; *see also* Outsourcing
  financing from, 170
  including in cross-functional teams, 230
  just-in-time inventory control, 260–261
  locations, 257
  relationships with, 259
  sustainability scorecards, 247
  sweatshop labor issue, 106–107
  use of Internet, 259
Supply, 37
Supply chain, 449; *see also* Marketing
      intermediaries
Supply chain management (SCM); *see also*
      Distribution
  careers in, 455–456
  complexity, 449–450

defined, 449
global, 450
outsourcing, 450
in service industries, 450
software, 449, 450
sustainability issues, 435
Supply curve, 37–38
Surcharges; see Tariffs
Surface transportation, 452–453
Surveys, marketing research, 385
Sustainability
recycling, 408
reports, 104
in supply chains, 247, 435
Sweatshop labor, 106–107, 343
SWFs; see Sovereign wealth funds
SWOT analysis, 196

T

Tabbedout, 405
Tactical planning, 197
Taft-Hartley Act; see Labor-Management
Relations Act
Tall organization structures, 223–224
Target costing, 423
Target marketing, 390, 391
Tariffs, 76, 77
TARP; see Troubled Assets Relief Program
Tax accountants, 502
Tax-deferred contributions, A2-13
Taxes
defined, A1-14
excise, A1-14
government policies, 50
income
corporate, 131–132, A1-14
deductions for homeowners, A2-7 to
A2-8
federal, A1-14
personal, 41, A1-14
rates, 41
on Internet transactions, A1-15
laws, A1-14 to A1-15
management of, 530
property, A1-14, A2-7
sales, 41, A1-14
sin, A1-14
Social Security, A2-12
types, A1-14
value-added, 41
Teams
compensation, 327–328
entrepreneurial, 158
global, 230
matrix organizations, 228–230
open communication and, 294
problem-solving, 199
self-managed cross-functional, 230, 294
Technical skills, 201
Technological environment, impact on
businesses, 14–16
Technology; see also Information technology;
Internet; Mobile technology; Networks;
Social media; Telecommuting
in banking, 603–605
benefits, 14–15
customer-responsiveness and, 16
defined, 14
digital video recorders, 469
effects on marketing, 387–388
jobs displaced by, 21
in manufacturing, 21, 259

predictions about, BA-4
product tracking, 412, 455, BA-5
productivity improvements, 15, 48,
252–253
Telecommunications Act of 1996, A1-18
Telecommunications deregulation, A1-18
Telecommuting
benefits to employee, 332, BA-17
benefits to employer, 331–332, BA-17
challenges, 332, BA-17 to BA-18
defined, 258
effects on facility location decisions, 258
nanobots, BA-18
Telemarketing, 446
Television
advertising, 466–467, 468, 469
digital video recorders, 469
infomercials, 470
product placement, 469
Spanish-language, 375
Temporary employees
hiring, 317, 319–320
number of, 319–320
Ten Commandments, 92
Term insurance, A2-10
Terminating employees, 333–334
Term-loan agreements, 543
Terrorism, 19, BA-20
Test marketing, 382
Testimonials, 483
Testing
drug, 362
of potential employees, 318
Test-taking hints, P-10
Text messaging, 483, 598
Thailand, 78, 81, 83
Theory X management, 285, 288
Theory Y management, 285–286, 288
Theory Z management, 286–288
Therbligs, 280
Third-party logistics, 452
Threats; see SWOT analysis
360-degree reviews, 325
Thrift institutions; see Savings and loan
associations
Time deposits, 597
Time management, P-10 to P-11
Time utility, 439
Time value of money, 535
Time-motion studies, 279
Title VII, Civil Rights Act of 1964, 312
Tobacco industry, A1-4, A1-5
Top management, 199–200
Tort law, A1-4 to A1-6
Torts, A1-4
Total fixed costs, 424
Total product offer, 406–407
Tourism, medical, 83; see also Travel industry
Trade; see also Exporting; Global markets;
Importing
balance of, 64
common markets, 77–79
comparative advantage theory, 62
dumping disputes, 66
financing, 605
free, 61–62
future issues, 80–82
growth, 18–19
importance, 18–19, 61
international agreements, 77–79
largest trading countries, 65
laws to ensure fairness, 66
measuring, 64–65

motives for, 62
opportunities, 63–64
organized labor and, 349
Trade barriers; see also Tariffs
embargoes, 76, 77
import quotas, 76, 77
nontariff, 77
Trade credit, 538
Trade deficits, 64, 65
Trade protectionism, 76–77
Trade shows, 480–481
Trade surpluses, 64
Trade unions; see Unions
Trademarks, 413, A1-7; see also Brand
names; Intellectual property protection
Trading blocs, 77–79
Trading securities; see Brokerage firms;
Securities markets
Training and development
activities, 320–322
apprentice programs, 322
benefits, 320
computer systems, 235, 322
defined, 320
by franchisors, 140
job rotation and, 292
job simulation, 322, 323
management development, 323–325
mentoring, 324
off-the-job, 322
online programs, 322
on-the-job, 321–322
outsourcing, BA-17
technical, BA-17
vestibule training, 322
Transfers, employee, 333
Translation apps, 201
Transparency, 203, 231–232
Transportation; see also Distribution;
Logistics
air, 454
costs, 435
energy consumption, 435
intermodal, 454
mode comparison, 452
pipelines, 454
railroads, 452–453
surface, 452–453
water, 453–454
Travel industry, 83
Treasurers, 528
Treasury bills, bonds, and notes, 564, 592–593
Trial balances, 504
Trial close, 476, 477
Triangle fire, 345
Troubled Assets Relief Program (TARP), 529,
579, 602
Trucking, 453
Truth-in-Lending Act (1968), A1-13

U

UCC; see Uniform Commercial Code
Uganda, microlending in, 36, 57
Umbrella policies, A2-12
Underemployed workers, 310
Unemployment, 46–47, 246, 299
Unemployment compensation, BB-5
Unemployment rate, 46–47
Unethical behavior; see Ethics
Uniform Commercial Code (UCC), 12, A1-8
to A1-9
Uniform Partnership Act (UPA), 125–126

Uninsurable risk, BB-5
Union security clause, 349
Union shop agreements, 350
Unions; *see also* Employee management
        relations
    apprentice programs, 322
    boycotts, 353
    certification, 347–348
    collective bargaining, 345, 346
    contracts, 349–350
    craft, 344
    decertification, 348
    decline of, 343, 345, 354
    defined, 342
    future of, 343, 350, 354–356
    givebacks, 354, 355
    history, 342–345
    industrial, 344
    membership by state, 355
    objectives, 349–350
    organizing campaigns, 347–348
    picketing, 352
    in professional sports, 341, 352
    public sector, 342, 345, 346
    resistance to management, 238
    shop stewards, 351
    strikes, 352–353
    tactics used in conflicts, 352–353
United Arab Emirates, 68, 544
United Nations, 107
United States
    comparative advantage, 62
    Constitution, A1-15, A1-17
    economic development, 20–21
    economic system
        business cycle, 49
        key economic indicators, 46–49
        mixed economy, 44
        productivity, 48–49
    exports, 61, 64, 65
    free trade agreements, 79
    imports, 61
    standard of living, 5–6
    trade deficits, 65
    trade laws, 66
    trading partners, 65
    unemployment, 46–47
U.S. dollar, 74, 591; *see also* Currencies
U.S. government
    administrative agencies, A1-3, A1-4
    assistance for exporters, 64, 68, 179
    budget deficits, 50
    corporate bailouts, 579
    debt, 50
    employees, 44
    insurance programs, BB-5
    revenues and expenditures, 50–51
    role in economy, 44
U.S. government bonds, 564, 592–593
United States v. American Tobacco, A1-11
United States v. AT&T, A1-11
United States v. E.I. du Pont de Nemours, A1-11
United States v. Microsoft, A1-11
United States v. Standard Oil, A1-11
Universal Product Codes (UPCs), 412, 455

Universities; *see* Colleges and universities
Unlimited liability, 124, 127
Unsecured bonds, 545, 564–565
Unsecured loans, 540
Unsought goods and services, 410
UPA; *see* Uniform Partnership Act
UPCs; *see* Universal Product Codes
Uruguay, 78
Uruguay Round, 77
USA Today, 576
Usage segmentation, 391, 392
Utilities
    cooperatives, 146
    deregulation of, 40, A1-18
    electric, 40
    monopolies, 40
    regulators, A1-4
    stock, 570
Utility
    defined, 439
    form, 251, 439
    information, 440
    place, 439
    possession, 440
    service, 440
    time, 439

V

Value, 404
Value chains, 449; *see also* Supply chain
Value enhancers, 406
Value package; *see* Total product offer
Value-added taxes, 41
Values, corporate, 203, 217, 236; *see also*
        Ethics
Variable costs, 424
Variable life insurance, A2-11
Vending machines, 446
Vendors; *see* Suppliers
Venture capital, 546–547
Venture capitalists, 172, 546–547
Vertical mergers, 136
Vestibule training, 322
Video games, 469–470
Vietnam, 42, 78, 81
Violence in workplace, 362–363
Viral marketing, 482–483
Virtual corporations, 231–232, 233
Virtual private networks (VPNs), BA-9
Virtualization, BA-14 to BA-15
Viruses, BA-19
Visions, 195, 203
Vocational Rehabilitation Act of 1973, 311
Volume, or usage, segmentation, 391, 392
Voluntary bankruptcy, A1-16
Volunteerism; *see* Community service;
        Nonprofit organizations
VPNs; *see* Virtual private networks

W

Wages, 328; *see also* Compensation
Wagner Act; *see* National Labor Relations Act
        of 1935

Wall Street Journal, 377, 571, 574, 576
Warehouse clubs, 441, 443
Warehouses, 435, 455
Warranties, A1-8 to A1-9
Wars, 19
Water transportation, 453–454
Weaknesses; *see* SWOT analysis
Wealth creation, by entrepreneurs, 9–10
Web 2.0, BA-12; *see also* Internet
Web 3.0, BA-12 to BA-13
Web-based businesses; *see* E-commerce;
        Internet companies
Webinars, 480–481
Western Europe; *see* Europe
Wheeler-Lea Amendment of 1938, A1-12
Whistleblowers, 96–97
Whole life insurance, A2-10 to A2-11
Wholesale prices, 48
Wholesalers; *see also* Marketing
        intermediaries
    cash-and-carry, 441
    defined, 435
    difference from retailers, 441
    full-service, 441, 442
    limited-function, 441
    merchant, 441
    stores sponsored by, 448
Wills, A2-16
Wireless technology; *see* Mobile
        technology
Wisconsin state government, 342, 343,
        345, 346
Women
    business owners, 9, 142–143
    comparable worth, 358
    discrimination against, 312
    in labor force, 358–359
    managers, 193, 324–325
    pay equity, 358–359
Word-of-mouth promotion, 481–483
Work teams; *see* Teams
Workers; *see* Employees; Labor
Workers' compensation insurance, BB-10
Workforce diversity; *see* Diversity
Workplace violence, 362–363
World Bank, 606, 607
World market; *see* Global markets
World trade; *see* Trade
World Trade Organization (WTO),
        77, 81
World Wide Web (WWW); *see* Internet
Wrongful discharge lawsuits, 334, 335
WTO; *see* World Trade Organization
WWW (World Wide Web); *see* Internet

Y

Yankee bonds, 564
Yellow Pages, 468
Yellow-dog contracts, 346, 347

Z

Zaire, 106
Zippers, 419